American Constitutional Law

D1411227

American Constitutional Law
by Louis Fisher and Katy J. Harriger
is available in two formats:

SINGLE VOLUME HARDCOVER EDITION
American Constitutional Law

TWO VOLUME PAPERBACK EDITION

VOLUME 1
Constitutional Structures
Separated Powers and Federalism

VOLUME 2
Constitutional Rights
Civil Rights and Civil Liberties

American Constitutional Law

Eighth Edition

VOLUME 1

Constitutional Structures
Separated Powers and Federalism

Louis Fisher

Katy J. Harriger

CAROLINA ACADEMIC PRESS
Durham, North Carolina

Copyright © 2009 by Louis Fisher and Katy J. Harriger.
All rights reserved.

ISBN 978-1-59460-624-3

Library of Congress Cataloging-in-Publication Data

Fisher, Louis.
  American constitutional law / Louis Fisher, Katy J. Harriger. — 8th ed.
     p. cm.
  Includes bibliographical references and index.
  ISBN 978-1-59460-624-3 (alk. paper)
  1. Constitutional law—United States. 2. Civil rights—United States. I. Harriger, Katy J.
(Katy Jean) II. Title.

KF4550.F568 2008
342.73—dc22   2008049726

Carolina Academic Press
700 Kent Street
Durham, North Carolina 27701
Telephone (919) 489-7486
Fax (919) 493-5668
e-mail cap@cap-press.com

Printed in the United States of America

To The Law Library — Louis Fisher

To my father, Russell E. Harriger — Katy J. Harriger

Summary of Contents

Contents

About the Authors

LOUIS FISHER received his B.S. from the College of William and Mary and his Ph.D. from the New School for Social Research. After teaching political science at Queens College, he joined the Congressional Research Service of the Library of Congress in 1970, where he served as Senior Specialist in Separation of Powers. On March 6, 2006, he joined the Law Library of the Library of Congress. He has testified before congressional committees on such issues as war powers, state secrets, NSA surveillance, Congress and the Constitution, executive lobbying, executive privilege, impoundment of funds, legislative vetoes, the item veto, the pocket veto, presidential reorganization authority, recess appointments, executive spending discretion, the congressional budget process, the Balanced Budget Amendment, biennial budgeting, covert spending, and CIA whistleblowing. During 1987 he served as Research Director for the House Iran-Contra Committee.

His books include *President and Congress* (1972), *Presidential Spending Power* (1975), *The Constitution between Friends* (1978), *The Politics of Shared Power* (4th ed., 1998), *Constitutional Conflicts between Congress and the President* (5th ed., 2007), *Constitutional Dialogues* (1988), *Political Dynamics of Constitutional Law* (with Neal Devins, 4th ed., 2006), the four-volume *Encyclopedia of the American Presidency* (with Leonard W. Levy, 1994), *Presidential War Power* (2d ed. 2004), *Congressional Abdication on War and Spending* (2000), *Religious Liberty in America: Political Safeguards* (2002), *Nazi Saboteurs on Trial: A Military Tribunal & American Law* (2003), *The Politics of Executive Privilege* (2004), *The Democratic Constitution* (with Neal Devins, 2004), *Military Tribunals and Presidential Power: American Revolution to the War on Terrorism* (2005), *In the Name of National Security: Unchecked Presidential Power and the* Reynolds *Case* (2006), *The Constitution and 9/11: Recurring Threats to America's Freedoms* (2008), and *Rival Interpretations: The Supreme Court and Congress* (2009).

Dr. Fisher has been active with CEELI (Central and East European Law Initiative) of the American Bar Association. He traveled twice to Bulgaria, twice to Albania, and to Hungary to lend assistance to constitution writers. In addition to these trips abroad, he participated in CEELI conferences in Washington, D.C., involving delegations from Lithuania, Romania, and Russia, and has served on CEELI "working groups" on Armenia and Belarus. He traveled to Russia in 1992 as part of a CRS delegation to assist on questions of separation of powers and federalism and to Ukraine in 1993 to participate in an election law conference.

Dr. Fisher's specialties include constitutional law, war powers, state secrets, budget policy, executive-legislative relations, and judicial-congressional relations. He is the author of more than 380 articles in law reviews, political science journals, encyclopedias, books, magazines, and newspapers. He has been invited to speak in Albania, Australia, Belgium, Bulgaria, Canada, the Czech Republic, China, England, France, Germany, Greece, Israel, Japan, Macedonia, Malaysia, Mexico, the Netherlands, Oman, the Philippines, Poland, Romania, Russia, Slovenia, South Korea, Taiwan, Ukraine, and United Arab Emirates.

KATY J. HARRIGER received her B.A. in Political Science from Edinboro State College in Pennsylvania and her M.A. and Ph.D in Political Science from the University of Connecticut. She is a Professor of Political Science and chair of that department at Wake Forest University where she teaches courses in American Constitutional Law, American politics, judicial process, and democracy and citizenship. She has testified before Congress and been a frequent media commentator on issues related to the use of independent counsel and political influences on the Department of Justice. Dr. Harriger is the editor of *Separation of Powers: Commentary and Documents,* (Congressional Quarterly Press 2003), the author of *The Special Prosecutor in American Politics.* 2nd ed., revised (University Press of Kansas, 2000), and *Independent Justice: The Federal Special Prosecutor in American Politics* (University Press of Kansas, 1992), as well as a number of articles about constitutional law issues in journals and law reviews. Most recently she co-authored, with Jill J. McMillan, *Speaking of Politics: Preparing College Students for Democratic Citizenship through Deliberative Dialogue* (Kettering Foundation Press, 2007). At Wake Forest, Harriger has been the recipient of the Reid Doyle Prize for Excellence in Teaching (1988), the John Reinhardt Distinguished Teaching Award (2002), and the Schoonmaker Award for Community Service (2006).

Acknowledgments

This book, in gestation for years, has many contributors and abettors. With the publication of the eighth edition, Katy J. Harriger joins as co-author. She brings to the task a strong background in constitutional law and separation of powers and many years of classroom experience and professional activity on legal issues. David Gray Adler, co-author of the seventh edition, offered extensive analytical contributions and in previous editions provided careful, thoughtful reviews.

Morton Rosenberg of the Congressional Research Service lent a guiding hand, giving encouragement and insightful observations. In reviewing the manuscript and selections for readings, he was the major source of counsel and enlightenment. Other friends and colleagues who offered important advice and comments include Susan Burgess, Phillip J. Cooper, Neal Devins, Murray Dry, Roger Garcia, Jerry Goldman, Nancy Kassop, Jacob Landynski, Leonard W. Levy, Robert Meltz, Ronald Moe, Christopher Pyle, Jeremy Rabkin, Harold Relyea, William Ross, Jay Shampansky, Gordon Silverstein, Mitchel Sollenberger, Charles Tiefer, and Stephen Wasby.

I joined the Law Library of the Library of Congress on March 6, 2006, after mining its wonderful collections over the past 35 years. It is my pleasure to dedicate the book to the Law Library. On the weekends, when I enter the building to pursue my writings, it is always a joy to place on the sign-in sheet my name, type of pass, and the division I work for: LAW.

Louis Fisher

After many years of teaching American Constitutional Law using this textbook, it has been a privilege and a pleasure to work with Lou Fisher on the eighth edition and to realize all that goes into keeping the book current and relevant. I have always been drawn to this text because it recognizes that constitutional law is made through a dynamic dialogic political process rather than simply by nine Supreme Court justices. This seems a particularly important lesson to understand, for political science and law students alike, in a time when the popular understandings of constitutional politics and issues are so shallow and, and often, misinformed. I dedicate the book to my father, Russell E. Harriger, who has always encouraged and supported my endeavors, even when he disagreed with me (which in the area of constitutional law was early and often).

Keith Sipe and Tim Colton, and the rest of the staff at Carolina Academic Press, were amiable, helpful and professional in bringing this project to fruition. We express our thanks and gratitude to them for all of their efforts.

Katy J. Harriger

Introduction

To accommodate the leading cases on constitutional law, textbooks concentrate on court decisions and overlook the political, historical, and social framework in which these decisions are handed down. Constitutional law is thus reduced to the judicial exercise of divining the meaning of textual provisions. The larger process, including judicial as well as nonjudicial actors, is ignored. The consequence, as noted by one law professor, is the absence of a "comprehensive course on constitutional law in any meaningful sense in American law schools."[1]

The political process must be understood because it establishes the boundaries for judicial activity and influences the substance of specific decisions, if not immediately then within a few years. This book keeps legal issues in a broad political context. Cases should not be torn from their environment. A purely legalistic approach to constitutional law misses the constant, creative interplay between the judiciary and the political branches. The Supreme Court is not the exclusive source of constitutional law. It is not the sole or even dominant agency in deciding constitutional questions. The Constitution is interpreted initially by a private citizen, legislator, or executive official. Someone from the private or public sector decides that an action violates the Constitution; political pressures build in ways to reshape fundamental constitutional doctrines.

Books on constitutional law usually focus exclusively on Supreme Court decisions and stress its doctrines, as though lower courts and elected officials are unimportant. Other studies describe constitutional decision making as lacking in legal principle, based on low-level political haggling by various actors. We see an open and vigorous system struggling to produce principled constitutional law. Principles are important. Constitutional interpretations are not supposed to be idiosyncratic events or the result of a political free-for-all. If they were, our devotion to the rule of law would be either absurd or a matter of whimsy.

It is traditional to focus on constitutional rather than statutory interpretation, and yet the boundaries between these categories are unclear. Issues of constitutional dimension usually form a backdrop to "statutory" questions. Preoccupation with the Supreme Court as the principal or final arbiter of constitutional questions fosters a misleading impression. A dominant business of the Court is statutory construction, and through that function it interacts with other branches of government in a process that refines the meaning of the Constitution.

This study treats the Supreme Court and lower courts as one branch of a political system with a difficult but necessary task to perform. They often share with the legislature and the executive the responsibility for defining political values, resolving political conflict, and protecting the political process. Through commentary and reading selections, we try to bridge the artificial gap in the literature that separates law from politics. Lord Radcliffe advised that "we cannot learn law by learning law." Law must be "a part of history, a part of economics and sociology, a part of ethics and a philosophy of life. It is not strong enough in itself to be a philosophy in itself."[2]

A Note on Citations. The introductory essays to each chapter contain many citations to court cases, public laws, congressional reports, and floor debates. The number of these citations may seem con-

---

1. W. Michael Reisman, "International Incidents: Introduction to a New Genre in the Study of International Law," 10 Yale J. Int'l L. 1, 8 n.13 (1984).
2. Lord Radcliffe, The Law & Its Compass 92-93 (1960).

fusing and even overwhelming. We want to encourage the reader to consult these documents and develop a richer appreciation of the complex process that shapes constitutional law. Repeated citations to federal statutes help underscore the ongoing role of Congress and the executive branch in constitutional interpretation. To permit deeper exploration of certain issues, either for a term paper or scholarly research, footnotes contain leads to supplementary cases. Bibliographies are provided for each chapter. The appendices include a glossary of legal terms and a primer on researching the law.

If the coverage is too detailed, the instructor may always advise students to skip some of the material. Another option is to ask the student to understand two or three departures from a general doctrine, such as the famous *Miranda* warning developed by the Warren Court but whittled away by the Burger and Rehnquist Courts. Even if a student is initially stunned by the complexity of constitutional law, it is better to be aware of the delicate shadings that exist than to believe that the Court paints with bold, permanent strokes.

At various points in the chapters, we give examples where state courts, refusing to follow the lead of the Supreme Court, conferred greater constitutional rights than available at the federal level. These are examples only. They could have been multiplied many times over. No one should assume that rulings from the Supreme Court represent the last word on constitutional law, even for lower courts.

Compared to other texts, this book offers much more in the way of citations to earlier decisions. We do this for several reasons. The citations allow the reader to research areas in greater depth. They also highlight the process of trial and error used by the Court to clarify constitutional principles. Concentration on contemporary cases would obscure the Court's record of veering down side roads, backtracking, and reversing direction. Focusing on landmark cases prevents the reader from understanding the *development* of constitutional law: the dizzying exceptions to "settled" doctrines, the laborious manner in which the Court struggles to fix the meaning of the Constitution, the twists and turns, the detours and dead ends. Describing major cases without these tangled patterns would presume an orderly and static system that mocks the dynamic, fitful, creative, and consensus-building process that exists. No one branch of government prevails. The process is polyarchal, not hierarchical. The latter, perhaps attractive for architectural structures, is inconsistent with our aspiration for self-government.

In all court cases and other documents included as readings, footnotes have been deleted. For the introductory essays, reference works are abbreviated as follows:

Comp. Gen.	Decisions of the Comptroller General.
Elliot	Jonathan Elliot, ed., The Debates in the Several State Conventions, on the Adoption of the Federal Constitution (5 vols., Washington, D.C., 1836–1845).
Farrand	Max Farrand, ed., The Records of the Federal Convention of 1787 (4 vols., New Haven: Yale University Press, 1937).
Fisher	Constitutional Conflicts between Congress and the President (4th ed. 1997).
Landmark Briefs	Landmark Briefs and Arguments of the Supreme Court of the United States: Constitutional Law. Gerald Gunther and Gerhard Casper, eds. University Publications of America.
O.L.C.	Office of Legal Counsel Opinions, U.S. Department of Justice.
Op. Att'y Gen.	Opinions of the Attorney General.
Richardson	James D. Richardson, ed., A Compilation of the Messages and Papers of the Presidents (20 vols., New York: Bureau of National Literature, 1897–1925).
Wkly Comp. Pres. Doc.	Weekly Compilation of Presidential Documents, published each week by the Government Printing Office since 1965.

American Constitutional Law

1

Constitutional Politics

For those who teach and study constitutional law, the relationship between the judiciary and politics remains an awkward issue. Technical details of a decision have a way of driving out the political events that generate a case and influence its disposition. To infuse law with dignity, majesty, and perhaps a touch of mystery, it is tempting to separate the courts from the rest of government and make unrealistic claims of judicial independence. Similarly, studies exaggerate the extent to which the Supreme Court supplies the "last word" on constitutional law. The elected branches and the general public necessarily share in that complex, sensitive task.

Legal scholars who explored the law-politics relationship early in the twentieth century did so against the warnings of traditional leaders of the legal profession. To speak the truth, or even search for it, threatened judicial symbols and concepts of long standing. In 1914, when legal philosopher Morris Raphael Cohen began describing how judges make law, his colleagues warned of dire consequences. The deans of major law schools advised him that his findings, although unquestionably correct, might invite even greater recourse to "judicial legislation."

Undeterred by these cautionary words, Cohen had "an abiding conviction that to recognize the truth and adjust oneself to it is in the end the easiest and most advisable course." He denied that the law is a "closed, independent system having nothing to do with economic, political, social, or philosophical science." If courts were in fact constantly making and remaking the law, it became "of the utmost social importance that the law should be made in accordance with the best available information, which it is the object of science to supply." Morris R. Cohen, Law and the Social Order 380–81 n.86 (1933).

Constitutional Principles

The chapter title "Constitutional Politics" is meant to underscore two values: the interplay between law and politics and the core principles that define constitutional government. Political judgments and accommodations must respect those principles and be subordinate to them. If public policy were merely the end result of compromises reached by the three branches of government, we would have politics but no constitution. The period after the terrorist attacks of 9/11 represents one period in American history where government pursued policies at the cost of constitutional liberties. In previous years, the country also lost sight of fundamental principles and violated the rights of citizens and aliens.

What are the overarching values of the U.S. Constitution? The framers were heavily influenced by the Enlightenment and its belief that individuals have the capacity to develop and participate in self-government. In America they would be citizens, not "subjects" of a monarch. A purpose of the U.S. Constitution is to protect the dignity and worth of individuals, enabling them to promote their skills and talents. James Madison believed that an individual "has property in his opinions and in the free communication of them." Property included religious opinions, personal safety and liberty, and the "free use of his faculties and free choice of the objects on which to employ them." Flowing from those fundamental, inherent values were the rights of free speech, free press, religious liberty, and protection against arbitrary arrest and seizure of property. Conscience, he said, "is the most sacred of all property." Invading someone's conscience was a greater violation than invading a person's home.

From British history, the framers held that individuals have a right to be tried in open court, upon specific charges, and with full access to evidence presented by prosecutors. Procedural safeguards were needed to curb arbitrary imprisonment. Secret trials and secret evidence were abhorrent. Defendants had the right to confront accusers and gain access to legal counsel. Juries and grand juries represented a potential check on government abuse. American colonies and states included the privilege against self-incrimination in their charters and constitutions. Evidence against the accused could not be obtained by coercive methods.

These rights and liberties were protected by the structure of government, including separation of powers and the system of checks and balances. The framers did not trust in human nature. Concentrating government authority in one place invited the abuse of power. In Federalist No. 4, John Jay explained why the power to place the country in a state of war was vested in Congress, not the President. A study of history demonstrated that executives regularly committed their country to military adventures not for national interest but for reasons of fame, glory, and ambition, leading to calamitous loss of life and treasure. It was the practice of an executive to engage in wars "not sanctified by justice or the voice and interests of his people." The period after World War II has underscored the dangers to constitutional democracy when unchecked power is concentrated in the executive branch.

Madison also depended on a self-checking mechanism within the regular political process. In Federalist No. 10, he analyzed what should be done about "factions," which he understood to mean citizens whose interests were adverse to that of the community. He rejected any effort to destroy the liberty that made factions possible, or attempt to make everyone think the same way. Some of the passions of factions would be filtered through a representative system. Another important check was to increase the size of the republic so that factions would tend to neutralize each other. These safeguards would help protect minority rights.

Mechanical Jurisprudence

For more than a century, the legal profession claimed that judges "found" the law rather than made it. This doctrine of mechanical jurisprudence, joined with the supposed nonpolitical nature of the judiciary, offered convenient reasons for separating courts from the rest of government. A perceptive essay by political scientist C. Herman Pritchett noted that the disciplines of law and political science drifted apart for semantic, philosophical, and practical reasons: "Law is a prestigious symbol, whereas politics tends to be a dirty word. Law is stability; politics is chaos. Law is impersonal; politics is personal. Law is given; politics is free choice. Law is reason; politics is prejudice and self-interest. Law is justice; politics is who gets there first with the most." Joel B. Grossman and Joseph Tanenhaus, eds., Frontiers of Judicial Research 31 (1969). With options drawn in that manner, no wonder courts looked attractive. A famous example of mechanical jurisprudence is the claim by Justice Roberts that when an act of Congress "is appropriately challenged in the courts as not conforming to the constitutional mandate the judicial branch of the Government has only one duty, — to lay the article of the Constitution which is invoked beside the statute which is challenged and to decide whether the latter squares with the former." United States v. Butler, 297 U.S. 1, 62 (1936).

Chief Justice Warren believed that law could be distinguished from politics. Progress in politics "could be made and most often was made by compromising and taking half a loaf where a whole loaf could not be obtained." He insisted that the "opposite is true so far as the judicial process was concerned." Through the judicial process, "and particularly in the Supreme Court, the basic ingredient of decision is principle, and it should not be compromised and parceled out a little in one case, a little more in another, until eventually someone receives the full benefit." The Memoirs of Earl Warren 6 (1977).

Yet the piecemeal approach applies quite well to the judicial process. The Supreme Court prefers to avoid general rules that exceed the necessities of a particular case. Especially in the realm of constitutional law, it recognizes the "embarrassment" that may result from formulating rules or deciding questions "beyond the necessities of the immediate issue." Euclid v. Ambler Co., 272 U.S. 365, 397 (1926). Compromise, expediency, and ad hoc action are no strangers to a multimember court that gropes incrementally toward a consensus and decision. The desegregation case, Brown v. Board of Education (1954), was preceded by two decades of halting progress toward the eventual abandonment of the "separate but equal" doctrine enunciated in 1896. After he left the Court, Potter Stewart reflected on the decision to exclude from the courtroom evidence that had been illegally obtained: "Looking back, the exclusionary rule seems a bit jerry-built—like a roller coaster track constructed while the roller coaster sped along. Each new piece of track was attached hastily and imperfectly to the one before it, just in time to prevent the roller coaster from crashing, but without an opportunity to measure the curves and dips preceding it or to contemplate the twists and turns that inevitably lay ahead." 83 Colum. L. Rev. 1365, 1366 (1983).

A. LITIGATION AS A POLITICAL PROCESS

Throughout the twentieth century, cases decided by federal courts embodied issues that were of vital importance to individual citizens, corporations and trade unions, and the elected branches of government. The Court moved from narrow nineteenth-century questions of private law (estates, trusts, admiralty, real property, contracts, and commercial law) to contemporary issues of public law (federal regulation, criminal law, individual liberties, equal protection, and federal taxation). The period after World War II is generally considered a high-water mark in judicial policymaking. Decisions with nationwide impact affected desegregation in 1954, reapportionment and school prayers in 1962, criminal justice in the 1960s, and abortion from 1973 onward.

Although members of Congress criticize "judicial activism," they do their part to encourage judicial policymaking. Congress passes statutes that give standing to litigants, provide fees for attorneys, and establish separate agencies (such as the Legal Services Corporation) to initiate suits on broad public issues. Instead of merely resolving private disputes between private individuals, courts develop and articulate public values on major social, economic, and political questions. Increasingly, their decisions are prospective rather than retrospective. Judges actively participate in negotiating a resolution and maintain their involvement after issuing an initial decree. Courts do more than resolve private disputes between litigants according to the principles of law. "As a result, courts are inevitably cast in an affirmative, political—activist, if you must—role, a role that contrasts with the passive umpireship we are taught to expect." Abram Chayes, "Public Law Litigation and the Burger Court," 96 Harv. L. Rev. 4, 4 (1982). This activist role has been criticized by those who believe that federal judges lack both the legitimacy and the capacity to decide questions of broad social policy (see box on next page).

Justices of the Supreme Court sometimes encourage the belief that a gulf separates law from politics. Chief Justice John Marshall insisted that "Questions in their nature political . . . can never be made in this court." Marbury v. Madison, 5 U.S. 137, 170 (1803). In that very same decision, however, he established a precedent of far-reaching political importance: the right of the judiciary to review and overturn the actions of Congress and the executive. As noted by one scholar, Marshall "more closely associated the art of judging with the positive qualities of impartiality and disinterestedness, and yet he had made his office a vehicle for the expression of his views about the proper foundations of American government." G. Edward White, The American Judicial Tradition 35 (1976).

During his days as law school professor, Felix Frankfurter referred to constitutional law as "applied politics." Archibald MacLeish and E. F. Prichard, eds., Law and Politics 6 (1962). "The simple truth of the matter," he said, "is that decisions of the Court denying or sanctioning the exercise of federal power, as in the first child labor case, largely involve a judgment about practical matters, and not at all any esoteric knowledge of the Constitution." Id. at 12. He regarded courts as "less than ever technical expounders of technical provisions of the Constitution. They are arbiters of the economic and

---

Judicial Capacity for Making Social Policy

[There is a] growing recognition that there are elements of overstatement in the case against judicial review. The courts are more democratically accountable, through a variety of formal and informal mechanisms, than they have been accused of being. Equally important, the other branches are in many ways less democratically accountable than they in turn were said to be by those who emphasized the special disabilities under which judges labor....

As the debate over the democratic character of judicial review wanes, there is another set of issues in the offing. It relates not to legitimacy but to capacity, not to whether the courts *should* perform certain tasks but to whether they *can* perform them competently.

Of course, legitimacy and capacity are related. A court wholly without capacity may forfeit its claim to legitimacy. A court wholly without legitimacy will soon suffer from diminished capacity....

[Judicial capacity is limited by five factors: (1) adjudication is so focused by the particular litigants that other alternatives and remedies are overlooked; (2) the piecemeal nature of adjudication leads to incremental decisionmaking that pushes to the side related issues; (3) judges must await the capricious timing of litigants; (4) fact-finding in adjudication is ill-adapted to the ascertainment of social facts and results in reduced understanding and abstract rulings; and (5) adjudication makes no provision for policy review and little for future consequences.]

SOURCE: Donald L. Horowitz, The Courts and Social Policy 18, 34–56 (1977).

---

social life of vast regions and at times of the whole country." Felix Frankfurter and James M. Landis, The Business of the Supreme Court 173 (1928).

Once on the bench, however, Frankfurter insisted that a dichotomy exists between law and politics. Refusing to take a reapportionment case in 1946, he said it was "hostile to a democratic system to involve the judiciary in the politics of the people." Colegrove v. Green, 328 U.S. 549, 553–54 (1946). In Baker v. Carr (1962) the Supreme Court liberated itself from this narrow holding and has demonstrated throughout its history an awareness of the political system in which it operates daily. Writing in 1921, Justice Cardozo dismissed the idea that judges "stand aloof" from the "great tides and currents" that engulf the rest of mankind (see box on next page). Although the Supreme Court is an independent branch, it is not isolated. It is buffeted by the same social winds that press upon the executive and legislative branches.

From the late nineteenth century to the 1930s, the courts struck down a number of federal and state efforts to ameliorate industrial conditions. Laws that established maximum hours or minimum wages were declared an unconstitutional interference with the "liberty of contract." Lawyers from the corporate sector helped translate the philosophy of laissez-faire into legal terms and constitutional doctrine. These judicial rulings were so spiced with conservative business values that Justice Holmes protested that cases were "decided upon an economic theory which a large part of the country does not entertain." He chided his brethren: "The Fourteenth Amendment does not enact Mr. Herbert Spencer's Social Statics." Lochner v. New York, 198 U.S. 45, 75 (1905). When it was evident that the country would no longer tolerate interference by the courts, the judiciary retreated. After retiring from the Court, Justice Roberts explained why the judiciary chose to step back and allow the expansion of national power over economic conditions: "Looking back, it is difficult to see how the Court could have resisted the popular urge for uniform standards throughout the country—for what in effect was a unified economy." Owen J. Roberts, The Court and the Constitution 61 (1951).

To associate litigation with economic and social forces is not meant to treat adjudication as just another form of politics. Judges make policy, but not in the same manner as legislators and executives. Unlike the elected branches, the judiciary is not expected to satisfy the needs of the majority. Although judges have an opportunity to engage in their own form of lobbying, they are not supposed to participate in ex parte meetings open to only one party—privileges routinely exercised by legisla-

---

Cardozo on Judicial Process

I do not doubt the grandeur of the conception which lifts [judges] into the realm of pure reason, above and beyond the sweep of perturbing and deflecting forces. None the less, if there is anything of reality in my analysis of the judicial process, they do not stand aloof on these chill and distant heights; and we shall not help the cause of truth by acting and speaking as if they do. The great tides and currents which engulf the rest of men do not turn aside in their course and pass the judges by. We like to figure to ourselves the processes of justice as coldly objective and impersonal. The law, conceived of as a real existence, dwelling apart and alone, speaks, through the voices of priests and ministers, the words which they have no choice except to utter. That is an ideal of objective truth toward which every system of jurisprudence tends. It is an ideal of which great publicists and judges have spoken as of something possible to attain.... It has a lofty sound; it is well and finely said; but it can never be more than partly true. [John] Marshall's own career is a conspicuous illustration of the fact that the ideal is beyond the reach of human faculties to attain. He gave to the constitution of the United States the impress of his own mind; and the form of our constitutional law is what it is, because he moulded it while it was still plastic and malleable in the fire of his own intense convictions.

SOURCE: Benjamin N. Cardozo, The Nature of the Judicial Process 168–70 (1921).

---

tors and administrators. Most lobbying of the executive and legislative branches is open and direct; lobbying the judiciary is filtered through legal briefs, professional meetings, and law review articles. The executive and legislative branches have elaborate mechanisms for handling public relations, self-promotion, and contacts with the press. For the most part, judges release their opinions and remain silent. If executive officials and legislators are criticized in the press, they can respond in kind. Judges, with rare exceptions, take their lumps without retaliation.

Operations of the political branches can resemble those of the courts. Although responsive to majoritarian pressures, Congress and the President are also sensitive to minority rights and can protect those rights as well as, if not better than, the courts. Since the days of President Franklin D. Roosevelt, executive orders and congressional statutes have advanced the cause of civil rights. Many religious freedoms are the result of statutes passed by Congress and the states. The political branches are more at liberty to engage in ad hoc actions, but they usually follow general principles and precedents of their own and feel an obligation to present a reasoned explanation for their decisions.

B. LOBBYING THE COURTS

Private organizations accept litigation as part of the political process. They may conclude that their interests will be better served through court action than through the legislative and executive branches. In 1963 Justice Brennan called litigation "a form of political expression." Groups unable to achieve their objectives through the electoral process often turn to the judiciary: "under the conditions of modern government, litigation may well be the sole practicable avenue open to a minority to petition for redress of grievances." NAACP v. Button, 371 U.S. 415, 429–30 (1963). It could also be said that under the conditions of modern government, appeals to the elected branches may well be the sole practicable avenue open to a minority after being rebuffed in the courts. For groups such as the National Association for the Advancement of Colored People (NAACP) and the American Civil Liberties Union (ACLU), litigation is not merely a technique for resolving private differences. It is a form of political action. In re Primus, 436 U.S. 412, 428 (1978). In an article in 1969, Justice Thurgood Marshall explained the importance of individual and group efforts to pressure courts and the elected branches (see box on next page).

The use of litigation in the 1940s and 1950s to shape social policy led to broader public participa-

Thurgood Marshall on Group Pressures

In last year's address, Justice Clark spoke to you of one of the most basic institutions for the attainment of justice—the courts. I speak to you tonight of another "institution" essential to the attainment of justice, an institution perhaps even more basic. No matter how solemn and profound the declarations of principle contained in our charter of government, no matter how dedicated and independent our judiciary, true justice can only be obtained through the actions of committed individuals, individuals acting both independently and through organized groups.

... As we move into the future, the role formerly filled for the most part by individuals will have to be filled to an increasingly large degree by organized group practice....

My message can be aptly illustrated by the history of the Civil War amendments, a history in which I was in recent years fortunate enough to have played a small part. That history demonstrates that mere declarations of rights have not been sufficient to secure justice. It further illustrates that true progress can only be made by organized effort. The rights guaranteed by our Constitution are not self-enforcing; they can be made meaningful only by legislative or judicial action. As we shall see, legislation does not pass itself and the courts cannot act in the absence of a controversy. Organized, committed effort is necessary to promote legislation and institute legal action on any significant scale.

SOURCE: Thurgood Marshall, "Group Action in the Pursuit of Justice," 44 N.Y.U. L. Rev. 661, 662–63 (1969).

tion and produced fundamental changes in the amicus curiae (friend of the court) brief. Originally, such briefs permitted third parties, without any direct interest in the case, to bring certain facts to the attention of the court to avoid judicial error. Over the years it lost this innocent quality and became an instrument used by private groups to advance their cause. The amicus curiae brief moved "from neutrality to partisanship, from friendship to advocacy." Samuel Krislov, 72 Yale L. J. 694 (1963). The briefs are now regularly used as part of the interest group struggle in the courts. The number of amicus briefs increased so rapidly that the Supreme Court adopted a rule in November 1949 to control their filing. With the exception of government units, all parties must consent to the filing of an amicus brief. If a party objects, the applicant must request the Court's permission to file.

The political nature of litigation is underscored by many familiar examples. Through dozens of court actions, the Jehovah's Witnesses secured such rights as the refusal to salute or pledge allegiance to the American flag, the right to solicit from house to house, and the right to preach in the streets without a license. The NAACP created a Legal Defense and Educational Fund to pursue rights denied blacks by Congress and state legislatures. A series of victories in the courts established basic rights for blacks in voting, housing, education, and jury service. The National Consumers' League channeled its resources into litigation and won important protections for factory workers. The American Liberty League, organized by conservative businessmen, turned to litigation in an effort to prevent the enactment of economic regulation by Congress.

Through the publication of articles, books, and commission reports, authors hope to influence a future court decision. Reliance on this body of literature has been of deep concern to many legislators who fear that the judiciary indiscriminately considers "unknown, unrecognized and nonauthoritative text books, law review articles, and other writings of propaganda artists and lobbyists." 103 Cong. Rec. 16160 (1957). The author of this statement, Congressman Wright Patman, complained that the Supreme Court had turned increasingly for guidance to private publications and studies promoted by the administration. The research was designed, he said, not to study an issue objectively but to advance the particular views of private interests trying, through the medium of publication, to influence the judiciary's disposition of public-policy questions. Experts have pointed out that the members of these study committees and commissions are aware that lawyers will cite the reports in their briefs "and that the real impact of this might very well be in the decisions made by courts and administrative agencies." Id. at 16167 (Prof. Louis B. Schwartz).

The practice of citing professional journals goes back at least to Justice Brandeis in the 1920s. Other Justices, like Cardozo and Stone, adopted this technique as a way of keeping law current with changes in American society. Brandeis's opinions introduced a new meaning to the word *authority*. He believed that an opinion "derives its authority, just as law derives its existence, from all the facts of life. The judge is free to draw upon these facts wherever he can find them, if only they are helpful." Chester A. Newland, 48 Geo. L. J. 105, 140 (1959).

C. THE EXECUTIVE IN COURT

The Judiciary Act of 1789 established an Attorney General to prosecute and conduct all suits in the Supreme Court concerning the government. This office represented Congress as well as the President. Despite some ambiguity in the original statute as to whether the Attorney General was an executive officer in the same sense as the heads of the State, Treasury, and War Departments, the first Attorney General (Edmund Randolph) attended Cabinet meetings and was early identified as an administrative official.

Unlike the heads of the executive departments, who received full-time salaries, the Attorney General received a nominal sum and was expected to maintain a private practice to supplement his income. Randolph complained that he was "a sort of mongrel between the State and the U.S.; called an officer of some rank under the latter, and yet thrust out to get a livelihood in the former,—perhaps in a petty mayor's or county court." Leonard D. White, The Federalists 164–65 (1948). The staff of the Attorney General was so small that outside counsel had to be hired to conduct the government's business in court. Partly to do away with this expense, in 1870 Congress established a Justice Department and created the office of Solicitor General to assist the Attorney General. To the Solicitor General fell the primary responsibility of representing the federal government in court.

The Solicitor General

Contemporary duties of the Solicitor General are broad-ranging. After consulting agency officials, the Solicitor General conducts (or assigns and supervises) Supreme Court cases, including appeals, petitions regarding certiorari, and the preparation of briefs and arguments; authorizes or declines to authorize appeals by the federal government to appellate courts; authorizes the filing of amicus briefs by the government in all appellate courts; and may authorize intervention by the government in cases involving the constitutionality of acts of Congress (see box on next page). The Supreme Court recognizes the Solicitor General's "traditional role in conducting and controlling all Supreme Court litigation on behalf of the United States and its agencies." FEC v. NRA Political Victory Fund, 513 U.S. 88, 93 (1994).

The cases that flow through the office of Solicitor General raise complex and specialized issues, but, as a former Solicitor General remarked, the incumbent "must try to discover the social tensions, the reverberations of strife and passion, the political issues, the clashes of interest that are dressed up in technical legal forms." Simon E. Sobeloff, 41 A.B.A.J. 229, 279 (1955). To discharge that responsibility, the Solicitor General juggles several conflicting assignments. As the federal government's lawyer, the Solicitor General is an advocate but is also positioned to play a somewhat detached role. By entering only at the appellate level, the Solicitor General does not begin with the same emotional attachment as do the original parties in district court (including agency attorneys). The Solicitor General must also decide, out of a multitude of cases requested by the agencies, which ones deserve the attention of the Supreme Court.

Because of the frequency of appearances before the Supreme Court, the Solicitor General has been characterized as the Court's "ninth-and-a-half" member and serves many functions for the Court:

The Supreme Court's frequent invitation to the Solicitor General to participate as amicus in constitutional cases is one indication of his useful role. The Solicitor General and his staff have

---

Duties of Solicitor General

The following-described matters are assigned to, and shall be conducted, handled, or supervised by, the Solicitor General, in consultation with each agency or official concerned:

(a) Conducting, or assigning and supervising, all Supreme Court cases, including appeals, petitions for and in opposition to certiorari, briefs and arguments, and ... settlement thereof.

(b) Determining whether, and to what extent, appeals will be taken by the Government to all appellate courts (including petitions for rehearing *en banc* and petitions to such courts for the issuance of extraordinary writs) and ... advising on the approval of settlements of cases in which he had determined that an appeal would be taken.

(c) Determining whether a brief *amicus curiae* will be filed by the Government, or whether the Government will intervene, in any appellate court.

(d) Assisting the Attorney General, the Deputy Attorney General and the Associate Attorney General in the development of broad Department program policy.

. . .

The Solicitor General may in consultation with each agency or official concerned, authorize intervention by the Government in cases involving the constitutionality of acts of Congress.

SOURCE: 28 C.F.R. §§0.20–0.21 (2003).

---

unparalleled experience in constitutional litigation. Their access to and knowledge of the government apparatus not only enable them to inform the Court of factors unknown to private parties, but also to proffer statutory grounds for a decision avoiding the constitutional issues raised. The Solicitor General may indicate the relationship of the case to others pending on the docket, or the particular infirmities or strengths of the case for resolving constitutional or statutory issues. Knowing the Justices' proclivities, the Solicitor General may be able to offer a compromise solution that can gain a majority vote of the Court. The Supreme Court, lacking an extensive staff of its own, often benefits from the Solicitor General's impartial and sophisticated analysis of such constitutional cases. 78 Yale L. J. 1442, 1480 (1969).

The long-term and "impartial" objectives of the Solicitor General compete with, and are sometimes subordinated to, the particular and immediate needs of the President. This relationship is especially common in the field of national security. In arguing cases involving the discharge of federal employees, exclusion and deportation of aliens, and actions against conscientious objectors, Solicitors General in the past have shown little sympathy for fundamental notions of individual liberties or due process. Kathryn Mickle Werdeger, "The Solicitor General and Administrative Due Process," 36 G.W. L. Rev. 481 (1968).

Attorneys General and Solicitors General are legal officers, operating as members of the bar and officers of the court. However, they are also executive officials responsible to the President. As underscored by the actions against Japanese-Americans during World War II, Justice Department attorneys at times swallow their doubts and defend government actions that seem to them not merely unwise but unconstitutional. Under these conditions, constitutional issues are subordinated to the task of behaving as the "President's lawyers." Peter H. Irons, Justice at War 350–61 (1982). Rex Lee, Solicitor General during the Reagan administration, said that one of his duties was "to represent his client, the president of the United States. One of the ways to implement the president's policies is through positions taken in court. When I have that opportunity, I'm going to take it." 69 A.B.A.J. 734, 736 (1983). If a Solicitor General becomes too partisan, there is risk of losing the trust and confidence of the Supreme Court.

There is often friction between the Justice Department and the White House. For example, during the Carter presidency, Attorney General Bell complained about White House interference in liti-

Justice Jackson on Public Opinion

The judge who would resolve uncertainties of interpretation by conscious deference to public opinion will find new pitfalls in his path. Is there any more reliable test of prevalence of a public opinion or will than the election returns? That certainly is its legal manifestation, and I see no reason to believe that judges have better understanding of it than those the public has elected to represent them. To the extent that public opinion of the hour is admitted to the process of constitutional interpretation, the basis for judicial review of legislative action disappears. If interpretation is not to be a mere following of election returns but a legal process, the utmost deference that courts can consciously pay to political trends is a strong, but rebuttable, presumption in favor of the constitutionality of action by the political branches.

Exclude as far as humanly possible the pressures of group opinion, but let us not deceive ourselves: long-sustained public opinion does influence the process of constitutional interpretation. Each new member of the ever-changing personnel of our courts brings to his task the assumptions and accustomed thought of a later period. The practical play of the forces of politics is such that judicial power has often delayed but never permanently defeated the persistent will of a substantial majority. Judicial review in practice therefore has proved less an obstacle to majority rule than the followers of Mr. Jefferson feared and less a guaranty of the *status quo* than the followers of Mr. Hamilton hoped.

SOURCE: Vital Speeches, No. 24, Vol. XIX, at 761 (October 1, 1953).

---

gation that involved questions of church-state separation, affirmative action, and civil rights. Vice President Mondale, his aide Bert Carp, domestic adviser Stuart Eizenstat, and other White House officials treated many of these matters as broad policy questions rather than technical legal issues. In one case, after the Justice Department had taken a position on a church-state question, President Carter responded to political considerations and personally intervened to overrule the decision. Griffin B. Bell, Taking Care of the Law 24–25 (1982).

The Tide of Public Opinion

Efforts to subordinate constitutional principles to political tactics can backfire against the President. Faced with a nationwide strike in 1952, President Truman decided to attack the steel companies and work informally with the labor unions rather than invoke the Taft-Hartley Act, which he had vetoed. When that strategy failed, he seized the steel mills and claimed that he could act "for whatever is for the best of the country." Public Papers of the Presidents, 1952, at 273. Realizing that his definition of presidential authority had shocked the country because it raised questions about his power to seize even the press and the radio, he hastily explained that his powers were derived from the Constitution and that individual rights were protected. Id. at 301.

In district court, however, the Justice Department told Judge Pine that the courts had no power to constrain the President. Presidential power could be curbed only by the ballot box or impeachment. This audacious and ill-advised presentation may have provoked the judiciary to act boldly to reject a sweeping and dangerous theory of inherent executive authority (see reading on Steel Seizure Case). The political climate invited a rebuff to presidential power. As Chief Justice Rehnquist noted in 1987, the Steel Seizure Case was "one of those celebrated constitutional issues where what might be called the tide of public opinion suddenly began to run against the government, for a number of reasons, and that this tide of public opinion had a considerable influence on the Court." William H. Rehnquist, The Supreme Court 95 (1987). Justice Robert Jackson spoke perceptively about the impact of public opinion (see box).

Control Over Litigation

The Justice Department has made a concerted effort to retain exclusive control over agency litigation policy. Loss of authority to the agencies can produce an incoherent and ineffective strategy in court. Some of the legal setbacks of the New Deal can be traced to the splintering of litigating authority in the Roosevelt administration. The Justice Department had to compete with autonomous efforts by the Interior Department and other agencies. Peter H. Irons, The New Deal Lawyers (1982).

The tremendous growth of litigation since the 1930s has made decentralization inevitable. Congress has given several agencies independent litigating authority and the Justice Department regularly enters into special agreements called Memoranda of Understanding (MOUs), which allow agencies to litigate certain types of cases at the district and appellate levels. In 1994 the Supreme Court held that the Federal Election Commission did not have general statutory authority to appeal its cases to the Supreme Court. Like other agencies, it must receive the Solicitor General's authorization. (The FEC does have statutory authority to seek appeal from the Supreme Court in the specific area of presidential election funds.) FEC v. NRA Political Victory Fund, 513 U.S. 88 (1994).

Steel Seizure Case of 1952:
Oral Argument Before the District Court

On April 24, 1952, in oral argument before U.S. District Judge David A. Pine, Assistant Attorney General Holmes Baldridge presented the government's case in defense of the seizure of steel companies by Secretary of Commerce Charles Sawyer. Judge Pine's decision, declaring the seizure illegal, was later affirmed by the Supreme Court. The following excerpt of the oral argument comes from House Document No. 534 (Part I), 82d Cong., 2d Sess. (1952), pp. 362–63, 371–73.

Mr. Baldridge: Our position is that there is no power in the Courts to restrain the President and, as I say, Secretary Sawyer is the alter ego of the President and not subject to injunctive order of the Court.

The Court: If the President directs Mr. Sawyer to take you into custody, right now, and have you executed in the morning you say there is no power by which the Court may intervene even by habeas corpus?

Mr. Baldridge: If there are statutes protecting me I would have a remedy.

The Court: What statute would protect you?

Mr. Baldridge: I do not recall any at the moment.

The Court: But on the question of the deprivation of your rights you have the Fifth Amendment; that is what protects you.

I would like an answer to that—what about that?

Mr. Baldridge: Well, as I was going to point out in a little while—

The Court (interposing): I will give you a chance to think about that overnight and you may answer me tomorrow....

The Court: Now, Mr. Attorney General, it is getting near the time when we shall have to stop. I won-

der if you would give me such assistance as you can before we stop so that I can think about your viewpoint overnight, as to your power, or as to your client's power.

As I understand it, you do not assert any statutory power.

Mr. Baldridge: That is correct.

The Court: And you do not assert any express constitutional power.

Mr. Baldridge: Well, your Honor, we base the President's power on Sections 1, 2 and 3 of Article II of the Constitution, and whatever inherent, implied or residual powers may flow therefrom.

We do not propose to get into a discussion of semantics with counsel for plaintiffs. We say that when an emergency situation in this country arises that is of such importance to the entire welfare of the country that something has to be done about it and has to be done now, and there is no statutory provision for handling the matter, that it is the duty of the Executive to step in and protect the national security and the national interests. We say that Article II of the Constitution, which provides that the Executive power of the Government shall reside in the President, that he shall faithfully execute the laws of the office and he shall be Commander-in-Chief of the Army and of the Navy and that he shall take care that the laws be faithfully executed, are sufficient to permit him to meet any national emergency that might arise, be it peace time, technical war time, or actual war time.

The Court: So you contend the Executive has unlimited power in time of an emergency?

Mr. Baldridge: He has the power to take such action as is necessary to meet the emergency.

The Court: If the emergency is great, it is unlimited, is it?

Mr. Baldridge: I suppose if you carry it to its logical conclusion, that is true. But I do want to point out that there are two limitations on the Executive power. One is the ballot box and the other is impeachment.

The Court: Then, as I understand it, you claim that in time of emergency the Executive has this great power.

Mr. Baldridge: That is correct.

The Court: And that the Executive determines the emergencies and the Courts cannot even review whether it is an emergency.

Mr. Baldridge: That is correct.

D. CONGRESSIONAL DUTIES

During the nineteenth century it was not unusual for members of Congress to maintain a flourishing business in the federal courts. Daniel Webster is the most prominent example of a member of Congress with a dual career as lawyer and legislator. While serving in Congress as a Representative and a Senator, he delivered forceful arguments in major cases before the Supreme Court, which at that time was located in a chamber beneath the Senate. Congressmen supplemented their incomes by "duck[ing] into the lower chamber, so to speak, for a lucrative hour or two. After all, should not those who made laws help interpret them?" Maurice G. Baxter, Daniel Webster & the Supreme Court 31 (1966).

Although Congress depends on the Justice Department to protect its interests, members of Congress may intervene on an individual basis. In a 1926 case, involving the President's power to remove executive officials, the Supreme Court invited Senator George Wharton Pepper to serve as amicus curiae. His oral argument and an extract of his brief, together with those of the appellant and the Solicitor General, are printed immediately before the Court's opinion. Myers v. United States, 272 U.S. 52, 65–88 (1926).

During the impoundment disputes of the Nixon administration, members of Congress submitted an amicus brief on behalf of the plaintiff suing the administration. State Highway Commission of Missouri v. Volpe, 479 F.2d 1099 n.1 (8th Cir. 1973). In the abortion case eventually decided by the Supreme Court in 1980, the district court permitted Senator James L. Buckley, Senator Jesse A. Helms, and Congressman Henry J. Hyde to intervene as defendants. Harris v. McRae, 448 U.S. 297, 303 (1980). The Ninth Circuit invited both the House and the Senate to submit briefs concerning a legislative veto used by Congress in deportation cases. When the case reached the Supreme Court, both Houses of Congress intervened to protect their interests and participated before the Court during oral argument. INS v. Chadha, 462 U.S. 919 (1983). The attorneys for Congress defended the legislative veto, but in a separate brief nine members of the House of Representatives urged the Supreme Court to declare the legislative veto unconstitutional.

Legislative precedents in the House and the Senate do not permit the Speaker or the Chair to rule on questions of constitutionality. Points of order, raising the issue of unconstitutional provisions, are referred to the full chamber for decision. In the Senate, a member may raise a point of order that a bill or an amendment is legislation that changes the Constitution. If there is substantial doubt within Congress concerning the constitutionality of a provision, legislators can place within the bill a procedure authorizing expedited review by the courts. Examples include the Federal Election Campaign Act amendments of 1974. 86 Stat. 1285, §315. Two years later the Supreme Court declared the contested provision unconstitutional. Buckley v. Valeo, 424 U.S. 1 (1976). A similar procedure was placed

POLITICAL DYNAMICS OF CONSTITUTIONAL LAW

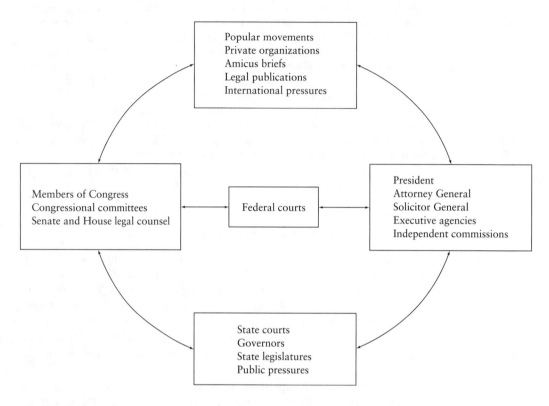

in the Gramm-Rudman-Hollings Act of 1985. 99 Stat. 1098, § 274 (1985). The provision in question was struck down a year later. Bowsher v. Synar, 478 U.S. 714 (1986).

Standing for Members

A striking development over the past decade is the frequency with which members of Congress take issues directly to the courts for resolution. Senator Edward M. Kennedy was successful at both the district court and appellate court levels in challenging Nixon's attempt to use the pocket veto during brief recesses of the House and Senate. Kennedy v. Sampson, 364 F.Supp. 1075 (D.D.C. 1973); Kennedy v. Sampson, 511 F.2d 430 (D.C. Cir. 1974). As a result of those lower court decisions, the Ford administration announced that it would use the pocket veto only during the final adjournment at the end of a Congress. 121 Cong. Rec. 41884 (1975); 122 Cong. Rec. 11202 (1976). Senator Kennedy was successful because his prerogative to vote (to override a presidential veto) had been denied by the pocket veto.

Other members of Congress have been unsuccessful when they have tried to achieve political goals from the courts that are available through the regular legislative process. In such cases the members have been told by the courts that (1) they lack standing to sue, (2) the issue is not ripe for adjudication, or (3) the matter is a "political question" to be decided by Congress and the President. Legislators must overcome the standing hurdles (faced by any litigant) by showing that (1) they have suffered injury, (2) the interests are within the zone protected by the statute or constitutional provision, (3) the injury is caused by the challenged action, and (4) the injury can be redressed by a favorable court decision. Legislators face an additional obstacle. If they suffer from an injury that can be redressed by colleagues acting through the regular legislative process, a court will instruct the lawmakers to use the institutional powers available to them.

Standing for Members

The item veto case was relatively easy for the Court to sidestep. To the extent that there was injury to Congress, it was self-administered. If surrendering some of its spending power to the President was repugnant, members of Congress had plenty of ways to recover the power: repeal the statute, add subsequent restrictions to the President's power, or write bills and committee reports in such a way that the President had fewer opportunities to cancel an item.

The item veto case was particularly weak for Congress. As the Court noted at the end of *Raines v. Byrd* (1997), Congress had not authorized Senator Byrd and his colleagues to bring the suit. In fact, both Houses of Congress had filed briefs opposing their action.

On other constitutional disputes, the President causes the injury and Congress has few or no institutional remedies. One example is the *Kennedy* pocket veto case. Because President Nixon did not return the vetoed bill to Congress, legislators had no options other than to pass the bill again and remain in session to prevent a pocket veto. Another dispute that might be litigated is the war power. Suppose Congress prohibited the President from engaging in a particular military action and the President vetoed the bill. If Congress lacked the two-thirds majority needed in each chamber to override the veto, could members bring the issue to the Court, having exhausted all legislative remedies? Without a judicial check, a President could initiate and continue a war so long as he retained a one-third plus one minority in either chamber to prevent the override. Would a court tackle that constitutional issue?

Throughout these cases, there is a general wariness on the part of judges that the controversy is really not between Congress and the executive. Rather, it is one group of legislators pitted against another. Federal judges may suspect that members of Congress turn to the courts because they have been unable to attract sufficient votes from colleagues to pass a bill. When judges believe that legislators have failed to make use of remedies available within Congress, they have been denied standing to resolve the issue in court. It was partly on that basis that the Supreme Court in 1997 denied standing to some members of Congress who had challenged the constitutionality of the Line Item Veto Act of 1996. RAINES v. BYRD, 521 U.S. 811 (1997). There may be other disputes that members of Congress could legitimately bring to court (see box).

Over the last half century, members of Congress have become concerned about the refusal of the Justice Department to defend the constitutionality of certain statutory provisions. Sometimes the Department took this position after deciding that a statute infringed on presidential power or was so patently unconstitutional that it could not be defended, as in the bill of attainder case in 1946. United States v. Lovett, 328 U.S. 303 (1946). Because of statutory language, the Attorney General must now report to Congress whenever the Justice Department does not intend to defend the constitutionality of a law passed by Congress. These reports specify the statutory provision and contain a detailed explanation by the Department for calling the provision unconstitutional.

Congress has always been able to hire private counsel to defend itself, as it did in the civil action brought against it by Congressman Adam Clayton Powell in the 1960s. Yet there was no established procedure for Congress to defend its statutes when the Justice Department chose not to do so. The institutional interests of Congress, as noted by the Senate Committee on Governmental Affairs in 1977, made it "inappropriate as a matter of principle and of the constitutional separation of powers for the legislative branch to rely upon and entrust the defense of its vital constitutional powers to the advocate for the executive branch, the Attorney General." S. Rept. No. 170, 95th Cong., 1st Sess. 11. The committee recalled that in two cases involving the power of Congress to investigate, the Justice Department withdrew its representation of Congress just as the litigation reached the Supreme Court, after having represented Congress in the district and appellate courts. Id. at 12.

As part of the Ethics in Government Act of 1978, the Senate established an Office of Senate Legal Counsel. The Senate Legal Counsel and the Deputy Legal Counsel are appointed by the President pro tempore of the Senate from among recommendations submitted by the majority and minority leaders of the Senate. The principal duty of the Counsel is to defend the Senate or a committee, subcommittee, member, officer, or employee of the Senate when directed by two-thirds of the members of the Joint Leadership Group or by the adoption of a Senate resolution. Individual Senators may initiate suits on their own. In the House of Representatives, the Office of General Counsel handles litigation that involves members, House officers, and staff.

Raines v. Byrd
521 U.S. 811 (1997)

The Line Item Veto Act of 1996 provided that any member of Congress may bring a lawsuit to challenge the constitutionality of the statute. Senator Robert C. Byrd and five other legislators sued under this provision, a district judge held that the statute violated the Constitution, and the matter was brought directly to the Supreme Court.

CHIEF JUSTICE REHNQUIST delivered the opinion of the Court.

The District Court for the District of Columbia declared the Line Item Veto Act unconstitutional. On this direct appeal, we hold that appellees lack standing to bring this suit, and therefore direct that the judgment of the District Court be vacated and the complaint dismissed....

II

Under Article III, § 2 of the Constitution, the federal courts have jurisdiction over this dispute between appellants and appellees only if it is a "case" or "controversy." This is a "bedrock requirement." ... As we said in *Simon v. Eastern Ky. Welfare Rights Organization*, 426 U.S. 26, 37 (1976), "No principle is more fundamental to the judiciary's proper role in our system of government than the constitutional limitation of federal-court jurisdiction to actual cases or controversies."

... In the light of this overriding and time-honored concern about keeping the judiciary's power within its proper constitutional sphere, we must put aside the natural urge to proceed directly to the merits of this important dispute and to "settle" it for the sake of convenience and efficiency. Instead, we must carefully inquire as to whether appellees have met their burden of establishing that their claimed injury is personal, particularized, concrete, and otherwise judicially cognizable.

III

We have never had occasion to rule on the question of legislative standing presented here. In *Powell v. McCormack*, 395 U.S. 486, 496, 512–514 (1969), we held that a Member of Congress' constitutional challenge to his exclusion from the House of Representatives (and his consequent loss of salary) presented an Article III case or controversy. But *Powell* does not help appellees. First, appellees have not been singled out for specially unfavorable treatment as opposed to other Members of their respective bodies. Their claim is that the Act causes a type of institutional injury (the diminution of legislative power), which necessarily damages all Members of Congress and both Houses of Congress equally.... Second, appellees do not claim that they have been deprived of something to which they *personally* are entitled — such as their seats as Members of Congress after their constituents had elected *them*. Rather, appellees' claim of standing is based on a loss of political power, not loss of any private right, which would make the injury more concrete. Unlike the injury claimed by Congressman Adam Clayton Powell, the injury claimed by the Members of Congress here is not claimed in any private capacity but solely because they are Members of Congress.... If one of the Members were to retire tomorrow, he would no longer have a claim; the claim would be possessed by his successor instead. The claimed injury thus runs (in a sense) with the Member's seat, a seat which the Member holds (it may quite arguably be said) as trustee for his constituents, not as a prerogative of personal power....

[The Court also distinguishes the item veto suit from an earlier case, Coleman v. Miller, 307 U.S. 433 (1939), in which the Court had upheld standing for state legislators who had claimed an institutional injury. But in this state case, twenty of Kansas' forty state senators voted not to ratify the proposed Child Labor Amendment to the Federal Constitution. With

the vote deadlocked 20 to 20, the amendment ordinarily would not have been ratified. However, the state's lieutenant governor, the presiding officer of the state senate, cast a deciding vote in favor of the amendment and it was deemed ratified. The twenty senators who had voted against the amendment, joined by a 21st senator and three state house members, filed an action to prevent ratification by the state. Senator Byrd and his colleagues could not argue that their votes on the Line Item Veto Act had not been given full effect. As the Court noted: "They simply lost that vote."]

There would be nothing irrational about a system which granted standing in these cases; some European constitutional courts operate under one or another variant of such a regime *[allowing legislators to take constitutional questions to the courts]*.... But it is obviously not the regime that has obtained under our Constitution to date. Our regime contemplates a more restricted role for Article III courts....

IV

In sum, appellees have alleged no injury to themselves as individuals (contra *Powell*), the institutional injury they allege is wholly abstract and widely dispersed (contra *Coleman*), and their attempt to litigate this dispute at this time and in this form is contrary to historical experience. We attach some importance to the fact that appellees have not been authorized to represent their respective Houses of Congress in this action, and indeed both Houses actively oppose their suit.... We also note that our conclusion neither deprives Members of Congress of an adequate remedy (since they may repeal the Act or exempt appropriations bills from its reach), nor forecloses the Act from constitutional challenge (by someone who suffers judicially cognizable injury as a result of the Act)....

JUSTICE SOUTER, concurring in the judgment, with whom JUSTICE GINSBURG joins, concurring.

. . .

JUSTICE STEVENS, dissenting.

The Line Item Veto Act purports to establish a procedure for the creation of laws that are truncated versions of bills that have been passed by the Congress and presented to the President for signature. If the procedure were valid, it would deny every Senator and every Representative any opportunity to vote for or against the truncated measure that survives the exercise of the President's cancellation authority. Because the opportunity to cast such votes is a right

guaranteed by the text of the Constitution, I think it clear that the persons who are deprived of that right by the Act have standing to challenge its constitutionality. Moreover, because the impairment of that constitutional right has an immediate impact on their official powers, in my judgment they need not wait until after the President has exercised his cancellation authority to bring suit. Finally, the same reason that the respondents have standing provides a sufficient basis for concluding that the statute is unconstitutional.

. . .

Assuming for the moment that this procedure is constitutionally permissible, and that the President will from time to time exercise the power to cancel portions of a just-enacted-law, it follows that the statute deprives every Senator and every Representative of the right to vote for or against measure that may become law. The appellees cast their challenge to the constitutionality of the Act in a slightly different way. Their complaint asserted that the Act "alter[s] the legal and practical effect of all votes they may cast on bills containing such separately vetoable items" and "divest[s] the[m] of their constitutional role in the repeal of legislation." Complaint ¶ 14. These two claimed injuries are at best the same as the injury on which I rest my analysis....

JUSTICE BREYER, dissenting.

. . .

I concede that there would be no case or controversy here were the dispute before us not truly adversary, or were it not concrete and focused. But the interests that the parties assert are genuine and opposing, and the parties are therefore truly adverse.... Moreover, as JUSTICE STEVENS points out, the harm that the plaintiffs suffer (on their view of the law) consists in part of the systematic abandonment of laws for which a majority voted, in part of the creation of other laws in violation of procedural rights which (they say) the Constitution provides them, and in part of the consequent and immediate impediment to their ability to do the job that the Constitution requires them to do....

In sum, I do not believe that the Court can find this case nonjusticiable without overruling *Coleman*. Since it does not do so, I need not decide whether the systematic nature, seriousness, and immediacy of the harm would make this dispute constitutionally justiciable even in *Coleman*'s absence. Rather, I can and would find this case justiciable on *Coleman*'s authority. I add that because the majority has decided that this dispute is not now justiciable and has expressed no view on the merits of the appeal, I shall not discuss the merits either, but reserve them for future argument.

E. JUDGE AS LAWMAKER

From the common law of England to the decisions of American courts, judge-made law has been a fact of life. Lawmaking by legislatures was a late development in our history, and one that judges opposed because of its blunt and imprecise quality. It is disingenuous to pretend that judges "find" the law rather than "make" it. Jeremiah Smith, who taught law at Harvard after a career on the New Hampshire Supreme Court, was refreshingly candid on this point. When asked "Do judges make law?" he responded: "'Course they do. Made some myself." Paul A. Freund, The Supreme Court of the United States 28 (1961). Few statutes or constitutional provisions are clear in meaning. Judicial interpretation, broadly exercised, becomes a substitute for legislation. Because judges fill in the "interstices" of law, Holmes said he recognized "without hesitation that judges do and must legislate." Southern Pacific Co. v. Jensen, 244 U.S. 205, 221 (1917).

There have been periods when judicial lawmaking became so flagrant and arbitrary that it provoked biting criticism. At the end of the nineteenth century, after legislative attempts to regulate the economy were frustrated by Supreme Court decisions, certain members of the Court condemned what they regarded as a judicial assumption of power. When the Court in 1890 decided that the judiciary, not the legislature, was the final arbiter in regulating railroad fares, freight rates, and other charges on the public, Justice Bradley's dissent considered this an arrogation of authority the Court had no right to make. Chicago, Milwaukee & St. Paul R.R. Co. v. Minnesota, 134 U.S. 418, 462–63 (1890). In the Income Tax Case of 1895, Justice White's dissent accused his brethren of amending the Constitution by judicial fiat. For more than a century the federal government and constitutional scholars had confined the definition of direct tax to capitation and land taxes. The Court decided to add a third category: the income tax. White said that the Constitution should have been amended directly rather than by the judiciary. Pollock v. Farmers' Home & Trust Col, 157 U.S. 429, 639 (1895). It took a constitutional amendment—the Sixteenth—to override the Court.

Dissenting in a 1904 case, Justice Harlan charged that the court "entrenches upon the domain of the legislative department…. It has made, not declared, law." Schick v. United States, 195 U.S. 65, 99 (1904). In an antitrust decision in 1911 he assailed the Court for converting the formula of the Sherman Act from restraint of trade to "rule of reason." Borrowing language from an earlier decision, he charged that the Court had read into the Act *by way of judicial legislation an exception that is not placed there by the lawmaking branch of the Government,* and this is to be done upon the theory that the impolicy of such legislation is so clear that it cannot be supposed Congress intended the natural import of the language it used. This *we cannot and ought not to do….*" By mere interpretation, he said, the Court had modified an act of Congress and deprived it of its force in combating monopoly practices. The most ominous part of the decision for Harlan was "the usurpation by the judicial branch of the Government of the functions of the legislative department." Standard Oil v. United States, 221 U.S. 1, 88, 99, 103 (1911).

Contemporary Issues

The judiciary plays an active legislative role by interpreting such general concepts as "equal protection" and "due process." The abortion decision of *Roe* v. *Wade* (1973) represents for many scholars a spectacular example of judicial legislation. Writing for the majority, Justice Blackmun declared that during the first three months (trimester) of pregnancy a physician, after consulting with the woman, is free to perform an abortion without interference by the state. During the second trimester, the state may regulate and even prevent abortion except where it is necessary to preserve the life or health of the mother. The state's interest expands during the third trimester. In one of the two dissents, Justice

Rehnquist said that the Court's "conscious weighing of competing factors … is far more appropriate to a legislative judgment than to a judicial one." Roe v. Wade, 410 U.S. at 173. After almost two decades of criticism, in 1992 the Court abandoned its trimester analysis. Planned Parenthood v. Casey, 505 U.S. 833 (1992).

If the weighing of competing factors constitutes an act of lawmaking, the courts do little else. Questions of federalism and the commerce power turn on the competing interests of the federal government and the states. The courts regularly balance the government's national security interests against the rights of individual freedom. The needs of law enforcement collide with the rights to privacy. A judge's decision to close a trial conflicts with the right of the press and the public to attend. The power of Congress to investigate the executive branch must be weighed against the President's privilege to withhold information.

In addition to this level of involvement, federal judges act on issues that are within the jurisdiction of Congress and could have been addressed through the regular legislative process. Justice Powell noted that much of the expanded role of the Warren Court "was a reaction to the sluggishness of the legislative branch in addressing urgent needs for reform." 62 A.B.A.J. 1454, 1455 (1976). There are other pressures on judges to legislate. If one section or provision of a statute is unconstitutional, courts may decide to "sever" that portion while retaining the balance of the statute. Such decisions require courts to judge whether the altered statute, as redesigned by the judiciary, is consistent with legislative objectives. Judicial rewriting can provoke comments from colleagues that the majority opinion erred by "simply deleting the crucial statutory language and using the words that remain as the raw materials for a new statute of his own making." Regan v. Time, Inc., 468 U.S. 641, 673 (1984). Justice Harlan once complained that the Court, in the name of interpreting the will of Congress, had resorted to "judicial surgery" to remove an offending section, so transforming the statute that the Court performed "a lobotomy." Welsh v. United States, 398 U.S. 333, 351 (1970).

F. JUDGE AS ADMINISTRATOR

Judicial lawmaking is a venerable and long-debated topic. A more contemporary issue, linked to the public-law litigation explosion, concerns judges who actually *administer* a political system to protect legal rights. Attorney General William French Smith offered this criticism in 1981:

> … federal courts have attempted to restructure entire school systems in desegregation cases— and to maintain continuing review over basic administrative decisions. They have asserted similar control over entire prison systems and public housing projects. They have restructured the employment criteria to be used by American business and government—even to the extent of mandating numerical results based upon race or gender. No area seems immune from judicial administration. At least one federal judge even attempted to administer a local sewer system. 21 Judges' Journal 4, 7 (Winter 1982).

Involvement in administrative affairs is not a totally new phenomenon for the courts. Nineteenth-century judges reviewed dismissals of federal employees, ordered administrators to carry out "ministerial" (nondiscretionary) duties, and decided questions about the liability of federal officials subjected to lawsuits. With the rise of federal regulatory commissions toward the end of the nineteenth century and the early decades of the twentieth, federal courts became involved in reviewing agency rulemaking and adjudication.

The Administrative Procedure Act (APA) of 1946 provides that any person suffering legal wrong because of agency action is entitled to judicial review. The reviewing court "shall decide all relevant questions of law, interpret constitutional and statutory provisions, and determine the meaning or applicability of the terms of any agency action." Courts shall hold unlawful and set aside agency actions found to be arbitrary, capricious, an abuse of discretion, or contrary to law; contrary to constitutional right, power, privilege, or immunity; or unsupported by substantial evidence in cases subject to formal rulemaking. Although courts often defer to agency expertise and grant a presumption of regularity in favor of the federal government, judges may also require agencies to take a "hard look" at the decisions entrusted to their jurisdiction and insist on adequate documentation to support the agency's determinations.

The breadth of judicial administration is reflected in the efforts of District Judge W. Arthur Garrity, Jr., to desegregate the Boston school system. In 1975 he placed South Boston High School in temporary receivership under a supervisor appointed by him. His ruling came after more than a decade of racial discrimination by the local school board. Barry Stuart Roberts, 12 N.E. L. Rev. 55 (1976). Another federal judge, seeking to promote school desegregation in Wilmington, Delaware, "set a tax rate for the school district, ordered state payments to the district, required new training programs for teachers and administrators, mandated specific curricular offerings, ordered the reassignment of staff and called for the development of an "appropriate human relations program'...." Terry W. Hartle, 41 Pub. Adm. Rev. 595, 599 (1981). Because of opposition from citizens and elected officials, judges gradually withdrew their involvement in school desegregation.

District Judge Frank M. Johnson, Jr., was deeply involved for more than a decade in administering certain institutions in Alabama. "The history of Alabama," he explained, "is replete with instances of state officials who could have chosen one of any number of courses to alleviate unconstitutional conditions but who chose instead to do nothing but punt the problem to the courts." Steven Brill, New York Magazine, April 26, 1976, at 38. Because of the failure of state officials to correct shocking deficiencies in state prisons, mental hospitals, and institutions for the retarded, Johnson repeatedly found violations of the Eighth and Fourteenth Amendments. He graphically described the conditions: "the evidence reflected that one resident was scalded to death when a fellow resident hosed water from one of the bath facilities on him; another died as a result of the insertion of a running water hose into his rectum by a working resident who was cleaning him; one died when soapy water was forced into his mouth; another died of a self-administered overdose of inadequately stored drugs; and authorities restrained another resident in a straightjacket for *nine years* to prevent him from sucking his hands and fingers." Frank M. Johnson, "The Constitution and the Federal District Judge," 54 Tex. L. Rev. 903 (1976).

Rather than devise specific steps to improve conditions, Johnson at first directed the state to design its own plan for upgrading the system to meet constitutional standards. After two deadlines passed without acceptable progress, Johnson intervened to define the minimal constitutional standards. The story suggests a solitary judge pitted against the state, but other parties intervened in the suit, including the Justice Department, the American Psychological Association, the American Orthopsychiatric Association, and the American Civil Liberties Union. Wyatt v. Stickney, 334 F.Supp. 1341 (M.D. Ala. 1971). Johnson was able to forge an effective alliance of state officials and private citizens to bring pressure on the legislature and the governor. A case of "judicial activism"? It is difficult to make that claim when the attorney for the state of Alabama admitted in open court that every prisoner in the state system was subjected to cruel and inhuman treatment within the meaning of the Eighth Amendment. Pugh v. Locke, 406 F.Supp. 318, 322, 329 & n.13 (M.D. Ala. 1976).

G. INDEPENDENT STATE ACTION

By interpreting their own constitutions and statutes, states can reach constitutional decisions that are markedly different from U.S. Supreme Court rulings. The federal Constitution provides only a minimum, or a floor, for the protection of individual rights and liberties. As noted by the U.S. Supreme Court, each state has the "sovereign right to adopt in its own Constitution individual liberties more expansive than those conferred by the Federal Constitution." PruneYard Shopping Center v. Robins, 447 U.S. 74, 81 (1980). When states want to express these independent views, they must make clear

A State Court Analyzes "Plain View"

In 1980 the Supreme Court of Washington held that a university police officer had exceeded his authority in seizing incriminating evidence in a student's room. The officer stopped the student who was carrying a bottle of gin and appeared to be under age. The student asked permission to return to his dormitory room to retrieve his identification card and the officer followed. From an open doorway the officer noticed what appeared to be marijuana seeds and a pipe. He entered the room, confirmed that the seeds were marijuana, and concluded that the pipe smelled of marijuana. The Supreme Court of Washington held that the evidence had been obtained illegally and could not be admitted at the trial. State v. Chrisman, 619 P.2d 971 (Wash. 1980).

The U.S. Supreme Court reversed the state court decision, holding that its "plain view" doctrine permits a law enforcement officer to seize incriminating evidence or contraband "when it is discovered in a place where the officer has a right to be." Washington v. Chrisman, 455 U.S. 1, 6 (1982). The case was returned to the state court for "further proceedings not inconsistent with this opinion."

In fact, on this next go-round the Supreme Court of Washington refused to accept the plain-view analysis offered by the U.S. Supreme Court. Whereas its 1980 decision had cited several federal decisions, this time the Supreme Court of Washington based its reasoning "solely and exclusively on the constitution and laws of the state of Washington." It concluded that it was right the first time and excluded the evidence. State v. Chrisman, 676 P.2d 419 (Wash. 1984).

---

that their rulings depend exclusively on the constitution and laws of the state. If state courts base their decisions on "bona fide separate, adequate and independent grounds," the U.S. Supreme Court will not undertake a review. Michigan v. Long, 463 U.S. 1032 (1983). Under these circumstances, the "final word" on state constitutional law rests with the states, not the U.S. Supreme Court (see box).

Many of the so-called innovations by the U.S. Supreme Court were established first at the state level. Thus, in 1914 the Court ruled that papers illegally seized by federal officers had to be excluded in federal court as evidence (the exclusionary rule). Some states had already adopted that policy. When the Court applied the exclusionary rule to all of the states in 1961, it acknowledged that states were moving increasingly in that direction anyway. Even now, the exclusionary rule leaves plenty of room for independent state action. Evidence admissible in federal court is not necessarily admissible in state court. In 1984, when the Supreme Court held that evidence resulting from a defective search warrant can be admitted if police believe they are acting in "good faith," this relaxed standard was later rejected by a number of state courts (see box in Chapter 14, Section E).

State independence is also strengthened by more explicit language in their constitutions. Although the Supreme Court has accepted the use of public funds for sectarian schools to pay for such expenses as transportation and textbooks, many state courts have denied this type of assistance because of highly restrictive language in their constitutions that prohibits the appropriation of public funds for any religious worship or instruction (see box in Chapter 12, Section D). Similarly, state constitutions are often far more explicit in protecting the rights of speech, assembly, and privacy. By interpreting this language, state courts can issue rulings that depart dramatically from U.S. Supreme Court doctrines. Independent constitutional interpretations by the states can satisfy the values we place on diversity, pluralism, representative government, and a distrust of centralized authority.

By participating in ballot initiatives in state elections, citizens regularly offer judgments on sensitive and controversial constitutional issues. In the state of Washington, voters in 1997 rejected a measure to legalize the medical use of marijuana, rejected a law requiring trigger locks on handguns and safety courses for owners, and rejected a proposal that barred job discrimination based on sexual orientation. Voters in Houston, Texas, rejected a measure to repeal affirmative action. Citizens in Or-ange County, California, supported a local school board's decision to drop bilingual education. The New York Times, November 11, 1997, at A28. In 1998, voters in California supported Proposition 227, which is designed to abolish bilingual education after no more than a year of intensive immersion in English. In a ballot initiative in 2000, California voters limited marriage to the union between man and woman, thereby excluding gay couples. In 2006, Arizonans rejected a similar amendment to their constitution. The issue of gay marriages returned to California in 2008, possibly pitting the courts against the voters.

H. WHO HAS THE "LAST WORD"?

The notion that the Constitution is somehow equivalent to Supreme Court decisions is a curious product of the twentieth century. One searches previous periods in vain for evidence that the judiciary enjoyed a monopoly on constitutional law. Nevertheless, students in undergraduate, graduate, and law schools are taught that the Court announces the "last word" on what the Constitution means. In 1992 Chief Justice Rehnquist wrote: "We rightly think of our courts as the final voice in the interpretation of our Constitution, and therefore tend to think of constitutional law in terms of cases decided by the courts." William H. Rehnquist, Grand Inquests 278 (1992). Law courses concentrate almost exclusively on case law, rather than exploring the complex (and far more interesting) process that involves the three branches of the national government, the states, and the general public.

This book develops the theme of coordinate construction—the opportunity for all three branches to interpret and shape the Constitution. That process is heavily influenced by pressures brought to bear by the public and organized interest groups, as well as by leadership and initiatives from state governments. The courts are an important element, but not the only one, in maintaining a constitutional order. Throughout this book there are many examples that explain the dynamic, open process of constitutional interpretation, which is constantly shaped by a combination of judicial and nonjudicial forces. If private organizations find the courts unreceptive to their arguments, they will turn to executive and legislative bodies, either at the federal or the state level.

The constitutionality of the Sedition Act of 1798 was never determined by the courts. Instead, it was decided by the people in the national elections of 1800, which drove the Federalist party out of office and into oblivion. President Jefferson called the Sedition Act a "nullity" and pardoned every person prosecuted under it (see box on next page). He believed that prosecution for seditious libel could be done only by the states, not the federal government. Later, Congress pronounced the statute "unconstitutional, null, and void," and appropriated funds to reimburse those who had been subjected to fines (see reading). The Supreme Court later acknowledged that the Sedition Act was struck down not by a court of law but by "the court of history." New York Times Co. v. Sullivan, 376 U.S. 254, 276 (1964).

President Andrew Jackson, who inherited some of the Jeffersonian distrust toward the judiciary, disagreed sharply with John Marshall on both personal and policy grounds. Every public officer, he said in 1832, took an oath to support the Constitution "as he understands it, and not as it is understood by others." The opinion of judges "has no more authority over Congress than the opinion of Congress has over the judges, and on that point the President is independent of both" (reading by Jackson). However, Jackson appreciated the value of judicial independence. He saw the courts as natural allies in his fight against the Nullifiers, who wanted to release the states from judgments of federal courts. Richard P. Longaker, 71 Pol. Sci. Q. 341, 358–61 (1956). Jackson's theory of the President's independent duty to interpret the Constitution provoked a sharp debate in the Senate (see reading).

In 1857, the Supreme Court held that Dred Scott (and all other black slaves and their descendants) was not a citizen of the United States or of Missouri. Chief Justice Taney refused to allow contemporary social beliefs to change the meaning of the constitution by making blacks citizens. Taney also

Jefferson and the Sedition Act

... I discharged every person under punishment or prosecution under the sedition law, because I considered, and now consider, that law to be a nullity, as absolute and as palpable as if Congress had ordered us to fall down and worship a golden image; and that it was as much my duty to arrest its execution in every stage, as it would have been to have rescued from the fiery furnace those who should have been cast into it for refusing to worship the image. It was accordingly done in every instance, without asking what the offenders had done, or against whom they had offended, but whether the pains they were suffering were inflicted under the pretended sedition law. (Jefferson to Mrs. John Adams, July 22, 1804).

You seem to think it devolved on the judges to decide on the validity of the sedition law. But nothing in the Constitution has given them a right to decide for the Executive, more than to the Executive to decide for them. Both magistrates are equally independent in the sphere of action assigned to them. The judges, believing the law constitutional, had a right to pass a sentence of fine and imprisonment; because the power was placed in their hands by the Constitution. But the executive, believing the law to be unconstitutional, were bound to remit the execution of it; because that power has been confided to them by the Constitution. That instrument meant that its co-ordinate branches should be checks on each other. But the opinion which gives to the judges the right to decide what laws are constitutional, and what not, not only for themselves in their own sphere of action, but for the legislature and executive also, in their spheres, would make the judiciary a despotic branch.... (Jefferson to Mrs. Adams, September 11, 1804).

ruled that Congress was without power to prevent the spread of slavery to the territories in the West. Dred Scott v. Sandford, 19 How. 393 (1857). During debates in a Senate race a year later, Abraham Lincoln repudiated the larger policy questions decided by the Court (see reading). In his first inaugural address, Lincoln acknowledged that Supreme Court rulings are binding on the parties to a suit and are "entitled to very high respect and consideration in all parallel cases by all other departments of the government." At the same time, he said that "if the policy of the Government upon vital questions affecting the whole people is to be irrevocably fixed by decisions of the Supreme Court, the instant they are made in ordinary litigation between parties in personal actions the people will have ceased to be their own rulers, having to that extent practically resigned their Government into the hands of that eminent tribunal."

These exchanges and volleys between the Court and the political system continue in our time. For example, during the 1970s and early 1980s, it appeared that courts were sympathetic to the arguments of those who were pro-choice on the issue of abortion. Consequently, the pro-choice community concentrated on litigation while the pro-life group appealed to the legislatures, the President, and governors. By the end of the 1980s, as a result of appointments by Presidents Nixon, Ford, Reagan, and Bush, the Supreme Court indicated that it would give less protection to the interests sought by the pro-choice organizations. Consequently, they now turned to Congress for support. On June 27, 1991, the National Abortion Rights Action League (NARAL) sent a "Supreme Court Alert" to its membership, calling attention to the abortion restrictions being enacted in the states and through regulations issued by the Bush administration. NARAL, which had relied on the courts in the past, now stated: "Clearly Congress is our Court of Last Resort. All hopes of protecting our constitutional right to choose depends upon our elected representatives in Congress responding to the will of the American people." The American Civil Liberties Union, which had also depended heavily on litigation, sounded a similar theme: "Congress is increasingly asked to look at these [constitutional] issues because there is nobody else. It is now the court of last resort." W. John Moore, "In Whose Court?," National Journal, Oct. 5, 1991, at 2400. The question "who shall interpret" the Constitution is explored in the final reading by Walter F. Murphy.

Congress Responds to the Sedition Act

The Federalists passed the Alien and Sedition Acts of 1798 to silence domestic opponents of governmental policy. Thomas Jefferson regarded the Sedition Act as unconstitutional, although federal judges did not find it so. After his election as President in 1800, he used his executive authority to discharge whoever had been punished or prosecuted under the Sedition Act. In 1840 Congress passed a private bill to reimburse the heirs of Matthew Lyon, who had been prosecuted under the Sedition Act (6 Stat. 802, c. 45). The committee report accompanying the bill stated that the Sedition Act was "unconstitutional, null, and void" (H. Rept. No. 86, 26th Cong., 1st Sess.).

That in the month of October, 1798, the late Matthew Lyon, the father of the petitioners, at the circuit court held at Rutland, in the State of Vermont, was indicted and found guilty of having printed and published what was alleged to be a libel against Mr. John Adams, the then President of the United States. The alleged libel was in the following words, to wit: "As to the Executive, when I shall see the effects of that power bent on the promotion of the comfort, the happiness, and accommodation of the people, that Executive shall have my zealous and uniform support. But whenever I shall, on the part of our Executive, see every consideration of public welfare swallowed up in a continual grasp for power, in an unbounded thirst for ridiculous pomp, foolish adulation, and selfish avarice—when I shall behold men of real merit daily turned out of office for no other cause than independency of sentiment—when I shall see men of firmness, merit, years, abilities, and experience, discarded in their applications for office, for fear they possess that independence, and men of meanness preferred for the ease with which they can take up and advocate opinions, the consequence of which they know but little of— when I shall see the sacred name of religion employed as a State engine to make mankind hate and persecute each other, I shall not be their humble advocate!" The second count in the indictment, on which the said Matthew Lyon was convicted, charged him with printing and publishing a seditious writing or libel, entitled "Copy of a letter from an American diplomatic character in France (Mr. Joel Barlow) to a member of Congress in Philadelphia," which was in the following words, to wit: "The misunderstanding between the two Governments has become extremely alarming; confidence is completely destroyed; mistrusts, jealousies, and a disposition to a wrong attribution of motives, are so apparent as to require the utmost caution in every word and action that are to come from your Executive—I mean if your object is to avoid hostilities. Had this truth been understood with you before the recall of Monroe—before the coming and second coming of Pinckney; had it guided the pens that wrote the bullying speech of your President, and stupid answer of your Senate, at the opening of Congress in November last, I should probably have had no occasion to address you this letter. But when we found him borrowing the language of Edmund Burke, and telling the world that, although he should succeed in treating with the French, there was no dependence to be placed in any of their engagements; that their religion and morality were at an end, and they had turned pirates and plunderers, and that it would be necessary to be perpetually armed against them, though you are at peace; we wondered that the answer of both Houses had not been an order to send him to the mad-house. Instead of this, the Senate have echoed the speech with more servility than ever George the Third experienced from either House of Parliament."

The court deemed both the publications above recited libellous, under the 2d section of the act commonly called the sedition law, passed the 4th July, 1798; which section is as follows, viz:"*And be it further enacted.* That if any person shall write, print, utter, or publish, or shall cause or procure to be written, printed, uttered, or published, or shall knowingly and wilfully assist or aid in writing, printing, uttering, or publishing, any false, scandalous, and malicious writing or writings, against the Government of the United States, or either House of the Congress of the United States, or of the President of the United States, with an intent to defame the said Government, or either House of the said Congress, or the President, or to bring them, or either of them, into contempt or disrespect, or to excite against them, or either or any of them, the hatred of the good people of the United States, &c., then such person, being thereof convicted before any court of the United States having jurisdiction thereof, shall be punished by a fine not exceeding two thousand dollars, and by imprisonment not exceeding two years."

Upon this indictment Matthew Lyon was convicted, and sentenced by the court to be imprisoned for four months; to pay a fine of one thousand dollars, and the costs of the prosecution, taxed at sixty dollars and ninety-six cents; and to stand committed until the fine and costs were paid: which were paid, as appears by the exemplification of the record of the said trial and proceedings, now in the archives of this House.

The committee are of opinion that the law above recited was unconstitutional, null, and void, passed under a mistaken exercise of undelegated power, and that the mistake ought to be corrected by returning the fine so obtained, with interest thereon, to the legal representatives of Matthew Lyon.

The committee do not deem it necessary to discuss at length the character of that law, or to assign all the reasons, however demonstrative, that have induced the conviction of its unconstitutionality. No question connected with the liberty of the press ever excited a more universal and intense interest — ever received so acute, able, long-continued, and elaborate investigation — was ever more generally understood, or so conclusively settled by the concurring opinions of all parties, after the heated political contests of the day had passed away. All that now remains to be done by the representatives of a people who condemned this act of their agents as unauthorized, and transcending their grant of power, to place beyond question, doubt, or cavil, that mandate of the constitution prohibiting Congress from abridging the liberty of the press, and to discharge an honest, just, moral, and honorable obligation, is to refund from the Treasury the fine thus illegally and wrongfully obtained from one of their citizens: for which purpose the committee herewith report a bill.

Jackson's Veto of the Bank Bill

President Andrew Jackson received a bill in 1832 to renew the Bank of the United States. Although the bill had been passed by Congress, and the constitutionality of the Bank had been upheld by the Supreme Court in *McCulloch* v. *Maryland* (1819), Jackson exercised his veto. His veto message of July 10, 1832, explains the independence of the President in determining constitutional questions notwithstanding the judgments reached by the legislative and judicial branches.

To the Senate:
The bill "to modify and continue" the act entitled "An act to incorporate the subscribers to the Bank of the United States" was presented to me on the 4th July instant. Having considered it with that solemn regard to the principles of the Constitution which the day was calculated to inspire, and come to the conclusion that it ought not to become a law, I herewith return it to the Senate, in which it originated, with my objections.

A bank of the United States is in many respects convenient for the Government and useful to the people. Entertaining this opinion, and deeply impressed with the belief that some of the powers and privileges possessed by the existing bank are unauthorized by the Constitution, subversive of the rights of the States, and dangerous to the liberties of the people, I felt it my duty at an early period of my Administration to call the attention of Congress to the practicability of organizing an institution combining all its advantages and obviating these objections.

I sincerely regret that in the act before me I can perceive none of those modifications of the bank charter which are necessary, in my opinion, to make it compatible with justice, with sound policy, or with the Constitution of our country.

[*Jackson states his objections that various features of the bill grant monopoly and exclusive privileges to the rich at the expense of the poor. He also regarded the Bank as injurious to the states.*]

It is maintained by the advocates of the bank that its constitutionality in all its features ought to be considered as settled by precedent and by the decision of the Supreme Court. To this conclusion I can not assent. Mere precedent is a dangerous source of authority, and should not be regarded as deciding questions of constitutional power except where the acquiescence of the people and the States can be considered as well settled. So far from this being the case on this subject, an argument against the bank might be based on precedent. One Congress, in 1791, decided in favor of a bank; another, in 1811, decided against it. One Congress, in 1815, decided against a bank; another, in 1816, decided in its favor.

SOURCE: The full veto message appears in 3 Messages and Papers of the Presidents 1139–43 (Richardson ed.)

Prior to the present Congress, therefore, the precedents drawn from that source were equal. If we resort to the States, the expressions of legislative, judicial, and executive opinions against the bank have been probably to those in its favor as 4 to 1. There is nothing in precedent, therefore, which, if its authority were admitted, ought to weigh in favor of the act before me.

If the opinion of the Supreme Court covered the whole ground of this act, it ought not to control the coordinate authorities of this Government. The Congress, the Executive, and the Court, must each for itself be guided by its own opinion of the Constitution. Each public officer who takes an oath to support the Constitution swears that he will support it as he understands it, and not as it is understood by others. It is as much the duty of the House of Representatives, of the Senate, and of the President to decide upon the constitutionality of any bill or resolution which may be presented to them for passage or approval as it is of the supreme judges when it may be brought before them for judicial decision. The opinion of the judges has no more authority over Congress than the opinion of Congress has over the judges, and on that point the President is independent of both. The authority of the Supreme Court must not, therefore, be permitted to control the Congress or the Executive when acting in their legislative capacities, but to have only such influence as the force of their reasoning may deserve.

. . .

The Senate Debates Jackson's Veto Message

President Jackson's veto of the Bank of the United States reached the Senate on July 10, 1832. Before sustaining the veto, the Senate engaged in a major debate on the substantive reasons given by Jackson in opposing the Bank. Several Senators also concentrated on the legitimacy of the veto itself. Did the President have the power to veto a proposal that had been previously passed by Congress, signed by a President (Madison), and upheld by the Supreme Court (in *McCulloch* v. *Maryland*)? Senator Daniel Webster argued that Jackson had no such right. Senator Hugh Lawson White strongly defended Jackson's action.

[*Senator Webster:*] Does the President, then, reject the authority of all precedent, except what is suitable to his own purposes to use? And does he use, without stint or measure, all precedents which may augment his own power, or gratify his wishes? But if the President thinks lightly of the authority of Congress, in construing the constitution, he thinks still more lightly of the authority of the Supreme Court. He asserts a right of individual judgment on constitutional questions, which is totally inconsistent with any proper administration of the Government, or any regular execution of the laws. Social disorder, entire uncertainty in regard to individual rights and individual duties, the cessation of legal authority, confusion, the dissolution of free Government — all these are the inevitable consequences of the principles adopted by the message, whenever they shall be carried to their full extent. Hitherto it has been thought that the final decision of constitutional questions belonged to the supreme judicial tribunal.

SOURCE: *Congressional Debates,* 22nd Cong. 1st Sess. 1231–44 (1832).

The very nature of free Government, it has been supposed, enjoins this: and our constitution, moreover, has been understood so to provide, clearly and expressly. It is true that each branch of the Legislature has an undoubted right, in the exercise of its functions, to consider the constitutionality of a law proposed to be passed. This is naturally a part of its duty, and neither branch can be compelled to pass any law, or do any other act, which it deems to be beyond the reach of its constitutional power. The President has the same right when a bill is presented for his approval; for he is, doubtless, bound to consider, in all cases, whether such bill be compatible with the constitution, and whether he can approve it consistently with his oath of office. But when a law has been passed by Congress, and approved by the President, it is now no longer in the power, either of the same President, or his successors, to say whether the law is constitutional or not. He is not at liberty to disregard it: he is not at liberty to feel or to affect "constitutional scruples," and to sit in judgment himself on the validity of a statute of the Government, and to nullify it if he so chooses. After a law has passed through all the requisite forms: after it has received the requisite legislative sanction and the Executive approval, the question of its constitutionality then becomes a judicial question, and a judicial question alone. In the courts, that question may be raised, argued, and adjudged; it can be adjudged nowhere else.

. . .

[*Senator White:*] The honorable Senator argues that the constitution has constituted the Supreme Court a tribunal to decide great constitutional questions, such as this, and that, when they have done so, the question is put at rest, and every other department of the Government must acquiesce. This doctrine I deny. The constitution vests "the judicial power in a Supreme Court, and in such inferior courts as Congress may from time to time ordain and establish." Whenever a suit is commenced and prosecuted in the courts of the United States, of which they have jurisdiction, and such suit is decided by the Supreme Court, as that is the court of the last resort, its decision is final and conclusive between the parties. But as an authority, it does not bind either the Congress or the President of the United States. If either of these co-ordinate departments is afterwards called upon to perform an official act, and conscientiously believe the performance of that act will be a violation of the constitution, they are not bound to perform it, but, on the con-trary, are as much at liberty to decline acting, as if no such decision had been made. In examining the extent of their constitutional power, the opinion of so enlightened a tribunal as our Supreme Court has been, and I hope ever will be, will always be entitled to great weight; and, without doubt, either Congress or the President would always be disposed, in a doubtful case, to think its decisions correct; but I hope neither will ever view them as authority binding upon them. They ought to examine the extent of their constitutional powers for themselves; and when they have had access to all sources of information within their reach, and given to every thing its due weight, if they are satisfied the constitution has not given a power to do the act required, I insist they ought to refrain from doing it.

… Each coordinate department, within its appropriate sphere of action, must judge of its own powers, when called upon to do its official duties; and if either blindly follows the others, without forming an opinion for itself, an essential check against the exercise of unconstitutional power is destroyed. A mistake by Congress in passing an act, inconsistent with the constitution, followed by a like mistake by the Supreme Court, in deciding such act to be constitutional, might be attended with the most fatal consequences. Let each department judge for itself, and we are safe. If different interpretations are put upon the constitution by the different departments, the people is the tribunal to settle the dispute.…

Lincoln's Critique of *Dred Scott*

On July 17, 1858, at Springfield, Illinois, Abraham Lincoln responded to the Supreme Court's decision in *Dred Scott* v. *Sandford* (1857). At the same time, he rejected the defense of that decision by his opponent for the U.S. Senate, Stephen A. Douglas. Lincoln carefully identified the portion of the decision he regarded as legally binding. He considered major parts of the decision a nullity, to be left to political resolution outside the courts.

Does Judge Douglas, when he says that several of the past years of his life have been devoted to the question of "popular sovereignty," and that all the remainder of his life shall be devoted to it, does he mean to say that he has been devoting his life to securing to the people of the territories the right to exclude slavery from the territories? If he means so to say, he means to deceive; because he and every one knows that the decision of the Supreme Court, which he approves and makes especial ground of attack upon me for disapproving, forbids the people of a territory to exclude slavery. This covers the whole ground, from the settlement of a territory till it reaches the degree of maturity entitling it to form a State Constitution. So far as all that ground is concerned, the Judge is not sustaining popular sovereignty, but absolutely opposing it.…

Now, as to the Dred Scott decision; for upon that he makes his last point at me. He boldly takes ground in favor of that decision.

This is one-half the onslaught, and one-third of the entire plan of the campaign. I am opposed to that decision in a certain sense, but not in the sense which he puts on it. I say that in so far as it decided in favor of Dred Scott's master and against Dred Scott and his family, I do not propose to disturb or resist the decision.

I never have proposed to do any such thing. I think, that in respect for judicial authority, my humble history would not suffer in a comparison with that of Judge Douglas. He would have the citizen conform his vote to that decision; the Member of Congress, his; the President, his use of the veto power. He would make it a rule of political action for the people and all the departments of the government. I would not. By resisting it as a political rule, I disturb no right of property, create no disorder, excite no mobs.

. . .

... I shall read from a letter written by Mr. Jefferson in 1820.... It seems he had been presented by a gentleman of the name of Jarvis with a book, or essay, or periodical, called the "Republican," and he was writing in acknowledgement of the present, and noting some of its contents. After expressing the hope that the work will produce a favorable effect upon the minds of the young, he proceeds to say:

"That it will have this tendency may be expected, and for that reason I feel an urgency to note what I deem an error in it, the more requiring notice as your opinion is strengthened by that of many others. You seem in pages 84 and 148, to consider the judges as the ultimate arbiters of all constitutional questions — a very dangerous doctrine indeed and one which would place us under the despotism of an oligarchy. Our judges are as honest as other men, and not more so. They have, with others, the same passions for party, for power, and the privilege of their corps. Their maxim is, "boni judicis est ampliare jurisdictionem'; and their power is the more dangerous as they are in office for life, and not responsible, as the other functionaries are, to the elective control. The Constitution has erected no such single tribunal, knowing that to whatever hands confided, with the corruptions of time and party, its members would become despots. It has more wisely made all

the departments co-equal and co-sovereign within themselves."

Thus we see the power claimed for the Supreme Court by Judge Douglas, Mr. Jefferson holds, would reduce us to the despotism of an oligarchy.

Now, I have said no more than this — in fact, never quite so much as this — at least I am sustained by Mr. Jefferson.

. . .

One more thing. Last night Judge Douglas tormented himself with horrors about my disposition to make negroes perfectly equal with white men in social and political relations. He did not stop to show that I have said any such thing, or that it legitimately follows from any thing I have said, but he rushes on with his assertions. I adhere to the Declaration of Independence. If Judge Douglas and his friends are not willing to stand by it, let them come up and amend it. Let them make it read that all men are created equal except negroes. Let us have it decided, whether the Declaration of Independence, in this blessed year of 1858, shall be thus amended.

. . .

My declarations upon this subject of negro slavery may be misrepresented, but can not be misunderstood. I have said that I do not understand the Declaration to mean that all men were created equal in all respects. They are not our equal in color; but I suppose that it does mean to declare that all men are equal in some respects; they are equal in their right to "life, liberty, and the pursuit of happiness." Certainly the negro is not our equal in color — perhaps not in many other respects; still, in the right to put into his mouth the bread that his own hands have earned, he is the equal of every other man, white or black. In pointing out that more has been given you, you can not be justified in taking away the little which has been given him. All I ask for the negro is that if you do not like him, let him alone. If God gave him but little, that little let him enjoy.

Walter F. Murphy
Who Shall Interpret?

So entrenched is the belief that the U.S. Supreme Court is the ultimate interpreter of the Constitution that the independent contributions of the other branches and the states are largely overlooked in the legal literature. In this essay, political scientist Walter Murphy explores the tradition of departmentalism: the responsibility of all three branches to interpret and apply the Constitution.

I. INTRODUCTION

... It is a fact of American political life that all public officials, from presidents to local police, often have to interpret the Constitution. Every public official takes an oath to uphold the Constitution, and the terms of the constitutional document are often broad. Deciding what policies government may legitimately pursue, whether to enact, sign, veto, or enforce a law, all create problems of interpretation. Even if one believes judges are the ultimate constitutional interpreters, government cannot halt and await a judicial decision whenever a constitutional problem arises.

The oath is also one that millions of private citizens have taken, and the Preamble lodges responsibility for the Constitution in "the people of the United States." Thus, it is fair for "the people," as its ultimate source of authority, to have an interpretive role. Indeed, one can plausibly argue, they have the duty, when they vote or utilize other means to influence public policy, to judge candidates' records and promises about constitutional interpretation.

. . .

II. WHO SHALL INTERPRET THE CONSTITUTION?

The plain words of the document contain several different messages about WHO shall interpret. In conferring on Congress authority to make "all laws necessary and proper" to carry out powers delegated to the national government, Article I, Sec. 8, clearly implies that Congress (with the participation of the president since he is part of the legislative process) shall make judgments about the Constitution's meaning, for what laws are "proper" under the Constitution are sometimes far from manifest. There are similar terms in the Thirteenth, Fourteenth, Fif-

teenth, Nineteenth, Twenty-third, Twenty-fourth, and Twenty-sixth amendments.

In requiring the president to "preserve, protect, and defend the Constitution," Article II adds to his interpretive responsibilities. He could hardly fulfill those tasks without interpreting the Constitution to determine if it was being threatened or how to protect it....

The logic of institutional history as well as the words of the constitutional document also enmesh judges in constitutional interpretation. By extending "the judicial power" "to all cases, in law and equity, arising under this Constitution," Article III commands courts to participate in the interpretive process, as judges before and since John Marshall have modestly conceded.

But there is not a word in these clauses about whose views should prevail if the branches disagree....

III. WHO IS THE AUTHORITATIVE INTERPRETER: THREE COMPETING THEORIES

Three principal theories claim to produce an answer to the question of WHO is the ultimate interpreter: judicial supremacy, legislative supremacy, and departmentalism. All, however, draw heavily on democratic theory; and much of the debate rests on the possibility of an appeal to "the people," though never so directly as in Jefferson's plan for national conventions.

A. Judicial Supremacy

Judicial supremacy is the most familiar theory. Its usual justification rests on the textual and functional grounds Marshall used in *Marbury v. Madison* (1803) for judicial review: (1) Article VI says the Constitution is law; (2) "it is emphatically the province and duty of the judicial department to say what the law is"; and thus (3) judicial review must be an integral part of the political system. Then follows a long step from judicial review—the authority of a court, when deciding cases, to refuse to give force to an act of a coordinate branch of govern-

---

Source: Walter F. Murphy, "Who Shall Interpret? The Quest for the Ultimate Constitutional Interpreter," 48 Review of Politics 401 (1986).

ment—to judicial supremacy, the obligation of co-ordinate officials not only to obey that ruling but to follow its reasoning in future deliberations....

On the other hand: (1) no constitutional text "expressly confine[s]" interpretation to the judiciary; (2) judicial review says nothing about the obligation of other branches of government to obey a court's decision or follow its reasoning; ...

B. Legislative Supremacy

Systematic assertions of legislative supremacy in constitutional interpretation have been infrequent, though they have at times been vigorously pushed, as after the Civil War when the Radical Republicans dominated Congress, impeached the president, and curbed the Court. Early on, some Jeffersonians had also pressed for congressional supremacy. Caesar Rodney of Delaware wrote in 1803: "Judicial supremacy may be made to bow before the strong arm of Legislative authority. We shall discover who is master of the ship." Threats of impeachment so frightened John Marshall that he was ready to modify judicial review:

[T]he modern doctrine of impeachment should yield to an appellate jurisdiction in the legislature. A reversal of those legal opinions deemed unsound by the legislature would certainly better comport with the mildness of our character than a removal of the Judge who has rendered them unknowing of his fault.

This proposal has been several times revised—usually with the appellate jurisdiction resting in the Senate alone—but, of course, has never been adopted.

At bottom, any claim that congressional interpretation should prevail over judicial rests on legislators' connections to the people....

On the other hand, constitutionalism is wary of arguments that allow popularly elected officials final authority to define substantive rights....

C. Departmentalism

No president has ever pressed a claim to su-premacy in constitutional interpretation. On the other hand, some presidents, like many legislators, have asserted equality.

Madison's position shifted as he faced various crises, but in the early days of the Republic he was clearly a departmentalist. His theory of allowing different social interests to dominate particular institutions and of pitting ambition against ambition and power against power pushes toward stalemates that can only be overcome by compromise, not adjudication. As he told the First Congress:

There is not one Government ... in the United States, in which provision is made for a particular authority to determine the limits of the constitutional division of power between the branches of the Government. In all systems, there are points which must be adjusted by the departments themselves, to which no one of them is competent.

. . .

V. CONCLUSION

The question of WHO shall interpret poses one of the fundamental problems with which any coherent constitutional theory must come to grips. The sort of analysis suggested here transforms the question from one that yields a universally applicable response, into a more complex set of queries about degrees of deference one institution owes another under varying circumstances. What emerges is a modified version of departmentalism.

. . .

There is a magnetic attraction to the notion of an ultimate constitutional interpreter, just as there is a magnetic pull to the idea of some passkey to constitutional interpretation that will, if properly turned, always open the door to truth, justice, and the American way. But finality, as Disraeli reminded us, "is not the language of politics." James Madison would have agreed.

NOTES AND QUESTIONS

1. Assume it is true, as Justice Robert H. Jackson observed in a speech on October 1, 1953 (fifth box in this chapter), that "long-sustained public opinion does influence the process of constitutional interpretation." Assume, as well, that Chief Justice Rehnquist was correct in his observation that the "tide of public opinion" had exerted "considerable influence" on the Court's ruling in the Steel Seizure Case. Do you think the Court should take account of public opinion in its deliberations? If so, how should the Court discern the state of public opinion? What are the implications of this interpretive approach for constitutional government?

2. Should majoritarian preferences outweigh minority rights? Does judicial consideration of public opinion promote republican values? Is it a desirable approach? Consider Justice Jackson's criticism: "To the extent that public opinion of the hour is admitted to the process of constitutional interpretation, the basis for judicial review of legislative action disappears."

3. On what basis did Thomas Jefferson and Abraham Lincoln subscribe to the doctrine of coordinate construction? What do you consider to be the strengths and weaknesses of their reasoning? How would you respond to Jefferson's warning of judicial supremacy: "[If the Supreme Court is the ultimate arbiter,] the constitution ... is a mere thing of wax in the hands of the judiciary, which they may twist and shape into any form they please."

4. If each of the three branches has the "right" and authority to interpret the constitution, who has the "last word"?

5. After the terrorist attacks of 9/11, Congress enacted some restrictions, such as prohibitions against torture. Should Presidents in their statements signing the bill be able to indicate that they may ignore the statutory language by relying on "inherent" powers available in Article II?

SELECTED READINGS

BAKER, NANCY. Conflicting Loyalties: Law and Politics in the Attorney General's Office, 1789–1990. Lawrence, Kansas: University Press of Kansas, 1992.

BALL, HOWARD. Courts and Politics: The Federal Judicial System. Englewood Cliffs, N.J.: Prentice-Hall, 1980.

BAMBURGER, MICHAEL A. Reckless Legislation: How Lawmakers Ignore the Constitution. New Brunswick, N.J.: Rutgers University Press, 2000.

CAMPBELL, TOM. Separation of Powers in Practice. Stanford, Cal.: Stanford University Press, 2004.

CAPLAN, LINCOLN. The Tenth Justice: The Solicitor General and the Rule of Law. New York: Knopf, 1987.

CHAYES, ABRAM. "The Role of the Judge in Public Law Litigation." 89 Harvard Law Review 1281 (1976).

CLAYTON, CORNELL W. The Politics of Justice: The Attorney General and the Making of Legal Policy. New York: M. E. Sharpe, Inc., 1992.

COOPER, PHILLIP J. Hard Judicial Choices: Federal District Court Judges and State and Local Officials. New York: Oxford University Press, 1988.

DEVINS, NEAL. Shaping Constitutional Values: Elected Government, the Supreme Court, and the Abortion Debate. Baltimore, Md.: Johns Hopkins University Press, 1996.

———, ed. Elected Branch Influences in Constitutional Decisionmaking, 56 Law & Contemporary. Problems (Autumn 1993).

——— and LOUIS FISHER. The Democratic Constitution. New York: Oxford University Press, 2004.

EPSTEIN, LEE. Conservatives in Court. Knoxville: University of Tennessee Press, 1985.

FISHER, LOUIS. "Social Influences on Constitutional Law." 15 Journal of Political Science 7 (1987).

———. "Constitutional Interpretation by Members of Congress." 63 North Carolina Law Review 707 (1985).

———. "Is the Solicitor General an Executive or a Judicial Agent? Caplan's Tenth Justice," 15 Law & Social Inquiry 305 (1990).

———. "The Judge as Manager," The Public Manager, Fall 1996, pp. 7–10.

———. Constitutional Dialogues: Interpretation as Political Process. Princeton, N.J.: Princeton University Press, 1988.

FISHER, LOUIS AND NEAL DEVINS. Political Dynamics of Constitutional Law. St. Paul, Minn.: Thomson-West Publishing, 4th ed. 2006.

GINGER, ANN FAGAN. "Litigation as a Form of Political Action." 9 Wayne Law Review 458 (1963).

GRIFFITH, J. A. G. The Politics of the Judiciary. Glasgow: Fontana Press, 1985.

HARRIMAN, LINDA, AND JEFFREY D. STRAUSSMAN. "Do Judges Determine Budget Decisions? Federal Court Decisions in Prison Reform and State Spending for Corrections." 43 Public Administration Review 343 (1983).

HODDER-WILLIAMS, RICHARD. The Politics of the U.S. Supreme Court. London: George Allen & Unwin, 1980.

KMIEC, DOUGLAS W. The Attorney General's Lawyer: Inside the Meese Justice Department. New York: Praeger, 1992.

LASSER, WILLIAM. The Limits of Judicial Power: The Supreme Court in American Politics. Chapel Hill: University of North Carolina Press, 1988.

LATHAM, EARL. "The Supreme Court as a Political Institution." 31 Minnesota Law Review 205 (1947).
MURPHY, WALTER, AND C. HERMAN PRITCHETT, eds.
Courts, Judges, and Politics. New York: Random
House, 2002.
NEIER, ARYEH. Only Judgment: The Limits of Litiga-
tion in Social Change. Middletown, Conn.: Wes-
leyan University Press, 1982.
O'BRIEN, DAVID M. Storm Center: The Supreme Court
in American Politics. New York: Norton, 1986.
O'CONNOR, KAREN, AND LEE EPSTEIN. "Amicus Cu-
riae Participation in U.S. Supreme Court Litiga-
tion: An Appraisal of Hakman's "Forklore."" 16 Law
and Society Review 311 (1981-1982).
PELTASON, JACK. Federal Courts in the Political
Process. New York: Random House, 1955.

PICKERILL, J. MITCHEL. Constitutional Deliberation
in Congress. Durham, N.C.: Duke University
Press, 2004.
ROSENBLUM, VICTOR G. Law as a Political Instrument.
New York: Random House, 1955.
SALOKAR, REBECCA MAE. The Solicitor General: The
Politics of Law. Philadelphia: Temple University
Press, 1992.
VOSE, CLEMENT E. Caucasians Only: The Supreme
Court, the NAACP, and the Restrictive Covenant
Cases. Berkeley: University of California Press,
1959.
WHITTINGTON, KEITH E. Constitutional Construc-
tion: Divided Powers and Constitutional Mean-
ing. Cambridge, Mass.: Harvard University Press,
1999.

2

The Doctrine of Judicial Review

Judicial review in America survives a number of nagging, unanswered questions. By what right do life-tenured judges invalidate policies adopted by popularly elected officials? If judicial review is of such crucial importance in safeguarding a written constitution, why did the framers omit it? Why is it based on implied, rather than explicit, power? If judicial review is essential to protect constitutional freedoms, how do other democratic nations survive without it?

At some point, judicial review assumes the characteristics of lawmaking. Constitutional interpretation is more than a technical exercise or display of judicial erudition. The power to interpret the law is the power to make the law. Judicial review can be another name for judicial legislation. As Bishop Hoadly announced in 1717: "Whoever hath an absolute authority to interpret any written or spoken laws, it is he who is truly the lawgiver, to all intents and purposes, and not the person who first wrote or spoke them." James Bradley Thayer, 7 Harv. L. Rev. 129, 152 (1893).

Judicial review includes many activities. Courts may overturn a government action, find support for it, or refuse to rule at all. Judicial review applies to Congress, the chief executive, administrative agencies, state legislatures, and rulings of state courts. Although the holding of the Supreme Court is of utmost importance, it often serves as but one stage of an ongoing constitutional process shared with lower courts, the executive branch, the legislature, and the general public.

A. SOURCES OF JUDICIAL REVIEW AUTHORITY

When the chief executive or legislators make unpopular decisions, the voters may jettison them at the next election. The ballot box represents a periodic test of the legitimacy of elected officers, a reaffirmation of authority they are quite happy to cite. The federal judiciary, however, cannot draw legitimacy from elections. When judges announce an unpopular decision, citizens want to know on what authority courts may overturn the judgments of elected officials who also take an oath to uphold the Constitution. Judges must be able to cite persuasive and authoritative sources: constitutional language, pre-*Marbury* precedents, principles announced by the Marshall Court, or convincing evidence that has accumulated since that time.

Constitutional Language

Article III, Section 1, of the Constitution provides that "The judicial Power of the United States, shall be vested in one Supreme Court, and in such inferior Courts as the Congress may from time to time ordain and establish." Section 2 extends the judicial power to various cases and controversies, but there is no specific grant of power to declare an act of Congress, the President, or state government unconstitutional. The absence of an explicit grant is not conclusive. An implied power may exist. For example, although the Constitution provides no authority for the President to assert executive privilege, remove appointees from office, issue executive orders with the force of law, or enter into international agreements without the advice and consent of the Senate, the Supreme Court has considered those powers implicit in Article II.[1] Similarly, the Court has found an implied power for Congress to investigate, issue subpoenas, and exercise the power of contempt.[2]

The power of judicial review might be drawn from three sources. First, courts need judicial review to strike down actions by the elected branches that threaten judicial independence. For example, suppose that Congress passed legislation that reduced the salary of judges, in direct violation of Article III, Section 1, which provides that federal judges shall receive a compensation "which shall not be diminished during their Continuance in Office." Invalidating such statutes would be consistent with the system of checks and balances that encourages each branch to fight off encroachments.

Second, under Article III, Section 2, the judicial power extends to all cases *"arising under this Constitution,* the Laws of the United States, and Treaties made" (emphasis added). In most of the early drafts of the Constitution, the language *arising under* applied only to laws passed by Congress. When William Samuel Johnson moved to insert the words *this Constitution and the* before the word *Laws,* James Madison objected, stating that he "doubted whether it was not going too far to extend the jurisdiction of the Court generally to cases arising Under the Constitution, & whether it ought to be limited to cases of a Judiciary Nature. The right of expounding the Constitution in cases of this nature ought not to be given to that Department." Johnson's motion was agreed to without further discussion, "it being generally supposed that the jurisdiction given was constructively limited to cases of a Judiciary nature." 2 Farrand 430.

An intriguing bit of legislative history, but what did the framers mean by cases of a "judiciary nature"? However defined, evidently it was something less than full-blown judicial review. At the Virginia ratifying convention, Madison interpreted "arising under" to justify judicial review only against the states. 3 Elliot 532. Alexander Hamilton made the same point in Federalist No. 80. Under these readings, the purpose of judicial review was to control the states and protect federalism. It was not intended to control Congress and the President.

Third, the power of judicial review might be drawn from the Supremacy Clause in Article VI, which provides that the Constitution, federal laws "made in Pursuance thereof," and all treaties shall be the supreme law of the land, and "the Judges in every State shall be bound thereby, any Thing in the Constitution or Laws of any State to the Contrary notwithstanding." At a minimum, the Supremacy Clause requires federal courts to review the actions of state governments. It might also invite review of congressional statutes that are not "in pursuance" of the Constitution. However, judicial review over the coequal branches of Congress and the President represents a major leap and demands greater evidence. Justice Holmes once remarked: "I do not think the United States would come to an end if [the Supreme Court] lost [its] power to declare an act of Congress void. I do think the Union would be imperiled if we could not make that declaration as to the laws of the several States." Collected Legal Papers 295–96 (1920).

The Pre-*Marbury* Precedents

Several precedents for judicial review, established in the years before *Marbury,* prepared the way for Marshall's famous statement in 1803 that it is "emphatically the province and duty of the judicial department to say what the law is." Marbury v. Madison, 5 U.S. (1 Cr.) 137, 177 (1803). British efforts in the 1760s to reestablish control over America provoked accusations by colonists that the laws of Parliament had violated the "common law" and the "law of reason" and were therefore void. Those

---

1. United States v. Nixon, 418 U.S. 683 (1974) (executive privilege); Myers v. United States, 272 U.S. 52 (1926) (removal power); Contractors Ass'n of Eastern Pa. v. Secretary of Labor, 442 F.2d 159 (3d Cir. 1971), cert. denied, 404 U.S. 854 (1971) (executive orders); and Dames & Moore v. Regan, 453 U.S. 654 (1981) (executive agreements).

2. McGrain v. Daugherty, 273 U.S. 135 (1927) (investigations); Eastland v. United States Servicemen's Fund, 421 U.S. 491, 505 (1975) (subpoenas); Anderson v. Dunn, 19 U.S. (6 Wheat.) 204, 228 (1821) (contempt power).

James Otis and Fundamental Law

This writ is against the fundamental principles of law. The privilege of the House. A man who is quiet, is as secure in his house, as a prince in his castle — notwithstanding all his debts and civil processes of any kind. But —

For flagrant crimes and in cases of great public necessity, the privilege may be infringed on. For felonies an officer may break, upon process and oath, that is, by a special warrant to search such a house, sworn to be suspected, and good grounds of suspicion appearing....

As to Acts of Parliament. An act against the Constitution is void; an act against natural equity is void; and if an act of Parliament should be made, in the very words of this petition, it would be void. The executive Courts must pass such acts in disuse.

SOURCE: The Works of John Adams (Charles Francis Adams, ed.), Vol. II, pp. 521–22. See also pp. 523–25.

---

arguments became important ingredients in the case presented to a "candid world" in the Declaration of Independence.

The best-known American challenge to an act of Parliament came in 1761 when James Otis argued the writs of assistance case in Boston. He claimed that British customs officials were not empowered by Parliament to use general search warrants. Even if Parliament had authorized the writs of assistance, Otis said that the statute would be "against the Constitution," "against natural equity," and therefore void (see box). In 1766 a Virginia court held the Stamp Act unconstitutional. On the eve of the Declaration of Independence, a Massachusetts judge instructed the jury to treat acts of Parliament that violated fundamental law as "void" and "inoperative." Edward S. Corwin, The Doctrine of Judicial Review 32 (1914).

The proposition that courts could void an act of Parliament appears in an opinion by Chief Justice Coke in 1610. He said that when an act of Parliament "is against common right and reason, or repugnant, or impossible to be performed, the common law will controul it, and adjudge such Act to be void." Dr. Bonham's Case, 77 Eng. Rep. 646, 652. A few British judges in the seventeenth and eighteenth centuries cited Coke's argument, but the principle of judicial review never took root on English soil. Day v. Savadge, 80 Eng. Rep. 235, 237 (1614); The City of London v. Wood, 88 Eng. Rep. 1592, 1602 (1702). In 1884 the Supreme Court noted: "notwithstanding what was attributed to Lord Coke in *Bonham's Case* ... the omnipotence of Parliament over the common law was absolute, even against common right and reason." Hurtado v. California, 110 U.S. 516, 531 (1884).

For their understanding of British law the framers relied mainly on Blackstone's *Commentaries,* which states the case for parliamentary supremacy with singular clarity. For those who believed that acts of Parliament contrary to reason were void, he offered this advice:

But if the parliament will positively enact a thing to be done which is unreasonable, I know of no power that can control it: and the examples usually alleged in support of this sense of the rule do none of them prove, that, where the main object of a statute is unreasonable, the judges are at liberty to reject it; for that were to set the judicial power above that of the legislature, which would be subversive of all government. Blackstone, Commentaries, Book One, § 3, at 91 (Oxford 1775).

Although *Dr. Bonham's Case* provides inadequate support for the American concept of judicial review, it was accepted as good law and precedent by those who wanted to break with England. Intellectual justifications were needed to neutralize the appearance of impetuous and impulsive behavior by the American colonists. However, "voiding" the acts of Parliament did not automatically deliver the power of judicial review to American courts, especially those at the national level.

From independence to the framing of the Constitution, some of the state judges challenged the acts of their legislatures. Although scholars disagree on the strength of those precedents, decisions providing support for the theory of judicial review were handed down by judges in Virginia, New Jersey, New York, Connecticut, Rhode Island, and North Carolina. The language used by judges in holding state laws invalid was often more bold than the results they achieved. Charles Grove Haines, The American Doctrine of Judicial Supremacy 88–120 (1932).

B. THE FRAMERS' INTENT

By the time of the convention, some of the framers expected judicial review to be part of the new government. In reading their statements at the convention and during the ratification debates, it is important to keep their thoughts in context and recognize conflicting statements. The framers did not have a clear or fully developed theory of judicial review.

The framers wanted to replace the Articles of Confederation to make the central government more effective, resolve disputes among the states over legal and monetary systems, and limit legislative abuses. Each goal depended on the structure and power of the federal judiciary. Instead of the legislative supremacy that prevailed under the Articles of Confederation, the new Congress would be only one of three coordinate and coequal branches. Both the Virginia Plan, presented by Edmund Randolph, and the New Jersey Plan, advocated by William Paterson, called for the creation of an independent judiciary headed by a Supreme Court. Although the new judicial article left undecided such questions as whether to create lower federal courts or rely solely on state courts, it did grant broad authority to the Supreme Court.

The framers were worried that 13 sets of state courts would announce contradictory rulings on matters of national concern. In Federalist No. 80, Alexander Hamilton said that 13 independent courts of final jurisdiction "over the same causes, arising upon the same laws, is a hydra in government from which nothing but contradiction and confusion can proceed." The convention responded to that problem by adopting the Supremacy Clause. Judicial review over presidential and congressional actions, however, was a subject of much greater delicacy. By 1787 the framers had become alarmed about legislative overreaching. In Federalist No. 48, James Madison wrote that the "legislative department is everywhere extending the sphere of its activity and drawing all power into its impetuous vortex." Several delegates to the Philadelphia Convention expressed the same concern. 1 Farrand 254 (Wilson) and 2 Farrand 35 (Madison), 110 (Madison), and 288 (Mercer). However, giving the courts the final say over congressional acts was an extremely radical notion.

A common pastime of constitutional scholars is counting the heads of framers who favored judicial review. Depending on which year he wrote, Edward S. Corwin vacillated on the statistics, ranging from a high of 17 framers to a low of five or six. Leonard D. Levy, ed., Judicial Review and the Supreme Court 3–4 (1967). Corwin uttered this scholar's lament in 1937 when he testified on the court-packing plan: "These people who say the framers intended [judicial review] are talking nonsense; and the people who say they did not intend it are talking nonsense. There is evidence on both sides." Senate Committee on the Judiciary, "Reorganization of the Federal Judiciary" (Part 2), 75th Cong., 1st Sess. 176 (1937). Other studies on the judiciary were flavored by a crusading spirit, designed either to "prove" the legitimacy of judicial review or to chop away at its foundations.[3] The issue remains unsettled; this very ambiguity adds some constraint to judicial activism.

---

3. For support of judicial review, see Charles A. Beard, The Supreme Court and the Constitution (1912), and Raoul Berger, Congress v. The Supreme Court (1969). Critics include Louis B. Boudin, Government by Judiciary (1932), and William W. Crosskey, Politics and the Constitution (1953).

Council of Revision

Judicial review was discussed at the convention as a means of checking Congress and the states. The most important debate was over the veto of legislation passed by Congress. Randolph proposed a Council of Revision consisting of the "Executive and a convenient number of the National Judiciary ... with authority to examine every act of the National Legislature before it shall operate, & every act of a particular Legislature before a Negative thereon shall be final; and that the dissent of the said Council shall amount to a rejection, unless the Act of the National Legislature be again passed...." 1 Farrand 21. Some commentators accept the elimination of the revisionary council as proof that the framers rejected judicial review. However, one of the arguments against the Council was the *availability* of judicial review. As reported by Madison: "Mr. Gerry doubts whether the Judiciary ought to form a part of it, as they will have a sufficient check agst. encroachments on their own department by their exposition of the laws, which involved a power of deciding on their Constitutionality. In some States the Judges had <actually> set aside laws as being agst. the Constitution. This was done too with general approbation." Id. at 97. Here is a clue of judicial review being exercised in cases of a "judiciary nature." The Court needed power to strike down congressional legislation that threatened the integrity or existence of the judiciary. Rufus King supported Gerry's argument after observing that the Justices of the Supreme Court "ought to be able to expound the law as it should come before them, free from the bias of having participated in its formation." This comment provides broader support for judicial review, whereas Gerry appeared to restrict it to legislative encroachments.

Congress Vetoing State Legislation

After debating a congressional veto over proposed state legislation, that idea was rejected for two reasons. The addition of the Supremacy Clause would presumably handle any conflicts between national law and state legislation. Moreover, the state courts could exercise judicial review to control legislative excesses. They "would not consider as valid any law contravening the Authority of the Union," and if such laws were not set aside by the judiciary they "may be repealed by a Nationl. law." 2 Farrand 27–28 (Sherman and Morris). Madison later said that a law "violating a constitution established by the people themselves, would be considered by the Judges as null & void." Id. at 93. These statements were clearly limited to judicial review at the *state,* not the national, level. A year later, writing to Thomas Jefferson, Madison denied that the Constitution empowered the Court to strike down acts of Congress (see box on next page). His comments support fluidity, not finality.

James Wilson, soon to be a member of the Supreme Court, defended the concept of judicial review at the Pennsylvania ratification convention. He said the legislature would be "kept within its prescribed bounds" by the judiciary. 2 Elliot 445. At the Connecticut ratifying convention, Oliver Ellsworth (destined to be the third Chief Justice of the Supreme Court) expected federal judges to void any legislative acts that were contrary to the Constitution. Id. at 196; see also Samuel Adams's comments in Massachusetts, id. at 131. At the Virginia ratifying convention, John Marshall anticipated that the federal judiciary would strike down unconstitutional legislative acts. Id. at 553; see also George Nicholas, id. at 443. The context of these remarks suggests that the availability of judicial review was used to reassure the states that national power would be held in check.

Federalists and Anti-Federalists

The *Federalist Papers* include several essays that speak strongly for judicial review. The principal essay, Hamilton's Federalist No. 78 (see reading), is designed partly to allay state fears about the power of the central government. The Antifederalists, as expressed in Letter XI of Brutus, worried that judicial

---

James Madison on Judicial Review

A revisionary power [by the Council of Revision] is meant as a check to precipitate, to unjust, and to unconstitutional laws. These important ends would it is conceded be more effectually secured, without disarming the Legislature of its requisite authority, by requiring bills to be separately communicated to the Exec. & Judic'y depts. If either of these object, let ⅔, if both ¾ of each House be necessary to overrule the objection; and if either or both protest agst a bill as violating the Constitution, let it moreover be suspended notwithstanding the overruling proportion of the [legislative] Assembly, until there shall have been a subsequent election of the [House of Deputies] and a re-passage of the bill by ⅔ or ¾ of both Houses as the case may be. It sd not be allowed the Judges or [the] Executive to pronounce a law thus enacted unconstitu'l & invalid.

In the State Constitutions & indeed in the Fed'l one also, no provision is made for the case of a disagreement in expounding them; and as the Courts are generally the last in making [the] decision, it results to them by refusing or not refusing to execute a law, to stamp it with its final character. This makes the Judiciary Dept paramount in fact to the Legislature, which was never intended and can never be proper.

SOURCE: 5 Writings of James Madison 294 (Hunt ed. 1904).

---

review at the national level would weaken the powers of the states, Congress, and the President. Any errors committed by federal courts could not be "corrected by any power above them, if any such power there be." From the decisions of federal courts there appeared to be "no appeal." How could Congress set aside a judgment if those courts "are authorized by the constitution to decide in the last resort"? The impeachment power, Brutus argued, would be an unlikely check on judicial errors. Herbert J. Storing, ed., The Anti-Federalist 163-65 (1985 ed.).

Hamilton's effort to rebut these concerns, in Federalist No. 78, were later borrowed by John Marshall to buttress his *Marbury* opinion. Hamilton's enthusiasm is somewhat suspect; he appears to have been a late convert to the cause of judicial review. His plan of government presented to the 1787 convention did not grant this power to the judiciary. 1 Farrand 282–93, 302–11; 3 Farrand 617–30. State laws contrary to the Constitution would be "utterly void," but the judiciary is not identified as the voiding agency. 1 Farrand 293.

The New Government

In the years between ratification and *Marbury* v. *Madison,* the issue of judicial review was debated often in Congress, but not with any consistency. When Madison introduced the Bill of Rights in the House of Representatives, he predicted that once they were incorporated into the Constitution, "independent tribunals of justice will consider themselves in a peculiar manner the guardians of those rights; they will be an impenetrable bulwark against every assumption of power in the Legislative or Executive." 1 Annals of Congress 439 (June 8, 1789). But nine days later, during debate on the President's removal power, Madison denied that Congress should defer to the courts on this constitutional issue. He begged to know on what principle could it be contended "that any one department draws from the Constitution greater powers than another, in marking out the limits of the powers of the several departments?" If questions arose on the boundaries between the branches, he did not see "that any one of these independent departments has more right than another to declare their sentiments on that point." Id. at 500 (June 17, 1789). In 1791, when proponents of a national bank cited judicial review as a possible check on unconstitutional legislation, Madison was unpersuaded and voted against the bank. 3 Annals of Congress 1978–79 (February 4, 1791).

Alexander Hamilton Federalist No. 78

We proceed now to an examination of the judiciary department of the proposed government.

In unfolding the defects of the existing Confederation, the utility and necessity of a federal judicature have been clearly pointed out....

Whoever attentively considers the different departments of power must perceive, that, in a government in which they are separated from each other, the judiciary, from the nature of its functions, will always be the least dangerous to the political rights of the Constitution; because it will be least in a capacity to annoy or injure them. The Executive not only dispenses the honors, but holds the sword of the community. The legislature not only commands the purse, but prescribes the rules by which the duties and rights of every citizen are to be regulated. The judiciary, on the contrary, has no influence over either the sword or the purse; no direction either of the strength or of the wealth of the society; and can take no active resolution whatever. It may truly be said to have neither FORCE nor WILL, but merely judgment; and must ultimately depend upon the aid of the executive arm even for the efficacy of its judgments....

The complete independence of the courts of justice is peculiarly essential in a limited Constitution. By a limited Constitution, I understand one which contains certain specified exceptions to the legislative authority; such, for instance, as that it shall pass no bills of attainder, no *ex-post-facto* laws, and the like. Limitations of this kind can be preserved in practice no other way than through the medium of courts of justice, whose duty it must be to declare all acts contrary to the manifest tenor of the Constitution void. Without this, all the reservations of particular rights or privileges would amount to nothing.

Some perplexity respecting the rights of the courts to pronounce legislative acts void, because contrary to the constitution, has arisen from an imagination that the doctrine would imply a superiority of the judiciary to the legislative power. It is urged that the authority which can declare the acts of another void, must necessarily be superior to the one whose acts may be declared void. As this doctrine is of great importance in all the American constitutions, a brief discussion of the ground on which it rests cannot be unacceptable.

There is no position which depends on clearer principles, than that every act of a delegated authority, contrary to the tenor of the commission under which it is exercised, is void. No legislative act, therefore, contrary to the Constitution, can be valid. To deny this, would be to affirm, that the deputy is greater than his principal; that the servant is above his master; that the representatives of the people are superior to the people themselves; that men acting by virtue of powers, may do not only what their powers do not authorize, but what they forbid.

If it be said that the legislative body are themselves the constitutional judges of their own powers, and that the construction they put upon them is conclusive upon the other departments, it may be answered, that this cannot be the natural presumption, where it is not to be collected from any particular provisions in the Constitution. It is not otherwise to be supposed, that the Constitution could intend to enable the representatives of the people to substitute their *will* to that of their constituents. It is far more rational to suppose, that the courts were designed to be an intermediate body between the people and the legislature, in order, among other things, to keep the latter within the limits assigned to their authority. The interpretation of the laws is the proper and peculiar province of the courts. A constitution is, in fact, and must be regarded by the judges, as a fundamental law. It therefore belongs to them to ascertain its meaning, as well as the meaning of any particular act proceeding from the legislative body. If there should happen to be an irreconcilable variance between the two, that which has the superior obligation and validity ought, of course, to be preferred; or, in other words, the Constitution ought to be preferred to the statute, the intention of the people to the intention of their agents.

Nor does this conclusion by any means suppose a superiority of the judicial to the legislative power. It only supposes that the power of the people is superior to both; and that where the will of the legislature, declared in its statutes, stands in opposition to that of the people, declared in the Constitution, the judges ought to be governed by the latter rather than the former. They ought to regulate their decisions by the fundamental laws, rather than by those which are not fundamental....

This independence of the judges is equally requisite to guard the Constitution and the rights of individuals from the effects of those ill humors, which the arts of designing men, or the influence of particular conjunctures, sometimes disseminate among the people themselves, and which, though they speedily give place to better information, and more deliberate reflection, have a tendency, in the meantime, to occasion dangerous innovations in the government, and serious oppressions of the minor party in the community.

Supreme Court Justices Inquire: May We Void a Legislative Act?

JUSTICE CHASE. Without giving an opinion, at this time whether this Court has jurisdiction to decide that any law made by Congress, contrary to the Constitution of the *United States* is void; I am fully satisfied that this court has no *jurisdiction* to determine that any law of any state *Legislature,* contrary to the Constitution of such *state,* is void....

I am under a necessity to give a *construction,* or explanation of the words, *"ex post facto law,"* because they have not any certain meaning attached to them. But I will not go farther than I feel myself bound to do; and if I ever exercise the jurisdiction I will not decide *any law to be void, but in a very clear case.*

JUSTICE IREDELL. If any act of Congress, or of the Legislature of a state, violates those constitutional provisions, it is unquestionably void; though, I admit, that as the authority to declare it void is of delicate and awful nature, the Court will never resort to that authority, but in a clear and urgent case.

SOURCE: Calder v. Bull, 3 Dall. 386, 392, 395, 399 (1798).

C. THE ROAD TO *MARBURY*

Federal courts reviewed both national and state legislation prior to the 1803 decision *Marbury.* In 1792, three circuit courts held divergent views on an act of Congress that appointed federal judges to serve as commissioners for claims settlement. Their decisions could be set aside by the Secretary of War. One of the courts agreed to serve. The other two believed that the statute was "unwarranted" because it required federal judges to perform nonjudicial duties and to render what was essentially an advisory(instead of binding) opinion. The Supreme Court postponed decision until the next term; by that time Congress had repealed the offending sections and removed the Secretary's authority to veto decisions rendered by judges. Hayburn's Case, 2 Dall. 409 (1792). See 1 Stat. 243 (1792) and 1 Stat. 324 (1793). In 1794, a year after Congress repaired the statute, the Supreme Court decided that the original statute would have been unconstitutional if it sought to place nonjudicial powers on the circuit courts. United States v. Yale Todd, 13 How. 52 (1794). The use of this case (not published until 1851) as a precedent for judicial review is rendered suspect by the fact that the statutory provision no longer existed.

Between 1791 and 1799, federal courts began to challenge and strike down a number of state laws. 1 Charles Warren, The Supreme Court in United States History 65–69 (1937). With regard to national legislation, in 1796 the Supreme Court *upheld* a congressional statute that imposed a tax on carriages. If the Court had authority to uphold an act of Congress, presumably it had authority to strike one down. Justice Chase said it was unnecessary"*at this time,* for me to determine, whether this court, *constitutionally* possesses the power to declare an act of Congress *void* ... but if the court have such power, I am free to declare, that I will never exercise it, *but in a very clear case."* Hylton v. United States, 3 Dall. 171, 175 (1796)(emphasis in original). Two years later the Court upheld the constitutionality of another congressional act, this time involving the process of constitutional amendment. Hollingsworth v. Virginia, 3 Dall. 378 (1798).

Three other cases between 1795 and 1800 explored the authority of federal judges to declare state acts unconstitutional. In the first case, a circuit court decided that a Pennsylvania law was unconstitutional and void. Vanhorne's Lessee v. Dorrance, 2 Dall. 304 (1795). In 1798, Supreme Court Justices offered differing views on the existence and scope of judicial review (see box). In the third case, Justice Chase said that even if it were agreed that a statute contrary to the Constitution would be void, "it still remains a question, where the power resides to declare it void?" The "general opinion," he said, is that the Supreme Court could declare an act of Congress unconstitutional, "but there is no adjudication of the Supreme Court itself upon the point." Cooper v. Telfair, 4 Dall. 14, 19 (1800).

From 1789 to 1802, eleven state judiciaries exercised judicial review over state statutes. Charles Grove Haines, The American Doctrine of Judicial Supremacy, at 148–64. The assertion of power by the national judiciary against coequal branches was much more cautious, and yet even the Jeffersonian Republicans rebuked the federal courts for not striking down the repressive Alien and Sedition Acts of 1798. 1 Warren, The Supreme Court in United States History, at 215. In that same year Jefferson looked to the courts to protect basic rights: "the laws of the land, administered by upright judges, would protect you from any exercise of power unauthorized by the Constitution of the United States." 10 Writings of Thomas Jefferson 61 (Memorial ed. 1903).

Marshall Court Foundations

By 1801 the Supreme Court had yet to solidify its powers. It had upheld the constitutionality of a congressional statute. In a series of dicta, it gingerly explored the theory that it could hold one unconstitutional. In four bold decisions from 1803 to 1821, the Court held that it had the power to determine the constitutionality of statutes passed by Congress and state legislatures, as well as authority to review judgments by state courts in cases raising federal questions.

The election of 1800 marked a pivotal point for the nation. Although formally neutral between Britain and France, America split into two warring camps. The Federalist party was pro-British; the Jeffersonian Republicans sympathized with the French. Efforts by the Adams administration to limit Republican criticism led to the Alien and Sedition Acts, further exacerbating partisan strife. When the Jeffersonians swept the elections of 1800, the Federalists looked for ways to salvage their dwindling political power.

Early in 1801, with a few weeks remaining for the Federalist Congress, two bills were passed to create a number of federal judges and justices of the peace in the District of Columbia. 2 Stat. 89, 103 (1801). Within a matter of days, President John Adams nominated Federalists to the new posts, much to the outrage of Republicans. John Marshall was at that point serving as Secretary of State, although he had already been appointed to the Supreme Court for the next term. The commissions of office were processed, sent to the Senate, and confirmed. Some of the commissions, William Marbury's among them, were never delivered.

In taking office as President, Thomas Jefferson ordered that the commissions be withheld. The administration also urged Congress to repeal the Circuit Court Act (with its additional judgeships) and to block the anticipated 1802 term of the Supreme Court. Congress complied. 2 Stat. 132, 156 (1802). Partisan bitterness increased in the spring of 1801 when two Federalist judges instructed a district attorney to prosecute a newspaper that had published an attack on the judiciary. The jury refused to indict, but the Republicans saw this as additional evidence that the Federalists were engaged in a national conspiracy.[4] As part of a counterattack, the House of Representatives impeached District Judge John Pickering (a Federalist) and the Senate removed him. Congress contemplated the removal of Justice Samuel Chase from the Supreme Court and seemed poised to remove other Federalist judges, including John Marshall.

In this tense political climate, William Marbury and his colleagues appealed to the former Attorney General, Charles Lee, for legal assistance. Lee brought the action directly to the Supreme Court under Section 13 of the Judiciary Act of 1789, which empowered the Court to issue writs of mandamus "in cases warranted by the principles and usages of law, to any courts appointed, or persons holding office, under the authority of the United States." Lee argued that the Court had jurisdiction under Section 13 because Madison was a person holding office (Secretary of State) under the authority

---

4. George Lee Haskins and Herbert A. Johnson, 2 History of the Supreme Court of the United States: Foundations of Power: John Marshall 161–62 (1981).

of the United States. He asked the Court to issue a writ of mandamus, ordering Madison to deliver the commissions.

Marshall's options were circumscribed by one overpowering fact: whatever technical ground he might use to rule against the administration, any order directing Madison to deliver the commissions was sure to be ignored. If the Court's order could be dismissed with impunity, the judiciary's power and prestige would suffer greatly. As Chief Justice Burger noted: "The Court could stand hard blows, but not ridicule, and the ale house would rock with hilarious laughter" had Marshall issued a mandamus ignored by Jefferson.[5] Marshall chose a tactic he used in future years. He would appear to absorb a short-term defeat in exchange for a long-term victory. The decision has been called "a masterwork of indirection, a brilliant example of Marshall's capacity to sidestep danger while seeking to court it, to advance in one direction while his opponents are looking in another." Robert G. McCloskey, The American Supreme Court 40 (1960).

The opinion acknowledged the merits of Marbury's case but denied that the Court had power to issue the mandamus. Through a strained reading, Marshall concluded that Section 13 expanded the original jurisdiction of the Court and thereby violated Article III of the Constitution. He maintained that Congress could alter the boundaries only of appellate jurisdiction and that if a statute conflicted with the Constitution it was the duty of judges, who took an oath to support the Constitution, to strike down the offending law. MARBURY v. MADISON, 5 U.S. (1 Cr.) 137 (1803).

The decision in *Marbury* has stimulated a number of critiques. Marshall's analysis of original and appellate jurisdiction is less than compelling. He could have read Section 13 to connect mandamus action to appellate jurisdiction. Even if he related it to original jurisdiction, the Constitution did not explicitly prohibit Congress from adding to original jurisdiction. Furthermore, if the Court did indeed lack jurisdiction, why did Marshall reach further and explore the merits of Marbury's claim and expound on novel questions of judicial authority? Finally, given his previous involvement in the matter, there were strong grounds for Marshall to disqualify himself (see reading by Van Alstyne).

Encircled by hostile political forces, Marshall decided to strike boldly for judicial independence. Instead of citing historical and legal precedents, all of which could have been challenged and picked apart by his opponents, Marshall reached to a higher plane and grounded his case on what appeared to be self-evident, universal principles. His decision seems to march logically and inexorably toward the only possible conclusion. *Marbury* v. *Madison* is famous for the proposition that the Court is supreme on constitutional questions, but it stands for a much more modest claim. Chief Justice Marshall stated that it is "emphatically the province and duty of the judicial department to say what the law is." 5 U.S. (1 Cr.) 137, 177 (1803). So it is, but the same can be said for Congress. Surely it is the province and duty of Congress to say what the law is. The Court in 1803 lacked the power to dictate to Congress or to the President.

Did Marshall believe that the Court was supreme on questions of constitutionality? Probably not. His behavior during the impeachment hearings of Judge Pickering and Justice Chase suggest that he was quite willing to share constitutional interpretations with the coequal branches. *Marbury* was issued on February 24, 1803. The House impeached Pickering on March 2, 1803, and the Senate convicted him on March 12, 1804. As soon as the House had impeached Pickering, it turned its guns on Chase. Under these precarious circumstances, Marshall wrote to Chase on January 23, 1805, suggesting that members of Congress did not have to impeach judges whenever they objected to their judicial opinions. Instead, Congress could simply review and reverse objectionable decisions through the legislative process. Marshall's letter to Chase is somewhat ambiguous. He could have been referring to reversals of statutory interpretation, not constitutional interpretation, but given the temper of the times the latter seems more likely (see box on next page).

---

5. Warren E. Burger, "The Doctrine of Judicial Review: Mr. Marshall, Mr. Jefferson, and Mr. Marbury," in Mark W. Cannon and David M. O'Brien, eds., Views From the Bench 14 (1985).

Marshall Writes to Chase

Jan. 23, 1805

My dear Sir

. . .

Admitting it to be true that on legal principles Colo. Taylors testimony was admissible, it certainly constitutes a very extraordinary ground for an impeachment. According to the antient doctrine a jury finding a verdict against the law of the case was liable to an attaint; & the amount of the present doctrine seems to be that a Judge giving a legal opinion contrary to the opinion of the legislature is liable to impeachment.

As, for convenience & humanity the old doctrine of attaint has yielded to the silent, moderate but not less operative influence of new trials, I think the modern doctrine of impeachment should yield to an appellate jurisdiction in the legislature. A reversal of those legal opinions deemed unsound by the legislature would certainly better comport with the mildness of our character than [would] a removal of the Judge who has rendered them unknowing of his fault.

. . .

J. Marshall

SOURCE: 3 Albert J. Beveridge, The Life of John Marshall 177 (1919). Marshall dated the letter January 23, 1804, but modern scholarship fixes the date a year later; 6 The Papers of John Marshall 348 n.1 (Hobson ed. 1990). Like the rest of us, Marshall forgot to switch to the new year.

Developments after *Marbury*

The power to strike down a congressional statute was not used again until 1857, when the Court tackled the issue of slavery. Dred Scott v. Sandford, 60 U.S. (19 How.) 393. Judicial review of state actions, however, was more frequent. In two sets of decisions, the Court established its authority to review state statutes and state judicial decisions.

United States v. *Peters* (1809) and *Fletcher* v. *Peck* (1810) were decided in a difficult political period. Some states, reacting against the growth of national power, threatened secession and nullification. Richard Peters, a federal judge in Pennsylvania, was unable to compel state officials to obey a decree he had issued. The state legislature passed a law declaring the decree a usurpation of power and ordered the governor to resist any attempt to enforce it. Chief Justice Marshall issued a mandamus, ordering enforcement on the ground that state legislatures cannot interfere with the operation of the federal judicial process. United States v. Peters, 9 U.S. (5 Cr.) 115 (1809). The governor called out the militia to prevent a federal marshal from executing the court order. He also sought President Madison's assistance, but the state's resistance collapsed when Madison replied that the President "is not only unauthorized to prevent the execution of a decree sanctioned by the Supreme Court of the United States, but is expressly enjoined, by statute, to carry into effect any such decree where opposition may be made to it." Annals of Congress, 11th Cong. 2269.

In *Fletcher* v. *Peck*, the Court struck down an act of a state legislature as unconstitutional. Several land companies had obtained a huge land grant at a bargain price from the Georgia legislature, offering bribes to a number of lawmakers. After elections, the new legislature revoked the land grant. In the meantime, innocent third parties had bought property from the corrupt land companies. Some of the purchasers challenged the revocation, claiming impairment of the obligations of a contract protected by Article I, Section 10, of the Constitution. Justice Marshall, recognizing the delicate task of reviewing state legislation, concluded that the revocation did constitute a violation of the Impairments Clause. Fletcher v. Peck, 10 U.S. (6 Cr.) 87, 136–39 (1810) (see reading in Chapter 9).

A second pair of cases was decided after the War of 1812, following a substantial change in the Supreme Court's membership. The most important addition was Joseph Story. Though appointed by James Madison, he became as ardent a defender of national interests as Marshall. He wrote the decision that established the Court's authority to review state court decisions involving federal questions. MARTIN v. HUNTER'S LESSEE, 1 Wheat. 304 (1816). The dispute in *Martin* was between two private parties. In 1821, with a state as one of the parties, Marshall solidified the relationship of the Court to state courts and breathed new life into the Supremacy Clause. COHENS v. VIRGINIA, 6 Wheat. 264 (1821).

Marbury v. Madison

5 U.S. (1 Cr.) 137 (1803)

William Marbury and several colleagues were nominated by President John Adams to be justices of the peace in the District of Columbia. The Senate confirmed their names. Adams signed their commissions, and the seal of the United States was affixed to the commissions. However, in the confusion of the remaining days of the Adams administration, some of the commissions, including Marbury's, were not delivered. When President Thomas Jefferson entered office, he ordered that the commissions not be delivered. Marbury sued the Secretary of State, James Madison. The opinion in this case is written by Chief Justice John Marshall.

Opinion of the Court.

At the last term on the affidavits then read and filed with the clerk, a rule was granted in this case, requiring the secretary of state to show cause why a *mandamus* should not issue, directing him to deliver to William Marbury his commission as a justice of the peace for the county of Washington, in the district of Columbia.

No cause has been shown, and the present motion is for a *mandamus*....

The first object of inquiry is,

1st. Has the applicant a right to the commission he demands?

. . .

It appears, from the affidavits, that ... a commission for William Marbury, as a justice of peace for the county of Washington, was signed by John Adams, then President of the United States; after which the seal of the United States was affixed to it; but the commission has never reached the person for whom it was made out....

The last act to be done by the president is the signature of the commission. He has then acted on the advice and consent of the senate to his own nomination. The time for deliberation has then passed. He has decided. His judgment, on the advice and consent of the senate concurring with his nomination, has been made, and the officer is appointed. This appointment is evidenced by an open, unequivocal act; and being the last act required from the person making it, necessarily excludes the idea of its being, so far as respects the appointment, an inchoate and incomplete transaction....

The commission being signed, the subsequent duty of the secretary of state is prescribed by law, and not to be guided by the will of the president. He is to affix the seal of the United States to the commission, and is to record it.

This is not a proceeding which may be varied, if the judgment of the executive shall suggest one more eligible; but is a precise course accurately marked out by law, and is to be strictly pursued. It is the duty of the secretary of state to conform to the law, and in this he is an officer of the United States, bound to obey the laws. He acts, in this respect, as has been very properly stated at the bar, under the authority of law, and not by the instructions of the president. It is a ministerial act which the law enjoins on a particular officer for a particular purpose....

Mr. Marbury, then, since his commission was signed by the president, and sealed by the secretary of state, was appointed; and as the law creating the office, gave the officer a right to hold for five years, independent of the executive, the appointment was not revocable, but vested in the officer legal rights, which are protected by the laws of his country.

To withhold his commission, therefore, is an act deemed by the court not warranted by law, but violative of a vested legal right.

This brings us to the second inquiry; which is,

2dly, If he has a right, and that right has been violated, do the laws of his country afford him a remedy?

The very essence of civil liberty certainly consists in the right of every individual to claim the protection of the laws, whenever he receives an injury. One of the first duties of government is to afford that protection....

The government of the United States has been emphatically termed a government of laws, and not of men. It will certainly cease to deserve this high appellation, if the laws furnish no remedy for the violation of a vested legal right....

By the constitution of the United States, the president is invested with certain important political powers, in the exercise of which he is to use his own discretion, and is accountable only to his country in his political character and to his own conscience. To aid him in the performance of these duties, he is authorized to appoint certain officers, who act by his authority, and in conformity with his orders.

In such cases, their acts are his acts; and whatever opinion may be entertained of the manner in which executive discretion may be used, still there exists, and can exist, no power to control that discretion. The subjects are political. They respect the nation, not individual rights, and being intrusted to the executive, the decision of the executive is conclusive.... The acts of such an officer, as an officer, can never be examinable by the courts.

But when the legislature proceeds to impose on that officer other duties; when he is directed peremptorily to perform certain acts; when the rights of individuals are dependent on the performance of those acts; he is so far the officer of the law; is amenable to the laws for his conduct; and cannot at his discretion sport away the vested rights of others.

The conclusion from this reasoning is, that where the heads of departments are the political or confidential agents of the executive, merely to execute the will of the president, or rather to act in cases in which the executive possesses a constitutional or legal discretion, nothing can be more perfectly clear than that their acts are only politically examinable. But where a specific duty is assigned by law, and individual rights depend upon the performance of that duty, it seems equally clear that the individual who considers himself injured, has a right to resort to the laws of his country for a remedy....

The question whether a right has vested or not, is, in its nature, judicial, and must be tried by the judicial authority....

It is, then, the opinion of the court,

1st. That by signing the commission of Mr. Marbury, the President of the United States appointed him a justice of peace for the county of Washington, in the district of Columbia; and that the seal of the United States, affixed thereto by the secretary of state, is conclusive testimony of the verity of the signature, and of the completion of the appointment; and that the appointment conferred on him a legal right to the office for the space of five years.

2dly. That, having this legal title to the office, he has a consequent right to the commission; a refusal to deliver which is a plain violation of that right, for which the laws of his country afford him a remedy.

It remains to be inquired whether,

3dly. He is entitled to the remedy for which he applies. This depends on,

1st. The nature of the writ applied for; and,

2dly. The power of this court.

1st. The nature of the writ.

Blackstone, in the 3d volume of his Commentaries, page 110, defines a *mandamus* to be "a command issuing in the king's name from the court of king's bench, and directed to any person, corporation, or inferior court of judicature within the king's dominions, requiring them to do some particular thing therein specified, which appertains to their office and duty, and which the court of king's bench has previously determined, or at least supposes, to be consonant to right and justice." ...

Still, to render the *mandamus* a proper remedy, the officer to whom it is to be directed, must be one to whom, on legal principles, such writ may be directed; and the person applying for it must be without any other specific and legal remedy.

1st. With respect to the officer to whom it would be directed. The intimate political relation subsisting between the President of the United States and the heads of departments, necessarily renders any legal investigation of the acts of one of those high officers peculiarly irksome, as well as delicate; and excites some hesitation with respect to the propriety of entering into such investigation. [*Judicial inquiry may*] be considered by some, as an attempt to intrude into the cabinet, and to intermeddle with the prerogatives of the executive.

It is scarcely necessary for the court to disclaim all pretensions to such a jurisdiction. An extravagance, so absurd and excessive, could not have been entertained for a moment. The province of the court is, solely, to decide on the rights of individuals, not to inquire how the executive, or executive officers, perform duties in which they have a discretion. Questions in their nature political, or which are, by the constitution and laws, submitted to the executive, can never be made in this court....

This, then, is a plain case for a *mandamus*, either to deliver the commission, or a copy of it from the record; and it only remains to be inquired,

Whether it can issue from this court.

The [1789] act to establish the judicial courts of the United States authorizes [in Section 13] the supreme court "to issue writs of *mandamus*, in cases warranted by the principles and usages of law, to any courts appointed, or persons holding office, under the authority of the United States."

The secretary of state, being a person holding an office under the authority of the United States, is precisely within the letter of the description; and if this court is not authorized to issue a writ of *mandamus* to such an officer, it must be because the law is unconstitutional, and therefore absolutely incapable of conferring the authority, and assigning the duties which its words purport to confer and assign.

The constitution vests the whole judicial power of the United States in one supreme court, and such inferior courts as congress shall, from time to time, ordain and establish. This power is expressly extended to all cases arising under the laws of the United States; and, consequently, in some form, may be exercised over the present case; because the right claimed is given by a law of the United States.

In the distribution of this power it is declared that "the supreme court shall have original jurisdiction in all cases affecting ambassadors, other public ministers and consuls, and those in which a state shall be a party. In all other cases, the supreme court shall have appellate jurisdiction."

It has been insisted, at the bar, that as the original grant of jurisdiction, to the supreme and inferior courts, is general, and the clause, assigning original jurisdiction to the supreme court, contains no negative or restrictive words, the power remains to the legislature, to assign original jurisdiction to that court in other cases than those specified in the article which has been recited; provided those cases belong to the judicial power of the United States.

If it had been intended to leave it in the discretion of the legislature to apportion the judicial power between the supreme and inferior courts according to the will of that body, it would certainly have been useless to have proceeded further than to have defined the judicial power, and the tribunals in which it should be vested. The subsequent part of the section is mere surplusage, is entirely without meaning, if such is to be the construction. If congress remains at liberty to give this court appellate jurisdiction, where the constitution has declared their jurisdiction shall be original; and original jurisdiction where the constitution has declared it shall be appellate; the distribution of jurisdiction, made in the constitution, is form without substance.

Affirmative words are often, in their operation, negative of other objects than those affirmed; and in this case, a negative or exclusive sense must be given to them, or they have no operation at all.

It cannot be presumed that any clause in the constitution is intended to be without effect; and, therefore, such a construction is inadmissible, unless the words require it.

If the solicitude of the convention, respecting our peace with foreign powers, induced a provision that the supreme court should take original jurisdiction in cases which might be supposed to affect them; yet the clause would have proceeded no further than to provide for such cases, if no further restriction on the powers of congress had been intended. That they should have appellate jurisdiction in all other cases, with such exceptions as congress might make, is no restriction; unless the words be deemed exclusive of original jurisdiction.

When an instrument organizing fundamentally a judicial system, divides it into one supreme, and so many inferior courts as the legislature may ordain and establish; then enumerates its powers, and proceeds so far to distribute them, as to define the jurisdiction of the supreme court by declaring the cases in which it shall take original jurisdiction, and that in others it shall take appellate jurisdiction; the plain import of the words seems to be, that in one class of cases its jurisdiction is original, and not appellate; in the other it is appellate, and not original. If any other construction would render the clause inoperative, that is an additional reason for rejecting such other construction, and for adhering to their obvious meaning.

To enable this court, then, to issue a *mandamus,* it must be shown to be an exercise of appellate jurisdiction, or to be necessary to enable them to exercise appellate jurisdiction.

It has been stated at the bar that the appellate jurisdiction may be exercised in a variety of forms, and that if it be the will of the legislature that a *mandamus* should be used for that purpose, that will must be obeyed. This is true, yet the jurisdiction must be appellate, not original.

It is the essential criterion of appellate jurisdiction, that it revises and corrects the proceedings in a cause already instituted, and does not create that cause. Although, therefore, a *mandamus* may be directed to courts, yet to issue such a writ to an officer for the delivery of a paper, is in effect the same as to sustain an original action for that paper, and, therefore, seems not to belong to appellate, but to original jurisdiction. Neither is it necessary in such a case as this, to enable the court to exercise its appellate jurisdiction.

The authority, therefore, given to the supreme court, by the act establishing the judicial courts of the United States, to issue writs of *mandamus* to public officers, appears not to be warranted by the constitution; and it becomes necessary to inquire whether a jurisdiction so conferred can be exercised.

The question, whether an act, repugnant to the constitution, can become the law of the land, is a question deeply interesting to the United States; but, happily, not of an intricacy proportioned to its interest. It seems only necessary to recognise certain principles, supposed to have been long and well established, to decide it.

That the people have an original right to establish, for their future government, such principles as, in their opinion, shall most conduce to their own happiness is the basis on which the whole American fabric has been erected. The exercise of this original right is a very great exertion; nor can it, nor ought it, to be frequently repeated. The principles, therefore, so established, are deemed fundamental. And as the authority from which they proceed is supreme, and can seldom act, they are designed to be permanent.

This original and supreme will organizes the government, and assigns to different departments their respective powers. It may either stop here, or establish certain limits not to be transcended by those departments.

The government of the United States is of the latter description. The powers of the legislature are defined and limited; and that those limits may not be mistaken, or forgotten, the constitution is written. To what purpose are powers limited, and to what purpose is that limitation committed to writing, if these limits may, at any time, be passed by those intended to be restrained? The distinction between a government with limited and unlimited powers is abolished, if those limits do not confine the persons on whom they are imposed, and if acts prohibited and acts allowed, are of equal obligation. It is a proposition too plain to be contested, that the constitution controls any legislative act repugnant to it; or, that the legislature may alter the constitution by an ordinary act.

Between these alternatives there is no middle ground. The constitution is either a superior paramount law, unchangeable by ordinary means, or it is on a level with ordinary legislative acts, and, like other acts, is alterable when the legislature shall please to alter it.

If the former part of the alternative be true, then a legislative act contrary to the constitution is not law: if the latter part be true, then written constitutions are absurd attempts, on the part of the people, to limit a power in its own nature illimitable.

Certainly all those who have framed written constitutions contemplate them as forming the fundamental and paramount law of the nation, and, consequently, the theory of every such government must be, that an act of the legislature, repugnant to the constitution, is void.

This theory is essentially attached to a written constitution, and, is consequently, to be considered, by this court, as one of the fundamental principles of our society. It is not therefore to be lost sight of in the further consideration of this subject.

If an act of the legislature, repugnant to the constitution, is void, does it, notwithstanding its invalidity, bind the courts, and oblige them to give it effect? Or, in other words, though it be not law, does it constitute a rule as operative as if it was a law? This would be to overthrow in fact what was established in theory; and would seem, at first view, an absurdity too gross to be insisted on. It shall, however, receive a more attentive consideration.

It is emphatically the province and duty of the judicial department to say what the law is. Those who apply the rule to particular cases, must of necessity expound and interpret that rule. If two laws conflict with each other, the courts must decide on the operation of each.

So if a law be in opposition to the constitution; if both the law and the constitution apply to a particular case, so that the court must either decide that case conformably to the law, disregarding the constitution; or conformably to the constitution, disregarding the law; the court must determine which of these conflicting rules governs the case. This is of the very essence of judicial duty.

If, then, the courts are to regard the constitution, and the constitution is superior to any ordinary act of the legislature, the constitution, and not such ordinary act, must govern the case to which they both apply.

Those, then, who controvert the principle that the constitution is to be considered, in court, as a paramount law, are reduced to the necessity of maintaining that courts must close their eyes on the constitution, and see only the law.

This doctrine would subvert the very foundation of all written constitutions. It would declare that an act which, according to the principles and theory of our government, is entirely void, is yet, in practice, completely obligatory. It would declare that if the legislature shall do what is expressly forbidden, such act, notwithstanding the express prohibition, is in reality effectual. It would be giving to the legislature a practical and real omnipotence, with the same breath which professes to restrict their powers within narrow limits. It is prescribing limits, and declaring that those limits may be passed at pleasure.

That it thus reduces to nothing what we have deemed the greatest improvement on political institutions, a written constitution, would of itself be sufficient, in America, where written constitutions have been viewed with so much reverence, for rejecting the construction. But the peculiar expressions of the constitution of the United States furnish additional arguments in favour of its rejection.

The judicial power of the United States is extended to all cases arising under the constitution.

Could it be the intention of those who gave this power, to say that in using it the constitution should not be looked into? That a case arising under the constitution should be decided without examining the instrument under which it arises?

This is too extravagant to be maintained.

In some cases, then, the constitution must be looked into by the judges. And if they can open it at all, what part of it are they forbidden to read or to obey?

There are many other parts of the constitution which serve to illustrate this subject.

It is declared that "no tax or duty shall be laid on articles exported from any state." Suppose a duty on the export of cotton, of tobacco, or of flour; and a suit instituted to recover it. Ought judgment to be rendered in such a case? ought the judges to close their eyes on the constitution, and only see the law?

The constitution declares "that no bill of attainder or *ex post facto* law shall be passed."

If, however, such a bill should be passed, and a person should be prosecuted under it; must the court condemn to death those victims whom the constitution endeavours to preserve?

"No person," says the constitution, "shall be convicted of treason unless on the testimony of two witnesses to the same overt act, or on confession in open court."

Here the language of the constitution is addressed especially to the courts. It prescribes, directly for them, a rule of evidence not to be departed from. If the legislature should change that rule, and declare *one* witness, or a confession *out* of court, sufficient for conviction, must the constitutional principle yield to the legislative act?

From these, and many other selections which might be made, it is apparent, that the framers of the constitution contemplated that instrument as a rule for the government of *courts*, as well as of the legislature.

Why otherwise does it direct the judges to take an oath to support it? This oath certainly applies in an especial manner, to their conduct in their official character. How immoral to impose it on them, if they were to be used as the instruments, and the knowing instruments, for violating what they swear to support!

The oath of office, too, imposed by the legislature, is completely demonstrative of the legislative opinion on this subject. It is in these words: "I do solemnly swear that I will administer justice without respect to persons, and do equal right to the poor and to the rich; and that I will faithfully and impartially discharge all the duties incumbent on me as * * * * * *, according to the best of my abilities and understanding, agreeably to *the constitution* and laws of the United States."

Why does a judge swear to discharge his duties agreeably to the constitution of the United States, if that constitution forms no rule for his government? if it is closed upon him, and cannot be inspected by him?

If such be the real state of things, this is worse than solemn mockery. To prescribe, or, to take this oath, becomes equally a crime.

It is also not entirely unworthy of observation, that in declaring what shall be the *supreme* law of the land, the *constitution* itself is first mentioned; and not the laws of the United States generally, but those only which shall be made in *pursuance* of the constitution, have that rank.

Thus, the particular phraseology of the constitution of the United States confirms and strengthens the principle, supposed to be essential to all written constitutions, that a law repugnant to the constitution is void; and that *courts*, as well as other departments, are bound by that instrument.

The rule must be discharged.

William W. Van Alstyne
A Critical Guide to *Marbury* v. *Madison*

The Court declares that the "first" issue presented by the case is: "Has the applicant a right to the commission he demands?" At least two criticisms of this beginning have been made. Both arise in answer to the question: Was Marbury's entitlement to the commission he demanded really the issue which the Court should have examined first? Arguably, it was not.

Surely the Court ought first determine whether

Source: 1969 Duke L. J. 1. Footnotes omitted.

it has any authority to decide any issues whatever respecting the merits of the case, *i.e.,* it should first resolve the preliminary question of its own jurisdiction. The Court's jurisdiction was ostensibly based on section 13 of the Judiciary Act of 1789 which Marbury alleged to empower the Court to issue a writ of mandamus in this sort of case. But if the Act did not in fact provide for such jurisdiction, or if it were invalid in attempting to provide for such jurisdiction, the Court would be without proper authority to consider the merits of Marbury's claim....

... [T]here is clearly an "issue" of sorts which preceded any of those touched upon in the opinion. Specifically, it would appear that Marshall should have recused himself in view of his substantial involvement in the background of this controversy. Remember, too, that the Court thought it important to establish whether Marbury's commission had already been signed and sealed before it was withdrawn — to determine whether Marbury's interest had "vested" and whether Madison was refusing to carry out a merely ministerial duty, or whether the commission was sufficiently incomplete that matters of executive discretion were involved. Proof of the status of Marbury's commission not only involved circumstances within the Chief Justice's personal knowledge, it was furnished in the Supreme Court by Marshall's own younger brother who had been with him in his office when, as Secretary of State, he had made out the commissions. Arguably the first issue, then, was the appropriateness of Marshall's participation in the decision.

MARBURY'S "RIGHT" TO THE COMMISSION

On the basis of the Act of 1801 providing for the appointment of justices of the peace for a five-year term plus findings of fact that the appointment had "vested," the Court held that Marbury had a "right" to the commission. The Act itself was based on the power of Congress granted by the Constitution in Article I, section 8, clause 17, "to exercise Legislation in all Cases whatsoever, over" the District of Columbia. Marshall concludes that once the commission had been signed and sealed by President Adams, Marbury's claim to the office was complete.

Marshall reasonably could have concluded, however, that no interest actually "vested" in Marbury prior to actual delivery of the commission. Jefferson evidently thought that the better conclusion, subsequently insisting that Marshall's decision on this point was a "perversion of law," and maintaining that "if there is any principle of law never yet contradicted, it is that delivery is one of the essentials to the validity of the deed." Even if Jefferson overstated the law, and even assuming authority could be found urging that certain interests "vest" prior to delivery, it would not necessarily be dispositive of this case. The Court is reviewing an aspect of executive power and passing judgment upon the propriety of conduct by a coordinate branch of government here, a consideration not present in an ordinary civil suit between private litigants....

STATUTORY INTERPRETATION

Certainly the first question is the following one of statutory interpretation which was just barely treated in the opinion: Did section 13 of the Judiciary Act authorize this action to originate in the Supreme Court? The section provides:

"And be it further enacted, That the Supreme Court shall have exclusive jurisdiction of all controversies of a civil nature, where a state is a party, except between a state and its citizens; and except also between a state and citizens of other states, or aliens, in which latter case it shall have original but not exclusive jurisdiction. And shall have exclusively all such jurisdiction of suits or proceedings against ambassadors, or other public ministers, or their domestics, or domestic servants, as a court of law can have or exercise consistently with the law of nations; and original, but not exclusive jurisdiction of all suits brought by ambassadors, or other public ministers, or in which a consul, or vice consul, shall be a party. And the trial of issues in fact in the Supreme Court, in all actions at law against citizens of the United States, shall be by jury. The Supreme Court shall also have appellate jurisdiction from the circuit courts and courts of the several states, in the cases herein after specially provided for; and shall have power to issue writs of prohibition to the district courts, when proceeding as courts of admiralty and maritime jurisdiction, and writs of *mandamus,* in cases warranted by the principles and usages of law, to any courts appointed, or persons holding office, under the authority of the United States."

Marshall quotes only the fragment at the end, perfunctorily notes that Madison holds office under the authority of the United States and therefore "is precisely within the letter of the description," and since he has already established that mandamus would otherwise be an appropriate remedy he quickly concludes that section 13 purports to authorize this case. But there is no discussion of whether this section *confers* original jurisdiction over suits seeking mandamus against persons holding office under the authority of the United States, or whether it merely authorizes mandamus to be so employed by the Court in cases properly *on appeal* or in aid of its original jurisdiction in cases involving foreign ministers or states. If it means only the latter, and if Marbury has no other basis for commencing his case in the Supreme Court, then the Court should simply dismiss the case for want of (statutory) jurisdiction and it need not, and ought not, examine the constitutionality of section 13 under some other construction. An argument can be made, of course, that section 13 did not attempt to grant original jurisdiction in Marbury's case.

The section opens by describing the Court's original jurisdiction and then moves on to describe appellate jurisdiction ("hereinafter specially provided for"). Textually, the provision regarding mandamus says nothing expressly as to whether it is part of original or appellate jurisdiction or both, and the clause itself does not speak at all of "conferring jurisdiction" on the court. The grant of "power" to issue the writ, however, is juxtaposed with the section of appellate jurisdiction and, in fact, follows the general description of appellate jurisdiction in the same sentence, being separated only by a semicolon. No textual mangling is required to confine it to appellate jurisdiction. Moreover, no mangling is required even if it attaches both to original and to appellate jurisdiction, not as an enlargement of either, but simply as a specification of power which the Court is authorized to use in cases which are *otherwise* appropriately under consideration. Since this case is not otherwise within the specified type of original jurisdiction (*e.g.,* it is not a case in which a state is a party or a case against an ambassador), it should be dismissed....

JUDICIAL REVIEW

Assuming that section 13 of the Judiciary Act of 1789 does confer original jurisdiction in this case, is its constitutionality subject to judicial review? Marshall initially responds to this question, which, of course, is the issue which has made the case of historic importance, by posing his own rhetorical question: "whether an Act repugnant to the Constitution can become the law of the land." That it

cannot is clear, he says, from the following considerations.

The people in an exercise of their "original right," established the government pursuant to a written constitution which defines and limits the powers of the legislature. A "legislative act contrary to the constitution is not law," therefore, as it is contrary to the original and supreme will which organized the legislature itself.

. . .

That the Constitution is a "written" one yields little or nothing as to whether acts of Congress may be given the force of positive law notwithstanding the opinion of judges, the executive, a minority or majority of the population, or even of Congress itself (assuming that Congress might sometimes be pressed by political forces to adopt a law against its belief that it lacked power to do so) that such Acts are repugnant to the Constitution. That this is so is clear enough simply from the fact that even in Marshall's time (and to a great extent today), a number of nations maintained written constitutions and yet gave national legislative acts the full force of positive law without providing any constitutional check to guarantee the compatibility of those acts with their constitutions.

This observation, moreover, leads to the conclusion that Marshall presents a false dilemma in insisting that "[t]he constitution is *either* a superior paramount law, unchangeable by ordinary means, *or* it is on a level with ordinary legislative acts, and, like other acts, is alterable when the legislature shall please to alter it." Remember, the question he has posed is "whether an Act repugnant to the Constitution can become the law of the land." The question is not whether Congress can alter the Constitution by means other than those provided by Article V, and the case raises no issue concerning an alteration of any provision in the Constitution. We may assume that Congress cannot, by simple act, alter the Constitution and still we may maintain that an act which the Court or someone else *believes* to be repugnant to the Constitution shall be given the full force of positive law until repealed. Again, this is the situation which prevails in many other countries, and no absurdity is felt to exist where such a condition obtains.

. . .

Martin v. Hunter's Lessee

14 U.S. (1 Wheat.) 304 (1816)

A state district court upheld Martin's land claim, which was based on a treaty between America and Great Britain. The Virginia Court of Appeals, the highest court in that state, regarded the issue as solely one of state law and reversed the district court. The conflict escalated when the U.S. Supreme Court set aside the state ruling and the state court refused to obey. The Virginia Court of Appeals claimed that the Supreme Court had no authority to review its judgment, and to the extent that Section 25 of the Judiciary Act of 1789 attempted to extend the appellate jurisdiction of the Supreme Court to the state courts, the statute was unconstitutional. Chief Justice Marshall did not participate since he had earlier served as attorney for one of the parties.

STORY, J., delivered the opinion of the court.

. . .

The constitution of the United States was ordained and established, not by the states in their sovereign capacities, but emphatically, as the preamble of the constitution declares, by "the People of the United States." There can be no doubt, that it was competent to the people to invest the general government with all the powers which they might deem proper and necessary; to extend or restrain these powers according to their own good pleasure, and to give them a paramount and supreme authority. As little doubt can there be, that the people had a right to prohibit to the states the exercise of any powers which were, in their judgment, incompatible with the objects of the general compact; to make the powers of the state governments, in given cases, subordinate to those of the nation, or to reserve to themselves those sovereign authorities which they might not choose to delegate to either. The constitution was not, therefore, necessarily carved out of existing state sovereignties, nor a surrender of powers already existing in state institutions, for the powers of the states depend upon their own constitutions; and the people of every state had the right to modify and restrain them, according to their own views of policy or principle. On the other hand, it is perfectly clear, that the sovereign powers vested in the state governments, by their respective constitutions, remained unaltered and unimpaired, except so far as they were granted to the government of the United States....

... The constitution was for a new government, organized with new substantive powers, and not a mere supplementary charter to a government already existing. The confederation was a compact between states; and its structure and powers were wholly unlike those of the national government. The constitution was an act of the people of the United States to supersede the confederation, and not to be engrafted on it, as a stock through which it was to receive life and nourishment....

This leads us to the consideration of the great question, as to the nature and extent of the appellate jurisdiction of the United States. We have already seen, that appellate jurisdiction is given by the constitution to the supreme court, in all cases where it has not original jurisdiction; subject, however, to such exceptions and regulations as congress may prescribe. It is, therefore, capable of embracing every case enumerated in the constitution, which is not exclusively to be decided by way of original jurisdiction. But the exercise of appellate jurisdiction is far from being limited, by the terms of the constitution, to the supreme court....

As, then, by the terms of the constitution, the appellate jurisdiction is not limited as to the supreme court, and as to this court, it may be exercised in all other cases than those of which it has original cognisance, what is there to restrain its exercise over state tribunals, in the enumerated cases? The appellate power is not limited by the terms of the third article to any particular courts. The words are, "the judicial power (which includes appellate power) shall extend to all cases," &c., and "in all other cases before mentioned the supreme court shall have appellate jurisdiction." It is the case, then, and not the court, that gives the jurisdiction....

If the constitution meant to limit the appellate jurisdiction to cases pending in the courts of the United States, it would necessarily follow, that the jurisdiction of these courts would, in all the cases enumerated in the constitution, be exclusive of state tribunals. How, otherwise, could the jurisdiction extend to *all* cases arising under the constitution, laws and treaties of the United States, or to *all* cases of admiralty and maritime jurisdiction? If some of these cases might be entertained by state tribunals, and no appellate jurisdiction as to them should exist, then the appellate power would not extend to *all*, but to *some*, cases....

But it is plain, that the framers of the constitution did contemplate that cases within the judicial cognisance of the United States, not only might, but would, arise in the state courts, in the exercise of their ordinary jurisdiction. With this view, the sixth article declares, that "this constitution, and the laws of the United States which shall be made in pursuance thereof, and all treaties made, or which shall be made, under the authority of the United States, shall be the supreme law of the land, and the judges in every state shall be bound thereby, anything in the constitution or laws of any state to the contrary notwithstanding." It is obvious, that this obligation is imperative upon the state judges, in their official, and not merely in their private, capacities. From the very nature of their judicial duties, they would be called upon to pronounce the law applicable to the case in judgment. They were not to decide merely according to the laws or constitution of the state, but according to the constitution, laws and treaties of the United States—"the supreme law of the land."...

. . .

It has been argued, that such an appellate jurisdiction over state courts is inconsistent with the genius of our governments, and the spirit of the constitution. That the latter was never designed to act upon state sovereignties, but only upon the people, and that if the power exists, it will materially impair the sovereignty of the states, and the independence of their courts. We cannot yield to the force of this reasoning; it assumes principles which we cannot admit, and draws conclusions to which we do not yield our assent.

... The courts of the United States can, without question, revise the proceedings of the executive and legislative authorities of the states, and if they are found to be contrary to the constitution, may declare them to be of no legal validity. Surely, the exercise of the same right over judicial tribunals is not a higher or more dangerous act of sovereign power.

Nor can such a right be deemed to impair the independence of state judges. It is assuming the very ground in controversy, to assert that they possess an absolute independence of the United States. In respect to the powers granted to the United States, they are not independent; they are expressly bound to obedience, by the letter of the constitution; and if they should unintentionally transcend their authority, or misconstrue the constitution, there is no more reason for giving their judgments an absolute and irresistible force, than for giving it to the acts of the other co-ordinate departments of state sovereignty....

It is further argued, that no great public mischief can result from a construction which shall limit the appellate power of the United States to cases in their own courts: first, because state judges are bound by an oath to support the constitution of the United States, and must be presumed to be men of learning and integrity; and secondly, because congress must have an unquestionable right [to] remove all cases within the scope of the judicial power from the state courts to the courts of the United States, at any time before final judgment, though not after final judgment. As to the first reason—admitting that the judges of the state courts are, and always will be, of as much learning, integrity and wisdom, as those of the courts of the United States (which we very cheerfully admit), it does not aid the argument. It is manifest, that the constitution has proceeded upon a theory of its own, and given or withheld powers according to the judgment of the American people, by whom it was adopted. We can only construe its powers, and cannot inquire into the policy or principles which induced the grant of them. The constitution has presumed (whether rightly or wrongly, we do not inquire), that state attachments, state prejudices, state jealousies, and state interests, might sometimes obstruct, or control, or be supposed to obstruct or control, the regular administration of justice....

This is not all. A motive of another kind, perfectly compatible with the most sincere respect for state tribunals, might induce the grant of appellate power over their decisions. That motive is the importance, and even necessity of uniformity of decisions throughout the whole United States, upon all subjects within the purview of the constitution. Judges of equal learning and integrity, in different states, might differently interpret the statute, or a treaty of the United States, or even the constitution itself: if there were no revising authority to control these jarring and discordant judgments, and harmonize them into uniformity, the laws, the treaties and the constitution of the United States would be different, in different states, and might, perhaps, never have precisely the same construction, obligation or efficiency, in any two states....

On the whole, the court are of opinion, that the appellate power of the United States does extend to cases pending in the state courts; and that the 25th section of the judiciary act, which authorizes the exercise of this jurisdiction in the specified cases, by a writ of error, is supported by the letter and spirit of the constitution. We find no clause in that instrument which limits this power; and we dare not interpose a limitation, where the people have not been disposed to create one.

. . .

It is the opinion of the whole court, that the judgment of the court of appeals of Virginia, rendered on the mandate in this cause, be reversed, and the judgment of the district court, held at Winchester, be, and the same is hereby affirmed.

Cohens v. Virginia

19 U.S. (6 Wheat.) 264 (1821)

This case involved the question of Supreme Court jurisdiction to review a criminal case in which the state itself was a party. The Cohen brothers were convicted by a Virginia court for selling lottery tickets, contrary to state law. The lottery had been established by an act of Congress to operate in the District of Columbia. The Cohens argued that state courts had no jurisdiction to review a congressional statute. The Virginia Court of Appeals, the state's highest court, rejected that defense and denied that the Supreme Court had power under the Constitution to review its ruling. Section 25 of the Judiciary Act of 1789 was again at issue.

Mr. Chief Justice MARSHALL delivered the opinion of the Court.

. . .

The counsel who opened the cause said, that the want of jurisdiction was shown by the subject matter of the case. The counsel who followed him said, that jurisdiction was not given by the judiciary act. The Court has bestowed all its attention on the arguments of both gentlemen, and supposes that their tendency is to show that this Court has no jurisdiction of the case, or, in other words, has no right to review the judgment of the State Court, because neither the constitution nor any law of the United States has been violated by that judgment.

The questions presented to the Court by the two first points made at the bar are of great magnitude, and may be truly said vitally to affect the Union. They exclude the inquiry whether the constitution and laws of the United States have been violated by the judgment which the plaintiffs in error seek to review; and maintain that, admitting such violation, it is not in the power of the government to apply a corrective. They maintain that the nation does not possess a department capable of restraining peaceably, and by authority of law, any attempts which may be made, by a part, against the legitimate powers of the whole; and that the government is reduced to the alternative of submitting to such attempts, or of resisting them by force. They maintain that the constitution of the United States has provided no tribunal for the final construction of itself, or of the laws or treaties of the nation; but that this power may be exercised in the last resort by the Courts of every State in the Union. That the constitution, laws, and treaties, may receive as many constructions as there are States; and that this is not a mischief, or, if a mischief, is irremediable. . . .

1st. The first question to be considered is, whether the jurisdiction of this Court is excluded by the character of the parties, one of them being a State, and the other a citizen of that State?

The second section of the third article of the constitution defines the extent of the judicial power of the United States. Jurisdiction is given to the Courts of the Union in two classes of cases. In the first, their jurisdiction depends on the character of the cause, whoever may be the parties. This class comprehends "all cases in law and equity arising under this constitution, the laws of the United States, and treaties made, or which shall be made, under their authority." This clause extends the jurisdiction of the Court to all the cases described, without making in its terms any exception whatever, and without any regard to the condition of the party. If there be any exception, it is to be implied against the express words of the article.

In the second class, the jurisdiction depends entirely on the character of the parties. In this are comprehended "controversies between two or more States, between a State and citizens of another State," "and between a State and foreign States, citizens or subjects." If these be the parties, it is entirely unimportant what may be the subject of controversy. Be it what it may, these parties have a constitutional right to come into the Courts of the Union.

. . .

When we consider the situation of the government of the Union and of a State, in relation to each other; the nature of our constitution; the subordination of the State governments to that constitution;

the great purpose for which jurisdiction over all cases arising under the constitution and laws of the United States, is confided to the judicial department; are we at liberty to insert in this general grant, an exception of those cases in which a State may be a party? Will the spirit of the constitution justify this attempt to control its words? We think it will not. We think a case arising under the constitution or laws of the United States, is cognizable in the Courts of the Union, whoever may be the parties to that case.

Had any doubt existed with respect to the just construction of this part of the section, that doubt would have been removed by the enumeration of those cases to which the jurisdiction of the federal Courts is extended, in consequence of the character of the parties.

... It would be hazarding too much to assert, that the judicatures of the States will be exempt from the prejudices by which the legislatures and people are influenced, and will constitute perfectly impartial tribunals. In many States the judges are dependent for office and for salary on the will of the legislature. The constitution of the United States furnishes no security against the universal adoption of this principle. When we observe the importance which that constitution attaches to the independence of judges, we are the less inclined to suppose that it can have intended to leave these constitutional questions to tribunals where this independence may not exist, in all cases where a State shall prosecute an individual who claims the protection of an act of Congress. These prosecutions may take place even without a legislative act. A person making a seizure under an act of Congress, may be indicted as a trespasser, if force has been employed, and of this a jury may judge. How extensive may be the mischief if the first decisions in such cases should be final! ...

It is most true that this Court will not take jurisdiction if it should not: but it is equally true, that it must take jurisdiction if it should. The judiciary cannot, as the legislature may, avoid a measure because it approaches the confines of the constitution. We cannot pass it by because it is doubtful. With whatever doubts, with whatever difficulties, a case may be attended, we must decide it, if it be brought before us. We have no more right to decline the exercise of jurisdiction which is given, than to usurp that which is not given. The one or the other would be treason to the constitution. Questions may occur which we would gladly avoid; but we cannot avoid them. All we can do is, to exercise our best judgment, and conscientiously to perform our duty. In doing this, on the present occasion, we find this tribunal invested with appellate jurisdiction in *all* cases

arising under the constitution and laws of the United States. We find no exception to this grant, and we cannot insert one....

2d. The second objection to the jurisdiction of the Court is, that its appellate power cannot be exercised, in any case, over the judgment of a State Court.

This objection is sustained chiefly by arguments drawn from the supposed total separation of the judiciary of a State from that of the Union, and their entire independence of each other. The argument considers the federal judiciary as completely foreign to that of a State; and as being no more connected with it in any respect whatever, than the Court of a foreign State....

That the United States form, for many, and for most important purposes, a single nation, has not yet been denied. In war, we are one people. In making peace, we are one people. In all commercial regulations, we are one and the same people. In many other respects, the American people are one, and the government which is alone capable of controlling and managing their interests in all these respects, is the government of the Union....

In a government so constituted, is it unreasonable that the judicial power should be competent to give efficacy to the constitutional laws of the legislature? That department can decide on the validity of the constitution or law of a State, if it be repugnant to the constitution or to a law of the United States. Is it unreasonable that it should also be empowered to decide on the judgment of a State tribunal enforcing such unconstitutional law? Is it so very unreasonable as to furnish a justification for controling the words of the constitution?

We think it is not. We think that in a government acknowledgedly supreme, with respect to objects of vital interest to the nation, there is nothing inconsistent with sound reason, nothing incompatible with the nature of government, in making all its departments supreme, so far as respects those objects, and so far as is necessary to their attainment. The exercise of the appellate power over those judgments of the State tribunals which may contravene the constitution or laws of the United States, is, we believe, essential to the attainment of those objects....

3d. We come now to the third objection, which, though differently stated by the counsel, is substantially the same. One gentleman has said that the judiciary act does not give jurisdiction in the case.

The cause was argued in the State Court, on a case agreed by the parties, which states the prosecution under a law for selling lottery tickets, which is set forth, and further states the act of Congress by which the City of Washington was authorized to establish the lottery. It then states that the lottery was regularly established by virtue of the act, and concludes with referring to the Court the questions, whether the act of Congress be valid? whether, on its just construction, it constitutes a bar to the prosecution? and, whether the act of Assembly, on which the prosecution is founded, be not itself invalid? These questions were decided against the operation of the act of Congress, and in favour of the operation of the act of the State.

If the 25th section of the judiciary act be inspected, it will at once be perceived that it comprehends expressly the case under consideration....

After having bestowed upon this question the most deliberate consideration of which we are capable, the Court is unanimously of opinion, that the objections to its jurisdiction are not sustained, and that the motion ought to be overruled.

Motion denied.

[*Having ruled against Virginia's motion to dismiss the case for want of jurisdiction, the Court heard arguments on the merits of the Cohens' claim that the congressional sponsorship of the lottery barred a state prosecution for the sale of tickets. The Court affirmed the Virginia conviction by reasoning that the congressional statute was not a piece of national legislation but rather an exercise of congressional power over the District of Columbia. As local legislation, the lottery law did not override state penal laws.*]

D. CONSTRAINTS ON JUDICIAL REVIEW

By the time he visited America in the 1830s, Alexis de Tocqueville could write of judicial review: "I am aware that a similar right has been sometimes claimed, but claimed in vain, by courts of justice in other countries, but in America it is recognized by all the authorities; and not a party, not so much as an individual, is found to contest it." 1 Alexis de Tocqueville, Democracy in America 100 (Bradley ed. 1951). In fact, judicial review was sharply challenged at every level of government and society. State courts and state legislatures regularly disputed the jurisdiction of the Supreme Court, not only up to the Civil War but afterward as well. Charles Warren, 47 Am. L. Rev. 1, 161 (1913).

Justice John Gibson's dissent in *Eakin* v. *Raub* (1825) represents a trenchant rebuttal of Marshall's position on judicial review. Gibson, a Pennsylvania judge, conceded that the Supremacy Clause required judges to strike down state laws in conflict with the federal Constitution, but he rejected judicial review as a means of policing Congress and the President. Although a constitution is superior to a statute, that fact alone did not elevate judges to be the sole interpreters. The oath to support the Constitution was not unique to judges. Political branches had an equal right to put a construction on the Constitution. If a legislature were to abuse its powers and overstep the boundaries established by the Constitution, Gibson preferred that correction come at the hands of the people. Judicial errors were more difficult to correct, for they required constitutional amendment or a change in the court's membership. EAKIN v. RAUB, 12 S. & R. 330, 343 (Pa. 1825). In subsequent years, Gibson resigned himself to a more generous definition of judicial review. Norris v. Clymer, 2 Pa. 277, 281 (1845).

Concern about judicial overreaching prompted some judges to advocate a philosophy of self-restraint. To temper criticism, they offered to presume the validity of government actions and to uphold the legislature in doubtful cases. Fletcher v. Peck, 10 U.S. 87, 128 (1810); Dartmouth College v. Woodward, 17 U.S. 517, 625 (1819). Similar guidelines were issued when reviewing lower court decisions. Judges comfortable with the legitimacy of judicial review wielded the power actively and aggressively. In a veto message in 1832, President Jackson vigorously asserted his own independent authority in interpreting the Constitution, even in the face of a contrary Supreme Court opinion. Similarly, President Lincoln sharply rejected the belief in judicial supremacy regarding constitutional analysis (see readings in Chapter 1, Section H).

A major challenge to judicial review arose late in the nineteenth century when federal judges began to impose their philosophies of economic laissez-faire. Repeatedly the courts struck down state and federal statutes designed to alleviate economic hardship. Legislative efforts to deal with monopoly, prices, minimum wages, maximum work hours, and organized labor were either rejected by the

Learned Hand on Judicial Restraint

... [W]hen the Constitution emerged from the Convention in September, 1787, the structure of the proposed government, if one looked to the text, gave no ground for inferring that the decisions of the Supreme Court, and *a fortiori* of the lower courts, were to be authoritative upon the Executive and the Legislature. Each of the three "departments" was an agency of a sovereign, the "People of the United States." Each was responsible to that sovereign, but not to one another; indeed, their "Separation" was still regarded as a condition of free government, whatever we may think of that notion now....

Each one of us must in the end choose for himself how far he would like to leave our collective fate to the wayward vagaries of popular assemblies. No one can fail to recognize the perils to which the last forty years have exposed such governments.... For myself it would be most irksome to be ruled by a bevy of Platonic Guardians, even if I knew how to choose them, which I assuredly do not. If they were in charge, I should miss the stimulus of living in a society where I have, at least theoretically, some part in the direction of public affairs. Of course I know how illusory would be the belief that my vote determined anything; but nevertheless when I go to the polls I have a satisfaction in the sense that we are all engaged in a common venture.

SOURCE: Learned Hand, The Bill of Rights 27–28, 73–74 (1958).

courts or severely restricted. The philosophy of judicial restraint, the presumption of legislative validity, and avoidance of decisions based on the wisdom of government action seemed virtually abandoned. The judges reached outside the Constitution to discover a "liberty of contract" that narrowed the scope of interstate commerce and the taxing power. These decisions stood in the path of progressive legislation and threatened effective government. Justice Stone lectured his colleagues in 1936 that courts "are not the only agency of government that must be assumed to have capacity to govern." United States v. Butler, 297 U.S. 1, 87 (1936).

Changes in the composition of the Supreme Court after 1937 removed the judicial impediment to economic regulation. The era of "substantive due process" appeared to be over. However, the Warren Court sparked another round of debate over judicial review, this time raising the claim that courts had tilted in a liberal direction. The opinions outlawing desegregation, requiring legislative reapportionment, providing right of counsel, and announcing novel constitutional rights of association and privacy—all supported the weak and politically disfranchised.

Activism vs. Self-Restraint

Critics who had called for judicial self-restraint during the 1930s now found themselves applauding the substantive results of the activist Warren Court. Others warned that the Court risked losing popular support by issuing broad decisions in social and political areas. Reacting against Judge Learned Hand's plea in 1958 for judicial restraint (see box), Herbert Wechsler maintained that the issue was not whether judges possessed judicial review but rather how they *exercised* that authority. He objected to what he regarded as idiosyncratic, ad hoc, and poorly reasoned decisions and urged the courts to follow principled rules, deciding on grounds of "adequate neutrality and generality, tested not only by the instant application but by others that the principles imply." 73 Harv. L. Rev. 1, 15 (1959).

Many scholars agree that the Warren Court's opinions should have been better crafted to clarify statements of principles. If a majority opinion simply announced a result without adequately explaining the underlying argument, the courts would rule by fiat and decree. However, the concept of "neutral principles" has remained elusive and confusing. It appears to run counter to Holmes's dictum: "The life of the law has not been logic: it has been experience." The Common Law 1 (1881). In

such areas as separation of church and state, separation of powers, and search-and-seizure operations, it is difficult to discover general principles that guide the Court. The judicial process has been
characterized by starts and stops, direction and redirection, trial and error. Others point out that an
insistence on principled decisions might prevent judges from discovering novel responses for unprecedented conditions. Charles E. Clark, 49 Va. L. Rev. 660, 665 (1963). Rigid adherence to fixed
principles would prevent the tactical use of threshold arguments (such as standing, mootness, and
ripeness) needed to protect the Court's prestige and effectiveness.

The post-Warren Court years were marked by continued controversy over the scope of judicial decisions. Presidents used rulings on such contentious issues as school desegregation, the death penalty,
criminal procedures, and abortion as political rallying points. Courts were accused of deciding too
many cases and overtaxing their institutional capacity. They were urged to limit court access in order
to divert issues from the courthouse to the legislative arena.

Despite President Nixon's vow to nominate "strict constructionists" to the bench, the Court continued to play an activist role. It created a constitutional right of "commercial free speech," struck
down death-penalty statutes, initiated busing to overcome segregated schools, began the process of
reversing sex discrimination, and authored the abortion decision of *Roe* v. *Wade*. Many commentators viewed the abortion case as a revival of the era of "substantive due process" that prevailed before 1937. The Court's decision against the legislative veto, Justice White noted, struck down in "one
fell swoop provisions in more laws enacted by Congress than the Court has cumulatively invalidated
in its history." INS v. Chadha, 462 U.S. 919, 1002 (1983). Conservatives were disappointed that the
Rehnquist Court, like the Burger Court, maintained an activist role. The conditions that encourage judicial activism were explored by Justice Powell in a revealing interview in 1979 (see Powell
reading).

Judicial Review and Democracy

Some critics of contemporary courts argue that the main objection to judicial review is that it runs
counter to American democratic values. One study advised judges to limit their work to supporting
broad participation in the democratic process and protecting minority rights. John Hart Ely, Democracy and Distrust (1980). Another study endorsed judicial review for protecting individual rights but
proposed that the courts withdraw from almost all areas of federalism and separation of powers. Jesse
H. Choper, Judicial Review and the National Political Process (1980).

It is tempting, but misleading, to call judicial review anti-democratic. The Constitution establishes
a limited republic, not a direct or pure democracy. Popular sentiment is filtered through a system of
representation. Majority vote is limited by various restrictions in the Constitution: candidates must
be a certain age, Presidents may not serve a third term—regardless of what the people want. Although
states range in population from less than a million to more than twenty million, each state receives
the same number of Senators. Filibusters conducted by a minority of Senators can prevent the Senate from acting. Majority rule is further constrained by checks and balances, separation of powers,
federalism, a bicameral legislature, and the Bill of Rights.

To the extent that the judiciary protects constitutional principles, it upholds the values of the people who drafted and ratified the Constitution. Throughout much of its history, however, the judiciary
gave little support to civil liberties or civil rights. The record of the first century and a half does provides little evidence of judicial support for individual liberties. Henry W. Edgerton, 22 Corn. L. Q.
299 (1937). In a number of contemporary cases on reapportionment, the right of association, and
the "white primary" cases, it can be argued that the Supreme Court opened the door to broader public participation in the political process. In many ways the contemporary judiciary has helped
strengthen democracy. Through its decisions, it performs an informing function previously associated with legislative bodies.

The judiciary performs other positive, legitimizing functions. Actions by executive and legislative officials are contested and brought before the courts for review. When upheld, citizens can see some standard at work other than the power of majorities and the raw force of politics. Alexander Bickel wrote: "The Court's prestige, the spell it casts as a symbol, enables it to entrench and solidify measures that may have been tentative in the conception or that are on the verge of abandonment in the execution." 75 Harv. L. Rev. 40, 48 (1961). But what happens when the Court faces a repressive executive or legislative action? If judges lend their support, as in the curfew and imprisonment of Japanese-Americans during World War II, the reputation of the judiciary as the guarantor of constitutional liberties is tarnished.

If the judiciary behaves in ways intolerable to the public, there are many methods available to legislators and executives to invoke court-curbing pressures. Presidential appointments and Senate confirmations supply a steady stream of influence by popularly elected public officials. Court decisions can be overturned by constitutional amendment, a process that is directly controlled by national and state legislatures. Short of such drastic remedies, judges remain sensitive and responsive to public opinion, notwithstanding traditional claims of judicial isolation from political forces(see the final chapter).

Statutory Restrictions on Judicial Review

By adopting explicit language in statutes, Congress may prohibit judicial review of agency actions. Thus, legislation in 1885 stated that decisions by the accounting officers of the Treasury Department regarding claims for property were to be treated as final determinations "and shall never thereafter be reopened or considered." A unanimous Court held that the statute conferred exclusive and final jurisdiction on the Treasury Department and that federal courts had no power to exercise judicial review over the agency's judgment. United States v. Babcock, 250 U.S. 328 (1919). Most decisions by the Secretary of Veterans Affairs on "questions of law and fact" affecting veterans' benefits "shall be final and conclusive and may not be reviewed by any other official or by any court...." 38 U.S.C. 511 (2000). The Court accepts the prohibition of judicial review on these questions of benefits or claims, providing there is no constitutional issue. Johnson v. Robison, 415 U.S. 361, 366–67 (1974). Legislation in 1988 subjected certain actions by the Department of Veterans Affairs to judicial review. 102 Stat. 4105 (1988). Under this authority, the Supreme Court decided a veteran's case in 1994. Brown v. Gardner, 513 U.S. 115 (1994).

The Administrative Procedure Act prohibits judicial review over agency action "committed to agency discretion by law." 5 U.S.C. 701(a)(2) (2000). When the Supreme Court determines that an agency action falls within that scope, it acknowledges that judicial review does not apply. Lincoln v. Vigil, 508 U.S. 182 (1993). If there is no explicit statutory language that precludes judicial review, courts will presume that federal court jurisdiction exists to hear challenges to agency procedures. McNary v. Haitian Refugee Center, Inc., 498 U.S. 479 (1991). Congress may authorize the Attorney General to make temporary orders that are not subject to judicial review. Touby v. United States, 500 U.S. 160 (1991).

In 1994 the Supreme Court again acknowledged the limits of judicial review. The Defense Base Closure and Realignment Act of 1990 established a commission to recommend the closing of unnecessary military bases. A unanimous Court ruled that commission recommendations were not a "final agency action" under the Administrative Procedure Act (APA) since the ultimate decision on closure rests with the President. Therefore the recommendations are not reviewable by the courts. "Where a statute, such as the 1990 Act, commits decisionmaking to the discretion of the President, judicial review of the President's action is not available." Dalton v. Specter, 511 U.S. 462, 477 (1994). An amendment by Senator Arlen Specter to subject base closures to judicial review was rejected a month later. 140 Cong. Rec. 14078–90, 14092–93 (1994). Two years earlier the Court had held that presidential actions are not reviewable under the APA because the President is not an "agency." Franklin v. Massachusetts, 505 U.S. 788 (1992).

Other executive actions are not subject to judicial review. When the Attorney General decides not to go to the special division of federal judges for the appointment of an independent counsel, that decision is not reviewable "in any court." 28 U.S.C. 592(f) (2000). See Dellums v. Smith, 797 F.2d 817, 823 (9th Cir. 1986); Banzhaf v. Smith, 737 F.2d 1167 (D.C. Cir. 1984). [In 1999, Congress decided not to reauthorize the independent counsel statute.]

Eakin v. Raub: Gibson's Dissent

12 S. & R. 330 (Pa. 1825)

In this case, the Supreme Court of Pennsylvania reviews the constitutionality of a law passed by the state legislature. In a dissenting opinion, Justice John Gibson acknowledged that the Supremacy Clause required federal and state judges to invalidate state laws in conflict with the U.S. Constitution, but denied that the same power gave judges the right to invalidate actions by the legislative and executive branches unrelated to the Supremacy Clause. Gibson's dissent represents one of the most coherent critiques of Chief Justice Marshall's reasoning in *Marbury* v. *Madison.*

GIBSON, J., dissenting. *[He questions the general power of courts to hold legislative acts unconstitutional.]* But it is said, that without*[the changes insisted on by the Supreme Court of Pennsylvania]*, the latter act would be unconstitutional; and, instead of controverting this, I will avail myself of it, to express an opinion which I have deliberately formed, on the abstract right of the judiciary to declare an unconstitutional act of the legislature void. It seems to me, there is a plain difference, hitherto unnoticed, between acts that are repugnant to the constitution of the particular state, and acts that are repugnant to the constitution of the *United States;* my opinion being, that the judiciary is bound to execute the former, but not the latter. I shall hereafter attempt to explain this difference, by pointing out the particular provisions in the constitution of the *United States,* on which it depends. I am aware, that a right to declare all unconstitutional acts void, without distinction as to either constitution, is generally held as a professional dogma; but I apprehend, rather as a matter of faith than of reason. I admit, that I once embraced the same doctrine, but without examination, and I shall, therefore, state the arguments that impelled me to abandon it, with great respect for those by whom it is still maintained. But I may premise, that it is not a little remarkable, that although the right in question has all along been claimed by the judiciary, no judge has ventured to discuss it, except Chief Justice MARSHALL (in *Marbury* v. *Madison,* 1 *Cranch* 176); and if the argument of a jurist so distinguished for the strength of his ratiocinative powers be found inconclusive, it may fairly be set down to the weakness of the position which he attempts to defend; ...

The constitution of *Pennsylvania* contains no express grant of political powers to the judiciary. But to establish a grant by implication, the constitution is said to be a law of superior obligation; and consequently, that if it were to come into collision with an act of the legislature, the latter would have to give way; this is conceded. But it is a fallacy, to suppose, that they can come into collision *before the judiciary....*

The constitution and the *right* of the legislature to pass the act, may be in collision; but is that a legitimate subject for judicial determination? If it be, the judiciary must be a peculiar organ, to revise the proceedings of the legislature, and to correct its mistakes; and in what part of the constitution are we to look for this proud preeminence? Viewing the matter in the opposite direction, what would be thought of an act of assembly in which it should be declared that the supreme court had, in a particular case, put a wrong construction on the constitution of the *United States,* and that the judgment should therefore be reversed? It would, doubtless, be thought a usurpation of judicial power. But it is by no means clear, that to declare a law void, which has been enacted according to the forms prescribed in the constitution, is not a usurpation of legislative power. It is an act of sovereignty; and sovereignty and legislative power are said by Sir William *Blackstone* to be convertible terms. It is the business of the judiciary, to interpret the laws, not scan the authority of the lawgiver; and without the latter, it cannot take cognisance of a collision between a law and the constitution. So that, to affirm that the judiciary has a right to judge of the existence of such collision, is to take for granted the very thing to be proved; ...

But it has been said to be emphatically the business of the judiciary, to ascertain and pronounce what the law is; and that this necessarily involves a consideration of the constitution. It does so: but how far? If the judiciary will inquire into anything beside the form of enactment, where shall it stop? ...

... [L]et it be supposed that the power to declare a law unconstitutional has been exercised. What is to be done? The legislature must acquiesce, although it may think the construction of the judiciary wrong. But why must it acquiesce? Only because it is bound to pay that respect to every other organ of the government, which it has a right to exact from each of them in turn. This is the argument. But it will not be pretended, that the legislature has not, at least, an equal right with the judiciary to put a construction on the constitution; nor that either of them is infallible; nor that either ought to be required to surrender its judgment to the other.... I take it, then, the legislature is entitled to all the deference that is due to the judiciary; that its acts are, in no case, to be treated as *ipso facto* void, except where they would produce a revolution in the government; and that, to avoid them, requires the act of some tribunal competent, under the constitution (if any such there be), to pass on their validity. All that remains, therefore, is, to inquire whether the judiciary or the people are that tribunal.

Now, as the judiciary is not expressly constituted for that purpose, it must derive whatever authority of the sort it may possess, from the reasonableness and fitness of the thing. But, in theory, all the organs of the government are of equal capacity; or, if not equal, each must be supposed to have superior capacity only for those things which peculiarly belong to it; and as legislation peculiarly involves the consideration of those limitations which are put on the law-making power, and the interpretation of the laws when made, involves only the construction of the laws themselves, it follows, that the construction of the constitution, in this particular, belongs to the legislature, which ought, therefore, to be taken to have superior capacity to judge of the constitutionality of its own acts. But suppose, all to be of equal capacity, in every respect, why should one exercise a controlling power over the rest? That the judiciary is of superior rank, has never been pretended, although it has been said to be co-ordinate....

But the judges are sworn to support the constitution, and are they not bound by it as the law of the land? ... The oath to support the constitution is not peculiar to the judges, but is taken indiscriminately by every officer of the government ... The official

oath, then, relates only to the official conduct of the officer, and does not prove that he ought to stray from the path of his ordinary business, to search for violations of duty in the business of others; nor does it, as supposed, define the powers of the officer.

· · ·

But it has been said, that this construction would deprive the citizen of the advantages which are peculiar to a written constitution, by at once declaring the power of the legislature, in practice, to be illimitable....

... I am of opinion, that it rests with the people, in whom full and absolute sovereign power resides, to correct abuses in legislation, by instructing their representatives to repeal the obnoxious act. What is wanting to plenary power in the government, is reserved by the people, for their own immediate use; and to redress an infringement of their rights in this respect, would seem to be an accessory of the power thus reserved. It might, perhaps, have been better to vest the power in the judiciary; as it might be expected, that its habits of deliberation, and the aid derived from the arguments of counsel, would more frequently lead to accurate conclusions. On the other hand, the judiciary is not infallible; and an error by it would admit of no remedy but a more distinct expression of the public will, through the extraordinary medium of a convention; whereas, an error by the legislature admits of a remedy by an exertion of the same will, in the ordinary exercise of the right of suffrage — a mode better calculated to attain the end, without popular excitement. It may be said, the people would probably not notice an error of their representatives. But they would as probably do so, as notice an error of the judiciary; and beside, it is a *postulate* in the theory of our government, and the very basis of the superstructure, that the people are wise, virtuous, and competent to manage their own affairs ...

· · ·

But in regard to an act of assembly, which is found to be in collision with the constitution, laws or treaties of the *United States,* I take the duty of the judiciary to be exactly the reverse. By becoming parties to the federal constitution, the states have agreed to several limitations of their individual sovereignty, to enforce which, it was thought to be absolutely necessary, to prevent them from giving effect to laws in violation of those limitations, through the instrumentality of their own judges. Accordingly, it is declared in the fifth article and second section of the federal constitution, that "This constitution, and the laws of the *United States* which shall be made in pursuance thereof, and all treaties made, or which shall be made under the authority of the *United States,* shall be the *supreme* law of the land; and the *judges* in every *state* shall be BOUND thereby; anything in the *laws* or *constitution* of any *state* to the contrary notwithstanding."

This is an express grant of a political power, and it is conclusive, to show that no law of inferior obligation, as every state law must necessarily be, can be executed at the expense of the constitution, laws or treaties of the *United States....*

The Boundaries of Judicial Review: Interview with Justice Powell

In an extraordinarily candid interview in 1979, Justice Lewis F. Powell discussed with Professor Harry M. Clor some of the considerations that determine the scope of judicial review and the reasons for judicial activism. The interview was published in the *Kenyon College Alumni Bulletin* (Summer 1979).

CLOR: I would like to begin with a rather broad and somewhat philosophic question. We can get more specific later on as you choose. This is a question about the role of the federal judiciary and particularly the Supreme Court in the American system of constitutional democracy. Do you see the Court as primarily a political institution, sharing responsibility for governing and making of public policy, or do you see it having a rather narrower function, simply to interpret the Constitution and the law?

POWELL: The judicial branch of government in the United States, of course, is a political branch in the broad sense. In view of the special role it has in our system, the Supreme Court is more than just an ordinary court. It is empowered to decide whether the other two branches of government live within the Constitution. You perhaps would know more accurately than I, but I do not think there is any other country in the world in which the judiciary has the power to invalidate decisions made by the legislative bodies of the country, both federal and state, and by the executive branch also. That's a rather awesome power and it's one that makes our system and our Court distinctive. A good many of the questions that involve constitutionality of statutes, and executive branch conduct, fairly can be viewed as political in the broadest sense. I suppose one could say our function, in that sense and to that degree, is politically oriented, yet basically we think of ourselves as judges guided by the Constitution as the law of the land.

CLOR: It is sometimes said that a certain judge or justice is a judicial statesman, or has acted in a states-manlike way, which seems to suggest that something more is involved than just reading or interpreting the text of the Constitution or a law. Do you think there is such a thing as judicial statesmanship?

POWELL: Possibly, though in a limited sense. The Constitution was framed in rather sweeping language, some of which is susceptible to interpretations that not only *may* change but *have* changed over the decades. The clauses that people think about more frequently in this connection are the due process and equal protection clauses, the commerce clause and a number of other quite general phrases. The Court has to give meaning to those provisions of the Constitution, particularly the Bill of Rights, and as history demonstrates the views taken by the Court in one era do not necessarily survive a different era. That has happened with a good deal of frequency. The Constitution has been described, properly I think, as a sort of living political organism. The Court has helped, by its decisions, to keep the Constitution abreast of the vast changes that occur in the life of our nation.

CLOR: Do you think that judicial statesmanship, to the extent that there is such a thing, consists primarily of insight into the needs or demands of the times or into the changing conditions to which Constitutional clauses are to be applied?

POWELL: I'd rather not phrase it quite that way. It's well to bear in mind that the Court is composed of judges who are elected for life. We, therefore, are not directly responsible to the people in any political sense. This is both an asset and perhaps a liability. It could mean that the Court could move too far away from our democratic system. I don't think the Court has done that. Perhaps on very rare occasions. Yet, our independence does give the Court a freedom to make decisions that perhaps are necessary for our society, decisions that the legislative branch may be reluctant to make. The classic case that comes to mind is *Brown* v. *Board of Education.* The Congress had adequate authority under the Constitution to enact the sort of legislation that has been adopted since *Brown.* But it was the Supreme Court that finally decided in 1954 that segregation in our society must come to an end....

CLOR: One thing that fascinates me about the desegregation decision of *Brown* v. *Board of Education* is that the Court interpreted the equal protection clause quite differently from the earlier interpretation in 1896 of *Plessy* v. *Ferguson.* The Court virtually reversed its interpretation of the equal protection clause. How do you do that, Mr. Justice Powell?

POWELL: The Court has felt far freer to reverse Constitutional decisions than it has to reverse the interpretation of statutes. The Court's peculiar responsibility is to decide what the Constitution means. This country had moved a long ways by 1954 from the public mores and public perceptions that existed at the time of *Plessy* v. *Ferguson.* If you read the history of the post-Civil War, civil rights legislation, legislation that enacted Section 1983 of the statute which now produces a vast amount of litigation, I think you would have a hard time justifying the decision of our Court in 1954. One would have to strain to find an intention on the part of the Congress in 1866, and again in 1870 and 1871, to provide that there should be integration in education.

Of course, there weren't very many public schools, but if the Court had gone strictly by what the Congress had intended, or probably intended, it would have reaffirmed *Plessy* v. *Ferguson.*

. . .

... The point I am making is that the Supreme Court perceived that vast changes had occurred not only in the United States but worldwide. It was long overdue to bring our Negro citizens into full citizenship.

CLOR: Does that mean the Court was remaking the Constitution, reading into the equal protection clause a meaning that it did not originally have?

POWELL: The Court cannot rely solely on what the founding fathers intended, or even on congressional intent when the Fourteenth Amendment was adopted. Conditions change as our country matures....

... As a matter of fact—and I don't assert this myself, but you've seen it in print—a good many people think the legislative branch bucks tough decisions to the judicial branch by drawing statutes in quite general and vague terms. Thus, a role sometimes viewed as legislative—I would not say "aristocratic"—is thrust upon us.

CLOR: The Congress hands the tough problem to the Court?

POWELL: It has been said a number of times that Congress does that, and perhaps if I were there I'd think it was a good idea on some issues. In this way members of Congress do not have to go on record on a tough issue.

. . .

E. METHODS OF CONSTITUTIONAL INTERPRETATION

Justice Jackson once remarked that "[n]othing has more perplexed generations of conscientious judges than the search in juridical science, philosophy and practice for objective and impersonal criteria for solution of politico-legal questions put to our courts." Vital Speeches, No. 24, Vol. XIX, at 759 (October 1, 1953). No completely satisfactory guide to judicial interpretation has ever been fashioned. Jerome Frank, in his classic, Law and the Modern Mind, 6th ed., XXIV (1963), wrote of a Freudian "yearning for an unattainable legal certainty," which resembled a "young child's father-dependence and the grown-up's resultant tendency to hanker after father-substitutes." Different techniques are available, including a dependence on foreign law, literalism, originalism, natural law, history, national consensus, and an eclectic approach.

Foreign Law

Decisions by federal courts are often influenced by foreign law and international pressures. In the Desegregation Case of 1954, both the State Department and the Justice Department urged the Supreme

Court to take the case and strike down the "separate but equal" doctrine. Much of their argument took into account the opportunity of the Soviet Union to highlight the hypocrisy of U.S. democracy to prevent black students from attending school with white students. As the government's brief explained to the Court, racial discrimination in the United States "furnishes grist for the Communist propaganda mills, and its raises doubts even among friendly nations as to the intensity of our devotion to the democratic faith" (reading in Chapter 15, Section C).

International pressures are well understood. Every nation lives in a fishbowl. Following decisions by courts in other countries, however, is more controversial. There is sharp disagreement on this practice. The House Judiciary Committee held hearings in 2005 on H. Res. 97, a resolution expressing the sense of the House that judicial determinations regarding the meaning of the U.S. Constitution should not be based on "judgments, laws, or pronouncements of foreign institutions unless such foreign judgments, laws, or pronouncements inform an understanding of the original meaning of the Constitution of the United States." The resolution singled out *Lawrence v. Texas*, 539 U.S. 558 (2003), which struck down Texas's ban on private consensual sex between adults of the same sex. In looking for authority, the Court cited a report submitted to the British Parliament in 1957, a decision by the European Court of Human Rights, and the European Convention on Human Rights. On March 1, 2005, in *Roper v. Simmons*, 543 U.S. 551 (2005), the Court held unconstitutional the death penalty for offenders under the age of 18, relying in part on a UN convention contained in other international convenants: "The opinion of the world community, while not controlling our outcome, does provide respected and significant confirmation for our own conclusions." Id. at 578.

Literalism

Advocates of strict constructionism argue that judges should enforce only those norms that are stated in the Constitution. Literalism is helpful on the easy issues (two Senators per state, minimum age of 35 for a President, and so forth), but those issues are so easy they do not provoke lawsuits. Other language in the Constitution is more vexing, such as the general phrases "due process" and "equal protection." Moreover, it would be inappropriate to take some phrases literally. In 1987 the Supreme Court noted that "it is well settled that the prohibition against impairing the obligation of contracts [Art. I, § 10] is not to be read literally." Keystone Bituminous Coal Assn. v. DeBenedictis, 480 U.S. 470, 502 (1987).

In fact, literalism may be self-defeating. The point is illustrated in Pufendorf's reference to an ancient Bolognian law which provided that "whoever drew blood in the streets should be punished with utmost severity." Enforcement of the statute would have punished the surgeon for his treatment of a man who had fallen in the street from a fit. Jerome Frank, Courts on Trial: Myth and Reality in American Justice 298 (1949). As Judge Learned Hand observed, it is "one of the surest indexes of a mature and developed jurisprudence not to make a fortress out of a dictionary; but to remember that statutes always have some purpose or object to accomplish, whose sympathetic and imaginative discovery is the surest guide to their meaning." Cabell v. Markham, 148 F. 2d 737, 739 (2d Cir. 1945). Linguistic precision is seldom attainable. In 1898, James Bradley Thayer wrote of a dream world, "that lawyer's paradise where all words have a fixed, precisely ascertained meaning; where men express their purposes not only with accuracy, but with fulness; and where, if the writer has been careful, a lawyer, having a document before him, may sit in his chair, inspect the text, and answer all questions without raising his eyes." Would that it were so, but as Jerome Frank observed, "there is no Paradise." Frank, Courts on Trial 299.

Although some politicians equate strict constructionism with conservative law-and-order views, it can be applied equally well to liberal support for individual rights and religious freedom. Likewise, strict constructionism does not always mean judicial restraint. It can be synonymous, and often is, with judicial activism. Arthur J. Goldberg, Equal Justice 35–63 (1971). An example is the legislative veto case of 1983, which used strict constructionism with a vengeance to invalidate dozens of statutory provisions. INS v. Chadha, 462 U.S. 919 (1983).

Marshall on Constitutional Interpretation

... A constitution, to contain an accurate detail of all the subdivisions of which its great powers will admit, and of all the means by which they may be carried into execution, would partake of the prolixity of a legal code, and could scarcely be embraced by the human mind. It would probably never be understood by the public. Its nature, therefore, requires, that only its great outlines should be marked, its important objects designated, and the minor ingredients which compose those objects be deduced from the nature of the objects themselves.... In considering this question, then, we must never forget, that it is *a constitution* we are expounding.

• • •

Let this be done in the case under consideration. The subject is the execution of those great powers on which the welfare of a nation essentially depends. It must have been the intention of those who gave these powers, to insure, as far as human prudence could insure, their beneficial execution. This could not be done by confiding the choice of means to such narrow limits as not to leave it in the power of Congress to adopt any

which might be appropriate, and which were conducive to the end. This provision is made in a constitution intended to endure for ages to come, and, consequently, to be adapted to the various *crises* of human affairs. To have prescribed the means by which government should, in all future time, execute its powers, would have been to change, entirely, the character of the instrument, and give it the properties of a legal code....

• • •

We admit, as all must admit, that the powers of the government are limited, and that its limits are not to be transcended. But we think the sound construction of the constitution must allow to the national legislature that discretion, with respect to the means by which the powers it confers are to be carried into execution, which will enable that body to perform the high duties assigned to it, in the manner most beneficial to the people. Let the end be legitimate, let it be within the scope of the constitution, and all means which are appropriate, which are plainly adapted to that end, which are not prohibited, but consist with the letter and spirit of the constitution, are constitutional.

Source: McCulloch v. Maryland, 17 U.S. 316, 407, 415, 421 (1819).

Extreme literalists demand that textual ambiguities be resolved solely by constitutional amendment instead of judicial interpretation. Although the literalist approach may have some superficial appeal, its impracticalities as Jerome Frank and Learned Hand pointed out, are immense. Madison went to great lengths in Federalist No. 44 to point out that a constitution, to survive, must be phrased in general terms. He offered his comments to support the Necessary and Proper Clause of Article I, Section 8, which had been attacked for its vague grant of power to Congress. He said that the framers might have copied the Articles of Confederation, which prohibited the exercise of any power not *expressly* delegated by the states, or they might have attempted to enumerate congressional powers. The first alternative risked leaving the national government with insufficient power, whereas the second meant "a complete digest of laws on every subject to which the Constitution relates; accommodated not only to the existing state of things, but to all the possible changes which futurity may produce...." In 1819 Chief Justice John Marshall advanced the same argument in *McCulloch* v. *Maryland* (see box).

Chief Justice Taney, in *Dred Scott*, authored what is widely regarded as one of the major self-inflicted wounds on the Supreme Court. He did so by insisting that the meaning of "citizens" in Article III was restricted to what it meant in 1787: "No one, we presume, supposes that any change in public opinion or feeling, in relation to this unfortunate race [of blacks], in the civilized nations of Europe or in this country, should induce the court to give to the words of the Constitution a more liberal construction in their favor than they were intended to bear when the instrument was framed and adopted.... [Constitutional language] must be construed now as it was understood at the time of its adoption. It is not only the same in words, but the same in meaning...." Dred Scott v. Sandford, 60 U.S. at 426 (1857).

Justice Holmes rejected that type of reasoning. To him, a word "is not a crystal, transparent and unchanged, it is the skin of a living thought and may vary greatly in color and content according to the circumstances and the time in which it is used." Towne v. Eisner, 245 U.S. 418, 425 (1918). Moreover, a literalist is at sea when two commands of the Constitution, such as free press and fair trial, collide. How is one constitutional principle to be balanced against another? What guides the Court in deciding between civil rights and state rights? When does government regulation give way to individual privacy? What weight should be given to protect a free press against searches and seizures by law enforcement officers? Where in the Constitution do we find answers to conflicts between workers and employers? Do certain rights, such as those enumerated in the First Amendment, have a "preferred" status?[6] Even if they do, are those rights subordinated to the needs of the government during time of national emergency?

Originalism

Attorney General Edwin Meese III, in a speech in 1985, advocated a "Jurisprudence of Original Intention." He argued that judges should restrict themselves to the original meaning of constitutional provisions. Justice Brennan, in a speech later that year, rejected the search for the framers' intent as "little more than arrogance cloaked as humility" (see reading).

Originalism, sometimes called interpretivism, involves a search for the intentions or purposes of those who wrote the Constitution. Judges generally try to interpret the Constitution in accordance with the framers' intent, so far as that is possible, but in sifting through conflicting evidence they may reach different conclusions. In 2008, all nine Justices of the Supreme Court looked to the intention of the Second Amendment in determining the constitutionality of a District of Columbia law that restricted handguns in the home. Yet the Court still split apart, 5 to 4, in interpreting the amendment. District of Columbia v. Heller, 554 U.S. ____ (2008).

How are the intentions of the framers determined? Are the records of the Constitutional Convention reliable? What weight should be attached to the remarks of the framers? How much importance should be attributed to the views of those who ratified the Constitution? Thomas Jefferson promised as President to administer the Constitution "according to the safe and *honest* meaning contemplated by the *plain understanding of the people at the time of its adoption*—a meaning to be found in the explanations of those who advocated, not those who opposed it." 4 Elliot 446 (emphasis in original).

In 1803, in *Stuart v. Laird*, Justice Paterson, himself a framer, held for the Court that a congressional interpretation of the Constitution, contemporaneous with the framing of the document fixed the meaning of the clause in question on the ground that early Congresses contained many members of the Philadelphia Convention who best knew the meaning of the Constitution. 1 Cranch 299 (1803). In *Ogden v. Saunders*, Justice William Johnson stated that the "contemporaries of the Constitution have claims to our deference ... because they had the best opportunities of informing ourselves of the understanding of the framers of the Constitution, and of the sense put upon it by the people, when it was adopted by them." 25 U.S. (12 Wheat.) 212, 270, 290 (1827). Yet advocates of Originalism are reminded that efforts by the Supreme Court to introduce historical evidence have been criticized by some historians as mere law-office efforts: special pleading for a particular point of view. Alfred H. Kelly, 1965 Sup. Ct. Rev. 119. Justice Jackson said despairingly at one point: "Just what our forefathers did envision, or would have envisioned had they foreseen modern conditions, must be divined from material almost as enigmatic as the dreams Joseph was called upon to interpret for Pharaoh." Youngstown Co. v. Sawyer, 343 U.S. 579, 624 (1952).

---

6. Palko v. Connecticut, 302 U.S. 319, 326–27 (1937); Marsh v. Alabama, 326 U.S. 501, 509 (1946); Kovacs v. Cooper, 336 U.S. 77, 106 (1949) (Rutledge, J., dissenting).

Justice Iredell on Natural Law

If, then, a government, composed of legislative, executive and judicial departments, were established, by a constitution which imposed no limits on the legislative power, the consequence would inevitably be, that whatever the legislative power chose to enact, would be lawfully enacted, and the judicial power could never interpose to pronounce it void. It is true, that some speculative jurists have held, that a legislative act against natural justice must, in itself, be void; but I cannot think that, under such a government any court of justice would possess a power to declare it so....

... If ... the legislature of the Union, or the legislature of any member of the Union, shall pass a law, within the general scope of their constitutional power, the court cannot pronounce it to be void, merely because it is, in their judgment, contrary to the principles of natural justice. The ideas of natural justice are regulated by no fixed standard: the ablest and the purest men have differed upon the subject; and all that the court could properly say, in such an event, would be, that the legislature (possessed of an equal right of opinion) had passed an act which, in the opinion of the judges, was inconsistent with the abstract principles of natural justice....

Source: Calder v. Bull, 3 U.S. at 398–99 (1798).

Natural Law

Judges sometimes reach outside the Constitution to discover fundamental or universal principles to guide their decisions. This natural law approach, however, remains a continuing source of dispute. Writing in *Calder* v. *Bull* (1798), Justice Iredell urged his colleagues to base their decisions on constitutional grounds rather than on mere declarations of opinions regarding the laws of nature, which "are regulated by no fixed standard" (see box).

Justices react defensively to the charge that they merely read their own predilections into the Constitution, especially when interpreting such vague phrases as "due process," "equal protection," "unreasonable searches and seizures," and "cruel and unusual punishments." Nevertheless, Justices who oppose the death penalty argue that it violates the "human dignity" protected by the Constitution and is "no longer morally tolerable in our civilized society."[7] The law of defamation has been drawn not just from the First Amendment but from "our basic concept of the essential dignity and worth of every human being—a concept at the root of any decent system of ordered liberty." Rosenblatt v. Baer, 383 U.S. 75, 92 (1966).

Justice Frankfurter, remembered as the champion of judicial restraint, objected to those who called the interpretation of "due process" a mere matter of judicial caprice. Notwithstanding his general doctrine, he struck down actions that "shock the conscience" and "offend the community's sense of fair play and decency." Justice Black, a perennial critic of these opinions, charged that Frankfurter derived his standards basically from natural law, not constitutional law, and that such methods allowed judges to propound their own personal philosophies (see readings). In fact, the Constitution does have a "higher law" heritage.[8] From the very start, federal judges recognized that "there are certain great principles of justice, whose authority is universally acknowledged, that ought not to be entirely disregarded." Fletcher v. Peck, 10 U.S. 87, 132 (1810).

---

7. Furman v. Georgia, 408 U.S. 238, 270 (1972) (Brennan, J., dissenting); Gregg v. Georgia, 428 U.S. 153, 229 (1976) (Brennan, J., dissenting).

8. Edward S. Corwin, The "Higher Law" Background of American Constitutional Law (1928); J. A. C. Grant, "The Natural Law Background of Due Process," 31 Colum. L. Rev. 56 (1931).

Historical Development

To shed further light on constitutional meaning, judges turn to historical analysis. Justice O'Connor has said that when the intent of the framers is unclear, "we must employ both history and reason in our analysis." Wallace v. Jaffree, 472 U.S. 38, 81 (1985). Legal historian Willard Hurst regarded the general political, economic, and social history of the United States as "legally competent and relevant evidence for the interpretation of the Constitution." Edmond Cahn, ed., Supreme Court and Supreme Law 56 (1954). The meaning of "interstate commerce" could not be restricted to the methods of commerce available at the time the Constitution was adopted. The phrase had to keep pace with the progress of the country, extending from stagecoaches to steamboats, from railroads to the telegraph. Pensacola Telegraph Co. v. Western Union Telegraph Co., 96 U.S. 1, 9 (1877).

More than a century of practice became a justification for supporting the exercise of presidential power over the public lands despite the absence of any express or statutory authority: "long continued practice, known to and acquiesced in by Congress, would raise a presumption ... of a recognised administrative power of the Executive in the management of the public lands."[9] Justice Holmes, writing in 1920, said that a case before the Court has to be considered "in the light of our whole experience and not merely in that of what was said a hundred years ago." Missouri v. Holland, 252 U.S. 416, 433 (1920). Holmes [also] remarked that "a page of history is worth a volume of logic." New York Trust Co. v. Eisner, 256 U.S. 345, 349 (1921). Death penalty cases are decided not by the meaning of the Eighth Amendment in 1791 but by "the evolving standards of decency that mark the progress of a maturing society." Trop v. Dulles, 356 U.S. 86, 101 (1958).

The judiciary has been influenced by the prevailing views of social scientists, be they conservative or liberal. It has been customary for the Court to go outside the legal record and take judicial notice of writings by experts. The philosophy of Social Darwinism in the late nineteenth and twentieth centuries supplied part of the theoretical justification for a laissez-faire state. This doctrine, reshaped in the hands of judges, helped support their opposition to social and economic regulation. In time, laissez-faire principles were challenged by the "Brandeis brief," which introduced social and economic facts to justify regulation of factory and working conditions. The use of extralegal data helped undermine the Court's reliance on abstract reasoning about "liberty of contract." Paul L. Rosen, The Supreme Court and Social Science 23–101 (1972). Eventually, lawyers on both sides learned how to put together a Brandeis brief to support their case. Today, it is not unusual in a particular case for dozens of individuals and groups to submit briefs that identify facts and precedents to guide the courts.

National Consensus

At times the Supreme Court will interpret the Constitution in terms of trends that develop in the states. It looks not to the text of the Constitution, framers' intent, or natural law, but rather to how *other people in the country* (particularly at the state level) are interpreting constitutional rights. For example, in 1977 the Court held that death is a disproportionate punishment for the crime of raping an adult woman. Coker v. Georgia, 433 U.S. 584 (1977). In deciding death penalty cases, it said that "attention must be given to the public attitudes concerning a particular sentence—history and precedent, legislative attitudes, and the response of juries reflected in their sentencing decisions." Id. at 592.

At no time in the past 50 years had a majority of states authorized death as a punishment for rape.

---

9. United States v. Midwest Oil Co., 236 U.S. 459, 472–74 (1915). See also Charles E. Miller, The Supreme Court and the Uses of History (1969); Paul Brest, "The Misconceived Quest for the Original Understanding," 60 B.U.L. Rev. 204 (1980); Frederick Bernays Wiener, Uses and Abuses of Legal History (1962); Sister Marie Carolyn Klinkhamer, "The Use of History in the Supreme Court, 1789–1935," 36 U. Det. L. J. 553 (1959); John Woodford, "The Blinding Light: The Uses of History in Constitutional Interpretation," 31 U. Chi. L. Rev. 502 (1964).

In 1925, 18 states, the District of Columbia, and the federal government authorized capital punishment for the rape of an adult female. By 1971, that number had declined to 16 states plus the federal government. When states had to rewrite death penalty laws after the Court in *Furman* v. *Georgia* (1972) invalidated existing laws on capital punishment, only three (Georgia, North Carolina, and Louisiana) decided to reinstate the death penalty for rape. Louisiana and North Carolina, responding to court challenges, reenacted the death penalty for murder but not for rape. This process of reconsideration by the states helped convince the Court that the penalty of death for rape was disproportionate.

In 1989, the Court was asked to decide whether a state could sentence to death someone who is mentally retarded. The individual sentenced to die argued that "there is an emerging national consensus against executing the mentally retarded." Penry v. Lynaugh, 492 U.S. 302, 329 (1989). However, only one state (Georgia) at the time this case was litigated banned the execution of retarded persons found guilty of a capital offense. A Maryland statute adopting the same policy was scheduled to take effect on July 1, 1989. In the Court's view, "the two state statutes prohibiting execution of the mentally retarded ... do not provide sufficient evidence at present of a natural consensus." Id. at 334.

By 2002, the Court decided that a sufficient number of states had moved toward prohibiting capital punishment for the retarded, making the practice no longer constitutional. Atkins v. Virginia, 536 U.S. 304 (2002). The two states that prohibited death penalties for the retarded had now grown to 18. Under pressure to reverse its 1989 ruling, the Court "asked whether there is reason to disagree with the judgment reached by the citizenry and its legislators." The Court said that "today our society views mentally retarded offenders as categorically less culpable than the average criminal." The practice of executing the retarded had declined to the point where the Court said "it is fair to say that a national consensus has developed against it." In 2008, the Court's relied on its understanding of "national consensus" to strike down the death penalty for someone convicted of raping an eight-year-old girl. Kennedy v. Louisiana, 554 U.S. ____(2008). What began as a process of the Court looking to individual state practices for guidance has gradually changed. Each time the Court "nationalizes" a constitutional value it inhibits states from making independent judgments. The decentralized and state-driven mechanism is increasingly centralized and made rigid by the Court.

Eclecticism

If the Constitution is to guide future generations, there must be some flexibility in applying its language. Speaking of a New Deal dispute over the Contract Clause, the Supreme Court observed:

> It is no answer to say that this public need was not apprehended a century ago, or to insist that what the provision of the Constitution meant to the vision of that day it must mean to the vision of our time. If by the statement that what the Constitution meant at the time of its adoption it means to-day, it is intended to say that the great clauses of the Constitution must be confined to the interpretation which the framers, with the conditions and outlook of their time, would have placed upon them, the statement carries its own refutation. Home Bldg. & Loan Ass'n v. Blaisdell, 290 U.S. 398, 442–43 (1934).

In interpreting the Constitution, we look partly at the "judicial gloss" added by the courts. It is the responsibility of the judiciary to interpret the law, and under the doctrine of stare decisis (stand by the precedents) judges try to honor prior rulings. Nevertheless, sufficient variations and discord among existing precedents allow any number of directions for future decisions. Which elements of an opinion were essential for the result and therefore binding on subsequent courts? Which were peripheral (obiter dicta)? At what point do we comb concurring and dissenting opinions?

Judges hold different views about the doctrine of stare decisis. Some are more willing than others to break with prior holdings. The Supreme Court's practice is to apply stare decisis less rigidly to constitutional than to nonconstitutional cases. Glidden Co. v. Zdanok, 370 U.S. 530, 543 (1962). If the

Court "errs" on nonconstitutional matters, legislatures may respond by passing a new statute. Errors of constitutional dimension, however, are more difficult to fix. Burnet v. Coronado Oil & Gas Co., 285 U.S. 393, 406–07 (1932). Continuity is important for statutory law, for it permits citizens to arrange their business and personal affairs with confidence. Courts should not disturb this sense of security and stability by needlessly disrupting the law. National Bank v. Whitney, 103 U.S. 99, 102 (1880). But errors of constitutional doctrine require correction. In the words of Justice Douglas, judges swear to support and defend the Constitution, "not the gloss which his predecessors may have put on it." 49 Colum. L. Rev. 735, 736 (1949).

Justice Owen Roberts once complained that the Court's change of views "tends to bring adjudications of this tribunal into the same class as a restricted railroad ticket, good for this day and train only." Smith v. Allwright, 321 U.S. 649, 669 (1944). Justice Stewart argued that even if he believed the Court decided wrongly and he dissented at the time, subsequent rulings should be governed by what the majority decided. Donovan v. Dewey, 452 U.S. 594, 609 (1981). Many judges, however, would consider it irresponsible if they failed to correct a previous decision containing a mistake in constitutional law. The initial embarrassment of having the Court reverse itself is more than offset by the enhanced reputation of a Court willing to acknowledge its own errors. Justice Jackson declined to bind himself "hand and foot" to prior decisions, even when they were his own. He saw "no reason why I should be consciously wrong today because I was unconsciously wrong yesterday." Massachusetts v. United States, 333 U.S. 611, 639–40 (1948). Two years later, he penned an elegant justification for rejecting prior opinions that have lost their persuasive quality (see Jackson reading).

Outright reversal of a ruling is rare. More frequent is the practice of ignoring a precedent or "distinguishing" it from the pending case. These silent or tacit overrulings prompted Justice Black to remark of such cases: "Their interment is tactfully accomplished, without ceremony, eulogy, or report of their demise." Hood & Sons v. Du Mond, 336 U.S. 525, 555 (1949). Judges may argue that the current facts are different or simply reinterpret the precedent. Such techniques avoid the costs of overruling a precedent but also produce conflicting case law and uncertainty for those who must obey, interpret, enforce, and practice law.

After reviewing the various approaches to constitutional interpretation, Justice Cardozo described the judge's task as an eclectic exercise that blends in varying proportions the methods of philosophy, history, tradition, logic, and sociology. Rules are replaced by working hypotheses. The Nature of the Judicial Process (1921). The pressure of deadlines eliminates many options. Time, political constraints, and other limitations often make it impossible for judges to examine the entire record, pursue promising leads, review all the precedents, and produce original research. For those and other reasons, judicial decisions should be treated not as final utterances but as works in progress.

Philip Bobbitt identified a broad range of techniques used by judges to interpret the Constitution. He suggested that if someone took colored pencils to mark through passages of a Supreme Court opinion, using a different color for each technique, the reader would end up with a multicolored document. Constitutional Fate 93–94 (1982).

The Doctrine of Original Intent:
Attorney General Meese versus Justice Brennan

Reliance on the framers' intent to interpret the Constitution has been debated almost continuously. A particularly interesting exchange of views occurred in 1985. Attorney General Edwin Meese III, in a speech to the American Bar Association on July 9, 1985, advocated a "Jurisprudence of Original Intention." He insisted that the only legitimate method of constitutional interpretation consists of resurrecting the original meaning of constitutional provisions. In a speech delivered at Georgetown University on October 12, 1985, Justice William J. Brennan, Jr., rejected primary dependence on original intent. The task of judges, he said, is to adapt the Constitution to current problems and current needs.

ATTORNEY GENERAL MEESE: The intended role of the judiciary generally, and the Supreme Court in particular, was to serve as the "bulwark of a limited constitution." The Founders believed that judges would not fail to regard the Constitution as fundamental law and would regulate their decisions by it. As the "faithful guardians of the Constitution," the judges were expected to resist any political effort to depart from the literal provisions of the Constitution. The standard of interpretation applied by the judiciary must focus on the text and the drafter's original intent.

. . .

In considering these areas of adjudication — Federalism, criminal law, and religion — one may conclude that far too many of the Court's opinions were, on the whole, mere policy choices rather than articulations of constitutional principle. The voting blocs and the arguments all reveal a greater allegiance to what the Court thinks constitutes sound public policy rather than a deference to what the Constitution, its text and intention, may demand.

One may also say that until there emerges a coherent jurisprudential stance, the work of the Court will continue in this ad hoc fashion. But that is not to argue for just *any* jurisprudence. In my opinion, a drift back toward the radical egalitarianism and expansive civil libertarianism of the Warren Court would once again be a threat to the notion of a limited but energetic government.

What, then, should a constitutional jurisprudence actually be? It should be a *jurisprudence of original intention.* By seeking to judge policies in light of principles, rather than remold principles in light of policies, the Court could avoid both the charge of incoherence *and* the charge of being either too conservative or too liberal.

A jurisprudence seriously aimed at the explication of original intention would produce defensible principles of government that would not be tainted by ideological predilection.

This belief in a *jurisprudence of original intention* also reflects a deeply rooted commitment to the idea of democracy. The Constitution represents the consent of the governed to the structures and powers of the government. The Constitution is the fundamental will of the people; that is the reason the Constitution is the fundamental law. To allow the courts to govern simply by what it views at the time as fair and decent, is a scheme of government no longer popular; the idea of democracy has suffered. The permanence of the Constitution has been weakened. A constitution that is viewed as only what the judges say it is, is no longer a constitution in the true sense of the term.

Those who framed the Constitution chose their words carefully; they debated at great length the most minute points. The language they chose meant something. It is incumbent upon the Court to determine what that meaning was. This is not a shockingly new theory; nor is it arcane or archaic.

. . .

Our belief is that only the sense in which the Constitution was accepted and ratified by the nation, and only the sense in which laws were drafted and passed provide a solid foundation for adjudication. Any other standard suffers the defect of pouring new meaning into old words, thus creating new powers and new rights totally at odds with the logic of our Constitution and its commitment to the rule of law.

JUSTICE BRENNAN:

The amended Constitution of the United States entrenches the Bill of Rights and the Civil War amendments and draws sustenance from the bedrock principles of another great text, the Magna Carta. So fashioned, the Constitution embodies the aspiration to social justice, brotherhood, and human dignity that brought this nation into being. The Declaration of Independence, the Constitution, and the Bill of Rights solemnly committed the United States to be a country where the dignity and rights of all persons were equal before all authority. In all candor we must concede that part of this egalitarianism in America has been more pretension than realized fact. But we are an aspiring people, a people with faith in progress. Our amended Constitution is the lodestar for our aspirations. Like every text worth reading, it is not crystalline. The phrasing is broad and the limitations of its provisions are

SOURCE: *South Texas Law Review,* Vol. 27, pp. 433–66 (1986). Footnotes omitted.

not clearly marked. Its majestic generalities and ennobling pronouncements are both luminous and obscure. This ambiguity, of course, calls forth interpretation, the interaction of reader and text. The encounter with the constitutional text has been, in many senses, my life's work. What is it we do when we interpret the Constitution? I will attempt to elucidate my approach to the text as well as my substantive interpretation.

. . .

… Our commitment to self-governance in a representative democracy must be reconciled with vesting in electorally unaccountable Justices the power to invalidate the expressed desires of representative bodies on the ground of inconsistency with higher law. Because judicial power resides in the authority to give meaning to the Constitution, the debate is really a debate about how to read the text, about constraints on what is legitimate interpretation.

There are those who find legitimacy in fidelity to what they call "the intentions of the Framers." In its most doctrinaire incarnation, this view demands that Justices discern exactly what the Framers thought about the question under consideration and simply follow that intention in resolving the case before them. It is a view that feigns self-effacing deference to the specific judgments of those who forged our original social compact. But in truth it is little more than arrogance cloaked as humility. It is arrogant to pretend that from our vantage we can gauge accurately the intent of the Framers on application of principle to specific, contemporary questions. All too often, sources of potential enlightenment such as records of the ratification debates provide sparse or ambiguous evidence of the original intention. Typically, all that can be gleaned is that the Framers themselves did not agree about the application or meaning of particular constitutional provisions and hid their differences in cloaks of generality. Indeed, it is far from clear whose intention is relevant—that of the drafters, the congressional disputants, or the ratifiers in the states—or even whether the idea of an original intention is a coherent way of thinking about a jointly drafted document drawing its authority from a general assent of the states. Apart from the problematic nature of the sources, our distance of two centuries cannot but work as a prism refracting all we perceive. One cannot help but speculate that the chorus of lamentations calling for interpretation faithful to "original intention"—and proposing nullification of interpretations that fail this quick litmus test—must inevitably come from persons who have no familiarity with the historical record.

. . .

Current Justices read the Constitution in the only way that we can: as twentieth-century Americans. We look to the history of the time of framing and to the intervening history of interpretation. But the ultimate question must be: What do the words of the text mean in our time? For the genius of the Constitution rests not in any static meaning it might have had in a world that is dead and gone, but in the adaptability of its great principles to cope with current problems and current needs....

The Natural Law Debate:
Frankfurter Against Black

In *Rochin* v. *California*, 342 U.S. 165 (1952), Justice Frankfurter overturned the actions of law enforcement officers who took a narcotics suspect to the hospital where an emetic was forced into his stomach against his will. He vomited two capsules containing morphine, and they were later admitted in evidence that led to his conviction. Frankfurter relied on the Due Process Clause of the Fourteenth Amendment to reverse the conviction. In a concurrence, Justice Black criticized Frankfurter for invoking natural law. Later, in *Griswold* v. *Connecticut*, 381 U.S. 479 (1965), in a case that struck down a state law banning contraceptives, Black's dissent summed up his views on the natural law approach.

MR. JUSTICE FRANKFURTER delivered the opinion of the Court.

… Regard for the requirements of the Due Process Clause "inescapably imposes upon this Court an exercise of judgment upon the whole course of the proceedings [resulting in a conviction] in order to ascertain whether they offend those canons of decency and fairness which express the notions of justice of English-speaking peoples even toward those charged with the most heinous offenses." *Malinski v. New York, supra,* at 416–417. These standards of justice are not authoritatively formulated anywhere as though they were specifics. Due process of law is a summarized constitutional guarantee of respect for those personal immunities which, as Mr. Justice Cardozo twice wrote for the Court, are "so rooted in the traditions and conscience of our people as to be ranked as fundamental" ... or are "implicit in the concept of ordered liberty." ...

The vague contours of the Due Process Clause do not leave judges at large. We may not draw on our merely personal and private notions and disregard the limits that bind judges in their judicial function. Even though the concept of due process of law is not final and fixed, these limits are derived from considerations that are fused in the whole nature of our judicial process. ...

Due process of law thus conceived is not to be derided as resort to a revival of "natural law." To believe that this judicial exercise of judgment could be avoided by freezing "due process of law" at some fixed stage of time or thought is to suggest that the most important aspect of constitutional adjudication is a function for inanimate machines and not for judges, for whom the independence safeguarded by Article III of the Constitution was designed and who are presumably guided by established standards of judicial behavior. Even cybernetics has not yet made that haughty claim. To practice the requisite detachment and to achieve sufficient objectivity no doubt demands of judges the habit of self-discipline and self-criticism, incertitude that one's own views are incontestable and alert tolerance toward views not shared. But these are precisely the presuppositions of our judicial process. They are precisely the qualities society has a right to expect from those entrusted with ultimate judicial power.

· · ·

Applying these general considerations to the circumstances of the present case, we are compelled to conclude that the proceedings by which this conviction was obtained do more than offend some fastidious squeamishness or private sentimentalism about combatting crime too energetically. This is conduct that shocks the conscience. Illegally breaking into the privacy of the petitioner, the struggle to open his mouth and remove what was there, the forcible extraction of his stomach's contents — this course of

proceeding by agents of government to obtain evidence is bound to offend even hardened sensibilities. They are methods too close to the rack and the screw to permit of constitutional differentiation. ...

MR. JUSTICE BLACK, concurring.

· · ·

What the majority hold is that the Due Process Clause empowers this Court to nullify any state law if its application "shocks the conscience," offends "a sense of justice" or runs counter to the "decencies of civilized conduct." The majority emphasize that these statements do not refer to their own consciences or to their senses of justice and decency. For we are told that "we may not draw on our merely personal and private notions"; our judgment must be grounded on "considerations deeply rooted in reason and in the compelling traditions of the legal profession." We are further admonished to measure the validity of state practices, not by our reason, or by the traditions of the legal profession, but by "the community's sense of fair play and decency"; by the "traditions and conscience of our people"; or by "those canons of decency and fairness which express the notions of justice of English-speaking peoples." These canons are made necessary, it is said, because of "interests of society pushing in opposite directions."

If the Due Process Clause does vest this Court with such unlimited power to invalidate laws, I am still in doubt as to why we should consider only the notions of English-speaking peoples to determine what are immutable and fundamental principles of justice. Moreover, one may well ask what avenues of investigation are open to discover "canons" of conduct so universally favored that this Court should write them into the Constitution? All we are told is that the discovery must be made by an "evaluation based on a disinterested inquiry pursued in the spirit of science, on a balanced order of facts." ...

MR. JUSTICE BLACK [*dissenting in* Griswold].

The due process argument which my Brothers HARLAN and WHITE adopt here is based, as their opinions indicate, on the premise that this Court is vested with power to invalidate all state laws that it considers to be arbitrary, capricious, unreasonable, or oppressive, or on this Court's belief that a particular state law under scrutiny has no "rational or justifying" purpose, or is offensive to a "sense of fairness and justice." If these formulas based on "natural justice," or others which mean the same thing, are to prevail, they require judges to determine what is or is not constitutional on the basis of their own appraisal of what laws are unwise or unnecessary. The power to make such decisions is of course that of a legislative body....

... And so, I cannot rely on the Due Process Clause or the Ninth Amendment or any mysterious and uncertain natural law concept as a reason for striking down this state law. The Due Process Clause with an "arbitrary and capricious" or "shocking to the conscience" formula was liberally used by this Court to strike down economic legislation in the early decades of this century, threatening, many people thought, the tranquility and stability of the Nation. See, *e.g., Lochner* v. *New York*, 198 U. S. 45. That formula, based on subjective considerations of "natural justice," is no less dangerous when used to enforce this Court's views about personal rights than those about economic rights....

Stare Decisis

In the interest of consistency and predictability, judges prefer to decide cases in accordance with past rulings. This doctrine of stare decisis (stand by the precedents) has particular force when applied to statutory interpretation, but decisions are regularly reviewed and revised to take into account recent developments, new information, and better understanding. In a concurring opinion in *McGrath* v. *Kristensen*, 340 U.S. 162 (1950), Justice Jackson offered a candid, personal, and amusing justification for parting company with opinions that seem, upon reflection, unconvincing.

MR. JUSTICE JACKSON, concurring.

I concur in the judgment and opinion of the Court. But since it is contrary to an opinion which, as Attorney General, I rendered in 1940, I owe some word of explanation. 39 Op. Atty. Gen. 504. I am entitled to say of that opinion what any discriminating reader must think of it — that it was as foggy as the statute the Attorney General was asked to interpret. It left the difficult borderline questions posed by the Secretary of War unanswered, covering its lack of precision with generalities which, however, gave off overtones of assurance that the Act applied to nearly every alien from a neutral country caught in the United States under almost any circumstances which required him to stay overnight.

The opinion did not at all consider aspects of our diplomatic history, which I now think, and should think I would then have thought, ought to be considered in applying any conscription Act to aliens.

· · ·

Precedent, however, is not lacking for ways by which a judge may recede from a prior opinion that has proven untenable and perhaps misled others. See Chief Justice Taney, *License Cases*, 5 How. 504, recanting views he had pressed upon the Court as Attorney General of Maryland in *Brown* v. *Maryland*, 12 Wheat. 419. Baron Bramwell extricated himself from a somewhat similar embarrassment by saying, "The matter does not appear to me now as it appears to have appeared to me then." *Andrews* v. *Styrap*, 26 L. T. R. (N.S.) 704, 706. And Mr. Justice Story, accounting for his contradiction of his own former opinion, quite properly put the matter: "My own error, however, can furnish no ground for its being adopted by this Court...." *United States* v. *Gooding*, 12 Wheat. 460, 478. Perhaps Dr. Johnson really went to the heart of the matter when he explained a blunder in his dictionary — "Ignorance, sir, ignorance." But an escape less self-depreciating was taken by Lord Westbury, who, it is said, rebuffed a barrister's reliance upon an earlier opinion of his Lordship: "I can only say that I am amazed that a man of my intelligence should have been guilty of giving such an opinion." If there are other ways of gracefully and good-naturedly surrendering former views to a better considered position, I invoke them all.

NOTES AND QUESTIONS

1. The omission in the text of the Constitution of any reference to the power of judicial review has triggered a great debate on several fronts. If the framers intended the courts to exercise the power, why didn't they enumerate it in the Constitution? Did they simply assume the availability of judicial re-

view? How do you compare the merits of Alexander Hamilton's Federalist No. 78 and the competing views of Brutus in his critique of judicial power?

2. In your view, did Chief Justice Marshall's opinion in *Marbury v. Madison* claim for the judiciary the final word on questions involving merely its own power, or did he assert the broader claim that the Court possessed the authority to rule on the constitutionality of the acts of coordinate departments as well?

3. Did Judge Gibson provide an effective critique of Marshall's reasoning in his dissent in *Eakin v. Raub*? Which of his arguments seem to you compelling?

4. In 1986, Attorney General Ed Meese III delivered a speech at Tulane University in which he challenged the last-word doctrine. His speech drew charges that he had exhibited disrespect for the Court, but which is more important: the text of the Constitution or the Court's interpretation of it? How would you answer that question?

5. Scholars have long debated the compatibility of judicial review and democracy. Is the promotion of democracy a responsibility of the judicial department? How should it best pursue that objective?

SELECTED READINGS

AGRESTO, JOHN. The Supreme Court and Constitutional Democracy. Ithaca, N.Y.: Cornell University Press, 1984.

ALFANGE, DEAN, JR. "On Judicial Policymaking and Constitutional Change: Another Look at the 'Original Intent' Theory of Constitutional Interpretation." 5 Hastings Constitutional Law Quarterly 603 (1978).

———. "Marbury v. Madison and Original Understandings of Judicial Review: In Defense of Traditional Wisdom," 1993 Supreme Court Review 329.

BERGER, RAOUL. Congress v. The Supreme Court. Cambridge, Mass.: Harvard University Press, 1969.

BICKEL, ALEXANDER M. The Least Dangerous Branch. New York: Bobbs-Merrill, 1962.

BISHIN, WILLIAM R. "Judicial Review in Democratic Theory." 50 Southern California Law Review 1099 (1977).

BLACK, CHARLES L., JR. The People and the Court. New York: Macmillan, 1960.

CARR, ROBERT K. The Supreme Court and Judicial Review. New York: Farrar and Rinehart, 1942.

COMMAGER, HENRY STEELE. Majority Rule and Minority Rights. New York: Oxford University Press, 1943.

CORWIN, EDWARD S. The Doctrine of Judicial Review. Princeton, N.J.: Princeton University Press, 1914.

———. Court over Constitution. Princeton, N.J.: Princeton University Press, 1938.

DAHL, ROBERT A. "Decision-Making in a Democracy: The Role of the Supreme Court as a National Policy-Maker." 6 Journal of Public Law 279 (1957).

DUCAT, CRAIG R. Modes of Constitutional Interpretation. St. Paul, Minn.: West, 1978.

FISHER, LOUIS. "Methods of Constitutional Interpretation: The Limits of Original Intent." 18 Cumberland Law Review 43 (1987-1988).

———. "The Curious Belief in Judicial Supremacy." 25 Suffolk University Law Review 85 (1991).

HAINES, CHARLES GROVES. The American Doctrine of Judicial Supremacy. Berkeley: University of California Press, 1932.

HENKIN, LOUIS. "Some Reflections on Current Constitutional Controversy." 109 University of Pennsylvania Law Review 637 (1961).

JAFFE, LOUIS L. "The Right to Judicial Review." 71 Harvard Law Review 401, 769 (1958).

KURLAND, PHILIP B. Politics, the Constitution, and the Warren Court. Chicago: University of Chicago Press, 1970.

LEVY, LEONARD W. Original Intent and the Framers' Constitution. New York: Macmillan, 1988.

MILLER, ARTHUR S., AND RONALD F. HOWELL. "The Myth of Neutrality in Constitutional Adjudication." 27 University of Chicago Law Review 661 (1960).

NELSON, WILLIAM E. "Changing Conceptions of Judicial Review: The Evolution of Constitutional Theory in the States, 1790–1860." 120 University of Pennsylvania Law Review 1166 (1972).

O'BRIEN, DAVID M. "Judicial Review and Constitutional Politics: Theory and Practice." 48 University of Chicago Law Review 1052 (1981).

POLLAK, LOUIS H. "Racial Discrimination and Judicial Integrity: A Reply to Professor Wechsler." 108 University of Pennsylvania Law Review 1 (1959).

ROSTOW, EUGENE V. The Sovereign Prerogative. New Haven, Conn.: Yale University Press, 1962.

SCALIA, ANTONIN. A Matter of Interpretation: Federal Courts and the Law. Princeton, N.J.: Princeton University Press, 1997.

SNOWISS, SYLVIA. Judicial Review and the Law of the Constitution. New Haven, Conn.: Yale University Press, 1990.

WELLINGTON, HARRY H. "The Nature of Judicial Review." 91 Yale Law Journal 486 (1982).

WOLFE, CHRISTOPHER. The Rise of Modern Judicial Review. New York: Basic Books, 1986.

WRIGHT, J. SKELLY. "The Role of the Supreme Court in a Democratic Society—Judicial Activism or Restraint." 54 Cornell Law Review 1 (1968).

———. "Professor Bickel, the Scholarly Tradition, and the Supreme Court." 84 Harvard Law Review 769 (1971).

3

Threshold Requirements: Husbanding Power and Prestige

The scope of judicial review is circumscribed by rules of self-restraint fashioned by judges. Various court doctrines sketch out the minimum conditions needed to adjudicate a case. These thresholds (or "gatekeeping rules") do more than limit access by litigants. They shield judges from cases that threaten their independence and institutional effectiveness. They ration scarce judicial resources and postpone or avoid decisions on politically sensitive issues.

Chief Justice Marshall suggested that the boundaries for judicial action were quite fixed: "It is most true that this Court will not take jurisdiction if it should not: but it is equally true, that it must take jurisdiction if it should." Cohens v. Virginia, 6 Wheat. 264, 404 (1821). The record of the judiciary, however, is quite different. What the Court should or should not accept is largely a matter of judicial discretion. Reflecting on his work at the Supreme Court, Justice Brandeis confided: "The most important thing we do is not doing." Alexander M. Bickel, The Unpublished Opinions of Mr. Justice Brandeis 17 (1957). The deliberate withholding of judicial power often reflects the fact that courts lack ballot-box legitimacy. While often couched in technical jargon, jurisdictional requirements implicate fundamental questions of democratic theory.

Judges invoke access rules to promote the adversary system, preserve public support, avoid conflicts with other branches of government, and provide flexibility of action for the judiciary. The doctrines used to pursue those goals include justiciability, standing, mootness, ripeness, political questions, and prudential considerations, all of which help protect an unelected and unrepresentative judiciary. Although efforts are made to distinguish these doctrines, inevitably they overlap. As noted by the Supreme Court: "The standing question thus bears close affinity to questions of ripeness — whether the harm asserted has matured sufficiently to warrant judicial intervention — and of mootness — whether the occasion for judicial intervention persists." Warth v. Seldin, 422 U.S. 490, 499 n.10 (1975).

A. CASES AND CONTROVERSIES

Article III of the Constitution limits the jurisdiction of federal courts to "cases" and "controversies." Courts must determine that they have jurisdiction to hear the case. Jurisdiction is granted both by the Constitution and by statute. Even after accepting jurisdiction, courts may decide that the subject matter is inappropriate for judicial consideration — what the courts call "nonjusticiable." This latter concept, at times synonymous with "political questions," is used to avoid collisions with Congress and the President. Baker v. Carr, 369 U.S. 186, 198, 208–34 (1962). It is also applied more broadly to cover issues outside the separation of powers. Flast v. Cohen, 392 U.S. 83, 95 (1968).

As a way to minimize error, miscalculation, and political conflict, courts adopt guidelines to avoid judgment on a large number of constitutional questions. These guidelines only provide very broad direction for judicial activity. If judges want to ignore them, they can. However, the rules supply a convenient list of justifications for refusing to decide a case. ASHWANDER v. TVA, 297 U.S. 288 (1936).

To resolve a legal claim, courts need to know that parties have been adversely affected. Abstract or hypothetical questions, removed from a concrete factual setting, prevent courts from reaching an informed judgment. The words "cases" and "controversies" limit the federal courts "to questions presented in an adversary context and in a form historically viewed as capable of resolution through the judicial process." Flast v. Cohen, 392 U.S. at 95.

Adverseness

The adversary system seeks truth by having judges and juries observe a contest between two sets of professional advocates. It assumes that two antagonistic parties, each with a sufficient stake in the outcome, will marshal the best arguments to defend their interests. This clash between rival parties "sharpens the presentation of issues upon which the court so largely depends for illumination of difficult constitutional questions." Baker v. Carr, 369 U.S. at 204. A case brought by two parties with the same interest loses its adversary character. South Spring Gold Co. v. Amador Gold Co., 145 U.S. 300 (1892). Nor is there adverseness when two attorneys bring a collusive or "friendly suit" or when both parties agree on a constitutional issue and want the same result.[1]

Courts occasionally consider a case even when both parties agree on the issue. In *United States* v. *Lovett* (1946), the Justice Department agreed with the plaintiff that a provision in a congressional statute was unconstitutional. To protect its interests, Congress passed legislation to create a special counsel. Functioning officially as amicus curiae, the counsel in effect served as counsel for Congress to assure adverseness. 328 U.S. 303, 304 (1946). In other cases the courts have appointed a special counsel to create an adversary proceeding. Granville-Smith v. Granville-Smith, 349 U.S. 1, 4 (1955).

During the battle over the Watergate tapes, President Nixon's lawyers argued in court that a case or controversy did not exist because Special Prosecutor Leon Jaworski "was an employee of the executive branch and Nixon was his boss." The judge in that trial, John Sirica, remarked: "any fool could see that a more genuine controversy couldn't be imagined." John J. Sirica, To Set the Record Straight 224 (1979).

There appeared to be lack of adverseness in the legislative veto case decided by the Supreme Court in 1983. The plaintiff, Jagdish Rai Chadha, sued the Immigration and Naturalization Service (INS), charging that its statutory procedure for deportation was unconstitutional. The government agreed with his position. The Ninth Circuit asked the House of Representatives and the Senate to file briefs as amici curiae. To the House, Chadha's case lacked adverseness because both parties found the statute invalid. Moreover, an appearance as amicus did not supply adverseness to create a case or controversy. The court rejected this reasoning because it would "implicitly approve the untenable result that all agencies could insulate unconstitutional orders and procedures from appellate review simply by agreeing that what they did was unconstitutional." Chadha v. INS, 634 F.2d 408, 420 (9th Cir. 1980).

In affirming the judgment of the Ninth Circuit, the Supreme Court also refused to regard the case as a "friendly, non-adversary, proceeding" between Chadha and the INS. As the Court noted, it would be "a curious result if, in the administration of justice, a person could be denied access to the courts because the Attorney General of the United States agreed with the legal arguments asserted by the individual." From the moment of Congress's formal intervention as amicus, adverseness was "beyond doubt." Even prior to intervention there was "adequate Art. III adverseness." INS v. Chadha, 462 U.S. 919, 939 (1983).

Advisory Opinions

The case or controversy requirement was tested in 1790 when Secretary of the Treasury Alexander Hamilton sought the advice of Chief Justice John Jay about a pending legal issue. Resolutions adopted

---

1. United States v. Johnson, 319 U.S. 302 (1943). See also Lord v. Veazie, 49 U.S. 251 (1850), in which the plaintiff and defendant had the same interest, and Moore v. Board of Education, 402 U.S. 47 (1971). In some cases the Court will allow a president to sue his or her own company because the board of directors, backed by stockholders, voted against the president to create adverseness. Carter v. Carter Coal Co., 298 U.S. 238, 286–87 (1936).

Chief Justice Jay Explains the Court's Position
on Issuing Advisory Opinions

We have considered the previous question stated in a letter written by your direction to us by the Secretary of State on the 18th of last month, [regarding] the lines of separation drawn by the Constitution between the three departments of the government. These being in certain respects checks upon each other, and our being judges of a court in the last resort, are considerations which afford strong arguments against the propriety of our extra-judicially deciding the questions alluded to, especially as the power given by the Constitu-

tion to the President, of calling on the heads of departments for opinions, seems to have been *purposely* as well as expressly united to the *executive* departments.

We exceedingly regret every event that may cause embarrassment to your administration, but we derive consolation from the reflection that your judgment will discern what is right, and that your usual prudence, decision, and firmness will surmount every obstacle to the preservation of the rights, peace, and dignity of the United States.

3 The Correspondence and Public Papers of John Jay 488–89 (H. Johnston ed. 1890) (emphasis in original). August 8, 1793.

---

by the Virginia House of Representatives had challenged the right of the national government to assume state debts. Hamilton regarded this resistance as "the first symptom of a spirit which must either be killed or it will kill the Constitution of the United States" and urged that the "collective weight" of the three branches be employed to repudiate the resolutions. Jay replied that it was inadvisable for the Court to join such action. 1 Charles Warren, Supreme Court in United States History 52–53 (1937). Similar efforts by Secretary of State Thomas Jefferson in 1793 to obtain advisory opinions were rebuffed by the Court. The Justices considered it improper to make extrajudicial decisions, noting that the Constitution gives the President the express power to obtain opinions from the heads of the executive departments (see box).

This same period, however, yields conflicting evidence. Chief Justice Jay and his colleagues on the Court advised President Washington in 1790 that the statutory requirement for them to "ride circuit" (travel around the country hearing appellate cases) was unconstitutional. Robert A. Dahlquist, 14 Sw. U. L. Rev. 46, 50–54 (1983). And in *Hayburn's Case* (1792), two circuit courts explained to President Washington their constitutional objections to a statute passed by Congress.[2] In both of these disputes, the interests of the courts were directly involved: having to ride circuit and perform nonjudicial duties.

The Supreme Court's formal position on advisory opinions appeared in 1911. Congress had authorized certain Indians to bring suit to determine the constitutionality of a statute. They were given expedited treatment by the Court of Claims and a right of appeal to the Supreme Court. Justice Day reviewed earlier instances in which federal judges decided that Congress could not impose nonjudicial duties on the courts. The suit, even though authorized by Congress, did not create a case or controversy between adverse parties. It was an effort to obtain the Court's opinion on the validity of congressional statutes. Day said it was inappropriate for the judiciary "to give opinions in the nature of advice concerning legislative action, a function never conferred upon it by the Constitution and against the exercise of which this court has steadily set its face from the beginning." Muskrat v. United

---

2. U.S. (2 Dall.) at 410–14 nn (1792). The statute was constitutionally objectionable because judicial decisions could be set aside by the Secretary of War, in effect converting a judicial decision into a mere advisory opinion. For similar reasons, the Court has opposed procedures that make its decisions dependent on executive and legislative actions before being carried out; Gordon v. United States, 117 U.S. 697 (1864).

States, 219 U.S. 346, 362 (1911). In 1948, the Court voiced constitutional objections to a statute that allowed the President to override the judgment of a federal court. The procedure amounted to "an advisory opinion in its most obnoxious form." C. & S. Air Lines v. Waterman Corp., 333 U.S. 103, 113–14 (1948).

Nevertheless, judges find ways to offer advice to the political branches. A number have met with Presidents, legislators, and agency administrators to discuss matters that were being, or could be, litigated. Walter Murphy, The Elements of Judicial Strategy 132–55 (1964). As a nonjudicial function, the Judicial Conference performs an advisory role by commenting on pending legislation. In their off-bench activities, federal judges have offered advice about the constitutionality of legislative proposals. After the Supreme Court in *INS* v. *Chadha* (1983) struck down the legislative veto, D.C. Circuit Judge Abner J. Mikva told a House committee that he did not think "there is any question" that a joint resolution of approval or disapproval, as a substitute for the discredited one-House and two-House vetoes, "would pass constitutional muster."[3]

Even in the course of writing an opinion, judges often resort to dicta to advise executive and legislative officers. In a 1978 case, Chief Justice Burger rejected a number of procedural attempts to postpone adjudication of the Price-Anderson Act. He said that any delay in interpreting the statute would frustrate one of its key purposes: "the elimination of doubts concerning the scope of private liability in the event of major nuclear accident." All parties would be adversely affected, he claimed, by deferring a decision. Duke Power Co. v. Carolina Environmental Study Group, 438 U.S. 59, 82 (1978). Justice Stevens admitted that the decision would serve the national interest by removing doubts concerning the constitutionality of the statute, but he did not include among judicial functions the duty to provide advisory opinions on important subjects:

> We are not statesmen; we are judges. When it is necessary to resolve a constitutional issue in the adjudication of an actual case or controversy, it is our duty to do so. But whenever we are persuaded by reasons of expediency to engage in the business of giving legal advice, we chip away a part of the foundation of our independence and our strength. Id. at 103 (concurring opinion).

A year later, Justice Stevens and three colleagues accused the Court of rendering an advisory opinion for the state of Massachusetts. In defense, Justice Powell explained that his decision merely provided "some guidance" to the state legislators. This exchange took place in two intriguing footnotes. See BELLOTTI v. BAIRD, 443 U.S. 622 (1979). In 1994, a concurrence by Justice O'Connor offered suggestions to New York State on how to create a school district for a religious minority without running into constitutional problems. Board of Ed. of Kiryas Joel v. Grumet, 512 U.S. 687, 717 (1994).

Declaratory Judgments

Parties uncertain of their legal rights want courts to determine those rights before injury is done. Otherwise, they might have to violate a law to bring a test case or forgo possible rights because of a fear of litigation. By issuing "declaratory judgments," courts can offer preventive relief. In 1928, Representative Ralph Gilbert explained the advantages of declaratory judgments: "Under the present law you take a step in the dark and then turn on the light to see if you stepped into a hole. Under the declaratory law you turn on the light and then take a step." 69 Cong. Rec. 2030 (1928). Unlike other judgments, declaratory relief decides only legal rights; it does not determine damages or the right to

---

3. "Legislative Veto After Chadha," hearings before the House Committee on Rules, 98th Cong., 2d Sess. 600 (1984).

coercive relief. To avoid the ban on advisory opinions, such judgments are limited to actual controversies. Also, declaratory judgments (unlike advisory opinions) are binding on the parties.

Before 1934, declaratory judgments had been issued by Great Britain, India, Scotland, Canada, Australia, and other nations. More than two dozen American states had adopted the practice. H. Rept. No. 1264, 73d Cong., 2d Sess. 1 (1934). Federal courts had also issued what were in effect declaratory judgments, because they determined rights and duties before a law was violated and even before a law had taken effect. Pierce v. Society of Sisters, 268 U.S. 510, 525 (1925); Village of Euclid v. Ambler Realty Co., 272 U.S. 365 (1926). To remove the legal uncertainty, Congress in 1934 passed the Declaratory Judgments Act. In "a case of actual controversy," it gives federal courts the power to declare "the rights and other legal relations of any interested party seeking such declaration, whether or not further relief is or could be sought. Any such declaration shall have the force and effect of a final judgment or decree and be reviewable as such." 48 Stat. 955 (1934); 28 U.S.C. § 2201 (2000). In a unanimous decision, the Supreme Court upheld the constitutionality of this statute. Aetna Life Insurance Co. v. Haworth, 300 U.S. 227 (1937).

Ashwander v. TVA
(The Brandeis Rules)
297 U.S. 288 (1936)

In a concurring opinion, Justice Brandeis reviewed the rules used by the courts to limit their exercise of judicial review. The rules are designed to avoid needless and potentially damaging (for the judiciary) conflicts with Congress.

The Court has frequently called attention to the "great gravity and delicacy" of its function in passing upon the validity of an act of Congress; and has restricted exercise of this function by rigid insistence that the jurisdiction of federal courts is limited to actual cases and controversies; and that they have no power to give advisory opinions. On this ground it has in recent years ordered the dismissal of several suits challenging the constitutionality of important acts of Congress....

The Court developed, for its own governance in the cases confessedly within its jurisdiction, a series of rules under which it has avoided passing upon a large part of all the constitutional questions pressed upon it for decision. They are:

1. The Court will not pass upon the constitutionality of legislation in a friendly, non-adversary, proceeding, declining because to decide such questions "is legitimate only in the last resort, and as a necessity in the determination of real, earnest and vital controversy between individuals. It never was the thought that, by means of a friendly suit, a party beaten in the legislature could transfer to the courts an inquiry as to the constitutionality of the legislative act."...

2. The Court will not "anticipate a question of constitutional law in advance of the necessity of deciding it."...

3. The Court will not "formulate a rule of constitutional law broader than is required by the precise facts to which it is to be applied."...

4. The Court will not pass upon a constitutional question although properly presented by the record, if there is also present some other ground upon which the case may be disposed of. This rule has found most varied application. Thus, if a case can be decided on either of two grounds, one involving a constitutional question, the other a question of statutory construction or general law, the Court will decide only the latter.... Appeals from the highest court of a state challenging its decision of a question under the Federal Constitution are frequently dismissed because the judgment can be sustained on an independent state ground....

5. The Court will not pass upon the validity of a statute upon complaint of one who fails to show that he is injured by its operation....

6. The Court will not pass upon the constitutionality of a statute at the instance of one who has availed himself of its benefits.

7. "When the validity of an act of the Congress is drawn in question, and even if a serious doubt of constitutionality is raised, it is a cardinal principle that this Court will first ascertain whether a construction of the statute is fairly possible by which the question may be avoided."...

Bellotti v. Baird (Advisory Opinions)

443 U.S. 622 (1979)

A Massachusetts statute required parental consent before an abortion could be performed on an unmarried woman under the age of eighteen. If one or both parents refused, a judge could order the abortion "for good cause shown." The Court held that the statute unduly burdened the right to seek an abortion because it gave a judge the right to disapprove an abortion for a mature minor and required parental consultation or notification in every instance. Writing for the Court, Justice Powell suggested to Massachusetts what would be an acceptable judicial by-pass procedure. Justice Stevens, joined by Justices Brennan, Marshall, and Blackmun, wrote a footnote that called Powell's opinion, in effect an advisory opinion. Powell prepared a footnote of his own to justify the direction he had given.

JUSTICE STEVENS:

Until and unless Massachusetts or another State enacts a less restrictive statutory scheme, this Court has no occasion to render an advisory opinion on the constitutionality of such a scheme. A real statute—rather than a mere outline of a possible statute—and a real case or controversy may well present questions that appear quite different from the hypothetical questions MR. JUSTICE POWELL has elected to address. Indeed, there is a certain irony in his suggestion that a statute that is intended to vindicate "the special interest of the State in encouraging an unmarried pregnant minor to seek the advice of her parents in making the important decision whether or not to bear a child," see *ante*, at 639, need not require notice to the parents of the minor's intended decision. That irony makes me wonder whether any legislature concerned with parental consultation would, in the absence of today's advisory opinion, have enacted a statute comparable to the one my Brethren have discussed.

JUSTICE POWELL:

The opinion of MR. JUSTICE STEVENS, concurring in the judgment, joined by three Members of the Court, characterizes this opinion as "advisory" and the questions it addresses as "hypothetical." Apparently, this is criticism of our attempt to provide some guidance as to how a State constitutionally may provide for adult involvement—either by parents or a state official such as a judge—in the abor-

tion decisions of minors. In view of the importance of the issue raised, and the protracted litigation to which these parties already have been subjected, we think it would be irresponsible simply to invalidate § 12S without stating our views as to the controlling principles.

The statute before us today is the same one that was here in *Bellotti I*. The issues it presents were not then deemed "hypothetical." In a unanimous opinion, we remanded the case with directions that appropriate questions be certified to the Supreme Judicial Court of Massachusetts "concerning the meaning of [§ 12S] and the procedure it imposes." 428 U.S., at 151. We directed that this be done because, as stated in the opinion, we thought the construction of § 12S urged by appellants would "avoid or substantially modify the federal constitutional challenge to the statute." *Id.*, at 148. The central feature of § 12S was its provision that a state-court judge could make the ultimate decision, when necessary, as to the exercise by a minor of the right to an abortion. See *id.*, at 145. We held that this "would be fundamentally different from a statute that creates a "'parental veto' [of the kind rejected in *Danforth*.]" *Ibid.* (footnote omitted). Thus, all Members of the Court agreed that providing for decisionmaking authority in a judge was not the kind of veto power held invalid in *Danforth*. The basic issues that were before us in *Bellotti I* remain in the case, sharpened by the construction of § 12S by the Supreme Judicial Court.

B. STANDING TO SUE

To satisfy the requirements of a case or controversy, parties bringing an action must have standing to sue. "Generalizations about standing to sue," Justice Douglas said with customary bluntness, "are largely worthless as such." Data Processing Service v. Camp, 397 U.S. 150, 151 (1970). Judges frequently accuse one another of circular reasoning. After the Supreme Court announced that the re-

---

The Elements of Standing

Lujan v. Defenders of Wildlife, 504 U.S. 555, 560–61 (1992): Over the years, our cases have established that the irreducible constitutional minimum of standing contains three elements. First, the plaintiff must have suffered an "injury in fact"—an invasion of a legally protected interest which is (a) concrete and particularized, see [Allen v. Wright, 468 U.S.] at 756; Warth v. Seldin, 422 U.S. 490, 508 (1975); Sierra Club v. Morton, 405 U.S. 727, 740–741, n. 16 (1972); and (b) "actual or imminent, not 'conjectural' or 'hypothetical,'" Whitmore [v. Arkansas], 495 U.S., at 155 (quoting Los Angeles v. Lyons, 461 U.S. 95, 102 (1983)). Second, there must be a causal connection between the injury and the conduct complained of—the injury has to be "fairly ... trace[able] to the challenged action of the defendant, and not ... th[e] result [of] the independent action of some third party not before the court." Simon v. Eastern Kentucky Welfare Rights Org., 426 U.S. 26, 41–42 (1976). Third, it must be "likely," as opposed to merely "speculative," that the injury will be "redressed by a favorable decision." Id., at 38, 43.

---

quirements of standing are met if a taxpayer has the "requisite personal stake in the outcome" of his or her suit, Justice Harlan chided the Court: "This does not, of course, resolve the standing problem; it merely restates it." Flast v. Cohen, 392 U.S. at 121 (dissenting opinion).

The reader forewarned, here are some generalizations. To demonstrate standing, parties must show injury to a legally protected interest, an injury that is real rather than abstract or hypothetical. O'Shea v. Littleton, 414 U.S. 488, 494 (1974). Injuries may be economic or noneconomic. Data Processing Service v. Camp, 397 U.S. at 154. They may be actual or threatened.[4] Injuries may afflict organizations as well as persons. Havens v. Realty Corp. v. Coleman, 455 U.S. 363, 379 n.19 (1982); Warth v. Seldin, 422 U.S. at 511. A "threatened" injury can be close cousin to the hypothetical. Five members of the Supreme Court in 1973 held that *allegations* of injury were sufficient to establish standing. Proof of actual injury was not necessary.[5] On the other hand, actual injury may be inadequate to establish standing if the Court wishes to defer to the states. City of Los Angeles v. Lyons, 461 U.S. 95 (1983). Occasionally, the Court summarizes the main elements of standing (see box).

Individuals, functioning in the role of private attorneys general, may have standing as "representatives of the public interest." Scenic Hudson Preservation Conf. v. FPC, 354 F.2d 608, 615–16 (2d Cir. 1965). This principle sometimes permits one party to assert the rights of third parties (jus tertii). Third-party suits (sometimes called "next-friend" standing) require special circumstances, such as someone intervening because a prisoner is mentally incompetent to represent himself. Coalition of Clergy, Lawyers & Professors v. Bush, 310 F.3d 1153, 1157–60 (9th Cir. 2002), citing Whitmore v. Arkansas, 495 U.S. 149, 161–64 (1990). Federal courts are reluctant to resolve a controversy on the basis of the rights of third persons who are not parties to the litigation. "The courts depend on effective advocacy, and therefore should prefer to construe legal rights only when the most effective advocates of those rights are before them." Singleton v. Wulff, 428 U.S. 106, 113–14 (1976). When genuine obstacles prevent a third party from appearing in court (such as the need to maintain anonymity to avoid the loss of rights), the courts allow exceptions.[6]

---

4. Linda R.S. v. Richard D., 410 U.S. 614, 617 (1973); Gladstone, Realtors v. Village of Bellwood, 441 U.S. 91, 99 (1979); Muller Optical Co. v. EEOC, 574 F.Supp. 946, 950 (W.D. Tenn. 1983).

5. United States v. SCRAP, 412 U.S. 669 (1973). Justice Stewart was satisfied with an "attenuated line of causation" linking litigant to an injury; id. at 688. Justices Blackmun and Brennan accepted allegations of harm as sufficient; id. at 699. Justice Douglas agreed with their position; id. at 703. Justice Marshall agreed with the holding on standing; id. at 724.

6. NAACP v. Alabama, 357 U.S. 449 (1958). See also Singleton v. Wulff, 428 U.S. at 114–16, and Note, "Standing to Assert Constitutional Jus Tertii," 88 Harv. L. Rev. 423 (1974). For a rejection of third-party suits, in this case involving one death row inmate attempting to intervene for another, see Whitmore v. Arkansas, 495 U.S. 149 (1990).

Courts recognize that Congress can, by statute, confer standing upon an individual or a group, and courts may defer to Congress on such matters.[7] "Citizen suits" may be brought by private individuals to enforce federal laws, such as the Clean Water Act. Friends of Earth v. Laidlaw Environmental Servs., 528 U.S. 167 (2000). However, such statutory phrases as "any person aggrieved" or "adversely affected" allow the courts broad discretion in interpreting what Congress means by *standing*. Furthermore, Congress cannot compel the courts to grant standing for a suit that, in the opinion of judges, lacks the necessary ingredients of a case or controversy. Congressional efforts to confer standing are limited by the judiciary's exclusive responsibility to determine Article III requirements.[8] There is a fundamental difference between Article I statutory standing and Article III constitutional standing. In addition to the standing requirements of Article III (injury, etc.), the Court adopts a "prudential standing" rule that can favor not only the plaintiff seeking relief but also judicial power to referee disputes.[9]

Courts raise and lower the standing barrier depending on circumstances. In 1923, an individual taxpayer was denied standing to challenge the constitutionality of a federal statute that provided appropriations to the states for maternal and infant care. The taxpayer claimed that Congress had exceeded its Article I powers and had invaded territory reserved to the states by the Tenth Amendment. The Supreme Court decided that a federal taxpayer's interest in financing the program was "comparatively minute and indeterminable," and the effect on future taxation "so remote, fluctuating and uncertain" that there was no possibility of a direct injury to confer standing. FROTHINGHAM v. MELLON, 262 U.S. 447, 487 (1923). As explained below, the Court found it necessary to revisit this reasoning.

The *Flast* Doctrine

The Court in *Frothingham* understood that any effort to lower the barrier for standing would mean increased casework for the judiciary. Other taxpayers could challenge federal statutes involving the outlay of public funds. Greater recourse to litigation might bring the administrative process to a standstill, as each disappointed party looked automatically to the courts for relief. Critics objected to the 1923 decision because it was unclear whether the Court had announced a constitutional bar to taxpayer suits (compelled by Article III limitations on federal court jurisdiction) or had temporarily imposed a rule of self-restraint to be lifted in the future. In later years the Supreme Court admitted that *Frothingham* could be read either way. Flast v. Cohen, 392 U.S. at 92–93.

The Justice Department interpreted *Frothingham* as an absolute prohibition on taxpayer suits. The Supreme Court discarded that notion in a 1968 suit that involved a taxpayer's challenge to the use of public funds for religious schools. An absolute prohibition would put the government in the position of conceding that a taxpayer lacked standing "even if Congress engaged in such palpably unconstitutional conduct as providing funds for the construction of churches for particular sects." FLAST v. COHEN, 392 U.S. 83, 98 n.17. The Court decided to liberalize the rule on standing but only at the cost of creating substantial doctrinal confusion. It claimed that standing focuses on the party, not the issue: "when standing is placed in issue in a case, the question is whether the person whose standing is challenged is a proper party to request an adjudication of a particular issue and not whether the issue is justiciable." Id. at 99–100. This distinction between party and issue was very

---

7. Sierra Club v. Morton, 405 U.S. 727, 732 n.3 (1972); Trafficante v. Metropolitan Life Ins., 409 U.S. 205, 209 (1972); Linda R.S. v. Richard D., 410 U.S. at 617 n.3; Warth v. Seldin, 422 U.S. at 501.

8. Data Processing Service v. Camp, 397 U.S. at 154; Simon v. Eastern Kentucky Welfare Rights Org., 426 U.S. 26, 41 n.22 (1976). For a strict reading of statutory authorization to bring suit, see Bread PAC v. FEC, 455 U.S. 577 (1982).

9. Here the courts determine whether the interest sought to be protected by the plaintiffs is *arguably* within the "zone of interests" to be protected by statute. The test is not whether a statute specifically intends to benefit a plaintiff; it is enough to find that the plaintiff's interests are arguably protected. National Credit Union Admin. v. First National Bank & Trust Co., 522 U.S. 479, 488–99 (1998); FEC v. Akins, 524 U.S. 11, 19–26 (1998).

The Party/Issue Dichotomy in *Flast*

The effort of the Court to distinguish between party and issue in *Flast* lost its crispness when the Justices tried to explain why Mrs. Flast had standing and Mrs. Frothingham did not. The Court looked to the substantive issues to determine whether a logical "nexus" existed between the status asserted and the claim adjudicated. The Court identified two aspects of nexus: "(1) the taxpayer must establish a logical link between his or her status and the legislative statute attacked, and (2) the taxpayer must connect his or her status with "the precise nature of the constitutional infringement alleged." 392 U.S. at 102. The Court concluded that both Frothingham and Flast satisfied the first but only Flast satisfied the second. Justice

Harlan dissented, unable to understand how the Court could classify the Article I/Tenth Amendment position in *Frothingham* as too general, while accepting the First Amendment/Establishment Clause in *Flast* as sufficiently "precise."

The Court decided that it was time to retreat from the absolute barrier of *Frothingham* even if it could not adequately explain why. The party/issue distinction was unpersuasive. Even the questions of party and injury had become muddled. Did Mrs. Flast have to be a taxpayer to bring suit? Could she have had standing if she lived on interest from tax-exempt bonds and was therefore unable to show injury or a monetary stake? Such fundamental questions were left unanswered.

unclear (see box). By lowering the barrier for standing, the Supreme Court not only encouraged more lawsuits but invited collisions with other branches of government. As noted in the next section, Supreme Court Justices regularly challenge the usefulness and value of *Flast*.

Separation of Powers Concerns

In 1972, the Burger Court raised the barrier to standing. It denied standing to an environmental group that wanted to prevent construction of a ski resort in a national park. The Court was deeply split, four Justices arrayed against three. Sierra Club v. Morton, 405 U.S. 727 (1972). In that same year it refused to decide whether the Army's surveillance of domestic activities constituted a chilling effect on First Amendment liberties. A majority of five Justices, with four dissenting, held that there was insufficient evidence of a direct injury to present a case for resolution in the courts.[10]

The close link between standing, issue, and limiting collisions with other branches is highlighted by a 1974 decision in which the Supreme Court denied standing to a taxpayer who challenged the constitutionality of covert spending by the Central Intelligence Agency. The Court specifically looked at the issues raised before dismissing the case on standing, even though the constitutional provision (the Statement and Account Clause) is quite as "precise" as the Establishment Clause at stake in *Flast*. More to the point, the Court noted that relief was available through the regular political process. What was dismissed on standing appeared to turn basically on questions of separation of power.[11] UNITED STATES v. RICHARDSON, 418 U.S. 166 (1974). In concurring in this 5 to 4 opinion, Justice Powell urged the Court to abandon *Flast*'s two-part "nexus" test as hopeless and warned that a failure by the judiciary to exercise self-restraint might provoke retaliation by the political branches. A relaxed standing policy, he said, would expand judicial power: "It seems to be inescapable that allowing unrestricted taxpayer or citizen standing would significantly alter the allocation of power at the national level, with a shift away from a democratic form of government." In 1997, under pressure of a lawsuit, the CIA

---

10. Laird v. Tatum, 408 U.S. 1 (1972). Curiously, a year later the Court gave standing to five law students to bring an environmental suit against the Interstate Commerce Commission; United States v. SCRAP, 412 U.S. 669 (1973). Evidently, standing *does* depend on the issue.

11. See also Schlesinger v. Reservists to Stop the War, 418 U.S. 208 (1974), which denied plaintiffs standing to challenge the constitutionality of members of Congress who served in the military reserves, in apparent conflict with the Ineligibility Clause.

released a figure of $26.6 billion for the budget of the intelligence community. Of that amount, the CIA portion was about $3 billion. In 1998, the CIA voluntarily released a figure of $26.7 billion for the community's budget, but in 1999 it again refused to disclose the aggregate budget. A lawsuit to obtain the budget total by invoking the Freedom of Information Act was dismissed in 1999. Aftergood v. CIA, Civ. No. 98-2107(TFH) (D.D.C. 1999). In 2007, Congress required the administration to disclose the aggregate budget of the intelligence community. 121 Stat. 335 (2007). On October 30, 2007, the administration released the aggregate amount of $43.5 billion for fiscal year 2007. Adding intelligence funds from the military services pushes the total beyond $50 billion.

The connection between standing and sensitive political issues was evident in 1975 when the Court announced that the inquiry into standing "involves both constitutional limitations on federal-court jurisdiction and prudential limitations on its exercise.... In both dimensions it is founded in concern about the proper—and properly limited—role of the courts in a democratic society." Warth v. Seldin, 422 U.S. at 498. Prudential rules of standing are not constitutionally required, but they "serve to limit the role of the courts in resolving public disputes." Id. at 500. In a dissenting opinion joined by Justices White and Marshall, Justice Brennan picked additional holes in the Court's doctrine that standing was unrelated to the issue being litigated:

> While the Court gives lip service to the principle, often repeated in recent years, that "standing in no way depends on the merits of the plaintiff's contention that particular conduct is illegal," ... in fact the opinion, which tosses out of court almost every conceivable kind of plaintiff who could be injured by the activity claimed to be unconstitutional, can be explained only by an indefensible hostility to the claim on the merits.

The *Flast* doctrine was further shaken by *Valley Forge College* v. *Americans United* (1982), which denied plaintiffs standing to challenge the transfer of federal property to a Christian college. Justice Rehnquist, writing for the Court, first argued that the plaintiffs could not sue as taxpayers because the land was transferred under the Property Clause, not the Taxing and Spending Clause. He then denied that the Establishment Clause gave citizens a personal constitutional right to bring suit. Four Justices dissented, accusing the majority of using a "threshold question" to decide substantive issues and obfuscate legal rights. Valley Forge College v. Americans United, 454 U.S. 464 (1982). In 1984, the Court relied on separation of powers analysis to deny standing to black parents who challenged the government's desegregation policy. ALLEN v. WRIGHT, 468 U.S. 737 (1984).

In 1997, the Supreme Court issued an important decision regarding standing for members of Congress. Senator Robert C. Byrd and five other legislators brought suit to challenge the constitutionality of the Line Item Veto Act of 1996. Although Congress had by statute authorized such a lawsuit by members of Congress, the Court unanimously held that the lawmakers lacked standing. The decision pointed out that Senator Byrd and his five colleagues were simply on the losing end of a vote to give the President a form of item-veto authority, and that both Houses of Congress had filed a brief upholding the constitutionality of the statute. The effect of the decision was to advise legislators who lose during the legislative process to seek remedies within Congress rather than turn to the courts for relief. Raines v. Byrd, 521 U.S. 811 (1997). See the reading for this case in Chapter One. A year later, when standing was established for two private plaintiffs, the Court declared the statute unconstitutional. Clinton v. City of New York, 524 U.S. 417 (1998). The reading for this decision appears in Chapter 6. Much of the confusion about the standing doctrine has its source in the Court's habit of spinning abstract theories that are, at bottom, techniques of pushing matters to the states and the elected branches.

In 2007, the Court appeared to partially revive *Frothingham* by placing strict limits on *Flast*. The case involved a presidential executive order that created a White House office to assist faith-based communities. The Court suggested that a plaintiff might have had standing if Congress had established the office, but not when the initiative came from the executive branch, even when the funds for the office came from congressional appropriations. Depending on how one wants to count the votes, the decision was either 5 to 4 or 3-2-4. Justices Scalia and Thomas concurred with the plurality of three but said it was time to overrule *Flast*. The plurality declined to go that far. Hein v. Freedom From Religion Foundation, 551 U.S. ____ (2007). This case is also discussed in Chapter 12.

Frothingham v. Mellon

262 U.S. 447 (1923)

The Commonwealth of Massachusetts and a taxpayer, Harriet Frothingham, challenged the constitutionality of a federal statute that provided funds [appropriations] to the states for maternal and infant care. They claimed that this use of the appropriations power exceeded the authority of Congress and invaded state power. The Court [determined] concluded that neither [whether either] party had sufficient standing to bring this type of lawsuit.

Mr. Justice Sutherland delivered the opinion of the Court.

These cases were argued and will be considered and disposed of together. The first is an original suit in this Court. The other was brought in the Supreme Court of the District of Columbia.... Both cases challenge the constitutionality of the Act of November 23, 1921, c. 135, 42 Stat. 224, commonly called the Maternity Act. Briefly, it provides for an initial appropriation and thereafter annual appropriations for a period of five years, to be apportioned among such of the several States as shall accept and comply with its provisions, for the purpose of coöperating with them to reduce maternal and infant mortality and protect the health of mothers and infants. It creates a bureau to administer the act in coöperation with state agencies, which are required to make such reports concerning their operations and expenditures as may be prescribed by the federal bureau. Whenever that bureau shall determine that funds have not been properly expended in respect of any State, payments may be withheld.

It is asserted that these appropriations are for purposes not national, but local to the States, and together with numerous similar appropriations constitute an effective means of inducing the States to yield a portion of their sovereign rights.... In the *Frothingham* case plaintiff alleges that the effect of the statute will be to take her property, under the guise of taxation, without due process of law.

We have reached the conclusion that the cases must be disposed of for want of jurisdiction without considering the merits of the constitutional questions.

In the first case, the State of Massachusetts presents no justiciable controversy either in its own behalf or as the representative of its citizens. The appellant in the second suit has no such interest in the subject-matter, nor is any such injury inflicted or threatened, as will enable her to sue.

First. The State of Massachusetts in its own behalf, in effect, complains that the act in question invades the local concerns of the State, and is a usurpation of power, viz: the power of local self government reserved to the States.

Probably, it would be sufficient to point out that the powers of the State are not invaded, since the statute imposes no obligation but simply extends an option which the State is free to accept or reject. But we do not rest here. Under Article III, § 2, of the Constitution, the judicial power of this Court extends "to controversies ... between a State and citizens of another State" and the Court has original jurisdiction "in all cases ... in which a State shall be party." The effect of this is not to confer jurisdiction upon the Court merely because a State is a party, but only where it is a party to a proceeding of judicial cognizance. Proceedings not of a justiciable character are outside the contemplation of the constitutional grant....

We come next to consider whether the suit may be maintained by the State as the representative of its citizens. To this the answer is not doubtful. We need not go so far as to say that a State may never intervene by suit to protect its citizens against any form of enforcement of unconstitutional acts of Congress; but we are clear that the right to do so does not arise here. Ordinarily, at least, the only way in which a State may afford protection to its citizens in such cases is through the enforcement of its own criminal statutes, where that is appropriate, or by opening its courts to the injured persons for the maintenance of civil suits or actions. But the citizens of Massachusetts are also citizens of the United States. It cannot be conceded that a State, as *parens patriae,* may institute judicial proceedings to protect citizens of the United States from the operation of the statutes thereof....

Second. The attack upon the statute in the *Froth-*

ingham case is, generally, the same, but this plaintiff alleges in addition that she is a taxpayer of the United States; and her contention, though not clear, seems to be that the effect of the appropriations complained of will be to increase the burden of future taxation and thereby take her property without due process of law. The right of a taxpayer to enjoin the execution of a federal appropriation act, on the ground that it is invalid and will result in taxation for illegal purposes, has never been passed upon by this Court. In cases where it was presented, the question has either been allowed to pass *sub silentio* or the determination of it expressly withheld....

... But the relation of a taxpayer of the United States to the Federal Government is very different. His interest in the moneys of the Treasury—partly realized from taxation and partly from other sources—is shared with millions of others; is comparatively minute and indeterminable; and the effect upon future taxation, of any payment out of the funds, so remote, fluctuating and uncertain, that no basis is afforded for an appeal to the preventive powers of a court of equity.

The administration of any statute, likely to produce additional taxation to be imposed upon a vast number of taxpayers, the extent of whose several liability is indefinite and constantly changing, is essentially a matter of public and not of individual concern. If one taxpayer may champion and litigate such a cause, then every other taxpayer may do the same, not only in respect of the statute here under review but also in respect of every other appropriation act and statute whose administration requires the outlay of public money, and whose validity may be questioned. The bare suggestion of such a result, with its attendant inconveniences, goes far to sustain the conclusion which we have reached, that a suit of this character cannot be maintained. It is of much significance that no precedent sustaining the right to maintain suits like this has been called to our attention, although, since the formation of the government, as an examination of the acts of Congress will disclose, a large number of statutes appropriating or involving the expenditure of moneys for non-federal purposes have been enacted and carried into effect.

The functions of government under our system are apportioned. To the legislative department has been committed the duty of making laws; to the executive the duty of executing them; and to the judiciary the duty of interpreting and applying them in cases properly brought before the courts. The general rule is that neither department may invade the province of the other and neither may control, direct or restrain the action of the other.... We have no power *per se* to review and annul acts of Congress on the ground that they are unconstitutional. That question may be considered only when the justification for some direct injury suffered or threatened, presenting a justiciable issue, is made to rest upon such an act.... Here the parties plaintiff have no such case. Looking through forms of words to the substance of their complaint, it is merely that officials of the executive department of the government are executing and will execute an act of Congress asserted to be unconstitutional; and this we are asked to prevent. To do so would be not to decide a judicial controversy, but to assume a position of authority over the governmental acts of another and co-equal department, an authority which plainly we do not possess.

No. 24, Original, dismissed.
No. 962 affirmed.

Flast v. Cohen

392 U.S. 83 (1968)

Taxpayers challenged the Elementary and Secondary Education Act of 1965 on the ground that it used federal funds to finance instruction and the purchase of educational materials for use in religious and sectarian schools, in violation of the Establishment and Free Exercise Clauses. A three-judge court ruled, on the basis of *Frothingham* v. *Mellon* (1923), that the taxpayers lacked standing to bring the suit. Florence Flast and other taxpayers brought this suit against Wilbur Cohen, Secretary of Health, Education and Welfare

MR. CHIEF JUSTICE WARREN delivered the opinion of the Court.

In *Frothingham* v. *Mellon*, 262 U.S. 447 (1923), this Court ruled that a federal taxpayer is without standing to challenge the constitutionality of a federal statute. That ruling has stood for 45 years as an impenetrable barrier to suits against Acts of Congress brought by individuals who can assert only the interest of federal taxpayers. In this case, we must decide whether the *Frothingham* barrier should be lowered when a taxpayer attacks a federal statute on the ground that it violates the Establishment and Free Exercise Clauses of the First Amendment.

Appellants filed suit in the United States District Court for the Southern District of New York to enjoin the allegedly unconstitutional expenditure of federal funds under Titles I and II of the Elementary and Secondary Education Act of 1965, ... The complaint alleged that the seven appellants had as a common attribute that "each pay[s] income taxes of the United States," and it is clear from the complaint that the appellants were resting their standing to maintain the action solely on their status as federal taxpayers....

The gravamen of the appellants' complaint was that federal funds appropriated under the Act were being used to finance instruction in reading, arithmetic, and other subjects in religious schools, and to purchase textbooks and other instructional materials for use in such schools. Such expenditures were alleged to be in contravention of the Establishment and Free Exercise Clauses of the First Amendment. Appellants' constitutional attack focused on the statutory criteria which state and local authorities must meet to be eligible for federal grants under the Act.... The specific criterion ... attacked by the appellants is the requirement

"that, to the extent consistent with the number of educationally deprived children in the school district of the local educational agency who are enrolled in private elementary and secondary schools, such agency has made provision for including special educational services and arrangements (such as dual enrollment, educational radio and television, and mobile educational services and equipment) in which such children can participate...." 20 U.S.C. §241e (a)(2).

... A State wishing to participate in the program must submit a plan to the Commissioner [*of Education*] for approval, and the plan must

"provide assurance that to the extent consistent with law such library resources, textbooks, and other instructional materials will be provided on an equitable basis for the use of children and teachers in private elementary and secondary schools in the State...."

· · ·

II.

This Court first faced squarely the question whether a litigant asserting only his status as a taxpayer has standing to maintain a suit in a federal court in *Frothingham* v. *Mellon, supra,* and that de-cision must be the starting point for analysis in this case.... The Court noted that a federal taxpayer's "interest in the moneys of the Treasury ... is comparatively minute and indeterminable" and that "the effect upon future taxation, of any payment out of the [Treasury's] funds, ... [is] remote, fluctuating and uncertain." *Id.,* at 487. As a result, the Court ruled that the taxpayer had failed to allege the type of "direct injury" necessary to confer standing. *Id.,* at 488.

Although the barrier *Frothingham* erected against federal taxpayer suits has never been breached, the decision has been the source of some confusion and the object of considerable criticism. The confusion has developed as commentators have tried to determine whether *Frothingham* establishes a constitutional bar to taxpayer suits or whether the Court was simply imposing a rule of self-restraint which was not constitutionally compelled. The conflicting viewpoints are reflected in the arguments made to this Court by the parties in this case. The Government has pressed upon us the view that *Frothingham* announced a constitutional rule, compelled by the Article III limitations on federal court jurisdiction and grounded in considerations of the doctrine of separation of powers. Appellants, however, insist that *Frothingham* expressed no more than a policy of judicial self-restraint which can be disregarded when compelling reasons for assuming jurisdiction over a taxpayer's suit exist. The opinion delivered in *Frothingham* can be read to support either position. The concluding sentence of the opinion states that, to take jurisdiction of the taxpayer's suit, "would be not to decide a judicial controversy, but to assume a position of authority over the governmental acts of another and co-equal department, an authority which plainly we do not possess." 262 U.S., at 489. Yet the concrete reasons given for denying standing to a federal taxpayer suggest that the Court's holding rests on something less than a constitutional foundation. For example, the Court conceded that standing had previously been conferred on municipal taxpayers to sue in that capacity. However, the Court viewed the interest of a federal taxpayer in total federal tax revenues as "comparatively minute and indeterminable" when measured against a municipal taxpayer's interest in a smaller city treasury. *Id.,* at 486–487. This suggests that the petitioner in *Frothingham* was denied standing not because she was a taxpayer but because her tax bill was not large enough. In addition, the Court spoke of the "attendant inconveniences" of entertaining that taxpayer's suit because it might open the door of federal courts to countless such suits "in respect of every other appropriation act and statute whose administration requires the outlay of public money, and whose validity may be questioned." *Id.*, at 487. Such a statement suggests pure policy considerations.

To the extent that *Frothingham* has been viewed as resting on policy considerations, it has been criticized as depending on assumptions not consistent with modern conditions. For example, some commentators have pointed out that a number of corporate taxpayers today have a federal tax liability running into hundreds of millions of dollars, and such taxpayers have a far greater monetary stake in the Federal Treasury than they do in any municipal treasury. To some degree, the fear expressed in *Frothingham* that allowing one taxpayer to sue would inundate the federal courts with countless similar suits has been mitigated by the ready availability of the devices of class actions and joinder under the Federal Rules of Civil Procedure, adopted subsequent to the decision in *Frothingham.* Whatever the merits of the current debate over *Frothingham,* its very existence suggests that we should undertake a fresh examination of the limitations upon standing to sue in a federal court and the application of those limitations to taxpayer suits.

III.

The jurisdiction of federal courts is defined and limited by Article III of the Constitution. In terms relevant to the question for decision in this case, the judicial power of federal courts is constitutionally restricted to "cases" and "controversies." As is so often the situation in constitutional adjudication, those two words have an iceberg quality, containing beneath their surface simplicity submerged complexities which go to the very heart of our constitutional form of government. Embodied in the words "cases" and "controversies" are two complementary but somewhat different limitations. In part those words limit the business of federal courts to questions presented in an adversary context and in a form historically viewed as capable of resolution through the judicial process. And in part those words define the role assigned to the judiciary in a tripartite allocation of power to assure that the federal courts will not intrude into areas committed to the other branches of government....

... [T]he Government's position is that the constitutional scheme of separation of powers, and the deference owed by the federal judiciary to the other two branches of government within that scheme, present an absolute bar to taxpayer suits challenging the validity of federal spending programs. The Government views such suits as involving no more than the mere disagreement by the taxpayer "with the uses to which tax money is put." According to the Government, the resolution of such disagreements is committed to other branches of the Federal Government and not to the judiciary. Consequently, the Government contends that, under no circumstances, should standing be conferred on federal taxpayers to challenge a federal taxing or spending program.*[At this point the Court observes, in a footnote: "The logic of the Government's argument would compel it to concede that a taxpayer would lack standing even if Congress engaged in such palpably unconstitutional conduct as providing funds for the construction of churches for particular sects."]* An analysis of the function served by standing limitations compels a rejection of the Government's position.

... The fundamental aspect of standing is that it focuses on the party seeking to get his complaint before a federal court and not on the issues he wishes to have adjudicated. The "gist of the question of standing" is whether the party seeking relief has "alleged such a personal stake in the outcome of the controversy as to assure that concrete adverseness which sharpens the presentation of issues upon which the court so largely depends for illumination of difficult constitutional questions." *Baker* v. *Carr,* 369 U.S. 186, 204 (1962). In other words, when standing is placed in issue in a case, the question is whether the person whose standing is challenged is a proper party to request an adjudication of a particular issue and not whether the issue itself is justiciable. Thus, a party may have standing in a particular case, but the federal court may nevertheless decline to pass on the merits of the case because, for example, it presents a political question....

When the emphasis in the standing problem is placed on whether the person invoking a federal court's jurisdiction is a proper party to maintain the action, the weakness of the Government's argument in this case becomes apparent. The question whether a particular person is a proper party to maintain the action does not, by its own force, raise separation of powers problems related to improper judicial interference in areas committed to other branches of the Federal Government. Such problems arise, if at all, only from the substantive issues the individual seeks to have adjudicated.... A taxpayer may or may not have the requisite personal stake in the outcome, depending upon the circumstances of the particular case. Therefore, we find no absolute bar in Article III to suits by federal taxpayers challenging allegedly unconstitutional federal taxing and spending programs. There remains, however, the problem of determining the circumstances under which a federal taxpayer will be deemed to have the personal stake and interest that impart the necessary concrete adverseness to such litigation so that standing can be conferred on the taxpayer *qua* taxpayer consistent with the constitutional limitations of Article III.

IV.

The various rules of standing applied by federal courts have not been developed in the abstract.... However, our decisions establish that, in ruling on standing, it is both appropriate and necessary to look to the substantive issues for another purpose, namely, to determine whether there is a logical nexus between the status asserted and the claim sought to be adjudicated....

The nexus demanded of federal taxpayers has two aspects to it. First, the taxpayer must establish a logical link between that status and the type of legislative enactment attacked.... Secondly, the taxpayer must establish a nexus between that status and the precise nature of the constitutional infringement alleged. Under this requirement, the taxpayer must show that the challenged enactment exceeds specific constitutional limitations imposed upon the exercise of the congressional taxing and spending power and not simply that the enactment is generally beyond the powers delegated to Congress by Art. I, § 8. When both nexuses are established, the litigant will have shown a taxpayer's stake in the outcome of the controversy and will be a proper and appropriate party to invoke a federal court's jurisdiction.

The taxpayer-appellants in this case have satisfied both nexuses to support their claim of standing under the test we announce today. Their constitutional challenge is made to an exercise by Congress of its power under Art. I, § 8, to spend for the general welfare, and the challenged program involves a substantial expenditure of federal tax funds. In addition, appellants have alleged that the challenged expenditures violate the Establishment and Free Exercise Clauses of the First Amendment. Our history vividly illustrates that one of the specific evils feared by those who drafted the Establishment Clause and fought for its adoption was that the taxing and spending power would be used to favor one religion over another or to support religion in general.

. . .

The allegations of the taxpayer in *Frothingham* v. *Mellon, supra,* were quite different from those made in this case, and the result in *Frothingham* is consistent with the test of taxpayer standing announced today. The taxpayer in *Frothingham* attacked a federal spending program and she, therefore, estab-

lished the first nexus required. However, she lacked standing because her constitutional attack was not based on an allegation that Congress, in enacting the Maternity Act of 1921, had breached a specific limitation upon its taxing and spending power. The taxpayer in *Frothingham* alleged essentially that Congress, by enacting the challenged statute, had exceeded the general powers delegated to it by Art. I, § 8, and that Congress had thereby invaded the legislative province reserved to the States by the Tenth Amendment. To be sure, Mrs. Frothingham made the additional allegation that her tax liability would be increased as a result of the allegedly unconstitutional enactment, and she framed that allegation in terms of a deprivation of property without due process of law. However, the Due Process Clause of the Fifth Amendment does not protect taxpayers against increases in tax liability, and the taxpayer in *Frothingham* failed to make any additional claim that the harm she alleged resulted from a breach by Congress of the specific constitutional limitations imposed upon an exercise of the taxing and spending power....

. . .

JUSTICE DOUGLAS, concurring.

While I have joined the opinion of the Court, I do not think that the test it lays down is a durable one for the reasons stated by my BROTHER HARLAN ... It would therefore be the part of wisdom, as I see the problem, to be rid of *Frothingham* here and now.

. . .

MR. JUSTICE STEWART, concurring.

I join the judgment and opinion of the Court, which I understand to hold only that a federal taxpayer has standing to assert that a specific expenditure of federal funds violates the Establishment Clause of the First Amendment....

MR. JUSTICE FORTAS, concurring.

I would confine the ruling in this case to the proposition that a taxpayer may maintain a suit to challenge the validity of a federal expenditure on the ground that the expenditure violates the Establishment Clause....

MR. JUSTICE HARLAN, dissenting.

The problems presented by this case are narrow and relatively abstract, but the principles by which they must be resolved involve nothing less than the proper functioning of the federal courts, and so run to the roots of our constitutional system. The nub of my view is that the end result of *Frothingham* v. *Mellon,* 262 U.S. 447, was correct, even though, like others, I do not subscribe to all of its reasoning and premises. Although I therefore agree with certain of the conclusions reached today by the Court, I cannot accept the standing doctrine that it substitutes for *Frothingham,* for it seems to me that this new doctrine rests on premises that do not withstand analysis. Accordingly, I respectfully dissent.

. . .

United States v. Richardson

418 U.S. 166 (1974)

William B. Richardson, a taxpayer, sued to obtain the expenditures of the Central Intelligence Agency, which are not publicly reported. He [The taxpayer] claimed that covert funding violated the Statement and Account Clause. In the majority opinion, which denied standing, Chief Justice Burger tried to preserve the doctrines set forth in *Flast* v. *Cohen.* Justice Powell, concurring, urged that the two-part "nexus" test in *Flast* be abandoned as intellectually incoherent.

Mr. Chief Justice Burger delivered the opinion of the Court.

We granted certiorari in this case to determine whether the respondent has standing to bring an action as a federal taxpayer alleging that certain provisions concerning public reporting of expenditures under the Central Intelligence Agency Act of 1949 ... violate Art. I, § 9, cl. 7, of the Constitution which provides:

"No Money shall be drawn from the Treasury, but in Consequence of Appropriations made by Law; and a regular Statement and Account of the Receipts and Expenditures of all public Money shall be published from time to time."

. . .

Although the recent holding of the Court in *Flast* v. *Cohen* ... is a starting point in an examination of respondent's claim to prosecute this suit as a taxpayer, that case must be read with reference to its principal predecessor, *Frothingham* v. *Mellon,* 262 U.S. 447 (1923). In *Frothingham,* the injury alleged was that the congressional enactment challenged as unconstitutional would, if implemented, increase the complainant's future federal income taxes. Denying standing, the *Frothingham* Court rested on the "comparatively minute[,] remote, fluctuating and uncertain," *id.,* at 487, impact on the taxpayer, and the failure to allege the kind of direct injury required for standing.

. . .

II

Although the Court made it very explicit in *Flast* that a "fundamental aspect of standing" is that it focuses primarily on the *party* seeking to get his complaint before the federal court rather than "on the issues he wishes to have adjudicated," *id.,* at 99, it made equally clear that

"in ruling on [taxpayer] standing, it is both appropriate and necessary to look to the substantive issues for another purpose, namely, to determine whether there is a logical nexus between the status asserted and the claim sought to be adjudicated." *Id.,* at 102.

We therefore turn to an examination of the issues sought to be raised by respondent's complaint to determine whether he is "a proper and appropriate party to invoke federal judicial power," *ibid.,* with respect to those issues.

We need not and do not reach the merits of the constitutional attack on the statute; our inquiry into the "substantive issues" is for the limited purpose indicated above. The mere recital of the respondent's claims and an examination of the statute under attack demonstrate how far he falls short of the standing criteria of *Flast* and how neatly he falls within the *Frothingham* holding left undisturbed....

Mr. Justice Powell, concurring.

I join the opinion of the Court because I am in accord with most of its analysis, particularly insofar as it relies on traditional barriers against federal taxpayer or citizen standing. And I agree that *Flast* v. *Cohen,* 392 U.S. 83 (1968), which set the boundaries for the arguments of the parties before us, is the most directly relevant precedent and quite correctly absorbs a major portion of the Court's attention. I write solely to indicate that I would go further than the Court and would lay to rest the approach undertaken in *Flast.* I would not overrule *Flast* on its facts, because it is now settled that federal taxpayer standing exists in Establishment Clause cases. I would not, however, perpetuate the doctrinal confusion inherent in the *Flast* two-part "nexus" test. That test is not a reliable indicator of when a federal taxpayer has standing, and it has no sound relationship to the question whether such a plaintiff, with no other interest at stake, should be allowed to bring suit against one of the branches of the Federal Government. In my opinion, it should be abandoned.

I

My difficulties with *Flast* are several. The opinion purports to separate the question of standing from the merits, *id.*, at 99–101, yet it abruptly returns to the substantive issues raised by a plaintiff for the purpose of determining "whether there is a logical nexus between the status asserted and the claim sought to be adjudicated." *Id.*, at 102. Similarly, the opinion distinguishes between constitutional and prudential limits on standing. *Id.*, at 92–94, 97. I find it impossible, however, to determine whether the two-part "nexus" test created in *Flast* amounts to a constitutional or a prudential limitation, because it has no meaningful connection with the Court's statement of the bare-minimum constitutional requirements for standing.

. . .

Relying on history, the Court [in *Flast*] identified the Establishment Clause as a specific constitutional limitation upon the exercise by Congress of the taxing and spending power conferred by Art. I, § 8. . . . On the other hand, the Tenth Amendment, and apparently the Due Process Clause of the Fifth Amendment, were determined not to be such "specific" limitations. The bases for these determinations are not wholly clear, but it appears that the Court found the Tenth Amendment addressed to the interests of the States, rather than of taxpayers, and the Due Process Clause no protection against increases in tax liability. *Id.*, at 105.

In my opinion, Mr. Justice Harlan's critique of the *Flast* "nexus" test is unanswerable. As he pointed out, "the Court's standard for the determination of standing [*i.e.*, sufficiently concrete adverseness] and its criteria for the satisfaction of that standard are entirely unrelated." *Id.*, at 122. . . .

The ambiguities inherent in the *Flast* "nexus" limitations on federal taxpayer standing are illustrated by this case. There can be little doubt about respondent's fervor in pursuing his case, both within administrative channels and at every level of the federal courts. The intensity of his interest appears to

bear no relationship to the fact that, literally speaking, he is not challenging directly a congressional exercise of the taxing and spending power. On the other hand, if the involvement of the taxing and spending power has some relevance, it requires no great leap in reasoning to conclude that the Statement and Account Clause, Art. I, § 9, cl. 7, on which respondent relies, is inextricably linked to that power. And that Clause might well be seen as a "specific" limitation on congressional spending. Indeed, it could be viewed as the most democratic of limitations. Thus, although the Court's application of *Flast* to the instant case is probably literally correct, adherence to the *Flast* test in this instance suggests, as does *Flast* itself, that the test is not a sound or logical limitation on standing.

The lack of real meaning and of principled content in the *Flast* "nexus" test renders it likely that it will in time collapse of its own weight, as Mr. Justice Douglas predicted in his concurring opinion in that case. 392 U.S., at 107. . . .

Relaxation of standing requirements is directly related to the expansion of judicial power. It seems to me inescapable that allowing unrestricted taxpayer or citizen standing would significantly alter the allocation of power at the national level, with a shift away from a democratic form of government. I also believe that repeated and essentially head-on confrontations between the life-tenured branch and the representative branches of government will not, in the long run, be beneficial to either. The public confidence essential to the former and the vitality critical to the latter may well erode if we do not exercise self-restraint in the utilization of our power to negative the actions of the other branches. We should be ever mindful of the contradictions that would arise if a democracy were to permit general oversight of the elected branches of government by a nonrepresentative, and in large measure insulated, judicial branch. Moreover, the argument that the Court should allow unrestricted taxpayer or citizen standing underestimates the ability of the representative branches of the Federal Government to respond to the citizen pressure that has been responsible in large measure for the current drift toward expanded standing. Indeed, taxpayer or citizen advocacy, given its potentially broad base, is precisely the type of leverage that in a democracy ought to be employed against the branches that were intended to be responsive to public attitudes about the appropriate operation of government. . . .

The power recognized in *Marbury* v. *Madison*, 1 Cranch 137 (1803), is a potent one. Its prudent use seems to me incompatible with unlimited notions of taxpayer and citizen standing. Were we to utilize this power as indiscriminately as is now being urged, we may witness efforts by the representative branches drastically to curb its use....

. . .

MR. JUSTICE DOUGLAS, dissenting.

. . .

From the history of the [Statement and Account Clause] it is apparent that the Framers inserted it in the Constitution to give the public knowledge of the way public funds are expended. No one has a greater "personal stake" in policing this protective measure than a taxpayer. Indeed, if a taxpayer may not raise the question, who may do so? The Court states that discretion to release information is in the first instance "committed to the surveillance of Congress," and that the right of the citizenry to information under Art. I, § 9, cl. 7, cannot be enforced directly, but only through the "[s]low, cumbersome, and unresponsive" electoral process. One has only to read

constitutional history to realize that statement would shock Mason and Madison. Congress of course has discretion; but to say that it has the power to read the clause out of the Constitution when it comes to one or two or three agencies is astounding....

MR. JUSTICE STEWART, with whom MR. JUSTICE MARSHALL, joins, dissenting.

... I believe that Richardson had standing to bring this action. Accordingly, I would affirm the judgment of the Court of Appeals.

MR. JUSTICE BRENNAN, dissenting [at 235].

... [Richardson's] complaint, properly construed, alleged that the violations caused him injury not only in respect of his right as a citizen to know how Congress was spending the public fisc, but also in respect of his right as a voter to receive information to aid his decision how and for whom to vote. These claims may ultimately fail on the merits, but Richardson has "standing" to assert them.

Allen v. Wright

468 U.S. 737 (1984)

Inez Wright and several other black parents had children attending public schools in districts that were undergoing desegregation. They brought this nationwide class action against the federal government, alleging that the Internal Revenue Service (1) had not adopted sufficient standards and procedures to fulfill its obligation to deny tax-exempt status to racially discriminatory private schools, and (2) had thereby harmed the parents and interfered with their children's opportunity to receive an education in desegregated public schools. W. Wayne Allen, the head of a private school identified in the complaint, intervened as a defendant. With an eye to the separation of powers doctrine, the Court held that the parents lacked standing to sue.

JUSTICE O'CONNOR delivered the opinion of the Court.

[II.A]

Article III of the Constitution confines the federal courts to adjudicating actual "cases" and "controversies." As the Court explained in *Valley Forge Christian College v. Americans United for Separation of Church and State, Inc.*, 454 U.S. 464, 471–476 (1982), the "case or controversy" requirement defines with respect to the Judicial Branch the idea of separation of powers on which the Federal Government is founded. The several doctrines that have grown up to elaborate that requirement are "founded in concern about the proper—and properly limited—role of the courts in a democratic society." *Warth v. Seldin*, 422 U.S. 490, 498 (1975).

"All of the doctrines that cluster about Article III—not only standing but mootness, ripeness, political question, and the like—relate in part, and in different though overlapping ways, to an idea, which is more than an intuition but less than a rigorous and explicit theory, about the constitutional and prudential limits to the powers of an unelected, unrepresentative judiciary in our kind of government." *Vander Jagt v. O'Neill*, 226 U.S. App. D.C. 14, 26–27, 699 F.2d 1166, 1178–1179 (1983) (Bork, J., concurring).

The case-or-controversy doctrines state fundamental limits on federal judicial power in our system of government.

The Art. III doctrine that requires a litigant to have "standing" to invoke the power of a federal court is perhaps the most important of these doctrines....

... [T]he law of Art. III standing is built on a single basic idea — the idea of separation of powers....

Determining standing in a particular case may be facilitated by clarifying principles or even clear rules developed in prior cases. Typically, however, the standing inquiry requires careful judicial examination of a complaint's allegations to ascertain whether the particular plaintiff is entitled to an adjudication of the particular claims asserted. Is the injury too abstract, or otherwise not appropriate, to be considered judicially cognizable? Is the line of causation between the illegal conduct and injury too attenuated? Is the prospect of obtaining relief from the injury as a result of a favorable ruling too speculative? These questions and any others relevant to the standing inquiry must be answered by reference to the Art. III notion that federal courts may exercise power only "in the last resort, and as a necessity," *Chicago & Grand Trunk R. Co. v. Wellman*, 143 U.S. 339, 345 (1892), and only when adjudication is "consistent with a system of separated powers and [the dispute is one] traditionally thought to be capable of resolution through the judicial process," *Flast v. Cohen*, 392 U.S. 83, 97 (1968). See *Valley Forge*, 454 U.S., at 472–473.

B

Respondents allege two injuries in their complaint to support their standing to bring this lawsuit. First, they say that they are harmed directly by the mere fact of Government financial aid to discriminatory private schools. Second, they say that the federal tax exemptions to racially discriminatory private schools in their communities impair their ability to have their public schools desegregated....

... We conclude that neither suffices to support respondents' standing. The first fails under clear precedents of this Court because it does not constitute judicially cognizable injury. The second fails because the alleged injury is not fairly traceable to the assertedly unlawful conduct of the IRS.

1

Respondent's first claim of injury can be interpreted in two ways. It might be a claim simply to have the Government avoid the violation of law alleged in respondents' complaint. Alternatively, it might be a claim of stigmatic injury, or denigration, suffered by all members of a racial group when the Government discriminates on the basis of race. Under neither interpretation is this claim of injury judicially cognizable.

. . .

The consequences of recognizing respondents'

standing on the basis of their first claim of injury illustrate why our cases plainly hold that such injury is not judicially cognizable. If the abstract stigmatic injury were cognizable, standing would extend nationwide to all members of the particular racial groups against which the Government was alleged to be discriminating by its grant of a tax exemption to a racially discriminatory school, regardless of the location of that school. All such persons could claim the same sort of abstract stigmatic injury respondents assert in their first claim of injury. A black person in Hawaii could challenge the grant of a tax exemption to a racially discriminatory school in Maine. Recognition of standing in such circumstances would transform the federal courts into "no more than a vehicle for the vindication of the value interest of concerned bystanders." *United States v. SCRAP*, 412 U.S. 669, 687 (1973). Constitutional limits on the role of the federal courts preclude such a transformation.

2

It is in their complaint's second claim of injury that respondents allege harm to a concrete, personal interest that can support standing in some circumstances. The injury they identify — their children's diminished ability to receive an education in a racially integrated school — is, beyond any doubt, not only judicially cognizable but, as shown by cases from *Brown v. Board of Education*, 347 U.S. 483 (1954), to *Bob Jones University v. United States*, 461 U.S. 574 (1983), one of the most serious injuries recognized in our legal system. Despite the constitutional importance of curing the injury alleged by respondents, however, the federal judiciary may not redress it unless standing requirements are met. In this case, respondents' second claim of injury cannot support standing because the injury alleged is not fairly traceable to the Government conduct respondents challenge as unlawful.

The illegal conduct challenged by respondents is the IRS's grant of tax exemptions to some racially discriminatory schools. The line of causation between that conduct and desegregation of respondents' schools is attenuated at best. From the perspective of the IRS, the injury to respondents is highly indirect and "results from the independent action of some third party not before the court," *Simon v. Eastern Kentucky Welfare Rights Org.*, 426 U.S., at 42. As the Court pointed out in *Warth v. Seldin*, 422 U.S., at 505, "the indirectness of the injury ... may make it substantially more difficult to meet the minimum requirement of Art. III...."

The diminished ability of respondents' children

to receive a desegregated education would be fairly traceable to unlawful IRS grants of tax exemptions only if there were enough racially discriminatory private schools receiving tax exemptions in respondents' communities for withdrawal of those exemptions to make an appreciable difference in public school integration. Respondents have made no such allegation. It is, first, uncertain how many racially discriminatory private schools are in fact receiving tax exemptions. Moreover, it is entirely speculative, as respondents themselves conceded in the Court of Appeals ... whether withdrawal of a tax exemption from any particular school would lead the school to change its policies. See 480 F.Supp., at 796. It is just as speculative whether any given parent of a child attending such a private school would decide to transfer the child to public school as a result of any changes in education or financial policy made by the private school once it was threatened with loss of tax-exempt status. It is also pure speculation whether, in a particular community, a large enough number of the numerous relevant school officials and parents would reach decisions that collectively would have a significant impact on the racial composition of the public schools.

The links in the chain of causation between the challenged Government conduct and the asserted injury are far too weak for the chain as a whole to sustain respondents' standing....

The idea of separation of powers that underlies standing doctrine explains why our cases preclude the conclusion that respondents' alleged injury "fairly can be traced to the challenged action" of the IRS. *Simon v. Eastern Kentucky Welfare Rights Org., supra,* at 41.

That conclusion would pave the way generally for suits challenging, not specifically identifiable Government violations of law, but the particular programs agencies establish to carry out their legal obligations. Such suits, even when premised on allegations of several instances of violations of law, are rarely if ever appropriate for federal-court adjudication.

"Carried to its logical end, [respondents'] approach would have the federal courts as virtually continuing monitors of the wisdom and soundness of Executive action; such a role is appropriate for the Congress acting through its committees and the 'power of the purse'; it is not the role of the judiciary, absent actual present of immediately threatened injury resulting from unlawful governmental action." *Laird v. Tatum,* 408 U.S., at 15.

... The Constitution, after all, assigns to the Executive Branch, and not to the Judicial Branch, the duty to "take Care that the Laws be faithfully executed." U.S. Const., Art. II, § 3. We could not recognize respondents' standing in this case without running afoul of that structural principle.

.   .   .

Justice Marshall took no part in the decision of these cases.

Justice Brennan, dissenting.

.   .   .

Justice Stevens, with whom Justice Blackmun joins, dissenting....

C. MOOTNESS

Litigants able to establish standing at the outset of a case may find their personal stake diluted or eliminated by subsequent events. Because of a change in law or facts, the case or controversy may disappear and leave insufficient adverseness to guide the courts. If the action that triggered the complaint ceases, a court may have no means of granting relief.[12]

A case is not mooted simply because one party discontinues a contested action. Judicial review cannot be circumvented merely through a strategy of starts and stops. If the controversy is likely to reappear, judicial scrutiny "ought not to be, as they might be, defeated, by short term orders, capa-

---

12. California v. San Pablo and Tulare Railroad Co., 149 U.S. 308 (1893); Jones v. Montague, 194 U.S. 147 (1904); Richardson v. McChesney, 218 U.S. 487 (1910). See also Sidney A. Diamond, "Federal Jurisdiction to Decide Moot Cases," 94 U. Pa. L. Rev. 125 (1946); United States v. Hamburg-American Co., 239 U.S. 466 (1916); United States v. Alaska S.S. Co., 253 U.S. 113 (1920); Brockington v. Rhodes, 396 U.S. 41 (1969); Hall v. Beals, 396 U.S. 45 (1969); Lewis v. Continental Bank Corp., 494 U.S. 472 (1990).

ble of repetition, yet evading review...."[13] Complaints about an election process, even after a particular election is over, may remain a continuing controversy that requires decision by the courts. Moore v. Ogilvie, 394 U.S. 814, 816 (1969).

If the judiciary is unprepared or unwilling to decide an issue, mootness is one avenue of escape. In 1952 the Supreme Court held that a public school Bible-reading case was moot because the child had graduated by the time the case had reached the Supreme Court. Although other students would be subjected to the same school policy in the future, the Court declared that "no decision we could render now would protect any rights she may once have had, and this Court does not sit to decide arguments after events have put them to rest." Doremus v. Board of Education, 342 U.S. 429, 433 (1952).

In a 1974 case, a white student denied admission to a law school claimed that the school's affirmative action policy discriminated against him, allowing minorities with lower test scores to enter. He was admitted after winning in trial court. By the time the case reached the Supreme Court he was in his third and final year. The school assured the Court that he would be allowed to complete his legal studies regardless of the disposition of the case. The Court refused to reach the merits of the case, considering it moot. Four Justices dissented, predicting (correctly) that the issue would inevitably return to the Supreme Court. DeFUNIS v. ODEGAARD, 416 U.S. 312 (1974). Within a few years another case challenging a university's affirmative action program found its way to the Supreme Court, and this time the Court confronted the merits. Regents of the University of California v. Bakke, 438 U.S. 265 (1978). For reading on *Bakke*, see Chapter 15.

In *Roe v. Wade* (1973), plaintiffs argued that the Texas criminal abortion laws were unconstitutionally vague and infringed upon their right of privacy. The laws prohibited abortion except on medical advice to save the mother's life. Texas responded that one of the suits, brought by a pregnant single woman, was moot because her pregnancy had terminated. Justice Blackmun, writing for the majority, rejected that position:

> But when, as here, pregnancy is a significant fact in the litigation, the normal 266-day human gestation period is so short that the pregnancy will come to term before the usual appellate process is complete. If that termination makes a case moot, pregnancy litigation seldom will survive much beyond the trial stage, and appellate review will be effectively denied. Our law should not be that rigid. Pregnancy often comes more than once to the same woman, and in the general population, if man is to survive, it will always be with us. Pregnancy provides a classic justification for a conclusion of nonmootness. It truly could be "capable of repetition, yet evading review." Roe v. Wade, 410 U.S. 113, 125 (1973).

In 1984, the Supreme Court had an opportunity to dismiss as moot an affirmative action case involving a court order for the dismissal or demotion of white employees who had more seniority than black employees who were retained. All white employees laid off as a result of the order were restored to duty a month later. Those demoted were later offered their old positions. Those facts did not prevent the Supreme Court from deciding the case and reversing the lower court actions. Firefighters v. Stotts, 467 U.S. 561, 568–72 (1984). Although some of the dissenters accused the majority of issuing an advisory opinion, the Court was evidently ready and willing to circumscribe the reach of affirmative action. The twists and turns of the mootness doctrine reflect the Court's effort to maintain a proper relationship with the other political branches.

In 2000, the Court held that the closing of a nude dancing club did not render the case moot. The city still needed to know whether its ordinance proscribing nudity in public places was constitutional and could be enforced. City of Erie v. Pap's A.M., 529 U.S. 277 (2000).

---

13. Southern Pacific Terminal Co. v. ICC, 219 U.S. 498, 515 (1911). See Washington v. Harper, 494 U.S. 210 (1990); United States v. Phosphate Export Corp., 393 U.S. 199, 203 (1968) and United States v. W. T. Grant Co., 345 U.S. 629, 632 (1953).

The Mootness Doctrine

Note, "The Mootness Doctrine in the Supreme Court," 88 Harv. L. Rev. 373, 374–76 (1974) (footnotes omitted). The Court's refusal to hear moot cases was initially grounded in the common law doctrine that courts lack power to decide abstract questions in cases where no dispute exists. Courts have traditionally declined to hear cases in which neither party stands to gain or lose by a decision, on the theory that the state should not "be burdened with the expense of trying such unsubstantial controversies." Over the past decade, however, the Court has based its mootness decisions specifically on the case or controversy requirement of article III of the Constitution, a broad limitation which maintains the separation of powers by "assur[ing] that the federal courts will not intrude into areas committed to the other branches of government." The doctrine that courts will not hear moot cases thus serves two complementary purposes: it prevents the useless expenditure of judicial resources and assures that the courts will not intrude prematurely into policymaking in a manner that will unnecessarily constrain the other branches of government.

DeFunis v. Odegaard

416 U.S. 312 (1974)

Marco DeFunis, Jr., was denied admission to the University of Washington Law School, although his test scores were higher than those of some of the minorities admitted. He was accepted after a trial court found in his favor and was in his third and final year when the case reached the Supreme Court. The question was whether the case should be dismissed on grounds of mootness.

PER CURIAM

In 1971 the petitioner Marco DeFunis, Jr., applied for admission as a first-year student at the University of Washington Law School, a state-operated institution. The size of the incoming first-year class was to be limited to 150 persons, and the Law School received some 1,600 applications for these 150 places. DeFunis was eventually notified that he had been denied admission. He thereupon commenced this suit in a Washington trial court, contending that the procedures and criteria employed by the Law School Admissions Committee invidiously discriminated against him on account of his race in violation of the Equal Protection Clause of the Fourteenth Amendment to the United States Constitution.

DeFunis brought the suit on behalf of himself alone, and not as the representative of any class, against the various respondents, who are officers, faculty members, and members of the Board of Regents of the University of Washington. He asked the trial court to issue a mandatory injunction commanding the respondents to admit him as a member of the first-year class entering in September 1971, on the ground that the Law School admissions policy had resulted in the unconstitutional denial of his application for admission. The trial court agreed with his claim and granted the requested relief. DeFunis was, accordingly, admitted to the Law School and began his legal studies there in the fall of 1971. On appeal, the Washington Supreme Court reversed the judgment of the trial court and held that the Law School admissions policy did not violate the Constitution. By this time DeFunis was in his second year at the Law School.

He then petitioned this Court for a writ of certiorari, and MR. JUSTICE DOUGLAS, as Circuit Justice, stayed the judgment of the Washington Supreme Court pending the "final disposition of the case by this Court." By virtue of this stay, DeFunis has remained in law school, and was in the first term of his third and final year when this Court first considered his certiorari petition in the fall of 1973. Because of our concern that DeFunis' third-year standing in the Law School might have rendered this case moot, we requested the parties to brief the question of mootness before we acted on the petition. In response, both sides contended that the case was not moot. The respondents indicated that, if the decision of the Washington Supreme Court were permitted to stand, the petitioner could complete the term for which he was then enrolled but would have to apply to the faculty for permission to continue in the school before he could register for another term.

We granted the petition for certiorari on November 19, 1973, 414 U.S. 1038. The case was in due course orally argued on February 26, 1974.

In response to questions raised from the bench during the oral argument, counsel for the petitioner has informed the Court that DeFunis has now registered "for his final quarter in law school." Counsel for the respondents have made clear that the Law School will not in any way seek to abrogate this registration. In light of DeFunis' recent registration for the last quarter of his final law school year, and the Law School's assurance that his registration is fully effective, the insistent question again arises whether this case is not moot, and to that question we now turn.

The starting point for analysis is the familiar proposition that "federal courts are without power to decide questions that cannot affect the rights of litigants in the case before them." *North Carolina* v. *Rice*, 404 U.S. 244, 246 (1971).... Although as a matter of Washington state law it appears that this case would be saved from mootness by "the great public interest in the continuing issues raised by this appeal," 82 Wash.2d 11, 23 n. 6, 507 P.2d 1169, 1177 n.6 (1973), the fact remains that under Art. III "[e]ven in cases arising in the state courts, the question of mootness is a federal one which a federal court must resolve before it assumes jurisdiction." *North Carolina* v. *Rice, supra,* at 246.

The respondents have represented that, without regard to the ultimate resolution of the issues in this case, DeFunis will remain a student in the Law School for the duration of any term in which he has already enrolled. Since he has now registered for his final term, it is evident that he will be given an opportunity to complete all academic and other requirements for graduation, and, if he does so, will receive his diploma regardless of any decision this Court might reach on the merits of this case. In short, all parties agree that DeFunis is now entitled to complete his legal studies at the University of Washington and to receive his degree from that institution. A determination by this Court of the legal issues tendered by the parties is no longer necessary to compel that result, and could not serve to prevent it. DeFunis did not cast his suit as a class action, and the only remedy he requested was an injunction commanding his admission to the Law School. He was not only accorded that remedy, but he now has also been irrevocably admitted to the final term of the final year of the Law School course. The controversy between the parties has thus clearly ceased to be "definite and concrete" and no longer "touch[es] the legal relations of parties having adverse legal interests." *Aetna Life Ins. Co.* v. *Haworth,* 300 U.S. 227, 240–241 (1937).

... [J]ust because this particular case did not reach the Court until the eve of the petitioner's graduation from law school, it hardly follows that the issue he raises will in the future evade review. If the admissions procedures of the Law School remain unchanged, there is no reason to suppose that a subsequent case attacking those procedures will not come with relative speed to this Court, now that the Supreme Court of Washington has spoken....

... [T]he judgment of the Supreme Court of Washington is vacated, and the cause is remanded for such proceedings as by that court may be deemed appropriate.

It is so ordered.

[Justice Douglas prepared a separate dissent.]

Mr. Justice Brennan, with whom Mr. Justice Douglas, Mr. Justice White, and Mr. Justice Marshall concur, dissenting.

I respectfully dissent. Many weeks of the school term remain, and petitioner may not receive his degree despite respondents' assurances that petitioner will be allowed to complete this term's schooling regardless of our decision. Any number of unexpected events—illness, economic necessity, even academic failure—might prevent his graduation at the end of the term. Were that misfortune to befall, and were petitioner required to register for yet another term, the prospect that he would again face the hurdle of the admissions policy is real, not fanciful; for respondents warn that "Mr. DeFunis would have to take some appropriate action to request continued admission for the remainder of his law school education, and *some discretionary action by the University on such request would have to be taken.*" Respondents' Memorandum on the Question of Mootness 3–4 (emphasis supplied). Thus, respondents' assurances have not dissipated the possibility that petitioner might once again have to run the gantlet of the University's allegedly unlawful admissions policy....

Moreover, in endeavoring to dispose of this case as moot, the Court clearly disserves the public interest. The constitutional issues which are avoided today concern vast numbers of people, organizations, and colleges and universities, as evidenced by the filing of twenty-six *amicus curiae* briefs. Few constitutional questions in recent history have stirred as much debate, and they will not disappear. They must inevitably return to the federal courts and ultimately again to this Court. Cf. *Richardson* v. *Wright,* 405 U.S. 208, 212 (1972) (dissenting opinion). Because avoidance of repetitious litigation serves the public interest, that inevitability counsels against mootness determinations, as here, not compelled by the record....

The Ripeness Doctrine

... The injunctive and declaratory judgment remedies are discretionary, and courts traditionally have been reluctant to apply them to administrative determinations unless these arise in the context of a controversy "ripe" for judicial resolution. Without undertaking to survey the intricacies of the ripeness doctrine it is fair to say that its basic rationale is to prevent the courts, through avoidance of premature adjudication, from entangling themselves in abstract disagreements over administrative policies, and also to protect the agencies from judicial interference until an administrative decision has been formalized and its effects felt in a concrete way by the challenging parties. The problem is best seen in a twofold aspect, requiring us to evaluate both the fitness of the issues for judicial decision and the hardship to the parties of withholding court consideration.

SOURCE: Abbott Laboratories v. Gardner, 387 U.S. 136, 148–49 (1967) (footnotes omitted).

D. RIPENESS

Just as a case brought too late can be moot, a case brought too early may not yet be ripe. Sometimes this results from a failure to exhaust administrative and state remedies. Plaintiffs must show that they have explored all avenues of relief before turning to the federal courts. Premature consideration by the courts does more than create unnecessary workload. It deprives judges of information needed for informed adjudication and forces them to deal at an abstract, speculative, and hypothetical level. The ripeness doctrine encourages settlement in the administrative arena (see box).

Ripeness was at issue in a 1947 case brought by twelve federal employees against the Civil Service Commission. They wanted to prevent the Commission from enforcing a section of the Hatch Act that prohibited them from taking "any active part in political management or in political campaigns." The federal workers complained that the statute deprived them of their First Amendment rights of speech, press, and assembly. The Supreme Court regarded the employees' fears of losing their jobs as too speculative:

> The power of courts, and ultimately of this Court, to pass upon the constitutionality of acts of Congress arises only when the interests of litigants require the use of this judicial authority for their protection against actual interference. A hypothetical threat is not enough. We can only speculate as to the kinds of political activity the appellants desire to engage in or as to the contents of their proposed public statements or the circumstances of their publication. It would not accord with judicial responsibility to adjudge, in a matter involving constitutionality, between the freedom of the individual and the requirements of public order except when definite rights appear upon the one side and definite prejudicial interferences upon the other. United Public Workers v. Mitchell, 330 U.S. 75, 90 (1947).

The situation of one of the federal employees, George P. Poole, was not hypothetical. He faced dismissal unless he could refute the charges of the Commission that his political activities had violated the Hatch Act. Accepting his suit as a justiciable case, the Court held that disciplinary action under the Hatch Act would not violate the Constitution. Justices Black and Douglas dissented, believing that the Court should have heard the cases of all twelve litigants. The threat of discharge, they said, was real rather than fanciful, immediate not remote. Douglas observed:

> ... [T]o require these employees first to suffer the hardship of a discharge is not only to make them incur a penalty; it makes inadequate, if not wholly illusory, any legal remedy which they might have. Men who must sacrifice their means of livelihood in order to test their rights to

their jobs must either pursue prolonged and expensive litigation as unemployed persons or pull up their roots, change their life careers, and seek employment in other fields.

The issue of preventive relief often splits the courts. Should judges rule on a statute before its sanctions are invoked? A decision might offer relief to threatened individuals, but it also requires the courts to rule in advance of a concrete case or controversy. It forces judgments on hypothetical situations that raise remote and abstract issues. And yet judicial inaction can lead to irreparable harm to individuals once the statute is enforced. Longshoremen's Union v. Boyd, 347 U.S. 222, 224–26 (1954). Judicial review may be both necessary and appropriate to protect individuals before an agency enforces a regulation.[14]

The extreme point is reached when a suit lingers so long in the courts that it becomes "overripe." Justice Black described a case that bounced around for ten years before the Supreme Court sent it back to the lower courts "because of the staleness of the record." Hugo L. Black, A Constitutional Faith 17 (1968).

Marking Time

As with mootness, disposing of a case on the ground of ripeness may delay but not necessarily avoid decision. In 1943 and 1961 the Supreme Court refused to rule on the constitutionality of Connecticut laws that prohibited married couples from using contraceptives or physicians from giving advice about their use. Tileston v. Ullman, 318 U.S. 44 (1943); Poe v. Ullman, 367 U.S. 497 (1961). Because the record suggested that the state was unlikely to prosecute offenders, the Court held that it lacked jurisdiction to decide hypothetical cases. In the 1961 case, the Court ignored the fact that the state had closed several birth control clinics. POE v. ULLMAN, 367 U.S. 497 (1961). After that decision, the state arrested physicians who had operated a birth control clinic in New Haven. They were found guilty and fined $100 each. In 1965 the Supreme Court held that they had standing and declared the Connecticut statute invalid under the "penumbra" of the Bill of Rights. Griswold v. Connecticut, 381 U.S. 479 (1965).

"Ripeness" may provide the means to sidestep momentarily a socially sensitive issue. Immediately after the Court had decided *Brown* v. *Board of Education* in 1954, it was faced with the constitutionality of a Virginia miscegenation statute. To strike down a law banning interracial marriages would stimulate the fears of critics of the decision who predicted that integrated schools would lead to "mongrelization" of the white race. The Court returned the case to the lower courts by citing the "inadequacy of the record" and the lack of a "properly-presented federal question." Naim v. Naim, 350 U.S. 891 (1955); 350 U.S. 985 (1956). In essence, the Court decided to buy some time. Years later, after the principle of desegregation had been safely established and Congress had passed the Civil Rights Act of 1964, the Court struck down the Virginia statute. Loving v. Virginia, 388 U.S. 1 (1967).

Judicial doctrine and political practicalities were joined in a 1978 case involving a congressional limitation on liability for accidents by private nuclear plants. A "hypothetical" issue, to be sure, but it was intuitively unappealing to insist that the courts await a nuclear catastrophe before deciding. The Court was satisfied that the test of ripeness had been met by two effects already evident from the operation of nuclear power plants: the emission of small quantities of radiation in the air and water, and an increase in the temperature of two lakes used for recreational purposes.[15]

---

14. Abbott Laboratories v. Gardner, 387 U.S. 136 (1967). See also Toilet Goods Assn. v. Gardner, 387 U.S. 158 (1967) and Gardner v. Toilet Goods Assn., 387 U.S. 167 (1967).

15. Duke Power Co. v. Carolina Environment Study Group, 438 U.S. 69, 72–74, 81–82 (1978). Also on the need for courts to avoid premature decisions: Renne v. Geary, 501 U.S. 312 (1991); Socialist Labor Party v. Gilligan, 406 U.S. 583 (1972); Adler v. Board of Education, 342 U.S. 485, 497–508 (Frankfurter, J., dissenting).

Poe v. Ullman

367 U.S. 497 (1961)

A married couple, a married woman, and a doctor sued for declaratory relief against the threatened enforcement of Connecticut's birth control laws that prohibited married couples from using contraceptives and physicians from advising married couples about their use. Paul and Pauline Poe are the fictitious names of the plaintiffs, threatened with prosecution by the state's attorney, Abraham S. Ullman.

MR. JUSTICE FRANKFURTER announced the judgment of the Court and an opinion in which THE CHIEF JUSTICE, MR. JUSTICE CLARK and MR. JUSTICE WHITTAKER join.

These appeals challenge the constitutionality, under the Fourteenth Amendment, of Connecticut statutes which, as authoritatively construed by the Connecticut Supreme Court of Errors, prohibit the use of contraceptive devices and the giving of medical advice in the use of such devices. In proceedings seeking declarations of law, not on review of convictions for violation of the statutes, that court has ruled that these statutes would be applicable in the case of married couples and even under claim that conception would constitute a serious threat to the health or life of the female spouse....

... The State's Attorney intends to prosecute offenses against the State's laws, and claims that the giving of contraceptive advice and the use of contraceptive devices would be offenses forbidden by Conn. Gen. Stat. Rev., 1958, §§ 53-32 and 54-196....

Appellants' complaints in these declaratory judgment proceedings do not clearly, and certainly do not in terms, allege that appellee Ullman threatens to prosecute them for use of, or for giving advice concerning, contraceptive devices. The allegations are merely that, in the course of his public duty, he intends to prosecute any offenses against Connecticut law, and that he claims that use of and advice concerning contraceptives would constitute offenses. The lack of immediacy of the threat described by these allegations might alone raise serious questions of non-justiciability of appellants' claims. See *United Public Workers v. Mitchell,* 330 U.S. 75, 88. But even were we to read the allegations to convey a clear threat of imminent prosecutions, we are not bound to accept as true all that is alleged on the face of the complaint and admitted, technically, by demurrer, any more than the Court is bound by stipulation of the parties. *Swift & Co. v. Hocking Valley R. Co.,* 243 U.S. 281, 289. Formal agreement between parties that collides with plausibility is too fragile a foundation for indulging in constitutional adjudication.

The Connecticut law prohibiting the use of contraceptives has been on the State's books since 1879. Conn. Acts 1879, c. 78. During the more than three-quarters of a century since its enactment, a prosecution for its violation seems never to have been initiated, save in *State v. Nelson,* 126 Conn. 412, 11 A.2d 856....

The fact that Connecticut has not chosen to press the enforcement of this statute deprives these controversies of the immediacy which is an indispensable condition of constitutional adjudication. This Court cannot be umpire to debates concerning harmless, empty shadows. To find it necessary to pass on these statutes now, in order to protect appellants from the hazards of prosecution, would be to close our eyes to reality....

Justiciability is of course not a legal concept with a fixed content or susceptible of scientific verification. Its utilization is the resultant of many subtle pressures, including the appropriateness of the issues for decision by this Court and the actual hardship to the litigants of denying them the relief sought. Both these factors justify withholding adjudication of the constitutional issue raised under the circumstances and in the manner in which they are now before the Court.

Dismissed.

MR. JUSTICE BLACK dissents because he believes that the constitutional questions should be reached and decided.

MR. JUSTICE BRENNAN, concurring in the judgment....

MR. JUSTICE DOUGLAS dissenting....

A public clinic dispensing birth-control information has indeed been closed by the State. Doctors and a nurse working in that clinic were arrested by the police and charged with advising married women on the use of contraceptives. That litigation produced *State v. Nelson,* 126 Conn. 412, 11 A.2d 856, which upheld these statutes. That same police raid on the clinic resulted in the seizure of a quantity of the clinic's contraception literature and medical equipment and supplies. The legality of that seizure was in question in *State* v. *Certain Contraceptive Materials,* 126 Conn. 428, 11 A.2d 863.

... At oral argument, counsel for appellants confirmed that the clinics are still closed. In response to a question from the bench, he affirmed that "no public or private clinic" has dared give birth-control advice since the decision in the *Nelson* case....

When the Court goes outside the record to determine that Connecticut has adopted "The undeviating policy of nullification ... of its anticontraceptive laws," it selects a particularly poor case in which to exercise such a novel power. This is not a law which is a dead letter. Twice since 1940, Connecticut has re-enacted these laws as part of general statutory revisions. Consistently, bills to remove the statutes from the books have been rejected by the legislature. In short, the statutes—far from being the accidental left-overs of another era—are the center of a continuing controversy in the State....

What are these people—doctor and patients—to do? Flout the law and go to prison? Violate the law surreptitiously and hope they will not get caught? By today's decision we leave them no other alternatives. It is not the choice they need have under the regime of the declaratory judgment and our constitutional system. It is not the choice worthy of a civilized society. A sick wife, a concerned husband, a conscientious doctor seek a dignified, discrete, orderly answer to the critical problem confronting them. We should not turn them away and make them flout the law and get arrested to have their constitutional rights determined....

Mr. Justice Harlan, dissenting.

I am compelled, with all respect, to dissent from the dismissal of these appeals. In my view the course which the Court has taken does violence to established concepts of "justiciability," and unjustifiably leaves these appellants under the threat of unconstitutional prosecution.

... Nor can I regard as "chimerical" the fear of enforcement of these provisions that seems to have caused the disappearance of at least nine birth-control clinics. In short, I fear that the Court has indulged in a bit of sleight of hand to be rid of this case....

. . .

Mr. Justice Stewart dissenting....

E. POLITICAL QUESTIONS

The "political question" doctrine survives partly on circular reasoning. Chief Justice Marshall claimed that "Questions in their nature political ... can never be made in this court." Marbury v. Madison, 5 U.S. (1 Cr.) 137, at 170 (1803). Yet every question that reaches a court is, by its very nature, political. Justice Holmes, hearing a litigant claim that a question concerning a party primary was nonjusticiable because of its political character, said that such an objection "is little more than a play upon words." Nixon v. Herndon, 273 U.S. 536, 540 (1927).

Definitional problems are legion. After refusing to decide a war powers case in 1968, a federal judge declared: "Though it is not always a simple matter to define the meaning of the term 'political question,' it is generally used to encompass all questions outside the sphere of judicial power." Velvel v. Johnson, 287 F.Supp. 846, 850 (D. Kans. 1968). That definition recalls this dictionary entry: "violins are small cellos, and cellos are large violins." Roche, 49 Am. Pol. Sci. Rev. 762, 768 (1955).

Beyond questions of definition, there is some doubt whether a political question doctrine even exists in the sense that courts refuse to adjudicate certain issues. After reviewing political question cases, Louis Henkin concluded: "the Court does not refuse judicial review; it exercises it. It is not dismissing the case or the issue as nonjusticiable; it adjudicates it. It is not refusing to pass on the power of the political branches; it passes upon it, only to affirm that they had the power which had been challenged and that nothing in the Constitution prohibited the particular exercise of it." Henkin, 85 Yale L. J. 597, 606 (1976). In 1962, the Court identified six areas that are generally classified as political questions. BAKER v. CARR, 369 U.S. 186 (1962). (see box on next page).

The first criterion is "a textually demonstrable constitutional commitment of the issue to a coordinate political department." However, the very question of whether an issue has been textually committed to a coordinate branch requires judicial interpretation. Powell v. McCormack, 395 U.S. 486,

Criteria for Political Questions

1. A textually demonstrable constitutional commitment of the issue to a coordinate political department.

2. A lack of judicially discoverable and manageable standards for resolving it.

3. The impossibility of deciding without an initial policy determination of a kind clearly for nonjudicial discretion.

4. The impossibility of a court's undertaking independent resolution without expressing lack of the respect due coordinate branches of government.

5. An unusual need for unquestioning adherence to a political decision already made.

6. The potentiality of embarrassment from multifarious pronouncements by various departments on one question.

Baker v. Carr, 369 U.S. 186, 217 (1962).

519 (1969). Moreover, the fact that an area *is* committed to Congress or the President does not automatically produce a political question. As the Supreme Court has noted, "virtually every challenge to the constitutionality of a statute would be a political question" under that reasoning. INS v. Chadha, 462 U.S. 919, 941 (1983). The Court further pointed out:

> It is correct that this controversy may, in a sense, be termed "political." But the presence of constitutional issues with significant political overtones does not automatically invoke the political question doctrine. Resolution of litigation challenging the constitutional authority of one of the three branches cannot be evaded by courts because the issues have political implications in the sense urged by Congress. *Marbury* v. *Madison,* 1 Cranch 137 (1803), was also a "political" case, involving as it did claims under a judicial commission alleged to have been duly signed by the President but not delivered. Id. at 942–43.

During the Vietnam War period, several students at Kent State University in Ohio were killed after the governor had called out the National Guard. The students sought injunctive relief to prevent the governor from taking such actions in the future and to prevent the Guard from future violations of students' constitutional rights. Basically, the students wanted the courts to supervise the future training and operations of the Guard. The Supreme Court regarded those duties as vested solely in Congress by Art. I, Sec. 8, Cl. 16, which empowers Congress to provide "for organizing, arming, and disciplining the Militia, and for governing such Part of them as may be employed in the Service of the United States, reserving to the States respectively, the Appointment of the Officers, and the Authority of training the Militia according to the discipline prescribed by Congress." The Court said that such actions were meant to be exercised by the political branches: "it is difficult to conceive of an area of governmental activity in which the courts have less competence." Gilligan v. Morgan, 413 U.S. 1, 10 (1973).

The Court agreed that the concept of political questions was not of fixed content, and that "nonjusticiable" voting rights cases came to be accepted by the courts. But those cases, it said, "represented the Court's efforts to strengthen the political system by assuring a higher level of fairness and responsiveness to the political processes, not the assumption of a continuing judicial review of substantive political judgments entrusted expressly to the coordinate branches of government." Id. at 11. The judiciary accepts the exclusive responsibility of Congress to determine whether a state satisfies the language of Article IV, Section 4, which requires that the United States "shall guarantee to every State in this Union a Republican Form of Government." Luther v. Borden, 7 How. 1 (1849). In 1993 the Court held that the particular procedure used by the Senate to try impeachments, including the use of a committee to take testimony and gather evidence, is a nonjusticiable political question. Some of the Justices, however, were reluctant to say that Senate procedures for trying impeachments could never be reviewed by the courts. NIXON v. UNITED STATES, 506 U.S. 224 (1993).

The second criterion in *Baker* v. *Carr* is "a lack of judicially discoverable and manageable standards for resolving" a dispute. One example comes from a 1939 case. Thirteen years had elapsed before Kansas ratified the Child Labor Amendment. Was that too long a time for state action? The Court decided that it lacked statutory and constitutional criteria for judicial determination. The question of a reasonable time involved "an appraisal of a great variety of relevant conditions, political, social and economic, which can hardly be said to be within the appropriate range of evidence receivable in a court of justice...." Coleman v. Miller, 307 U.S. 433, 453 (1939).

Certain matters of foreign policy are too sensitive for the courts to handle. When President Carter terminated the defense treaty with Taiwan, Senator Goldwater asked the courts to declare the termination invalid. The case reached the Supreme Court a few weeks before the scheduled termination. Justice Rehnquist attracted three other colleagues to his position that the issue represented a nonjusticiable political question. The Court was being asked to settle a dispute between the executive and legislative branches, "each of which has resources available to protect and assert its interests, resources not available to private litigants outside the judicial forum." Goldwater v. Carter, 444 U.S. 996, 1004 (1979). (See the reading on *Goldwater* v. *Carter* in Chapter 7.)

In 2001, a federal appellate court was asked to decide whether the North American Free Trade Agreement (NAFTA) was a "treaty" requiring Senate ratification pursuant to the Treaty Clause. It had been passed as a regular bill and submitted to the President for his signature. The court held that there were no standards available to the judiciary to decide whether one procedure was superior to the other. The issue represented a nonjusticiable political question. Made in the USA Foundation v. United States, 242 F.3d 1300 (11th Cir. 2001), cert. denied, sub nom. United Steelworkers of America, AFL-CIO, CLC, et al., 534 U.S. 1039 (2001).

The third criterion is "the impossibility of deciding without an initial policy determination of a kind clearly for nonjudicial discretion." This criterion is laced with circularity and basically restates the issue. It would cover reapportionment in 1946 but not after 1962 (Colegrove v. Green, 328 U.S. 549 and Baker v. Carr, 369 U.S. 186).

The fourth criterion: "the impossibility of a court's undertaking independent resolution without expressing lack of the respect due coordinate branches of government." This factor offers little guidance in resolving particular controversies. Whether in the Nixon tapes case(*United States* v. *Nixon)* or the exclusion of Adam Clayton Powell by the House of Representatives(*Powell* v. *McCormack)*, the Court's judgment often challenges and overrides decisions made by coordinate branches (see box on next page). Disrespect, in that sense, cannot be sufficient reason for creating a political question: "If it were, *every* judicial resolution of a constitutional challenge to a congressional enactment would be impermissible." United States v. Munoz-Flores, 495 U.S. 385, 390–91 (1990) (emphasis in original).

Criterion five: "an unusual need for unquestioning adherence to a political decision already made." Professor Henkin said that he did not know "of any case from which Justice Brennan might have derived such a principle." 85 Yale L. J. at 605–06 n.26. Some recent possibilities might include President Carter's termination of the Taiwan defense treaty and his handling of Iranian assets.[16]

The sixth criterion: "the potentiality of embarrassment from multifarious pronouncements by various departments on one question." Despite this guideline, the Supreme Court told the House of Representatives that Adam Clayton Powell should be seated. However, this criterion retains usefulness in

---

16. Goldwater v. Carter, 444 U.S. 996 (1979); Dames & Moore v. Regan, 453 U.S. 654 (1981). See also Idaho v. Freeman, 529 F.Supp. 1107, 1140–41 (D. Idaho 1981), regarding Idaho's rescission of its vote to ratify the Equal Rights Amendment.

The Exclusion of Adam Clayton Powell

Adam Clayton Powell, a black Democrat from New York, served for 22 years in Congress and chaired the House Education and Labor Committee. He was re-elected in 1966 by a three-to-one majority, despite press reports that he had misallocated public funds and was unlawfully abusing the privileges of his office. He had also been held in criminal contempt of New York state courts in connection with a defamation suit against him.

Rather than expel Powell, a constitutional procedure that requires a two-thirds majority, the House decided on January 10, 1967 to postpone the seating of Powell until a special committee could investigate his conduct. On March 1, the committee unanimously recommended that Powell be seated and then publicly censured and fined. The committee proposed this intermediate solution rather than risk an almost certain confrontation with the courts by excluding Powell.

In a fighting mood, the House decided that the courts would not intervene because of the political question. The committee's proposal failed by a vote of 202 to 222. A vote to exclude Powell passed by the overwhelming margin of 307 to 115.

The D.C. Circuit upheld the exclusion. Writing for the court was Warren Burger, who a year later would become Chief Justice of the Supreme Court. Burger wanted to avoid a collision course with Congress. That courts "encounter some problems for which they can supply no solution is not invariably an occasion for regret or concern; this is an essential limitation in a system of divided powers." Powell v. McCormack, 395 F.2d 577, 605 (D.C. Cir. 1968).

When the case was taken to the Supreme Court, the House claimed "exclusive power" over the seating of members. In oral argument, House counsel Bruce Bromley insisted that the Court had no authority to restrain House action, no matter how audacious or unconstitutional. He claimed that "clearly unconstitutional, clearly improper" action would not be subject to judicial review. Yet in this confrontation the Supreme Court declared that Congress had overstepped its authority by excluding someone on factors other than the three qualifications specified in the Constitution: age, citizenship, and residency requirements. Powell v. McCormack, 395 U.S. 486 (1969). (See reading in Chapter 6.)

matters regarding the recognition of foreign governments, political boundaries, envoys, the dates for beginning and ending wars, calling out the militia, and an alien's eligibility for federal benefits.[17]

Rules of self-restraint are part of the complex process of drawing limits on judicial power. Some scholars argue that prudence dictates restrictions on judicial activity. Others warn that the contemporary Court has confused the concept of justiciability and abdicated its duty to decide proper cases and controversies. The use of threshold requirements to avoid or delay judicial decision has sparked a number of lively debates, particularly one between Alexander M. Bickel and Gerald Gunther (see reading).

Baker v. Carr

369 U.S. 186 (1962)

In this case, in which the Supreme Court accepts jurisdiction over the apportionment of legislative seats, the Court offers criteria for determining whether a case falls within the category of a "political question."

---

17. Recognizing foreign governments: Rose v. Himely, 4 Cr. 241 (1808); Gelston v. Hoyt, 3 Wheat. 246 (1818). Political boundaries: Foster v. Neilson, 2 Pet. 253 (1829); Williams v. Suffolk Insurance Co., 13 Pet. 415 (1839). Envoys: Ex parte Hitz, 111 U.S. 766 (1884). Beginning and ending wars: Martin v. Mott, 12 Wheat. 19 (1827); Commercial Trust Co. v. Miller, 262 U.S. 51 (1923). Calling out the militia: Martin v. Mott, 12 Wheat. 19 (1827). Federal benefits: Mathews v. Diaz, 426 U.S. 67, 81–84 (1976).

MR. JUSTICE BRENNAN delivered the opinion of the Court....

Our discussion, even at the price of extending this opinion, requires review of a number of political question cases, in order to expose the attributes of the doctrine—attributes which, in various settings, diverge, combine, appear, and disappear in seeming disorderliness. Since that review is undertaken solely to demonstrate that neither singly nor collectively do these cases support a conclusion that this apportionment case is nonjusticiable, we of course do not explore their implications in other contexts. That review reveals that in the Guaranty Clause cases and in the other "political question" cases, it is the relationship between the judiciary and the coordinate branches of the Federal Government, and not the federal judiciary's relationship to the States, which gives rise to the "political question."

We have said that "In determining whether a question falls within [the political question] category, the appropriateness under our system of government of attributing finality to the action of the political departments and also the lack of satisfactory criteria for a judicial determination are dominant considerations." *Coleman* v. *Miller,* 307 U. S. 433, 454–455. The nonjusticiability of a political question is primarily a function of the separation of powers. Much confusion results from the capacity of the "political question" label to obscure the need for case-by-case inquiry. Deciding whether a matter has in any measure been committed by the Constitution to another branch of government, or whether the action of that branch exceeds whatever authority has been committed, is itself a delicate exercise in constitutional interpretation, and is a responsibility of this Court as ultimate interpreter of the Constitution. To demonstrate this requires no less than to analyze representative cases and to infer from them the analytical threads that make up the political question doctrine. We shall then show that none of those threads catches this case.

Foreign relations: There are sweeping statements to the effect that all questions touching foreign relations are political questions. Not only does resolution of such issues frequently turn on standards that defy judicial application, or involve the exercise of a discretion demonstrably committed to the executive or legislature; but many such questions uniquely demand single-voiced statement of the Government's views. Yet it is error to suppose that every case or controversy which touches foreign relations lies beyond judicial cognizance....

While recognition of foreign governments so strongly defies judicial treatment that without executive recognition a foreign state has been called "a republic of whose existence we know nothing," and the judiciary ordinarily follows the executive as to which nation has sovereignty over disputed territory, once sovereignty over an area is politically determined and declared, courts may examine the resulting status and decide independently whether a statute applies to that area. Similarly, recognition of belligerency abroad is an executive responsibility, but if the executive proclamations fall short of an explicit answer, a court may construe them seeking, for example, to determine whether the situation is such that statutes designed to assure American neutrality have become operative. *The Three Friends,* 166 U.S. 1, 63, 66....

Dates of duration of hostilities: Though it has been stated broadly that "the power which declared the necessity is the power to declare its cessation, and what the cessation requires," *Commercial Trust Co.* v. *Miller,* 262 U.S. 51, 57, here too analysis reveals isolable reasons for the presence of political questions, underlying this Court's refusal to review the political departments' determination of when or whether a war has ended. Dominant is the need for finality in the political determination, for emergency's nature demands "A prompt and unhesitating obedience," *Martin* v. *Mott,* 12 Wheat. 19, 30 (calling up of militia). Moreover, "the cessation of hostilities does not necessarily end the war power. It was stated in *Hamilton* v. *Kentucky Distilleries & W. Co.,* 251 U.S. 146, 161, that the war power includes the power 'to remedy the evils which have arisen from its rise and progress' and continues during that emergency. *Stewart* v. *Kahn,* 11 Wall, 493, 507." *Fleming* v. *Mohawk Wrecking Co.,* 331 U.S. 111, 116. But deference rests on reason, not habit....

Validity of enactments: In *Coleman* v. *Miller, supra,* this Court held that the questions of how long a proposed amendment to the Federal Constitution remained open to ratification, and what effect a prior rejection had on a subsequent ratification, were committed to congressional resolution and involved criteria of decision that necessarily escaped the judicial grasp. Similar considerations apply to the enacting process: "The respect due to coequal and independent departments," and the need for finality and certainty about the status of a statute contribute to judicial reluctance to inquire whether, as passed, it complied with all requisite formalities. *Field* v. *Clark,* 143 U.S. 649, 672, 676–677; see *Leser* v. *Garnett,* 258 U.S. 130, 137. But it is not true that courts will never delve into a legislature's records upon such a quest: If the enrolled statute lacks an effective date, a court will not hesitate to seek it in the legislative journals in order to preserve the enactment. *Gardner* v. *The Collector,* 6 Wall. 499. The political question doctrine, a tool of maintenance of governmental order, will not be so applied as to promote only disorder.

The status of Indian tribes: This Court's deference to the political departments in determining whether Indians are recognized as a tribe, while it reflects familiar attributes of political questions, *United States* v. *Holliday,* 3 Wall. 407, 419, also has a unique element in that "the relation of the Indians to the United States is marked by peculiar and cardinal distinctions which exist no where else.... [The Indians are] domestic dependent nations ... in a state of pupilage. Their relation to the United States resembles that of a ward to his guardian." *The Cherokee Nation* v. *Georgia,* 5 Pet. 1, 16, 17. Yet, here too, there is no blanket rule.... [I]t is not meant ... that Congress may bring a community or body of people within the range of this power by arbitrarily calling them an Indian tribe...." *United States* v. *Sandoval,* 231 U.S. 28, 46. Able to discern what is "distinctly Indian," *ibid.,* the courts will strike down any heedless extension of that label. They will not stand impotent before an obvious instance of a manifestly unauthorized exercise of power.

It is apparent that several formulations which vary slightly according to the settings in which the questions arise may describe a political question, although each has one or more elements which identify it as essentially a function of the separation of powers. Prominent on the surface of any case held to involve a political question is found a textually demonstrable constitutional commitment of the issue to a coordinate political department; or a lack of judicially discoverable and manageable standards for resolving it; or the impossibility of deciding without an initial policy determination of a kind clearly for nonjudicial discretion; or the impossibility of a court's undertaking independent resolution without expressing lack of the respect due coordinate branches of government; or an unusual need for unquestioning adherence to a political decision already made; or the potentiality of embarrassment from multifarious pronouncements by various departments on one question.

Unless one of these formulations is inextricable from the case at bar, there should be no dismissal for nonjusticiability on the ground of a political question's presence. The doctrine of which we treat is one of "political questions," not one of "political cases." The courts cannot reject as "no law suit" a bona fide controversy as to whether some action denominated "political" exceeds constitutional authority. The cases we have reviewed show the necessity for discriminating inquiry into the precise facts and posture of the particular case, and the impossibility of resolution by any semantic cataloguing.

But it is argued that this case shares the characteristics of decisions that constitute a category not yet considered, cases concerning the Constitution's guaranty, in Art. IV, ' 4, of a republican form of government....

Republican form of government: Luther v. *Borden,* 7 How. 1, though in form simply an action for damages for trespass was, as Daniel Webster said in opening the argument for the defense, "an unusual case." The defendants, admitting an otherwise tortious breaking and entering, sought to justify their action on the ground that they were agents of the established lawful government of Rhode Island, which State was then under martial law to defend itself from active insurrection; that the plaintiff was engaged in that insurrection; and that they entered under orders to arrest the plaintiff....

Clearly, several factors were thought by the Court in *Luther* to make the question there "political": the commitment to the other branches of the decision as to which is the lawful state government; the unambiguous action by the President, in recognizing the charter government as the lawful authority; the need for finality in the executive's decision; and the lack of criteria by which a court could determine which form of government was republican.

Nixon v. United States

506 U.S. 224 (1993)

Walter L. Nixon, Jr., a federal district judge, was convicted of federal crimes and sentenced to prison. The House of Representatives adopted articles of impeachment against him and the Senate, following Rule XI, sent the matter to a committee of Senators to hear evidence and report that evidence to the full Senate. After the Senate voted to convict Nixon, he sued on the ground that Senate Rule XI violates the constitutional language that places upon the Senate, and not a committee of the Senate, to "have the sole Power to try all Impeachments." A district court and appellate court held that his claim was nonjusticiable.

CHIEF JUSTICE REHNQUIST delivered the opinion of the Court.

. . .

A controversy is nonjusticiable—*i.e.*, involves a political question—where there is "a textually demonstrable constitutional commitment of the issue to a coordinate political department; or a lack of judicially discoverable and manageable standards for resolving it...." *Baker v. Carr*, 369 U.S. 186, 217 (1962). But the courts must, in the first instance, interpret the text in question and determine whether and to what extent the issue is textually committed. See *ibid.; Powell v. McCormack*, 396 U.S. 486, 519 (1969). As the discussion that follows makes clear, the concept of a textual commitment to a coordinate political department is not completely separate from the concept of a lack of judicially discoverable and manageable standards for resolving it; the lack of judicially manageable standards may strengthen the conclusion that there is a textually demonstrable commitment to a coordinate branch.

In this case, we must examine Art I, § 3, cl. 6, to determine the scope of authority conferred upon the Senate by the Framers regarding impeachment. It provides:

"The Senate shall have the sole Power to try all Impeachments. When sitting for that Purpose, they shall be on Oath or Affirmation. When the President of the United States is tried, the Chief Justice shall preside: And no Person shall be convicted without the Concurrence of two thirds of the Members present."

The language and structure of this Clause are revealing. The first sentence is a grant of authority to the Senate, and the word "sole" indicates that this authority is reposed in the Senate and nowhere else. The next two sentences specify requirements to which the Senate proceedings shall conform: The Senate shall be on oath or affirmation, a two-thirds vote is required to convict, and when the President is tried the Chief Justice shall preside.

Petitioner argues that the word "try" in the first sentence imposes by implication an additional requirement on the Senate in that the proceedings must be in the nature of a judicial trial. From there petitioner goes on to argue that this limitation precludes the Senate from delegating to a select committee the task of hearing the testimony of witnesses, as was done pursuant to Senate Rule XI. "'[T]ry' means more than simply 'vote on' or 'review' or

'judge.' In 1787 and today, trying a case means hearing the evidence, not scanning a cold record." Brief for Petitioner 25. Petitioner concludes from this that courts may review whether or not the Senate "tried" him before convicting him.

There are several difficulties with this position which lead us ultimately to reject it. The word "try," both in 1787 and later, has considerably broader meanings than those to which petitioner would limit it. Older dictionaries define try as "[t]o examine" or "[t]o examine as a judge." See 2 S. Johnson, A Dictionary of the English Language (1785). In more modern usage the term has various meanings. For example, try can mean "to examine or investigate judicially," "to conduct the trial of," or "to put to the test by experiment, investigation, or trial." Webster's Third New International Dictionary 2457 (1971). Petitioner submits that "try," as contained in T. Sheridan, Dictionary of the English Language (1796), means "to examine as a judge; to bring before a judicial tribunal." Based on the variety of definitions, however, we cannot say that the Framers used the word "try" as an implied limitation on the method by which the Senate might proceed in trying impeachments....

... We think that the word "sole" is of considerable significance. Indeed, the word "sole" appears only one other time in the Constitution—with respect to the House of Representatives' "*sole* Power of Impeachment." Art. I, § 2, cl. 5 (emphasis added). The commonsense meaning of the word "sole" is that the Senate alone shall have authority to determine whether an individual should be acquitted or convicted. The dictionary definition bears this out. "Sole" is defined as "having no companion," "solitary," "being the only one," and "functioning ... independently and without assistance or interference." Webster's Third New International Dictionary 2168 (1971). If the courts may review the actions of the Senate in order to determine whether that body "tried" an impeached official, it is difficult to see how the Senate would be "functioning ... independently and without assistance or interference."

. . .

The Framers labored over the question of where the impeachment power should lie. Significantly, in at least two considered scenarios the power was placed with the Federal Judiciary. See 1 Farrand 21–22 (Virginia Plan); *id.*, at 244 (New Jersey Plan). Indeed, James Madison and the Committee of Detail proposed that the Supreme Court should have the power to determine impeachments. See 2 *id.*, at 551 (Madison); *id.*, at 178–179, 186 (Committee of Detail). Despite these proposals, the Convention ultimately decided that the Senate would have "the sole Power to try all Impeachments." Art. I, § 3, cl. 6. According to Alexander Hamilton, the Senate was the "most fit depositary of this important trust" because its Members are representatives of the people. See The Federalist No. 65, p. 440 (J. Cooke ed. 1961). The Supreme Court was not the proper body because the Framers "doubted whether the members of that tribunal would, at all times, be endowed with so eminent a portion of fortitude as would be called for in the execution of so difficult a task" or whether the Court "would possess the degree of credit and authority" to carry out its judgment if it conflicted with the accusation brought by the Legislature—the people's representative. See *id.*, at 441. In addition, the Framers believed the Court was too small in number: "The awful discretion, which a court of impeachments must necessarily have, to doom to honor or to infamy the most confidential and the most distinguished characters of the community, forbids the commitment of the trust to a small number of persons." Id., at 441–442.

There are two additional reasons why the Judiciary, and the Supreme Court in particular, were not chosen to have any role in impeachments. First, the Framers recognized that most likely there would be two sets of proceedings for individuals who commit impeachable offenses—the impeachment trial and a separate criminal trial. In fact, the Constitution explicitly provides for two separate proceedings. See Art. I, § 3, cl. 7. The Framers deliberately separated the two forums to avoid raising the specter of bias and to ensure independent judgments....

Second, judicial review would be inconsistent with the Framers' insistence that our system be one of checks and balances. In our constitutional system, impeachment was designed to be the *only* check on the Judicial Branch by the Legislature....

... Nixon's argument would place final reviewing authority with respect to impeachments in the hands of the same body that the impeachment process is meant to regulate.

. . .

In addition to the textual commitment argument, we are persuaded that the lack of finality and the difficulty of fashioning relief counsel against justiciability. See *Baker v. Carr*, 369 U.S., at 210. We agree with the Court of Appeals that opening the door of judicial review to the procedures used by the Senate in trying impeachments would "expose the political life of the country to months, or perhaps years, of chaos." ... This lack of finality would manifest itself most dramatically if the President were impeached. The legitimacy of any successor, and hence his effectiveness, would be impaired severely, not merely while the judicial process was running its course, but during any retrial that a differently constituted Senate might conduct if its first judgment of conviction were invalidated. Equally uncertain is the question of what relief a court may give other than simply setting aside the judgment of conviction. Could it order the reinstatement of a convicted federal judge, or order Congress to create an additional judgeship if the seat had been filled in the interim?

. . .

For the foregoing reasons, the judgment of the Court of Appeals is

Affirmed

JUSTICE STEVENS, concurring.

For me, the debate about the strength of the inferences to be drawn from the use of the words "sole" and "try" is far less significant than the central fact that the Framers decided to assign the impeachment power to the Legislative Branch.... Respect for a coordinate branch of the Government forecloses any assumption that improbable hypotheticals like those mentioned by JUSTICE WHITE and JUSTICE BLACKMUN will ever occur....

JUSTICE WHITE, with whom JUSTICE BLACKMUN joins, concurring in the judgment.

Petitioner contends that the method by which the Senate convicted him on two articles of impeachment violates Art. I, § 3, cl. 6, of the Constitution, which mandates that the Senate "try" impeachments. The Court is of the view that the Constitution forbids us even to consider his contention. I find no such prohibition and would therefore reach the merits of the claim. I concur in the judgment because the Senate fulfilled its constitutional obligation to "try" petitioner.

I

... I would prefer not to announce an unreviewable discretion in the Senate to ignore completely the constitutional direction to "try" impeachment cases. When asked at oral argument whether that direction would be satisfied if, after a House vote to impeach, the Senate, without any procedure whatsoever, unanimously found the accused guilty of being "a bad guy," counsel for the United States answered that the Government's theory "leads me to answer that question yes." Tr. of Oral Arg. 51. Especially in light of this advice from the Solicitor General, I would not issue an invitation to the Senate to find an excuse, in the name of other pressing business, to be dismissive of its critical role in the impeachment process....

[II. A]

... While the majority rejects petitioner's justiciability argument as espousing a view "inconsistent with the Framers' insistence that our system be one of checks and balances," *ante*, at 234, it is the Court's finding of nonjusticiability that truly upsets the Framers' careful design. In a truly balanced system, impeachments tried by the Senate would serve as a means of controlling the largely unaccountable Judiciary, even as judicial review would ensure that the Senate adhered to a minimal set of procedural standards in conducting impeachment trials.

B

The majority also contends that the term "try"

does not present a judicially manageable standard....

... Were the Senate, for example, to adopt the practice of automatically entering a judgment of conviction whenever articles of impeachment were delivered from the House, it is quite clear that the Senate will have failed to "try" impeachments....

JUSTICE SOUTER, concurring in the judgment.

. . .

[Although Souter regards the Court as correct in dismissing this particular dispute as a political question, he can] envision different and unusual circumstances that might justify a more searching review of impeachment proceedings. If the Senate were to act in a manner seriously threatening the integrity of its results, convicting, say, upon a coin toss, or upon a summary determination that an officer of the United States was simply "'a bad guy,'" *ante*, at 239 (White, J., concurring in judgment), judicial interference might well be appropriate....

Virtues and Vices: Bickel versus Gunther

In a foreword entitled "The Passive Virtues," written for the 1960 term of the Supreme Court and published in the *Harvard Law Review* in 1961, Alexander M. Bickel urged the Court to avoid adjudication by making greater use of its doctrines on standing, case and controversy, ripeness, and political questions. A rebuttal, "The Subtle Vices of the 'Passive Virtues' — A Comment on Principle and Expediency in Judicial Review," was prepared by Gerald Gunther and published in the January 1964 issue of the *Columbia Law Review*.

ALEXANDER M. BICKEL:

. . .

It would seem ... to follow from *Marbury* v. *Madison* that, except as stated, "all Cases" are justiciable and must be heard. Indeed Marshall, assuming the tone of absolute assertion that he deemed suitable when the Court's basic powers were in issue, said in *Cohens* v. *Virginia*:

"It is most true that this court will not take jurisdiction if it should not; but it is equally true, that it must take jurisdiction if it should. The judiciary cannot, as the legislature may, avoid a measure because it approaches the confines of the constitution. We cannot pass it by because it is doubtful. With whatever doubts, with whatever difficulties, a case may be attended, we must decide it if it be brought before us. We have no more right to decline the exercise of jurisdiction which is given, than to usurp

that which is not given. The one or the other would be treason to the constitution."

But the doctrines of standing and case and controversy have in time come to mean also something entirely unrelated to the reasoning of *Marbury* v. *Madison*. They have encompassed numerous instances in which the Court did nothing else but to "decline the exercise of jurisdiction which is given...." And to this end they have been abetted by, or used interchangeably (and rather unanalytically) with, other doctrines, such as "ripeness" and "political question." This has caused great difficulties for those who would rest the institution of judicial review on the foundation of the opinion in *Marbury* v. *Madison*, or even on an independent, more scrupulous but quite similar process of deduction from the constitutional text.

. . .

... [O]nly by means of a play on words can the

broad discretion that the courts have in fact exercised be turned into an act of constitutional interpretation. The political-question doctrine simply resists being domesticated in this fashion. There is something different about it, in kind, not in degree, from the general "interpretive process"; something greatly more flexible, something of prudence, not construction and not principle. And it is something that cannot exist within the four corners of *Marbury v. Madison.*

. . .

I have tried to show that the Supreme Court's well-established if imperfectly understood practice of declining on occasion to exercise the power of judicial review is difficult to reconcile with the strict-constructionist conception of the foundation of that power. If this were all what is called merely academic, it would be none the worse for it. Actually, however, important consequences are in play. Of course, no concept, strict-, loose-, or medium-constructionist, can get around the sheer necessity of limiting each year's business to what nine men can fruitfully deal with. But strict-constructionist compunctions cause the techniques for meeting this necessity to be viewed with misgiving and to be encumbered with fictive explanations. So are other techniques of avoiding adjudication, and I would suggest that herein lies at least part of the reason for the confusion and lack of direction that has characterized their development. Some of the confusion may be in the eye of the beholder, but not all....

Quite obviously, no society, certainly not a large and heterogeneous one, can fail in time to explode if it is deprived of the arts of compromise, if it knows no ways to muddle through. No good society can be unprincipled; and no viable society can be principle-ridden. But it is not true in our society that we are generally governed wholly by principle in some matters and indulge a rule of expediency exclusively in others. There is no such neat dividing line. There are exceptions, some of which are delineated by the political-question doctrine. Most often, however, and as often as not in matters of the widest and deepest concern such as the racial problem, both requirements exist most imperatively side by side: guiding principle and expedient compromise. The role of principle, when it cannot be the inflexible governing rule, is to affect the tendency of policies of expediency. And it is a potent role....

It follows that the techniques and allied devices for staying the Court's hand, as is avowedly true at least of certiorari, cannot themselves be principled in the sense in which we have a right to expect adjudications on the merits to be principled. They mark the point at which the Court gives the electoral institutions their head and itself stays out of politics, and there is nothing paradoxical in finding that here the Court is most a political animal. But this is not to concede unchanneled, undirected, unchartered discretion. It is not to concede judgment proceeding from impulse, hunch, sentiment, predilection, inarticulable and unreasoned. The antithesis of principle in an institution that represents decency and reason is not whim, nor even expediency, but prudence....

GERALD GUNTHER:

. . .

Principle and reason are hard taskmasters. Insistence on these essential ingredients is Bickel's starting point; but, as he contemplates their impact on the judicial process, unpalatable consequences loom ever larger. He cannot bear to abandon the requirement of principle in constitutional adjudication; he cannot bear the inexpedient results of unflinching adherence to principle. He is put to an excruciating choice; his response is to avoid the choice, to seek escape routes.

He derives the philosophic basis for his ingenious solution from his contemplation of American democracy at large: "No good society can be unprincipled; and no viable society can be principle-ridden.... Our democratic system of government exists in this Lincolnian tension between principle and expediency, and within its judicial review must play its role." These cosmic observations may be sound; but their relevance and utility as applied to a specific process and institution, to judicial review and the Supreme Court, are questionable. And the inferences Bickel draws ultimately fail to satisfy: they rest on faulty perceptions of the adjudicatory process; and they yield guidelines which invite not accommodation but surrender of principle to expediency....

Bickel's ambitious survey of the avoidance techniques, his "passive virtues," is the most comprehensive we have had, and his examination of this tangled field is of significance quite independent of his purposes....

The result is a strange mixture. He covers an enormous range of techniques; he describes and applies his concepts with skill; he offers some fresh insights and much helpful clarification; yet the total product is essentially unpersuasive, profoundly disturbing, and ultimately subversive of the very values it professes to serve. Two major flaws, I submit, help to explain why so many superior parts add up to such an unsatisfying whole. First, the discrete analyses of the varied avoidance devices are too much influenced by Bickel's underlying premises and overriding purposes: in his anxiety to enlarge Court discretion not to adjudicate, some of the techniques are subjected to greater strains than they can bear. Second, as Bickel criticized some commentators as neo-realists, so it can be said that he suffers from the neo-Brandeisian fallacy: invoking the well-known *Ashwander* statement by Brandeis, regarding avoidance of constitutional questions in adjudication, to assert an amorphous authority to withhold adjudication altogether — a power far broader than any suggested by the examples given by Brandeis, a discretion far wider than any that can be independently justified....

Of course the Court often may and should avoid "passing upon a large part of all of the constitutional questions pressed upon it for decision." Four of the seven Brandeis rules involve well-known instances of such avoidance — avoidance only of some or all of the constitutional questions argued, *not* avoidance of all decision on the merits of the case. Thus, when the Court does not "formulate a rule of constitutional law broader than is required by the precise facts," it merely narrows the constitutional ground of decision, but does not even avoid all constitutional decision. Similarly, when the Court does not decide a constitutional question presented by the case because there is a nonconstitutional ground "upon which the case may be disposed of," it only avoids constitutional decision, not a decision on the merits of the case. Nor, of course, does the Court withhold adjudication of the case when it makes a ruling on the constitutionality of a federal law unnecessary by finding a construction of the statute which is "fairly possible" and which avoids the constitutional doubts. These are all in a sense avoidance devices, and Bickel includes these and similar ones in his catalogue of techniques — but they are devices which go to the choice of the ground of decision of a case, not devices which avoid decision on the merits, not devices which "decline to exercise" the jurisdiction to decide....

F. EQUITABLE DISCRETION

As Justice Brennan observed in *Baker v. Carr*, the political question doctrine is "essentially a function of the separation of powers," designed to restrain courts "from inappropriate interference in the business of the other branches of Government." See also Nixon v. United States, 506 U.S. 224, 252 (1993); United States v. Munoz-Flores, 495 U.S. 385, 394 (1990). The same may be said of the doctrine of equitable discretion, often invoked by courts as a "companion" to the political question doctrine. Equitable discretion has been utilized by courts, particularly in foreign affairs cases, to dismiss claims against the executive brought by members of Congress, when members have an effective in-House remedy for their alleged injuries.

Congressional lawsuits may arise if a disappointed minority in either the House or the Senate is unable to move its chamber to act against a claimed presidential usurpation, and seeks relief from the Court. The doctrine of equitable discretion may be invoked to deny relief. Justice Powell provided the rationale in a concurring opinion in *Goldwater v. Carter*: "If the Congress chooses not to confront the President, it is not our task to do so." 444 U.S. 996, 998 (1979). See also Crockett v. Reagan, 558 F.Supp. 893, 898–99 (D.D.C. 1982); aff'd per curiam, 720 F.2d 1355 (D.C. Cir. 1983); Riegle v. FOMC, 656 F.2d 873, 879 (D.C. Cir. 1981), cert. denied, 454 U.S. 1082 (1981).

NOTES AND QUESTIONS

1. Suppose, for the sake of argument that Chief Justice Marshall really did assert, in *Marbury v. Madison*, that the Supreme Court is the "final arbiter" of the meaning of the Constitution. Is the "final word" principle reconcilable with the political question doctrine? Does the political question doctrine leave the last word to the courts or to the political branches?

2. Louis Henkin concluded that there is no political question "doctrine." Henkin, "Is there a Political Question Doctrine?" 85 Yale L. J. 597, 622–23 (1976). Is he correct? If so, what are the courts doing when they characterize a case as a "nonjusticiable" political question?

3. Should the Court abstain from ruling in a case in which a remedy seems unavailing or likely to invite sharp conflict with a coordinate branch? Was there a remedy in *Nixon v. United States*?

Could the Court have ordered reinstatement of Judge Nixon if it had determined that the Senate had abused its powers? Charles Black observed: "If the Supreme Court [were] to order reinstatement of an impeached and convicted president there would be [a] very grave and quite legitimate doubt whether that decree had any title to being obeyed, or whether it was [as] widely outside judicial jurisdiction as would be a judicial order to Congress to increase the penalty for counterfeiting. To cite the most frightening consequence, our military commanders would have to decide for themselves which president they were bound to obey. [It] would be most unfortunate if the notion got about that the Senate's verdict was somewhat tentative." Charles Black, Jr., Impeachment: A Handbook 61–62 (1974).

4. In *Cohens v. Virginia* (1821), Chief Justice Marshall wrote: "It is most true that this Court will not take jurisdiction if it should not: but it is equally true, that it must take jurisdiction if it should." He said the Court had "no more right to decline the exercise of jurisdiction which is given, than to usurp that which is not given." What exceptions to that policy did the Court later develop? What insights were provided by Alexander Bickel and Gerald Gunther?

SELECTED READINGS

ALBERT, LEE A. "Justiciability and Theories of Judicial Review: A Remote Relationship." 50 Southern California Law Review 1139 (1977).

BRILMAYER, LEA. "The Jurisprudence of Article III: Perspectives on the 'Case or Controversy' Requirement." 93 Harvard Law Review 297 (1979).

CONDON, DANIEL PATRICK. "The Generalized Grievance Restriction: Prudential Restraint or Constitutional Mandate?" 70 Georgetown Law Journal 1157 (1982).

HUGHES, GRAHAM. "Civil Disobedience and the Political Question Doctrine." 43 New York University Law Review 1 (1968).

JACKSON, R. BROOKE. "The Political Question Doctrine: Where Does It Stand After Powell v. McCormack, O'Brien v. Brown, and Gilligan v. Morgan?" 44 University of Colorado Law Review 477 (1973).

KATES, DON B., JR., AND WILLIAM T. BARKER. "Mootness in Judicial Proceedings: Toward a Coherent Theory." 62 California Law Review 1385 (1974).

LOGAN, DAVID A. "Standing to Sue: A Proposed Separation of Powers Analysis." 1984 Wisconsin Law Review 37.

MONAGHAN, HENRY P. "Constitutional Adjudication: The Who and When." 82 Yale Law Journal 1363 (1973).

MORRISON, HENRY P. "Rights Without Remedies: The Burger Court Takes the Federal Courts Out of the Business of Protecting Federal Rights." 30 Rutgers Law Review 841 (1977).

MOURTADA-SABBAH AND BRUCE E. CAIN, EDS. The Political Question Doctrine and the Supreme Court of the United States. Lanham, Md.: Lexington Books, 2007.

NAGEL, ROBERT F. "Political Law, Legalistic Politics: A Recent History of the Political Question Doctrine." 56 University of Chicago Law Review 643 (1989).

NICHOL, GENE R., JR. "Causation as a Standing Requirement: The Unprincipled Use of Judicial Restraint." 69 Kentucky Law Journal 185 (1980).

ORREN, KAREN." Standing to Sue: Interest Group Conflict in the Federal Courts." 70 American Political Science Review 723 (1976).

POST, CHARLES GORDON, JR. The Supreme Court and Political Questions. Baltimore: The Johns Hopkins Press, 1936.

RADCLIFFE, JAMES E. The Case-or-Controversy Provision. University Park: Pennsylvania State University Press, 1978.

ROSENBLUM, VICTOR G. "Justiciability and Justice: Elements of Restraint and Indifference." 15 Catholic University Law Review 141 (1966).

SCALIA, ANTONIN. "The Doctrine of Standing as an Essential Element of the Separation of Powers." 17 Suffolk University Law Review 881 (1983).

SCHARPF, FRITZ W. "Judicial Review and the Political Question: A Functional Analysis." 75 Yale Law Journal 517 (1966).

SCOTT, KENNETH E. "Standing in the Supreme Court—A Functional Analysis." 86 Harvard Law Review 645 (1973).

SEDLER, ROBERT ALLEN. "Standing and the Burger Court: An Analysis and Some Proposals for Legislative Reform." 30 Rutgers Law Review 863 (1977).

STRUM, PHILIPPA. The Supreme Court and "Political Questions." University: University of Alabama Press, 1974.

Tigar, Michael E. "Judicial Power, the 'Political Question Doctrine,' and Foreign Relations." 17 UCLA Law Review 1135 (1970).

Tucker, Edwin W. "The Metamorphosis of the Standing to Sue Doctrine." 17 New York Law Forum 911 (1972).

Tushnet, Mark V. "The Sociology of Article III: A Response to Professor Brilmayer." 93 Harvard Law Review 1698 (1980).

4

Judicial Organization

Questions of judicial organization may seem overly technical and unrelated to constitutional law. However, organizational issues ultimately present questions of power. This chapter identifies the tangible constraints that operate on the judiciary: the power of Congress to create and monitor the federal court system, including the creation of legislative and specialized courts; the President's power to appoint judges and the Senate's power to confirm; questions of tenure, removal, and compensation of federal judges; and the extent to which judges can lobby for their causes.

A. FEDERAL COURT SYSTEM

Long before the American colonies declared their separation from England, the idea of an independent judiciary had secured a firm foothold among the framers. The Act of Settlement, passed by England in 1701, contributed to judicial autonomy by guaranteeing tenure for judges during good behavior. The power to constitute courts in the American colonies, however, was vested in the governor and council (creatures of the King). The assemblies were allowed to create courts only for small causes, subject always to the King's veto.[1]

The principle of judicial independence appears in several sections of the Declaration of Independence. The American framers accused the King of "obstruct[ing] the Administration of Justice, by refusing his Assent to Laws for establishing Judiciary Powers." Because of disputes between the British Crown and several of the colonies, laws establishing courts of justice were struck down repeatedly, sometimes eliminating courts for long stretches of time. Edward Dumbauld, The Declaration of Independence and What It Means Today 108–12 (1950). The Declaration of Independence criticized the King for making judges "dependent on his Will alone, for the Tenure of their Offices, and the Amount and Payment of Their Salaries." The policy of colonial judges serving at the King's pleasure provoked bitter resistance in New York, New Jersey, Pennsylvania, North Carolina, South Carolina, and Massachusetts, where colonial legislatures wanted judges to have tenure during good behavior. Id. at 112–15. Following the break with England, several American colonies included tenure and salary provisions in their constitutions to secure judicial independence.

Setting Up Federal Courts

After the colonies cut ties with England, state governments authorized vessels to prey on British shipping. A judicial system was needed to dispose of "prizes"(property captured at sea). State admiralty courts made the initial determination, but appeals beyond that level required the attention of the Continental Congress. From 1776 to 1780, appeals were handled first by temporary committees and then by a standing committee, until Congress, in May 1780, created a "Court of Appeals in Cases of Capture." This tribunal, the first national judiciary, took direction from the Continental Congress and

---

1. Julius Goebel, Jr., 1 History of the Supreme Court of the United States: Antecedents and Beginnings 12–13 (1971).

even from the Secretary for Foreign Affairs.[2] The Court of Appeals continued to function until delegates arrived at Philadelphia in May 1787 to draft a new constitution.

The delegates to the Philadelphia Convention recognized the need for executive and judicial independence. They explored the possibility of setting up a Council of Revision, consisting of the executive and "a convenient number of the National Judiciary," to examine all bills from the legislature before they became law. Rejection by the Council could be overridden by the legislature. 1 Farrand 21. The convention turned down the proposal because the delegates wanted the Supreme Court to interpret the law without any prior participation. Id. at 97–98. The framers decided to vest the veto power exclusively in the President.

Article III of the Constitution created a separate judicial branch. The judges, both of the Supreme and inferior courts, "shall hold their Offices during good Behaviour, and shall, at stated Times, receive for their Services, a Compensation, which shall not be diminished during their Continuance in Office." The Constitution vests the judicial power of the United States "in one supreme Court, and in such inferior Courts as the Congress may from time to time ordain and establish." The word "may" implies that the establishment of lower courts is discretionary, and some members of the First Congress proposed to do only the minimum: staff and fund the Supreme Court and rely on the states for trial courts. The Judiciary Bill of 1789, as first drafted by the Senate, opted for federal trial (district) courts. An amendment to restrict those courts to cases of admiralty and maritime matters (like the Court of Appeals in Cases of Capture) was rejected. Warren, 37 Harv. L. Rev. 49, 67 (1923).

There were similar efforts in the House of Representatives to limit inferior courts to questions of admiralty. 1 Annals of Cong. 762, 777–78. These proposals, too, were unsuccessful. Although there was some resistance to federal district courts, the House rejected the idea of relying on state courts. Id. at 783. Madison warned that the courts in many states "cannot be trusted with the execution of Federal laws." Because of limited tenure and possible salary reductions, some courts were too dependent on state legislatures. Making federal laws dependent on these courts, Madison said, "would throw us back into all the embarrassments which characterized our former situation." Id. at 812–13. By a vote of 31 to 11, the House decisively rejected a motion to establish only State Courts of Admiralty with no federal district courts. Id. at 834.

Creating Circuit Courts

The Judiciary Act of 1789 provided for a Chief Justice and five Associate Justices for the Supreme Court. It divided the United States into thirteen districts, with a federal judge for each district, and created three circuits to handle appellate cases: the eastern, middle, and southern circuits. The circuit courts met twice a year in each district and consisted of any two Justices of the Supreme Court and one district judge from that circuit. District judges could not vote in any case of appeal or error from their own decisions. Section 25 of the Judiciary Act solidified federal control over the states by conferring upon the Supreme Court a supervisory role over state courts.

The Justices of the Supreme Court complained bitterly about their circuit court duties. In addition to handling cases on the Court's docket, Justices had to "ride circuit" by traveling around the country to hear appellate cases in the circuit courts. Riding circuit was an arduous and hazardous enterprise. Participation in circuit cases had another drawback: a Justice might have to review his own decision if the case reached the Supreme Court. All six Justices appealed to President Washington and Congress to reduce their labors. Congress offered modest relief in 1793 by allowing the attendance of only one Justice for the holding of circuit court. 1 Am. State Papers 24, 52 (1834); 1 Stat. 333 (1793).

With six Justices to cover three circuits, each Justice now had to ride circuit only once a year. Pressure for relief resulted in the controversial Judiciary Act of 1801, which divided the country into six

---

2. Id. at 178–79; Henry J. Bourguignon, The First Federal Court: The Federal Appellate Prize Court of the American Revolution (1977).

Congress "Fixes" the Meaning of the Constitution

[Congress passed legislation in 1802 to repeal the Judiciary Act of the previous year, in effect abolishing sixteen circuit judges and their salaries. A case challenging the right of Congress to abolish the circuit courts reached the Supreme Court in 1803, but Justice Paterson, writing for the Court, declined to overturn the statute.]

... Congress have constitutional authority to establish, from time to time, such inferior tribunals as they may think proper; and to transfer a cause from one such tribunal to another. In this last particular, there are no words in the constitution to prohibit or restrain the exercise of legislative power....

2d. Another reason for reversal is, that the judges of the supreme court have no right to sit as circuit judges, not being appointed as such, or, in other words, that they ought to have distinct commissions for that purpose. To this objection, which is of recent date, it is sufficient to observe, that practice, and acquiescence under it, for a period of several years, commencing with the organization of the judicial system, affords an irresistible answer, and has indeed fixed the construction. It is a contemporary interpretation of the most forcible nature. This practical exposition is too strong and obstinate to be shaken or controlled. Of course, the question is at rest, and ought not now to be disturbed.

SOURCE: Stuart v. Laird, 5 U.S. (1 Cr.) 298, 308 (1803).

---

circuits and promised to terminate circuit riding by creating sixteen circuit judges. Following the election of Thomas Jefferson as the next President, President John Adams elevated six district judges to those positions and named three Senators and one Representative to the vacant district judgeships. Farrand, 5 Am. Hist. Rev. 682 (1900); 2 Stat. 89, §7 (1801).

Although the creation of circuit judges had been proposed for several years, the statute creating them was not signed until the closing days of the Adams administration. After President Adams hastily filled the positions and allotted them to loyal Federalists, the Jeffersonians condemned the "midnight judges bill" as unconscionable. They accused the Federalists of trying to accomplish through judicial appointments what had just been denied them in the national election. The Judiciary Act of 1801 reduced the number of Supreme Court Justices from six to five, effective with the next vacancy. The reduction might have been justified because the work of the Justices had been cut back by eliminating circuit duties. Moreover, five Justices would avoid the possibility of tie votes. The Jeffersonians interpreted the statute less charitably. The reduction decreased Jefferson's opportunity to appoint his own candidate to the High Court. The new Congress promptly repealed the Judiciary Act of 1801 (see box).

Changes in the Number of Justices

The size of the Supreme Court fluctuated throughout the nineteenth century, keeping pace with the addition of new circuits. A seventh Justice was added in 1807 after the creation of a new judicial circuit. The size of the Supreme Court rose to nine in 1837, reflecting the westward expansion, and to ten by 1863 (to accommodate the Pacific Circuit). Three years later Congress lowered the permanent size of the Court to seven, although the membership never fell below eight. The reduction is often interpreted as a slap against President Andrew Johnson, depriving him of an opportunity to fill vacancies. The Radical Republicans feared that his appointees to the Court would oppose Reconstruction policies. S. Rept. No. 711, 75th Cong., 1st Sess. 13 (1937). His nomination of Henry Stanbery as an Associate Justice had to be withdrawn because Congress reduced the Court's size. However, Johnson signed the bill, and its legislative history does not suggest an attack on the Court. In fact, Chief Jus-

THE THIRTEEN FEDERAL JUDICIAL COURTS

tice Salmon P. Chase, in pursuit of higher salaries for the Supreme Court, supported a reduction to seven members.[3] Legislation in 1869 brought the Court back to its present size of nine members.

Appellate Courts

A major step in judicial reorganization occurred in 1891 when Congress created a separate system of appellate courts, producing three tiers: district (trial) courts, circuit (appellate) courts, and the Supreme Court. A comprehensive "Judges Bill" in 1925 gave the Supreme Court greater discretion to grant or deny petitions of appeal from the lower courts.

In 1891 there were nine circuit courts of appeals. The Tenth Circuit, split from the Eighth, appeared in 1929. When the workload of the Fifth Circuit grew too large, Congress divided it in 1981, forming the Eleventh Circuit. Together with the D.C. Circuit, that made twelve courts of appeals. In 1982 Congress established the Court of Appeals for the Federal Circuit (CAFC), which inherited the work of the Court of Customs and Patent Appeals and reviewed cases coming from the U.S. Claims Court (later renamed Court of Federal Claims). Unlike the other twelve circuits, which cover a specific geographical area and possess general jurisdiction, the CAFC is nationwide and limited in subject matter jurisdiction (see map).

---

3. Charles Fairman, 6 History of the Supreme Court of the United States: Reconstruction and Reunion 163–71 (1971); Cong. Globe, 39th Cong. 3909 (July 18, 1866); Stanley I. Kutler, Judicial Power and Reconstruction Politics 48–63 (1968). As a U.S. Senator, Chase had proposed that no vacancies be filled until the Court's membership fell to six. He justified this smaller number because of reduced duties once Justices were relieved of their responsibilities for riding circuit. Cong. Globe, 33d Cong., 2d Sess. 216–17 (1855).

Three-Judge Courts

As a means of expediting action, Congress submits some disputes to a three-judge court consisting of a mix of district and appellate judges. 28 U.S.C. § 2284 (2000). Initially, these courts were established to limit the interference of federal courts with state statutes. Instead of allowing a single federal district judge to nullify a state law, Congress required three federal judges (including at least one circuit judge) to hear applications to enjoin the enforcement of state statutes on constitutional grounds. Their determinations are appealable directly to the Supreme Court. Three-judge courts place an administrative burden on the federal judiciary, requiring three judges to do what might be done by one. In 1976 Congress eliminated three-judge courts for certain disputes. 90 Stat. 1119. Over the years, the jurisdiction of three-judge courts has been cut substantially. Gressman, Geller, Shapiro, Bishop, and Hartnett, Supreme Court Practice 89-92, 99-121 (9th ed. 2007).

Other Judicial Bodies

Congress has established several organizations to help the judiciary. In 1922, it created the Judicial Conference to coordinate the legislative requests and administrative actions of the federal courts. It had been the responsibility of the Justice Department to handle the administrative needs of the courts (including their budgets), creating an obvious separation of powers problem. In 1939, Congress established the Administrative Office of the United States Courts to take care of the managerial, research, statistical, and budgetary needs of the national judiciary. Also in 1939, Congress created judicial councils in each circuit to supervise the work of judges. In 1967, Congress created a Federal Judicial Center to study methods of improving judicial administration.

B. LEGISLATIVE AND SPECIALIZED COURTS

In addition to "constitutional courts" established by Congress pursuant to Article III of the Constitution, Congress creates Article I courts to carry out legislative duties. Drawing on various sections of the Constitution, Congress has set up territorial courts, legislative courts, military courts, and the courts of the District of Columbia. Judges sitting on those courts are not entitled to the rights of life tenure and irreducible compensation guaranteed to Article III federal judges.

Territorial Courts

Section 3 of Article IV gives Congress the power "to dispose of and make all needful Rules and Regulations respecting the Territory or other Property belonging to the United States." After Spain ceded Florida to the United States in 1819, Congress established a territorial government in Florida and its legislature created a court system that gave judges a term of four years. This system was challenged as a violation of the requirement in Article III that judges serve for life "during good Behaviour." The Supreme Court ruled that the territorial courts of Florida were not constitutional courts; they were legislative courts.[4]

Under its authority to govern territories, Congress established district courts in Puerto Rico, Guam, the Virgin Islands, the former Canal Zone, and the Northern Mariana Islands. The district court of Puerto Rico is classified as an Article III federal district court. Its judges hold office during

---

4. American Ins. Co. v. Canter, 26 U.S. (1 Pet.) 511, 545 (1828). Also on territorial courts see Benner v. Porter, 9 How. 235 (1850); Hornbuckle v. Toombs, 18 Wall. 648 (1874); Reynolds v. United States, 98 U.S. 145 (1878); The "City of Panama," 101 U.S. 453 (1880); and Romeu v. Todd, 206 U.S. 358 (1907).

Is It Legislative or Judicial?

Two centuries of statutory activity illustrate the broad range of options available to Congress in handling the adjudication of certain federal questions. It may choose to resolve disputes within its own chambers, as it did initially with federal claims. In legislating on claims, it can create outside bodies and call on them to investigate and make nonbinding recommendations. Congress may decide to shift adjudicatory issues to executive agencies, as it did with the Board of General Appraisers. Finally, it can vest them in adjudicatory bodies and designate whether those courts should have Article I or Article III status. In cases brought before them, federal courts monitor these designations to assure that they comply with constitutional principles. Functions of government therefore float from one branch to another as Congress searches for the most effective means of discharging its duties. What is "legislative" at one stage becomes "administrative" at another and "judicial" still later.

good behavior; territorial judges serve eight-year terms. Similar to territorial courts are the consular courts established by Congress to carry out the constitutional powers regarding treaties and commerce with foreign nations. Ex parte Bakelite Corp., 279 U.S. 438, 451 (1929).

Legislative Courts

Congress has established a number of Article I legislative courts. It created the Court of Claims in 1855 to help Congress handle the large number of claims presented by citizens against the United States. The responsibility for determining these claims "belongs primarily to Congress as an incident of its power to pay the debts of the United States." Ex parte Bakelite, 279 U.S. at 452. Initially, the Court of Claims performed an advisory role but subsequent statutes made some of its judgments binding. Gradually, the Court of Claims changed from an investigative to an adjudicatory body. In 1953 Congress made the Court of Claims an Article III court, giving it the constitutional protections of tenure and salary. 67 Stat. 226 (1953). However, legislation in 1982 gave the judges of the Claims Court a 14-year term, returning them to the status of an Article I Court. 96 Stat. 25 (1982). Legislation in 1992 changed its name to the Court of Federal Claims.

The United States Customs Court also illustrates the congressional need to delegate some of its constitutional responsibilities to judicial bodies. In 1890 Congress established within the Department of Treasury a Board of General Appraisers to review the decisions of appraisers and collectors at U.S. ports. In 1926 the Board was replaced by the United States Customs Court and in 1956 Congress made the Customs Court an Article III court. Its name was changed in 1980 to the Court of International Trade. 70 Stat. 532 (1956); 94 Stat. 1727 (1980).

Congress created a Court of Customs Appeal in 1909 to review final decisions of the Board of General Appraisers. The Court was established pursuant to the power of Congress to lay and collect duties on imports. Ex parte Bakelite, 279 U.S. at 458–59. The statute had been silent about judicial tenure. Congress granted the judges life tenure in 1930. 46 Stat. 590, 762 (1930). In 1958 Congress changed the court (by now called the Court of Customs and Patent Appeals) to an Article III court. Legislation in 1982 folded this court into the Court of Appeals for the Federal Circuit. 72 Stat. 848 (1958); 96 Stat. 25 (1982). These statutes illustrate the choices available to Congress in handling adjudicatory issues (see box).

The United States Tax Court was created in 1924 as the Board of Tax Appeals, placed within the Treasury Department as "an independent agency in the executive branch of the Government." 43 Stat. 338 (1924). Legislation in 1942 and 1969 changed the name of the Board to the "Tax Court of the United States" and gave it Article I status, 56 Stat. 957 (1942); 83 Stat. 30 (1969). All decisions of the

Tax Court, other than small tax cases, are subject to review by the United States Court of Appeals and by the Supreme Court.

Military Courts

A third class of specialized courts derives from the power of Congress under Article I, Section 8, to "make Rules for the Government and Regulation of the land and naval Forces." Congress decided that criminal behavior in the military shall be tried by court-martial proceedings, not by courts established under Article III. The United States Court of Military Appeals, composed of five judges with 15-year terms, is an Article I court. Military courts need not satisfy all of the procedural protections offered by Article III courts.[5]

In 1969, the Supreme Court attempted to subject certain military questions to the jurisdiction of civilian courts. It held that a crime must be "service connected" to be under military jurisdiction. O'-Callahan v. Parker, 395 U.S. 258 (1969). The service-connected doctrine became so confusing that the Court abandoned it in 1987. Jurisdiction of a court-martial now depends solely on the accused's status as a member of the armed forces. Solorio v. United States, 483 U.S. 435 (1987). Thus, the rights of servicemen result from action by Congress, not the courts. (For additional material on military courts, see Chapter 7.)

Article II Courts

The executive branch has created a number of courts to administer justice in territories occupied by U.S. armed forces. Frequently these take the form of military tribunals (discussed in Chapter 7). The President's power to establish these courts is subject to legislative and judicial checks. A recent example of an Article II court is the United States Court for Berlin, created in 1955 but not activated until 1979. The case produced a major collision between the State Department, which regarded the court as an instrument of American foreign policy, and the Article III judge who presided and insisted on full independence. United States v. Tiede, 86 F.R.D. 227 (U.S. Ct. Berlin 1979). See also Louis Fisher, "Hijack in Berlin," Legal Times, July 2, 2004, at 50–51, and David J. Bederman, "Article II Courts," 44 Mercer L. Rev. 825 (1993).

District of Columbia Courts

Under Article I, Section 8, Congress exercises "exclusive Legislation in all Cases whatsoever, over such District." Initially, the Supreme Court regarded the District of Columbia courts as legislative, not constitutional.[6] In 1933 the Court reasoned that because the District was formed from territory belonging to Maryland and Virginia, District inhabitants should continue to enjoy their former constitutional rights and protections. D.C. courts were therefore considered constitutional courts established under Article III. O'Donoghue v. United States, 289 U.S. 516 (1933). There are two types of D.C. courts: federal courts (the U.S. District Court for the District of Columbia and the U.S. Court of Appeals for the D.C. Circuit) and local courts for the District (the Superior Court and the D.C. Court of Appeals). The former are Article III Courts; the latter can have Article I characteristics. The Court compared a District resident to that of a citizen in any other state charged with violating a state criminal law. Citizens in the D.C. courts are "no more disadvantaged and no more entitled to an Art. III

---

5. Palmore v. United States, 411 U.S. 389, 404 (1973). See Toth v. Quarles, 350 U.S. 11, 17–18 (1955).

6. Keller v. Potomac Electric Power Co., 261 U.S. 428, 441–43 (1923); Postum Cereal Co. v. Calif. Fig Nut Co., 272 U.S. 693, 700 (1927); Ex parte Bakelite Corp., 279 U.S. 438, 450 (1929); Federal Radio Comm'n v. Gen'l Elec. Co., 281 U.S. 464, 468 (1930).

ROUTES TO THE SUPREME COURT

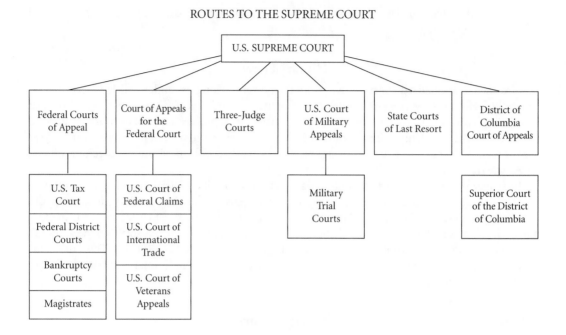

judge than any other citizen of any of the 50 States who is tried for a strictly local crime." Palmore v. United States, 411 U.S. 389, 410 (1973).

Bankruptcy Courts

The demarcation between Article I and Article III courts remains a source of disagreement among Justices of the Supreme Court. In 1978, in an effort to handle thousands of bankruptcy cases, Congress established a bankruptcy court in each federal district. The judges of those courts were appointed by the President (subject to Senate advice and consent) for 14-year terms and could be removed by the judicial council of the circuit. Their salaries could be decreased by Congress.

In 1982, the Supreme Court denied that Congress could establish specialized courts to carry out every one of its Article I powers. Although Congress has constitutional authority under Article I, Section 8, to establish "uniform Laws on the subject of Bankruptcies throughout the United States," this authority did not permit Congress to rely on a non-Article III court. Such reasoning, said the Court, "threatens to supplant completely our system of adjudication in independent Art. III tribunals and replace it with a system of 'specialized' legislative courts." The Court concluded that the Bankruptcy Act of 1978 had removed essential attributes of judicial power from the Article III district court and vested them in a non-Article III body. Northern Pipeline Const. Co. v. Marathon Pipe Line Co., 458 U.S. 50 (1982). Two years later, Congress passed legislation to reinstate the bankruptcy courts. The bankruptcy judges were made adjuncts of the district courts and given 14-year terms. 98 Stat. 2704 (1984).

The strict ruling on bankruptcy judges should not obscure the extent of adjudication that takes place outside Article III courts. In 1985 a unanimous Court upheld the arbitration provision of the Federal Insecticide, Fungicide, and Rodenticide Act. The Court decided that agency adjudication posed only a minimum threat to Article III judicial powers: "practical attention to substance rather than doctrinaire reliance on formal categories should inform application of Article III." Thomas v. Union Carbide Agric. Products Co., 473 U.S. 568, 587 (1985). A year later, the Court upheld another case of agency adjudication, again declining to "adopt formalistic and unbending rules." Commodity Futures Trading Comm'n v. Schor, 478 U.S. 833, 851 (1986).

Magistrates

In 1976 Congress created the office of U.S. magistrate to replace the earlier office of U.S. commissioner. Magistrates are appointed by district judges to serve for fixed terms. Their salaries, set by the Judicial Conference pursuant to statute, may be diminished by Congress. Magistrates are not Article III judges; they serve "as an integral part" of the U.S. District Court to hear and determine procedural motions, to hear motions for dismissal and for summary judgment, and to serve as special masters to research particular issues. In 1980 the Supreme Court upheld the authority of magistrates to conduct an evidentiary hearing, provided that the district judge makes a de novo (new) determination when the magistrate's findings or recommendations are contested. United States v. Raddatz, 447 U.S. 667 (1980).

C. THE APPOINTMENT PROCESS

The delegates at the Constitutional Convention condemned the British system of executive appointment, associating it with official corruption and debasement of the judiciary. At first they placed the power to select judges with Congress. Next, they considered vesting that responsibility solely in the Senate. Only late in the convention did they settle on joint action by the President and the Senate. 1 Farrand 21, 63, 119–28, 232–33; 2 Farrand 41–44, 80–83, 121. The President, under Article II of the Constitution, shall nominate "and by and with the Advice and Consent of the Senate, shall appoint ... Judges of the supreme Court." The Constitution also permits Congress to vest the appointment of "inferior officers" in the President alone, in the courts, or in the heads of the executive departments.

Subjecting federal judges to presidential nomination and Senate confirmation creates an intensely political process. From an early date, Senators wielded considerable power in choosing nominees for federal judgeships. Members of the Supreme Court (especially Chief Justice Taft) have lobbied vigorously for their candidates. Other sectors of government are active. Private organizations participate. The American Bar Association (ABA) plays a key role. Its influence increased during the Truman administration when it established a special committee to judge the professional qualifications of candidates submitted by the Attorney General. In 2001, the Bush White House advised the ABA that it would no longer receive advance notice of judicial nominees. However, the Senate Judiciary Committee continues to rely on ABA evaluations. At face value, the Constitution appears to give the President the exclusive power over nominations ("he shall nominate"). However, many public officials and private citizens participate actively and influentially in the pre-nomination process. Mitchel A. Sollenberger, The President Shall Nominate: How Congress Trumps Executive Power (2008).

Nominating Panels

President Carter altered the selection process for appellate judges by establishing nominating panels. They were directed to recommend five candidates for each vacancy, allowing the President to select the nominee. As part of an accommodation, Senators continued to control nominations for district judges, although some opted for a panel system. When President Reagan took office, he abolished the judicial nominating commissions for appellate judges. During subsequent administrations, the nominating process for selecting federal judges followed a variety of practices: screening committees or panels to help Senators choose a nominee, recommendations from the state bar or lawyers associations, and an informal structure for interviewing and recommending candidates for judgeships.

How Nominations Affect Judicial Policy

The power to nominate Supreme Court Justices can produce sudden shifts in judicial policy. Slight changes in the composition of the Supreme Court have reversed previous rulings. In 1870 the Court reviewed a congressional statute that treated paper money as legal tender for discharging prior debts. Voting 4 to 3, the Court declared the statute unconstitutional. The partisanship that raged throughout the post-Civil War period did not bypass the courts. The four Justices in the majority were Democrats; the three dissenters were Republicans. In the lower federal courts, almost every Democratic judge pronounced the statute unconstitutional; nearly every Republican judge sustained it. Hepburn v. Griswold, 8 Wall. (75 U.S.) 603 (1870); Fairman, 54 Harv. L. Rev. 1128, 1131 (1941).

The retirement of Justice Grier and the authorization by Congress the previous year of a new Justice allowed President Grant to appoint **two** new members. His first appointments were ill-starred. The Senate rejected his Attorney General, Ebenezer Hoar, while his second nominee, Edwin Stanton, died four days after being confirmed. Those nominations were made before the Court's decision. Grant had reason to believe that his next two appointments, submitted after the decision, would support the statute. William Strong, as a member of the Supreme Court of Pennsylvania, had already sustained the Legal Tender Act. Joseph P. Bradley appeared to be no less sympathetic. Fifteen months after the Legal Tender Act had been declared unconstitutional, the reconstituted Court upheld the Act by a 5–4 margin. Strong and Bradley joined the original three dissenters to form the majority; the four Justices who decided the case in 1870 now found themselves in the minority. Legal Tender Cases, 12 Wall. (79 U.S.) 457 (1871).

The transition from the Warren Court to the Burger Court also produced reversals of prior decisions (or efforts by the Court to "distinguish" prior holdings from current judicial policy). In 1971 a 5 to 4 majority—including two newcomers, Chief Justice Burger and Justice Blackmun—upheld a statutory procedure that stripped an individual of citizenship. The Court thus narrowed earlier holdings that citizenship could not be taken away unless voluntarily renounced. Justice Black objected that protections for American citizenship "should not be blown around by every passing political wind that changes the composition of this Court." Rogers v. Bellei, 401 U.S. 815, 837 (1971). No doubt Black was frustrated by policy shifts from the Warren Court to the Burger Court, but he himself had been part of the Roosevelt nominations after 1937 that helped chart a new course in constitutional interpretation. Changes in the Court's composition enable it to incorporate contemporary ideas and attitudes.

The Senate's Confirmation Record

The Senate has refused to confirm almost one out of every five presidential nominations to the Supreme Court. Twenty-five nominees have either been rejected, had their names submitted without Senate action, or been forced to withdraw. Most of those actions (eighteen) occurred before 1900. After the Senate rejected John J. Parker in 1930, confirmation of Supreme Court nominees seemed an automatic step. That pattern ended in 1968 when the Senate refused to advance Associate Justice Abe Fortas to the position of Chief Justice. Fortas, subjected to embarrassing questions about his acceptance of fees from private parties, eventually asked President Johnson to withdraw his nomination. Homer Thornberry, picked by Johnson to fill Fortas's seat as Associate Justice, then withdrew his name. A year later, with impeachment proceedings gearing up against him amidst charges of financial and personal improprieties, Fortas resigned from the Court.

The Supreme Court remained embroiled in political controversy in 1969 when the Senate rejected Nixon's nomination of Clement F. Haynsworth, Jr., to the Supreme Court. The ethical test applied by Republicans against Fortas was now used by Democrats against Haynsworth. A year later, the Senate rejected Nixon's next nominee, G. Harrold Carswell, who lacked the qualifications needed for Associate Justice. Nixon finally nominated Harry A. Blackmun, who was confirmed by a unanimous vote.

Probing a Nominee's Views

The emphasis given by Nixon to the sociopolitical views of judicial candidates helps underscore the entanglement of law and politics. Senators, too, in expressing their advice and consent, feel at liberty

Ruth Bader Ginsburg on Abortion

Judge GINSBURG.... you asked me about my thinking on equal protection versus individual autonomy. My answer is that both are implicated. The decision whether or not to bear a child is central to a woman's life, to her well-being and dignity. It is a decision she must make for herself. When Government controls that decision for her, she is being treated as less than a fully adult human responsible for her own choices.

Senator [Hank] BROWN.... With regard to the equal protection argument, though, since this may well confer a right to choose on the woman, or could, would it also follow that the father would be entitled to a right to choose in this regard or [possess] some rights in this regard?

Judge GINSBURG. That was an issue left open in *Roe v. Wade* (1973). But if I recall correctly, it was put to rest in *Casey* (1992). In that recent decision, the Court dealt with a series of regulations. It upheld most of them, but it struck down one requiring notice to the husband....

The *Casey* majority understood that marriage and family life is not always all we might wish them to be. There are women whose physical safety, even their lives, would be endangered, if the law required them to notify their partner....

Senator BROWN. I was concerned that if the equal protection argument were relied on to ensure a right to choose, then looking for a sex-blind standard in this regard might also then convey rights in the father to this decision. Do you see that as following logically from the rights that can be conferred on the mother?

Judge GINSBURG. I will rest my answer on the *Casey* decision, which recognizes that it is her body, her life, and men, to that extent, are not similarly situated. They don't bear the child.

Senator BROWN. So the rights are not equal in this regard, because the interests are not equal?

Judge GINSBURG. It is essential to woman's equality with man that she be the decisionmaker, that her choice be controlling....

SOURCE: "Nomination of Ruth Bader Ginsburg, To Be Associate Justice of the Supreme Court of the United States," hearings before the Senate Committee on the Judiciary, 103d Cong., 1st Sess. 207 (1993).

to evaluate a nominee's political and constitutional philosophy in order to maintain a balance of views on the Court.[7]

As shown by the 1981 hearings on the nomination of Sandra Day O'Connor to the Court, her personal and judicial philosophy on the exceedingly sensitive issue of abortion became a matter of recurrent interest to Senators and one on which she was willing to state her views (see reading). O'Connor's willingness to discuss her opposition to abortion "as a matter of birth control or otherwise" can be compared to very different responses from Clarence Thomas and Ruth Bader Ginsburg during their confirmation hearings. At his hearings in 1991, Thomas was asked to comment on the position in *Roe* v. *Wade* that it is a woman's right to decide to terminate a pregnancy. He declined to discuss the issue: "I do not think that at this time that I could maintain my impartiality as a member of the judiciary and comment on that specific case" (page 127, Part 1, of hearings). Most nominees offer similar responses, regarding it as improper to discuss an issue that is likely to come before the Court. However, in hearings in 1993, Ruth Bader Ginsburg did not hesitate to express her view about a woman's right to choose (see box).

The Senate's rejection of two nominees by Nixon to the Supreme Court was duplicated in 1987. President Reagan nominated Judge Robert H. Bork, a conservative member of the D.C. Circuit, to replace the more moderate Justice Powell. Everyone recognized the nomination as pivotal, especially

---

7. Senate Committee on the Judiciary, "Advice and Consent on Supreme Court Nominations," 94th Cong., 2d Sess. (Committee Print 1976). See L. A. Powe, Jr., "The Senate and the Court: Questioning a Nominee," 54 Tex. L. Rev. 891 (1976).

after Reagan's selection of O'Connor in 1981, Antonin Scalia in 1986, and the elevation of Rehnquist as Chief Justice in 1986. Powell, a centrist, had supplied a swing vote on the Burger Court. The addition of Bork threatened to reverse a number of important decisions.

Major groups in the country mounted an intensive campaign against Bork, whose writings and speeches contained provocative views on civil rights, women's rights, the First Amendment, abortion, privacy, reapportionment, and criminal law. Four members of the ABA committee found him "not qualified." One voted "not opposed" (meaning minimally qualified and not among the best available). Bork did not fare well during the hearings, and the White House committed a number of tactical blunders, such as trying to paint Bork as a moderate. The Senate voted 58 to 42 to reject him.

To replace Bork, Reagan turned to Judge Douglas H. Ginsburg of the D.C. Circuit. The nomination unraveled almost hour by hour because of Ginsburg's modest credentials and questions about conflicts of interest while he served in the Justice Department. When he admitted smoking marijuana into his thirties, as a professor of law, conservative support for his nomination took flight. The disclosure was particularly damaging because of Reagan's strong campaign against drugs and the administration's heavy emphasis on law and order. Within nine days of the nomination, Reagan received Ginsburg's request to withdraw his name. The next nominee, Judge Anthony Kennedy of the Ninth Circuit, sailed through the confirmation process without difficulty.

Another bruising battle occurred in 1991, when President George H. W. Bush nominated Clarence Thomas to replace Justice Thurgood Marshall. After sensational hearings in which Anita F. Hill testified on alleged sexual harassment by Thomas when he served as chairman of the Equal Employment Opportunity Commission, the Senate confirmed him by the close vote of 52 to 48. Clinton's nominees encountered little opposition. Ruth Bader Ginsburg was confirmed by a vote of 96 to 3 and Stephen Breyer by a vote of 87 to 9.

Two nominations by George W. Bush encountered greater opposition. John Roberts was confirmed as Chief Justice with a vote of 78-22; the margin for Samuel Alito as Associate Justice was 58-42. During his confirmation hearing, Roberts' prepared statement said that judges "are like umpires. Umpires don't make the rules, they apply them. The role of an umpire and a judge is critical. They make sure everybody plays by the rules, but it is a limited role. Nobody ever went to a ball game to see the umpire.... I will remember that it's my job to call balls and strikes, and not to pitch or bat." "Confirmation Hearing on the Nomination of John G. Robert, Jr. to be Chief Justice of the United States," hearing before the Senate Committee on the Judiciary, 109th Cong., 1st Sess. 55-56 (2005). For comments on the baseball analogy by Senators, see pp. 46, 184-86, 256-57, 266-67, 279.

In baseball, the strike zone is defined by the width of the home plate and the height from the shoulders down to the knees. The U.S. Constitution has some clear strike zones, including a two-thirds majority for veto overrides, the age of at least 35 to be President, a six-year term for Senators, and the requirement of two witnesses to prove treason. What is the strike zone for equal protection of the laws, freedom of speech, free exercise of religion, due process of law, unreasonable searches and seizures, cruel and unusual punishments, and other constitutional values?

Recess Appointments

The Senate is denied a role in the confirmation process when the President makes recess appointments, including to the Supreme Court. Under Article II, Section 2, the President "shall have Power to fill up all Vacancies that may happen during the Recess of the Senate, by granting Commissions which may expire at the End of their next Session." During the 1950s, President Eisenhower placed three men on the Supreme Court while the Senate recessed: Earl Warren, William J. Brennan, Jr., and Potter Stewart. All three joined the Court and participated in decisions before the Senate had an opportunity to review their qualifications and vote on their confirmation. In each case, the Senate gave its advice and consent, but the experience convinced most Senators that the procedure was unhealthy both for the Senate and the Court. How could federal judges serving under a recess appointment maintain total independence of mind? The anticipation of questions by a Senate committee during confirmation hearings might influence the direction and content of a nominee's decision. Similarly, a recess appointee could shade an opinion to attract White House support for a lifetime appointment.

In 1960, Senator Philip Hart introduced a resolution to discourage recess appointments to the courts. The Senate passed the resolution, 48 to 37, voting essentially along party lines. The resolution stated that the making of recess appointments to the Supreme Court may be inconsistent with the interests of the Court, the nominee, litigants before the Court, and the people of the United States. Such appointments should "not be made except under unusual circumstances and for the purpose of preventing or ending a demonstrable breakdown in the administration of the Court's business." 106 Cong. Rec. 18130–45 (1960). Although the resolution is not legally binding, no President after Eisenhower has made recess appointments to the Supreme Court.

The President's constitutional authority to make recess appointments to federal courts was upheld in 1985. United States v. Woodley, 751 F.2d 1008 (9th Cir. 1985), cert. denied, 475 U.S. 1048 (1986). However, the dissenters noted that although there have been approximately 300 judicial recess appointments since 1789, there had been only one such appointment since 1964. A second recess appointment of a federal judge occurred on December 27, 2000, when President Clinton placed Roger L. Gregory on the Fourth Circuit. President George W. Bush nominated Gregory for a life term on July 20, 2001, and the Senate confirmed him. President Bush made two recess appointments to federal appellate courts: Charles Pickering to the Fifth Circuit on January 16, 2004, and William Pryor to the Eleventh Circuit on February 20, 2004.

The fact that courts sanction the use of judicial recess appointments does not mean that the elected branches are obliged to accept the practice as constitutionally acceptable. The decision of the appellate court in 1985 functions more like an advisory opinion: It is constitutional if the elected branches want to do it. The final word on whether judges are placed on the courts on a recess basis lies with the President and the Senate. The Senate has a powerful role because it can decide to automatically deny a life term to any judge who receives a recess appointment.

Nomination Hearings of Sandra Day O'Connor

During the 1981 hearings on the nomination of Sandra Day O'Connor to be Associate Justice of the Supreme Court, Senators were interested in learning about the personal and philosophical views of the first woman nominated to the High Bench. Although the Senators wanted a nominee who would possess certain general qualities—integrity, honesty, technical knowledge, and proper judicial temperament—they also probed her position on the highly controversial issue of abortion, a question that had been decided already by the Court and was likely to be relitigated in the future. The selections below come from "Nomination of Sandra Day O'Connor," hearings before the Senate Committee on the Judiciary, 97th Cong., 1st Sess., September 9, 1981, pp. 60–63.

The CHAIRMAN [Strom Thurmond]. Judge O'-Connor, there has been much discussion regarding your views on the subject of abortion. Would you discuss your philosophy on abortion, both personal and judicial, and explain your actions as a State senator in Arizona on certain specific matters: First, your 1970 committee vote in favor of House bill No. 20, which would have repealed Arizona's felony statutes on abortion. Then I have three other instances I will inquire about.

Judge O'CONNOR. Very well. May I preface my response by saying that the personal views and philosophies, in my view, of a Supreme Court Justice and indeed any judge should be set aside insofar as it is possible to do that in resolving matters that come before the Court.

Issues that come before the Court should be resolved based on the facts of that particular case or matter and on the law applicable to those facts, and any constitutional principles applicable to those facts. They should not be based on the personal views and ideology of the judge with regard to that particular matter or issue.

Now, having explained that, I would like to say

that my own view in the area of abortion is that I am opposed to it as a matter of birth control or otherwise. The subject of abortion is a valid one, in my view, for legislative action subject to any constitutional restraints or limitations.

I think a great deal has been written about my vote in a Senate Judiciary Committee in 1970 on a bill called House bill No. 20, which would have repealed Arizona's abortion statutes. Now in reviewing that, I would like to state first of all that that vote occurred some 11 years ago, to be exact, and was one which was not easily recalled by me, Mr. Chairman. In fact, the committee records when I looked them up did not reflect my vote nor that of other members, with one exception.

It was necessary for me, then, to eventually take time to look at news media accounts and determine from a contemporary article a reflection of the vote on that particular occasion. The bill did not go to the floor of the Senate for a vote; it was held in the Senate Caucus and the committee vote was a vote which would have taken it out of that committee with a recommendation to the full Senate.

The bill is one which concerned a repeal of Arizona's then statutes which made it a felony, punishable by from 2 to 5 years in prison, for anyone providing any substance or means to procure a miscarriage unless it was necessary to save the life of the mother. It would have, for example, subjected anyone who assisted a young woman who, for instance, was a rape victim in securing a D. & C. procedure within hours or even days of that rape.

At that time I believed that some change in Arizona statutes was appropriate, and had a bill been presented to me that was less sweeping than House bill No. 20, I would have supported that. It was not, and the news accounts reflect that I supported the committee action in putting the bill out of committee, where it then died in the caucus.

I would say that my own knowledge and awareness of the issues and concerns that many people have about the question of abortion has increased since those days. It was not the subject of a great deal of public attention or concern at the time it came before the committee in 1970. I would not have voted, I think, Mr. Chairman, for a simple repeal thereafter.

The CHAIRMAN. Now the second instance was your cosponsorship in 1973 of Senate bill No. 1190, which would have provided family planning services, including surgical procedures, even for minors without parental consent.

Judge O'CONNOR. Senate bill No. 1190 in 1973 was a bill in which the prime sponsor was from the city of Tucson, and it had nine other cosigners on the bill. I was one of those cosigners.

I viewed the bill as a bill which did not deal with abortion but which would have established as a State policy in Arizona, a policy of encouraging the availability of contraceptive information to people generally. The bill at the time, I think, was rather loosely drafted, and I can understand why some might read it and say, "What does this mean?"

That did not particularly concern me at the time because I knew that the bill would go through the committee process and be amended substantially before we would see it again....

The CHAIRMAN. The third instance, your 1974 vote against House Concurrent Memorial No. 2002, which urged Congress to pass a constitutional amendment against abortion.

Judge O'CONNOR. Mr. Chairman, as you perhaps recall, the *Rowe* [sic] v. *Wade* decision was handed down in 1973. I would like to mention that in that year following that decision, when concerns began to be expressed, I requested the preparation in 1973 of Senate bill No. 1333 which gave hospitals and physicians and employees the right not to participate in or contribute to any abortion proceeding if they chose not to do so and objected, notwithstanding their employment. That bill did pass the State Senate and became law.

The following year, in 1974, less than a year following the *Rowe* [sic] v. *Wade* decision, a House Memorial was introduced in the Arizona House of Representatives. It would have urged Congress to amend the Constitution to provide that the word person in the 5th and 14th amendments applies to the unborn at every stage of development, except in an emergency when there is a reasonable medical certainty that continuation of the pregnancy would cause the death of the mother. The amendment was further amended in the Senate Judiciary Committee.

I did not support the memorial at that time, either in committee or in the caucus.

. . .

I voted against it, Mr. Chairman, because I was not sure at that time that we had given the proper amount of reflection or consideration to what action, if any, was appropriate by way of a constitutional amendment in connection with the *Rowe* [sic] v. *Wade* decision.

. . .

The CHAIRMAN. Now the last instance is concerning a vote in 1974 against a successful amendment to a stadium construction bill which limited the availability of abortions.

Judge O'CONNOR. Also in 1974, which was an active year in the Arizona Legislature with regard to the issue of abortion, the Senate had originated a bill that allowed the University of Arizona to issue bonds to expand its football stadium. That bill passed the State Senate and went to the House of Representatives.

In the House it was amended to add a nongermane rider which would have prohibited the performance of abortions in any facility under the jurisdiction of the Arizona Board of Regents. When the measure returned to the Senate, at that time I was the Senate majority leader and I was very concerned because the whole subject had become one that was controversial within our own membership.

I was concerned as majority leader that we not encourage a practice of the addition of nongermane riders to Senate bills which we had passed without that kind of a provision. Indeed, Arizona's constitution has a provision which prohibits the putting together of bills or measures or riders dealing with more than one subject. I did oppose the addition by the House of the nongermane rider when it came back.

It might be of interest, though, to know, Mr. Chairman, that also in 1974 there was another Senate bill which would have provided for a medical assistance program for the medically needy. That was Senate bill No. 1165. It contained a provision that no benefits would be provided for abortions except when deemed medically necessary to save the life of the mother, or where the pregnancy had resulted from rape, incest, or criminal action. I supported that bill together with that provision and the measure did pass and become law....

D. TENURE, REMOVAL, AND COMPENSATION

Under Article III of the Constitution, judges "both of the supreme and inferior Courts, shall hold their Offices during good Behaviour." Article I gives the House of Representatives the sole power of impeachment and the Senate the sole power to try all impeachments. A two-thirds majority of the Senate is required for conviction. Judges may be removed from office "on Impeachment for, and Conviction of, Treason, Bribery, or other high Crimes and Misdemeanors."

The impeachment process is cumbersome and suitable only for grave offenses. However, the need to remove judges for lesser offenses has long been recognized. In Federalist No. 79, Alexander Hamilton said that "insanity, without any formal or express provision, may be safely pronounced to be a virtual disqualification" for federal judges. If insanity is a basis for removal, what of senility, incompetence, disability, alcoholism, laziness, and other deficiencies that may fall short of an impeachable offense?

19th Century Removal Efforts

The first example of a federal judge impeached and removed from office occurred in 1803 in the case of John Pickering. He was charged with misconduct in a trial and for being on the bench while intoxicated. Supreme Court Justice Samuel Chase was impeached in 1804 but acquitted. Actions were brought against a number of other federal judges, many of whom preferred to resign from office rather than defend themselves against the charges. Shipley, 35 Law & Contemp. Prob. 178, 190–91 (1970). Still other federal judges withdrew quietly from the bench before prosecutors could launch a full-scale investigation. Joseph Borkin, The Corrupt Judge (1962).

To encourage aged and infirm judges to leave the bench, Congress passed legislation in 1869 to authorize the payment of full salary to any federal judge who resigned at or after age 70 with at least ten years' service on the bench. 16 Stat. 44, § 5 (1869). For Justices with less than ten years, Congress has passed special statutes to provide full retirement benefits. 22 Stat. 2 (1882); Fairman, 51 Harv. L. Rev. 397 (1938).

Article I judges, such as territorial judges, have been removed by Presidents; these judges are not entitled to life tenure.[8] Article III judges are immune from removal, other than by impeachment. Nev-

---

8. United States v. Guthrie, 58 U.S. (17 How.) 284, 288–89 (1854); 5 Op. Att'y Gen. 288, 291 (1851); and McAllister v. United States, 141 U.S. 174 (1891).

ertheless, they are subject to prosecution by the Justice Department for criminal offenses. The First Congress passed legislation providing that judges convicted of accepting a bribe "shall forever be disqualified to hold any office of honour, trust or profit under the United States." 1 Stat. 117, § 21 (1790). Moreover, any federal judge who engages in the practice of law "is guilty of a high misdemeanor." 28 U.S.C. § 454 (2000).

20th Century Removals

Criminal prosecutions have been used to drive corrupt judges from the bench. In 1973 Judge Otto Kerner, Jr., of the Seventh Circuit was found guilty of bribery, perjury, tax evasion, and other crimes, most of which occurred during his previous service as governor of Illinois. On appeal, Kerner argued that the Constitution provides only one way to remove a judge: impeachment. The Seventh Circuit decided that judicial immunity does not exempt judges from the operation of criminal laws and affirmed Kerner's conviction. United States v. Isaacs, 493 F.2d 1124 (7th Cir. 1974).

Kerner's prosecution largely concerned his actions before joining the bench. A different issue arose in the early 1980s when the Justice Department charged U.S. District Judge Alcee L. Hastings with criminal activities while sitting as a judge. The Eleventh Circuit decided in 1982 that Hastings could be prosecuted. United States v. Hastings, 681 F.2d 706 (11th Cir. 1982), cert. denied, 459 U.S. 1203 (1983). After a jury acquitted Hastings in 1983, a judicial inquiry panel conducted its own investigation into charges of misconduct. Hastings claimed that this inquiry undermined his independence as a federal judge, but the investigative and disciplinary procedure was upheld by the courts.[9]

As explained later in this section, Hastings was impeached and removed by Congress. In 1984 U.S. District Judge Harry Claiborne was found guilty of income tax evasion. Two years later he was impeached and removed. In 1986 U.S. District Judge Walter L. Nixon, Jr., of Mississippi was convicted of lying to a federal grand jury; in 1989 he was impeached and removed.

Ineligibility Clause

Once nominated and appointed to the bench, a few judges have been vulnerable to the charge that they violated the "ineligibility clause" of the Constitution. Article I, Section 6, Clause 2, provides that no Senator or Representative "shall, during the Time for which he was elected, be appointed to any Civil Office under the Authority of the United States, which shall have been created, or the Emoluments whereof shall have been encreased during such time." Hugo Black's nomination to the Supreme Court in 1937 was challenged because a retirement system for the judiciary had been enacted that year while Black served as U.S. Senator. The Supreme Court avoided the constitutional issue by holding that the plaintiff lacked standing to bring suit. Ex parte Levitt, 302 U.S. 633 (1937).

A more recent challenge concerned Abner Mikva, a member of Congress nominated by President Carter to the D.C. Circuit. Working through Senator James McClure, who served as plaintiff, the National Rifle Association argued that the salaries of federal judges had been increased during Mikva's term in Congress. A three-judge court ruled that McClure lacked standing to challenge the validity of an appointment of a federal judge. The court said that McClure and his colleagues had an opportunity to vote against Mikva's confirmation. Senators on the losing side could not then ask the judiciary to reverse the Senate's action. McClure v. Carter, 513 F.Supp. 265 (D. Idaho 1981), aff'd sub nom. McClure v. Reagan, 454 U.S. 1025 (1981).

---

9. Hastings v. Judicial Conference of United States, 593 F.Supp. 1371 (D.D.C. 1984); In the Matter of Certain Complaints Under Investigation, 783 F.2d 1488 (11th Cir. 1986).

Judicial Council Sanctions

Statutory procedures are available for judges to retire on grounds of disability. If a judge fails to certify to the President his disability, a majority of the members of the judicial council of his circuit may sign a certificate of disability and submit it to the President. Once the President finds that the judge is "unable to discharge efficiently all the duties of his office by reason of permanent mental or physical disability," and that an additional judge is needed, the President may make the appointment with the advice and consent of the Senate. 28 U.S.C. § 372(b) (2000). Under this procedure the "disabled" judge remains in office.

Each judicial council is authorized to make all necessary orders for the effective administration of court business. Judges "shall promptly carry into effect all orders of the judicial council." 28 U.S.C. § 332(d)(2) (2000). The judicial council for the Tenth Circuit relied on this provision in the 1960s to order Judge Stephen S. Chandler of the Western District of Oklahoma to "take no action whatsoever in any case or proceeding now or hereafter pending in his court." The order did not remove Chandler from office; instead, it removed the office from him. In 1966 the Supreme Court denied an application to stay the council's order. Chandler v. Judicial Council, 382 U.S. 1003 (1966). The judicial council later modified its order, allowing Chandler to retain his cases but withholding any new assignments. The Supreme Court denied a motion by Chandler to nullify the new order. Chandler v. Judicial Council, 398 U.S. 74 (1970).

By 1979 all judicial councils had implemented rules for the processing of complaints against federal judges. Building on this system, Congress passed legislation in 1980 that assigns to the councils the responsibility for investigating charges against judges. The statute contemplates charges of inefficiency or ineffectiveness resulting from mental or physical disability (conditions that may not be impeachable). The legislation does not encompass complaints regarding the merits of a decision or the conduct of judges unconnected with their judicial duties.[10] The 1980 statute was upheld by a district court in 1984 and by the Eleventh Circuit in 1986. The latter court argued that investigation by judicial councils *increased* judicial independence (see box on next page).[11]

The statute also allows a judicial council, after determining that a judge has engaged in conduct constituting one or more grounds for impeachment, to certify this determination for the Judicial Conference, which may then present a report to the House of Representatives for possible impeachment proceedings. This statutory procedure was upheld by a federal appellate court in 1987. Hastings v. Judicial Conference of United States, 829 F.2d 91 (D.C. Cir. 1987). The Judicial Conference invoked the statute in 1987 to vote unanimously for a recommendation to the House of Representatives that it consider impeaching U.S. District Court Judge Hastings. A year later, the House acted to impeach him, and in 1989 he was removed by the Senate.

Judges Nixon and Hastings continued to challenge their removals. Nixon brought an action claiming that his conviction in the Senate was void because he was not granted a trial before the full Senate. Instead, he was first examined by a twelve-member Senate committee. The lower courts held that the Senate's procedure was not justiciable. Nixon v. United States, 744 F.Supp. 9 (D.D.C. 1990); Nixon v. United States, 938 F.2d 239 (D.C. Cir. 1991). To the surprise of many, the Supreme Court granted cert to hear the case. Later, a federal district judge reviewed a similar complaint by Judge Hastings and de-

---

10. 94 Stat. 2035 (1980). See S. Rept. No. 362, 96th Cong., 1st Sess. (1979) and H. Rept. No. 1313, 96th Cong., 2d Sess. (1980).

11. Hastings v. Judicial Conference of the United States, 593 F.Supp. 1371 (D.D.C. 1984). This decision was vacated in part and remanded in Hastings v. Judicial Conference of the United States, 770 F.2d 1093 (D.C. Cir. 1985). The appellate court ruled that the question of constitutionality of the 1980 statute was premature. The Eleventh Circuit not only upheld the statute but regarded it as a means of protecting judicial independence. In the Matter of Certain Complaints Under Investigation, 783 F.2d 1488 (11th Cir. 1986).

Judicial Councils Investigating Judges

... [W]e believe that Congress [in the 1980 statute] could reasonably have determined that some internal procedure for investigating complaints against members of the judiciary was not only in the public interest but was important to the continued independence of the judiciary as a whole. Judges have very substantial powers and are supported at public expense. Today, some kind of complaint procedure exists with respect to state judges in every state in the union. The judiciary as a whole, including the colleagues of complained-against judges, has an interest in seeing that non-frivolous complaints are looked into, to the end that the judge, and the system he exemplifies, be exonerated or, if not, that the public perceive that the system has undertaken to police itself, within constitutional limits, of course. Absent any form of judicial complaint procedure, courts would be virtually alone among public and professional oc-cupations in lacking a means to clean house. The increase in the number of judges coupled with the increase in the complexity of judicial work and of courts, all suggest that some mechanism for looking into complaints is necessary and reasonable, if only to enable the courts themselves to sort out their own shortcomings and make the necessary administrative adjustments. In fact, a credible internal complaint procedure can be viewed as essential to maintaining the institutional independence of the courts. If judges cannot or will not keep their own house in order, pressures from the public and legislature might result in withdrawal of needed financial support or in the creation of investigatory mechanisms outside the judicial branch which, to a greater degree than the Act, would threaten judicial independence. Considerations of this sort were at the heart of the present legislation.

SOURCE: In the Matter of Certain Complaints Under Investigation, 783 F.2d 1488, 1507 (11th Cir. 1986).

---

cided that the Senate procedure violated elementary notions of fairness and due process associated with a trial. Hastings v. United States, 802 F.Supp. 491 (D.D.C. 1992). In 1993 the Supreme Court held that the Senate had sole discretion to choose the procedures to be used for impeachment, including the use of a committee to take testimony and gather evidence. Nixon v. United States, 506 U.S. 224 (1993). (This decision appears as a reading in Chapter 3, in the section on political questions.)

U.S. District Court Judge Robert Aguilar was convicted of illegally disclosing a wiretap. Although an appellate court reversed that conviction, Aguilar's conviction was reinstated by the Supreme Court in 1995. United States v. Aguilar, 515 U.S. 593 (1995). In 1996, the Justice Department dropped the charges in return for Aguilar's resignation. Legal Times, July 8, 1996, at 8.

In 2002, the Supreme Court denied cert to a case involving an action by the Judicial Council of the Fifth Circuit, which reprimanded a federal district judge and suspended him from hearing new cases for a year because of "intemperate, abusive and intimidating" treatment of lawyers and other judges. McBryde v. Committee to Review Circuit Council Conduct, 264 F.3d 52 (D.C. Cir. 2001), cert. denied, 537 U.S. 821 (2002).

Compensation

Judicial independence would count for little if the salaries of judges could be cut by legislators. Federal judges appointed to Article III courts are entitled to a compensation "which shall not be diminished during their Continuance in Office." In Federalist No. 79, Hamilton said that next to permanency in office "nothing can contribute more to the independence of the judges than a fixed provision for their support.... In the general course of human nature, a power over a man's subsistence amounts to a power over his will." That principle had been embodied in the Declaration of Independence, which attacked the British King for making colonial judges "dependent on his Will alone, for the Tenure of their Offices, and the Amount and Payment of their Salaries."

The No-Diminution Clause of the Constitution was challenged in 1802 when Congress repealed the Judiciary Act of the previous year. The effect was to abolish 16 circuit judges and their salaries. Supporters of the repeal argued that it was irrational to expect a judge to hold office during good behavior and to continue receiving payment if the office no longer existed. A salary could not exist without an office. A case challenging the right of Congress to abolish the circuit courts reached the Supreme Court in 1803, but the Court declined to overturn the statute. Stuart v. Laird, 5 U.S. (1 Cr.) 298 (1803).

In 1920, the Supreme Court held that a federal income tax levied against Article III judges unconstitutionally diminished their salaries. Justice Holmes, in a dissent that would later become the majority position, denied that the No-Diminution Clause relieved federal judges "from the ordinary duties of a citizen." To require someone from the judicial branch to pay taxes like other people "cannot possibly be made an instrument to attack his independence as a judge." Evans v. Gore, 253 U.S. 245, 265 (1920). Nineteen years later the Supreme Court held that a federal tax could be applied to Article III judges. O'Malley v. Woodrough, 307 U.S. 277 (1939).

Nothing in this line of cases prevents Congress from giving judges a smaller pay raise than other federal employees or no increase at all. In 1964 members of Congress raised their pay by $7,500 while limiting the increase for Supreme Court Justices to $4,500. The legislative debate suggests that some members of Congress may have wanted to use the power of the purse to penalize the Court for its recent decisions. However, the smaller raise for the judiciary could be justified on other grounds: the more generous retirement system for the courts, the need for members of Congress to maintain two residences, and the extra costs they bear in traveling home to see constituents. 110 Cong. Rec. 17912, 18032–33 (1964).

As a way to protest their salary levels, 140 federal judges brought an action in the 1970s to argue that their salaries had been diminished unconstitutionally because pay had not kept pace with inflation. The courts dismissed this claim as meritless. Atkins v. United States, 556 F.2d 1028 (Ct. Cl. 1977), cert. denied, 434 U.S. 1009 (1978). Another case arose when Congress, in four consecutive years (1976–1979), passed statutes to stop or reduce scheduled cost-of-living increases for all federal employees, including judges. A number of federal judges filed suit, claiming that these actions violated the No-Diminution Clause. In 1980 the Supreme Court held that Congress, under the provisions of the salary statutes, could disapprove scheduled pay increases for the judiciary provided it acted before October 1 of a new fiscal year (when they automatically took effect). The Court allowed two of the statutory actions taken prior to October 1 and struck down two others that came too late. United States v. Will, 449 U.S. 200 (1980).

As a result of this decision, judicial salaries moved well ahead of executive and legislative pay schedules. Congress retaliated in 1981 by passing legislation to require specific congressional authorization before any future pay raise for federal judges could take effect. The language effectively eliminated future automatic increases for the judiciary. 95 Stat. 1200, § 140 (1981). A subsequent statute allowed judicial salaries to be increased unless Congress, within a 30-day period, passed a joint resolution of disapproval. 99 Stat. 1322, § 135 (1985). Congress used that procedure in 1989 to defeat a substantial raise for all federal officials, including judges. Later that year, however, it passed legislation that authorized pay increases for all three branches. 103 Stat. 1763–71 (1989).

Beginning in 1994, members of Congress denied themselves a cost-of-living increase. Since federal district judges are tied to the same salary as a member of Congress, the effect was to deny increases for the judiciary as well. Congress denied itself those increases in 1995 and 1996. When Congress voted itself a pay raise in 1997, it neglected to include judges. "Congress, but Not Judiciary, Receives an Increase in Pay," The New York Times, October 21, 1997, at A23. The following month Congress included a cost-of-living increase for federal judges. 111 Stat. 2493, § 306 (1997).

In 1998, federal judges went to court to win a cost-of-living pay increase and prevailed in district court. Williams v. United States, 48 F.Supp.2d 52 (D.D.C. 1999). However, that victory was overturned two years later by the U.S. Court of Appeals for the Federal Circuit. The Supreme Court denied cert on March 4, 2002. Williams v. United States, 240 F.3d 1019 (Fed. Cir. 2001), cert. denied, 535 U.S. 911 (2002).

State judges are also under pressure to receive regular pay increases. On June 11, 2008, a New York court reviewed the record of the governor's office and the legislative branch in depriving the judiciary of a salary adjustment for almost a decade. It decided that the refusal to act demonstrated an abuse of power and an unconstitutional interference with the independence of the judiciary. Inaction amounted to a 30% decrease in judicial salaries. Having so held, the court expected the two elected branches to take the appropriate remedial steps within 90 days. Larabee v. Governor of the State of New York, 2008 N.Y., Slip Op 28217.

E. JUDICIAL LOBBYING

To preserve their reputation for impartiality, objectivity, and independence, judges traditionally abstain from political activities that are the daily fare of executives and legislators. Judicial activities, both on and off the bench, are expected to be free from impropriety and the *appearance* of impropriety.

This principle is strained by the manner of recruiting judges. Before coming to the bench, most judges have been active in legislatures, government agencies, and other political activities. They are unlikely, upon confirmation, to behave like a cloistered judge. Nor should they. Legislation often has a direct bearing on the courts, justifying the active participation of judges at the bill-drafting and congressional-hearing stages. Canon 4 of the American Bar Association's Code of Judicial Conduct permits a judge to "appear at a public hearing before an executive or legislative body or official on matters concerning the law, the legal system, and the administration of justice," and they may "otherwise consult with an executive or legislative body or official, but only on matters concerning the administration of justice" and never by casting doubt on their capacity to decide impartially any issue that may come before them. See 2 O.L.C. 30 (1978).

Frankfurter's Activities

With the 1982 release of *The Brandeis/Frankfurter Connection* by Bruce Allen Murphy, the public learned that Justice Brandeis, over a period of years, had secretly paid more than $50,000 to Felix Frankfurter to advance Brandeis's political agenda. The financial arrangement ended when Brandeis left the Court in 1939. Frankfurter joined the Court that year and remained deeply enmeshed in politics. He drafted legislative proposals for the Roosevelt administration, helped staff the upper echelons of the War Department, and assisted Roosevelt's reelection campaign in 1940.

The details of Frankfurter's activities were particularly ironic. As a member of the Court, he described himself as a "political eunuch," claiming that the Court "has no excuse for being unless it's a monastery." In 1944 he confided to a friend that "I have an austere and even sacerdotal view of the position of a judge on this Court, and that means I have nothing to say on matters that come within a thousand miles of what may fairly be called politics." Murphy, The Brandeis/Frankfurter Connection 9, 259–69. In a dissenting opinion, Frankfurter insisted that the authority of the Supreme Court depended on its "complete detachment, in fact and in appearance, from political entanglements." Baker v. Carr, 369 U.S. 186, 267 (1962). Despite such protestations, few Justices have been as politically active as Frankfurter.

Other Justices also participated in off-the-bench activities. The contacts between Brandeis and President Franklin D. Roosevelt had already been noted in the literature.[12] Taft, Frankfurter, Byrnes,

---

12. Philippa Strum, "Justice Brandeis and President Roosevelt," reprinted in Walter F. Murphy and C. Herman Pritchett, eds., Courts, Judges, and Politics 187–90 (1979).

and Fortas, while on the Court, met frequently with Presidents and discussed public issues.[13]

Other Political Actions

Much earlier examples illustrate the difficulty that some members of the Supreme Court have had in drawing a line between law and politics. During the Court's first two decades, individual Justices campaigned for political candidates, ran for political office, and accepted political duties that came their way. Chief Justice John Jay was sent as special envoy to negotiate a treaty with England. Chief Justice Oliver Ellsworth followed that precedent by negotiating a treaty with France. Murphy, The Brandeis/Frankfurter Connection 345–63.

After Chief Justice Marshall issued his decision in *McCulloch* v. *Maryland* (1819), arguing in favor of broad implied powers for the federal government, a series of anonymous articles appeared in a Richmond newspaper attacking the decision and championing states' rights. The first few critiques were probably written by William Brockenbrough, a state judge from Virginia. Marshall could not bear to let the charges go unanswered. Working through his colleague Justice Bushrod Washington, Marshall penned a number of anonymous rebuttals (signed "A Friend of the Union") and published them in a Philadelphia newspaper. Four more critiques appeared in the Richmond newspaper, this time by Judge Spencer Roane of the Virginia Court of Appeals (using the pseudonym Hampden). Marshall answered those as well, signing them "A Friend of the Constitution." Gerald Gunther, ed., John Marshall's Defense of *McCulloch* v. *Maryland* (1969). Justice Story, while serving for more than 20 years as president of a Massachusetts branch of the United States Bank, tried to influence Treasury Department officials to secure large deposits in his bank and helped Daniel Webster draft a reply to President Jackson's veto of the Bank's charter in 1832.[14]

Many avenues are available to Justices who want to affect the course of political events. Public addresses, law review articles, and contacts with reporters, scholars, and magazine writers are methods of extending judicial influence beyond official actions. The Chief Justice prepares an annual "year-ender," summing up the problems, needs, and accomplishments of federal courts. He also delivers an annual report on the state of the judiciary, sometimes using these forums to criticize Congress for its actions and inactions. Proposals have been introduced for an annual "State of the Judiciary" address, to be delivered by the Chief Justice to a joint session of Congress. This proposal passed the Senate in 1980, but the House took no action. 126 Cong. Rec. 23397 (1980).

Judicial Conference

The Judicial Conference is the principal institutional body for preparing a legislative agenda. The organization dates back to 1922, when Congress directed the Chief Justice to call an annual conference of the senior circuit judges. The objective was to make a comprehensive survey of cases pending before the federal courts: their number and character, cases disposed of, and backlog. The potential for judicial lobbying did not go unnoticed. Representative Clarence F. Lea predicted that the Conference "will become the propaganda organization for legislation for the benefit of the Federal judiciary." 62 Cong. Rec. 203 (1921).

As the law now reads, the Chief Justice submits to Congress "an annual report of the proceedings

---

13. See Max Freedman, ed., Roosevelt and Frankfurter: Their Correspondence (1967); John P. MacKenzie, The Appearance of Justice 1–33 (1974); and "Nonjudicial Activities of Supreme Court Justices and Other Federal Judges," hearings before the Senate Committee on the Judiciary, 91st Cong., 1st Sess. (1969).

14. G. Edward White, The American Political Tradition 41 (1976); Gerald T. Dunne, Justice Joseph Story and the Rise of the Supreme Court 301–02, 328–31 (1970).

of the Judicial Conference and its recommendations for legislation." 28 U.S.C. § 331 (2000). These reports are prepared for the spring and fall meetings of the Conference. Because the meetings are largely devoted to administrative and legislative matters rather than judicial duties, there has been pressure to open them to the public. Opponents of this reform proposal concede that the Conference is a creature of Congress and subject to further statutory change, but they argue that the principle of judicial independence should protect the proceedings of the Judicial Conference. The Conference came under fire in 1984 for improper lobbying, including a private group called the Federal Judges Association, but a GAO investigation found no legal violation. 63 Comp. Gen. 624 (1984).

Chief Justice Initiatives

The lobbying activities of Chief Justice Burger attracted press attention in 1978. On the eve of a Senate vote on the bankruptcy bill, he called Senator Dennis DeConcini and several other members of the Senate Judiciary Committee. DeConcini told reporters that Burger accused him of being "irresponsible" for supporting the legislation and said that the bill "was a political sale and he was going to the President and have him veto it." Calling the charge "a slap in the face of the entire Senate," DeConcini described Burger as being "very, very irate and rude." He "just screamed at me" and "not only lobbied, but pressured and attempted to be intimidating."[15] Representative Don Edwards, head of the House subcommittee responsible for the bankruptcy bill, said that he welcomed the views of judges but only when presented in "a scholarly, judicious way, in writing or in hearings, not in telephone calls once a bill has gone to the floor."[16]

Within a month, while accepting an award in New York City, Burger defended his participation in the legislative process (see Burger reading). He also resisted activities he viewed as inappropriate. In 1981, a number of federal judges wanted to form an association to lobby Congress for higher salaries and fringe benefits. Interested judges would contribute $200 and list the members of Congress they felt comfortable contacting about judicial salaries. Burger advised the judges that the position of the federal judiciary should be expressed through the Judicial Conference.[17]

Chief Justice Rehnquist took a leading role in advocating legislation to reform appellate procedures for the death penalty. In 1989, instead of waiting for the Judicial Conference to submit its report and recommendations to Congress, Rehnquist took the initiative in sending to Congress a report prepared by a committee of federal judges he had appointed. Some judges interpreted his move as an end run around the Judicial Conference. Rehnquist's effort to expedite the legislative process was unsuccessful; serious divisions continued within Congress and the Judicial Conference on the proper legislative remedy. In 1991, Rehnquist intervened to ask members of the House of Representatives to reject a handgun bill because it would strain the federal courts (see box on next page). In 2000, he urged Congress to end an eleven-year ban on speaking honoraria for federal judges.

Burger on Judicial Lobbying

On October 25, 1978, while accepting the Fordham-Stein Award in New York City, Chief Justice Burger delivered the following remarks on the proper boundaries of judicial intervention in the legislative process.

· · ·

From time to time the question comes up as to

whether the activities of those of our profession who are judges and who try to see that the needs of the

---

15. "Senator Slams Burger on Move to Thwart Bill," National Law Journal, October 16, 1978; "Burger Wants Judges to Speak Up to Congress," Washington Post, October 26, 1978, at A13.

16. "Lobbying by Burger Provokes Criticism," New York Times, November 19, 1978, at 39.

17. "U.S. Judges Want Lobby; Burger Against Proposal," National Law Journal, June 29, 1981, at 2, 10.

Rehnquist Lobbies the House

Chief Justice William H. Rehnquist yesterday took the unusual step of asking House members to reject a Senate-passed provision that would make most handgun murders a federal crime that carries the death penalty.

Rehnquist's lobbying effort against two provisions of the Senate's crime bill came as the House Judiciary Committee prepared for a drafting session Monday on its version of anti-crime legislation.

The Senate bill would authorize prosecution of handgun murders as federal crimes punishable by death. The provision introduced by Sen. Alfonse D'Amato (R-N.Y.) would apply to all murders committed with handguns that moved across state lines....

A statement accompanying Rehnquist's letter said the D'Amato amendments "will swamp the federal courts with routine cases that states are better equipped to handle, and will weaken the ability of the federal courts effectively to deal with difficult criminal cases that present uniquely federal issues."...

SOURCE: "Rehnquist Asks House Members to Reject Senate Handgun Bill," Washington Post, September 21, 1991, at A2.

---

courts are met in some way violate the concept of separation of powers.

I hope that you will not mind if I reflect with you tonight on the real meaning of the separation of powers in our tripartite constitutional system—and what it does not mean.

Justice Jackson had some relevant observations on this subject:

"While the Constitution diffuses power the better to secure liberty, it also contemplates that practice will integrate the dispersed powers into a workable government. It enjoins upon its branches separateness but interdependence, autonomy but reciprocity."

The separation of powers concept was never remotely intended to preclude cooperation, coordination, communication and joint efforts by the members of each branch with the members of the others. Examples of this are legion: The executive, represented by the Solicitor General, volunteers, or is invited by the Supreme Court, to file briefs advising the Supreme Court on questions of law. This happens countless times each term. Members of the Congress—sometimes singly, sometimes a dozen or more of them together—file briefs *amicus curiae* before the Court, advising us how a matter should be decided. These briefs are always welcomed by the Court.

We all remember that President Washington formally asked the Supreme Court for advice on certain policy questions but wisely the Court decided that it would not advise him on such matters. Justices have come to realize that they should avoid advising Presidents and the Congress on substantive policy questions but on matters relating to the courts there must be joint consultation. The separation of powers does not preclude such consultation.

From the beginning of the republic, members of the Congress have appeared as advocates before the Supreme Court. Indeed, they have been some of our great advocates, from Daniel Webster, Henry Clay and John Quincy Adams, and later William Seward. Webster was a Senator when he argued the famous *Dartmouth College* case. In more recent times other Senators, including Sam Ervin and William Saxbe, have appeared.

To be sure, there is a great and necessary tradition of insulation of judges and Justices from political activities generally. But participation in legislative and executive decisions which affect the judicial system is an absolute obligation of judges, as it is of lawyers. One manifestation of the desirable aloofness of judges from controversy is found in the tradition that they do not answer criticism or respond to attacks, no matter how scurrilous or unwarranted. But reasons for refusing to answer attacks must not be used as reasons to abdicate responsibility when Congress is legislating on matters directly affecting the courts. Indeed, the contrary is most emphatically true.

It is entirely appropriate for judges to comment upon issues which affect the courts. The Judicial Conference of the United States and the Administrative Office of the United States Courts receive requests from Congress from fifty to one hundred times each year to comment on pending bills.

Historically, the most valuable judicial improvements are made when the judiciary makes proposals and consults with Congress. Indeed, even after Congress acts, the President regularly requests the views of the Judicial Conference before he passes on legislation which relates to the federal courts. This has been going on for nearly two hundred years. It was more than forty years ago that Congress created the Judicial Conference of the United States, which as you know is made up of twenty-five judges from district courts, courts of appeals and special courts. It made the Chief Justice of the United States the chairman of that Conference. It meets approximately five or six days each year. It has committees dealing with special subjects — a committee on court administration, a committee on appellate rules, on criminal rules, on civil rules, on bankruptcy, on magistrates and similar subjects. These committees regularly confer with Congress and its staffs and the executive branch.

In creating the Judicial Conference, it was contemplated that the Conference would comment on legislation directly affecting the operation of the federal judicial system. The Conference has been doing that routinely for more than forty years. Any notion, therefore, that each of these branches should remain in solitary isolation or logic-tight compartments has no basis in reason, law, history or tradition....

NOTES AND QUESTIONS

1. The framers of the Constitution provided structural mechanisms such as tenure during "good Behavior" and protection from salary cuts as a means of promoting judicial independence. Still, the combination of presidential nomination and Senate confirmation of judges assures an intensely political process. Should Senators "defer" to presidential choices? If not, what independent standards should the Senate impose?

2. What degree of judicial independence is appropriate in a democratic republic? Given the confirmation process and the type of cases decided by the judiciary, can it be anything other than a "political" branch? When should federal judges, lacking ballot-box legitimacy, push legal and constitutional issues to the elected branches and the public for resolution?

3. Various individuals and organizations influence the selection of judges. Do you believe it is appropriate for a sitting member of the Court to suggest to the President names of potential nominees? May it be argued that, by reason of their experience and expertise, that sitting Justices are better equipped than most to make such suggestions?

4. In recent confirmation hearings, nominees to the Supreme Court typically claim they will approach issues with "an open mind" and they have "no agenda." Yet Presidents routinely search for nominees to promote specific values and principles. How realistic is it to expect nominees, once on the Bench, to treat each legal dispute independently and without reference to a broader framework?

5. What level of judicial lobbying is appropriate? When does it undermine the reputation and integrity of the judiciary?

SELECTED READINGS

ABRAHAM, HENRY J. Justices and Presidents: A Political History of Appointments to the Supreme Court. New York: Oxford University Press, 1974.

BALL, HOWARD. Courts and Politics: The Federal Judicial System. Englewood Cliffs, N.J.: Prentice-Hall, 1980.

BLACK, CHARLES L., JR. "A Note on Senatorial Consideration of Supreme Court Nominees." 79 Yale Law Journal 657 (1970).

BUSHNELL, ELEANORE. Crimes, Follies, and Misfortunes: The Federal Impeachment Trials. Champaign, Ill.: University of Illinois Press, 1992.

CARP, ROBERT A., AND C. K. ROWLAND. Policymaking and Politics in the Federal District Courts. Knoxville: University of Tennessee Press, 1983.

CHASE, HAROLD W. Federal Judges: The Appointing Process. Minneapolis: University of Minnesota, 1972.

DANELSKI, DAVID J. A Supreme Court Justice Is Appointed. New York: Random House, 1964.

EARLY, STEPHEN T., JR. Constitutional Courts of the U.S. Totowa, N.J.: Littlefield, Adams, 1977.

FISH, PETER GRAHAM. The Politics of Federal Judicial Administration. Princeton, N.J.: Princeton University Press, 1973.

GERHARDT, MICHAEL J. The Federal Impeachment Process: A Constitutional and Historical Analysis. Princeton University Press, 1996.

GROSSMAN, JOEL B. Lawyers and Judges: The ABA and the Politics of Judicial Selection. New York: Wiley, 1965.

HARRIS, JOSEPH P. The Advice and Consent of the Senate. Berkeley: University of California Press, 1953.

HAYNES, EVAN. The Selection and Tenure of Judges. Newark, N.J.: National Conference of Judicial Councils, 1944.

HOWARD, J. WOODFORD, JR. Courts of Appeals in the Federal Judicial System. Princeton, N.J.: Princeton University Press, 1981.

HULBARY, WILLIAM E., AND THOMAS G. WALKER. "The Supreme Court Selection Process: Presidential Motivations and Judicial Performance." 33 Western Political Quarterly 185 (1980).

KAHN, MICHAEL A. "The Politics of the Appointment Process: An Analysis of Why Learned Hand Was Never Appointed to the Supreme Court." 25 Stanford Law Review 251 (1973).

KURLAND, PHILIP B. "The Constitution and the Tenure of Federal Judges: Some Notes From History." 36 University of Chicago Law Review 665 (1969).

MASON, ALPHEUS THOMAS. "Extra-Judicial Work for Judges: The Views of Chief Justice Stone." 67 Harvard Law Review 193 (1953).

MURPHY, WALTER. "In His Own Image: Mr. Chief Justice Taft and Supreme Court Appointments." 1961 Supreme Court Review 159.

REHNQUIST, WILLIAM H. Grand Inquests: The Historical Impeachments of Justice Samuel Chase and President Andrew Johnson. New York: Morrow & Co., 1992.

SCHMIDHAUSER, JOHN R. "The Justices of the Supreme Court: A Collective Portrait." 3 Midwest Journal of Political Science 1 (1959).

———. Judges and Justices: The Federal Appellate Judiciary. Boston: Little, Brown, 1979.

SCIGLIANO, ROBERT. The Supreme Court and the Presidency. New York: The Free Press, 1971.

TRIBE, LAURENCE H. God Save This Honorable Court. New York: Random House, 1985.

WHEELER, RUSSELL. "Extrajudicial Activities of the Early Supreme Court." 1973 Supreme Court Review 123.

WINTERS, GLENN R., ed. Selected Readings: Judicial Selection and Tenure. Chicago: American Judicature Society, 1973.

5

Decision Making:
Process and Strategy

Publication of *The Brethren: Inside the Supreme Court* in 1979 promised a rare glimpse into the inner sanctum of the Supreme Court. The authors claimed that for nearly two centuries the Supreme Court had made its decisions "in absolute secrecy." In fact, the deliberative process of the Court has been studied and scrutinized for years. Scholars have access to internal memoranda, conference notes, diaries, draft opinions, and correspondence by the Justices. Members of the Court and their law clerks publish widely. Drawing on those materials, we have a fairly detailed picture of the process that Justices use to make decisions.[1]

The Supreme Court begins its term on the first Monday in October and ends in late June or early July of the following year. A term is designated by the October date. For example, the 2008 term began October 6, 2008. During these approximately nine months, the Court selects cases, hears oral argument, writes opinions, and announces decisions. After recessing for the summer, the Justices continue to review petitions in preparation for the new term and decide emergency petitions brought to their attention. Although decisions by the Supreme Court require a quorum of six, in certain cases individual Justices may stay the enforcement of lower court orders and give aggrieved parties time to petition the full Court for review. Each Justice performs other duties when assigned to one of the judicial circuits.

On rare occasions the Court convenes in the summer in special session to deal with urgent matters. For example, the Court met on July 29–30, 1942, to hear argument for nine hours on the Nazi saboteur case. Ex parte Quirin, 317 U.S. 1 (1942). On June 18, 1953, it considered Justice Douglas' stay in the execution of Ethel and Julius Rosenberg, convicted of delivering atomic bomb information to the then Soviet Union. On the following day the Court vacated the stay and the Rosenbergs were executed hours later. Another special session occurred on August 28, 1958, when the Court convened to consider a lower court order enforcing a desegregation plan for Little Rock High School. The Court unanimously upheld the lower court on September 12, three days before the school's scheduled opening. Cooper v. Aaron, 358 U.S. 1 (1958). On July 8, 1974, the Court held oral argument on the Watergate tapes case, deciding on July 24 that President Nixon had to surrender the tapes to prosecutors. United States v. Nixon, 418 U.S. 683 (1974). He resigned from office on August 9.

---

1. Bob Woodward and Scott Armstrong, The Brethren: Inside the Supreme Court 1 (1979). Of many commendable studies published before *The Brethren,* special note should be made of J. Woodford Howard, Jr., Mr. Justice Murphy 231–496 (1968); Walter F. Murphy, Elements of Judicial Strategy (1964); and Alpheus Thomas Mason, Harlan Fiske Stone: Pillar of the Law (1956). See also H. W. Perry, Jr., Deciding to Decide: Agenda Setting in the United States Supreme Court (1991); Bernard Schwartz, Decision: How the Supreme Court Decides Cases (1996); Edward Lazarus, Closed Chambers: The First Eyewitness Account of the Epic Struggles Inside the Supreme Court (1998); Jeffrey Toobin, The Nine: Inside the Secret World of the Supreme Court (2007).

A. JURISDICTION: ORIGINAL AND APPELLATE

The Constitution assigns to the Supreme Court judicial power in "all Cases, in Law and Equity, arising under this Constitution, the Laws of the United States, and Treaties made, or which shall be made under their Authority...." The types of cases identified in the Constitution affect (1) ambassadors, other public ministers, and consuls; (2) admiralty and maritime controversies; (3) controversies in which the United States is a party; and (4) controversies between two or more states, between a state and a citizen of another state, between citizens of different states, between citizens of the same state claiming lands under grants of different states, and between a state (or its citizens) and foreign states, citizens, or subjects.

This jurisdiction is divided between original and appellate. In all cases affecting ambassadors, other public ministers, and consuls, and those in which a state is a party, the Supreme Court has original jurisdiction. These cases may be taken directly to the Court without action by lower courts. Only rarely does a case of original jurisdiction concern ambassadors, diplomats, and consuls. Most of the cases involve litigation between states, such as disputes over boundaries and water rights. In the early days, original cases were tried before a jury in the Supreme Court. Georgia v. Brailsford, 3 U.S. (3 Dall.) 1 (1794). That practice was soon abandoned.

"Original" appears to imply exclusivity, suggesting that what is granted by the Constitution cannot be abridged or altered by Congress. Nevertheless, Congress has passed legislation that divides original jurisdiction into two categories: (1) original and exclusive jurisdiction, and (2) original but not exclusive jurisdiction. 28 U.S.C. § 1251 (2000). For the latter, lower federal courts share concurrent jurisdiction.

Congress has restricted the jurisdiction of federal courts by establishing criteria for "federal questions." Until 1980, certain federal court cases required at least $10,000 in dispute. The purpose was to reduce case congestion in federal courts. That amount was eliminated in 1980. 94 Stat. 2369. Congress wanted to resolve the anomaly faced by persons whose rights had been violated but were barred from the courts because they had not suffered a sufficient economic injury. Congress has established a dollar threshold of $75,000 for "diversity" jurisdiction (where federal courts consider cases involving state law if the parties are from different states). 28 U.S.C. § 1332 (2000).

Court jurisdiction may seem like a technical matter of interest only to specialists and practitioners of the law, but jurisdiction translates into political power. A question of jurisdiction provoked the first constitutional amendment adopted after the Bill of Rights. In 1793 the Court held that states could be sued in federal courts by citizens of another state. Chisholm v. Georgia, 2 Dall. (2 U.S.) 419. The public outcry was so deep and swift that the Eleventh Amendment, overriding *Chisholm,* passed both Houses of Congress in 1794 and was ratified in 1798. (Congressional efforts to withdraw jurisdiction from the courts are covered in the final chapter, "Efforts to Curb the Court.")

Dockets

Each year the Supreme Court receives about 7,000 petitions for review. A few cases concern original jurisdiction and are placed on the Original Docket. Original jurisdiction is used sparingly to protect the Court's workload with its appellate docket. The Court is especially reluctant to become a court of first instance and assume the fact-finding function of a trial court, a task for which the Court considers itself "ill-equipped." Ohio v. Wyandotte, 401 U.S. 493, 498 (1971). To assist in the handling of its original jurisdiction docket, the Court usually appoints special masters to study an issue and present recommendations.

Cases reach the Supreme Court by one of four routes. First, some parties come to the Court as a matter of statutory right. Congress has passed a number of statutes that provide for direct appeal, preferred treatment, and expedited action. In recent years, however, Congress has begun converting some of these statutes to discretionary review. H. Rept. No. 824 (Part 1), 97th Cong., 2d Sess. 6 (1982).

After the Court urged Congress to grant even greater discretion, Congress passed legislation in 1988 to substantially eliminate the Court's mandatory or obligatory jurisdiction. 102 Stat. 662 (1988). To handle its workload, the Court often disposes of cases without written opinion.

Writs of certiorari are a second route to the Supreme Court. By "granting cert" the Court calls up the records of a lower court, a decision that is wholly discretionary.

Third, petitions for review are submitted by indigents, including prison inmates, sometimes in the form of handwritten notes. These requests, called *in forma pauperis* (in the manner of a pauper), numbered a few dozen in 1930 but now range in the thousands each term. To discourage nuisance suits by indigents who file dozens of petitions and motions, the Court can require indigents to pay the normal $300 filing fee when they seek "extraordinary writs" in excess of normal requests. In re Sindram, 498 U.S. 177 (1991). Subsequently, the Court changed its rules to allow it to reject filings by indigents if filings are frivolous or malicious (Rule 39.8).

Fourth, an appellate court may submit a writ of certification to seek instruction on a question of law. 28 U.S.C. § 1254 (2000). This procedure is seldom used, for it forces the Court to decide questions of law without the guidance of findings and conclusions by the lower courts.

B. THE WRIT OF CERTIORARI

The Supreme Court controls its workload largely by exercising discretionary authority over cases coming to it for review. The discretionary writ of certiorari was initiated by the Evarts Act of 1891 and the Judicial Code of 1911, but the primary source of discretion awaited the "Judges Bill" of 1925. That statute eliminated direct review by the Supreme Court of decisions in the district courts and greatly expanded the use of the writ of certiorari. 43 Stat. 936 (1925).

Most of the decisions of the Supreme Court involve "cert" denials. Under Rule 10 of the Supreme Court, a review on writ of certiorari "is not a matter of right, but of judicial discretion" and will be granted "only for compelling reasons." Among the reasons listed in Rule 10 are conflicts among federal courts of appeals, between a federal court of appeals and a state court of last resort, and over federal questions decided by different state courts of last resort. Justices look for cases that pose questions of general importance: broad issues on the administration of the law, substantive constitutional questions, the construction of important federal statutes, and serious questions of public law. In a 1949 address, Chief Justice Vinson advised lawyers who prepare cert petitions to spend "a little less time discussing the merits of their cases and a little more time demonstrating why it is important that the Court should hear them.... If [a petition for certiorari] only succeeds in demonstrating that the decision below may be erroneous, it has not fulfilled its purpose." 69 S.Ct. vi (1949). Lawyers learn how to get the Court's attention (reading by Lauter).

Other factors explain why the Court grants cert. The literature on "cue theory" points to a key ingredient: the federal government's decision to seek review. The Court relies heavily on the seasoned judgment of the Solicitor General to bring only those cases that merit appeal. When that factor combines with other elements (the presence of a civil liberty issue, conflict between circuits, a lower court decision in which judges are divided), granting a petition is even more likely (see box on next page).

At various times in its history, the Court has accepted an issue from a lower court because it appeared that the executive and legislative branches were unwilling to act. An appellate judge said that "waiting for the legislature is not productive. The legislature doesn't legislate. Courts have had to do a good deal of stuff that would be better for the legislature to have done. But it's better for courts to do them than no one." J. Woodford Howard, Jr., Courts of Appeals in the Federal Judicial System 163 n. (1981). Presumably the same attitude prevailed on the Supreme Court, but only recently have its members publicly admitted this function. Justice Powell said that judicial independence gives the Court "a freedom to make decisions that perhaps are necessary for our society, decisions that the legislative branch may be reluctant to make." Kenyon College Alumni Bulletin, Summer 1979, at 15. Jus-

---

Major Reasons for Granting Cert

1. Conflicts among federal appellate courts.

2. Conflicts between federal courts and state courts.

3. State or federal court's holding congressional statute unconstitutional.

4. Substantial constitutional, legal, or political issue.

5. Construction of important federal statute.

6. Submission of a petition by the Solicitor General.

7. Flagrant or egregious abuse of justice in the lower courts.

---

tice Blackmun elaborated on that point in 1982. Asked whether desegregation was an example of where the courts had to do more because other branches did less, he replied:

> Well, one can come up with a lot of possible examples. That is one. One man, one vote is another one. And many of the sex discrimination cases perhaps are others. If one goes back twenty-five years, certainly things are different because of judicial intervention. I can remember when I was a law clerk a case came up concerning the possibility of a federal judge intervening in the administration of a prison and it was unheard of in those days. That was a problem for the prison administrative authorities. And now, of course, in recent years—and by that I mean twenty years anyway—there have been many instances where the courts, in effect, have taken constitutional rights inside the prison doors...."A Justice Speaks Out: A Conversation with Harry A. Blackmun," Cable News Network, Inc., conducted November 25, 1982, at 10–11.

Of the approximately 7,000 cases received each year, less than one hundred are accepted for oral argument and full opinions. In other words, more than 95 percent of all petitions are denied. In evaluating the petitions, Justices dismiss many as frivolous and "dead-list" them (deny them "cert") without further deliberation. In recent years the Court has replaced the "dead list" with a "discuss list," which includes the cases deemed worthy of discussion. Any Justice can request that a case be added to the discuss list. Examples of frivolous petitions include: "Are Negroes in fact Indians and therefore entitled to Indians' exemptions from federal income taxes?"; "Are the federal income tax laws unconstitutional insofar as they do not provide a deduction for depletion of the human body?"; and "Does a ban on drivers turning right on a red light constitute an unreasonable burden on interstate commerce?" Brennan, 40 U. Chi. L. Rev. 473, 478 (1973). When an appeal or petition for writ of certiorari is frivolous, the Supreme Court may award appropriate damages or costs to the party sued (Rule 42.2).

Screening Cert Petitions

Justices try to avoid cases where the legal issue is overpowered by emotional ingredients. When the Court reviewed cert petitions in 1975 to clarify the rights available to criminal defendants, it deliberately passed over the petition of someone who had been convicted of strangling, raping, and beheading a woman, followed by an attempt to skin her. Liva Baker, Miranda 105 (1983). It would have been poor judgment for the Court to announce legal principles in the midst of such gruesome circumstances.

Justices depend on their law clerks to prepare memoranda that summarize the facts of a case and recommend acceptance or rejection. All of the Justices, with the exception of Samuel Alito and John Paul Stevens, participate in a "cert pool" to divvy up the work. They meet at a Friday conference to discuss and vote on the petitions that survive initial review. A single Justice may set a case for decision at conference. As a symbol of unity, Justices shake hands upon entering the conference room.

These gestures preserve an atmosphere of civility in an institution compelled to deal with some of the most fractious issues in society. Maintaining a measure of collegiality among nine strong personalities is no small feat.

To preserve confidentiality in the conference room, only the Justices are present. The junior Justice sits closest to the door, receiving and delivering messages that flow in and out of the room. Some political scientists reported that the rectangular table in the conference room had been chopped into three pieces by Chief Justice Burger and converted into an inverted U, supposedly to prevent the liberal Douglas from sitting opposite him in direct confrontation. Justice Powell reassured his readers in 1975 that the conference table "retains its pristine shape; there has been no hacking or sawing; the justices occupy their seats in the traditional order of seniority."[2] Visitors to the room find the table intact.

The Chief Justice begins the discussion of each case. He summarizes the facts, analyzes the law, and announces his proposed vote. He is followed by the other Justices, in order of seniority, from the senior Associate Justice down to the newest Justice. Before the Warren Court, voting was done in the opposite manner: the junior Justice voted first and the Chief Justice last. Toward the end of his service, Warren persuaded the Justices to vote in the same order as they had spoken.[3] Four votes are needed to grant certiorari. There have been cases where the Court grants cert and later, on the basis of changed circumstances, dismisses the writ of certiorari as "improvidently granted." Dismissing a case in this manner is sometimes called "digging a case" (dig—dismissed as improvidently granted).

Granting cert involves some tactical decisions by Justices. If five Justices are rigidly opposed, the four in favor of granting cert may decide against hearing the case because they know they will lose on the merits. If three Justices feel strongly that cert should be granted, sometimes another Justice will add the fourth vote ("join three"). For "defensive denials," Justices prefer to let some cases at lower levels, even if decided badly, remain as a precedent only for a single circuit, instead of compounding the legal situation with a decision by the Supreme Court. If the Court is in transition from a liberal to a conservative body, a remaining liberal Justice may engage in defensive denials to prevent the Court from overturning liberal precedents. H. W. Perry, Jr., Deciding to Decide 98, 166–70, 198–207 (1991).

Justices address a wide range of complex cases at each conference. They keep a docket sheet to record each step of the process from deciding to hear a case to postconference voting. Conference notes provide a summary record of the arguments of each Justice on the merits of the case. Whoever is selected to draft the opinion can review the conference notes and weave an argument that will attract the maximum number of votes. At any point, however, votes may be changed before the opinion of the Court reaches its final stage.

In denying cert, the Court seldom offers an explanation. When it does, the reason is usually brief if not cryptic. More light is shed when Justices write a dissenting opinion on cert denials. This practice, which has grown significantly in recent decades, complicates the Court's traditional position that cert denial means a refusal to take a case and nothing more. Darr v. Burford, 339 U.S. 200, 226 (1950). If dissenting Justices strongly voice their reasons and argue the merits, it may appear that the major-

---

2. Lewis F. Powell, Jr., "Myths and Misconceptions About the Supreme Court," 61 A.B.A.J. 1344 (1975). See Glendon Schubert, Judicial Policy Making 134 (1977) and Howard Ball, Courts and Politics 254 (1980). For a discussion of some of the practices in conference, see William H. Rehnquist, "Sunshine in the Third Branch," 16 Washburn L. J. 559 (1977).

3. Walter F. Murphy and C. Herman Pritchett, eds., Courts, Judges, and Politics 657 (1979). This account is supported by a 1982 interview with Justice Blackmun; "A Justice Speaks Out: A Conversation with Harry A. Blackmun," Cable News Network, Inc., conducted November 25, 1982, at 21. In a 1963 article, Justice Brennan stated that voting began with the junior Justice; William J. Brennan, Jr., "Inside View of the High Court," New York Times Magazine, October 6, 1963, at 100. Justice Clark, in 1956, also said that the junior Justice voted first, 19 F.R.D. 303, 307, as did Justice Frankfurter in 1953, "Chief Justices I Have Known," 39 Va. L. Rev. 883, 903.

ity denying cert considered and rejected those arguments. Justices often differ on the significance to be attached to dissents on cert denials.[4] Speculation as to intent is hazardous. Even when Justices think that a lower court is wrong, they may vote to deny an application simply because they regard the federal question as insubstantial, poorly timed for review, or inappropriate because of the need for judicial restraint.

David Lauter
Certiorari Strategies

In the following article, "The Fine Art of Creating a Certiorari Petition," Lauter explains the considerations of obtaining four votes for a successful cert petition. The article appeared in the *National Law Journal*, December 10, 1984.

Several years ago, Bruce J. Ennis, then legal director of the American Civil Liberties Union, wrote a law review article about how to write a brief for the Supreme Court.

The theme of the piece was that a lawyer should not write for an abstract court, but should concentrate on catching the attention of each of the nine justices who actually will be reviewing the case.

Last week, Mr. Ennis ... provided an object lesson on how the job is done, persuading the Supreme Court to grant certiorari in a libel case involving a candidate for U.S. attorney, a man who didn't like him and a letter to President Reagan. *McDonald* v. *Smith*, 84476.

The letter, written in 1980 by Robert McDonald, Mr. Ennis' client, told the president that he should not appoint David I. Smith to the U.S. attorney's job in Greensboro, N.C. Mr. Smith did not get the job, found out about the letter and sued for libel.

Mr. Ennis' argument, so far unsuccessful in federal district court and the 4th U.S. Circuit Court of Appeals, is that Mr. McDonald should be absolutely immune from civil liability for the letter under the First Amendment right to "petition the Government for a redress of grievances." The decisions rejecting that argument appear to be the first times the issue has been considered in federal court.

Mr. Ennis started out with the assumption that Justices William J. Brennan Jr. and Thurgood Marshall, who have been sympathetic to defense claims in libel cases, might be interested in hearing the case. Then he set about trying to find two more votes.

First, he noted, "the court has sort of gotten interested in libel issues again. From a law clerk's per-

spective it's a very juicy question and I thought the law clerks would push it."

The petition for certiorari made a particular point of emphasizing the venerable nature of the petition clause, arguing that the right to petition is far older than the rights of free speech and press. That argument, Mr. Ennis noted, was specially designed to appeal to the interest that several of the justices have in history. Justices John Paul Stevens and Lewis F. Powell Jr. frequently mention historical antecedents in their opinions as does Chief Justice Warren E. Burger.

In addition, the case posed an unusual conflict between state- and federal-court interpretations of constitutional law that Mr. Ennis hoped would appeal to several other justices.

Two state high courts within the 4th Circuit—West Virginia and Maryland—have held that petitions to the government cannot be the basis for a civil suit. With the 4th Circuit holding the other way, Mr. Ennis' petition argued, federal district courts in those two states sitting in diversity actions would be forced to follow the law of the circuit, rejecting the law of the state, implying "a premise that federal courts have greater wisdom, or at least authority, in interpreting the federal Constitution than do state courts."

"Justice [Sandra Day] O'Connor has written law review articles about the need to allow state court judges to make decisions," Mr. Ennis noted, hoping that argument might particularly appeal to her. In addition, Justice William H. Rehnquist might be interested in the federalism aspect of the argument, he said.

---

4. See differing views of Justices Blackmun and Marshall in United States v. Kras, 409 U.S. 434, 443, 460–61 (1973). Justices Stevens, Brennan, and Stewart objected when the Court gave a brief reason for denying cert ("for failure to file petition within time provided"); County of Sonoma v. Isbell, 439 U.S. 996 (1978). See also Peter Linzer, "The Meaning of Certiorari Denials," 79 Colum. L. Rev. 1127 (1979).

Having now gotten the court's attention, Mr. Ennis, of course, faces the more difficult matter of winning the case. "It's a long way to go to convince this court to grant a new absolute right," he said.

C. FROM ORAL ARGUMENT TO DECISION

After a case receives four votes from Justices, it is transferred to the oral argument list. If Justices conclude that a question is clearly controlled by one of the Court's earlier decisions, they may summarily dispose of a lower court decision without oral argument or full briefing. One form of summary disposition is a per curiam opinion that grants cert but disposes of the merits without giving parties an opportunity to file briefs or argue before the Court. In 1980, for example, the Court decided a case involving press and speech restrictions on former government employees without hearing oral argument. Snepp v. United States, 444 U.S. 507. Summary disposition carries the risk of depriving the Court of crucial information. It can also suggest a "rush to judgment."

The Pentagon papers case of 1971 moved through the courts with extraordinary speed. Beginning with the New York Times's publication of a secret Pentagon study on the origins and conduct of the Vietnam War, only 17 days were consumed for action by two district courts, two appellate courts, and the Supreme Court. The New York Times's petitions and motions were filed with the Supreme Court on June 24 at about 11 A.M. The government filed its motion later that evening. Oral argument took place on June 26. The record in the Times case did not arrive until 7 or 8 P.M. the previous evening. The briefs of the parties were received less than two hours before oral argument. Four days later the Court announced its decision, upholding the right of the press to publish material from the Pentagon study. Despite protests from several Justices, the Court moved quickly to protect the First Amendment right of the press to publish without prior restraint. New York Times v. United States, 403 U.S. 713 (1971).

Oral Argument

In preparation for oral argument, counsel for each side submits briefs and records that are distributed to each Justice. The Court hears oral argument in public session from Monday through Thursday, listening to cases from 10 A.M. to noon and from 1 to 3 P.M. On some days it is only from 10 to noon. Usually one hour is set aside for each case. Although briefs are important, members of the judiciary have noted that there are some judges "who listen better than they read and who are more receptive to the spoken than the written word." Harlan, 41 Corn. L. Q. 6 (1955). The impressions they receive during oral argument often carry with them into the conference room at the end of the week. Oral argument allows judges to explore with counsel key issues left undeveloped in the briefs.

During oral argument, the Chief Justice sits in the center of a raised bench with the senior Associate Justice to his right and the next ranking Justice to his left. Other Justices are arrayed by seniority alternately to his right and left, leaving the most junior Justice positioned farthest to his left. Some Justices rely on a "bench memorandum" prepared by law clerks to digest the facts and arguments of both sides and provide guidance during the questioning of counsel. Judicial styles differ at oral argument. Justice Douglas asked few questions and regarded many of the ones put forth by colleagues as attempts to lobby Justices for votes rather than to illuminate issues. William O. Douglas, The Court Years 181 (1981). On the current Court, Justice Clarence Thomas is known for keeping silent while Justices Antonin Scalia and Ruth Bader Ginsburg participate actively.

Writing Opinions

The number of full opinions each year is now about 80, down from the 150 annual rate of the 1980s (see figure on workload on the next page). To divide the time between hearing cases and writing opinions, the Court alternates between several weeks of oral argument and several weeks of recess to write

SUPREME COURT'S WORKLOAD (2006–2007 TERM)

```
                        ┌─────────────────────────┐
                        │   10,256 cases on docket │
                        └─────────────────────────┘
         ┌────────────────────┼────────────────────┐
┌──────────────────┐ ┌──────────────────┐ ┌──────────────────┐
│  Original: 6     │ │ In forma pauperis:│ │  Other (paid):   │
│  (including 2    │ │  8,181           │ │  2,069           │
│  from prior term)│ │ (including 1,049 │ │ (including 346   │
│                  │ │  from prior term)│ │  from prior term)│
└──────────────────┘ └──────────────────┘ └──────────────────┘
```

| Original: 6 (including 2 from prior term) | In forma pauperis: 8,181 (including 1,049 from prior term) | Other (paid): 2,069 (including 346 from prior term) |

| 1 case disposed of | 15 cases granted review | 239 cases summarily decided | 24 cases granted review | 39 cases summarily decided |

78 cases decided

| 74 disposed of by signed opinion | 4 disposed of by per curiam opinion |

Source: 76 LW 3016 (July 10, 2007)

opinions and study appeals and cert petitions. If the Chief Justice has voted with the majority in conference, he assigns the majority opinion either to himself or to another Justice. When the Chief Justice is in the minority, the senior Justice voting with the majority assigns the case. The decision by William Rehnquist to dissent in many cases during his first year as Chief Justice allowed Justice Brennan, a liberal colleague, to control assignment. The dissenters decide who shall write the dissenting opinion. Each Justice may write a separate opinion, concurrence, or dissent.

The assignment of opinions recognizes the need to distribute workload fairly, the different speeds with which Justices complete their research and writing, and the availability of expertise within the Court. Chief Justice Vinson, a former member of the House Ways and Means Committee and Secretary of the Treasury, preferred to handle tax cases. 49 Nw. U. L. Rev. 26, 31–32 (1954).

Although Justices are appointed for life and are immune from periodic campaigning for electoral office, they know that the ability to write acceptable opinions depends on sensitivity to the public. This consideration affects the assignment of opinions. In 1944, Chief Justice Stone initially assigned the Texas "white primary" case to Justice Frankfurter. Justice Jackson shared his misgivings with both Frankfurter and Stone, suggesting that because of "Southern sensibilities" it was unwise to have a Vienna-born Jew, raised in New England (the seat of the abolition movement), write the majority opinion striking down the Texas statute. With Frankfurter's consent, Stone transferred the assignment to

Stanley Reed, a native-born Protestant and old-line Kentuckian. Reed was a Democrat of long-standing, whereas Frankfurter's past ties to the Democratic party were suspect. Alpheus T. Mason, Harlan Fiske Stone: Pillar of the Law 614–15 (1968).

Recusal

Under English common law, judges could be disqualified for direct interest in a case but never for bias. Such an admission would have conceded the capacity for partiality or favoritism in a judge. Frank, 56 Yale L. J. 605, 609–10 (1947); Forer, 73 Harv. L. Rev. 1325, 1327 (1960). Many of the early Justices on the Supreme Court failed to recuse (remove) themselves from cases that, under today's standards, would call for disqualification. Justice Story decided cases involving the Bank of the United States while serving as president of a Massachusetts branch of it. Chief Justice Marshall wrote *Marbury* v. *Madison* after serving as the Secretary of State who had neglected to deliver the commission of office. However, Marshall withdrew from *Stuart* v. *Laird* (1803) because he had tried the case earlier in the circuit court.

Based on statutory guidelines, court decisions, judicial codes, and personal standards, judges withdraw from certain cases when they have a personal bias, when they previously served as counsel in the matter in controversy, and for other stated (and unstated) reasons. 28 U.S.C. §§ 144, 455 (2000). Judges disqualify themselves to maintain the appearance of impartiality and due process. Chief Justice Stone and Justice Jackson did not take part in a 1942 decision because as former Attorneys General they had helped prosecute the case. United States v. Bethlehem Steel Corp., 315 U.S. 289, 309 (1942).

Justice Jackson shocked the country in June 1946 by issuing a blistering attack on Justice Black. This extraordinary public revelation of a bitter feud between two members of the Supreme Court had its origins in a 1945 decision in which Black was part of a 5 to 4 majority upholding the right of coal miners. Jewell Ridge Coal Corp. v. Local No. 6167, 325 U.S. 161 (1945). Jackson's dissent in that case quoted from a Senate debate in 1937 to show that Black, as a Senator, provided legislative history contrary to the majority's decision. It was also known that the chief counsel for the miners in the 1945 case was Black's former law partner.

The coal company petitioned for a rehearing, asking whether Black could render impartial justice given his connection with the legislation and the chief counsel. All members of the Court agreed that the motion for a rehearing should be denied, because the decision to disqualify oneself is purely a personal judgment to be made by each Justice. However, Jackson did not want to imply, by silence, that everyone on the Court supported Black's decision. When the Court denied the motion, Jackson wrote a concurring opinion, explaining that disqualification was not a decision for the full Court. Each Justice had to make that determination for himself. Frankfurter joined Jackson's concurrence. Jewell Ridge Coal Corp. v. Local No. 6167, 325 U.S. 897 (1945). Black's supporters were outraged by the concurrence because it drew attention to the issue of disqualification.

A newspaper article in May 1946 reported that Black regarded Jackson's concurrence as a gratuitous insult and a slur on Black's honor. The dispute intensified with the pending selection of a Chief Justice. Jackson hoped to be named; Black was dead-set against it. According to the newspaper story, Black threatened to resign if President Truman selected Jackson as Chief Justice. Fleeson, "Supreme Court Feud," [Washington] Evening Star, May 16, 1946, at A15. Black refused to comment on these newspaper stories.

While Jackson was in Nuremberg serving as Special Prosecutor for the Nazi trials, Truman nominated Fred Vinson to be Chief Justice. Jackson believed that Black played a hand in denying him the promotion. From Nuremberg, Jackson cabled the Judiciary Committees to elaborate on the 1945 dispute. He said that after he announced his decision to write a concurrence on the petition for a rehearing, Black became "very angry" and said that any opinion that discussed the subject at all would mean "a declaration of war." Jackson told Black that he would "not stand for any more of his bullying and that, whatever I would otherwise do, I would now have to write my opinion to keep self-respect in the face of threats." Alluding to rumors that had been published critical of his role, Jackson remarked: "If war is declared on me I propose to wage it with the weapons of the open warrior, not those of the stealthy assassin." Jackson warned that if Black failed to disqualify himself in comparable situations in the future, "I will make my Jewell Ridge opinion look like a letter of recommendation by comparison." New York Times, June 11, 1946, at 2.

Justice Rehnquist was asked to recuse himself from a case because he had earlier testified on the subject while serving as an official in the Justice Department. In a highly unusual memorandum, Rehnquist agreed that disqualification would have been required had he signed a pleading or brief in the case or actively participated in it. In two earlier cases he withdrew for those reasons. Laird v. Tatum, 409 U.S. 824, 828–29 (1972). However, he disagreed that testimony or the expression of one's views were adequate grounds for recusal. He also pointed out that disqualification of a Supreme Court Justice presents problems that do not exist in a lower court where one judge may substitute for another. Id. at 837–38. This issue resurfaced in 1986 during Rehnquist's nomination hearings to be Chief Justice.

In 2004, Justice Scalia was pressured to recuse himself from a case involving Vice President Cheney. The two had gone duck hunting together, and Scalia had traveled on Cheney's government plane to the hunting camp in Louisiana. Scalia did not save any money from Cheney's offer, because Scalia bought a round-trip ticket and returned home by commercial aircraft. Scalia reasoned that recusal would be appropriate if the personal fortune or personal freedom of a friend was at stake, but not when a case concerned Cheney's *official* action. Cheney v. U.S. District Court, 541 U.S. 913 (2004).

Drafting Opinions

The process of writing opinions begins with the briefs prepared by opposing counsel, research by law clerks and library staff, and the knowledge that Justices acquire from decades of experience in public and private life. Drafts are printed within the Court building and circulated among the Justices. Comments are written on the drafts; memorandums are exchanged. Often, a forceful dissent may persuade members of the majority to change their position, creating a new majority from the old dissenting position. Chief Justice Vinson once remarked that an opinion circulated as a dissent "sometimes has so much in logic, reason, and authority to support it that it becomes the opinion of the Court." 69 S.Ct. x (1949). Draft opinions may be so influential in modifying the Court's final decision that they are never published. Alexander M. Bickel, The Unpublished Opinions of Mr. Justice Brandeis (1967). The threat of a dissent can force changes in the majority opinion.

The role of law clerks is sometimes described in lavish terms, as though they function as the actual judge. Because of the growing importance of law clerks, Senator John Stennis suggested (perhaps whimsically) that it might be appropriate to subject them to confirmation by the Senate. 104 Cong. Rec. 8107–08 (1958). Publication of *The Brethren: Inside the Supreme Court* in 1979 catapulted clerks to a seemingly pivotal role in making judicial policy. However, this study depended heavily on interviews with clerks who no doubt found it irresistible to magnify their contributions to public law. Edward Lazarus, a former Supreme Court law clerk, claimed that Justices "yield great and excessive power to immature, ideologically driven clerks, who in turn use that power to manipulate their bosses and the institution they ostensibly serve." Edward Lazarus, Closed Chambers 6 (1998).

Judges in the prime of life are unlikely to defer to the opinions of clerks fresh out of law school, however much the clerks may stimulate new ideas and approaches. Clerks come and go, but the persistence in decisions of a unique writing style is compelling evidence that judges do their own work. Nevertheless, clerks do more than check footnotes, review cert petitions, and perform minor editing tasks. Depending on the judge they work for, they might be asked to prepare a "prototype or aspirant opinion" to guide the thinking of the court. Frank M. Coffin, The Ways of a Judge 69 (1980). Because of heavy court workload, judges usually ask clerks to write the preliminary draft of an opinion (see Coffin reading).

Personal Values and Attitudes

The legal profession no longer seriously argues that it is the duty of a judge to place a constitutional provision next to a challenged statute to see whether the latter squares with the former. United States v. Butler, 297 U.S. 1, 62 (1936). Still, the belief that judges, in the act of deciding, are able to put aside their personal value systems retains a following. Justice Frankfurter made an eloquent plea for this concept of judicial deliberation:

> It is asked with sophomoric brightness, does a man cease to be himself when he becomes a Justice? Does he change his character by putting on a gown? No, he does not change his character. He brings his whole experience, his training, his outlook, his social, intellectual and moral environment with him when he takes a seat on the Supreme Bench. But a judge worth his salt is in the grip of his function. The intellectual habits of self-discipline which govern his mind are as much a part of him as the influence of the interest he may have represented at the bar, often much more so. 98 Proceedings Am. Phil. Soc. 233, 238 (1954).

It would be superficial to suggest that judges use their office simply to disseminate personal views, but decisions of individual judges flow at least in part from their own values and attitudes. Justice Miller, who served on the Supreme Court from 1862 to 1890, despaired of the fixed views and predispositions of those on the bench: "It is vain to contend with judges who have been at the bar the advocates for forty years of rail road companies, and all the forms of associated capital, when they are called upon to decide cases where such interests are in contest. All their training, all their feelings are from the start in favor of those who need no such influence." Charles Fairman, Mr. Justice Miller and the Supreme Court 374 (1939).

Although the votes of judges cannot be predicted with mathematical accuracy, attorneys are sophisticated enough to engage in "forum shopping" to find the court or circuit that augurs best for their client. Judicial independence and objectivity remain important values in the administration of justice, but by now it is routine to recognize definite alignments and alliances among judges. Even members of the judiciary acknowledge the existence of blocs. When Justice Blackmun joined the Supreme Court, he calculated that there were two Justices on the right, two on the left, and "five of us in the center." "A Justice Speaks Out: A Conversation with Harry A. Blackmun," Cable News Network, Inc., conducted November 25, 1982, at 22. Justice O'Connor's appearance in 1981 added another conservative voice to that of Chief Justice Burger and Justice Rehnquist. Blackmun, meanwhile, now found himself voting more frequently with the liberal bloc of Justices Brennan and Marshall. Blocs are not necessarily stable. They change over time and vary with the issue. During the Burger Court, Justices Blackmun, Powell, Stevens, and White formed part of a "floating center," casting the votes necessary to build a majority by joining either with the liberal votes of Brennan and Marshall or the conservative wing of Burger, O'Connor, and Rehnquist.

By the early 1990s, O'Connor was often associated with a moderate center consisting of Kennedy and Souter. Blackmun and Stevens formed a more liberal bloc, while Scalia and Thomas were identified as conservatives. After President Clinton's appointments of Ruth Bader Ginsburg and Stephen Breyer, the Court divided largely along the lines of five conservatives (Rehnquist, O'Connor, Scalia, Kennedy, and Thomas) and four moderate-liberals (Stevens, Souter, Ginsburg, and Breyer). Several Justices operated in the center, adding a fifth vote with one side to form a majority. O'Connor played that role on the Rehnquist Court; Kennedy functions that way with the Roberts Court.

Communicating Clearly

Members of the judiciary sometimes complain that their decisions are distorted by the press. Mistakes and misconceptions by reporters are likely, given the time pressures between the announcement of a decision and the deadlines imposed by newspapers, magazines, and broadcast services. These pressures have been partly relieved by several changes over the past few decades. In 1965 the Supreme Court, instead of handing down all opinions on "Decision Monday," began delivering some of its decisions on other days of the week. The Court also started meeting at 10 A.M. rather than noon; these extra hours eased deadlines for reporters. To assure more accurate and sophisticated coverage, major newspapers and wire services began selecting reporters with law degrees or special training in the law.

Some of the "distortions" in the press come from Justices who use careless language in their opinions. When the Supreme Court announced the School Prayer Decision in 1962, Justice Douglas's concurrence suggested that the decision would cover ceremonial observances of a religious nature, such as the Court's traditional invocation when it convenes and the offering of a daily prayer by a chaplain in Congress. Engel v. Vitale, 370 U.S. 421, 439–42 (1962). Such speculations, well beyond the issue before the Court, helped fuel public confusion and outrage. When opinions contain sharp crossfire between Justices, "news reporters and the public at large are likely to lose sight of the law in what appears (to the uninitiated at least) to be a battle of men and not of law." Newland, 17 West. Pol. Q. 15, 24–25 (1964). The prayer case was also grossly misrepresented by the president of the American Bar Association, who weighed in with the warning that the decision would require elimination of the motto "In God We Trust" from all coins. Id. at 28.

The judiciary's ability to communicate accurately to the public requires a writing style that is precise and economical. Opinion writers should use familiar words and short sentences, emphasizing simplicity, clarity, brevity, and a direct and vigorous style. Justice Jackson gloried in the "short Saxon word that pierces the mind like a spear and the simple figure that lights the understanding." 37 A.B.A.J. 801, 863–64 (1951). Nevertheless, judges have personal idiosyncrasies that produce affectation, ornate prose, and verbosity. Ambiguity is also likely when several strong-minded individuals must agree on a single statement.

In deciding a particular case, judges often stray from the central issue and add extraneous matter in the form of obiter dicta. Because these remarks are not necessary to the basic decision, they are not binding as legal precedent. Nevertheless, they can serve as the functional equivalent of an advisory opinion, supplying guidance to the future direction of legal thinking. It is not unusual for dicta, over time, to be treated as the decision.

Coherence and "principled decision making" are difficult virtues to achieve for a multi-membered Court that operates necessarily as a committee, attempting to stitch together a decision that can attract a majority. Compromises are needed. The difficulty is compounded by the practice of moving a step at a time, responding to the concrete case at hand. As noted by one scholar, the Court "is in the unenviable posture of a committee attempting to draft a horse by placing very short lines on a very large drawing-board at irregular intervals during which the membership of the committee constantly changes." Amsterdam, 58 Minn. L. Rev. 349, 350 (1974).

Finality of Decisions

Decisions by federal courts may embody broad policies of commerce, slavery and other issues that provoke other branches to restrict and reverse judicial judgments. The general rule is that the outcome of an individual case—for a particular litigant—is accepted by Congress and the President, but not necessarily the larger public policy. For example, Abraham Lincoln challenged the political judgments in *Dred Scott* v. *Sandford* without proposing to "disturb or resist the decision" regarding Dred Scott or Dred Scott's master (see reading in Chapter 1). The overarching issue—such as slavery or abortion—requires continuing debate in a democratic society.

Writing in 2003, Justice O'Connor challenged the notion that a decision by the Supreme Court on a controversial issue settles it. Instead, she described a "dynamic dialogue" between the Court and the American public: "No one, it seems, considers the Supreme Court decision in *Roe* v. *Wade* to have settled the issue for all time. Such intense debate by citizens is as it should be. A nation that docilely and unthinkingly approved every Supreme Court decision as infallible and immutable would, I believe, have severely disappointed our founders." Sandra Day O'Connor, The Majesty of the Law 45 (2003).

Frank M. Coffin
The Process of Writing a Decision

Every important appellate court decision is made by a group of equals. This fact reflects the shrewd judgment of the architects of our state and federal judicial systems that an appellate judge is no wiser than a trial judge. His only claim to superior judgment lies in numbers; three, five, seven, or nine heads are usually better than one....

There is intimacy, continuity, and dynamism in the relations among judges, at least on the smaller courts. They do not come together just to vote. They interact with each other, influence each other, and have each other in mind almost from the time they first read briefs for the next session of court. In a sense, the relationship among judges who differ in their values and views is a bargaining one, yet it is a continuing negotiation, where each player lays his cards on the table just as soon as he discovers what cards he has. There is, on a serene court, no suggestion that anyone seeks to manipulate anyone else.

In short, there is a difference between arriving at a yes or no decision through majority vote and working up an opinion on a close case so that three or more judges of different sensitivities, values, and backgrounds can join not only in the result, but in the rationale, tone, nuances, and reservations. Although the task of building toward a unanimous opinion, or even of carpentering a majority, demands a certain amount of sacrifice of ego and substantive concession, collegiality has its solid satisfactions. One quickly realizes that he is not the only source of useful insights. He learns to rejoice when he sees an opinion he has written measurably strengthened by the suggestion of one of his colleagues. Then, too, decisions are sometimes unpleasant, hard, risky, controversial, when the public and the press are hot and quick in their criticism. On such occasions, the comfort of collegiality is a pearl of no little worth.

THE INTENSITY OF INDIVIDUAL INVOLVEMENT

One of the paradoxes about appellate courts is

that there can coexist the kind of intimate collegiality I have sketched and a profound, almost antique individualism. Indeed, perhaps the collegiality is the more enduring because it feeds on, cherishes, and respects the individualism nourished by appellate courts. In any case I make so bold as to say that in this supertechnical, industrialized, computerized, organized age, appellate courts are among the last redoubts of individual work.

While reliance on machines and staff proliferates apace in corporations, legislatures, and executive bureaucracies, the appellate judge still lives and works in his chamber with his law clerks. Although, unlike his predecessor, he can no longer write the first draft of every opinion, he is, as we shall see, in the very heart of creation of every opinion at every stage.

The kind of individualism I refer to is not the individualism of style, flair, or color, though these, happily, are not absent. Rather, every work product of an appellate court, a judicial opinion, bears the individual trademarks of, and is freighted with, the personal scrutiny and reflection of each member to a greater extent than that of any other collegial body....

Perhaps there are appellate judges who, on hearing the essential facts of such a case, can confidently announce a sound decision without pause. I have seen professors in the classroom so respond; also panelists, lecturers, and cocktail-party pundits. But I am thankful that nothing said under such circumstances affects the rights of parties. Judges do have their share of excellent talkers. The best of them are called brilliant. Brilliance, however, seems to me more associated with the pyrotechnics of speech and writing; as the word suggests, it has to do with how thoughts can be made to shine and sparkle. Sound decision, on the other hand, is more than result; it is an edifice made up of rationale, tone, and direction. It is faithful to the past, settles the present, and foreshadows the future. Such a decision is rarely made quickly.

I see decision-making as neither a process that results in an early conviction based on instant exposure to competing briefs nor one in which the judge keeps an open mind through briefs, discussion in chambers, argument, and conference, and then summons up the will to decide. I see the process,

---

Source: From Frank M. Coffin, The Ways of a Judge: Reflections from the Federal Appellate Bench (Boston: Houghton Mifflin, 1980), pp. 57–63. When this book was published, Coffin was Chief Judge of the First Circuit.

rather, as a series of shifting biases. It is much like tracing the source of a river, following various minor tributaries, which are found to rise in swamps, returning to the channel, which narrows as one goes upstream.

One reads a good brief from the appellant; the position seems reasonable. But a good brief from appellee, bolstered perhaps by a trial judge's opinion, seems incontrovertible. Discussion with the law clerks in chambers casts doubt on any tentative position. Any such doubt may be demolished by oral argument, only to give rise to a new bias, which in turn may be shaken by the postargument conference among the judges. As research and writing reveal new problems, the tentative disposition of the panel of judges may appear wrong. The opinion is written and circulated, producing reactions from the other judges, which again change the thrust, the rationale, or even the result. Only when the process has ended can one say that the decision has been made, after as many as seven turns in the road. The guarantee of a judge's impartiality lies not in suspending judgment throughout the process but in recognizing that each successive judgment is tentative, fragile, and likely to be modified or set aside as a consequence of deepened insight. The nonlawyer looks on the judge as a model of decisiveness. The truth is more likely that the appellate judge in a difficult case is committed to the unpleasant state of prolonged indecisiveness.

D. UNANIMITY AND DISSENT

The Supreme Court initially followed the British practice of allowing each Justice to write opinions seriatim (in a series). Rather than announce a single opinion representing the collective position of the majority, the Justices delivered separate statements. Before John Marshall's appointment as Chief Justice, the Court had begun to deliver an opinion for the entire Court rather than a string of seriatim opinions. Marshall reinforced that direction, believing that a single decision strengthened the Court's power and dignity. He selected one Justice (often himself) to write the majority opinion. Dissents were rare. Jefferson delivered a stinging rebuke to the Chief Justice for departing from seriatim decisions: "An opinion is huddled up in conclave, perhaps by a majority of one, delivered as if unanimous, and with the silent acquiescence of lazy or timid associates, by a crafty chief judge, who sophisticates the law to his own mind, by the turn of his own reasoning." 15 Writings of Thomas Jefferson 298 (Memorial ed. 1904).

Jefferson's critique was written in 1820, about two decades after Marshall had joined the Court, and appeared to be triggered by Marshall's broad nationalist ruling in *McCulloch* v. *Maryland* (1819). Seriatim opinions had offered a definite benefit: each Justice was accountable for articulating the rationale behind a decision. However, Marshall wanted the Court to develop an institutional view, moving away from personal positions to a more generalized principle for the majority.

Dissents became more frequent in later years of the Marshall Court and under future Chief Justices. At various times throughout history, however, members of the Court have placed a premium on unanimity. In 1922 Justice McReynolds wrote a majority opinion that provoked dissents from Brandeis, Clarke, and Pitney. Chief Justice Taft scheduled a reargument, and by the time he wrote the new majority opinion, Clarke and Pitney had retired. Taft sought Brandeis's views and eventually produced a unanimous opinion, with which McReynolds concurred.[5]

Concurrences and Per Curiams

At the urging of colleagues who fear that dissents will damage the corporate reputation of the Supreme Court, Justices have been willing to convert a dissent into a concurring opinion. Labeling it a con-

---

5. Alpheus Thomas Mason, "William Howard Taft," in Leon Friedman and Fred L. Israel, eds., 3 The Justices of the United States Supreme Court 2114 (1969), and Alexander M. Bickel, The Unpublished Opinions of Mr. Justice Brandeis, at 11–113. The case was Sonneborn Bros. v. Cureton, 262 U.S. 506 (1923).

currence, however, is often an inadequate mask to cover the dissenting view.[6] It is not unusual for Justices to concur in the judgment or result while shredding the logic, reasoning, and precedents contained in the opinion of the Court.[7] Justices also withhold dissents when the case is less significant to them. Such accommodations create a reservoir of good will, promote institutional harmony, and allow the acquiescent Justice to call upon a colleague at some future time for reciprocal favors—perhaps a fourth vote to grant certiorari. Walter F. Murphy, Elements of Judicial Strategy 52–53 (1964).

During preparation for *Brown* v. *Board of Education*, members of the Court felt strongly that unanimity was crucial in building public acceptance for desegregation. Discreet pressure was applied to Justices to ward off concurring and dissenting opinions. Chief Justice Warren realized that once a Justice had announced his position, it would be more difficult for him to change his thinking, "so we decided that we could dispense with our usual custom of formally expressing our individual views at the first conference and would confine ourselves for a time to informal discussion of the briefs, the arguments made at the hearing, and our own independent research for each conference day, reserving our final opinions until the discussions were concluded." Warren, 239 Atlantic Monthly 35–36 (April 1977). By following this process, the Court agreed unanimously that the "separate but equal" doctrine had no place in public education.

In earlier rulings, the Court relied on per curiam opinions (unsigned opinions "for the court") to reduce friction. This technique permitted the Justices to present a united front and avoid details or legal interpretations that might have fractured the Court and communicated more information to the public than the Court thought prudent. In one of the early racial discrimination cases before *Brown*, Justice Frankfurter explained in a letter to Chief Justice Vinson that the per curiam "should set forth as briefly and as unargumentatively as possible" the Court's position. "In short," Frankfurter wrote, "our *per cur.* should avoid every possibility of serving as a target for contention...." Hutchinson, 68 Geo. L. J. 1, 9 (1979).

In the Nazi Saboteur Case of 1942, the Supreme Court chose to issue a per curiam upholding the jurisdiction of a military tribunal, leading to the execution of six men. Not until three months later did the Court release a full decision setting forth the legal reasoning. Ex parte Quirin, 317 U.S. 1 (1942). This two-step procedure so damaged the Court's reputation that when it had an opportunity in 1953 to follow that precedent with the case of Julius and Ethel Rosenberg, it chose not to. Louis Fisher, Nazi Saboteurs on Trial 68-79, 108-34 (2003).

Unanimity to Make a Point

When Governor Orval Faubus and the Arkansas legislature fought to retain the state's system of segregated schools, the Supreme Court reaffirmed the principle it had enunciated in 1954. To underscore its unanimity, the names of all nine Justices were listed, including the three who had joined the Court since 1954. Frankfurter frustrated this strategy by insisting on a separate concurrence, agreeing to file it a week after the Court released its opinion. Cooper v. Aaron, 358 U.S. 1 (1958). Warren, Black, and Brennan were furious. Frankfurter's only justification for the extra statement was that he felt a special responsibility to lecture Southern lawyers and law professors who had been his students at Harvard Law School. Bernard Schwartz, Super Chief 302–03 (1983).

In 1974, with President Nixon threatening to defy any judicial effort to make him surrender the Watergate tapes, the Supreme Court once again produced a unanimous ruling. United States v. Nixon, 418 U.S. 683 (1974). By forging a united front and rejecting Nixon's broad claim of executive privi-

---

6. Justice Murphy, under the urgings of colleagues, changed his dissent in *Hirabayashi* v. *United States* to a concurrence. See Murphy, supra note 1, at 46–47, and Howard, supra note 1, at 302–09.

7. Murphy v. Waterfront Comm'n, 378 U.S. 52, 80–92 (Harlan, J., concurring) (1964); Warden v. Hayden, 387 U.S. 294, 310–12 (Fortas, J., and Warren, C. J., concurring) (1967); Argersinger v. Hamlin, 407 U.S. 25, 41–44 (Burger, C. J., concurring) and 44–46 (Powell, J., concurring, joined by Rehnquist, J.) (1972).

lege, the Court played a crucial role in bringing about his resignation. However, the very process of generating a unanimous opinion invited generalization at so high a plane, accompanied by wholly unnecessary dicta, that the result obfuscated the law of executive privilege.[8] This is an ever-present risk. Attracting a few additional votes may dilute legal principles to such an extent that some Justices in the original majority may decide to write concurring or even dissenting opinions.

Unanimity can help prepare the public for important rulings. In other situations, however, a multiplicity of opinions may be enlightening. In *Youngstown Co. v. Sawyer* (1952), every member of the six-man majority wrote a separate opinion discussing the limits of presidential power in time of emergency. The country was therefore privy to nuances and complexities that would have been obscured by a broad ruling satisfactory to the majority. Multiplicity gave room for sophisticated explorations of the source and scope of executive powers but also added uncertainty about constitutional principles. Concurring opinions may anticipate future developments in the direction of law.

Plurality Opinions

With the growth in the number of cases that determine constitutional issues, separate concurring and dissenting opinions have increased dramatically. Justice Rehnquist suggested that it "may well be that the nature of constitutional adjudication invites, at least, if it does not require, more separate opinions than does adjudication of issues of law in other areas." Rehnquist, 59 A.B.A.J. 361, 363 (1973). Of special concern is the Court's inability to prepare a decision that attracts a majority of the Justices. Instead, the Court delivers a plurality opinion that creates confusion in the lower courts and other branches of government. The number of plurality opinions by the Burger Court exceeded the number of all previous Courts. Note, 94 Harv. L. Rev. 1127 (1981); Davis & Reynolds, 1974 Duke L. J. 59.

In 1977, the Supreme Court announced a rule for determining the meaning of a plurality holding. Borrowing language from *Gregg v. Georgia* (1976), the Court stated: "When a fragmented Court decides a case and no single rationale explaining the result enjoys the assent of five Justices, 'the holding of the Court may be viewed as that position taken by those Members who concurred in the judgments on the narrowest grounds.... '" Marks v. United States, 430 U.S. 188, 193 (1977). A scholar, after studying the application of the *Marks* rule, concluded that it was "insupportable and should be rejected." Mark Allen Thurmon, "When the Supreme Court Divides: Reconsidering the Precedential Value of Supreme Court Plurality Decisions," 42 Duke L. J. 419 (1992).

Dissents

Shortly before returning to the Supreme Court, this time as Chief Justice, Charles Evans Hughes wrote eloquently on the deliberative process of the judiciary. He recognized that a dissenting opinion can damage the appearance of justice that the public needs in a court of last resort. However, he felt it far more injurious to obtain unanimity by concealing genuine differences and personal convictions (see box on next page). Following this tradition, Justice Douglas said that "[c]ertainty and unanimity in the law are possible both under the fascist and communist systems. They are not only possible; they are indispensable...." (see Douglas reading).

Dissents may force the majority to clarify and tighten its opinion. They can also serve as a precursor for a future majority holding. Justice Harlan's dissents in the *Civil Rights Cases* (1883), in *Plessy v. Ferguson* (1895), and in other race cases offered a broad interpretation of the Fourteenth Amendment in protecting the rights of blacks. His doctrine gained strength in some of the lower courts more than a half century later and foreshadowed the eventual overruling of *Plessy*. The dissents of Justice Holmes, especially in economic regulation cases, later carried the day for the Court. Justice Stone was a lone

---

8. Louis Henkin, "Executive Privilege: Mr. Nixon Loses but the Presidency Largely Prevails," 22 UCLA L. Rev. 40 (1974); William Van Alstyne, "A Political and Constitutional Review of *United States* v. *Nixon*," 22 UCLA L. Rev. 116 (1974).

Charles Evans Hughes on Dissent

There are some who think it desirable that dissents should not be disclosed as they detract from the force of the judgment. Undoubtedly, they do. When unanimity can be obtained without sacrifice of conviction, it strongly commends the decision to public confidence. But unanimity which is merely formal, which is recorded at the expense of strong, conflicting views, is not desirable in a court of last resort, whatever may be the effect upon public opinion at the time. This is so because what must ultimately sustain the court in public confidence is the character and independence of the judges. They are not there simply to decide cases, but to decide them as they think they should be decided, and while it may be regrettable that they cannot always agree, it is better that their independence should be maintained and recognized than that unanimity should be secured through its sacrifice. This does not mean that a judge should be swift to dissent, or that he should dissent for the sake of self-exploitation or because of a lack of that capacity for cooperation which is of the essence of any group action, whether judicial or otherwise. Independence does not mean cantankerousness and a judge may be a strong judge without being an impossible person. Nothing is more distressing on any bench than the exhibition of a captious, impatient, querulous spirit. We are fortunately free from this in our highest courts in Nation and State, much freer than in some of the days gone by. Dissenting opinions enable a judge to express his individuality. He is not under the compulsion of speaking for the court and thus of securing the concurrence of a majority. In dissenting, he is a free lance. A dissent in a court of last resort is an appeal to the brooding spirit of the law, to the intelligence of a future day, when a later decision may possibly correct the error into which the dissenting judge believes the court to have been betrayed.

SOURCE: Charles Evans Hughes, The Supreme Court of the United States 67–68 (1928).

dissenter in the first flag-salute case in 1940, involving the religious freedoms of Jehovah's Witnesses. Two years later, three Justices from the majority (Black, Douglas, and Murphy) publicly announced that the decision "was wrongly decided." The following year, the Court reversed its 1940 ruling, vindicating Stone's position.[9] In 1942 the Court split 6 to 3, deciding that indigent defendants did not have a right to counsel in state court for all felonies. By 1963 the position of the three dissenters had been elevated to the majority position. Betts v. Brady, 316 U.S. 455, 474 (1942); Gideon v. Wainwright, 372 U.S. 335 (1963).

For a judicial body, dissent carries substantial costs. Justice Edward D. White, himself dissenting in an 1895 opinion, said that the "only purpose which an elaborate dissent can accomplish, if any, is to weaken the effect of the opinion of the majority, and thus engender want of confidence in the conclusions of courts of last resort." Pollock v. Farmers' Loan & Trust Co., 157 U.S. 429, 608 (1895). Dissents detract from institutional unity and may exacerbate tensions within a court, which is by nature a collegial body. Those tensions are heightened by sarcastic dissents that question the integrity or intellectual ability of a fellow judge. Dissents can be especially irresponsible when they confuse or distort the holding of the Court (see Jackson reading).

Some members of the judiciary feel a special obligation to express their dissent when constitutional questions are at stake. Said Justice Moody in a 1908 dissent:

Under ordinary circumstances, where the judgment rests exclusively, as it does here, upon a mere interpretation of the words of a law, which may be readily changed by the lawmaking

---

9. Minersville School District v. Gobitis, 310 U.S. 586 (1940); Jones v. Opelika, 316 U.S. 584, 624 (1942); West Virginia Board of Education v. Barnette, 319 U.S. 624 (1943).

branches of the Government, if they be so minded, a difference of opinion may well be left without expression. But where the judgment is a judicial condemnation of an act of a coordinate branch of our Government it is so grave a step that no member of the court can escape his own responsibility, or be justified in suppressing his own views, if unhappily they have not found expression in those of his associates. The Employers' Liability Cases, 207 U.S. 463, 504–05 (1908).

The choice between writing a dissent and joining the majority remains an individual matter. Although Justice Harlan dissented in *Miranda* v. *Arizona* (1966), the principle of stare decisis and the goal of institutional continuity and cohesiveness prompted him to acquiesce in future applications of *Miranda*. Orozco v. Texas, 394 U.S. 324, 328 (1969). Other Justices persist with their dissents.

William O. Douglas
The Dissent: A Safeguard of Democracy

All of us in recent years have heard and read many criticisms of the dissenting or concurring opinion. Separate opinions have often been deplored. Courts have been severely criticized for tolerating them. And that is why I rise to their defense.

. . .

SEARCH FOR CERTAINTY

Holmes, perhaps better than anyone either before or after him, pointed out how illusory was the lawyer's search for certainty. Law is not what has been or is—law in the lawyer's sense is the prediction of things to come, the prediction of what decree will be written by designated judges on specified facts. In layman's language law is the prediction of what will happen to you if you do certain things. This was the lesson Holmes taught; and every lawyer on reflection knows that it is sound.

There are many reasons why this is so. No matter how clear and precise the code or other legal rule may be, the proof may be surrounded with doubt. And even though the proof is clear to the advocate, the credibility of the witnesses may raise serious questions for judge or jury. Uncertainty is increased when new and difficult problems under ambiguous statutes arise....

These are the things that Holmes summed up when he described the lawyer's continuing and uncertain search for certainty. They indeed suggest why philosophers of the democratic faith will rejoice in the uncertainty of the law and find strength and glory in it.

Certainty and unanimity in the law are possible both under the fascist and communist systems. They are not only possible; they are indispensable; for complete subservience to the political regime is a *sine qua non* to judicial survival under either system. One cannot imagine the courts of Hitler engaged in a public debate over the principles of Der Fuehrer, with a minority of one or four deploring or denouncing the principles themselves. One cannot imagine a judge of a Communist court dissenting against the decrees of the Kremlin.

Disagreement among judges is as true to the character of democracy as freedom of speech itself. The dissenting opinion is as genuinely American as Otis' denunciation of the general warrants, as Thomas Paine's, Thomas Jefferson's, or James Madison's briefs for civil liberties....

LEGISLATIVE PROCESS ONE OF COMPROMISE

Those who have followed the legislative process can produce examples on end. That process is one of compromise—of qualifying absolutes, of creating exceptions to general rules. At times the process of compromise or conciliation involves well-nigh impossible adjustments. The clash of ideas may be so violent that a meeting of the minds seems out of the question. Where such cleavage is great and involves major issues, it may even tear a society apart. By the same token it can stop the legislative process or render it impotent, and thus deprive society of lawful and nonviolent means and methods of solving its problems. When the breach between the *pros* and *cons* is not too great, the legislative process functions. Even then, the compromise between compet-

Source: Journal of the American Judicature Society, Vol. 32, pp. 104–07 (December 1948). Justice Douglas served on the Supreme Court from 1939 to 1975.

ing ideas that emerges in the final legislation may be more apparent than real. For the legislative solution is often to write two opposing ideas into a statute. Without that solution enactment of the measure might, indeed, be impossible.

INTERPRETATION HAS LEGISLATIVE CHARACTERISTICS

And so the bill becomes the law and the law arrives before judges for interpretation. The battle that raged before the legislature is now transferred to the court. The passage of the legislation quieted the conflict only temporarily. It breaks out anew in the process of interpretation in the courts. A storm hits the court room, and the advocates take up the fight where the legislators left off. The same cleavage that appeared in legislative halls now shows up among the judges. Each side has eminent authority for its view since two conflicting ideas found their way into the legislation. It is therefore easy for judge or lawyer or editor to accuse the judge, who takes the opposing view, of usurping the role of the legislature. A more honest, a more objective view would concede that interpretation has legislative as well as judicial

characteristics. It cannot be otherwise where the legislature has left the choice of competing theories or ideas to the judges.

. . .

STARE DECISIS HAS SMALL PLACE IN CONSTITUTIONAL LAW

When we move to constitutional questions, uncertainty necessarily increases. A judge who is asked to construe or interpret the Constitution often rejects the gloss which his predecessors have put on it. For the gloss may, in his view, offend the spirit of the Constitution or do violence to it. That has been the experience of this generation and of all those that have preceded. It will likewise be the experience of those which follow. And so it should be. For it is the Constitution which we have sworn to defend, not some predecessor's interpretation of it. *Stare decisis* has small place in constitutional law. The Constitution was written for all time and all ages. It would lose its great character and become feeble, if it were allowed to become encrusted with narrow, legalistic notions that dominated the thinking of one generation.

Robert H. Jackson
The Limitation of Dissent

In argued cases, conferences are followed by the preparation and circulation of opinions by Justices designated by the Chief Justice when he is with the prevailing view and, if not, by the senior Associate who is. But any Justice is free to write as he will, and there may be one or more opinions concurring in the result but reaching it by different reasons, and there may be a dissenting opinion or opinions....

The dissenting opinion strives to undermine the Court's reasoning and discredit its result. At its best, the dissent, as Mr. Hughes said, is "an appeal to the brooding spirit of the law, to the intelligence of a future day...." But Judge Cardozo has written:

"... Comparatively speaking at least, the dissenter is irresponsible. The spokesman of the court is cautious, timid, fearful of the vivid word, the heightened phrase. He dreams of an unworthy brood of

scions, the spawn of careless *dicta*, disowned by the *ratio decidendi*, to which all legitimate offspring must be able to trace their lineage. The result is to cramp and paralyze. One fears to say anything when the peril of misunderstanding puts a warning finger to the lips. Not so, however, the dissenter.... For the moment, he is the gladiator making a last stand against the lions. The poor man must be forgiven a freedom of expression, tinged at rare moments with a touch of bitterness, which magnanimity as well as caution would reject for one triumphant."

Dissent has a popular appeal, for it is an underdog judge pleading for an underdog litigant. Of course, one party or the other must always be underdog in a lawsuit, the purpose of which really is to determine which one it shall be. But the tradition of great dissents built around such names as Holmes, Brandeis, Cardozo, and Stone is not due to the frequency or multiplicity of their dissents, but to their quality and the importance of the few cases in which they carried their disagreement beyond the conference table. Also, quite contrary to the popular notion, relatively few of all the dissents recorded in the

---

SOURCE: From Justice Jackson's book, The Supreme Court in the American System of Government 16–19 (1955). Footnotes omitted.

Supreme Court have later become law, although some of these are of great importance.

There has been much undiscriminating eulogy of dissenting opinions. It is said they clarify the issues. Often they do the exact opposite. The technique of the dissenter often is to exaggerate the holding of the Court beyond the meaning of the majority and then to blast away at the excess. So the poor lawyer with a similar case does not know whether the majority opinion meant what it seemed to say or what the minority said it meant. Then, too, dissenters frequently force the majority to take positions more extreme than was originally intended. The classic example is the *Dred Scott Case,* in which Chief Justice Taney's extreme statements were absent in his original draft and were inserted only after Mr. Justice McLean, then a more than passive candidate for the presidency, raised the issue in dissent.

The *right of dissent* is a valuable one. Wisely used on well-chosen occasions, it has been of great service to the profession and to the law. But there is nothing good, for either the Court or the dissenter, in dissenting per se. Each dissenting opinion is a confession of failure to convince the writer's colleagues, and the true test of a judge is his influence in leading, not in opposing, his court.

E. CASELOAD BURDENS

The number of cases submitted to the Supreme Court increased dramatically in the twentieth century. In this era of "rights consciousness," individuals and organizations went to court either to secure rights or to enforce rights already established by statute. The creation of additional district and appellate judgeships allows more plaintiffs and attorneys to enter the courts. Further aggravating the workload are dozens of statutes passed by Congress creating new causes of action, providing expedited methods of appeal, imposing duties on the judiciary, and awarding fees for attorneys.

In 1971, Chief Justice Burger appointed a group to study the growing caseload of the Supreme Court. Called the Freund Committee, the group recommended that Congress establish a seven-member National Court of Appeals to screen petitions filed with the Supreme Court and to certify 400 or so cases considered the most worthy. The Supreme Court would select from that list, but no appeal would be permitted from the cases rejected by the National Court of Appeals. The Committee's recommendation paralleled those announced earlier by Burger. U.S. News & World Report, December 14, 1970, at 43. The previous Chief Justice, Earl Warren, criticized the Committee's screening idea as a naive proposal from people who were unfamiliar with the Court's decisional process. He also objected to giving the National Court limited power to resolve conflicting decisions among the circuits. Warren, 28 Record Ass'n Bar of the City of N.Y. 627, 637, 642 (1973).

A second study, prepared by the Hruska Commission, was released in 1975. It, too, proposed a National Court of Appeals, but not to screen cases for the Supreme Court. A new court would be established to handle cases referred to it by the Supreme Court or appellate courts. In 1983 Chief Justice Burger offered his own version of a National Court of Appeals. He suggested a temporary court, drawn from appellate judges in each circuit, to resolve conflicts between appellate courts. A major restructuring of the judicial system, he warned, was necessary to "avoid a breakdown of the system — or of some of the justices." Washington Post, February 7, 1983, at A1.

The Court's docket is largely discretionary; to that extent its workload is self-imposed and self-inflicted. Workload increases when the Court reaches out to decide matters that might have been left to state courts or to the regular political process. In 1985 Justice Stevens (joined by Justices Brennan and Marshall) noted in dissent:

> Much of the Court's "burdensome" workload is a product of its own aggressiveness in this area [*of Fourth Amendment cases*]. By promoting the Supreme Court of the United States as the High Magistrate for every warrantless search and seizure, this practice has burdened the argument docket with cases presenting fact bound errors of minimal significance. It has also encouraged state legal officers to file petitions for certiorari in even the most frivolous search and seizure cases. California v. Carney, 471 U.S. 386, 396 (1985).

TABLE 5.1 CASES DECIDED BY THE SUPREME COURT 1984–2008

	Disposed of by Signed Opinion	Disposed of by Per Curiam Opinion
1984–1985	159	11
1985–1986	161	10
1986–1987	164	10
1987–1988	151	9
1988–1989	156	12
1989–1990	143	3
1990–1991	121	4
1991–1992	120	3
1992–1993	111	4
1993–1994	93	6
1994–1995	91	3
1995–1996	87	3
1996–1997	87	3
1997–1998	93	1
1998–1999	84	4
1999–2000	81	2
2000–2001	87	4
2001–2002	85	3
2002–2003	79	5
2003–2004	89	2
2004–2005	85	2
2005–2006	82	5
2006–2007	74	4
2007–2008	72	2

Justice Stevens made a similar point in two cases decided in 1990. Florida v. Wells, 495 U.S. 1, 12–13 (1990); Minnesota v. Olson, 495 U.S. 91, 101–02 (1990).

Justice Brennan consistently criticized proposals to allow a special court to screen cases for the Supreme Court. He called the screening function "second to none in importance." Brennan, 40 U. Chi. L. Rev. 473, 477 (1973). From his perspective, the dissenting opinions in denying cert represent an important foundation for the development of legal doctrine and the formation of future majority positions. He would not delegate to a separate court the responsibility for screening cases, a process he called "inherently subjective" in nature and one that helps educate Justices on contemporary issues. Id. at 480–81.

Workload problems could be relieved by withdrawing some nonjudicial duties from the Court. At present, the Chief Justice is a member of the Board of Regents of the Smithsonian Institution. He is also a trustee of the National Gallery of Art and of the Joseph H. Hirshhorn Museum and Sculpture Garden. He is responsible for appointing someone from the judicial branch to the National Historical Publications and Records Commission. Carrying out these extraneous duties seems to belie the claim that the Court is pressed to the limit with its caseload. In recent years, the Court decides fewer cases than in the past (see Table 5.1) and does not use the full amount of time available for oral argument.

NOTES AND QUESTIONS

1. Considerable debate surrounds the question of the relevance and utility of oral argument. Justice William O. Douglas believed "oral arguments win or lose a case," while Chief Justice Earl Warren thought they were "not highly persuasive." Quoted in Henry Abraham, The Judicial Process 203 (4th ed. 1980). What do you see as the purpose of oral argument?

2. Scholars agree that when it comes to the Court's opinion that the choice of the opinion writer is crucial to the result, for any one of several reasons. Lee Epstein and Jack Knight, The Choices Justices Make 125–37 (1998). By tailoring an opinion narrowly or broadly, how might that establish the initial legal and policy preferences over which Justices will negotiate, bargain and fight?

3. An opinion may be made more "palatable" to the public if it is written by a particular Justice. For example, Chief Justice Harlan Fiske Stone assigned to Justice Hugo Black, a prominent civil libertarian, the task of writing the opinion in *Korematsu v. United States*, in which the Court authorized the exclusion of Japanese-Americans from a West Coast Military area. Chief Justice Warren assigned *Mapp v. Ohio*, in which the Court created the exclusionary rule, to Justice Tom Clark, a former attorney general. David M. O'Brien, Storm Center 303–04 (4th ed.1996).

4. Chief Justice John Marshall sought to build the Court's prestige. Toward that end, he abandoned the Court's practice of issuing seriatim opinions and implemented the practice of issuing a majority opinion, that is, an institutional opinion. He also discouraged dissenting opinions as a means of creating consensus on the Court. To what extent do individual opinions, particularly dissents, help shape constitutional law?

5. Do dissenting and concurring opinions undermine public respect for the Court as an institution? Dissents represent a method of undercutting the Court's opinion. Do you suppose that the threat of a dissent is an effective tool for judicial bargaining? Consider the dissent as a means of persuading the majority to narrow its holding. How often do dissents later become the "law of the land" or provoke legislative action? Justice John Marshall Harlan's famous dissent in *Plessy v. Ferguson* (1896) was vindicated in *Brown v. Board of Education* (1954). Justice James Iredell's dissent in *Chisholm v. Georgia* (1793) encouraged adoption of the Eleventh Amendment, which overturned the Court's opinion.

SELECTED READINGS

BARTH, ALAN. Prophets with Honor: Great Dissents and Great Dissenters in the Supreme Court. New York: Knopf, 1974.

CASPER, GERHARD, AND RICHARD A. POSNER. The Workload of the Supreme Court. Chicago: American Bar Foundation, 1976.

EPSTEIN, LEE AND JACK KNIGHT. The Choices Justices Make. Washington, D.C.: CQ Press, 1998.

ESTREICHER, SAMUEL, AND JOHN SEXTON. Redefining the Supreme Court's Role. New Haven: Yale University Press, 1986.

FRANK, JOHN P. Marble Palace: The Supreme Court in American Life. New York: Knopf, 1958.

HART, HENRY M., JR. "Foreword: The Time Chart of the Justices." 73 Harvard Law Review 84 (1959).

HARTNETT, EDWARD A. "Questioning Certiorari: Some Reflections Seventy-Five Years After the Judges' Bill." 100 Columbia Law Review 1643 (2000).

HELLMAN, ARTHUR D. "Caseload, Conflicts, and Decisional Capacity: Does the Supreme Court Need Help?" 67 Judicature 29 (1983).

HOWARD, J. WOODFORD, JR. Mr. Justice Murphy. Princeton, N.J.: Princeton University Press, 1968.

LAZARUS, EDWARD. Closed Chambers. New York: Times Books (1998).

MASON, ALPHEUS THOMAS. Harlan Fiske Stone: Pillar of the Law. New York: Viking, 1956.

MILLER, ARTHUR SELWYN, AND D. S. SASTRI. "Secrecy and the Supreme Court—On the Need for Piercing the Red Velour Curtain." 22 Buffalo Law Review 799 (1973). See also accompanying comments by Eugene Gressman; Joel B. Grossman; J. Woodford Howard, Jr.; Walter Probert; Glendon Schubert; and Roland Young.

MURPHY, WALTER F. Elements of Judicial Strategy. Chicago: University of Chicago Press, 1964.

NEWLAND, CHESTER A. "Personal Assistants to Supreme Court Justices: The Law Clerks." 40 Oregon Law Review 299 (1961).

O'BRIEN, DAVID M. Storm Center: The Supreme Court in American Politics. New York: Norton, 6th ed., 2002.

————, ed. Judges on Judging: Views from the Bench. Chatham, N.J.: Chatham House Publishers, 2d ed., 2004.

PELTASON, JACK W. Federal Courts in the Political Process. New York: Random House, 1955.

PERRY, H. W., JR. Deciding to Decide: Agenda Setting in the United States Supreme Court. Cambridge: Harvard University Press, 1991.

PROVINE, DORIS MARIE. Case Selection in the United States Supreme Court. Chicago: University of Chicago Press, 1980.

RICHARDSON, RICHARD J., AND KENNETH N. VINES. The Politics of Federal Courts: Lower Courts in the United States. Boston: Little, Brown, 1970.

ROHDE, DAVID W., AND HAROLD J. SPAETH. Supreme Court Decision Making. San Francisco: W. H. Freeman, 1976.

SCHWARTZ, BERNARD. Decision: How the Supreme Court Decides Cases. New York: Oxford University Press, 1996.

SEGAL, JEFFREY A. AND HAROLD J. SPAETH. The Supreme Court and the Attitudinal Model Revisited. Cambridge: Cambridge University Press, 2002.

SPAETH, HAROLD J. Supreme Court Policy Making. San Francisco: W. H. Freeman, 1979.

STERN, ROBERT L., EUGENE GRESSMAN, AND STEPHEN M. SHAPIRO. Supreme Court Practice, 7th ed. Washington, D.C.: The Bureau of National Affairs, 1993.

SUNSTEIN, CASS. One Case at a Time: Judicial Minimalism on the Supreme Court. Cambridge, Mass.: Harvard University Press, 1999.

ULMER, S. SIDNEY. "Bricolage and Assorted Thoughts on Working in the Papers of the Supreme Court Justices." 35 Journal of Politics 286 (1973).

WESTIN, ALAN F., ed. The Supreme Court: Views from Inside. New York: Norton, 1961.

————. An Autobiography of the Supreme Court. New York: Macmillan, 1963.

WILKINSON, J. HARVIE, III. Serving Justice: A Supreme Court Clerk's View. New York: Charterhouse, 1974.

WOODWARD, BOB, AND SCOTT ARMSTRONG. The Brethren: Inside the Supreme Court. New York: Simon and Schuster, 1979.

6

Separation of Powers: Domestic Conflicts

The doctrine of separation of powers, as applied in the United States, is difficult to grasp. In both theory and practice it teems with subtleties, ironies, and apparent contradictions. Just what the framers intended remains a subject of continuing dispute, spawning a vast literature with varying interpretations. Even if we could agree on the "framers' intent," the relationships among the three branches of government have changed fundamentally in two centuries to produce novel arrangements and peculiar overlappings. Chapters 6 and 7 cover these general principles as well as specific clashes and controversies.

A. THE SEPARATION DOCTRINE

Critics of separated powers in America claim that this political system produces intolerable deadlocks and inefficiency, especially for a twenty-first-century government expected to exercise worldwide responsibilities. However, there is no necessary link between separated powers and inefficiency. The framers did not adopt a separation of powers to obstruct government. They wanted to create a system in 1787 that would operate more effectively and efficiently than the discredited Articles of Confederation, written in 1777 and ratified in 1781.

From One Branch to Three

Only one branch of national government existed before 1787: the Continental Congress. There was no executive or judiciary. Members of the Congress had to legislate and then serve on committees to administer and adjudicate what they had passed. Within a few years, the system proved to be so exhausting, inept, and embarrassing that it became necessary to delegate administrative and judicial duties to outside bodies. To relieve committees of administrative details, Congress turned to boards staffed by people outside the legislature. When those multiheaded boards failed to supply energy and accountability, Congress appointed single executive officers in 1781 to run the executive departments. These departments supplied a vital link in administrative structures between the Continental Congress and the national government established in 1787. Louis Fisher, President and Congress 1–27, 253–70 (1972).

The Continental Congress also established the beginnings of a national judiciary by setting up Courts of Admiralty to decide all controversies over naval captures and the distribution of war prizes. In 1780 Congress created the Court of Appeals in Cases of Capture, which functioned until its last session on May 16, 1787, at the State House in Philadelphia across the hall from the room in which delegates were assembling for the Constitutional Convention.

Separation for Efficiency and Liberty

This separation of legislative, executive, and judicial functions reflects the framers' search for more efficient government. The separation was driven principally by events, not theory. In a striking phrase, the historian Francis Wharton said that the Constitution "did not make this distribution of power. It would be more proper to say that this distribution of power made the Constitution of the United States." 1 Francis Wharton, The Revolutionary Correspondence of the United States 663 (1889). Justice Brandeis spoke a half-truth when he claimed that the doctrine of separated powers was "adopted by the Convention of 1787, not to promote efficiency but to preclude the exercise of arbitrary power." Myers v. United States, 272 U.S. 52, 293 (1926). Efficiency was a key objective.

It is often said that powers are separated to preserve liberties. It is equally true that a rigid separation can *destroy* liberties. The historic swings in France between executive and legislative dominance demonstrate the danger of extreme separation. The French constitutions of 1791 and 1848, based on a pure separation of powers, ended in absolutism and reaction. M.J.C. Vile, Constitutionalism and the Separation of Powers 176–211 (1967). The framers wanted to avoid political fragmentation and paralysis of power. They knew that a rigid adherence to separated powers "in all cases would be subversive of the efficiency of the government, and result in the destruction of the public liberties." 2 Joseph Story, Commentaries on the Constitution of the United States 12 (1970 ed.). Justice Jackson described the complex elements that coexist in America's separation doctrine: "While the Constitution diffuses power the better to secure liberty, it also contemplates that practice will integrate the dispersed powers into a workable government. It enjoins upon its branches separateness but interdependence, autonomy but reciprocity." Youngstown Co. v. Sawyer, 343 U.S. 579, 635 (1952).

Implied Separation

Although the separation of powers doctrine is not expressly stated in the Constitution, it is implied in the allocation of legislative powers to the Congress in Article I, executive powers to the President in Article II, and judicial powers to the Supreme Court in Article III. Several provisions help reinforce the separation. Article I, Section 6, prohibits members of either House of Congress from holding any other civil office (the *Incompatibility Clause*). This provision has been difficult to litigate. In 1974 the Court denied standing to plaintiffs who challenged the right of members of Congress to hold a commission in the armed forces reserves. Schlesinger v. Reservists to Stop the War, 418 U.S. 208 (1974). The meaning of that clause is therefore left to the elected branches. Article I, Section 6, also prohibits members of Congress from being appointed to any federal office created during their term of office, or to any federal position whose salary has been increased during their term of office (the *Ineligibility Clause*). The framers were aware that members of the British Parliament had been corrupted by appointments to office from the Crown, but they were reluctant to exclude qualified and able people from public office. 1 Farrand 379–82, 386–90; 2 Farrand 283–84, 489–92.

To reconcile these conflicting goals, Congress has at times reduced the salary of an executive position to permit someone from the House or the Senate to be appointed to the post. For example, after Congress had increased the salary of the Secretary of State from $8,000 to $12,000, President Taft wanted to name Senator Philander Knox to that office in 1909. A special bill was drafted to reduce the compensation of the Secretary of State to the original figure. The bill inspired heated debate in the House of Representatives, 43 Cong. Rec. 2390–2404, 2408–15, but was enacted into law. 35 Stat. 626. Knox was then nominated by President Taft and confirmed by the Senate. A similar situation arose in 1973 concerning the nomination of Senator William Saxbe as Attorney General after Congress had increased the salary of that office from $35,000 to $60,000. Legislation was enacted to keep Saxbe's compensation at $35,000. 87 Stat. 697 (1973). Floor debate illustrates how Congress engages in constitutional interpretation (see reading on Ineligibility Clause). Building on these precedents, Congress passed legislation in 1980 (94 Stat. 343) and in 1993 (107 Stat. 4) to permit Senator Ed Muskie to become Secretary of State and Senator Lloyd Bentsen to become Secretary of the Treasury.

Other safeguards for the separation doctrine exist. Congress is prohibited from reducing the compensation of the President and members of the judiciary. United States v. Will, 449 U.S. 200 (1980).

The Speech or Debate Clause, covered later in this chapter, provides legislative immunity to protect members of Congress from executive or judicial harassment and intimidation.

Explicit Sharing

Several sections of the Constitution produce combinations, not separations, of the branches. The President may veto legislation, subject to a two-thirds override vote of each House. Some of the Anti-Federalists objected that the veto allowed the President to encroach upon the legislature. Alexander Hamilton, in Federalist No. 73, defended the qualified veto on two grounds: it protected the President's office against legislative "depredations," and it served as a check on bad laws. In signing legislation into law, Presidents often interpret provisions of a bill to avoid what they consider to be constitutional infirmities. This practice is not without controversy. Critics of President George W. Bush objected to the frequency of his signing statements asserting broad claims of presidential power (see readings on signing statements).

Presidents also exercise a "pocket veto." The Constitution provides that any bill not returned by the President within ten days (Sundays excepted) shall become law unless the adjournment by Congress prevents the bill's return. In such cases, the bill does not become law and is pocket vetoed. Several decisions effectively eliminated the use of a pocket veto *during* a congressional session.[1] The power to pocket veto a bill *between* the first and second sessions reached the Supreme Court but was dismissed in 1987 as moot. Barnes v. Kline, 759 F.2d 21 (D.C. Cir. 1985); Burke v. Barnes, 479 U.S. 361 (1987). This is another constitutional issue that requires interpretation by the elected branches. Of course there is no question about the President's power to invoke the pocket veto at the end of the second session when Congress adjourns.

The Constitution contains other overlappings of power. The President nominates officers and judges, but the Senate confirms. The President submits treaties that the Senate must approve. The House of Representatives may impeach executive and judicial officers, subject to the Senate's conviction in a trial presided over by the Chief Justice (for presidential impeachment). The courts decide criminal cases, but the President may pardon offenders. These mixtures led to complaints by several delegates at the state ratifying conventions. They objected that the branches of government had been intermingled instead of being kept separate. By the time of the Philadelphia Convention, however, the doctrine of separated powers had been overtaken by the system of checks and balances. One contemporary pamphleteer dismissed the separation doctrine, in its pure form, as a "hackneyed principle" and a "trite maxim." M.J.C. Vile, Constitutionalism and the Separation of Powers 153.

Madison devoted several of the essays in his *Federalist Papers* to the need for overlapping powers, claiming that the concept was superior to the impracticable partitioning of powers demanded by some of the Anti-Federalists (see readings). Alexander Hamilton, in Federalist No. 75, defended the combination of the executive with the Senate in the treaty process and bristled at "the trite topic of the intermixture of powers." Opponents were not satisfied. Three states—Virginia, North Carolina, and Pennsylvania—wanted a separation clause added to the national Bill of Rights. They proposed that neither branch could exercise the powers vested in the others. Congress rejected that proposal as well as a substitute amendment to make the three departments "separate and distinct."[2]

---

1. Kennedy v. Sampson, 511 F.2d 430 (D.C. Cir. 1974); Wright v. United States, 302 U.S. 583 (1938). See also The Pocket Veto Case, 279 U.S. 655 (1929).

2. Proposed by three states: 3 Elliot 280; 4 Elliot 116, 121; John Bach McMaster and Frederick D. Stone, eds., Pennsylvania and the Federal Constitution 475–77 (1888). Amendment language: Edward Dumbauld, The Bill of Rights and What It Means Today 174–75, 183, 199 (1957). Rejection: 1 Annals of Congress 435–36 (June 8, 1789) and 789–90 (August 18, 1789); 1 Senate Journals 64, 73–74 (1820).

Is the Federal Government One of Enumerated Powers?

In exercising its power of judicial review, the Supreme Court frequently claims that the federal government is one of enumerated powers. In 1995, while striking down a congressional effort to regulate guns in schoolyards, it said: "We start with first principles. The Constitution creates a Federal Government of enumerated powers." United States v. Lopez, 514 U.S. 549, 552 (1995). Two years later, in invalidating the Religious Freedom Restoration Act, the Court announced: "Under our Constitution, the Federal Government is one of enumerated powers." Boerne v. Flores, 521 U.S. 507, 516 (1997).

Yet the federal government clearly exercises powers that are not enumerated, including the Court's own power of judicial review. Over the years, the Court has recognized a number of implied powers for all three branches. A more accurate statement would be that the federal government is one of enumerated powers plus those that are implied in the enumeration or consid-

ered necessary for the effective functioning of government.

Article I, Section 5, provides that each House of Congress "may determine the Rules of its Proceedings [and] punish its Members for disorderly Behaviour." Article II, Section 2, states that the President "may require the Opinion, in writing, of the principal Officer in each of the executive Departments." Does any one doubt that Congress and the President could exercise those powers even if not enumerated?

Why does the Court speak about enumerated powers? Is it to impress upon the public that the federal government is subject to limits and that the Court is available to police the boundaries? Wouldn't that goal be satisfied by saying that the federal government is one of limited powers, which is surely the case? In these assertions about enumerated powers, is there risk that the Court may mislead the public and appear to be simplistic and false about fundamental principles?

Enumerated and Implied Powers

Strict constructionists treat the American Constitution as one of enumerated powers. They oppose the notion of implied powers, powers derived from custom, or any other power not explicitly granted to one of the three branches. Although there is legitimate concern about the scope of implied powers, all three branches find it necessary to exercise powers not stated in the Constitution. Congress has the power to investigate as a necessary function of its legislative power; the President has the power to remove certain administrative officials to maintain executive accountability and responsibility; the Supreme Court has acquired the power to review legislative, executive, and state actions on questions of federal constitutionality. Nevertheless, the Court frequently insists that the federal government "is one of enumerated powers" (see box).

The framers recognized the need for implied powers. Madison noted in Federalist No. 44: "No axiom is more clearly established in law, or in reason, than that whenever the end is required, the means are authorized; whenever a general power to do a thing is given, every particular power necessary for doing it is included." Congress is granted not merely the enumerated powers found within Article I but is also authorized to "make all Laws which shall be necessary and proper for carrying into Execution the foregoing Powers, and all other Powers vested by this Constitution in the Government of the United States, or in any Department or Officer thereof." The history of the Tenth Amendment underscores the need for implied powers (see section "Tenth Amendment" early in Chapter 8).[3]

The boundaries between the three branches of government are also strongly affected by the role of custom and acquiescence. When one branch engages in a certain practice and the other branches ac-

---

3. Implied powers have been upheld in such cases as In re Neagle, 135 U.S. 1 (1890), which recognized the President's authority to assign a U.S. marshal to protect a threatened federal judge, and In re Debs, 158 U.S. 1 (1895), supporting presidential use of military force to break a railroad strike.

quiesce, the practice gains legitimacy and can fix the meaning of the Constitution. Stuart v. Laird, 5 U.S. (1 Cr.) 299, 309 (1803). The President's power to remove officials was upheld in a 1903 ruling based largely on the "universal practice of the government for over a century." Shurtleff v. United States, 189 U.S. 311, 316 (1903). See also United States v. Midwest Oil Co., 236 U.S. 459, 469–71 (1915). Justice Frankfurter explained how executive power can grow when unchallenged: "A systematic, unbroken executive practice, long pursued to the knowledge of the Congress and never before questioned, engaged in by Presidents who have also sworn to uphold the Constitution, making as it were such exercise of power part of the structure of our government, may be treated as a gloss on 'executive Power' vested in the President by § 1 of Art. II." Youngstown Co. v. Sawyer, 343 U.S. 579, 610–11 (1952) (concurring opinion).[4]

Congress Interprets the Ineligibility Clause

During debate in 1973, Congress interpreted the Ineligibility (or Emoluments) Clause, which provides that no Senator or Representative shall, during the time for which he or she is elected, be appointed to any civil office "the Emoluments whereof shall have been increased during such time." President Nixon wanted to nominate Senator William Saxbe to be Attorney General. Because of the constitutional prohibition, legislation was introduced with the support of the administration. The debate is an excellent example of the choice between the literal language of the Constitution and going behind the language to determine the framers' intent. The debate below occurred in the Senate on November 28, 1973, and can be found at 119 Cong. Rec. 38315–49. Senator Hiram Fong defended the bill; Senator Robert C. Byrd opposed it.

Mr. FONG. Mr. President, S. 2673 is a very simple bill. It merely sets the compensation and emoluments of the Office of Attorney General at that which existed on January 1, 1969. The proposed nomination of our colleague, Senator WILLIAM SAXBE, to the office of Attorney General has raised the question of the eligibility of a Member of Congress for appointment to a high executive office when the emoluments of that office have been increased during the term of the Member.

Senator SAXBE was elected a Senator from the State of Ohio. He took his oath January 4, 1969, and commenced his term of office....

The President transmitted to Congress on January 15, 1969, recommendations which included the increase of the salary of the Attorney General from $35,000 to $60,000 a year. On February 4, 1969, the Senate defeated Senate Resolution No. 82, which would have disapproved the Presidential recommendation. Senator SAXBE voted with the majority.

The pay raise, including that of the Attorney General, became effective shortly thereafter.

This is the increased emolument now making Senator SAXBE ineligible for appointment to the Office of Attorney General.

S. 2673 is designed to reduce the emolument of the Office of Attorney General to what it was at the time Senator SAXBE took office as Senator in 1969 and thus remove his ineligibility for appointment to that office.

· · ·

2. APPOINTMENT TO OFFICE WHERE EMOLUMENT INCREASED

The relevant portion of the clause where an emolument has been increased states:

"No Senator or Representative shall, during the Time for which he was elected, be appointed to any civil Office under the Authority of the United

4. The failure of Congress to repeal or revise a grant of statutory authority in the face of administrative interpretation has been held by the courts as "persuasive evidence" that the interpretation was intended by Congress. Zemel v. Rusk, 381 U.S. 1, 11 (1965). See also Dames & Moore v. Regan; 453 U.S. 654, 678–88 (1981); Norwegian Nitrogen Co. v. United States, 288 U.S. 294, 313 (1933); Costanzo v. Tillinghast, 287 U.S. 341, 345 (1932).

States ... the Emoluments whereof shall have been increased during such time;" ...

What has been permissible under this portion of this clause?

[Senator Fong explains that in two earlier instances, Senators were permitted to accept a Cabinet position although the salary of the Cabinet position had been increased during their term in office. In one case, Senator Morrill was confirmed for Secretary of State in 1876 after Congress had increased Cabinet officers from $8,000 to $10,000 in 1873 and reduced the salary a year later to $8,000. There was no challenge to his eligibility to serve. In 1909, Senator Knox was appointed Secretary of State after the salary for that position had been increased from $8,000 to $12,000 while Knox served as Senator. The Senate reduced Knox's salary as Secretary of State to what it was before his Senate term commenced and before the increase in pay.]

. . .

The *[Ineligibility Clause]* ... was intended mainly to prevent two evils:

First. To protect legislators from unscrupulous executives using the enticement of public office to influence the actions of the legislators, and

Second. To avoid legislators viewing their election to Congress as a stepping stone to lucrative public office and utilizing their positions in the legislature as a means of creating offices or increasing the compensation of the offices they seek.

This being so, clearly the intent was not to prevent able and qualified Members of Congress from taking civil office.

Surely, the action of this Congress in reducing the emolument of the office of Attorney General from $60,000 to $35,000 cannot be said to be corruptive of the Members of this Congress nor can it be said that Senator SAXBE used his $42,500 Senate office as a stepping stone to a $35,000 office of Attorney General.

. . .

Mr. ROBERT C. BYRD. Mr. President, I yield myself such time as I may require.

... it seems clear beyond doubt that the proposed nomination of Mr. SAXBE, would fly squarely into the face of the prohibition contained in article I, section 6, clause 2 of the Constitution ...

Clearly, the emoluments of the Office of Attorney General were increased from $35,000 to $60,000 during the term for which Mr. SAXBE was elected — which term will not expire until January 3, 1975.

. . .

We, as legislators, have a responsibility to consider the constitutional aspects of the actions we take in the performance of our senatorial duties. We cannot be fully responsive to the high calling of our office by simply saying, "We will act to do thus and so; leave it to the courts to determine the constitutional rectitude of what we have done."

Ours is a higher duty. It is a duty that requires us — especially when great constitutional questions confront us in the first instance and on the first impression — to examine and to determine, according to our best lights, the constitutionality of actions we are called upon to take.

The nomination of Mr. SAXBE, under the circumstances peculiar to the nomination, fits almost squarely as a constitutional question heretofore essentially untested and unexplored.

Returning now to the matter before us: Can the constitutional bar be lifted by legislation? I say not.

. . .

[The Senate passed the bill, 75 to 16, and the House passed it on December 3. It became law on December 10, 1973 (P.L. 93-178, 87 Stat. 697)].

Presidential Signing Statements

When signing a bill into law, Presidents have adopted the practice of offering interpretations of various provisions in the bill to bring about what the President and his advisers consider a constitutional result. In 2006 a controversy erupted when a reporter for the Boston Globe published an article detailing the extensive use by President George W. Bush of signing statements asserting broad presidential powers. Below is a statement by President Bush on December 30, 2005, signing a defense appropriation bill that prohibited cruel, inhuman, or degrading treatment or punishment of persons held in U.S. custody. The purpose of the legislation was to prohibit torture of detainees. Following that is a bill proposed in the House of Representatives in response to the practice.

· · ·

Today, I have signed into law H.R. 2863, the "Department of Defense, Emergency Supplemental Appropriations to Address Hurricanes in the Gulf of Mexico, and Pandemic Influenza Act, 2006." The Act provides resources needed to fight the war on terror, help citizens of the Gulf States recover from devastating hurricanes, and protect Americans from a potential influenza pandemic.

Sections 8007, 8011, and 8093 of the Act prohibit the use of funds to initiate a special access program, a new overseas installation, or a new start program, unless the congressional defense committees receive advance notices. The Supreme Court of the United States has stated that the President's authority to classify and control access to information bearing on the national security flows from the Constitution and does not depend upon a legislative grant of authority. Although the advance notice contemplated by sections 8007, 8011, and 8093 can be provided in most situations as a matter of comity, situations may arise, especially in wartime, in which the President must act promptly under his constitutional grants of

executive power and authority as Commander in Chief of the Armed Forces while protecting certain extraordinarily sensitive national security information. The executive branch shall construe these sections in a manner consistent with the constitutional authority of the President.

· · ·

The executive branch shall construe Title X in Division A of the Act, relating to detainees, in a manner consistent with the constitutional authority of the President to supervise the unitary executive branch and as Commander in Chief and consistent with the constitutional limitations on the judicial power, which will assist in achieving the shared objective of the Congress and the President, evidenced in Title X, of protecting the American people from further terrorist attacks. Further, in light of the principles enunciated by the Supreme Court of the United States in 2001 in *Alexander v. Sandoval*, and noting that the text and structure of Title X do not create a private right of action to enforce Title X, the executive branch shall construe Title X not to create a private right of action.

· · ·

Response in Congress to Signing Statement Controversy

Congresswoman Sheila Jackson Lee of Texas introduced the following bill in 2007 objecting to the President's use of signing statements to assert his authority:

110TH CONGRESS
1ST SESSION
H. R. 264

To prevent the President from encroaching upon the Congressional prerogative to make laws, and for other purposes.

· · ·

A BILL

To prevent the President from encroaching upon the Congressional prerogative to make laws, and for other purposes.

Be it enacted by the Senate and House of Representatives of the United States of America in Congress assembled,

SECTION 1. SHORT TITLE.

This Act may be cited as the 'Congressional Lawmaking Authority Protection Act of 2007'.

SEC. 2. FINDINGS AND PURPOSES.

(a) Findings- The Congress makes the following findings:

(1) The Framers of the Constitution understood that the power to make laws is such an awesome power that they intended it to be exercised by the most democratic branch of government.

(2) To ensure that the lawmaking power would be exercised by the branch of government that is the closest and most accountable to the people the Constitution provides that 'All legislative power herein granted shall be vested in a Congress of the United States, which shall consist of

a Senate and House of Representatives.'

(3) The Constitution limits the role of the President in the lawmaking process to—

(A) giving Congress information on the State of the Union;

(B) recommending to Congress for consideration such measures as the President deems necessary and expedient; and

(C) approving or vetoing bills and joint resolutions presented to him for signature.

(4) Statements made by the President contemporaneously with the signing of a bill or joint resolution that express the President's interpretation of the scope, constitutionality, and intent of Congress in enacting the bill or joint resolution presented for signature encroach upon the power to make laws that the Framers vested solely in the Congress.

(5) According to a May 5, 2006, editorial in the New York Times, the current President of the United States has issued more than 750 'presidential signing statements' declaring he would not do what the laws required, the most notorious example of which is the signing statement issued by the President asserting he was not bound by the Congressional ban on the torture of prisoners.

(6) On June 5, 2006, the American Bar Association created a 10-member Blue-Ribbon Task Force on Presidential Signing Statements and the Separation of Powers Doctrine' to take a balanced, scholarly look at the use and implications of signing statements, and to propose appropriate ABA policy consistent with the ABA's commitment to safeguarding the rule of law and the separation of powers in our system of government.

(7) On July 24, 2006, the Task Force determined that signing statements that signal the president's intent to disregard laws adopted by Congress undermine the separation of powers by depriving Congress of the opportunity to override a veto, and by shutting off policy debate between the two branches of government. According to the Task Force, such presidential signing statements operate as a 'line item veto,' which the U.S. Supreme Court has ruled unconstitutional. The Task Force strongly recommended the Congress to enact appropriate legislation to ensure that such presidential signing statements do not undermine the rule of law and the constitutional system of separation of powers.

(b) Purposes- The purposes of this Act are—

(1) to preserve the separation of powers intended by the Framers by preventing the President from encroaching upon the Congressional prerogative to make law; and

(2) to ensure that no Federal or State executive or independent agency, and no Federal or State judge, can attach legal significance to any presidential signing statement when construing any law enacted by the Congress.

SEC. 3. LIMITATION ON USE OF FUNDS.

(a) Limitation on Use of Funds- None of the funds made available to the Executive Office of the President, or to any Executive agency (as defined in section 105 of title 5 of the United States Code), from any source may be used to produce, publish, or disseminate any statement made by the President contemporaneously with the signing of any bill or joint resolution presented for signing by the President.

(b) Application of Limitation- Subsection (a) shall apply only to statements made by the President regarding the bill or joint resolution presented for signing that contradict, or are inconsistent with, the intent of Congress in enacting the bill or joint resolution or that otherwise encroach upon the Congressional prerogative to make laws.

SEC. 4. CONSTRUCTION AND APPLICATION OF ACTS OF CONGRESS.

For purposes of construing or applying any Act enacted by the Congress, a governmental entity shall not take into consideration any statement made by the President contemporaneously with the President's signing of the bill or joint resolution that becomes such Act.

Madison's Analysis of the Separation Doctrine

Some Anti-Federalists were astonished to find in the draft Constitution a variety of overlappings among the three branches of government: the President's power to veto legislation, the Senate's involvement in treaties and appointments, and other features of what we now call the system of checks and balances. In Federalist Nos. 47, 48, and 51, James Madison refutes these objections by reviewing the British Constitution, the theory of Montesquieu, and the practices adopted by the American states, all for the purpose of demonstrating that checks and balances are necessary to give the three branches adequate power to resist encroachments.

FEDERALIST NO. 47

Having reviewed the general form of the proposed government and the general mass of power allotted to it, I proceed to examine the particular structure of this government, and the distribution of this mass of power among its constituent parts.

One of the principal objections inculcated by the more respectable adversaries to the Constitution, is its supposed violation of the political maxim, that the legislative, executive, and judiciary departments ought to be separate and distinct. In the structure of the federal government, no regard, it is said, seems to have been paid to this essential precaution in favor of liberty. The several departments of power are distributed and blended in such a manner as at once to destroy all symmetry and beauty of form, and to expose some of the essential parts of the edifice to the danger of being crushed by the disproportionate weight of other parts.

No political truth is certainly of greater intrinsic value, or is stamped with the authority of more enlightened patrons of liberty, than that on which the objection is founded. The accumulation of all powers, legislative, executive, and judiciary, in the same hands, whether of one, a few, or many, and whether hereditary, self-appointed, or elective, may justly be pronounced the very definition of tyranny. Were the federal Constitution, therefore, really chargeable with the accumulation of power, or with a mixture of powers, having a dangerous tendency to such an accumulation, no further arguments would be necessary to inspire a universal reprobation of the system. I persuade myself, however, that it will be made apparent to every one, that the charge cannot be supported, and that the maxim on which it relies has been totally misconceived and misapplied....

The oracle who is always consulted and cited on this subject is the celebrated Montesquieu. If he be not the author of this invaluable precept in the science of politics, he has the merit at least of displaying and recommending it most effectually to the attention of mankind. Let us endeavor, in the first place, to ascertain his meaning on this point.

The British Constitution was to Montesquieu what Homer has been to the didactic writers on epic poetry....

On the slightest view of the British Constitution, we must perceive that the legislative, executive, and judiciary departments are by no means totally separate and distinct from each other. The executive magistrate forms an integral part of the legislative authority. He alone has the prerogative of making treaties with foreign sovereigns, which, when made, have, under certain limitations, the force of legislative acts. All the members of the judiciary department are appointed by him, can be removed by him on the address of the two Houses of Parliament, and form, when he pleases to consult them, one of his constitutional councils. One branch of the legislative department forms also a great constitutional council to the executive chief, as, on another hand, it is the sole depositary of judicial power in cases of impeachment, and is invested with the supreme appellate jurisdiction in all other cases. The judges, again, are so far connected with the legislative department as often to attend and participate in its deliberations, though not admitted to a legislative vote.

From these facts, by which Montesquieu was guided, it may clearly be inferred that, in saying "There can be no liberty where the legislative and executive powers are united in the same person, or body of magistrates," or, "if the power of judging be not separated from the legislative and executive powers," he did not mean that these departments ought to have no *partial agency* in, or no *control* over, the acts of each other. His meaning, as his own words import, and still more conclusively as illustrated by the example in his eye, can amount to no more than this, that where the *whole* power of one department is exercised by the same hands which possess the *whole* power of another department, the fundamental principles of a free constitution are subverted....

If we look into the constitutions of the several States, we find that, notwithstanding the emphatical and, in some instances, the unqualified terms in which this axiom has been laid down, there is not a single instance in which the several departments of power have been kept absolutely separate and distinct.

[Here Madison proceeds, state by state, to explain how the state constitutions mix the three powers of government.]

FEDERALIST NO. 48

It was shown in the last paper that the political apothegm there examined does not require that the legislative, executive, and judiciary departments should be wholly unconnected with each other. I shall undertake, in the next place, to show that unless these departments be so far connected and blended as to give to each a constitutional control over the others, the degree of separation which the maxim requires, as essential to a free government, can never in practice be duly maintained.

It is agreed on all sides, that the powers properly belonging to one of the departments ought not to be directly and completely administered by either of the other departments. It is equally evident, that none of them ought to possess, directly or indirectly, an overruling influence over the others, in the administration of their respective powers. It will not be denied, that power is of an encroaching nature, and that it ought to be effectually restrained from passing the limits assigned to it. After discriminating, therefore, in theory, the several classes of power, as they may in their nature be legislative, executive, or judiciary, the next and most difficult task is to provide some practical security for each, against the invasion of the others. What this security ought to be, is the great problem to be solved.

Will it be sufficient to mark, with precision, the boundaries of these departments, in the constitution of the government, and to trust to these parchment barriers against the encroaching spirit of power? This is the security which appears to have been principally relied on by the compilers of most of the American constitutions. But experience assures us, that the efficacy of the provision has been greatly overrated; and that some more adequate defence is indispensably necessary for the more feeble, against the more powerful, members of the government. The legislative department is everywhere extending the sphere of its activity, and drawing all power into its impetuous vortex.

[Starting with Virginia, Madison details various examples of legislative usurpations of executive and judicial power. He also cites instances of executive encroachments.]

FEDERALIST NO. 51

To what expedient, then, shall we finally resort, for maintaining in practice the necessary partition of power among the several departments, as laid down in the Constitution? The only answer that can be given is, that as all these exterior provisions are found to be inadequate, the defect must be supplied, by so contriving the interior structure of the government as that its several constituent parts may, by their mutual relations, be the means of keeping each other in their proper places....

In order to lay a due foundation for that separate and distinct exercise of the different powers of government, which to a certain extent is admitted on all hands to be essential to the preservation of liberty, it is evident that each department should have a will of its own; and consequently should be so constituted that the members of each should have as little agency as possible in the appointment of the members of the others....

It is equally evident, that the members of each department should be as little dependent as possible on those of the others, for the emoluments annexed to their offices. Were the executive magistrate, or the judges, not independent of the legislature in this particular, their independence in every other would be merely nominal.

But the great security against a gradual concentration of the several powers in the same department, consists in giving to those who administer each department the necessary constitutional means and personal motives to resist encroachments of the others. The provision for defence must in this, as in all other cases, be made commensurate to the danger of attack. Ambition must be made to counteract ambition. The interest of the man must be connected with the constitutional rights of the place. It may be a reflection on human nature, that such devices should be necessary to control the abuses of government. But what is government itself, but the greatest of all reflections on human nature? If men were angels, no government would be necessary. If angels were to govern men, neither external nor internal controls on government would be necessary. In framing a government which is to be administered by men over men, the great difficulty lies in this: you must first enable the government to control the governed; and in the next place oblige it to control itself. A dependence on the people is, no doubt, the primary control on the government; but experience has taught mankind the necessity of auxiliary precautions.

B. PRESIDENTIAL POWER

Scholars have long debated the nature of executive power, viewing it in historical, philosophical, political, and constitutional terms. Do the words "executive power" in Article II suggest a grant to the President of broad, discretionary authority, of all powers conceivably executive in nature? Or is the executive power clause a reference to the subsequent enumeration of presidential power? In Federalist Nos. 69 and 70, Alexander Hamilton offered his views on the nature of executive power and compared it to the more comprehensive grant of power for the English king (see reading).

In a concurring opinion, Justice Robert H. Jackson denied that the executive power "is a grant in bulk of all conceivable power." Youngstown Co. v. Sawyer, 343 U.S. 579, 641 (1952). Yet it is widely acknowledged that the President possesses powers beyond those that are enumerated. For functional purposes, he enjoys some implied powers. As part of his administrative responsibilities and his duty to faithfully execute the laws under the Take Care Clause of Article II, he may exercise the power to remove executive officials. Myers v. United States, 272 U.S. 52 (1926). Similarly, the Court has recognized a limited executive privilege to retain information within the executive branch, as an attribute of the President's duties and responsibilities. United States v. Nixon, 418 U.S. 683 (1974).

Prerogative

Quite apart from the concept of enumerated and implied powers, as properly grounded in the Constitution, do Presidents possess an extraconstitutional authority or prerogative power? May they act in response to an emergency—in the absence of law or even in conflict with it—for the public good? In 1936, Justice George Sutherland asserted that authority over foreign affairs is not dependent upon a grant from the Constitution since the powers of external sovereignty are derived from the English Crown. United States v. Curtiss-Wright, 299 U.S. 304, 315–16 (1936). When President Harry S. Truman seized the steel mills in 1952, he invoked emergency powers and claimed that he could act "for whatever is for the best of the country." Public Papers of the Presidents, 1952–53, at 273. That interpretation was emphatically rejected by the Supreme Court. Youngstown Co. v. Sawyer, 343 U.S. 579 (1952).

Some scholars, embracing the claim of extraconstitutional executive powers, have located its modern expression in the Lockean Prerogative. Edward S. Corwin, The President: Office and Powers, 1787–1948, at 10, 15–16, 6–7, 182 (3rd rev. ed. 1948), In the second of his *Two Treatises of Government* published in 1690, John Locke stated that prerogative was the power "to act according to discretion, for the public good, without the prescription of the law and sometimes even against it." The executive does not possess the legal authority to act, but because he is perhaps best-positioned and best-equipped to act, he may choose to respond to the emergency, much like the man who pulls down "an innocent Man's House to stop the Fire, when the next to it is burning." Locke, Second Treatise, § 159. Neither the good citizen nor the executive acts under the color of law in the case of emergency; they simply act and accept the consequences. They can be spared punishment through exoneration from the legislature in the way of retroactive authorization or by a pardon. If a President's explanation is unsatisfactory he may be impeached.

The method of retroactive authorization or indemnity maintains constitutional government: the legislature and not the executive is the lawmaker. There is no evidence that the framers of the Constitution intended to incorporate the Lockean Prerogative in the Constitution. When President Lincoln took extraordinary actions at the start of the Civil War while Congress was in recess, he acknowledged that some of his actions may have lacked legal authority and therefore turned to Congress for retroactive approval (see "Lincoln's Initiatives" in Chapter 7).

Hamilton on Executive Power

In several essays in *The Federalist,* Alexander Hamilton hoped to allay the fears that the framers had defined executive power too broadly. In Federalist No. 69, he compared the power of the President to the much larger prerogatives of the King of England. How does contemporary presidential power compare with Hamilton's analysis? In Federalist No. 70, he defended energy in the executive as not only a leading characteristic of good government but also consistent with republican principles.

FEDERALIST NO. 69

I PROCEED now to trace the real characters of the proposed Executive, as they are marked out in the plan of the convention. This will serve to place in a strong light the unfairness of the representations which have been made in regard to it.

. . .

That magistrate is to be elected for *four* years; and is to be reeligible as often as the people of the United States shall think him worthy of their confidence. In these circumstances there is a total dissimilitude between *him* and a king of Great Britain, who in an *hereditary* monarch, possessing the crown as a patrimony descendible to his heirs forever; but there is a close analogy between *him* and a governor of New York, who is elected for *three* years, and is reeligible without limitation or intermission....

The President of the United States would be liable to be impeached, tried, and, upon conviction of treason, bribery, or other high crimes or misdemeanors, removed from office; and would afterwards be liable to prosecution and punishment in the ordinary course of law. The person of the king of Great Britain is sacred and inviolable; there is no constitutional tribunal to which he is amenable; no punishment to which he can be subjected without involving the crisis of a national revolution....

The President of the United States is to have power to return a bill, which shall have passed the two branches of the legislature, for reconsideration; and the bill so returned is to become a law, if, upon that reconsideration, it be approved by two thirds of both houses. The king of Great Britain, on his part, has an absolute negative upon the acts of the two houses of Parliament....

The President is to be the "commander-in-chief of the army and navy of the United States, and of the militia of the several States, when called into the actual service of the United States.... In most of these particulars, the power of the President will resemble equally that of the king of Great Britain and of the governor of New York. The most material points of difference are these: — *First*. The President will have only the occasional command of such part of the militia of the nation as by legislative provision may be called into the actual service of the Union. The king of Great Britain and the governor of New York have at all times the entire command of all the militia within their several jurisdictions. In this article, therefore, the power of the President would be inferior to that of either the monarch or the governor. *Second*. The President is to be commander-in-chief of the army and navy of the United States. In this respect his authority would be nominally the same with that of the king of Great Britain, but in substance much inferior to it. It would amount to nothing more than the supreme command and direction of the military and naval forces, as first General and admiral of the Confederacy; while that of the British king extends to the *declaring* of war and to the *raising* and *regulating* of fleets and armies, — all which, by the Constitution under consideration, would appertain to the legislature....

The President is to have power, with the advice and consent of the Senate, to make treaties, provided two thirds of the senators present concur. The king of Great Britain is the sole and absolute representative of the nation in all foreign transactions. He can of his own accord make treaties of peace, commerce, alliance, and of every other description....

The President is also to be authorized to receive ambassadors and other public ministers. This, though it has been a rich theme of declamation, is more a matter of dignity than of authority....

The President is to nominate, and, *with the advice and consent of the Senate,* to appoint ambassadors and other public ministers, judges of the Supreme Court, and in general all officers of the United States established by law, and whose appointments are not otherwise provided for by the Constitution. The king of Great Britain is emphatically and truly styled the fountain of honor. He not only appoints to all offices, but can create offices. He can confer titles of nobility at pleasure; and has the disposal of an immense number of church preferments. There is evidently a great inferiority in the power of the President, in this particular, to that of the British king; ...

FEDERALIST NO. 70

THERE is an idea, which is not without its advocates, that a vigorous Executive is inconsistent with the genius of republican government. The enlightened well-wishers to this species of government must at least hope that the supposition is destitute of foundation; since they can never admit its truth, without at the same time admitting the condemnation of their own principles. Energy in the Executive is a leading character in the definition of good government. It is essential to the protection of the community against foreign attacks; it is not less essential to the steady administration of the laws; to the protection of property against those irregular and high-handed combinations which sometimes interrupt the ordinary course of justice; to the security of liberty against the enterprises and assaults of ambition, of faction, and of anarchy....

There can be no need, however, to multiply arguments or examples on this head. A feeble Executive implies a feeble execution of the government. A feeble execution is but another phrase for a bad execution; and a government ill executed, whatever it may be in theory, must be, in practice, a bad government.

Taking it for granted, therefore, that all men of sense will agree in the necessity of an energetic Executive, it will only remain to inquire, what are the ingredients which constitute this energy? ...

The ingredients which constitute energy in the Executive are, unity; duration; an adequate provision for its support; competent powers.

The ingredients which constitute safety in the republican sense are, a due dependence on the people; a due responsibility.

. . .

That unity is conducive to energy will not be disputed. Decision, activity, secrecy, and despatch will generally characterize the proceedings of one man in a much more eminent degree than the proceedings of any greater number; and in proportion as the number is increased, these qualities will be diminished.

C. CREATING THE EXECUTIVE DEPARTMENTS

The Constitution established only a shell for government. It was left to the First Congress, by statute, to create executive departments and lower federal courts. In so doing, it necessarily debated and decided a number of fundamental constitutional issues. At that time, there was neither a functioning judiciary nor federal judicial precedents. From 1789 to the present, it has been primarily the responsibility of Congress to determine the structure of government, the powers and functions of agencies, limitations on the President's power, the qualifications of appointees, and the level of funding. But as presidential power expanded, so too did efforts to resist congressional attempts to limit presidential control of executive officers. Contemporary advocates for a strong presidency argue that the Framers intended to create a "unitary executive" without the divided control that is characteristic of the modern administrative state. Calabresi and Yoo, The Unitary Executive (2008). Other scholars have challenged this notion, characterizing the theory as one that undermines the separation of powers. MacKenzie, Absolute Power: How the Unitary Executive is Undermining the Constitution (2008). The history of the development of the federal government administrative structure tends to support the claims for congressional authority.

Since each department had to be created by statute, the First Congress could have placed departments under a single individual or a board of commissioners. The experience under the Articles of Confederation convinced most legislators that the board system lacked responsibility, energy, and order. The House of Representatives in 1789 voted for single executives to head the departments. Congress treated the Secretary of Foreign Affairs and the Secretary of War as executive officials, which had been the practice under the Articles. In contrast, Congress regarded the Secretary of the Treasury partly as a *legislative* agent, reflecting the mixed record during the Articles when the duties shifted back and forth between a Superintendent of Finance and a Board of Treasury. However, the first Secretary of the Treasury, Alexander Hamilton, performed essentially as an arm of the President, not Congress, and so it has been ever since. Under President Andrew Jackson, Congress tried to treat the Secretary of the Treasury as a legislative agent. Jackson eventually prevailed by arguing that the Secretary was "wholly an executive officer," but he had to remove two Secretaries of the Treasury to effectuate his policy and was censured by the Senate for his action. Three years later the Senate ordered its resolution of censure expunged from the record. Louis Fisher, Constitutional Conflicts Between Congress and the President 54 (2007).

Hybrid Officers

Some of the officers within the Treasury Department had duties that were not wholly executive in nature. During debate on the Department in 1789, Madison admitted that the comptroller's office

Madison Describing Independence of Comptroller's Office

It will be necessary, said he, to consider the nature of this office, to enable us to come to a right decision on the subject; in analyzing its properties, we shall discover they are not purely of an Executive nature. It seems to me that they partake of a Judiciary quality as well as Executive; perhaps the latter obtains in the greater degree. The principal duty seems to be deciding upon the lawfulness and justice of the claims and accounts subsisting between the United States and particular citizens; this partakes strongly of a judicial character, and there may be strong reasons why an officer of this kind should not hold his office at the pleasure of the Executive branch of the Government.

... I question very much whether [the President] can or ought to have any interference in the settling and adjusting the legal claims of individuals against the United States. The necessary examination and decision in such cases partake too much of the Judicial capacity to be blended with the Executive....

Source: 1 Annals of Congress 611–12, 614 (1789).

"seemed to bear a strong affinity" to the legislative branch, while its settlement and adjustment of legal claims "partake too much of the Judicial capacity to be blended with the Executive" (see box). When Congress created the General Accounting Office (GAO) in 1921, it transferred to it not merely the powers and duties of the comptroller but even the personnel. GAO has been called a mixed agency: "legislative" when it audits accounts and investigates programs, and "executive" when it approves payments and settles and adjusts accounts.[5]

This hybrid status was attacked by the Reagan administration in 1985 when it challenged the Comptroller General's authority to determine "bid protests." Disappointed bidders of government contracts could appeal to GAO and have the award of the contract delayed while GAO studied the dispute. The Justice Department regarded GAO as part of the legislative branch and therefore without authority to participate in executive duties. However, GAO's bid-protest powers were upheld in the lower courts.[6]

The confrontation heightened at the end of 1985 when Congress passed the Gramm-Rudman-Hollings Act. The statute, which attempted to reduce federal deficits, authorized the Comptroller General under certain circumstances to order program cuts to be carried out by the President through a "sequestration" process. The administration claimed that Congress could not give executive duties to a legislative officer. The Supreme Court in 1986 agreed that the Comptroller General's sequestration duties were unconstitutional because Congress could not vest executive functions in an officer removable by Congress. BOWSHER v. SYNAR, 478 U.S. 714 (1986).

Take Care Clause

What is the President's authority to supervise officers within the executive branch? A careless reading of the Constitution gives the President the power to execute the laws. In fact, he is to "take Care that the Laws be faithfully executed" (Article II, Section 3). What happens if a statute places the execution of a program outside his control? Does this violate the principle of responsibility and ac-

---

5. United States ex rel. Brookfield Const. Co., Inc. v. Stewart, 234 F.Supp. 94, 99–100 (D.D.C. 1964), aff'd, 339 F.2d 754 (D.C. Cir. 1964).

6. See Ameron, Inc. v. U.S. Army Corps of Engineers, 607 F.Supp. 962 (D. N.J. 1985); 610 F.Supp. 750 (D. N.J. 1985); 787 F.2d 875 (3d Cir. 1986); 809 F.2d 979 (3d Cir. 1986). The statute was also upheld in Lear Siegler, Inc. v. Lehman, 842 F.2d 1102 (9th Cir. 1988). In response to a Justice Department request, the Supreme Court agreed to dismiss its writ of certiorari. 488 U.S. 918 (1988).

countability vested in a single executive? The short answer is that the heads of executive departments function only in part as political agents of the President. They also perform legal duties assigned to them by Congress.

In 1803, Chief Justice Marshall distinguished between two types of duties for a Cabinet head: ministerial and discretionary. The first duty allows Congress to direct a Secretary to carry out certain activities. The second duty is owed to the President alone. When a Secretary performs the first duty he is bound to obey the laws: "He acts ... under the authority of law, and not by the instructions of the president. It is a ministerial act which the law enjoins on a particular officer for a particular purpose." Marbury v. Madison, 5 U.S. (1 Cr.) 137, 157 (1803). The dispute over ministerial duties reappeared in 1838. Congress could mandate that certain payments be made, and neither the head of the executive department nor the President could deny or control these ministerial acts. Kendall v. United States, 37 U.S. 522 (1838).[7]

In 1854, the Attorney General stated that when laws "define what is to be done by a given head of department, and how he is to do it, there the President's discretion stops...." 6 Op. Att'y Gen. 326, 341. Opinions by Attorneys General advised various Presidents of substantial political and legal constraints on their ability to intervene in certain departmental matters (see Attorney General reading). The President is responsible for seeing that administrative officers faithfully perform their duties, "but the statutes regulate and prescribe these duties, and he has no more power to add to, or subtract from, the duties imposed upon subordinate executive and administrative officers by the law, than those officers have to add or subtract from his duties."[8] Departmental heads recognize the limitations that prevent them from interfering with decisions by administrative law judges (ALJs). Nash v. Califano, 613 F.2d 10 (2d Cir. 1980).

Federal courts invoked the ministerial-discretionary distinction on a regular basis during the Nixon administration to force the release of impounded funds. Cabinet heads were ordered to allocate or obligate funds. Berends v. Butz, 357 F.Supp. 143 (D. Minn. 1973); Train v. City of New York, 420 U.S. 35 (1975). Statutory duties also apply to the President. In 1974 an appellate court held that President Nixon had violated the law by refusing to carry out a statute on federal pay. He was directed to either submit to Congress the pay plan proposed by a salary commission or his own alternative plan. National Treasury Employees Union v. Nixon, 492 F.2d 587 (D.C. Cir. 1974).

The Department of Justice offers a classic case study of the tensions inherent in executive control of law enforcement. As presidential appointees, officers like the Attorney General and U.S. Attorneys serve at the pleasure of the President and are expected to advance the policy objectives of the President. On the other hand, as key federal law enforcement officers they are also expected to "take care" that the laws are faithfully executed regardless of political considerations. The controversy that erupted in 2007 over the firing of a number of U.S. Attorneys illustrated this tension. While everyone acknowledged that the President had the authority to remove these attorneys at his discretion, the concern that they were removed for illegitimate political reasons led to extensive press coverage, congressional hearings, and ultimately, the resignation of Attorney General Alberto Gonzales.

Independent Commissions

Beginning in 1887, Congress created independent regulatory commissions and gave them some autonomy from presidential control. The Interstate Commerce Commission (ICC) was the first of these

---

7. See also United States v. Schurz, 102 U.S. 378 (1880); United States v. Price, 116 U.S. 43 (1885); United States v. Louisville, 169 U.S. 249 (1898); and Clackamus County, Ore. v. McKay, 219 F.2d 479, 496 (D.C. Cir. 1954), vacated as moot, 349 U.S. 909 (1955).

8. 19 Op. Att'y Gen. 685, 686–87 (1890). See also 1 Op. Att'y Gen. 624 (1823); 1 Op. Att'y Gen. 636 (1824); 1 Op. Att'y Gen. 678 (1824); 1 Op. Att'y Gen. 705 (1825); 1 Op. Att'y Gen. 706 (1825); 2 Op. Att'y Gen. 480 (1831); 2 Op. Att'y Gen. 507 (1832); 2 Op. Att'y Gen. 544 (1832); 4 Op. Att'y Gen. 515 (1846); 5 Op. Att'y Gen. 287 (1851); 10 Op. Att'y Gen. 526 (1863); 11 Op. Att'y Gen. 14 (1864); 13 Op. Att'y Gen. 28 (1869); 18 Op. Att'y Gen. 31 (1884).

creatures, and since that time Congress has established other independent bodies, including the Federal Reserve System (1913), the Federal Trade Commission (1914), the Securities and Exchange Commission (1934), and the Commodity Futures Trading Commission (1975).

Compared to the single administrators who head the executive departments, commissions are multimember (collegial) bodies that are headed by at least three commissioners. Independence is secured in three ways: (1) the terms of the commissioners are staggered to insulate them from presidential elections, (2) the President's power to remove commissioners is limited by specified statutory grounds, and (3) restrictions are placed on the number of commissioners who may belong to the same political party.

Independent commissions often carry out judicial duties, which helps explain why commissions are collegial bodies. Just as we want appellate courts to consist of more than one judge to protect against "the idiosyncracies of a single individual," so do we want agencies that adjudicate to be multimember. Kenneth Culp Davis, Administrative Law of the Seventies 15 (1976). Even if the functions of these commissions were transferred to the regular executive departments, the judicial functions would still be set apart and insulated from presidential control.

Another odd body created by Congress is the U.S. Sentencing Commission, established in 1984 "as an independent commission in the judicial branch of the United States." Because of serious disparities among the sentences imposed by federal judges for similar offenses, this commission is responsible for devising more equitable sentencing guidelines. The seven voting members are appointed by the President with the advice and consent of the Senate. At least three members are federal judges. The chairman of the Commission and other members are subject to removal by the President "only for neglect of duty or malfeasance in office or for other good cause shown." Of course, the President may only remove judges from the Commission, not from their judicial positions. The Supreme Court, voting 8 to 1, upheld the Commission against a number of challenges. It concluded that Congress had not delegated excessive legislative power to the Commission, nor had it violated separation of power principles by placing the Commission in the judicial branch and requiring federal judges to serve on the Commission and share their authority with nonjudges. Furthermore, it was not a constitutional violation to limit presidential removal for cause only. Mistretta v. United States, 488 U.S. 361 (1989).

Independent Counsel

Following the scandals of the Watergate period, Congress passed legislation in 1978 to establish an independent "special prosecutor" to investigate charges against the President, the Vice President, and high-level executive branch officials. Congress concluded that the Attorney General, as a key member of the President's cabinet, might face a conflict of interest in trying to prosecute a suspected top official. The special prosecutor, later called independent counsel, could be removed by the President only for "good cause" and was appointed by a special panel of federal judges.

The Justice Department attacked the statute as unconstitutional because it vested part of law enforcement in an officer not appointed by the President. Moreover, the removal feature was seen as an impermissible restriction on presidential power. However, the Supreme Court voted 7 to 1 to sustain the independent counsel. MORRISON v. OLSON, 487 U.S. 654 (1988). Although the independent counsel statute was reauthorized by Congress in 1994 for five years, objections continued to be voiced, both on policy and constitutional grounds. If Congress reauthorized the statute, could the President veto the bill on constitutional grounds after the procedure had been upheld by the Court in *Morrison* (see box on next page)?

Each time Congress reauthorized the independent counsel statute—in 1983, 1987, and 1994—substantial reforms were adopted. Even with these changes, no doubt the potential for abuse is great for any prosecutor, including those in the Justice Department. When the office of independent counsel expired in 1999, Congress did not renew it.

The record of the independent counsel law does not support the general claim that these individ-

---

Could the President Use Constitutional Grounds to Veto an Independent Counsel Bill?

Suppose you work in the White House Counsel office and the President receives a bill to reauthorize the independent counsel statute. He tells you he has serious reservations about the bill, not merely policy concerns but constitutional issues as well. He concludes that the exercise of prosecuting authority by the independent counsel encroaches upon executive power and his obligations under the Constitution.

You remind him that the Supreme Court considered those issues in *Morrison* and yet upheld the statute on constitutional grounds. He reminds you that President Jackson vetoed the U.S. Bank bill despite *McCulloch* and says he does not feel bound by Court rulings when it comes to invoking the veto power to protect the prerogatives of his office. He feels an obligation to defend his own institution, regardless of what Congress or the courts do. In drafting his veto message, can you use constitutional arguments or has that issue already been settled by the Court's decision? For that matter, could Congress, in considering a bill to reauthorize the independent counsel, vote it down on constitutional grounds?

---

uals inevitably target a particular person and use unlimited funds to indict him. From 1978 to 1999, independent counsels conducted 20 investigations. No indictments were brought in twelve of the cases. When indictments and convictions were obtained, as with probes into corruption in executive departments (Housing and Urban Development, Agriculture) or the Iran-Contra affair, the abuses were great and needed correction. Complaints have been made about the time that some investigations take and the level of expenditures (especially Lawrence Walsh's investigation of Iran-Contra and Kenneth Starr's investigation of Whitewater and other matters), but much of the delay and cost come from the complexity of the issues and the withholding of key documents by the administration. Some form of independent counsel — whether statutory or not — is needed because there are activities (particularly White House and presidential) that cannot be investigated by the Justice Department without creating an unacceptable conflict of interest.

On December 30, 2003, Acting Attorney General James B. Comey appointed Patrick J. Fitzgerald as special counsel to investigate the leak from the Bush White House of the name of a CIA employee, Valerie Plame. In 2005 a grand jury indicted I. Lewis "Scooter" Libby, assistant to the Vice President, for perjury and making false statements in the investigation and in 2007 a jury found him guilty. Later that year President Bush, in the exercise of his pardon power, commuted Libby's prison sentence, leaving in place the conviction. Although Special Counsel Fitzgerald had been appointed by the executive, he was nonetheless criticized in the same way independent counsels had been under the Ethics Act provisions. Given the high political stakes in criminal investigations of top-level executive branch officials, it seems inevitable that prosecutors of these investigations will face challenges to their authority. Katy Harriger, "Executive Power and Prosecution: Lessons from the Libby Trial and the U.S. Attorney Firings," 38 Pres. Stud. Q. 491 (2008).

Bowsher v. Synar

478 U.S. 714 (1986)

In an effort to control the budget deficits that had mushroomed during the Reagan administration, Congress passed the Gramm-Rudman-Hollings Act in 1985. The statute established a multiyear schedule designed to bring the federal deficit to zero by 1991. If Congress and the President failed to abide by the statutory schedule, automatic cuts (called "sequestration") would occur. Under the sequestration process, the Comptroller General would receive budget estimates from the Office of Management and Budget (OMB) and the Congressional Budget Office (CBO) and proceed to draft the sequestration order, to be signed and issued by the President without change. The principal constitutional question was whether Congress could use the Comptroller General, generally thought to be within the legislative branch, to play a role in the execution of the laws. A three-judge federal court in 1986 held that the statute was unconstitutional as a violation of the separation of powers doctrine because the Comptroller General is removable only by a joint resolution initiated by Congress or by impeachment. Congressman Mike Synar filed the suit attacking the constitutionality of the Act. One of the defendants was Charles A. Bowsher, the Comptroller General.

CHIEF JUSTICE BURGER delivered the opinion of the Court.

The question presented by these appeals is whether the assignment by Congress to the Comptroller General of the United States of certain functions under the Balanced Budget and Emergency Deficit Control Act of 1985 violates the doctrine of separation of powers.

I

A

On December 12, 1985, the President signed into law the Balanced Budget and Emergency Deficit Control Act of 1985, ... popularly known as the "Gramm-Rudman-Hollings Act." The purpose of the Act is to eliminate the federal budget deficit. To that end, the Act sets a "maximum deficit amount" for federal spending for each of fiscal years 1986 through 1991. The size of that maximum deficit amount progressively reduces to zero in fiscal year 1991. If in any fiscal year the federal budget deficit exceeds the maximum deficit amount by more than a specified sum, the Act requires across-the-board cuts in federal spending to reach the targeted deficit level, with half of the cuts made to defense programs and the other half made to non-defense programs. The Act exempts certain priority programs from these cuts. § 255.

These "automatic" reductions are accomplished through a rather complicated procedure, spelled out in § 251, the so-called "reporting provisions" of the Act. Each year, the Directors of the Office of Management and Budget (OMB) and the Congressional Budget Office (CBO) independently estimate the amount of the federal budget deficit for the upcoming fiscal year. If that deficit exceeds the maximum targeted deficit amount for that fiscal year by more than a specified amount, the Directors of OMB and CBO independently calculate, on a program-by-program basis, the budget reductions necessary to ensure that the deficit does not exceed the maximum deficit amount. The Act then requires the Directors to report jointly their deficit estimates

and budget reduction calculations to the Comptroller General.

The Comptroller General, after reviewing the Directors' reports, then reports his conclusions to the President. § 251(b). The President in turn must issue a "sequestration" order mandating the spending reductions specified by the Comptroller General....

. . .

III

We noted recently that "[t]he Constitution sought to divide the delegated powers of the new Federal Government into three defined categories, Legislative, Executive, and Judicial." *INS* v. *Chadha*, 462 U.S. 919, 951 (1983). The declared purpose of separating and dividing the powers of government, of course, was to "diffus[e] power the better to secure liberty." *Youngstown Sheet & Tube Co.* v. *Sawyer*, 343 U.S. 579, 635 (1952) (Jackson, J., concurring). Justice Jackson's words echo the famous warning of Montesquieu, quoted by James Madison in The Federalist No. 47, that "'there can be no liberty where the legislative and executive powers are united in the same person, or body of magistrates'...." ...

The Constitution does not contemplate an active role for Congress in the supervision of officers charged with the execution of the laws it enacts. The President appoints "Officers of the United States" with the "Advice and Consent of the Senate...." Article II, § 2. Once the appointment has been made and confirmed, however, the Constitution explicitly provides for removal of Officers of the United States by Congress only upon impeachment by the House of Representatives and conviction by the Senate. An impeachment by the House and trial by the Senate can rest only on "Treason, Bribery or other high Crimes and Misdemeanors." Article II, § 4. A direct congressional role in the removal of officers charged with the execution of the laws beyond this limited one is inconsistent with separation of powers.

This was made clear in debate in the First Congress in 1789. *[The Court summarizes the holdings in Myers v. United States, 272 U.S. 52 (1926), Humphrey's Executor v. United States, 295 U.S. 602 (1935), and Weiner v. United States, 357 U.S. 349 (1958).]*

In light of these precedents, we conclude that Congress cannot reserve for itself the power of removal of an officer charged with the execution of the laws except by impeachment. To permit the execution of the laws to be vested in an officer answerable only to Congress would, in practical terms, reserve in Congress control over the execution of the laws....

. . .

IV

Appellants urge that the Comptroller General performs his duties independently and is not subservient to Congress. We agree with the District Court that this contention does not bear close scrutiny.

The critical factor lies in the provisions of the statute defining the Comptroller General's office relating to removability. Although the Comptroller General is nominated by the President from a list of three individuals recommended by the Speaker of the House of Representatives and the President pro tempore of the Senate, see 31 U.S.C. §703(a)(2), and confirmed by the Senate, he is removable only at the initiative of Congress. He may be removed not only by impeachment but also by Joint Resolution of Congress "at any time" resting on any one of the following bases:

"(i) permanent disability;

"(ii) inefficiency;

"(iii) neglect of duty;

"(iv) malfeasance; or

"(v) a felony or conduct involving moral turpitude." 31 U.S.C. §703(e)(1).

. . .

... The statute permits removal for "inefficiency," "neglect of duty," or "malfeasance." These terms are very broad and, as interpreted by Congress, could sustain removal of a Comptroller General for any number of actual or perceived transgressions of the legislative will....

... In constitutional terms, the removal powers over the Comptroller General's office dictate that he will be subservient to Congress.

. . .

Against this background, we see no escape from the conclusion that, because Congress had retained removal authority over the Comptroller General,

he may not be entrusted with executive powers. The remaining question is whether the Comptroller General has been assigned such powers in the Balanced Budget and Emergency Deficit Control Act of 1985.

V

The primary responsibility of the Comptroller General under the instant Act is the preparation of a "report." This report must contain detailed estimates of projected federal revenues and expenditures. The report must also specify the reductions, if any, necessary to reduce the deficit to the target for the appropriate fiscal year. The reductions must be set forth on a program-by-program basis.

. . .

... [W]e view these functions as plainly entailing execution of the law in constitutional terms. Interpreting a law enacted by Congress to implement the legislative mandate is the very essence of "execution" of the law. Under §251, the Comptroller General must exercise judgment concerning facts that affect the application of the Act. He must also interpret the provisions of the Act to determine precisely what budgetary calculations are required. Decisions of that kind are typically made by officers charged with executing a statute.

... [A]s *Chadha* makes clear, once Congress makes its choice in enacting legislation, its participation ends. Congress can thereafter control the execution of its enactment only indirectly—by passing new legislation. *Chadha*, 462 U.S., at 958. By placing the responsibility for execution of the Balanced Budget and Emergency Deficit Control Act in the hands of an officer who is subject to removal only by itself, Congress in effect has retained control over the execution of the Act and has intruded into the executive function. The Constitution does not permit such intrusion.

VI

[Appellants argued that rather than strike down the sequestration powers of the Comptroller General, the Court should nullify the provision of the Budget and Accounting Act of 1921 giving Congress authority to remove the Comptroller General. The Court rejected this option, concluding that this might make the Comptroller General subservient to the President, a result not intended by Congress.]

VII

No one can doubt that Congress and the President are confronted with fiscal and economic problems of unprecedented magnitude, but "the fact that a given law or procedure is efficient, convenient, and useful in facilitating functions of government, standing alone, will not save it if it is contrary to the Constitution. Convenience and efficiency are not the primary objectives—or the hallmarks—of democratic government …" *Chadha, supra,* 462 U.S., at 944.

We conclude the District Court correctly held that the powers vested in the Comptroller General under § 251 violate the command of the Constitution that the Congress play no direct role in the execution of the laws. Accordingly, the judgment and order of the District Court are affirmed.

Our judgment is stayed for a period not to exceed 60 days to permit Congress to implement the fallback provisions.

JUSTICE STEVENS, with whom JUSTICE MAR-SHALL joins, concurring in the judgment.

[They disagree that the power of Congress to remove the Comptroller General "represents the primary constitutional evil." They disagree also on the attempt to label the functions assigned to the Comptroller General as "executive." They view the statute as unconstitutional because it allows Congress, through the agency of the Comptroller General, to make policy that binds the nation without following the procedures mandated by Article I: passage of a bill by both Houses and presentment of the bill to the President. Stevens and Marshall also reject the premise in the majority opinion that a definite line distinguishes executive power from legislative power.]

· · ·

JUSTICE WHITE dissenting.

The Court, acting in the name of separation of powers, takes upon itself to strike down the Gramm-Rudman-Hollings Act, one of the most novel and far-reaching legislative responses to a national crisis since the New Deal. The basis of the Court's action is a solitary provision of another statute that was passed over sixty years ago and has lain dormant since that time. I cannot concur in the Court's action. Like the Court, I will not purport to speak to the wisdom of the policies incorporated in the legislation the Court invalidates; that is a matter for the Congress and the Executive, *both* of which expressed their assent to the statute barely half a year ago. I will, however, address the wisdom of the Court's willingness to interpose its distressingly formalistic view of separation of powers as a bar to the attainment of governmental objectives through the means chosen by the Congress and the President in the legislative process established by the Constitution. Twice in the past four years I have expressed my view that the Court's recent efforts to police the separation of powers have rested on untenable constitutional propositions leading to regrettable results. See *Northern Pipeline Construction Co.* v. *Marathon Pipe Line Co.,* 458 U.S. 50, 92–118 (1982) (WHITE, J., dissenting); *INS* v. *Chadha,* 462 U.S. 919, 967–1003. (WHITE, J., dissenting). Today's result is even more misguided.…

JUSTICE BLACKMUN dissenting.

The Court may be correct when it says that Congress cannot constitutionally exercise removal authority over an official vested with the budget-reduction powers that § 251 of the Balanced Budget and Emergency Deficit Control Act of 1985 gives to the Comptroller General. This, however, is not because "the removal powers over the Comptroller General's office dictate that he will be subservient to Congress," *ante,* at 730; I agree with JUSTICE WHITE that any such claim is unrealistic. Furthermore, I think it is clear under *Humphrey's Executor* v. *United States,* 295 U.S. 602 (1935), that "executive" powers of the kind delegated to the Comptroller General under the Deficit Control Act need not be exercised by an officer who serves at the President's pleasure; Congress certainly could prescribe the standards and procedures for removing the Comptroller General.…

Attorney General Opinion on Ministerial Duties

As early as *Marbury* v. *Madison* (1803), the Supreme Court distinguished between two types of executive duties: ministerial and discretionary. For the latter, the duty of an executive official and adviser is to the President alone. For ministerial actions, the duty is to the statute. Beginning in 1823, Attorneys General regularly informed Presidents that they had no authority to interfere with certain statutory duties assigned by Congress to executive officers. The opinion below, by Attorney General William Wirt in 1823 (1 Op. Att'y Gen. 624), explains the law on ministerial duties to President Monroe.

Sir: I have examined the case of Major Joseph Wheaton, submitted by you for my opinion; and would proceed at once to the expression of an opinion on the merits of his claims, but that there is a preliminary inquiry which must be first made, and as to which I beg leave to ask your direction; and that is, whether it is proper for you to interfere in this case at all? I will suggest the considerations which strike me as rendering it improper.

I. It appears to me that you have no power to interfere.

The constitution of the United States requires the President, in general terms, to take care that the laws be faithfully executed; that is, it places the officers engaged in the execution of the laws under his general superintendence: he is to see that they do their duty faithfully; and on their failure, to cause them to be displaced, prosecuted, or impeached, according to the nature of the case. In case of forcible resistance to the laws, too, so as to require the interposition of the power of the government to overcome the illegal resistance, he is to see that that power be furnished. But it could never have been the intention of the constitution, in assigning this general power to the President to take care that the laws be executed, that he should in person execute the laws himself. For example: if a marshal should either refuse to serve process altogether, or serve it irregularly, that the President should correct the irregularity, or supply the omission, by executing the process in person. To interpret this clause of the constitution so as to throw upon the President the duty of a personal interference in every specific case of an alleged or defective execution of the laws, and to call upon him to perform such duties himself, would be not only to require him to perform an impossibility himself, but to take upon himself the responsibility of all the subordinate executive officers of the government — a construction too absurd to be seriously contended for. But the requisition of the constitution is, that he shall *take care* that the *laws* be executed. If the laws, then, require a particular officer by name to perform a duty, not only is that officer bound to perform it, but no other officer can perform it without a violation of the law; and were the President to perform it, he would not only be not taking care that the laws were faithfully executed, but he would be violating them himself. The constitution assigns to Congress the power of designating the duties of particular officers: the President is only required to take care that they execute them faithfully....

Let us carry this principle to the laws which regulate the settlement of public accounts. In the original organization of the Treasury Department (vol. 2, Laws U.S., p. 48,) the duties of the officers are designated specifically. There was one Auditor and one Comptroller. The duty of the Auditor is declared to be to receive all public accounts; and, after examination, to certify the balance, and transmit the accounts, with the vouchers and certificate, to the Comptroller, for his decision thereon; with this *proviso:* that if any person be dissatisfied therewith, he may within six months appeal to the Comptroller against such settlement. Here the right of appeal stops; there is no proviso for an appeal to the President. With regard to the Comptroller, it directs that it shall be his duty to superintend the adjustment and preservation of all public accounts; to examine all accounts settled by the Auditor, and certify the balances arising thereon to the Register: no right of appeal from his decision to the President....

It would be strange, indeed, if it were otherwise. The office of President is ordained for very different purposes than that of settling individual accounts. The constitution has committed to him the care of the great interests of the nation, in all its foreign and domestic relations. *[For example, the President is charged with being the Commander in Chief, granting pardons, selecting ambassadors, making treaties, and so forth.]* How will it be possible for the President to perform these great duties, if he is also to exercise the appellate power of revising and correcting the settlement of all the individual accounts which pass through the hands of the accounting officers? ...

Morrison v. Olson

487 U.S. 654 (1988)

The Ethics in Government Act of 1978, as amended, created an "independent counsel" to investigate high-ranking officials in the executive branch. Under the provisions of the statute, if the Attorney General concluded that the actions of an official exceeded a certain threshold that required additional investigation, he or she applied to a panel of three federal judges who were

authorized to appoint an independent counsel and to define the counsel's prosecutorial jurisdiction. The Attorney General could remove the independent counsel only "for cause." The
statute was challenged in court on a number of constitutional grounds: the appointment power,
the removal power, the separation of powers doctrine, and the President's obligation to see that
the laws are faithfully executed. In this lawsuit, Independent Counsel Alexia Morrison investigated Theodore B. Olson, a former official with the Department of Justice. He was accused of
giving false and misleading testimony to Congress. The statute was declared unconstitutional
by a divided (2 to 1) panel of the D.C. Circuit.

CHIEF JUSTICE REHNQUIST delivered the opinion
of the Court.

This case presents us with a challenge to the independent counsel provisions of the Ethics in Government Act of 1978, 28 U.S.C.A. §§ 49, 591 *et seq.*
(1982 ed., Supp. V). We hold today that these provisions of the Act do not violate the Appointments
Clause of the Constitution, Art. II, § 2, cl. 2, or the
limitations of Article III, nor do they impermissibly
interfere with the President's authority under Article II in violation of the constitutional principle of
separation of powers.

I

Briefly stated, Title VI of the Ethics in Government Act ... allows for the appointment of an "independent counsel" to investigate and, if appropriate, prosecute certain high ranking government
officials for violations of federal criminal laws. The
Act requires the Attorney General, upon receipt of
information that he determines is "sufficient to constitute grounds to investigate whether any person
[covered by the Act] may have violated any Federal
criminal law," to conduct a preliminary investigation
of the matter. When the Attorney General has completed this investigation, or 90 days has elapsed, he
is required to report to a special court (the Special
Division) created by the Act "for the purpose of appointing independent counsels." ... If the Attorney
General determines that "there are no reasonable
grounds to believe that further investigation is warranted," then he must notify the Special Division of
this result. In such a case, "the division of the court
shall have no power to appoint an independent
counsel." § 592(b)(1). If, however, the Attorney General has determined that there are "reasonable
grounds to believe that further investigation or prosecution is warranted," then he "shall apply to the division of the court for the appointment of an independent counsel." The Attorney General's
application to the court "shall contain sufficient information to assist the [court] in selecting an independent counsel and in defining that independent
counsel's prosecutorial jurisdiction." § 592(d). Upon
receiving this application, the Special Division "shall

appoint an appropriate independent counsel and
shall define that independent counsel's prosecutorial jurisdiction." § 593(b).

With respect to all matters within the independent
counsel's jurisdiction, the Act grants the counsel "full
power and independent authority to exercise all investigative and prosecutorial functions and powers of
the Department of Justice, the Attorney General, and
any other officer or employee of the Department of
Justice." § 594(a). The functions of the independent
counsel include conducting grand jury proceedings
and other investigations, participating in civil and
criminal court proceedings and litigation, and appealing any decision in any case in which the counsel
participates in an official capacity. §§ 594(a)(1)(3)....

Two statutory provisions govern the length of an
independent counsel's tenure in office. The first defines the procedure for removing an independent
counsel. Section 596(a)(1) provides:

"An independent counsel appointed under this
chapter may be removed from office, other than by
impeachment and conviction, only by the personal
action of the Attorney General and only for good
cause, physical disability, mental incapacity, or any
other condition that substantially impairs the performance of such independent counsel's duties."

If an independent counsel is removed pursuant to
this section, the Attorney General is required to submit a report to both the Special Division and the Judiciary Committees of the Senate and the House
"specifying the facts found and the ultimate grounds
for such removal." § 596(a)(2)....

The other provision governing the tenure of the
independent counsel defines the procedures for "terminating" the counsel's office. Under § 596(b)(1),
the office of an independent counsel terminates
when he notifies the Attorney General that he has
completed or substantially completed any investigations or prosecutions undertaken pursuant to the
Act. In addition, the Special Division, acting either
on its own or on the suggestion of the Attorney General, may terminate the office of an independent
counsel at any time if it finds that "the investigation

of all matters within the prosecutorial jurisdiction of such independent counsel ... have been completed or so substantially completed that it would be appropriate for the Department of Justice to complete such investigations and prosecutions." § 596(b)(2).

...

III

The Appointments Clause of Article II reads as follows:

"[The President] shall nominate, and by and with the Advice and Consent of the Senate, shall appoint Ambassadors, other public Ministers and Consuls, Judges of the Supreme Court, and all other Officers of the United States, whose Appointments are not herein otherwise provided for, and which shall be established by Law: but the Congress may by Law vest the Appointment of such inferior Officers, as they think proper, in the President alone, in the Courts of Law, or in the Heads of Departments." U.S. Const., Art. II, § 2, cl. 2.

The parties do not dispute that "[t]he Constitution for purposes of appointment ... divides all its officers into two classes." *United States* v. *Germaine,* 99 U.S. (9 Otto) 508, 509 (1879). As we stated in *Buckley* v. *Valeo,* 424 U.S. 1, 132 (1976), "[p]rincipal officers are selected by the President with the advice and consent of the Senate. Inferior officers Congress may allow to be appointed by the President alone, by the heads of departments, or by the Judiciary." The initial question is, accordingly, whether appellant is an "inferior" or a "principal" officer. If she is the latter, as the Court of Appeals concluded, then the Act is in violation of the Appointments Clause.

The line between "inferior" and "principal" officers is one that is far from clear, and the Framers provided little guidance into where it should be drawn.... We need not attempt here to decide exactly where the line falls between the two types of officers, because in our view appellant clearly falls on the "inferior officer" side of that line. Several factors lead to this conclusion.

First, appellant is subject to removal by a higher Executive Branch official. Although appellant may not be "subordinate" to the Attorney General (and the President) insofar as she possesses a degree of independent discretion to exercise the powers delegated to her under the Act, the fact that she can be removed by the Attorney General indicates that she is to some degree "inferior" in rank and authority. Second, appellant is empowered by the Act to perform only certain, limited duties. An independent counsel's role is restricted primarily to investigation

and, if appropriate, prosecution for certain federal crimes.... [T]his grant of authority does not include any authority to formulate policy for the Government or the Executive Branch....

Third, appellant's office is limited in jurisdiction. Not only is the Act itself restricted in applicability to certain federal officials suspected of certain serious federal crimes, but an independent counsel can only act within the scope of the jurisdiction that has been granted by the Special Division pursuant to a request by the Attorney General. Finally, appellant's office is limited in tenure. There is concededly no time limit on the appointment of a particular counsel. Nonetheless, the office of independent counsel is "temporary" in the sense that an independent counsel is appointed essentially to accomplish a single task, and when that task is over the office is terminated, either by the counsel herself or by action of the Special Division.... In our view, these factors relating to the "ideas of tenure, duration ... and duties" of the independent counsel, *Germaine, supra,* at 511, are sufficient to establish that appellant is an "inferior" officer in the constitutional sense.

. . .

This does not, however, end our inquiry under the Appointments Clause. Appellees argue that even if appellant is an "inferior" officer, the Clause does not empower Congress to place the power to appoint such an officer outside the Executive Branch. They contend that the Clause does not contemplate congressional authorization of "interbranch appointments," in which an officer of one branch is appointed by officers of another branch. The relevant language of the Appointments Clause is worth repeating. It reads: " ... but the Congress may by Law vest the Appointment of such inferior Officers, as they think proper, in the President alone, in the courts of Law, or in the Heads of Departments." On its face, the language of this "excepting clause" admits of no limitation on interbranch appointments. Indeed, the inclusion of "as they think proper" seems clearly to give Congress significant discretion to determine whether it is "proper" to vest the appointment of, for example, executive officials in the "courts of Law." ...

We do not mean to say that Congress' power to provide for interbranch appointments of "inferior officers" is unlimited. In addition to separation of powers concerns, which would arise if such provisions for appointment had the potential to impair the constitutional functions assigned to one of the branches, *Siebold* itself suggested that Congress' decision to vest the appointment power in the courts would be improper if there was some "incongruity" between the functions normally performed by the courts and the performance of their duty to appoint....

IV

Appellees next contend that the powers vested in the Special Division by the Act conflict with Article III of the Constitution.... As a general rule, we have broadly stated that "executive or administrative duties of a nonjudicial nature may not be imposed on judges holding office under Art. III of the Constitution." *Buckley,* 424 U.S., at 123.... The purpose of this limitation is to help ensure the independence of the Judicial Branch and to prevent the judiciary from encroaching into areas reserved for the other branches....

Most importantly, the Act vests in the Special Division the power to choose who will serve as independent counsel and the power to define his or her jurisdiction. § 593(b). Clearly, once it is accepted that the Appointments Clause gives Congress the power to vest the appointment of officials such as the independent counsel in the "courts of Law," there can be no Article III objection to the Special Division's exercise of that power, as the power itself derives from the Appointments Clause, a source of authority for judicial action that is independent of Article III....

We are more doubtful about the special Division's power to terminate the office of the independent counsel pursuant to § 596(b)(2). As appellees suggest, the power to terminate, especially when exercised by the Division on its own motion, is "administrative" to the extent that it requires the Special Division to monitor the progress of proceedings of the independent counsel and come to a decision as to whether the counsel's job is "completed." § 596(b)(2). It also is not a power that could be considered typically "judicial," as it has few analogues among the court's more traditional powers. Nonetheless, we do not, as did the Court of Appeals, view this provision as a significant judicial encroachment upon executive power or upon the prosecutorial discretion of the independent counsel.

... As we see it, "termination" may occur only when the duties of the counsel are truly "completed" or "so substantially completed" that there remains no need for any continuing action by the independent counsel. It is basically a device for removing from the public payroll an independent counsel who has served her purpose, but is unwilling to acknowledge the fact. So construed, the Special Division's power to terminate does not pose a sufficient threat

of judicial intrusion into matters that are more properly within the Executive's authority to require that the Act be invalidated as inconsistent with Article III.

. . .

V

We now turn to consider whether the Act is invalid under the constitutional principle of separation of powers. Two related issues must be addressed: The first is whether the provision of the Act restricting the Attorney General's power to remove the independent counsel to only those instances in which he can show "good cause," taken by itself, impermissibly interferes with the President's exercise of his constitutionally appointed functions. The second is whether, taken as a whole, the Act violates the separation of powers by reducing the President's ability to control the prosecutorial powers wielded by the independent counsel.

A

Two Terms ago we had occasion to consider whether it was consistent with the separation of powers for Congress to pass a statute that authorized a government official who is removable only by Congress to participate in what we found to be "executive powers." *Bowsher* v. *Synar,* 478 U.S. 714, 730 (1986). We held in *Bowsher* that "Congress cannot reserve for itself the power of removal of an officer charged with the execution of the laws except by impeachment." *Id.,* at 726. A primary antecedent for this ruling was our 1926 decision in *Myers* v. *United States* ...

Unlike both *Bowsher* and *Myers,* this case does not involve an attempt by Congress itself to gain a role in the removal of executive officials other than its established powers of impeachment and conviction. The Act instead puts the removal power squarely in the hands of the Executive Branch; an independent counsel may be removed from office, "only by the personal action of the Attorney General, and only for good cause." ... In our view, the removal provisions of the Act make this case more analogous to *Humphrey's Executor* v. *United States,* 295 U.S. 602 (1935), and *Wiener* v. *United States,* 357 U.S. 349 (1958), than to *Myers* or *Bowsher.*

. . .

Considering for the moment the "good cause" removal provision in isolation from the other parts of the Act at issue in this case, we cannot say that the imposition of a "good cause" standard for removal by itself unduly trammels on executive authority ...

Although the counsel exercises no small amount of discretion and judgment in deciding how to carry out her duties under the Act, we simply do not see how the President's need to control the exercise of that discretion is so central to the functioning of the Executive Branch as to require as a matter of constitutional law that the counsel be terminable at will by the President.

. . .

B

The final question to be addressed is whether the Act, taken as a whole, violates the principle of separation of powers by unduly interfering with the role of the Executive Branch....

We observe first that this case does not involve an attempt by Congress to increase its own powers at the expense of the Executive Branch.... Unlike some of our previous cases, most recently *Bowsher v. Synar,* this case simply does not pose a "dange[r] of congressional usurpation of Executive Branch functions." 478 U.S., at 727; see also *INS v. Chadha,* 462 U.S. 919, 958 (1983)....

Similarly, we do not think that the Act works any *judicial* usurpation of properly executive functions. As should be apparent from our discussion of the Appointments Clause above, the power to appoint inferior officers such as independent counsels is not in itself an "executive" function in the constitutional sense, at least when Congress has exercised its power to vest the appointment of an inferior office in the "courts of Law." ...

Finally, we do not think that the Act "impermissibly undermine[s]" the powers of the Executive Branch, *Schor, supra,* 478 U.S., at 856, or "disrupts the proper balance between the coordinate branches [by] prevent[ing] the Executive Branch from accomplishing its constitutionally assigned functions," *Nixon v. Administrator of General Services, supra,* 433 U.S., at 443. It is undeniable that the Act reduces the amount of control or supervision that the Attorney General and, through him, the President exercises over the investigation and prosecution of a certain class of alleged criminal activity. The Attorney General is not allowed to appoint the individual of his choice; he does not determine the counsel's jurisdiction; and his power to remove a counsel is limited. Nonetheless, the Act does give the Attorney General several means of supervising or controlling the prosecutorial powers that may be wielded by an independent counsel. Most importantly, the Attorney General retains the power to remove the counsel for "good cause," ... Notwithstanding the fact that the counsel is to some degree "independent" and free from Executive supervision to a greater extent than other federal prosecutors, in our view these features of the Act give the Executive Branch sufficient control over the independent counsel to ensure that the President is able to perform his constitutionally assigned duties.

. . .

Reversed.

JUSTICE KENNEDY took no part in the consideration or decision of this case.

JUSTICE SCALIA, dissenting.

... [T]he founders conspicuously and very consciously declined to sap the executive's strength in the same way they had weakened the legislature: by dividing the executive power. Proposals to have multiple executives, or a council of advisors with separate authority were rejected.... Thus, while "[a]ll legislative Powers herein granted shall be vested in a Congress of the United States, which shall consist of a Senate *and* House of Representatives," U.S. Const., Art I, § 1 (emphasis added), "[t]he executive Power shall be vested in *a President of the United States,*" Art. II, § 1, cl. 1 (emphasis added).

That is what this suit is about. Power. The allocation of power among Congress, the President and the courts in such fashion as to preserve the equilibrium the Constitution sought to establish—so that "a gradual concentration of the several powers in the same department," Federalist No. 51, p. 321 (J. Madison), can effectively be resisted. Frequently an issue of this sort will come before the Court clad, so to speak, in sheep's clothing: the potential of the asserted principle to effect important change in the equilibrium of power is not immediately evident, and must be discerned by a careful and perceptive analysis. But this wolf comes as a wolf.

I

[In this section, Justice Scalia reviews the history of Congress' investigation of the EPA scandal and concludes that the Attorney General, as a "practical matter," had no choice but to seek the appointment of an independent counsel to prosecute Olson.]

II

. . .

"The executive Power shall be vested in a President of the United States."

As I described at the outset of this opinion, this does not mean *some of* the executive power, but *all of* the executive power. It seems to me, therefore, that the decision of the Court of Appeals invalidating the present statute must be upheld on fundamental separation-of-powers principles if the following two questions are answered affirmatively: (1) Is the conduct of a criminal prosecution (and of an investigation to decide whether to prosecute) the exercise of purely executive power? (2) Does the statute deprive the President of the United States of exclusive control over the exercise of that power? Surprising to say, the Court appears to concede an affirmative answer to both questions, but seeks to avoid the inevitable conclusion that since the statute vests some purely executive power in a person who is not the President of the United States it is void.

. . .

As for the second question, whether the statute before us deprives the President of exclusive control over that quintessentially executive activity: The Court does not, and could not possibly, assert that it does not. That is indeed the whole object of the statute. Instead, the Court points out that the President, through his Attorney General, has at least *some* control. That concession is alone enough to invalidate the statute....

... It is not for us to determine, and we have never presumed to determine, how much of the purely executive powers of government must be within the full control of the President. The Constitution prescribes that they *all* are....

[In Sections III and IV, Scalia concludes that the independent counsel is a principal (not inferior) officer and, therefore, must be nominated by the President and confirmed by the Senate, and he agrees with the lower court's decision that the restrictions placed on the removal of the independent counsel violate established precedent.]

V

The purpose of the separation and equilibration of powers in general, and of the unitary Executive in particular, was not merely to assure effective government but to preserve individual freedom. Those who hold or have held offices covered by the Ethics in Government Act are entitled to that protection as much as the rest of us, and I conclude my discussion by considering the effect of the Act upon the fairness of the process they receive.

Only someone who has worked in the field of law enforcement can fully appreciate the vast power and the immense discretion that are placed in the hands of a prosecutor with respect to the objects of his investigation....

Under our system of government, the primary check against prosecutorial abuse is a political one. The prosecutors who exercise this awesome discretion are selected and can be removed by a President, whom the people have trusted enough to elect. Moreover, when crimes are not investigated and prosecuted fairly, nonselectively, with a reasonable sense of proportion, the President pays the cost in political damage to his administration....

... How frightening it must be to have your own independent counsel and staff appointed, with nothing else to do but to investigate you until investigation is no longer worthwhile—with whether it is worthwhile not depending upon what such judgments usually hinge on, competing responsibilities. And to have that counsel and staff decide, with no basis for comparison, whether what you have done is bad enough, willful enough, and provable enough, to warrant an indictment. How admirable the constitutional system that provides the means to avoid such a distortion. And how unfortunate the judicial decision that has permitted it.

D. APPOINTMENTS AND REMOVALS

Three steps are required to fill offices created by Congress: (1) nomination by the President, (2) confirmation by the Senate, and (3) commissioning of the appointee by the President. For lesser officers, the Constitution permits Congress to dispense with the confirmation process and place the power of appointment directly in the President, the courts, or department heads.

In legal theory, the power to nominate is the "sole act of the president" and "completely voluntary." Marbury v. Madison, 5 U.S. at 155. Theoretically, Congress cannot designate the person to fill the office it creates. United States v. Ferreira, 54 U.S. (13 How.) 39, 50–51 (1852); Myers v. United States, 272 U.S. at 128. Nevertheless, it can stipulate the qualifications of appointees, and legislators frequently select the names of judges, U.S. attorneys, and marshals for their state. In such cases, the roles are reversed: Congress nominates and the President "advises and consents." If the names submitted

Congressional Appointment of Executive Officials That Investigate

[*President Reagan's statement on signing the U.S. Commission on Civil Rights Act of 1983*]:

I have signed today H.R. 2230, establishing a new Commission on Civil Rights....

The bill I have signed today is, of course, a product of negotiation and compromise. While, as noted, I am pleased that the Commission has been re-created so that it may continue the missions assigned to it, the Department of Justice has raised concerns as to the constitutional implications of certain provisions of this legislation. I have appended a recitation of these reservations.

. . .

Statement by the Department of Justice
... The basic purpose of the old Commission on Civil Rights—to investigate, study, appraise, and report on discrimination—would be maintained, and most of its current authorities would remain intact. However, because half of the members of the Commission will be appointed by the Congress, the Constitution does not permit the Commission to exercise responsibilities that may be performed only by "Officers of the United States" who are appointed in accordance with the Appointments Clause of the United States Constitution (Article II, Section 2, clause 2). Therefore, it should be clear that although the Commission will continue to perform investigative and informative functions, it may not exercise enforcement, regulatory, or other executive responsibilities that may be performed only by officers of the United States.

SOURCE: Public Papers of the Presidents, 1983 (II), at 1634–35.

by Congress are unacceptable, the White House and the Justice Department can insist on substitute recommendations. Interest groups and professional organizations are also active in submitting names for consideration and evaluating those who are nominated.

There are limits to congressional intervention. In 1976, the Supreme Court reviewed a statute giving Congress the power to appoint four members to the Federal Election Commission, which monitors the financing and conduct of congressional and presidential elections. All six voting members (including two nominated by the President) required confirmation by the majority of *both* Houses of Congress. The Court ruled that Congress could not select officers responsible for carrying out executive and judicial duties. Such functions could be exercised only by "Officers of the United States" appointed pursuant to Article II, Section 2, Clause 2. For the Court, this meant either one of two constitutional options: nomination by the President, subject to the advice and consent of the Senate; or vesting the appointment power in the President alone, in the courts of law, or in department heads. Congress took the first option when it rewrote the statute. The decision explains how the appointment process is related to presidential responsibility and the separation doctrine. BUCKLEY v. VALEO, 424 U.S. 1 (1976).[9]

In *Buckley* v. *Valeo*, the Court noted that if an agency's powers are "essentially of an investigative and informative nature," Congress can appoint the agency officials. In reauthorizing the Civil Rights Commission in 1983, Congress passed legislation that gave it the right to appoint four of the eight members of the Commission. The President appointed the remaining four. 97 Stat. 1301 (1983). In signing the bill, President Reagan acknowledged that Congress operated within its powers because the essential functions of the Civil Rights Commission were investigative (see box).

Recess Appointments

The framers recognized that the Senate would not always be in session to give advice and consent to presidential nominations. To cover these periods, the President is authorized to make recess ap-

---

9. For subsequent analyses of the Appointments Clause, see Olympic Federal Savings and Loan Assn. v. Director, Office of Thrift Supervision, 732 F.Supp. 1183 (D.D.C. 1990), Freytag v. Commissioner, 501 U.S. 868 (1991), and Edmond v. United States, 520 U.S. 661 (1997).

pointments: "The President shall have Power to fill up all Vacancies that may happen during the Recess of the Senate, by granting Commissions which shall expire at the End of their next Session" (Article II, Section 3, Clause 3). "Happen" is interpreted broadly to mean "happen to exist," even if a vacancy occurs while the Senate is in session. 1 Op. Att'y Gen. 631 (1823). The meaning of "recess" remains uncertain. The Justice Department has stated that adjournments "for 5 or even 10 days" are too short to justify the use of the recess power. 3 Op. Att'y Gen. 20, 25 (1921); 3 O.L.C. 311, 314 (1979). In recent years, however, the department has argued in briefs that recess appointments might be justified for recesses in excess of three days.

In 1863, when it appeared that Presidents were abusing the power to make recess appointments and were deliberately circumventing the Senate's confirmation role, Congress passed legislation to prohibit the use of funds to pay the salary of anyone appointed during a Senate recess to fill a vacancy that existed "while the Senate was in session and is by law required to be filled by and with the advice and consent of the Senate, until such appointee shall have been confirmed by the Senate." 12 Stat. 646 (1863). The law was liberalized in 1940 to permit payment under three conditions. 54 Stat. 751 (1940); 5 U.S.C. § 5503 (2004). Legislation has also been passed to prohibit funds to pay the salary of any recess appointee who is later rejected by the Senate. E.g., 113 Stat. 467, § 609 (1999); Fisher, Constitutional Conflicts between Congress and the President 38–45. See also the section, "Recess Appointments" in Chapter 4.

Removing Officials

Although the Constitution provides no express authority for the President to remove officials in the executive branch, it was agreed by the First Congress that responsible government requires the President to dismiss incompetent, corrupt, or unreliable administrators. If anything by nature is executive, Madison said, "it must be that power which is employed in superintending and seeing that the laws are faithfully executed." 1 Annals of Congress 500 (June 17, 1789).

The debates of 1789 were interpreted by Chief Justice Taft to leave not the "slightest doubt" that the power to remove officers appointed by the President and confirmed by the Senate is "vested in the President alone." MYERS v. UNITED STATES, 272 U.S. at 114. Taft reached too far; the debates reveal deep divisions among House members and close votes on the Senate side. Fisher, Constitutional Conflicts between Congress and the President, 49–54. Moreover, the debates in 1789 focused on the President's power to remove the Secretary of Foreign Affairs, which Congress conceded to be an agent of the President and executive in nature. Madison anticipated other types of officers in the executive branch who might have a mix of legislative and judicial duties, requiring greater independence from the President. 1 Annals of Congress 611–14 (June 29, 1789). See box in Section C of this chapter. Congress can place statutory limitations on the removal power. Before Taft made his sweeping claim, the Supreme Court had recognized that Congress could specify the grounds for removal. Shurtleff v. United States, 189 U.S. 311 (1903).

A balance must be struck between the President's authority to remove executive officials and Congress's power under the Necessary and Proper Clause to create an office and attach conditions to it. Taft's decision was later modified to permit Congress to limit the President's power to remove commissioners with quasi-legislative and quasi-judicial powers. HUMPHREY'S EXECUTOR v. UNITED STATES 295 U.S. 602 (1935); Wiener v. United States, 357 U.S. 349 (1958). Depending on statutory language or commitments by the President and his subordinates to maintain an officer's independence, presidential power to remove officers may face other constraints.[10]

Beyond the occasional lawsuit are the more frequent interventions by Congress. Congress may re-

---

10. Nader v. Bork, 366 F.Supp. 104 (D.D.C. 1973); Borders v. Reagan, 518 F.Supp. 250 (D.D.C. 1981); Stephen Gettinger, "The Power Struggle Over Federal Parole," 8 Corrections Magazine 41 (1982); Berry v. Reagan, Civil Action No. 83-3182 (D.D.C. November 14, 1983).

move an individual by abolishing the office. A term of office created by one statute can be reduced or eliminated by a subsequent statute, requiring the discharge of a federal employee. Crenshaw v. United States, 134 U.S. 99 (1890). Through the passage of nonbinding resolutions, committee investigations, the contempt power, and other pressures, Congress can precipitate a person's resignation or removal. Congress also intervenes to *protect* an officeholder, particularly a "whistleblower" who alerts Congress to agency deficiencies. Lawmakers intervene for reasons of simple justice and to keep open the channels of communication between agencies and Congress. Louis Fisher, "Congress and the Removal Power," 10 Congress & the Presidency 63 (1983).

Buckley v. Valeo

424 U.S. 1 (1976)

As part of the Federal Election Campaign Act amendments of 1974, which responded to the scandals during the presidential election of 1972, Congress enacted a number of reforms, including the creation of the Federal Election Commission (FEC). Because Congress appointed some of the commissioners, the Supreme Court reviewed the framers' intent with respect to the Appointments Clause and the separation of powers theory. The case also involved First Amendment challenges to the limits placed on campaign spending, although that part of the opinion is not excerpted here. Senator James Buckley was one of several plaintiffs who brought this action against Francis Valeo, Secretary of the Senate.

PER CURIAM.

These appeals present constitutional challenges to the key provisions of the Federal Election Campaign Act of 1971 (Act), and related provisions of the Internal Revenue Code of 1954, all as amended in 1974.

. . .

IV. THE FEDERAL ELECTION COMMISSION

The 1974 amendments to the Act create an eight-member Federal Election Commission (Commission) and vest in it primary and substantial responsibility for administering and enforcing the Act. The question that we address in this portion of the opinion is whether, in view of the manner in which a majority of its members are appointed, the Commission may under the Constitution exercise the powers conferred upon it....

... the Commission is given extensive rulemaking and adjudicative powers....

The body in which this authority is reposed consists of eight members. The Secretary of the Senate and the Clerk of the House of Representatives are *ex officio* members of the Commission without the right to vote. Two members are appointed by the President *pro tempore* of the Senate "upon the recommendations of the majority leader of the Senate and the minority leader of the Senate." Two more are to be appointed by the Speaker of the House of Representatives, likewise upon the recommendations of its respective majority and minority leaders. The remaining two members are appointed by the President. Each of the six voting members of the Commission must be confirmed by the majority of both Houses of Congress, and each of the three appointing authorities is forbidden to choose both of their appointees from the same political party.

. . .

[After concluding that the Commission's composition was ripe for review, the Court analyzed the substantive issues.]

B. The Merits

Appellants urge that since Congress has given the Commission wide-ranging rulemaking and enforcement powers with respect to the substantive provisions of the Act, Congress is precluded under the principle of separation of powers from vesting in itself the authority to appoint those who will exercise such authority. Their argument is based on the language of Art. II, § 2, cl. 2, of the Constitution, which provides in pertinent part as follows:

"[The President] shall nominate, and by and with the Advice and Consent of the Senate, shall appoint ... all other Officers of the United States, whose Appointments are not herein otherwise provided for, and which shall be established by Law: but the Congress may by Law vest the Appointment of such inferior Officers, as they think proper, in the President alone, in the Courts of Law, or in the Heads of Departments."

Appellants' argument is that this provision is the exclusive method by which those charged with executing the laws of the United States may be chosen. Congress, they assert, cannot have it both ways. If the Legislature wishes the Commission to exercise all of the conferred powers, then its members are in fact "Officers of the United States" and must be appointed under the Appointments Clause. But if Congress insists upon retaining the power to appoint, then the members of the Commission may not discharge those many functions of the Commission which can be performed only by "Officers of the United States," as that term must be construed within the doctrine of separation of powers.

Appellee Commission and *amici* in support of the Commission urge that the Framers of the Constitution, while mindful of the need for checks and balances among the three branches of the National Government, had no intention of denying to the Legislative Branch authority to appoint its own officers. Congress, either under the Appointments Clause or under its grants of substantive legislative authority and the Necessary and Proper Clause in Art. I, is in their view empowered to provide for the appointment to the Commission in the manner which it did because the Commission is performing "appropriate legislative functions."

. . .

1. SEPARATION OF POWERS

... Our inquiry of necessity touches upon the fundamental principles of the Government established by the Framers of the Constitution, and all litigants and all of the courts which have addressed themselves to the matter start on common ground in the recognition of the intent of the Framers that the powers of the three great branches of the National Government be largely separate from one another.

... [T]he Constitution by no means contemplates total separation of each of these three essential branches of Government.... The men who met in Philadelphia in the summer of 1787 were practical statesmen, experienced in politics, who viewed the principle of separation of powers as a vital check against tyranny. But they likewise saw that a hermetic sealing off of the three branches of Government from one another would preclude the establishment of a Nation capable of governing itself effectively.

. . .

2. THE APPOINTMENTS CLAUSE

The principle of separation of powers was not simply an abstract generalization in the minds of the Framers: it was woven into the document that they drafted in Philadelphia in the summer of 1787....

The Appointments Clause could, of course, be read as merely dealing with etiquette or protocol in describing "Officers of the United States," but the drafters had a less frivolous purpose in mind....

We think that the term "Officers of the United States" ... is a term intended to have substantive meaning. We think its fair import is that any appointee exercising significant authority pursuant to the laws of the United States is an "Officer of the United States," and must, therefore, be appointed in the manner prescribed by § 2, cl. 2, of that Article.

. . .

Although two members of the Commission are initially selected by the President, his nominations are subject to confirmation not merely by the Senate, but by the House of Representatives as well. The remaining four voting members of the Commission are appointed by the President *pro tempore* of the Senate and by the Speaker of the House. While the second part of the Clause authorizes Congress to vest the appointment of the officers described in that part in "the Courts of Law, or in the Heads of Departments," neither the Speaker of the House nor the President *pro tempore* of the Senate comes within this language.

The phrase "Heads of Departments," used as it is in conjunction with the phrase "Courts of Law," suggests that the Departments referred to are themselves in the Executive Branch or at least have some connection with that branch. While the Clause expressly authorizes Congress to vest the appointment of certain officers in the "Courts of Law," the absence of similar language to include Congress must mean that neither Congress nor its officers were included within the language "Heads of Departments" in this part of cl. 2.

Thus with respect to four of the six voting members of the Commission, neither the President, the head of any department, nor the Judiciary has any voice in their selection.

. . .

An interim version of the draft Constitution had vested in the Senate the authority to appoint Ambassadors, public Ministers, and Judges of the Supreme Court, and the language of Art. II as finally adopted is a distinct change in this regard. We believe that it was a deliberate change made by the Framers with the intent to deny Congress any authority itself to appoint those who were "Officers of the United States."...

3. THE COMMISSION'S POWERS

… Our previous description of the statutory provisions … disclosed that the Commission's powers fall generally into three categories: functions relating to the flow of necessary information—receipt, dissemination, and investigation; functions with respect to the Commission's task of fleshing out the statute—rulemaking and advisory opinions; and functions necessary to ensure compliance with the statute and rules—informal procedures, administrative determinations and hearings, and civil suits.

Insofar as the powers confided in the Commission are essentially of an investigative and informative nature, falling in the same general category as those powers which Congress might delegate to one of its own committees, there can be no question that the Commission as presently constituted may exercise them.…

But when we go beyond this type of authority to the more substantial powers exercised by the Commission, we reach a different result. The Commission's enforcement power, exemplified by its discretionary power to seek judicial relief, is authority that cannot possibly be regarded as merely in aid of the legislative function of Congress. A lawsuit is the ultimate remedy for a breach of the law, and it is to the President, and not to the Congress, that the Constitution entrusts the responsibility to "take Care that the Laws be faithfully executed." Art. II, § 3.

. . .

We hold that these provisions of the Act, vesting in the Commission primary responsibility for conducting civil litigation in the courts of the United States for vindicating public rights, violate Art. II, § 2, cl. 2, of the Constitution. Such functions may be discharged only by persons who are "Officers of the United States" within the language of that section.

. . .

MR. JUSTICE STEVENS took no part in the consideration or decision of these cases.

. . .

MR. CHIEF JUSTICE BURGER, concurring in part and dissenting in part.

. . .

MR. JUSTICE WHITE, concurring in part and dissenting in part.

. . .

[Justices Marshall, Blackmun, and Rehnquist wrote separate opinions, concurring in part and dissenting in part, but concurred in the Court's opinion on FEC appointments.]

Myers v. United States

272 U.S. 52 (1926)

A statute of 1876 provided that postmasters of the first, second, and third classes shall be appointed and may be removed by the President "by and with the advice and consent of the Senate." President Wilson removed Frank S. Myers, a postmaster of the first class, without seeking or obtaining Senate approval. The constitutional question was whether Congress could interfere with or restrict the President's power of removal, which the Solicitor General [and the heirs of Myers argued] was essential to preserve the President's responsibility as chief executive officer. The issue of the removal power was limited to officers subject to Senate confirmation.

MR. CHIEF JUSTICE TAFT delivered the opinion of the Court.

This case presents the question whether under the Constitution the President has the exclusive power of removing executive officers of the United States whom he has appointed by and with the advice and consent of the Senate.

Myers, appellant's intestate, was on July 21, 1917, appointed by the President, by and with the advice and consent of the Senate, to be a postmaster of the first class at Portland, Oregon, for a term of four years. On January 20, 1920, Myers' resignation was demanded. He refused the demand. On February 2, 1920, he was removed from office by order of the Postmaster General, acting by direction of the President.…

By the 6th section of the Act of Congress of July 12, 1876, 19 Stat. 80, 81, c. 179, under which Myers was appointed with the advice and consent of the Senate as a first-class postmaster, it is provided that

"Postmasters of the first, second and third classes shall be appointed and may be removed by the President by and with the advice and consent of the Senate and shall hold their offices for four years unless sooner removed or suspended according to law."

The Senate did not consent to the President's removal of Myers during his term....

The question where the power of removal of executive officers appointed by the President by and with the advice and consent of the Senate was vested, was presented early in the first session of the First Congress. There is no express provision respecting removals in the Constitution, except as Section 4 of Article II ... provides for removal from office by impeachment. The subject was not discussed in the Constitutional Convention. Under the Articles of Confederation, Congress was given the power of appointing certain executive officers of the Confederation, and during the Revolution and while the Articles were given effect, Congress exercised the power of removal....

Consideration of the executive power was initiated in the Constitutional Convention by the seventh resolution in the Virginia Plan, introduced by Edmund Randolph. 1 Farrand, Records of the Federal Convention, 21. It gave to the Executive "all the executive powers of the Congress under the Confederation," which would seem therefore to have intended to include the power of removal which had been exercised by that body as incident to the power of appointment.

[Later modifications vested executive power in a single person, elected by an electoral college, with the power to appoint officers and the duty to see that all laws are faithfully observed.]

In the House of Representatives of the First Congress, on Tuesday, May 18, 1789, Mr. Madison moved in the Committee of the Whole that there should be established three executive departments — one of Foreign Affairs, another of the Treasury, and a third of War — at the head of each of which there should be a Secretary, to be appointed by the President by and with the advice and consent of the Senate, and to be removable by the President. The committee agreed to the establishment of a Department of Foreign Affairs, but a discussion ensued as to making the Secretary removable by the President. 1 Annals of Congress, 370, 371. "The question was now taken and carried, by a considerable majority, in favor of declaring the power of removal to be in the President." 1 Annals of Congress, 383.

On June 16, 1789, the House resolved itself into a Committee of the Whole on a bill proposed by Mr. Madison for establishing an executive department to be denominated the Department of Foreign Affairs, in which the first clause, after stating the title of the officer and describing his duties, had these words: "to be removable from office by the President of the United States." 1 Annals of Congress, 455. After a very full discussion the question was put: shall the words "to be removable by the President" be struck out? It was determined in the negative — yeas 20, nays 34. 1 Annals of Congress, 576.

On June 22, in the renewal of the discussion, "Mr. Benson moved to amend the bill, by altering the second clause, so as to imply the power of removal to be in the President alone.... 1 Annals of Congress, 578.

"Mr. Benson stated that his objection to the clause 'to be removable by the President' arose from an idea that the power of removal by the President hereafter might appear to be exercised by virtue of a legislative grant only, and consequently be subjected to legislative instability, when he was well satisfied in his own mind that it was fixed by a fair legislative construction of the Constitution." ...

Mr. Madison admitted the objection made by the gentleman near him (Mr. Benson) to the words in the bill. He said: "They certainly may be construed to imply a legislative grant of the power. He wished everything like ambiguity expunged, and the sense of the House explicitly declared, and therefore seconded the motion." ...

Mr. Benson's first amendment ... was then approved by a vote of thirty to eighteen. 1 Annals of Congress, 580. Mr. Benson then moved to strike out in the first clause the words "to be removable by the President," in pursuance of the purpose he had already declared, and this second motion of his was carried by a vote of thirty-one to nineteen. 1 Annals of Congress, 585.

The bill as amended was ordered to be engrossed, and read the third time the next day, June 24, 1789, and was then passed by a vote of twenty-nine to twenty-two, and the Clerk was directed to carry the bill to the Senate and desire their concurrence. 1 Annals of Congress, 591.

It is very clear from this history that the exact question which the House voted upon was whether it should recognize and declare the power of the President under the Constitution to remove the Secretary of Foreign Affairs without the advice and consent of the Senate. That was what the vote was taken for. Some effort has been made to question whether the decision carries the result claimed for it, but there is not the slightest doubt, after an examination of the record, that the vote was, and was intended to be, a legislative declaration that the power to remove officers appointed by the President and the Senate vested in the President alone, and until the Johnson Impeachment trial in 1868, its meaning was not doubted even by those who questioned its soundness.

... After the bill as amended had passed the House, it was sent to the Senate, where it was discussed in secret session, without report. The critical vote there was upon the striking out of the clause recognizing and affirming the unrestricted power of the President to remove. The Senate divided by ten to ten, requiring the deciding vote of the Vice-President, John Adams, who voted against striking out, and in favor of the passage of the bill as it had left the House. Ten of the Senators had been in the Constitutional Convention, and of them six voted that the power of removal was in the President alone. The bill having passed as it came from the House was signed by President Washington and became a law. Act of July 27, 1789, 1 Stat. 28, c.4.

[Taft summarizes the reasons advanced by Madison and his associates for vesting the removal power in the President: the need to separate the legislature from the executive functions; the intention to create a strong President; the use of the removal power to permit the President to take responsibility for the conduct of the executive branch and to see that the laws are faithfully executed; the intention to make the power of removal incident to the power of appointment; and the need for the President to have full confidence in his subordinates. Nevertheless, Taft acknowledges that Congress can place certain duties in executive officers to make presidential removal inappropriate:]

... Of course there may be duties so peculiarly and specifically committed to the discretion of a particular officer as to raise a question whether the President may overrule or revise the officer's interpretation of his statutory duty in a particular instance. Then there may be duties of a quasi-judicial character imposed on executive officers and members of executive tribunals whose decisions after hearing affect interests of individuals, the discharge of which the President can not in a particular case properly influence or control. But even in such a case he may consider the decision after its rendition as a reason for removing the officer, on the ground that the discretion regularly entrusted to that officer by statute has not been on the whole intelligently or wisely exercised. Otherwise he does not discharge his own constitutional duty of seeing that the laws be faithfully executed.

· · ·

For the reasons given, we must therefore hold that the provision of the law of 1876, by which the unrestricted power of removal of first class postmasters is denied to the President, is in violation of the Constitution, and invalid. This leads to an affirmance of the judgment of the Court of Claims.

· · ·

MR. JUSTICE HOLMES, dissenting.

My brothers MCREYNOLDS and BRANDEIS have discussed the question before us with exhaustive research and I say a few words merely to emphasize my agreement with their conclusion.

The arguments drawn from the executive power of the President, and from his duty to appoint officers of the United States (when Congress does not vest the appointment elsewhere), to take care that the laws be faithfully executed, and to commission all officers of the United States, seem to me spider's webs inadequate to control the dominant facts.

We have to deal with an office that owes its existence to Congress and that Congress may abolish tomorrow. Its duration and the pay attached to it while it lasts depend on Congress alone. Congress alone confers on the President the power to appoint to it and at any time may transfer the power to other hands. With such power over its own creation, I have no more trouble in believing that Congress has power to prescribe a term of life for it free from any interference than I have in accepting the undoubted power of Congress to decree its end. I have equally little trouble in accepting its power to prolong the tenure of an incumbent until Congress or the Senate shall have assented to his removal. The duty of the President to see that the laws be executed is a duty that does not go beyond the laws or require him to achieve more than Congress sees fit to leave within his power.

The separate opinion of MR. JUSTICE MCREYNOLDS.

[In this 62-page dissent, McReynolds reviews the succession of statutes that have limited the President's power of removal: civil service reforms; the laws creating commissions, boards, the Comptroller General, and the Board of Tax Appeals; and the general history of congressional control over postal affairs. He also refutes Taft's claim that a majority of the First Congress believed that the President's removal power was a constitutional grant. McReynolds pulls together his critique in the following section:]

X.

Congress has long and vigorously asserted its

right to restrict removals and there has been no common executive practice based upon a contrary view. The President has often removed, and it is admitted that he may remove, with either the express or implied assent of Congress; but the present theory is that he may override the declared will of that body. This goes far beyond any practice heretofore approved or followed; it conflicts with the history of the Constitution, with the ordinary rules of interpretation, and with the construction approved by Congress since the beginning and emphatically sanctioned by this court. To adopt it would be revolutionary.

MR. JUSTICE BRANDEIS, dissenting.

[Brandeis followed with a 56-page dissent, spelling out in great detail the power of Congress to fix the tenure of inferior officers and to limit the President's power of removal. Some of the statutes provided that removal shall be made only for specified causes. Others provided for removal only after a hearing. Congress also passed legislation restricting the President's power of nomination.]

. . .

The separation of the powers of government did not make each branch completely autonomous. It left each, in some measure, dependent upon the others, as it left to each power to exercise, in some respects, functions in their nature executive, legislative and judicial. Obviously the President cannot secure full execution of the laws, if Congress denies to him adequate means of doing so. Full execution may be defeated because Congress declines to create offices indispensable for that purpose. Or, because Congress, having created the office, declines to make the indispensable appropriation. Or, because Congress, having both created the office and made the appropriation, prevents, by restrictions which it imposes, the appointment of officials who in quality and character are indispensable to the efficient execution of the law.

. . .

Checks and balances were established in order that this should be "a government of laws and not of men." ... The doctrine of the separation of powers was adopted by the Convention of 1787, not to promote efficiency but to preclude the exercise of arbitrary power. The purpose was, not to avoid friction, but, by means of the inevitable friction incident to the distribution of the governmental powers among three departments, to save the people from autocracy....

Humphrey's Executor v. United States

295 U.S. 602 (1935)

William E. Humphrey, nominated by President Hoover for the Federal Trade Commission in 1931, was confirmed by the Senate. The Federal Trade Commission (FTC) Act allowed the President to remove a commissioner only for "inefficiency, neglect of duty, or malfeasance in office." In 1933 President Franklin D. Roosevelt asked Humphrey to resign, explaining that the administration's policies could be carried out only with commissioners supportive of Roosevelt's goals. When Humphrey refused to resign, Roosevelt removed him for policy reasons rather than the "for cause" reasons specified in the FTC Act. Humphrey's heirs brought suit to recover his salary. In this decision, the Court reviews and qualifies its broad ruling in *Myers* regarding the scope of the President's removal power.

MR. JUSTICE SUTHERLAND delivered the opinion of the Court.

Plaintiff brought suit in the Court of Claims against the United States to recover a sum of money alleged to be due the deceased for salary as a Federal Trade Commissioner from October 8, 1933, when the President undertook to remove him from office, to the time of his death on February 14, 1934....

William E. Humphrey, the decedent, on December 10, 1931, was nominated by President Hoover to succeed himself as a member of the Federal Trade Commission, and was confirmed by the United States Senate. He was duly commissioned for a term of seven years expiring September 25, 1938; and, after taking the required oath of office, entered upon his duties. On July 25, 1933, President Roosevelt addressed a letter to the commissioner asking for his resignation, on the ground "that the aims and purposes of the Administration with respect to the work of the Commission can be carried out most effectively with personnel of my own selection," but disclaiming any reflection upon the commissioner personally or upon his services. The commissioner replied, asking time to consult his friends. After some further correspondence upon the subject, the President on August 31, 1933, wrote the commissioner expressing the hope that the resignation would be forthcoming and saying:

"You will, I know, realize that I do not feel that your mind and my mind go along together on either the policies or the administering of the Federal Trade Commission, and, frankly, I think it is best for the people of this country that I should have a full confidence."

The commissioner declined to resign; and on October 7, 1933, the President wrote him:

"Effective as of this date you are hereby removed from the office of Commissioner of the Federal Trade Commission."

Humphrey never acquiesced in this action, but continued thereafter to insist that he was still a member of the commission, entitled to perform its duties and receive the compensation provided by law at the rate of $10,000 per annum....

The Federal Trade Commission Act ... creates a commission of five members to be appointed by the President by and with the advice and consent of the Senate, and § 1 provides *[that a commissioner]* "may be removed by the President for inefficiency, neglect of duty, or malfeasance in office...."

First. The question first to be considered is whether, by the provisions of § 1 of the Federal Trade Commission Act already quoted, the President's power is limited to removal for the specific causes enumerated therein. The negative contention of the government is based principally upon the decision of this court in *Shurtleff* v. *United States*, 189 U. S. 311. [*That case involved the President's power to remove a general appraiser of merchandise. An 1890 statute provided for the appointment of nine general appraisers of merchandise, who "may be removed from office at any time by the President for inefficiency, neglect of duty, or malfeasance in office." The President removed Shurtleff without giving a reason. The Court of Claims dismissed Shurtleff's petition to recover salary, upholding the President's power to remove for causes other than those stated in the law. The Supreme Court acknowledged that Congress can restrict the President's removal power to specified causes, but only if the statute used "plain language" to limit the President's general power of removal. An uncertainly in the 1890 statute was the lack of a fixed term for the general appraiser.*]

... The situation here presented is plainly and wholly different. The statute fixes a term of office, in accordance with many precedents. The first com-

missioners appointed are to continue in office for terms of three, four, five, six, and seven years, respectively; and their successors are to be appointed for terms of seven years—any commissioner being subject to removal by the President for inefficiency, neglect of duty, or malfeasance in office. The words of the act are definite and unambiguous.

... [I]f the intention of Congress that no removal should be made during the specified term except for one or more of the enumerated causes were not clear upon the face of the statute, as we think it is, it would be made clear by a consideration of the character of the commission and the legislative history which accompanied and preceded the passage of the act.

The commission is to be non-partisan; and it must, from the very nature of its duties, act with entire impartiality. It is charged with the enforcement of no policy except the policy of the law. Its duties are neither political nor executive, but predominantly quasi-judicial and quasi-legislative....

[The legislative reports in both Houses reflected the view that a fixed term was necessary to the effective and fair administration of the law. The term of office at seven years anticipated commissioners who would have experience and knowledge of both the public requirements and the practical affairs of industry. The long terms gave commissioners an opportunity to acquire expertise. Unlike the Bureau of Corporations (an executive subdivision in the Department of Commerce abolished by the act), the FTC would be independent and less open to the suspicion of partisan direction.]

The debates in both houses demonstrate that the prevailing view was that the commission was not to be "subject to anybody in the government but ... only to the people of the United States"; free from "political domination or control" or the "probability or possibility of such a thing"; to be "separate and apart from any existing department of the government—not subject to the orders of the President."

More to the same effect appears in the debates, which were long and thorough and contain nothing to the contrary....

Thus, the language of the act, the legislative reports, and the general purposes of the legislation as reflected by the debates, all combine to demonstrate the Congressional intent to create a body of experts who shall gain experience by length of service—a body which shall be independent of executive authority, *except in its selection,* and free to exercise its judgment without the leave or hindrance of any other official or any department of the government. To the accomplishment of these purposes, it is clear that Congress was of opinion that length and certainty of tenure would vitally contribute. And to hold that, nevertheless, the members of the commission continue in office at the mere will of the President, might be to thwart, in large measure, the very ends which Congress sought to realize by definitely fixing the term of office.

We conclude that the intent of the act is to limit the executive power of removal to the causes enumerated, the existence of none of which is claimed here; and we pass to the second question.

Second. To support its contention that the removal provision of § 1, as we have just construed it, is an unconstitutional interference with the executive power of the President, the government's chief reliance is *Myers* v. *United States,* 272 U.S. 52 ... [T]he narrow point actually decided was only that the President had power to remove a postmaster of the first class, without the advice and consent of the Senate as required by act of Congress....

The office of a postmaster is so essentially unlike the office now involved that the decision in the *Myers* case cannot be accepted as controlling our decision here. A postmaster is an executive officer restricted to the performance of executive functions. He is charged with no duty at all related to either the legislative or judicial power....

The Federal Trade Commission is an administrative body created by Congress to carry into effect legislative policies embodied in the statute in accordance with the legislative standard therein prescribed, and to perform other specified duties as a legislative or as a judicial aid. Such a body cannot in any proper sense be characterized as an arm or an eye of the executive. Its duties are performed without executive leave and, in the contemplation of the statute, must be free from executive control. In administering the provisions of the statute ... the commission acts in part quasi-legislatively and in part quasi-judicially. In making investigations and reports thereon for the information of Congress under

§ 6, in aid of the legislative power, it acts as a legislative agency....

We think it plain under the Constitution that illimitable power of removal is not possessed by the President in respect of officers of the character of those just named ...

... A reading of the debates [*in 1789*] shows that the President's illimitable power of removal was not considered in respect of other than executive officers....

The result of what we now have said is this: Whether the power of the President to remove an officer shall prevail over the authority of Congress to condition the power by fixing a definite term and precluding a removal except for cause, will depend upon the character of the office; the *Myers* decision, affirming the power of the President alone to make the removal, is confined to purely executive officers; and as to officers of the kind here under consideration, we hold that no removal can be made during the prescribed term for which the officer is appointed, except for one or more of the causes named in the applicable statute.

To the extent that, between the decision in the *Myers* case, which sustains the unrestrictable power of the President to remove purely executive officers, and our present decision that such power does not extend to an office such as that here involved, there shall remain a field of doubt, we leave such cases as may fall within it for future consideration and determination as they may arise.

In accordance with the foregoing, the questions submitted are answered.

Question No. 1, Yes. Question No. 2, Yes.

Mr. Justice McReynolds agrees that both questions should be answered in the affirmative. A separate opinion in *Myers* v. *United States,* 272 U. S. 178, states his views concerning the power of the President to remove appointees.

E. DELEGATION OF LEGISLATIVE POWER

The boundaries between the legislative and executive branches are often obscured by large grants of power delegated by Congress. This delegation supposedly violates a fundamental principle, dating back to John Locke. The legislature "cannot transfer the power of making laws to any other hands, for it being but a delegated power from the people, they who have it cannot pass it over to others." John Locke, Second Treatise on Civil Government, § 141. This concept is embodied in the ancient maxim *delegata potestas non potest delegari* ("delegated power cannot be delegated").

The non-delegation principle is essential at least in preventing Congress from transferring its legislative power to private groups. In 1936 the Supreme Court struck down a statute partly because it delegated power to representatives of the coal industry to set up a code of mandatory regulations. This

Standardless Delegations

Broad delegations have been upheld in many cases because of the structure provided for independent commissions. They operate on a multimember (collegial) basis, which supplies a check on possible abuses. Moreover, the term of commissioners are lengthy and staggered. Congress limits the number of commissioners who may belong to the same political party and restricts the ability of the President to remove commissioners. Finally, standardless delegations have been upheld when the accumulated customs of a regulated industry and the practices developed by states have served to narrow the discretion of a federal agency. Fahey v. Mallonee, 332 U.S. 245, 250, 253 (1947). See also Chapter 5 of Louis Fisher, The Politics of Shared Power (1998).

Standardless delegations have been upheld when the legislative history supplies guidelines for administrative action. A massive delegation of wage-price controls to President Nixon in 1970 was justified by guidelines placed in committee reports and the legislative history. A three-judge court claimed that whether legislative purposes are included in committee reports or the public law "is largely a matter of drafting style." Amalgamated Meat Cutters & Butcher Work. v. Connally, 337 F.Supp. 737, 750 (D.D.C. 1971) (three-judge court). However, agencies are not as tightly bound by legislative history and nonstatutory controls.

was "legislative delegation in its most obnoxious form; for it is not even delegation to an official or an official body, presumptively disinterested, but to private persons whose interests may be and often are adverse to the interests of others in the same business." Carter v. Carter Coal Co., 298 U.S. 238, 311 (1936).

With the exception of two cases handed down in 1935, Congress has encountered little opposition from the courts in delegating legislative power to the President, executive agencies, and independent commissions. In sustaining these delegations, the judiciary typically waxes eloquent about the serious breach were Congress ever to transfer its legislative power to other parties, after which it finds a way to uphold the delegation. Field v. Clark, 143 U.S. 649, 692 (1891) and HAMPTON & CO. v. UNITED STATES 276 U.S. 394, 406 (1928).

The courts justify vast delegations of legislative power after satisfying themselves that the powers are confined either by congressional guidelines or procedural safeguards. Statutory guidelines are often absent, however, when Congress orders the Interstate Commerce Commission to protect the "public interest," directs the Federal Trade Commission to police "unfair methods of competition," supplies the standard of "public convenience, interest, or necessity" for the Federal Communications Commission, and requires the Securities and Exchange Commission to ensure that corporations do not "unduly or unnecessarily complicate the structure" or "unfairly or inequitably distribute voting power among security holders."[11] The structure of these commissions supplies some built-in safeguards (see box).

The NIRA Cases

On two occasions the Supreme Court struck down a delegation of legislative authority to the President. Both cases involved the National Industrial Recovery Act (NIRA), which authorized industrial and trade associations to draw up codes that minimized competition, raised prices, and restricted production. If the President found the codes unacceptable, he could prescribe his own and enforce

---

11. The "public interest" guideline was upheld in ICC v. Goodrich Transit Co., 224 U.S. 194, 214–15 (1912), Intermountain Rate Cases, 234 U.S. 476, 486–88 (1914), Avent v. United States, 266 U.S. 127, 130 (1924), and N.Y. Central Securities Co. v. United States, 287 U.S. 12, 24–25 (1932). "Unfair method of competition" passed muster in FTC v. Gratz, 253 U.S. 421, 427–28 (1920), while "public convenience" survived judicial scrutiny in FCC v. Pottsville Broadcasting Co., 309 U.S. 134, 137–88 (1940). The SEC guideline was upheld in American Power Co. v. SEC, 329 U.S. 90, 104–06 (1946).

them as law. In the first case, the Court held that Congress had failed to establish guidelines or congressional policy to control the President's actions. Panama Refining v. Ryan, 293 U.S. 388 (1935). Although Justice Cardozo argued in the first decision that Congress had supplied adequate standards, in the second he protested: "This is delegation running riot." SCHECHTER CORP. v. UNITED STATES, 295 U.S. at 553. The drafting of the NIRA was dominated by industries and trade associations; executive officials appeared to have little interest in constitutional questions or procedural safeguards. Peter H. Irons, The New Deal Lawyers 22–107 (1982).

During the course of this litigation, the Court discovered that the government had brought an indictment and taken an appeal only to learn, to its embarrassment, that the regulation justifying this action had been repealed by an executive order. Panama Refining Co. v. Ryan, 293 U.S. at 412–13. The House Judiciary Committee in 1935 condemned the "utter chaos" regarding the publication and distribution of administrative rules and pronouncements. H. Rept. No. 280, 74th Cong., 1st Sess. 1–2 (1935). Congress passed legislation that year to provide for publication in a "Federal Register" of all presidential and agency documents having the effect of law. 49 Stat. 500 (1935).

Other reforms are embodied in the Administrative Procedure Act (APA) of 1946, which establishes standards for agency rulemaking to assure fairness and openness. Agencies are required to give notice and a hearing before issuing a rule or regulation. Findings of fact are supplied for the record; procedures exist for appeal. Through such procedural standards, Congress tries to eliminate or minimize the opportunity for executive caprice and arbitrariness. The APA relies on the doctrine of separated powers by prohibiting investigative or prosecuting personnel from participating in agency adjudications. 5 U.S.C. §§ 553–54 (2000).

The standards for delegation need not be stricter when the power to tax is involved. Skinner v. Mid-America Pipeline Co., 490 U.S. 212 (1989). Also in 1989, all nine Justices rejected a claim that Congress had delegated excessively in creating the U.S. Sentencing Commission. Mistretta v. United States, 488 U.S. 361 (1989). Unanimous decisions in 1991 and 1996 dismissed the argument that Congress had unconstitutionally delegated its legislative power. Touby v. United States, 500 U.S. 160 (1991); Loving v. United States, 517 U.S. 748 (1996).

In 1999, the D.C. Circuit held that language in the Clean Air Act resulted in an unconstitutional delegation of legislative power to the Environmental Protection Agency. American Trucking Associations v. U.S. E.P.A., 175 F.3d 1027 (D.C. Cir. 1999). After the EPA issued final rules, the D.C. Circuit could not yet determine whether the nondelegation doctrine had been satisfied. American Trucking Associations, Inc. v. E.P.A., 195 F.3d 4 (D.C. Cir. 1999). When the Supreme Court decided the case in 2001, it ruled that the transfer of authority to EPA was not an unconstitutional delegation of legislative power. Whitman v. American Trucking Associations, 531 U.S. 457 (2001).

Presidential Legislation

Agency regulations are not supposed to be a substitute for the general policy-making that Congress supplies in the form of a public law. 6 Op. Att'y Gen. 10 (1853). Agency rulemaking draws its authority from power granted directly or indirectly by Congress.[12] The situation may be different when the President "legislates" by issuing executive orders and proclamations. Here the President draws not necessarily on statutory authority but on power he believes is his under the Constitution.

Executive orders and proclamations are subject to legislative and judicial controls. When Congress objected to an executive order used by President Nixon to rejuvenate the Subversive Activities Control Board, Congress used its power of the purse to prohibit the agency from using any funds to carry

---

12. Chrysler Corp. v. Brown, 441 U.S. 281, 306–08 (1979). See Lincoln Electric Co. v. Commissioner of Int. Rev., 190 F.2d 326, 330 (6th Cir. 1951); American Broadcasting Co. v. United States, 110 F.Supp. 374, 384 (S.D. N.Y. 1953), aff'd, 347 U.S. 284 (1954); and Independent Meat Packers Ass'n v. Butz, 526 F.2d 228, 234–36 (8th Cir. 1975), cert. denied, 424 U.S. 966 (1976).

out the order. As a result, the agency eventually disappeared. Fisher, Constitutional Conflicts between Congress and the President, 112–13. The federal courts have also been active in declaring proclamations and executive orders illegal.[13]

Hampton & Co. v. United States

276 U.S. 394 (1928)

The Tariff Act of 1922 empowered the President to increase or decrease duties in order to equalize the differences between the costs of production at home and the costs in competing foreign countries. The Act established certain criteria to be taken into account in determining the differences, fixed the limits for increases and decreases, and required the Tariff Commission to first investigate before any duties could be changed. The major issue before the Court was whether the Act constituted an invalid delegation of legislative power to the President. J.W. Hampton, Jr. & Company, an importer, challenged the Constitutionality of this statute.

MR. CHIEF JUSTICE TAFT delivered the opinion of the Court.

J. W. Hampton, Jr., & Company made an importation into New York of barium dioxide, which the collector of customs assessed at the dutiable rate of six cents per pound. This was two cents per pound more than that fixed by statute.... The rate was raised by the collector by virtue of the proclamation of the President ... issued under, and by authority of, § 315 of Title III of the Tariff Act of September 21, 1922 ... which is the so-called flexible tariff provision. Protest was made and an appeal was taken under § 514, ... The pertinent parts of § 315 of Title III ... are as follows:

"Section 315(a). That in order to regulate the foreign commerce of the United States and to put into force and effect the policy of the Congress by this Act intended, whenever the President, upon investigation of the differences in costs of production of articles wholly or in part the growth or product of the United States and of like or similar articles wholly or in part the growth or product of competing foreign countries, shall find it thereby shown that the duties fixed in this Act do not equalize the said differences in costs of production in the United States and the principal competing country he shall, by such investigation, ascertain said differences and determine and proclaim the changes in classifications or increases or decreases in any rate of duty provided in

this Act shown by said ascertained differences in such costs of production necessary to equalize the same. Thirty days after the date of such proclamation or proclamations, such changes in classification shall take effect, ... the total increase or decrease of such rates of duty shall not exceed 50 per centum of the rates specified in Title I of this Act, or in any amendatory Act....

"(c). That in ascertaining the differences in costs of production, under the provisions of subdivisions (a) and (b) of this section, the President, in so far as he finds it practicable, shall take into consideration (1) the differences in conditions in production, including wages, costs of material, and other items in costs of production of such or similar articles in the United States and in competing foreign countries; (2) the differences in the wholesale selling prices of domestic and foreign articles in the principal markets of the United States; (3) advantages granted to a foreign producer by a foreign government, or by a person, partnership, corporation, or association in a foreign country; and (4) any other advantages or disadvantages in competition.

"Investigations to assist the President in ascertaining differences in costs of production under this section shall be made by the United States Tariff Commission, and no proclamation shall be issued under this section until such investigation shall have been made. The commission shall give reasonable public notice of its hearings and shall give reasonable

13. Chamber of Commerce of U.S. v. Reich, 74 F.3d 1322 (D.C. Cir. 1996); Independent Gasoline Marketers Council v. Duncan, 492 F.Supp. 614, 620–21 (D.D.C. 1980); Kaplan v. Johnson, 409 F.Supp. 190, 206 (N.D.Ill. 1976); Cole v. Young, 351 U.S. 536, 555 (1956); Youngstown Co. v. Sawyer, 343 U.S. 579 (1952); Schechter Corp. v. United States, 295 U.S. 495, 525–26 (1935); Panama Refining Co. v. Ryan, 293 U.S. 388, 433 (1935); United States v. Symonds, 120 U.S. 46 (1887); Little v. Barreme, 6 U.S. (2 Cr.) 170 (1804). See Adam L. Warber, Executive Orders and the Modern Presidency (2006); Phillip J. Cooper, By Order of the President (2002); Kenneth R. Mayer, With the Stroke of a Pen (2001); Louis Fisher, Constitutional Conflicts Between Congress and the President 102–14 (2007).

opportunity to parties interested to be present, to produce evidence, and to be heard. The commission is authorized to adopt such reasonable procedure, rules, and regulations as it may deem necessary."

. . .

[*The petitioners*] argue that the section is invalid in that it is a delegation to the President of the legislative power, which by Article I, § 1 of the Constitution, is vested in Congress, the power being that declared in § 8 of Article I, that the Congress shall have power to lay and collect taxes, duties, imposts and excises....

First. It seems clear what Congress intended by § 315. Its plan was to secure by law the imposition of customs duties on articles of imported merchandise which should equal the difference between the cost of producing in a foreign country the articles in question and laying them down for sale in the United States, and the cost of producing and selling like or similar articles in the United States, so that the duties not only secure revenue but at the same time enable domestic producers to compete on terms of equality with foreign producers in the markets of the United States. It may be that it is difficult to fix with exactness this difference, but the difference which is sought in the statute is perfectly clear and perfectly intelligible. Because of the difficulty in practically determining what that difference is, Congress seems to have doubted that the information in its possession was such as to enable it to make the adjustment accurately, and also to have apprehended that with changing conditions the difference might vary in such a way that some readjustments would be necessary to give effect to the principle on which the statute proceeds....

The well-known maxim *"Delegata potestas non potest delegari,"* applicable to the law of agency in the general and common law, is well understood and has had wider application in the construction of our Federal and State Constitutions than it has in private law. The Federal Constitution and State Constitutions of this country divide the governmental power into three branches.... [I]t is a breach of the National fundamental law if Congress gives up its legislative power and transfers it to the President, or to the Judicial branch, or if by law it attempts to invest itself or its members with either executive power or judicial power....

The field of Congress involves all and many varieties of legislative action, and Congress has found it frequently necessary to use officers of the Executive Branch, within defined limits, to secure the exact effect intended by its acts of legislation, by vesting discretion in such officers to make public regulations interpreting a statute and directing the details of its execution, even to the extent of providing for penalizing a breach of such regulations....

Congress may feel itself unable conveniently to determine exactly when its exercise of the legislative power should become effective, because dependent on future conditions, and it may leave the determination of such time to the decision of an Executive, ...

Again, one of the great functions conferred on Congress by the Federal Constitution is the regulation of interstate commerce and rates to be exacted by interstate carriers for the passenger and merchandise traffic. The rates to be fixed are myriad. If Congress were to be required to fix every rate, it would be impossible to exercise the power at all....

... If Congress shall lay down by legislative act an intelligible principle to which the person or body authorized to fix such rates is directed to conform, such legislative action is not a forbidden delegation of legislative power....

... What the President was required to do was merely in execution of the act of Congress. It was not the making of law. He was the mere agent of the law-making department to ascertain and declare the event upon which its expressed will was to take effect.

. . .

Affirmed.

Schechter Corp. v. United States

295 U.S. 495 (1935)

In *Panama Refining Co. v. Ryan*, 293 U.S. 388 (1935), the Supreme Court struck down part of the National Industrial Recovery Act as an invalid delegation of legislative power from Congress to the President. The statute placed upon industrial and trade associations the responsibility for drawing up codes to minimize competition, raise prices, and restrict production. If the President regarded the codes as unacceptable, he could prescribe his own codes and enforce them by law. *Panama Refining* held that a section of the statute governing controls on petroleum production failed to establish criteria to govern the President's course. Only Justice Cardozo dissented. In *Schechter,* the "sick chicken" case, the Court examines the constitutionality of the rest of the statute.

Mr. Chief Justice Hughes delivered the opinion of the Court.

Petitioners ... were convicted in the District Court of the United States for the Eastern District of New York on eighteen counts of an indictment charging violations of what is known as the "Live Poultry Code," and on an additional count for conspiracy to commit such violations. By demurrer to the indictment and appropriate motions on the trial, the defendants contended (1) that the Code had been adopted pursuant to an unconstitutional delegation by Congress of legislative power; (2) that it attempted to regulate intrastate transactions which lay outside the authority of Congress; and (3) that in certain provisions it was repugnant to the due process clause of the Fifth Amendment.

[*The Court described New York City as the largest live-poultry market in the United States, with 96 percent of the poultry coming from other states. The Schechter Corporation usually purchased their live poultry from a market in New York City or at the railroad terminals serving the City, but occasionally they bought in Philadelphia. They trucked the poultry to their slaughterhouse markets in Brooklyn for sale to retail dealers and butchers. They did not sell the poultry in interstate commerce.*]

The "Live Poultry Code" was promulgated under § 3 of the National Industrial Recovery Act. That section ... authorizes the President to approve "codes of fair competition." Such a code may be approved for a trade or industry, upon application by one or more trade or industrial associations or groups, if the President finds (1) that such associations or groups "impose no inequitable restrictions on admission to membership therein and are truly representative," and (2) that such codes are not designed "to promote monopolies or to eliminate or oppress small enterprises and will not operate to discriminate against them, and will tend to effectuate the policy" of Title I of the Act. Such codes "shall not permit monopolies or monopolistic practices." ... Where such a code has not been approved, the President may prescribe one, either on his own motion or on complaint. Violation of any provision of a code (so approved or prescribed) "in any transaction in or affecting interstate or foreign commerce" is made a misdemeanor punishable by a fine of not more than

$500 for each offense, and each day the violation continues is to be deemed a separate offense.

The "Live Poultry Code" was approved by the President on April 13, 1934....

[*The Code fixed the number of hours for workdays, the minimum pay, the minimum number of employees, and prohibited the employment of any person under 16 years of age. The Code was administered through an "industry advisory committee" selected by trade associations and members of the industry. A "code supervisor" was appointed with the approval of the committee by agreement between the Secretary of Agriculture and the Administrator for Industrial Recovery.*]

First. Two preliminary points are stressed by the Government with respect to the appropriate approach to the important questions presented. We are told that the provision of the statute authorizing the adoption of codes must be viewed in the light of the grave national crisis with which Congress was confronted. Undoubtedly, the conditions to which power is addressed are always to be considered when the exercise of power is challenged. Extraordinary conditions may call for extraordinary remedies. But the argument necessarily stops short of an attempt to justify action which lies outside the sphere of constitutional authority. Extraordinary conditions do not create or enlarge constitutional power. The Constitution established a national government with powers deemed to be adequate, as they have proved to be both in war and peace, but these powers of the national government are limited by the constitutional grants....

The further point is urged that the national crisis demanded a broad and intensive coöperative effort by those engaged in trade and industry, and that this necessary coöperation was sought to be fostered by permitting them to initiate the adoption of codes. But the statutory plan is not simply one for voluntary effort. It does not seek merely to endow voluntary trade or industrial associations or groups with privileges or immunities. It involves the coercive exercise of the lawmaking power....

Second. The question of the delegation of legislative power. We recently had occasion to review the pertinent decisions and the general principles which govern the determination of this question. *Panama Refining Co.* v. *Ryan,* 293 U.S. 388.... The Congress is not permitted to abdicate or to transfer to others the essential legislative functions with which it is thus vested. We have repeatedly recognized the necessity of adapting legislation to complex conditions involving a host of details with which the national legislature cannot deal directly. We pointed out in the *Panama Company* case that the Constitution has never been regarded as denying to Congress the necessary resources of flexibility and practicality, which will enable it to perform its function in laying down policies and establishing standards, while leaving to selected instrumentalities the making of subordinate rules within prescribed limits and the determination of facts to which the policy as declared by the legislature is to apply. But we said that the constant recognition of the necessity and validity of such provisions, and the wide range of administrative authority which has been developed by means of them, cannot be allowed to obscure the limitations of the authority to delegate, if our constitutional system is to be maintained. *Id.*, p. 421.

Accordingly, we look to the statute to see whether Congress has overstepped these limitations, — whether Congress in authorizing "codes of fair competition" has itself established the standards of legal obligation, thus performing its essential legislative function, or, by the failure to enact such standards, has attempted to transfer that function to others.

The aspect in which the question is now presented is distinct from that which was before us in the case of the *Panama Company*. There, the subject of the statutory prohibition was defined. National Industrial Recovery Act, § 9 (c). That subject was the transportation in interstate and foreign commerce of petroleum and petroleum products which are produced or withdrawn from storage in excess of the amount permitted by state authority. The question was with respect to the range of discretion given to the President in prohibiting that transportation. *Id.*, pp. 414, 415, 430. As to the "codes of fair competition," under § 3 of the Act, the question is more fundamental. It is whether there is any adequate definition of the subject to which the codes are to be addressed.

What is meant by "fair competition" as the term is used in the Act? Does it refer to a category established in the law, and is the authority to make codes limited accordingly? Or is it used as a convenient designation for whatever set of laws the formulators of a code for a particular trade or industry may propose and the President may approve (subject to certain restrictions), or the President may himself prescribe, as being wise and beneficent provisions for the government of the trade or industry in order to

accomplish the broad purposes of rehabilitation, correction and expansion which are stated in the first section of Title I?

The Act does not define "fair competition." ...

... [W]ould it be seriously contended that Congress could delegate its legislative authority to trade or industrial associations or groups so as to empower them to enact the laws they deem to be wise and beneficent for the rehabilitation and expansion of their trade or industries? Could trade or industrial associations or groups be constituted legislative bodies for that purpose because such associations or groups are familiar with the problems of their enterprises? And, could an effort of that sort be made valid by such a preface of generalities as to permissible aims as we find in section 1 of title I? The answer is obvious. Such a delegation of legislative power is unknown to our law and is utterly inconsistent with the constitutional prerogatives and duties of Congress.

... Section 3 of the Recovery Act is without precedent. It supplies no standards for any trade, industry or activity. It does not undertake to prescribe rules of conduct to be applied to particular states of fact determined by appropriate administrative procedure. Instead of prescribing rules of conduct, it authorizes the making of codes to prescribe them. For that legislative undertaking, § 3 sets up no standards, aside from the statement of the general aims of rehabilitation, correction and expansion described in section one. In view of the scope of that broad declaration, and of the nature of the few restrictions that are imposed, the discretion of the President in approving or prescribing codes, and thus enacting laws for the government of trade and industry throughout the country, is virtually unfettered. We think that the code-making authority thus conferred is an unconstitutional delegation of legislative power.

· · ·

Mr. Justice Cardozo, concurring.

The delegated power of legislation which has found expression in this code is not canalized within banks that keep it from overflowing. It is unconfined and vagrant, if I may borrow my own words in an earlier opinion. *Panama Refining Co.* v. *Ryan*, 293 U.S. 388, 440.

This court has held that delegation may be unlawful though the act to be performed is definite and single, if the necessity, time and occasion of performance have been left in the end to the discretion of the delegate. *Panama Refining Co.* v. *Ryan, supra.* I thought that ruling went too far. I pointed out in an opinion that there had been "no grant to the Executive of any roving commission to inquire into evils and then, upon discovering them, do anything he pleases." ... Here, in the case before us, is an attempted delegation not confined to any single act nor to any class or group of acts identified or described by reference to a standard. Here in effect is a roving commission to inquire into evils and upon discovery correct them.

... This is delegation running riot. No such plenitude of power is susceptible of transfer....

I am authorized to state that Mr. Justice Stone joins in this opinion.

F. CONGRESSIONAL OVERSIGHT

Congress maintains control over delegated power through a variety of methods: the power to appropriate funds, changes in authorization language, reliance on nonstatutory controls, and different forms of the "legislative veto" (which retains some vitality even after the Supreme Court declared it unconstitutional in 1983). Another form of control, the power to investigate, is covered in the next section.

Power of the Purse

In Federalist No. 58, James Madison regarded the power of the purse as the "most complete and effectual weapon with which any constitution can arm the immediate representatives of the people, for obtaining a redress of every grievance, and for carrying into effect every just and salutary measure." Article I, Section 9, of the Constitution places this weapon squarely in the hands of Congress: "No Money shall be drawn from the Treasury, but in Consequence of Appropriations made by Law."

There are relatively few restrictions on this power of the purse. Congress cannot lawfully use its funding power to establish a religion.[14] It may not diminish the compensation of federal judges. It may neither increase nor decrease the compensation of the President during his term in office. It may not include language in appropriations bills to deny funds to named "subversives," for such legislative punishment is a bill of attainder prohibited by Article III, Section 3. United States v. Lovett, 328 U.S. 303 (1946); Blitz v. Donovan, 538 F.Supp. 1119 (D.D.C. 1982). A proviso in an appropriations bill may not interfere with the President's power to issue a pardon or prescribe for the judiciary the effect of a pardon. United States v. Klein, 13 Wall. 128 (1872); Hart v. United States, 118 U.S. 62 (1886).

For the most part, Congress may invoke the power of the purse to control almost every facet of executive activity. Appropriations can be lump sum or itemized. If lump sum (to give administrators discretion), congressional committees can insist on an informal veto over certain agency actions. Congress can attach "riders" or conditions to appropriations bills to prohibit the use of funds for specified purposes. Executive officials may object to "micromanagement" by legislators, but Congress has the constitutional authority to control administrative activity in minute detail.

Presidents share the power of the purse in several ways. The Budget and Accounting Act of 1921 directed the President to submit a national budget each year. Through this submission the President has an important means of setting the legislative agenda for Congress. Moreover, Presidents and their assistants are generally given some discretion in withholding funds (impoundment), transferring funds from one appropriation account to another, and "reprogramming" funds within an account. Louis Fisher, Presidential Spending Power (1975).

In response to abuses by the Nixon administration, Congress passed the Impoundment Control Act of 1974 to limit presidential actions to two types of impoundment: *rescission* (terminating funds),

---

14. U.S. Constitution, Amend. I; Flast v. Cohen, 392 U.S. 83, 104–05 (1968). However, plaintiffs who challenge federal assistance to religious institutions may be unable to establish standing as a litigant; Valley Forge College v. Americans United, 454 U.S. 464 (1982).

The Item Veto: Will It Return?

By a 6–3 vote, the Supreme Court decided that the Line Item Veto Act of 1996 was unconstitutional because it violated the Presentment Clause. Clinton v. City of New York, 524 U.S. 417 (1998). That central part of the decision suggests that the issue was essentially procedural: to cancel law, the two branches have to follow the standard legislative process, including presentment of a bill to the President for his signature or veto. In a sense, the Court adhered to language in *Chadha*: "Amendment and repeal of statutes, no less than enactment, must conform with Art. I." 462 U.S. at 954. But *Chadha* was about Congress intervening in the executive process without complying with the lawmaking requirements of bicameralism and presentment. The item veto statute represented a grant of power to the President with no congressional interference other than an opportunity to disapprove the President's cancellations, and the disapproval measure complied fully with bicameralism and presentment.

The Court admitted, as it had to, that previous legislation had delegated to the President substantial authority to suspend and alter statutory language, particularly in tariffs and duties. Conceding the point, the Court noted that the statutes identified "all relate to foreign trade, and this Court has recognized that in the foreign affairs arena" the President has considerable discretion. The argument appears to turn from strict procedural matters (Presentment Clause) to the substance of law being altered (foreign versus domestic policy).

The Court ends by saying that any presidential power to alter legislation must come not by legislation but by constitutional amendment. However, there are a number of statutory options to create a new type of "item veto" that would comply fully with presentment. One is "separate enrollment" (breaking large appropriations bills into separate pieces). Another is to appropriate sums "not exceeding" a specified amount, allowing the President to withhold much or all of the money. Another option: a statute directs the President to carry out a program unless he certifies that it is unnecessary or not in the national interest.

which requires the approval of Congress within 45 days of continuous session, and *deferral* (delay of spending), subject to disapproval by either House. When the legislative veto was invalidated by INS v. CHADHA, 462 U.S. 919, in 1983, it was later decided that the President's authority to make policy deferrals disappeared with the legislative veto because the authority and the veto were inseverable. City of New Haven v. United States, 809 F.2d 900 (D.C. Cir. 1987). This decision restricted the President to submitting routine deferrals to Congress.

The Item Veto

In 1996, Congress passed the Line Item Veto Act to strengthen the President's power to rescind funds. Instead of requiring the approval of Congress (the procedure established in 1974), presidential rescissions would take effect within 30 days unless Congress passed a bill or joint resolution of disapproval. The President could then veto the disapproval legislation, forcing each House to muster a two-thirds majority to override the veto. It is actually a misnomer to call this statute an "item veto." Presidents would still be left with the same choice they have had since 1789: either sign the whole bill or veto the whole bill. If the President signed a bill, the new procedure became available to cancel not only appropriated funds but also new entitlements and limited tax benefits.

In 1997, a constitutional challenge to the statute was turned back by the Supreme Court, which held that the plaintiffs (members of Congress) lacked standing to bring the suit. Raines v. Byrd, 521 U.S. 811 (1997). (See the reading on this decision in Chapter 1.) A year later the Court granted standing to other plaintiffs and ruled that the Line Item Veto Act violated the Presentment Clause. CLINTON v. CITY OF NEW YORK, 524 U.S. 417 (1998). The item veto could return in some other form (see box). Both the House and the Senate were active in 2006 and 2007 in considering item veto legislation that would survive the *Clinton* test.

Enactment of Authorizations

With the exception of the offices of the President, the Vice President, and the Supreme Court, every other agency of government depends on Congress for its existence. In creating an agency, Congress determines its mission, structure, personnel, and ceilings for appropriations. It is for Congress to decide whether the agency has a permanent authorization or must return to Congress every year or every few years for reauthorization. Through its action on authorization bills, Congress can redirect agency activities, require reports to Congress, redefine missions, or reorganize the agency out of existence.

Nonstatutory Controls

Although agencies are subject to authorization and appropriation actions through public law, much of the congressional control is maintained outside the statutory process. Committee reports, committee hearings, correspondence from review committees, and other nonstatutory techniques allow Congress to monitor and direct agency activity without passing another public law. Because these controls are informal and not legally binding, the system functions on a "keep the faith" attitude. Agencies receive lump-sum funds and broad authority from Congress; in return, they acquiesce to a multitude of nonstatutory controls. Agencies follow these controls for practical, not legal, reasons. Violation of congressional trust may result in budget cutbacks, restrictive statutory language, and line-item appropriations.

Legislative Vetoes

During the 1930s, executive officials wanted to "make law" without passage of a statute. President Hoover obtained authority to reorganize the executive branch without having to submit a bill to Congress for hearings, amendments, and enactment by both Houses. Congress agreed only on the condition that either House could reject a reorganization plan by passing a resolution of disapproval. Through this accommodation was born the "legislative veto." Congress experimented with the one-House veto, the two-House veto (passage of a concurrent resolution), and even a committee veto. Fisher, Constitutional Conflicts between Congress and the President, at 137–45 (5th ed.).

This procedure obviously departs from the Presentment Clause in Article I, Section 7, which provides that "Every Order, Resolution, or Vote to which the Concurrence of the Senate and House of Representatives may be necessary (except on a question of Adjournment)" shall be presented to the President. Legislative vetoes are not presented to the President. President Hoover accepted the compromise because it facilitated executive reorganization. This quid pro quo was extended to other areas, including immigration, arms sales, the war power, impoundment, and agency regulations. Eventually, the Justice Department and the White House decided that the bargain no longer favored the executive branch. A test case, involving an immigration statute, was soon on its way to the Supreme Court.

In the 1930s the executive branch had prevailed upon Congress to delegate discretionary authority over the deportation of aliens. Congress agreed to allow the Attorney General to suspend deportations provided that the suspensions were subject to a one-House legislative veto. Congress exercised this power on numerous occasions. The test case arose in 1975 when the House of Representatives disapproved the suspension of deportation for six aliens, including Jagdish Rai Chadha. After exhausting his administrative remedies in the Immigration and Naturalization Service, he won a court victory in the Ninth Circuit in 1980. The Supreme Court granted cert and twice heard the case on oral argument.

INS v. Chadha

In a sweeping decision issued in 1983, the Supreme Court declared the legislative veto unconstitutional. All legislative vetoes were unconstitutional because they violated the Presentment Clause. In

The Baker Accord

April 28, 1989

Dear Mr. Speaker:

Pursuant to the bipartisan agreement on Central America between the Executive and the Congress, the Congress has now voted to extend humanitarian assistance to the Nicaraguan Resistance at current levels through February 28, 1990. This assistance has been authorized and appropriated but will not be obligated beyond November 30, 1989, except in the context of consultation among the Executive, the Senate Majority and Minority leaders, the Speaker of the House of Representatives and the Majority and Minority leaders, and the relevant authorization and appropriation committees, and only if affirmed via letters from the Bipartisan Leadership of Congress and the relevant House and Senate authorization and appropriations committees.

This bipartisan accord on Central America represents a unique agreement between the Executive and Legislative Branches. Thus, it is the intention of the parties that this agreement in no way establishes any precedent for the Executive or the Legislative Branch regarding the authorization and appropriation process.

Sincerely yours,
James A. Baker, III

addition, the one-House veto was unconstitutional because it violated the principle of bicameralism (which requires action by both Houses). Chief Justice Burger, writing for the majority, said that whenever congressional action has the "purpose and effect of altering the legal rights, duties and relations of persons" outside the legislative branch, Congress must act through both Houses in a bill presented to the President. INS v. CHADHA, 462 U.S. 919 (1983).

The Court's opinion is shallow in many ways. It claimed that the convenience of the legislative veto could not overcome the framers' view that efficiency was not a primary objective or hallmark of democratic government, and yet the framers ranked efficiency highly. The Court also argued that the legislative veto threatened the independence of the President by evading his veto power, but Presidents encouraged the legislative veto to obtain greater authority. Under the legislative veto procedure, Congress could not amend a President's proposal. The general veto was therefore not needed for presidential self-defense. More importantly, the decision did not, and could not, eliminate the political conditions that gave rise to the legislative veto: the desire of executive officials for broad delegations of power, and the insistence of Congress that it control those delegations without having to pass another public law. The executive-legislative accommodations that prevailed before *Chadha* continue to exist, sometimes in forms that are indistinguishable from the legislative veto supposedly struck down by the Court (see Fisher reading).

Disputes after Chadha

In 1989, the Bush administration entered into an accommodation with Congress which was criticized as an unconstitutional legislative veto. To obtain funds for the Nicaraguan contras, Secretary of State James A. Baker, III agreed to give four committees of Congress and congressional leaders a veto power over the release of some of the funds. White House Counsel C. Boyden Gray objected that the agreement appeared to be unconstitutional under *Chadha,* as did former federal judge Robert H. Bork. However, Baker's agreement did not appear in a public law. It was an informal, nonstatutory, "side agreement" that is not covered by *Chadha* (see box). Four members of the House of Representatives challenged the "Baker Accord" as unconstitutional, but their suit was dismissed by a federal district court. Burton v. Baker, 723 F.Supp. 1550 (D.D.C. 1990).

In 1991, the Court relied on *Chadha* to strike down a statutory provision enacted by Congress that gave a board of review (composed of nine members of Congress) a veto over decisions made by a regional authority responsible for two airports serving the District of Columbia. The Court held that the veto power violated the doctrine of separation of powers. Metropolitan Washington Airports Auth. v. Noise Abatement Citizens, 501 U.S. 252 (1991). Congress enacted remedial legislation later that year, reconstituting the board of review and giving it the power to recommend but not to veto. The new statute authorized Congress to pass a joint resolution of disapproval to reject actions by the regional authority. Joint resolutions satisfy the requirements of *Chadha* (bicameralism and presentment). 105 Stat. 2197, Title VII (1991). This new law didn't satisfy the courts either. The D.C. Circuit held that the board of review acted as an agent of Congress and that it exercised federal power in violation of the separation of powers doctrine. When this ruling was appealed to the Supreme Court, cert was denied. Hechinger v. Metro. Wash. Airports Authority, 36 F.3d 97 (D.C. Cir. 1994), cert. denied, 513 U.S. 1126 (1995).

Clinton v. City of New York

524 U.S. 417 (1998)

After President Clinton had exercised his authority under the Line Item Veto Act by canceling certain items, two plaintiffs claiming injury challenged the constitutionality of the statute. A district court ruled that the Act's cancellation procedures violated the Presentment Clause. Having granted the plaintiffs standing, the Supreme Court turned to the constitutional question: May Congress grant the President discretionary authority to amend or cancel certain provisions in budget legislation?

JUSTICE STEVENS delivered the opinion of the Court.

The Line Item Veto Act (Act) ... was enacted in April 1996 and became effective on January 1, 1997....

[In Sections I, II, and III, Stevens reviews the canceled items that were at issue in this case, states the injuries claimed by the plaintiffs, decides that the plaintiffs (the City of New York and a farmers' cooperative) were "individuals" entitled to bring an expedited matter to the Court, and concludes that the plaintiffs had standing.]

IV

The Line Item Veto Act gives the President the power to "cancel in whole" three types of provisions that have been signed into law: "(1) any dollar amount of discretionary budget authority; (2) any item of new direct spending; or (3) any limited tax benefit." ... It is undisputed that the New York case involves an "item of new direct spending" and that the Snake River case involves a "limited tax benefit" as those terms are defined in the Act....

The Act requires the President to adhere to precise procedures whenever he exercises his cancellation authority. In identifying items for cancellation he must consider the legislative history, the purposes, and other relevant information about the items.... He must determine, with respect to each cancellation, that it will "(i) reduce the Federal budget deficit; (ii) not impair any essential Government functions; and (iii) not harm the national interest." ... Moreover, he must transmit a special message to Congress notifying it of each cancellation within five calendar days (excluding Sundays) after the enactment of the canceled provision....

A cancellation takes effect upon receipt by Congress of the special message from the President.... If, however, a "disapproval bill" pertaining to a special message is enacted into law, the cancellations set forth in that message become "null and void." ...

The effect of a cancellation is plainly stated in § 691e, which defines the principal terms used in the Act. With respect to both an item of new direct spending and a limited tax benefit, the cancellation prevents the item "from having legal force or effect." ...

In both legal and practical effect, the President has amended two Acts of Congress by repealing a portion of each. "[R]epeal of statutes, no less than enactment, must conform with Art. I." *INS v. Chadha*, 462 U.S. 919, 954 (1983). There is no provision in the Constitution that authorizes the President to enact, to amend, or to repeal statutes. Both Article I and Article II assign responsibilities to the President that directly relate to the lawmaking process, but neither addresses the issue presented by these cases....

There are important differences between the President's "return" of a bill pursuant to Article I, § 7, and the exercise of the President's cancellation authority pursuant to the Line Item Veto Act. The constitutional return takes place *before* the bill becomes law; the statutory cancellation occurs *after* the bill becomes law. The constitutional return is of the entire bill; the statutory cancellation is of only a part. Although the Constitution expressly authorizes the President to play a role in the process of enacting statutes, it is silent on the subject of unilateral Presidential action that either repeals or amends parts of duly enacted statutes.

There are powerful reasons for construing constitutional silence on this profoundly important issue as equivalent to an express prohibition. The procedures governing the enactment of statutes set forth in the text of Article I were the product of the great debates and compromises that produced the Constitution itself. Familiar historical materials provide abundant support for the conclusion that the power to enact statutes may only "be exercised in accord with a single, finely wrought and exhaustively considered, procedure." *Chadha*, 462 U.S., at 951. Our first President understood the text of the Presentment Clause as requiring that he either "approve all the parts of a Bill, or reject it in toto." What has emerged in these cases from the President's exercise of his statutory cancellation powers, however, are truncated versions of two bills that passed both Houses of Congress. They are not the product of the "finely wrought" procedure that the Framers designed....

V

The Government advances two related arguments to support its position that despite the unambiguous provisions of the Act, cancellations do not amend or repeal properly enacted statutes in violation of the Presentment Clause. First, relying primarily on *Field v. Clark*, 143 U.S. 649 (1892), the Government contends that the cancellations were merely exercises of discretionary authority granted to the President by the Balanced Budget Act and the Taxpayer Relief Act read in light of the previously enacted Line Item Veto Act. Second, the Government submits that the substance of the authority to cancel tax and spending items "is, in practical effect, no more and no less than the power to 'decline to spend' specified sums of money, or to 'decline to implement' specified tax measures." ... Neither argument is persuasive.

In *Field v. Clark*, the Court upheld the constitutionality of the Tariff Act of 1890. *[The statute contained a "free list" of almost 300 specific articles that were exempted from import duties, but authorized the*

President to suspend the exemption for certain articles whenever he decided that the country exporting those products imposed duties on the agricultural products of the United States that he deemed to be "reciprocally unequal and unreasonable." Stevens identifies what he considered to be three critical differences between the President's power to suspend the exemption from import duties and the President's power under the Line Item Veto Act.] First, the exercise of the suspension power was contingent upon a condition that did not exist when the Tariff Act was passed: the imposition of "reciprocally unequal and unreasonable" import duties by other countries. In contrast, the exercise of the cancellation power within five days after the enactment of the Balanced Budget and Tax Reform Acts necessarily was based on the same conditions that Congress evaluated when it passed those statutes. Second, under the Tariff Act, when the President determined that the contingency had arisen, he had a duty to suspend; in contrast, while it is true that the President was required by the Act to make three determinations before he canceled a provision, ... those determinations did not qualify his discretion to cancel or not to cancel. Finally, whenever the President suspended an exemption under the Tariff Act, he was executing the policy that Congress had embodied in the statute. In contrast, whenever the President cancels an item of new direct spending or a limited tax benefit he is rejecting the policy judgment made by Congress and relying on his own policy judgment....

The cited statutes all relate to foreign trade, and this Court has recognized that in the foreign affairs arena, the President has "a degree of discretion and freedom from statutory restriction which would not be admissible were domestic affairs alone involved." *United States v. Curtiss-Wright Export Corp.*, 299 U.S. 304, 320 (1936)....

Neither are we persuaded by the Government's contention that the President's authority to cancel new direct spending and tax benefit items is no greater than his traditional authority to decline to spend appropriated funds. The Government has reviewed in some detail the series of statutes in which Congress has given the Executive broad discretion over the expenditure of appropriated funds. For example, the First Congress appropriated "sum[s] not exceeding" specified amounts to be spent on various Government operations.... In those statutes, as in later years, the President was given wide discretion with respect to both the amounts to be spent and how the money would be allocated among different functions. It is argued that the Line Item Veto Act merely confers comparable discretionary authority over the expenditure of appropriated funds. The critical difference between this statute and all of its predecessors, however, is that unlike any of them, this Act gives the President the unilateral power to change the text of duly enacted statutes. None of the Act's predecessors could even arguably have been construed to authorize such a change.

VI

. . .

If there is to be a new procedure in which the President will play a different role in determining the final text of what may "become a law," such change must come not by legislation but through the amendment procedures set forth in Article V of the Constitution....

The judgment of the District Court is affirmed.

It is so ordered.

JUSTICE KENNEDY, concurring.

[Kennedy emphasized the structural issues present in this case. "Liberty is always at stake when one or more of the branches seek to transgress the separation of powers." Concentration of power in the hands of a single branch "is a threat to liberty." Liberty is protected not only by the Bill of Rights but by the principles of separation of powers, federalism, and checks and balances.]

It is no answer, of course, to say that Congress surrendered its authority by its own hand; nor does it suffice to point out that a new statute, signed by the President or enacted over his veto, could restore to Congress the power it now seeks to relinquish. That a congressional cession of power is voluntary does not make it innocuous. The Constitution is a compact enduring for more than our time, and one Congress cannot yield up its own powers, much less those of other Congresses to follow.... Abdication of responsibility is not part of the constitutional design....

JUSTICE SCALIA, with whom JUSTICE O'CONNOR joins, and with whom JUSTICE BREYER joins as to Part III, concurring in part and dissenting in part.

... [U]nlike the Court I find the President's cancellation of spending items to be entirely in accord with the Constitution.

. . .

Insofar as the degree of political, "law-making" power conferred upon the Executive is concerned, there is not a dime's worth of difference between Congress's authorizing the President to *cancel* a spending item, and Congress's authorizing money to be spent on a particular item at the President's discretion. And the latter has been done since the Founding of the Nation. From 1789–1791, the First Congress made lump-sum appropriations for the entire Government—"sum[s] not exceeding" specified amounts for broad purposes.... From a very early date Congress also made permissive individual appropriations, leaving the decision whether to spend the money to the President's unfettered discretion....

The short of the matter is this: Had the Line Item Veto Act authorized the President to "decline to spend" any item of spending contained in the Balanced Budget Act of 1997, there is not the slightest doubt that authorization would have been constitutional. What the Line Item Veto Act does instead—authorizing the President to "cancel" an item of spending—is technically different. But the technical difference does *not* relate to the technicalities of the Presentment Clause, which have been fully complied with; and the doctrine of unconstitutional delegation, which *is* at issue here, is preeminently *not* a doctrine of technicalities. The title of the Line Item Veto Act, which was perhaps designed to simplify for public comprehension, or perhaps merely to comply with the terms of a campaign pledge, has succeeded in faking out the Supreme Court. The President's action it authorizes in fact is not a line-item veto and thus does not offend Art. I, § 7; and insofar as the substance of that action is concerned, it is no different from what Congress has permitted the President to do since the formation of the Union....

JUSTICE BREYER, with whom JUSTICE O'CONNOR and JUSTICE SCALIA join as to Part III, dissenting.

I agree with the Court that the parties have standing, but I do not agree with its ultimate conclusion. In my view the Line Item Veto Act does not violate any specific textual constitutional command, nor does it violate any implicit Separation of Powers principle. Consequently, I believe that the Act is constitutional....

III

... When the President "canceled" the two appropriation measures now before us, he did not *repeal* any law nor did he *amend* any law. He simply *followed* the law, leaving the statutes, as they are literally written, intact....

INS v. Chadha

462 U.S. 919 (1983)

Congress authorized the Attorney General to suspend the deportation of aliens. Suspensions, however, were subject to the disapproval of either House. Along with a list of 340 names, the Attorney General suspended the deportation of Jagdish Rai Chadha, an East Indian born in Kenya and who held a British passport. In 1975 the House of Representatives adopted a resolution disapproving six names, including that of Chadha. He moved to suspend the deportation proceedings on the ground that the portion of the statute giving Congress a one-House veto was unconstitutional. In 1980 the Ninth Circuit held that the legislative veto violated the doctrine of separation of powers. The Supreme Court twice held oral argument before deciding the case.

CHIEF JUSTICE BURGER delivered the opinion of the Court.

We granted certiorari [*to consider*] a challenge to the constitutionality of the provision in § 244(c)(2) ... authorizing one House of Congress, by resolution, to invalidate the decision of the Executive Branch, pursuant to authority delegated by Congress to the Attorney General of the United States, to allow a particular deportable alien to remain in the United States.

I

Chadha is an East Indian who was born in Kenya and holds a British passport. He was lawfully admitted to the United States in 1966 on a nonimmigrant student visa. His visa expired on June 30, 1972. On October 11, 1973, the District Director of the Immigration and Naturalization Service ordered Chadha to show cause why he should not be deported for having "remained in the United States for a longer time than permitted." ... Chadha conceded that he was deportable for overstaying his visa and the hearing was adjourned to enable him to file an application for suspension of deportation under § 244(a)(1) of the Act....

[The immigration judge suspended Chadha's deportation, and a report of the suspension was transmitted. Acting under § 244(c)(2), and without debate or recorded vote, the House of Representatives disapproved Chadha's suspension. Before addressing the constitutionality of the one-House veto, the Court concluded that (1) it had jurisdiction to entertain the INS appeal, (2) the legislative veto could be severed from the Act without affecting the Attorney General's authority to suspend deportations, (3) Chadha had standing to bring the suit, (4) there was no reason to avoid the constitutional issue because Chadha might have alternative means of relief, (5) the Ninth Circuit had jurisdiction to decide the case, (6) the case represented a genuine case or controversy with the necessary

concrete adverseness, and (7) the case did not constitute a nonjusticiable political question.]

III
A

We turn now to the question whether action of one House of Congress under § 244(c)(2) violates strictures of the Constitution. We begin, of course, with the presumption that the challenged statute is valid....

By the same token, the fact that a given law or procedure is efficient, convenient, and useful in facilitating functions of government, standing alone, will not save it if it is contrary to the Constitution. Convenience and efficiency are not the primary objectives—or the hallmarks—of democratic government and our inquiry is sharpened rather than blunted by the fact that congressional veto provisions are appearing with increasing frequency in statutes which delegate authority to executive and independent agencies:

"Since 1932, when the first veto provision was enacted into law, 295 congressional veto-type procedures have been inserted in 196 different statutes as follows: from 1932 to 1939, five statutes were affected; from 1940–49, nineteen statutes; between 1950–59, thirty-four statutes; and from 1960–69, forty-nine. From the year 1970 through 1975, at least one hundred sixty-three such provisions were included in eighty-nine laws." Abourezk, The Congressional Veto: A Contemporary Response to Executive Encroachment on Legislative Prerogatives, 52 Ind. L. Rev. 323, 324 (1977).

. . .

Explicit and unambiguous provisions of the Constitution prescribe and define the respective functions of the Congress and of the Executive in the legislative process. Since the precise terms of those familiar provisions are critical to the resolution of these cases, we set them out verbatim. Article I provides:

"All legislative Powers herein granted shall be vested in a Congress of the United States, which shall consist of a Senate *and* House of Representatives." Art. I, § 1. (Emphasis added.)

"Every Bill which shall have passed the House of Representatives *and* the Senate, *shall,* before it becomes a law, be presented to the President of the United States ..." Art. I, § 7, cl. 2. (Emphasis added.)

"*Every* Order, Resolution, or Vote to which the Concurrence of the Senate and House of Representatives may be necessary (except on a question of Adjournment) *shall be* presented to the President of the United States; and before the Same shall take Effect, *shall be* approved by him, or being disapproved by him, *shall be* repassed by two thirds of the Senate and House of Representatives, according to the Rules and Limitations prescribed in the Case of a Bill." Art. I, § 7, cl. 3. (Emphasis added.)

. . .

B

THE PRESENTMENT CLAUSES

The records of the Constitutional Convention reveal that the requirement that all legislation be presented to the President before becoming law was uniformly accepted by the Framers. Presentment to the President and the Presidential veto were considered so imperative that the draftsmen took special pains to assure that these requirements could not be circumvented. During the final debate on Art. I, § 7, cl. 2, James Madison expressed concern that it might easily be evaded by the simple expedient of calling a proposed law a "resolution" or "vote" rather than a "bill." 2 Farrand 301–302. As a consequence, Art. I, § 7, cl. 3 ... was added....

C

BICAMERALISM

The bicameral requirement of Art. I, §§ 1, 7, was of scarcely less concern to the Framers than was the Presidential veto and indeed the two concepts are interdependent. By providing that no law could take effect without the concurrence of the prescribed majority of the Members of both Houses, the Framers reemphasized their belief, already remarked upon in connection with the Presentment Clauses, that legislation should not be enacted unless it has been carefully and fully considered by the Nation's elected officials....

... It emerges clearly that the prescription for legislative action in Art. I, §§ 1, 7, represents the Framers' decision that the legislative power of the Federal Government be exercised in accord with a single, finely wrought and exhaustively considered, procedure.

IV

. . .

Examination of the action taken here by one House pursuant to § 244(c)(2) reveals that it was essentially legislative in purpose and effect. In purporting to exercise power defined in Art. I, § 8, cl. 4, to "establish an uniform Rule of Naturalization," the House took action that had the purpose and effect of altering the legal rights, duties, and relations of persons, including the Attorney General, Executive Branch officials and Chadha, all outside the Legislative Branch. Section 244(c)(2) purports to authorize one House of Congress to require the Attorney General to deport an individual alien whose deportation otherwise would be canceled under § 244. The one-House veto operated in these cases to overrule the Attorney General and mandate Chadha's deportation; absent the House action, Chadha would remain in the United States. Congress has *acted* and its action has altered Chadha's status.

[The Court acknowledges that the Constitution in some cases authorizes one House of Congress to act alone without the check of the President's veto: the power of the House of Representatives to initiate impeachment, the Senate's power to try impeachments, the Senate's action on appointments, and the Senate's action on treaties.]

The veto authorized by § 244(c)(2) doubtless has been in many respects a convenient shortcut; the "sharing" with the Executive by Congress of its authority over aliens in this manner is, on its face, an appealing compromise. In purely practical terms, it is obviously easier for action to be taken by one House without submission to the President; but it is crystal clear from the records of the Convention, contemporaneous writings and debates, that the Framers ranked other values higher than efficiency. The records of the Convention and debates in the states preceding ratification underscore the common desire to define and limit the exercise of the newly created federal powers affecting the states and the people. There is unmistakable expression of a determination that legislation by the national Congress be a step-by-step, deliberate and deliberative process.

The choices we discern as having been made in the Constitutional Convention impose burdens on governmental processes that often seem clumsy, inefficient, even unworkable, but those hard choices were consciously made by men who had lived under a form of government that permitted arbitrary governmental acts to go unchecked. There is no support in the Constitution or decisions of this Court for the proposition that the cumbersomeness and delays often encountered in complying with explicit constitutional standards may be avoided, either by the Congress or by the President. See *Youngstown Sheet & Tube Co.* v. *Sawyer*, 343 U.S. 579 (1952). With all the obvious flaws of delay, untidiness, and potential for abuse, we have not yet found a better way to preserve freedom than by making the exercise of power subject to the carefully crafted restraints spelled out in the Constitution.

V

We hold that the congressional veto provision in § 244(c)(2) is severable from the Act and that it is unconstitutional. Accordingly, the judgment of the Court of Appeals is

Affirmed.

JUSTICE POWELL, concurring in the judgment.

The Court's decision, based on the Presentment Clauses, Art. I, § 7, cls. 2 and 3, apparently will invalidate every use of the legislative veto. The breadth of this holding gives one pause. Congress has included the veto in literally hundreds of statutes, dating back to the 1930's. Congress clearly views this procedure as essential to controlling the delegation of power to administrative agencies. One reasonably may disagree with Congress' assessment of the veto's utility, but the respect due its judgment as a coordinate branch of Government cautions that our holdings should be no more extensive than necessary to decide these cases. In my view, the cases may be decided on a narrower ground. When Congress finds that a particular person does not satisfy the statutory criteria for permanent residence in this country it has assumed a judicial function in violation of the principle of separation of powers. Accordingly, I concur only in the judgment.

· · ·

JUSTICE WHITE, dissenting.

Today the Court not only invalidates § 244(c)(2) of the Immigration and Nationality Act, but also sounds the death knell for nearly 200 other statutory provisions in which Congress has reserved a "legislative veto." For this reason, the Court's decision is of surpassing importance. And it is for this reason that the Court would have been well advised to de-

cide the cases, if possible, on the narrower grounds of separation of powers, leaving for full consideration the constitutionality of other congressional review statutes operating on such varied matters as war powers and agency rulemaking, some of which concern the independent regulatory agencies.

The prominence of the legislative veto mechanism in our contemporary political system and its importance to Congress can hardly be overstated. It has become a central means by which Congress secures the accountability of executive and independent agencies. Without the legislative veto, Congress is faced with a Hobson's choice: either to refrain from delegating the necessary authority, leaving itself with a hopeless task of writing laws with the requisite specificity to cover endless special circumstances across the entire policy landscape, or in the alternative, to abdicate its lawmaking function of the Executive Branch and independent agencies. To choose the former leaves major national problems unresolved; to opt for the latter risks unaccountable policymaking by those not elected to fill that role. Accordingly, over the past five decades, the legislative veto has been placed in nearly 200 statutes. The device is known in every field of governmental concern: reorganization, budgets, foreign affairs, war powers, and regulation of trade, safety, energy, the environment, and the economy.

I

[White explains that the legislative veto arose in 1929 when President Hoover sought authority to reorganize the executive branch and expressed willingness to have Congress check his actions by exercising a one-House veto. In subsequent actions, the two branches applied this quid pro quo to other areas. The result was that the President gained new authority and Congress held a legislative veto to control the delegated authority.]

... While the President has often objected to particular legislative vetoes, generally those left in the hands of congressional Committees, the Executive has more often agreed to legislative review as the price for a broad delegation of authority. To be sure, the President may have preferred unrestricted power, but that could be precisely why Congress thought it essential to retain a check on the exercise of delegated authority.

· · ·

V

I regret that I am in disagreement with my colleagues on the fundamental questions that these cases present. But even more I regret the destructive scope of the Court's holding. It reflects a profoundly different conception of the Constitution than that held by the courts which sanctioned the modern administrative state. Today's decision strikes down in one fell swoop provisions in more laws enacted by Congress than the Court has cumulatively invalidated in its history....

JUSTICE REHNQUIST, with whom JUSTICE WHITE joins, dissenting.

[Rehnquist states his belief that Congress did not intend the one-House veto to be severable from § 244(c)(2). Because the Court had held the legislative veto unconstitutional, Rehnquist would strike down the delegated authority as well.]

Louis Fisher
Legislative Vetoes After *Chadha*

After the Supreme Court in *INS* v. *Chadha* (1983) held the legislative veto unconstitutional, Congress continued to place legislative vetoes in bills and Presidents continued to sign them into law. Many of these new statutory controls required executive agencies to seek the approval of specific congressional committees before implementing an agency action. The various methods available to Congress for finding substitutes for the legislative veto, and in fact for using legislative vetoes, are explored by Louis Fisher in "Judicial Misjudgments About the Lawmaking Process: The Legislative Veto Case," 45 Pub. Adm. Rev. 705 (Special Issue, November 1985). A later analysis appears in Louis Fisher, "The Legislative Veto: Invalidated, It Survives," 56 Law & Contemp. Prob. 273 (Autumn 1993).

In past years the Supreme Court has damaged its reputation by issuing decisions based on misconceptions about the political and economic system. After trying to impose archaic and mechanical concepts about federalism, the taxing power, the commerce power, and other clauses of the Constitution, the court was forced to retreat from pronouncements that were simply unacceptable for a developing nation. To minimize what Charles Evans Hughes once called the court's penchant for "self-inflicted wounds," justices evolved a number of rules to limit their exercise of judicial review. One mainstay is the principle that the court will not "formulate a rule of constitutional law broader than is required by the precise facts to which it is to be applied."

That guideline was not followed in 1983 when the Supreme Court issued *INS* v. *Chadha*, which declared the legislative veto unconstitutional in all its forms. The court announced that future congressional efforts to alter "the legal rights, duties and relations of persons" outside the legislative branch must follow the full lawmaking process: passage of a bill or joint resolution by both Houses and presentment of that measure to the president for his signature or veto. The court lectured Congress that it could no longer rely on the legislative veto as "a convenient shortcut" to control executive agencies. Instead, "legislation by the national Congress [must] be a step-by-step, deliberate and deliberative

process." According to the court, the framers insisted that "the legislative power of the Federal Government be exercised in accord with a single, finely wrought and exhaustively considered, procedure."

A HISTORY OF ACCOMMODATIONS

All three branches reached agreement long ago that the step-by-step, deliberate and deliberative process is not appropriate for each and every exercise of the legislative power. Despite occasional invocations of the non-delegation doctrine, the court itself has accepted the inevitable delegation of legislative power to executive agencies and independent commissions. Administrative bodies routinely "make law" through the rulemaking process. Efforts are made to subject this lawmaking activity to procedural safeguards, but the persistence of the Administrative State is ample proof that the theoretical model of legislative action envisioned by the framers applies only in the most general sense to the 20th [now 21st] century.

. . .

THE PERSISTENCE OF LEGISLATIVE VETOES

It came as a surprise to some observers that Congress continued to place legislative vetoes in bills after the court's decision and President Reagan continued to sign the bills into law. In the 16 months between *Chadha* and the adjournment of the 98th Congress, an additional 53 legislative vetoes were added to the books.

[By the end of the 110th Congress, which adjourned at the end of 2008, the list of new legislative vetoes exceeded six hundred.]

A flagrant case of non-compliance? A sign of disrespect for the courts? An alarming challenge to the time-honored belief that the Supreme Court has the last word on constitutional questions? Perhaps, but the court painted with too broad a brush and offered a simplistic solution that is unacceptable to the political branches. Its decision will be eroded by open defiance and subtle evasion. Neither consequence is attractive, but much of the responsibility for this condition belongs on the doorstep of the court.

Some of the legislative vetoes enacted since *Chadha* are easy to spot. Most of them vest control in the appropriations committees. For example, construction grants by the Environmental Protection Agency are subject to the approval of the appropriations committees (97 Stat. 226). The approval of the appropriations committees is required before exceeding certain dollar amounts in the National Flood Insurance Fund (97 Stat. 227)....

Other legislative vetoes are more subtle. A continuing resolution provided that foreign assistance funds allocated to each country "shall not exceed those provided in fiscal year 1983 or those provided in the budget estimates for each country, whichever are lower, unless submitted through the regular reprogramming procedures of the Committees on Appropriations" (97 Stat. 736). Those procedures provide for committee prior-approval. The District of Columbia Appropriation Act for fiscal 1984 prohibited funds from being obligated or spent by reprogramming "except pursuant to advance approval of the reprogramming granted according to the procedure set forth" in two House reports, both of which require prior approval by the appropriations committees (97 Stat. 827).

One year after *Chadha*, President Reagan received the HUD-Independent Agencies Appropriations bill which contained a number of committee vetoes. In his signing statement, he took note of those vetoes and asked Congress to stop adding provisions that the Supreme Court had held to be unconstitutional. He said that "the time has come, with more than a year having passed since the Supreme Court's decision in *Chadha*, to make clear that legislation containing legislative veto devices that comes to me for my approval or disapproval will be implemented in a manner consistent with the *Chadha* decision." The clear import was that the administration

did not feel bound by the statutory requirements to seek the approval of congressional committees before implementing certain actions.

The House Appropriations Committee responded to the president's statement by reviewing an agreement it had entered into with NASA four years previously. Caps were set on various NASA programs, usually at the level requested in the president's budget. The agreement allowed NASA to exceed the caps with the approval of the appropriations committees. The House Appropriations Committee thought that the procedure had "worked well during the past four years, and has provided a mechanism by which the Congress and the Committee can be assured that funds are used solely for the purpose for which they were appropriated." Because of Reagan's statement and the threat to ignore committee controls, the committee said it was necessary to repeal the accommodation that had lasted for four years. Repeal language was inserted in the second supplemental bill for fiscal 1984. Both sides stood to lose. The appropriations committees would not be able to veto NASA proposals; NASA would not be able to exceed ceilings without enacting new language in a separate appropriation bill.

Neither NASA nor the appropriations committees wanted to enact a separate public law just to exceed a cap. To avoid this kind of administrative rigidity, NASA Administrator James M. Beggs wrote to both committees on August 9, 1984. His letter reveals the pragmatic sense of give-and-take that is customary between executive agencies and congressional committees. His letter also underscores the impracticality and unreality of the doctrines enunciated by the Supreme Court in *Chadha*:

"We have now operated under the present operating plan and reprogramming procedures for several years and have found them to be workable. In light of the constitutional questions raised concerning the legislative veto provisions included in P.L. 98-371 [the HUD-Independent Agencies Appropriations Act], however, the House Committee on Appropriations has proposed in H.R. 6040, the FY 1984 general supplemental, deletion of all Committee approval provisions, leaving inflexible, binding funding limitations on several programs. Without some procedure for adjustment, other than a subsequent separate legislative enactment, these ceilings could seriously impact the ability of NASA to meet unforeseen technical changes or problems that are inherent in challenging R&D programs. We believe that the present legislative procedure could be converted by this letter into an informal agreement by

NASA not to exceed amounts for Committee designated programs without the approval of the Committees on Appropriations. This agreement would assume that both the statutory funding ceilings and the Committee approval mechanisms would be deleted from the FY 1985 legislation, and that it would not be the normal practice to include either mechanism in future appropriations bills. Further, the agreement would assume that future program ceiling amounts would be identified by the Committees in the Conference Report accompanying NASA's annual appropriations act and confirmed by NASA in its submission of the annual operating plan. NASA would not expend any funds over the ceilings identified in the Conference Report for these programs without the prior approval of the Committees."

In short, the agency would continue to honor legislative vetoes. But they would be informal rather than statutory. Beggs ended his letter by assuring the appropriations committees that NASA "will comply with any ceilings imposed by the Committees without the need for legislative ceilings which could cause serious damage to NASA's ongoing programs." By converting the legislative veto to an informal and non-statutory status, NASA is not legally bound by the agreement. Violation of the agreement, however, could provoke the appropriations committees to place caps in the appropriation bill and force the agency to lift them only through the enactment of another public law.

. . .

CONCLUSIONS

Through its misreading of history, congressional procedures, and executive-legislative relations, the Supreme Court has commanded the political branches to follow a lawmaking process that is impracticable and unworkable. Neither agencies nor committees want the static model of government offered by the court. The inevitable result is a record of non-compliance, subtle evasion, and a system of lawmaking that is now more convoluted, cumbersome, and covert than before. In many cases the court's decision simply drives underground a set of legislative and committee vetoes that had previously operated in plain sight. No one should be misled if the number of legislative vetoes placed in statutes gradually declines over the years. Fading from view will not mean disappearance. In one form or another legislative vetoes will remain an important method for reconciling legislative and executive interests.

G. INVESTIGATIONS AND EXECUTIVE PRIVILEGE

The impact of implied powers is nowhere more evident than in the struggle for information. Although the Constitution does not expressly give Congress the power to investigate, the Supreme Court has noted that a legislative body "cannot legislate wisely or effectively in the absence of information respecting the conditions which the legislation is intended to affect or change." McGrain v. Daugherty, 273 U.S. 135, 175 (1927). Similarly, the Constitution does not give the President the privilege of withholding information from Congress, and yet in 1974 the Court decided that the President's interest in withholding information to protect confidentiality with his advisers is implied in the Constitution: "to the extent this interest relates to the effective discharge of a President's powers, it is constitutionally based." UNITED STATES v. NIXON, 418 U.S. 683, 711 (1974).

There is an inevitable collision when Congress attempts to carry out its investigative function and the President invokes executive privilege. Which branch should surrender to the other? Major confrontations require some type of compromise, prodded by Congress's power to punish for contempt and the judiciary's ability to steer both branches toward an acceptable accommodation.

Congressional Investigations

Congress relies on its investigative power to enact legislation; to oversee the administration of programs; to inform the public; and to protect its integrity, dignity, reputation, and privileges. To enforce each of these responsibilities, each House of Congress possesses the power to punish for contempt. Without that power, Congress would be left "exposed to every indignity and interruption that rudeness, caprice, or even conspiracy, may mediate against it." Anderson v. Dunn, 6 Wheat. 204, 228 (1821).

This decision in 1821 limited the power of Congress to punish for contempt. Each House had to exercise the least possible power adequate to the end proposed (in this case the power to imprison) and the duration of punishment could not exceed the life of the legislative body (that is, imprisonment had to terminate with congressional adjournment). Because of those restrictions, Congress decided in 1857 to use the judiciary to enforce its investigative power. Failure to appear or refusal to answer pertinent questions can lead to a contempt vote in either House, which requires a U.S. attorney to seek an indictment by a grand jury and conviction in the courts. 11 Stat. 155 (1857), codified at 2 U.S.C. §§ 192–94 (2004). This law, as amended, was upheld by the Court. In re Chapman, 166 U.S. 661 (1897). Congress created a third option in 1978. If an individual from the private sector refuses to comply with a Senate subpoena (an order requiring certain action under threat of punishment), the Senate may request a court order to require compliance with the subpoena. Failure to obey the court order can lead to civil contempt. The sanction is lifted once the individual complies with the Senate's request. 28 U.S.C. § 1364 (2004).

Because of such spectacles as the McCarthy hearings of the 1950s, which deteriorated into a witch hunt for "subversives," congressional investigations are often associated with careless and damaging intrusions into personal lives. Most investigations, however, are conducted in a responsible manner and pose no threat to individual liberties or the separation of powers. In fact, congressional investigations often enhance individual liberties by challenging and exposing abuses by the executive branch or the private sector.

Prodded by the adverse publicity from the 1950s, Congress adopted a set of procedures for committee investigations to assure fairness. The courts also insisted that committee hearings be properly authorized by Congress and their scope defined. United States v. Rumely, 345 U.S. 41 (1953); Gojack v. United States, 384 U.S. 702 (1966). In 1957, in what was considered a sharp rebuke to Congress, the Court held that fundamental fairness demanded that a witness be given adequate guidance in deciding the pertinency of a question. There was no congressional power "to expose for the sake of exposure." WATKINS v. UNITED STATES, 354 U.S. 178 (1957). The tone of the decision, together with other judicial rulings during that period, triggered a groundswell of opposition from legislators. Various bills were introduced to curb the Court. In the face of this political pressure, the Supreme Court, two years later, retreated from its position. It now adopted a generous "balancing test" that allowed the government's interest in self-preservation to outweigh the individual's right to remain silent. BARENBLATT v. UNITED STATES, 360 U.S. 109 (1959).

When the activities of an organization did not raise questions of subversion and communism, at least directly, the courts were more likely to protect the rights of association. This is the teaching of a 1958 case, in which a state's attorney general attempted to obtain the membership list of a civil rights organization, the NAACP. Such publicity could have discouraged individuals from joining and participating in exposed groups. The principles announced in this case give greater support to the rights of speech, assembly, and association. NAACP v. Alabama, 357 U.S. 449 (1958). See also Gibson v. Florida Legislative Investigation Committee, 372 U.S. 539 (1963).

Immunity for Witnesses

Witnesses may invoke the Fifth Amendment privilege against self-incrimination. Quinn v. United States, 349 U.S. 155 (1955) and Emspak v. United States, 349 U.S. 190 (1955). An immunity procedure is available to force testimony while at the same time recognizing Fifth Amendment rights. Witnesses may receive full immunity or partial immunity. For the latter, a witness can be compelled to testify and later be prosecuted so long as the witness's testimony (or evidence derived from it) is not used in the prosecution.[15]

---

15. 18 U.S.C. §§ 6001–05 (2004). The immunity procedure, as a substitute for the Fifth Amendment, was upheld in Ullmann v. United States, 350 U.S. 422 (1956); Kastigar v. United States, 406 U.S. 441 (1972); and Application of U.S. Senate Select Com. on Pres. Cam. Act., 361 F.Supp. 1270 (D.D.C. 1973).

Evolving Judicial Standards for Congressional Investigations

Congress could not conduct "fruitless" inquiries without the prospect for legislation. Kilbourn v. Thompson, 103 U.S. 168, 194–95 (1881)

"Potential" for legislation is sufficient. McGrain v. Daugherty, 273 U.S. 135, 177 (1927)

Witnesses must understand the pertinency of a question. Watkins v. United States, 354 U.S. 178 (1957)

A "balancing test" permits the government's interest in self-preservation to outweigh an individual's right to remain silent. Barenblatt v. United States, 360 U.S. 109 (1959)

Investigation can lead up "blind alleys" with no predictable legislative result. Eastland v. United States Servicemen's Fund, 421 U.S. 491, 509 (1975)

Colonel Oliver North received partial immunity—also called "use immunity"—when he testified before the Iran-Contra hearings in 1987. He was later convicted of three felonies: obstructing the investigation by Congress, mutilating government documents, and taking an illegal gratuity. The charges were subsequently dismissed because of new and more stringent standards imposed by the courts. Prosecutors now had to show that a defendant's testimony could have had no influence on the witnesses called to a trial. Otherwise, the witnesses are "tainted" and their remarks may not be used to convict (see section "Immunity" in Chapter 13).

Limits on Investigations

Over the years, the Court has attempted to establish guidelines for congressional investigations. It struck down an investigation and a contempt action because the matter was already pending before a court. Kilbourn v. Thompson, 103 U.S. 168, 182 (1881). Such a doctrine would put congressional investigations on the back burner for years while awaiting the outcome of a lawsuit. Executive agencies could sidetrack an embarrassing committee hearing simply by filing suit and pursuing appeals. Congress may decide to defer its investigation until the completion of a criminal trial or refuse to wait for the results of long, drawn-out litigation. The latter course was followed during the Reagan administration when Congress investigated corruption within the Environmental Protection Agency. In such circumstances, Congress has the right to proceed, even at the cost of postponing or jeopardizing a trial.[16]

Initially, the courts held that congressional investigations must relate to some legislative purpose. Congress should not conduct "fruitless" inquiries without the prospect of legislation. Kilbourn v. Thompson, 103 U.S. at 194–95. Later, however, the Court admitted that a "potential" for legislation is sufficient. McGrain v. Daugherty, 273 U.S. at 177. Even this is too restrictive a test. Committee efforts to oversee executive agencies may take researchers up "blind alleys" and into nonproductive enterprises: "To be a valid legislative inquiry there need be no predictable end result." Eastland v. United States Servicemen's Fund, 421 U.S. 491, 509 (1975) (see box). Attorney General William French Smith incorrectly stated that congressional requests for information are on stronger ground if Congress has specific legislation in mind than when it simply probes as part of a general oversight effort.[17] Oversight is not subordinate to legislation. Even if that position could be argued, lawmakers could simply introduce a bill to justify an oversight investigation.

---

16. Delaney v. United States, 199 F.2d 107, 114–15 (1st Cir. 1952). See also Hutcheson v. United States, 369 U.S. 599, 612–13, 623–24 (1962), Sinclair v. United States, 279 U.S. 263, 295 (1929), and Fisher, Constitutional Conflicts Between Congress and the President 155–66 (2007).

17. "Executive Privilege: Legal Opinions Regarding Claim of President Ronald Reagan in Response to a Subpoena Issued to James G. Watt, Secretary of the Interior," prepared for the use of the House Committee on Energy and Commerce, 97th Cong., 1st Sess. 3 (Comm. Print November 1981).

A decision by the Supreme Court in 1995 limited the ability of the Justice Department to prosecute lawmakers and government officials for lying to Congress. Section 1001 of Title 18 criminalizes unsworn false statements in any matter within the jurisdiction of any "department or agency" of the United States. In holding that Section 1001 did not apply to federal courts, the Court also overruled a 1955 case that had applied Section 1001 to a former member of Congress who had made a false statement to the Disbursing Office of the House of Representatives. The effect of the 1995 ruling was to limit the Justice Department's ability to prosecute only those individuals who committed perjury to Congress (for lying under oath). Hubbard v. United States, 514 U.S. 695 (1995). Congress responded to *Hubbard* by enacting legislation a year later that reinstated criminal penalties for making false statements to Congress. 110 Stat. 3459 (1996).

Impeachment

The ultimate form of the investigative power is impeachment. The President, Vice President, and all civil officers of the United States shall be removed from office upon "Impeachment for, and Conviction of, Treason, Bribery, or other high Crimes and Misdemeanors" (Article II, Section 4). Treason is defined in Article III, Section 3, while bribery has a fairly clear statutory meaning. What constitutes "other high Crimes and Misdemeanors"? The framers rejected vague grounds for impeachment, such as "maladministration," because this would be equivalent to having the President serve at the pleasure of Congress. 3 Farrand 65–66, 550. However, impeachment need not require indictable crimes or specific statutory offenses. In Federalist No. 65, Alexander Hamilton included "political crimes" (abuses in office or violation of the public trust) as legitimate grounds for impeachment. Madison also supported impeachment for political abuses or neglect of office. 1 Annals of Congress 372–73 (May 19, 1789). The purpose of impeachment is to remove someone from office, not to punish for a crime. Impeachable conduct need not be criminal. That was the conclusion of the House Committee on the Judiciary during the impeachment proceedings of Richard Nixon. In 1993 the Supreme Court upheld the Senate's practice of conducting an impeachment trial in two stages: fact-finding by a 12-member committee followed by action by the full Senate. Nixon v. United States, 506 U.S. 224 (1993). For a reading on this decision, see chapter 3.

The impeachment of President Bill Clinton highlighted several issues about the process. The House of Representatives, voting largely along party lines on December 19, 1998, adopted two articles of impeachment, one on perjury and the other on obstruction of justice. Voting on February 12, 1999, the Senate "acquitted" Clinton on both articles. With regard to the perjury article, 45 Senators voted "guilty" and 55 voted "not guilty." The vote on obstruction of justice was 50 to 50, far short of the two-thirds required for removal.

The votes were distorted because the Senate currently votes simultaneously on two separate issues: guilt and removal. From 1789 to 1936, the Senate voted first for guilt and next for removal, allowing Senators to hold someone guilty of the charges brought against them but then decide that the person should not be removed from office. After 1936 the two issues were collapsed into a single vote. Many Senators who voted "not guilty" explained that Clinton was indeed guilty.

For example, Senator Robert C. Byrd (D-W.Va.) voted "not guilty" on both articles although he thought that Clinton's behavior constituted "an impeachable offense, a political high crime or misdemeanor against the state." Not wanting to remove Clinton, Byrd had only one choice: to vote "not guilty," after judging him guilty on both counts. Other Senators, including Susan Collins (R-Me.), Olympia Snowe (R-Me.), James Jeffords (R-Vt.), Fred Thompson (R-Tenn.), Ted Stevens (R-Alas.), and Slade Gorton (R-Wash.), concluded that Clinton was guilty on one or both articles but voted "not guilty" because they thought removal was unwarranted.

Senator Snowe put it this way: "Acquittal is not exoneration." John Breaux, a Democrat from Louisiana, voted against the articles but cautioned that his vote "is not a vote on the innocence of this President. He is not innocent." Bob Kerrey, Democrat from Nebraska, added: "While there is plenty of blame to go around in this case, the person responsible for it going this far is the President of the United States."

Secondly, the votes on the two articles turned on factors that had nothing to do with the evidence presented. Some legislators cited public polls of Clinton's popularity as reason to vote against impeachment and removal. Had Clinton been less popular, would that factor (unrelated to the evidence) have been adequate grounds for supporting his impeachment and removal? Moreover, lawmakers pointed to the buoyant stock market, low unemployment, and modest inflation as reasons for keeping Clinton in office. Had economic conditions turned sour, would that have justified Clinton's impeachment and removal from office? Obviously many lawmakers found it difficult to focus on the substance of the two articles.

Executive Privilege

President George Washington and his cabinet complied with a request by the House of Representatives in 1792 for papers regarding a military defeat but also concluded that it would be appropriate in the future to refuse documents "the disclosure of which would injure the public." 1 Writings of Thomas Jefferson 303–05 (Mem. ed. 1903). In general, Presidents agree to make papers and documents available for impeachment inquiries or congressional investigations into administrative corruption. While upholding a very broad theory of executive privilege in 1982, Attorney General Smith said he would not try to "shield documents [from Congress] which contain evidence of criminal or unethical conduct by agency officials from proper review." H. Rept. No. 968, 97th Cong., 2d Sess. 41 (1982).

If executive officials refuse congressional requests for information, a move by Congress to cite the person for contempt is often an effective way to get the official's attention and cooperation. For example, in 1982 the House of Representatives voted 259 to 105 to hold Anne Gorsuch, administrator of the Environmental Protection Agency, in contempt. In an unprecedented action, the U.S. Attorney did not take the contempt citation to the grand jury, as required by statute. Instead, the administration asked a district court to declare the House action an unconstitutional intrusion into the President's authority to withhold information from Congress. After this tactic failed, the documents were released. United States v. House of Representatives, 556 F. Supp. 150 (D.D.C. 1983). Use of subpoenas and threats of contempt citations led to the release of several documents by the Clinton administration. Louis Fisher, The Politics of Executive Privilege (2004).

The major executive privilege case — United States v. Nixon — did not involve a congressional request for executive documents. The request came from the courts as part of the effort to prosecute Watergate crimes. A unanimous Court rejected the argument that the decision to release such documents is up to the President, not the courts. To permit Nixon absolute control over the documents would have prevented the judiciary from carrying out its duties. UNITED STATES v. NIXON, 418 U.S. 683 (1974).

Conflicts between the executive and legislative branches are sometimes resolved with the assistance of federal judges. A deadlock between a House committee and the Justice Department during the 1970s, regarding the release of "national security" information, was eventually broken through the efforts of Judge Harold Leventhal. He convinced each branch that a compromise worked out between them would be better than a solution dictated by the courts. Practical accommodations are required instead of rigid abstractions about the power of Congress to investigate or the power of the President to withhold information (see readings for AT&T cases). In 2008, several claims of executive privilege led to congressional contempt citations and litigation before the courts. Former presidential advisors Karl Rove and Harriet Miers were subpoenaed to appear before hearings about the decisionmaking behind the 2007 firings of U. S. Attorneys. Also, the House Judiciary Committee subpoenaed documents from White House Chief of Staff Joshua Bolten, who provided no materials. The House held Miers and Bolten in contempt. When Attorney General Mukasey refused to refer the matter to the grand jury for possible indictment, the House filed suit in federal court. On July 31, 2008, District

Judge John D. Bates rejected the administration's claim that senior White House officials have absolute immunity from congressional process. He ordered Miers to appear before the committee and Bolten to produce privilege logs.

Presidential Immunity

Although the Constitution does not provide an express immunity for the President, the courts have developed a doctrine of official immunity for executive officials and the President. Unless executive employees enjoyed an immunity for their official actions, they could not be expected to administer laws vigorously and effectively. Barr v. Matteo, 360 U.S. 564 (1959); Gregoire v. Biddle, 177 F.2d 579 (2d Cir. 1949). In 1982, the Supreme Court held that the President is entitled to absolute immunity, in civil suits, regarding all of his official acts. Nixon v. Fitzgerald, 457 U.S. 731 (1982). A qualified immunity is available for presidential aides. Harlow v. Fitzgerald, 457 U.S. 800 (1982); Mitchell v. Forsyth, 472 U.S. 511 (1985).

A separate question is whether the President is entitled to immunity from civil liability for *unofficial* acts: acts committed in a personal capacity rather than as President. This issue arose when Paula Corbin Jones brought a lawsuit against Bill Clinton for an incident that occurred before he became President. She claimed that in 1991, at a conference held at a hotel in Little Rock, Clinton (at that time governor of Arkansas) sexually harassed and assaulted her. Clinton's attorneys argued that the President should have a temporary immunity while serving in office and that the case should not go forward until he left office. In 1997, a unanimous Court decided that the Constitution did not afford the President temporary immunity in this case. CLINTON v. JONES, 520 U.S. 681 (1997). The case was dismissed in 1998 when a district judge held that there were "no genuine issues for trial in this case." After Jones appealed, Clinton agreed to settle the case by giving her $850,000.

The Supreme Court's prediction that the case could go forward without substantially burdening President Clinton has been much maligned. However, the resulting burden had less to do with Jones than to new allegations concerning Clinton's relationship with White House intern Monica Lewinsky and serious charges of his efforts to lie, suborn witnesses, and obstruct justice.

The scope of presidential immunity was explored in two lawsuits aimed at Vice President Dick Cheney. Both cases involved efforts to obtain documents related to the energy task force he chaired. Members of Congress and private groups wanted to understand how much influence nongovernmental officials had on the energy bill that the administration drafted and presented to Congress. GAO initiated the first suit, which a district court dismissed on the ground that the Comptroller General lacked standing. Walker v. Cheney, 230 F.Supp.2d 51 (D.D.C. 2002); Fisher, The Politics of Executive Privilege, at 183–98. GAO decided not to appeal.

The second case came from two private groups, Judicial Watch and the Sierra Club. The D.C. Circuit rejected the administration's argument that the President and the Vice President possessed a broad immunity against any effort, through litigation, to determine how they formulated legislative proposals. It directed the two groups to narrow their request for documents. The Supreme Court declined to accept the administration's broad doctrine, preferring to return the case to the D.C. Circuit with instructions to seek an accommodation to protect the President from litigation that might distract from the performance of constitutional duties. Cheney v. United States District Court for D.C., 542 U.S. 367 (2004).

Watkins v. United States

354 U.S. 178 (1957)

Beginning in the early 1950s, congressional committees conducted searching inquiries into left-wing activities of American citizens. The atmosphere of the cold war permitted little toleration

for "disloyal" thoughts and conduct. In this case, the House Committee on Un-American Activities called John Watkins, a labor organizer, to testify. He agreed to describe his past participation in the Communist party and identify current members, but declined to answer questions about those who had left the movement. His refusal led to conviction for contempt of Congress. A panel of the D.C. Circuit reversed the conviction, but the full bench, sitting *en banc*, affirmed the conviction.

MR. CHIEF JUSTICE WARREN delivered the opinion of the Court.

This is a review by certiorari of a conviction under 2 U.S.C. § 192 for "contempt of Congress." The misdemeanor is alleged to have been committed during a hearing before a congressional investigating committee. It is not the case of a truculent or contumacious witness who refuses to answer all questions or who, by boisterous or discourteous conduct, disturbs the decorum of the committee room. Petitioner was prosecuted for refusing to make certain disclosures which he asserted to be beyond the authority of the committee to demand. The controversy thus rests upon fundamental principles of the power of the Congress and the limitations upon that power. We approach the questions presented with conscious awareness of the far-reaching ramifications that can follow from a decision of this nature.

On April 29, 1954, petitioner appeared as a witness in compliance with a subpoena issued by a Subcommittee of the Committee on Un-American Activities of the House of Representatives. The Subcommittee elicited from petitioner a description of his background in labor union activities....

[Watkins's name had been mentioned by two witnesses who testified that he had been active with the Communist Party. He admitted to the subcommittee that "from approximately 1942 to 1947 I cooperated with the Communist Party and participated in Communist activities to such a degree that some persons may honestly believe that I was a member of the party. I have made contributions upon occasions to Communist causes. I have signed petitions for Communist causes. I attended caucuses at an FE [Farm Equipment] convention at which Communist Party officials were present." However, Watkins refused to talk about other people who might have been members of the Party.]:

"I am not going to plead the fifth amendment, but I refuse to answer certain questions that I believe are outside the proper scope of your committee's activities. I will answer any questions which this committee puts to me about myself. I will also answer questions about those persons whom I knew to be members of the Communist Party and whom I believe still are. I will not, however, answer any questions with respect to others with whom I associated in the past. I do not believe that any law in this country requires me to testify about persons who may in the past have been Communist Party members or otherwise engaged in Communist Party activity but who to my best knowledge and belief have long since removed themselves from the Communist movement.

"I do not believe that such questions are relevant to the work of this committee nor do I believe that this committee has the right to undertake the public exposure of persons because of their past activities. I may be wrong, and the committee may have this power, but until and unless a court of law so holds and directs me to answer, I most firmly refuse to discuss the political activities of my past associates."

[Watkins was held in contempt by the House and sentenced to a fine of $100 and one year in prison, which was suspended. He was placed on probation. The conviction was reversed by the D.C. Circuit.]

We start with several basic premises on which there is general agreement. The power of the Congress to conduct investigations is inherent in the legislative process. That power is broad. It encompasses inquiries concerning the administration of existing laws as well as proposed or possibly needed statutes. It includes surveys of defects in our social, economic or political system for the purpose of enabling the Congress to remedy them. It comprehends probes into departments of the Federal Government to expose corruption, inefficiency or waste. But, broad as is this power of inquiry, it is not unlimited. There is no general authority to expose the private affairs of individuals without justification in terms of the functions of the Congress. This was freely conceded by the Solicitor General in his argument of this case. Nor is the Congress a law enforcement or trial agency. These are functions of the executive and judicial departments of government. No inquiry is an end in itself; it must be related to, and in furtherance of, a legitimate task of the Congress. Investigations conducted solely for the personal aggrandizement of the investigators or to "punish" those investigated are indefensible.

It is unquestionably the duty of all citizens to cooperate with the Congress in its efforts to obtain the facts needed for intelligent legislative action. It is their unremitting obligation to respond to subpoenas, to respect the dignity of the Congress and its committees and to testify fully with respect to matters within the province of proper investigation. This, of course, assumes that the constitutional rights of witnesses will be respected by the Congress as they are in a court of justice. The Bill of Rights is applicable to investigations as to all forms of governmental action. Witnesses cannot be compelled to give evidence against themselves. They cannot be subjected to unreasonable search and seizure. Nor can the First Amendment freedoms of speech, press, religion, or political belief and association be abridged.

[*The Court describes the English Parliament's abuse of its contempt power, which was immune even from judicial review. Citizens who made comments critical of Parliament could be punished, fined, and imprisoned. Parliamentary probes were eventually replaced by investigations conducted by Royal Commissions of Inquiry, comprised of experts who rarely had the authority to compel the testimony of witnesses or the production of documents.*]

The history of contempt of the legislature in this country is notably different from that of England. In the early days of the United States, there lingered the direct knowledge of the evil effects of absolute power. Most of the instances of use of compulsory process by the first Congresses concerned matters affecting the qualification or integrity of their members or came about in inquiries dealing with suspected corruption or mismanagement of government officials. Unlike the English practice, from the very outset the use of contempt power by the legislature was deemed subject to judicial review.

. . .

It is not surprising, from the fact that the Houses of Congress so sparingly employed the power to conduct investigations, that there have been few cases requiring judicial review of the power. The Nation was almost one hundred years old before the first case reached this Court to challenge the use of compulsory process as a legislative device [*Kilbourn v. Thompson, 103 U.S. 168 (1881). Relatively few congressional investigations thereafter were contested in the courts.*] ...

In the decade following World War II, there appeared a new kind of congressional inquiry unknown in prior periods of American history. Principally this was the result of the various investigations into the threat of subversion of the United States Government, but other subjects of congressional interest also contributed to the changed scene. This new phase of legislative inquiry involved a broad-scale intrusion into the lives and affairs of private citizens. It brought before the courts novel questions of the appropriate limits of congressional inquiry....

We have no doubt that there is no congressional power to expose for the sake of exposure. The public is, of course, entitled to be informed concerning the workings of its government. That cannot be inflated into a general power to expose where the predominant result can only be an invasion of the private rights of individuals....

The authorizing resolution of the Un-American Activities Committee was adopted in 1938.... It defines the Committee's authority as follows:

"The Committee on Un-American Activities, as a whole or by subcommittee, is authorized to make from time to time investigations of (1) the extent, character, and objects of un-American propaganda activities in the United States, (2) the diffusion within the United States of subversive and un-American propaganda that is instigated from foreign countries or of a domestic origin and attacks the principle of the form of government as guaranteed by our Constitution, and (3) all other questions in relation thereto that would aid Congress in any necessary remedial legislation."

It would be difficult to imagine a less explicit authorizing resolution. Who can define the meaning of "un-American"? What is that single, solitary "principle of the form of government as guaranteed by our Constitution"? There is no need to dwell upon the language, however. At one time, perhaps, the resolution might have been read narrowly to confine the Committee to the subject of propaganda. The events that have transpired in the fifteen years before the interrogation of petitioner make such a construction impossible at this date.

The members of the Committee have clearly demonstrated that they did not feel themselves restricted in any way to propaganda in the narrow sense of the word. Unquestionably the Committee conceived of its task in the grand view of its name. Un-American activities were its target, no matter how or where manifested....

Combining the language of the resolution with the construction it has been given, it is evident that the preliminary control of the Committee exercised by the House of Representatives is slight or non-existent. No one could reasonably deduce from the charter the kind of investigation that the Committee was directed to make.

[The Court offers these guidelines: In order for a reviewing court to determine whether a committee investigation is fulfilling a legislative purpose, the committee's activity must be properly authorized by resolution. In order for a witness to understand the pertinency of a question directed by a committee member or committee staff, and to avoid being held in contempt, the witness must have knowledge of the subject of the inquiry and the pertinency of a question to that inquiry. This knowledge can come from the authorizing resolution, remarks by committee members, and the nature of the proceedings.]

... Unless the subject matter has been made to appear with undisputable clarity, it is the duty of the investigative body, upon objection of the witness on grounds of pertinency, to state for the record the subject under inquiry at that time and the manner in which the propounded questions are pertinent thereto. To be meaningful, the explanation must describe what the topic under inquiry is and the connective reasoning whereby the precise questions asked relate to it.

The statement of the Committee Chairman in this case, in response to petitioner's protest, was woefully inadequate to convey sufficient informa-

tion as to the pertinency of the questions to the subject under inquiry. Petitioner was thus not accorded a fair opportunity to determine whether he was within his rights in refusing to answer, and his conviction is necessarily invalid under the Due Process Clause of the Fifth Amendment.

The judgment of the Court of Appeals is reversed, and the case is remanded to the District Court with instructions to dismiss the indictment.

It is so ordered.

Mr. Justice Burton and Mr. Justice Whittaker took no part in the consideration or decision of this case.

Mr. Justice Frankfurter, concurring.

. . .

Mr. Justice Clark, dissenting.

As I see it the chief fault in the majority opinion is its mischievous curbing of the informing function of the Congress. While I am not versed in its procedures, my experience in the Executive Branch of the Government leads me to believe that the requirements laid down in the opinion for the operation of the committee system of inquiry are both unnecessary and unworkable....

Barenblatt v. United States

360 U.S. 109 (1959)

The Court's "lecture" to Congress in *Watkins* v. *United States* (1957) was one of several cases that convinced many members of Congress that the judiciary was overstepping its bounds. A number of court-curbing bills were introduced and acted upon. There is reason to believe that the Court recognized a serious collision with Congress and moved in this case, as well as others, to reduce the friction. Lloyd Barenblatt, a college professor, refused to answer certain questions put to him by a subcommittee of the House Committee on Un-American Activities. For his refusal he was convicted, fined, and sentenced to six months in prison.

Mr. Justice Harlan delivered the opinion of the Court.

. . .

We here review petitioner's conviction under 2 U.S.C. § 192 for contempt of Congress, arising from his refusal to answer certain questions put to him by a Subcommittee of the House Committee on Un-American Activities during the course of an inquiry concerning alleged Communist infiltration into the field of education.

[Section 192 provides: "Every person who having been summoned as a witness by the authority of either House of Congress to give testimony or to produce papers upon any matter under inquiry before either House, or any joint committee established by a joint or concurrent resolution of the two Houses of Congress, or any committee of either House of Congress, willfully makes default, or who, having appeared, refuses to answer any question pertinent to the question under inquiry, shall be deemed guilty of a misdemeanor, punishable by a fine of not more than $1,000 nor less than

$100 and imprisonment in a common jail for not less than one month nor more than twelve months."]

Pursuant to a subpoena, and accompanied by counsel, petitioner on June 28, 1954, appeared as a witness before this congressional Subcommittee. After answering a few preliminary questions and testifying that he had been a graduate student and teaching fellow at the University of Michigan from 1947 to 1950 and an instructor in psychology at Vassar College from 1950 to shortly before his appearance before the Subcommittee, petitioner objected generally to the right of the Subcommittee to inquire into his "political" and "religious" beliefs or any "other personal and private affairs" or "associational activities," upon grounds set forth in a previously prepared memorandum which he was allowed to file with the Subcommittee. Thereafter petitioner specifically declined to answer each of the following five questions:

"Are you now a member of the Communist Party? [Count One.]

"Have you ever been a member of the Communist Party? [Count Two.]

"Now, you have stated that you knew Francis Crowley. Did you know Francis Crowley as a member of the Communist Party? [Count Three.]

"Were you ever a member of the Haldane Club of the Communist Party while at the University of Michigan? [Count Four.]

"Were you a member while a student of the University of Michigan Council of Arts, Sciences, and Professions?" [Count Five.]

In each instance the grounds of refusal were those set forth in the prepared statement. Petitioner expressly disclaimed reliance upon "the Fifth Amendment."

… As we conceive the ultimate issue in this case to be whether petitioner could properly be convicted of contempt for refusing to answer questions relating to his participation in or knowledge of alleged Communist Party activities at educational institutions in this country, we find it unnecessary to consider the validity of his conviction under the Third and Fifth Counts, the only ones involving questions which on their face do not directly relate to such participation or knowledge.

Petitioner's various contentions resolve themselves into three propositions: First, the compelling of testimony by the Subcommittee was neither legislatively authorized nor constitutionally permissible because of the vagueness of Rule XI of the House of Representatives, Eighty-third Congress, the charter of authority of the parent Committee. Second, petitioner was not adequately apprised of the pertinency of the Subcommittee's questions to the subject matter of the inquiry. Third, the questions petitioner refused to answer infringed rights protected by the First Amendment.

[After deciding that Rule XI was not constitutionally infirm on the ground of vagueness, that the questions put to Barenblatt were clearly pertinent, and that he had been adequately informed, the Court turns to the First Amendment issue.]

CONSTITUTIONAL CONTENTIONS.

… Where First Amendment rights are asserted to bar governmental interrogation resolution of the issue always involves a balancing by the courts of the competing private and public interests at stake in the particular circumstances shown. These principles were recognized in the *Watkins* case, where, in speaking of the First Amendment in relation to congressional inquiries, we said (at p. 198): "It is manifest that despite the adverse effects which follow upon compelled disclosure of private matters, not all such inquiries are barred.… The critical element is the existence of, and the weight to be ascribed to, the interest of the Congress in demanding disclosures from an unwilling witness." …

… [I]n stating in the *Watkins* case, p. 200, that "there is no congressional power to expose for the sake of exposure," we at the same time declined to inquire into the "motives of committee members," and recognized that their "motives alone would not vitiate an investigation which had been instituted by a House of Congress if that assembly's legislative purpose is being served." Having scrutinized this record we cannot say that the unanimous panel of the Court of Appeals which first considered this case was wrong in concluding that "the primary purposes of the inquiry were in aid of legislative processes." 240 F.2d, at 881. Certainly this is not a case like *Kilbourn* v. *Thompson*, 103 U.S. 168, 192, where "the House of Representatives not only exceeded the limit of its own authority, but assumed a power which could only be properly exercised by another branch of the government, because it was in its nature clearly judicial." See *McGrain* v. *Daugherty*, 273 U.S. 135, 171. The constitutional legislative power of Congress in this instance is beyond question.

. . .

We conclude that the balance between the individual and the governmental interests here at stake must be struck in favor of the latter, and that therefore the provisions of the First Amendment have not been offended.

We hold that petitioner's conviction for contempt of Congress discloses no infirmity, and that the judgment of the Court of Appeals must be

Affirmed.

Mr. Justice Black, with whom The Chief Justice and Mr. Justice Douglas concur, dissenting.

... I cannot agree with this disposition of the case for I believe that the resolution establishing the House Un-American Activities Committee and the questions that Committee asked Barenblatt violate the Constitution in several respects. (1) Rule XI creating the Committee authorizes such a sweeping, unlimited, all-inclusive and undiscriminating compulsory examination of witnesses in the field of speech, press, petition and assembly that it violates the procedural requirements of the Due Process Clause of the Fifth Amendment. (2) Compelling an answer to the questions asked Barenblatt abridges freedom of speech and association in contravention of the First Amendment. (3) The Committee proceedings were part of a legislative program to stigmatize and punish by public identification and exposure all witnesses considered by the Committee to be guilty of Communist affiliations, as well as all witnesses who refused to answer Committee questions on constitutional grounds; the Committee was thus improperly seeking to try, convict, and punish suspects, a task which the Constitution expressly denies to Congress and grants exclusively to the courts, to be exercised by them only after indictment and in full compliance with all the safeguards provided by the Bill of Rights....

II.

... I do not agree that laws directly abridging First Amendment freedoms can be justified by a congressional or judicial balancing process....

To apply the Court's balancing test under such circumstances is to read the First Amendment to say "Congress shall pass no law abridging freedom of speech, press, assembly and petition, unless Congress and the Supreme Court reach the joint conclusion that on balance the interest of the Government in stifling these freedoms is greater than

the interest of the people in having them exercised." ...

But even assuming what I cannot assume, that some balancing is proper in this case, I feel that the Court after stating the test ignores it completely. At most it balances the right of the Government to preserve itself, against Barenblatt's right to refrain from revealing Communist affiliations. Such a balance, however, mistakes the factors to be weighed. In the first place, it completely leaves out the real interest in Barenblatt's silence, the interest of the people as a whole in being able to join organizations, advocate causes and make political "mistakes" without later being subjected to governmental penalties for having dared to think for themselves. It is this right, the right to err politically, which keeps us strong as a Nation. For no number of laws against communism can have as much effect as the personal conviction which comes from having heard its arguments and rejected them, or from having once accepted its tenets and later recognized their worthlessness. Instead, the obloquy which results from investigations such as this not only stifles "mistakes" but prevents all but the most courageous from hazarding any views which might at some later time become disfavored. This result, whose importance cannot be overestimated, is doubly crucial when it affects the universities, on which we must largely rely for the experimentation and development of new ideas essential to our country's welfare. It is these interests of society, rather than Barenblatt's own right to silence, which I think the Court should put on the balance against the demands of the Government, if any balancing process is to be tolerated....

Ultimately all the questions in this case really boil down to one—whether we as a people will try fearfully and futilely to preserve democracy by adopting totalitarian methods, or whether in accordance with our traditions and our Constitution we will have the confidence and courage to be free.

I would reverse this conviction.

Mr. Justice Brennan, dissenting.

I would reverse this conviction. It is sufficient that I state my complete agreement with my Brother Black that no purpose for the investigation of Barenblatt is revealed by the record except exposure purely for the sake of exposure....

United States v. Nixon

418 U.S. 683 (1974)

The Special Prosecutor investigating the Watergate affair filed a motion for a subpoena to produce certain tapes and documents relating to conversations and meetings between President Nixon and others. President Nixon, claiming executive privilege, filed a motion to quash the subpoena. A district judge rejected that motion and issued an order for an *in camera* examination of the subpoenaed material. This order was stayed pending appellate review.

MR. CHIEF JUSTICE BURGER delivered the opinion of the Court.

This litigation presents for review the denial of a motion, filed in the District Court on behalf of the President of the United States, in the case of *United States* v. *Mitchell* (D. C. Crim. No. 74-110), to quash a third-party subpoena *duces tecum* issued by the United States District Court for the District of Columbia, pursuant to Fed. Rule Crim. Proc. 17 (c). The subpoena directed the President to produce certain tape recordings and documents relating to his conversations with aides and advisers....

On March 1, 1974, a grand jury of the United States District Court for the District of Columbia returned an indictment charging seven named individuals*[Attorney General John N. Mitchell, White House aides H. R. Haldeman and John D. Ehrlichman, Charles W. Colson, Robert C. Mardian, Kenneth W. Parkinson, and Gordon Strachan. The latter four were either on the White House staff or with the Committee for the Re-election of the President.]* with various offenses, including conspiracy to defraud the United States and to obstruct justice. Although he was not designated as such in the indictment, the grand jury named the President, among others, as an unindicted coconspirator. On April 18, 1974, upon motion of the Special Prosecutor, see n. 8, *infra,* a subpoena *duces tecum* was issued pursuant to Rule 17(c) to the President by the United States District Court and made returnable on May 2, 1974. This subpoena required the production, in advance of the September 9 trial date, of certain tapes, memoranda, papers, transcripts, or other writings relating to certain precisely identified meetings between the President and others. The Special Prosecutor was able to fix the time, place, and persons present at these discussions because the White House daily logs and appointment records had been delivered to him. On April 30, the President publicly released edited transcripts of 43 conversations; portions of 20 conversations subject to subpoena in the present case were included. On May 1, 1974, the President's counsel filed a "special appearance" and a motion to quash the subpoena under Rule 17 (c). This motion was accompanied by a formal claim of privilege.

. . .

II. JUSTICIABILITY

In the District Court, the President's counsel argued that the court lacked jurisdiction to issue the subpoena because the matter was an intrabranch dispute between a subordinate and superior officer of the Executive Branch and hence not subject to judicial resolution. That argument has been renewed in this Court with emphasis on the contention that the dispute does not present a "case" or "controversy" which can be adjudicated in the federal courts. The President's counsel argues that the federal courts should not intrude into areas committed to the other branches of Government. He views the present dispute as essentially a "jurisdictional" dispute within the Executive Branch which he analogizes to a dispute between two congressional committees. Since the Executive Branch has exclusive authority and absolute discretion to decide whether to prosecute a case, ... it is contended that a President's decision is final in determining what evidence is to be used in a given criminal case. Although his counsel concedes that the President has delegated certain specific powers to the Special Prosecutor, he has not "waived nor delegated to the Special Prosecutor the President's duty to claim privilege as to all materials ... which fall within the President's inherent authority to refuse to disclose to any executive officer." ... The Special Prosecutor's demand for the items therefore presents, in the view of the President's counsel, a political question under *Baker* v. *Carr,* 369 U.S. 186 (1962), since it involves a "textually demonstrable" grant of power under Art. II.

The mere assertion of a claim of an "intrabranch dispute," without more, has never operated to defeat federal jurisdiction; justiciability does not depend on such a surface inquiry....

[The Court reviewed the following facts: under authority of Article II, Section 2, Congress vested in the Attorney General the power to conduct criminal liti-

gation and to appoint subordinate officers; acting pursuant to statutory authority, the Attorney General delegated authority to a Special Prosecutor with unique authority and tenure; the regulation delegating this authority gave the Special Prosecutor explicit power to contest claims of executive privilege; this regulation had the force of law and had not been amended or revoked.]

In light of the uniqueness of the setting in which the conflict arises, the fact that both parties are officers of the Executive Branch cannot be viewed as a barrier to justiciability. It would be inconsistent with the applicable law and regulation, and the unique facts of this case to conclude other than that the Special Prosecutor has standing to bring this action and that a justiciable controversy is presented for decision....

IV. THE CLAIM OF PRIVILEGE
A

... [W]e turn to the claim that the subpoena should be quashed because it demands "confidential conversations between a President and his close advisors that it would be inconsistent with the public interest to produce." App. 48a. The first contention is a broad claim that the separation of powers doctrine precludes judicial review of a President's claim of privilege. The second contention is that if he does not prevail on the claim of absolute privilege, the court should hold as a matter of constitutional law that the privilege prevails over the subpoena *duces tecum*.

In the performance of assigned constitutional duties each branch of the Government must initially interpret the Constitution, and the interpretation of its powers by any branch is due great respect from the others. The President's counsel, as we have noted, reads the Constitution as providing an absolute privilege of confidentiality for all Presidential communications. Many decisions of this Court, however, have unequivocally reaffirmed the holding of *Marbury* v. *Madison,* 1 Cranch 137 (1803), that "[i]t is emphatically the province and duty of the judicial department to say what the law is." *Id.*, at 177.

No holding of the Court has defined the scope of judicial power specifically relating to the enforcement of a subpoena for confidential Presidential communications for use in a criminal prosecution, but other exercises of power by the Executive Branch and the Legislative Branch have been found invalid as in conflict with the Constitution. *Powell* v. *McCormack,* 395 U.S. 486 (1969); *Youngstown Sheet & Tube Co.* v. *Sawyer,* 343 U.S. 579 (1952). Notwithstanding the deference each branch must

accord the others, the "judicial Power of the United States" vested in the federal courts by Art. III, § 1, of the Constitution can no more be shared with the Executive Branch than the Chief Executive, for example, can share with the Judiciary the veto power, or the Congress share with the Judiciary the power to override a Presidential veto. Any other conclusion would be contrary to the basic concept of separation of powers and the checks and balances that flow from the scheme of a tripartite government....

B

In support of his claim of absolute privilege, the President's counsel urges two grounds, one of which is common to all governments and one of which is peculiar to our system of separation of powers. The first ground is the valid need for protection of communications between high Government officials and those who advise and assist them in the performance of their manifold duties; the importance of this confidentiality is too plain to require further discussion. Human experience teaches that those who expect public dissemination of their remarks may well temper candor with a concern for appearances and for their own interests to the detriment of the decision-making process. Whatever the nature of the privilege of confidentiality of Presidential communications in the exercise of Art. II powers, the privilege can be said to derive from the supremacy of each branch within its own assigned area of constitutional duties. Certain powers and privileges flow from the nature of enumerated powers; the protection of the confidentiality of Presidential communications has similar constitutional underpinnings.

The second ground asserted by the President's counsel in support of the claim of absolute privilege rests on the doctrine of separation of powers. Here it is argued that the independence of the Executive Branch within its own sphere, ... insulates a President from a judicial subpoena in an ongoing criminal prosecution, and thereby protects confidential Presidential communications.

However, neither the doctrine of separation of powers, nor the need for confidentiality of high-level communications, without more, can sustain an absolute, unqualified Presidential privilege of immunity from judicial process under all circumstances. The President's need for complete candor and objectivity from advisers calls for great deference from the courts. However, when the privilege depends solely on the broad, undifferentiated claim of public interest in the confidentiality of such conversations, a confrontation with other values arises. Absent a claim of need to protect military, diplomatic, or sensitive national security secrets, we find it difficult to accept the argument that even the very important interest in confidentiality of Presidential communications is significantly diminished by production of such material for *in camera* inspection with all the protection that a district court will be obliged to provide.

The impediment that an absolute, unqualified privilege would place in the way of the primary constitutional duty of the Judicial Branch to do justice in criminal prosecutions would plainly conflict with the function of the courts under Art. III....

C

Since we conclude that the legitimate needs of the judicial process may outweigh Presidential privilege, it is necessary to resolve those competing interests in a manner that preserves the essential functions of each branch....

The expectation of a President to the confidentiality of his conversations and correspondence, like the claim of confidentiality of judicial deliberations, for example, has all the values to which we accord deference for the privacy of all citizens and, added to those values, is the necessity for protection of the public interest in candid, objective, and even blunt or harsh opinions in Presidential decisionmaking. A President and those who assist him must be free to explore alternatives in the process of shaping policies and making decisions and to do so in a way many would be unwilling to express except privately. These are the considerations justifying a presumptive privilege for Presidential communications. The privilege is fundamental to the operation of Government and inextricably rooted in the separation of powers under the Constitution....

But this presumptive privilege must be considered in light of our historic commitment to the rule of law. This is nowhere more profoundly manifest than in our view that "the twofold aim [of criminal justice] is that guilt shall not escape or innocence suffer." *Berger* v. *United States,* 295 U.S., at 88. We have elected to employ an adversary system of criminal justice in which the parties contest all issues before a court of law. The need to develop all relevant facts in the adversary system is both fundamental and comprehensive. The ends of criminal justice would be defeated if judgments were to be founded on a partial or speculative presentation of the facts. The very integrity of the judicial system and public confidence in the system depend on full disclosure of all the facts, within the framework of the rules of evidence. To ensure that justice is done, it is imperative to the function of courts that compulsory process be available for the production of evidence needed either by the prosecution or by the defense.

. . .

In this case the President challenges a subpoena served on him as a third party requiring the production of materials for use in a criminal prosecution; he does so on the claim that he has a privilege against disclosure of confidential communications. He does not place his claim of privilege on the ground they are military or diplomatic secrets. As to these areas of Art. II duties the courts have traditionally shown the utmost deference to Presidential responsibilities....

. . .

In this case we must weigh the importance of the general privilege of confidentiality of Presidential communications in performance of the President's responsibilities against the inroads of such a privilege on the fair administration of criminal justice. *[The Court, in a footnote, adds: "We are not here concerned with the balance between the President's generalized interest in confidentiality and the need for relevant evidence in civil litigation, nor with that between the confidentiality interest and congressional demands for information, nor with the President's interest in preserving state secrets. We address only the conflict between the President's assertion of a generalized privilege of confidentiality and the constitutional need for relevant evidence in criminal trials."]* The interest in preserving confidentiality is weighty indeed and entitled to great respect. However, we cannot conclude that advisers will be moved to temper the candor of their remarks by the infrequent occasions of disclosure because of the possibility that such conversations will be called for in the context of a criminal prosecution.

On the other hand, the allowance of the privilege to withhold evidence that is demonstrably relevant in a criminal trial would cut deeply into the guarantee of due process of law and gravely impair the basic function of the courts. A President's acknowledged need for confidentiality in the communications of his office is general in nature, whereas the constitutional need for production of relevant evidence in a criminal proceeding is specific and central to the fair adjudication of a particular criminal case in the administration of justice. Without access to specific facts a criminal prosecution may be totally frustrated. The President's broad interest in confidentiality of communications will not be vitiated by disclosure of a limited number of conversations preliminarily shown to have some bearing on the pending criminal cases.

We conclude that when the ground for asserting privilege as to subpoenaed materials sought for use in a criminal trial is based only on the generalized interest in confidentiality, it cannot prevail over the fundamental demands of due process of law in the fair administration of criminal justice. The generalized assertion of privilege must yield to the demonstrated, specific need for evidence in a pending criminal trial.

· · ·

Since this matter came before the Court during the pendency of a criminal prosecution, and on representations that time is of the essence, the mandate shall issue forthwith.

Affirmed.

Mr. Justice Rehnquist took no part in the consideration or decision of these cases.

Negotiating Executive Privilege: The AT&T Cases

Executive documents are routinely shared with Congress, including documents that are highly classified and confidential. When there is a conflict between the executive and legislative branches, accommodations are usually discovered that avoid litigation. Even when a case is brought to court, the usual resolution is to force the two branches to find an intermediate position that will satisfy executive as well as congressional interests. The two cases below, involving national-security wiretaps, illustrate the practical efforts to iron out executive-legislative collisions. In a series of steps, Judge Harold Leventhal helped resolve a dispute between the Justice Department and a congressional committee. The two cases are *United States* v. *AT&T,* 551 F.2d 384 (D.C. Cir. 1976) and *United States* v. *AT&T,* 567 F.2d 121 (D.C. Cir. 1977). The first selection is from the 1976 case.

LEVENTHAL, Circuit Judge.

This unusual case involves a portentous clash between the executive and legislative branches, the executive branch asserting its authority to maintain tight control over information related to our national security, and the legislative branch asserting its authority to gather information necessary for the formulation of new legislation.

In the name of the United States, the Justice Department sued to enjoin the American Telephone and Telegraph Co. (AT&T) from complying with a subpoena of a subcommittee of the House of Representatives issued in the course of an investigation into warrantless "national security" wiretaps. Congressman Moss, chairman of the subcommittee, intervened on behalf of the House, the real defendant in interest since AT&T, while prepared to comply with the subpoena in the absence of a protective court order, has no stake in the controversy beyond knowing whether its legal obligation is to comply with the subpoena or not. The District Court issued the injunction requested by plaintiff and Chairman Moss appeals.

The case presents difficult problems, preliminary questions of jurisdiction and justiciability (application of the political question doctrine) and the ultimate issue on the merits of resolving or balancing the constitutional powers asserted by the legislative and executive branches.

In order to avoid a possibly unnecessary constitutional decision, we suggest the outlines of a possible settlement which may meet the mutual needs of the congressional and executive parties, without requiring a judicial resolution of a head-on confrontation, and we remand without decision at this time in order to permit exploration of this solution by the parties, under District Court guidance if needed.

If the parties reach an impasse this will be reported to us by the District Court. We would then be confronted with the need to enter an order disposing of the appeal pending.

I. BACKGROUND

The controversy arose out of an investigation by the Subcommittee on Oversight and Investigations of the House Committee on Interstate and Foreign Commerce. The Subcommittee was interested in determining the nature and extent of warrantless wiretapping in the United States for asserted national security purposes. It was concerned with the possible abuse of that power and its effect on privacy and other interests of U.S. citizens, and with the possible need for limiting legislation.

The warrantless wiretaps which became the focus of this part of the investigation used facilities provided by AT&T upon its receipt from the FBI of "request" letters. Each request letter specified a target line to be tapped, identified by telephone number, address, or other numerical designation. The letter requested a "leased line" to carry the tapped communications from the target location to a designated monitoring station manned by federal agents.

On June 22, 1976, the Subcommittee authorized and the Committee Chairman issued a subpoena requiring the president of AT&T to turn over to the Subcommittee copies of all national security request letters sent to AT&T and its subsidiaries by the FBI as well as records of such taps prior to the time when the practice of sending such letters was initiated. After the subpoena was issued, AT&T stood ready to comply.

At this point the White House approached Subcommittee Chairman John Moss in search of an alternative arrangement meeting the Subcommittee's information needs. The basic thrust of the ensuing negotiations between the Subcommittee and the Justice Department was to substitute, for the request letters, expurgated copies of the backup memoranda upon which the Attorney General based his decision to authorize the warrantless taps. These memoranda, providing information on the purpose and nature of the surveillance, might have been more informative to Congress than the request letters, which merely contained numerical identification of the line to be tapped. The Justice Department agreed, at least informally and tentatively, to provide the Subcommittee staff expurgated copies of the backup memo pertaining to foreign intelligence taps, with all information which would identify the target replaced by generic description, such as "Middle Eastern diplomat." The negotiations came close to success, but broke down over the issue of verification by the Subcommittee of the accuracy of the executive's generic descriptions by inspection of a sample of the original memoranda.

[Judge Leventhal reviewed the powers of Congress to investigate, and the President's national security powers. "Each branch of government claims that as long as it is exercising its authority for a legitimate purpose, its actions are unreviewable by the courts."]

F. BALANCING BY THE COURTS

A court seeking to balance the legislative and executive interests asserted here would face severe problems in formulating and applying standards. Granted that the subpoenas are clearly within the proper legislative investigatory sphere, it is difficult to "weigh" Congress's need for the request letters. Congress's power to monitor executive actions is implicit in the appropriations power. Here, for instance, if the President has the inherent power claimed to block the subpoena, how is Congress to assure that appropriated funds are not being used for illegal warrantless domestic electronic surveillance?

As to the danger to national security, a court would have to consider the Subcommittee's track record for security, the likelihood of a leak if other members of the House sought access to the material. In addition to this delicate and possibly unseemly determination, the court would have to weigh the effect of a leak on intelligence activities and diplomatic relations. Finally, the court would have to consider the reasonableness of the alternatives offered by the parties and decide which would better reconcile the competing constitutional interests.

IV. REASONS FOR EXPLORATION OF SETTLEMENT

Before moving on to a decision of such nerve-center constitutional questions, we pause to allow for further efforts at a settlement. We think that suggestion is particularly appropriate in this case and may well be productive.... The legislative and executive branches have a long history of settlement of disputes that seemed irreconcilable. There was almost a settlement in 1976. It may well be attainable in 1977.

Furthermore, our own reflections may be of some assistance. As a prelude to settlement conference, it may be helpful if we review pertinent considerations:

1. This dispute between the legislative and executive branches has at least some elements of the political-question doctrine. A court decision selects a victor, and tends thereafter to tilt the scales. A compromise worked out between the branches is most likely to meet their essential needs and the country's constitutional balance.

[1977 decision:]

LEVENTHAL, Circuit Judge:

This case brings to us for a second time conflicting assertions by the executive and legislative branches, contentions that require the third branch to decide whether its constitutional mandate to decide controversies extends to such a conflict, and if so what measure of judicial resolution is sound and appropriate.

. . .

When we first came to the case, we developed a

novel and somewhat gingerly approach for the delicate problem of accommodating the needs and powers of two coordinate branches in a situation where each claimed absolute authority.... To the extent possible, we wished to avoid a resolution that might disturb the balance of power between the two branches and inaccurately reflect their true needs....

Negotiation has narrowed but not bridged the gap between the parties. Accordingly, we must adopt a somewhat more traditional approach. We begin by deciding that complete judicial abstention on political question grounds is not warranted. In addressing the merits, however, we continue to move cautiously. Taking full account of the negotiating positions, we have chartered the course that we think is most likely to accommodate the substantial needs of the parties. Doubtless, neither will be satisfied. But in our view there is good reason to believe that the procedure set forth in this opinion will prove feasible in practice, with such adjustments and refinements as may be evolved by the parties and the district court....

The framers, rather than attempting to define and allocate all governmental power in minute detail, relied, we believe, on the expectation that where conflicts in scope of authority arose between the coordinate branches, a spirit of dynamic compromise would promote resolution of the dispute in the manner most likely to result in efficient and effective functioning of our governmental system. Under this view, the coordinate branches do not exist in an exclusively adversary relationship to one another when a conflict in authority arises. Rather, each branch should take cognizance of an implicit constitutional mandate to seek optimal accommodation through a realistic evaluation of the needs of the conflicting branches in the particular fact situation. This aspect of our constitutional scheme avoids the mischief of polarization of disputes....

[The case was dismissed on December 21, 1978, after the Justice Department and the subcommittee amicably resolved their differences.]

Clinton v. Jones

520 U.S. 681 (1997)

Paula Corbin Jones sued President Clinton for sexual harassment and assault for an incident that occurred in 1991, when Clinton served as governor of Arkansas. While recognizing that she would have a right to pursue the lawsuit after he left the presidency, Clinton moved to dismiss the case on grounds of presidential immunity. A federal appellate court held that a President enjoys absolute immunity only for official, not unofficial, acts. Jones v. Clinton, 72 F.3d 1354 (8th Cir. 1996). The Supreme Court agreed to hear the case.

JUSTICE STEVENS delivered the opinion of the Court.

This case raises a constitutional and a prudential question concerning the Office of the President of the United States. Respondent, a private citizen, seeks to recover damages from the current occupant of that office based on actions allegedly taken before his term began. The President submits that in all but the most exceptional cases the Constitution requires federal courts to defer such litigation until his term ends and that, in any event, respect for the office warrants such a stay. Despite the force of the arguments supporting the President's submissions, we conclude that they must be rejected.

I

Petitioner, William Jefferson Clinton, was elected to the Presidency in 1992, and reelected in 1996. His term of office expires on January 20, 2001. In 1991 he was the Governor of the State of Arkansas. Re-

spondent, Paula Corbin Jones, is a resident of California. In 1991 she lived in Arkansas, and was an employee of the Arkansas Industrial Development Commission.

On May 6, 1994, she commenced this action in the United States District Court for the Eastern District of Arkansas by filing a complaint naming petitioner and Danny Ferguson, a former Arkansas State Police officer, as defendants....

Those allegations principally describe events that are said to have occurred on the afternoon of May 8, 1991, during an official conference held at the Excelsior Hotel in Little Rock, Arkansas. The Governor delivered a speech at the conference; respondent—working as a state employee—staffed the registration desk. She alleges that Ferguson persuaded her to leave her desk and to visit the Governor in a business suite at the hotel, where he made "abhorrent" sexual advances that she vehemently rejected. She further claims that her superiors at work subsequently dealt with her in a hostile and rude manner, and changed her duties to punish her for rejecting those advances. Finally, she alleges that after petitioner was elected President, Ferguson defamed her by making a statement to a reporter that implied she had accepted petitioner's alleged overtures, and that various persons authorized to speak for the President publicly branded her a liar by denying that the incident had occurred.

Respondent seeks actual damages of $75,000, and punitive damages of $100,000. Her complaint contains four counts. The first charges that petitioner, acting under color of state law, deprived her of rights protected by the Constitution, in violation of Rev. Stat. § 1979, 42 U.S.C. § 1983. The second charges that petitioner and Ferguson engaged in a conspiracy to violate her federal rights, also actionable under federal law. See Rev. Stat. § 1980, 42 U.S.C. § 1985. The third is a state common law claim for intentional infliction of emotional distress, grounded primarily on the incident at the hotel. The fourth count, also based on state law, is for defamation, embracing both the comments allegedly made to the press by Ferguson and the statements of petitioner's agents....

II

In response to the complaint, petitioner promptly advised the District Court that he intended to file a motion to dismiss on grounds of Presidential immunity, and requested the court to defer all other pleadings and motions until after the immunity issue was resolved....

IV

Petitioner's principal submission — that "in all but the most exceptional cases"... the Constitution affords the President temporary immunity from civil damages litigation arising out of events that occurred before he took office — cannot be sustained on the basis of precedent.

Only three sitting Presidents have been defendants in civil litigation involving their actions prior to taking office. Complaints against Theodore Roosevelt and Harry Truman had been dismissed before they took office; the dismissals were affirmed after their respective inaugurations. Two companion cases arising out of an automobile accident were filed against John F. Kennedy in 1960 during the Presidential campaign. After taking office, he unsuccessfully argued that his status as Commander in Chief gave him a right to a stay under the Soldiers' and Sailors' Civil Relief Act of 1940, 50 U.S.C.App. §§ 501–525. The motion for a stay was denied by the

District Court, and the matter was settled out of court. Thus, none of those cases sheds any light on the constitutional issue before us.

The principal rationale for affording certain public servants immunity from suits for money damages arising out of their official acts is inapplicable to unofficial conduct. In cases involving prosecutors, legislators, and judges we have repeatedly explained that the immunity serves the public interest in enabling such officials to perform their designated functions effectively without fear that a particular decision may give rise to personal liability....

This reasoning provides no support for an immunity for *unofficial* conduct....

VI

Petitioner's strongest argument supporting his immunity claim is based on the text and structure of the Constitution. He does not contend that the occupant of the Office of the President is "above the law," in the sense that his conduct is entirely immune from judicial scrutiny. The President argues merely for a postponement of the judicial proceedings that will determine whether he violated any law. His argument is grounded in the character of the office that was created by Article II of the Constitution, and relies on separation of powers principles that have structured our constitutional arrangement since the founding.

As a starting premise, petitioner contends that he occupies a unique office with powers and responsibilities so vast and important that the public interest demands that he devote his undivided time and attention to his public duties. He submits that — given the nature of the office — the doctrine of separation of powers places limits on the authority of the Federal Judiciary to interfere with the Executive Branch that would be transgressed by allowing this action to proceed.

We have no dispute with the initial premise of the argument. Former presidents, from George Washington to George Bush, have consistently endorsed petitioner's characterization of the office....

... As a factual matter, petitioner contends that this particular case — as well as the potential additional litigation that an affirmance of the Court of Appeals judgment might spawn — may impose an unacceptable burden on the President's time and energy, and thereby impair the effective performance of his office.

Petitioner's predictive judgment finds little support in either history or the relatively narrow compass of the issues raised in this particular case. As we have already noted, in the more than 200-year history of the Republic, only three sitting Presidents have been subjected to suits for their private actions.... If the past is any indicator, it seems unlikely that a deluge of such litigation will ever engulf the Presidency. As for the case at hand, if properly managed by the District Court, it appears to us highly unlikely to occupy any substantial amount of petitioner's time.

Of greater significance, petitioner errs by presuming that interactions between the Judicial Branch and the Executive, even quite burdensome interactions, necessarily rise to the level of constitutionally forbidden impairment of the Executive's ability to perform its constitutionally mandated functions. "[O]ur ... system imposes upon the Branches a degree of overlapping responsibility, a duty of interdependence as well as independence the absence of which 'would preclude the establishment of a Nation capable of governing itself effectively.'" *Mistretta*, 488 U.S., at 381 (quoting *Buckley*, 424 U.S., at 121). As Madison explained, separation of powers does not mean that the branches "ought to have no *partial agency* in, or no *controul* over the acts of each other." ...

First, we have long held that when the President takes official action, the Court has the authority to determine whether he has acted within the law. Perhaps the most dramatic example of such a case is our holding that President Truman exceeded his constitutional authority when he issued an order directing the Secretary of Commerce to take possession of and operate most of the Nation's steel mills in order to avert a national catastrophe. *Youngstown Sheet & Tube Co. v. Sawyer* 343 U.S. 579 (1952)....

Second, it is also settled that the President is subject to judicial process in appropriate circumstances....

Sitting Presidents have responded to court orders to provide testimony and other information with sufficient frequency that such interactions between the Judicial and Executive Branches can scarcely be thought a novelty. President Monroe responded to written interrogatories, ... President Nixon — as noted above — produced tapes in response to a subpoena *duces tecum,* see *United States v. Nixon*, President Ford complied with an order to give a deposition in a criminal trial, *United States v. Fromme*, 405 F.Supp. 578 (E.D.Cal.1975), and President Clinton has twice given videotaped testimony in criminal proceedings.... Moreover, sitting Presidents have also voluntarily complied with judicial requests for testimony. President Grant gave a lengthy deposition in a criminal case under such circumstances, ... and President Carter similarly gave videotaped testimony for use at a criminal trial, *ibid.*

... We therefore hold that the doctrine of separation of powers does not require federal courts to stay all private actions against the President until he leaves office.

... [W]e turn to the question whether the District Court's decision to stay the trial until after petitioner leaves office was an abuse of discretion.

VII

... Although we have rejected the argument that the potential burdens on the President violate separation of powers principles, those burdens are appropriate matters for the District Court to evaluate in its management of the case. The high respect that is owed to the office of the Chief Executive, though not justifying a rule of categorical immunity, is a matter that should inform the conduct of the entire proceeding, including the timing and scope of discovery.

Nevertheless, we are persuaded that it was an abuse of discretion for the District Court to defer the trial until after the President leaves office. Such a lengthy and categorical stay takes no account whatever of the respondent's interest in bringing the case to trial. The complaint was filed within the statutory limitations period — albeit near the end of that period — and delaying trial would increase the danger of prejudice resulting from the loss of evidence, including the inability of witnesses to recall specific facts, or the possible death of a party.

... We think the District Court may have given undue weight to the concern that a trial might generate unrelated civil actions that could conceivably hamper the President in conducting the duties of his office. If and when that should occur, the court's discretion would permit it to manage those actions in such fashion (including deferral of trial) that interference with the President's duties would not occur. But no such impingement upon the President's conduct of his office was shown here.

VIII

We add a final comment on two matters that are discussed at length in the briefs: the risk that our decision will generate a large volume of politically motivated harassing and frivolous litigation, and the danger that national security concerns might prevent the President from explaining a legitimate need for a continuance.

We are not persuaded that either of these risks is serious. Most frivolous and vexatious litigation is terminated at the pleading stage or on summary judgment, with little if any personal involvement by the defendant.... Moreover, the availability of sanctions provides a significant deterrent to litigation directed at the President in his unofficial capacity for purposes of political gain or harassment. History indicates that the likelihood that a significant number of such cases will be filed is remote....

If Congress deems it appropriate to afford the President stronger protection, it may respond with appropriate legislation....

The Federal District Court has jurisdiction to decide this case. Like every other citizen who properly invokes that jurisdiction, respondent has a right to an orderly disposition of her claims. Accordingly, the judgment of the Court of Appeals is affirmed.

It is so ordered.

[Justice Breyer prepared a lengthy concurring opinion in which he discussed the specific situation when a President "sets forth and explains a conflict between judiciary proceeding and public duties." Under this circumstance, a federal district judge might schedule a trial in such a way that it interferes with the President's discharge of his public duties. Breyer's concurrence emphasizes the importance of the President's office and the danger of having a single judge "second guess" a President's needs.]

H. CONGRESSIONAL MEMBERSHIP AND PREROGATIVES

Under Article I, Section 5, each House of Congress "may determine the rules of its proceedings, punish its members for disorderly behavior, and, with the concurrence of two thirds, expel a member." Each House is also "the judge of the elections, returns and qualifications of its own members." Qualifications for office are set forth in Article I, Sections 2 and 3: age (25 for Representatives and 30 for Senators), citizenship (seven years for Representatives and nine years for Senators), and residency (members must be "inhabitants" of the state in which they are chosen). The custom is for Representatives to also reside in the district for which they are elected.

On a few occasions the House of Representatives has refused to seat someone elected to office. A prominent example was Victor Berger of Wisconsin, a Socialist denied his seat in 1919 because he had been convicted for opposing World War I. A case that eventually reached the Supreme Court involved Adam Clayton Powell, a controversial black Congressman from New York. He was reelected in 1966 but the House refused to seat him, in part because of criminal proceedings against him. Many observers thought that the issue was clearly a political question to be decided solely by the House, but in 1969 the Supreme Court held that neither House could deny a seat to a duly elected member who satisfied the qualifications for office specified in the Constitution: age, citizenship, and residency. Congress could not add to that list of qualifications. POWELL v. McCORMACK, 395 U.S. 486 (1969). (See box on "The Exclusion of Adam Clayton Powell" in Chapter 3).

If the House wanted to exclude Powell, it had to first seat him and then expel him by the two-thirds majority required by the Constitution. Previously, the Court had held that the Georgia legislature had violated Julian Bond's First Amendment rights by refusing to seat him because he had expressed his opposition to the Vietnam War. Bond v. Floyd, 385 U.S. 116 (1966). In addition to expulsion, Congress may censure a member for dishonorable or disreputable behavior.

Term Limits

A number of states adopted constitutional amendments and other measures to place term limits on legislators not only in state government but in Congress as well. An amendment to the Arkansas Constitution, limiting members of Congress to three terms in the House of Representatives and two terms in the Senate, was declared unconstitutional by the Supreme Court in 1995. Relying primarily on *Powell v. McCormack*, the court held that the Arkansas provision violated the U.S. Constitution by adding to the qualifications established for members of Congress. U.S. Term Limits, Inc. v. Thornton, 514 U.S. 779 (1995).

Also in 1995, the U.S. House of Representatives voted on a constitutional amendment to limit Representatives and Senators to a certain number of terms. Some of the proposals would have limited the terms of Representatives to six years and Senators to twelve, while others imposed limits of twelve

---

Speech or Debate Clause

Covers	*Does Not Cover*
Words spoken in debate and anything in relation to legislative business. Kilbourn v. Thompson, 103 U.S. 168, 204 (1881).	Criminal actions that are peripherally related to some legislative function. United States v. Brewster, 408 U.S. 501, 521 (1972).
Remarks in committee hearings and committee reports. Gravel v. United States, 408 U.S. 606 (1972); Doe v. McMillan, 412 U.S. 306 (1973).	"Errands" for constituents, making appointments with executive agencies, and assistance in securing federal contracts. United States v. Brewster, at 513.
Speeches in *Congressional Record,* whether delivered or not. Hutchinson v. Proxmire, 433 U.S. 111, 116 n.3 (1979).	Newsletters to constituents, news releases, and speeches delivered outside Congress. United States v. Brewster, at 513; Hutchinson v. Proxmire.
Congressional aides when carrying out legislative tasks. Gravel v. United States, 408 U.S. 606 (1972).	Private publications by members of Congress. Gravel v. United States, at 625; Doe v. McMillan, at 314–15.
Judges may not inquire into the motivation for a Congressman's speech. United States v. Johnson, 383 U.S. 169, 176–77 (1966).	Contacts with executive branch. United States v. Johnson, at 172; Gravel v. United States, at 625.

---

years on both chambers. All of these amendments were voted down, including the basic Republican amendment (a lifetime limit of twelve years for both Houses), which lost on a vote of 227 to 204 — a two-thirds majority being required for a constitutional amendment. A constitutional amendment stalled in the Senate in 1996 because of a filibuster. Another House effort in 1997 to amend the Constitution to impose term limits attracted the support of only 217 to 211.

In 2001, the Supreme Court struck down a 1996 amendment to the Missouri constitution that required special ballot language next to the names of candidates for the U.S. Congress who did not support term limits. A unanimous Court held that the notations put the candidates at a political disadvantage and represented an unconstitutional attempt to dictate electoral outcomes. Cook v. Gralike, 531 U.S. 510 (2001).

Speech or Debate Clause

Article I, Section 6, provides that "for any Speech or Debate in either House," Senators and Representatives "shall not be questioned in any other Place." The courts have consistently held that the immunities offered by this Clause exist not simply for the personal or private benefit of members "but to protect the integrity of the legislative process by insuring the independence of individual legislators." United States v. Brewster, 408 U.S. 501, 507 (1972). It protects members from executive or judicial harassment. United States v. Johnson, 383 U.S. 177 (1966). The Clause covers not only words spoken in debate but also anything required to conduct legislative business: remarks made in the course of committee hearings; speeches printed in the *Congressional Record,* even when not delivered; and information acquired by congressional staff. Other activities, which the courts call "political" rather than "legislative," are not protected: contacts with executive agencies, assistance to constituents seeking federal contracts, the preparation of news releases and newsletters, and speeches or documents delivered outside the Congress (see box). See Gravel v. United States, 408 U.S. 606 (1972).

To protect its prerogatives, Congress has not hesitated to engage in direct confrontations with the judiciary. In 1970, the House Committee on Internal Security prepared a report entitled "Limited Survey of Honoraria Given Guest Speakers for Engagements at Colleges and Universities." By including the names of leftist or antiwar speakers and the amounts they received, the committee hoped that alumni would complain about the use of college funds and threaten to withhold future contributions. The ACLU obtained a copy of the galleys of the committee report and asked a federal judge to issue an injunction prohibiting its publication. U.S. District Judge Gesell did just that, ordering the Public Printer and the Superintendent of Documents not to print the report or even any "fascimile" of it. He suggested that Congress could print the report in the *Congressional Record* if it wanted to. Hentoff v. Ichord, 318 F.Supp. 1175 (D.D.C. 1970).

The House of Representatives responded with a resolution that told everyone, including the courts, to get out of the way. During debate on the resolution, it was pointed out that Congress does not print committee reports in the *Congressional Record*. Supporters of the resolution argued that Judge Gesell's order violated the Speech and Debate Clause and interfered with the authority of each House to determine the rules of its proceedings and to publish them. After the resolution passed by a large bipartisan margin of 302 to 54, the report was printed without any further judicial involvement. 116 Cong. Rec. 41358–74 (1970); H. Rept. No. 1732, 91st Cong., 2d Sess. (1970).

Article I, Section 6, also provides that members of Congress "shall in all cases, except treason, felony and breach of the peace, be privileged from arrest during their attendance at the session of their respective houses, and in going to and returning from the same." Immunity from arrest during sessions of the legislature can be traced back to struggles between the English Parliament and the King.

On May 20, 2006 the Justice Department triggered a major Speech or Debate Clause issue by obtaining a search warrant and entering the Capitol Hill office of Rep. William J. Jefferson (D-La.). The search continued for 18 hours, until Sunday morning. The FBI threatened to pick the office door lock if not given immediate entry. Once inside, the FBI agents refused to permit the House General Counsel or Capitol Police to enter the office while the search was proceeding. The execution of the warrant was the first ever carried out on a congressional office in over 200 years.

The initial media issue was whether a member of Congress "was above the law." The deeper issue, however, was the use of a search warrant by the executive branch on Capitol Hill and the damage that did to the independence and coequal status of Congress. In a case brought by Jefferson and the Bipartisan Legal Advisory Group of the United States House of Representatives, a district court judge found the raid to be legal. He rejected the claim that the search violated the Constitution's Speech and Debate Clause and the separation of powers, holding that a Congressman is "generally bound to the operation of the criminal laws as are ordinary persons," and the Speech or Debate Clause does not "make Members of Congress super-citizens, immune from criminal responsibility." An appellate panel overturned this decision, ruling that the Department of Justice could not review the seized files until Jefferson had the chance to determine which ones pertained to his work as a legislator. U.S. v. Rayburn House, Rm 2113, Washington, DC, 497 F.3d 654 (D.C. Cir. 2007). In 2008 the Supreme Court denied further review.

Powell v. McCormack

395 U.S. 486 (1969)

Adam Clayton Powell had served New York's 18th Congressional District since 1945. After his reelection in 1966, the House of Representatives passed a resolution refusing to seat him. By that point Powell had been charged with a number of offenses, including misappropriation of public funds and illegal salary payments for his wife. Also, he had been held in contempt in a New York defamation suit. After the exclusion vote, Powell and 13 voters of his congressional district sued John W. McCormack, Speaker of the House, and several other House officials. A district court said it lacked jurisdiction to hear the case; the D.C. Circuit held that it had jurisdiction but that the case was nonjusticiable.

MR. CHIEF JUSTICE WARREN delivered the opinion of the Court.

In November 1966, petitioner Adam Clayton Powell, Jr., was duly elected from the 18th Congressional District of New York to serve in the United States House of Representatives for the 90th Congress. However, pursuant to a House resolution, he was not permitted to take his seat. Powell (and some of the voters of his district) then filed suit in Federal District Court, claiming that the House could exclude him only if it found he failed to meet the standing requirements of age, citizenship, and residence contained in Art. I, § 2, of the Constitution — requirements the House specifically found Powell met — and thus had excluded him unconstitutionally. The District Court dismissed petitioners' complaint "for want of jurisdiction of the subject matter." A panel of the Court of Appeals affirmed the dismissal, although on somewhat different grounds, each judge filing a separate opinion. We have determined that it was error to dismiss the complaint and that petitioner Powell is entitled to a declaratory judgment that he was unlawfully excluded from the 90th Congress.

I. FACTS.

During the 89th Congress, a Special Subcommittee on Contracts of the Committee on House Administration conducted an investigation into the expenditures of the Committee on Education and Labor, of which petitioner Adam Clayton Powell, Jr., was chairman. The Special Subcommittee issued a report concluding that Powell and certain staff employees had deceived the House authorities as to travel expenses. The report also indicated there was strong evidence that certain illegal salary payments had been made to Powell's wife at his direction.... No formal action was taken during the 89th Congress. However, prior to the organization of the 90th Congress, the Democratic members-elect met in caucus and voted to remove Powell as chairman of the Committee on Education and Labor....

When the 90th Congress met to organize in January 1967, Powell was asked to step aside while the oath was administered to the other members-elect. Following the administration of the oath to the remaining members, the House discussed the procedure to be followed in determining whether Powell was eligible to take his seat. After some debate, by a vote of 363 to 65 the House adopted House Resolution No. 1, which provided that the Speaker appoint a Select Committee to determine Powell's eligibility. 113 Cong. Rec. 26–27. Although the resolution prohibited Powell from taking his seat until the House acted on the Select Committee's report, it did provide that he should receive all the pay and allowances due a member during the period.

... [O]n February 23, 1967, the Committee issued its report, finding that Powell met the standing qualifications of Art. I § 2.... However, the Committee further reported that Powell had asserted an unwarranted privilege and immunity from the processes of the courts of New York; that he had wrongfully diverted House funds for the use of others and himself; and that he had made false reports on expenditures of foreign currency to the Committee on House Administration.... The Committee recommended that Powell be sworn and seated as a member of the 90th Congress but that he be censured by the House, fined $40,000 and be deprived of his seniority....

The report was presented to the House on March 1, 1967, and the House debated the Select Committee's proposed resolution. At the conclusion of the debate, by a vote of 222 to 202 the House rejected a motion to bring the resolution to a vote. An amendment to the resolution was then offered; it called for the exclusion of Powell and a declaration that his seat was vacant. The Speaker ruled that a majority vote of the House would be sufficient to pass the resolution if it were so amended. 113 Cong. Rec. 5020. After further debate, the amendment was adopted by a vote of 248 to 176. Then the House adopted by a vote of 307 to 116 House Resolution No. 278 in its amended form, thereby excluding Powell and directing that the Speaker notify the Governor of New York that the seat was vacant.

... While the case was pending on our docket, the 90th Congress officially terminated and the 91st Congress was seated. In November 1968, Powell was again elected as the representative of the 18th Congressional District of New York and he was seated by the 91st Congress. The resolution seating Powell also fined him $25,000....

Respondents press upon us a variety of arguments to support the court below; they will be considered in the following order. (1) Events occurring subsequent to the grant of certiorari have rendered this litigation moot. (2) The Speech or Debate Clause of the Constitution, Art. I, § 6, insulates respondents' action from judicial review. (3) The decision to exclude petitioner Powell is supported by the power granted to the House of Representatives to expel a member. (4) This Court lacks subject matter jurisdiction over petitioners' action. (5) Even if subject matter jurisdiction is present, this litigation is not justiciable either under the general criteria established by this Court or because a political question is involved.

II. MOOTNESS.

[The House argued that the case was moot because Powell was seated as a member of the 91st Congress. The Court, however, decided that the salary withheld from Powell after his exclusion from the 90th Congress made the dispute a "case or controversy."]

III. SPEECH OR DEBATE CLAUSE.

Respondents assert that the Speech or Debate Clause of the Constitution, Art. I, § 6, is an absolute bar to petitioners' action. This Court has on four prior occasions—*Dombrowski* v. *Eastland,* 387 U. S. 82 (1967); *United States* v. *Johnson,* 383 U.S. 169 (1966); *Tenney* v. *Brandhove,* 341 U.S. 367 (1951); and *Kilbourn* v. *Thompson,* 103 U.S. 168 (1881)—been called upon to determine if allegedly unconstitutional action taken by legislators or legislative employees is insulated from judicial review by the Speech or Debate Clause....

The Speech or Debate Clause, adopted by the Constitutional Convention without debate or opposition, finds its roots in the conflict between Parliament and the Crown culminating in the Glorious Revolution of 1688 and the English Bill of Rights of 1689. Drawing upon this history, we concluded in *United States* v. *Johnson* ... that the purpose of this clause was "to prevent intimidation [of legislators] by the executive and accountability before a possibly hostile judiciary." ...

Our cases make it clear that the legislative immunity created by the Speech or Debate Clause performs an important function in representative government. It insures that legislators are free to represent the interests of their constituents without fear that they will be later called to task in the courts for that representation....

Legislative immunity does not, of course, bar all judicial review of legislative acts....

That House employees are acting pursuant to express orders of the House does not bar judicial review of the constitutionality of the underlying legislative decision. *Kilbourn* decisively settles this question, since the Sergeant at Arms was held liable for false imprisonment even though he did nothing more than execute the House Resolution that Kilbourn be arrested and imprisoned.... [T]hough this action may be dismissed against the Congressmen petitioners are entitled to maintain their action against House employees and to judicial review of the propriety of the decision to exclude petitioner Powell....

IV. EXCLUSION OR EXPULSION.

The resolution excluding petitioner Powell was adopted by a vote in excess of two-thirds of the 434 Members of Congress—307 to 116. 113 Cong. Rec. 5037–5038. Article I, § 5, grants the House authority to expel a member "with the Concurrence of two thirds." Respondents assert that the House may expel a member for any reason whatsoever and that, since a two-thirds vote was obtained, the procedure by which Powell was denied his seat in the 90th Congress should be regarded as an expulsion, not an exclusion....

[The Court reviewed the legislative proceedings of Powell's exclusion. The chairman of the Select Committee posed a parliamentary inquiry to determine whether a two-thirds vote was necessary. The Speaker replied that action by a majority vote would be in accordance with the rules. The Court also notes that the House has determined that a member should not be expelled for action taken during a prior Congress.]

VI. B. *POLITICAL QUESTION DOCTRINE.*

1. Textually Demonstrable Constitutional Commitment.

[The Court concludes that the House may not exclude someone who meets the requirements for membership expressly prescribed by the Constitution. After seating such a person, the House may expel, but only after securing the two-thirds majority required by the Constitution.]

2. *OTHER CONSIDERATIONS.*

Respondents' alternate contention is that the case presents a political question because judicial resolution of petitioners' claim would produce a "potentially embarrassing confrontation between coordinate branches" of the Federal Government. But, as our interpretation of Art. I, § 5, discloses, a determination of petitioner Powell's right to sit would require no more than an interpretation of the Constitution. Such a determination falls within the traditional role accorded courts to interpret the law, and does not involve a "lack of the respect due [a] coordinate [branch] of government," nor does it involve an "initial policy determination of a kind clearly for nonjudicial discretion." *Baker* v. *Carr,* 369 U.S. 186, at 217. Our system of government requires that federal courts on occasion interpret the Constitution in a manner at variance with the construction given the document by another branch. The alleged conflict that such an adjudication may cause cannot justify the courts' avoiding their constitutional responsibility. See *United States* v. *Brown,* 381 U.S. 437, 462 (1965); *Youngstown Sheet & Tube Co.* v. *Sawyer,* 343 U.S. 579, 613–614 (1952) (Frankfurter,

J., concurring); *Myers* v. *United States,* 272 U.S. 52, 293 (1926) (Brandeis, J., dissenting).

... For, as we noted in *Baker* v. *Carr, supra,* at 211, it is the responsibility of this Court to act as the ultimate interpreter of the Constitution. *Marbury* v. *Madison,* 1 Cranch 137 (1803). Thus, we conclude that petitioners' claim is not barred by the political question doctrine, and, having determined that the claim is otherwise generally justiciable, we hold that the case is justiciable.

Mr. Justice Douglas*[concurring]*....

MR. JUSTICE STEWART, dissenting.

I believe that events which have taken place since certiorari was granted in this case on November 18, 1968, have rendered it moot, and that the Court should therefore refrain from deciding the novel, difficult, and delicate constitutional questions which the case presented at its inception. ···

CONCLUSIONS

Most of the conflicts between Congress and the President are resolved through informal negotiations and accommodations. Rarely does an issue enter the judicial arena. When it does, the courts are reluctant to set hard-and-fast rules in such complex areas as executive privilege, delegation, and congressional investigations. An emphasis is placed on middle-ground remedies that protect the essential interests of each branch. Beyond the statutory framework agreed to by executive and legislative officials, the two branches have evolved an elaborate system of informal, nonstatutory agreements that satisfy the competing needs of executive flexibility and congressional control. In this important sense, the meaning of separation of powers depends heavily on nonjudicial interpretations by the executive and legislative branches. Louis Fisher, "Separation of Powers: Interpretation Outside the Courts," 18 Pepperdine L. Rev. 57 (1990).

NOTES AND QUESTIONS

1. What types of separation of powers issues are likely to be resolved without need of litigation, thus challenging the notion that federal courts are the ultimate voice in deciding the meaning of the Constitution?

2. The framers decided on a single Executive to help assure accountability and effectiveness. But in what ways is the theory of a "unitary executive" undercut by statutes that place certain executive decisions beyond the reach of the President?

3. Chief Justice Taft, in *Myers* v. *United States* (1926), recognized a broad removal power for the President, but at the same time acknowledged that certain duties within the executive branch could be appropriately shielded from presidential influence or control. What type of duties?

4. Congress exercises substantial control over executive decisions by means of nonstatutory controls, such as committee and subcommittee vetoes. Are those types of congressional controls likely to be successfully challenged in court? If not, why not?

SELECTED READINGS

ADLER, DAVID GRAY AND MICHAEL A. GENOVESE, eds. The Presidency and the Law: The Clinton Legacy. Lawrence: University Press of Kansas, 2002.

BARBER, SOTIRIOS A. The Constitution and the Delegation of Congressional Power. Chicago: University of Chicago Press, 1975.

BESSETTE, JOSEPH M., AND JEFFREY TULIS, eds. The Presidency in the Constitutional Order. Baton Rouge: Louisiana State University Press, 1981.

BRECKENRIDGE, ADAM CARLYLE. The Executive Privilege, Lincoln: University of Nebraska Press, 1974.

CALABRESI, STEVEN G. AND CHRISTOPHER S. YOO. The Unitary Executive: Presidential Power from Washington to Bush. New Haven: Yale University Press, 2008.

CRAIG, BARBARA HINKSON. Chadha. New York: Oxford University Press, 1988.

FISHER, LOUIS. The Politics of Shared Power: Congress and the Executive. College Station, Tex.: Texas A&M University Press, 4th ed., 1998.

———. Constitutional Conflicts Between Congress and the President. Lawrence: University Press of Kansas, 5th ed., 2007.

———. The Politics of Executive Privilege. Durham: Carolina Academic Press, 2004.

GLENNON, MICHAEL J. "The Use of Custom in Resolving Separation of Powers Disputes." 64 Boston University Law Review 109 (1984).

GOLDWIN, ROBERT A. AND ART KAUFMAN, eds. Separation of Powers—Does It Still Work? Washington, D.C.: American Enterprise Institute, 1986.

GWYN, W.B. "The Meaning of Separation of Powers." Tulane Series in Political Science, Vol. IX (1965).

HAMILTON, JAMES. The Power to Probe: A Study of Congressional Investigations. New York: Random House, 1976.

HARRIGER, KATY J. The Special Prosecutor in American Politics. Lawrence: University Press of Kansas, 2nd ed., rev., 2000.

———. "Executive Power and Prosecution: Lessons from the Libby Trial and the U.S. Attorney Firings." 38 Presidential Studies Quarterly 491 (2008).

HARRIS, JOSEPH P. The Advice and Consent of the Senate: A Study of the Confirmation of Appointments by the United States Senate. Berkeley: University of California Press, 1953.

KADEN, ALAN SCOTT. "Judicial Review of Executive Action in Domestic Affairs." 80 Columbia Law Review 1535 (1980).

KAISER, FREDERICK M. "Congressional Control of Executive Actions in the Aftermath of the *Chadha* Decision." 36 Administrative Law Review 239 (1984).

MACKENZIE, JOHN P. Absolute Power: How the Unitary Executive is Undermining the Constitution. Washington, DC: Century Foundation Press, 2008.

McGOWAN, CARL "Congress, Court and Control of Delegated Powers." 77 Columbia Law Review 1119 (1977).

POSNER, RICHARD A. An Affair of State; The Investigation, Impeachment, and Trial of President Clinton. Cambridge: Harvard University Press, 1999.

ROSENBERG, MORTON. "Beyond the Limits of Executive Power: Presidential Control of Agency Rulemaking Under Executive Order 12,291." 80 Michigan Law Review 193 (1981).

ROZELL, MARK J. Executive Privilege. Lawrence: University Press of Kansas, 2002.

ROZELL, MARK J. AND CLYDE WILCOX, eds. The Clinton Scandal and the Future of American Government. Washington, D.C.: Georgetown University Press, 2000.

STATHIS, STEPHEN W. "Executive Cooperation: Presidential Recognition of the Investigative Authority of Congress and the Courts." 3 Journal of Law & Politics 183 (1986).

VILE, M.J.C. Constitutionalism and the Separation of Powers. London: Oxford University Press, 1967.

WINTERTON, GEORGE. "The Concept of Extra-Constitutional Executive Power in Domestic Affairs." 7 Hastings Constitutional Law Quarterly 1 (1979).

7

Separation of Powers: Emergencies and Foreign Affairs

The doctrine of separated powers has its share of subtleties and puzzles in domestic disputes. Even more enigmatic is the doctrine's application to external affairs and emergency powers. This chapter begins by examining efforts to distinguish between external and internal affairs. It next analyzes the scope of the "executive prerogative," which some Presidents cite as authority to exercise powers not expressly stated in the Constitution, even when their actions are contrary to laws passed by Congress. Subsequent sections explore the scope of treaties and executive agreements, the war power, and questions of citizenship.

A. EXTERNAL AND INTERNAL AFFAIRS

Those who believe that the lion's share of authority in foreign affairs belongs with the President rely heavily on Justice Sutherland's decision in *United States* v. *Curtiss-Wright Corp.* (1936). The case could have been confined to a single question: May Congress delegate to the President the authority to prohibit the shipment of arms or munitions to any country in South America whenever he decided that the material would promote domestic violence? At every stage the case was about congressional power, not presidential power. The Court agreed that legislation over the international field may accord to the President greater discretion than would be admissible for domestic affairs. But Sutherland went beyond the issue of delegation to add pages of obiter dicta to describe the far-reaching dimensions of executive power in foreign affairs. He assigned to the President a number of powers not found in the Constitution. *Curtiss-Wright* is cited frequently to justify not only broad grants of legislative power to the President but also the exercise of inherent, extraconstitutional powers. UNITED STATES v. CURTISS-WRIGHT CORP., 299 U.S. 304 (1936).

Curtiss-Wright echoed positions Sutherland had taken as a United States Senator and member of the Senate Foreign Relations Committee. It closely tracks his article, "The Internal and External Powers of the National Government," printed as Senate Document No. 417 in 1910. The article claimed that national sovereignty "inhered in the United States from the beginning" rather than in the colonies or the states. His book, *Constitutional Power and World Affairs* (1919), promoted the same themes.

In *Curtiss-Wright,* Sutherland refers to Congressman John Marshall's remark in 1800 that the President is the "sole organ of the nation in its external relations," implying that the President makes foreign policy unilaterally. That would be powerful evidence, given Marshall's elevation a year later to be Chief Justice of the Supreme Court. However, when read in context, Marshall only meant that the President communicates to other nations U.S. foreign policy *after* it has been adopted jointly by the executive and legislative branches (either by treaty or statute). Marshall clearly meant that the President was the "sole organ" in *implementing,* not formulating, foreign policy (see box on next page).

Sutherland believed that foreign and domestic affairs were fundamentally different because the powers of external sovereignty passed from the Crown "not to the colonies severally, but to the

Marshall's "Sole Organ" Remark

[The following statement by Congressman John Marshall, during legislative debate in 1800, came in response to a proposal to impeach President John Adams for interfering with judicial proceedings underway in the trial of Jonathan Robbins. Pursuant to an extradition treaty, Adams had agreed to return Robbins to England.]

The [dispute] was in its nature a national demand made upon the nation. The parties were the two nations. They cannot come into court to litigate their claims, nor can a court decide on them. Of consequence, the demand is not a case for judicial cognizance.

The President is the sole organ of the nation in its external relations, and its sole representative with foreign nations. Of consequence, the demand of a foreign nation can only be made on him.

He possesses the whole Executive power. He holds and directs the force of the nation. Of consequence, any act to be performed by the force of the nation is to be performed through him.

He is charged to execute the laws. A treaty is declared to be a law. He must then execute a treaty, where he, and he alone, possesses the means of executing it.

The treaty, which is a law, enjoins the performance of a particular object. The person who is to perform this object is marked out by the Constitution, since the person is named who conducts the foreign intercourse, and is to take care that the laws be faithfully executed. The means by which it is to be performed, the force of the nation, are in the hands of this person. Ought not this person to perform the object, although the particular mode of using the means has not been prescribed? Congress, unquestionably, may prescribe the mode, and Congress may devolve on others the whole execution of the contract; but, till this be done, it seems the duty of the Executive department to execute the contract by any means it possesses.

SOURCE: Annals of Cong., 6th Cong. 613–14 (1800).

colonies in their collective and corporate capacity as the United States of America." However, from 1774 to 1788 the colonies and states operated as sovereign entities, not as parts of a collective body. They acted free and independent of one another. The creation of the Continental Congress did not disturb the sovereign capacity of the states to make treaties, borrow money, solicit arms, lay embargoes, collect tariff duties, and conduct separate military campaigns.

Even if the power of external sovereignty had somehow passed intact from the Crown to the "United States," the Constitution divides that power between Congress and the President. The President and the Senate share the treaty power. Congress has the responsibility to raise and support military forces, to lay and collect duties on foreign trade, to regulate commerce with foreign nations, and to fund the armed services. Contemporary conditions make it increasingly difficult to draw a crisp line between external and internal affairs. Oil embargoes imposed by foreign governments immediately impact America's economy, raising the price at home and producing long lines at the neighborhood gas station. The President's decision to ship or withhold wheat from a foreign nation has a major effect on farming communities. Trade policies are both international and domestic in scope. As President Bush noted in 1991: "I guess my bottom line ... is you can't separate foreign policy from domestic." Public Papers of the Presidents, 1991, II, at 1629. President Clinton, in his first inaugural address in 1993, similarly remarked: "There is no longer a clear division between what is foreign and what is domestic." There never was.

The contemporary Supreme Court continues to look more sympathetically on delegation that involves external affairs. Even Chief Justice Rehnquist, a strong advocate of the nondelegation doctrine, adopted a different standard for international crises, "the nature of which Congress can hardly have been expected to anticipate in any detail." Dames & Moore v. Regan, 453 U.S. 654, 669 (1981). He agreed that Congress "is permitted to legislate both with greater breadth and with greater flexibility" when a statute governs military affairs. Rostker v. Goldberg, 453 U.S. 57, 66 (1981), quoting Parker v. Levy, 417 U.S. 733, 756 (1974). More importantly, *Curtiss-Wright* is used to support the existence of independent, implied, and inherent powers for the President.[1]

Officials of the Reagan administration took a number of actions known collectively as the Iran-Contra affair: sending arms to Iran, diverting funds to the Contras in Nicaragua, and soliciting funds from private donors and foreign countries because Congress refused to appropriate funds for the Contras. Some defenders of these executive actions pointed to *Curtiss-Wright* as legal justification. A report, prepared jointly by the House and the Senate, rejects this reliance on *Curtiss-Wright* (see reading "Congress Interprets *Curtiss-Wright:* The Iran-Contra Report"). In the period following the terrorist attacks of 9/11, the Bush administration relied repeatedly on what it considered "inherent" presidential powers to act in the absence of law and sometimes against it, citing the "sole organ" doctrine of *Curtiss-Wright* among other arguments (discussed later in this chapter).

Right to Travel

Claiming both constitutional and statutory authority, Presidents and their administrations use the control over passports and visas to restrict travel by foreigners to this country and by Americans to other countries. Administrations advance a number of foreign policy and national security justifications, while opponents of restraints on foreign travel raise First Amendment issues of access to information and right of association. There is broad agreement among both groups that the government is justified in banning travel to regions affected by pestilence or war.

The interesting fact about these cases is that the Court generally decides them on statutory grounds. This keeps the door fully open for participation by Congress and the President in shaping the law on the right to travel. In 1958 the Supreme Court reviewed the State Department's action in withholding passports from several Americans because of their alleged association with the Communist Party. Although the Court referred to the right to travel as part of a citizen's constitutional "liberty" that could not be denied without due process of law, it avoided the constitutional issue and held that the Secretary of State had exceeded the authority delegated to him by Congress. Kent v. Dulles, 357 U.S. 116 (1958); Dayton v. Dulles, 357 U.S. 144 (1958). Legislation was introduced to strengthen the authority of the Secretary of State, but none of the bills passed Congress.

In 1964 the Court struck down a congressional provision that prevented individuals from applying for a passport if they belonged to a "Communist-action" or "Communist-front" organization. If they already held a passport, it would be revoked. The Court decided that the provision was too broad and indiscriminate in restricting the right to travel. Aptheker v. United States, 378 U.S. 500 (1964). A year later, the Court upheld the authority of the State Department to impose *area* restrictions (in this case, involving Cuba). The Court argued that it was permissible to deny all citizens the right to travel to a certain country, in contrast to the 1958 case which involved an individual's belief or association. Zemel v. Rusk, 381 U.S. 1 (1965).

Subsequent cases circumscribed the State Department's authority to impose area restrictions.[2] In 1978 Congress passed legislation to limit area restrictions. In the spirit of the Helsinki Accords of 1975, which encouraged the free movement of people and ideas, Congress adopted the following amendment to the Passport Act: "Unless authorized by law, a passport may not be designated as restricted for travel to or for use in any country other than a country with which the United States is at war, where armed hostilities are in progress, or where there is imminent danger to the public health or the

---

1. United States v. Pink, 315 U.S. 203, 229 (1942); Knauff v. Shaughnessy, 338 U.S. 537, 542 (1950); United States v. Mazurie, 419 U.S. 544, 566–67 (1975). See Louis Fisher, "Presidential Inherent Power: The 'Sole Organ' Doctrine," 37 Pres. Stud. Q. 139 (2007).

2. On area restrictions, see also United States v. Laub, 385 U.S. 475 (1967); Travis v. United States, 385 U.S. 491 (1967); Lynd v. Rusk, 389 F.2d 940 (D.C. Cir. 1967). Congress can limit welfare payments to recipients who travel abroad for 30 days or more; Califano v. Aznavorian, 439 U.S. 170 (1978).

physical safety of United States travelers." 92 Stat. 971, §124 (1978); 22 U.S.C. §211a (2004).

Recent cases have given broad support to executive restrictions on foreign travel. In 1981 the Court upheld the authority of the Secretary of State to revoke the passport of Philip Agee, a former CIA employee who had announced his intention to identify undercover CIA agents and intelligence sources in foreign countries. The Court said that the revocation inhibited Agee's actions, not his speech. The Secretary's decision was based on a departmental regulation, a broad interpretation of the 1978 amendments, and the "silence" of Congress in acquiescing to the Department's action. Specific authorization from Congress, said the Court, was not required. HAIG v. AGEE, 453 U.S. 280 (1981). The broadness of this ruling suggests that an administration may prevent the foreign travel of anyone who is apt to question or embarrass the President's foreign policy.

In 1984, the Court upheld (5 to 4) a Treasury Department regulation that prohibited general tourist and business travel to Cuba. The Reagan administration decided to retaliate against Cuba for its political and military interventions in Latin America and in Africa. Congress had passed the International Emergency Economic Powers Act in 1977 to limit the President's power, but the Court read the Act broadly to permit the sanctions against Cuba. Regan v. Wald, 468 U.S. 222 (1984).

In recent years Congress has revisited the McCarran-Walter Act of 1952, which kept aliens out of the country because of their political and economic beliefs. 66 Stat. 184–86 (1952). Under that authority, a number of noted writers and political figures have been denied entrance into the United States to speak. In 1990 Congress revised McCarran-Walter to make it more difficult to exclude aliens for their beliefs, statements, and associations. 104 Stat. 5071 (1990).

United States v. Curtiss-Wright Corp.

299 U.S. 304 (1936)

In 1935, in the *Panama Refining* and *Schechter* cases, the Supreme Court struck down the National Industrial Recovery Act and its delegation of legislative power to the President. The *Curtiss-Wright* case involves the delegation of legislative power to the President in foreign rather than domestic affairs. In 1934 Congress authorized the President to place an embargo on the sale of arms and munitions to countries engaged in armed conflict in South America if the President determined that an embargo would contribute to the establishment of peace. Justice Sutherland, writing for the Court, upheld the statute partly on the distinction he drew between external and internal affairs.

MR. JUSTICE SUTHERLAND delivered the opinion of the Court.

On January 27, 1936, an indictment was returned in the court below, the first count of which charges that appellees, beginning with the 29th day of May, 1934, conspired to sell in the United States certain arms of war, namely fifteen machine guns, to Bolivia, a country then engaged in armed conflict in the Chaco, in violation of the Joint Resolution of Congress approved May 28, 1934, and the provisions of a proclamation issued on the same day by the President of the United States pursuant to authority conferred by §1 of the resolution....

First. It is contended that by the Joint Resolution, the going into effect and continued operation of the resolution was conditioned (a) upon the President's judgment as to its beneficial effect upon the reestablishment of peace between the countries engaged in armed conflict in the Chaco; (b) upon the making of a proclamation, which was left to his unfettered discretion, thus constituting an attempted substitution of the President's will for that of Congress; (c) upon the making of a proclamation putting an end to the operation of the resolution, which again was left to the President's unfettered discretion; and (d) further, that the extent of its operation in particular cases was subject to limitation and exception by the President, controlled by no standard. In each of these particulars, appellees urge that Congress abdicated its essential functions and delegated them to the Executive.

Whether, if the Joint Resolution had related solely to internal affairs it would be open to the challenge that it constituted an unlawful delegation of legislative power to the Executive, we find it unnecessary to determine. The whole aim of the resolution is to affect a situation entirely external to the United

States, and falling within the category of foreign affairs. The determination which we are called to make, therefore, is whether the Joint Resolution, as applied to that situation, is vulnerable to attack under the rule that forbids a delegation of the lawmaking power. In other words, assuming (but not deciding) that the challenged delegation, if it were confined to internal affairs, would be invalid, may it nevertheless be sustained on the ground that its exclusive aim is to afford a remedy for a hurtful condition within foreign territory?

It will contribute to the elucidation of the question if we first consider the differences between the powers of the federal government in respect of foreign or external affairs and those in respect of domestic or internal affairs. That there are differences between them, and that these differences are fundamental, may not be doubted.

The two classes of powers are different, both in respect of their origin and their nature. The broad statement that the federal government can exercise no powers except those specifically enumerated in the Constitution, and such implied powers as are necessary and proper to carry into effect the enumerated powers, is categorically true only in respect of our internal affairs. In that field, the primary purpose of the Constitution was to carve from the general mass of legislative powers *then possessed by the states* such portions as it was thought desirable to vest in the federal government, leaving those not included in the enumeration still in the states. *Carter v. Carter Coal Co.*, 298 U.S. 238, 294. That this doctrine applies only to powers which the states had, is self evident. And since the states severally never possessed international powers, such powers could not have been carved from the mass of state powers but obviously were transmitted to the United States from some other source. During the colonial period, those powers were possessed exclusively by and were entirely under the control of the Crown. By the Declaration of Independence, "the Representatives of the United States of America" declared the United [not the several] Colonies to be free and independent states, and as such to have "full Power to levy War, conclude Peace, contract Alliances, establish Commerce and to do all other Acts and Things which Independent States may of right do."

As a result of the separation from Great Britain by the colonies acting as a unit, the powers of external sovereignty passed from the Crown not to the colonies severally, but to the colonies in their collective and corporate capacity as the United States of America. Even before the Declaration, the colonies were a unit in foreign affairs, acting through a common agency—namely the Continental Congress, composed of delegates from the thirteen colonies. That agency exercised the powers of war and peace, raised an army, created a navy, and finally adopted the Declaration of Independence. Rulers come and go; governments end and forms of government change; but sovereignty survives. A political society cannot endure without a supreme will somewhere. Sovereignty is never held in suspense. When, therefore, the external sovereignty of Great Britain in respect of the colonies ceased, it immediately passed to the Union. *See Penhallow* v. *Doane*, 3 Dall. 54, 80–81. That fact was given practical application almost at once. The treaty of peace, made on September 23, 1783, was concluded between his Brittanic Majesty and the "United States of America." 8 Stat.—European Treaties—80.

The Union existed before the Constitution, which was ordained and established among other things to form "a more perfect Union." Prior to that event, it is clear that the Union, declared by the Articles of Confederation to be "perpetual," was the sole possessor of external sovereignty and in the Union it remained without change save in so far as the Constitution in express terms qualified its exercise....

[*Sutherland neglected to point out that American states did indeed exercise sovereign powers after the break with England. The creation of the Continental Congress did not disturb the sovereign power of states to make treaties, borrow money, solicit arms, lay embargoes, collect tariff duties, and conduct separate military campaigns. The Supreme Court has recognized that the American colonies, upon their separation from England, exercised the powers of a sovereign and independent government. United States v. California, 332 U.S. 19, 31 (1947); Texas v. White, 74 U.S. 700, 725 (1869); M'Ilvaine v. Coxe's Lessee, 8 U.S. (4 Cr.) 209, 212 (1808); Ware v. Hylton, 3 U.S. (3 Dall.) 199, 222-24 (1796).*]

Not only, as we have shown, is the federal power over external affairs in origin and essential character different from that over internal affairs, but participation in the exercise of the power is significantly limited. In this vast external realm, with its important, complicated, delicate and manifold problems, the President alone has the power to speak or listen as a representative of the nation. He *makes* treaties with the advice and consent of the Senate; but he alone negotiates. Into the field of negotiation the Senate cannot intrude; and Congress itself is powerless to invade it. As Marshall said in his great argument of March 7, 1800, in the House of Representatives, "The President is the sole organ of the nation in its external relations, and its sole representative with foreign nations." Annals, 6th Cong., col. 613....

[Sutherland exaggerates the President's exclusive power to negotiate treaties. In his book, Constitutional Powers and World Affairs (1919), he recognized that Senators did in fact participate in the negotiation phase and that Presidents had often acceded to this "practical construction" (p. 123). Far from being a "presidential monopoly," treaty negotiation frequently includes not only Senators but members of the House. Fisher, 39 Pres. Stud. Q. 144 (2008).]

It is important to bear in mind that we are here dealing not alone with an authority vested in the President by an exertion of legislative power, but with such an authority plus the very delicate, plenary and exclusive power of the President as the sole organ of the federal government in the field of international relations—a power which does not require as a basis for its exercise an act of Congress, but which, of course, like every other governmental power, must be exercised in subordination to the applicable provisions of the Constitution. It is quite apparent that if, in the maintenance of our international relations, embarrassment—perhaps serious embarrassment—is to be avoided and success for our aims achieved, congressional legislation which is to be made effective through negotiation and inquiry within the international field must often accord to the President a degree of discretion and freedom from statutory restriction which would not be admissible were domestic affairs alone involved. Moreover, he, not Congress, has the better opportunity of knowing the conditions which prevail in foreign countries, and especially is this true in time of war....

The judgment of the court below must be reversed and the cause remanded for further proceedings in accordance with the foregoing opinion.

Reversed.

MR. JUSTICE MCREYNOLDS does not agree. He is of opinion that the court below reached the right conclusion and its judgment ought to be affirmed.

MR. JUSTICE STONE took no part in the consideration or decision of this case.

Congress Interprets *Curtiss-Wright*: The Iran-Contra Report

Several witnesses before the Iran-Contra Committees in 1987 testified that the actions by the Reagan administration could be justified in terms of *United States* v. *Curtiss-Wright Corp.* (1936), which they claimed recognized broad powers for the President in foreign affairs. The majority report rejected this position. The passage below appeared in *Iran-Contra Affair,* H. Rept. No. 100-433, S. Rept. No. 100-216, 100th Cong., 1st Sess., 388–90 (November 1987).

In urging a broad interpretation of presidential power, various witnesses before these Committees invoked the Supreme Court's 1936 decision in *United States* v. *Curtiss-Wright Export Corporation.* Their reliance on this case is misplaced.

In *Curtiss-Wright,* Congress, by statute, had delegated to the President the power to prohibit the sale of arms to countries in an area of South America if the President believed the prohibition would promote peace. The Curtiss-Wright Corporation claimed that the power to make this determination was a legislative power that Congress could not delegate to the President.

Witnesses at the hearings misread this case to justify their claim that the President had broad inherent foreign policy powers to the virtual exclusion of Congress. *Curtiss-Wright* did not present any such issue. The case involved the question of the powers of the President in foreign policy where Congress expressly authorizes him to act; it did not involve the question of the President's foreign policy powers when Congress expressly forbids him to act.

In *Curtiss-Wright,* the Court upheld broad delegations by Congress of power to the President in matters of foreign affairs. Writing for the Court, Justice Sutherland said that legislation within "the international field must often accord to the President a degree of discretion and freedom from statutory restriction which would not be admissible were domestic affairs alone involved."

In language frequently seized on by those seeking to claim that the President's role in foreign policy is exclusive, Justice Sutherland noted that the President was acting not only with a delegation of power by the legislature, but also with certain powers the Constitution gave directly to him:

"It is important to bear in mind that we are here dealing not alone with an authority vested in the President by an exertion of legislative power, but with such an authority plus the very delicate, plenary and exclusive power of the President as the sole organ of the federal government in the field of international relations—a power which does not require as a basis for its exercise an act of Congress, but which, of course, like every other governmental power, must be exercised in subordination to applicable provisions of the Constitution."

Some have tried to interpret this passage as stating that the President may act in foreign affairs against the will of Congress. But that is not what it says. As Justice Jackson later observed, the most that can be drawn from Justice Sutherland's language is the intimation "that the President might act in external affairs without congressional authority, but not that he might act contrary to an Act of Congress." More recently, in *Dames & Moore* v. *Regan,* the Supreme Court cautioned that the broad language in *Curtiss-Wright* must be viewed only in context of that case. Writing for the majority, Justice (now Chief Justice) Rehnquist expressed the Court's view of the appropriate relationship between the executive and the legislative branches in the conduct of foreign policy:

"When the President acts pursuant to an express or implied authorization from Congress, he exercises not only his powers but also those delegated by Congress. In such a case the executive action 'would be supported by the strongest presumptions and widest latitude of judicial interpretation, and the burden of persuasion would rest heavily upon any who might attack it.'... When the President acts in the absence of congressional authorization he may enter a 'zone of twilight in which he and Congress may have concurrent authority, or in which its distribution is uncertain.'... In such a case, the analysis becomes more complicated, and the validity of the President's action, at least so far as separation-of-powers principles are concerned, hinges on a con-

sideration of all the circumstances which might shed light on the views of the Legislative Branch toward such action, including 'congressional inertia, indifference or quiescence.'... Finally, when the President acts in contravention of the will of Congress, 'his power is at its lowest ebb' and the Court can sustain his actions 'only by disabling the Congress from action on the subject.'"

Similarly, in 1981, the D.C. Circuit cautioned against undue reliance on the quoted passage from *Curtiss-Wright:* "To the extent that denominating the President as the 'sole organ' of the United States in international affairs constitutes a blanket endorsement of plenary Presidential power over any matter extending beyond the borders of this country, we reject that characterization."

In calling the President the "sole organ" of the Nation in its relations with other countries, Justice Sutherland quoted from a speech by John Marshall in 1800 when Marshall was a Member of the House of Representatives: "As Marshall said in his great argument of March 7, 1800, in the House of Representatives, 'The President is the sole organ of the nation in its external relations, and its sole representative with foreign nations.' Annals, 6th Cong., col. 613."

The reader might assume from this passage that Marshall advocated an exclusive, independent power for the President in the area of foreign affairs, free from legislative control. When his statement is placed in the context of the "great argument of March 7, 1800," however, it is clear that Marshall regarded the President as simply carrying out the law as established by statute or treaty. The House had been debating a decision by President John Adams to turn over to England a person charged with murder. Some members thought the President should be impeached for encroaching upon the judiciary, since the case was already pending in court. Marshall replied that President Adams was executing a treaty approved by the Senate that had the force of law.

Haig v. Agee

453 U.S. 280 (1981)

In this case, the "right to travel" collides with the President's interests over foreign policy and national security. Philip Agee, a former employee of the Central Intelligence Agency, had announced a campaign to expose CIA officers and agents. His activities abroad resulted in the identification of CIA agents and intelligence sources in foreign countries. After Secretary of State Alexander Haig revoked his passport, Agee filed suit claiming that the regulation cited by Haig had not been authorized by Congress and was impermissibly overbroad. Agee also argued that the passport revocation violated his freedom to travel and his First Amendment right to criticize governmental policies. Moreover, he charged that the failure to accord him a hearing before the revocation constituted a violation of procedural due process under the Fifth Amendment. The district court and the D.C. Circuit agreed that the regulation exceeded Haig's authority.

CHIEF JUSTICE BURGER delivered the opinion of the Court.

The question presented is whether the President, acting through the Secretary of State, has authority to revoke a passport on the ground that the holder's activities in foreign countries are causing or are likely to cause serious damage to the national security or foreign policy of the United States.

I

A

Philip Agee, an American citizen, currently resides in West Germany. From 1957 to 1968, he was employed by the Central Intelligence Agency. He held key positions in the division of the Agency that is responsible for covert intelligence gathering in foreign countries. In the course of his duties at the Agency. Agee received training in clandestine operations, including the methods used to protect the identities of intelligence employees and sources of the United States overseas. He served in undercover assignments abroad and came to know many Government employees and other persons supplying information to the United States. The relationships of many of these people to our Government are highly confidential; many are still engaged in intelligence gathering.

In 1974, Agee called a press conference in London to announce his "campaign to fight the United States CIA wherever it is operating." He declared his intent "to expose CIA officers and agents and to take the measures necessary to drive them out of the countries where they are operating." Since 1974, Agee has, by his own assertion, devoted consistent effort to that program, and he has traveled extensively in other countries in order to carry it out. To identify CIA personnel in a particular country, Agee goes to the target country and consults sources in local diplomatic circles whom he knows from his prior service in the United States Government. He recruits collaborators and trains them in clandestine techniques designed to expose the "cover" of CIA employees and sources. Agee and his collaborators have repeatedly and publicly identified individuals and organizations located in foreign countries as undercover CIA agents, employees, or sources. The record reveals that the identifications divulge classi-

fied information, violate Agee's express contract not to make any public statements about Agency matters without prior clearance by the Agency, have prejudiced the ability of the United States to obtain intelligence, and have been followed by episodes of violence against the persons and organizations identified.

In December 1979, the Secretary of State revoked Agee's passport and delivered an explanatory notice to Agee in West Germany. The notice states in part:

"The Department's action is predicated upon a determination made by the Secretary under the provisions of [22 CFR] Section 51.70 (b)(4) that your activities abroad are causing or are likely to cause serious damage to the national security or the foreign policy of the United States...."

The notice also advised Agee of his right to an administrative hearing and offered to hold such a hearing in West Germany on 5 days' notice.

Agee at once filed suit against the Secretary. He alleged that the regulation invoked by the Secretary, 22 CFR § 51.70 (b)(4) (1980), has not been authorized by Congress and is invalid; that the regulation is impermissibly overbroad; that the revocation prior to a hearing violated his Fifth Amendment right to procedural due process; and that the revocation violated a Fifth Amendment liberty interest in a right to travel and a First Amendment right to criticize Government policies. He sought declaratory and injunctive relief, and he moved for summary judgment on the question of the authority to promulgate the regulation and on the constitutional claims.

[The district court held that the regulation exceeded the statutory powers of the Secretary under the Passport Act and ordered the Secretary to restore Agee's passport. The D.C. Circuit held that the Secretary was required to show that Congress had authorized the regulation either by an express delegation or by an implied approval. The Court found that the regulation exceeded authority granted by Congress.]

II

The principal question before us is whether the statute authorizes the action of the Secretary pursuant to the policy announced by the challenged regulation.

A

1

Although the historical background that we develop later is important, we begin with the language of the statute.... The Passport Act of 1926 provides in pertinent part:

"The Secretary of State may grant and issue passports, and cause passports to be granted, issued, and verified in foreign countries by diplomatic representatives of the United States ... under such rules as the President shall designate and prescribe for and on behalf of the United States, and no other person shall grant, issue, or verify such passports." 22 U.S.C. § 211a (1976 ed., Supp. IV).

This language is unchanged since its original enactment in 1926.

The Passport Act does not in so many words confer upon the Secretary a power to revoke a passport. Nor, for that matter, does it expressly authorize denials of passport applications. Neither, however, does any statute expressly limit those powers. It is beyond dispute that the Secretary has the power to deny a passport for reasons not specified in the statutes. For example, in *Kent v. Dulles*, 357 U.S. 116 (1958), the Court recognized congressional acquiescence in Executive policies of refusing passports to applicants "participating in illegal conduct, trying to escape the toils of the law, promoting passport frauds, or otherwise engaging in conduct which would violate the laws of the United States." *Id.*, at 127. In *Zemel*, the Court held that "the weightiest considerations of national security" authorized the Secretary to restrict travel to Cuba at the time of the Cuban missile crisis. 381 U.S., at 16. Agee concedes that if the Secretary may deny a passport application for a certain reason, he may revoke a passport on the same ground.

2

Particularly in light of the "broad rule-making authority granted in the [1926] Act," *Zemel*, 381 U.S., at 12, a consistent administrative construction of that statute must be followed by the courts "'unless there are compelling indications that it is wrong.'" *E. I. du Pont de Nemours & Co. v. Collins*, 432 U.S. 46, 55 (1977), quoting *Red Lion Broadcasting Co. v. FCC*, 395 U.S. 367, 381 (1969); see *Zemel*, *supra*, at 11. This is especially so in the areas of foreign policy and national security, where congressional silence is not to be equated with congressional disapproval. In *United States v. Curtiss-Wright Export Corp.*, 299 U.S. 304 (1936), the volatile nature of problems confronting the Executive in foreign policy and national defense was underscored....

Matters intimately related to foreign policy and national security are rarely proper subjects for judicial intervention. In *Harisiades v. Shaughnessy*, 342 U.S. 580 (1952), the Court observed that matters relating "to the conduct of foreign relations ... are so exclusively entrusted to the political branches of government as to be largely immune from judicial inquiry or interference." *Id.*, at 589; accord, *Chicago & Southern Air Lines, Inc. v. Waterman S.S. Corp.*, 333 U.S. 103, 111 (1948).

III

. . .

Revocation of a passport undeniably curtails travel, but the freedom to travel abroad with a "letter of introduction" in the form of a passport issued by the sovereign is subordinate to national security and foreign policy considerations; as such, it is subject to reasonable governmental regulation....

We reverse the judgment of the Court of Appeals and remand for further proceedings consistent with this opinion.

Reversed and remanded.

JUSTICE BLACKMUN, concurring....

JUSTICE BRENNAN, with whom JUSTICE MARSHALL joins, dissenting....

II

This is not a complicated case. The Court has twice articulated the proper mode of analysis for determining whether Congress has delegated to the Executive Branch the authority to deny a passport under the Passport Act of 1926. *Zemel v. Rusk*, 381 U.S. 1 (1965); *Kent v. Dulles*, 357 U.S. 116 (1958). The analysis is hardly confusing, and I expect that had the Court faithfully applied it, today's judgment would affirm the decision below.

... [C]learly neither *Zemel* nor *Kent* holds that a longstanding Executive *policy* or *construction* is sufficient proof that Congress has implicitly authorized the Secretary's action. The cases hold that an administrative *practice* must be demonstrated; in fact *Kent* unequivocally states that mere *construction* by the Executive—no matter how longstanding and consistent—is *not* sufficient....

... Only when Congress had maintained its silence in the face of a consistent and substantial pattern of actual passport denials or revocations—where the parties will presumably object loudly, perhaps through legal action, to the Secretary's exercise of discretion — can this Court be sure that

Congress is aware of the Secretary's actions and has implicitly approved that exercise of discretion....

B. AN EXECUTIVE PREROGATIVE?

Theodore Roosevelt and William Howard Taft supposedly championed rival theories of presidential power. Roosevelt claimed that it was the President's right and duty to do "anything that the needs of the Nation demanded, unless such action was forbidden by the Constitution or by the laws." 20 Works of Theodore Roosevelt 347 (1926). Through this theory the President could enter and occupy any vacuum. In contrast, Taft maintained that the President "can exercise no power which cannot be fairly and reasonably traced to some specific grant of power or justly implied and included within such express grant as proper and necessary to its exercise. Such specific grant must be either in the Federal Constitution or in an act of Congress passed in pursuance thereof." William Howard Taft, Our Chief Magistrate and His Powers 139–40 (1916).

This passage appears to make Taft an advocate of enumerated powers, but he did not believe that every use of presidential power required a specific constitutional or statutory grant. He recognized the need for implied powers: powers that can be "fairly and reasonably traced" or "justly implied." He even adds a "necessary and proper" clause for the President. His book on the presidency promotes a broad view of executive power: incidental powers to remove officers, inferable powers to protect the lives and property of American citizens living abroad, powers created by custom, and emergency powers (such as Lincoln's suspension of the writ of habeas corpus during the Civil War). Taft concluded that executive power was limited "so far as it is possible to limit such a power consistent with that discretion and promptness of action that are essential to preserve the interests of the public in times of emergency, or legislative neglect or inaction."

Lincoln's Initiatives

Taft's formulation follows what is known as the Lockean prerogative: the executive's power to act for the public good in the absence of law and sometimes even against it. Lincoln claimed this authority in April 1861 while Congress was in recess. He issued proclamations calling forth state militias, suspended the writ of habeas corpus, and placed a blockade on the rebellious states. He told Congress that his actions, "whether strictly legal or not," were necessary for the public good. 7 Richardson, Messages and Papers of the Presidents 3225. Congress subsequently passed a statute legalizing his proclamations "as if they had been issued and done under the previous express authority and direction of the Congress of the United States." 12 Stat. 326 (1861). Legislative sanction is an essential ingredient of the prerogative. In times of emergency, the executive may act outside the law but must submit his case to the legislature and the people for approval (see box on next page).

Lincoln's suspension of the writ of habeas corpus ran directly counter to a decision by Chief Justice Taney, sitting as a circuit judge in Baltimore. Taney concluded that Lincoln had no power to issue the writ and that the prisoner, John Merryman, should be set free. But Taney recognized that he could not prevail in a direct confrontation with the President on this issue during an emergency period. With some resignation, Taney said he exercised "all the power which the constitution and laws confer upon me, but that power has been resisted by a force too strong for me to overcome." Ex parte Merryman, 17 Fed. Case No. 9,487 (1861), at 153. Lincoln had the legal support of his Attorney General. 10 Op. Att'y Gen. 74, 81 (1861).

Lincoln's use of emergency power to justify the blockade on Southern states was upheld by a sharply divided Supreme Court. In a 5 to 4 decision, the Court held that Lincoln could take the actions he did despite the absence of a declaration of war by Congress. The President was bound to meet the emergency "in the shape it presented itself, without waiting for Congress to baptize it with a name;

Lincoln's Exercise of the Emergency Power

... These measures, whether strictly legal or not, were ventured upon under what appeared to be a popular demand and a public necessity; trusting then as now that Congress would readily ratify them. It is believed that nothing has been done beyond the constitutional competency of Congress.

Soon after the first call for militia, it was considered a duty to authorize the commanding general in proper cases, according to his discretion, to suspend the privilege of the writ of *habeas corpus,* or, in other words, to arrest and detain, without resort to the ordinary processes and forms of law, such individuals as he might deem dangerous to the public safety. This authority has purposely been exercised but very sparingly. Nevertheless, the legality and propriety of what has been done under it are questioned, and the attention of the country has been called to the proposition that one who is sworn to "take care that the laws be faithfully executed" should not himself violate them. Of course some consideration was given to the questions of power and propriety before this matter was acted upon. The whole of the laws which were required to be faithfully executed were being resisted, and

failing of execution in nearly one third of the States. Must they be allowed to finally fail of execution, even had it been perfectly clear that by the use of the means necessary to their execution some single law, made in such extreme tenderness of the citizen's liberty, that practically it relieves more of the guilty than of the innocent, should to a very limited extent be violated? To state the question more directly: are all the laws *but one* to go unexecuted, and the Government itself go to pieces, lest that one be violated? Even in such a case, would not the official oath be broken if the government should be overthrown, when it was believed that disregarding the single law would tend to preserve it? [*Here Lincoln explains why it was appropriate for him to suspend the writ of habeas corpus, in a "dangerous emergency," even though the language for suspension appears in Article I.*]

No more extended argument is now offered, as an opinion, at some length, will probably be presented by the Attorney General. Whether there shall be any legislation upon the subject, and if any, what, is submitted entirely to the better judgment of Congress.

Source: Message to Congress, July 4, 1861.

and no name given to it by him or them could change the fact." THE PRIZE CASES, 2 Black (67 U.S.) 635, 669 (1863). Justice Grier in the decision and White House Counsel during oral argument both understood that the power to *initiate war against another country* was vested solely in Congress (see excerpts from the case reading).

Not until the war was over and Lincoln dead did the Supreme Court breathe some life into the privilege of the writ of habeas corpus. EX PARTE MILLIGAN, 4 Wall. (71 U.S.) 2 (1866). *Milligan* announced the principle that U.S. citizens may not be tried in military courts when civil courts are open and operating. That principle was undercut somewhat by the World War II case of *Ex parte Quirin* (see the section "Military Tribunals" under Section D in this chapter).

Although *Milligan* in contemporary times is generally considered a landmark case in defense of civil liberties, it was severely criticized at the time as a judicial threat to congressional actions taken after the Civil War as part of Reconstruction of the Southern states. In response to *Milligan,* Congress passed legislation to limit the Court's jurisdiction to hear cases involving martial law and military trials (see the section on withdrawing jurisdiction in the final chapter "Efforts to Curb the Court"). In the years immediately following the Civil War, the Court was somewhat reluctant to challenge the powers of commander in chief. Mississippi v. Johnson, 4 Wall. 475 (1867).

FDR, Truman, and Nixon

A notorious use of emergency power was President Roosevelt's decision during World War II to put a curfew on more than 100,000 Americans of Japanese descent (about two-thirds of them natural-born U.S. citizens) and later place them in detention camps. A unanimous Supreme Court sustained the curfew, although Justice Murphy remarked that it "bears a melancholy resemblance to the treatment accorded to the members of the Jewish race in Germany and in other parts of Europe." Hirabayashi v. United States, 320 U.S. 81 (1943). Putting Japanese-Americans in detention camps split the Court, the Justices voting 6–3 to uphold this action. The dissents by Murphy and Jackson, objecting that the exclusion order resulted from racism, were particularly vehement. KOREMATSU v. UNITED STATES, 323 U.S. 214, 243 (1944).[3] Congress passed legislation in 1988 to offer the nation's apology for this tragic episode and to provide cash reparations to survivors and their families. 102 Stat. 903 (1988).

President Truman used the emergency power in 1952 to seize steel mills during the Korean War. The Supreme Court overturned his action, but the 6 to 3 decision revealed as many positions as there were Justices. All six Justices in the majority wrote separate opinions, each taking a slightly different view of emergency power. Only Justices Black and Douglas advocated a doctrine of express and enumerated powers. The other seven Justices, in four concurrences and three dissents, recognized that implied and emergency powers may be appropriately invoked. Jackson developed a theory of constitutional powers that had three scenarios. Presidential authority reaches its highest level when the President acts pursuant to congressional authorization. His power is at its "lowest ebb" when he takes measures incompatible with the will of Congress. In between these two categories lay a "zone of twilight" in which Congress neither grants nor denies authority. In such circumstances, "congressional inertia, indifference or quiescence may sometimes, at least as a practical matter, enable, if not invite, measures of independent presidential responsibility." YOUNGSTOWN CO. v. SAWYER, 343 U.S. 579, 637 (1952). Jackson's opinion underscores the fact that the Constitution is often shaped not by textual interpretations from the courts but by a political dialectic among the branches.

The concept of "national security" often becomes an umbrella term to justify a broad range of emergency actions by the President. The Nixon administration was especially active in invoking the term. It asked the courts to enjoin two newspapers from publishing the Pentagon Papers, a confidential report that the administration had prepared to study the origins and conduct of the Vietnam War. The report had been leaked to the newspapers, raising the question of prior restraint on a free press. The Supreme Court decided against the administration. The word "security," warned Justice Black, "is a broad, vague generality whose contours should not be invoked to abrogate the fundamental law embodied in the First Amendment." NEW YORK TIMES CO. v. UNITED STATES, 403 U.S. 713, 719 (1971). Erwin N. Griswold, who served as Solicitor General at the time of the Pentagon Papers case, and who claimed in oral argument that publication of the documents would damage national security, admitted in 1989 that no such damage had occurred (see Griswold reading). Although First Amendment freedoms were protected in the Pentagon Papers case, the Court upheld the right of the Central Intelligence Agency to require its employees to sign secrecy agreements promising not to publish information about the agency without the Director's prior approval. Snepp v. United States, 444 U.S. 507 (1980).

National Security Wiretaps

Beginning in the 1920s, a succession of administrations resorted to wiretapping for the purpose of controlling domestic crime and protecting national security. The Communications Act of 1934 made it a crime to intercept and divulge wire or radio communications, but President Roosevelt in 1940 instructed his Attorney General that wiretapping should continue for "grave matters involving the de-

---

3. See also Yasui v. United States, 320 U.S. 115 (1943); Ex parte Endo, 323 U.S. 283 (1944); Eugene V. Rostow, "The Japanese American Cases—A Disaster," 54 Yale L. J. 489 (1945); Nanette Dembitz, "Racial Discrimination and the Military Judgment: The Supreme Court's Korematsu and Endo Decisions," 45 Colum. L. Rev. 175 (1945); Peter Irons, Justice at War: The Story of the Japanese American Internment Cases (1983).

fense of the nation." Francis Biddle, In Brief Authority 167 (1962). The tension between the statute and Roosevelt's instruction was relieved in part by the practice of intercepting but not divulging communications or using them in court for evidence.

The Omnibus Crime Control Act of 1968 allowed domestic wiretaps if authorized by judicial warrants. The government claimed that warrantless surveillances for "national security" purposes were lawful as a reasonable exercise of presidential power. A section of the 1968 Act stated that nothing in the statute limited the President's constitutional power to protect against the overthrow of the government or against "any other clear and present danger to the structure or existence of the Government." A unanimous decision by the Supreme Court in 1972 held that the section merely disclaimed congressional intent to define presidential powers in matters affecting national security and did not authorize warrantless national security surveillances. Moreover, the Fourth Amendment required prior judicial approval for surveillances of *domestic* organizations. The Court carefully avoided the question of surveillances over foreign powers, whether within or outside the country. United States v. United States District Court, 407 U.S. 297 (1972).

Congress passed the Foreign Intelligence Surveillance Act (FISA) of 1978 to clarify the scope of presidential power. A court order was now required to engage in electronic surveillance within the United States for purposes of obtaining foreign intelligence information. A special surveillance court (the FISA Court), appointed by the Chief Justice, reviews applications submitted by government attorneys. 93 Stat. 1783 (1978).

Following the terrorists attacks of 9/11 on the World Trade Center and the Pentagon, the Bush Administration requested new authority to protect the nation. The USA Patriot Act, enacted on October 26, 2001, gave federal officials new powers to track and intercept communications, both for law enforcement and foreign intelligence gathering purposes. In secret, the Administration ordered the National Security Agency (NSA) to work with private telecommunications companies to conduct a surveillance program outside of FISA, claiming inherent powers under Article II. The existence of this program was revealed by the *New York Times* in December 2005, precipitating a number of lawsuits in federal courts around the country. Congress passed legislation in 2008 to revise FISA and grant immunity to the telecoms that had cooperated with the illegal program.

The Prize Cases

2 Black (67 U.S.) 635 (1863)

Among other emergency actions in 1861, President Lincoln declared a blockade of ports controlled by persons in armed rebellion against the government. The owners of the captured ships and cargo (prize, or captured property), brought suit in federal court. To justify the blockade and seizure of neutral vessels, a state of war had to exist, but Congress had made no such declaration. Under what constitutional authority did Lincoln act? Does a state of war require a formal declaration by Congress? Three Lincoln appointees—Swayne, Miller, and Davis—joined Grier and Wayne to uphold presidential power.

Mr. Justice GRIER. There are certain propositions of law which must necessarily affect the ultimate decision of these cases, and many others, which it will be proper to discuss and decide before we notice the special facts peculiar to each.

They are, 1st. Had the President a right to institute a blockade of ports in possession of persons in armed rebellion against the Government, on the

principles of international law, as known and acknowledged among civilized States?

2d. Was the property of persons domiciled or residing within those States a proper subject of capture on the sea as "enemies' property?"

I. Neutrals have a right to challenge the existence of a blockade *de facto,* and also the authority of the party exercising the right to institute it. They have a right to enter the ports of a friendly nation for the purposes of trade and commerce, but are bound to recognize the rights of a belligerent engaged in actual war, to use this mode of coercion, for the purpose of subduing the enemy.

That a blockade *de facto* actually existed, and was formally declared and notified by the President on the 27th and 30th of April, 1861, is an admitted fact in these cases.

That the President, as the Executive Chief of the Government and Commander-in-chief of the Army and Navy, was the proper person to make such notification, has not been, and cannot be disputed.

The right of prize and capture has its origin in the *"jus belli,"* and is governed and adjudged under the law of nations. To legitimate the capture of a neutral vessel or property on the high seas, a war must exist *de facto,* and the neutral must have a knowledge or notice of the intention of one of the parties belligerent to use this mode of coercion against a port, city, or territory, in possession of the other.

Let us enquire whether, at the time this blockade was instituted, a state of war existed which would justify a resort to these means of subduing the hostile force.

War has been well defined to be, "That state in which a nation prosecutes its right by force."

... A civil war is never solemnly declared; it becomes such by its accidents — the number, power, and organization of the persons who originate and carry it on. When the party in rebellion occupy and hold in a hostile manner a certain portion of territory; have declared their independence; have cast off their allegiance; have organized armies; have commenced hostilities against their former sovereign, the world acknowledges them as belligerents, and the contest a *war....*

As a civil war is never publicly proclaimed, *eo nomine,* against insurgents, its actual existence is a fact in our domestic history which the Court is bound to notice and to know.

The true test of its existence, as found in the writings of the sages of the common law, may be thus summarily stated: "When the regular course of justice is interrupted by revolt, rebellion, or insurrection, so that the Courts of Justice cannot be kept open, *civil war exists* and hostilities may be prosecuted on the same footing as if those opposing the Government were foreign enemies invading the land."

By the Constitution, Congress alone has the power to declare a national or foreign war. It cannot declare war against a State, or any number of States, by virtue of any clause in the Constitution. The Constitution confers on the President the whole Ex-

ecutive power. He is bound to take care that the laws be faithfully executed. He is Commander-in-chief of the Army and Navy of the United States, and of the militia of the several States when called into the actual service of the United States. He has no power to initiate or declare a war either against a foreign nation or a domestic State. [During oral argument, Richard Henry Dana, Jr. for the White House agreed that the President's power did not include "the right *to initiate a war, as a voluntary act of sovereignty.* That is vested only in Congress." 67 U.S. at 660.] But by the Acts of Congress of February 28th, 1795, and 3d of March, 1807, he is authorized to call out the militia and use the military and naval forces of the United States in case of invasion by foreign nations, and to suppress insurrection against the government of a State or of the United States.

If a war be made by invasion of a foreign nation, the President is not only authorized but bound to resist force by force. He does not initiate the war, but is bound to accept the challenge without waiting for any special legislative authority. And whether the hostile party be a foreign invader, or States organized in rebellion, it is none the less a war, ...

This greatest of civil wars was not gradually developed by popular commotion, tumultuous assemblies, or local unorganized insurrections. However long may have been its previous conception, it nevertheless sprung forth suddenly from the parent brain, a Minerva in the full panoply of *war.* The President was bound to meet it in the shape it presented itself, without waiting for Congress to baptize it with a name; and no name given to it by him or them could change the fact.

. . .

Whether the President in fulfilling his duties, as Commander-in-chief, in suppressing an insurrection, has met with such armed hostile resistance, and a civil war of such alarming proportions as will compel him to accord to them the character of belligerents, is a question to be decided *by him,* and this Court must be governed by the decisions and acts of the political department of the Government to which this power was entrusted....

If it were necessary to the technical existence of a war, that it should have a legislative sanction, we find it in almost every act passed at the extraordinary session of the Legislature of 1861, which was wholly employed in enacting laws to enable the Government to prosecute the war with vigor and efficiency. And finally, in 1861, we find Congress "ex majore cautela" and in anticipation of such astute objections, passing an act "approving, legalizing, and making valid all the acts, proclamations, and orders of the President, &c., as if they had been *issued and done under the previous express authority* and direction of the Congress of the United States."

. . .

The objection made to this act of ratification, that it is *expost facto,* and therefore unconstitutional and void, might possibly have some weight on the trial of an indictment in a criminal Court. But precedents from that source cannot be received as authoritative in a tribunal administering public and international law.

On this first question therefore we are of the opinion that the President had a right, *jure belli,* to institute a blockade of ports in possession of the States in rebellion, which neutrals are bound to regard.

[The Court then decides whether the property of all persons residing within the territory of the states in rebellion, captured on the high seas, is to be treated as "enemies' property" whether the owner be in arms against the government or not.]

Mr. Justice NELSON dissenting.

. . .

This power *[of announcing war]* in all civilized nations is regulated by the fundamental laws or municipal constitution of the country.

By our Constitution this power is lodged in Congress. Congress shall have power "to declare war, grant letters of marque and reprisal, and make rules concerning captures on land and water."

... But we are asked, what would become of the peace and integrity of the Union in case of an insurrection at home or invasion from abroad if this power could not be exercised by the President in the recess of Congress, and until that body could be assembled?

The framers of the Constitution fully comprehended this question, and provided for the contingency. Indeed, it would have been surprising if they had not, as a rebellion had occurred in the State of Massachusetts while the Convention was in session, and which had become so general that it was quelled only by calling upon the military power of the State. The Constitution declares that Congress shall have power "to provide for calling forth the militia to execute the laws of the Union, suppress insurrections, and repel invasions." Another clause, "that the President shall be Commander-in-chief of the Army and Navy of the United States, and of the militia of the several States when called into the actual service of the United States;" and, again, "He shall take care that the laws shall be faithfully executed." Congress passed laws on this subject in 1792 and 1795. 1 United States Laws, pp. 264, 424.

[In 1807 Congress passed additional legislation authorizing the President to call forth the militia to suppress insurrection.]

The Acts of 1795 and 1807 did not, and could not under the Constitution, confer on the President the power of declaring war against a State of this Union, or of deciding that war existed, and upon that ground authorize the capture and confiscation of the property of every citizen of the State whenever it was found on the waters.... This great power over the business and property of the citizen is reserved to the legislative department by the express words of the Constitution. It cannot be delegated or surrendered to the Executive....

... [T]his power belongs exclusively to the Congress of the United States, and, consequently, that the President had no power to set on foot a blockade under the law of nations, and that the capture of the vessel and cargo in this case, and in all cases before us in which the capture occurred before the 13th of July, 1861, for breach of blockade, or as enemies' property, are illegal and void, and that the decrees of condemnation should be reversed and the vessel and cargo restored.

Mr. Chief Justice TANEY, Mr. Justice CATRON and Mr. Justice CLIFFORD, concurred in the dissenting opinion of Mr. Justice NELSON.

Ex parte Milligan

4 Wall. (71 U.S.) 2 (1866)

Lambdin P. Milligan, a U.S. citizen from Indiana, was arrested by the military in 1864 on charges of conspiracy, found guilty before a military tribunal, and sentenced to be hanged. He presented a petition of habeas corpus to the federal courts, asking to be discharged from unlawful imprisonment because the military had no jurisdiction over him. He insisted that he was entitled to trial by jury in a civilian court. The question was whether the President, in times of

emergency, could suspend the writ of habeas corpus and declare martial law, and whether the tribunal had legal authority to punish Milligan.

Mr. Justice DAVIS delivered the opinion of the court.

On the 10th day of May, 1865, Lambdin P. Milligan presented a petition to the Circuit Court of the United States for the District of Indiana, to be discharged from an alleged unlawful imprisonment....

The controlling question in the case is this: Upon the *facts* stated in Milligan's petition, and the exhibits filed, had the military commission mentioned in it *jurisdiction*, legally, to try and sentence him? Milligan, not a resident of one of the rebellious states, or a prisoner of war, but a citizen of Indiana for twenty years past, and never in the military or naval service, is, while at his home, arrested by the military power of the United States, imprisoned, and, on certain criminal charges preferred against him, tried, convicted, and sentenced to be hanged by a military commission, organized under the direction of the military commander of the military district of Indiana. Had this tribunal the *legal* power and authority to try and punish this man?

[The Court reviews such fundamental constitutional rights as grand jury, trial by jury, confrontation of witnesses against the accused, obtaining witnesses in the accused's favor, and assistance of counsel.]

Time has proven the discernment of our ancestors; for even these provisions, expressed in such plain English words, that it would seem the ingenuity of man could not evade them, are *now,* after the lapse of more than seventy years, sought to be avoided. Those great and good men foresaw that troublous times would arise, when rulers and people would become restive under restraint, and seek by sharp and decisive measures to accomplish ends deemed just and proper; and that the principles of constitutional liberty would be in peril, unless established by irrepealable law. The history of the world had taught them that what was done in the past might be attempted in the future. The Constitution of the United States is a law for rulers and people, equally in war and in peace, and covers with the shield of its protection all classes of men, at all times, and under all circumstances. No doctrine, involving more pernicious consequences, was ever invented by the wit of man than that any of its provisions can be suspended during any of the great exigencies of government. Such a doctrine leads directly to anarchy or despotism, but the theory of necessity on which it is based is false; for the government, within the Constitution, has all the powers granted to it, which are necessary to preserve its existence; as has been happily proved by the result of the great effort to throw off its just authority.

. . .

This court has judicial knowledge that in Indiana the Federal authority was always unopposed, and its courts always open to hear criminal accusations and redress grievances; and no usage of war could sanction a military trial there for any offence whatever of a citizen in civil life, in nowise connected with the military service. Congress could grant no such power; and to the honor of our national legislature be it said, it has never been provoked by the state of the country even to attempt its exercise. One of the plainest constitutional provisions was, therefore, infringed when Milligan was tried by a court not ordained and established by Congress, and not composed of judges appointed during good behavior.

. . .

This nation, as experience has proved, cannot always remain at peace, and has no right to expect that it will always have wise and humane rulers, sincerely attached to the principles of the Constitution. Wicked men, ambitious of power, with hatred of liberty and contempt of law, may fill the place once occupied by Washington and Lincoln; and if this right is conceded, and the calamities of war again befall us, the dangers to human liberty are frightful to contemplate....

It is essential to the safety of every government that, in a great crisis, like the one we have just passed through, there should be a power somewhere of suspending the writ of *habeas corpus....* The Constitution ... does not say after a writ of *habeas corpus* is denied a citizen, that he shall be tried otherwise than by the course of the common law; if it had intended this result, it was easy by the use of direct words to have accomplished it....

... Martial rule can never exist where the courts are open, and in the proper and unobstructed exercise of their jurisdiction....

The CHIEF JUSTICE delivered the following opinion.

[He agrees that the civil court in Indiana had jurisdiction over Milligan, he was entitled to be released from military custody, and that the military commission had no jurisdiction.]

But the opinion which has just been read goes further; and as we understand it, asserts not only that the military commission held in Indiana was not authorized by Congress, but that it was not in the power of Congress to authorize it; from which it may be thought to follow, that Congress has no power to indemnify the officers who composed the commission against liability in civil courts for acting as members of it.

We cannot agree to this.

We agree in the proposition that no department of the government of the United States — neither President, nor Congress, nor the Courts — possesses any power not given by the Constitution.

We assent, fully, to all that is said, in the opinion, of the inestimable value of the trial by jury, and of the other constitutional safeguards of civil liberty. And we concur, also, in what is said of the writ of *habeas corpus,* and of its suspension, with two reservations: (1.) That, in our judgment, when the writ is suspended, the Executive is authorized to arrest as well as to detain; and (2.) that there are cases in which, the privilege of the writ being suspended, trial and punishment by military commission, in states where civil courts are open, may be authorized by Congress, as well as arrest and detention.

We think that Congress had power, though not exercised, to authorize the military commission which was held in Indiana....

Mr. Justice WAYNE, Mr. Justice SWAYNE, and Mr. Justice MILLER concur with me in these views.

Korematsu v. United States

323 U.S. 214 (1944)

Under authority of President Roosevelt's Executive Order 9066 and a congressional statute enacted in 1942, the Commanding General of the Western Defense Command issued an order directing the exclusion of all Japanese-Americans from a West Coast military area. Exclusion meant imprisonment in barbed wire stockades, called assembly centers, until the individuals could be transported inland to "relocation centers" under military guard. The military order, covering both aliens and U.S. citizens, was based on the belief of Commanding General J.L. DeWitt that all individuals of Japanese descent were "subversive" and belonged to an "enemy race" whose "racial strains are undiluted." Fred Korematsu, an American citizen of Japanese descent, was convicted for violating the exclusion order. His conviction was affirmed by the Ninth Circuit.

MR. JUSTICE BLACK delivered the opinion of the Court.

The petitioner, an American citizen of Japanese descent, was convicted in a federal district court for remaining in San Leandro, California, a "Military Area," contrary to Civilian Exclusion Order No. 34 of the Commanding General of the Western Command, U. S. Army, which directed that after May 9, 1942, all persons of Japanese ancestry should be excluded from that area. No question was raised as to petitioner's loyalty to the United States. The Circuit Court of Appeals affirmed, and the importance of the constitutional question involved caused us to grant certiorari.

It should be noted, to begin with, that all legal restrictions which curtail the civil rights of a single racial group are immediately suspect. That is not to say that all such restrictions are unconstitutional. It is to say that courts must subject them to the most rigid scrutiny. Pressing public necessity may sometimes justify the existence of such restrictions; racial antagonism never can.

. . .

Exclusion Order No. 34, which the petitioner knowingly and admittedly violated, was one of a number of military orders and proclamations, all of which were substantially based upon Executive Order No. 9066, 7 Fed. Reg. 1407. That order, issued after we were at war with Japan, declared that "the successful prosecution of the war requires every possible protection against espionage and against sabotage to national-defense material, national-defense premises, and national-defense utilities...."

One of the series of orders and proclamations, a curfew order, which like the exclusion order here was promulgated pursuant to Executive Order 9066, subjected all persons of Japanese ancestry in prescribed West Coast military areas to remain in their residences from 8 P.M. to 6 A.M. As is the case with the exclusion order here, that prior curfew order was designed as a "protection against espionage and against sabotage." In *Hirabayashi* v. *United States,* 320 U.S. 81, we sustained a conviction obtained for violation of the curfew order. The Hirabayashi con- viction and this one thus rest on the same 1942 Con- gressional Act and the same basic executive and mil- itary orders, all of which orders were aimed at the twin dangers of espionage and sabotage.

… We upheld the curfew order as an exercise of the power of the government to take steps necessary to prevent espionage and sabotage in an area threat- ened by Japanese attack.

In the light of the principles we announced in the *Hirabayashi* case, we are unable to conclude that it was beyond the war power of Congress and the Ex- ecutive to exclude those of Japanese ancestry from the West Coast war area at the time they did. True, exclusion from the area in which one's home is lo- cated is a far greater deprivation than constant con- finement to the home from 8 P.M. to 6 A.M. Nothing short of apprehension by the proper military au- thorities of the gravest imminent danger to the pub- lic safety can constitutionally justify either. But ex- clusion from a threatened area, no less than curfew, has a definite and close relationship to the preven- tion of espionage and sabotage. The military au- thorities, charged with the primary responsibility of defending our shores, concluded that curfew pro- vided inadequate protection and ordered exclusion. They did so, as pointed out in our *Hirabayashi* opin- ion, in accordance with Congressional authority to the military to say who should, and who should not, remain in the threatened areas.

… [W]e are not unmindful of the hardships im- posed by it upon a large group of American citizens. Cf. *Ex parte Kawato*, 317 U.S. 69, 73. But hardships are part of war, and war is an aggregation of hard- ships. All citizens alike, both in and out of uniform, feel the impact of war in greater or lesser measure. Citizenship has its responsibilities as well as its priv- ileges, and in time of of war the burden is always heavier….

It is said that we are dealing here with the case of imprisonment of a citizen in a concentration camp solely because of his ancestry, without evidence or in- quiry concerning his loyalty and good disposition to- wards the United States. Our task would be simple, our duty clear, were this a case involving the impris- onment of a loyal citizen in a concentration camp be- cause of racial prejudice. Regardless of the true na- ture of the assembly and relocation centers—and we deem it unjustifiable to call them concentration camps with all the ugly connotations that term im- plies—we are dealing specifically with nothing but an exclusion order. To cast this case into outlines of racial prejudice, without reference to the real military dangers which were presented, merely confuses the

issue. Korematsu was not excluded from the Military Area because of hostility to him or his race. He *was* excluded because we are at war with the Japanese Empire, because the properly constituted military authorities feared an invasion of our West Coast and felt constrained to take proper security measures, be- cause they decided that the military urgency of the situation demanded that all citizens of Japanese an- cestry be segregated from the West Coast temporar- ily, and finally, because Congress, reposing its confi- dence in this time of war in our military leaders—as inevitably it must—determined that they should have the power to do just this. There was evidence of disloyalty on the part of some, the military authori- ties considered that the need for action was great, and time was short. We cannot—by availing ourselves of the calm perspective of hindsight—now say that at that time these actions were unjustified.

Affirmed.

MR. JUSTICE FRANKFURTER, concurring.

· · ·

MR. JUSTICE ROBERTS.

I dissent, because I think the indisputable facts exhibit a clear violation of Constitutional rights.

This is not a case of keeping people off the streets at night as was *Hirabayashi* v. *United States,* 320 U.S. 81, nor a case of temporary exclusion of a citizen from an area for his own safety or that of the com- munity, nor a case of offering him an opportunity to go temporarily out of an area where his presence might cause danger to himself or to his fellows. On the contrary, it is the case of convicting a citizen as a punishment for not submitting to imprisonment in a concentration camp, based on his ancestry, and solely because of his ancestry, without evidence or inquiry concerning his loyalty and good disposition towards the United States.…

MR. JUSTICE MURPHY, dissenting.

This exclusion of "all persons of Japanese ances- try, both alien and non-alien," from the Pacific Coast area on a plea of military necessity in the absence of martial law ought not to be approved. Such exclu- sion goes over "the very brink of constitutional power" and falls into the ugly abyss of racism.

In dealing with matters relating to the prosecu- tion and progress of a war, we must accord great re- spect and consideration to the judgments of the military authorities who are on the scene and who have full knowledge of the military facts. The scope of their discretion must, as a matter of necessity and common sense, be wide. And their judgments ought not to be overruled lightly by those whose training and duties ill-equip them to deal intelligently with matters so vital to the physical security of the nation.

At the same time, however, it is essential that there be definite limits to military discretion, especially where martial law has not been declared. Individuals must not be left impoverished of their constitutional rights on a plea of military necessity that has neither substance nor support. Thus, like other claims conflicting with the asserted constitutional rights of the individual, the military claim must subject itself to the judicial process of having its reasonableness determined and its conflicts with other interests reconciled....

That this forced exclusion was the result in good measure of this erroneous assumption of racial guilt rather than bona fide military necessity is evidenced by the Commanding General's Final Report on the evacuation from the Pacific Coast area. In it he refers to all individuals of Japanese descent as "subversive," as belonging to "an enemy race" whose "racial strains are undiluted," and as constituting "over 112,000 potential enemies ... at large today" along the Pacific Coast. In support of this blanket condemnation of all persons of Japanese descent, however, no reliable evidence is cited to show that such individuals were generally disloyal, ...

I dissent, therefore, from this legalization of racism....

MR. JUSTICE JACKSON, dissenting.

Korematsu was born on our soil, of parents born in Japan. The Constitution makes him a citizen of the United States by nativity and a citizen of California by residence. No claim is made that he is not loyal to this country. There is no suggestion that apart from the matter involved here he is not law-abiding and well disposed. Korematsu, however, has been convicted of an act not commonly a crime. It consists merely of being present in the state whereof he is a citizen, near the place where he was born, and where all his life he has lived.

. . .

Now, if any fundamental assumption underlies our system, it is that guilt is personal and not inheritable. Even if all of one's antecedents had been convicted of treason, the Constitution forbids its penalties to be visited upon him, for it provides that "no attainder of treason shall work corruption of blood, or forfeiture except during the life of the person attained." But here is an attempt to make an otherwise innocent act a crime merely because this prisoner is the son of parents as to whom he had no choice, and belongs to a race from which there is no way to resign....

Youngstown Co. v. Sawyer

343 U.S. 579 (1952)

In April 1952, to avert a nationwide strike of steelworkers that threatened U.S. military needs in the Korean War, President Truman issued an executive order directing Secretary of Commerce Sawyer to seize and operate most of the steel mills. The order was not based on specific statutory authority. In fact, Truman decided not to use the statutory remedy available in the Taft-Hartley Act of 1947, which was enacted into law over his veto. In court, the administration justified the executive order on the basis of inherent presidential power (oral argument, as a reading, in Chapter 1). The district court issued a preliminary injunction against the seizure, rejecting the theory of inherent power, but the D.C. Circuit stayed this injunction pending review by the Supreme Court.

MR. JUSTICE BLACK delivered the opinion of the Court.

We are asked to decide whether the President was acting within his constitutional power when he issued an order directing the Secretary of Commerce to take possession of and operate most of the Nation's steel mills. The mill owners argue that the President's order amounts to lawmaking, a legisla-

tive function which the Constitution has expressly confided to the Congress and not to the President. The Government's position is that the order was made on findings of the President that his action was necessary to avert a national catastrophe which would inevitably result from a stoppage of steel production, and that in meeting this grave emergency the President was acting within the aggregate of his constitutional powers as the Nation's Chief Executive and the Commander in Chief of the Armed Forces of the United States....

I.

[The Court rejects the administration's argument that the case should be resolved on nonconstitutional grounds. The constitutional question is "ripe for determination on the record presented."]

II.

The President's power, if any, to issue the order must stem either from an act of Congress or from the Constitution itself. There is no statute that expressly authorizes the President to take possession of property as he did here. Nor is there any act of Congress to which our attention has been directed from which such a power can fairly be implied. Indeed, we do not understand the Government to rely on statutory authorization for this seizure....

Moreover, the use of the seizure technique to solve labor disputes in order to prevent work stoppages was not only unauthorized by any congressional enactment; prior to this controversy, Congress had refused to adopt that method of settling labor disputes. When the Taft-Hartley Act was under consideration in 1947, Congress rejected an amendment which would have authorized such governmental seizures in cases of emergency. Apparently it was thought that the technique of seizure, like that of compulsory arbitration, would interfere with the process of collective bargaining. Consequently, the plan Congress adopted in that Act did not provide for seizure under any circumstances....

It is clear that if the President had authority to issue the order he did, it must be found in some provision of the Constitution. And it is not claimed that express constitutional language grants this power to the President. The contention is that presidential power should be implied from the aggregate of his powers under the Constitution. Particular reliance is placed on provisions in Article II which say that "The executive Power shall be vested in a President ..."; that "he shall take Care that the Laws be faithfully executed"; and that he "shall be Commander in Chief of the Army and Navy of the United States."

The order cannot properly be sustained as an exercise of the President's military power as Commander in Chief of the Armed Forces. The Government attempts to do so by citing a number of cases upholding broad powers in military commanders engaged in day-to-day fighting in a theater of war. Such cases need not concern us here. Even though "theater of war" be an expanding concept, we cannot with faithfulness to our constitutional system hold that the Commander in Chief of the Armed Forces has the ultimate power as such to take possession of private property in order to keep labor disputes from stopping production. This is a job for the Nation's lawmakers, not for its military authorities.

Nor can the seizure order be sustained because of the several constitutional provisions that grant executive power to the President. In the framework of our Constitution, the President's power to see that the laws are faithfully executed refutes the idea that he is to be a lawmaker. The Constitution limits his functions in the lawmaking process to the recommending of laws he thinks wise and the vetoing of laws he thinks bad. And the Constitution is neither silent nor equivocal about who shall make laws which the President is to execute. The first section of the first article says that "All legislative Powers herein granted shall be vested in a Congress of the United States...." After granting many powers to the Congress, Article I goes on to provide that Congress may "make all Laws which shall be necessary and proper for carrying into Execution the foregoing Powers, and all other Powers vested by this Constitution in the Government of the United States, or in any Department or Officer thereof."

... The power of Congress to adopt such public policies as those proclaimed by the order is beyond question. It can authorize the taking of private property for public use. It can make laws regulating the relationships between employers and employees, prescribing rules designed to settle labor disputes, and fixing wages and working conditions in certain fields of our economy. The Constitution does not subject this lawmaking power of Congress to presidential or military supervision or control.

It is said that other Presidents without congressional authority have taken possession of private business enterprises in order to settle labor disputes. But even if this be true, Congress has not thereby lost its exclusive constitutional authority to make laws necessary and proper to carry out the powers vested by the Constitution "in the Government of the United States, or any Department or Officer thereof."

The Founders of this Nation entrusted the lawmaking power to the Congress alone in both good and bad times. It would do no good to recall the historical events, the fears of power and the hopes for freedom that lay behind their choice. Such a review would but confirm our holding that this seizure order cannot stand.

The judgment of the District Court is

Affirmed.

. . .

Mr. Justice Frankfurter, concurring.

... Not so long ago it was fashionable to find our system of checks and balances obstructive to effective government. It was easy to ridicule that system as outmoded — too easy. The experience through which the world has passed in our own day has made vivid the realization that the Framers of our Constitution were not inexperienced doctrinaires. These long-headed statesmen had no illusion that our people enjoyed biological or psychological or sociological immunities from the hazards of concentrated power. It is absurd to see a dictator in a representative product of the sturdy democratic traditions of the Mississippi Valley. The accretion of dangerous power does not come in a day. It does come, however slowly, from the generative force of unchecked disregard of the restrictions that fence in even the most disinterested assertion of authority.

... It is an inadmissibly narrow conception of American constitutional law to confine it to the words of the Constitution and to disregard the gloss which life has written upon them. In short, a systematic, unbroken, executive practice, long pursued to the knowledge of the Congress and never before questioned, engaged in by Presidents who have also sworn to uphold the Constitution, making as it were such exercise of power part of the structure of our government, may be treated as a gloss on "executive Power" vested in the President by § 1 of Art. II.

. . .

Mr. Justice Douglas, concurring. ...

. . .

Mr. Justice Jackson, concurring in the judgment and opinion of the Court.

. . .

A judge, like an executive adviser, may be surprised at the poverty of really useful and unambiguous authority applicable to concrete problems of executive power as they actually present themselves. Just what our forefathers did envision, or would have envisioned had they foreseen modern conditions, must be divined from materials almost as enigmatic as the dreams Joseph was called upon to interpret for Pharaoh. A century and a half of partisan debate and scholarly speculation yields no net result but only supplies more or less apt quotations from respected sources on each side of any question. They largely cancel each other. And court decisions are indecisive because of the judicial practice of dealing with the largest questions in the most narrow way.

The actual art of governing under our Constitution does not and cannot conform to judicial definitions of the power of any of its branches based on isolated clauses or even single Articles torn from context. While the Constitution diffuses power the better to secure liberty, it also contemplates that practice will integrate the dispersed powers into a workable government. It enjoins upon its branches separateness but interdependence, autonomy but reciprocity. Presidential powers are not fixed but fluctuate, depending upon their disjunction or conjunction with those of Congress. We may well begin by a somewhat over-simplified grouping of practical situations in which a President may doubt, or others may challenge, his powers, and by distinguishing roughly the legal consequences of this factor of relativity.

1. When the President acts pursuant to an express or implied authorization of Congress, his authority is at its maximum, for it includes all that he possesses in his own right plus all that Congress can delegate. ...

2. When the President acts in absence of either a congressional grant or denial of authority, he can only rely upon his own independent powers, but there is a zone of twilight in which he and Congress may have concurrent authority, or in which its distribution is uncertain. Therefore, congressional inertia, indifference or quiescence may sometimes, at least as a practical matter, enable, if not invite, measures on independent presidential responsibility. In this area, any actual test of power is likely to depend on the imperatives of events and contemporary imponderables rather than on abstract theories of law.

3. When the President takes measures incompatible with the expressed or implied will of Congress, his power is at its lowest ebb, for then he can rely only upon his own constitutional powers minus any constitutional powers of Congress over the matter. ...

We should not use this occasion to circumscribe, much less to contract, the lawful role of the President as Commander in Chief. I should indulge the widest latitude of interpretation to sustain his exclusive function to command the instruments of national force, at least when turned against the outside world for the security of our society. But, when it is turned inward, not because of rebellion but because of a lawful economic struggle between industry and labor, it should have no such indulgence. ...

... I have no illusion that any decision by this Court can keep power in the hands of Congress if it is not wise and timely in meeting its problems. A crisis that challenges the President equally, or perhaps primarily, challenges Congress. If not good law, there was worldly wisdom in the maxim attributed to Napoleon that "The tools belong to the man who can use them." We may say that power to legislate for emergencies belongs in the hands of Congress, but only Congress itself can prevent power from slipping through its fingers.

... With all its defects, delays and inconveniences, men have discovered no technique for long preserving free government except that the Executive be under the law, and that the law be made by parliamentary deliberations.

Such institutions may be destined to pass away. But it is the duty of the Court to be last, not first, to give them up.

MR. JUSTICE BURTON, concurring in both the opinion and judgment of the Court.

... The present situation is not comparable to that of an imminent invasion or threatened attack. We do not face the issue of what might be the President's constitutional power to meet such catastrophic situations....

MR. JUSTICE CLARK, concurring in the judgment of the Court.

... [T]he Constitution does grant to the President extensive authority in times of grave and imperative national emergency. In fact, to my thinking, such a grant may well be necessary to the very existence of the Constitution itself....

I conclude that where Congress has laid down specific procedures to deal with the type of crisis confronting the President, he must follow those procedures in meeting the crisis; but that in the absence of such action by Congress, the President's independent power to act depends upon the gravity of the situation confronting the nation. I cannot sustain the seizure in question because here ... Congress had prescribed methods to be followed by the President in meeting the emergency at hand.

. . .

MR. CHIEF JUSTICE VINSON, with whom MR. JUSTICE REED and MR. JUSTICE MINTON join, dissenting.

. . .

I.

... In 1950, when the United Nations called upon member nations "to render every assistance" to repel aggression in Korea, the United States furnished its vigorous support. For almost two full years, our armed forces have been fighting in Korea, suffering casualties of over 108,000 men. Hostilities have not abated. The "determination of the United Nations to continue its action in Korea to meet the aggression" has been reaffirmed. Congressional support of the action in Korea has been manifested by provisions for increased military manpower and equipment and for economic stabilization, as hereinafter described.

. . .

Congress recognized the impact of these defense programs upon the economy. Following the attack in Korea, the President asked for authority to requisition property and to allocate and fix priorities for scarce goods. In the Defense Production Act of 1950, Congress granted the powers requested and, *in addition,* granted power to stabilize prices and wages and to provide for settlement of labor disputes arising in the defense program. The Defense Production Act was extended in 1951, a Senate Committee noting that in the dislocation caused by the programs for purchase of military equipment "lies the seed of an economic disaster that might well destroy the military might we are straining to build." Significantly, the Committee examined the problem "in terms of just one commodity, steel," and found "a graphic picture of the over-all inflationary danger growing out of reduced civilian supplies and rising incomes." ...

New York Times Co. v. United States

403 U.S. 713 (1971)

The Nixon administration brought action in federal court to prevent publication in the *New York Times* and the *Washington Post* of certain materials collectively called the Pentagon Papers. The documents consisted of a classified study prepared by the Defense Department, entitled "History of U.S. Decision-Making Process on Viet Nam Policy." The administration claimed that

publication of the materials would be injurious to national security. The newspapers argued that the First Amendment protected against prior restraint on the right to publish.

PER CURIAM.

We granted certiorari in these cases in which the United States seeks to enjoin the New York Times and the Washington Post from publishing the contents of a classified study entitled "History of U.S. Decision-Making Process on Viet Nam Policy." ...

"Any system of prior restraints of expression comes to this Court bearing a heavy presumption against its constitutional validity." *Bantam Books, Inc.* v. *Sullivan,* 372 U.S. 58, 70 (1963); see also *Near* v. *Minnesota,* 283 U.S. 697 (1931). The Government "thus carries a heavy burden of showing justification for the imposition of such a restraint." *Organization for a Better Austin* v. *Keefe,* 402 U.S. 415, 419 (1971). The District Court for the Southern District of New York in the *New York Times* case and the District Court for the District of Columbia and the Court of Appeals for the District of Columbia Circuit in the *Washington Post* case held that the Government had not met that burden. We agree.

The judgment of the Court of Appeals for the District of Columbia Circuit is therefore affirmed. The order of the Court of Appeals for the Second Circuit is reversed and the case is remanded with directions to enter a judgment affirming the judgment of the District Court for the Southern District of New York. The stays entered June 25, 1971, by the Court are vacated. The judgments shall issue forthwith.

So ordered.

MR. JUSTICE BLACK, with whom MR. JUSTICE DOUGLAS joins, concurring.

I adhere to the view that the Government's case against the Washington Post should have been dismissed and that the injunction against the New York Times should have been vacated without oral argument when the cases were first presented to this Court. I believe that every moment's continuance of the injunctions against these newspapers amounts to a flagrant, indefensible, and continuing violation of the First Amendment....

... Madison and the other Framers of the First Amendment, able men that they were, wrote in language they earnestly believed could never be misunderstood: "Congress shall make no law ... abridging the freedom ... of the press...." Both the history and language of the First Amendment support the view that the press must be left free to publish news, whatever the source, without censorship, injunctions, or prior restraints.

In the First Amendment the Founding Fathers gave the free press the protection it must have to fulfill its essential role in our democracy. The press was to serve the governed, not the governors. The Government's power to censor the press was abolished so that the press would remain forever free to censure the Government. The press was protected so that it could bare the secrets of government and inform the people. Only a free and unrestrained press can effectively expose deception in government. And paramount among the responsibilities of a free press is the duty to prevent any part of the government from deceiving the people and sending them off to distant lands to die of foreign fevers and foreign shot and shell....

The word "security" is a broad, vague generality whose contours should not be invoked to abrogate the fundamental law embodied in the First Amendment. The guarding of military and diplomatic secrets at the expense of informed representative government provides no real security for our Republic....

MR. JUSTICE DOUGLAS, with whom MR. JUSTICE BLACK joins, concurring....

MR. JUSTICE BRENNAN, concurring....

MR. JUSTICE STEWART, with whom MR. JUSTICE WHITE joins, concurring.

... If the Constitution gives the Executive a large degree of unshared power in the conduct of foreign affairs and the maintenance of our national defense, then under the Constitution the Executive must have the largely unshared duty to determine and preserve the degree of internal security necessary to exercise that power successfully. It is an awesome responsibility, requiring judgment and wisdom of a high order. I should suppose that moral, political, and practical considerations would dictate that a very first principle of that wisdom would be an insistence upon avoiding secrecy for its own sake. For when everything is classified, then nothing is classified, and the system becomes one to be disregarded by the cynical or the careless, and to be manipulated by those intent on self-protection or self-promotion....

... I am convinced that the Executive is correct with respect to some of the documents involved. But I cannot say that disclosure of any of them will surely result in direct, immediate, and irreparable damage to our Nation or its people. That being so, there can under the First Amendment be but one judicial resolution of the issues before us. I join the judgments of the Court.

MR. JUSTICE WHITE, with whom MR. JUSTICE STEWART joins, concurring....

MR. JUSTICE MARSHALL, concurring....

MR. CHIEF JUSTICE BURGER, dissenting.

... In these cases, the imperative of a free and unfettered press comes into collision with another imperative, the effective functioning of a complex modern government and specifically the effective exercise of certain constitutional powers of the Executive. Only those who view the First Amendment as an absolute in all circumstances—a view I respect, but reject—can find such cases as these to be simple or easy.

These cases are not simple for another and more immediate reason. We do not know the facts of the cases. No District Judge knew all the facts. No Court of Appeals judge knew all the facts. No member of this Court knows all the facts.

Why are we in this posture, in which only those judges to whom the First Amendment is absolute and permits of no restraint in any circumstances or for any reason, are really in a position to act?

I suggest we are in this posture because these cases have been conducted in unseemly haste....

MR. JUSTICE HARLAN, with whom THE CHIEF JUSTICE and MR. JUSTICE BLACKMUN join, dissenting.

These cases forcefully call to mind the wise admonition of Mr. Justice Holmes, dissenting in *Northern Securities Co.* v. *United States,* 193 U.S. 197, 400–401 (1904):

"Great cases like hard cases make bad law. For great cases are called great, not by reason of their real importance in shaping the law of the future, but because of some accident of immediate overwhelming interest which appeals to the feelings and distorts the judgment. These immediate interests exercise a kind of hydraulic pressure which makes what previously was clear seem doubtful, and before which even well settled principles of law will bend."

With all respect, I consider that the Court has been almost irresponsibly feverish in dealing with these cases.

Both the Court of Appeals for the Second Circuit and the Court of Appeals for the District of Columbia Circuit rendered judgment on June 23. The New York Times' petition for certiorari, its motion for accelerated consideration thereof, and its application for interim relief were filed in this Court on June 24 at about 11 A.M. The application of the United States for interim relief in the *Post* case was also filed here on June 24 at about 7:15 P.M. This Court's order setting a hearing before us on June 26 at 11 A.M., a course which I joined only to avoid the possibility of even more peremptory action by the Court, was issued less than 24 hours before. The record in the *Post* case was filed with the Clerk shortly before 1 P.M. on June 25; the record in the *Times* case did not arrive until 7 or 8 o'clock that same night. The briefs of the parties were received less than two hours before argument on June 26.

This frenzied train of events took place in the name of the presumption against prior restraints created by the First Amendment. Due regard for the extraordinarily important and difficult questions involved in these litigations should have led the Court to shun such a precipitate timetable.

. . .

MR. JUSTICE BLACKMUN, dissenting....

Erwin N. Griswold
How Sensitive Were the "Pentagon Papers"?

In the administration's brief to the Supreme Court on *New York Times Co.* v. *United States,* Solicitor General Erwin N. Griswold described all of the materials in the 47 volumes as classified "Top Secret-Sensitive," "Top Secret," or "Secret." By the time the case reached the Court, the administration wanted to bar only the publication of a smaller number of documents, the disclosure of which would pose a "grave and immediate danger to the security of the United States." During oral argument, Griswold told the Court that the broaching of one of the documents "would be of extraordinary seriousness to the security of the United States." Publication of the documents, according to Griswold, "will affect lives. It will affect the process of the termination of the war. It will affect the process of recovering prisoners of war." Later in the oral argument he warned the Court that publication would interfere with the conduct of "delicate negotiations now in process, or contemplated for the future." Yet in an article for the *Washington Post* on February 15, 1989, entitled "Secrets Not Worth Keeping" (p. A25), he admits that publication produced no trace of a threat to the national security. As he explains, the principal concern of classifiers "is not with national security, but rather with government embarrassment of one sort or another."

It may be relevant at this time to recount some details of events which attracted widespread attention several years ago. The occasion was the presentation of the Pentagon Papers case *(New York Times* v. *United States* and *United States* v. *Washington Post)* before the United States Supreme Court, and the year was 1971.

At that time, I held the office of solicitor general of the United States. The government then in office, under the presidency of Richard Nixon, was determined to do everything in its power to prevent the press from publishing some 47 volumes of mimeographed papers preserved primarily in the office of the Secretary of Defense in the Pentagon, and thus known as the Pentagon Papers. These papers were *in toto* classified as Top Secret....

It was my responsibility to represent the interests of the United States before the Supreme Court. Everything happened very fast. The U.S. Court of Appeals for the District of Columbia decided the case on Thursday, June 24, 1971. On Friday, at noon, I was advised by Chief Justice Warren Burger that the case would be heard by the Supreme Court on Saturday morning, June 26, and that "briefs will be exchanged between the parties in the courtroom immediately before the argument."

At that time, no briefs had been written, and, indeed, I had never seen the *outside* of the Pentagon Papers. I immediately arranged for a set of the papers to be brought to my office. It was obvious that I could not read all of the materials in the time available. In this situation, I arranged to have three high officials, one each from the Defense Department, the State Department and the National Security Agency come to my office. I asked them to tell me what items in the 47 volumes were really bad — what items, if disclosed, would be a real threat to the security of the United States.

This produced a total of about 40 items over which these officers expressed concern. I then read each of these items, but quickly came to the conclusion that most of them presented no serious threat to national security, and that there was simply no prospect that the Supreme Court would ban the publication of all of these items. Eventually, I reduced the list to a total of 11 items. My deputy, Daniel M. Friedman, wrote the main or "open" brief for the United States, while I wrote the "secret" brief, contending that these 11 items presented a threat to the national security.

. . .

So, I went ahead and presented the case before the court, relying only on the 11 items. As is well known, we lost, by a six-to-three vote, with three members of the majority saying there could never be a prior restraint, while three others said that a prior restraint would be appropriate in a proper case, but that there was no adequate threat to national security in this case.

Accordingly, the newspapers printed many items from the Pentagon Papers. And within a few weeks, under the auspices of Sen. Mike Gravel of Alaska, the entire contents of all the papers were printed. I have never seen any trace of a threat to the national security from the publication. Indeed, I have never seen it even suggested that there was such an actual threat....

It quickly becomes apparent to any person who has considerable experience with classified material that there is massive overclassification and that the principal concern of the classifiers is not with national security, but rather with governmental embarrassment of one sort or another. There may be some basis for short-term classification while plans are being made, or negotiations are going on, but apart from details of weapons systems, there is very rarely any real risk to current national security from the publication of facts relating to transactions in the past, even the fairly recent past....

C. TREATIES AND EXECUTIVE AGREEMENTS

Under Article VI of the Constitution, federal statutes made pursuant to the Constitution and all treaties "shall be the supreme Law of the Land." State judges are bound by those actions, "any Thing in the Constitution or Laws of any State to the Contrary Notwithstanding." Much depends on whether the treaty is "self-executing" (does not require implementing legislation or other action) or is not self-executing. In passing legislation to carry out a treaty, Congress may act in ways that might not have been sustained in the form of a freestanding statute. See Missouri v. Holland in Chapter 8.

The President makes treaties "by and with the Advice and Consent of the Senate." The process of treaty-making need not be divided into two exclusive and sequential stages: negotiation solely by the President, followed by Senate advice and consent. When President Washington first communicated with the Senate regarding the appropriate procedure for treaties, he considered oral communications with Senators "indispensably necessary." Treaties seemed to him "of a legislative nature," inviting deliberation in the Senate's chamber. 30 Writings of Washington 373, 378. On August 22, 1789, he met with Senators to secure their advice and consent to an Indian treaty. The Senators felt uncomfortable in his presence and disliked having to rely solely on information provided by the Secretary of War, who was present. Washington returned two days later and obtained the Senate's consent, but he decided against a repeat performance.

This incident has been misinterpreted to suggest that Washington negotiated all future treaties without Senate involvement. In fact, he continued to seek the Senate's advice by written communications rather than personal appearances. Senators were asked to approve the appointment of treaty negotiators and even advise on their negotiating instructions. Far from being a "presidential monopoly," the negotiation of treaties has often been shared with the Senate in order to obtain legislative guidance, understanding, and support. Presidential insistence to "go it alone" in negotiating treaties has often had disastrous results. Fisher, Constitutional Conflicts Between Congress and the President 221-26 (2007 ed.); Fisher, 38 Pres. Stud. Q. 144 (2008).

Role of the House

Although the Senate is the only chamber of Congress with an express constitutional duty in the treaty process, the House of Representatives plays a crucial role in funding treaties. As early as 1796, members of the House of Representatives insisted that the House possessed "a discretionary power of carrying the Treaty into effect, or refusing it their sanction." Annals of Congress, 4th Cong., 1st Session. 426–28. Lawmakers decided that certain powers delegated to Congress as a whole, such as the authority to regulate foreign commerce or to set tariffs, could not be exercised through the treaty-making power. The general power of appropriating funds to execute a treaty represents a substantial constraint on the President and the Senate.

When two-thirds of the Senate fails to ratify a treaty, Presidents have at times turned to Congress as a whole to accomplish the same purpose by obtaining a simple majority vote in both Houses for a joint resolution. The annexation of Texas and Hawaii and the adoption of the St. Lawrence Seaway plan were accomplished in this manner. The position of the House of Representatives is enhanced when treaties contain language requiring that funds be made available through the normal procedures of Congress, including prior authorization and annual appropriations. This language requires action not only by the Senate Foreign Relations Committee and the House Foreign Affairs Committee but also by both Appropriations Committees.

Treaty Termination

The constitutional issue of treaty termination was raised in 1978 when President Jimmy Carter terminated a defense treaty with Taiwan. The Senate considered a resolution that would have required the approval of the Senate or both Houses of Congress before the President could terminate any defense treaty, but final action was never taken on the measure. A federal district judge decided that some form of congressional concurrence was required, either the approval of a majority of both Houses or the consent of two-thirds of the Senate. Goldwater v. Carter, 481 F.Supp. 949, 963–64

(D.D.C. 1979). This decision was rejected by an appellate court and the Supreme Court, in part because of the failure of Congress to confront the President in a direct and final way. In the words of Justice Jackson from the Steel Seizure Case of 1952, Carter had acted in a "zone of twilight." Goldwater v. Carter, 617 F.2d 697 (D.C. Cir. 1979); GOLDWATER v. CARTER, 444 U.S. 996 (1979). The Justices of the Supreme Court split along so many lines that their opinions shed little light on future treaty terminations. Congress has yet to pass legislation to define executive and legislative roles in this matter.

In 2001, President George W. Bush terminated the 1972 ABM treaty between the United States and Russia. A lawsuit, challenging his authority to terminate a treaty without congressional approval, was turned aside on grounds of standing and the political question doctrine. Kucinich v. Bush, 236 F.Supp.2d 1 (D.D.C. 2002). For further analysis of the ABM dispute, see David Gray Adler, 34 Pres. Stud. Q. 156-167 (2004).

Executive Agreements

Treaties differ from executive agreements in several regards. Treaties require the advice and consent of the Senate; executive agreements do not. Treaties (unlike executive agreements) may supersede prior conflicting statutes. United States v. Schooner Peggy, 5 U.S. (1 Cr.) 103 (1801). Otherwise, officials in the executive branch have considerable latitude in entering into international compacts either by treaty or by executive agreement. Among the more controversial executive agreements are the destroyers-bases deal with Great Britain in 1940, the Yalta and Potsdam agreements of 1945, the Vietnam peace agreement of 1973, the Sinai agreements of 1975, and military-base agreements with Spain, Diego Garcia, and Bahrain. The Bush administration in 2008 raised constitutional issues when it attempted to enter into an agreement with Iraq concerning future U.S. military bases and other matters.

The vast majority of executive agreements are based on statutory authority or treaty language. Although these agreements may lack what the Supreme Court calls the "dignity" of a treaty, since they do not require Senate approval, they are nevertheless valid international compacts. Altman & Co. v. United States, 224 U.S. 583, 600–01 (1912).[4] In addition to statutory and treaty authority, the executive branch claims four sources of constitutional authority that allow the President to enter into executive agreements: (1) his duty as chief executive to represent the nation in foreign affairs, (2) his authority to receive ambassadors and other public ministers, (3) his authority as commander in chief, and (4) his duty to "take care that the laws be faithfully executed." 11 FAM [Foreign Affairs Manual] 721.2(b)(3). The scope of these unilateral initiatives has been narrowed by judicial and congressional actions.

The President has broad constitutional authority to recognize foreign governments. President Roosevelt's recognition of Soviet Russia led to the "Litvinov Assignment" in 1933 and subsequent property claims in the courts. His decision was upheld by the Supreme Court. United States v. Belmont, 301 U.S. 324 (1937); United States v. Pink, 315 U.S. 203 (1942). Left undecided is the President's power to enter into agreements that violate such constitutional provisions as the Due Process and Just Compensation Clauses of the Fifth Amendment. Under certain circumstances, the use of the recognition power by the President may invade the war prerogatives of Congress. President Andrew Jackson made that argument in declining to recognize the independence of Texas, fearing that such action would result in war with Mexico and undercut the legitimate constitutional role of Congress. Louis Fisher, Presidential War Power 39 (2d ed. 2004).

---

4. In United States v. Pink, 315 U.S. 203, 230 (1942), the Court regarded executive agreements as having a "similar dignity" with treaties. For an opinion by Acting Attorney General McGranery in 1946 upholding the legality of an executive agreement made pursuant to a joint resolution, see 40 Op. Att'y Gen. 469. In 2003, the Court divided 5 to 4 to uphold an executive agreement by noting that Congress had not taken steps to disapprove it. American Ins. Assn. v. Garamendi, 539 U.S. 396 (2003).

The State Department concedes that an executive agreement cannot be "inconsistent with legislation enacted by the Congress in the exercise of its constitutional authority." 11 FAM 721.2(b)(3). For example, an agreement cannot survive if it conflicts with a commercial statute concerning another country. Foreign commerce is "subject to regulation, so far as this country is concerned, by Congress alone." United States v. Guy W. Capps, Inc., 204 F.2d 655, 660 (4th Cir. 1953), aff'd on other grounds, 348 U.S. 296 (1955). Other executive agreements have been struck down because they violate the Just Compensation Clause or deprive an accused of trial by jury. Seery v. United States, 127 F.Supp. 601 (Ct. Cl. 1955); Reid v. Covert, 354 U.S. 1 (1957).

The Iranian hostage crisis of 1979 produced a series of extraordinary moves by President Carter, including the freezing of Iran's assets in America and the suspension of claims pending in American courts. Although the Supreme Court found no specific authority for the suspension of claims, legal justifications were discovered somewhere in the combination of past presidential practices to settle claims by executive agreement, the history of "implicit" congressional approval, and the failure of Congress to contest the Iranian agreement. The Court, straining to uphold an agreement it was unlikely to overturn, limited the reach of its opinion by confining it to the specific circumstances in the case. DAMES & MOORE v. REGAN, 453 U.S. 654 (1981).

In 2008, the Court decided a complex case that blended many elements: international law, presidential power, and federalism. Texas had prosecuted a Mexican foreign national and found him guilty of a crime punishable by the death penalty. It did not comply with a treaty calling for countries to notify the consulate of a foreign national. A decision by the World Court (the International Court of Justice) and a memorandum signed by President George W. Bush urged Texas not to execute the prisoner without offering him a second habeas hearing, which is not allowed under Texas law. Divided 6 to 3, the Court held that the treaty in dispute (Vienna Convention on Consular Relations) was not self-executing and therefore not binding on U.S. domestic courts. Congress would have to pass legislation making the treaty binding on the states. Thus, neither the decision by the World Court nor a presidential memorandum could preempt limitations in state law that prohibited the filing of successive habeas petitions. Medellin v. Texas, 552 U.S. ____ (2008). With regard to the reach of executive agreements, the decision did much to cut back on such decisions as *Belmont*, *Pink*, *Dames & Moore*, and *Garamendi*.

A number of secret agreements have been entered into without the knowledge of Congress. Many of these agreements were of an economic or military nature, committing the United States to various obligations (see box on next page). Legislation in 1972 (the Case Act) requires the Secretary of State to transmit to Congress within 60 days the text of "any international agreement, other than a treaty," to which the United States is a party. If the President decides that publication would be prejudicial to national security, he may transmit an agreement to the Senate Committee on Foreign Relations and the House Committee on Foreign Affairs under an injunction of secrecy removable only by the President. 86 Stat. 619 (1972); 1 U.S.C. §112b (2000). When the executive branch circumvented the statute by calling some agreements "arrangements," Congress passed legislation to tighten the reporting statute. 91 Stat. 224, §5 (1977); 92 Stat. 993, §708 (1978). Legislative control is strengthened even more by requiring that Congress approve certain agreements or appropriate funds to carry them out.

Goldwater v. Carter

444 U.S. 996 (1979)

On December 15, 1978, President Carter terminated a defense treaty with Taiwan. Under the terms of the treaty, either party could end the pact after giving the other country a year's notice. By the time the case had traveled through the district court and the appellate court, the treaty was about to be terminated. Senator Barry Goldwater argued that a treaty, being law, required

Congressional Oversight of Executive Agreements

The Committee on Foreign Relations, to which was referred the bill (S. 596) to require that international agreements other than treaties, hereafter entered into by the United States, be transmitted to the Congress within 60 days after the execution thereof, having considered the same, reports favorably thereon without amendment and recommends that the bill do pass.

. . .

As the committee has discovered, there have been numerous agreements contracted with foreign governments in recent years, particularly agreements of a military nature, which remain wholly unknown to Congress and to the people. A number of these agreements have been uncovered by the Symington Subcommittee on Security Agreements and Commitments Abroad, including, for example, an agreement with Ethiopia in 1960, agreements with Laos in 1963, with Thailand in 1964 and again in 1967, with Korea in 1966, and certain secret annexes to the Spanish bases agreement.

Section 112(a) of title I of the United States Code now requires the Secretary of State to com- pile and publish all international agreements other than treaties concluded by the United States during each calendar year. The executive, however, has long made it a practice to withhold those agreements which, in its judgment, are of a "sensitive" nature. Such agreements, often involving military arrangements with foreign countries, are frequently not only "sensitive" but exceedingly significant as broadened commitments for the United States. Although they are sometimes characterized as "contingency plans," they may in practice involve the United States in war. For this reason the committee attaches the greatest importance to the establishment of a legislative requirement that all such agreements be submitted to Congress.

… Whatever objection on security grounds the executive might have to the submission of such information to Congress is met by the provision of the bill which authorizes the President, at his option, to transmit certain agreements not to the Congress as a whole, but to the two foreign affairs committees "under an appropriate injunction of secrecy to be removed only upon due notice from the President."

SOURCE: S. Rept. No. 92-591, 92d Cong., 2d Sess. (1972).

legislative action for its repeal. Acting without oral argument, the Court dismissed the complaint by Goldwater. Having disposed of the issue in summary fashion, several Justices filed separate statements setting forth their individual views.

MR. JUSTICE POWELL, concurring in the judgment.

Although I agree with the result reached by the Court, I would dismiss the complaint as not ripe for judicial review.

I

This Court has recognized that an issue should not be decided if it is not ripe for judicial review. *Buckley* v. *Valeo,* 424 U.S. 1, 113–114 (1976)*(per curiam).* Prudential considerations persuade me that a dispute between Congress and the President is not ready for judicial review unless and until each branch has taken action asserting its constitutional authority. Differences between the President and the Congress are commonplace under our system. The differences should, and almost invariably do, turn on political rather than legal considerations. The Ju- dicial Branch should not decide issues affecting the allocation of power between the President and Congress until the political branches reach a constitutional impasse. Otherwise, we would encourage small groups or even individual Members of Congress to seek judicial resolution of issues before the normal political process has the opportunity to resolve the conflict.

In this case, a few Members of Congress claim that the President's action in terminating the treaty with Taiwan has deprived them of their constitutional role with respect to a change in the supreme law of the land. Congress has taken no official action. In the present posture of this case, we do not know whether there ever will be an actual confrontation between the Legislative and Executive Branches. Although the Senate has considered a resolution declaring that Senate approval is necessary for the termination of any mutual defense treaty, see 125 Cong. Rec. 13672, 13695–13697 (1979), no final vote has been taken on the resolution. See *id.*, at 32522–32531. Moreover, it is unclear whether the resolution would have retroactive effect. See *id.*, at 13711–13721; *id.*, at 15210. It cannot be said that either the Senate or the House has rejected the President's claim. If the Congress chooses not to confront the President, it is not our task to do so. I therefore concur in the dismissal of this case.

II

Mr. Justice Rehnquist suggests, however, that the issue presented by this case is a nonjusticiable political question which can never be considered by this Court. I cannot agree.

[Justice Powell concludes that if this case were ready for review, it would satisfy the criteria established by Baker v. Carr (1962) for cases that the Court may properly decide.]

III

In my view, the suggestion that this case presents a political question is incompatible with this Court's willingness on previous occasions to decide whether one branch of our Government has impinged upon the power of another. See *Buckley* v. *Valeo,* 424 U.S., at 138; *United States* v. *Nixon, supra,* at 707; *The Pocket Veto Case,* 279 U.S. 655, 676–678 (1929); *Myers* v. *United States,* 272 U.S. 52 (1926). Under the criteria enunciated in *Baker* v. *Carr,* we have the responsibility to decide whether both the Executive and Legislative Branches have constitutional roles to play in termination of a treaty. If the Congress, by appropriate formal action, had challenged the President's authority to terminate the treaty with Taiwan, the resulting uncertainty could have serious consequences for our country. In that situation, it would be the duty of this Court to resolve the issue.

Mr. Justice Rehnquist, with whom The Chief Justice, Mr. Justice Stewart, and Mr. Justice Stevens join, concurring in the judgment.

I am of the view that the basic question presented by the petitioners in this case is "political" and therefore nonjusticiable because it involves the authority of the President in the conduct of our country's foreign relations and the extent to which the Senate or the Congress is authorized to negate the action of the President....

The present case differs in several important respects from *Youngstown Sheet & Tube Co.* v. *Sawyer,* 343 U.S. 579 (1952), cited by petitioners as author-

ity both for reaching the merits of this dispute and for reversing the Court of Appeals. In *Youngstown,* private litigants brought a suit contesting the President's authority under his war powers to seize the Nation's steel industry, an action of profound and demonstrable domestic impact. Here, by contrast, we are asked to settle a dispute between coequal branches of our Government, each of which has resources available to protect and assert its interests, resources not available to private litigants outside the judicial forum....

Mr. Justice Blackmun, with whom Mr. Justice White joins, dissenting in part.

In my view, the time factor and its importance are illusory; if the President does not have the power to terminate the treaty (a substantial issue that we should address only after briefing and oral argument), the notice of intention to terminate surely has no legal effect. It is also indefensible, without further study, to pass on the issue of justiciability or on the issues of standing or ripeness. While I therefore join in the grant of the petition for certiorari, I would set the case for oral argument and give it the plenary consideration it so obviously deserves.

Mr. Justice Brennan, dissenting.

I respectfully dissent from the order directing the District Court to dismiss this case, and would affirm the judgment of the Court of Appeals in-so-far as it rests upon the President's well-established authority to recognize, and withdraw recognition from, foreign governments....

In stating that this case presents a nonjusticiable "political question," Mr. Justice Rehnquist, in my view, profoundly misapprehends the political-question principle as it applies to matters of foreign relations. Properly understood, the political-question doctrine restrains courts from reviewing an exercise of foreign policy judgment by the coordinate political branch to which authority to make that judgment has been "constitutional[ly] commit[ted]." *Baker* v. *Carr,* 369 U.S. 186, 211–213, 217 (1962). But the doctrine does not pertain when a court is faced with the *antecedent* question whether a particular branch has been constitutionally designated as the repository of political decisionmaking power. Cf. *Powell* v. *McCormack,* 395 U.S. 486, 519–521 (1969). The issue of decisionmaking authority must be resolved as a matter of constitutional law, not political discretion; accordingly, it falls within the competence of the courts.

The constitutional question raised here is prudently answered in narrow terms. Abrogation of the defense treaty with Taiwan was a necessary incident to Executive recognition of the Peking Government, because the defense treaty was predicated upon the now-abandoned view that the Taiwan Government was the only legitimate political authority in China.

Our cases firmly establish that the Constitution commits to the President alone the power to recognize, and withdraw recognition from, foreign regimes.... That mandate being clear, our judicial inquiry into the treaty rupture can go no further....

Dames & Moore v. Regan

453 U.S. 654 (1981)

After Iran seized American hostages in 1979, President Carter declared a national emergency and blocked the removal or transfer of all Iranian property subject to the jurisdiction of the United States. He also authorized certain judicial proceedings to handle resulting disputes brought by private parties seeking access to Iranian assets. When the American hostages were released on January 20, 1981, the United States and Iran entered into an agreement that required the termination of all legal proceedings in U.S. courts involving claims of U.S. nationals against Iran. Those claims would be submitted to binding arbitration before an Iran-United States Claims Tribunal. In this case, a private party seeks to prevent enforcement of various executive orders and regulations issued to implement the agreement with Iran. The basic question of this case is whether the administration exceeded statutory and constitutional powers. A private company, Dames & Moore, sued Secretary of the Treasury Donald Regan.

JUSTICE REHNQUIST delivered the opinion of the Court.

The questions presented by this case touch fundamentally upon the manner in which our Republic is to be governed....

[This] dispute involves various Executive Orders and regulations by which the President nullified attachments and liens on Iranian assets in the United States, directed that these assets be transferred to Iran, and suspended claims against Iran that may be presented to an International Claims Tribunal. This action was taken in an effort to comply with an Executive Agreement between the United States and Iran....

But before turning to the facts and law which we believe determine the result in this case, we stress that the expeditious treatment of the issues involved by all of the courts which have considered the President's actions makes us acutely aware of the necessity to rest decision on the narrowest possible ground capable of deciding the case. *Ashwander* v. *TVA*, 297 U.S. 288, 347 (1936) (Brandeis, J., concurring)....

I

On November 4, 1979, the American Embassy in Tehran was seized and our diplomatic personnel were captured and held hostage. In response to that crisis, President Carter, acting pursuant to the International Emergency Economic Powers Act, ... (hereinafter IEEPA), declared a national emergency on November 14, 1979, and blocked the removal or transfer of "all property and interests in property of

the Government of Iran, its instrumentalities and controlled entities and the Central Bank of Iran which are or become subject to the jurisdiction of the United States...."... On November 15, 1979, the Treasury Department's Office of Foreign Assets Control issued a regulation providing that "[u]nless licensed or authorized ... any attachment, judgment, decree, lien, execution, garnishment, or other judicial process is null and void with respect to any property in which on or since [November 14, 1979,] there existed an interest of Iran."...

On November 26, 1979, the President granted a general license authorizing certain judicial proceedings against Iran but which did not allow the "entry of any judgment or of any decree or order of similar or analogous effect...." § 535.504 (a). On December 19, 1979, a clarifying regulation was issued stating that "the general authorization for judicial proceedings contained in § 535.504 (a) includes pre-judgment attachment." § 535.418.

On December 19, 1979, petitioner Dames & Moore filed suit in the United States District Court for the Central District of California against the Government of Iran, the Atomic Energy Organization of Iran, and a number of Iranian banks. In its complaint, petitioner alleged that its wholly owned subsidiary, Dames & Moore International, S. R. L., was a party to a written contract with the Atomic Energy Organization, and that the subsidiary's entire interest in the contract had been assigned to petitioner. Under the contract, the subsidiary was to conduct site studies for a proposed nuclear power plant in Iran. As provided in the terms of the contract, the Atomic Energy Organization terminated the agreement for its own convenience on June 30, 1979. Petitioner contended, however, that it was owed $3,436,694.30 plus interest for services performed under the contract prior to the date of termination. The District Court issued orders of attachment directed against property of the defendants, and the property of certain Iranian banks was then attached to secure any judgment that might be entered against them.

On January 20, 1981, the Americans held hostage were released by Iran pursuant to an Agreement entered into the day before.... The Agreement stated that "[i]t is the purpose of [the United States and Iran] ... to terminate all litigation as between the Government of each party and the nationals of the other, and to bring about the settlement and termination of all such claims through binding arbitration."...

On January 19, 1981, President Carter issued a series of Executive Orders implementing the terms of the agreement.

[On February 24, 1981, President Reagan issued an executive order in which he "ratified" the January 19 executive orders. Meanwhile, a federal district court awarded Dames & Moore the amount claimed under the contract plus interest. Later, the company filed an action seeking to prevent enforcement of the executive orders and Treasury Department regulations implementing the agreement with Iran.]

II

[In this section, Justice Rehnquist finds Justice Jackson's concurring opinion in Youngstown Co. v. Sawyer (1952), classifying presidential actions into three general categories, to be analytically useful but too general to apply. Presidential action in any particular case does not fall "neatly in one of three pigeonholes, but rather at some point along a spectrum running from explicit congressional authorization to explicit congressional prohibition. This is particularly true as respects cases such as the one before us...."]

III

In nullifying post-November 14, 1979, attachments and directing those persons holding blocked Iranian funds and securities to transfer them to the Federal Reserve Bank of New York for ultimate transfer to Iran, President Carter cited five sources of express or inherent power. The Government,

however, has principally relied on § 203 of the IEEPA....

[Dames and Moore argued that the Court should ignore the plain language of this statute and examine its legislative history and the history of the Trading With the Enemy Act (TWEA), which reveals that IEEPA "was not intended to give the President such extensive power over the assets of a foreign state during times of national emergency." The Court disagreed, refusing to read out of IEEPA the meaning of certain words. To the Court, nothing in the history of that statute or of the TWEA requires such a result.] To the contrary, we think both the legislative history and cases interpreting the TWEA fully sustain the broad authority of the Executive when acting under this congressional grant of power....

IV

Although we have concluded that the IEEPA constitutes specific congressional authorization to the President to nullify the attachments and order the transfer of Iranian assets, there remains the question of the President's authority to suspend claims pending in American courts. Such claims have, of course, an existence apart from the attachments which accompanied them. In terminating these claims through Executive Order No. 12294, the President purported to act under authority of both the IEEPA and 22 U. S. C. § 1732, the so-called "Hostage Act." 46 Fed. Reg. 14111 (1981).

We conclude that although the IEEPA authorized the nullification of the attachments, it cannot be read to authorize the suspension of the claims. The claims of American citizens against Iran are not in themselves transactions involving Iranian property or efforts to exercise any rights with respect to such property.... *[The Court also concludes that the Hostage Act does not provide specific authorization to the President to suspend claims in American courts.]*

Concluding that neither the IEEPA nor the Hostage Act constitutes specific authorization of the President's action suspending claims, however, is not to say that these statutory provisions are entirely irrelevant to the question of the validity of the President's action. We think both statutes highly relevant in the looser sense of indicating congressional acceptance of a broad scope for executive action in circumstances such as those presented in this case. As noted in Part III, ... the IEEPA delegates broad authority to the President to act in times of national emergency with respect to property of a foreign country. The Hostage Act similarly indicates congressional willingness that the President have broad discretion when responding to the hostile acts of foreign sovereigns....

Although we have declined to conclude that the IEEPA or the Hostage Act directly authorizes the President's suspension of claims for the reasons noted, we cannot ignore the general tenor of Congress' legislation in this area in trying to determine whether the President is acting alone or at least with the acceptance of Congress. As we have noted, Congress cannot anticipate and legislate with regard to every possible action the President may find it necessary to take or every possible situation in which he might act. Such failure of Congress specifically to delegate authority does not, "especially ... in the areas of foreign policy and national security," imply "congressional disapproval" of action taken by the Executive. *Haig* v. *Agee, ante,* at 291. On the contrary, the enactment of legislation closely related to the question of the President's authority in a particular case which evinces legislative intent to accord the President broad discretion may be considered to "invite" "measures on independent presidential responsibility." *Youngstown,* 343 U. S., at 637 (Jackson, J., concurring). At least this is so where there is no contrary indication of legislative intent and when, as here, there is a history of congressional acquiescence in conduct of the sort engaged in by the President....

... Consistent with that principle, the United States has repeatedly exercised its sovereign authority to settle the claims of its nationals against foreign countries. Though those settlements have sometimes been made by treaty, there has also been a longstanding practice of settling such claims by executive agreement without the advice and consent of the Senate....

Crucial to our decision today is the conclusion that Congress has implicitly approved the practice of claim settlement by executive agreement....

... [T]he legislative history of the IEEPA further reveals that Congress has accepted the authority of the Executive to enter into settlement agreements. Though the IEEPA was enacted to provide for some limitation on the President's emergency powers, Congress stressed that "[n]othing in this act is intended ... to interfere with the authority of the President to [block assets], or to impede the settlement of claims of U. S. citizens against foreign countries." S. Rep. No. 95-466, p. 6 (1977); 50 U. S. C. § 1706 (a)(1) (1976 ed., Supp. III).

... [W]e do not believe that the President has attempted to divest the federal courts of jurisdiction. Executive Order No. 12294 purports only to "suspend" the claims, not divest the federal court of "jurisdiction." As we read the Executive Order, those claims not within the jurisdiction of the Claims Tribunal will "revive" and become judicially enforceable in United States courts....

In light of all of the foregoing—the inferences to be drawn from the character of the legislation Congress has enacted in the area, such as the IEEPA and the Hostage Act, and from the history of acquiescence in executive claims settlement—we conclude that the President was authorized to suspend pending claims pursuant to Executive Order No. 12294....

Just as importantly, Congress has not disapproved of the action taken here.... We are thus clearly not confronted with a situation in which Congress has in some way resisted the exercise of Presidential authority.

Finally, we re-emphasize the narrowness of our decision. We do not decide that the President possesses plenary power to settle claims, even as against foreign governmental entities....

JUSTICE STEVENS, concurring in part.

. . .

JUSTICE POWELL, concurring in part and dissenting in part.

. . .

D. THE WAR POWER

The framers broke decisively with the British political model, which gave the Executive exclusive authority over external affairs, including the power to initiate war. Under the U.S. Constitution, the power to take the country from a state of peace to a state of war against another country is placed in Congress, not the President. Congress is given specific power to declare war and to provide for the armed forces. Congress has declared war in five conflicts: the War of 1812 against England, the Mexican War in 1846, the Spanish-American War in 1898, World War I in 1917, and World War II in

1941.[5] Congress may also pass legislation to *authorize* military action against another nation, as it did with the Quasi-War against France in 1798, the war against Iraq in 1991, the war against Afghanistan in 2001, and the Iraq Resolution in 2002. The Supreme Court recognizes the constitutionality of undeclared wars, which it calls limited, partial, imperfect, or "quasi" wars. Bas v. Tingy, 4 U.S. (4 Dall.) 36 (1800); Talbot v. Seeman, 5 U.S. (1 Cr.) 1 (1801). In the second case, Chief Justice Marshall acknowledged the broad constitutional authority of Congress to decide to *initiate* hostilities, whether by declaration or not: "The whole powers of war being, by the constitution of the United States, vested in congress, the acts of that body can alone be resorted to as our guides in this inquiry." 5 U.S. at 28.

Article I, Section 2, makes the President "Commander in Chief of the Army and Navy of the United States, and of the Militia of the several States, when called into the actual Service of the United States." Scholars disagree whether this merely confers a title (Commander in Chief) or implies additional powers for the President. At a minimum, the title provides for unity of control. The Justice Department has also argued that the President is Commander in Chief not because he is necessarily skilled in the art of war but because it preserves civilian supremacy over the military. 10 Op. Att'y Gen. 74, 79 (1861).

The delegates at the Philadelphia Convention recognized an implied power for the President to "repel sudden attacks." When it was proposed that Congress be empowered to "make war," Charles Pinckney objected that legislative proceedings "were too slow" for the safety of the country in an emergency. Madison and Elbridge Gerry successfully inserted "declare" for "make," thereby "leaving to the Executive the power to repel sudden attacks" (see box on next page). The President's independent power was therefore limited to *defensive* actions. Offensive actions were reserved to Congress, to be decided through its deliberative processes. At the Pennsylvania ratifying convention, James Wilson expressed the prevailing sentiment that the system of checks and balances "will not hurry us into war; it is calculated to guard against it. It will not be in the power of a single man, or a single body of men, to involve us in such distress; for the important power of declaring war is vested in the legislature at large." 2 Elliot 528.

Presidents and their military advisers recognized that the decision to take the country to war lay with Congress. As President Jefferson told Congress on December 8, 1801, anything "beyond the line of defense" depended on legislative judgment. Fisher, Presidential War Power, at 32–37. Court decisions during this period acknowledged the supremacy of Congress in authorizing war and setting boundaries for the President. Little v. Barreme, 6 U.S. (2 Cr.) 169, 179 (1804); United States v. Smith, 27 Fed. Cas. 1192, 1229–30 (C.C.N.Y. 1806)(No. 16,342).

When Congress delegates to the President its power to call forth the militia to suppress insurrections or to repel invasions, the decision to use force belongs to the President, but Congress can add constraints. The Militia Act of 1792 required the President to obtain the approval of a Supreme Court Justice or a district judge before calling out the militia. In time of emergencies, Presidents must take effective action. Martin v. Mott, 25 U.S. (12 Wheat.) 19 (1827). The Supreme Court has noted that the President as Commander in Chief "is authorized to direct the movements of the naval and military forces placed by law at his command, and to employ them in the manner he may deem most effectual to harass and conquer and subdue the enemy." Fleming v. Page, 50 U.S. (9 How.) 602, 614 (1850). Notice that the power to move forces is "placed by *law* at his command." How much does the President depend on Congress to provide the authorizations and appropriations necessary for military action? Under the Constitution, it is the responsibility of Congress to raise and support the military forces, to make military regulations, to provide for calling up the militia to suppress insurrections and to repel invasions, and to provide for the organization and disciplining of the militia. Art. I, §8.

---

5. Actually, there were multiple declarations during the two world wars: two declarations for World War I (against Germany and Austria-Hungary) and six declarations for World War II (Japan, Germany, Italy, Bulgaria, Hungary, and Rumania).

The Framers Debating to "Declare War"

[*On August 17, 1787, the delegates at the Constitutional Convention debated giving Congress the power to "make war."*]

Mr Pinkney opposed the vesting this power in the Legislature. Its proceedings were too slow. It wd. meet but once a year. The Hs. of Reps. would be too numerous for such deliberations. The Senate would be the best depositary, being more acquainted with foreign affairs, and most capable of proper resolutions. If the States are equally represented in Senate, so as to give no advantage to large States, the power will notwithstanding be safe, as the small have their all at stake in such cases as well as the large States. It would be singular for one—authority to make war, and another peace.

Mr Butler. The Objections agst the Legislature lie in a great degree agst the Senate. He was for vesting the power in the President, who will have all the requisite qualities, and will not make war but when the Nation will support it.

Mr. M<adison> and Mr Gerry moved to insert "*declare*," striking out "*make*" war; leaving to the Executive the power to repel sudden attacks.

Mr Sharman thought it stood very well. The Executive shd. be able to repel and not to commence war. "Make" better than "declare" the latter narrowing the power too much.

Mr Gerry never expected to hear in a republic a motion to empower the Executive alone to declare war.

Mr Elseworth. there is a material difference between the cases of making *war,* and making *peace.* It shd. be more easy to get out of war, than into it. War also is a simple and overt declaration. peace attended with intricate & secret negociations.

Mr. Mason was agst giving the power of war to the Executive, because not <safely> to be trusted with it; or to the Senate, because not so constructed as to be entitled to it. He was for clogging rather than facilitating war; but for facilitating peace. He preferred "*declare*" to "*make*".

On the Motion to insert *declare*—in place of *Make,* <it was agreed to.>

N. H. no. Mas. abst. Cont. no.* Pa ay. Del. ay. Md. ay. Va. ay. N. C. ay. S. C. ay. Geo—ay. [Ayes—7; noes—2; absent—I.]

*On the remark by Mr. King that "*make*" war might be understood to "conduct" it which was an Executive function, Mr. Elseworth gave up his objection (and the vote of Cont was changed to—ay.)

Article I, Section 8, assigns to Congress and the states different responsibilities over the militia (the part-time fighting force). Congress provides for organizing, arming, and disciplining the militia, while the states appoint the officers and retain authority for training the militia "according to the discipline prescribed by Congress." Congress may authorize the President to order members of the National Guard to active duty for purposes of training outside the United States, during time of peace, without either the consent of state governors or the declaration of a national emergency. Perpich v. Department of Defense, 496 U.S. 334 (1990).

Military Tribunals/Guantánamo

The use of military courts during the Civil War in states where federal courts were open and operating had been curbed by *Ex parte Milligan.* The issue returned during and after World War II. A unanimous Court in 1942 held that aliens and U.S. citizens who entered the country as "unlawful combatants" could be tried by military tribunal. Those who enter in civilian clothing on behalf of an enemy are not entitled to trial by jury before a civilian court. Ex parte Quirin, 317 U.S. 1 (1942).

When looked at closely, *Quirin* provides an unattractive precedent. The Roosevelt administration, reflecting on what it did in 1942 with eight German saboteurs, decided not to follow the same procedures two years later when two more unlawful combatants arrived. Louis Fisher, Nazi Saboteurs on Trial (2003). Moreover, Court decisions upholding military tribunals during World War II are almost uniformly condemned today. For example, In re Yamishita, 327 U.S. 1 (1946). *Quirin* did not allow state governors to operate under martial law and substitute military for judicial trials of civilians who were not charged with violations of the law of war. Duncan v. Kahanamoku, 327 U.S. 304 (1946). Nor may the military arrest someone who has been honorably discharged and try that person before a court-martial. Prosecution must be conducted by civilian courts. Toth v. Quarles, 350 U.S. 11 (1955).

In 1969, the Supreme Court attempted to subject certain military questions to the jurisdiction of civilian courts. It held that to be under military jurisdiction, a crime must be "service connected." Otherwise, members of the military were entitled to a civilian trial, including the constitutional right to indictment by grand jury and trial by jury. O'Callahan v. Parker, 395 U.S. 258 (1969). So confusing was the service-connected doctrine that the Court abandoned it in 1987. Jurisdiction of a court-martial now depends solely on the accused's status as a member of the armed forces. The Court announced that Congress "has primary responsibility for the delicate task of balancing the rights of servicemen against the needs of the military." Solorio v. United States, 483 U.S. 435, 447 (1987).

On November 13, 2001, in response to terrorist attacks on the United States, President George W. Bush issued a military order authorizing the use of military tribunals. Three national security cases reached the Supreme Court in 2004, testing the limits of presidential power to detain U.S. citizens and foreign nationals without trial or some kind of process to separate the guilty from the innocent. Two of the cases involved U.S. citizens: Yaser Esam Hamdi and Jose Padilla. The third affected aliens held at the U.S. naval base in Guantánamo, Cuba. In the Padilla case, the Court divided 5–4 in deciding that his habeas petition had been filed with the wrong court. Rumsfeld v. Padilla, 542 U.S. 426 (2004). Although the Fourth Circuit ruled in favor of the government in 2005, the government switched course by bringing charges against Padilla in a criminal court in Florida. The indictment made no mention of serious charges earlier made by the government, such as a "dirty bomb" plot by Padilla. In 2007, a jury convicted him of terrorism conspiracy charges and he was sentenced to 17 years in prison.

For Hamdi, eight Justices rejected the government's central argument that the detention was quintessentially a presidential decision, not to be reevaluated or second-guessed by the courts. Four members of the plurality, joined by Justices Souter and Ginsburg, held that an enemy combatant "must receive notice of the factual basis for his classification, and a fair opportunity to rebut the Government's factual assertions before a neutral decisionmaker." The plurality emphasized such terms as "an independent tribunal," an "independent review," and an "impartial adjudication," expressing satisfaction that the review could be within the executive branch and perhaps take the form of "an appropriately authorized and properly constituted military tribunal." The plurality seemed to lose sight of how Hamdi became an "enemy combatant." The person who made that designation was President Bush. No review panel within the executive branch, much less within the military, could possibly possess the sought-for qualities of neutrality, detachment, independence, and impartiality in having to pass judgment to possibly reverse a presidential decision. HAMDI v. RUMSFELD, 542 U.S. 507 (2004). Following this decision, the government decided to transfer Hamdi to Saudi Arabia in October 2004.

The third case involved the Guantánamo detainees. The government argued that the naval base was outside the jurisdiction of federal courts to give habeas relief. A 6–3 decision rejected that position, identifying a number of differences between the prisoners at the base and those held abroad in a ruling decided a half century earlier. Johnson v. Eisentrager, 339 U.S. 763 (1950). Consequently, federal courts have jurisdiction to consider challenges to the legality of the Guantánamo detainees. Rasul v. Bush, 542 U.S. 466 (2004).

As a result of *Rasul*, dozens of legal challenges were filed by detainees in Guantánamo Bay. A major case, *Hamdan* v. *Rumsfeld*, reached the Supreme Court and was decided there on June 29, 2006. Salim Ahmed Hamdan, a driver for Osama bin Laden, had been captured on the battlefield in Afghanistan and turned over to the U.S. military base in Guantánamo. During oral argument before the Court, his attorney focused on the procedures adopted for the military tribunal that was to try Hamdan: "if the military commission complied with the rules of courts-martial, we wouldn't be here." That issue was prominent among those decided by the Court, which held that the Bush administration lacked authority to proceed with the military commission it had devised. HAMDAN v. RUMSFELD, 548

U.S. 557 (2006). The decision rejected the administration's reliance on presidential "inherent" powers to conduct the war on terrorism.

Congress responded to *Hamdan* by passing the Military Commissions Act (MCA) of 2006, providing for the first time a statutory basis for the tribunals. Lawsuits against the administration claimed that the detainees at Guantánamo were entitled to submit habeas petitions to federal courts. The D.C. Circuit denied that such rights existed for the detainees, but a dissenting judge raised the question whether the MCA offended the constitutional requirement that habeas must be formally suspended and that the Suspension Clause made no distinction between citizens and non-citizens. Boumediene v. Bush, 476 F.3d 981 (D.C. Cir. 2007). On June 12, 2008, the Supreme Court held that both the MCA and the Detainee Treatment Act of 2005 operated as an unconstitutional suspension of the writ. BOUMEDIENE v. BUSH, 553 U.S. ____ (2008).

War Powers Resolution

Presidential war powers have expanded because of several developments. The idea of "defensive war" was originally limited to protective actions against the borders of the United States or ships at sea. After World War II, defensive war assumed a much broader meaning. American bases were spread throughout the world; military commitments were added to defense pacts and treaties. Under these agreements, a President could interpret an attack on an ally as an attack on the United States. Presidents also used military force on numerous occasions to protect American lives and property, often stretching those objectives to achieve foreign policy or military objectives, as in the Dominican Republic in 1965, Cambodia in 1970, Grenada in 1983, and Panama in 1989. The bombing of Libya in 1986 was defended as an antiterrorist response.

The exercise of presidential war power by Lyndon Johnson and Richard Nixon provoked Congress to pass legislation in an effort to curb executive initiatives and promote collective efforts between Congress and the President. The War Powers Resolution of 1973 has three main provisions: presidential consultation with Congress, presidential reports to Congress, and congressional termination of military action. The purpose of the Resolution, as stated in § 2(a), is "to insure that the collective judgment" of both branches will apply to the introduction of U.S. forces into hostilities. Yet an examination of other sections, together with executive interpretations, judicial decisions, and congressional behavior, supplies ample evidence that the statute does not assure collective judgment. WAR POWERS RESOLUTION.

The President is to consult with Congress "in every possible instance." The language obviously leaves considerable discretion to the President on both the form and timing of consultation. The framers of the resolution did not expect the President to consult with 535 legislators, but who should be contacted? The leadership? The chairmen and ranking members of designated committees? Selected advisers? It is agreed that consultation means more than being briefed. Consultation means an opportunity to influence a pending decision. H. Rept. No. 287, 93d Cong., 1st Sess. 6–7 (1973).

The resolution requires that the President, after introducing forces into hostilities, report to Congress within 48 hours. Precisely what conditions require a report is unclear from the legislation, and if a report is delayed, so are the mechanisms for congressional control. Under the Resolution, military action must terminate within 60 days after the report unless Congress (1) declares war or enacts a specific authorization, (2) extends by law the 60-day period, or (3) is physically unable to meet as a result of an armed attack on the United States. The President may extend the period by an additional 30 days if he determines that force is needed to protect and remove American troops.

Congress has two means of control: (1) a decision not to support the President during the 60-to-90 day period or (2) passage of a concurrent resolution at any time to direct the President to remove forces engaged in hostilities. The first mechanism has little meaning because the clock for the 60-to-90 day period begins to run only when the President reports under a very specific section: Section 4(a)(1). President Ford was the only President to report under that section—in the *Mayaguez* capture in 1975—but by the time he reported the operation was over. Thus, the clock that was intended to limit the President never ticks.

The force of a concurrent resolution has been weakened by two developments. The executive branch takes the position that if the President has power to put men into combat, "that power could not be taken away by concurrent resolution because the power is constitutional in nature." "War Powers: A Test of Compliance," hearings before the House Committee on International Relations, 94th Cong., 1st Sess. 91 (1975). Executive officials argue that the President has a number of constitutional powers to use military force without congressional approval, such as rescuing Americans living abroad, rescuing foreign nationals under certain circumstances, and protecting U.S. embassies and legations. Id. at 90–91.

Moreover, the Supreme Court struck down all one-House and two-House (concurrent) resolutions as "legislative vetoes" that have no binding effect on the executive branch. INS v. Chadha, 462 U.S. 919 (1983). Still, passage of a concurrent resolution would mean that a majority of legislators in each House opposed the President's actions. It is difficult to conceive of a President persisting after that vote. Also, if Congress complied with *Chadha* by passing a joint resolution of disapproval, the President could veto that and Congress would now need a two-thirds majority in each House to stop a presidential war.

Members of Congress have gone to court to contest military initiatives by the President, but these efforts are regularly turned aside by federal judges on the ground that the determination of what constitutes hostilities or imminent hostilities is essentially a fact-finding matter reserved to Congress, not the courts. Crockett v. Reagan, 558 F.Supp. 893 (D.D.C. 1982), aff'd, 720 F.2d 1355 (D.C. Cir. 1983), cert. denied, 467 U.S. 1251 (1984).[6] When President Reagan sent ships into the Persian Gulf in 1987 without reporting to Congress under the War Powers Resolution, 110 members of the House of Representatives took the matter to court. Similar to the other cases, a district court declined to accept jurisdiction and dismissed the case. Lowry v. Reagan, 676 F.Supp. 333 (D.D.C. 1987).

The War Powers Resolution does not cover "paramilitary" (covert) operations. Beginning in 1974 and continuing through the Reagan years, Congress enacted a number of statutes and amendments to restrict covert actions. Part of the accommodation of a 1980 statute required the President to fully inform the House and Senate Intelligence Committees in a "timely fashion" of covert operations in foreign countries. Congress discovered in November 1986 that President Reagan had been sending arms to Iran for ten months, without any notification to Congress. As a result, the Senate passed legislation in 1988 to tighten the requirement so that notification could be delayed for no more than 48 hours, but the House of Representatives did not act on the bill. Legislation in 1991 clarified the reporting requirements for covert operations. Presidents are now expected to inform the intelligence committees in advance on almost all such operations. 105 Stat. 441–45 (1991).

Military Actions from 1990 to 2000

The principle of "collective judgment" contemplated in § 2(a) of the War Powers Resolution was sorely tested in 1990, when President George H. W. Bush claimed that he could mount an offensive operation against Iraq without any congressional authorization. After Iraq's invasion of Kuwait on August 2, 1990, he sent U.S. troops to Saudi Arabia to defend that country, assembled a 28-nation coalition against Iraq, and obtained a number of UN resolutions condemning Iraq. In November, Bush announced a substantial increase in the number of U.S. troops, giving him the capability of acting offensively against Iraq. The Bush administration argued that it could shift from a defensive posture to an offensive operation without first obtaining authorization from Congress. Two lawsuits challeng-

---

6. See also Sanchez-Espinoza v. Reagan, 568 F.Supp. 596 (D.D.C. 1983), aff'd, Sanchez-Espinoza v. Reagan, 770 F.2d 202 (D.C. Cir. 1985) (Nicaragua); Conyers v. Reagan, 578 F.Supp. 324 (D.D.C. 1984), dismissed as moot, Conyers v. Reagan, 765 F.2d 1124 (D.C. Cir. 1985) (Grenada).

ing the constitutionality of Bush's action were avoided by [**two**] federal courts. Ange v. Bush, 752 F.Supp. 509 (D.D.C. 1990); DELLUMS v. BUSH, 752 F.Supp. 1141 (D.D.C. 1990). The latter, however, rejected many of the ambitious arguments advanced by the Justice Department with regard to presidential war powers. Perhaps with an eye to that decision, on January 8, 1991, Bush asked Congress to pass legislation supporting military action in the Persian Gulf. After three days of intense debate, Congress passed the bill. 105 Stat. 3 (1991). Because of the authorizing statute, a major constitutional crisis was averted.

In his eight years in office, President Clinton engaged in a remarkable amount of military activity without ever seeking authority from Congress. He sent cruise missiles into Iraq, conducted military operations in Somalia, threatened to invade Haiti, ordered air strikes in Bosnia, dispatched 20,000 ground troops to Bosnia, sent cruise missiles into Sudan and Afghanistan, and went to war against Yugoslavia. In each case he argued that he had no constitutional obligation other than to consult with members of Congress before taking military action. Like Bush in Iraq, he sometimes pointed to "authority" obtained from resolutions passed by the UN Security Council. In addition, he cited "authorizing" actions by the North Atlantic Council (NATO) for ordering air strikes in Bosnia. Louis Fisher, "Sidestepping Congress: Presidents Acting Under the UN and NATO," 47 Case Western Reserve L. Rev. 1237 (1997).

Clinton's major military initiative was against Yugoslavia in 1999. Here there was no claim of acting in a defensive manner or to protect American lives. It was an unambiguous, unvarnished example of taking the country from a state of peace to a state of war, without ever asking Congress for authority. Congress took a number of votes; none authorized what Clinton did and none prohibited him from doing what he did. An effort by a member of Congress to litigate the constitutionality of the war in Yugoslavia was unsuccessful. CAMPBELL v. CLINTON, 203 F.3d 19 (D.C. Cir. 2000). The federal appellate court revealed different views by judges on a member's standing to bring such a case and the competence of courts to decide questions of war.

Attempts to Reform or Repeal the WPR

The War Powers Resolution has been criticized ever since it was enacted. An effort by the House of Representatives in 1995 to repeal most of it failed on a vote of 201 to 217. 142 Cong. Rec. 15209–10 (1995). Only two provisions would have been kept (consultation and reporting). Much of the motivation behind that attempt reflected the belief that the resolution interferes with the President's constitutional duties. However, some scholars support repeal because the resolution delegates to the President powers that the Constitution lodges with Congress, especially the decision to initiate war.[7]

In 2008, a private war powers commission recommended the repeal of the WPR and its replacement by a statute creating a Joint Congressional Consultation Committee consisting of 20 senior lawmakers. Headed by former Secretaries of State James A. Baker III and Warren Christopher, the commission report proposed a "practical solution" to help future Presidents and members of Congress deal with war power disputes. According to the report, the proposal "avoids clearly favoring one branch over the other." In fact, the commission recommended a procedure that would allow the President to initiate military operations simply by consulting with the committee. If Congress had not enacted a formal declaration of war or expressly authorized the military action, the consultation committee would introduce a concurrent resolution of approval within 30 days. Several weeks would elapse for the two houses to report and act on this measure. If it passed, it would have no legal effect because concurrent resolutions are not submitted to the President. In the event the resolution of approval did not pass, a joint resolution of disapproval would be acted on. Additional time would be

---

7. Louis Fisher & David Gray Adler, "The War Powers Resolution: Time to Say Goodbye," 113 Pol. Sci. Q. 1 (1998); Michael J. Glennon, "Too Far Apart: Repeal the War Powers Resolution," 50 U. Miami L. Rev. 17 (1995); Edward Keynes, "The War Powers Resolution: A Bad Idea Whose Time Has Come and Gone," 23 U. Toledo L. Rev. 343 (1992).

consumed with this procedure and joint resolutions must be presented to the President. Presumably the President would veto it, requiring Congress now to muster a two-thirds majority in each house to override the veto. In other words, the President could begin and continue a war provided he maintained the support of one-third plus one in a single house.

Response to the 9/11 Attacks

On September 11, 2001, terrorists flew two planes into the World Trade Center in New York City. Under the intense heat from interior burning the two buildings collapsed, as did a third nearby. Another aircraft hit the Pentagon in Washington, D.C., and a fourth—probably destined for the White House or the Capitol—crashed in Pennsylvania. Approximately 3,000 people, of almost every nationality, died. Congress responded with legislation that authorized U.S. armed forces against those responsible for the attacks. 115 Stat. 224 (2001). In addition, Congress passed legislation strengthening airport security and expanding the authority of law enforcement officials to deal with terrorists. The major bill, the USA Patriot Act, gave the federal government major powers over the accused. Changes in the rights of the accused and electronic surveillance are discussed in Chapters 13 and 14. On November 13, 2001, President George W. Bush issued a military order allowing the use of military tribunals to try captured terrorists.

Regarding the war power, the issue debated in 2002 was whether the statute enacted the previous year (AUMF), authorizing the use of military force against the terrorists, was sufficient authority to enable President Bush to go to war against Iraq. The 2001 statute required the President to determine that a nation, organization, or person aided in the 9/11 attacks, a link the Bush administration had not been able to establish with Iraq. However, even if a link could be determined, the financial implications of a war against Iraq (hundreds of billions of dollars) and the impact on Middle East stability convinced many members of Congress that Bush needed to return to Congress for supplemental authority before mounting a war against Iraq. That legislation was enacted. 116 Stat. 1498 (2002).

State Secrets Privilege

In addition to the NSA surveillance conducted after 9/11 – brought to light by the *New York Times* in December 2005 – the Bush administration carried out another secret program called "extraordinary rendition" (sending suspected terrorists to other countries for interrogation and torture). Efforts to challenge the NSA and rendition operations in court were met by administration claims that the cases could not proceed without the risk of disclosing sensitive "national security" information. The state secrets privilege had been recognized by the Supreme Court in *United States* v. *Reynolds*, 345 U.S. 1 (1953), but cases on state secrets in the past had not addressed major initiatives by the executive branch that credibly violated statutes, treaties, and the Constitution. Louis Fisher, The Constitution and 9/11 (2008).

Hamdi v. Rumsfeld

542 U.S. 507 (2004)

The father of Yaser Esam Hamdi filed a writ of habeas corpus to challenge the government's custody of his son "without access to legal counsel or notice of any charges pending against him." The petition argued that Hamdi's detention was not legally authorized and that detention without charges, access to an impartial tribunal, or assistance of counsel violated the Fifth and Fourteenth Amendments. The lawsuit was directed against Secretary of Defense Donald Rumsfeld.

JUSTICE O'CONNOR announced the judgment of the Court and delivered an opinion, in which THE CHIEF JUSTICE, JUSTICE KENNEDY, and JUSTICE BREYER join.

At this difficult time in our Nation's history, we are called upon to consider the legality of the Government's detention of a United States citizen on United States soil as an "enemy combatant" and to address the process that is constitutionally owed to one who seeks to challenge his classification as such.... We hold that although Congress authorized the detention of combatants in the narrow circumstances alleged here, due process demands that a citizen held in the United States as an enemy combatant be given a meaningful opportunity to contest the factual basis for that detention before a neutral decisionmaker.

I

[Justice O'Connor describes the enactment by Congress of the Authorization for Use of Military Force (the AUMF), which authorized the President to "use all necessary and appropriate force against those nations, organizations, or persons he determines planned, authorized, committed, or aided the terrorist attacks" of 9/11 or "harbored such organizations or persons, in order to prevent any future acts of international terrorism against the United States by such nations, organizations or persons." On the basis of that authority, President Bush ordered U.S. forces to Afghanistan, with a mission to subdue al Qaeda and quell the Taliban regime. Yaser Esam Hamdi, born in Louisiana, was seized by members of the Northern Alliance, a coalition of military groups opposed to the Taliban government, and turned over to the U.S. military. After being taken to Guantánamo Bay he was transferred to a naval brig in Norfolk, Va., and later to a brig in Charlestown, S.C. The government designated Hamdi an "enemy combatant" who could be held indefinitely, without formal charges or proceedings.]

II

The threshold question before us is whether the Executive has the authority to detain citizens who qualify as "enemy combatants"....

The Government maintains that no explicit congressional authorization is required, because the Executive possesses plenary authority to detain pursuant to Article II of the Constitution. We do not reach the question whether Article II provides such authority, however, because we agree with the Government's alternative position, that Congress has in fact authorized Hamdi's detention, through the AUMF.

[Justice O'Connor summarizes Hamdi's argument that his detention is forbidden by 18 U.S.C. § 4001(a), enacted in 1971, providing that "[n]o citizen shall be imprisoned or otherwise detained by the United States except pursuant to an Act of Congress." She concludes that AUMF is "explicit congressional authorization for the detention of individuals in the narrow category we describe." Detention of individuals in this category "is so fundamental and accepted as an incident to war as to be an exercise of the 'necessary and appropriate force' Congress has authorized the President to use." Detention, she says, is not punishment but simply a means of preventing "the captured individual from serving the enemy."]

Hamdi contends that the AUMF does not authorize indefinite or perpetual detention. Certainly, we agree that indefinite detention for the purpose of interrogation is not authorized....

Ex parte Milligan, 4 Wall. 2, 125 (1866), does not undermine our holding about the Government's authority to seize enemy combatants, as we define that term today. In that case, the Court made repeated reference to the fact that its inquiry into whether the military tribunal had jurisdiction to try and punish Milligan turned in large part on the fact that Milligan was not a prisoner of war, but a resident of Indiana arrested while at home there.... Had Milligan been captured while he was assisting Confederate soldiers by carrying a rifle against Union troops on a Confederate battlefield, the holding of the Court might well have been different....

Quirin ... both postdates and clarifies *Milligan*, providing us with the most apposite precedent we have on the question of whether citizens may be detained in such circumstances....

III

[In this section, O'Connor analyzes the writ of habeas corpus, pointing out that all sides agree that the writ—absent suspension of the writ (which "has not occurred here")—remains available to every individual detained within the United States. It is thus "undisputed that Hamdi was properly before an Article III court to challenge his detention." The Government argued that because it is "undisputed" that Hamdi's seizure took place in a combat zone, no further hearing of factfinding was necessary to settle the habeas determination. She rejects that position because the circumstances of Hamdi's seizure in Afghanistan "cannot in any way be characterized as 'undisputed.'" Hamdi was not permitted to speak for himself or even through counsel. She also rejects the argument that, under the circumstances of the case, the federal judiciary should defer to the findings of the executive branch. After weighing the government's interests against those of Hamdi, she concludes that the risk of erroneous deprivation of a detainee's liberty interest

is "unacceptably high" under the Government's proposed rule.]

We therefore hold that a citizen-detainee seeking to challenge his classification as an enemy combatant must receive notice of the factual basis for his classification, and a fair opportunity to rebut the Government's factual assertions before a neutral decisionmaker....

At the same time, the exigencies of the circumstances may demand that, aside from these core elements, enemy combatant proceedings may be tailored to alleviate their uncommon potential to burden the Executive at a time of ongoing military conflict. Hearsay, for example, may need to be accepted as the most reliable available evidence from the Government in such a proceeding. Likewise, the Constitution would not be offended by a presumption in favor of the Government's evidence, so long as that presumption remained a rebuttable one and fair opportunity for rebuttal were provided....

... The parties agree that initial captures on the battlefield need not receive the process we have discussed here; that process is due only when the determination is made to *continue* to hold those who have been seized....

In so holding, we necessarily reject the Government's assertion that separation of powers principles mandate a heavily circumscribed role for the courts in such circumstances.... We have long since made clear that a state of war is not a blank check for the President when it comes to the rights of the Nation's citizens.... Whatever power the United States Constitution envisions for the Executive in its exchanges with other nations or with enemy organizations in times of conflict, it most assuredly envisions a role for all three branches when individual liberties are at stake.... Likewise, we have made clear that, unless Congress acts to suspend it, the Great Writ of habeas corpus allows the Judicial Branch to play a necessary role in maintaining this delicate balance of governance, serving as an important judicial check on the Executive's discretion in the realm of detentions....

There remains the possibility that the standards we have articulated could be met by an appropriately authorized and properly constituted military tribunal....

IV

Hamdi asks us to hold that the Fourth Circuit also erred by denying him immediate access to counsel upon his detention and by disposing of the case without permitting him to meet with an attorney.... He unquestionably has the right to access to counsel in connection with the proceedings on remand....

The judgment of the United States Court of Appeals for the Fourth Circuit is vacated, and the case is remanded for further proceedings.

It is so ordered.

JUSTICE SOUTER, with whom JUSTICE GINSBURG, joins, concurring in part, dissenting in part, and concurring in the judgment.

[*The plurality accepted the Government's argument that the AUMF is authority under the Non-Detention Act.*] Here, I disagree and respectfully dissent. The Government has failed to demonstrate that the Force Resolution authorizes the detention complained of here even on the facts the Government claims. If the Government raises nothing further than the record now shows, the Non-Detention act entitles Hamdi to be released.

... I do not adopt the plurality's resolution of constitutional issues that I would not reach.... [N]or, of course, could I disagree with the plurality's affirmation of Hamdi's right to counsel.... On the other hand, I do not mean to imply agreement that the Government could claim an evidentiary presumption casting the burden of rebuttal on Hamdi, ... or that an opportunity to litigate before a military tribunal might obviate or truncate enquiry by a court on habeas....

JUSTICE SCALIA, with whom JUSTICE STEVENS joins, dissenting....

The very core of liberty secured by our Anglo-Saxon system of separated powers has been freedom from indefinite imprisonment at the will of the Executive....

... When the writ is suspended, the Government is entirely free from judicial oversight. It does not claim such total liberation here, but argues that it need only produce what it calls "some evidence" to satisfy a habeas court that a detained individual is an enemy combatant. [*Scalia rejects the Government's position, concluding that the "only constitutional alternatives are to charge the crime or suspend the writ."*]....

The proposition that the Executive lacks indefinite wartime detention authority over citizens is consistent with the Founders' general mistrust of military power permanently at the Executive's disposal....

IV

The Government argues that our more recent jurisprudence ratifies its indefinite imprisonment of a citizen within the territorial jurisdiction of federal courts. It places primary reliance upon *Ex parte*

Quirin, 317 U.S. 1 (1942), ... The case was not this Court's finest hour....

... In *Quirin* it was uncontested that the petitioners were members of enemy forces. They were *admitted* enemy invaders," 317 U.S., at 47 (emphasis added), and it was "undisputed" that they had landed in the United States in service of German forces, ... [P]etitioner insists that he is *not* a belligerent....

V

It follows from what I have said that Hamdi is entitled to a habeas decree requiring his release unless (1) criminal proceedings are promptly brought, or

(2) Congress has suspended the writ of habeas corpus....

JUSTICE THOMAS, dissenting.

The Executive Branch, acting pursuant to the powers vested in the President by the Constitution and with explicit congressional approval, has determined that Yaser Hamdi is an enemy combatant and should be detained. This detention falls squarely within the Federal Government's war powers, and we lack the expertise and capacity to second-guess that decision. [*Justice Thomas agrees with the plurality that the AUMF authorized the President to detain U.S. citizens.*]

Hamdan v. Rumsfeld

548 U.S. 557 (2006)

Salim Ahmed Hamdan was picked up by military forces in Afghanistan after 9/11 and taken to the American naval base in Guantánamo. President George W. Bush designated him an "enemy combatant" eligible for trial by military commission. Hamdan charged that the commission lacked authority to try him and its procedures prevented him from mounting an effective defense. Bringing his action against Secretary of Defense Donald H. Rumsfeld, he prevailed in district court but lost in the D.C. Circuit.

JUSTICE STEVENS announced the judgment of the Court and delivered the opinion of the Court with respect to Parts I through IV, Parts VI through VI-D-iii, Part VI-D-v, and Part VII, and an opinion with respect to Parts V and Vi-D-iv, in which JUSTICE SOUTER, JUSTICE GINSBURG, and JUSTICE BREYER join.

Petitioner Salim Ahmed Hamdan, a Yemeni national, is in custody at an American prison in Guantanamo Bay, Cuba. In November 2001, during hostilities between the United States and the Taliban (which then governed Afghanistan), Hamdan was captured by militia forces and turned over to the U.S. military. In June 2002, he was transported to Guantanamo Bay. Over a year later, the President deemed him eligible for trial by military commission for then-unspecified crimes. After another year had passed, Hamdan was charged with one count of conspiracy "to commit ... offenses triable by military commission." ...

Hamdan filed petitions for writs of habeas corpus and mandamus to challenge the Executive Branch's intended means of prosecuting this charge. He concedes that a court-martial constituted in accordance with the Uniform Code of Military Justice

(UCMJ) ... would have authority to try him. His objection is that the military commission the President has convened lacks such authority, for two principal reasons: First, neither congressional Act nor the common law of war supports trial by this commission for the crime of conspiracy—an offense that, Hamdan says, is not a violation of the law of war. Second, Hamdan contends, the procedures that the President had adopted to try him violate the most basic tenets of military and international law, including the principle that a defendant must be permitted to see and hear the evidence against him.

... [W]e conclude that the military commission convened to try Hamdan lacks power to proceed because its structure and procedures violate both the UCMJ and the Geneva Conventions. Four of us also conclude, see Part V, *infra*, that the offense with which Hamdan has been charged is not an "offens[e] that by ... the law of war may be tried by military commissions." 10 U.S.C. § 821.

I

[*The charging documents contain 13 numbered paragraphs, the last two entitled "Charge: Conspiracy," containing allegations against Hamdan.*] There is no allegation that Hamdan had any command responsibilities, played a leadership role, or participated in the planning of any activity....

II-III

[In these sections, Justice Stevens analyzed language in the Detainee Treatment Act (DTA) that prohibited federal courts from hearing habeas petitions from Guantánamo detainees, other than giving the D.C. Circuit "exclusive jurisdiction" over "any final decision" of a Combatant Status Review Tribunal (CSRT). Did the jurisdictional restrictions apply only to new claims by detainees or also to claims pending on the date the bill became law? Justice Stevens rejected the government's argument that the statute stripped the Court of jurisdiction to review a decision on Hamdan by the D.C. Circuit. He also rejected the government's contention that prior case law dictated that the Court abstain from hearing Hamdan's case until there had been a final outcome of on-going military proceedings. Concluding that none of the abstention precedents applied to Hamdan, he moved to the merits of his challenge.]

IV

... [W]hile we assume that the AUMF activated the President's war powers, ... and that those powers include the authority to convene military commissions in appropriate circumstances, ... there is nothing in the text or legislative history of the AUMF even hinting that Congress intended to expand or alter the authorization set forth in Article 21 of the UCMJ [which provides: "The provisions of this code conferring jurisdiction upon courts-martial shall not be construed as depriving military commissions, provost courts, or other military tribunals of concurrent jurisdiction in respect of offenders or offenses that by statute or by the law of war may be tried by such military commissions, provost courts, or other military tribunals."].…

Likewise, the DTA cannot be read to authorize this commission.... [I]t contains no language authorizing that tribunal [for Hamdan] or any other at Guantanamo Bay....

V

[Stevens reviews the types of military commissions previously used to try defendants who violated the law of war. He finds that "[n]one of the overt acts that Hamdan is alleged to have committed violates the law of war. These facts alone cast doubt on the legality of the charge and, hence, the commission.... The offense it alleges is not triable by law-of-war military commission.... There is no suggestion that Congress has, in exercise of its constitutional authority to 'define and

punish ... Offences against the Law of Nations,' U.S. Const., Art. I, § 8, cl. 10, positively identified 'conspiracy' as a war crime." ... [Without explicit authority from Congress there is risk of] concentrating in military hands a degree of adjudicative and punitive power in excess of that contemplated either by statute or by the Constitution."]

VI

[This section focuses on several procedural deficiencies of the commission created to try Hamdan. "The accused and his civilian counsel may be excluded from, and precluded from ever learning what evidence was presented during, any part of the proceeding that either the Appointing Authority or the presiding officer decides to 'close.'... neither live testimony nor witnesses' written statements need be sworn.... a presiding officer's determination that evidence 'would not have probative value to a reasonable person' may be overridden by a majority of the other commission members." If the government relied on a confidential informant, Hamdan would not be permitted to hear the testimony, see the witness's face, or learn his name."]

[Stevens finds that "the procedures governing trials by military commission historically have been the same as those governing courts-martial.... The uniformity principle is not an inflexible one; it does not preclude all departures from the procedures dictated for use by courts-martial. But any departure must be tailored to the exigency that necessitates it.... The rules set forth in the Manual for Courts-Martial must apply to military commissions unless impracticable.... Nothing in the record before us demonstrates that it would be impracticable to apply court-martial rules in this case."]

[Finally, Stevens concludes that Common Article 3 of the Geneva Conventions "requires that Hamdan be tried by a 'regularly constituted court affording all the judicial guarantees which are recognized as indispensable by civilized peoples.'... Common Article 3 obviously tolerates a great degree of flexibility in trying individuals captured during armed conflict; its requirements are general ones, crafted to accommodate a wide variety of legal systems. But requirements they are nonetheless. The commission that the President has convened to try Hamdan does not meet those requirements."]

VII

... Hamdan does not challenge, and we do not today address, the Government's power to detain him for the duration of active hostilities in order to prevent such harm. But in undertaking to try Hamdan and subject him to criminal punishment, the

Executive is bound to comply with the Rule of Law that prevails in this jurisdiction.

The judgment of the Court of Appeals is reversed, and the case is remanded for further proceedings.

It is so ordered.

THE CHIEF JUSTICE took no part in the consideration or decision of this case *[because he participated in the case before the Court of Appeals].*

[Justice Breyer wrote a concurrence, joined by Kennedy, Souter, and Ginsburg. Kennedy wrote a separate concurrence, joined in part by Souter, Ginsburg, and Breyer.]

JUSTICE SCALIA, with whom JUSTICE THOMAS and JUSTICE ALITO join, dissenting.

[Scalia finds that the DTA "unambiguously" stripped the courts of jurisdiction to hear this case. He sharply criticizes Stevens for relying on legislative history of the DTA "to buttress its implausible reading" of the statute. Scalia concludes that under the doctrine of abstention the Court should not have exercised jurisdiction over the Hamdan case until all proceedings by military authorities and lower federal courts had been exhausted.]

JUSTICE THOMAS, with whom JUSTICE SCALIA joins, and with whom JUSTICE ALITO joins in all but Parts I, II-C-1, and III-B-2, dissenting.

[Thomas agrees with Scalia and Alito that "this Court lacks jurisdiction" to hear Hamdan's case. He also argues that the Court "openly flouts our well-established duty to respect the Executive's judgment in matters of military operations and foreign affairs." He recognizes that Congress, "to be sure, has a substantial and essential role in both foreign affairs and national security," but having gone to Congress to obtain the AUMF, President Bush had sufficient statutory and constitutional authority to act as he did with military commissions.]

JUSTICE ALITO, with whom JUSTICE SCALIA and JUSTICE THOMAS join in Parts I-III, dissenting.

… There is no reason why a court that differs in structure or composition from an ordinary military court must be viewed as having been improperly constituted.… The commission in *Quirin* was certainly no more independent from the Executive than the commissions at issue here …

Boumediene v. Bush

553 U.S. ____ (2008)

Detainees in Guantánamo had been designated as "enemy combatants" by Combatant Status Review Tribunals at the naval base. Although captured in Afghanistan and elsewhere, they denied membership in the al Qaeda terrorist network and the Taliban regime that supported al Qaeda. They sought a writ of habeas corpus in federal court. While their appeals were pending, Congress passed the Detainee Treatment Act (DTA) of 2005 to deny habeas relief. After the Supreme Court in *Hamdan* v. *Rumsfeld* (2006) held that the DTA was inapplicable to their case, Congress passed the Military Commissions Act (MCA) of 2006 to deny the courts jurisdiction over habeas actions by detainees who had been determined to be enemy combatants.

JUSTICE KENNEDY delivered the opinion of the Court.

Petitioners are aliens designated as enemy combatants and detained at the United States Naval Station at Guantanamo Bay, Cuba. There are others detained there, also aliens, who are not parties to this suit.

Petitioners present a question not resolved by our earlier cases relating to the detention of aliens at Guantanamo: whether they have the constitutional privilege of habeas corpus, a privilege not to be withdrawn except in conformance with the Suspension Clause, Art. I, § 9, cl. 2. We hold these petitioners do have the habeas corpus privilege. Congress has enacted a statute, the Detainee Treatment Act of 2005 (DTA), 119 Stat. 2739, that provides certain procedures for review of the detainees' status. We hold that those procedures are not an adequate and effective substitute for habeas corpus. Therefore § 7 of the Military Commissions Act of 2006 (MCA), 28 U.S.C.A. § 2241(e) (Supp. 2007), operates as an unconstitutional suspension of the writ. We do not address whether the President has authority to detain these petitioners nor do we hold that the writ must issue. These and other questions regarding the legality of the detention are to be resolved in the first instance by the District Court.

I

[*Justice Kennedy explains that after the Court's decision in* Hamdi, *Congress established Combatant Status Review Tribunals (CSRTs) to determine whether individuals detained at Guantanamo were "enemy combatants" as defined by the Defense Department. The administration adopted procedures to implement the CSRTs, maintaining that the procedures were designed to comply with the due process requirements identified by the plurality in* Hamdi. *Although each of the detainees in this case denied that they are a member of al Qaeda or the Taliban regime, the CSRT determined them to be an enemy combatant. Their effort to seek a writ of habeas corpus began in February 2002. Federal courts reached different conclusions on their access to habeas. While their appeals were pending, Congress passed the DTA, providing that "no court, justice, or judge shall have jurisdiction to hear or consider ... an application for a writ of habeas corpus filed by or on behalf of an alien detained by the Department of Defense at Guantanamo Bay, Cuba." The statute also provided that the D.C. Circuit would have exclusive jurisdiction to review decisions of the CSRTs. In* Hamdan, *the Court held that this provision did not apply to cases (like the one here) that were pending when Congress passed the DTA. Congress responded by passing the MCA. The D.C. Circuit concluded in the* Boumediene *case that the MCA stripped from it, and all federal courts, jurisdiction to consider the habeas petitions presented by the petitioners.*]

II

As a threshold matter, we must decide whether MCA §7 denies the federal courts jurisdiction to hear habeas corpus actions pending at the time of its enactment. We hold that statute does deny that jurisdiction so that, if the statute is valid, petitioners' cases must be dismissed. [*Kennedy first rejects the argument of the petitioners that the MCA is not a sufficiently clear statement of congressional intent to strip the federal courts of jurisdiction in pending cases. MCA, he notes, was "a direct response to* Hamdan's *holding that the DTA's jurisdiction-stripping provision had no application to pending cases."*]

III

In deciding the constitutional questions now presented we must determine whether petitioners are barred from seeking the writ or invoking the protections of the Suspension Clause either because of their status, *i.e.*, petitioners' designation by the Executive Branch as enemy combatants, or their physical location, *i.e.*, their presence at Guantanamo Bay. The Government contends that non-citizens designated as enemy combatants and detained in territory located outside our Nation's borders have no constitutional rights and no privilege of habeas corpus....

We begin with a brief account of the history and origins of the writ. Our account proceeds from two propositions. First, protection for the privilege of habeas corpus was one of the few safeguards of liberty specified in a Constitution that, at the outset, had no Bill of Rights. In the system conceived by the Framers the writ had a centrality that must inform proper interpretation of the Suspension Clause. Second, to the extent there were settled precedents or legal commentaries in 1789 regarding the extra-territorial scope of the writ or its application to enemy aliens, those authorities can be instructive for the present case.

... The Framers viewed freedom from unlawful restraint as a fundamental precept of liberty, and they understood the writ of habeas corpus as a vital instrument to secure that freedom. [*Because the writ had frequently been abused by monarchical power, the Framers recognized the need for securing it in the Constitution. After the Magna Carta supposedly placed some constraints on the king, Parliament found it necessary in 1679 to enact additional legislation to secure the writ against executive abuse.*] The Framers' inherent distrust of governmental power was the driving force behind the constitutional plan that allocated powers among the three independent branches. [*The Constitution's structure*] protects persons as well as citizens.... We know that at common law a petitioner's status as an alien was not a categorical bar to habeas corpus relief. [*Although in England, courts were prevented from issuing the writ to such places as Scotland,*] [w]e have no reason to believe an order from a federal court would be disobeyed at Guantanamo.... [W]e take notice of the obvious and uncontested fact that the United States, by virtue of its complete jurisdiction and control over the base, maintains *de facto* sovereignty over this territory.... The Government presents no credible arguments that the military mission at Guantanamo would be compromised if habeas corpus courts had jurisdiction to hear the detainees' claims.... It is true that before today the Court has never held that noncitizens detained by our Government in territory over which another country maintains *de jure* sovereignty have any rights under our Constitution.... We hold that Art. I, §9, cl. 2, of the Constitution has full effect at Guantanamo Bay.

If the privilege of habeas corpus is to be denied to the detainees now before us, Congress must act in accordance with the requirements of the Suspension Clause.

[Kennedy argues that a detainee needs "a meaningful opportunity" to demonstrate that he is being held erroneously and must have the right to introduce evidence to clear him. Elementary procedural safeguards, including assistance of counsel, protect both citizens and non-citizens. Because of the DTA and MCA, detainees at Guantanamo face restrictions on their access to classified evidence against them and can be found guilty on the basis of hearsay evidence. The CSRTs run "considerable risk of error in the tribunal's findings of fact." Detention at Guantanamo "may last a generation or more." Congress has allowed detainee access to the D.C. Circuit, but it appears that the court cannot consider any evidence "outside the CSRT record." On those grounds, Kennedy decides that the DTA and MCA effect "an unconstitutional suspension of the writ."]

[His concluding observations]: Security subsists, too, in fidelity to freedom's first principles. Chief among these are freedom from arbitrary and unlawful restraint and the personal liberty that is secured by adherence to the separation of powers.... The laws and Constitution are designed to survive, and remain in force, in extraordinary times. Liberty and security can be reconciled; and in our system they are reconciled within the framework of the law. The Framers decided that habeas corpus, a right of first importance, must be a part of that framework, a part of that law.

JUSTICE SOUTER, with whom JUSTICE GINSBURG and JUSTICE BREYER join, concurring.

... [T]he Court in *Rasul* directly answered the very historical question that JUSTICE SCALIA says is dispositive.... But whether one agrees or disagrees with today's decision, it no bolt from the blue....

It is in fact the very lapse of four years from the time *Rasul* put everyone on notice that habeas process was available to Guantanamo detainees.... [T]oday's decision is no judicial victory, but an act of perseverance in trying to make habeas review, and the obligation of the courts to provide it, mean something of value both to prisoners and to the Nation....

CHIEF JUSTICE ROBERTS, with whom JUSTICE SCALIA, JUSTICE THOMAS, and JUSTICE ALITO join, dissenting.

Today, the Court strikes down as inadequate the most generous set of procedural protections ever afforded aliens detained by this country as enemy combatants. The political branches crafted these procedures amidst an ongoing military conflict, after much careful investigation and thorough debate. The Court rejects them today out of hand, without bothering to say what due process rights the detainees possess, without explaining how the statute fails to vindicate those rights, and before a single petitioner has even attempted to avail himself of the law's operation. And to what effect? The majority merely replaces a review system designed by the people's representatives with a set of shapeless procedures to be defined by federal courts at some future date. One cannot help but think, after surveying the modest practical results of the majority's ambitious opinion, that this decision is not really about the detainees at all, but about control of federal policy regarding enemy combatants.

... How the detainee's claims will be decided now that the DTA is gone is anybody's guess....

It is grossly premature to pronounce on the detainees' right to habeas without first assessing whether the remedies the DTA system provides vindicate whatever rights petitioners may claim....

... If the majority were truly concerned about delay, it would have required petitioners to use the DTA process that has been available to them for 22 years, with its Article III review in the D.C. Circuit....

For all its eloquence about the detainees' right to the writ, the Court makes no effort to elaborate how exactly the remedy it prescribes will differ from the procedural protections detainees enjoy under the DTA. The Court objects to the detainees' limited access to witnesses and classified material, but proposes no alternatives of its own....

So who has won? Not the detainees. The Court's analysis leaves them with only the prospect of further litigation ... Not Congress, whose attempt to "determine — through democratic means — how best" to balance the security of the American people with the detainees' liberty interests ... has been unceremoniously brushed aside. Not the Great Writ, whose majesty is hardly enhanced by its extension to a jurisdictionally quirky outpost, with no tangible benefit to anyone. Not the rule of law, unless by that is meant the rule of lawyers, who will now arguably have a greater role than military and intelligence officials in shaping policy for alien enemy combatants. And certainly not the American people, who today lose a bit more control over the conduct of this Nation's foreign policy to unelected, politically unaccountable judges.

I respectfully dissent.

JUSTICE SCALIA, with whom THE CHIEF JUSTICE, JUSTICE THOMAS, and JUSTICE ALITO join, dissenting.

Today, for the first time in our Nation's history, the Court confers a constitutional right to habeas corpus on alien enemies detained abroad by our military forces in the course of an ongoing war. THE CHIEF JUSTICE's dissent, which I join, shows that the procedures prescribed by Congress in the Detainee Treatment Act provide the essential protections that habeas corpus guarantees; there has thus been no suspension of the writ, and no basis exists for judicial intervention beyond what the Act allows. My problem with today's opinion is more fundamental still: The writ of habeas corpus does not, and never has, run in favor of aliens abroad; the Suspension Clause thus has no application, and the Court's intervention in this military matter is entirely *ultra vires....*

The game of bait-and-switch that today's opinion plays upon the Nation's Commander in Chief will make the war harder on us. It will almost certainly cause more Americans to be killed. That consequence would be tolerable if necessary to preserve a time-honored legal principle vital to our constitutional Republic. But it is this Court's blatant *abandonment* of such a principle that produces the decision today. The President relied on our settled precedent in *Johnson* v. *Eisentrager*, 339 U.S. 763 (1950), when he established the prison at Guantanamo Bay for enemy aliens.

... What competence does the Court have to second-guess the judgment of Congress and the President on such a point? None whatever. But the Court blunders in nonetheless. Henceforth, as today's opinion makes unnervingly clear, how to handle enemy prisoners in this war will ultimately lie with the branch that knows least about the national security concerns that the subject entails....

The Nation will live to regret what the Court has done today. I dissent.

War Powers Resolution

After several years of hearings and floor action, Congress passed legislation in 1973 to provide a framework for "collective judgment" between Congress and the President in the exercise of the war power. Although President Nixon vetoed the bill, he was overridden by both Houses and the bill became law. It establishes procedures for the introduction of U.S. forces into combat and sets forth a number of important policies in Section 8. The legislation, P.L. 93-148, is found at 87 Stat. 555 (1973) and 50 U.S.C. § 1541–48 (2000).

JOINT RESOLUTION

Concerning the war powers of Congress and the President.

Resolved by the Senate and House of Representatives of the United States of America in Congress assembled,

SHORT TITLE

Section 1. This joint resolution may be cited as the "War Powers Resolution".

PURPOSE AND POLICY

Sec. 2. (a) It is the purpose of this joint resolution to fulfill the intent of the framers of the Constitution of the United States and insure that the collective judgment of both the Congress and the President will apply to the introduction of United States Armed Forces into hostilities, or into situations where imminent involvement in hostilities is clearly indicated by the circumstances, and to the continued use of such forces in hostilities or in such situations.

(b) Under article I, section 8, of the Constitution, it is specifically provided that the Congress shall have the power to make all laws necessary and proper for carrying into execution, not only its own powers but also all other powers vested by the Constitution in the Government of the United States, or in any department or officer thereof.

(c) The constitutional powers of the President as Commander-in-Chief to introduce United States Armed Forces into hostilities, or into situations where imminent involvement in hostilities is clearly indicated by the circumstances, are exercised only pursuant to (1) a declaration of war, (2) specific statutory authorization, or (3) a national emergency created by attack upon the United States, its territories or possessions, or its armed forces.

CONSULTATION

Sec. 3. The President in every possible instance shall consult with Congress before introducing

United States Armed Forces into hostilities or into situations where imminent involvement in hostilities is clearly indicated by the circumstances, and after every such introduction shall consult regularly with the Congress until United States Armed Forces are no longer engaged in hostilities or have been removed from such situations.

REPORTING

Sec. 4. (a) In the absence of a declaration of war, in any case in which United States Armed Forces are introduced—

(1) into hostilities or into situations where imminent involvement in hostilities is clearly indicated by the circumstances;

(2) into the territory, airspace or waters of a foreign nation, while equipped for combat, except for deployments which relate solely to supply, replacement, repair, or training of such forces; or

(3) in numbers which substantially enlarge United States Armed Forces equipped for combat already located in a foreign nation;

the President shall submit within 48 hours to the Speaker of the House of Representatives and to the President pro tempore of the Senate a report, in writing, setting forth—

(A) the circumstances necessitating the introduction of United States Armed Forces;

(B) the constitutional and legislative authority under which such introduction took place; and

(C) the estimated scope and duration of the hostilities or involvement....

CONGRESSIONAL ACTION

Sec. 5. (a) Each report submitted pursuant to section 4(a) (1) shall be transmitted to the Speaker of the House of Representatives and to the President pro tempore of the Senate on the same calendar day....

(b) Within sixty calendar days after a report is submitted or is required to be submitted pursuant to section 4(a) (1), whichever is earlier, the President shall terminate any use of United States Armed Forces with respect to which such report was submitted (or required to be submitted), unless the Congress (1) has declared war or has enacted a specific authorization for such use of United States Armed Forces, (2) has extended by law such sixty-day period, or (3) is physically unable to meet as a result of an armed attack upon the United States. Such sixty-day period shall be extended for not more than an additional thirty days if the President determines and certifies to the Congress in writing that unavoidable military necessity respecting the safety of United States Armed Forces requires the continued use of such armed forces in the course of bringing about a prompt removal of such forces.

(c) Notwithstanding subsection (b), at any time that United States Armed Forces are engaged in hostilities outside the territory of the United States, its possessions and territories without a declaration of war or specific statutory authorization, such forces shall be removed by the President if the Congress so directs by concurrent resolution.

CONGRESSIONAL PRIORITY PROCEDURES FOR JOINT RESOLUTION OR BILL

Sec. 6 *[Provides for expedited consideration of a joint resolution or bill introduced pursuant to Section 5(b). Deadlines are established for committee and floor action, unless the House or Senate determine otherwise by yeas and nays. The objective is to complete action not later than the expiration of the 60-day period.]*

CONGRESSIONAL PRIORITY PROCEDURES FOR CONCURRENT RESOLUTION

Sec. 7. *[Provides for expedited consideration of a concurrent resolution introduced pursuant to Section 5(c). Deadlines are established for committee and floor action, unless the House or Senate determine otherwise by yeas and nays. The objective is to complete action within 48 days.]*

INTERPRETATION OF JOINT RESOLUTION

Sec. 8. (a) Authority to introduce United States Armed Forces into hostilities or into situations wherein involvement in hostilities is clearly indicated by the circumstances shall not be inferred—

(1) from any provision of law (whether or not in effect before the date of the enactment of this joint resolution), including any provision contained in any appropriation Act, unless such provision specifically authorizes the introduction of United States Armed Forces into hostilities or into such situations and states that it is intended to constitute specific statutory authorization within the meaning of this joint resolution; or

(2) from any treaty heretofore or hereafter ratified unless such treaty is implemented by legislation specifically authorizing the introduction of United States Armed Forces into hostilities or into such situations and stating that it is intended to constitute specific statutory authorization within the meaning of this joint resolution.

(b) Nothing in this joint resolution shall be construed to require any further specific statutory authorization to permit members of United States Armed Forces to participate jointly with members of the armed forces of one or more foreign countries in the headquarters operations of high-level military commands which were established prior to the date of enactment of this joint resolution and pursuant to the United Nations Charter or any treaty ratified by the United States prior to such date.

(c) For purposes of this joint resolution, the term "introduction of United States Armed Forces" includes the assignment of members of such armed forces to command, coordinate, participate in the movement of, or accompany the regular or irregular military forces of any foreign country or government when such military forces are engaged, or there exists an imminent threat that such forces will become engaged, in hostilities.

(d) Nothing in this joint resolution—

(1) is intended to alter the constitutional au-

thority of the Congress or of the President, or the provisions of existing treaties; or

(2) shall be construed as granting any authority to the President with respect to the introduction of United States Armed Forces into hostilities or into situations wherein involvement in hostilities is clearly indicated by the circumstances which authority he would not have had in the absence of this joint resolution.

SEPARABILITY CLAUSE

Sec. 9. If any provision of this joint resolution or the application thereof to any person or circumstance is held invalid, the remainder of the joint resolution and the application of such provision to any other person or circumstance shall not be affected thereby.

EFFECTIVE DATE

Sec. 10. This joint resolution shall take effect on the date of its enactment.

Dellums v. Bush

752 F.Supp. 1141 (D.D.C. 1990)

After President George H. W. Bush introduced U.S. troops into the Persian Gulf to create the potential for taking offensive action against Iraq, Congressman Ron Dellums and 53 other members of Congress brought suit requesting an injunction to prevent him from going to war without first securing a declaration of war or other explicit congressional authorization. Although the district court declined to issue the injunction, it issued a significant opinion rejecting many of the theories of presidential power advanced by the administration.

HAROLD H. GREENE, District Judge.

This is a lawsuit by a number of members of Congress who request an injunction directed to the President of the United States to prevent him from initiating an offensive attack against Iraq without first securing a declaration of war or other explicit congressional authorization for such action.

I

The factual background is, briefly, as follows. On August 2, 1990, Iraq invaded the neighboring country of Kuwait. President George Bush almost immediately sent United States military forces to the Persian Gulf area to deter Iraqi aggression and to preserve the integrity of Saudi Arabia. The United States, generally by presidential order and at times with congressional concurrence, also took other steps, including a blockade of Iraq, which were approved by the United Nations Security Council, and participated in by a great many other nations.

On November 8, 1990, President Bush an-

nounced a substantial increase in the Persian Gulf military deployment, raising the troop level significantly above the 230,000 then present in the area. At the same time, the President stated that the objective was to provide "an adequate *offensive* military option" should that be necessary to achieve such goals as the withdrawal of Iraqi forces from Kuwait. Secretary of Defense Richard Cheney likewise referred to the ability of the additional military forces "to conduct *offensive* military operations."

The House of Representatives and the Senate have in various ways expressed their support for the President's past and present actions in the Persian Gulf. However, the Congress was not asked for, and it did not take, action pursuant to Article I, Section 8, Clause 11 of the Constitution "to declare war" on Iraq. On November 19, 1990, the congressional plaintiffs brought this action, which proceeds on the premise that the initiation of offensive United States military action is imminent, that such action would be unlawful in the absence of a declaration of war by the Congress, and that a war without concurrence by the Congress would deprive the congressional plaintiffs of the voice to which they are entitled under the Constitution....

II POLITICAL QUESTION

It is appropriate first to sketch out briefly the constitutional and legal framework in which the current controversy arises. Article, I, Section 8, Clause 11 of the Constitution grants to the Congress the power "To declare War." To the extent that this unambiguous direction requires construction or explanation, it is provided by the framers' comments that they felt it to be unwise to entrust the momentous power to involve the nation in a war to the President alone; Jefferson explained that he desired "an effectual check to the Dog of war"; James Wilson similarly expressed the expectation that this system would guard against hostilities being initiated by a single man. Even Abraham Lincoln, while a Congressman, said more than half a century later that *"no one man* should hold the power of bringing" war upon us.

The congressional power to declare war does not stand alone, however, but it is accompanied by powers granted to the President. Article II, Section 1, Clause 1 and Section 2 provide that "[t]he executive powers shall be vested in a President of the United States of America," and that "[t]he President shall be Commander in Chief of the Army and Navy...."

It is the position of the Department of Justice on behalf of the President that the simultaneous existence of all these provisions renders it impossible to isolate the war-declaring power....

... Indeed, the Department contends that there are no judicially discoverable and manageable standards to apply....

This claim on behalf of the Executive is far too sweeping to be accepted by the courts. If the Executive had the sole power to determine that any particular offensive military operation, no matter how vast, does not constitute war-making but only an offensive military attack, the congressional power to declare war will be at the mercy of a semantic decision by the Executive. Such an "interpretation" would evade the plain language of the Constitution, and it cannot stand.

... [T]he Department goes on the suggest that the issue in this case is still political rather than legal, because in order to resolve the dispute the Court would have to inject itself into foreign affairs, a subject which the Constitution commits to the political branches. That argument, too, must fail.

While the Constitution grants to the political branches, and in particular to the Executive, responsibility for conducting the nation's foreign affairs, it does not follow that the judicial power is excluded from the resolution of cases merely because they may touch upon such affairs. The court must instead look at "the particular question posed" in the case. *Baker v. Carr,* 369 U.S. at 211.... In fact, courts are routinely deciding cases that touch upon or even have a substantial impact on foreign and defense policy....

... [T]he Court has no hesitation in concluding that an offensive entry into Iraq by several hundred thousand United States servicemen under the conditions described above could be described as a "war" within the meaning of Article I, Section 8, Clause 11, of the Constitution. To put it another way: the Court is not prepared to read out of the Constitution the clause granting to the Congress, and to it alone, the authority "to declare war."

III STANDING

The Department of Justice argues next that the plaintiffs lack "standing" to pursue this action.

. . .

With close to 400,000 United States troops stationed in Saudi Arabia, with all troop rotation and leave provisions suspended, and with the President having acted vigorously on his own as well as through the Secretary of State to obtain from the United Nations Security Council a resolution authorizing the use of all available means to remove Iraqi forces from Kuwait, including the use of force, it is disingenuous for the Department to characterize plaintiffs' allegations as to the imminence of the threat of offensive military action for standing purposes as "remote and conjectural,".... For these reasons, the Court concludes that the plaintiffs have adequately alleged a threat of injury in fact necessary to support standing.

IV REMEDIAL DISCRETION

Another issue raised by the Department which must be addressed briefly is the application to this case of the doctrine of "remedial" discretion developed by the Court of Appeals for this Circuit.*[i.e., courts will dismiss a case brought by a congressional plaintiff who could obtain substantial relief from fellow legislators through the enactment, repeal, or amendment of a statute.]* Judge Greene concludes that the "plaintiffs in this case do not have a remedy available from their fellow legislators."

V RIPENESS

. . .

No one knows the position of the Legislative Branch on the issue of war or peace with Iraq; certainly no one, including this Court, is able to ascertain the congressional position on that issue on the basis of this lawsuit brought by fifty-three members of the House of Representatives and one member of the U.S. Senate. It would be both premature and presumptuous for the Court to render a decision on the issue of whether a declaration of war is required at this time or in the near future when the Congress itself has provided no indication whether it deems such a declaration either necessary, on the one hand, or imprudent, on the other.

... In short, unless the Congress as a whole, or by a majority, is heard from, the controversy here cannot be deemed ripe; it is only if the majority of the Congress seeks relief from an infringement on its constitutional war-declaration power that it may be entitled to receive it.

... [A]n injunction will be issued only if, the Court could find that the controversy is ripe for judicial decision. That situation does not, or at least not yet, prevail, and plaintiffs' request for a preliminary injunction will therefore not be granted.

For the reasons stated, it is this 13th day of December, 1990

ORDERED that plaintiffs' motion for preliminary injunction be and it is hereby denied.

Campbell v. Clinton

203 F.3d 19 (D.C. Cir. 2000)

Congressman Tom Campbell, joined by several other members of Congress, filed a lawsuit seeking a declaration that President Clinton violated the War Powers Clause of the Constitution and the War Powers Resolution by committing U.S. forces to hostilities in Yugoslavia without obtaining authority from Congress. After a district court granted the President's motion to dismiss, Campbell brought this appeal. The D.C. circuit considered several issues, including Campbell's standing to bring the suit and the competence of courts to decide questions of war.

SILBERMAN, Circuit Judge: ...

On March 24, 1999, President Clinton announced the commencement of NATO air and cruise missile attacks on Yugoslav targets. Two days later he submitted to Congress a report, "consistent with the War Powers Resolution," detailing the circumstances necessitating the use of armed forces, the deployment's scope and expected duration, and asserting that he had "taken these actions pursuant to [his] authority ... as Commander in Chief and Chief Executive." On April 28, Congress voted on four resolutions related to the Yugoslav conflict: It voted down a declaration of war 427 to 2 and an "authorization" of the air strikes 213 to 213, but it also voted against requiring the President to immediately end U.S. participation in the NATO operation and voted to fund that involvement. The conflict between NATO and Yugoslavia continued for 79 days, ending on June 10 with Yugoslavia's agreement to withdraw its forces from Kosovo and allow deployment of a NATO-led peacekeeping force....

... Since we agree with the district court that the congressmen lack standing it is not necessary to decide whether there are other jurisdictional defects.

... Congress certainly could have passed a law forbidding the use of U.S. forces in the Yugoslav campaign; indeed, there was a measure—albeit only a concurrent resolution—introduced to require the President to withdraw U.S. troops. Unfortunately, however, for those congressmen who, like appellants, desired an end to U.S. involvement in Yugoslavia, this measure was *defeated* by a 139 to 290 vote. Of course, Congress always retains appropriations authority and could have cut off funds for the American role in the conflict. Again there was an effort to do so but it failed; appropriations were authorized. And there always remains the possibility of impeachment should a President act in disregard of Congress' authority on these matters.

. . .

Accordingly, the district court is affirmed; appellants lack standing.

The text for this case was obtained in electronic form from Westlaw and is reproduced by permission of the West Group.

SILBERMAN, Circuit Judge, concurring:

... [I]n my view, no one is able to bring this challenge because the two claims are not justiciable. We lack "judicially discoverable and manageable standards" for addressing them, and the War Powers Clause claim implicates the political question doctrine. See *Baker* v. *Carr*, 369 U.S. 186, 217 (1962).

... It has been held that the statutory threshold standard is not precise enough and too obviously calls for a political judgment to be one suitable for judicial determinations.... I think that is correct....

RANDOLPH, Circuit Judge, concurring in the judgment:

The majority opinion [*by Silberman and Tatel, on standing*] does not, I believe, correctly analyze plaintiffs' standing to sue. It misconceives the holding of *Raines v. Byrd* ... and conflicts with the law of this circuit. I believe plaintiffs lack standing, at least to litigate their constitutional claim, but for reasons the majority opinion neglects. I also believe that the case is moot, an optional disposition of the appeal....

TATEL, Circuit Judge, concurring:

Although I agree with Judge Silberman that *Raines v. Byrd* ... as interpreted by this court in *Chenoweth v. Clinton* ... deprives plaintiffs of standing to bring this action, I do not share his view that the case poses a nonjusticiable political question....

To begin with, I do not agree that courts lack judicially discoverable and manageable standards for "determining the existence of a 'war.'" ... Whether the military activity in Yugoslavia amounted to "war" within the meaning of the Declare War Clause ... is no more standardless than any other question regarding the constitutionality of government action. Precisely what police conduct violates the Fourth Amendment guarantee "against unreasonable searches and seizures?" When does government action amount to "an establishment of religion" prohibited by the First Amendment? When is an election district so bizarrely shaped as to violate the Fourteenth Amendment guarantee of "equal protection of the laws?" Because such constitutional terms are not self-defining, standards for answering these questions have evolved, as legal standards always do, through years of judicial decisionmaking. Courts have proven no less capable of developing standards to resolve war powers challenges.

Since the earliest years of the nation, courts have not hesitated to determine when military action constitutes "war." In *Bas v. Tingy*, 4 U.S. (4 Dall.) 37 (1800), the Supreme Court had to decide whether hostilities between France and the United States amounted to a state of war in order to resolve disputes over captured ships....

... [C]ourts are competent to adjudge the existence of war and the allocation of war powers between the President and Congress....

E. RIGHTS OF CITIZENSHIP

All three branches have been active in determining questions of citizenship and aliens. Article I, Section 8, Clause 4, gives Congress the power to establish a "uniform Rule of Naturalization." Congress has conferred jurisdiction upon the courts to naturalize aliens as citizens, and the executive branch has been active in asserting its notion of prerogatives concerning both citizenship and aliens.

Part of the controversy concerns the ability of aliens to obtain citizenship if they oppose war. In 1929 the Supreme Court held that the government was entitled to deny a woman an application for naturalization because, as a pacifist, she answered that she "would not take up arms personally" to defend the country. The Court said that the duty of citizens to defend the country against enemies was a "fundamental principle" of the Constitution. United States v. Schwimmer, 279 U.S. 644, 650 (1929). In one of his famous dissents, Justice Holmes noted that the woman was more than fifty years of age and could not bear arms if she wanted to. He added:

... [I]f there is any principle of the Constitution that more imperatively calls for attachment than any other it is the principle of free thought—not free thought for those who agree with us but freedom for the thought that we hate.... I would suggest that the Quakers have done their share to make the country what it is, that many citizens agree with the applicant's belief and that I had not supposed hitherto that we regretted our inability to expel them because they believe more than some of us do in the teachings of the Sermon on the Mount.

Two years later, the Court again upheld the government's action in denying an application for citizenship from someone who would not promise to bear arms in defense of the United States unless he believed the war to be morally justified. He based his belief not on pacifism but on the principles of Christianity. The Court acknowledged that Congress could, as it had, relieve the conscientious objector from the obligation to bear arms, but this policy applied only to citizens, not to aliens seeking citizenship. The dissenters in this 5 to 4 decision argued that Congress had never expressly required that aliens promise to bear arms as a condition of obtaining citizenship and that courts should not act on the basis of implications. United States v. Macintosh, 283 U.S. 605, 623–24 (1931); United States v. Bland, 283 U.S. 636 (1931).

These decisions were shaken and finally overturned by cases in the 1940s. The first concerned someone who had been granted citizenship in 1927 but the government began proceedings in 1939 to cancel the citizenship, claiming that during the five years before naturalization the man had been affiliated with certain Communist organizations. The government charged that he had obtained citizenship by "fraud." The Court held that it was not enough for the government to prevail on a bare preponderance of the evidence. The evidence had to be clear, unequivocal, and convincing. The government could not sustain this higher burden. Schneiderman v. United States, 320 U.S. 118 (1943).

In 1946 the Court overruled its earlier decisions in *Schwimmer, Macintosh,* and *Bland.* It held that an alien who is willing to take the oath of allegiance and to serve in the army as a noncombatant but who, because of religious beliefs, is unwilling to bear arms in defense of the country, may be admitted nonetheless to citizenship. The Court pointed out that many citizens — nurses, engineers, doctors, chaplains, litter bearers — contribute to the war effort without bearing arms. Girouard v. United States, 328 U.S. 61, 64 (1946).

The Loss of Citizenship

In 1958, the Court decided whether a native-born American could be stripped of his citizenship because he had been convicted by court-martial for wartime desertion. The Army had sentenced him to three years of hard labor, forfeited his pay and allowances, and gave him a dishonorable discharge. When he later applied for a passport, it was denied because a congressional statute required loss of citizenship for wartime desertion or a dishonorable discharge. The Court held that a person must voluntarily renounce or abandon citizenship. Citizenship was not "a license that expires upon misbehavior." Trop v. Dulles, 356 U.S. 86, 92 (1958). Denationalization violated the Eighth Amendment because it resulted in "the total destruction of the individual's status in organized society. It is a form of punishment more primitive than torture, for it destroys for the individual the political existence that was centuries in the development." Id. at 101.

The Court divided 5 to 4 on this case and split by the same margin in a companion case that upheld the power of Congress to strip someone of citizenship if he or she votes in a foreign political election. The Court deferred to Congress on this occasion because of foreign policy considerations and the possibility of serious international embarrassment. Perez v. Brownell, 356 U.S. 44 (1958). The dissenters maintained that citizenship "*is* man's basic right for it is nothing less than the right to have rights. Remove this priceless possession and there remains a stateless person, disgraced and degraded in the eyes of his countrymen."

Another 5–4 decision in 1963 held that Congress could not use expatriation as punishment for draft evaders without providing for the procedural safeguards in the Fifth and Sixth Amendments: indictment, notice, confrontation, jury trial, assistance of counsel, and compulsory process for obtaining witnesses. Kennedy v. Mendoza-Martinez, 372 U.S. 144 (1963). Obviously, this decision was inconsistent with the result five years before in *Perez,* which permitted expatriation without criminal trial, and the Court was parting company from earlier decisions that had ruled expatriation unconstitutional under the Eighth Amendment. Another ruling in 1964 struck down a statutory provision because it favored native-born citizens over naturalized citizens. Schneider v. Rusk, 377 U.S. 163 (1964).

The confusion continued in 1967 with a 5–4 decision overruling *Perez*. This brought the Court back to where it was in 1958: citizenship could be renounced only voluntarily. Even acting under the foreign affairs power, Congress has no power to divest a person of his or her citizenship. Afroyim v. Rusk, 387 U.S. 253 (1967). However, this decision and *Schneider* were "distinguished" in 1971 when the Court allowed citizenship to be lost under certain conditions. If someone acquires citizenship by being born abroad to parents, one of whom is an American citizen, citizenship can be retained only by satisfying residency requirements established by Congress. Rogers v. Bellei, 401 U.S. 815 (1971).[8]

CONCLUSIONS

Much of the debate on the allocation of foreign affairs powers between Congress and the President revolves around two competing models. Under *Curtiss-Wright*, the President is blessed with extra-constitutional, inherent powers. The necessities of international affairs and diplomacy make the President the dominant figure. On the other hand, the *Steel Seizure Case* assumes that Congress is the basic lawmaker in both domestic and foreign affairs. Inherent powers are denied, although congressional inertia, silence, or acquiescence may invite independent and conclusive actions by the executive.

The lesson to be drawn from either model is that Congress has ample powers to legislate for emergencies, at home or abroad, but those powers must be exercised. Congressional influence depends on its willingness to act and take responsibility. Presidential influence, at least for long-term commitments, cannot survive on assertions of inherent power. The President needs the support and understanding of both Congress and the public. Another lesson regards the role of federal courts in participating in matters of war and foreign policy. Like Congress, judges need to show a willingness to act and take responsibility. Otherwise, presidential power operates with few checks and balances.

NOTES AND QUESTIONS

1. The framers vested in Congress the constitutional authority to take the country from a state of peace to a state of war against another country. How do the doctrines developed by Justice Sutherland in *Curtiss-Wright* undermine that constitutional value of republican government? What were his sources for inherent presidential power?

2. If his comments were dicta, why are they considered relevant and influential? Did he characterize John Marshall's "sole organ" doctrine correctly? Do dicta, if repeated often enough, become the holding?

3. The framers understood that constitutional text alone would not preserve the system of checks and balances that is so critical in protecting individual rights and liberties. How is that lesson revealed in such examples as the detention of Japanese-Americans during World War II, Justice Jackson's concurrence in the Steel Seizure Case, and the treaty termination case of *Goldwater v. Carter*?

4. What basic judicial checks operated on the creation of military tribunals by President George W. Bush after 9/11? Do courts have authority and competence to participate on questions of foreign relations, the war power, and national security?

---

8. See also Fedorenko v. United States, 449 U.S. 490 (1981); John P. Roche, "The Expatriation Cases: 'Breathes There the Man, With Soul So Dead ...'?" 1963 Sup. Ct. Rev. 325; P. Allan Dionisopoulos, "Afroyim v. Rusk: The Evolution, Uncertainty and Implications of a Constitutional Principle," 55 Minn. L. Rev. 235 (1970).

SELECTED READINGS

ADLER, DAVID GRAY, AND LARRY N. GEORGE, eds. The Constitution and the Conduct of American Foreign Policy. Lawrence, Kans.: University Press of Kansas, 1996.

BOROSAGE, ROBERT L. "Para-Legal Authority and Its Perils." 40 Law and Contemporary Problems 166 (1976).

COHEN, RICHARD. "Self-Executing Executive Agreements: A Separation of Powers Problem." 24 Buffalo Law Review 137 (1974).

EDGAR, HAROLD, AND BENNO C. SCHMIDT, JR. "Curtiss-Wright Comes Home: Executive Power and National Security Secrecy." 21 Harvard Civil Rights — Civil Liberties Law Review 349 (1986).

ELY, JOHN HART. War and Responsibility: Constitutional Lessons of Vietnam and Its Aftermath. Princeton: Princeton University Press, 1993.

FARBER, DANIEL A. "National Security, the Right to Travel, and the Courts." 1981 Supreme Court Review 263.

FISHER, LOUIS. Presidential War Power. Lawrence: University Press of Kansas, 2d ed. 2004.

———. Military Tribunals and Presidential Power. Lawrence: University Press of Kansas, 2005.

———. The Constitution and 9/11: Recurring Threats to America's Freedoms. Lawrence: University Press of Kansas, 2008.

FRANCK, THOMAS M., AND EDWARD WEISBAND. Foreign Policy by Congress. New York: Oxford University Press, 1979.

——— and Michael J. Glennon. Foreign Relations and National Security Law. St. Paul, Minn.: West, 1987.

GLENNON, MICHAEL J. Constitutional Diplomacy. Princeton: Princeton University Press, 1990.

GOLDSMITH, JACK. The Terror Presidency: Law and Judgment Inside the Bush Administration. New York: Norton, 2007.

HENKIN, LOUIS. Foreign Affairs and the Constitution. New York: Oxford University Press, 1996.

HESS, GARY R. Presidential Decisions for War: Korea, Vietnam, and the Persian Gulf. Baltimore: Johns Hopkins University Press, 2001.

HURTGEN, JAMES R. "The Case for Presidential Prerogative." 7 University of Toledo Law Review 59 (1975).

KOH, HAROLD HONGJU. The National Security Constitution. New Haven: Yale University Press, 1990.

LOFGREN, CHARLES A. "U.S. v. Curtiss-Wright Export Corporation: An Historical Reassessment." 83 Yale Law Journal 1 (1973).

———. "War-Making Under the Constitution: The Original Understanding." 81 Yale Law Journal 672 (1972).

MARCUS, MAEVA. Truman and the Steel Seizure Case: The Limits of Presidential Power. New York: Columbia University Press, 1977.

MURPHY, JOHN F. "Treaties and International Agreements Other Than Treaties: Constitutional Allocation of Power and Responsibility Among the President, the House of Representatives, and the Senate." 23 University of Kansas Law Review 221 (1975).

O'DONNELL, THOMAS A. "Illumination or Elimination of the "Zone of Twilight'? Congressional Acquiescence and Presidential Authority in Foreign Affairs." 51 Cincinnati Law Review 95 (1982).

OHLY, D. CHRISTOPHER. "Advice and Consent: International Executive Claims Settlement Agreements." 5 Californian Western International Law Journal 271 (1975).

PAUST, JORDAN J. "Is the President Bound by the Supreme Law of the Land? — Foreign Affairs and National Security Reexamined." 9 Hastings Constitutional Law Quarterly 719 (1982).

POWELL, A. JEFFERSON. The President's Authority Over Foreign Affairs. Durham: Carolina Academic Press, 2002.

REVELEY, W. TAYLOR, III. War Powers of the President and Congress. Charlottesville: University Press of Virginia, 1981.

ROVINE, ARTHUR W. "Separation of Powers and International Executive Agreements." 52 Indiana Law Review 297 (1977).

SILVERSTEIN, GORDON. Imbalance of Powers: Constitutional Interpretation and the Making of American Foreign Policy. New York: Oxford University Press, 1997.

SOFAER, ABRAHAM D. War, Foreign Affairs and Constitutional Power: The Origins. Cambridge, Mass.: Ballinger Publishing, 1976.

STEVENS, CHARLES J. "The Use and Control of Executive Agreements: Recent Congressional Initiatives." 20 Orbis 905 (1977).

YOO, JOHN. The Powers of War and Peace: The Constitution and Foreign Affairs after 9/11. Chicago: University of Chicago Press, 2005.

8

Federal-State Relations

Federalism divides constitutional authority and political power between the national government and the states. Theories of federalism cut across almost every constitutional issue, including law enforcement, civil liberties, civil rights, sex discrimination, voting rights, reapportionment, privacy, and welfare payments. This chapter focuses on six topics: the principle of federalism, state immunity against suits, the Commerce Clause, the spending and taxing power, the doctrines of preemption and abstention, and the Incorporation Doctrine (applying the Bill of Rights to the states).

Under Chief Justice Marshall, the Supreme Court extended broad support to congressional efforts to exercise its commerce powers. By the end of the nineteenth century, the Court attempted to restrain Congress, but a variety of judicial doctrines did little more than slow the growth of national power. Congress developed its own independent view of federal-state relations. The meaning of federalism has been shaped more by Congress than by the courts. As the Supreme Court noted in 1946: "the history of judicial limitation of congressional power over commerce, when exercised affirmatively, has been more largely one of retreat than of ultimate victory." Prudential Ins. Co. v. Benjamin, 328 U.S. 408, 415.

A. THE PRINCIPLE OF FEDERALISM

In Federalist No. 39, James Madison responded to criticism that the Constitution had improperly created a national government instead of a federal form (a confederation of sovereign states). Madison identified some features of the Constitution that gave it a national character; other provisions vested power directly in the states. He concluded that the proposed Constitution "is, in strictness, neither a national nor a federal Constitution, but a composition of both."

Independence from England left the 13 American states without a central government. Under the Articles of Confederation, drafted in 1777 and ratified in 1781, each state retained "its sovereignty, freedom and independence" except for a few powers *expressly* delegated to the national government. The weakness of the confederation became of increasing concern, forcing the states to seek some form of regional cooperation to deal with commercial problems. Representatives of Virginia and Maryland met in 1785 at the home of George Washington, but it was decided that an interstate compact would be of more value if it included additional states. Consequently, all states were invited to Annapolis in 1786 to discuss commercial issues. Poor attendance and the need to address other problems led to the convention at Philadelphia the following year "to devise such further provisions as shall appear to them necessary to render the constitution of the Federal Government adequate to the exigencies of the Union."

What emerged from Philadelphia was an entirely new structure of government that divided power functionally (among three separate branches) and spatially (between the national government and the states). The Constitution rejected Montesquieu's theory that republican government could flourish only in small countries. He believed that as the size of the country increased, popular control had to be surrendered, yielding power to aristocracies in moderate-sized countries and to monarchies in large countries. Madison turned this theory on its head in Federalist No. 10 by arguing that republican government was unlikely to survive in a small territory, because a dominant faction would most likely oppress the minority. "Extend the sphere," however, "and you take in a greater variety of parties

TABLE 8.1 NATIONAL AND STATE POWERS UNDER THE CONSTITUTION*

National Powers	State Powers	Prohibited State Powers	State Powers if Congress Consents
Tax	Tax	—	—
Lay duties on imports and exports	Exercise police power	Tax articles from other states	Lay duties on imports and exports
Borrow money	Borrow money	—	—
Regulate foreign commerce	—	—	—
Regulate interstate commerce	Regulate intrastate commerce	—	—
Establish courts	Establish courts	—	—
Make treaties	—	Make treaties	Make compacts with other states
Coin money	—	Coin money	—
Emit bills of credit	—	Emit bills of credit	—
Declare war	—	Declare war	Engage in war
Raise and support military	—	—	Keep troops in time of peace
Grant letters of marque and reprisal	—	Grant letters of marque and reprisal	—

*The national powers identified above are found in Art. I, § 8, and Art. II. State powers are proscribed by Art. I, § 10. Under Art. I, §§ 9 and 10, both Congress and the states are prohibited from passing bills of attainder, ex post facto laws, and laws that grant titles of nobility. In addition, states may not pass laws that impair obligation of contracts.

and interests; you make it less probable that a majority of the whole will have a common motive to invade the rights of other citizens." Dividing this large territory into distinct states added further stability. As Hamilton said in Federalist No. 28, the national government and the states could check the usurpations of each other: "The people, by throwing themselves into either scale, will infallibly make it preponderate. If their rights are invaded by either, they can make use of the other as the instrument of redress."

The Virginia Plan

The Virginia Plan submitted to the Philadelphia Convention called for a strong central government. The rival New Jersey Plan, espousing a confederation with power left largely to the states, attracted little support. The eventual compromise gave the central government power to collect taxes, regulate commerce, declare war, and other express functions, including the Necessary and Proper Clause to carry into effect the enumerated powers. The power of Congress was divided between two chambers: a House of Representatives elected by the people, with its membership based on population; and a Senate elected by state legislatures, with two Senators for each state. This struck an accommodation between the preference of the big states (representation by population) and the demand of the small states (equal voting power for each state).

The Virginia Plan proposed a congressional veto over all state laws "contravening in the opinion of the National Legislature the articles of Union." Although this provision was initially agreed to without debate or dissent, it was later eliminated. 1 Farrand 21, 54. Instead, the Constitution assigns specific powers to Congress, expressly prohibits the states from exercising certain powers, and allows states to exercise other powers if Congress consents (see Table 8.1).

New States and Territories

The Constitution provides for the admission of new states in Article IV, Section 3: "[N]o new State shall be formed or erected within the Jurisdiction of any other State; nor any State be formed by the Junction of two or more States, or Parts of States, without the consent of the legislatures of the States concerned as well as of the Congress." An exception to this provision occurred in 1861, after South Carolina fired on Fort Sumter. Several states, including Virginia, voted to secede from the Union. The western counties of Virginia nullified the Virginia ordinance of secession and agreed to form a new state. In 1863 President Lincoln issued a proclamation making West Virginia the 35th state. For territory acquired from other countries (such as from the Louisiana Purchase or the Mexican War), Congress converted those lands to territories and later to states.

The Supremacy Clause

National powers are further reinforced by the Supremacy Clause in Article IV, Section 2: "This Constitution, and the laws of the United States which shall be made in pursuance thereof; and all treaties made, or which shall be made, under the authority of the United States, shall be the supreme law of the land; and the judges in every State shall be bound thereby, anything in the constitution or laws of any State to the contrary notwithstanding." Early in its history, the Supreme Court decided that in cases of conflict between state law and a treaty, the latter prevails. Ware v. Hylton, 3 U.S. (3 Dall.) 198 (1796).

In 2000, the Supreme Court applied the Supremacy Clause to a Massachusetts law that barred state entities from buying goods or services from companies doing business with Burma (Myanmar). Congress later imposed sanctions on the country, but delegated to the President substantial discretion to lift the sanctions if the regime made progress in human rights and democracy. A nonprofit corporation, representing several companies affected by the state law, sued on the basis that Massachusetts infringed on the federal foreign affairs power, violated the Foreign Commerce Clause, and was preempted by the federal statute. The Supreme Court held that the state law was invalid under the Supremacy Clause. Crosby v. National Foreign Trade Council, 530 U.S. 363 (2000).

The Property Clause

State power is qualified by the authority of Congress under the Property Clause "to dispose of and make all needful Rules and Regulations respecting the Territory or other Property belonging to the United States" (Art. IV, § 3, Cl. 2). Under this grant of authority, Congress exercises control over vast stretches of public land located inside the states, particularly those in the West. Kleppe v. New Mexico, 426 U.S. 529 (1976).

Privileges and Immunities

State sovereignty is also limited by the Privileges and Immunities Clause: "The Citizens of each State shall be entitled to all Privileges and Immunities of Citizens in the several States" (Art. IV, § 2). Along with the Commerce Clause, this was intended to create a "national economic union." Supreme Court of New Hampshire v. Piper, 470 U.S. 274, 280 (1985).[1]

The protection of privileges and immunities also appears in Section 1 of the Fourteenth Amendment: "No State shall make or enforce any law which shall abridge the privileges or immunities of citizens of the United States." In 1999, the Supreme Court resurrected that provision by striking down a California statute that limited the maximum welfare benefits available to a family that had resided

---

1. See also Hicklin v. Orbeck, 437 U.S. 518 (1978); Baldwin v. Montana Fish and Game Comm'n, 436 U.S. 371 (1978); Austin v. New Hampshire, 420 U.S. 656 (1975); Toomer v. Witsell, 334 U.S. 385 (1948).

in the state for less than twelve months. Such families would receive the amount paid by the state of their prior residence. Voting 7 to 2, the Court ruled that this durational residence requirement discriminated against citizens who were entitled to enjoy the privileges and immunities of citizens in the states that they visit. Saenz v. Roe, 526 U.S. 489 (1999). Dissenting in this case, Chief Justice Rehnquist objected to the Court "unearthing from its tomb" the Privileges and Immunities Clause of the Fourteenth Amendment.

The Privileges and Immunities Clause of the Fourteenth Amendment had little use after the Court decided the *Slaughter-House Cases* in 1873. The Court at times struck down durational residency requirements for welfare benefits, but only by finding a "right to travel" in the equal protection guarantee of the Fourteenth Amendment. Shapiro v. Thompson, 394 U.S. 618 (1969). Thirteen years later, in a concurring opinion, Justice O'Connor found a right to travel in the privileges and immunities protection of Article IV, § 2. Zobel v. Williams, 457 U.S. 55 (1982).

The National Guard

Questions of federalism also affect National Guard units. Under Article I, Section 8, Congress may call forth the "militia" (part-time military forces) to suppress insurrections and repel invasions. Congress may also provide for "organizing, arming, and disciplining" the militia and "for governing such Part of them" when called into service for the federal government. The states appoint the officers and have authority for "training the Militia according to the discipline prescribed by Congress." In 1990 a unanimous Court held that a state governor's consent is not needed for training the National Guard in foreign countries. Perpich v. Department of Defense, 496 U.S. 334 (1990). The issue of state v. federal control over the National Guard surfaced again in the aftermath of the disaster caused by Hurricane Katrina in 2005, as the state of Louisiana and the federal government argued over their deployment.

Nullification and Secession

Early in U.S. history, national powers were regularly threatened by state efforts to secede from the Union or to assert the doctrines of interposition and nullification. After the Federalist party passed the Alien and Sedition Acts, the Jeffersonian Republicans protested this exercise of national power. Jefferson's draft of the Kentucky Resolutions of 1798 stated that unauthorized actions by the federal government were "void, and of no force." Here was the doctrine of nullification. The Virginia Resolutions of 1798, which Madison helped write, used somewhat softer language. In cases where the federal government overstepped its powers, the states "have the right and are in duty bound to interpose for arresting the progress of the evil, and for maintaining within their respective limits the authorities, rights, and liberties appertaining to them." Some years later the Federalists complained about Republican policies in the national government. Meeting at the Hartford Convention of 1814, Federalists considered secession and registered the opposition of New England states to the measures taken by Republicans. In 1832 South Carolina's ordinance of nullification maintained that the tariff acts enacted by Congress were "null, void, and no law."

The spirit of nullification led eventually to the South's secession from the Union and the start of the Civil War. After the war, the Supreme Court determined that the rebel states never left the Union: "The Constitution, in all its provisions, looks to an indestructible Union, composed of indestructible States." Texas v. White, 7 Wall. (74 U.S.) 700, 725 (1869). In admitting new states to the Union, Congress cannot impose conditions that would make a state unequal to others. It cannot, for example, dictate to a state the location of its capital. Coyle v. Oklahoma, 221 U.S. 559 (1911).

The Tenth Amendment

Throughout the nineteenth and twentieth centuries, there have been efforts to promote the notion of sovereign states by misconstruing the Tenth Amendment, which provides that the powers "not dele-

Nonjudicial Officials Determine Constitutionality of U.S. Bank

Responding to a request by the House of Representatives, Secretary of the Treasury Alexander Hamilton prepared a report on the establishment of a national bank and submitted it on December 13, 1790. 2 Annals of Cong. 2082–2112. Much of the legislative debate the following year focused on the constitutional authority of Congress to use implied powers to create the bank. The Senate acted first, passing the bank bill on January 20, 1791.

During House debate, Madison argued against the constitutionality of the bank on the ground that it was not an enumerated power of Congress, although this contradicted his position two years earlier on the Tenth Amendment. Fisher Ames challenged this theory of enumerated powers by saying that if the power to raise armies had not been given expressly to Congress, it would have been implied by other parts of the Constitution. Theodore Sedgwick reminded the House that Madison, in 1789, had convinced a majority of members that the President had the power to remove executive officials, even though that power is not specifically stated in the Constitution. 2 Annals of Cong. 1955, 1960. Elias Boudinot pointed

to Madison's essay in Federalist No. 44, which offered a broad interpretation of the Necessary and Proper Clause available to Congress to discharge its powers. Id. at 1977. The House passed the bill, 39 to 20.

After the bill cleared Congress, President George Washington asked Cabinet members to comment on the constitutionality of the legislation. Attorney General Edmund Randolph and Secretary of State Thomas Jefferson concluded that Congress lacked the constitutional power to grant a corporate charter for a national bank. Secretary of the Treasury Hamilton prepared a detailed analysis, defending the power of Congress to act in this area. Having drafted the bank bill, he was hardly in a position to claim detachment or objectivity, but Madison, Randolph, and Jefferson also had well-formed attachments and predilections. Washington decided to sign the bill. When the issue was later taken to the Supreme Court, Chief Justice Marshall borrowed wholesale from Hamilton's interpretation of implied powers, sovereignty, and the Necessary and Proper Clause. See 8 The Papers of Alexander Hamilton 97–134 (Harold C. Syrett ed. 1965).

gated to the United States by the Constitution, nor prohibited by it to the States, are reserved to the States respectively, or to the people." The Articles of Confederation had given greater protection to the states, which retained all powers except those "expressly delegated" to the national government. When that phrase was proposed for the Tenth Amendment, Madison objected to the word "expressly" because the functions and responsibilities of the federal government could not be delineated with such precision. It was impossible to confine a government to the exercise of express powers, for there "must necessarily be admitted powers by implication, unless the Constitution descended to recount every minutiae." 1 Annals of Cong. 761 (Aug. 18, 1789). On the strength of his argument, Congress eliminated the word "expressly." Moreover, the Necessary and Proper Clause affords Congress the power to pass laws to carry into execution the express powers.

Chief Justice Marshall relied on this legislative history and constitutional text when he upheld the power of Congress to establish a national bank, even though such power is not expressly included in the Constitution. This endorsement of incidental or implied powers signaled a major advance for both national and congressional powers. McCULLOCH v. MARYLAND, 17 U.S. (4 Wheat.) 315 (1819). In upholding the national bank, Marshall followed closely the reasoning and justification first set forth by legislative and executive officials when they developed constitutional grounds for the bank in 1791 (see box).

The idea that the Tenth Amendment contains substantive powers for the states is revived on occasion when the Supreme Court tries to rewrite the Constitution by shoehorning the word "expressly" into the Tenth Amendment. Lane County v. Oregon, 74 U.S. (7 Wall.) 71, 76 (1868); Hammer v. Dagenhart, 247 U.S. 251, 275 (1918). Most decisions, however, accept the Amendment as merely declaratory of a general relationship between the federal government and the states. In 1920, the Court denied that the treaty power was restricted in any way "by some invisible radiation from the general terms of the Tenth Amendment." MISSOURI v. HOLLAND, 252 U.S. 416, 434. A decade later, the Court held that the Tenth Amendment added nothing to the Constitution as originally ratified. United States v. Sprague, 282 U.S. 716, 733 (1931). After another decade, Justice Stone dismissed the Tenth Amendment as a "truism," rephrasing it to read "that all is retained which has not been surrendered." United States v. Darby, 312 U.S. 100, 124 (1941). As a declaratory statement, however, the Amendment "is not without significance." Fry v. United States, 421 U.S. 542, 547 n.7 (1975). The Tenth Amendment has been cited in recent cases to uphold state powers (Section F).

The Eleventh Amendment

States feared lawsuits by citizens from other states or citizens from foreign countries. At the Virginia ratifying convention, Madison insisted that the Supreme Court's jurisdiction over controversies between a state and citizens of another state did not give individuals the power to call any state into court. A citizen might initiate an action, but federal courts would have jurisdiction only if a state consented to be a party. 3 Elliot 533. In Federalist No. 81, Hamilton claimed that states would be shielded by the general principle of immunity: "It is inherent in the nature of sovereignty not to be amenable to the suit of an individual *without its consent.*"

One of the first cases brought to the Supreme Court involved a suit by Dutch bankers to recover funds from Maryland. In this case, the state's Attorney General voluntarily appeared. Vanstophorst v. Maryland, 2 Dall. 401 (1791). The issue of state immunity reached explosive proportions when two citizens from South Carolina, acting as executors of a British creditor, filed suit against Georgia. In 1793 the Supreme Court decided that the suit was consistent with Article III, Section 2, which gave the federal courts jurisdiction over controversies "between a State and Citizens of another State." Chisholm v. Georgia, 2 U.S. (2 Dall.) 419. To prevent a rash of citizen suits, Congress and the states promptly overturned the Court's ruling by ratifying the Eleventh Amendment: "The Judicial power of the United States shall not be construed to extend to any suit in law or equity, commenced or prosecuted against one of the United States by Citizens of another State, or by Citizens or Subjects of any foreign state." Although the Amendment does not expressly bar suits against a state by its own citizens, the Court has consistently held that a state is subject to such suits if it consents.[2]

As interpreted by the Court, however, the Eleventh Amendment does not give states total immunity from suits filed by citizens from other states. The doctrine that a state may not be sued in its own courts without its consent does not provide absolute immunity from suits in the courts of another state. Nevada v. Hall, 440 U.S. 410 (1979). Moreover, the Eleventh Amendment has been substantially narrowed by the Fourteenth Amendment. The Eleventh Amendment only prohibits suits directed against the *states.* Suits are allowed against state *officers* who are charged with denying due process or equal protection under the Fourteenth Amendment. The theory is that an officer acting illegally is functioning as an individual rather than a state official. Ex parte Young, 209 U.S. 123 (1908); Smyth v. Ames, 169 U.S. 466, 518–519 (1898).[3]

---

2. Blatchford v. Native Village of Noatak, 501 U.S. 775 (1991). Employees v. Missouri Public Health Dept., 411 U.S. 279, 280 (1973); Great Northern Life Ins. Co. v. Read, 322 U.S. 47, 51 (1944); Duhne v. New Jersey, 251 U.S. 311 (1920); Hans v. Louisiana, 134 U.S. 1 (1890). The theory that the Eleventh Amendment forbids federal courts to hear suits against a state by a citizen of that state was rejected by four Justices in Atascadero State Hospital v. Scanlon, 473 U.S. 234 (1985) and Welch v. Texas Dept. of Highways, 483 U.S. 468 (1987).

3. See Truax v. Raich, 239 U.S. 33 (1915); William A. Fletcher, "A Historical Interpretation of the Eleventh Amendment: A Narrow Construction of an Affirmative Grant of Jurisdiction Rather than a Prohibition Against Jurisdiction," 35 Stan. L. Rev. 1033 (1983); Doyle Mathis, "The Eleventh Amendment: Adoption and Interpretation," 2 Ga. L. Rev. 207 (1968).

State Budgets

This theory of liability does not support a suit against a state official who is used simply as a conduit to recover money from the state. Even if not named in such a case, the state is the real party and is entitled to sovereign immunity. Ford Motor Co. v. Department of Treasury, 323 U.S. 459 (1945); Alabama v. Pugh, 438 U.S. 781 (1978).

State governments regularly invoke sovereign immunity to protect their budgets. In 1974, the Supreme Court held that a suit could not force a state to make retroactive payments for a program it administered for the aged, blind, and disabled. Although the suit was filed against various state officials who administered the program, the funds for retroactive payments would come from the state. The fact that the program was funded equally by state and federal funds was insufficient to establish state consent to be sued in federal courts. Edelman v. Jordan, 415 U.S. 651, 673 (1974). Two years later the Court decided that whenever there is a collision between the Eleventh Amendment and Section 5 of the Fourteenth Amendment, which grants Congress authority to enforce "by appropriate legislation" the substantive provisions of the Fourteenth Amendment, the congressional statute prevails. This policy allows suits against states even for retroactive payments from their treasuries. Fitzpatrick v. Bitzer, 427 U.S. 445 (1976).

Other Factors

Principles of federalism "that might otherwise be an obstacle to congressional authority are necessarily overridden by the power to enforce the Civil War Amendments 'by appropriate legislation.' Those Amendments were specifically designed as an expansion of federal power and an intrusion on state sovereignty." Rome v. United States, 446 U.S. 156, 179 (1980). Unless Congress expresses in unmistakable terms its intent to abrogate the Eleventh Amendment, states may not be sued in federal court without their consent. Atascadero State Hospital v. Scanlon, 473 U.S. 234 (1985); Dellmuth v. Muth, 491 U.S. 223 (1989).

Other than its enforcement powers under the Fourteenth Amendment, may Congress use its Article I powers to abrogate the Eleventh Amendment? The Court has held that Congress may use the Commerce Clause to set aside the sovereign immunity of states. Dennis v. Higgins, 498 U.S. 439 (1991); Pennsylvania v. Union Gas Co., 491 U.S. 1 (1989). As explained later in this chapter (Section F), the Court began to place some limits on the Commerce Clause during the 1990s. The Court has also ruled that the Bankruptcy Code, based on the Article I power of Congress to establish uniform laws for bankruptcies, does not abrogate the states' Eleventh Amendment immunity. Hoffman v. Connecticut Income Maint. Dept., 492 U.S. 96 (1989). A series of decisions in the 1980s and 1990s revealed a Court sharply split over the meaning and application of the Eleventh Amendment, with the Court often divided 5 to 4 (Section F).

McCulloch v. Maryland

17 U.S. (4 Wheat.) 315 (1819)

Congress passed legislation in 1816 to create a Bank of the United States. The power to incorporate a national bank is not expressly granted in the Constitution. On the issue whether an implied power existed, Chief Justice Marshall supplies a broad interpretation of the meaning of the Constitution. In 1818 Maryland passed legislation to impose a tax on all banks or branches of banks in the state not chartered by the legislature. James W. McCulloch, the Bank's cashier in Baltimore, refused to pay the tax. The dispute gave Marshall an opportunity to explore the extent of state sovereignty, interpret the Necessary and Proper Clause, and judge the validity of a state tax on a federal instrumentality.

March 7th, 1819. MARSHALL Ch. J., delivered the opinion of the court.—In the case now to be determined, the defendant, a sovereign state, denies the obligation of a law enacted by the legislature of the Union, ...

The first question made in the cause is—has congress power to incorporate a bank? It has been truly said, that this can scarcely be considered as an open question, entirely unprejudiced by the former proceedings of the nation respecting it....

The power now contested was exercised by the first congress elected under the present constitution. The bill for incorporating the Bank of the United States did not steal upon an unsuspecting legislature, and pass unobserved. Its principle was completely understood, and was opposed with equal zeal and ability. After being resisted, first, in the fair and open field of debate, and afterwards, in the executive cabinet, with as much persevering talent as any measure has ever experienced, and being supported by arguments which convinced minds as pure and as intelligent as this country can boast, it became a law. The original act was permitted to expire; but a short experience of the embarrassments to which the refusal to revive it exposed the government, convinced those who were most prejudiced against the measure of its necessity, and induced the passage of the present law....

In discussing this question, the counsel for the state of Maryland have deemed it of some importance, in the construction of the constitution, to consider that instrument, not as emanating from the people, but as the act of sovereign and independent states. The powers of the general government, it has been said, are delegated by the states, who alone are truly sovereign; and must be exercised in subordination to the states, who alone possess supreme dominion. It would be difficult to sustain this proposition. The convention which framed the constitution was indeed elected by the state legislatures. But the instrument, when it came from their hands, was a mere proposal, without obligation, or pretensions to it. It was reported to the then existing congress of the United States, with a request that it might "be submitted to a convention of delegates, chosen in each state by the people thereof, under the recommendation of its legislature, for their assent and ratification." This mode of proceeding was adopted; and by the convention, by congress, and by the state legislatures, the instrument was submitted to the *people.* They acted upon it in the only manner in which they can act safely, effectively and wisely, on such a subject, by assembling in convention. It is true, they assembled in their several states—and where else should they have assembled? ...

From these conventions, the constitution derives its whole authority. The government proceeds directly from the people; is "ordained and established," in the name of the people; and is declared to be ordained, "in order to form a more perfect union, establish justice, insure domestic tranquility, and secure the blessings of liberty to themselves and to their posterity." The assent of the states, in their sovereign capacity, is implied, in calling a convention, and thus submitting that instrument to the people. But the people were at perfect liberty to accept or reject it; and their act was final. It required not the affirmance, and could not be negatived, by the state governments. The constitution, when thus adopted, was of complete obligation, and bound the state sovereignties.

. . .

This government is acknowledged by all, to be one of enumerated powers. The principle, that it can exercise only the powers granted to it, would seem too apparent, to have required to be enforced by all those arguments, which its enlightened friends, while it was depending before the people, found it necessary to urge; that principle is now universally admitted. But the question respecting the extent of the powers actually granted, is perpetually arising, and will probably continue to arise, so long as our system shall exist....

Among the enumerated powers, we do not find that of establishing a bank or creating a corporation. But there is no phrase in the instrument which, like the articles of confederation, excludes incidental or implied powers; and which requires that everything granted shall be expressly and minutely described. Even the 10th amendment, which was framed for the purpose of quieting the excessive jealousies which had been excited, omits the word "expressly," and declares only, that the powers "not delegated to the United States, nor prohibited to the states, are reserved to the states or to the people;" thus leaving the question, whether the particular power which may become the subject of contest, has been delegated to the one government, or prohibited to the other, to depend on a fair construction of the whole instrument. The men who drew and adopted this amendment had experienced the embarrassments resulting from the insertion of this word in the articles of confederation, and probably omitted it, to avoid those embarrassments. A constitution, to contain an accurate detail of all the subdivisions of which its great powers will admit, and of all the means by which they may be carried into execution, would partake of the prolixity of a legal code, and could scarcely be embraced by the human mind. It would, probably, never be understood by the public. Its nature, therefore, requires, that only its great outlines should be marked, its important objects designated, and the minor ingredients which compose those objects, be deduced from the nature of the objects themselves. That this idea was entertained by the framers of the American constitution, is not only to be inferred from the nature of the instrument, but from the language. Why else were some of the limitations, found in the 9th section of the 1st article, introduced? It is also, in some degree, warranted by their having omitted to use any restrictive term which might prevent its receiving a fair and just interpretation. In considering this question, then, we must never forget that it is a *constitution* we are expounding.

Although, among the enumerated powers of government, we do not find the word "bank" or "incorporation," we find the great powers, to lay and collect taxes; to borrow money; to regulate commerce; to declare and conduct a war; and to raise and support armies and navies. The sword and the purse, all the external relations, and no inconsiderable portion of the industry of the nation, are intrusted to its government. It can never be pretended, that these vast powers draw after them others of inferior importance, merely because they are inferior. Such an idea can never be advanced. But it may with great reason be contended, that a government, intrusted with such ample powers, on the due execution of which the happiness and prosperity of the nation so vitally depends, must also be intrusted with ample means for their execution....

... [T]he constitution of the United States has not left the right of congress to employ the necessary means, for the execution of the powers conferred on the government, to general reasoning. To its enumeration of powers is added, that of making "all laws which shall be necessary and proper, for carrying into execution the foregoing powers, and all other powers vested by this constitution, in the government of the United States, or in any department thereof." The counsel for the state of Maryland have urged various arguments, to prove that this clause, though, in terms, a grant of power, is not so, in effect; but is really restrictive of the general right, which might otherwise be implied, of selecting means for executing the enumerated powers. In support of this proposition, they have found it necessary to contend, that this clause was inserted for the purpose of conferring on congress the power of making laws. That, without it, doubts might be entertained, whether congress could exercise its powers in the form of legislation.

But could this be the object for which it was inserted? A government is created by the people, having legislative, executive and judicial powers. Its legislative powers are vested in a congress, which is to consist of a senate and house of representatives.... Could it be necessary to say, that a legislature should exercise legislative powers, in the shape of legislation? After allowing each house to prescribe its own course of proceeding, after describing the manner in which a bill should become a law, would it have entered into the mind of a single member of the convention, that an express power to make laws was necessary, to enable the legislature to make them? That a legislature, endowed with legislative powers, can legislate, is a proposition too self-evident to have been questioned.

But the argument on which most reliance is placed, is drawn from that peculiar language of this clause. Congress is not empowered by it to make all laws, which may have relation to the powers conferred on the government, but such only as may be *"necessary and proper"* for carrying them into execution. The word *"necessary"* is considered as controlling the whole sentence, and as limiting the right to pass laws for the execution of the granted powers, to such as are indispensable, and without which the power would be nugatory. That it excludes the choice of means, and leaves to congress, in each case, that only which is most direct and simple.

Is it true, that this is the sense in which the word "necessary" is always used? Does it always import an absolute physical necessity, so strong, that one thing to which another may be termed necessary, cannot exist without that other? We think it does not. If reference be had to its use, in the common affairs of the world, or in approved authors, we find that it frequently imports no more than that one thing is convenient, or useful, or essential to another. To employ the means necessary to an end, is generally understood as employing any means calculated to produce the end, and not as being confined to those single means, without which the end would be entirely unattainable....

... This provision is made in a constitution, intended to endure for ages to come, and consequently, to be adapted to the various *crises* of human affairs. To have prescribed the means by which government should, in all future time, execute its powers, would have been to change, entirely, the character of the instrument, and give it the properties of a legal code. It would have been an unwise attempt to provide, by immutable rules, for exigencies which, if foreseen at all, must have been seen dimly, and which can be best provided for as they occur....

[*Marshall proceeds to reject Maryland's argument that the Necessary and Proper Clause was intended to abridge the powers of Congress.*]

1st. The clause is placed among the powers of congress, not among the limitations on those powers. 2d. Its terms purport to enlarge, not to diminish the powers vested in the government. It purports to be an additional power, not a restriction on those already granted. No reason has been, or can be assigned, for thus concealing an intention to narrow the discretion of the national legislature, under words which purport to enlarge it....

We admit, as all must admit, that the powers of the government are limited, and that its limits are not to be transcended. But we think the sound construction of the constitution must allow to the national legislature that discretion, with respect to the means by which the powers it confers are to be carried into execution, which will enable that body to perform the high duties assigned to it, in the manner most beneficial to the people. Let the end be legitimate, let it be within the scope of the constitution, and all means which are appropriate, which are plainly adapted to that end, which are not prohibited, but consist with the letter and spirit of the constitution, are constitutional.

. . .

It being the opinion of the court, that the act incorporating the bank is constitutional; and that the power of establishing a branch in the state of Maryland might be properly exercised by the bank itself, we proceed to inquire—

2. Whether the state of Maryland may, without violating the constitution, tax that branch? That the power of taxation is one of vital importance; that it is retained by the states; that it is not abridged by the grant of a similar power to the government of the Union; that it is to be concurrently exercised by the two governments—are truths which have never been denied....

... [T]he counsel for the bank places its claim to be exempted from the power of a state to tax its operations. There is no express provision for the case, but the claim has been sustained on a principle which so entirely pervades the constitution, is so intermixed with the materials which compose it, so interwoven with its web, so blended with its texture, as to be incapable of being separated from it, without rending it into shreds. This great principle is, that the constitution and the laws made in pursuance thereof are supreme; that they control the constitution and laws of the respective states, and cannot be

controlled by them. From this, which may be almost termed an axiom, other propositions are deduced as corollaries, on the truth or error of which, and on their application to this case, the cause has been supposed to depend. These are, 1st. That a power to create implies a power to preserve: 2d. That a power to destroy, if wielded by a different hand, is hostile to, and incompatible with these powers to create and to preserve: 3d. That where this repugnancy exists, that authority which is supreme must control, not yield to that over which it is supreme.

... That the power of taxing [*the bank*] by the states may be exercised so as to destroy it, is too obvious to be denied. But taxation is said to be an absolute power, which acknowledges no other limits than those expressly prescribed in the constitution, and like sovereign power of every other description, is intrusted to the discretion of those who use it. But the very terms of this argument admit, that the sovereignty of the state, in the article of taxation itself, is subordinate to, and may be controlled by the constitution of the United States. How far it has been controlled by that instrument, must be a question of construction. In making this construction, no principle, not declared, can be admissible, which would defeat the legitimate operations of a supreme government. It is of the very essence of supremacy, to remove all obstacles to its action within its own sphere, and so to modify every power vested in subordinate governments, as to exempt its own operations from their own influence. This effect need not be stated in terms. It is so involved in the declaration of supremacy, so necessarily implied in it, that the expression of it could not make it more certain. We must, therefore, keep it in view, while construing the constitution.

. . .

The sovereignty of a state extends to everything which exists by its own authority, or is introduced by its permission; but does it extend to those means which are employed by congress to carry into execution powers conferred on that body by the people of the United States? We think it demonstrable, that it does not. Those powers are not given by the people of a single state. They are given by the people of the United States, to a government whose laws, made in pursuance of the constitution, are declared to be supreme. Consequently, the people of a single state cannot confer a sovereignty which will extend over them.

. . .

The court has bestowed on this subject its most

deliberate consideration. The result is a conviction that the states have no power, by taxation or otherwise, to retard, impede, burden, or in any manner control, the operations of the constitutional laws enacted by congress to carry into execution the powers vested in the general government. This is, we think, the unavoidable consequence of that supremacy which the constitution has declared. We are unanimously of opinion, that the law passed by the legislature of Maryland, imposing a tax on the Bank of the United States, is unconstitutional and void.

. . .

Missouri v. Holland

252 U.S. 416 (1920)

The United States and Great Britain entered into a treaty in 1916 to protect migratory birds in the United States and Canada. Congress passed legislation in 1918 to enforce the treaty, providing for prohibitions on the killing, capturing, or selling of any of the migratory birds included within the terms of the treaty, except as permitted by regulations compatible with the treaty. Ray P. Holland, U.S. Game Warden, threatened to arrest and prosecute citizens of Missouri for violating the Migratory Bird Treaty Act. Missouri claimed that the treaty and the statute invaded the rights reserved to the states by the Tenth Amendment. A federal district court upheld the congressional act.

MR. JUSTICE HOLMES delivered the opinion of the court.

This is a bill in equity brought by the State of Missouri to prevent a game warden of the United States from attempting to enforce the Migratory Bird Treaty Act of July 3, 1918, c. 128, 40 Stat. 755, and the regulations made by the Secretary of Agriculture in pursuance of the same. The ground of the bill is that the statute is an unconstitutional interference with the rights reserved to the States by the Tenth Amendment, and that the acts of the defendant done and threatened under that authority invade the sovereign right of the State and contravene its will manifested in statutes. The State also alleges a pecuniary interest, as owner of the wild birds within its borders and otherwise, admitted by the Government to be sufficient, but it is enough that the bill is a reasonable and proper means to assert the alleged quasi sovereign rights of a State....

... It is unnecessary to go into any details, because, as we have said, the question raised is the general one whether the treaty and statute are void as an interference with the rights reserved to the States.

To answer this question it is not enough to refer to the Tenth Amendment, reserving the powers not delegated to the United States, because by Article II, § 2, the power to make treaties is delegated expressly, and by Article VI treaties made under the authority of the United States, along with the Constitution and laws of the United States made in pursuance thereof, are declared the supreme law of the land. If the treaty is valid there can be no dispute about the validity of the statute under Article I, § 8, as a necessary and proper means to execute the powers of the Government. The language of the Constitution as to the supremacy of treaties being general, the question before us is narrowed to an inquiry into the ground upon which the present supposed exception is placed.

It is said that a treaty cannot be valid if it infringes the Constitution, that there are limits, therefore, to the treatymaking power, and that one such limit is that what an act of Congress could not do unaided, in derogation of the powers reserved to the States, a treaty cannot do. An earlier act of Congress that attempted by itself and not in pursuance of a treaty to regulate the killing of migratory birds within the States had been held bad in the District Court. *United States* v. *Shauver,* 214 Fed. Rep. 154. *United States* v. *McCullagh,* 221 Fed. Rep. 288. Those decisions were supported by arguments that migratory birds were owned by the States in their sovereign capacity for the benefit of their people, and that under cases like *Geer* v. *Connecticut,* 161 U. S. 519, this control was one that Congress had no power to displace. The same argument is supposed to apply now with equal force.

Whether the two cases cited were decided rightly or not they cannot be accepted as a test of the treaty power. Acts of Congress are the supreme law of the land only when made in pursuance of the Constitution, while treaties are declared to be so when made under the authority of the United States. It is open to question whether the authority of the United

States means more than the formal acts prescribed to make the convention. We do not mean to imply that there are no qualifications to the treaty-making power; but they must be ascertained in a different way. It is obvious that there may be matters of the sharpest exigency for the national well being that an act of Congress could not deal with but that a treaty followed by such an act could, and it is not lightly to be assumed that, in matters requiring national action, "a power which must belong to and somewhere reside in every civilized government" is not to be found. *Andrews* v. *Andrews,* 188 U.S. 14, 33. What was said in that case with regard to the powers of the States applies with equal force to the powers of the nation in cases where the States individually are incompetent to act. We are not yet discussing the particular case before us but only are considering the validity of the test proposed. With regard to that we may add that when we are dealing with words that also are a constituent act, like the Constitution of the United States, we must realize that they have called into life a being the development of which could not have been foreseen completely by the most gifted of its begetters. It was enough for them to realize or to hope that they had created an organism; it has taken a century and has cost their successors much sweat and blood to prove that they created a nation. The case before us must be considered in the light of our whole experience and not merely in that of what was said a hundred years ago. The treaty in question does not contravene any prohibitory words to be found in the Constitution. The only question is whether it is forbidden by some invisible radiation from the general terms of the Tenth Amendment. We must consider what this country has become in deciding what that Amendment has reserved.

The State as we have intimated founds its claim of exclusive authority upon an assertion of title to migratory birds, an assertion that is embodied in statute. No doubt it is true that as between a State and its inhabitants the State may regulate the killing and sale of such birds, but it does not follow that its authority is exclusive of paramount powers. To put the claim of the State upon title is to lean upon a slender reed. Wild birds are not in the possession of anyone; and possession is the beginning of ownership. The whole foundation of the State's rights is the presence within their jurisdiction of birds that yesterday had not arrived, tomorrow may be in another State and in a week a thousand miles away. If we are to be accurate we cannot put the case of the State upon higher ground than that the treaty deals with creatures that for the moment are within the state borders, that it must be carried out by officers of the United States within the same territory, and that but for the treaty the State would be free to regulate this subject itself.

As most of the laws of the United States are carried out within the States and as many of them deal with matters which in the silence of such laws the State might regulate, such general grounds are not enough to support Missouri's claim. Valid treaties of course "are as binding within the territorial limits of the States as they are elsewhere throughout the dominion of the United States." *Baldwin* v. *Franks,* 120 U. S. 678, 683. No doubt the great body of private relations usually fall within the control of the State, but a treaty may override its power....

Here a national interest of very nearly the first magnitude is involved. It can be protected only by national action in concert with that of another power. The subject-matter is only transitorily within the State and has no permanent habitat therein. But for the treaty and the statute there soon might be no birds for any powers to deal with. We see nothing in the Constitution that compels the Government to sit by while a food supply is cut off and the protectors of our forests and our crops are destroyed. It is not sufficient to rely upon the States. The reliance is vain, and were it otherwise, the question is whether the United States is forbidden to act. We are of opinion that the treaty and statute must be upheld. *Carey* v. *South Dakota,* 250 U. S. 118.

Decree affirmed.

Mr. Justice Van Devanter and Mr. Justice Pitney dissent.

B. THE COMMERCE CLAUSE

The Commerce Clause has produced many collisions between the legislative and judicial branches, often pitting the power of Congress to advance its national agenda against judicial constraints that favored business or state interests. Although the Court in many instances blocked national efforts to regulate the economy, over the long run a persistent Congress prevailed with its independent interpretation of the Commerce Clause. Today, the scope of the commerce power is left largely to Congress. Over the past half century, Congress has invoked the Commerce Clause to enact civil rights legislation, treated in Chapter 15.

Commercial friction among the states during the 1770s and 1780s generated pressure for stronger national powers. The Continental Congress had no power to raise revenue or to regulate commerce among the states. Its power to conclude treaties with foreign nations meant little unless it could control commerce coming into state ports. With each state guarding its sphere of sovereignty, 13 conflicting systems of commercial regulation and duty schedules governed trade in the country. These commercial disputes led to the Annapolis Convention in 1786 and the Philadelphia Convention a year later. Among the enumerated duties given to Congress was the power to "regulate commerce with foreign nations, and among the several States, and with the Indian tribes." Art. I, §8, Cl. 2.

The scope of the Commerce Clause reached the Supreme Court in *Gibbons v. Ogden* (1824). The decision by Chief Justice Marshall is significant for three reasons. First, although Marshall was a strong defender of private property and contractual rights, he advanced a broad interpretation of the power of Congress to regulate commerce. Commerce was more than discrete transactions; it was intercourse. Congress had the power to regulate economic life in the nation to promote the free flow of interstate commerce, including actions within state borders that interfered with that flow. Second, his decision averted potential economic warfare among the states, which would have revived the destructive practices operating before the Constitution. Third, the decision represents one of the most articulate rebuttals of "strict constructionism." GIBBONS v. OGDEN, 22 U.S. (9 Wheat.) 1 (1824).

Three years later, Marshall again supported national power by striking down a Maryland statute because it violated two constitutional provisions: the prohibition on states to lay a duty on imports and the power of Congress to regulate interstate commerce. To distinguish between congressional and state powers, Marshall developed the "original package" concept. States could not tax an import in its original form or package, but after the imported article became "incorporated and mixed up with the mass of property in the country," it was vulnerable to state taxes. Brown v. Maryland, 25 U.S. (12 Wheat.) 419, 441 (1827). Those decisions recognized that the national government did not have exclusive control over the commerce power. In areas where Congress had not exercised its commerce power, Marshall supported the authority of states to regulate commerce within their own borders. Willson v. Black-bird Creek Marsh Co., 27 U.S. (2 Pet.) 244 (1829).

Concurrent Powers

Other cases explored jurisdictional boundaries between the national and state governments. The broad nationalistic interpretation of Marshall was supplanted by more restrictive rulings from the Taney Court. A decision in 1837 permitted states to adopt regulations for passengers arriving from foreign countries. The Court considered packages, not people, as subjects of commerce for congressional control. States could exercise the "police power" to protect the general welfare of their citizens. New York v. Miln, 36 U.S. (11 Pet.) 102 (1837). Under this doctrine of concurrent powers, states could regulate commerce within their borders unless preempted by Congress. If Congress authorized the importation of liquor from foreign countries, states had to accept the liquor in its "original package." Once the cask became part of retail or domestic traffic, the state police power justified the imposition of taxes, licenses, or total prohibition of liquor. The same reasoning applied to liquor shipped from neighboring states. License Cases, 46 U.S. (5 How.) 504 (1847). The Supreme Court allowed states to collect "fees" from foreign vessels by distinguishing fees from the imposts and duties forbidden by Article I, Section 10. States could exercise concurrent jurisdiction over portions of the power over foreign commerce, especially when invited by Congress. COOLEY v. BOARD OF WARDENS, 53 U.S. (12 How.) 299 (1852). During this same period, however, the Court denied states the right to impose taxes on alien passengers arriving at state ports, even when states used "health" as a justification. Passenger Cases, 48 U.S. (7 How.) 282 (1849).

In some cases the Supreme Court recognized exclusive jurisdictions. Under the theory of "dual federalism," the states and the national government exercised mutually exclusive powers. "The powers which one possesses, the other does not." United States v. Cruikshank, 92 U.S. (2 Otto.) 542, 550 (1876). In 1890, the Court ruled that a state's prohibition of intoxicating liquors could not be applied to original packages or kegs. The power of Congress over commerce, even if not expressly stated in a statute, appeared to override state police powers and local options. The Court qualified its opinion by saying that the states could not exclude incoming articles "without congressional permission." Leisy v. Hardin, 135 U.S. 100, 125 (1890).

Congress promptly overturned the decision by passing legislation that made intoxicating liquors, upon their arrival in a state or territory, subject to the police powers "to the same extent and in the same manner as though such liquids or liquors had been produced in such State or Territory, and shall not be exempt therefrom by reason of being introduced therein in original packages or otherwise." 26 Stat. 313 (1890). The Supreme Court upheld the constitutionality of this statute. In re Rahrer, 140 U.S. 545 (1891). Excerpts from the congressional debate are reprinted at the end of this section. Three years later, the Court reviewed a state statute that prohibited the sale of oleomargarine that had been colored to look like butter, including oleomargarine manufactured outside the state. The Court supported the statute even though Congress had previously legislated on oleomargarine. Plumley v. Massachusetts, 155 U.S. 461 (1894).

Dormant Commerce Clause

In cases where Congress does not exercise its commerce power, that authority is silent or dormant. In such situations the Court may decide that a state action is forbidden by the Commerce Clause. However, if Congress then enacts legislation to permit the state action, the Court will acquiesce to the congressional policy. For example, in 1852 the Supreme Court held that the height of a bridge in Pennsylvania made it "a nuisance." Congress quickly passed legislation declaring the bridges at issue to be "lawful structures" and the Court subsequently ruled that the bridge was no longer an unlawful obstruction.[4] In separate dissents, Justices McLean, Grier, and Wayne argued that Congress could not annul or vacate a court decree and that the 1852 statute was improperly an exercise of judicial, not legislative, power (see box on next page).

Those positions have never been adopted by the Court, which noted in 1946: "whenever Congress' judgment has been uttered affirmatively to contradict the Court's previously expressed view that specific action taken by the states in Congress' silence was forbidden by the commerce clause, this body has accommodated its previous judgment to Congress' expressed approval." Prudential Ins. Co. v. Benjamin, 326 U.S. 408, 425 (1946). In 1985, the Court said that when Congress "so chooses, state actions which it plainly authorizes are invulnerable to constitutional attack under the Commerce Clause."[5]

The give-and-take between Congress and the judiciary is illustrated by the insurance cases. In 1869, the Supreme Court held that states could regulate insurance because it was not a "transaction of commerce." Paul v. Virginia, 8 Wall. 168. That holding, along with 150 years of precedents, was overturned in 1944 when the Court interpreted the transaction of insurance business across state lines as interstate commerce subject to congressional regulation. The Court said that Congress had not intended to exempt the insurance business from the Sherman Antitrust Act. United States v. South-Eastern Underwriters Assn., 322 U.S. 533 (1944). Congress quickly passed the McCarran Act, reversing the Court

---

4. Pennsylvania v. Wheeling &c. Bridge Co., 13 How. (54 U.S.) 518 (1852); 10 Stat. 112, § 6 (1852); Pennsylvania v. Wheeling and Belmont Bridge Co., 18 How. (59 U.S.) 421 (1856).

5. Northeast Bancorp v. Board of Governors, FRS, 472 U.S. 159, 174 (1985). In a concurrence in 1995, Justices Kennedy and O'Connor conceded that "if we invalidate a state law, Congress can in effect overturn our judgment." United States v. Lopez, 514 U.S. 549, 580 (1995). See also Julian N. Eule, "Laying the Dormant Commerce Clause to Rest," 91 Yale L. J. 425 (1982); William Cohen, "Congressional Power to Validate Unconstitutional State Laws: A Forgotten Solution to an Old Enigma," 35 Stan. L. Rev. 387 (1983).

May Congress Annul a Court Decision?

Mr. Justice McLEAN dissenting....

After a very tedious and minute investigation of the facts of the case, which embraced the reports of practical engineers, depositions from the most experienced river men, statements of the stages of water in the river throughout the year, and also after a full consideration of the legal principles applicable to the matter in controversy, six of the members of this tribunal, two only dissenting, were brought to the conclusion that the bridge was a material obstruction to the navigation of the river....

The decree in the Wheeling bridge case was the result of a judicial investigation, founded upon facts ascertained in the course of the hearing. It was strictly a judicial question. The complaint was an obstruction of commerce, by the bridge, to the injury of the complainant, and the court found the fact to be as alleged in the bill. It was said by Chief Justice Marshall, many years ago, that congress could do many things, but that it could not alter a fact. This it has attempted to do in the above act....

From the organization of the legislative power, it is unfitted for the discharge of judicial duties; and the same may be said of this court in regard to legislation. It may therefore happen, that, when either trenches upon the appropriate powers of the other, their acts are inoperative and void....

Mr. Justice GRIER....

I concur with my brother McLean, that congress cannot annul or vacate any decree of this court; that the assumption of such a power is without precedent, and, as a precedent for the future, it is of dangerous example.

Mr. Justice WAYNE....

... Whatever congress may have intended by the act of August, 1852, I do not think it admits of the interpretation given to it by the majority of the court; and if it does, then my opinion is that the act would be unconstitutional....

SOURCE: Pennsylvania v. Wheeling and Belmont Bridge Co., 18 How. (59 U.S.) 421, 437–40, 449, 450 (1856).

by authorizing states to regulate insurance. 59 Stat. 33 (1945). Acting under cover of this statute, states were once again allowed to regulate and tax the business of insurance. Prudential Ins. Co. v. Benjamin, 328 U.S. 408 (1946).

Antitrust Policy

In an effort to curb the concentration of economic power after the Civil War, Congress passed the Sherman Antitrust Act in 1890 to prohibit combinations and conspiracies that restrained trade. Through a series of rulings, the Supreme Court largely nullified the law's effectiveness. In 1895 the Court held that the Act did not apply to monopolies engaged in the *manufacture* of items necessary for life. Through this reasoning the Act exempted (by judicial fiat) the "Sugar Trust": the American Sugar Refining Company, which was incorporated in New Jersey and controlled about 98 percent of the sugar refining business in the country. The Court argued that manufacturing precedes commerce and is not part of it and that the power to regulate the manufacture of a "necessary of life" belongs to the police power of the states. The Court regarded the sugar monopoly's restraint on trade as "indirect," not direct. United States v. E.C. Knight Co., 156 U.S. 1 (1895).

The Court narrowly upheld the application of the Sherman Antitrust Act to holding companies that competing railroad companies had established to combine their forces and restrain interstate commerce. Northern Securities Co. v. United States, 193 U.S. 197 (1904). The Act was gravely weakened in 1911 when the Court adopted the "rule of reason" doctrine. Previously, the Court had applied the literal and strict language of the Act, which made no exceptions. It prohibited *every* contract, combination, or conspiracy in restraint of interstate or foreign trade. *Every* person engaged in such activity was guilty of a misdemeanor. Initially the Court refused to limit the Act to "unreasonable" restraints of trade. United States v. Trans-Missouri Freight Assn., 166 U.S. 290, 327–41 (1897); United

States v. Joint Traffic Assn., 171 U.S. 505, 573–78 (1898). If companies entered into contracts that restrained interstate or foreign commerce to any extent, Congress could nullify the contracts. Addyston Pipe & Steel Co. v. United States, 175 U.S. 211 (1899).

Matters changed abruptly in 1911 with the "rule of reason." The Sherman Act was judicially amended to prohibit only *unreasonable* or *undue* restraints. In a dissent, Justice Harlan condemned the use of judicial construction to amend the Constitution and rewrite statutes. Standard Oil Co. v. United States, 221 U.S. 1, 105 (1911); United States v. American Tobacco Co., 221 U.S. 106 (1911). Judgments of "reasonable" rates are now exercised by administrative agencies, not the judiciary. Moreover, the Court has long since abandoned the artificial separation between "manufacturing" and "commerce." Mandeville Farms v. Sugar Co., 334 U.S. 219, 229 (1948).

Gibbons v. Ogden

22 U.S. (9 Wheat.) 1 (1824)

New York granted to Robert R. Livingston and Robert Fulton the exclusive privilege to operate steamboats on all waters within the jurisdiction of the state. Other states enacted similar laws, and soon friction emerged as states required out-of-state boats to pay substantial fees to be admitted. The retaliation that resulted was similar to the commercial warfare among the states prior to the adoption of the Constitution. This case involved the issue of whether New York could require a steamboat operating between New York and New Jersey to secure a New York license. Was this within the power of a state or did it infringe on the commerce power given to Congress? Thomas Gibbons and Aaron Ogden had been partners, operating a steamboat between New Jersey and New York, but they became antagonists in this tangled suit.

March 2d, 1824. MARSHALL, Ch. J., ... The appellant contends, that this decree [*by New York*] is erroneous, because the laws which purport to give the exclusive privilege it sustains, are repugnant to ... that clause in the constitution which authorizes congress to regulate commerce [*and*] to that which authorizes congress to promote the progress of science and useful arts.

... [R]eference has been made to the political situation of these states, anterior to its formation. It has been said, that they were sovereign, were completely independent, and were connected with each other only by a league. This is true. But when these allied sovereigns converted their league into a government, when they converted their congress of ambassadors, deputed to deliberate on their common concerns, and to recommend measures of general utility, into a legislature, empowered to enact laws on the most interesting subjects, the whole character in which the states appear, underwent a change, the extent of which must be determined by a fair consideration of the instrument by which that change was effected.

This instrument contains an enumeration of powers expressly granted by the people to their government. It has been said, that these powers ought to be construed strictly. But why ought they to be so construed? Is there one sentence in the constitution

which gives countenance to this rule? In the last of the enumerated powers, that which grants, expressly, the means for carrying all others into execution, congress is authorized "to make all laws which shall be necessary and proper" for the purpose. But this limitation on the means which may be used, is not extended to the powers which are conferred; nor is there one sentence in the constitution, which has been pointed out by the gentlemen of the bar, or which we have been able to discern, that prescribes this rule. We do not, therefore, think ourselves justified in adopting it. What do gentlemen mean, by a strict construction? If they contend only against that enlarged construction, which would extend words beyond their natural and obvious import, we might question the application of the term, but should not controvert the principle. If they contend for that narrow construction which, in support of some theory not to be found in the constitution, would deny to the government those powers which the words of the grant, as usually understood, import, and which are consistent with the general views and objects of the instrument—for that narrow construction, which would cripple the government, and render it unequal to the objects for which it is declared to be instituted, and to which the powers given, as fairly understood, render it competent—then we cannot perceive the propriety of this strict construction, nor adopt it as the rule by which the constitution is to be expounded....

The words are, "congress shall have power to regulate commerce with foreign nations, and among the several states, and with the Indian tribes."

The subject to be regulated is commerce; and our constitution being, as was aptly said at the bar, one of enumeration, and not of definition, to ascertain the extent of the power, it becomes necessary to settle the meaning of the word. The counsel for the appellee would limit it to traffic, to buying and selling, or the interchange of commodities, and do not admit that it comprehends navigation. This would restrict a general term, applicable to many objects, to one of its significations. Commerce, undoubtedly, is traffic, but it is something more—it is intercourse. It describes the commercial intercourse between nations, and parts of nations, in all its branches, and is regulated by prescribing rules for carrying on that intercourse. The mind can scarcely conceive a system for regulating commerce between nations, which shall exclude all laws concerning navigation, which shall be silent on the admission of the vessels of the one nation into the ports of the other.... All America understands, and has uniformly understood, the word "commerce," to comprehend navigation. It was so understood, and must have been so understood, when the constitution was framed. The power over commerce, including navigation, was one of the primary objects for which the people of America adopted their government, and must have been contemplated in forming it. The convention must have used the word in that sense, because all have understood it in that sense; and the attempt to restrict it comes too late.

If the opinion that "commerce," as the word is used in the constitution, comprehends navigation also, requires any additional confirmation, that additional confirmation is, we think, furnished by the words of the instrument itself.... The 9th section of the last article declares, that "no preference shall be given, by any regulation of commerce or revenue, to the ports of one state over those of another." This clause cannot be understood as applicable to those laws only which are passed for the purposes of revenue, because it is expressly applied to commercial regulations; and the most obvious preference which can be given to one port over another, in regulating commerce, relates to navigation. But the subsequent part of the sentence is still more explicit. It is, "nor shall vessels bound to or from one state, be obliged to enter, clear or pay duties in another." These words have a direct reference to navigation.

The universally acknowledged power of the government to impose embargoes, must also be considered as showing, that all America is united in that construction which comprehends navigation in the word commerce. Gentlemen have said, in argument, that this is a branch of the war-making power, and that an embargo is an instrument of war, not a regulation of trade. That it may be, and often is, used as an instrument of war, cannot be denied.... But all embargoes are not of this description.... When congress imposed that embargo which, for a time, engaged the attention of every man in the United States, the avowed object of the law was, the protection of commerce, and the avoiding of war. By its friends and its enemies, it was treated as a commercial, not as a war measure....

The word used in the constitution, then, comprehends, and has been always understood to comprehend, navigation within its meaning; and a power to regulate navigation, is as expressly granted, as if that term had been added to the word "commerce."

To what commerce does this power extend? The constitution informs us, to commerce "with foreign nations, and among the several states, and with the Indian tribes."

It has, we believe, been universally admitted, that these words comprehend every species of commercial intercourse between the United States and foreign nations. No sort of trade can be carried on between this country and any other, to which this power does not extend. It has been truly said, that commerce, as the word is used in the constitution, is a unit, every part of which is indicated by the term.

If this be the admitted meaning of the word, in its application to foreign nations, it must carry the same meaning throughout the sentence, and remain a unit, unless there be some plain intelligible cause which alters it.

The subject to which the power is next applied, is to commerce, "among the several states." The word "among" means intermingled with. A thing which is among others, is intermingled with them. Commerce among the states, cannot stop at the external boundary line of each state, but may be introduced into the interior.

... [I]n regulating commerce with foreign nations, the power of congress does not stop at the jurisdictional lines of the several states. It would be a very useless power, if it could not pass those lines. The commerce of the United States with foreign nations, is that of the whole United States; every district has a right to participate in it. The deep streams which penetrate our country in every direction, pass through the interior of almost every state in the Union, and furnish the means of exercising this right.

If congress has the power to regulate it, that power must be exercised whenever the subject exists. If it exists within the states, if a foreign voyage may commence or terminate at a port within a state, then the power of congress may be exercised within a state.

... Commerce among the states must, of necessity, be commerce with the states....

We are now arrived at the inquiry—what is this power?

It is the power to regulate; that is, to prescribe the rule by which commerce is to be governed. This power, like all others vested in congress, is complete in itself, may be exercised to its utmost extent, and acknowledges no limitations, other than are prescribed in the constitution. These are expressed in plain terms, and do not affect the questions which arise in this case, or which have been discussed at the bar....

The power of congress, then, comprehends navigation, within the limits of every state in the Union; so far as that navigation may be, in any manner, connected with "commerce with foreign nations, or among the several states, or with the Indian tribes." It may, of consequence, pass the jurisdictional line of New York, and act upon the very waters to which the prohibition now under consideration applies.

[Marshall concludes that the licenses for the steamboats operated by Gibbons, which were granted under an act of Congress, gave full authority to those vessels to navigate the waters of the United States, notwithstanding any law of New York to the contrary. Conflicting New York laws were unconstitutional and void.]

Powerful and ingenious minds, taking, as postulates, that the powers expressly granted to the government of the Union, are to be contracted, by construction, into the narrowest possible compass, and that the original powers of the states are retained, if any possible construction will retain them, may, by a course of well-digested, but refined and metaphysical reasoning, founded on these premises, explain away the constitution of our country, and leave it, a magnificent structure, indeed, to look at, but totally unfit for use.

JOHNSON, Justice.—The judgment entered by the court in this cause, has my entire approbation; but having adopted my conclusions on views of the subject materially different from those of my brethren, I feel it incumbent on me to exhibit those views....

The "power to regulate commerce" here meant to be granted was that power to regulate commerce which previously existed in the States. But what was that power? The States were unquestionably supreme, and each possessed that power over commerce which is acknowledged to reside in every sovereign State. The definition and limits of that power are to be sought among the features of international law, and, as it was not only admitted but insisted on by both parties in argument that, "unaffected by a state of war, by treaties, or by municipal regulations, all commerce among independent States was legitimate," there is no necessity to appeal to the oracles of the *jus commune* for the correctness of that doctrine. The law of nations, regarding man as a social animal, pronounces all commerce legitimate in a state of peace until prohibited by positive law. The power of a sovereign state over commerce therefore amounts to nothing more than a power to limit and restrain it at pleasure. And since the power to prescribe the limits to its freedom necessarily implies the power to determine what shall remain unrestrained, it follows that the power must be exclusive; it can reside but in one potentate, and hence the grant of this power carries with it the whole subject, leaving nothing for the State to act upon....

When speaking of the power of Congress over navigation, I do not regard it as a power incidental to that of regulating commerce; I consider it as the thing itself, inseparable from it as vital motion is from vital existence.

Cooley v. Board of Wardens

53 U.S. 299 (1852)

A Pennsylvania law provided that all vessels of a certain description coming into state port should employ pilots to assure safety. If they refused they were required to pay a pilotage fee. Aaron Cooley argued that the state law was a regulation of foreign commerce and therefore an action solely within the authority of Congress, which had passed legislation in 1789 regarding the regulation of ports. Was this area of commerce within the exclusive domain of Congress, or could states exercise concurrent jurisdiction? Did foreign commerce demand uniformity or permit local diversity?

Mr. Justice CURTIS delivered the opinion of the court.

. . .

We think this particular regulation concerning half-pilotage fees, is an appropriate part of a general system of regulations of this subject. Testing it by the practice of commercial States and countries legislating on this subject, we find it has usually been deemed necessary to make similar provisions. Numerous laws of this kind are cited in the learned argument of the counsel for the defendant in error; and their fitness, as a part of a system of pilotage, in many places, may be inferred from their existence in so many different States and countries. Like other laws they are framed to meet the most usual cases, *quœ frequentius accidunt;* they rest upon the propriety of securing lives and property exposed to the perils of a dangerous navigation, by taking on board a person peculiarly skilled to encounter or avoid them; …

That the power to regulate commerce includes the regulation of navigation, we consider settled. And when we look to the nature of the service performed by pilots, to the relations which that service and its compensations bear to navigation between the several States, and between the ports of the United States and foreign countries, we are brought to the conclusion, that the regulation of the qualifications of pilots, of the modes and times of offering and rendering their services, of the responsibilities which shall rest upon them, of the powers they shall possess, of the compensation they may demand, and of the penalties by which their rights and duties may be enforced, do constitute regulations of navigation, and consequently of commerce, within the just meaning of this clause of the Constitution.

. . .

It becomes necessary, therefore, to consider whether this law of Pennsylvania, being a regulation of commerce, is valid.

The act of Congress of the 7th of August, 1789, sect. 4, is as follows:

"That all pilots in the bays, inlets, rivers, harbors, and ports of the United States shall continue to be regulated in conformity with the existing laws of the States, respectively, wherein such pilots may be, or with such laws as the States may respectively hereafter enact for the purpose, until further legislative provision shall be made by Congress."

If the law of Pennsylvania, now in question, had been in existence at the date of this act of Congress, we might hold it to have been adopted by Congress, and thus made a law of the United States, and so valid. Because this act does, in effect, give the force of an act of Congress, to the then existing State laws on this subject, so long as they should continue unrepealed by the State which enacted them.

But the law on which these actions are founded was not enacted till 1803. What effect then can be attributed to so much of the act of 1789, as declares, that pilots shall continue to be regulated in conformity, "with such laws as the States may respectively hereafter enact for the purpose, until further legislative provision shall be made by Congress"?

. . .

It is the opinion of a majority of the court that the mere grant to Congress of the power to regulate commerce, did not deprive the States of power to regulate pilots, and that although Congress has legislated on this subject, its legislation manifests an intention, with a single exception, not to regulate this subject, but to leave its regulation to the several States. …

We are of opinion that this State law was enacted by virtue of a power, residing in the State to legislate; that it is not in conflict with any law of Congress; that it does not interfere with any system which Congress has established by making regulations, or by intentionally leaving individuals to their own unrestricted action; that this law is therefore valid, and the judgment of the Supreme Court of Pennsylvania in each case must be affirmed.

Mr. Justice McLean and Mr. Justice Wayne dissented; and Mr. Justice Daniel, although he concurred in the judgment of the court, yet dissented from its reasoning.

Mr. Justice McLEAN.

It is with regret that I feel myself obliged to dissent from the opinion of a majority of my brethren in this case.

. . .

Why did Congress pass the act of 1789, adopting the pilot-laws of the respective States? Laws they unquestionably were, having been enacted by the States before the adoption of the Constitution. …

Congress adopted the pilot-laws of the States, because it was well understood, they could have had no force, as regulations of foreign commerce or of commerce among the States, if not so adopted. By their adoption they were made acts of Congress, and ever since they have been so considered and enforced.

Each State regulates the commerce within its limits; which is not within the range of federal powers. So far, and no farther could effect have been given to the pilot laws of the States, under the Constitution. But those laws were only adopted "until further legislative provisions shall be made by Congress."

This shows that Congress claimed the whole commercial power on this subject, by adopting the pilot laws of the States, making them acts of Congress; ...

I think the charge of half-pilotage is correct under the circumstances, and I only object to the power of the State to pass the law. Congress, to whom the subject peculiarly belongs, should have been applied to, and no doubt it would have adopted the act of the State.

Mr. Justice DANIEL.

... The true question here is, whether the power to enact pilot-laws is appropriate and necessary, or rather most appropriate and necessary to the State or the federal governments. It being conceded that this power has been exercised by the States from their very dawn of existence; that it can be practically and beneficially applied by the local authorities only; it being conceded, as it must be, that the power to pass pilot-laws, as such, has not been in any express terms delegated to Congress, and does not necessarily conflict with the right to establish commercial regulations, I am forced to conclude that this is an original and inherent power in the States, and not one to be merely tolerated, or held subject to the sanction of the federal government.

. . .

Congress Overturns *Leisy v. Hardin*

In *Leisy* v. *Hardin,* 135 U.S. 100 (1890), the Supreme Court held that an Iowa law violated the Commerce Clause by prohibiting the sale of intoxicating liquors except for pharmaceutical, medicinal, chemical, or sacramental purposes. The law applied to "original packages" or kegs, unbroken and unopened, from the importer. Under the decision, based on Chief Justice Marshall's decision in *Brown* v. *Maryland* (1827), states were forbidden from regulating commerce between the states "without congressional permission." Within a matter of months, Congress passed legislation to override the Court. Portions of the Senate debate are reproduced here (21 Cong. Rec. 4642, 4954–55, 4964) as well as the statute (26 Stat. 313). The statute was upheld in *In re Rahrer,* 140 U.S. 545 (1891).

Mr. WILSON, of Iowa. From the Committee on the Judiciary I report favorably, with an amendment, the bill (S. 398) subjecting imported liquors to the provisions of the laws of the several States....

Mr. HOAR. I desire to make a brief statement in regard to the matter. This bill is rendered necessary, in the opinion of the committee, by the late decision of the Supreme Court of the United States, which holds, as I understand it, that intoxicating liquor manufactured in one State, conveyed into another, and there sold by the manufacturer or his agent, is protected by the Constitution of the United States from any regulation or prohibition of that sale by the State law on the ground that such prohibition or regulation is an interference with the regulation of commerce between the States. The court, in their opinion, say that the States can not pass such prohibitory or regulating statutes without the permission of Congress, which is understood to imply an opinion on the part of the court that Congress may give that permission, and that with that permission

the States may pass the regulation or prohibitory enactment which they see fit.

. . .

[Mr. WILSON, of Iowa.]

... Mr. President, that State, which I in part represent in this body, elected as its policy the prohibition of the manufacture and sale of intoxicating liquors. The people of the State are satisfied with it; they desire the enforcement of their law; but, since the decision from which I have read an extract was announced, agents of distilleries and breweries in other States of the Union are already traversing Iowa and organizing "the original-package saloon" within the State, and there is no limitation as to what "the original package" may be. It may be a pint or a half-pint bottle of whisky; it may be a bottle or a keg of beer; it may be in any quantity and whatsoever form of package agreed upon between the manufacturer of another State and the agent that he may send to transact his business in Iowa.

All the States of this Union do not want prohibition. Some of them want license; some of them want local option; they have various desires in this respect. Some of them may want unrestrained traffic in the sale of intoxicants. The State of Iowa does not want that. She wants her present policy; at least, she should have an opportunity to administer it until her people determine to adopt something else in its place; and so with all the States.

Mr. BUTLER. The Senator from Iowa will allow me to interrupt him for an inquiry.

Mr. WILSON, of Iowa. Certainly.

Mr. BUTLER. Does the Senator hold that under the decision of the Supreme Court the State of Iowa would have the right, after the package gets into that State, to prevent the sale or take control of it in any way after it crosses the line?

Mr. WILSON, of Iowa. Undoubtedly the decision of the Supreme Court protects every package that may be transported into that State from abroad, from foreign countries or from other States, until it shall have passed from the hands of the importer and thereby become mingled with the common property of the State.

Mr. BUTLER. Then the State has the right to interpose by its laws and prevent the sale or any disposition of the article imported?

Mr. WILSON, of Iowa. After it shall have passed from the hands of the importer or his agent. But under this decision, whatever package may be introduced there—for instance, the brewer in Illinois, the distiller in Illinois or any other State may arrange to send his package in there, even in the shape of a vial containing a single drink, and organize his saloon on that basis, the importer holding possession, protected by the decision of the Supreme Court, until that package shall pass from his possession into the hands of his customer and that customer may drink a single drink of whisky in that original-package saloon in the good State of Iowa, and in spite of her laws.

. . .

Mr. EDMUNDS....

Now, let us begin with the Supreme Court. The Supreme Court of the United States is an independent and co-ordinate branch of the Government. Its mission is to decide causes between parties, and its decision of causes between parties all good order and government require shall be carried out and respected as between parties. But, as it regards the Congress of the United States, its opinions are of no more value to us than ours are to it. We are just as in-dependent of the Supreme Court of the United States as it is of us, and every judge will admit it.

Suppose we think that this court has gone wrong and has made a mistake in deciding a given case between A and B that involves the safety and happiness of all the people of the United States in their respective States covering a continent, and that an internal policy may be good for the Pacific coast and bad for a State on the Atlantic coast, are we to stop and say that is the end of the law and the mission of civilization in the United States for that reason? I take it not. It may be that when the next case comes up on a further and wider consideration the very gentlemen who now compose the court, differing as some of them did with the majority, may come to the conclusion that they had been led into an error and that they may still hold that the States of the United States in respect of what shall be done in those States and not among them is a matter that the Constitution leaves to those States to regulate as they will.

So I do not feel absolutely condemned and over-persuaded and feel myself as put in a box by what the Supreme Court of the United States have so recently said. It is their mission to decide causes between parties as they think they ought to be decided; and, as they have often done, it may be their mission next year to change their opinion and say that the rule ought to be the other way. So I do not feel deeply embarrassed by the fact that the Supreme Court of the United States has taken the largest step that in the whole hundred years of the Republic has ever been taken toward the centralization of power somewhere, either in the Supreme Court or in Congress, one or the other.

I do not believe, for one, in the centralization of power. I believe in its segregation and separation in every respect that concerns the internal affairs of the body of the people in every one of the States, leaving out of the question those universal human rights that everybody agrees are intrinsic in man and citizen.

So I am not greatly disturbed in respect of what the Supreme Court of the United States have said and done, except so far as it makes it now the mission of Congress to exert its power upon the subjects according to the light that it thought it had shone upon it, in order to preserve the internal policy and police of every State for itself, whether you call it an independent right or the execution of a national power under agencies that Congress provides, whichever way you choose to state it.

[Statute (26 Stat. 313)]:

Be it enacted by the Senate and House of Representatives of the United States of America in Congress as-

sembled, That all fermented, distilled, or other intoxicating liquors or liquids transported into any State or Territory or remaining therein for use, consumption, sale or storage therein, shall upon arrival in such State or Territory be subject to the operation and effect of the laws of such State or Territory enacted in the exercise of its police powers, to the same extent and in the same manner as though such liquids or liquors had been produced in such State or Territory, and shall not be exempt therefrom by reason of being introduced therein in original packages or otherwise.

Approved, August 8, 1890.

C. NATIONALIZATION OF THE ECONOMY

Fundamental changes in economic structures after the Civil War gradually washed away many traditional boundaries between intrastate and interstate commerce. Judicial doctrines of dual federalism and concurrent powers lost ground to a gradual centralization of authority in the national government.

In 1886, the Supreme Court struck down an Illinois railroad statute because it affected, even for the part of the journey within the state, commerce among the states. Wabash, &c., Railway Co. v. Illinois, 118 U.S. 557 (1886). This decision made national regulation imperative, and Congress responded a year later by creating the Interstate Commerce Commission. Another decision allowed Congress to prohibit national and interstate traffic in lottery tickets even if its motivation—such as morality—competed with the state police power. CHAMPION v. AMES (Lottery Case), 188 U.S. 321 (1903). Two years later, a unanimous Court upheld a congressional statute that prevented a company from restraining trade even when the company's cattle came to rest within a stockyard of a particular state. The movement of cattle from state to state created a "current of commerce" subject to congressional control. Swift & Co. v. United States, 196 U.S. 375, 399 (1905). In later years, the Court evoked a similar image, calling the stockyards a temporary resting place for cattle moving interstate, serving as "a throat through which the current of commerce flows." Stafford v. Wallace, 258 U.S. 495, 516 (1922).

These decisions supported congressional regulation only in selected areas: railroads, morals, and health. For example, in 1914 the Supreme Court rejected artificial distinctions between *intrastate* and *interstate* by holding that Congress could regulate actions inside a state that were *related* to interstate commerce. Through this reasoning, it allowed a congressional commission to set railroad rates within a state. Shreveport Rate Case, 234 U.S. 342 (1914). Under the Commerce Clause, Congress could establish an eight-hour day for all railroad workers engaged in interstate commerce, especially when needed to resolve a nationwide strike. Wilson v. New, 243 U.S. 332 (1917). Other decisions upheld the power of Congress to seize and condemn prohibited articles, to forbid the interstate transportation of women engaged in prostitution, and to make it a crime to transport stolen motor vehicles in interstate or foreign commerce.[6] During time of war, many commercial operations normally regulated by the states fall within the domain of the national government.[7]

Child Labor Legislation

This pattern of sustaining congressional power did not apply to factory conditions, hours, or wages. In 1916 Congress passed legislation to prevent the products of child labor from being shipped interstate. Legislators concluded that the bill was constitutional and consistent with recent Supreme Court rulings that permitted Congress to use the Commerce Clause to regulate public health and morals.

---

6. Hipolite Egg Co. v. United States, 220 U.S. 45 (1911) (seizing and condemning articles); Hoke v. United States, 227 U.S. 308 (1913) and Caminetti v. United States, 242 U.S. 470 (1917) (White Slave Traffic Act); Brooks v. United States, 267 U.S. 432 (1925) (stolen cars). See also Atlantic Coast Line v. Riverside Mills, 219 U.S. 186 (1911).

7. Case v. Bowles, 327 U.S. 92, 102 (1946); Dakota Cent. Tel. Co. v. South Dakota, 250 U.S. 163 (1919); Northern Pac. Ry. Co. v. North Dakota, 250 U.S. 135 (1919).

Solicitor General Beck Defends Child Labor Bill

The belief that the judiciary is fully empowered to sit in judgment upon the motives or objectives of other branches of the Government is a mischievous one, in that it so lowers the sense of constitutional morality among the people that neither in the legislative branch of the Government nor among the people is there as strong a purpose as formerly to maintain their constitution form of Government.

. . .

The erroneous idea that this court is the sole guardian and protector of our constitutional form of government has inevitably led to an impairment, both with the people and with their representatives, of what may be called the constitutional conscience.

... The prevalent disposition seems to be to ignore constitutional questions by shifting them to the Supreme Court, in the belief that that court will exercise the full powers of revision, which I have tried to show the Framers of the Constitution did not intend this court to have. The result may be an exaltation of this court, as a tribunal of extraordinary power; but, in the matter of constitutionalism, it inevitably leads to an impairment of the powers and duties of Congress and, above all, to the impairment of the popular conscience; for, in the last analysis, the Constitution will last in substance as long as the people believe in it and are willing to struggle for it.

SOURCE: Brief on Behalf of Appellants and Plaintiff in Error, Bailey v. Drexel Furniture Co., Nos. 590, 657, U.S. Supreme Court, October Term, 1921, at 54–55; 21 Landmark Briefs 59–60.

However, the Court held that the law exceeded the commerce power and invaded responsibilities left to the states. HAMMER v. DAGENHART, 247 U.S. 251 (1918). Within a matter of days, members of Congress confronted the Court by introducing new measures to regulate child labor. 56 Cong. Rec. 8341 (1918). The strategy this time was to use the taxing power by levying an excise tax on the net profits of persons employing child labor. Id. at 11560. Some members of Congress thought that the Court's decision had settled the issue and that Congress had no business reopening it. Senator Henry Cabot Lodge (R-Mass.), a leading conservative, denied that another legislative attempt at ending the "great evil" of child labor was inappropriate. 57 Cong. Rec. 611 (1918).

When this statute was brought before the Supreme Court, Solicitor General James M. Beck prepared a brief that defended the tax. He also urged the Court to exercise political prudence when reviewing, and possibly overturning, the considered efforts of the coequal branches, Congress and the President (see box). Nevertheless, the Court struck down this second statute as well. BAILEY v. DREXEL FURNITURE CO. [Child Labor Tax Case], 259 U.S. 20 (1922). Not until 1941, after the composition of the Court had been drastically altered and restrictive judicial doctrines abandoned, was child labor legislation upheld. UNITED STATES v. DARBY, 312 U.S. 100 (1941).

Judicial efforts to curb other economic reforms adopted by Congress and the states are treated in Chapter 9. Courts restricted state use of the "police power," relied on a fictional "liberty of contract" to invalidate other statutes, and used substantive due process to strike down legislative efforts to establish maximum hours and minimum wages. These judicial doctrines came to an end in 1937.

Champion v. Ames (Lottery Case)

188 U.S. 321 (1903)

Many of the states tried to suppress the buying and selling of lottery tickets but found themselves helpless in controlling lotteries in interstate commerce. Congress passed legislation in 1895 to prohibit lottery tickets from interstate or foreign commerce. Charles Champion was charged with violating the act. The Court confronted three principal issues. Is the selling of lottery tickets subject to regulation under the Commerce Clause? Does the power to regulate commerce include the authority to prohibit it? May Congress exercise a national "police power" to protect citizens from immoral transactions, or is that responsibility reserved to the states?

MR. JUSTICE HARLAN, after making the foregoing statement of facts, delivered the opinion of the court.

The appellant insists that the carrying of lottery tickets from one State to another State by an express company engaged in carrying freight and packages from State to State, although such tickets may be contained in a box or package, does not constitute, and cannot by any act of Congress be legally made to constitute, *commerce* among the States within the meaning of the clause of the Constitution of the United States providing that Congress shall have power "to regulate commerce with foreign nations, and among the several States, and with the Indian tribes;" consequently, that Congress cannot make it an offence to cause such tickets to be carried from one State to another.

. . .

It was said in argument that lottery tickets are not of any real or substantial value in themselves, and therefore are not subjects of commerce. If that were conceded to be the only legal test as to what are to be deemed subjects of the commerce that may be regulated by Congress, we cannot accept as accurate the broad statement that such tickets are of no value. Upon their face they showed that the lottery company offered a large capital prize, to be paid to the holder of the ticket winning the prize at the drawing advertised to be held at Asuncion, Paraguay. Money was placed on deposit in different banks in the United States to be applied by the agents representing the lottery company to the prompt payment of prizes. These tickets were the subject of traffic; they could have been sold; and the holder was assured that the company would pay to him the amount of the prize drawn.…

We are of opinion that lottery tickets are subjects of traffic and therefore are subjects of commerce, and the regulation of the carriage of such tickets from State to State, at least by independent carriers, is a regulation of commerce among the several States.

But it is said that the statute in question does not regulate the carrying of lottery tickets from State to State, but by punishing those who cause them to be so carried Congress in effect prohibits such carrying; that in respect of the carrying from one State to another of articles or things that are, in fact, or according to usage in business, the subjects of commerce, the authority given Congress was not to *prohibit*, but only to *regulate.*…

… Are we prepared to say that a provision which is, in effect, a *prohibition* of the carriage of such articles from State to State is not a fit or appropriate mode for the *regulation* of that particular kind of commerce? If lottery traffic, *carried on through interstate commerce,* is a matter of which Congress may take cognizance and over which its power may be exerted, can it be possible that it must tolerate the traffic, and simply regulate the manner in which it may be carried on? Or may not Congress, for the protection of the people of all the States, and under the power to regulate interstate commerce, devise such means, within the scope of the Constitution, and not prohibited by it, as will drive that traffic out of commerce among the States?

. . .

If a State, when considering legislation for the suppression of lotteries within its own limits, may properly take into view the evils that inhere in the raising of money, in that mode, why may not Congress, invested with the power to regulate commerce among the several States, provide that such commerce shall not be polluted by the carrying of lottery tickets from one State to another? In this connection it must not be forgotten that the power of Congress to regulate commerce among the States is plenary, is complete in itself, and is subject to no limitations except such as may be found in the Constitution. What provision in that instrument can be regarded as limiting the exercise of the power granted? What clause can be cited which, in any degree, countenances the suggestion that one may, of right, carry or cause to be carried from one State to another that which will harm the public morals? *[The Court dismisses the argument that the constitutional provision that no person shall be deprived of liberty without due process of law implies the right to introduce into commerce an article that is injurious to the public morals.]*

If it be said that the act of 1895 is inconsistent with the Tenth Amendment, reserving to the States respectively or to the people the powers not delegated to the United States, the answer is that the power to regulate commerce among the States has been expressly delegated to Congress.

Besides, Congress, by that act, does not assume to interfere with traffic or commerce in lottery tickets carried on exclusively within the limits of any State, but has in view only commerce of that kind among the several States. It has not assumed to interfere with the completely internal affairs of any State, and has only legislated in respect of a matter which concerns the people of the United States....

... We decide nothing more in the present case than that lottery tickets are subjects of traffic among those who choose to sell or buy them; that the carriage of such tickets by independent carriers from one State to another is therefore interstate commerce; that under its power to regulate commerce among the several States Congress—subject to the limitations imposed by the Constitution upon the exercise of the powers granted—has plenary authority over such commerce, and may prohibit the carriage of such tickets from State to State; and that legislation to that end, and of that character, is not inconsistent with any limitation or restriction imposed upon the exercise of the powers granted to Congress.

The judgment is

Affirmed.

Mr. Chief Justice Fuller, with whom concur Mr. Justice Brewer, Mr. Justice Shiras and Mr. Justice Peckham, dissenting.

. . .

The power of the State to impose restraints and burdens on persons and property in conservation and promotion of the public health, good order and prosperity is a power originally and always belonging to the States, not surrendered by them to the General Government nor directly restrained by the Constitution of the United States, and essentially exclusive, and the suppression of lotteries as a harmful business falls within this power, commonly called of police. *Douglas* v. *Kentucky,* 168 U.S. 488.

It is urged, however, that because Congress is empowered to regulate commerce between the several States, it, therefore, may suppress lotteries by prohibiting the carriage of lottery matter. Congress may indeed make all laws necessary and proper for carrying the powers granted to it into execution, and doubtless an act prohibiting the carriage of lottery matter would be necessary and proper to the execution of a power to suppress lotteries; but that power belongs to the States and not to Congress. To hold that Congress has general police power would be to hold that it may accomplish objects not entrusted to the General Government, and to defeat the operation of the Tenth Amendment, declaring that: "The powers not delegated to the United States by the Constitution, nor prohibited by it to the States, are reserved to the States respectively, or to the people."

. . .

Hammer v. Dagenhart

247 U.S. 251 (1918)

In 1916, Congress passed legislation to prohibit the transportation in interstate commerce of goods made at a factory where children under the age of 14 years worked, or children between the ages of 14 and 16 worked more than eight hours a day, or more than six days a week, or after 7p.m. or before 6a.m. Roland H. Dagenhart filed this suit on his own behalf and for his two minor sons who were employed in a cotton mill. After a district court declared the statute unconstitutional, the U.S. Attorney, W.C. Hammer, brought an appeal to the Supreme Court.

Mr. Justice Day delivered the opinion of the court.

. . .

The attack upon the act rests upon three propositions: First: It is not a regulation of interstate and foreign commerce; Second: It contravenes the Tenth Amendment to the Constitution; Third: It conflicts with the Fifth Amendment to the Constitution.

The controlling question for decision is: Is it within the authority of Congress in regulating commerce among the States to prohibit the transporta-

tion in interstate commerce of manufactured goods, the product of a factory in which, within thirty days prior to their removal therefrom, children ... have been employed....

The power essential to the passage of this act, the Government contends, is found in the commerce clause of the Constitution which authorizes Congress to regulate commerce with foreign nations and among the States.

In *Gibbons* v. *Ogden,* 9 Wheat. 1, Chief Justice Marshall, speaking for this court, and defining the extent and nature of the commerce power, said, "It is the power to regulate; that is, to prescribe the rule by which commerce is to be governed." In other words, the power is one to control the means by which commerce is carried on, which is directly the contrary of the assumed right to forbid commerce from moving and thus destroy it as to particular commodities. But it is insisted that adjudged cases in this court establish the doctrine that the power to regulate given to Congress incidentally includes the authority to prohibit the movement of ordinary commodities and therefore that the subject is not open for discussion. The cases demonstrate the contrary. They rest upon the character of the particular subjects dealt with and the fact that the scope of governmental authority, state or national, possessed over them is such that the authority to prohibit is as to them but the exertion of the power to regulate.

The first of these cases is *Champion* v. *Ames,* 188 U.S. 321, the so-called *Lottery Case,* in which it was held that Congress might pass a law having the effect to keep the channels of commerce free from use in the transportation of tickets used in the promotion of lottery schemes. In *Hipolite Egg Co.* v. *United States,* 220 U.S. 45, this court sustained the power of Congress to pass the Pure Food and Drug Act which prohibited the introduction into the States by means of interstate commerce of impure foods and drugs. In *Hoke* v. *United States,* 227 U.S. 308, this court sustained the constitutionality of the so-called "White Slave Traffic Act" whereby the transportation of a woman in interstate commerce for the purpose of prostitution was forbidden....

In each of these instances the use of interstate transportation was necessary to the accomplishment of harmful results. In other words, although the power over interstate transportation was to regulate, that could only be accomplished by prohibiting the use of the facilities of interstate commerce to effect the evil intended.

This element is wanting in the present case. The thing intended to be accomplished by this statute is the denial of the facilities of interstate commerce to those manufacturers in the States who employ children within the prohibited ages. The act in its effect does not regulate transportation among the States, but aims to standardize the ages at which children may be employed in mining and manufacturing within the States. The goods shipped are of themselves harmless....

The grant of power to Congress over the subject of interstate commerce was to enable it to regulate such commerce, and not to give it authority to control the States in their exercise of the police power over local trade and manufacture.

The grant of authority over a purely federal matter was not intended to destroy the local power always existing and carefully reserved to the States in the Tenth Amendment to the Constitution.

. . .

In our view the necessary effect of this act is, by means of a prohibition against the movement in interstate commerce of ordinary commercial commodities, to regulate the hours of labor of children in factories and mines within the States, a purely state authority. Thus the act in a twofold sense is repugnant to the Constitution. It not only transcends the authority delegated to Congress over commerce but also exerts a power as to a purely local matter to which the federal authority does not extend. The far reaching result of upholding the act cannot be more plainly indicated than by pointing out that if Congress can thus regulate matters entrusted to local authority by prohibition of the movement of commodities in interstate commerce, all freedom of commerce will be at an end, and the power of the States over local matters may be eliminated, and thus our system of government be practically destroyed.

For these reasons we hold that this law exceeds the constitutional authority of Congress. It follows that the decree of the District Court must be

Affirmed.

Mr. Justice Holmes, dissenting.

… The objection urged against the power*[of Congress]* is that the States have exclusive control over their methods of production and that Congress cannot meddle with them, and taking the proposition in the sense of direct intermeddling I agree to it and suppose that no one denies it. But if an act is within the powers specifically conferred upon Congress, it seems to me that it is not made any less constitutional because of the indirect effects that it may have, however obvious it may be that it will have those effects, and that we are not at liberty upon such grounds to hold it void.

The first step in my argument is to make plain what no one is likely to dispute—that the statute in question is within the power expressly given to Congress if considered only as to its immediate effects and that if invalid it is so only upon some collateral ground. The statute confines itself to prohibiting the carriage of certain goods in interstate or foreign commerce. Congress is given power to regulate such commerce in unqualified terms. It would not be argued today that the power to regulate does not include the power to prohibit....

The question then is narrowed to whether the exercise of its otherwise constitutional power by Congress can be pronounced unconstitutional because of its possible reaction upon the conduct of the States in a matter upon which I have admitted that they are free from direct control....

The notion that prohibition is any less prohibition when applied to things now thought evil I do not understand. But if there is any matter upon which civilized countries have agreed — far more unanimously than they have with regard to intoxicants and some other matters over which this country is now emotionally aroused — it is the evil of premature and excessive child labor. I should have thought that if we were to introduce our own moral conceptions where in my opinion they do not belong, this was preëminently a case for upholding the exercise of all its powers by the United States.

But I had thought that the propriety of the exercise of a power admitted to exist in some cases was for the consideration of Congress alone and that this Court always had disavowed the right to intrude its judgment upon questions of policy or morals. It is not for this Court to pronounce when prohibition is necessary to regulation if it ever may be necessary — to say that it is permissible as against strong drink but not as against the product of ruined lives.

The act does not meddle with anything belonging to the States. They may regulate their internal affairs and their domestic commerce as they like. But when they seek to send their products across the state line they are no longer within their rights. If there were no Constitution and no Congress their power to cross the line would depend upon their neighbors. Under the Constitution such commerce belongs not to the States but to Congress to regulate. It may carry out its views of public policy whatever indirect effect they may have upon the activities of the States....

Mr. Justice McKenna, Mr. Justice Brandeis and Mr. Justice Clarke concur in this opinion.

Bailey v. Drexel Furniture Co. (Child Labor Tax Case)

259 U.S. 20 (1922)

After the Supreme Court in *Hammer* v. *Dagenhart* (1918) struck down the attempt by Congress to use the Commerce Clause to regulate child labor, Congress passed legislation in 1919 to levy a tax on goods produced by child labor. The Court in this case reviews the power of Congress to use its taxing power as a regulatory device to eliminate the evils of child labor. J.W. Bailey, an IRS collector, assessed the Drexel Furniture Company $6,312.79 for employing a boy under the age of 14 during the 1919 tax year.

Mr. Chief Justice Taft delivered the opinion of the court.

This case presents the question of the constitutional validity of the Child Labor Tax Law....

The law is attacked on the ground that it is a regulation of the employment of child labor in the States — an exclusively state function under the Federal Constitution and within the reservations of the Tenth Amendment. It is defended on the ground that it is a mere excise tax levied by the Congress of the United States under its broad power of taxation conferred by § 8, Article I, of the Federal Constitution....

... If it were an excise on a commodity or other thing of value we might not be permitted under previous decisions of this court to infer solely from its heavy burden that the act intends a prohibition instead of a tax. But this act is more. It provides a heavy exaction for a departure from a detailed and specified course of conduct in business. That course of business is that employers shall employ in mines and quarries, children of an age greater than sixteen years; in mills and factories, children of an age greater than fourteen years, and shall prevent children of less than sixteen years in mills and factories from working more than eight hours a day or six days in the week. If an employer departs from this prescribed course of business, he is to pay to the Government one-tenth of his entire net income in the business for a full year....

... In the light of these features of the act, a court must be blind not to see that the so-called tax is imposed to stop the employment of children within the age limits prescribed. Its prohibitory and regulatory effect and purpose are palpable. All others can see and understand this. How can we properly shut our minds to it?

It is the high duty and function of this court in cases regularly brought to its bar to decline to recognize or enforce seeming laws of Congress, dealing with subjects not entrusted to Congress but left or committed by the supreme law of the land to the control of the States. We can not avoid the duty even though it require us to refuse to give effect to legislation designed to promote the highest good. The good sought in unconstitutional legislation is an insidious feature because it leads citizens and legislators of good purpose to promote it without thought of the serious breach it will make in the ark of our covenant or the harm which will come from breaking down recognized standards. In the maintenance of local self government, on the one hand, and the national power, on the other, our country has been able to endure and prosper for near a century and a half.

Out of a proper respect for the acts of a coördinate branch of the Government, this court has gone far to sustain taxing acts as such, even though there has been ground for suspecting from the weight of the tax it was intended to destroy its subject. But, in the act before us, the presumption of validity cannot prevail, because the proof of the contrary is found on the very face of its provisions. Grant the validity of this law, and all that Congress would need to do, hereafter, in seeking to take over to its control any one of the great number of subjects of public interest, jurisdiction of which the States have never parted with, and which are reserved to them by the Tenth Amendment, would be to enact a detailed measure of complete regulation of the subject and enforce it by a so-called tax upon departures from it. To give such magic to the word "tax" would be to break down all constitutional limitation of the powers of Congress and completely wipe out the sovereignty of the States.

. . .

The analogy of the *Dagenhart Case* is clear. The congressional power over interstate commerce is, within its proper scope, just as complete and unlimited as the congressional power to tax, and the legislative motive in its exercise is just as free from judicial suspicion and inquiry. Yet when Congress threatened to stop interstate commerce in ordinary and necessary commodities, unobjectionable as subjects of transportation, and to deny the same to the people of a State in order to coerce them into compliance with Congress's regulation of state concerns, the court said this was not in fact regulation of interstate commerce, but rather that of State concerns and was invalid. So here the so-called tax is a penalty to coerce people of a State to act as Congress wishes them to act in respect of a matter completely the business of the state government under the Federal Constitution....

For the reasons given, we must hold the Child Labor Tax Law invalid and the judgment of the District Court is

Affirmed.

MR. JUSTICE CLARKE dissents.

United States v. Darby

312 U.S. 100 (1941)

The Fair Labor Standards Act of 1938 provided for minimum wages and maximum hours for employees engaged in the production of goods for interstate commerce. The statute forced the Court to rethink its doctrine on "manufacture." If manufacture is not of itself interstate commerce, would the shipment of manufactured goods interstate bring it within the authority of Cobngress to regulate? The statute also excluded the products of child labor from interstate commerce, requiring the Court to revisit its holding in *Hammer* v. *Dagenhart* (1918), which had struck down the use of the Commerce Clause to regulate child labor. In this case, the government prosecutes Fred W. Darby, owner of a lumber company, for violating the 1938 statute.

MR. JUSTICE STONE delivered the opinion of the Court.

The two principal questions raised by the record in this case are, *first,* whether Congress has constitutional power to prohibit the shipment in interstate commerce of lumber manufactured by employees whose wages are less than a prescribed minimum or whose weekly hours of labor at that wage are greater than a prescribed maximum, and, *second,* whether it has power to prohibit the employment of workmen in the production of goods "for interstate commerce" at other than prescribed wages and hours. A subsidiary question is whether in connection with such prohibitions Congress can require the employer subject to them to keep records showing the hours worked each day and week by each of his employees including those engaged "in the production and manufacture of goods to-wit, lumber, for 'interstate commerce.'"

. . .

The indictment charges that appellee is engaged, in the State of Georgia, in the business of acquiring raw materials, which he manufactures into finished lumber with the intent, when manufactured, to ship it in interstate commerce to customers outside the state, and that he does in fact so ship a large part of the lumber so produced. There are numerous counts charging appellee with the shipment in interstate commerce from Georgia to points outside the state of lumber in the production of which, for interstate commerce, appellee has employed workmen at less than the prescribed minimum wage or more than the prescribed maximum hours without payment to them of any wage for overtime. Other counts charge the employment by appellee of workmen in the production of lumber for interstate commerce at wages at less than 25 cents an hour or for more than the maximum hours per week without payment to them of the prescribed overtime wage. Still another count charges appellee with failure to keep records showing the hours worked each day a week by each of his employees....

The demurrer, so far as now relevant to the appeal, challenged the validity of the Fair Labor Standards Act under the Commerce Clause and the Fifth and Tenth Amendments. The district court quashed the indictment in its entirety upon the broad grounds that the Act, which it interpreted as a regulation of manufacture within the states, is unconstitutional. It declared that manufacture is not interstate commerce and that the regulation by the Fair Labor Standards Act of wages and hours of employment of those engaged in the manufacture of goods which it is intended at the time of production "may or will be" after production "sold in interstate commerce in part or in whole" is not within the congressional power to regulate interstate commerce.

. . .

The prohibition of shipment of the proscribed goods in interstate commerce....

While manufacture is not of itself interstate commerce, the shipment of manufactured goods interstate is such commerce and the prohibition of such shipment by Congress is indubitably a regulation of the commerce. The power to regulate commerce is the power "to prescribe the rule by which commerce is governed." *Gibbons* v. *Ogden,* 9 Wheat. 1, 196. It extends not only to those regulations which aid, fos-

ter and protect the commerce, but embraces those which prohibit it.... It is conceded that the power of Congress to prohibit transportation in interstate commerce includes noxious articles, ... stolen articles, ... kidnapped persons, ... and articles such as intoxicating liquor or convict made goods, traffic in which is forbidden or restricted by the laws of the state of destination....

But it is said that the present prohibition falls within the scope of none of these categories; that while the prohibition is nominally a regulation of the commerce its motive or purpose is regulation of wages and hours of persons engaged in manufacture, the control of which has been reserved to the states and upon which Georgia and some of the states of destination have placed no restriction; ...

... Congress, following its own conception of public policy concerning the restrictions which may appropriately be imposed on interstate commerce, is free to exclude from the commerce articles whose use in the states for which they are destined it may conceive to be injurious to the public health, morals or welfare, even though the state has not sought to regulate their use....

Such regulation is not a forbidden invasion of state power merely because either its motive or its consequence is to restrict the use of articles of commerce within the states of destination; and is not prohibited unless by other Constitutional provisions. It is no objection to the assertion of the power to regulate interstate commerce that its exercise is attended by the same incidents which attend the exercise of the police power of the states....

In the more than a century which has elapsed since the decision of *Gibbons* v. *Ogden,* these principles of constitutional interpretation have been so long and repeatedly recognized by this Court as applicable to the Commerce Clause, that there would be little occasion for repeating them now were it not for the decision of this Court twenty-two years ago in *Hammer* v. *Dagenhart,* 247 U.S. 251. In that case it was held by a bare majority of the Court over the powerful and now classic dissent of Mr. Justice Holmes setting forth the fundamental issues involved, that Congress was without power to exclude the products of child labor from interstate commerce. The reasoning and conclusion of the Court's opinion there cannot be reconciled with the conclusion which we have reached, that the power of Congress under the Commerce Clause is plenary to exclude any article from interstate commerce subject only to the specific prohibitions of the Constitution.

Hammer v. *Dagenhart* has not been followed. The distinction on which the decision was rested that Congressional power to prohibit interstate commerce is limited to articles which in themselves have some harmful or deleterious property — a distinction which was novel when made and unsupported by any provision of the Constitution — has long since been abandoned. . . .

The conclusion is inescapable that *Hammer* v. *Dagenhart* was a departure from the principles which have prevailed in the interpretation of the Commerce Clause both before and since the decision and that such vitality, as a precedent, as it then had has long since been exhausted. It should be and now is overruled.

. . .

Our conclusion is unaffected by the Tenth Amendment which provides: "The powers not delegated to the United States by the Constitution, nor prohibited by it to the States, are reserved to the States respectively, or to the people." The amendment states but a truism that all is retained which has not been surrendered. There is nothing in the history of its adoption to suggest that it was more than declaratory of the relationship between the national and state governments as it had been established by the Constitution before the amendment or that its purpose was other than to allay fears that the new national government might seek to exercise powers not granted, and that the states might not be able to exercise fully their reserved powers. . . .

Reversed.

D. THE NEW DEAL WATERSHED

During the New Deal, the Supreme Court at first resisted, but eventually capitulated, to a wholesale expansion of congressional power over commerce. Initially the Court prohibited Congress from regulating commercial activities that were regarded as production and manufacture, as "local" or intrastate, or that affected commerce only "indirectly." Those formulas were variations of dual federalism. By 1936 the Court began to embrace what it had accepted intermittently in the past: Congress could regulate intrastate activities that had a substantial relation to interstate commerce.

In two cases in 1935, the Court declared unconstitutional the National Industrial Recovery Act (NIRA) of 1933. A provision involving production quotas for petroleum products was struck down as an excessive delegation of legislative power to the President. Panama Refining Co. v. Ryan, 293 U.S. 388 (1935). The remainder of the NIRA was invalidated a few months later when a unanimous Court decided that the statute violated the delegation doctrine and exceeded Congress's power to regulate commerce. The Court refused to apply the "current of commerce" concept to intrastate commerce that involved purchases or transportation of goods outside the state. Once a commodity became "commingled with the mass of property within the State," the flow of interstate commerce ceased. Schechter Corp. v. United States, 295 U.S. 495, 543 (1935). A reading of *Schechter* appears in Chapter 6.

The Court struck down the Railroad Retirement Act, which transferred funds from railroad carriers to retirees. The Court, refusing to justify the statute under the Commerce Clause, treated it as a taking of property requiring just compensation. Railroad Retirement Board v. Alton R. Co., 295 U.S. 330 (1935). Also invalidated was the Bituminous Coal Conservation Act of 1935, which relied on the Commerce Clause to regulate mining and the distribution of coal. The Court said that the commerce power did not permit Congress to control the conditions in which coal is produced (such as labor conditions) before coal became an article of commerce. Labor conditions affected commerce only "indirectly." Production and manufacture did not constitute commerce, said the Court, even when done with intent to sell or transport the commodities out of the state. CARTER v. CARTER COAL CO., 298 U.S. 238 (1936). The processing tax of the Agricultural Adjustment Act was declared unconstitutional in *United States* v. *Butler* (see discussion later in this chapter).

The Court Switches

After Roosevelt's election in 1936 and his unsuccessful attempt to pack the judiciary, the Supreme Court began to accommodate New Deal legislation. Without a change in the Court's composition,

Stages of Federalism

1. Nationalism (1789–1835). National powers are read broadly to include implied as well as explicit powers. Generous interpretation of Commerce Clause. Dominated by *McCulloch v. Maryland* (1819) and *Gibbons v. Ogden* (1824). Opportunity for states in some areas to exercise concurrent power over commerce.

2. Dual Federalism (1835–1937). National and state governments have mutually exclusive powers. Within their own spheres they are supreme and independent. Congress may not exercise power over production or manufacturing because they are "local" and intrastate. Congress could not regulate economic activities that affected commerce only "indirectly."

3. Cooperative Federalism (1937–1990). Businesses "affected with a public interest" or with a substantial relation to interstate commerce may be regulated by Congress. Relying on the spending power, Congress makes grants to states and imposes conditions on those funds. Congress may preempt state regulation but, until it does, states may regulate with standards that differ from federal requirements.

4. Dual Federalism Revived (1990– ?). Beginning in the 1990s, the Supreme Court handed down a number of decisions that revitalized dual federalism. As a 5–4 decision noted in 2002: "Dual sovereignty is a defining feature of our Nation's constitutional blueprint." Fed. Maritime Com'n v. S.C. State Ports Auth., 535 U.S. 743, 751 (2002). Some decisions in 2003, 2004, and 2005 seemed to suggest that this era was waning as the makeup of the Court changed.

but with Chief Justice Hughes and Justice Roberts now solidly supporting the three liberals (Brandeis, Cardozo, and Stone), the Court upheld the National Labor Relations Act. The Court accepted Congress's argument that labor disputes directly burdened or obstructed interstate or foreign commerce and could be regulated by the Commerce Clause. The Act gave employees in industry a fundamental right to organize and engage in collective bargaining. Any intrastate activity that had a close and substantial relationship to interstate commerce could be brought within the control of Congress. To enforce the Act, Congress established a National Labor Relations Board (NLRB) with the power to prevent any person from engaging in unfair labor practices "affecting commerce." NLRB v. JONES & LAUGHLIN, 301 U.S. 1 (1937).

In 1939 the Court sustained the Agricultural Adjustment Act, which used marketing controls to limit the amount of commodities that could be sold. Through the use of quotas, Congress hoped to stabilize prices and limit production. Farmers who exceeded their allotment had to pay a penalty at the warehouses, the "throat" where commodities entered "the stream of commerce." Mulford v. Smith, 307 U.S. 38, 47 (1939). Wheat marketing quotas, even for wheat not intended for commerce but for consumption on the farm, were upheld three years later by a unanimous Court. WICKARD v. FILBURN, 317 U.S. 111 (1942). The Fair Labor Standards Act of 1938 was upheld, allowing Congress to regulate the wages and hours of manufacturing employees. The Court rejected the argument that manufacturing was an intrastate activity and therefore outside the Commerce Clause. Congress could regulate intrastate activities where they have a "substantial effect" on interstate commerce. United States v. Darby, 312 U.S. 100, 119 (1941).

Through these decisions the United States entered into its third stage of "cooperative federalism" (see box). Although by the late 1930s the Court had largely bowed to the judgments of Congress on economic regulation and the scope of the Commerce Clause, the new Roosevelt Court signaled its intention to give greater scrutiny to constitutional provisions that protect individual rights and liberties. In a famous footnote written by Justice Stone in a 1938 case, the Court suggested that it might have a special responsibility to protect "discrete and insular minorities," especially when the political processes that supposedly safeguard minority rights have been curtailed. United States v. Carolene Products Co., 304 U.S. 144, 153 n.4 (1938). This footnote foreshadowed the Court's later activism in such areas as religious liberty, racial discrimination, and criminal rights. (The *Carolene* footnote appears in Chapter 15, Section C.)

After the Court's retreat in 1937, it continued to monitor federal-state legislation over the economy. State efforts to limit the length of railroad cars traveling interstate could not be justified for reasons of safety or the police power. Even when Congress had not regulated an area, state actions that interfered with interstate commerce were not permitted under the Commerce Clause. Southern Pacific Co. v. Arizona 325 U.S. 761 (1945). Although states may impose burdensome regulations in the interest of local health and safety, they may not restrain interstate commerce for the purpose of advancing their own commercial interests or promoting local economic advantages. Hood v. Du Mond, 336 U.S. 525 (1949). The Supreme Court has developed a number of criteria to indicate when state actions burden interstate commerce, but the enforcement and implementation of these judicial tests depend largely on congressional action. Commonwealth Edison Co. v. Montana, 453 U.S. 609 (1981).

Scope of Independent State Action

These decisions did not permit Congress to preempt every area of commerce that might affect interstate activities. States could still control local conditions and affect interstate commerce incidentally while protecting their citizens' welfare. Milk Board v. Eisenberg Co., 306 U.S. 346 (1939). Even when 90 to 95 percent of a state's product was shipped in interstate or foreign commerce, states could adopt marketing and price-stabilization programs in the interest of the "safety, health and well-being of local communities," especially when the activity "may never be adequately dealt with by Congress." Parker v. Brown, 317 U.S. 341, 362–63 (1943).[8] To protect their environmental and natural resources, states may enact regulations even when the incidental effect creates some burden on interstate commerce. Minnesota v. Clover Leaf Creamery Co., 449 U.S. 456 (1981).

The commerce power allows Congress to control such local activity as "loan sharking" (using threats and extortion to collect loans). Although local, these techniques are part of organized crime that affect interstate and foreign commerce. Perez v. United States, 402 U.S. 146 (1971). The breadth of the New Deal revolution is reflected in two decisions in 1981 that upheld congressional regulation of surface coal mining. The statute authorized states to propose a program of environmental protection to meet minimum federal standards. If states failed to prepare a program, they would be forced to adopt a federal plan. A unanimous Court upheld the statute. Hodel v. Virginia Surface Mining & Recl. Assn., 452 U.S. 264 (1981); Hodel v. Indiana, 452 U.S. 314 (1981). [As explained later in Section F, several decisions by the Court beginning in the 1990s limited congressional power over the states.]

Other decisions gave states substantial leeway to look for new sources of revenue. The Supreme Court held in 1991 that states may adopt a single business tax (a value-added tax) without violating the Due Process Clause or the Commerce Clause. Trinova Corp. v. Michigan Dept. of Treasury, 498 U.S. 358 (1991). A 1992 ruling marked a first step toward allowing states to force mail-order companies to collect taxes from out-of-state shoppers. Quill Corp. v. North Dakota, 504 U.S. 298 (1992). The mail-order business had grown from $2.4 billion a year in 1967, when the Court first blocked state taxes on such sales, to an estimated $183 billion by 1989. In 1994, the Court ruled that states could tax corporations not merely on their earnings within the state but also on their worldwide income. Barclays Bank v. Franchise Tax Bd. of Cal., 512 U.S. 298 (1994).

While the Court and Congress supported these state initiatives, some state activities still run afoul of the Commerce Clause. Two decisions in 1992 limited the authority of states to dispose of hazardous waste and other materials. Chemical Waste Management, Inc. v. Hunt, 504 U.S. 334 (1992); Fort Gra-

---

8. See also Carter v. Virginia, 321 U.S. 131 (1944) for the power of states to regulate shipments entering into and passing out of their borders, and Milk Board v. Eisenberg Co., 306 U.S. 346, 351 (1939) for the ability of states to regulate local conditions even when they incidentally or indirectly involve interstate commerce.

tiot Landfill v. Mich. Dept. of Nat. Res., 504 U.S. 353 (1992). A 1994 decision held that an Oregon law—subjecting waste generated in other states to a discriminatory surcharge approximately three times higher than that imposed on waste generated within the state—was invalid under the Commerce Clause. Oregon Waste Systems v. Dept. of Env. Quality, 511 U.S. 93 (1994). In that same year, the Court ruled that a local ordinance on solid waste discriminated against interstate commerce because it favored the local station and squelched competition. C&A Carbone, Inc. v. Clarkstown, 511 U.S. 383 (1994). A unanimous Court in 1996 ruled that a North Carolina "intangibles tax" discriminated against interstate commerce by favoring purely domestic corporations over those involved in interstate commerce. Fulton Corp. v. Faulkner, 516 U.S. 325 (1996). Another unanimous ruling in 1999 held that an Alabama franchise tax violated the Commerce Clause. South Central Bell Telephone Co. v. Alabama, 526 U.S. 160 (1999).

Carter v. Carter Coal Co.
298 U.S. 238 (1936)

After the Supreme Court in 1935 struck down the National Industrial Recovery Act, Congress relied on the Commerce Clause to pass legislation to regulate mining and the distribution of coal. The legislation authorized a commission to determine maximum and minimum prices of coal and regulate the workers engaged in coal production. Could Congress control the conditions in which coal was produced before it became an article of interstate commerce, or were production and manufacturing purely within the control of states?

MR. JUSTICE SUTHERLAND delivered the opinion of the Court.

The purposes of the "Bituminous Coal Conservation Act of 1935," involved in these suits, as declared by the title, are to stabilize the bituminous coal-mining industry and promote its interstate commerce; to provide for cooperative marketing of bituminous coal; to levy a tax on such coal and provide for a drawback under certain conditions; to declare the production, distribution, and use of such coal to be affected with a national public interest; to conserve the national resources of such coal; to provide for the general welfare, and for other purposes.... The constitutional validity of the act is challenged in each of the suits.

. . .

The general rule with regard to the respective powers of the national and the state governments under the Constitution, is not in doubt. The states were before the Constitution; and, consequently, their legislative powers antedated the Constitution. Those who framed and those who adopted that instrument meant to carve from the general mass of legislative powers, then possessed by the states, only such portions as it was thought wise to confer upon the federal government; and in order that there should be no uncertainty in respect of what was taken and what was left, the national powers of legislation were not aggregated but enumerated—with the result that what was not embraced by the enumeration remained vested in the states without change or impairment....

... Since the validity of the act depends upon whether it is a regulation of interstate commerce, the nature and extent of the power conferred upon Congress by the commerce clause becomes the determinative question in this branch of the case....

As used in the Constitution, the word "commerce" is the equivalent of the phrase "intercourse for the purposes of trade," and includes transportation, purchase, sale, and exchange of commodities between the citizens of the different states. And the power to regulate commerce embraces the instruments by which commerce is carried on....

That commodities produced or manufactured within a state are intended to be sold or transported outside the state does not render their production or manufacture subject to federal regulation under the commerce clause....

We have seen that the word "commerce" is the equivalent of the phrase "intercourse for the purposes of trade." Plainly, the incidents leading up to and culminating in the mining of coal do not constitute such intercourse. The employment of men, the fixing of their wages, hours of labor and working conditions, the bargaining in respect of these things—whether carried on separately or collectively—each and all constitute intercourse for the purposes of production, not of trade....

A consideration of the foregoing, and of many cases which might be added to those already cited, renders inescapable the conclusion that the effect of the labor provisions of the act, including those in respect of minimum wages, wage agreements, collective bargaining, and the Labor Board and its powers, primarily falls upon production and not upon commerce; and confirms the further resulting conclusion that production is a purely local activity. It follows that none of these essential antecedents of production constitutes a transaction in or forms any part of interstate commerce.... Everything which moves in interstate commerce has had a local origin. Without local production somewhere, interstate commerce, as now carried on, would practically disappear. Nevertheless, the local character of mining, of manufacturing and of crop growing is a fact, and remains a fact, whatever may be done with the products.

. . .

Whether the effect of a given activity or condition is direct or indirect is not always easy to determine. The word "direct" implies that the activity or condition invoked or blamed shall operate proximately—not mediately, remotely, or collaterally—to produce the effect. It connotes the absence of an efficient intervening agency or condition. And the extent of the effect bears no logical relation to its character. The distinction between a direct and an indirect effect turns, not upon the magnitude of either the cause or the effect, but entirely upon the manner in which the effect has been brought about. If the production by one man of a single ton of coal intended for interstate sale and shipment, and actually so sold and shipped, affects interstate commerce indirectly, the effect does not become direct by multiplying the tonnage, or increasing the number of men employed, or adding to the expense or complexities of the business, or by all combined. It is quite true that rules of law are sometimes qualified by considerations of degree, as the government argues. But the matter of degree has no bearing upon the question here, since that question is not—What is the *extent* of the local activity or condition, or the *extent* of the effect produced upon interstate commerce? but—What is the *relation* between the activity or condition and the effect?

Much stress is put upon the evils which come from the struggle between employers and employees over the matter of wages, working conditions, the right of collective bargaining, etc., and the resulting strikes, curtailment and irregularity of production and effect on prices; and it is insisted that interstate commerce is *greatly* affected thereby. But, in addition to what has just been said, the conclusive answer is that the evils are all local evils over which the federal government has no legislative control. The relation of employer and employee is a local relation. At common law, it is one of the domestic relations. The wages are paid for the doing of local work. Working conditions are obviously local conditions....

Separate opinion of Mr. Chief Justice Hughes.

I agree that the stockholders were entitled to bring their suits; that, in view of the question whether any part of the Act could be sustained, the suits were not premature; that the so-called tax is not a real tax, but a penalty; that the constitutional power of the Federal Government to impose this penalty must rest upon the commerce clause, as the Government concedes; that production—in this case mining—which precedes commerce, is not itself commerce; and that the power to regulate commerce among the several States is not a power to regulate industry within the State.

. . .

But that is not the whole case. The Act also provides for the regulation of the prices of bituminous coal sold in interstate commerce and prohibits unfair methods of competition in interstate commerce. Undoubtedly transactions in carrying on interstate commerce are subject to the federal power to regulate that commerce and the control of charges and the protection of fair competition in that commerce are familiar illustrations of the exercise of the power, as the Interstate Commerce Act, the Packers and Stockyards Act, and the Anti-Trust Acts abundantly show....

Whether the policy of fixing prices of commodities sold in interstate commerce is a sound policy is not for our consideration. The question of that policy, and of its particular applications, is for Congress. The exercise of the power of regulation is subject to the constitutional restriction of the due process clause, and if in fixing rates, prices or conditions of competition, that requirement is transgressed, the judicial power may be invoked to the end that the constitutional limitation may be maintained....

Upon what ground, then, can it be said that this plan for the regulation of transactions in interstate commerce in coal is beyond the constitutional power of Congress? The Court reaches that conclusion in the view that the invalidity of the labor provisions requires us to condemn the Act in its entirety. I am unable to concur in that opinion. I think that the express provisions of the Act preclude such a finding of inseparability.

. . .

MR. JUSTICE CARDOZO (dissenting in Nos. 636, 649 and 650, and in No. 651 concurring in the result).

. . .

First: I am satisfied that the Act is within the power of the central government in so far as it provides for minimum and maximum prices upon sales of bituminous coal in the transactions of interstate commerce and in those of intrastate commerce where interstate commerce is directly or intimately affected. Whether it is valid also in other provisions that have been considered and condemned in the opinion of the court, I do not find it necessary to determine at this time.…

Congress was not condemned to inaction in the face of price wars and wage wars so pregnant with disaster. Commerce had been choked and burdened; its normal flow had been diverted from one state to another; there had been bankruptcy and waste and ruin alike for capital and for labor. The liberty protected by the Fifth Amendment does not include the right to persist in this anarchic riot.… There is testimony in these records, testimony even by the assailants of the statute, that only through a system of regulated prices can the industry be stabilized and set upon the road of orderly and peaceful progress.… An evil existing, and also the power to correct it, the lawmakers were at liberty to use their own discretion in the selection of the means.

. . .

I am authorized to state that MR. JUSTICE BRANDEIS and MR. JUSTICE STONE join in this opinion.

NLRB v. Jones & Laughlin

301 U.S. 1 (1937)

In the National Labor Relations Act of 1935, Congress concluded that labor disputes had a direct burden on interstate or foreign commerce and could be regulated by the Commerce Clause. Even activities taking place within a state, if they had a close and substantial relationship to interstate commerce, could be brought within the control of Congress. Under the shadow of Roosevelt's court-packing plan, the Court decided whether this exertion of national power invaded the rights reserved to the states.

MR. CHIEF JUSTICE HUGHES delivered the opinion of the Court.

In a proceeding under the National Labor Relations Act of 1935, the National Labor Relations Board found that the respondent, Jones & Laughlin Steel Corporation, had violated the Act by engaging in unfair labor practices affecting commerce.… The unfair labor practices charged were that the corporation was discriminating against members of the union with regard to hire and tenure of employment, and was coercing and intimidating its employees in order to interfere with their self-organization. The discriminatory and coercive action alleged was the discharge of certain employees.

The National Labor Relations Board, sustaining the charge, ordered the corporation to cease and desist from such discrimination and coercion, to offer reinstatement to ten of the employees named, to make good their losses in pay, and to post for thirty days notices that the corporation would not discharge or discriminate against members, or those desiring to become members, of the labor union.…

Contesting the ruling of the Board, the respondent argues (1) that the Act is in reality a regulation of labor relations and not of interstate commerce; (2) that the Act can have no application to the respondent's relations with its production employees because they are not subject to regulation by the federal government; and (3) that the provisions of the Act violate § 2 of Article III and the Fifth and Seventh Amendments of the Constitution of the United States.

… Jones & Laughlin Steel Corporation … is organized under the laws of Pennsylvania and has its principal office at Pittsburgh. It is engaged in the business of manufacturing iron and steel in plants situated in Pittsburgh and nearby Aliquippa, Pennsylvania. It manufactures and distributes a widely diversified line of steel and pig iron, being the fourth largest producer of steel in the United States. With its subsidiaries—nineteen in number—it is a completely integrated enterprise, owning and operating ore, coal and limestone properties, lake and river transportation facilities and terminal railroads located at its manufacturing plants. It owns or controls mines in Michigan and Minnesota. It operates four ore steamships on the Great Lakes, used in the transportation of ore to its factories. It owns coal mines in Pennsylvania. It operates towboats and steam barges used in carrying coal to its factories. It owns limestone properties in various places in Pennsylvania and West Virginia. It owns the Monongahela connecting railroad which connects the plants of the Pittsburgh works and forms an interconnection with the Pennsylvania, New York Central and Baltimore and Ohio Railroad systems. It owns the Aliquippa and Southern Railroad Company which connects the Aliquippa works with the Pittsburgh and Lake Erie, part of the New York Central system. Much of its product is shipped to its warehouses in Chicago, Detroit, Cincinnati and Memphis,—to the last two places by means of its own barges and transportation equipment. In Long Island City, New York, and in New Orleans it operates structural steel fabricating shops in connection with the warehousing of semi-finished materials sent from its works. Through one of its wholly-owned subsidiaries it owns, leases and operates stores, warehouses and yards for the distribution of equipment and supplies for drilling and operating oil and gas wells and for pipe lines, refineries and pumping stations. It has sales offices in twenty cities in the United States and a wholly-owned subsidiary which is devoted exclusively to distributing its product in Canada. Approximately 75 per cent. of its product is shipped out of Pennsylvania.

Summarizing these operations, the Labor Board concluded that the works in Pittsburgh and Aliquippa "might be likened to the heart of a self-contained, highly integrated body. They draw in the raw materials from Michigan, Minnesota, West Virginia, Pennsylvania in part through arteries and by means controlled by the respondent; they transform the materials and then pump them out to all parts of the nation through the vast mechanism which the respondent has elaborated."

. . .

First. The scope of the Act. — The Act is challenged in its entirety as an attempt to regulate all industry, thus invading the reserved powers of the States over their local concerns....

There can be no question that the commerce thus contemplated by the Act (aside from that within a Territory or the District of Columbia) is interstate and foreign commerce in the constitutional sense. The Act also defines the term "affecting commerce" (§ 2 (7)):

"The term 'affecting commerce' means in commerce, or burdening or obstructing commerce or the free flow of commerce, or having led or tending to lead to a labor dispute burdening or obstructing commerce or the free flow of commerce."

This definition is one of exclusion as well as inclusion. The grant of authority to the Board does not purport to extend to the relationship between all industrial employees and employers. Its terms do not impose collective bargaining upon all industry regardless of effects upon interstate or foreign commerce. It purports to reach only what may be deemed to burden or obstruct that commerce and, thus qualified, it must be construed as contemplating the exercise of control within constitutional bounds. It is a familiar principle that acts which directly burden or obstruct interstate or foreign commerce, or its free flow, are within the reach of the congressional power....

Second. The unfair labor practices in question. — The unfair labor practices found by the Board are those defined in § 8, subdivisions (1) and (3). These provide:

Sec. 8. It shall be an unfair labor practice for an employer—

"(1) To interfere with, restrain, or coerce employees in the exercise of the rights guaranteed in section 7."

"(3) By discrimination in regard to hire or tenure of employment or any term or condition of employment to encourage or discourage membership in any labor organization: ..."

Section 8, subdivision (1), refers to § 7, which is as follows:

"Sec. 7. Employees shall have the right to self-organization, to form, join, or assist labor organizations, to bargain collectively through representatives of their own choosing, and to engage in concerted activities, for the purpose of collective bargaining or other mutual aid or protection."

Thus, in its present application, the statute goes no further than to safeguard the right of employees to self-organization and to select representatives of their own choosing for collective bargaining or other mutual protection without restraint or coercion by their employer.

That is a fundamental right. Employees have as clear a right to organize and select their representatives for lawful purposes as the respondent has to organize its business and select its own officers and agents. Discrimination and coercion to prevent the free exercise of the right of employees to self-organization and representation is a proper subject for condemnation by competent legislative authority. Long ago we stated the reason for labor organizations. We said that they were organized out of the necessities of the situation; that a single employee was helpless in dealing with an employer; that he was dependent ordinarily on his daily wage for the maintenance of himself and family; that if the employer refused to pay him the wages that he thought fair, he was nevertheless unable to leave the employ and resist arbitrary and unfair treatment; that union was essential to give laborers opportunity to deal on an equality with their employer....

Third. The application of the Act to employees engaged in production. — The principle involved. — Respondent says that whatever may be said of employees engaged in interstate commerce, the industrial relations and activities in the manufacturing department of respondent's enterprise are not subject to federal regulation. The argument rests upon the proposition that manufacturing in itself is not commerce....

... Although activities may be intrastate in character when separately considered, if they have such a close and substantial relation to interstate commerce that their control is essential or appropriate to protect that commerce from burdens and obstructions, Congress cannot be denied the power to exercise that control....

Fourth. Effects of the unfair labor practice in respondent's enterprise. — Giving full weight to respondent's contention with respect to a break in the complete continuity of the "stream of commerce" by reason of respondent's manufacturing operations, the fact remains that the stoppage of those operations by industrial strife would have a most serious effect upon interstate commerce. In view of respondent's far-flung activities, it is idle to say that the effect would be indirect or remote. It is obvious that it would be immediate and might be catastrophic. We are asked to shut our eyes to the plainest facts of our national life and to deal with the question of direct and indirect effects in an intellectual vacuum....

Experience has abundantly demonstrated that the recognition of the right of employees to self-organization and to have representatives of their own choosing for the purpose of collective bargaining is often an essential condition of industrial peace. Refusal to confer and negotiate has been one of the most prolific causes of strife. This is such an outstanding fact in the history of labor disturbances that it is a proper subject of judicial notice and requires no citation of instances....

Our conclusion is that the order of the Board was within its competency and that the Act is valid as here applied. The judgment of the Circuit Court of Appeals is reversed and the cause is remanded for further proceedings in conformity with this opinion.

Reversed.

[On the same day, the Court handed down other decisions that upheld actions by the National Labor Relations Board. The dissents below are directed against this cluster of rulings.]

MR. JUSTICE McREYNOLDS delivered the following dissenting opinion in the cases preceding:

MR. JUSTICE VAN DEVANTER, MR. JUSTICE SUTHERLAND, MR. JUSTICE BUTLER and I are unable to agree with the decisions just announced.

. . .

The Constitution still recognizes the existence of states with indestructible powers; the Tenth Amendment was supposed to put them beyond controversy.

We are told that Congress may protect the "stream of commerce" and that one who buys raw material without the state, manufactures it therein, and ships the output to another state is in that stream. Therefore it is said he may be prevented from doing anything which may interfere with its flow.

This, too, goes beyond the constitutional limitations heretofore enforced. If a man raises cattle and regularly delivers them to a carrier for interstate shipment, may Congress prescribe the conditions under which he may employ or discharge helpers on the ranch? The products of a mine pass daily into interstate commerce; many things are brought to it from other states. Are the owners and the miners within the power of Congress in respect of the miners' tenure and discharge? May a mill owner be prohibited from closing his factory or discontinuing his business because so to do would stop the flow of products to and from his plant in interstate commerce? May employees in a factory be restrained from quitting work in a body because this will close the factory and thereby stop the flow of commerce? May arson of a factory be made a Federal offense whenever this would interfere with such flow? If the business cannot continue with the existing wage scale, may Congress command a reduction? If the ruling of the Court just announced is adhered to these questions suggest some of the problems certain to arise.

. . .

Wickard v. Filburn

317 U.S. 111 (1942)

In 1941 Congress amended the Agricultural Adjustment Act of 1938 to increase the penalty on excess production. Roscoe Filburn, a farmer, received a wheat allotment of 11 acres for his 1941 crop but sowed 23 acres, planning to use the extra crop for home consumption. He was penalized for the excess production and brought suit against Secretary of Agriculture Claude Wickard. This case examines the power of Congress to control production, even within a state, to increase the price of wheat.

Mr. Justice Jackson delivered the opinion of the Court.

. . .

II

It is urged that under the Commerce Clause of the Constitution, Article I, § 8, clause 3, Congress does not possess the power it has in this instance sought to exercise. The question would merit little consideration since our decision in *United States* v. *Darby,* 312 U.S. 100, sustaining the federal power to regulate production of goods for commerce, except for the fact that this Act extends federal regulation to production not intended in any part for commerce but wholly for consumption on the farm. The Act includes a definition of "market" and its derivatives, so that as related to wheat, in addition to its conventional meaning, it also means to dispose of "by feeding (in any form) to poultry or livestock which, or the products of which, are sold, bartered, or exchanged, or to be so disposed of." Hence, marketing quotas not only embrace all that may be sold without penalty but also what may be consumed on the premises. Wheat produced on excess acreage is designated as "available for marketing" as so defined, and the penalty is imposed thereon. Penalties do not depend upon whether any part of the wheat, either within or without the quota, is sold or intended to be sold. The sum of this is that the Federal Government fixes a quota including all that the farmer may harvest for sale or for his own farm needs, and declares that wheat produced on excess acreage may neither be disposed of nor used except upon payment of the penalty, or except it is stored as required by the Act or delivered to the Secretary of Agriculture.

Appellee says that this is a regulation of production and consumption of wheat. Such activities are, he urges, beyond the reach of Congressional power under the Commerce Clause, since they are local in character, and their effects upon interstate commerce are at most "indirect." In answer the Government argues that the statute regulates neither pro-

duction nor consumption, but only marketing; and, in the alternative, that if the Act does go beyond the regulation of marketing it is sustainable as a "necessary and proper" implementation of the power of Congress over interstate commerce.

The Government's concern lest the Act be held to be a regulation of production or consumption, rather than of marketing, is attributable to a few dicta and decisions of this Court which might be understood to lay it down that activities such as "production," "manufacturing," and "mining" are strictly "local" and, except in special circumstances which are not present here, cannot be regulated under the commerce power because their effects upon interstate commerce are, as matter of law, only "indirect." Even today, when this power has been held to have great latitude, there is no decision of this Court that such activities may be regulated where no part of the product is intended for interstate commerce or intermingled with the subjects thereof. We believe that a review of the course of decision under the Commerce Clause will make plain, however, that questions of the power of Congress are not to be decided by reference to any formula which would give controlling force to nomenclature such as "production" and "indirect" and foreclose consideration of the actual effects of the activity in question upon interstate commerce.

At the beginning Chief Justice Marshall described the federal commerce power with a breadth never yet exceeded. *Gibbons* v. *Ogden,* 9 Wheat. 1, 194–195. He made emphatic the embracing and penetrating nature of this power by warning that effective restraints on its exercise must proceed from political rather than from judicial processes. *Id.* at 197.

For nearly a century, however, decisions of this Court under the Commerce Clause dealt rarely with questions of what Congress might do in the exercise of its granted power under the Clause, and almost entirely with the permissibility of state activity which it was claimed discriminated against or burdened interstate commerce. During this period there was perhaps little occasion for the affirmative exercise of the commerce power, and the influence of the Clause on American life and law was a negative one, resulting almost wholly from its operation as a restraint upon the powers of the states. In discussion and decision the point of reference, instead of being what was "necessary and proper" to the exercise by Congress of its granted power, was often some concept of sovereignty thought to be implicit in the status of statehood. Certain activities such as "production," "manufacturing," and "mining" were occasionally said to be within the province of state governments and beyond the power of Congress under the Commerce Clause.

It was not until 1887, with the enactment of the Interstate Commerce Act, that the interstate commerce power began to exert positive influence in American law and life. This first important federal resort to the commerce power was followed in 1890 by the Sherman Anti-Trust Act and, thereafter, mainly after 1903, by many others. These statutes ushered in new phases of adjudication, which required the Court to approach the interpretation of the Commerce Clause in the light of an actual exercise by Congress of its power thereunder.

When it first dealt with this new legislation, the Court adhered to its earlier pronouncements, and allowed but little scope to the power of Congress. *United States* v. *Knight Co.,* 156 U.S. 1. These earlier pronouncements also played an important part in several of the five cases in which this Court later held that Acts of Congress under the Commerce Clause were in excess of its power.

Even while important opinions in this line of restrictive authority were being written, however, other cases called forth broader interpretations of the Commerce Clause destined to supersede the earlier ones, and to bring about a return to the principles first enunciated by Chief Justice Marshall in *Gibbons* v. *Ogden, supra.*

Not long after the decision of *United States* v. *Knight Co., supra,* Mr. Justice Holmes, in sustaining the exercise of national power over intrastate activity, stated for the Court that "commerce among the States is not a technical legal conception, but a practical one, drawn from the course of business." *Swift & Co.* v. *United States,* 196 U.S. 375, 398. It was soon demonstrated that the effects of many kinds of intrastate activity upon interstate commerce were such as to make them a proper subject of federal regulation. In some cases sustaining the exercise of federal power over intrastate matters the term "direct" was used for the purpose of stating, rather than of reaching, a result; in others it was treated as synonymous with "substantial" or "material"; and in others it was

not used at all. Of late its use has been abandoned in cases dealing with questions of federal power under the Commerce Clause.

In the *Shreveport Rate Cases,* 234 U.S. 342, the Court held that railroad rates of an admittedly intrastate character and fixed by authority of the state might, nevertheless, be revised by the Federal Government because of the economic effects which they had upon interstate commerce. The opinion of Mr. Justice Hughes found federal intervention constitutionally authorized because of "matters having such a close and substantial relation to interstate traffic that the control is essential or appropriate to the security of that traffic, to the efficiency of the interstate service, and to the maintenance of conditions under which interstate commerce may be conducted upon fair terms and without molestation or hindrance." *Id.* at 351.

The Court's recognition of the relevance of the economic effects in the application of the Commerce Clause, exemplified by this statement, has made the mechanical application of legal formulas no longer feasible. Once an economic measure of the reach of the power granted to Congress in the Commerce Clause is accepted, questions of federal power cannot be decided simply by finding the activity in question to be "production," nor can consideration of its economic effects be foreclosed by calling them "indirect." …

Whether the subject of the regulation in question was "production," "consumption," or "marketing" is, therefore, not material for purposes of deciding the question of federal power before us. That an activity is of local character may help in a doubtful case to determine whether Congress intended to reach it. The same consideration might help in determining whether in the absence of Congressional action it would be permissible for the state to exert its power on the subject matter, even though in so doing it to some degree affected interstate commerce. But even if appellee's activity be local and though it may not be regarded as commerce, it may still, whatever its nature, be reached by Congress if it exerts a substantial economic effect on interstate commerce, and this irrespective of whether such effect is what might at some earlier time have been defined as "direct" or "indirect."

.   .   .

It is well established by decisions of this Court that the power to regulate commerce includes the power to regulate the prices at which commodities in that commerce are dealt in and practices affecting such prices. One of the primary purposes of the Act in question was to increase the market price of wheat, and to that end to limit the volume thereof that could affect the market. It can hardly be denied that a factor of such volume and variability as home-consumed wheat would have a substantial influence on price and market conditions. This may arise because being in marketable condition such wheat overhangs the market and, if induced by rising prices, tends to flow into the market and check price increases. But if we assume that it is never marketed, it supplies a need of the man who grew it which would otherwise be reflected by purchases in the open market. Home-grown wheat in this sense competes with wheat in commerce. The stimulation of commerce is a use of the regulatory function quite as definitely as prohibitions or restrictions thereon. This record leaves us in no doubt that Congress may properly have considered that wheat consumed on the farm where grown, if wholly outside the scheme of regulation, would have a substantial effect in defeating and obstructing its purpose to stimulate trade therein at increased prices.

. . .

E. FROM *NATIONAL LEAGUE* TO *GARCIA*

A contentious issue of federalism in recent decades involved the extension of federal hours-and-wages standards to state employees. The Supreme Court halted this trend toward national control in *National League of Cities* v. *Usery* (1976) but reversed itself nine years later in *Garcia* v. *San Antonio Metropolitan Transit Authority* (1985), giving Congress almost total power under the Commerce Clause. In *Garcia*, the Court announced that the protection of federalism depends largely on the political process operating within Congress.

The Fair Labor Standards Act of 1938 expressly exempted all states and their political divisions from the federal minimum-wage and overtime provisions. In 1966, Congress extended federal minimum wages and overtime pay to state-operated hospitals and schools. Two years later the Court upheld that legislation as rationally based, deciding that Congress had properly taken into account the effect on interstate competition and the promotion of labor peace. Maryland v. Wirtz, 392 U.S. 183 (1968). Building on that decision, in 1975 the Court upheld the short-term power of the President to stabilize wages and salaries of state employees. Fry v. United States, 421 U.S. 542, 549–59 (1975).

A year later, however, Justice Rehnquist attracted four other votes to his position that federal minimum-wage and maximum-hour provisions could not displace state powers in such "traditional governmental functions" as fire prevention, police protection, sanitation, public health, and parks and recreation. Amendments to the Fair Labor Standards Act in 1974 had extended the wage-and-hour provisions to almost all state employees. The 5–4 decision by Rehnquist overruled *Wirtz* by holding that the 1974 amendments threatened the independent existence of states. Justice Blackmun, in a tentative concurrence, supplied the fifth vote. The dissents were sharply worded. For the first time in four decades, the Court had invalidated a statute passed by Congress pursuant to the Commerce Clause. NATIONAL LEAGUE OF CITIES v. USERY, 426 U.S. 833 (1976).

Rehnquist's bifurcation between traditional and nontraditional governmental functions could not be applied with confidence or consistency either in the lower courts or in the Supreme Court itself. When lower courts found a function to be "traditional" and thus within the realm of state sovereignty, the Court would frequently reverse on the ground that the function was actually nontraditional and beyond the protection offered in *National League* (see box on next page).

One of the curious facts about *National League* is that when the Supreme Court remanded the case to a three-judge district court, the district court did not try to determine the difference between traditional and nontraditional functions. Instead, it asked the Labor Department to identify nontraditional state functions. It did so, providing a list of traditional functions as well. Included in the Department's list of nontraditional functions was "local mass transit systems," a decision that prompted new litigation and a challenge to *National League*.

The Hapless, Hopeless Effort to Implement *National League*

In 1981, a unanimous Court rejected a district court's argument that land use regulation was a "traditional governmental function" reserved to the states under *National League*. The Court held that *National League* applied to "states as states" and not to private business operations within a state. Hodel v. Virginia Surface Mining & Recl. Assn., 452 U.S. 264 (1981). A year later, a 5–4 Court rejected a district court's attempt to use *National League* to prohibit Congress from regulating retail sales of electricity and natural gas. The district court said this area of economic regulation was traditional; the Court said it was not. FERC v. Mississippi, 456 U.S. 742 (1982). In that same year, the Court rejected a Second Circuit's conclusion that a state-owned railroad engaged in interstate commerce represented a traditional governmental function. A unanimous Court said that the operation of railroads "has traditionally been a function of private industry, not state or local governments." United Transportation Union v. Long Island R. Co., 455 U.S. 678, 686 (1982).

In 1981, a federal district court held that the Age Discrimination in Employment Act passed by Congress in 1967 violated the Tenth Amendment theory articulated in *National League*. The case involved Wyoming's mandatory retirement of game wardens at the age of 55. Game wardens seemed to fit the categories of police protection, parks, and recreation, all of which *National League* specifically classified as a traditional state function. Nevertheless, a 5–4 Court reversed the district court. EEOC v. Wyoming, 460 U.S. 226 (1983). Significantly, Justice Blackmun (who had given Rehnquist a fifth vote in *National League*) provided the fifth vote in this case. Although the Wyoming case did not override *National League*, many Court-watchers concluded that little life remained in the 1976 ruling.

National League Is Overturned

Justice Blackmun's majority opinion in the mass transit case nullified the decision with which he had concurred less than ten years before. He pointed to the difficulty that courts had experienced in distinguishing between "traditional" and "nontraditional" state functions. The effect of his 5–4 decision was to leave the protection of federalism largely to the political process of Congress. GARCIA v. SAN ANTONIO METROPOLITAN TRANSIT AUTHORITY, 469 U.S. 528 (1985).

Garcia threatened the states with massive budgetary obligations. Most state employees were already receiving at least the minimum wage, but the cost of meeting the overtime provisions of the Fair Labor Standards Act could have reached several billion dollars, much of it for firefighters and police in local government. To prevent that cost from being transferred to the states, Congress passed legislation to postpone the effective date of *Garcia* (decided February 19, 1985) to April 15, 1986, and permitted the use of compensatory time as a substitute for paying overtime. 99 Stat. 787 (1985).

National League of Cities v. Usery
426 U.S. 833 (1976)

This case marks an effort by Justice Rehnquist to devise a doctrine to protect states' rights against federal intrusion. In 1974 Congress amended the Fair Labor Standards Act to extend minimum wage and maximum hour provisions to cover almost all employees of states and their political divisions. The National League of Cities, supported by a number of cities and states, brought an action against Secretary of Labor W.J. Usery, Jr., challenging the validity of the 1974 amendments and seeking declaratory and injunctive relief. A three-judge district court dismissed the complaint for failure to state a claim upon which relief might be granted.

Mr. Justice Rehnquist delivered the opinion of the Court.

Nearly 40 years ago Congress enacted the Fair Labor Standards Act, and required employers covered by the Act to pay their employees a minimum hourly wage and to pay them at one and one-half times their regular rate of pay for hours worked in excess of 40 during a workweek....

The original Fair Labor Standards Act passed in 1938 specifically excluded the States and their political subdivisions from its coverage....

I

[Rehnquist reviews congressional changes in the Act across a period of fifteen years.]

... In 1974, Congress again broadened the coverage of the Act.... ... The Act thus imposes upon almost all public employment the minimum wage and maximum hour requirements previously restricted to employees engaged in interstate commerce....

II

It is established beyond peradventure that the Commerce Clause of Art. I of the Constitution is a grant of plenary authority to Congress. That authority is, in the words of Mr. Chief Justice Marshall in *Gibbons* v. *Ogden*, 9 Wheat. 1 (1824), "the power to regulate; that is, to prescribe the rule by which commerce is to be governed." *Id.*, at 196....

Appellants in no way challenge these decisions establishing the breadth of authority granted Congress under the commerce power. Their contention, on the contrary, is that when Congress seeks to regulate directly the activities of States as public employers, it transgresses an affirmative limitation on the exercise of its power akin to other commerce power affirmative limitations contained in the Constitution....

This Court has never doubted that there are limits upon the power of Congress to override state sovereignty, even when exercising its otherwise plenary powers to tax or to regulate commerce which are conferred by Art. I of the Constitution. In *Wirtz*, for example, the Court took care to assure the appellants that it had "ample power to prevent ... 'the utter destruction of the State as a sovereign political entity,'" which they feared. 392 U.S., at 196....

One undoubted attribute of state sovereignty is the States' power to determine the wages which shall be paid to those whom they employ in order to carry out their governmental functions, what hours those persons will work, and what compensation will be provided where these employees may be called upon to work overtime. The question we must resolve here, then, is whether these determinations are "'functions essential to separate and independent existence,'" ... so that Congress may not abrogate the States' otherwise plenary authority to make them....

[Rehnquist observes that the Act will significantly increase the costs of state programs, including police and fire protection.]

... Our examination of the effect of the 1974 amendments, as sought to be extended to the States and their political subdivisions, satisfies us that both the minimum wage and the maximum hour provisions will impermissibly interfere with the integral governmental functions of these bodies.... [E]ven if we accept appellee's assessments concerning the impact of the amendments, their application will nonetheless significantly alter or displace the States' abilities to structure employer-employee relationships in such areas as fire prevention, police protection, sanitation, public health, and parks and recreation. These activities are typical of those performed by state and local governments in discharging their dual functions of administering the public law and furnishing public services. Indeed, it is functions such as these which governments are created to provide, services such as these which the States have traditionally afforded their citizens. We hold that insofar as the challenged amendments operate to directly displace the States' freedom to structure integral operations in areas of traditional governmental functions, they are not within the authority granted Congress by Art. I, § 8, cl. 3....

The judgment of the District Court is accordingly reversed, and the cases are remanded for further proceedings consistent with this opinion.

So ordered.

Mr. Justice Blackmun, concurring.

The Court's opinion and the dissents indicate the importance and significance of this litigation as it bears upon the relationship between the Federal Government and our States. Although I am not untroubled by certain possible implications of the Court's opinion — some of them suggested by the dissents — I do not read the opinion so despairingly as does my Brother Brennan. In my view, the result with respect to the statute under challenge here is necessarily correct. I may misinterpret the Court's opinion, but it seems to me that it adopts a balancing approach, and does not outlaw federal power in areas such as environmental protection, where the federal interest is demonstrably greater and where state facility compliance with imposed federal standards would be essential.... With this understanding on my part of the Court's opinion, I join it.

MR. JUSTICE BRENNAN, with whom MR. JUSTICE WHITE and MR. JUSTICE MARSHALL join, dissenting.

The Court concedes, as of course it must, that Congress enacted the 1974 amendments pursuant to its exclusive power under Art. I, § 8, cl. 3, of the Constitution "[t]o regulate Commerce ... among the several States." It must therefore be surprising that my Brethren should choose this bicentennial year of our independence to repudiate principles governing judicial interpretation of our Constitution settled since the time of Mr. Chief Justice John Marshall, discarding his postulate that the Constitution contemplates that restraints upon exercise by Congress of its plenary commerce power lie in the political process and not in the judicial process. For 152 years ago Mr. Chief Justice Marshall enunciated that principle to which, until today, his successors on this Court have been faithful.

"[T]he power over commerce ... is vested in Congress as absolutely as it would be in a single government, having in its constitution the same restrictions on the exercise of the power as are found in the constitution of the United States. *The wisdom and the discretion of Congress, their identity with the people, and the influence which their constituents possess at elections, are ... the sole restraints on which they have relied, to secure them from its abuse. They are the restraints on which the people must often rely solely, in all representative governments.*" *Gibbons* v. *Ogden,* 9 Wheat. 1, 197 (1824) (emphasis added).

. . .

Today's repudiation of this unbroken line of precedents that firmly reject my Brethren's ill-conceived abstraction can only be regarded as a transparent cover for invalidating a congressional judgment with which they disagree. The only analysis even remotely resembling that adopted today is found in a line of opinions dealing with the Commerce Clause and the Tenth Amendment that ultimately provoked a constitutional crisis for the Court in the 1930's. *E.g., Carter* v. *Carter Coal Co.,* 298 U.S. 238 (1936); *United States* v. *Butler,* 297 U.S. 1 (1936); *Hammer* v. *Dagenhart,* 247 U.S. 251 (1918).... It may have been the eventual abandonment of that overly restrictive construction of the commerce power that spelled defeat for the Court-packing plan, and preserved the integrity of this institution....

MR. JUSTICE STEVENS, dissenting.

The Court holds that the Federal Government may not interfere with a sovereign State's inherent right to pay a substandard wage to the janitor at the state capitol. The principle on which the holding rests is difficult to perceive.

The Federal Government may, I believe, require the State to act impartially when it hires or fires the janitor, to withhold taxes from his paycheck, to observe safety regulations when he is performing his job, to forbid him from burning too much soft coal in the capitol furnace, from dumping untreated refuse in an adjacent waterway, from overloading a state-owned garbage truck, or from driving either the truck or the Governor's limousine over 55 miles an hour. Even though these and many other activities of the capitol janitor are activities of the State *qua* State, I have no doubt that they are subject to federal regulation.

I agree that it is unwise for the Federal Government to exercise its power in the ways described in the Court's opinion....

My disagreement with the wisdom of this legislation may not, of course, affect my judgment with respect to its validity. On this issue there is no dissent from the proposition that the Federal Government's power over the labor market is adequate to embrace these employees....

Garcia v. San Antonio Metro. Transit Auth.

469 U.S. 528 (1985)

The federalism doctrine of *National League of Cities* (1976) rested on a narrow 5 to 4 decision, with Justice Blackmun's concurrence supplying the fifth vote. The doctrine's attempt to distinguish between "traditional" and "nontraditional" governmental functions produced vast confusion in the lower courts. Blackmun eventually concluded that the doctrine was unsound and unworkable. By switching sides, he created a new 5 to 4 majority to overturn *National League of Cities*. The *Garcia* case began in 1979 when the Department of Labor issued an opinion that the operations of the San Antonio Metropolitan Transit Authority (SAMTA) were not immune from the minimum-wage and overtime requirements of the Fair Labor Standards Act. SAMTA filed an action in federal district court, seeking declaratory relief. On the same day, Joe G. Garcia and several other SAMTA employees brought suit against SAMTA for overtime pay under the Fair Labor Standards Act.

JUSTICE BLACKMUN delivered the opinion of the Court....

In the present cases, a Federal District Court concluded that municipal ownership and operation of a mass-transit system is a traditional governmental function and thus, under *National League of Cities,* is exempt from the obligations imposed by the FLSA. Faced with the identical question, three Federal Courts of Appeals and one state appellate court have reached the opposite conclusion.

Our examination of this "function" standard applied in these and other cases over the last eight years now persuades us that the attempt to draw the boundaries of state regulatory immunity in terms of "traditional governmental function" is not only unworkable but is also inconsistent with established principles of federalism and, indeed, with those very federalism principles on which *National League of Cities* purported to rest. That case, accordingly, is overruled.

I

[Justice Blackmun reviews the history of public transportation in San Antonio and the funding sources that supported it.]

II

... The District Court voiced a common concern: "Despite the abundance of adjectives, identifying which particular state functions are immune *[from regulation under the Fair Labor Standards Act]* remains difficult." 557 F. Supp., at 447. Just how troublesome the task has been is revealed by the results reached in other federal cases.... We find it difficult, if not impossible, to identify an organizing principle that places each of the cases in the first group*[protected under National League of Cities]* on one side of a line and each of the cases in the second group*[not protected]* on the other side. The constitutional distinction between licensing drivers*[protected]* and regulating traffic*[not protected]*, for example, or between operating a highway authority*[protected]* and operating a mental health facility*[not protected]*, is elusive at best....

We believe, however, that there is a more fundamental problem at work here.... The essence of our federal system is that within the realm of authority left open to them under the Constitution, the States must be equally free to engage in any activity that their citizens choose for the common weal, no matter how unorthodox or unnecessary anyone else— including the judiciary—deems state involvement to be. Any rule of state immunity that looks to the "traditional," "integral," or "necessary" nature of governmental functions inevitably invites an unelected federal judiciary to make decisions about which state policies it favors and which ones it dislikes.... In the words of Justice Black:

"There is not, and there cannot be, any unchanging line of demarcation between essential and non-essential governmental functions. Many governmental functions of today have at some time in the past been nongovernmental. The genius of our government provides that, within the sphere of constitutional action, the people—acting not through the courts but through their elected legislative representatives—have the power to determine as conditions demand, what services and functions the public welfare requires." *Helvering* v. *Gerhardt,* 304 U.S., at 427 (concurring opinion).

We therefore now reject, as unsound in principle and unworkable in practice, a rule of state immunity from federal regulation that turns on a judicial appraisal of whether a particular governmental function is "integral" or "traditional."...

IV

This analysis makes clear that Congress' action in affording SAMTA employees the protections of the wage and hour provisions of the FLSA contravened no affirmative limit on Congress' power under the Commerce Clause. The judgment of the District Court therefore must be reversed.

Of course, we continue to recognize that the States occupy a special and specific position in our constitutional system and that the scope of Congress' authority under the Commerce Clause must reflect that position. But the principal and basic limit on the federal commerce power is that inherent in all congressional action—the built-in restraints that our system provides through state participation in federal governmental action. The political process ensures that laws that unduly burden the States will not be promulgated. In the factual setting of these cases the internal safeguards of the political process have performed as intended.

. . .

National League of Cities v. *Usery,* 426 U.S. 833 (1976), is overruled. The judgment of the District Court is reversed, and these cases are remanded to that court for further proceedings consistent with this opinion.

It is so ordered.

JUSTICE POWELL, with whom THE CHIEF JUSTICE, JUSTICE REHNQUIST, and JUSTICE O'CONNOR join, dissenting....

I

There are, of course, numerous examples over the history of this Court in which prior decisions have been reconsidered and overruled. There have been few cases, however, in which the principle of *stare decisis* and the rationale of recent decisions were ignored as abruptly as we now witness....

Whatever effect the Court's decision may have in weakening the application of *stare decisis,* it is likely to be less important than what the Court has done to the Constitution itself. A unique feature of the United States is the *federal* system of government guaranteed by the Constitution and implicit in the very name of our country. Despite some genuflecting in the Court's opinion to the concept of federalism, today's decision effectively reduces the Tenth Amendment to meaningless rhetoric

when Congress acts pursuant to the Commerce Clause....

[II.B]

Today's opinion does not explain how the States' role in the electoral process guarantees that particular exercises of the Commerce Clause power will not infringe on residual state sovereignty. Members of Congress are elected from the various States, but once in office they are Members of the Federal Government....

More troubling than the logical infirmities in the Court's reasoning is the result of its holding, *i.e.,* that federal political officials, invoking the Commerce Clause, are the sole judges of the limits of their own power. This result is inconsistent with the fundamental principles of our constitutional system. See, *e.g.,* The Federalist No. 78 (Hamilton). At least since *Marbury* v. *Madison,* 1 Cranch 137, 177 (1803), it has been the settled province of the federal judiciary "to say what the law is" with respect to the constitutionality of Acts of Congress....

JUSTICE REHNQUIST, dissenting....

JUSTICE O'CONNOR, with whom JUSTICE POWELL and JUSTICE REHNQUIST join, dissenting.

The Court today surveys the battle scene of federalism and sounds a retreat. Like JUSTICE POWELL, I would prefer to hold the field and, at the very least, render a little aid to the wounded....

... With the abandonment of *National League of Cities,* all that stands between the remaining essentials of state sovereignty and Congress is the latter's underdeveloped capacity for self-restraint.

. . .

F. STATE POWERS REVIVED

Although *Garcia* shifted much of the guardian role of federalism to Congress, the Supreme Court continued to use the Tenth Amendment and other constitutional provisions to protect state powers. Whereas the Court in *Garcia* was willing to leave federalism largely to the political process, in the 1990s the Court moved aggressively to curb congressional authority and reinforce state sovereignty.

In 1991 the Court held that Missouri's constitution—providing a mandatory retirement age of 70 for most state judges—did not violate the Age Discrimination in Employment Act (ADEA) of 1967. As a sovereign state, Missouri's range of action is protected by the Tenth Amendment and the Guarantee Clause of Art. IV, § 4. The authority of states to determine the qualification of their officials lies at the heart of representative government. This decision seemed to rest largely on constitutional grounds, and yet the Court was also involved in statutory interpretation, leaving the door open for Congress to rewrite the ADEA so that it explicitly covers state judges. Gregory v. Ashcroft, 501 U.S. 452, 467 (1991).

A year later, the Court relied on the Tenth Amendment to invalidate part of a 1985 congressional statute designed to force states to find disposal sites for low-level radioactive waste. The 6–3 decision ruled that the statutory provision (forcing states to take possession of the waste if they failed to discover other solutions) represented an invalid effort by Congress to commandeer the states' legislative processes and thus inconsistent with the Tenth Amendment. The Court said that states are not "mere political subdivisions" of the United States, nor are state governments regional offices or administrative agencies of the federal government. New York v. United States, 505 U.S. 144, 188 (1992). In terms of public policy, the decision was not too significant. Rather than draft new legislation to satisfy the Court, Congress decided to rely on the existing compacts that states had created to dispose of low-level radioactive waste.

Gun Controls

In 1995, the Supreme Court struck down a congressional statute that banned guns within 1,000 feet of a school. Divided 5 to 4, the Court ruled that Congress had exceeded its authority under the Commerce Clause. The majority held that the statute had nothing to do with commerce or any sort of economic enterprise. UNITED STATES v. LOPEZ, 514 U.S. 549 (1995). Some commentators regarded the decision as one of the most important rulings in recent decades, but it may have been a case where Congress simply failed to present adequate findings to show an interstate commerce link with guns on school playgrounds.

Within two weeks of the Court's decision, President Clinton submitted legislation to Congress to amend the earlier statute by requiring the federal government to prove that the firearm has "moved in or the possession of such firearm otherwise affects interstate or foreign commerce." Public Papers of the Presidents, 1995, I, at 678. Congress enacted legislation in 1996, finding that crime at the local level "is exacerbated by the interstate movement of drugs, guns, and criminal gangs," that the occurrence of violent crime in school zones has resulted in a decline in the quality of education, and that it has the power under the interstate commerce clause to enact the legislation. The statutory language provides: "It shall be unlawful for any individual knowingly to possess a firearm that has moved in or that otherwise affects interstate or foreign commerce at a place that the individual knows, or has reasonable cause to believe, is a school zone." 110 Stat. 3009-369, § 657 (1996). There have been no legal challenges to this legislation.

Term Limits and Indian Casinos

Federalism was an issue in the term limits case decided by the Supreme Court in 1995. A number of states had adopted constitutional amendments or other measures to place term limits on legislators not only from the states but in Congress as well. Arkansas, for example, amended its constitution to limit members of Congress to three terms in the House of Representatives and to two terms in the Senate. Relying primarily on *Powell* v. *McCormack*, 395 U.S. 486 (1969), the Court held that the Arkansas provision violated the U.S. Constitution by adding to the qualifications established for members of Congress. U.S. Term Limits, Inc. v. Thornton, 514 U.S. 779 (1995). The fifth vote in this 5 to 4 decision was supplied in a concurrence by Justice Kennedy, who invoked principles of federalism to strike down the Arkansas amendment: "That the States may not invade the sphere of federal sovereignty is as incontestable, in my view, as the corollary proposition that the Federal Government must be held within the boundaries of its own power when it intrudes upon matters reserved to the States." Id. at 841.

Again divided 5 to 4, the Court in 1996 ruled that Congress lacked authority under the Indian Commerce Clause to abrogate the states' Eleventh Amendment immunity from lawsuits. At issue was the Indian Gaming Regulatory Act, which allowed Indian tribes to sue states in federal court in disputes between tribes and states regarding gaming operations. Gambling in Indian casinos had grown to a $4 billion a year business. While overruling the opinion in *Pennsylvania* v. *Union Gas Co.* (1989)

that the Commerce Clause can trump state sovereign immunity, the Court left in place the holding in *Fitzpatrick* v. *Bitzer* (1976) that Congress can override state immunity when it legislates pursuant to the Fourteenth Amendment. Four Justices joined two lengthy dissents. Seminole Tribe of Florida v. Florida, 517 U.S. 44 (1996).

Gun Controls Again

In another 5 to 4 ruling, the Court in 1997 relied largely on its understanding of federalism to strike down a key portion of the 1993 Brady gun control law. That statute required state and local law enforcement officers to conduct background checks on prospective handgun purchasers. Relying heavily on its 1992 decision in *New York,* the Court held that state legislatures "are *not* subject to federal direction." Printz v. United States, 521 U.S. 898 (1997). The Court cited the Tenth Amendment as ground for invalidating the statutory provision. Id. at 919. It also pointed to *New York*'s standard that Congress cannot compel the states to enact or enforce a federal regulatory program and cannot "circumvent that prohibition by conscripting the States's officers directly." Id. at 935. Concurrences by Justices O'Connor and Thomas agreed that the Brady Act violated the Tenth Amendment. The dissenters looked to Hamilton's essay in Federalist No. 27 and to statutes of the early Congresses as evidence that Congress may require state courts and other state officials to implement federal law.

The Court's decision is not expected to have a substantial effect on governmental policy. Most states already require background checks and the federal government is developing a system that can do the work currently left to local law enforcement officials. Beginning on November 30, 1998, gun dealers were required to check the names of prospective buyers against a computerized list of offenders prepared by the FBI.

Lawsuits Against the States

A trio of 5–4 decisions on June 23, 1999, placed additional curbs on congressional power to expose states to private lawsuits without state consent. Although the rulings attracted broad attention, much of the interest was directed to the continued division of Justices on federalism. Split along political lines, the majority consisted of the conservative-moderate wing (Rehnquist, O'Connor, Kennedy, Scalia, and Thomas), while the dissents came from moderate-liberals (Stevens, Souter, Ginsburg, and Breyer). Writing for the *New York Times,* Linda Greenhouse remarked that "the fault line that runs through the current Court as an all but unbridgeable gulf has to do not with the higher-profile issues of race, religion, abortion or due process, but with federalism." N.Y. Times, June 24, 1999, at A22.

Two of the decisions affected the application of federal law to states. In the first, Congress had amended the Lanham Act to subject states to suits for false and misleading advertising. The Court ruled that the statute abrogated state sovereign immunity because Florida had not expressly consented to being sued in federal court and Congress had not acted validly under its enforcement powers under the Fourteenth Amendment. College Savings Bank v. Florida Prepaid Postsecondary, 527 U.S. 666 (1999).

The second decision covered a 1992 amendment to federal law that expressly abrogated the states' sovereign immunity from claims of patent infringement. The Court ruled that this amendment could not be upheld as an exercise of Congress' power under the Fourteenth Amendment because it was not properly "remedial" and it lacked proportionality. To invoke the Fourteenth Amendment, Congress must identify state conduct that transgresses the substantive provisions of the Amendment. Florida Prepaid Postsecondary v. College Sav., 527 U.S. 627 (1999). Legislation has been introduced to allow holders of intellectual property to sue states for infringement damages. 147 Cong. Rec. S11364–68 (daily ed. Nov. 1, 2001); 148 Cong. Rec. S2078–82 (daily ed. March 19, 2002).

The decision that drew most of the interest involved a suit brought against a state for violating the overtime provision of the Fair Labor Standards Act. The Court held that any effort by Congress to authorize private actions against the states *in state court*, without the consent of the states, is an unconstitutional abrogation of state sovereign immunity. In an exceptionally long and complex decision, five members of the majority and four dissenters often cited identical historical materials but came to entirely different conclusions. Alden v. Maine, 527 U.S. 706 (1999).

Continuing its string of 5–4 decisions on federalism, in 2000 the Court ruled that state workers— discriminated against because of their age — could not sue under federal law in the states. The Eleventh Amendment, said the majority, prevented such suits against state employers. The Court held that Congress, in the Age Discrimination in Employment Act of 1967 (ADEA), had stated a clear intent to abrogate the states' immunity but that the abrogation exceeded congressional authority under Section 5 of the Fourteenth Amendment. Kimel v. Florida Bd. of Regents, 528 U.S. 62 (2000).

On the following day, in a rare unanimous decision involving federalism, the Court upheld a congressional statute (the Driver's Privacy Protection Act of 1994) that prohibited states from disclosing the personal information that drivers provide when obtaining a license. As a result of the decision, states may not sell addresses, telephone numbers, and other information included in the license application. Congress passed the 1994 statute after the death of a woman who had been killed by a stalker who had obtained her address from the motor vehicles division. The Court held that Congress acted properly under its powers to regulate interstate commerce. Reno v. Condon, 528 U.S. 141 (2000).

Another blow to congressional power came in 2000 when the Court held that a provision in the Violence Against Women Act of 1994 could not be sustained under the Commerce Clause or Section 5 of the Fourteenth Amendment. The provision permitted victims of rape, domestic violence and other crimes "motivated by gender" to sue their attackers in federal court. The Court ruled that Congress may not regulate "noneconomic, violent criminal conduct based solely on that conduct's aggregate effect on interstate commerce." Unlike the Guns in the Schoolyard Act, Congress had amassed findings and compiled a record to demonstrate the scope of the problem. Similar to other federalism rulings, the Court was split 5 to 4. UNITED STATES v. MORRISON, 529 U.S. 598 (2000).

Federalism was at stake in 2000 when the Court reversed the Supreme Court of Florida's order for a manual recount to decide the presidential election. Although critics accused the majority of inconsistently championing federalism in most matters but not in this one, the Court was faced with issues of Art. II, § 1, cl. 2, of the United States Constitution and compliance with 3 U.S.C. § 5 (see Chapter 18 for further details). As Chief Justice Rehnquist and Justices Scalia and Thomas noted in their concurrence, the Court's "inquiry does not imply a disrespect for state *courts* but rather a respect for the constitutionally prescribed role of state *legislatures*." Bush v. Gore, 531 U.S. 98, 115 (2000).

Two other decisions, in 2001 and 2002, gave further protection to the states. In 2001, split along its usual 5–4 axis, the Supreme Court ruled that state immunity prevents state employees from suing state agencies for money damages under the federal Americans With Disabilities Act (ADA). The Court decided that Congress in such cases lacked power under Section 5 of the Fourteenth Amendment to abrogate state immunity under the Eleventh Amendment. The ADA's legislative record, said the Court, failed to identify a history and pattern of irrational employment discrimination by the states against the disabled. The Court concluded that the ADA was aimed primarily at employment discrimination in the private sector. The dissenters found about 300 examples of discrimination by state governments in the legislative record. Board of Trustees of Univ. of Ala. v. Garrett, 531 U.S. 356 (2001).

In 2002, another 5–4 decision held that the principle of state sovereignty protected states from having to respond to private complaints before federal agencies, in this case the Federal Maritime Commission. The decision applies only to agency actions against the states based on private complaints. Agencies may still go to court based on their own investigations of the states. Fed. Maritime Com'n v. S.C. State Ports Auth., 535 U.S. 743 (2002).

[Also struck down largely on grounds of federalism was the Religious Freedom Restoration Act of 1993, treated in Chapter 12; Boerne v. Flores, 521 U.S. 507 (1997).]

More Fine-Tuning

The pattern of 5–4 decisions dominated by conservatives broke in two cases decided in 2003 and 2004. In the first, a 6–3 Court ruled that states can be sued if they violate a worker's federally guaranteed right to take time off for family emergencies. Nevada had claimed constitutional immunity from being sued under the Family and Medical Leave Act. Curiously, the author of the majority opinion was Chief Justice Rehnquist, joined by O'Connor and the liberal-moderate wing of Souter, Ginsburg, Breyer, and Stevens. Rehnquist concluded that the family leave act was more "narrowly targeted" than federal statutes challenged in previous rulings. Neither proponents nor opponents of the decision could discover much coherence or consistency in the Court's federalism rulings, especially cases concerning state immunity from lawsuit. Although the congressional statute in this case was upheld, the Court could use the occasion to highlight its belief that "it falls to this Court, not Congress, to define the substance of constitutional guarantees." Nevada Dept. of Human Resources v. Hibbs, 538 U.S. 721, 728 (2003).

Some interpreters thought the decision could be explained by the Court's "heightened scrutiny" of gender-based discrimination. However, in 2004 the Court upheld the right of disabled individuals to sue state governments that fail to provide ramps and other forms of access to their courthouses. Tennessee tried to dismiss the suit by relying on the Eleventh Amendment. The Court returned to its customary 5–4 division, but this time O'Connor joined the four liberal-moderate Justices to form the majority, with Rehnquist, Kennedy, Thomas, and Scalia dissenting. The majority ruled that the Americans With Disabilities Act provides a proper basis to allow individuals to seek money damages from states that do not accommodate their access to courthouses. O'Connor may have joined the majority decision because it was limited to "the fundamental right of access to the court" and did not involve access to other state facilities, such as hockey rinks or voting booths. Moreover, in renovating courthouses, states were not expected to assume "an undue financial or administrative burden" or threaten historic preservation interests. Tennessee v. Lane, 541 U.S. 509 (2004).

Linda Greenhouse, long-time Supreme Court reporter for *The New York Times,* suggested in 2008 that the Court had backed off from its formalistic pro-state analysis of federalism because it was "out of sync with the prevailing mood" after the events of September 11, 2001. "Suddenly, the federal government looked useful, even necessary," wrote Greenhouse. "The Supreme Court's federalism revolution had been overtaken by events." "2,691 Decisions," New York Times, July 13, 2008, at WK 4.

State Moral Issues: Wine, Marijuana, and Assisted Suicide

The ambiguity about the Court's direction in the federalism realm was heightened by decisions made in 2005-2006. State attempts to regulate the sale of wine and the use of marijuana for medical purposes were rebuffed by the Court during the 2005 Term as violations of the Commerce Clause. The Court, in a 5-4 ruling, struck down Michigan and New York laws that permitted in-state, but not out-of-state, wineries to sell directly to consumers in the state. Justice Kennedy wrote for the Court that, "in all but the narrowest circumstances, state laws violate the Commerce Clause if they mandate differential treatment of in-state and out-of-state economic interests that benefits the former and burdens the latter." The Court held that the discrimination was "neither authorized nor permitted by the Twenty-first Amendment," which grants to states the authority to regulate the importation of liquor. GRANHOLM v. HEALD, 544 U.S. 460 (2005).

In *Gonzales v. Raich,* the Court, in a 6–3 ruling, upheld congressional authority and the federal prosecution of California residents who, under state law, used medically-prescribed marijuana, in a challenge that claimed Congress had violated the Commerce Clause and the boundaries of federalism. In an opinion that relied on the reasoning of Wickard v. Filburn, 317 U.S. 111 (1942), Justice Stevens held that Congress possesses the authority to prohibit the "local cultivation and use of marijuana" as a means of regulating "purely local activities that are part of an economic "class of activities' that have a substantial effect on interstate commerce." GONZALES v. RAICH, 545 U.S. 1 (2005).

But in 2006 the Court upheld Oregon's Death with Dignity Act, concluding that the U.S. Attorney General had overstepped his authority under the Controlled Substances Act in issuing a regulation designed to stop implementation of the state act. Justice Kennedy, writing for the six- person majority, argued that if Congress had intended to preempt the traditional state regulation of the medical profession it would have done so more clearly. The new Chief Justice Roberts joined Scalia and Thomas in dissent, finding that the congressional act was sufficiently pervasive to allow the federal regulation. GONZALES v. OREGON, 546 U.S. 243 (2006). At the very least, the loss of Rehnquist and O'Connor, two strong advocates of state power, and their replacement by Roberts and Alito, two men whose careers were largely centered in the federal government, suggests that the Court may be less "aggressive" going forward in pursuing a "rigid" notion of American federalism. Banks and Blakeman, 38 Publius 576-600 (2008).

United States v. Lopez

514 U.S. 549 (1995)

Congress enacted legislation in 1990 [§ 922(q)] to forbid "any individual knowingly to possess a firearm at a place that [he] knows … is a school zone." The Fifth Circuit held that, in light of what it characterized as insufficient congressional findings and legislative history, the provision was invalid because it exceeded Congress' power under the Commerce Clause. Alfonso Lopez, Jr., a 12th-grade student, arrived at his high school carrying a concealed handgun and five bullets.

CHIEF JUSTICE REHNQUIST delivered the opinion of the Court.

In the Gun-Free School Zones Act of 1990, Congress made it a federal offense "for any individual knowingly to possess a firearm at a place that the individual knows, or has reasonable cause to believe, is a school zone."… The Act neither regulates a commercial activity nor contains a requirement that the possession be connected in any way to interstate commerce. We hold that the Act exceeds the authority of Congress "[t]o regulate Commerce … among the several States.…" U. S. Const., Art. I, § 8, cl. 3.

. . .

We start with first principles. The Constitution creates a Federal Government of enumerated powers. See Art. I, § 8. As James Madison wrote, "[t]he powers delegated by the proposed Constitution to the federal government are few and defined. Those which are to remain in the State governments are numerous and indefinite." The Federalist No. 45, pp. 292–293 (C. Rossiter ed. 1961). This constitutionally mandated division of authority "was adopted by the Framers to ensure protection of our fundamental liberties." *Gregory v. Ashcroft,* 501 U. S. 452, 458 (1991) (internal quotation marks omitted).…

The Constitution delegates to Congress the power "[t]o regulate Commerce with foreign Nations, and among the several States, and with the Indian Tribes." Art. I, § 8, cl. 3. The Court, through Chief Justice Marshall, first defined the nature of

Congress' commerce power in *Gibbons v. Ogden,* 9 Wheat. 1, 189–190 (1824):

"Commerce, undoubtedly, is traffic, but it is something more: it is intercourse. It describes the commercial intercourse between nations, and parts of nations, in all its branches, and is regulated by prescribing rules for carrying on that intercourse."

The commerce power "is the power to regulate; that is, to prescribe the rule by which commerce is to be governed. This power, like all others vested in congress, is complete in itself, may be exercised to its utmost extent, and acknowledges no limitations, other than are prescribed in the constitution." *Id.,* at 196. The *Gibbons* Court, however, acknowledged that limitations on the commerce power are inherent in the very language of the Commerce Clause.

"It is not intended to say that these words comprehend that commerce, which is completely internal, which is carried on between man and man in a State, or between different parts of the same State, and which does not extend to or affect other States. Such a power would be inconvenient, and is certainly unnecessary.

"Comprehensive as the word 'among' is, it may very properly be restricted to that commerce which concerns more States than one.… The enumeration presupposes something not enumerated; and that something, if we regard the language, or the subject of the sentence, must be the exclusively internal commerce of a State." *Id.*, at 194–195.

For nearly a century thereafter, the Court's Commerce Clause decisions dealt but rarely with the extent of Congress' power, and almost entirely with the Commerce Clause as a limit on state legislation that discriminated against interstate commerce [*Chief Justice Rehnquist summarizes the Court's holdings in cases that recognized a broad power in Congress to regulate commerce, including NLRB v. Jones & Laughlin Steel Corp. (1937), United States v. Darby (1941), and Wickard v. Filburn (1942).*]

... [W]e have identified three broad categories of activity that Congress may regulate under its commerce power.... First, Congress may regulate the use of the channels of interstate commerce.... Second, Congress is empowered to regulate and protect the instrumentalities of interstate commerce, or persons or things in interstate commerce, even though the threat may come only from intrastate activities.... Finally, Congress' commerce authority includes the power to regulate those activities having a substantial relation to interstate commerce, ... *i.e.*, those activities that substantially affect interstate commerce, ...

Within this final category, admittedly, our case law has not been clear whether an activity must "affect" or "substantially affect" interstate commerce in order to be within Congress' power to regulate it under the Commerce Clause.... We conclude, consistent with the great weight of our case law, that the proper test requires an analysis of whether the regulated activity "substantially affects" interstate commerce.

We now turn to consider the power of Congress, in the light of this framework, to enact § 922(q). The first two categories of authority may be quickly disposed of: § 922(q) is not a regulation of the use of the channels of interstate commerce, nor is it an attempt to prohibit the interstate transportation of a commodity through the channels of commerce; nor can § 922(q) be justified as a regulation by which Congress has sought to protect an instrumentality of interstate commerce or a thing in interstate commerce. Thus, if § 922(q) is to be sustained, it must be under the third category as a regulation of an activity that substantially affects interstate commerce.

. . .

Section 922(q) is a criminal statute that by its terms has nothing to do with "commerce" or any sort of economic enterprise, however broadly one might define those terms. Section 922(q) is not an essential part of a larger regulation of economic ac-

tivity, in which the regulatory scheme could be undercut unless the intrastate activity were regulated. It cannot, therefore, be sustained under our cases upholding regulations of activities that arise out of or are connected with a commercial transaction, which viewed in the aggregate, substantially affects interstate commerce.

. . .

Although as part of our independent evaluation of constitutionality under the Commerce Clause we of course consider legislative findings, and indeed even congressional committee findings, regarding effect on interstate commerce, ... the Government concedes that "[n]either the statute nor its legislative history contain[s] express congressional findings regarding the effects upon interstate commerce of gun possession in a school zone." ... We agree with the Government that Congress normally is not required to make formal findings as to the substantial burdens that an activity has on interstate commerce.... But to the extent that congressional findings would enable us to evaluate the legislative judgment that the activity in question substantially affected interstate commerce, even though no such substantial effect was visible to the naked eye, they are lacking here.

. . .

The Government's essential contention, *in fine*, is that we may determine here that § 922(q) is valid because possession of a firearm in a local school zone does indeed substantially affect interstate commerce.... The Government argues that possession of a firearm in a school zone may result in violent crime and that violent crime can be expected to affect the functioning of the national economy in two ways. First, the costs of violent crime are substantial, and, through the mechanism of insurance, those costs are spread throughout the population.... Second, violent crime reduces the willingness of individuals to travel to areas within the country that are perceived to be unsafe.... The Government also argues that the presence of guns in schools poses a substantial threat to the educational process by threatening the learning environment. A handicapped educational process, in turn, will result in a less productive citizenry. That, in turn, would have an adverse effect on the Nation's economic well-being As a result, the Government argues that Congress could rationally have concluded that § 922(q) substantially affects interstate commerce.

We pause to consider the implications of the Government's arguments. The Government admits, under its "costs of crime" reasoning, that Congress could regulate not only all violent crime, but all activities that might lead to violent crime, regardless of how tenuously they relate to interstate commerce.... Similarly, under the Government's "national productivity" reasoning, Congress could regulate any activity that it found was related to the economic productivity of individual citizens: family law (including marriage, divorce, and child custody), for example. Under the theories that the Government presents in support of § 922(q), it is difficult to perceive any limitation on federal power, even in areas such as criminal law enforcement or education where States historically have been sovereign. Thus, if we were to accept the Government's arguments, we are hard pressed to posit any activity by an individual that Congress is without power to regulate.

Although JUSTICE BREYER argues that acceptance of the Government's rationales would not authorize a general federal police power, he is unable to identify any activity that the States may regulate but Congress may not....

For the foregoing reasons the judgment of the Court of Appeals is

Affirmed.

JUSTICE KENNEDY, with whom JUSTICE O'CONNOR joins, concurring....

The statute now before us forecloses the States from experimenting and exercising their own judgment in an area to which States lay claim by right of history and expertise, and it does so by regulating an activity beyond the realm of commerce in the ordinary and usual sense of that term. The tendency of this statute to displace state regulation in areas of traditional state concern is evident from its territorial operation. There are over 100,000 elementary and secondary schools in the United States....

JUSTICE THOMAS, concurring.

... Although I join the majority, I write separately to observe that our case law has drifted far from the original understanding of the Commerce Clause. In a future case, we ought to temper our Commerce Clause jurisprudence in a manner that both makes sense of our more recent case law and is more faithful to the original understanding of that Clause....

JUSTICE STEVENS, dissenting....

JUSTICE SOUTER, dissenting.

In reviewing congressional legislation under the Commerce Clause, we defer to what is often a merely implicit congressional judgment that its reg-

ulation addresses a subject substantially affecting interstate commerce "if there is any rational basis for such a finding...."

... The modern respect for the competence and primacy of Congress in matters affecting commerce developed only after one of this Court's most chastening experiences, when it perforce repudiated an earlier and untenably expansive conception of judicial review in derogation of congressional commerce power. A look at history's sequence will serve to show how today's decision tugs the Court off course....

II

... [I]f it seems anomalous that the Congress of the United States has taken to regulating school yards, the Act in question is still probably no more remarkable than state regulation of bake shops 90 years ago....

JUSTICE BREYER, with whom JUSTICE STEVENS, JUSTICE SOUTER, and JUSTICE GINSBURG join, dissenting.

The issue in this case is whether the Commerce Clause authorizes Congress to enact a statute that makes it a crime to possess a gun in, or near, a school.... In my view, the statute falls well within the scope of the commerce power as this Court has understood that power over the last half century.

I

In reaching this conclusion, I apply three basic principles of Commerce Clause interpretation. First, the power to "regulate Commerce ... among the several States," U. S. Const., Art. I, § 8, cl. 3, encompasses the power to regulate local activities insofar as they significantly affect interstate commerce....

... I use the word "significant" because the word "substantial" implies a somewhat narrower power than recent precedent suggests.... But to speak of "substantial effect" rather than "significant effect" would make no difference in this case.

Second, in determining whether a local activity will likely have a significant effect upon interstate commerce, a court must consider, not the effect of an individual act (a single instance of gun possession), but rather the cumulative effect of all similar instances (*i.e.*, the effect of all guns possessed in or near schools)....

Third, the Constitution requires us to judge the connection between a regulated activity and interstate commerce, not directly, but at one remove. Courts must give Congress a degree of leeway in determining the existence of a significant factual connection between the regulated activity and interstate commerce—both because the Constitution delegates the commerce power directly to Congress and because the determination requires an empirical judgment of a kind that a legislature is more likely than a court to make with accuracy. The traditional words "rational basis" capture this leeway....

II

... Numerous reports and studies—generated both inside and outside government—make clear that Congress could reasonably have found the empirical connection that its law, implicitly or explicitly, asserts. [Breyer supplies an Appendix of materials to document this point.]

United States v. Morrison

529 U.S. 598 (2000)

Christy Brzonkala, a student at the Virginia Polytechnic Institute, charged two students with assaulting and raping her in 1994. Although the school's Judicial Committee initially found one of the students, Antonio Morrison, guilty of sexual assault (later changing the charge to "using abusive language") and sentenced him to suspension for two semesters, the university later set aside Morrison's punishment. Brzonkala sued the students and Virginia Tech in federal court, complaining that the attack violated 42 U.S.C. § 13981 (part of the Violence Against Women Act of 1994). She also charged that Virginia Tech violated Title IX. A district court dismissed the Title IX claim and concluded that Congress lacked authority under either the Commerce Clause or Section 5 of the Fourteenth Amendment to enact § 13981. The Fourth Circuit, sitting en banc, affirmed the district court's conclusion that Congress lacked constitutional authority to enact § 13981.

CHIEF JUSTICE REHNQUIST delivered the opinion of the Court.

In these cases we consider the constitutionality of 42 U.S.C. § 13981, which provides a federal civil remedy for the victims of gender-motivated violence.... Believing that these cases are controlled by our decisions in *United States* v. *Lopez*, 514 U.S. 549 (1995), *United States* v. *Harris*, 106 U.S. 629 (1883), and the *Civil Rights Cases*, 109 U.S. 3 (1883), we affirm.

I

Petitioner Christy Brzonkala enrolled at Virginia Polytechnic Institute (Virginia Tech) in the fall of 1994. In September of that year, Brzonkala met respondents Antonio Morrison and James Crawford, who were both students at Virginia Tech and members of its varsity football team. Brzonkala alleges that, within 30 minutes of meeting Morrison and Crawford, they assaulted and repeatedly raped her....

[*Brzonkala filed a complaint against the two students. After several actions by the university's judicial committee, Virginia Tech's senior vice president and provost set aside any punishment for Morrison. After learning that Morrison would be returning to Virginia*

Tech, Brzonkala dropped out of the university and sued Morrison, Crawford, and Virginia Tech, claiming a violation of § 13981 and Title IX.]

Section 13981 was part of the Violence Against Women Act of 1994.... It states that "[a]ll persons within the United States shall have the right to be free from crimes of violence motivated by gender."...

Section 13981 defines a "crim[e] of violence motivated by gender" as "a crime of violence committed because of gender or on the basis of gender, and due, at least in part, to an animus based on the victim's gender."...

... [S]ubsection (e)(3) provides a § 13981 litigant with a choice of forums: Federal and state courts "shall have concurrent jurisdiction" over complaints brought under the section.

... Congress explicitly identified the sources of federal authority on which it relied in enacting § 13981. It said that a "federal civil rights cause of action" is established "[p]ursuant to the affirmative power of Congress ... under section 5 of the Fourteenth Amendment to the Constitution, as well as under section 8 of Article I of the Constitution."...

II

... Brzonkala and the United States rely upon the third clause of [*section 8*], which gives Congress

---

The text for this case, obtained in electronic form from Westlaw, is reproduced by permission of the West Group.

power "[t]o regulate Commerce with foreign Nations, and among the several States, and with the Indian Tribes."...

As we observed in *Lopez*, modern Commerce Clause jurisprudence has "identified three broad categories of activity that Congress may regulate under its commerce power." ..."First, Congress may regulate the use of the channels of interstate commerce." ..."Second, Congress is empowered to regulate and protect the instrumentalities of interstate commerce, or persons or things in interstate commerce, even though the threat may come only from intrastate activities." ..."Finally, Congress' commerce authority includes the power to regulate those activities having a substantial relation to interstate commerce, ... *i.e.*, those activities that substantially affect interstate commerce." ...

Petitioners do not contend that these cases fall within either of the first two of these categories of Commerce Clause regulation. They seek to sustain § 13981 as a regulation of activity that substantially affects interstate commerce.... [W]e agree that this is the proper inquiry.

Since *Lopez* most recently canvassed and clarified our case law governing this third category of Commerce Clause regulation, it provides the proper framework for conducting the required analysis of § 13981....

With these principles underlying our Commerce Clause jurisprudence as reference points, the proper resolution of the present cases is clear. Gender-motivated crimes of violence are not, in any sense of the phrase, economic activity....

Like the Gun-Free School Zones Act at issue in *Lopez*, § 13981 contains no jurisdictional element establishing that the federal cause of action is in pursuance of Congress' power to regulate interstate commerce. Although *Lopez* makes clear that such a jurisdictional element would lend support to the argument that § 13981 is sufficiently tied to interstate commerce, Congress elected to cast § 13981's remedy over a wider, and more purely intrastate, body of violent crime.

In contrast with the lack of congressional findings that we faced in *Lopez*, § 13981 is supported by numerous findings regarding the serious impact that gender-motivated violence has on victims and their families.... But the existence of congressional findings is not sufficient, by itself, to sustain the constitutionality of Commerce Clause legislation.... "'[w]hether particular operations affect interstate commerce sufficiently to come under the constitutional power of Congress to regulate them is ultimately a judicial rather than a legislative question,

and can be settled finally only by this Court.'" 514 U.S., at 557, n. 2 (quoting *Heart of Atlanta Motel*, 379 U.S., at 273 (Black, J., concurring)).

In these cases, Congress' findings are substantially weakened by the fact that they rely so heavily on a method of reasoning that we have already rejected as unworkable if we are to maintain the Constitution's enumeration of powers. Congress found that gender-motivated violence affects interstate commerce

"by deterring potential victims from traveling interstate, from engaging in employment in interstate business, and from transacting with business, and in places involved in interstate commerce; ... by diminishing national productivity, increasing medical and other costs, and decreasing the supply of and the demand for interstate products." ...

... If accepted, petitioners' reasoning would allow Congress to regulate any crime as long as the nationwide, aggregated impact of that crime has substantial effects on employment, production, transit, or consumption. Indeed, if Congress may regulate gender-motivated violence, it would be able to regulate murder or any other type of violence since gender-motivated violence, as a subset of all violent crime, is certain to have lesser economic impacts than the larger class of which it is a part.

Petitioners' reasoning, moreover, will not limit Congress to regulating violence but may, as we suggested in *Lopez*, be applied equally as well to family law and other areas of traditional state regulation since the aggregate effect of marriage, divorce, and childrearing on the national economy is undoubtedly significant. Congress may have recognized this specter when it expressly precluded § 13981 from being used in the family law context....

We accordingly reject the argument that Congress may regulate noneconomic, violent criminal conduct based solely on that conduct's aggregate effect on interstate commerce. The Constitution requires a distinction between what is truly national and what is truly local.... The regulation and punishment of intrastate violence that is not directed at the instrumentalities, channels, or goods involved in interstate commerce has always been the province of the States....

III

[W]e address petitioners' alternative argument that the section's civil remedy should be upheld as an exercise of Congress' remedial power under § 5 of the Fourteenth Amendment.... The principles governing an analysis of congressional legislation under § 5 are well settled. Section 5 states that Congress may "'enforce,' by 'appropriate legislation' the constitutional guarantee that no State shall deprive any person of 'life, liberty or property, without due process of law,' nor deny any person 'equal protection of the laws.'" *City of Boerne* v. *Flores*, 521 U.S. 507, 517 (1997)....

Petitioners' § 5 argument is founded on an assertion that there is pervasive bias in various state justice systems against victims of gender-motivated violence. This assertion is supported by a voluminous congressional record....

... However, the language and purpose of the Fourteenth Amendment place certain limitations on the manner in which Congress may attack discriminatory conduct. These limitations are necessary to prevent the Fourteenth Amendment from obliterating the Framers' carefully crafted balance of power between the States and the National Government. Foremost among these limitations is the time-honored principle that the Fourteenth Amendment, by its very terms, prohibits only state action. [*Here Rehnquist discusses* United States v. Harris, *106 U.S. 629 (1883) and the* Civil Rights Cases, *109 U.S. 3 (1883) for the proposition that Congress' § 5 power cannot be directed exclusively against the actions of private persons. He rejects the argument that* United States v. Guest, *383 U.S. 745 (1966) and* District of Columbia v. Carter, *409 U.S. 418 (1973) overruled these longstanding limitations on Congress' § 5 authority.*]

For these reasons, we conclude that Congress' power under § 5 does not extend to the enactment of § 13981.

IV

Petitioner Brzonkala's complaint alleges that she was the victim of a brutal assault. But Congress' effort in § 13981 to provide a federal civil remedy can be sustained neither under the Commerce Clause nor under § 5 of the Fourteenth Amendment. If the allegations here are true, no civilized system of justice could fail to provide her a remedy for the conduct of respondent Morrison. But under our federal system that remedy must be provided by the Commonwealth of Virginia, and not by the United States. The judgment of the Court of Appeals is

Affirmed.

Justice Thomas, concurring....

Justice Souter, with whom Justice Stevens, Justice Ginsburg, and Justice Breyer join, dissenting.

The Court says both that it leaves Commerce Clause precedent undisturbed and that the Civil Rights Remedy of the Violence Against Women Act of 1994 ... exceeds Congress's power under that Clause. I find the claims irreconcilable and respectfully dissent. [*In a footnote, Souter explains that by finding the law a valid exercise of Commerce Clause power, he has no occasion to analyze the Fourteenth Amendment claim.*]

I

Our cases, which remain at least nominally undisturbed, stand for the following propositions. Congress has the power to legislate with regard to activity that, in the aggregate, has a substantial effect on interstate commerce....

One obvious difference from *United States* v. *Lopez* ... is the mountain of data assembled by Congress, here showing the effects of violence against women on interstate commerce. Passage of the Act in 1994 was preceded by four years of hearings, which included testimony from physicians and law professors; from survivors of rape and domestic violence; and from representatives of state law enforcement and private business. The record includes reports on gender bias from task forces in 21 States, and we have the benefit of specific factual findings in the eight separate Reports issued by Congress and its committees over the long course leading to enactment....

With respect to domestic violence, Congress received evidence for the following findings: [*The facts disclosed that three out of four American women will be victims of violent crimes sometime during their life; violence is the leading cause of injuries to women ages 15 to 44; an estimated four million American women are battered each year by their husbands or partners; and over one million women in America seek medical assistance each year for injuries sustained from their husbands or other partners.*]

The evidence as to rape was similarly extensive, supporting these conclusions: [*The incidence of rape rose four times as fast as the total national crime rate over the past ten years; one study concluded that close to half a million girls now in high school will be raped before they graduate; and 125,000 college women can expect to be raped during any year.*]

Congress thereby explicitly stated the predicate for the exercise of its Commerce Clause power.... [T]he sufficiency of the evidence before Congress to provide a rational basis for the finding cannot seriously be questioned....

II

The Act would have passed muster at any time between *Wickard* in 1942 and *Lopez* in 1995, a period in which the law enjoyed a stable understanding that congressional power under the Commerce Clause, complemented by the authority of the Necessary and Proper Clause, Art. I. § 8 cl. 18, extended to all activity that, when aggregated, has a substantial effect on interstate commerce....

The fact that the Act does not pass muster before the Court today is therefore proof, to a degree that *Lopez* was not, that the Court's nominal adherence to the substantial effects test is merely that. Although a new jurisprudence has not emerged with any distinctness, it is clear that some congressional conclusions about obviously substantial, cumulative effects on commerce are being assigned lesser values than the once-stable doctrine would assign them. These devaluations are accomplished not by any express repudiation of the substantial effects test or its application through the aggregation of individual conduct, but by supplanting rational basis scrutiny with a new criterion of review....

A

... In the half century following the modern ac-

tivation of the commerce power with passage of the Interstate Commerce Act in 1887, this Court from time to time created categorical enclaves beyond congressional reach by declaring such activities as "mining," "production," "manufacturing," and union membership to be outside the definition of "commerce" and by limiting application of the effects test to "direct" rather than "indirect" commercial consequences....

Since adherence to these formalistically contrived confines of commerce power in large measure provoked the judicial crisis of 1937, one might reasonably have doubted that Members of this Court would ever again toy with a return to the days before *NLRB* v. *Jones & Laughlin Steel Corp.*, 301 U.S. 1 (1937), which brought the earlier and nearly disastrous experiment to an end. And yet today's decision can only be seen as a step toward recapturing the prior mistakes....

JUSTICE BREYER, with whom JUSTICE STEVENS joins, and with whom JUSTICE SOUTER and JUSTICE GINSBURG join as to Part I-A, dissenting....

Granholm v. Heald

544 U.S. 460 (2005)

State laws in Michigan and New York permitted in-state, but not out-of-state, wineries to sell wine directly to consumers in the state. Out-of-state wineries were required to work through in-state wholesalers and retailers, a regulatory feature that increased the sales price of their wine. This "differential treatment" raised questions about the scope of state authority under the Twenty-first Amendment to regulate the sale of liquor without infringing on the power of Congress to regulate interstate commerce (Art. § 8, cl. 3). The Healds, wine critics and consultants, joined Michigan residents in an action against Governor Jennifer Granholm challenging the validity of the law. The Michigan statute was declared invalid by the Sixth Circuit as a violation of the Commerce Clause, while the New York law was upheld by the Second Circuit as falling within the ambit of the state's powers under the Twenty-first Amendment.

JUSTICE KENNEDY delivered the opinion of the Court.

These consolidated cases present challenges to state laws regulating the sale of wine from out-of-state wineries to consumers in Michigan and New York. The details and mechanics of the two regulatory schemes differ, but the object and effect of the laws are the same: to allow in-state wineries to sell wine directly to consumers in that State but to prohibit out-of-state wineries from doing so, or, at the least, to make direct sales impractical from an economic standpoint. It is evident that the object and design of the Michigan and New York statutes is to grant in-state wineries a competitive advantage over wineries located beyond the States' borders.

We hold that the laws in both States discriminate against interstate commerce in violation of the Commerce Clause, Art. I, § 8, cl. 3, and that the discrimination is neither authorized nor permitted by the Twenty-first Amendment. Accordingly, we affirm the judgment of the Court of Appeals for the Sixth Circuit, which invalidated the Michigan laws; and we reverse the judgment of the Court of Appeals for the Second Circuit, which upheld the New York laws.

I

Like many other States, Michigan and New York regulate the sale and importation of alcoholic beverages, including wine, through a three-tier distribution system. Separate licenses are required for producers, wholesalers, and retailers.... As relevant to today's cases, though, the three-tier system is, in broad terms and with refinements to be discussed, mandated by Michigan and New York only for sales from out-of-state wineries. In-state wineries, by contrast, can obtain a license for direct sales to consumers. The differential treatment between in-state and out-of-state wineries constitutes explicit discrimination against interstate commerce.

This discrimination substantially limits the direct sale of wine to consumers, an otherwise emerging and significant business....

The wine producers in the cases before us are small wineries that rely on direct consumer sales as an important part of their businesses. Domaine Alfred, one of the plaintiffs in the Michigan suit, is a small winery located in San Luis Obispo, California. It produces 3,000 cases of wine per year. Domaine Alfred has received requests for its wine from Michigan consumers but cannot fill the orders because of the State's direct-shipment ban. Even if the winery could find a Michigan wholesaler to distribute its wine, the wholesaler's markup would render shipment through the three-tier system economically infeasible.

[Similarly, two plaintiffs in the New York suit operate small wineries in Virginia and California and face limits imposed by New York on direct wine shipments. In the sections that follow, the respondents from the Michigan challenge and the petitioners in the New York challenge are referred to collectively as the wineries. The opposing parties (Michigan, New York, and the wholesalers and retailers) are referred to as the states.]

II

A

Time and again this Court has held that, in all but the narrowest circumstances, state laws violate the Commerce Clause if they mandate "differential treatment of in-state and out-of-state economic interests that benefits the former and burdens the latter." *Oregon Waste Systems, Inc. v. Department of Environmental Quality of Ore.*, 511 U.S. 93, 99 (1994).... This rule is essential to the foundations of the Union. The mere fact of nonresidence should not foreclose a producer in one State from access to markets in other States....

The rule prohibiting state discrimination against interstate commerce follows also from the principle that States should not be compelled to negotiate with each other regarding favored or disfavored status for their own citizens. States do not need, and may not attempt, to negotiate with other States regarding their mutual economic interests. Cf. U.S. Const., Art. I, § 10, cl. 3. Rivalries among the States

are thus kept to a minimum, and a proliferation of trade zones is prevented....

Laws of the type at issue in the instant cases contradict these principles. They deprive citizens of their right to have access to the markets of other States on equal terms. The perceived necessity for reciprocal sale privileges risks generating the trade rivalries and animosities, the alliances and exclusivity, that the Constitution and, in particular, the Commerce Clause were designed to avoid....

[The Court reviews the regulatory features of the Michigan and New York laws and concludes that they discriminate against interstate commerce through their direct shipping laws.]

III

State laws that discriminate against interstate commerce face "a virtually *per se* rule of invalidity." *Philadelphia v. New Jersey*, 437 U.S. 617, 624 (1978). The Michigan and New York laws by their own terms violate this proscription. The two States, however, contend their statutes are saved by § 2 of the Twenty-first Amendment, which provides:

"The transportation or importation into any State, Territory, or possession of the United States for delivery or use therein of intoxicating liquors, in violation of the laws thereof, is hereby prohibited."

The States' position is inconsistent with our precedents and with the Twenty-first Amendment's history. Section 2 does not allow States to regulate the direct shipment of wine on terms that discriminate in favor of in-state producers.

A

[The Opinion reviews prior rulings in which the Court, relying on the Commerce Clause, invalidated various state liquor regulations that discriminated against imported liquor. It also discusses federal measures in which Congress required equal treatment of in-state and out-of-state liquor.]

[B]

The aim of the Twenty-first Amendment was to allow States to maintain an effective and uniform system for controlling liquor by regulating its transportation, importation, and use. The Amendment did not give States the authority to pass nonuniform laws in order to discriminate against out-of-state goods, a privilege they had not enjoyed at any earlier time....

Our more recent cases, furthermore, confirm that the Twenty-first Amendment does not supersede other provisions of the Constitution and, in particular, does not displace the rule that States may not give a discriminatory preference to their own producers....

IV

[The States offered two reasons for restricting direct shipments from out-of-state wineries: Keeping alcohol away from minors and facilitating tax collection. The Court found little evidence to support the argument that minors through credit cards and the Internet can obtain alcohol illegally from out of state. Nor had the states provided sufficient concrete evidence about problems of tax collection.]

V

States have broad power to regulate liquor under § 2 of the Twenty-first Amendment. This power, however, does not allow States to ban, or severely limit, the direct shipment of out-of-state wine while simultaneously authorizing direct shipment by in-state producers. If a State chooses to allow direct shipment of wine, it must do so on evenhanded terms. Without demonstrating the need for discrimination, New York and Michigan have enacted regulations that disadvantage out-of-state wine producers. Under our Commerce Clause jurisprudence, these regulations cannot stand.

We affirm the judgment of the Court of Appeals for the Sixth Circuit; and we reverse the judgment of the Court of Appeals for the Second Circuit and remand the case for further proceedings consistent with our opinion.

It is so ordered.

JUSTICE STEVENS, with whom JUSTICE O'CON-NOR joins, dissenting.

Congress' power to regulate commerce among the States includes the power to authorize the States to place burdens on interstate commerce.... Absent such congressional approval, a state law may violate the unwritten rules described as the "dormant Commerce Clause" either by imposing an undue burden on both out-of-state and local producers engaged in interstate activities or by treating out-of-state producers less favorably than their local competitors....

The New York and Michigan laws challenged in these cases would be patently invalid under well settled dormant Commerce Clause principles if they regulated sales of an ordinary article of commerce rather than wine. But ever since the adoption of the Eighteenth Amendment and the Twenty-first Amendment, our Constitution has placed commerce in alcoholic beverages in a special category....

... *[In a footnote, Justice Stevens invoked Justice Black:]* According to Justice Black, who participated in the passage of the Twenty-first Amendment in the Senate, § 2 was intended to return " 'absolute control' of liquor traffic to the States, free of all restrictions which the Commerce Clause might before that time have imposed." *Hostetter v. Idlewild Bon Voyage Liquor Corp.*, 377 U.S. 324, 338 (1964) (dissenting opinion)....

My understanding (and recollection) of the historical context reinforces my conviction that the text of § 2 should be "broadly and colloquially interpreted." ... Indeed, the fact that the Twenty-first Amendment was the only Amendment in our history to have been ratified by the people in state conventions, rather than by state legislatures, provides further reason to give its terms their ordinary meaning. Because the New York and Michigan laws regulate the "transportation or importation" of "intoxicating liquors" for "delivery or use therein," they are exempt from dormant Commerce Clause scrutiny....

JUSTICE THOMAS, with whom THE CHIEF JUSTICE, JUSTICE STEVENS, and JUSTICE O'CONNOR join, dissenting....

Gonzales v. Raich

545 U.S. 1 (2005)

The federal Controlled Substances Act (CSA) generally criminalizes the manufacture, distribution, or possession of marijuana. California law imposed similar prohibitions but it created an exemption from prosecution for possession for (1) physicians who recommended marijuana to patients for medical purposes, and (2) patients, and their primary caregivers, who possessed or cultivated marijuana for patients' personal medical purposes upon recommendation or approval by a physician. Angel Raich used physician-recommended marijuana for serious medical conditions and sought injunctive and declaratory relief to prohibit U.S. Attorney General

Alberto Gonzales from enforcing the CSA to prevent the medical use of marijuana. She asserted that enforcement of the CSA in this context would violate the Commerce Clause. The District Court denied Raich's motion, but the Ninth Circuit reversed, holding that Congress exceeded its authority under the Commerce Clause. Note the prominence of *Wickard v. Filburn* in the Supreme Court's Opinion.

JUSTICE STEVENS delivered the opinion of the Court.

California is one of at least nine States that authorize the use of marijuana for medicinal purposes. The question presented in this case is whether the power vested in Congress by Article I, § 8, of the Constitution "[t]o make all Laws which shall be necessary and proper for carrying into Execution" its authority to "regulate Commerce with foreign Nations, and among the several States" includes the power [*through the Controlled Substances Act, or CSA*] to prohibit the local cultivation and use of marijuana in compliance with California law.

I

... In 1996, California voters passed Proposition 215, now codified as the Compassionate Use Act of 1996. The proposition was designed to ensure that "seriously ill" residents of the State have access to marijuana for medical purposes....

Respondents Angel Raich and Diane Monson are California residents who suffer from a variety of serious medical conditions and have sought to avail themselves of medical marijuana pursuant to the terms of the Compassionate Use Act. They are being treated by licensed, board-certified family practitioners, who have concluded, after prescribing a host of conventional medicines to treat respondents' conditions and to alleviate their associated symptoms, that marijuana is the only drug available that provides effective treatment....

... The case is made difficult by respondents' strong arguments that they will suffer irreparable harm because, despite a congressional finding to the contrary, marijuana does have valid therapeutic purposes. The question before us, however, is not whether it is wise to enforce the statute in these circumstances; rather, it is whether Congress' power to regulate interstate markets for medicinal substances encompasses the portions of those markets that are supplied with drugs produced and consumed locally. Well-settled law controls our answer. The CSA is a valid exercise of federal power, even as applied to the troubling facts of this case. We accordingly vacate the judgment of the Court of Appeals....

III

... [R]espondents' challenge is actually quite lim-

ited; they argue that the CSA's categorical prohibition of the manufacture and possession of marijuana as applied to the intrastate manufacture and possession of marijuana for medical purposes pursuant to California law exceeds Congress' authority under the Commerce Clause....

Our case law firmly establishes Congress' power to regulate purely local activities that are part of an economic "class of activities" that have a substantial effect on interstate commerce.... *Wickard v. Filburn*, 317 U.S. 111, 128-128 (1942). As we stated in *Wickard*, "even if appellee's activity be local and though it may not be regarded as commerce, it may still, whatever its nature, be reached by Congress if it exerts a substantial economic effect on interstate commerce."...

The similarities between this case and *Wickard* are striking. Like the farmer in *Wickard*, respondents are cultivating, for home consumption, a fungible commodity for which there is an established, albeit illegal, interstate market. Just as the Agricultural Adjustment Act was designed "to control the volume [*of wheat*] moving in interstate and foreign commerce in order to avoid surpluses ..." and consequently control the market price, ... a primary purpose of the CSA is to control the supply and demand of controlled substances in both lawful and unlawful drug markets.... In *Wickard*, we had no difficulty concluding that Congress had a rational basis for believing that, when viewed in the aggregate, leaving home-consumed wheat outside the regulatory scheme would have a substantial influence on price and market conditions. Here too, Congress had a rational basis for concluding that leaving home-consumed marijuana outside federal control would similarly affect price and market conditions.

More concretely, one concern prompting inclusion of wheat grown for home consumption in the 1938 Act was that rising market prices could draw such wheat into the interstate market, resulting in lower market prices.... The parallel concern making it appropriate to include marijuana grown for home consumption in the CSA is the likelihood that the high demand in the interstate market will draw such marijuana into that market....

In assessing the scope of Congress' authority under the Commerce Clause, we stress that the task before us is a modest one. We need not determine whether respondents' activities, taken in the aggregate, substantially affect interstate commerce in fact, but only whether a "rational basis" exists for so concluding.... Given the enforcement difficulties that attend distinguishing between marijuana cultivated locally and marijuana grown elsewhere, ... and concerns about diversion into illicit channels, we have no difficulty concluding that Congress had a rational basis for believing that failure to regulate the intrastate manufacture and possession of marijuana would leave a gaping hole in the CSA....

IV

[In this section, Stevens reasoned that unlike United States v. Lopez (1995) *and* United States v. Morrison (2000), *the activities regulated by the CSA "are quintessentially economic." Economics refers to "the production, distribution, and consumption of commodities." Because the CSA directly regulates economic and commercial activity, Morrison "casts no doubt on its constitutionality." The CSA designated marijuana "as contraband for any purpose. Congress "expressly found that the drug has no acceptable medical uses." The CSA imposed controls beyond what was required by California law. The Supremacy Clause "unambiguously provides that if there is any conflict between federal and state law, federal law shall prevail."]*

... Thus the case for the exemption comes down to the claim that a locally cultivated product that is used domestically rather than sold on the open market is not subject to federal regulation. Given the findings in the CSA and the undisputed magnitude of the commercial market for marijuana, our decisions in *Wickard v. Filburn* and the later cases endorsing its reasoning foreclose that claim....

JUSTICE SCALIA, concurring in the judgment....

JUSTICE O'CONNOR, with whom THE CHIEF JUSTICE and Justice Thomas join as to all but Part III, dissenting....

This case exemplifies the role of States as laboratories. The States' core police powers have always included authority to define criminal law and to protect the health, safety, and welfare of their citizens.... Exercising those powers, California (by ballot initiative and then by legislative codification) has come to its own conclusion about the difficult and sensitive question of whether marijuana should be available to relieve severe pain and suffering. Today the Court sanctions an application of the federal Controlled Substances Act that extinguishes that experiment, without any proof that the personal cultivation, possession, and use of marijuana for medicinal purposes, if economic activity in the first place, has a substantial effect on interstate commerce and is therefore an appropriate subject of federal regulation....

[II A]

... If the Court is right, then *Lopez* stands for nothing more than a drafting guide: Congress should have described the relevant crime as "transfer or possession of a firearm anywhere in the nation" — thus including commercial and noncommercial activity, and clearly encompassing some activity with assuredly substantial effect on interstate commerce. Had it done so, the majority hints, we would have sustained its authority to regulate possession of firearms in school zones....

[B]

Even assuming that economic activity is at issue in this case, the Government has made no showing in fact that the possession and use of homegrown marijuana for medical purposes, in California or elsewhere, has a substantial effect on interstate commerce....

JUSTICE THOMAS, dissenting....

Gonzales v. Oregon

546 U. S. 243 (2006)

In 1994, Oregon voters approved a ballot measure entitled the Oregon Death With Dignity Act (ODWDA), legalizing assisted suicide. It exempted state-licensed physicians who followed a set of procedural safeguards from civil or criminal liability for dispensing or prescribing a lethal dose of drugs at the request of a terminally ill patient. In 2001, Attorney General John Ashcroft (who had been replaced by Alberto Gonzales by the time the case reached the Supreme Court) issued an "interpretive rule" based on his authority under the Controlled Substances Act, finding that the dispensing of controlled drugs for the purposes of assisting suicide was not a legitimate medical practice and was forbidden under the Act. A district court upheld the Attorney General's action but the Court of Appeals overturned that decision.

JUSTICE KENNEDY delivered the opinion of the Court.

The question before us is whether the Controlled Substances Act allows the United States Attorney General to prohibit doctors from prescribing regulated drugs for use in physician-assisted suicide, notwithstanding a state law permitting the procedure. As the Court has observed, "Americans are engaged in an earnest and profound debate about the morality, legality, and practicality of physician-assisted suicide." *Washington* v. *Glucksberg*, 521 U. S. 702, 735 (1997). The dispute before us is in part a product of this political and moral debate, but its resolution requires an inquiry familiar to the courts: interpreting a federal statute to determine whether Executive action is authorized by, or otherwise consistent with, the enactment....

The drugs Oregon physicians prescribe under ODWDA are regulated under a federal statute, the Controlled Substances Act (CSA or Act).... The CSA allows these particular drugs to be available only by a written prescription from a registered physician. In the ordinary course the same drugs are prescribed in smaller doses for pain alleviation.

A November 9, 2001 Interpretive Rule issued by the Attorney General addresses the implementation and enforcement of the CSA with respect to ODWDA. It determines that using controlled substances to assist suicide is not a legitimate medical practice and that dispensing or prescribing them for this purpose is unlawful under the CSA. The Interpretive Rule's validity under the CSA is the issue before us.

[I.A]

We turn first to the text and structure of the CSA. Enacted in 1970 with the main objectives of combating drug abuse and controlling the legitimate and illegitimate traffic in controlled substances, the CSA creates a comprehensive, closed regulatory regime criminalizing the unauthorized manufacture, distribution, dispensing, and possession of substances classified in any of the Act's five schedules.... Congress classified a host of substances when it enacted the CSA, but the statute permits the Attorney General to add, remove, or reschedule substances. He may do so, however, only after making particular findings, and on scientific and medical matters he is required to accept the findings of the Secretary of Health and Human Services (Secretary) ...

The present dispute involves controlled substances listed in Schedule II, substances generally available only pursuant to a written, non-refillable prescription by a physician. 21 U. S. C. § 829(a). A 1971 regulation promulgated by the Attorney General requires that every prescription for a controlled substance "be issued for a legitimate medical purpose by an individual practitioner acting in the usual course of his professional practice." 21 CFR § 1306.04(a) (2005).

To prevent diversion of controlled substances with medical uses, the CSA regulates the activity of physicians. To issue lawful prescriptions of Schedule II drugs, physicians must "obtain from the Attorney General a registration issued in accordance with the rules and regulations promulgated by him." 21 U. S. C. § 822(a)(2). The Attorney General may deny, suspend, or revoke this registration if, as relevant here, the physician's registration would be "inconsistent with the public interest." § 824(a)(4); § 822(a)(2)....

The CSA explicitly contemplates a role for the States in regulating controlled substances, as evidenced by its preemption provision.

"No provision of this subchapter shall be construed as indicating an intent on the part of the Congress to occupy the field in which that provision operates ... to the exclusion of any State law on the same subject matter which would otherwise be within the authority of the State, unless there is a positive conflict between that provision ... and that State law so that the two cannot consistently stand together." § 903.

B

[Here Kennedy describes the procedures required by ODWDA in order for an Oregon citizen to be eligible for a lethal prescription, including a diagnosis that the disease will be terminal within six months, insurance of informed consent, a second opinion by another physician, and detailed record keeping to be reviewed by the state's Department of Human Services.] In 2004, 37 patients ended their lives by ingesting a lethal dose of medication prescribed under ODWDA. Oregon Dept. of Human Servs., Seventh Annual Report on Oregon's Death with Dignity Act 20 (Mar. 10, 2005).

C

. . .

In 2001, John Ashcroft was appointed Attorney General....

On November 9, 2001, without consulting Oregon or apparently anyone outside his Department, the Attorney General issued an Interpretive Rule announcing his intent to restrict the use of controlled substances for physician-assisted suicide. Incorporating the legal analysis of a memorandum he had solicited from his Office of Legal Counsel, the Attorney General ruled "assisting suicide is not a 'legitimate medical purpose' within the meaning of 21 CFR 1306.04 (2001), and that prescribing, dispensing, or administering federally controlled substances to assist suicide violates the Controlled Substances Act. Such conduct by a physician registered to dispense controlled substances may 'render his registration ... inconsistent with the public interest' and therefore subject to possible suspension or revocation under 21 U. S. C. 824(a)(4). The Attorney General's conclusion applies regardless of whether state law authorizes or permits such conduct by practitioners or others and regardless of the condition of the person whose suicide is assisted." 66 Fed. Reg. 56608 (2001).

There is little dispute that the Interpretive Rule would substantially disrupt the ODWDA regime. Respondents contend, and petitioners do not dispute, that every prescription filled under ODWDA has specified drugs classified under Schedule II. A physician cannot prescribe the substances without DEA registration, and revocation or suspension of the registration would be a severe restriction on medical practice. Dispensing controlled substances without a valid prescription, furthermore, is a federal crime. See, e.g., 21 U. S. C. § 841(a)(1) (2000 ed., Supp. II); United States v. Moore, 423 U. S. 122 (1975)....

II

Executive actors often must interpret the enactments Congress has charged them with enforcing and implementing. The parties before us are in sharp disagreement both as to the degree of deference we must accord the Interpretive Rule's substantive conclusions and whether the Rule is authorized by the statutory text at all. Although balancing the necessary respect for an agency's knowledge, expertise, and constitutional office with the courts' role as interpreter of laws can be a delicate matter, familiar principles guide us. An administrative rule may receive substantial deference if it interprets the issuing agency's own ambiguous regulation. *Auer* v. *Robbins*, 519 U. S. 452, 461–463 (1997). An interpretation of an ambiguous statute may also receive substantial deference. *Chevron U. S. A. Inc.* v. *Natural Resources Defense Council, Inc.*, 467 U. S. 837, 842–845 (1984). Deference in accordance with

Chevron, however, is warranted only "when it appears that Congress delegated authority to the agency generally to make rules carrying the force of law, and that the agency interpretation claiming deference was promulgated in the exercise of that authority." *United States* v. *Mead Corp.*, 533 U. S. 218, 226–227 (2001). Otherwise, the interpretation is "entitled to respect" only to the extent it has the "power to persuade." *Skidmore* v. *Swift & Co.*, 323 U. S. 134, 140 (1944).

A

The Government first argues that the Interpretive Rule is an elaboration of one of the Attorney General's own regulations, 21 CFR § 1306.04 (2005), which requires all prescriptions be issued "for a legitimate medical purpose by an individual practitioner acting in the usual course of his professional practice." As such, the Government says, the Interpretive Rule is entitled to considerable deference in accordance with *Auer*.

In our view *Auer* and the standard of deference it accords to an agency are inapplicable here....

In *Auer*, the underlying regulations gave specificity to a statutory scheme the Secretary was charged with enforcing and reflected the considerable experience and expertise the Department of Labor had acquired over time with respect to the complexities of the Fair Labor Standards Act. Here, on the other hand, the underlying regulation does little more than restate the terms of the statute itself. The language the Interpretive Rule addresses comes from Congress, not the Attorney General, and the near equivalence of the statute and regulation belies the Government's argument for *Auer* deference.... It gives little or no instruction on a central issue in this case: Who decides whether a particular activity is in "the course of professional practice" or done for a "legitimate medical purpose"? Since the regulation gives no indication how to decide this issue, the Attorney General's effort to decide it now cannot be considered an interpretation of the regulation. Simply put, the existence of a parroting regulation does not change the fact that the question here is not the meaning of the regulation but the meaning of the statute. An agency does not acquire special authority to interpret its own words when, instead of using its expertise and experience to formulate a regulation, it has elected merely to paraphrase the statutory language....

B

Just as the Interpretive Rule receives no deference under *Auer*, neither does it receive deference under *Chevron*. If a statute is ambiguous, judicial review of administrative rulemaking often demands *Chevron* deference; and the rule is judged accordingly. All would agree, we should think, that the statutory phrase "legitimate medical purpose" is a generality, susceptible to more precise definition and open to varying constructions, and thus ambiguous in the relevant sense. *Chevron* deference, however, is not accorded merely because the statute is ambiguous and an administrative official is involved. To begin with, the rule must be promulgated pursuant to authority Congress has delegated to the official....

The Attorney General has rulemaking power to fulfill his duties under the CSA. The specific respects in which he is authorized to make rules, however, instruct us that he is not authorized to make a rule declaring illegitimate a medical standard for care and treatment of patients that is specifically authorized under state law....

The CSA gives the Attorney General limited powers, to be exercised in specific ways.... Congress did not delegate to the Attorney General authority to carry out or effect all provisions of the CSA. Rather, he can promulgate rules relating only to "registration" and "control," and "for the efficient execution of his functions" under the statute.... The Interpretive Rule now under consideration does not concern the scheduling of substances and was not issued after the required procedures for rules regarding scheduling, so it cannot fall under the Attorney General's "control" authority....

We turn, next, to the registration provisions of the CSA.... The CSA was amended in 1984 to allow the Attorney General to deny registration to an applicant "if he determines that the issuance of such registration would be inconsistent with the public interest." 21 U. S. C. § 823(f).... In determining consistency with the public interest, the Attorney General must ... consider five factors, including: the State's recommendation; compliance with state, federal, and local laws regarding controlled substances; and public health and safety. § 823(f).

The Interpretive Rule cannot be justified under this part of the statute. It does not undertake the five-factor analysis and concerns much more than registration. Nor does the Interpretive Rule on its face purport to be an application of the registration provision in § 823(f).... It begins by announcing that assisting suicide is not a "legitimate medical purpose" under § 1306.04, and that dispensing controlled substances to assist a suicide violates the CSA. 66 Fed. Reg. 56608 (2001). Violation is a criminal offense, and often a felony, under 21 U. S. C. § 841 (2000 ed. and Supp. II). The Interpretive Rule thus purports to declare that using controlled substances for physi-

cian-assisted suicide is a crime, an authority that goes well beyond the Attorney General's statutory power to register or deregister.... The explanation the Government seems to advance is that the Attorney General's authority to decide whether a physician's actions are inconsistent with the "public interest" provides the basis for the Interpretive Rule.

By this logic, however, the Attorney General claims extraordinary authority. If the Attorney General's argument were correct, his power to deregister necessarily would include the greater power to criminalize even the actions of registered physicians, whenever they engage in conduct he deems illegitimate. This power to criminalize—unlike his power over registration, which must be exercised only after considering five express statutory factors—would be unrestrained. It would be anomalous for Congress to have so painstakingly described the Attorney General's limited authority to deregister a single physician or schedule a single drug, but to have given him, just by implication, authority to declare an entire class of activity outside "the course of professional practice," and therefore a criminal violation of the CSA....

The structure of the CSA, then, conveys unwillingness to cede medical judgments to an Executive official who lacks medical expertise....

The idea that Congress gave the Attorney General such broad and unusual authority through an implicit delegation in the CSA's registration provision is not sustainable....

III

. . .

In deciding whether the CSA can be read as prohibiting physician-assisted suicide, we look to the statute's text and design. The statute and our case law amply support the conclusion that Congress regulates medical practice insofar as it bars doctors from using their prescription-writing powers as a means to engage in illicit drug dealing and trafficking as conventionally understood. Beyond this, however, the statute manifests no intent to regulate the practice of medicine generally. The silence is understandable given the structure and limitations of federalism, which allow the States "'great latitude under their police powers to legislate as to the protection of the lives, limbs, health, comfort, and quiet of all persons.'" *Medtronic, Inc.* v. *Lohr*, 518 U. S. 470, 475 (1996) (quoting *Metropolitan Life Ins. Co.* v. *Massachusetts*, 471 U. S. 724, 756 (1985)).

The structure and operation of the CSA presume and rely upon a functioning medical profession regulated under the States' police powers.... Further cautioning against the conclusion that the CSA effectively displaces the States' general regulation of medical practice is the Act's pre-emption provision, which indicates that, absent a positive conflict, none of the Act's provisions should be "construed as indicating an intent on the part of the Congress to occupy the field in which that provision operates ... to the exclusion of any State law on the same subject matter which would otherwise be within the authority of the State." § 903.

Oregon's regime is an example of the state regulation of medical practice that the CSA presupposes.... Just as the conventions of expression indicate that Congress is unlikely to alter a statute's obvious scope and division of authority through muffled hints, the background principles of our federal system also belie the notion that Congress would use such an obscure grant of authority to regulate areas traditionally supervised by the States' police power....

IV

The Government, in the end, maintains that the prescription requirement delegates to a single Executive officer the power to effect a radical shift of authority from the States to the Federal Government to define general standards of medical practice in every locality. The text and structure of the CSA show that Congress did not have this far-reaching intent to alter the federal-state balance and the congressional role in maintaining it.

The judgment of the Court of Appeals is

Affirmed.

Justice Scalia, with whom Chief Justice Roberts and Justice Thomas join, dissenting....

The Court's decision today is perhaps driven by a feeling that the subject of assisted suicide is none of the Federal Government's business. It is easy to sympathize with that position. The prohibition or deterrence of assisted suicide is certainly not among the enumerated powers conferred on the United States by the Constitution, and it is within the realm of public morality (*bonos mores*) traditionally addressed by the so-called police power of the States. But then, neither is prohibiting the recreational use of drugs or discouraging drug addiction among the enumerated powers. From an early time in our national history, the Federal Government has used its enumerated powers, such as its power to regulate interstate commerce, for the purpose of protecting public morality—for example, by banning the interstate shipment of lottery tickets, or the interstate transport of women for immoral purposes. See *Hoke* v. *United States*, 227 U. S. 308, 321–323 (1913); *Lottery Case*, 188 U. S. 321, 356 (1903). Unless we are to repudiate a long and well-established principle of our jurisprudence, using the federal commerce power to prevent assisted suicide is unquestionably permissible. The question before us is not whether Congress can do this, or even whether Congress *should* do this; but simply whether Congress *has* done this in the CSA. I think there is no doubt that it has. If the term "*legitimate* medical purpose" has any meaning, it surely excludes the prescription of drugs to produce death....

Justice Thomas, dissenting.

When Angel Raich and Diane Monson challenged the application of the Controlled Substances Act (CSA), 21 U. S. C. § 801 *et seq.*, to their purely intrastate possession of marijuana for medical use as authorized under California law, a majority of this Court (a mere seven months ago) determined that the CSA effectively invalidated California's law because "the CSA is a comprehensive regulatory regime specifically designed to regulate which controlled substances can be utilized for medicinal purposes, *and in what manner.*" *Gonzales* v. *Raich*, 545 U. S. ___, ___ (2005) (slip op., at 24) (emphasis added)....

Today the majority beats a hasty retreat from these conclusions....

... The majority's newfound understanding of the CSA as a statute of limited reach is all the more puzzling because it rests upon constitutional principles that the majority of the Court rejected in *Raich*....

... While the scope of the CSA and the Attorney General's power there under are sweeping, and perhaps troubling, such expansive federal legislation and broad grants of authority to administrative agencies are merely the inevitable and inexorable consequence of this Court's Commerce Clause and separation-of-powers jurisprudence....

I agree with limiting the applications of the CSA in a manner consistent with the principles of federalism and our constitutional structure. *Raich, supra,* at ___ (Thomas, J., dissenting); ... But that is now water over the dam. The relevance of such considerations was at its zenith in *Raich*, when we considered whether the CSA could be applied to the intrastate possession of a controlled substance consistent with the limited federal powers enumerated by the Constitution. Such considerations have little, if any, relevance where, as here, we are merely presented with a question of statutory interpretation, and not the extent of constitutionally permissible federal power.... The Court's reliance upon the constitutional principles that it rejected in *Raich*—albeit under the guise of statutory interpretation—is perplexing to say the least. Accordingly, I respectfully dissent.

G. THE SPENDING AND TAXING POWERS

The pattern of federal spending and taxing powers has been similar to the Commerce Clause. The courts initially placed constraints on congressional power and offered protection to "local" activities in the states. Over time, however, these constraints have been largely removed because the judiciary recognizes the need for national powers and regulation.

The Constitution speaks clearly on only one aspect of the taxing power: "No tax or duty shall be laid on articles exported from any State" (Art. I, §9). Other tax questions have provoked extensive litigation. Difficulties in distinguishing between direct and indirect taxes created major conflicts between Congress and the judiciary. Indirect taxes must follow the rule of uniformity: "The Congress shall have Power to lay and collect Taxes, Duties, Imposts, and Excises, to pay the Debts and provide for the common Defense and general Welfare of the United States; but all Duties, Imposts and Excises shall be uniform throughout the United States" (Art. I, §8). The rule of uniformity protects states from discriminatory actions by the national government, although federal taxes do not have to fall equally on each state, nor is Congress barred from adopting tax exemptions for certain regions. United States v. Psasynski, 462 U.S. 74 (1983).

Direct taxes are covered in Article I, Section 9: "No capitation, or other direct, tax shall be laid, unless in proportion to the census or enumeration herein before directed to be taken." Capitation taxes, or "head taxes," have never been enacted by Congress. Other direct taxes must be levied among the states in accordance with the rule of apportionment. The question of a direct tax was first decided by the Supreme Court in 1796. A carriage tax imposed by Congress was attacked as a direct tax, requiring that it be apportioned among the states on the basis of population. A unanimous Court, however, ruled that the tax was indirect. The decision appeared to limit direct taxes to two kinds: a capitation or poll tax, imposed without regard to property, and a tax on land. Hylton v. United States, 3 Dall. 171, 175 (1796). From 1798 to 1816 the federal government imposed direct taxes on real estate and slaves. In 1861 the federal tax applied to real estate only. Veazie Bank v. Fenno, 75 U.S. (8 Wall.) 533, 543 (1869). Federal taxes on currency and bank circulation were not considered a direct tax. Id. at 546–47.

Income Tax

In 1881, a unanimous Court again limited the meaning of direct taxes to capitation taxes and taxes on real estate. The Court interpreted the federal income tax of 1864, as amended in 1865, as an indirect tax. Springer v. United States, 102 U.S. 586 (1881). In 1895, after a hundred years of agreement on the meaning of direct taxes, the Court reversed direction and struck down a federal income tax, treating it as a direct tax to be apportioned on the basis of population. The statute was invalidated in two steps. The first decision held that the tax on rents or income of real estate was a direct tax and violated the Constitution by not following the apportionment rule. Pollock v. Farmers' Loan & Trust Co., 157 U.S. 429 (1895). A second decision struck down the income tax, in part because the Court concluded that invalidation of the other taxes left a tax scheme that Congress could not have intended. Pollock v. Farmers' Loan and Trust Co., 158 U.S. 601, 637 (1895).

The Court acted under the shadow of class warfare and threats of socialism. During oral argument, Joseph H. Choate warned the Justices that the tax was "communistic in its purposes and tendencies." 157 U.S. at 532. After the first hearing, the Court split 4 to 4 on the question of the income tax. Upon rehearing, a 5 to 4 decision invalidated the tax. The member missing from the first decision, Justice

Jackson, voted to *sustain* the tax in the second case. All things being equal, this should have yielded a 5–4 tally supporting the income tax. One Justice obviously switched his vote. Who he was, and why he switched, has never been revealed. Because of the vote switching and razor-thin majority, the decision became known as one of three "self-inflicted wounds" on the Court (the other two being *Dred Scott* in 1857 and the Legal Tender Cases of 1871). Charles Evans Hughes, The Supreme Court of the United States 54 (1928). It was not until 1913 that Congress and the states overrode *Pollock* by passing the Sixteenth Amendment.

The income tax cases marked an unusual setback for the power of Congress to tax. In 1904 the Court held that the judiciary would not limit the taxing power simply because it had been exercised in an unwise, oppressive, or injurious manner. Nor could the courts inquire into the motive or purpose of Congress in passing a tax, or discover a limitation in the Due Process Clause of the Fifth Amendment. Congressional abuses in such cases had to be corrected by the voters. McCray v. United States, 195 U.S. 27 (1904). In 1911 a unanimous Court upheld a corporation income tax passed by Congress. The Court called it an excise, not a direct, tax and said it complied with the rule of uniformity. Flint Stone Tracy Co., 220 U.S. 107 (1911). When Congress tried to use the taxing power to regulate matters the Court considered within the police power of the states, the congressional statute was declared invalid. Bailey v. Drexel Furniture Co. (Child Labor Tax Case), 259 U.S. 20 (1922); Hill v. Wallace, 259 U.S. 44 (1922).

New Deal Cases

The question of Congress intruding upon "local" matters within the jurisdiction of the states resulted in the invalidation of several New Deal statutes. In 1936, the Supreme Court struck down a so-called excise tax in the Bituminous Coal Conservation Act of 1935 because it coerced coal producers to submit to the price-fixing and labor provisions of the Act. Carter v. Carter Coal Co., 298 U.S. 238, 288–89 (1936). Also in 1936, the Court declared unconstitutional a "processing tax" enacted by Congress as part of the Agricultural Adjustment Act. In return for limiting their acreage and crops, farmers received payments from this tax. The Court held that the power of taxation exists to support government, not to expropriate money from one group to benefit another as part of a general regulatory scheme. Moreover, the Court held that the tax was coercive on farmers and invaded state powers by trying to regulate the "local" matter of agriculture. The decision suggests that had Congress explicitly invoked its commerce power, the Act might have been sustained. In writing the opinion for the Court, Justice Owen Roberts unveiled his famous mechanical formula for determining the constitutionality of a statute, arguing that the Court's job is to "lay the article of the Constitution which is invoked beside the statute which is challenged and to decide whether the latter squares with the former." United States v. Butler, 297 U.S. 1, 62 (1936).

Spending and Regulatory Power

Roberts abandoned his conservative brethren a year later by joining a 5 to 4 decision upholding Title IX of the Social Security Act. Congress imposed a tax on employers to support a national unemployment compensation plan. Funds from state unemployment laws were paid over to the Secretary of the Treasury and credited to an unemployment trust fund. Title IX was upheld even though it seemed to conflict with *Butler* by pressuring states to adopt unemployment compensation laws as part of a regulatory, and not merely revenue-raising, effort. STEWARD MACHINE CO. v. DAVIS, 301 U.S. 548 (1937). Congress responded to *Butler* by passing the Soil Conservation and Domestic Allotment Act of 1936 and the Agricultural Adjustment Act of 1938. Those statutes avoided the processing tax but pursued the same objective of controlling production by relying on the federal appropriations power and the Commerce Clause.

By attaching conditions to federal funds, Congress can regulate certain state activities. States acquiesce by accepting federal strings with the funds. Oklahoma v. CSC, 330 U.S. 127, 143–44 (1947).

Federal grants to states have grown over the years, representing a substantial percentage of state budgets. In 1955, for example, federal grants made up about 10 percent of state budgets while they are now, on average, around 20 percent. This gives the federal government the ability to induce the states to follow national policy goals. Thus, Congress may direct the Secretary of Transportation to withhold a percentage of federal highway funds from states that allow persons under 21 to buy alcoholic beverages. SOUTH DAKOTA v. DOLE, 483 U.S. 203 (1987). The Court has accepted the use of the spending power to impose racial and ethnic criteria as a condition attached to federal grants (a 10 percent "set-aside" for minority businesses). Fullilove v. Klutznick, 448 U.S. 448 (1980), reprinted in Chapter 15. If the conditions are offensive to state interests or its constitutional values, there is no obligation to accept the funds.

The states and the federal government are generally free to exercise their taxing power if they proceed on a rational basis and do not resort to classifications that are "palpably arbitrary." Allied Stores of Ohio v. Bowers, 358 U.S. 522, 527 (1959); Lehnhausen v. Lake Shore Auto Parts Co., 410 U.S. 356 (1973). Congress has had mixed results in using the taxing power to regulate narcotics, gambling, liquor, and firearms. The application of the taxing power to narcotics has been repeatedly upheld.[9] The Court has ruled that because a federal liquor tax operated not as a tax but as a penalty, it usurped the police powers of the states. United States v. Constantine, 296 U.S. 287 (1935); United States v. Kesterson, 296 U.S. 299 (1935).

The taxing power has been used to regulate firearms, with the Court pointing out that every tax "is in some measure regulatory." Sonzinsky v. United States, 300 U.S. 506, 513 (1937). Such statutes, however, cannot force gun dealers to incriminate themselves. Haynes v. United States, 390 U.S. 85 (1968). The same issue applies to federal taxes on gambling. At first, the Court determined that federal taxes and requirements to register with the Internal Revenue Service did not violate the Self-Incrimination Clause. United States v. Kahriger, 345 U.S. 22 (1953); Lewis v. United States, 348 U.S. 419 (1955). The Court later held that such statutes unconstitutionally compel gamblers to incriminate themselves. Marchetti v. United States, 390 U.S. 39 (1968); Grosso v. United States, 390 U.S. 62 (1968).

Intergovernmental Tax Immunity

The theory of dual federalism, which created exclusive jurisdictions for the federal government and the states, spawned the sister doctrine of intergovernmental tax immunity. Chief Justice Marshall struck down a state tax on the U.S. Bank by arguing extravagantly that the power to tax is the power to destroy. McCulloch v. Maryland, 17 U.S. (4 Wheat.) 315 (1819). If states could not tax federal instrumentalities, presumably the federal government could not tax state activities, and indeed the Court reached that conclusion in 1871 by holding that Congress could not tax the salary of a state judge. Justice Bradley, in a solitary dissent, objected to the doctrine that "the general government is to be regarded in any sense foreign or antagonistic to the State governments, their officers, or people." He correctly predicted that the decision would lead to impractical and mischievous results. Collector v. Day, 78 U.S. (11 Wall.) 113, 128–29 (1871).

The doctrine of intergovernmental tax immunity did not exempt state activities from federal taxation when states entered the field of ordinary business operations. Nongovernmental functions are taxed in the same manner as private businesses. South Carolina v. United States, 199 U.S. 437 (1905). The doctrine was shaken in 1928 when four Justices dissented against a rigid application of reciprocal tax immunity. In one of the dissents, Justice Holmes remarked: "The power to tax is not

---

9. United States v. Doremus, 249 U.S. 86 (1919); Nigro v. United States, 276 U.S. 332 (1928); United States v. Sanchez, 340 U.S. 42 (1950). Questions have been raised in some cases as to whether compliance with these laws automatically exposes someone to the risk of self-incrimination. Leary v. United States, 395 U.S. 6 (1969); United States v. Covington, 395 U.S. 57 (1969); Minor v. United States, 396 U.S. 87 (1969).

the power to destroy while this Court sits." Panhandle Oil Co. v. Knox, 277 U.S. 218, 223 (1928). By 1939 the Court decided to overrule *Collector* v. *Day* to the extent that it recognized "an implied constitutional immunity from income taxation of the salaries of officers or employees of the national or a state government or their instrumentalities." Graves v. N.Y. ex rel. O'Keefe, 306 U.S. 466, 486 (1939).

Congressional legislation also changed the substance of intergovernmental tax immunity. Beginning in 1864, Congress allowed the states to tax certain activities of national banks. 13 Stat. 111 (1864); see 12 U.S.C. § 548 (2000). Any changes in state taxation of national banks must come from Congress, not from the courts. First Agricultural Nat'l Bank v. State Tax Comm'n, 392 U.S. 339, 346 (1968). Recent decisions have struck down state taxes on military installations operated by the federal government, but the judgment in these cases turned not on abstract constitutional doctrines but on congressional intent (the Buck Act of 1940).[10]

A decision in 1989 struck down state laws that impose discriminatory taxes on state and federal workers. Michigan taxed federal government pensions but exempted state and local government retirees. The 8–1 ruling affected more than a dozen states, especially Virginia. Davis v. Michigan Dept. of Treasury, 489 U.S. 803 (1989). Virginia changed its law to treat all pensions the same, but federal and military pensioners sued the state to recover taxes paid earlier. In 1993 the Court ruled that the *Davis* decision must be applied retroactively, exposing Virginia and 15 other states to a potential cost of $1.8 billion in refunds. Harper v. Virginia Dept. of Taxation, 509 U.S. 86 (1993). Also relying on the *Davis* precedent, a unanimous Court in 1992 held invalid a Kansas law that taxed federal military retirement benefits while exempting benefits received by other retirees. Barker v. Kansas, 503 U.S. 594 (1992). A decision in 1994 made it more difficult for states to avoid paying tax refunds to federal retirees. Reich v. Collins, 513 U.S. 106 (1994).[11]

Steward Machine Co. v. Davis

301 U.S. 548 (1937)

Title IX of the Social Security Act of 1935 imposed an "excise tax" on employers, the proceeds to go into the U.S. Treasury to establish an unemployment compensation fund. Credit against the tax (up to 90 percent) would be given to employers who contributed under a state unemployment law. Questions: Did the tax unconstitutionally attempt to coerce the states to adopt their own unemployment compensation legislation, to be approved by the Federal Government? Could Title IX be interpreted as a "cooperative plan" into which states freely entered because of benefits available to them? If the credit gave the states motive and temptation, was that the same as coercion? The Steward Machine Company brought this action against Harwell G. Davis, Collector of Internal Revenue.

---

10. United States v. Tax Comm'n of Mississippi, 421 U.S. 599 (1975); United States v. State Tax Comm'n of Mississippi, 412 U.S. 363 (1973). Massachusetts v. United States, 435 U.S. 444 (1978), held that a registration tax by Congress in the Airport and Airway Revenue Act of 1970 did not violate the tax immunity of states. South Carolina v. Baker, 485 U.S. 505 (1988), upheld a congressional statute that removed the federal tax exemption for interest earned on nonregistered (bearer) state and local bonds. A state sales or use tax on a federal bankruptcy liquidation sale has been upheld. California Equalization Bd. v. Sierra Summit, 490 U.S. 844 (1989).

11. Tax liabilities of states were also affected by two decisions in 1990. In the first decision, a unanimous Court held that states must pay refunds or make adjustments for taxes that were collected unconstitutionally. Due process requires a state to give taxpayers a meaningful opportunity to obtain relief from such taxes. McKesson Corp. v. Florida Alcohol & Tobacco Div., 496 U.S. 18 (1990). In the second decision, a 5–4 Court ruled that a 1987 decision striking down a Pennsylvania tax as discriminatory could not be applied retroactively to force Arkansas (with a similar law) to repay taxes collected before the 1987 decision. The Court reasoned that Arkansas had no way of foreseeing the 1987 ruling. American Trucking Assns., Inc. v. Smith, 496 U.S. 167 (1990).

MR. JUSTICE CARDOZO delivered the opinion of the Court.

The validity of the tax imposed by the Social Security Act on employers of eight or more is here to be determined....

The assault on the statute proceeds on an extended front. Its assailants take the ground that the tax is not an excise; that it is not uniform throughout the United States as excises are required to be; that its exceptions are so many and arbitrary as to violate the Fifth Amendment; that its purpose was not revenue, but an unlawful invasion of the reserved powers of the states; and that the states in submitting to it have yielded to coercion and have abandoned governmental functions which they are not permitted to surrender.

The objections will be considered seriatim with such further explanation as may be necessary to make their meaning clear.

First. The tax, which is described in the statute as an excise, is laid with uniformity throughout the United States as a duty, an impost or an excise upon the relation of employment....

The subject matter of taxation open to the power of the Congress is as comprehensive as that open to the power of the states, though the method of apportionment may at times be different. "The Congress shall have power to lay and collect taxes, duties, imposts and excises." Art. 1, § 8. If the tax is a direct one, it shall be apportioned according to the census or enumeration. If it is a duty, impost, or excise, it shall be uniform throughout the United States. Together, these classes include every form of tax appropriate to sovereignty.... Whether the tax is to be classified as an "excise" is in truth not of critical importance. If not that, it is an "impost" ... or a "duty".... A capitation or other "direct" tax it certainly is not....

2. The tax being an excise, its imposition must conform to the canon of uniformity. There has been no departure from this requirement. According to the settled doctrine the uniformity exacted is geographical, not intrinsic....

Second. The excise is not invalid under the provisions of the Fifth Amendment by force of its exemptions.

The statute does not apply, as we have seen, to employers of less than eight. It does not apply to agricultural labor, or domestic service in a private home or to some other classes of less importance. Petitioner contends that the effect of these restrictions is an arbitrary discrimination vitiating the tax....

The classifications and exemptions directed by the statute now in controversy have support in considerations of policy and practical convenience that cannot be condemned as arbitrary....

Third. The excise is not void as involving the coercion of the States in contravention of the Tenth Amendment or of restrictions implicit in our federal form of government....

To draw the line intelligently between duress and inducement there is need to remind ourselves of facts as to the problem of unemployment that are now matters of common knowledge.... During the years 1929 to 1936, when the country was passing through a cyclical depression, the number of the unemployed mounted to unprecedented heights. Often the average was more than 10 million; at times a peak was attained of 16 million or more. Disaster to the breadwinner meant disaster to dependents. Accordingly the roll of the unemployed, itself formidable enough, was only a partial roll of the destitute or needy. The fact developed quickly that the states were unable to give the requisite relief. The problem had become national in area and dimensions. There was need of help from the nation if the people were not to starve. It is too late today for the argument to be heard with tolerance that in a crisis so extreme the use of the moneys of the nation to relieve the unemployed and their dependents is a use for any purpose narrower than the promotion of the general welfare.... The nation responded to the call of the distressed....

... Before Congress acted, unemployment compensation insurance was still, for the most part, a project and no more. Wisconsin was the pioneer. Her statute was adopted in 1931. At times bills for such insurance were introduced elsewhere, but they did not reach the stage of law. In 1935, four states (California, Massachusetts, New Hampshire and New York) passed unemployment laws on the eve of the adoption of the Social Security Act, and two others did likewise after the federal act and later in the year. The statutes differed to some extent in type, but were directed to a common end. In 1936, twenty-eight other states fell in line, and eight more the present year. But if states had been holding back before the passage of the federal law, inaction was not owing, for the most part, to the lack of sympathetic interest. Many held back through alarm lest, in laying such a toll upon their industries, they would place themselves in a position of economic disadvantage as compared with neighbors or competitors.... Two consequences ensued. One was that the freedom of a state to contribute its fair share to the solution of a national problem was paralyzed by fear. The other was that in so far as there was failure by the states to contribute relief according to the measure of their capacity, a disproportionate burden, and a mountainous one, was laid upon the resources of the Government of the nation.

The Social Security Act is an attempt to find a method by which all these public agencies may work together to a common end. Every dollar of the new taxes will continue in all likelihood to be used and needed by the nation as long as states are unwilling, whether through timidity or for other motives, to do what can be done at home....

Who then is coerced through the operation of this statute? Not the taxpayer. He pays in fulfilment of the mandate of the local legislature. Not the state. Even now she does not offer a suggestion that in passing the unemployment law she was affected by duress.... For all that appears she is satisfied with her choice, and would be sorely disappointed if it were now to be annulled. The difficulty with the petitioner's contention is that it confuses motive with coercion.... In like manner every rebate from a tax when conditioned upon conduct is in some measure a temptation. But to hold that motive or temptation is equivalent to coercion is to plunge the law in endless difficulties....

Fourth. The statute does not call for a surrender by the states of powers essential to their quasi-sovereign existence....

... The states are at liberty, upon obtaining the consent of Congress, to make agreements with one another. Constitution, Art. I, § 10, par. 3.... We find no room for doubt that they may do the like with Congress if the essence of their statehood is maintained without impairment....

Separate opinion of MR. JUSTICE MCREYNOLDS.

That portion of the Social Security legislation here under consideration, I think, exceeds the power granted to Congress. It unduly interferes with the orderly government of the State by her own people and otherwise offends the Federal Constitution....

Separate opinion of MR. JUSTICE SUTHERLAND.

With most of what is said in the opinion just handed down, I concur....

But the question with which I have difficulty is whether the administrative provisions of the act invade the governmental administrative powers of the several states reserved by the Tenth Amendment. A state may enter into contracts; but a state cannot, by contract or statute, surrender the execution, or a share in the execution, of any of its governmental powers either to a sister state or to the federal government, any more than the federal government can surrender the control of any of its governmental powers to a foreign nation....

MR. JUSTICE VAN DEVANTER joins in this opinion.

MR. JUSTICE BUTLER, dissenting.

I think that the objections to the challenged enactment expressed in the separate opinions of MR. JUSTICE MCREYNOLDS and MR. JUSTICE SUTHERLAND are well taken. I am also of opinion that, in principle and as applied to bring about and to gain control over state unemployment compensation, the statutory scheme is repugnant to the Tenth Amendment ...

South Dakota v. Dole

483 U.S. 203 (1987)

Congress passed legislation in 1984 directing the Secretary of Transportation to withhold a percentage of federal highway funds from states that refuse to adopt age 21 as the minimum drinking age. An issue before the Court was the extent to which Congress can use its spending power, and more particularly conditions attached to federal funds, to achieve national objectives. South Dakota challenged the constitutionality of the statute and brought suit against Secretary of Transportation Elizabeth Dole. A district court dismissed the complaint and the Eighth Circuit affirmed.

CHIEF JUSTICE REHNQUIST delivered the opinion of the Court....

In this Court, the parties direct most of their efforts to defining the proper scope of the Twenty-first Amendment. Relying on our statement in *California Retail Liquor Dealers Assn.* v. *Midcal Aluminum, Inc.,* 445 U.S. 97, 110 (1980), that the "Twenty-first Amendment grants the States virtually complete control over whether to permit importation or sale of liquor and how to structure the liquor distribution system," South Dakota asserts that the setting of minimum drinking ages is clearly within the "core powers" reserved to the States under § 2 of the Amendment....

... Despite the extended treatment of the question by the parties, however, we need not decide in this case whether that Amendment would prohibit an attempt by Congress to legislate directly a national minimum drinking age. Here, Congress has acted indirectly under its spending power to encourage uniformity in the States' drinking ages. As we explain below, we find this legislative effort within constitutional bounds even if Congress may not regulate drinking ages directly.

The Constitution empowers Congress to "lay and collect Taxes, Duties, Imposts, and Excises, to pay the Debts and provide for the common Defence and general Welfare of the United States." Art. I, § 8, cl. 1. Incident to this power, Congress may attach conditions on the receipt of federal funds, and has repeatedly employed the power "to further broad policy objectives by conditioning receipt of federal moneys upon compliance by the recipient with federal statutory and administrative directives." *Fullilove* v. *Klutznick,* 448 U.S. 448, 474 (1980) (Opinion of Burger, C.J.).... The breadth of this power was made clear in *United States* v. *Butler,* 297 U.S. 1, 66 (1936), where the Court, resolving a longstanding debate over the scope of the Spending Clause, determined that "the power of Congress to authorize expenditure of public moneys for public purposes is not limited by the direct grants of legislative power found in the Constitution." Thus, objectives not thought to be within Article I's "enumerated legislative fields," *id.,* at 65, may nevertheless be attained through the use of the spending power and the conditional grant of federal funds.

The spending power is of course not unlimited, *Pennhurst State School and Hospital* v. *Halderman,* 451 U.S. 1, 17, and n. 13 (1981), but is instead subject to several general restrictions articulated in our cases. The first of these limitations is derived from the language of the Constitution itself: the exercise of the spending power must be in pursuit of "the general welfare." ... In considering whether a particular expenditure is intended to serve general public purposes, courts should defer substantially to the judgment of Congress.... Second, we have required that if Congress desires to condition the States' receipt of federal funds, it "must do so unambiguously..., enabl[ing] the States to exercise their choice knowingly, cognizant of the consequences of their participation." ... Third, our cases have suggested (without significant elaboration) that conditions on federal grants might be illegitimate if they are unrelated "to the federal interest in particular national projects or programs." ... Finally, we have noted that other constitutional provisions may provide an independent bar to the conditional grant of federal funds....

South Dakota does not seriously claim that § 158 is inconsistent with any of the first three restrictions mentioned above.... Congress found that the differing drinking ages in the States created particular incentives for young persons to combine their desire to drink with their ability to drive, and that this interstate problem required a national solution. The means it chose to address this dangerous situation were reasonably calculated to advance the general welfare. The conditions upon which States receive the funds, moreover, could not be more clearly stated by Congress. See 23 U.S.C. § 158 (1982 ed., Supp. III). And the State itself, rather than challenging the germaneness of the condition to federal purposes, admits that it "has never contended that the congressional action was ... unrelated to a national concern in the absence of the Twenty-first Amendment." ... Indeed, the condition imposed by Congress is directly related to one of the main purposes for which highway funds are expended—safe interstate travel. See 23 U.S.C. § 101(b). This goal of the interstate highway system had been frustrated by varying drinking ages among the States. A presidential commission appointed to study alcohol-related accidents and fatalities on the Nation's highways concluded that the lack of uniformity in the States' drinking ages created "an incentive to drink and drive" because "young persons commut[e] to border States where the drinking age is lower." ...

The remaining question about the validity of § 158—and the basic point of disagreement between the parties—is whether the Twenty-first Amendment constitutes an "independent constitutional bar" to the conditional grant of federal funds....

[*Previous*] cases establish that the "independent constitutional bar" limitation on the spending power is not, as petitioner suggests, a prohibition on the indirect achievement of objectives which Congress is not empowered to achieve directly. Instead, we think that the language in our earlier opinions stands for the unexceptional proposition that the power may not be used to induce the States to engage in activities that would themselves be unconstitutional. Thus, for example, a grant of federal funds conditioned on invidiously discriminatory state action or the infliction of cruel and unusual punishment would be an illegitimate exercise of the Congress' broad spending power. But no such claim can be or is made here. Were South Dakota to succumb to the blandishments offered by Congress and raise its drinking age to 21, the State's action in so doing would not violate the constitutional rights of anyone.

Our decisions have recognized that in some circumstances the financial inducement offered by Congress might be so coercive as to pass the point at which "pressure turns into compulsion." *Steward Machine Co.* v. *Davis, supra,* 301 U.S., at 590. Here, however, Congress has directed only that a State desiring to establish a minimum drinking age lower than 21 lose a relatively small percentage of certain federal highway funds. Petitioner contends that the coercive nature of this program is evident from the degree of success it has achieved. We cannot conclude, however, that a conditional grant of federal money of this sort is unconstitutional simply by reason of its success in achieving the congressional objective.

When we consider, for a moment, that all South Dakota would lose if she adheres to her chosen course as to a suitable minimum drinking age is 5% of the funds otherwise obtainable under specified highway grant programs, the argument as to coercion is shown to be more rhetoric than fact....

JUSTICE BRENNAN, dissenting.

I agree with JUSTICE O'CONNOR that regulation of the minimum age of purchasers of liquor falls squarely within the ambit of those powers reserved to the States by the Twenty-first Amendment.... Since States possess this constitutional power, Congress cannot condition a federal grant in a manner that abridges this right. The Amendment, itself, strikes the proper balance between federal and state authority. I therefore dissent.

JUSTICE O'CONNOR, dissenting.

[The National Minimum Drinking Age Amendment] is an attempt to regulate the sale of liquor, an attempt that lies outside Congress' power to regulate commerce because it falls within the ambit of § 2 of the Twenty-first Amendment....

... [T]he Court's application of the requirement that the condition imposed be reasonably related to the purpose for which the funds are expended, is cursory and unconvincing....

... [I]f the purpose of § 158 is to deter drunken driving, it is far too over- and under-inclusive. It is over-inclusive because it stops teenagers from drinking even when they are not about to drive on interstate highways. It is under-inclusive because teenagers pose only a small part of the drunken driving problem in this Nation. See, *e.g.,* 130 Cong. Rec. S8216 (June 26, 1984) (remarks of Sen. Humphrey) ("Eighty-four percent of all highway fatalities involving alcohol occur among those whose ages exceed 21"); *id.,* at S8219 (remarks of Sen. McClure)....

H. PREEMPTION AND ABSTENTION

Federal-state relationships are shaped by two cross-cutting doctrines. Under the preemption doctrine, certain matters have such a national character that federal laws must supersede state laws. The abstention doctrine works in the opposite direction. As an exercise of discretionary authority, federal courts relinquish jurisdiction under various circumstances in order to avoid needless friction with the administration of state affairs. Both doctrines are complex and change over time.

The Preemption Doctrine

The preemption doctrine draws its force from the Supremacy Clause of Article VI of the Constitution, which declares that all laws made in pursuance to the Constitution and all treaties made under the authority of the United States shall be the "supreme Law of the Land." Federal actions of this character are superior to any conflicting provision of a state constitution or law. When Congress exercises its express powers, as it does by adopting uniform laws of bankruptcy, national legislation preempts state legislation. Perez v. Campbell, 402 U.S. 637 (1971). If compliance with both federal and state regulations in interstate commerce is a physical impossibility, federal law also preempts state law. Florida Lime & Avocado Growers, Inc. v. Paul, 373 U.S. 132, 142–43 (1963). Some of the enumerated powers of Congress are obviously exclusive, such as the power to exercise "exclusive Legislation" over the District of Columbia and the power "to coin money," which Art. I, § 10, expressly prohibits for the states.

The preemption doctrine also covers powers not expressly stated. In the area of foreign affairs, in-

Smith Reacts to Court Decisions

Mr. [*Howard*] SMITH of Virginia.... I do want to make 1 or 2 comments on ... a bill of which I am an author, H.R. 3, to correct a decision of the Supreme Court of the United States in the Steve Nelson and other cases....

... [T]he Supreme Court has assumed out of a clear sky to say what the Congress intended when the Congress has not said it. If anything is to be done upon this subject, I think it is very important that we have a general law which will simply say that when Congress means to do away with State laws the Congress shall say so. [102 Cong. Rec. 6385 (1956)]

Mr. SMITH of Virginia.... This bill ... just does two things. It says to the Supreme Court—

First. Do not undertake to read the minds of the Congress; we, in the Congress, think ourselves more capable of knowing our minds than the

Supreme Court has proved itself capable of in the past; and we will do our own mind reading; and we are telling you that when we get ready to repeal a State law or preempt a field, we will say so and we will not leave it to the Supreme Court to guess whether we are or not. That is No. 1.

Second. The other thing this bill does is to say that the Supreme Court must not knock down State laws unless they are in irreconcilable conflict with a Federal law.... [104 Cong. Rec. 14139–40 (1958)]

[The House of Representatives passed legislation of this nature in 1958, but no action was taken by the Senate. The House again passed legislation in 1959, but by that time the Supreme Court, in Uphaus v. Wyman, *360 U.S. 72, had decided that states could proceed with prosecutions for sedition against the state itself.]*

cluding regulation of aliens, state statutes may not stand "as an obstacle to the accomplishment and execution of the full purposes and objectives of Congress." Hines v. Davidowitz, 312 U.S. 52, 67 (1941). In 1956, the Supreme Court invalidated a state sedition law because the Smith Act, passed by Congress, regulated the same subject. The Court concluded that it had been the intent of Congress to occupy the whole field of sedition. PENNSYLVANIA v. NELSON, 350 U.S. 497, 504. As an illustration of Congress—not the Court—protecting state sovereignty, the author of the Smith Act promptly denied that he had ever intended the result reached by the Court (see box).

Congressional committees reported legislation to permit federal-state concurrent jurisdiction in the area of sedition and subversion and to prohibit courts from using intent or implication to decide preemption.[12] Although these bills were never enacted, in the midst of their consideration the Court held that a state could investigate subversive activities against itself. To this extent state and federal sedition laws could coexist. Uphaus v. Wyman, 360 U.S. 72, 76 (1959). A potential legislative-judicial clash was thus averted.

In matters affecting foreign affairs and international relations, the courts have excluded state involvement. Zschernig v. Miller, 389 U.S. 429, 436 (1968); Crosby v. National Foreign Trade Council, 530 U.S. 363 (2000). State governments maintain direct contact with both private and government officials in foreign countries in order to promote export trade and foreign investments. But a state may not use its power to regulate insurance companies in a way that interferes with federal foreign policy making, as California discovered when it attempted to require insurance companies to assist Holocaust survivors in tracing their former property. American Ins. Assn. v. Garamendi, 539 U.S. 396 (2003).

Congress has used its preemption power to regulate major areas of environmental law. The Water

---

12. H. Rept. No. 2576, 84th Cong., 2d Sess. (1956); S. Rept. No. 2117, 84th Cong., 2d Sess. (1956); S. Rept. No. 2230, 84th Cong., 2d Sess. (1956); H. Rept. No. 1878, 85th Cong., 2d Sess. (1958); 104 Cong. Rec. 13844–65, 13993–14023, 14138–62 (1958); H. Rept. No. 422, 86th Cong., 1st Sess. (1959); 105 Cong. Rec. 11486–508, 11625–67, 11789–808 (1959).

Quality Act of 1965, the Air Quality Act of 1967, and the Clean Water Act of 1972 illustrate this trend toward national standards. States can attempt to forestall federal controls by forming interstate compacts to handle problems of a regional nature. These compacts, however, require the approval of Congress if they tend to increase the political power of the states or encroach upon the Supremacy Clause. Cuyler v. Adams, 449 U.S. 433, 440 (1981).

The field of nuclear energy has been largely preempted by Congress, especially over questions of safety and plant construction. States retain authority over economic questions, such as the need for additional plants, the type of facility to be licensed, land use, and setting rates. Pacific Gas & Elec. v. Energy Resources Comm'n, 461 U.S. 190, 212 (1983). The exclusive authority of the federal government over safety questions was compromised a year later when the Court allowed a jury to award punitive damages against a company in a case where Karen Silkwood, a laboratory analyst, was contaminated by plutonium. Silkwood v. Kerr-McGee Corp., 464 U.S. 238 (1984). State law claims were also allowed in a later nuclear-safety case; English v. General Electric Co., 496 U.S. 72 (1990).

In 2002, Congress used an interesting procedure in the Nuclear Waste Policy Act of 1982 to approve using Yucca Mountain, Nevada, as the site for storing high-level radioactive waste. The statute allows the governor or the state legislature to disapprove a site selected by the President. Congress then has 90 days to pass a joint resolution of approval, overriding the state. In 2002, Nevada exercised its veto, both the House and the Senate passed a resolution of approval, and President Bush signed it into law. P.L. 107-200 (July 23, 2002). Yucca Mountain continued to be a controversial issue in the presidential campaign of 2004.

A number of preemption cases involve pension plans. In response to pension benefits lost by employees because of bankruptcies, mergers, and theft, Congress passed the Employee Retirement Income Security Act of 1974 (ERISA). With certain exceptions, the statute preempts all state laws that "relate to" any employee benefit plan. The Supreme Court has given a broad reading to the statute's preemption clause.[13]

The dominant role of Congress in determining preemption was emphasized by Justice Rehnquist in 1986 during his confirmation hearings to be Chief Justice. He said that Congress "is probably the ultimate decider as to what the proper relationship between State and Federal law is in most situations.... How much is going to be Federal law in any area in which the Congress power reaches and how much is going to be State law, really in the last analysis, depends upon Congress." "Nomination of Justice William Hubbs Rehnquist," hearings before the Senate Committee on the Judiciary, 99th Cong., 2d Sess., 131 (1986). His judgment has been supported by subsequent cases.[14]

---

13. Ingersoll-Rand Co. v. McClendon, 498 U.S. 133 (1990); FMC v. Holliday, 498 U.S. 52 (1990); Metropolitan Life Ins. Co. v. Massachusetts, 471 U.S. 724 (1985); Shaw v. Delta Air Lines, 463 U.S. 85 (1983); Alessi v. Raybestos-Manhattan, Inc., 451 U.S. 504 (1981). Other preemption cases include California Coastal Comm'n v. Granite Rock Co., 480 U.S. 572 (1987); Exxon Corp. v. Governor of Maryland, 437 U.S. 117 (1978); Ray v. Atlantic Richfield Co., 435 U.S. 151 (1978). For a case in which federal regulations did not preempt state and local regulation because Congress had not expressed that intent, see Hillsborough County v. Automated Medical Labs, 471 U.S. 707 (1985).

14. American Ins. Assn. v. Garamendi, 539 U.S. 396 (2003); United States v. Locke, 529 U.S. 89 (2000) (federal law preempts state regulation of oil tankers); Barnett Bank of Marion County, N.A. v. Nelson, 517 U.S. 25 (1996) (federal statute preempts state statute that prevented a national bank from selling insurance in a small town); Cipollone v. Liggett Group, Inc., 505 U.S. 504 (1992) (federal legislation does not preempt state law damages actions, although it does preempt state mandates for particular warnings on cigarette labels or in cigarette advertisements); Gade v. National Solid Wastes Management Assn., 505 U.S. 88 (1992) (federal law prohibits states from adopting additional training requirements for workers handling hazardous waste); Morales v. Trans World Airlines, Inc., 504 U.S. 374 (1992) (federal law preempts state regulation of airline fare advertising to protect consumers); Wisconsin Public Intervenor v. Mortier, 504 U.S. 374 (1991) (federal law does not preempt regulation of pesticides by local governments); United Steelworkers of America v. Rawson, 495 U.S. 362 (1990) (federal labor law preempts tort claim in state court); California v. FERC, 495 U.S. 490 (1990) (federal law preempts states from requiring flow rates for water in hydroelectric projects that are higher than federal standards, even for the purpose of protecting fish and wildlife).

The Abstention Doctrine

The abstention doctrine helps puncture the periodic, apocalyptic announcement that "federalism is dead." To cultivate comity and mutual respect between the national and state levels, federal courts abstain in some areas. It would be impossible and self-destructive for federal courts to intervene in every state matter. The policy of abstention can be traced back to a congressional statute in 1793: "nor shall a writ of injunction [by federal courts] be granted to stay proceedings in any court of a state." 1 Stat. 335, §5.

The Fourteenth Amendment opened the door to a much larger federal role. After the Supreme Court in *Ex parte Young* (1908) suggested that federal courts would intervene extensively in state affairs, Congress acted to limit judicial interference. Instead of allowing a single federal judge to strike down a state statute or enjoin its operation, Congress required a three-judge court to hear and decide such actions.[15] The policy of abstention crystallized as court doctrine in 1941. A unanimous Supreme Court held that it should withhold judgment until state courts reach a definitive construction of a state statute. Federal courts should avoid "needless friction with state policies" and promote "harmonious relation between state and federal authority" by waiting until the highest state court has disposed of a constitutional issue. Railroad Commission v. Pullman, 312 U.S. 496, 500–01 (1941). Acting under this authority, the Supreme Court has returned cases to state courts to permit interpretation of questions that were not considered or resolved.[16]

Abstention is a general policy and can be waived. Abstention is inappropriate where state statutes are vulnerable on their face for abridging free expression or discouraging protected activities. Federal courts intervene in these cases to prevent state officials from invoking a statute in bad faith, with no hope for success, simply to harass minorities or their organizations. This exception to the abstention doctrine is aimed at statutes that are so vague or overbroad that they threaten First Amendment freedoms. Dombrowski v. Pfister, 380 U.S. 479 (1965); Zwickler v. Koota, 389 U.S. 241 (1967). In the case of a pending state criminal proceeding, federal courts intervene only under extraordinary circumstances: where the danger of irreparable loss is both great and immediate and where the threat to federally protected rights cannot be eliminated during the course of the trial. Younger v. Harris, 401 U.S. 37 (1971); Samuels v. Mackell, 401 U.S. 66 (1971). The policy of noninterference also applies to certain state civil proceedings. Huffman v. Pursue, Ltd., 420 U.S. 592 (1975).

Noninterference by the Supreme Court in state matters often provokes biting dissents that regard federalism as a cloak used to cover constitutional violations by state officials. Justice Brennan, for example, remarked: "Under the banner of vague, undefined notions of equity, comity, and federalism, the Court has embarked upon the dangerous course of condoning both isolated ... and systematic ... violations of civil liberties." Juidice v. Vail, 430 U.S. 327, 346 (1977). See also the dissents in Paul v. Davis, 424 U.S. 693 (1976), and Rizzo v. Goode, 423 U.S. 362 (1976).

Pennsylvania v. Nelson

350 U.S. 497 (1956)

Steve Nelson was convicted for violating the Pennsylvania Sedition Act. The question here is whether Congress, by passing the Smith Act of 1940, preempted the enforcement of state sedition acts.

---

15. 36 Stat. 557, §17 (1910); 36 Stat. 1162, §266 (1911); 37 Stat. 1013 (1913); 38 Stat. 220 (1913). These statutes are codified at 28 U.S.C. §2284 (2000).

16. Reetz v. Bozanich, 397 U.S. 82 (1970); Henry v. Mississippi, 379 U.S. 443 (1965); Meridian v. Southern Bell T. & T. Co., 358 U.S. 639 (1959); Musser v. Utah, 333 U.S. 95 (1948).

Mr. Chief Justice Warren delivered the opinion of the Court.

The respondent Steve Nelson, an acknowledged member of the Communist Party, was convicted in the Court of Quarter Sessions of Allegheny County, Pennsylvania, of a violation of the Pennsylvania Sedition Act and sentenced to imprisonment for twenty years and to a fine of $10,000 and to costs of prosecution in the sum of $13,000. The Superior Court affirmed the conviction. 172 Pa. Super. 125, 92 A.2d 431. The Supreme Court of Pennsylvania, recognizing but not reaching many alleged serious trial errors and conduct of the trial court infringing upon respondent's right to due process of law, decided the case on the narrow issue of supersession of the state law by the Federal Smith Act. In its opinion, the court stated:

"And, while the Pennsylvania statute proscribes sedition against either the Government of the United States or the Government of Pennsylvania, it is only alleged sedition against the United States with which the instant case is concerned. Out of all the voluminous testimony, we have not found, nor has anyone pointed to, a single word indicating a seditious act or even utterance directed against the Government of Pennsylvania."

The precise holding of the court, and all that is before us for review, is that the Smith Act of 1940, as amended in 1948, which prohibits the knowing advocacy of the overthrow of the Government of the United States by force and violence, supersedes the enforceability of the Pennsylvania Sedition Act which proscribes the same conduct....

It should be said at the outset that the decision in this case does not affect the right of States to enforce their sedition laws at times when the Federal Government has not occupied the field and is not protecting the entire country from seditious conduct. The distinction between the two situations was clearly recognized by the court below. Nor does it limit the jurisdiction of the States where the Constitution and Congress have specifically given them concurrent jurisdiction, as was done under the Eighteenth Amendment and the Volstead Act. *United States* v. *Lanza,* 260 U.S. 377. Neither does it limit the right of the State to protect itself at any time against sabotage or attempted violence of all kinds. Nor does it prevent the State from prosecuting where the same act constitutes both a federal offense and a state offense under the police power....

... In this case, we think that each of several tests of supersession is met.

First, "[t]he scheme of federal regulation [is] so pervasive as to make reasonable the inference that Congress left no room for the States to supplement it." *Rice* v. *Santa Fe Elevator Corp.,* 331 U.S., at 230. The Congress determined in 1940 that it was necessary for it to re-enter the field of antisubversive legislation, which had been abandoned by it in 1921. In that year, it enacted the Smith Act which proscribes advocacy of the overthrow of any government—federal, state or local—by force and violence and organization of and knowing membership in a group which so advocates.*[The Court also summarizes the Internal Security Act of 1950 and the Communist Control Act of 1954.]*

We examine these Acts only to determine the congressional plan. Looking to all of them in the aggregate, the conclusion is inescapable that Congress has intended to occupy the field of sedition. Taken as a whole, they evince a congressional plan which makes it reasonable to determine that no room has been left for the States to supplement it....

Second, the federal statutes "touch a field in which the federal interest is so dominant that the federal system [must] be assumed to preclude enforcement of state laws on the same subject." *Rice* v. *Santa Fe Elevator Corp.,* 331 U.S., at 230, citing *Hines* v. *Davidowitz, supra.* Congress has devised an all-embracing program for resistance to the various forms of totalitarian aggression....

Third, enforcement of state sedition acts presents a serious danger of conflict with the administration of the federal program. Since 1939, in order to avoid a hampering of uniform enforcement of its program by sporadic local prosecutions, the Federal Government has urged local authorities not to intervene in such matters, but to turn over to the federal authorities immediately and unevaluated all information concerning subversive activities....

The judgment of the Supreme Court of Pennsylvania is

Affirmed.

Mr. Justice Reed, with whom Mr. Justice Burton and Mr. Justice Minton join, dissenting....

Congress has not, in any of its statutes relating to sedition, specifically barred the exercise of state power to punish the same Acts under state law. And, we read the majority opinion to assume for this case that, absent federal legislation, there is no constitutional bar to punishment of sedition against the United States by both a State and the Nation....

First, the Court relies upon the pervasiveness of the antisubversive legislation embodied in the Smith

Act of 1940, 18 U.S.C. § 2385, the Internal Security Act of 1950, 64 Stat. 987, and the Communist Control Act of 1954, 68 Stat. 775. It asserts that these Acts in the aggregate mean that Congress has occupied the "field of sedition" to the exclusion of the States....

We cannot agree that the federal criminal sanctions against sedition directed at the United States are of such a pervasive character as to indicate an intention to void state action.

Secondly, the Court states that the federal sedition statutes touch a field "in which the federal interest is so dominant" they must preclude state laws on the same subject. This concept is suggested in a comment on *Hines* v. *Davidowitz*, 312 U.S. 52, in the *Rice* case, at 230. The Court in *Davidowitz* ruled that federal statutes compelling alien registration preclude enforcement of state statutes requiring alien registration. We read *Davidowitz* to teach nothing more than that, when the Congress provided a single nation-wide integrated system of regulation so complete as that for aliens' registration (with fingerprinting, a scheduling of activities, and continuous information as to their residence), the Act bore so directly on our foreign relations as to make it evident that Congress intended only one uniform national alien registration system....

Thirdly, the Court finds ground for abrogating Pennsylvania's antisedition statute because, in the Court's view, the State's administration of the Act may hamper the enforcement of the federal law.... The Court's attitude as to interference seems to us quite contrary to that of the Legislative and Executive Departments. Congress was advised of the existing state sedition legislation when the Smith Act was enacted and has been kept current with its spread. No declaration of exclusiveness followed....

Finally, and this one point seems in and of itself decisive, there is an independent reason for reversing the Pennsylvania Supreme Court. The Smith Act appears in Title 18 of the United States Code, which Title codifies the federal criminal laws. Section 3231 of that Title provides:

"Nothing in this title shall be held to take away or impair the jurisdiction of the courts of the several States under the laws thereof."

That declaration springs from the federal character of our Nation. It recognizes the fact that maintenance of order and fairness rests primarily with the States. The section was first enacted in 1825 and has appeared successively in the federal criminal laws since that time. This Court has interpreted the section to mean that States may provide concurrent legislation in the absence of explicit congressional intent to the contrary....

I. NATIONALIZATION OF THE BILL OF RIGHTS

Two months before the first Congress met, James Madison supported constitutional amendments to provide "for all essential rights, particularly the rights of Conscience in the fullest latitude, the freedom of the press, trials by jury, security against general warrants &c." 5 The Writings of James Madison 320 (letter to George Eve, January 2, 1789). The responsibility for moving these amendments through the House of Representatives fell to Madison, who argued that a Bill of Rights would remove apprehensions that the people felt toward the new national government. 1 Annals of Congress 431–33 (1789). He also wanted to place restrictions on the states and proposed that "[n]o State shall violate the equal rights of conscience, of the freedom of the press, or the trial by jury in criminal cases." Id. at 435. The states "are as liable to attack these invaluable privileges as the General Government...." Id. at 441. As finally drafted and ratified, however, the first ten amendments to the Constitution — the Bill of Rights — limited only the federal government.

In 1833, the Supreme Court reaffirmed that the Bill of Rights restrained only the federal government, not the states. At issue was the Just Compensation Clause of the Fifth Amendment. Barron v. Baltimore, 32 U.S. (7 Pet.) 243. The same conclusion was reached by the Court 25 years later. Withers v. Buckley, 20 How. (61 U.S.) 84, 89–90 (1858). However, the Civil War and passage of the Fourteenth Amendment in 1868 worked a fundamental change in federal-state relations. The Amendment prohibited states from making or enforcing any law "which shall abridge the privileges or immunities of citizens of the United States; nor shall any State deprive any person of life, liberty, or property, without due process of law; nor deny to any person within its jurisdiction the equal protection of the laws." The Due Process Clause would become the vehicle for applying most of the Bill of Rights to the states.

The idea of imposing a national standard on the states was rejected by the Supreme Court in 1873 when it held that the primary purpose of the Civil War amendments (the Thirteenth, Fourteenth, and Fifteenth Amendments) was to guarantee freedom for blacks. Moreover, privileges and immunities were to be protected by the states, not the national government. Slaughter-House Cases, 16 Wall. 36, 77–79. Other decisions during this period also refused to apply the Bill of Rights to the states.[17] However, the Equal Protection Clause of the Fourteenth Amendment was available to prevent states from acting in a discriminatory or arbitrary manner. Yick Wo v. Hopkins, 118 U.S. 356 (1886).

The Incorporation Doctrine

By the end of the century, the Court had decided that certain portions of the Bill of Rights should be applied to the states. The Court began with the Just Compensation Clause of the Fifth Amendment, reflecting the judiciary's commitment at that time to business and corporate interests. Missouri Pacific Railway Co. v. Nebraska, 164 U.S. 403 (1896); Chicago, B. & Q. Railway Co. v. Chicago, 166 U.S. 226 (1897). Thus began the process of "incorporating" the Bill of Rights into the Due Process Clause of the Fourteenth Amendment and extending these guarantees to the states. Although in 1904 the Court held that the Confrontation Clause of the Sixth Amendment did not apply to the states (West v. Louisiana, 194 U.S. 258), and four years later refused to extend the Self-Incrimination Clause of the Fifth Amendment to the states (Twining v. New Jersey, 211 U.S. 78), within a few decades the Court began the step-by-step process of bringing the states under the Bill of Rights. Almost every provision of the Bill of Rights now covers the states (see Table 8.2). This process is sometimes called the doctrine of absorption or the selective incorporation of the Bill of Rights.

Selective incorporation reflects a contest between two schools of thought. The second Justice Harlan believed that courts have a duty to see that due process follows principles consistent with the people's "traditions and conscience." In re Gault, 387 U.S. 1, 67 (1967). Justice Black opposed this philosophy because it requires judges to impose personal notions of natural law. Duncan v. Louisiana, 391 U.S. 145, 168 (1968). To limit judicial activism, at least in the incremental form supported by Harlan, Black promoted the wholesale incorporation of the Bill of Rights. ADAMSON v. CALIFORNIA, 332 U.S. 46, 75 (1947). Ironically, Black's activism probably exceeded Harlan's. Almost all of the Bill of Rights has been incorporated, with little opposition from contemporary members of the Supreme Court (see Rehnquist's testimony).

The selective incorporation of the Bill of Rights does not always mean that a national standard has been forced upon the states. For example, the First Amendment applies to all states, and yet court rulings on obscenity allow wide discretion to accommodate local community standards. Miller v. California, 413 U.S. 15, 30–34 (1973). The right to a jury trial applies to the states, but states are at liberty to depart from federal standards by establishing juries with less than twelve members and by accepting nonunanimous verdicts (chapter 13). Also, state courts can insulate themselves from national standards by basing their rulings not on the U.S. Constitution but on rights guaranteed in their state constitutions. State courts are able to interpret individual liberties more expansively than the federal government. PruneYard Shopping Center v. Robins, 447 U.S. 74, 81 (1980); Collins et al., 13 Hast. Const. L. Q. 599 (1986). Other chapters offer specific examples in which state courts, relying on their own constitutions, reject constitutional doctrines advanced by the U.S. Supreme Court.

---

17. Pervear v. Commonwealth, 5 Wall. (72 U.S.) 475 (1867); Twitchell v. The Commonwealth, 7 Wall. (74 U.S.) 321 (1869); The Justices v. Murray, 9 Wall. (76 U.S.) 274 (1870); Walker v. Sauvinet, 92 U.S. (2 Otto.) 90, 92 (1876); United States v. Cruikshank, 92 U.S. 542, 552 (1876); Hurtado v. California, 110 U.S. 516, 538 (1884); Presser v. Illinois, 116 U.S. 252, 265 (1886); Spies v. Illinois, 123 U.S. 131, 166 (1887); In re Kemmler, 136 U.S. 436, 446 (1890); McElvaine v. Brush, 142 U.S. 155, 158 (1891); O'Neil v. Vermont, 144 U.S. 323, 332 (1892). See also Maxwell v. Dow, 176 U.S. 581 (1900), which declined to apply the guarantees of the Fifth and Sixth Amendments to the states.

TABLE 8.2   INCORPORATION OF BILL OF RIGHTS

Amendment	Clause	Decision
First	Congress shall make no law respecting an establishment of religion,...	Everson v. Board of Education, 330 U.S. 1, 15 (1947).
	or prohibiting the free exercise thereof;...	Cantwell v. Connecticut, 310 U.S. 296, 303 (1940).
	or abridging the freedom of speech,...	Gitlow v. New York, 268 U.S. 652, 666 (1925); Fiske v. Kansas, 274 U.S. 380, 387 (1927).
	or of the press;...	Near v. Minnesota, 283 U.S. 697, 707 (1931). See also Gitlow v. New York, 268 U.S. 652, 666 (1925).
	or the right of the people peaceably to assemble, and to petition the Government for a redress of grievances.	DeJonge v. Oregon, 299 U.S. 352, 364 (1937).
Second	A well regulated Militia, being necessary to the security of a free State, the right of the people to keep and bear arms, shall not be infringed.	—
Third	No soldier shall, in time of peace be quartered in any house, without the consent of the Owner, nor in time of war, but in a manner to be prescribed by law.	—
Fourth	The right of the people to be secure in their persons, houses, papers, and effects, against unreasonable searches and seizures, shall not be violated, and no Warrants shall issue, but upon probable cause, supported by Oath or affirmation, and particularly describing the place to be searched, and the persons or things to be seized.	Wolf v. Colorado, 338 U.S. 25, 27–28 (1949); Mapp v. Ohio, 367 U.S. 643, 655 (1961); Ker v. California, 374 U.S. 23 (1963).
Fifth	No person shall be held to answer for a capital, or otherwise infamous crime, unless on a presentment or indictment of a Grand Jury, except in cases arising in the land or naval forces, or in the Militia, when in actual service in time of War or public danger;...	—
	nor shall any person be subject for the same offence to be twice put in jeopardy of life or limb;...	Benton v. Maryland, 395 U.S. 784, 787 (1969).
	nor shall be compelled in any Criminal Case to be a witness against himself;...	Malloy v. Hogan, 378 U.S. 1, 3 (1964).
	nor be deprived of life, liberty, or property, without due process of law;...	[Parallel to Fourteenth Amendment.]
	nor shall private property be taken for public use, without just compensation.	Missouri Pacific Railway Co. v. Nebraska, 164 U.S. 403, 417 (1896); Chicago, B. & Q. R.R. Co. v. Chicago, 166 U.S. 226, 241 (1897).

TABLE 8.2   INCORPORATION OF BILL OF RIGHTS CONTINUED

Amendment	Clause	Decision
Sixth	In all criminal prosecutions, the accused shall enjoy the right to a speedy and public trial,...	In re Oliver, 333 U.S. 257, 273 (1948) [right to public trial] and Klopfer v. North Carolina, 386 U.S. 213, 222 (1967) [right to speedy trial].
	by an impartial jury of the State and district wherein the crime shall have been committed, which district shall have been previously ascertained by law, and to be informed of the nature and cause of the accusation;...	Duncan v. Louisiana, 391 U.S. 145, 149 (1968); Parker v. Gladden, 385 U.S. 363–64 (1966). See also Irvin v. Dowd, 366 U.S. 717 (1961) and Turner v. Louisiana, 379 U.S. 466 (1965).
	to be confronted with the witness against him;...	Pointer v. Texas, 380 U.S. 400, 403 (1965).
	to have compulsory process for obtaining witnesses in his favor;...	Washington v. Texas, 388 U.S. 14, 19 (1967).
	and to have the Assistance of Counsel for his defence.	Powell v. Alabama, 287 U.S. 45, 67–68 (1932) [counsel for young and illiterate in a capital case]; Gideon v. Wainright, 372 U.S. 335, 344 (1963) [counsel for felony trials]; Douglas v. California, 372 U.S. 353, 357–58 (1963) [counsel for first appeals]; Argersinger v. Hamlin, 407 U.S. 25 (1972) [counsel for felony or misdemeanor trials involving jail term].
Seventh	In suits at common law, where the value in Controversy shall exceed twenty dollars, the right of trial by jury shall be preserved, and no fact tried by a jury, shall be otherwise re-examined in any Court of the United States, than according to the rules of the common law.	—
Eighth	Excessive bail shall not be required...	Schilb v. Kuebel, 404 U.S. 357, 365 (1971).
	nor excessive fines imposed...	—
	nor cruel and unusual punishment inflicted.	Robinson v. California, 370 U.S. 660, 666 (1962).
Ninth	The enumeration in the Constitution, of certain rights, shall not be construed to deny or disparage others retained by the people.	Griswold v. Connecticut, 381 U.S. 479 484 (1965) [also invoked other parts of the Bill of Rights].
Tenth	The powers not delegated to the United States by the Constitution, nor prohibited by it to the States, are reserved to the States respectively, or to the people.	—

Adamson v. California

332 U.S. 46 (1947)

Admiral Dewey Adamson was convicted of a murder charge and sentenced to death. Under California's constitution and its penal laws, Adamson's failure to explain or to deny evidence against him could be commented on by the court and by counsel and considered by the court and the jury. The immediate question was whether this procedure violated the guaranty in the Fifth Amendment that no person "shall be compelled in any criminal case to be a witness against himself." The Court held that his privilege is not inherent in the right to a fair trial and is not protected by the Due Process Clause of the Fourteenth Amendment. In his dissent, Justice Black lays the groundwork for arguing that the entire Bill of Rights should be incorporated in the Due Process Clause of the Fourteenth Amendment and applied against the states.

MR. JUSTICE REED delivered the opinion of the Court.

... The provisions of California law which were challenged in the state proceedings as invalid under the Fourteenth Amendment to the Federal Constitution are those of the state constitution and penal code.... They permit the failure of a defendant to explain or to deny evidence against him to be commented upon by court and by counsel and to be considered by court and jury. The defendant did not testify....

In the first place, appellant urges that the provision of the Fifth Amendment that no person "shall be compelled in any criminal case to be a witness against himself" is a fundamental national privilege or immunity protected against state abridgment by the Fourteenth Amendment or a privilege or immunity secured, through the Fourteenth Amendment, against deprivation by state action because it is a personal right, enumerated in the federal Bill of Rights.

Secondly, appellant relies upon the due process of law clause of the Fourteenth Amendment to invalidate the provisions of the California law....

... It is settled law that the clause of the Fifth Amendment, protecting a person against being compelled to be a witness against himself, is not made effective by the Fourteenth Amendment as a protection against state action on the ground that freedom from testimonial compulsion is a right of national citizenship, or because it is a personal privilege or immunity secured by the Federal Constitution as one of the rights of man that are listed in the Bill of Rights.

The reasoning that leads to those conclusions starts with the unquestioned premise that the Bill of Rights, when adopted, was for the protection of the individual against the federal government and its provisions were inapplicable to similar actions done by the states. *Barron* v. *Baltimore*, 7 Pet. 243; *Feld-man* v. *United States*, 322 U.S. 487, 490. With the adoption of the Fourteenth Amendment, it was suggested that the dual citizenship recognized by its first sentence ["All persons born or naturalized in the United States, and subject to the jurisdiction thereof, are citizens of the United States and of the State wherein they reside"] secured for citizens federal protection for their elemental privileges and immunities of state citizenship. The *Slaughter-House Cases* decided, contrary to the suggestion, that these rights, as privileges and immunities of state citizenship, remained under the sole protection of the state governments....

Appellant secondly contends that if the privilege against self-incrimination is not a right protected by the privileges and immunities clause of the Fourteenth Amendment against state action, this privilege, to its full scope under the Fifth Amendment, inheres in the right to a fair trial. A right to a fair trial is a right admittedly protected by the due process clause of the Fourteenth Amendment. Therefore, appellant argues, the due process clause of the Fourteenth Amendment protects his privilege against self-incrimination. The due process clause of the Fourteenth Amendment, however, does not draw all the rights of the federal Bill of Rights under its protection. That contention was made and rejected in *Palko* v. *Connecticut*, 302 U.S. 319, 323 ...

MR. JUSTICE FRANKFURTER, concurring....

Between the incorporation of the Fourteenth Amendment into the Constitution and the beginning of the present membership of the Court—a period of seventy years—the scope of that Amendment was passed upon by forty-three judges. Of all these judges, only one, who may respectfully be called an eccentric exception, ever indicated the belief that the Fourteenth Amendment was a shorthand summary of the first eight Amendments theretofore limiting only the Federal Government, and that due process incorporated those eight Amendments as restrictions upon the powers of the States....

Indeed, the suggestion that the Fourteenth Amendment incorporates the first eight Amendments as such is not unambiguously urged. Even the boldest innovator would shrink from suggesting to more than half the States that they may no longer initiate prosecutions without indictment by grand jury, or that thereafter all the States of the Union must furnish a jury of twelve for every case involving a claim above twenty dollars. There is suggested merely a selective incorporation of the first eight Amendments into the Fourteenth Amendment. Some are in and some are out, but we are left in the dark as to which are in and which are out. Nor are we given the calculus for determining which go in and which stay out. If the basis of selection is merely that those provisions of the first eight Amendments are incorporated which commend themselves to individual justices as indispensable to the dignity and happiness of a free man, we are thrown back to a merely subjective test....

Mr. Justice Black, dissenting....

This decision reasserts a constitutional theory spelled out in *Twining* v. *New Jersey*, 211 U.S. 78, that this Court is endowed by the Constitution with boundless power under "natural law" periodically to expand and contract constitutional standards to conform to the Court's conception of what at a particular time constitutes "civilized decency" and "fundamental liberty and justice." Invoking this *Twining* rule, the Court concludes that although comment upon testimony in a federal court would violate the Fifth Amendment, identical comment in a state court does not violate today's fashion in civilized decency and fundamentals and is therefore not prohibited by the Federal Constitution as amended.

· · ·

My study of the historical events that culminated in the Fourteenth Amendment, and the expressions of those who sponsored and favored, as well as those who opposed its submission and passage, persuades me that one of the chief objects that the provisions of the Amendment's first section, separately, and as a whole, were intended to accomplish was to make the Bill of Rights applicable to the states. With full knowledge of the import of the *Barron* decision, the framers and backers of the Fourteenth Amendment proclaimed its purpose to be to overturn the constitutional rule that case had announced. This historical purpose has never received full consideration or

exposition in any opinion of this Court interpreting the Amendment....

... I am attaching to this dissent an appendix which contains a résumé, by no means complete, of the Amendment's history. In my judgment that history conclusively demonstrates that the language of the first section of the Fourteenth Amendment, taken as a whole, was thought by those responsible for its submission to the people, and by those who opposed its submission, sufficiently explicit to guarantee that thereafter no state could deprive its citizens of the privileges and protections of the Bill of Rights. Whether this Court ever will, or whether it now should, in the light of past decisions, give full effect to what the Amendment was intended to accomplish is not necessarily essential to a decision here. However that may be, our prior decisions, including *Twining*, do not prevent our carrying out that purpose, at least to the extent of making applicable to the states, not a mere part, as the Court has, but the full protection of the Fifth Amendment's provision against compelling evidence from an accused to convict him of crime. And I further contend that the "natural law" formula which the Court uses to reach its conclusion in this case should be abandoned as an incongruous excrescence on our Constitution. I believe that formula to be itself a violation of our Constitution, in that it subtly conveys to courts, at the expense of legislatures, ultimate power over public policies in fields where no specific provision of the Constitution limits legislative power....

... I fear to see the consequences of the Court's practice of substituting its own concepts of decency and fundamental justice for the language of the Bill of Rights as its point of departure in interpreting and enforcing that Bill of Rights. If the choice must be between the selective process of the *Palko* decision applying some of the Bill of Rights to the States, or the *Twining* rule applying none of them, I would choose the *Palko* selective process. But rather than accept either of these choices, I would follow what I believe was the original purpose of the Fourteenth Amendment — to extend to all the people of the nation the complete protection of the Bill of Rights. To hold that this Court can determine what, if any, provisions of the Bill of Rights will be enforced, and if so to what degree, is to frustrate the great design of a written Constitution....

Mr. Justice Douglas joins in this opinion.

[At this point, Black inserts a 31-page appendix describing the origin and legislative history of the Fourteenth Amendment, concluding that the Bill of Rights applies to the states. He also quotes from Jus-

tices who believed that the Privileges and Immunities Clause of the Fourteenth Amendment applies to the states.]

Mr. Justice Murphy, with whom Mr. Justice Rutledge concurs, dissenting....

The Incorporation Doctrine:
Testimony by Justice Rehnquist

In 1986, during Senate hearings for his nomination for Chief Justice of the Supreme Court, Justice Rehnquist was asked by Senator Arlen Specter about the "incorporation doctrine": the gradual incorporation of the Bill of Rights into the Due Process Clause of the Fourteenth Amendment to be applied against the states. Originally, the Bill of Rights restricted only the federal government. Attorney General Edwin Meese III, as one of the more vocal critics of the incorporation doctrine, had written that "nowhere else has the principle of Federalism been dealt such a politically violent and constitutionally suspect blow as by the theory of incorporation." Meese, "The Supreme Court of the United States: Bulwark of a Limited Constitution," 27 So. Tex. L. Rev. 455, 463–64 (1986). The testimony below comes from "Nomination of Justice William Hubbs Rehnquist," hearings before the Senate Committee on the Judiciary, 99th Cong., 2d Sess., 191–92, 350–51, 356 (1986).

Justice Rehnquist.... [I]f you are looking at the language of the due process clause, as I recall it, Senator, it says: "No State shall deprive any person of life, liberty or property without due process of law."

And the question then becomes, you know, as you know perfectly well, what is included under liberty, or, what provisions from the Bill of Rights are carried over by that language? And I would say that, from the language itself, it is not evident that any particular provisions are carried over, not inexorable; but if you look at the word liberty, and you wonder what kind of liberty are they talking about, surely one liberty was freedom of speech, freedom of the press.

So, it seems to me it is quite natural to carry those over. But I do not know that the language of the due process clause, nor necessarily, what I happen to recall about the debates, and that sort of thing, necessarily indicates that the full rigors of the first amendment as applied to Congress, necessarily were to be applied to the States.

Senator Specter. Well, the difficulty with that, it seems to me—and I am just probing to get your line of reasoning on it—is that it is so speculative. If you are picking out a portion of the first amendment, the freedom of speech—if you seek to avoid putting your own personal views, as they arise in a case, which I know you have testified in the 1971 proceedings, that you are very much opposed to—how can you really separate the various aspects of something as fundamental as speech?

Isn't it really all in there? Once you say that the due process clause incorporates freedom of speech under the first amendment, isn't that all there is to it? How can you separate any of it out as not incorporated?

Justice Rehnquist. Well, if you say that the due process clause incorporates and makes applicable against the States, the first amendment in haec verba, so to speak, the question is answered. If it does that, it does carry it over in precisely the terms that it is applicable to Congress against the State.

But I think the argument on the other side, is that—and I think this is made very well in Justice Jackson's dissent in the *Beauharnais* case—is that there was a good deal of understanding of what freedom of speech meant at the time the Constitution was adopted, that was undoubtedly applicable against the States, but that there were perhaps slightly more latitude allowed to the States than were allowed to the Federal Government.

Justice Harlan took that position in his opinion in the *Roth* case. That the States could proscribe certain kinds of obscenity but that the Federal Government could not.

Senator Specter. Mr. Justice Rehnquist, at the risk of asking questions which may come before the Court, I think these are pretty well established principles, but, there is considerable concern on the part of this Senator about the applicability of the due process clause of the 14th amendment to certain fundamental liberties, as embodied in the first 10 amendments.

And I would like to ask your view as to the inclusion of the free exercise of religion in *Cantwell* v. *Connecticut.* It was a unanimous opinion. Does that matter rest, so far as you are concerned?

Justice REHNQUIST. Most certainly, yes.

Senator SPECTER. And the establishment clause in *Everson* v. *Board of Education?*

Justice REHNQUIST. No. I think I criticized the *Everson* case in my dissent in Wallace against Jaffrey, not for the result it reached at all, but for its use of the term "wall of separation between church and state," which I felt was simply not historically justified....

Senator SPECTER.... Is there any question in your mind that the due process clause of the 14th amendment incorporates freedom of speech?

Justice REHNQUIST. Other than the point I made yesterday. It, obviously, incorporates freedom of speech. I took the position in a couple of opinions I wrote in following Justice Jackson and Justice Harlan that some of the details might be different as applied against the States as opposed to the Federal Government.

Senator SPECTER. Would you repeat the distinction you see as to the scope of the due process clause incorporating the establishment clause of the first amendment?

Justice REHNQUIST. No; I think that is settled by the *Everson* case.

Senator SPECTER. All right.

There is no question that the due process clause of the 14th amendment incorporates freedom of the press under the first amendment?

Justice REHNQUIST. I do not think so.

Senator SPECTER. Are the rights of assembly and petition incorporated by the due process clause of the 14th amendment?

Justice REHNQUIST. Yes; I think they are.

Senator SPECTER. Is the search and seizure clause of the fourth amendment incorporated by the due process clause of the fourteenth amendment?

Justice REHNQUIST. That was held in *Mapp* v. *Ohio.*

Senator SPECTER. Do you agree with that? Do you believe it is a decided matter?

Justice REHNQUIST. It is certainly a settled matter, yes.

Senator SPECTER. Is double jeopardy under the fifth amendment incorporated in the due process clause of the 14th amendment?

Justice REHNQUIST. I think that was in the—Senator, I am going to draw back a little. Because in a case like *Benton* v. *Maryland* that came to the Court

where—before I got there. I did not participate in that case. I have followed *Benton* v. *Maryland* many times when I have been on the Court. But to say whether I agree with a case that was decided before I came on the Court, I think it is better to phrase it that my record in voting on the case has certainly shown that I have followed that case.

Senator SPECTER. Well, I am not asking whether you agree with it. I am asking whether you consider it a settled issue that the incorporation doctrine covers that issue.

The concern I have is whether the incorporation doctrine is going to be undercut. Although I do not think that you and I have any difference of opinion on this, I just want to be sure.

Justice REHNQUIST. I think in a case—I cannot remember—a case coming up from Montana, I took the—Justice Stewart joined my opinion, I joined Justice Stewart's opinion—saying that some of the nuances of the double jeopardy clause should not apply the same to the States as to the Federal Government.

I think this was a case involving when the trial started, for the purposes of—when jeopardy attached. And the rule in the Federal cases was when a witness is first sworn. But Montana had a wholly different procedure. And it just seemed that a fair translation of the Federal rule to the State rule would not give you an identical situation....

Senator SPECTER.... I had gone through a number of the provisions of the Bill of Rights on the incorporation doctrine, Mr. Justice Rehnquist, because I think it is important to lay to rest the conclusion that the 14th amendment due process clause does incorporate certain provisions of the Bill of Rights.

I have only gone over the ones which have been incorporated. I have not gone into the ones which have not been, because I do not want to move into a lot of areas of the law which are not settled.

There are two remaining areas I want to ask you about. Do you regard it as settled law that the speedy trial provision is incorporated under the due process clause of the 14th amendment?

Justice REHNQUIST. Yes, I think that is settled law, and my opinions reflect it.

Senator SPECTER. What about the cruel and unusual punishment provision of the eighth amendment, is that incorporated into the due process clause of the 14th amendment?

Justice REHNQUIST. Again, my opinions reflect the fact.

CONCLUSIONS

Areas in which state and local governments were once virtually supreme, including agriculture, mining, manufacturing, and labor, eventually gave way to federal controls when transportation systems and economic markets assumed a national character. Over time, much of intrastate commerce became interstate commerce. Issues long identified with local government, including education, health, welfare, and law enforcement, are now largely a matter of federal-state cooperation. The federal taxing power, magnified by the Sixteenth Amendment and the income tax, ushered in hundreds of federal grant programs.

The Supreme Court likes to characterize itself as a guardian of federalism, but its doctrines in this area are often vague and unworkable. One scholar, Mark Tushnet, remarked: "Every time the Supreme Court has wandered into the federalism forest, it has gotten lost." 47 Vand. L. Rev. 1623, 1624 (1994). Moreover, the Court's incorporation doctrine has done much to undermine state independence and to centralize national power.

Although litigation continues to define federal-state relations, it operates mostly at the margins. Basic questions of federalism are left to the determination of Congress. During his confirmation hearings in 1986 to be Associate Justice to the Supreme Court, Antonin Scalia testified that "the primary defender of the constitutional balance, the Federal Government versus the states ... the primary institution to strike the right balance is the Congress.... On the basis of the court's past decisions ... the main protection for that is in the policymaking area, is in the Congress. The court's struggles to prescribe what is the proper role of the Federal Government vis-à-vis the State have essentially been abandoned for quite a while." "Nomination of Judge Antonin Scalia," hearings before the Senate Committee on the Judiciary, 99th Cong., 2d Sess., 8182 (1986).

Scalia testified one year after the Court, in *Garcia,* seemed to signal that it would no longer intervene to police the boundaries between the national government and the states, but would leave that determination chiefly to Congress. Nonetheless, beginning in the 1990s, the Court reentered the field to challenge congressional statutes and to breathe new life into the Tenth Amendment and the Eleventh Amendment. A new era of "dual federalism" appeared to have begun, although the Court was closely divided on these questions. When Chief Justice Rehnquist died and Justice O'Connor retired, the Court lost perhaps its two strongest advocates for state power and in recent years has seemed more favorably inclined toward federal power.

NOTES AND QUESTIONS

1. How should we understand the "elastic nature" of the Necessary and Proper Clause, as viewed by Marshall in *McCulloch v. Maryland*? What are the implications for federalism?

2. *Gibbons v. Ogden* has been referred to as the "Magna Carta of Interstate Commerce." What accounts for its stature? Have Marshall's definitions of "commerce" weathered the passage of time? Why or why not?

3. Is *Wickard v. Filburn* consistent with Marshall's reasoning in *Gibbons* v. *Ogden*? Do both rulings rest on the concept of "plenary" congressional power over commerce, or did *Filburn* represent a departure from *Gibbons v. Ogden*?

4. Explain the concept of "dual federalism." What role has it played in Supreme Court decisions? In your view, does it possess constitutional merit? What is its currency today?

5. What does it mean to say, as Chief Justice Stone does in *United States v. Darby,* that the Tenth Amendment is a "truism"?

6. Can the majority opinions in *Gonzales v. Raich* and *Gonzales v. Oregon* be reconciled? Why might traditional defenders of state's rights like Justice Scalia support federal regulation of marijuana and assisted suicide?

SELECTED READINGS

ABRAMS, KATHRYN. "On Reading and Using the Tenth Amendment." 93 Yale Law Journal 723 (1984).

ADLER, MATTHEW D. AND SETH F. KREIMER. "The New Etiquette of Federalism: New York, Printz, and Yeskey." 1998 Supreme Court Review 71.

ALFANGE, DEAN, JR. "Congressional Regulation of the 'States Qua States': From National League of Cities to EEOC v. Wyoming." 1983 Supreme Court Review 215.

ANDERSON, WILLIAM. The Nation and the States: Rivals or Partners? Minneapolis: University of Minnesota Press, 1955.

BANKS, CHRISTOPHER AND JOHN BLAKEMAN. "Chief Justice Roberts, Justice Alito, and New Federalism Jurisprudence." 38 Publius: The Journal of Federalism 576 (2008).

BENSON, PAUL R., JR. The Supreme Court and the Commerce Clause, 1937–1970. New York: Dunellen, 1970.

BRENNAN, WILLIAM J., JR. "The Bill of Rights and the States." 36 New York University Law Review 761 (1961).

BRIGHTON, ROBERT CHARLES, JR. "Separating Myth from Reality in Federalism Decisions: A Perspective of American Federalism—Past and Present." 35 Vanderbilt Law Review 161 (1982).

CORWIN, EDWARD S. The Commerce Power Versus States' Rights. Princeton, N.J.: Princeton University Press, 1936.

———. "The Passing of Dual Federalism." 36 Virginia Law Review 1 (1950).

FISHER, LOUIS. "How the States Shape Constitutional Law." 15 State Legislatures 37 (August 1989).

GIBBONS, JOHN J. "The Eleventh Amendment and State Sovereign Immunity: A Reinterpretation." 83 Columbia Law Review 1889 (1983).

HOWARD, A.E. DICK. "The States and the Supreme Court." 31 Catholic University Law Review 380 (1982).

KRAMER, LARRY D. "Putting the Politics Back into the Political Safeguards of Federalism." 100 Columbia Law Review 215 (2000).

LESSIG, LAWRENCE. "Translating Federalism: United States v. Lopez," 1995 Supreme Court Review 125.

LOFGREN, CHARLES A. "The Origins of the Tenth Amendment: History, Sovereignty, and the Problem of Constitutional Intention," in Ronald K.L. Collins, ed., Constitutional Government in America. Durham, N.C.: Carolina Academic Press, 1980.

MERRITT, DEBORAH JONES. "Commerce!," 94 Michigan Law Review 674 (1995).

MICHELMAN, FRANK I. "States' Rights and States' Roles: Permutations of 'Sovereignty' in National League of Cities v. Usery." 86 Yale Law Journal 1165 (1977).

MORRISON, STANLEY. "Does the Fourteenth Amendment Incorporate the Bill of Rights?" 2 Stanford Law Review 140 (1949).

NAGEL, ROBERT F. "Federalism as a Fundamental Value: National League of Cities in Perspective." 1981 Supreme Court Review 81.

NEUBORNE, BURT. "The Myth of Parity." 90 Harvard Law Review 1105 (1977).

SCHMIDHAUSER, JOHN R. The Supreme Court as Final Arbiter in Federal-State Relations, 1789–1957. Chapel Hill: University of North Carolina Press, 1958.

SHAPIRO, DAVID L. "Wrong Terms: The Eleventh Amendment and the Pennhurst Case." 98 Harvard Law Review 61 (1984).

VILE, M.J.C. The Structure of American Federalism. London: Oxford University Press, 1961.

WELLS, MICHAEL. "The Role of Comity in the Law of Federal Courts." 60 North Carolina Law Review 59 (1981).

WISE, CHARLES AND ROSEMARY O'LEARY. "Is Federalism Dead or Alive in the Supreme Court? Implications for Public Administrators." 52 Public Administration Review 559 (1992).

9

Economic Liberties

From the late nineteenth century to the 1930s, the courts struck down efforts by Congress and state legislatures to ease the harshness of industrial conditions. Statutes that established maximum hours or minimum wages were declared unconstitutional interferences with property rights, due process, and the judicially created "liberty of contract." State legislatures had relied on the "police power" to protect public health and safety. In many of these cases the courts held that government existed to protect life, liberty, and property, with property accorded the greatest protection. Over those decades the judiciary promoted a narrow definition of property and restricted the government's ability to protect the health and safety of citizens. This chapter analyzes two other issues involving economic rights: the Contract Clause (prohibiting states from impairing the obligation of contracts) and the Taking Clause (providing that private property shall not be taken for public use without just compensation).

A. THE MEANING OF PROPERTY

Few words evoke more powerful emotions than *property*. Pierre Proudhon, the French anarchist of the nineteenth century, equated property with theft. Jesus warned that it would be easier for a camel to pass through the eye of a needle than for a rich man to enter the kingdom of God. Others elevated property to a position of reverence and respect. Machiavelli advised a prince not to take property, for "men forget more easily the death of their father than the loss of their patrimony."

We are taught from childhood to think of property as tangible objects: land, buildings, personal property, business, and wealth. The word itself, however, suggests a larger meaning. It derives from *proprius,* which means something private or peculiar to oneself. This general concept embraces intangible possessions, including reputation, ideas, and religious opinions. As a result of court decisions in recent decades, property rights have expanded to cover welfare payments, job rights, garnishment procedures, unemployment compensation, and environmental rights. Property in America acquires specific meaning from custom, statutes, and court decisions.

Property, as a legal creation, fluctuates in meaning over time. Before the War of Independence, a landed aristocracy in America gained protection from *entail* (making land inalienable) and *primogeniture* (transferring land to the eldest son). Gradually those laws were abolished. Up until the Civil War, property extended to black slaves, who were auctioned off at the market, bought and sold as human merchandise. Congress enacted fugitive slave laws to return "property" to its owners. In the *Dred Scott* case, Chief Justice Taney said that the right of property in a slave was "distinctly and expressly affirmed in the Constitution. The right to traffic in it, like an ordinary article of merchandise and property, was guaranteed to the citizens of the United States, in every State that might desire it, for twenty years." Dred Scott v. Sandford, 60 U.S. 393, 451(1857).

Well into the twentieth century, the courts continued to treat wives as the property of the husband. The concept of *coverture,* described by Blackstone more than two centuries ago, maintained its influence. Upon marriage, a woman's legal existence was submerged into that of the husband. Marriage made husband and wife "one person in law." Under the husband's "wing, protection, and *cover,* she performs every thing." Performance included availability for sex, making it legally impossible in some

389

states for a man to rape his wife. Adultery with a man's wife was considered a violation of the *husband's* property rights. Tinker v. Colwell, 193 U.S. 473 (1904).

Locke and Madison

To the framers of the Constitution, property had a broad meaning. They knew that when John Locke spoke of property, he meant "lives, liberties and estates"—not simply the latter. To Locke, individuals possessed property in their persons as well as in their goods. Every man had a property in the labor of his body and the work of his hands. The act of labor invested part of one's personality in an object.

James Madison developed a comprehensive view of property. In Federalist No. 10, he spoke of the "diversity in the faculties of men, from which the rights of property originate." Because mankind consists of different and unequal faculties, different and unequal kinds of property result. But Madison did not say that the most important function of government was to protect property. Rather, the "protection of these faculties is the first object of government." Consistent with that notion, the Constitution authorizes Congress to "promote the progress of science and useful arts, by securing for limited times to authors and inventors the exclusive right to their respective writings and discoveries." Art. I, §8, Cl. 8. Madison expanded on his views in an essay written in 1792. People had property in their opinions, in the free communication of ideas, in religious beliefs, and the free use of faculties and "free choice of the objects on which to employ them." Because conscience is the "most sacred of all property," it is a greater violation to invade a man's conscience than to invade his home (see Madison reading).

This broad view of property rights was obscured by the Supreme Court during America's industrial growth in the nineteenth century. The Court invoked the Due Process Clause of the Fifth and Fourteenth Amendments to control the substantive content of federal and state legislation. In upholding the right of business to operate free of government control, the Court was said to protect property. But it did not protect property in its larger sense, including the community's interest in health and safety. Walton Hamilton and Irene Till explained that it is "incorrect to say that the judiciary protected property; rather they called that property to which they accorded protection." 12 Encycl. Soc. Sci. 536 (1934).

Property has come to represent a "bundle of rights." Kaiser Aetna v. United States, 444 U.S. 164, 176 (1979). These rights have little in common except that they are asserted by persons and enforced by government. Felix S. Cohen, for many years a gifted lecturer at the Yale Law School, underscored the enforcement aspect by proposing that the following label be affixed to all property: "To the world: 'Keep off X unless you have my permission, which I may grant or withhold.' Signed: Private citizen. Endorsed: The state." 9 Rutgers L. Rev. 347, 374 (1954). Although legislative actions and judicial decisions help determine the boundaries of property, the state does not create interests. The active, driving force behind property is the individual who remains conscious of rights and insists on their protection.

Madison's Essay on Property

This term in its particular application means "that dominion which one man claims and exercises over the external things of the world, in exclusion of every other individual."

In its larger and juster meaning, it embraces every thing to which a man may attach a value and have a right; and *which leaves to every one else the like advantage.*

SOURCE: This essay, by James Madison, appeared in *The National Gazette*, March 29, 1792, and is reprinted in 6 The Writings of James Madison 101–03 (Gaillard Hunt ed.).

In the former sense, a man's land, or merchandize, or money is called his property.

In the latter sense, a man has property in his opinions and the free communication of them.

He has a property of peculiar value in his religious opinions, and in the profession and practice dictated by them.

He has property very dear to him in the safety and liberty of his person.

He has an equal property in the free use of his faculties and free choice of the objects on which to employ them.

In a word, as a man is said to have a right to his

property, he may be equally said to have a property in his rights.

Where an excess of power prevails, property of no sort is duly respected. No man is safe in his opinions, his person, his faculties or his possessions.

Where there is an excess of liberty, the effect is the same, tho' from an opposite cause.

Government is instituted to protect property of every sort; as well that which lies in the various rights of individuals, as that which the term particularly expresses. This being the end of government, that alone is a *just* government, which *impartially* secures to every man, whatever is his *own.*

According to this standard of merit, the praise of affording a just security to property, should be sparingly bestowed on a government which, however scrupulously guarding the possessions of individuals, does not protect them in the enjoyment and communication of their opinions, in which they have an equal, and in the estimation of some, a more valuable property.

More sparingly should this praise be allowed to a government, where a man's religious rights are violated by penalties, or fettered by tests, or taxed by a hierarchy. Conscience is the most sacred of all property; other property depending in part on positive law, the exercise of that, being a natural and inalienable right. To guard a man's house as his castle, to pay public and enforce private debts with the most exact faith, can give no title to invade a man's conscience which is more sacred than his castle, or to withhold from it that debt of protection, for which the public faith is pledged, by the very nature and original conditions of the social pact.

That is not a just government, nor is property secure under it, where the property which a man has in his personal safety and personal liberty, is violated by arbitrary seizures of one class of citizens for the service of the rest. A magistrate issuing warrants to a press gang, would be in his proper functions in Turkey or Indostan, under appellations proverbial of the most compleat despotism.

That is not a just government, nor is property secure under it, where arbitrary restrictions, exemptions, and monopolies deny to part of its citizens that free use of their faculties, and free choice of their occupations, which not only constitute their property in the general sense of the word; but are the means of acquiring property strictly so called. What must be the spirit of legislation where a manufacturer of linen cloth is forbidden to bury his own child in a linen shroud, in order to favour his neighbor who manufactures woolen cloth; where the manufacturer and wearer of woolen cloth are again forbidden the economical use of buttons of that material, in favor of the manufacturer of buttons of other materials!

A just security to property is not afforded by that government under which unequal taxes oppress one species of property and reward another species: where arbitrary taxes invade the domestic sanctuaries of the rich, and excessive taxes grind the faces of the poor; where the keenness and competitions of want are deemed an insufficient spur to labor, and taxes are again applied by an unfeeling policy, as another spur; in violation of that sacred property, which Heaven, in decreeing man to earn his bread by the sweat of his brow, kindly reserved to him, in the small repose that could be spared from the supply of his necessities.

If there be a government then which prides itself on maintaining the inviolability of property; which provides that none shall be taken *directly* even for public use without indemnification to the owner, and yet *directly* violates the property which individuals have in their opinions, their religion, their persons, and their faculties; nay more, which *indirectly* violates their property, in their actual possessions, in the labor that acquires their daily subsistence, and in the hallowed remnant of time which ought to relieve their fatigues and soothe their cares, the inference will have been anticipated, that such a government is not a pattern for the United States.

If the United States mean to obtain or deserve the full praise due to wise and just governments, they will equally respect the rights of property, and the property in rights: they will rival the government that most sacredly guards the former; and by repelling its example in violating the latter, will make themselves a pattern to that and all other governments.

B. THE CONTRACT CLAUSE

The Constitution prohibits any state from passing any law "impairing the Obligation of Contracts." Art. I, § 10. Objections were raised at the Philadelphia Convention that this provision was far too broad and impractical, 2 Farrand 439-40, and so it has proven to be. Madison stated in Federalist No. 44 that the constitutional prohibitions against bills of attainder, ex post facto laws, and laws impair-

Doctrine of Vested Rights

... [L]egislative acts interfering with an individual's property or diminishing its value were constitutionally suspect, and this led to the third main contribution of *Fletcher* v. *Peck,* the instrumental conclusion that courts had a duty to void state laws tampering with either private or public contracts. Marshall's opinion, to be sure, made much of the great "delicacy" of voiding a law, but it did not flinch from the "solemn obligation" to declare the repeal act unconstitutional. Together, these three assumptions—the inclusion of public grants under the limitations of the contract clause, the primacy of vested property as a constitutional value, and the judicial duty to void legislative impairments of contract rights—summarize one of the most influential doctrines of American constitutionalism. Edward S. Corwin called it the "Doctrine of Vested Rights." "Setting out with the assumption that the property right is fundamental," Corwin wrote, it "treats any law impairing *vested rights,* whatever its intention, as a bill of pains and penalties, and so, void." This doctrine, which was fully asserted for the first time in the case that grew out of the Yazoo land fraud, dominated American constitutional law during much of the nineteenth century and the first third of the twentieth.

SOURCE: C. Peter Magrath, Yazoo, Law and Politics in the New Republic: The Case of *Fletcher* v. *Peck* 103 (1966).

ing the obligation of contracts were added in the interest of "personal security and private rights" and to protect the people from the "fluctuating policy which had directed the public councils." However, under the police power and emergency conditions, state actions that impair the obligation of contracts have been upheld repeatedly by the courts. As the Supreme Court noted in 1987, "it is well settled that the prohibition against impairing the obligation of contracts is not to be read literally." Keystone Bituminous Coal Assn. v. DeBenedictis, 480 U.S. 470, 502 (1987). The Contract Clause is invoked only when there has been a *substantial* impairment of a contractual relationship.[1]

The prohibition against ex post facto laws might have been used to protect contracts and property rights, but in 1798 the Court restricted this constitutional provision to criminal statutes. To the Court: "Every *ex post facto* law must necessarily be retrospective; but every retrospective law is not an *ex post facto* law." CALDER v. BULL, 3 U.S. (3 Dall.) 385, 390 (1798).

The first major case involving the Contract Clause arose in Georgia. The state legislature, in what became known as the "Yazoo Land Fraud," sold vast tracts of land in 1795 to four companies. With a single exception, every legislator voting for the measure sold his vote either for money or for shares of stock in the companies. In response to this blatant bribery, a mob marched on the state capital and threatened the lives of the lawmakers. Benjamin Wright, The Contract Clause of the Constitution 21 (1938). Public outrage forced the new legislature a year later to rescind the statute. Did this repeal of a corrupt statute violate the contractual rights of speculators and prospective settlers who purchased land from the companies?

Writing for the Supreme Court, Chief Justice Marshall held that the legislature of 1795 possessed constitutional authority to pass the initial statute. The innocent third parties who bought land from the companies, he said, were not responsible for legislative corruption or fraud. On a good-faith basis they had entered into contracts with the companies. Marshall further pointed out that it was inappropriate to expect courts to annul a statute by inquiring into the purity of legislative motives. FLETCHER v. PECK, 10 U.S. (6 Cr.) 87 (1810). This decision made it clear that the Contract Clause covered not only "private contracts" but "state contracts" as well (see box). Another reading of the

---

1. General Motors Corp. v. Romein, 503 U.S. 181, 186 (1992); Energy Reserves Group, Inc. v. Kansas Power & Light Co., 459 U.S. 400, 411 (1983); Allied Structural Steel Co. v. Spannaus, 438 U.S. 234, 244 (1978).

Contract Clause in defense of property rights was announced in 1812, extending the contract clause to grants of tax immunity. New Jersey v. Wilson, 11 U.S. (7 Cr.) 164 (1812). The overriding theme over history has been a balancing between the right of private property and the right of government to regulate property for the general public.

The Dartmouth College case of 1819 stands as a famous legal landmark. The college had been created in 1754 as a charity school to instruct Indians in the Christian religion. In 1769 it was chartered by the British crown as a private corporation. The college continued to be funded entirely by private donations. In 1816 New Hampshire passed legislation to increase the number of trustees in the college and thereby transfer control to appointees of the governor.

In his decision for the Court, Chief Justice Marshall said that the British parliament could have annulled the charter at any time. New Hampshire could have altered the charter after the break with England and before ratification of the U.S. Constitution. However, the Contract Clause prohibited the state from impairing the contract of a "private eleemosynary institution": an institution created by private parties, sustained by private funds, and devoted to charitable goals. Marshall explained that had the college been created by the legislature and supported by public funds, the state could have altered the contract. Under those circumstances the college would have existed as a public corporation to satisfy a public purpose. Dartmouth, however, had a right to continue under its private charter without interference by the state. Otherwise, Marshall warned, all charitable and educational institutions would fall under the control of government. DARTMOUTH COLLEGE v. WOODWARD, 17 U.S. (4 Wheat.) 517 (1819).

This case has few applications today. The line between "public" and "private" is less clear, and even private institutions are subject to state regulation and control. Henry J. Friendly, The Dartmouth College Case and the Public-Private Penumbra (1969). Nevertheless, the case established important limits on the power of government to interfere with academic freedom and acts of incorporation. It also reassured Federalist property holders who feared the reach of majority rule and state legislatures.

Rights of the Community

The Charles River Bridge case of 1837 illustrates that the right of contract is never absolute. In 1785 the legislature of Massachusetts incorporated a company to build a bridge and take tolls. About four decades later it created another company to build a bridge nearby. The second bridge took tolls for a few years and then became free. Travelers, of course, switched to the new bridge and proprietors of the first bridge complained that the legislature had impaired the obligations of a contract. The Supreme Court, balancing the rights of property against the rights reserved to the states, held that a state law may be retrospective in character and alter rights formerly vested by law without violating the Contract Clause. Although corporations are given certain rights by law, the community also has rights in a dynamic economy that offers improvements in public accommodations and travel. CHARLES RIVER BRIDGE v. WARREN BRIDGE, 36 U.S. (11 Pet.) 420 (1837).

The principle of *Charles River* has been affirmed in many cases. The Contract Clause does not prevent a state from granting a right and repealing or modifying that right in future years. A legislature may grant a monopoly and decide at a later time that it is in the interest of the state to abolish the monopoly and allow other companies to enter the field. Slaughter-House Cases, 83 U.S. (16 Wall.) 36 (1873); Butchers' Union Co. v. Crescent City Co., 111 U.S. 746 (1884). In matters affecting public health, public safety, or public morals, one legislature may not bind future legislatures.[2]

Private contracts are subject to government control. The right of an owner of a building to contract with tenants may be limited by rent-control laws. Block v. Hirsh, 256 U.S. 135 (1921). Although contracts may create rights of property, when they concern a subject matter within the control of Con-

---

2. Stone v. Mississippi, 101 U.S. 814 (1880); Fertilizing Co. v. Hyde Park, 97 U.S. 659 (1879); Beer Co. v. Massachusetts, 97 U.S. 25 (1878).

gress "they have a congenital infirmity." Norman v. Baltimore & Ohio R. Co., 294 U.S. 240, 307–08 (1935), cited in Connolly v. Pension Benefit Guaranty Corp., 475 U.S. 211, 223–24 (1986).

If a state passes a bankruptcy law to relieve debtors of their liabilities, does this impair the obligation of contracts? The Supreme Court in an early case decided that states are not prevented from passing bankruptcy laws unless Congress preempts the field by passing a uniform law authorized by Article I, Section 8, Clause 4. In this particular case, the Court determined that the state law did impair the obligation of contracts. Sturges v. Crowninshield, 17 U.S. (4 Wheat.) 120 (1819). The following decade the Court again held that congressional inaction on uniform bankruptcy laws permitted the states to legislate on the subject. Moreover, states could pass laws discharging a debtor from liability if the law preceded the contract. If a bankruptcy act operated prospectively, it did not violate the Contract Clause. Ogden v. Saunders, 25 U.S. (12 Wheat.) 212 (1827). Contracts are then entered into in light of the bankruptcy policy established by law.

The Minnesota Moratorium

The question of a retrospective law was decided by the Supreme Court in 1934. A 5 to 4 decision upheld a Minnesota law, passed during the Great Depression, that gave homeowners a delay of up to two years in meeting their mortgage payments. Although the law clearly impaired contracts entered into prior to the statute, both the state court and the Supreme Court agreed that the police power had sufficient scope in an emergency to set aside, for a limited period, the Contract Clause. HOME BLDG. & LOAN ASSN. v. BLAISDELL, 290 U.S. 398 (1934). A year later, by a 5 to 4 vote, the Court upheld the power of Congress to abrogate the "gold clauses" in private contracts. To prevent a run on the banks and the hoarding of gold, President Franklin D. Roosevelt and Congress had taken emergency actions in 1933 to prevent individuals from requiring payment in gold or a particular kind of coin.[3] In several other cases, where state actions were not restricted to an emergency period, statutes were declared invalid under the Contract Clause.[4]

The Contract Clause does not carry the same importance today as it did in the era of *Fletcher* and *Dartmouth College*. As a limitation on state power, it has been largely replaced by the Due Process and Equal Protection Clauses of the Fourteenth Amendment. There are still circumstances, however, where the Contract Clause is successfully invoked to strike down a state statute. A contemporary case involved the Port Authority of New York and New Jersey. In 1962 the two states passed a statutory covenant that prevented the Authority from subsidizing rail passenger transportation by using revenues and reserves pledged as security for bonds issued by the Authority. In 1974 the two states repealed the statutory covenant. Although the New Jersey courts upheld the repeal as a valid exercise of the police power, the Supreme Court in 1977 ruled that the repeal violated the Contract Clause by eliminating an important security provision for bondholders. United States Trust Co. v. New Jersey, 431 U.S. 1 (1977).

The dissenters in this 4–3 decision accused the Court of "dusting off" the Contract Clause and giving it a meaning broader than intended by the framers. According to their analysis and some other studies, the Contract Clause was conceived of "primarily as protection for economic transactions entered into by purely private parties, rather than obligations involving the State itself." Id. at 45. This philosophy would allow each new legislature to rescind the policies of the previous legislature. The problem is that state obligations frequently involve investments by private parties, as in the Port Authority case.

---

3. Norman v. B.&O. R. Co., 294 U.S. 240 (1935). For other "gold clause" cases, see Nortz v. United States, 294 U.S. 317 (1935) and Perry v. United States, 294 U.S. 330 (1935).

4. Treigle v. Acme Homestead Assn., 297 U.S. 189 (1936); Worthen Co. v. Kavanaugh, 295 U.S. 56 (1935); Worthen Co. v. Thomas, 292 U.S. 426 (1934). But see also El Paso v. Simmons, 379 U.S. 497 (1965); East New York Bank v. Hahn, 326 U.S. 230 (1945); Faitoute Co. v. Asbury Park, 316 U.S. 502 (1942); Veix v. Sixth Ward Assn., 310 U.S. 32 (1940).

A year later, the Court struck down a Minnesota law for violating the Contract Clause, pointing out that the police power did not give the states unlimited authority to abridge existing contractual relationships. Moreover, the Minnesota law did not deal with grave economic or social emergencies, as in the 1934 *Blaisdell* case. Justices Brennan, White, and Marshall dissented from what they regarded as the Court's extension of the Contract Clause beyond its original intent. Allied Structural Steel Co. v. Spannaus, 438 U.S. 234 (1978).

Calder v. Bull

3 U.S. (3 Dall.) 385 (1798)

The Constitution prohibits any state from passing any law "impairing the Obligation of Contracts." The Constitution also prohibits states from passing ex post facto laws, which might apply to protect contracts and property rights. The issue in this case was [is] whether the prohibition against ex post facto laws applied[s] only to criminal statutes. Caleb Bull and his wife attempted to appeal a probate court ruling over a will, only to find that the time for their appeal had expired. After they convinced the Connecticut legislature to revise the law and lengthen the time for appeal, and prevailed in the lawsuit, John Calder and his wife protested that the new law violated the Ex Post Facto Clause. The opinion remains prominent for the conflicting views of the Court on the role of "natural justice" in limiting and defining [as a limitation on] governmental power.

CHASE, Justice. — The decision of one question determines (in my opinion) the present dispute....

The counsel for the plaintiffs in error contend, that the said resolution or law of the legislature of Connecticut, granting a new hearing, in the above case, is an *ex post facto* law, prohibited by the constitution of the United States; that any law of the federal government, or of any of the state government, contrary to the constitution of the United States, is void; and that this court possesses the power to declare such law void.

. . .

The effect of the resolution or law of Connecticut, above stated, is to revise a decision of one of its inferior courts, ...

Whether the legislature of any of the states can revise and correct by law, a decision of any of its courts of justice, although not prohibited by the constitution of the state, is a question of very great importance, and not necessary now to be determined; because the resolution or law in question does not go so far. I cannot subscribe to the omnipotence of a state legislature, or that it is absolute and without control; ... An act of the legislature (for I cannot call it a law), contrary to the great first principles of the social compact, cannot be considered a rightful exercise of legislative authority. The obligation of a law, in governments established on express compact, and on republican principles, must be determined by the nature of the power on which it is founded.

. . .

I shall endeavor to show what law is to be considered an *ex post facto* law, within the words and meaning of the prohibition in the federal constitution. The prohibition, "that no state shall pass any *ex post facto* law," necessarily requires some explanation; for, naked and without explanation, it is unintelligible, and means nothing.... [T]he plain and obvious meaning and intention of the prohibition is this: that the legislatures of the several states, shall not pass laws, after a fact done by a subject or citizen, which shall have relation to such fact, and shall punish him for having done it. The prohibition, considered in this light, is an additional bulwark in favor of the personal security of the subject, to protect his person from punishment by legislative acts, having a retrospective operation. I do not think it was inserted, to secure the citizen in his private rights of either property or contracts. The prohibitions not to make anything but gold and silver coin a tender in payment of debts, and not to pass any law impairing the obligation of contracts, were inserted to secure private rights; but the restriction not to pass any *ex post facto* law, was to secure the person of the subject from injury or punishment, in consequence of such law. If the prohibition against making *ex post facto* laws was intended to secure personal rights from being affected or injured by such laws, and the prohibition is sufficiently extensive for that object, the other restraints I have enumerated, were unnecessary, and therefore, improper; for both of them are retrospective.

I will state what laws I consider *ex post facto* laws, within the words and the intent of the prohibition. 1st. Every law that makes an action done before the passing of the law, and which was innocent when done, criminal; and punishes such action. 2d. Every law that aggravates a crime, or makes it greater than it was, when committed. 3d. Every law that changes the punishment, and inflicts a greater punishment, than the law annexed to the crime, when committed. 4th. Every law that alters the legal rules of evidence, and receives less, or different testimony, than the law required at the time of the commission of the offence, in order to convict the offender. All these, and similar laws, are manifestly unjust and oppressive. In my opinion, the true distinction is between *ex post facto* laws, and retrospective laws. Every *ex post facto* law must necessarily be retrospective; but every retrospective law is not an *ex post facto* law: the former only are prohibited. Every law that takes away or impairs rights vested, agreeable to existing laws, is retrospective, and is generally unjust, and may be oppressive; and it is a good general rule, that a law should have no retrospect: but there are cases in which laws may justly, and for the benefit of the community, and also of individuals, relate to a time antecedent to their commencement; as statutes of oblivion or of pardon. They are certainly retrospective, and literally both concerning and after the facts committed. But I do not consider any law *ex post facto,* within the prohibition, that mollifies the rigor of the criminal law: but only those that create or aggravate the crime; or increase the punishment, or change the rules of evidence, for the purpose of conviction....

I am of opinion, that the decree of the supreme court of errors of Connecticut be affirmed, with costs.

PATERSON, Justice.—

... [The framers of the Constitution] understood and used the words in their known and appropriate signification, as referring to crimes, pains and penalties, and no further....

IREDELL, Justice.—Though I concur in the general result of the opinions which have been delivered, I cannot entirely adopt the reasons that are assigned upon the occasion.

... [T]hough, I admit, that as the authority to declare it void is of a delicate and awful nature, the court will never resort to that authority, but in a clear and urgent case. If, on the other hand, the legislature of the Union, or the legislature of any member of the Union, shall pass a law, within the general scope of their constitutional power, the court cannot pronounce it to be void, merely because it is, in their judgment, contrary to the principles of natural justice. The ideas of natural justice are regulated by no fixed standard: the ablest and the purest men have differed upon the subject; ...

CUSHING, Justice.—The case appears to me to be clear of all difficulty, taken either way. If the act is a judicial act, it is not touched by the federal constitution: and if it is a legislative act, it is maintained and justified by the ancient and uniform practice of the state of Connecticut.

Judgment affirmed.

Fletcher v. Peck

10 U.S. (6 Cr.) 87 (1810)

In 1803 John Peck sold to Robert Fletcher a tract of land lying along the Mississippi River. The land dated back to an act of the Georgia legislature in 1795 and had changed hands often since that time. Because of corruption associated with the statute, a new legislature in 1796 rescinded the land grant. Fletcher went to court in Massachusetts, claiming a breach of contract because the legislature never had authority to sell and dispose of the land. Did the rescinding legislation nullify the contractual rights of innocent third parties who had purchased land and sold it, or were they protected by the Contract Clause?

MARSHALL, Ch. J. delivered the opinion of the court as follows:

. . .

The 2d count assigns, in substance, as a breach of this covenant, that the original grantees from the

state of Georgia promised and assured divers members of the legislature, then sitting in general assembly, that if the said members would assent to, and vote for, the passing of the act, and if the said bill should pass, such members should have a share of, and be interested in, all the lands purchased from the said state by virtue of such law. And that divers of the said members, to whom the said promises were made, were unduly influenced thereby, and, under such influence, did vote for the passing of the said bill; by reason whereof the said law was a nullity, &c. and so the title of the state of Georgia did not pass to the said Peck, &c.

· · ·

That corruption should find its way into the governments of our infant republics, and contaminate the very source of legislation, or that impure motives should contribute to the passage of a law, or the formation of a legislative contract, are circumstances most deeply to be deplored. How far a court of justice would, in any case, be competent, on proceedings instituted by the state itself, to vacate a contract thus formed, and to annul rights acquired, under that contract, by third persons having no notice of the improper means by which it was obtained, is a question which the court would approach with much circumspection. It may well be doubted how far the validity of a law depends upon the motives of its framers, and how far the particular inducements, operating on members of the supreme sovereign power of a state, to the formation of a contract by that power, are examinable in a court of justice. If the principle be conceded, that an act of the supreme sovereign power might be declared null by a court, in consequence of the means which procured it, still would there be much difficulty in saying to what extent those means must be applied to produce this effect. Must it be direct corruption, or would interest or undue influence of any kind be sufficient? Must the vitiating cause operate on a majority, or on what number of the members? Would the act be null, whatever might be the wish of the nation, or would its obligation or nullity depend upon the public sentiment?

If the majority of the legislature be corrupted, it may well be doubted, whether it be within the province of the judiciary to control their conduct, and, if less than a majority act from impure motives, the principle by which judicial interference would be regulated, is not clearly discerned.

... It would be indecent, in the extreme, upon a private contract, between two individuals, to enter into an inquiry respecting the corruption of the sovereign power of a state. If the title be plainly deduced from a legislative act, which the legislature might constitutionally pass, if the act be clothed with all the requisite forms of a law, a court, sitting as a court of law, cannot sustain a suit brought by one individual against another founded on the allegation that the act is a nullity, in consequence of the impure motives which influenced certain members of the legislature which passed the law.

· · ·

In this case the legislature may have had ample proof that the original grant was obtained by practices which can never be too much reprobated, and which would have justifed its abrogation so far as respected those to whom crime was imputable. But the grant, when issued, conveyed an estate in fee-simple to the grantee, clothed with all the solemnities which law can bestow. This estate was transferrable; and those who purchased parts of it were not stained by that guilt which infected the original transaction....

The principle asserted is, that one legislature is competent to repeal any act which a former legislature was competent to pass; and that one legislature cannot abridge the powers of a succeeding legislature....

It is, then, the unanimous opinion of the court, that, in this case, the estate having passed into the hands of a purchaser for a valuable consideration, without notice, the state of Georgia was restrained, either by general principles which are common to our free institutions, or by the particular provisions of the constitution of the United States, from passing a law whereby the estate of the plaintiff in the premises so purchased could be constitutionally and legally impaired and rendered null and void....

JOHNSON, J. In this case I entertain, on two points, an opinion different from that which has been delivered by the court.

I do not hesitate to declare that a state does not possess the power of revoking its own grants. But I do it on a general principle, on the reason and nature of things: a principle which will impose laws even on the deity....

Dartmouth College v. Woodward

17 U.S. (4 Wheat.) 517 (1819)

Dartmouth College functioned as a private school, funded entirely by private donations. New Hampshire passed legislation in 1816 to increase the number of trustees at the college and thereby transfer control to appointees of the governor. The constitutional question was whether the Contract Clause prohibited the state from impairing the contract of a "private eleemosynary institution." The old trustees of Dartmouth College brought this suit against William H. Woodward, the secretary-treasurer of Dartmouth who sided with the new trustees. The "old" trustees appealed to the Supreme Court.

February 2d, 1819. The opinion of the court was delivered by MARSHALL, Ch. J.

. . .

It can require no argument to prove, that the circumstances of this case constitute a contract. An application is made to the crown for a charter to incorporate a religious and literary institution. In the application, it is stated, that large contributions have been made for the object, which will be conferred on the corporation, as soon as it shall be created. The charter is granted, and on its faith the property is conveyed. Surely, in this transaction every ingredient of a complete and legitimate contract is to be found. The points for consideration are, 1. Is this contract protected by the constitution of the United States? 2. Is it impaired by the acts under which the defendant holds?

1. On the first point, it has been argued, that the word "contract," in its broadest sense, would comprehend the political relations between the government and its citizens, would extend to offices held within a state, for state purposes, and to many of those laws concerning civil institutions, which must change with circumstances, and be modified by ordinary legislation; which deeply concern the public, and which, to preserve good government, the public judgment must control. That even marriage is a contract, and its obligations are affected by the laws respecting divorces. That the clause in the constitution, if construed in its greatest latitude, would prohibit these laws. Taken in its broad, unlimited sense, the clause would be an unprofitable and vexatious interference with the internal concerns of a state, would unnecessarily and unwisely embarrass its legislation, and render immutable those civil institutions, which are established for purposes of internal government, and which, to subserve those purposes, ought to vary with varying circumstances. That as the framers of the constitution could never have intended to insert in that instrument, a provision so unnecessary, so mischievous, and so repugnant to its

general spirit, the term "contract" must be understood in a more limited sense. That it must be understood as intended to guard against a power, of at least doubtful utility, the abuse of which had been extensively felt; and to restrain the legislature in future from violating the right to property....

... If the act of incorporation be a grant of political power, if it create a civil institution, to be employed in the administration of the government, or if the funds of the college be public property, or if the state of New Hampshire, as a government, be alone interested in its transactions, the subject is one in which the legislature of the state may act according to its own judgment, unrestrained by any limitation of its power imposed by the constitution of the United States.

But if this be a private eleemosynary institution, endowed with a capacity to take property, for objects unconnected with government, whose funds are bestowed by individuals, on the faith of the charter; if the donors have stipulated for the future disposition and management of those funds, in the manner prescribed by themselves; there may be more difficulty in the case....

[After determining that the funds of Dartmouth College consisted entirely of private donations, Chief Justice Marshall raises broader issues.]

... Are the trustees and professors public officers, invested with any portion of political power, partaking in any degree in the administration of civil government, and performing duties which flow from the sovereign authority? That education is an object of national concern, and a proper subject of legislation, all admit. That there may be an institution, founded by government, and placed entirely under its immediate control, the officers of which would be public officers, amenable exclusively to government, none will deny. But is Dartmouth College such an institution? Is education altogether in the hands of government? Does every teacher of youth become a public officer, and do donations for the purpose of education necessarily become public property, so far that the will of the legislature, not the will of the donor, becomes the law of the donation? These questions are of serious moment to society, and deserve to be well considered....

From this review of the charter, it appears, that Dartmouth College is an eleemosynary institution, incorporated for the purpose of perpetuating the application of the bounty of the donors, to the specified objects of that bounty; that its trustees or governors were originally named by the founder, and invested with the power of perpetuating themselves; that they are not public officers, nor is it a civil institution, participating in the administration of government; but a charity school, or a seminary of education, incorporated for the preservation of its property, and the perpetual application of that property to the objects of its creation.

. . .

The opinion of the court, after mature deliberation, is, that this is a contract, the obligation of which cannot be impaired, without violating the constitution of the United States. This opinion appears to us to be equally supported by reason, and by the former decisions of this court.

2. We next proceed to the inquiry, whether its obligation has been impaired by those acts of the legislature of New Hampshire, to which the special verdict refers?

From the review of this charter, which has been taken, it appears that the whole power of governing the college, of appointing and removing tutors, of fixing their salaries, of directing the course of study to be pursued by the students, and of filling up vacancies created in their own body, was vested in the trustees. On the part of the crown, it was expressly stipulated, that this corporation, thus constituted, should continue for ever; and that the number of trustees should for ever consist of twelve, and no more. By this contract, the crown was bound, and

could have made no violent alteration in its essential terms, without impairing its obligation.

By the revolution, the duties, as well as the powers, of government devolved on the people of New Hampshire. It is admitted, that among the latter was comprehended the transcendent power of parliament, as well as that of the executive department. It is too clear, to require the support of argument, that all contracts and rights respecting property, remained unchanged by the revolution. The obligations, then, which were created by the charter to Dartmouth College, were the same in the new, that they had been in the old government. The power of the government was also the same. A repeal of this charter, at any time prior to the adoption of the present constitution of the United States, would have been an extraordinary and unprecedented act of power, but one which could have been contested only by the restrictions upon the legislature, to be found in the constitution of the state. But the constitution of the United States has imposed this additional limitation, that the legislature of a state shall pass no act "impairing the obligation of contracts."...

It results from this opinion, that the acts of the legislature of New Hampshire, which are stated in the special verdict found in this cause, are repugnant to the constitution of the United States; and that the judgment on this special verdict ought to have been for the plaintiffs. The judgment of the state court must, therefore, be reversed.

WASHINGTON, Justice. — *[Concurred.]*

JOHNSON, Justice, concurred, for the reasons stated by the Chief Justice.

LIVINGSTON, Justice, concurred, for the reasons stated by the Chief Justice, and Justices WASHINGTON and STORY.

Story, Justice. — *[Concurred.]*

DUVALL, Justice, dissented.

Charles River Bridge v. Warren Bridge

36 U.S. (11 Pet.) 420 (1837)

In 1650, the Massachusetts legislature granted to Harvard College authority to set up a ferry from Charleston to Boston, passing over Charles River. In 1785, the legislature incorporated a company ("The Proprietors of the Charles River Bridge") to build a bridge and accept tolls. Decades later it established "The Proprietors of the Warren Bridge" to build a bridge nearby; over the course of time this bridge became free to travelers. The first bridge company filed a lawsuit, claiming that the legislature had impaired the obligation of a contract by violating the company's implied right of exclusivity to operate a bridge across the Charles River. This significant decision by Chief Justice Taney balances the rights of private property against the public's need for economic development.

TANEY, Ch. J., delivered the opinion of the court. —

. . .

[U]pon what ground can the plaintiffs in error contend, that the ferry-rights of the college [*Harvard*] have been transferred to the proprietors of the bridge? If they have been thus transferred, it must be by some mode of transfer known to the law; and the evidence relied on to prove it, can be pointed out in the record. How was it transferred? It is not suggested, that there ever was, in point of fact, a deed of conveyance executed by the college to the bridge company. Is there any evidence in the record, from which such a conveyance may, upon legal principle, be presumed? The testimony before the court, so far from laying the foundation for such a presumption, repels it, in the most positive terms....

This brings us to the act of the legislature of Massachusetts, of 1785, by which the plaintiffs were incorporated by the name of "The Proprietors of the Charles River Bridge;" and it is here, and in the law of 1792, prolonging their charter, that we must look for the extent and nature of the franchise conferred upon the plaintiffs. Much has been said in the argument of the principles of construction by which this law is to be expounded, and what undertakings, on the part of the state, may be implied. The court think there can be no serious difficulty on that head. It is the grant of certain franchises, by the public, to a private corporation, and in a matter where the public interest is concerned....

... [T]he object and end of all government is to promote the happiness and prosperity of the community by which it is established; and it can never be assumed, that the government intended to diminish its power of accomplishing the end for which it was created. And in a country like ours, free, active and enterprising, continually advancing in numbers and wealth, new channels of communication are daily found necessary, both for travel and trade, and are essential to the comfort, convenience and prosperity of the people. A state ought never to be presumed to surrender this power, because, like the taxing power, the whole community have an interest in preserving it undiminished. And when a corporation alleges, that a state has surrendered, for seventy years, its power of improvement and public accommodation, in a great and important line of travel, along which a vast number of its citizens must daily

pass, the community have a right to insist, in the language of this court, above quoted, "that its abandonment ought not to be presumed, in a case, in which the deliberate purpose of the state to abandon it does not appear." The continued existence of a government would be of no great value, if, by implications and presumptions, it was disarmed of the powers necessary to accomplish the ends of its creation, and the functions it was designed to perform, transferred to the hands of privileged corporations.... While the rights of private property are sacredly guarded, we must not forget, that the community also have rights, and that the happiness and well-being of every citizen depends on their faithful preservation.

Adopting the rule of construction above stated as the settled one, we proceed to apply it to the charter of 1785, to the proprietors of the Charles River bridge. This act of incorporation is in the usual form, and the privileges such as are commonly given to corporations of that kind. It confers on them the ordinary faculties of a corporation, for the purpose of building the bridge; and establishes certain rates of toll, which the company are authorized to take: this is the whole grant. There is no exclusive privilege given to them over the waters of Charles river, above or below their bridge; no right to erect another bridge themselves, nor to prevent other persons from erecting one; no engagement from the state, that another shall not be erected; and no undertaking not to sanction competition, nor to make improvements that may diminish the amount of its income....

The relative position of the Warren bridge has already been described. It does not interrupt the passage over the Charles River bridge, nor make the way to it, or from it, less convenient. None of the faculties or franchises granted to that corporation, have been revoked by the legislature; and its right to take the tolls granted by the charter remains unaltered. In short, all the franchises and rights of property, enumerated in the charter, and there mentioned to have been granted to it, remain unimpaired. But its income is destroyed by the Warren bridge; which, being free, draws off the passengers and property which would have gone over it, and renders their franchise of no value. This is the gist of the complainant; for it is not pretended, that the erection of the Warren bridge would have done them any injury, or in any degree affected their right of property, if it had not diminished the amount of their tolls. In order, then, to entitle themselves to relief, it is necessary to show, that the legislature contracted not to do the act of which they complain; and that they impaired, or in other words, violated, that contract, by the erection of the Warren bridge.

The inquiry, then, is, does the charter contain such a contract on the part of the state? Is there any such stipulation to be found in that instrument? It must be admitted on all hands, that there is none; no words that even relate to another bridge, or to the diminution of their tolls, or to the line of travel....

Indeed, the practice and usage of almost every state in the Union, old enough to have commenced the work of internal improvement, is opposed to the doctrine contended for on the part of the plaintiffs in error. Turnpike roads have been made in succession, on the same line of travel; the later ones interfering materially with the profits of the first. These corporations have, in some instances, been utterly ruined by the introduction of newer and better modes of transportation and traveling. In some cases, railroads have rendered the turnpike roads on the same line of travel so entirely useless, that the franchise of the turnpike corporation is not worth preserving. Yet in none of these cases have the corporation supposed that their privileges were invaded, or any contract violated on the part of the state....

The judgment of the supreme judicial court of the commonwealth of Massachusetts, dismissing the plaintiffs' bill, must, therefore, be affirmed, with costs.

McLEAN, Justice. *[Favored dismissing the case for lack of jurisdiction.]*

BALDWIN, Justice. — *[Concurred.]*

STORY, Justice. *(Dissenting.)*

. . .

But it has been argued, and the argument has been pressed in every form which ingenuity could suggest, that if grants of this nature are to be construed liberally, as conferring any exclusive rights on the grantees, it will interpose an effectual barrier against all general improvements of the country. For myself, I profess not to feel the cogency of this argument, either in its general application to the grant of franchises, or in its special application to the present grant. This is a subject upon which different minds may well arrive at different conclusions, both as to policy and principle.... For my own part, I can conceive of no surer plan to arrest all public improvements, founded on private capital and enterprise, than to make the outlay of that capital uncertain and questionable, both as to security and as to productiveness. No man will hazard his capital in any enterprise, in which, if there be a loss, it must be borne exclusively by himself; and if there be success, he has not the slightest security of enjoying the rewards of that success, for a single moment. If the government means to invite its citizens to enlarge the public comforts and conveniences, to establish bridges, or turnpikes, or canals, or railroads, there must be some pledge, that the property will be safe; that the enjoyment will be co-extensive with the grant; and that success will not be the signal of a general combination to overthrow its rights and to take away its profits....

Upon the whole, my judgment is, that the act of the legislature of Massachusetts granting the charter of Warren Bridge, is an act impairing the obligation of the prior contract and grant to the proprietors of Charles River bridge; and, by the constitution of the United States, it is, therefore, utterly void....

THOMPSON, Justice. — The opinion delivered by my brother, Mr. Justice STORY, I have read over and deliberately considered. On this full consideration, I concur entirely in all the principles and reasonings contained in it; and I am of opinion, the decree of the supreme judicial court of Massachusetts should be reversed.

Home Bldg. & Loan Assn. v. Blaisdell

290 U.S. 398 (1934)

A Minnesota statute, enacted in 1933, declared that the Great Depression created an emergency demanding an exercise of the police power to protect the public and promote the general welfare. It temporarily extended the time allowed by existing law for redeeming real property from foreclosure and sale under existing mortgages. It became known as the Minnesota Mortgage Moratorium Law. At issue was Article I, § 10, of the U.S. Constitution, which provides that no state shall pass any law "impairing the Obligation of Contracts." Could this constitutional prohibition be waived during time of emergency? A married couple, John H. and Rosella Blaisdell, won a court order under the act, extending the period of redemption from the foreclosure on their property. Under the order, the Blaisdells were required to pay Home Building and Loan Assn. $40 per month. Home Building and Loan appealed to the U.S. Supreme Court claiming the act violated the Contract Clause. A key underlying question: Does the Constitution change in time of emergency?

MR. CHIEF JUSTICE HUGHES delivered the opinion of the Court.

. . .

In determining whether the provision for this temporary and conditional relief exceeds the power of the State by reason of the clause in the Federal Constitution prohibiting impairment of the obligations of contracts, we must consider the relation of emergency to constitutional power, the historical setting of the contract clause, the development of the jurisprudence of this Court in the construction of that clause, and the principles of construction which we may consider to be established.

Emergency does not create power. Emergency does not increase granted power or remove or diminish the restrictions imposed upon power granted or reserved. The Constitution was adopted in a period of grave emergency. Its grants of power to the Federal Government and its limitations of the power of the States were determined in the light of emergency and they are not altered by emergency. What power was thus granted and what limitations were thus imposed are questions which have always been, and always will be, the subject of close examination under our constitutional system.

While emergency does not create power, emergency may furnish the occasion for the exercise of power. "Although an emergency may not call into life a power which has never lived, nevertheless emergency may afford a reason for the exertion of a living power already enjoyed." *Wilson* v. *New,* 243 U.S. 332, 348.... [E]mergency would not permit a State to have more than two Senators in the Congress, or permit the election of President by a general popular vote without regard to the number of electors to which the States are respectively entitled, or permit the States to "coin money" or to "make anything but gold and silver coin a tender in payment of debts." But where constitutional grants and limitations of power are set forth in general clauses, which afford a broad outline, the process of construction is essential to fill in the details. That is true of the contract clause....

In the construction of the contract clause, the debates in the Constitutional Convention are of little aid. But the reasons which led to the adoption of that clause, and of the other prohibitions of Section 10 of Article I, are not left in doubt and have frequently been described with eloquent emphasis. The widespread distress following the revolutionary period, and the plight of debtors, had called forth in the States an ignoble array of legislative schemes for the defeat of creditors and the invasion of contractual obligations. Legislative interferences had been so numerous and extreme that the confidence essential to prosperous trade had been undermined and the utter destruction of credit was threatened. "The sober people of America" were convinced that some "thorough reform" was needed which would "inspire a general prudence and industry, and give a regular course to the business of society." *The Federalist,* No. 44. It was necessary to interpose the restraining power of a central authority in order to secure the foundations even of "private faith." ...

But full recognition of the occasion and general purpose of the clause does not suffice to fix its precise scope. Nor does an examination of the details of prior legislation in the States yield criteria which can be considered controlling. To ascertain the scope of the constitutional prohibition we examine the course of judicial decisions in its application. These put it beyond question that the prohibition is not an absolute one and is not to be read with literal exactness like a mathematical formula....

Not only is the constitutional provision qualified by the measure of control which the State retains over remedial processes, but the State also continues to possess authority to safeguard the vital interests of its people. It does not matter that legislation appropriate to that end "has the result of modifying or abrogating contracts already in effect." *Stephenson* v. *Binford,* 287 U.S. 251, 276.... The policy of protecting contracts against impairment presupposes the maintenance of a government by virtue of which contractual relations are worth while, — a government which retains adequate authority to secure the peace and good order of society....

While the charters of private corporations constitute contracts, a grant of exclusive privilege is not to be implied as against the State. *Charles River Bridge* v. *Warren Bridge,* 11 Pet. 420. And all contracts are subject to the right of eminent domain.

West River Bridge v. *Dix,* 6 How. 507. The reservation of this necessary authority of the State is deemed to be a part of the contract....

It is no answer to say that this public need was not apprehended a century ago, or to insist that what the provision of the Constitution meant to the vision of that day it must mean to the vision of our time. If by the statement that what the Constitution meant at the time of its adoption it means to-day, it is intended to say that the great clauses of the Constitution must be confined to the interpretation which the framers, with the conditions and outlook of their time, would have placed upon them, the statement carries its own refutation. It was to guard against such a narrow conception that Chief Justice Marshall uttered the memorable warning—"We must never forget that it is a *constitution* we are expounding" (*McCulloch* v. *Maryland,* 4 Wheat. 316, 407)—"a constitution intended to endure for ages to come, and consequently, to be adapted to the various *crises* of human affairs." *Id.,* p. 415. When we are dealing with the words of the Constitution, said this Court in *Missouri* v. *Holland,* 252 U.S. 416, 433, "we must realize that they have called into life a being the development of which could not have been foreseen completely by the most gifted of its begetters.... The case before us must be considered in the light of our whole experience and not merely in that of what was said a hundred years ago."

. . .

We are of the opinion that the Minnesota statute as here applied does not violate the contract clause of the Federal Constitution. Whether the legislation is wise or unwise as a matter of policy is a question with which we are not concerned.

. . .

Mr. Justice Sutherland, dissenting.

... The effect of the Minnesota legislation, though serious enough in itself, is of trivial significance compared with the far more serious and dangerous inroads upon the limitations of the Constitution which are almost certain to ensue as a consequence naturally following any step beyond the boundaries fixed by that instrument....

A provision of the Constitution, it is hardly necessary to say, does not admit of two distinctly opposite interpretations. It does not mean one thing at one time and an entirely different thing at another time. If the contract impairment clause, when framed and adopted, meant that the terms of a contract for the payment of money could not be altered *in invitum* by a state statute enacted for the relief of hardly pressed debtors to the end and with the effect of postponing payment or enforcement during and because of an economic or financial emergency, it is but to state the obvious to say that it means the same now....

The provisions of the Federal Constitution, undoubtedly, are pliable in the sense that in appropriate cases they have the capacity of bringing within their grasp every new condition which falls within their meaning. But, their *meaning* is changeless; it is only their *application* which is extensible....

. . .

I am authorized to say that Mr. Justice Van Devanter, Mr. Justice McReynolds and Mr. Justice Butler concur in this opinion.

C. THE TAKING CLAUSE

Under the Fifth Amendment, private property shall not "be taken for public use, without just compensation." This is referred to variously as the Taking Clause, the Public Use Clause, or the Just Compensation Clause. Under the Due Process Clause of the Fourteenth Amendment, as well as under their own constitutions, states are also forbidden from taking private property for public use without just compensation. Chicago, B. & Q. R.R. Co. v. Chicago, 166 U.S. 226, 236–37, 241 (1897). The taking of property constitutes an exercise of the power of eminent domain, which gives the sovereign the right to condemn or expropriate private property for a public purpose upon payment of just compensation.

The decision to invoke the power of eminent domain is purely a legislative function. Whether compensation is "just" or whether property has been taken for "public use" are questions that might be taken to the courts. Every deprivation of property does not require compensation. PruneYard Shopping Center v. Robins, 447 U.S. 74, 82 (1980). Even when compensation must be paid, a plethora of

5–4 decisions by the Supreme Court demonstrate fundamental disagreements about the proper method of calculating what is "just."[5]

The Scope of Property

The protections available for land are of broad and changing scope. The ancient *ad coelum* doctrine gave landowners control of their property downward to the core of the earth and upward to the heavens. A landowner's rights to the column of air above the land led to successful actions against overhanging eaves, protruding structures, and firing projectiles or stringing wires across the property. Portsmouth Co. v. United States, 260 U.S. 327 (1922). One case involved a deed under which a coal company conveyed land surface to homeowners but reserved the right to remove coal under the property. Any damages to the surface resulting from mining were waived. The homeowners tried to prevent the company from burrowing under their property and removing supporting structures for their house and land. Despite the existence of a state statute passed after the deed, forbidding mining that would cause land under a home to sink, an 8–1 decision by the Supreme Court held that the police power could not protect shortsighted homeowners who acquired only surface rights. Pennsylvania Coal Co. v. Mahon, 260 U.S. 393 (1922).

Homeowners in the vicinity of transportation systems may be entitled to some compensation for damages. Those who lived next to a railroad tunnel had no right to be compensated for normal operations (vibration from trains and the emission of smoke, cinders, and gases). However, they were entitled to the recovery of some damages if fans within the tunnel pumped additional smoke and gases onto their property. Richards v. Washington Terminal Co., 233 U.S. 546 (1914). If military bombers skim so close to a person's home and chicken farm that chickens are killed by crashing into the walls from fright and homeowners are unable to sleep, the flights constitute a "taking" of property requiring just compensation. United States v. Causby, 328 U.S. 256 (1946). See also Griggs v. Allegheny County, 369 U.S. 84 (1962).[6]

The Court remains divided on issues involving private property and environmental law. In *Rapanos* v. *United States*, 547 U.S. 715 (2006), the Court split 5–4 on the question of whether wetlands adjacent to tributaries of traditionally navigable waters are "waters of the United States" within the meaning of the Clean Water Act. 86 Stat. 816 (1972). The Army Corps of Engineers had refused to issue a permit to John Rapanos to backfill wetlands that had surface connections to tributaries of navigable waters. In the opinion of the Court, Justice Scalia denounced the federal regulators' policy towards the wetlands as "beyond parody." Justice Kennedy joined the majority, but wrote a concurring opinion that set forth a standard that seemed closer to the dissenters who, in an opinion by Justice Stevens, would have deferred to federal regulators.

War, Regulation, and Zoning

Under conditions of war, private property may be demolished to prevent use by the enemy. Compensation need not be given to the owner. United States v. Caltex, 344 U.S. 149 (1952). Through its power to regulate commerce and other matters, Congress may diminish the value of private property without triggering the Taking Clause. The Supreme Court noted in 1986 that Congress "routinely creates burdens for some that directly benefit others." In setting minimum wages, controlling prices, or

---

5. United States v. Fuller, 409 U.S. 488 (1973); Almota Farmers Elevator & Whse. Co. v. United States, 409 U.S. 470 (1973); United States v. Cors, 337 U.S. 325 (1949); United States ex rel. TVA v. Powelson, 319 U.S. 266 (1943).

6. Other "taking" cases include Andrus v. Allard, 444 U.S. 51 (1979); United States v. Reynolds, 397 U.S. 14 (1970); YMCA v. United States, 395 U.S. 85 (1969); Goldblatt v. Hempstead, 369 U.S. 590 (1962); Armstrong v. United States, 364 U.S. 40 (1960); United States v. Central Eureka Mining Co., 357 U.S. 155 (1958); Berman v. Parker, 348 U.S. 26 (1954); United States v. Petty Motor Co., 327 U.S. 372 (1946); Miller v. Schoene, 276 U.S. 272 (1928); Hadacheck v. Sebastian, 239 U.S. 394 (1915).

regulating other actions, "it cannot be said that the Taking Clause is violated whenever legislation requires one person to use his or her assets for the benefit of another." Connolly v. Pension Benefit Guaranty Corp., 475 U.S. 211, 223 (1986). Statutes may be interpreted as merely regulatory rather than a taking. FCC v. Florida Power Corp., 480 U.S. 245 (1987).

Zoning laws that restrict, diminish, or destroy the value of property do not necessarily represent a taking. Communities use zoning ordinances as part of the police power to promote public health, safety, and morals. Restrictions are placed on the height of buildings and the materials and methods of construction. Certain industries are excluded from residential areas. These regulations usually do not represent unconstitutional deprivations of property or takings.[7] Zoning ordinances that attempted to segregate neighborhoods on the basis of race have been struck down as unconstitutional. Buchanan v. Warley, 245 U.S. 60 (1917). Moreover, zoning ordinances that arbitrarily or unreasonably interfere with a family's right to remain as a unit within their home have been declared unconstitutional. Moore v. East Cleveland, 431 U.S. 494 (1977).

Zoning ordinances apply equally to all property owners in a designated area. However, laws passed to preserve historic buildings and neighborhoods affect only particular property owners. Any alterations to these structures must be approved by local officials or commissions. In a case decided by the Supreme Court in 1978, a company claimed that the application of New York City's landmarks law to the Grand Central Terminal constituted a taking of property in violation of the Fifth and Fourteenth Amendments. The decision, which denied that property had been taken, reveals the difficulty the Court encounters when it attempts to define the meaning of the Taking Clause. Penn Central Transp. Co. v. New York City, 438 U.S. 104 (1978).

Although the Taking Clause of the Fifth Amendment applies to the states, state courts may reach a different result by deciding cases entirely upon their own constitutions. Twenty-five states have Taking Clauses that require compensation for property that is "taken or damaged." The last two words can offer a heightened or different level of constitutional protection. Robert Meltz, Dwight H. Merriam, and Richard M. Frank. The Takings Issue 20–21 (1999).

Contemporary Disputes

Recent cases highlight the complexity and broad reach of the Taking Clause (see box on next page). In a controversial case in 1984, the Court held that the use of eminent domain to condemn land as a means of redistributing private property and combating oligarchy represented a valid "public use." HAWAII HOUSING AUTHORITY v. MIDKIFF, 467 U.S. 229 (1984). The decision underscores the degree to which the judiciary will defer to constitutional judgments by national and state legislatures.

Several cases in 1992 promised to provide greater protection to property owners under the Taking Clause, but the merits were not squarely reached. In one case a unanimous Court merely held that a rent-control ordinance did not amount to a *physical* taking of the property of owners of a mobile home park. The Court concluded that the ordinance might have caused a *regulatory* taking, but that issue was not properly before the Court. Yee v. Escondido, 503 U.S. 519 (1992). A more significant ruling that year narrowed the rights of states to rely on regulatory takings that completely deprive individuals of the economic use of their property. In this case an individual bought two oceanfront lots with the intent to build homes on them, but two years later the South Carolina legislature passed environmental regulations that prohibited development of the property. As a result of the Court's ruling, South Carolina had to identify nuisance and property laws in force at the time the oceanfront lots

---

7. San Diego Gas & Electric Co. v. San Diego, 450 U.S. 621 (1981); Agins v. City of Tiburon, 447 U.S. 255 (1980); Village of Belle Terre v. Boraas, 416 U.S. 1 (1974); Zahn v. Bd. of Public Works, 274 U.S. 325 (1927); Euclid v. Ambler Co., 272 U.S. 365 (1926); Welch v. Swasey, 214 U.S. 91 (1909). See also MacDonald, Sommer & Frates v. Yolo County, 477 U.S. 340 (1986) and Williamson Planning Comm'n v. Hamilton Bank, 473 U.S. 172 (1985), for the ripeness hurdle that can prevent courts from reaching the taking issue.

Other Taking Cases

A state may not force landlords to permit a company to install cable television in return for nominal payments (such as a one-time one-dollar payment). The permanent physical occupation of an owner's property constitutes a taking and requires just compensation.	Loretto v. Teleprompter Manhattan CATV Corp., 458 U.S. 419 (1972).
If a private developer deepens a pond to form a marina and connects it to a navigable bay used by the public, the marina loses its character as a private property. However, if the government wishes to make the marina a public aquatic park, it must pay just compensation.	Kaiser Aetna v. United States, 444 U.S. 164 (1979).
Company data supplied to the government in the form of trade secrets can be treated as property entitled to protection under the Taking Clause.	Ruckelshaus v. Monsanto Co., 467 U.S. 986 (1984).
Coal companies failed to show that a taking had occurred when a state required that 50 percent of the coal beneath statutorily protected structures had to be kept in place to provide surface support.	Keystone Bituminous Coal Assn. v. DeBenedictis, 480 U.S. 470 (1987).
"Temporary" takings are impermissible. Once a taking has been determined, government must compensate the owner for the period during which the taking was effective.	First English Evangelical Lutheran Church v. Los Angeles County, 482 U.S. 304 (1987).
As a condition for permitting someone to replace a small bungalow on their beachfront lot with a larger house, a state may not insist that the owners allow the public to pass across their beach, which was located between two public beaches.	Nollan v. California Coastal Commission, 483 U.S. 825 (1987).

were purchased. To be exempt from compensating a property owner, the state would have to claim more than a general public interest or an interest in preventing serious public harm. Lucas v. South Carolina Coastal Council, 505 U.S. 1003 (1992). As explained in the next section, this case took odd turns when it went back to South Carolina.

A 1994 ruling by the Supreme Court broadened property rights by announcing that land use requirements may be "takings." The 5–4 decision dealt with the practice of local governments giving property owners a permit for building a development only on the condition that they donate part of their land for parks, bike paths, and other public purposes. These conditions will now be valid only if the local government makes "some sort of individualized determination that the required dedication is related both in nature and extent to the impact of the proposed development." Dolan v. City of Tigard, 512 U.S. 374, 391 (1994). Other recent decisions on the taking of property include Babbitt v. Youpee, 519 U.S. 234 (1997); Suitum v. Tahoe Regional Planning Agency, 520 U.S. 725 (1997); Phillips v. Washington Legal Foundation, 524 U.S. 156 (1998); Eastern Enterprises v. Apfel, 524 U.S. 498 (1998); and City of Monterey v. Del Monte Dunes, 526 U.S. 687 (1999). The last three were 5–4 decisions, underscoring the Court's inability to agree on constitutional principles.

Deep disagreements also flavored two property cases decided by the Supreme Court in 2001 and 2002. In the first case, it ruled 5 to 4 that the owner of waterfront property in Rhode Island had a right to challenge in court some development restrictions even though the restrictions existed when he bought the property. The Court held that land-use restrictions that are unreasonable "do not become less so through passage of time or title." Future generations "have a right to challenge unreasonable limitations on the use and value of land." The Court remanded under the principles set forth in *Penn Central*. Palazzolo v. Rhode Island, 533 U.S. 606, 627 (2001).

A 6–3 decision in 2002 strengthened environmental regulators against legal challenges from the property-rights movement. The Court ruled that the Constitution does not automatically require governments to pay compensation to landowners when planning agencies temporarily prohibit them from developing their property. Such disputes are to be decided case by case, weighing such factors as the length of the moratorium and the reasons offered by the government. Writing for the majority, Justice Stevens said that "the extreme categorical rule that any deprivation of all economic use, no matter how brief, constitutes a compensable taking surely cannot be sustained." Tahoe-Sierra Preserv. v. Tahoe Reg. Planning, 535 U.S. 302, 334 (2002). He confined *Lucas* to "the 'extraordinary case' in which a regulation permanently deprives property of all value." Id. at 332. Interestingly, he said that many of the key decisions on takings "should be the product of legislative rulemaking rather than adjudication." Id. at 335.

The *Kelo* Decision

A landmark 5–4 ruling in 2005 triggered nationwide controversy. The Supreme Court upheld the exercise of the governmental power of eminent domain to condemn and take, with just compensation, private property for the public purpose of advancing economic development of the community. In an opinion with major implications for city planners and homeowners, Justice John Paul Stevens wrote for the Court that "public use" includes "promoting economic development," even if property was seized and sold for development by private developers. KELO v. CITY OF NEW LONDON, 545 U.S. 469 (2005). He added: "we emphasize that nothing in our opinion precludes any state from placing further restrictions on its exercise of the takings power." Id. at 19.

Reaction to the ruling was fast and heated. More than three dozen states accepted the Court's "invitation" and imposed restrictions on the ability of local governments to seize property and turn it over to private developers. A number of voter referendums and propositions were approved in the states, placing similar restrictions on the right of eminent domain. Pamela A. MacLean, "The 'Kelo' Effect," Nat'l L. J., March 31, 2008, at 1.

The Court's decision had the effect of uniting conservatives (who viewed it as a threat to private property rights) and liberals (who expressed concern about urban renewal projects displacing minority neighborhoods). Republicans and Democrats provided overwhelming support for H. Res. 340, which took sharp exception to the Court's interpretation of the Takings Clause: "eminent domain should never be used to advantage one private party over another." The measure also stated: "Congress maintains the prerogative and reserves the right to address through legislation any abuses of eminent domain by State and local government in light of the ruling in Kelo et al. v. City of New London et al." The House adopted the resolution 365 to 33, but it merely expressed the sense of the House and had no legal force. Congress considered other binding measures (H.R. 3135 and H.R. 4128) but they did not become law.

In an example of coordinate construction, President George W. Bush, on June 23, 2006 — the first anniversary of *Kelo* — issued an executive order that prohibits federal agencies from seizing private property, except for public projects such as medical facilities, roads, parks, and government office building and institutes.

In another takings case, Lingle v. Chevron, 544 U.S. 528 (2005), the Court, in a unanimous opinion by Justice O'Connor, upheld a Hawaiian statute that capped the rent paid by gasoline dealers who lease company-owned service stations, and ruled that the legislation had not effected an unconstitutional taking. The Ninth Circuit had relied on the Court's "substantially advance" test set forth in *Agins*

v. *City of Tiburon*, 447 U.S. 255, 260 (1980), to affirm a lower court ruling that declared the cap an unconstitutional taking. The *Agins* test provided that a regulation effects a Fifth Amendment taking if it does not "substantially advance" legitimate state interests. But Justice O'Connor ruled that the test was dictum and that it was not a valid method for determining whether a regulation constitutes a taking of private property. As an alternative, the Court affirmed its adherence to precedents, such as *Penn Central*, which emphasize multiple factors in determining whether a taking had been effected.

Following the Trail

As with other Supreme Court decisions, one never knows what gap will emerge between what the Court says and what happens next. *Lucas* v. *South Carolina Coastal Council* (1992) supposedly featured a collision between two forces, with the state ("the Environmentalist") preventing David Lucas from doing any construction on his two beachfront lots. After the Court reversed and remanded, South Carolina was unable to prove that the building contemplated by Lucas would constitute a common law nuisance. A settlement of $1.5 million paid Lucas $425,000 for each lot and covered his interest and legal fees. After deducting mortgage and costs, he walked away with less than $100,000. What did South Carolina do with the two lots? Keep them pristine and untouched by the worker's hand? Not at all. First it rejected a bid from one of Lucas's neighbors, who offered $315,000 for one of the lots to prevent any building on it. The state then accepted $392,500 per lot from a construction company which intended to develop the property, precisely what the state had prohibited Lucas from doing. Thus, a case that started out with South Carolina adamantly opposed to any construction on oceanfront property did a full reverse after the Court's opinion. Gideon Kanner, "Not with a Bang, but a Giggle: The Settlement of the Lucas Case," in David L. Callies, ed., Takings 308–11 (1996).

Congressional Action

Congress has considered legislation in recent years to require federal agencies to determine whether their regulatory activities amount to a taking of private property. The purpose is either to compel government to compensate property owners or to force agencies to scale back their regulations. The Senate passed this type of requirement in 1991, building on Executive Order 12630 issued by President Reagan in 1988, but the Senate language was not enacted. 137 Cong. Rec. 14446–54, 14456–67 (1991); 53 Fed. Reg. 8859 (1988).

The "Contract with America," announced by more than 300 Republican candidates for the U.S. House of Representatives on September 27, 1994, called for a number of reforms to limit government and expand individual rights. One of the provisions sought to protect private property owners by compensating them for all but very small reductions in the value of their property that were caused by government regulation. The draft bill provided that a private property owner "is entitled" to receive compensation and the head of an agency "shall pay" a private property owner any compensation required.

However, when it became apparent that full compensation for such losses would add massive amounts to the federal deficit and jeopardize other Republican goals (such as a balanced budget), the bill was modified by removing the concept of an entitlement. As passed by the House, the private property bill stated that the federal government "shall" compensate anyone whose private property had been diminished in value by at least 20 percent. Yet the government's liability was sharply reduced by other language in the bill. No compensation would be made if an agency's primary purpose was to prevent an identifiable hazard to public health or safety, or if the owner's proposed use of land would have been a nuisance. Moreover, if a citizen presented a claim, the agency had the option of paying the amount or seeking reimbursement from another agency that shared responsibility. If an agency said that it had no money to pay the claim, the only obligation at that point would be for the agency head to ask Congress for an appropriation. Congress would have no obligation (except perhaps a moral one) to appropriate anything. The Senate never acted on the bill or any variation of it.

In 1997, the House passed a bill to expedite access to the federal courts for private parties claiming a violation of the Taking Clause. 143 Cong. Rec. 22509–34 (1997). The Senate did not bring the bill up for a vote. In 1998, the House passed another version of this legislation. 144 Cong. Rec. 3329–39, 3393–98 (1998). The Senate failed to act on this bill either. Opponents objected that federal courts would end up making decisions better left to local zoning authorities and state courts. In 2000, the House passed legislation for expedited access to federal courts to challenge deprivations of private property by governmental actions. 146 Cong. Rec. H1089–114 (daily ed. March 16, 2000). The Senate took no action on the bill.

Hawaii Housing Authority v. Midkiff

467 U.S. 229 (1984)

How much may legislatures exercise their police powers without "taking" property in violation of the Fifth and Fourteenth Amendments? Such questions necessarily involve a sharing of judgments and jurisdiction by legislatures and courts. In this case, the Hawaii Legislature enacted a land reform act in 1967 in an effort to reduce the social and economic evils of a land oligopoly that could be traced back to the early high chiefs of the Hawaiian Islands. The statute created a land condemnation scheme and provoked a suit that claimed a violation of constitutional rights. Frank Midkiff, a landowner, filed suit to have the land reform act declared unconstitutional as a violation of the Taking Clause. The Ninth Circuit agreed that it was a taking.

JUSTICE O'CONNOR delivered the opinion of the Court.

. . .

[I.A]

The Hawaiian Islands were originally settled by Polynesian immigrants from the western Pacific. These settlers developed an economy around a feudal land tenure system in which one island high chief, the ali'i nui, controlled the land and assigned it for development to certain subchiefs. The subchiefs would then reassign the land to other lower ranking chiefs, who would administer the land and govern the farmers and other tenants working it. All land was held at the will of the ali'i nui and eventually had to be returned to his trust. There was no private ownership of land....

Beginning in the early 1800's, Hawaiian leaders and American settlers repeatedly attempted to divide the lands of the kingdom among the crown, the chiefs, and the common people. These efforts proved largely unsuccessful, however, and the land remained in the hands of a few. In the mid-1960's, after extensive hearings, the Hawaii Legislature discovered that, while the State and Federal Governments owned almost 49% of the State's land, another 47% was in the hands of only 72 private landowners.... The legislature further found that 18 landholders, with tracts of 21,000 acres or more,

owned more than 40% of this land and that on Oahu, the most urbanized of the islands, 22 landowners owned 72.5% of the fee simple titles.... The legislature concluded that concentrated land ownership was responsible for skewing the State's residential fee simple market, inflating land prices, and injuring the public tranquility and welfare.

To redress these problems, the legislature decided to compel the large landowners to break up their estates.... To accommodate the needs of both lessors and lessees, the Hawaii Legislature enacted the Land Reform Act of 1967 (Act), Haw. Rev. Stat., ch. 516, which created a mechanism for condemning residential tracts and for transferring ownership of the condemned fees simple to existing lessees. By condemning the land in question, the Hawaii Legislature intended to make the land sales involuntary, thereby making the federal tax consequences less severe while still facilitating the redistribution of fees simple....

Under the Act's condemnation scheme, tenants living on single-family residential lots within developmental tracts at least five acres in size are entitled to ask the Hawaii Housing Authority (HHA) to condemn the property on which they live.... When 25 eligible tenants, or tenants on half the lots in the tract, whichever is less, file appropriate applications, the Act authorizes HHA to hold a public hearing to determine whether acquisition by the State of all or part of the tract will "effectuate the public purposes" of the Act.... If HHA finds that these public purposes will be served, it is authorized to designate some or all of the lots in the tract for acquisition. It then acquires, at prices set either by condemnation trial or by negotiation between lessors and lessees, the former fee owners' full "right, title, and interest" in the land....

After compensation has been set, HHA may sell the land titles to tenants who have applied for fee simple ownership.... If HHA does not sell the lot to the tenant residing there, it may lease the lot or sell it to someone else, provided that public notice has been given....

. . .

III

The majority of the Court of Appeals next determined that the Act violates the "public use" requirement of the Fifth and Fourteenth Amendments. On this argument, however, we find ourselves in agreement with the dissenting judge in the Court of Appeals.

A

The starting point for our analysis of the Act's constitutionality is the Court's decision in *Berman v. Parker,* 348 U.S. 26 (1954). In *Berman,* the Court held constitutional the District of Columbia Redevelopment Act of 1945. That Act provided both for the comprehensive use of the eminent domain power to redevelop slum areas and for the possible sale or lease of the condemned lands to private interests. In discussing whether the takings authorized by that Act were for a "public use," *id.,* at 31, the Court stated:

"We deal, in other words, with what traditionally has been known as the police power. An attempt to define its reach or trace its outer limits is fruitless, for each case must turn on its own facts. The definition is essentially the product of legislative determinations addressed to the purposes of government, purposes neither abstractly nor historically capable of complete definition. Subject to specific constitutional limitations, when the legislature has spoken, the public interest has been declared in terms well-nigh conclusive. In such cases the legislature, not the judiciary, is the main guardian of the public needs to be served by social legislation, whether it be Congress legislating concerning the District of Columbia ... or the States legislating concerning local affairs.... This principle admits of no exception merely because the power of eminent domain is involved...." *Id.,* at 32 (citations omitted).

. . .

There is, of course, a role for courts to play in reviewing a legislature's judgment of what constitutes a public use, even when the eminent domain power is equated with the police power. But the Court in *Berman* made clear that it is "an extremely narrow" one. *Id.,* at 32. The Court in *Berman* cited with approval the Court's decision in *Old Dominion Co. v. United States,* 269 U.S. 55, 66 (1925), which held that deference to the legislature's "public use" determination is required "until it is shown to involve an impossibility."...

To be sure, the Court's cases have repeatedly stated that "one person's property may not be taken for the benefit of another private person without a justifying public purpose, even though compensation be paid." *Thompson v. Consolidated Gas Corp.,* 300 U.S. 55, 80 (1937).... Where the exercise of the eminent domain power is rationally related to a conceivable public purpose, the Court has never held a compensated taking to be proscribed by the Public Use Clause....

On this basis, we have no trouble concluding that the Hawaii Act is constitutional. The people of Hawaii have attempted, much as the settlers of the original 13 Colonies did, to reduce the perceived social and economic evils of a land oligopoly traceable to their monarchs. The land oligopoly has, according to the Hawaii Legislature, created artificial deterrents to the normal functioning of the State's residential land market and forced thousands of individual homeowners to lease, rather than buy, the land underneath their homes. Regulating oligopoly and the evils associated with it is a classic exercise of a State's police powers.... We cannot disapprove of Hawaii's exercise of this power.

. . .

B

... The fact that a state legislature, and not the Congress, made the public use determination does not mean that judicial deference is less appropriate. Judicial deference is required because, in our system of government, legislatures are better able to assess what public purposes should be advanced by an exercise of the taking power. State legislatures are as capable as Congress of making such determinations within their respective spheres of authority. See *Berman v. Parker,* 348 U.S., at 32. Thus, if a legislature, state or federal, determines there are substantial reasons for an exercise of the taking power, courts must defer to its determination that the taking will serve a public use.

IV

The State of Hawaii has never denied that the Constitution forbids even a compensated taking of property when executed for no reason other than to confer a private benefit on a particular private party. A purely private taking could not withstand the scrutiny of the public use requirement; it would serve no legitimate purpose of government and would thus be void. But no purely private taking is involved in these cases.... Accordingly, we reverse the judgment of the Court of Appeals, and remand these cases for further proceedings in conformity with this opinion.

It is so ordered.

JUSTICE MARSHALL took no part in the consideration or decision of these cases.

Kelo v. City of New London

545 U.S. 469 (2005)

In an effort to revitalize its ailing economy, the City of New London (through its development agent) purchased most of the property earmarked for an economic development project from willing sellers, but initiated condemnation proceedings when petitioners, the owners of the rest of the property, refused to sell. Susette Kelo and other homeowners brought a state-court action claiming that the taking of their properties would violate the "public use" restriction in the Fifth Amendment Takings Clause since their properties would not be used for a "public purpose." A trial court issued a restraining order prohibiting New London from taking some of the property, but the Connecticut Supreme Court upheld the takings. The U.S. Supreme Court's opinion is noteworthy for its emphasis on judicial self-restraint.

JUSTICE STEVENS delivered the opinion of the Court.

[II]

We granted certiorari to determine whether a city's decision to take property for the purpose of economic development satisfies the "public use" requirement of the Fifth Amendment....

III

Two polar propositions are perfectly clear. On the one hand, it has long been accepted that the sovereign may not take the property of *A* for the sole purpose of transferring it to another private party *B*, even though *A* is paid just compensation. On the other hand, it is equally clear that a State may transfer property from one private party to another if future "use by the public" is the purpose of the taking; the condemnation of land for a railroad with common-carrier duties is a familiar example. Neither of these propositions, however, determines the disposition of this case.

As for the first proposition, the City would no doubt be forbidden from taking petitioners' land for the purpose of conferring a private benefit on a particular private party. See *[Hawaii Housing Authority v.] Midkiff,* 467 U.S., [229] at 245.... Nor would the City be allowed to take property under the mere pretext of a public purpose, when its actual purpose was

to bestow a private benefit. The takings before us, however, would be executed pursuant to a "carefully considered" development plan.... The trial judge and all the members of the Supreme Court of Connecticut agreed that there was no evidence of an illegitimate purpose in this case....

. . .

The disposition of this case therefore turns on the question whether the City's development plan serves a "public purpose." Without exception, our cases have defined that concept broadly, reflecting our longstanding policy of deference to legislative judgments in this field.

In *Berman v. Parker,* 348 U.S. 26 (1954), this Court upheld a redevelopment plan targeting a blighted area of Washington, D. C., in which most of the housing for the area's 5,000 inhabitants was beyond repair. Under the plan, the area would be condemned and part of it utilized for the construction of streets, schools, and other public facilities. The remainder of the land would be leased or sold to private parties for the purpose of redevelopment, including the construction of low-cost housing.

The owner of a department store located in the area challenged the condemnation, pointing out that his store was not itself blighted and arguing that the creation of a "better balanced, more attractive community" was not a valid public use.... Writing for a unanimous Court, Justice Douglas refused to evaluate this claim in isolation, deferring instead to the legislative and agency judgment that the area "must be planned as a whole" for the plan to be successful....

. . .

IV

Those who govern the City were not confronted with the need to remove blight in the Fort Trumbull area, but their determination that the area was sufficiently distressed to justify a program of economic rejuvenation is entitled to our deference. The City has carefully formulated an economic development plan that it believes will provide appreciable benefits to the community, including—but by no means limited to—new jobs and increased tax revenue. As with other exercises in urban planning and development, the City is endeavoring to coordinate a variety of commercial, residential, and recreational uses of land, with the hope that they will form a whole greater than the sum of its parts. To effectuate this plan, the City has invoked a state statute that specifically authorizes the use of eminent domain to promote economic development.... Because that plan unquestionably serves a public purpose, the takings challenged here satisfy the public use requirement of the Fifth Amendment.

To avoid this result, petitioners urge us to adopt a new bright-line rule that economic development does not qualify as a public use. Putting aside the unpersuasive suggestion that the City's plan will provide only purely economic benefits, neither precedent nor logic supports petitioners' proposal. Promoting economic development is a traditional and long accepted function of government. There is, moreover, no principled way of distinguishing economic development from the other public purposes that we have recognized....

Petitioners contend that using eminent domain for economic development impermissibly blurs the boundary between public and private takings. Again, our cases foreclose this objection. Quite simply, the government's pursuit of a public purpose will often benefit individual private parties. For example, in *Midkiff*, the forced transfer of property conferred a direct and significant benefit on those lessees who were previously unable to purchase their homes....

It is further argued that without a bright-line rule nothing would stop a city from transferring citizen A's property to citizen B for the sole reason that cit-

izen *B* will put the property to a more productive use and thus pay more taxes. Such a one-to-one transfer of property, executed outside the confines of an integrated development plan, is not presented in this case. While such an unusual exercise of government power would certainly raise a suspicion that a private purpose was afoot, the hypothetical cases posited by petitioners can be confronted if and when they arise....

In affirming the City's authority to take petitioners' properties, we do not minimize the hardship that condemnations may entail, notwithstanding the payment of just compensation. We emphasize that nothing in our opinion precludes any State from placing further restrictions on its exercise of the takings power. Indeed, many States already impose "public use" requirements that are stricter than the federal baseline. Some of these requirements have been established as a matter of state constitutional law, while others are expressed in state eminent domain statutes that carefully limit the grounds upon which takings may be exercised....

The judgment of the Supreme Court of Connecticut is affirmed.

Justice Kennedy, concurring....

Justice O'Connor, with whom The Chief Justice, Justice Scalia, and Justice Thomas join, dissenting.

Over two centuries ago, just after the Bill of Rights was ratified, Justice Chase wrote:

"An ACT of the Legislature (for I cannot call it a law) contrary to the great first principles of the social compact, cannot be considered a rightful exercise of legislative authority.... A few instances will suffice to explain what I mean.... [A] law that takes property from A. and gives it to B: It is against all reason and justice, for a people to entrust a Legislature with SUCH powers; and, therefore, it cannot be presumed that they have done it." *Calder v. Bull,* 3 Dall. 386, 388 (1798) (emphasis deleted).

Today the Court abandons this long-held, basic limitation on government power. Under the banner of economic development, all private property is now vulnerable to being taken and transferred to another private owner, so long as it might be upgraded—*i.e.*, given to an owner who will use it in a way that the legislature deems more beneficial to the public—in the process. To reason, as the Court does, that the incidental public benefits resulting from the subsequent ordinary use of private property render economic development takings "for public use" is to wash out any distinction between private and public use of property—and thereby effectively to delete the words "for public use" from the Takings Clause of the Fifth Amendment. Accordingly I respectfully dissent.

. . .

II

... [W]e have read the Fifth Amendment's language to impose two distinct conditions on the exercise of eminent domain: "the taking must be for a 'public use' and 'just compensation' must be paid to the owner." ...

These two limitations serve to protect "the security of Property," which Alexander Hamilton described to the Philadelphia Convention as one of the "great obj[ects] of Gov[ernment]." 1 Records of the Federal Convention of 1787, p. 302 (M. Farrand ed. 1934). Together they ensure stable property ownership by providing safeguards against excessive, unpredictable, or unfair use of the government's eminent domain power—particularly against those owners who, for whatever reasons, may be unable to protect themselves in the political process against the majority's will.

While the Takings Clause presupposes that government can take private property without the owner's consent, the just compensation requirement spreads the cost of condemnations and thus "prevents the public from loading upon one individual more than his just share of the burdens of government." ... The public use requirement, in turn, imposes a more basic limitation, circumscribing the very scope of the eminent domain power: Government may compel an individual to forfeit her property for the *public's* use, but not for the benefit of another private person. This requirement promotes fairness as well as security....

Where is the line between "public" and "private" property use? We give considerable deference to legislatures' determinations about what governmental activities will advantage the public. But were the political branches the sole arbiters of the public-private distinction, the Public Use Clause would amount to little more than hortatory fluff. An external, judicial check on how the public use requirement is interpreted, however limited, is necessary if this constraint on government power is to retain any meaning....

In moving away from our decisions sanctioning the condemnation of harmful property use, the Court today significantly expands the meaning of public use. It holds that the sovereign may take private property currently put to ordinary private use, and give it over for new, ordinary private use, so long as the new use is predicted to generate some secondary benefit for the public—such as increased tax revenue, more jobs, maybe even aesthetic pleasure. But nearly any lawful use of real private property can be said to generate some incidental benefit to the public. Thus, if predicted (or even guaranteed) positive side-effects are enough to render transfer from one private party to another constitutional, then the words "for public use" do not realistically exclude *any* takings, and thus do not exert any constraint on the eminent domain power.

. . .

Any property may now be taken for the benefit of another private party, but the fallout from this decision will not be random. The beneficiaries are likely to be those citizens with disproportionate influence and power in the political process, including large corporations and development firms. As for the victims, the government now has license to transfer property from those with fewer resources to those with more. The Founders cannot have intended this perverse result. "[T]hat alone is a *just* government," wrote James Madison, "which *impartially* secures to every man, whatever is his *own*." ...

JUSTICE THOMAS, dissenting....

D. THE POLICE POWER

The courts of the nineteenth century permitted legislatures and municipalities broad discretion to use the "police power" to regulate public health and safety. The power of states to "impose restraints and burdens upon persons and property in conservation and promotion of the public health, good order and prosperity, is a power originally and always belonging to the States, not surrendered by them to the general government nor directly restrained by the Constitution of the United States, and essentially exclusive." In re Rahrer, 140 U.S. 545, 554 (1891). The police power may serve malign as well as benign purposes. In 1896, the Supreme Court held that Louisiana could use its police power

The Police Power

... While this [police] power is inherent in all governments, it has doubtless been greatly expanded in its application during the past century, owing to an enormous increase in the number of occupations that are dangerous, or so far detrimental to the health of employés as to demand special precautions for their well-being and protection, or the safety of adjacent property. While this court has held ... that the police power cannot be put forward as an excuse for oppressive and unjust legislation, it may be lawfully resorted to for the purpose of preserving the public health, safety or morals, or the abatement of public nuisances, and a large discretion "is necessarily vested in the legislature to determine not only what the interests of the public require, but what measures are necessary for the protection of such interests." ...

While this power is necessarily inherent in every form of government, it was, prior to the adoption of the Constitution, but sparingly used in this country. As we were then almost purely an agricultural people, the occasion for any special protection of a particular class did not exist. Certain profitable employments, such as lotteries and the sale of intoxicating liquors, which were then considered to be legitimate, have since fallen under the ban of public opinion, and are now either altogether prohibited, or made subject to stringent police regulations. The power to do this has been repeatedly affirmed by this court....

While the business of mining coal and manufacturing iron began in Pennsylvania as early as 1716, and in Virginia, North Carolina and Massachusetts even earlier than this, both mining and manufacturing were carried on in such a limited way and by such primitive methods that no special laws were considered necessary, prior to the adoption of the Constitution, for the protection of the operatives; but, in the vast proportions which these industries have since assumed, it has been found that they can no longer be carried on with due regard to the safety and health of those engaged in them, without special protection against the dangers necessarily incident to these employments....

SOURCE: Holden v. Hardy, 169 U.S. 366, 391–93 (1898).

to provide for "separate but equal" accommodations for whites and blacks in railway coaches. Plessy v. Ferguson, 163 U.S. 537, 544 (1896).

In a major case in 1873, a 5 to 4 decision by the Supreme Court upheld a monopoly that Louisiana had granted to a slaughterhouse. The Court ruled that the statute represented a valid police regulation for the health and comfort of the people. The decision proved pivotal for two other reasons. First, it concluded that the privileges and immunities under the Fourteenth Amendment were to be protected by the states, not the national government. Second, the powerful dissents influenced future proponents of property rights and liberty of contract. SLAUGHTER-HOUSE CASES, 83 U.S. (16 Wall.) 36 (1873). Just as the police power could justify a monopoly, so could the same state a few years later invoke that power to abolish the monopoly and reintroduce competition. Butchers' Union Co. v. Crescent City Co., 111 U.S. 746 (1884).

There were some hints at the state level that legislative efforts to control business activities could be curbed by the courts. Wynehamer v. People, 13 N.Y. 378 (1856). However, the Supreme Court provided broad support for state regulatory efforts. An Illinois law setting maximum charges for storing grain in warehouses and elevators was upheld in 1877 as a legitimate exercise of state authority to regulate businesses affected with a public interest. MUNN v. ILLINOIS, 94 U.S. 113 (1877). Other cases during this period supported use of the police power for economic regulation. Fertilizing Co. v. Hyde Park, 97 U.S. 659 (1879); Patterson v. Kentucky, 97 U.S. 501 (1879); Beer Co. v. Massachusetts, 97 U.S. 25 (1878).

A unanimous decision in 1885 upheld a law prohibiting public laundries from operating from 10 P.M. to 6 A.M. Barbier v. Connolly, 113 U.S. 27. A year later, the Court upheld the power of a state railroad commission to fix freight and passenger rates. Railroad Commission Cases, 116 U.S. 307, 347, 353 (1886). A unanimous ruling in 1887 allowed states to prohibit the manufacture and sale of intoxicating liquors within the state. It belonged to the legislative branch "to exert what are known as the police powers of the State, and to determine, primarily, what measures are appropriate or needful for the protection of the public morals, the public health, or the public safety." Mugler v. Kansas, 123 U.S. 623, 661 (1887).

Judicial Limits

In 1890, the Supreme Court declared unconstitutional a Minnesota law not because it exceeded the police power but because the judiciary of that state had decided that the reasonableness of rates established by a railroad and warehouse commission was final and conclusive, prohibiting review by the courts. This case did not prevent regulation by the state. It merely required the courts to determine whether the rates satisfied due process of law. Chicago, Milwaukee and St. Paul Railway Co. v. Minnesota, 134 U.S. 418 (1890). Also that year, the Court invalidated a Minnesota police power statute because it interfered with commerce among the states and thus invaded the province of Congress. Minnesota v. Barber, 136 U.S. 313 (1890).

In 1897 a unanimous Supreme Court, using the magic phrase "liberty to contract," spoke strongly about a citizen's right to be free to earn his livelihood. Allgeyer v. Louisiana, 165 U.S. 578, 589, 591 (1897). This general philosophy did not prevent the Court the next year from upholding an eight-hour day for workers in coal mines and smelters. The Court flatly rejected the idea that workers and employers stood on equal footing in reaching a contract. Holden v. Hardy, 169 U.S. 366, 397 (1898). The Court perceptively noted that the police power had been greatly expanded in the nineteenth century because of the growth of dangerous occupations (see box). In 1903, the Court upheld an eight-hour law in Kansas covering all persons employed by the state or local governments, including work contracted by the state. Atkin v. Kansas, 191 U.S. 207 (1903).

Slaughter-House Cases

16 Wall. 36 (1873)

The legislature of Louisiana passed an act granting to a corporation, which it created, the exclusive right for 25 years to operate slaughterhouses. The corporation operated within three parishes, including the city of New Orleans, and prohibited other persons from competing with the corporation. The constitutional issue was whether this exclusive grant of monopoly privilege was a police regulation for the health and comfort of the people or whether it violated the constitutional rights of other citizens to exercise their trade and occupation. The Supreme Court's decision is significant because it marks the first interpretation of the Civil War Amendments, especially the reach and purpose of the Fourteenth Amendment and the power of the federal government to direct state activities.

Mr. Justice MILLER, now, April 14th, 1873, delivered the opinion of the court.

. . .

It is ... the slaughter-house privilege, which is mainly relied on to justify the charges of gross injustice to the public, and invasion of private right.

It is not, and cannot be successfully controverted, that it is both the right and the duty of the legislative body—the supreme power of the State or municipality—to prescribe and determine the localities where the business of slaughtering for a great city may be conducted. To do this effectively it is indispensable that all persons who slaughter animals for food shall do it in those places *and nowhere else.*

The statute under consideration defines these localities and forbids slaughtering in any other. It does not, as has been asserted, prevent the butcher from doing his own slaughtering. On the contrary, the Slaughter-House Company is required, under a heavy penalty, to permit any person who wishes to do so, to slaughter in their houses; and they are bound to make ample provision for the convenience of all the slaughtering for the entire city. The butcher then is still permitted to slaughter, to prepare, and to sell his own meats; but he is required to slaughter at a specified place and to pay a reasonable compensation for the use of the accommodations furnished him at that place.

. . .

It cannot be denied that the statute under consideration is aptly framed to remove from the more densely populated part of the city, the noxious slaughter-houses, and large and offensive collections of animals necessarily incident to the slaughtering business of a large city, and to locate them where the convenience, health, and comfort of the people require they shall be located. And it must be conceded that the means adopted by the act for this purpose are appropriate, are stringent, and effectual....

The plaintiffs in error accepting this issue, allege that the statute is a violation of the Constitution of the United States in these several particulars:

That it creates an involuntary servitude forbidden by the thirteenth article of amendment;

That it abridges the privileges and immunities of citizens of the United States;

That it denies to the plaintiffs the equal protection of the laws; and,

That it deprives them of their property without due process of law; contrary to the provisions of the first section of the fourteenth article of amendment....

. . .

[The Court summarizes the adoption of the Fourteenth Amendment, as a response to the "black codes" used by southern states to suppress blacks, and the Fifteenth Amendment.]

The first section of the fourteenth article, to which our attention is more specially invited, opens with a definition of citizenship....

"All persons born or naturalized in the United States, and subject to the jurisdiction thereof, are citizens of the United States and of the State wherein they reside."

. . .

It is quite clear, then, that there is a citizenship of the United States, and a citizenship of a State, which are distinct from each other, and which depend upon different characteristics or circumstances in the individual.

We think this distinction and its explicit recogni-

tion in this amendment of great weight in this argument, because the next paragraph of this same section, which is the one mainly relied on by the plaintiffs in error, speaks only of privileges and immunities of citizens of the United States, and does not speak of those of citizens of the several States. The argument, however, in favor of the plaintiffs rests wholly on the assumption that the citizenship is the same, and the privileges and immunities guaranteed by the clause are the same.

The language is, "No State shall make or enforce any law which shall abridge the privileges or immunities of citizens of *the United States*." It is a little remarkable, if this clause was intended as a protection to the citizen of a State against the legislative power of his own State, that the word citizen of the State should be left out when it is so carefully used, and used in contradistinction to citizens of the United States, in the very sentence which precedes it....

Fortunately we are not without judicial construction of this clause of the Constitution. The first and the leading case on the subject is that of *Corfield* v. *Coryell*, decided by Mr. Justice Washington in the Circuit Court for the District of Pennsylvania in 1823.

"The inquiry," he says, "is, what are the privileges and immunities of citizens of the several States? We feel no hesitation in confining these expressions to those privileges and immunities which are *fundamental;* which belong of right to the citizens of all free governments, and which have at all times been enjoyed by citizens of the several States which compose this Union, from the time of their becoming free, independent, and sovereign. What these fundamental principles are, it would be more tedious than difficult to enumerate. They may all, however, be comprehended under the following general heads: protection by the government, with the right to acquire and possess property of every kind, and to pursue and obtain happiness and safety, subject, nevertheless, to such restraints as the government may prescribe for the general good of the whole."

... Was it the purpose of the fourteenth amendment, by the simple declaration that no State should make or enforce any law which shall abridge the privileges and immunities of *citizens of the United States,* to transfer the security and protection of all the civil rights which we have mentioned, from the States to the Federal government? And where it is declared that Congress shall have the power to enforce that article, was it intended to bring within the power of Congress the entire domain of civil rights heretofore belonging exclusively to the States?

... [S]uch a construction followed by the reversal

of the judgments of the Supreme Court of Louisiana in these cases, would constitute this court a perpetual censor upon all legislation of the States, on the civil rights of their own citizens, with authority to nullify such as it did not approve as consistent with those rights, as they existed at the time of the adoption of this amendment. The argument we admit is not always the most conclusive which is drawn from the consequences urged against the adoption of a particular construction of an instrument. But when, as in the case before us, these consequences are so serious, so far-reaching and pervading, so great a departure from the structure and spirit of our institutions; when the effect is to fetter and degrade the State governments by subjecting them to the control of Congress, in the exercise of powers heretofore universally conceded to them of the most ordinary and fundamental character; when in fact it radically changes the whole theory of the relations of the State and Federal governments to each other and of both these governments to the people; the argument has a force that is irresistible, in the absence of language which expresses such a purpose too clearly to admit of doubt.

We are convinced that no such results were intended by the Congress which proposed these amendments, nor by the legislatures of the States which ratified them.

. . .

[*Section 1 of the Fourteenth Amendment provides:*] "No State shall make or enforce any law which shall abridge the privileges or immunities of citizens of the United States; nor shall any State deprive any person of life, liberty, or property without due process of law, nor deny to any person within its jurisdiction the equal protection of its laws."

... The first of these paragraphs has been in the Constitution since the adoption of the fifth amendment, as a restraint upon the Federal power. It is also to be found in some form of expression in the constitutions of nearly all the States, as a restraint upon the power of the States. This law, then, has practically been the same as it now is during the existence of the government, except so far as the present amendment may place the restraining power over the States in this matter in the hands of the Federal government.

We are not without judicial interpretation, therefore, both State and National, of the meaning of this clause. And it is sufficient to say that under no construction of that provision that we have ever seen, or any that we deem admissible, can the restraint im-

posed by the State of Louisiana upon the exercise of their trade by the butchers of New Orleans be held to be a deprivation of property within the meaning of that provision....

The judgments of the Supreme Court of Louisiana in these cases are

Affirmed.

Mr. Justice FIELD, dissenting:

. . .

The act of Louisiana presents the naked case, unaccompanied by any public considerations, where a right to pursue a lawful and necessary calling, previously enjoyed by every citizen, and in connection with which a thousand persons were daily employed, is taken away and vested exclusively for twenty-five years, for an extensive district and a large population, in a single corporation, or its exercise is for that period restricted to the establishments of the corporation, and there allowed only upon onerous conditions ...

[*After reviewing a number of judicial rulings, Field concludes:*] In all these cases there is a recognition of the equality of right among citizens in the pursuit of the ordinary avocations of life, and a declaration that all grants of exclusive privileges, in contravention of this equality, are against common right, and void.

This equality of right, with exemption from all disparaging and partial enactments, in the lawful pursuits of life, throughout the whole country, is the distinguishing privilege of citizens of the United States. To them, everywhere, all pursuits, all professions, all avocations are open without other restrictions than such as are imposed equally upon all others of the same age, sex, and condition.... [I]t is to me a matter of profound regret that its validity is not recognized by a majority of this court, for by it the right of free labor, one of the most sacred and imprescriptible rights of man, is violated....

I am authorized by the CHIEF JUSTICE, Mr. Justice SWAYNE, and Mr. Justice BRADLEY, to state that they concur with me in this dissenting opinion.

Mr. Justice BRADLEY, also dissenting:

... [I]n my judgment, the right of any citizen to follow whatever lawful employment he chooses to adopt (submitting himself to all lawful regulations) is one of his most valuable rights, and one which the legislature of a State cannot invade, whether restrained by its own constitution or not.

. . .

... [T]he Declaration of Independence, which was the first political act of the American people in their independent sovereign capacity, lays the foundation of our National existence upon this broad proposition: "That all men are created equal; that they are endowed by their Creator with certain inalienable rights; that among these are life, liberty, and the pursuit of happiness." Here again we have the great threefold division of the rights of freemen, asserted as the rights of man. Rights to life, liberty, and the pursuit of happiness are equivalent to the rights of life, liberty, and property. These are the fundamental rights which can only be taken away by due process of law, ...

Mr. Justice SWAYNE, dissenting:

. . .

Munn v. Illinois

94 U.S. 113 (1877)

This case illustrates the need to balance two conflicting interests: the property rights of private individuals against the duty of the state to regulate economic conditions for the public good. Although economic regulation is sometimes regarded as a phenomenon of the twentieth century, this case makes clear that it has been customary "from time immemorial." Statutes regulating private property do not necessarily deprive an owner of his property without due process of law. When the owner of property devotes it to a use "in which the public has an interest," the owner must submit to some degree of public control. Ira Munn, owner of a number of grain warehouses, challenged a state law.

MR. CHIEF JUSTICE WAITE delivered the opinion of the court.

The question to be determined in this case is whether the general assembly of Illinois can, under the limitations upon the legislative power of the States imposed by the Constitution of the United States, fix by law the maximum of charges for the storage of grain in warehouses at Chicago and other places in the State....

It is claimed that such a law is repugnant—

1. To that part of sect. 8, art. 1, of the Constitution of the United States which confers upon Congress the power "to regulate commerce with foreign nations and among the several States;"

2. To that part of sect. 9 of the same article which provides that "no preference shall be given by any regulation of commerce or revenue to the ports of one State over those of another;" and

3. To that part of amendment 14 which ordains that no State shall "deprive any person of life, liberty, or property, without due process of law, nor deny to any person within its jurisdiction the equal protection of the laws."

We will consider the last of these objections first.

Every statute is presumed to be constitutional. The courts ought not to declare one to be unconstitutional, unless it is clearly so. If there is doubt, the expressed will of the legislature should be sustained.

The Constitution contains no definition of the word "deprive," as used in the Fourteenth Amendment. To determine its signification, therefore, it is necessary to ascertain the effect which usage has given it, when employed in the same or a like connection.

While this provision of the amendment is new in the Constitution of the United States, as a limitation upon the powers of the States, it is old as a principle of civilized government. It is found in Magna Charta, and, in substance if not in form, in nearly or quite all the constitutions that have been from time to time adopted by the several States of the Union. By the Fifth Amendment, it was introduced into the Constitution of the United States as a limitation upon the powers of the national government, and by the Fourteenth, as a guaranty against any encroachment upon an acknowledged right of citizenship by the legislatures of the States.

... Under these *[police]* powers the government regulates the conduct of its citizens one towards another, and the manner in which each shall use his own property, when such regulation becomes necessary for the public good. In their exercise it has been customary in England from time immemorial, and in this country from its first colonization, to regulate ferries, common carriers, hackmen, bakers, millers, wharfingers, innkeepers, &c., and in so doing to fix a maximum of charge to be made for services rendered, accommodations furnished, and articles sold....

From this it is apparent that, down to the time of the adoption of the Fourteenth Amendment, it was not supposed that statutes regulating the use, or even the price of the use, of private property necessarily deprived an owner of his property without due process of law. Under some circumstances they may, but not under all....

... Looking, then, to the common law, from whence came the right which the Constitution protects, we find that when private property is "affected with a public interest, it ceases to be *juris privati* only."... Property does become clothed with a public interest when used in a manner to make it of public consequence, and affect the community at large. When, therefore, one devotes his property to a use in which the public has an interest, he, in effect, grants to the public an interest in that use, and must submit to be controlled by the public for the common good, to the extent of the interest he has thus created....

... It remains only to ascertain whether the warehouses of these plaintiffs in error, and the business which is carried on there, come within the operation of this principle.

For this purpose we accept as true the statements of fact contained in the elaborate brief of one of the counsel of the plaintiffs in error. From these it appears that "the great producing region of the West and North-west sends its grain by water and rail to Chicago, where the greater part of it is shipped by vessel for transportation to the seaboard by the Great Lakes, and some of it is forwarded by railway to the Eastern ports.... Vessels, to some extent, are loaded in the Chicago harbor, and sailed through the St. Lawrence directly to Europe.... The quantity [of grain] received in Chicago has made it the greatest grain market in the world. This business has created a demand for means by which the immense quantity of grain can be handled or stored, and these have been found in grain warehouses, which are commonly called elevators, because the grain is elevated from the boat or car, by machinery operated by steam, into the bins prepared for its reception, and elevated from the bins, by a like process, into the vessel or car which is to carry it on...."

... [I]t is apparent that all the elevating facilities through which these vast productions "of seven or eight great States of the West" must pass on the way "to four or five of the States on the sea-shore" may be a "virtual" monopoly.

Under such circumstances it is difficult to see why, if the common carrier, or the miller, or the ferryman, or the innkeeper, or the wharfinger, or the baker, or the cartman, or the hackney-coachman, pursues a public employment and exercises "a sort of public office," these plaintiffs in error do not.

They stand, to use again the language of their counsel, in the very "gateway of commerce," and take toll from all who pass. Their business most certainly "tends to a common charge, and is become a thing of public interest and use."... Certainly, if any business can be clothed "with a public interest, and cease to be *juris privati* only," this has been. It may not be made so by the operation of the Constitution of Illinois or this statute, but it is by the facts.

We also are not permitted to overlook the fact that, for some reason, the people of Illinois, when they revised their Constitution in 1870, saw fit to make it the duty of the general assembly to pass laws "for the protection of producers, shippers, and receivers of grain and produce," art. 13, sect. 7; ... This indicates very clearly that during the twenty years in which this peculiar business had been assuming its present "immense proportions," something had occurred which led the whole body of the people to suppose that remedies such as are usually employed to prevent abuses by virtual monopolies might not be inappropriate here.... Of the propriety of legislative interference within the scope of legislative power, the legislature is the exclusive judge....

We know that *[the police power]* is a power which may be abused; but that is no argument against its existence. For protection against abuses by legislatures the people must resort to the polls, not to the courts....

We come now to consider the effect upon this statute of the power of Congress to regulate commerce.

... The warehouses of these plaintiffs in error are situated and their business carried on exclusively within the limits of the State of Illinois.... Incidentally they may become connected with inter-state commerce, but not necessarily so. Their regulation is a thing of domestic concern, and, certainly, until Congress acts in reference to their inter-state relations, the State may exercise all the powers of government over them, even though in so doing it may indirectly operate upon commerce outside its immediate jurisdiction....

Judgment affirmed.

Mr. Justice Field and Mr. Justice Strong dissented.

Mr. Justice Field....

... [I]t would seem from its opinion that the court holds that property loses something of its private character when employed in such a way as to be generally useful....

If this be sound law, if there be no protection, either in the principles upon which our republican government is founded, or in the prohibitions of the Constitution against such invasion of private rights, all property and all business in the State are held at the mercy of a majority of its legislature. The public has no greater interest in the use of buildings for the storage of grain than it has in the use of buildings for the residences of families, nor, indeed, any thing like so great an interest; and, according to the doctrine announced, the legislature may fix the rent of all tenements used for residences, without reference to the cost of their erection.... indeed, there is hardly an enterprise or business engaging the attention and labor of any considerable portion of the community, in which the public has not an interest in the sense in which that term is used by the court in its opinion; ...

Mr. Justice Strong....

E. SUBSTANTIVE DUE PROCESS

By 1903, the Court had sustained an eight-hour day for the public sector and for certain industries in the private sector (coal mining and smelting). Over the next three decades the courts regularly invalidated legislative efforts to establish maximum hours or minimum wages — efforts the judiciary regarded as an unconstitutional interference with the "liberty of contract." Lawyers from the corporate sector helped translate the philosophy of laissez-faire into legal terms and constitutional doctrine. One of the intellectual pillars of this movement was Thomas M. Cooley, whose *Constitutional Limitations* appeared in 1868. Cooley emphasized limits on legislative authority in order to protect personal liberty and private property. Herbert Spencer's *Social Statics* (1851) counseled against government efforts to protect the weak, preferring instead a kind of Darwinian struggle for survival of the "fittest." Christopher G. Tiedeman's *Treatise on the Limitations of the Police Power* (1886) also developed the theory of laissez-faire and liberty of contract. See Benjamin R. Twiss, Lawyers and the Constitution (1942).

The climate of the years following the Civil War promoted the pursuit of material goals, especially after the heavy sacrifices demanded by the war. Elitism by corporate leaders could not be justified on tradition (feudalism) or the will of God (Calvinism). Neither belief system fitted an age devoted to materialist thinking, scientific discovery, and industrial capitalism. Justification took the form of Social Darwinism: the belief in ruthless individualism in which only the strongest were entitled to survive. Material success became the overriding value. The American Bar Association, founded in 1878, campaigned to limit legislative interference with property rights. The specter of "socialism" and "communism" gave added force and urgency to these efforts.

The *Lochner* Era

Judicial tolerance of the police power came to an abrupt halt in 1905 when the Supreme Court invalidated a New York law limiting bakery workers to sixty hours a week or ten hours a day. Justice Peckham, writing for a 5 to 4 majority, converted the general right to make a contract into laissez-faire rigidity. He found no "reasonable ground" to interfere with the liberty of a person to contract for as many hours of work as desired. LOCHNER v. NEW YORK, 198 U.S. 45, 57 (1905). The statute seemed to him to serve no purpose in safeguarding public health or the health of the worker. Such laws were "mere meddlesome interferences" with the rights of an individual to enter into contracts. Lawyers who opposed the law argued that it was not a health measure but rather "a labor law" to promote paternalism.

In their dissent, Justices Harlan, White, and Day reviewed previous holdings of the Court that had interpreted the police power generously to support economic regulation. They cited statistical studies to show the need for remedial legislation. Peckham's opinion was so flavored with conservative business doctrines that Justice Holmes, in his dissent, accused the majority of deciding "upon an economic theory which a large part of the country does not entertain." The Constitution, he said, is "not intended to embody a particular economic theory, whether of paternalism and the organic relation of the citizen to the state or of *laissez faire*." The doctrine of laissez-faire never meant a pure free market. Corporations were busily involved in forming pools, trusts, "community of interests," and other devices to protect themselves from competition. The marketplace of many competing units was becoming a relic of the past.

Sociological Data

The Court equivocated on the principle of laissez-faire. In 1908 it struck down a congressional statute that made it unlawful for the railroads to fire workers because of their union membership. A 6–2 decision maintained the fiction of *Lochner* that the employer and employee had "equality of right" to enter into a contract, "and any legislation that disturbs that equality is an arbitrary interference with the liberty of contract over which no government can legally justify in a free land." Adair v. United States, 208 U.S. 161, 175 (1908). See also Coppage v. Kansas, 236 U.S. 1 (1915).

Also in 1908, however, the Court sustained Oregon's ten-hour day for women. The statistical record referred to by the dissenters in *Lochner* supplied a good tactical clue for Louis D. Brandeis, who argued the case for Oregon. His sister-in-law, Josephine Goldmark, was closely associated with the National Consumers' League, which had long advocated improved working conditions. She supervised an intensive search of library holdings and helped produce a brief of 113 pages, almost all of which consisted of copious data extracted from sociological studies supporting the need for limiting working hours for women. The Court called attention to what is now known as the "Brandeis brief": a compilation of state and foreign statutes that imposed restrictions on the hours of labor required of women, followed by extracts from more than 90 reports of committees, bureaus of statistics, commissioners of hygiene, and inspectors of factories. These studies, drawn primarily from Europe, concluded that long hours of labor "are dangerous for women, primarily because of their special physical organization." Muller v. Oregon, 208 U.S. 412, 419–20 n.1 (1908).

Could the constitutional principle announced in *Lochner* be displaced by public opinion and sociological data? The Court indulged in a bit of judicial doubletalk:

> The legislation and opinions referred to in the margin may not be, technically speaking, authorities, and in them is little or no discussion of the constitutional question presented to us for determination, yet they are significant of a widespread belief that woman's physical structure, and the functions she performs in consequence thereof, justify special legislation restricting or qualifying the conditions under which she should be permitted to toil. Constitutional questions, it is true, are not settled by even a consensus of present public opinion, for it is the peculiar value of a written constitution that it places in unchanging form limitations upon legislative action, and thus gives a permanence and stability to popular government which otherwise would be lacking. At the same time, when a question of fact is debated and debatable, and the extent to which a special constitutional limitation goes is affected by the truth in respect to that fact, a widespread and long continued belief concerning it is worthy of consideration. We take judicial cognizance of all matters of general knowledge.[8]

"Liberty of contract" did not prevent the Court in 1911 from unanimously upholding an Iowa statute that prohibited certain contracts by railroad companies, or delivering another unanimous opinion three years later to sustain a New York law requiring certain industries to pay employees semimonthly and in cash. Chicago, Burlington & Quincy R.R. Co. v. McGuire, 219 U.S. 543 (1911) and

---

8. Muller v. Oregon, 208 U.S. 412, 420–21 (1908). For unanimous rulings that upheld other state statutes setting maximum hours for women, see Bosley v. McLaughlin, 236 U.S. 385 (1915); Miller v. Wilson, 236 U.S. 373 (1915); and Riley v. Massachusetts, 232 U.S. 671 (1914). A 5–4 Court upheld a congressional statute setting an eight-hour day for railroad workers engaged in interstate commerce; Wilson v. New, 243 U.S. 332 (1917).

Erie R.R. Co. v. Williams, 233 U.S. 685 (1914). Rent-control laws were also upheld, preventing a landlord from freely contracting with his or her tenants. Block v. Hirsh, 256 U.S. 135 (1921).

In 1917, the Court upheld the constitutionality of Oregon's ten-hour day for men and women, including a provision for overtime pay. Brandeis was now on the Court as an Associate Justice. Because of his previous involvement in litigating this type of case, he did not participate in the decision. Felix Frankfurter of the Harvard Law School argued the case for Oregon and prepared a "Brandeis brief" that contained an array of facts and statistics to demonstrate the effects of overtime on the physical and moral health of the worker. His brief reviewed industrial conditions and labor experiences in England and the United States. A 5–3 Court sustained the statute. Bunting v. Oregon, 243 U.S. 426 (1917).

Frankfurter was again lead counsel in defending a congressional statute that provided for minimum wages for women and children in the District of Columbia. Despite his lengthy sociological brief, the Court held the statute invalid. Writing for a 5–3 majority, Justice Sutherland found the mass of data compiled by Frankfurter "interesting but only mildly persuasive." ADKINS v. CHILDREN'S HOSPITAL, 261 U.S. 525, 560 (1923). Because of progress in contractual, political, and civil status of women since the *Muller* decision of 1908, Sutherland said that the continuation of protective legislation could not be justified. Although the Court had sustained statutes setting maximum hours, the minimum wage law seemed dangerous territory to the majority. What was next, Sutherland asked, maximum wages? In one of the dissents, Chief Justice Taft thought that the line drawn between hours and wages was imaginary. Justice Holmes's dissent described how the phrase "due process of law" had evolved into the "dogma, Liberty of Contract."

The Great Depression

Between 1923 and 1934, the Court repeatedly struck down statutes on the ground that the activity regulated was not "affected with a public interest."[9] At the same time, new areas of economic life were becoming national in scope and gradually brought within Congress' power over interstate commerce (see Chapter 8). Finally, the onset of the Great Depression of 1929 shattered the theory of a self-correcting free economy.

The philosophy of *Adkins* survived as late as 1936, although a decision that year striking down New York's minimum wage law for women and children could muster only a 5–4 majority. "Freedom of contract," said the Court, "is the general rule and restraint the exception." Morehead v. N.Y. ex rel. Tipaldo, 298 U.S. 587, 610–11 (1936). Chief Justice Hughes dissented, joined by Brandeis, Stone, and Cardozo. Stone, in a separate dissent, criticized the basis on which the majority had declared the New York law invalid: "It is difficult to imagine any grounds, other than our own personal economic predilections, for saying that the contract of employment is any the less an appropriate subject of legislation than are scores of others, in dealing with which this Court has held that legislatures may curtail individual freedom in the public interest." Stone emphasized the changes that had occurred in economic conditions: "In the years that have intervened since the *Adkins* case we have had opportunity to learn that a wage is not always the resultant of free bargaining between employers and employees; that it may be one forced upon employees by their economic necessities and upon employers by the most ruthless of their competitors.... Because of their nature and extent these are public problems. A generation ago they were for the individual to solve; today they are the burden of the nation."

Liberty-of-Contract Doctrine Abandoned

Adkins was finally overruled in 1937. Sutherland, Van Devanter, McReynolds, and Butler, who had provided four of the majority votes in *Morehead*, dissented. Roberts, the fifth member of that ma-

---

9. New State Ice Co. v. Liebmann, 285 U.S. 262 (1932); Williams v. Standard Oil Co., 278 U.S. 235 (1929); Ribnik v. McBride, 277 U.S. 350 (1928); Tyson & Brother v. Banton, 273 U.S. 418 (1927); Wolff Co. v. Industrial Court, 262 U.S. 522 (1923).

Political Reaction to *West Coast Hotel*

The effect of this decision was far-reaching in law and in economics, but its immediate repercussions were political. The Administration forces had to like the decision, for it was what they had long contended the law to be. It stimulated the movement in both state and nation to "put a floor under wages" and a "ceiling over hours," and a law to prescribe minimum wages and maximum hours in interstate commerce was soon proposed to Congress. But the liberals had a good deal to say about judicial strangling for fifteen years of such legislation in both state and nation by what was now conceded to be a blunder of the Court....

The conservatives liked the decision. They knew the former one [*Adkins*] took ground too reactionary to be held. The timing of the yielding was a boon to them. It removed a great deal of pressure for reform of the Court, and they made much of the argument that the Court did not need reforming, but could and would reform itself. At any rate the Court had made a bold turn in direction. The doctrine of "freedom of contract," which had menaced all types of legislation to regulate the master and servant relation, had been uprooted so definitely that it could hardly be expected to thrive again. Labor was free from the shackles of a fictitious freedom.

SOURCE: Robert H. Jackson, The Struggle for Judicial Supremacy 211–12 (1941).

jority, now joined the four dissenters from *Morehead* to uphold a minimum wage law for women and minors in the state of Washington. WEST COAST HOTEL CO. v. PARRISH, 300 U.S. 379 (1937). Since the Washington case was decided about two months after President Franklin D. Roosevelt had unveiled his court-packing plan (see the section on the court-packing plan in the concluding chapter), much has been made of Roberts's "switch in time that saved nine." However, Roberts had already broken with his doctrinaire laissez-faire colleagues. He wrote the 5–4 opinion in *Nebbia* v. *New York*, 291 U.S. 502 (1934), which upheld a price-setting statute. With his support, the Court was prepared to sustain minimum wage legislation in the fall of 1936 but had delayed its ruling because Justice Stone was ill.[10]

Justice Sutherland, speaking for the four dissenters in *West Coast Hotel*, assailed the theory that decisions of the Supreme Court should be reconsidered because of economic conditions: "the meaning of the Constitution does not change with the ebb and flow of economic events." His phrase "ebb and flow" suggests a seasonal if not spasmodic quality, which seems offensive to a constitution grounded on fundamental principles. However, the record of the Court on economic regulation was decidedly one of ebb and flow. Over a period of about four decades, the Court had tried to impose a liberty-of-contract theory at a time when power was shifting dramatically from the employee to the employer. A countervailing force was needed, and the elected branches intervened to redress the imbalance. Liberals welcomed the decision in *West Coast Hotel* as did conservatives, because it averted a serious threat to the Court's independence and prestige (see box).

By 1941 the composition of the Court had been radically altered, especially with Reed, Murphy, and Black replacing Sutherland, Butler, and Van Devanter. A unanimous Court that year upheld a congressional statute setting minimum wages and maximum hours for men and women. The statute was within the power of Congress to regulate interstate commerce and to protect public health, morals, and welfare. No conflict was found with the due process of law or with the rights of states

10. Felix Frankfurter, "Mr. Justice Roberts," 104 U. Pa. L. Rev. 311 (1955); 2 Merlo J. Pusey, Charles Evans Hughes 757 (1963). For a challenge to Roberts' recollection of key events in 1936, see Clement E. Vose, Constitutional Change 228–34 (1972). See also Marian C. McKenna, Franklin Roosevelt and the Great Constitutional War 418–19, 422–23, 435–37, 536 (2002).

under the Tenth Amendment. United States v. Darby, 312 U.S. 100 (1941). Another unanimous decision in 1941 overruled the laissez-faire doctrine of *Ribnik* v. *McBride.* Olsen v. Nebraska, 313 U.S. 236 (1941). A combination of social, economic, and political forces had finally reversed the constitutional doctrines of the Court. In the future, decisions about economic or social philosophy would be left largely to legislatures, not to the courts. FERGUSON v. SKRUPA, 372 U.S. 726 (1963). See also Williamson v. Lee Optical Co., 348 U.S. 483, 488 (1955) and Day-Brite Lighting, Inc. v. Missouri, 342 U.S. 421 (1952).

Lochner v. New York

198 U.S. 45 (1905)

New York passed a law prohibiting employees from working in bakeries more than 60 hours a week or ten hours a day. The statute, sustained by the state courts, was similar to other labor laws passed by states to protect workers from industrial conditions that threatened health and safety. The case represented a conflict between two values: the police power of the state to regulate economic activities versus the "liberty" protected by the Fourteenth Amendment to contract without unreasonable interference by the state. Joseph Lochner, a bakery owner, claimed that the New York law violated the U.S. Constitution.

MR. JUSTICE PECKHAM, after making the foregoing statement of the facts, delivered the opinion of the court.

The indictment, it will be seen, charges that the plaintiff in error violated the one hundred and tenth section of article 8, chapter 415, of the Laws of 1897, known as the labor law of the State of New York, in that he wrongfully and unlawfully required and permitted an employé working for him to work more than sixty hours in one week.... The mandate of the statute that "no employé shall be required or permitted to work," is the substantial equivalent of an enactment that "no employé shall contract or agree to work," more than ten hours per day, and as there is no provision for special emergencies the statute is mandatory in all cases. It is not an act merely fixing the number of hours which shall constitute a legal day's work, but an absolute prohibition upon the employer, permitting, under any circumstances, more than ten hours work to be done in his establishment. The employé may desire to earn the extra money, which would arise from his working more than the prescribed time, but this statute forbids the employer from permitting the employé to earn it.

The statute necessarily interferes with the right of contract between the employer and employés, concerning the number of hours in which the latter may labor in the bakery of the employer. The general right to make a contract in relation to his business is part of the liberty of the individual protected by the Fourteenth Amendment of the Federal Constitution. *Allgeyer* v. *Louisiana,* 165 U.S. 578. Under that provision no State can deprive any person of life, liberty or property without due process of law. The right to purchase or to sell labor is part of the liberty protected by this amendment, unless there are circumstances which exclude the right. There are, however, certain powers, existing in the sovereignty of each State in the Union, somewhat vaguely termed police powers, the exact description and limitation of which have not been attempted by the courts. Those powers, broadly stated and without, at present, any attempt at a more specific limitation, relate to the safety, health, morals and general welfare of the public....

The State, therefore, has power to prevent the individual from making certain kinds of contracts, and in regard to them the Federal Constitution offers no protection. If the contract be one which the State, in the legitimate exercise of its police power, has the right to prohibit, it is not prevented from prohibiting it by the Fourteenth Amendment. Contracts in violation of a statute, either of the Federal or state government, or a contract to let one's property for immoral purposes, or to do any other unlawful act, could obtain no protection from the Federal Constitution, as coming under the liberty of person or of free contract....

It must, of course, be conceded that there is a limit to the valid exercise of the police power by the State. There is no dispute concerning this general proposition. Otherwise the Fourteenth Amendment would have no efficacy and the legislatures of the States would have unbounded power, and it would be enough to say that any piece of legislation was enacted to conserve the morals, the health or the safety of the people; such legislation would be valid, no matter how absolutely without foundation the claim might be. The claim of the police power would be a mere pretext—become another and delusive name for the supreme sovereignty of the State to be exercised free from constitutional restraint. This is not contended for. In every case that comes before this court, therefore, where legislation of this character is concerned and where the protection of the Federal Constitution is sought, the question necessarily arises: Is this a fair, reasonable and appropriate exercise of the police power of the State, or is it an unreasonable, unnecessary and arbitrary interference with the right of the individual to his personal liberty or to enter into those contracts in relation to labor which may seem to him appropriate or necessary for the support of himself and his family? Of course the liberty of contract relating to labor includes both parties to it. The one has as much right to purchase as the other to sell labor.

This is not a question of substituting the judgment of the court for that of the legislature. If the act be within the power of the State it is valid, although the judgment of the court might be totally opposed to the enactment of such a law. But the question would still remain: Is it within the police power of the State? and that question must be answered by the court.

The question whether this act is valid as a labor law, pure and simple, may be dismissed in a few words. There is no reasonable ground for interfering with the liberty of person or the right of free contract, by determining the hours of labor, in the occupation of a baker. There is no contention that bakers as a class are not equal in intelligence and capacity to men in other trades or manual occupations, or that they are not able to assert their rights and care for themselves without the protecting arm of the State, interfering with their independence of judgment and of action. They are in no sense wards of the State. Viewed in the light of a purely labor law, with no reference whatever to the question of health, we think that a law like the one before us involves neither the safety, the morals nor the welfare of the public, and that the interest of the public is not in the slightest degree affected by such an act. The law must be upheld, if at all, as a law pertaining to the health of the individual engaged in the occupation of a baker. It does not affect any other portion of the public than those who are engaged in that occupation. Clean and wholesome bread does not depend upon whether the baker works but ten hours per day or only sixty hours a week....

· · ·

We think that there can be no fair doubt that the trade of a baker, in and of itself, is not an unhealthy one to that degree which would authorize the legislature to interfere with the right to labor, and with the right of free contract on the part of the individual, either as employer or employé. In looking through statistics regarding all trades and occupations, it may be true that the trade of a baker does not appear to be as healthy as some other trades, and is also vastly more healthy than still others. To the common understanding the trade of a baker has never been regarded as an unhealthy one....

... The act is not, within any fair meaning of the term, a health law, but is an illegal interference with the rights of individuals, both employers and employés, to make contracts regarding labor upon such terms as they may think best, or which they may agree upon with the other parties to such contracts. Statutes of the nature of that under review, limiting the hours in which grown and intelligent men may labor to earn their living, are mere meddlesome interferences with the rights of the individual, and they are not saved from condemnation by the claim that they are passed in the exercise of the police power....

Mr. Justice Harlan, with whom Mr. Justice White and Mr. Justice Day concurred, dissenting.

... Whether or not this be wise legislation it is not the province of the court to inquire. Under our systems of government the courts are not concerned with the wisdom or policy of legislation.... I submit that this court will transcend its functions if it assumes to annul the statute of New York. [*Justice Harlan summarizes a number of studies that describe the health hazards of working in a bakery, including the inhalation of flour dust that causes inflammation of the lungs and the bronchial tubes.*]

Mr. Justice Holmes dissenting.

· · ·

This case is decided upon an economic theory which a large part of the country does not entertain. If it were a question whether I agreed with that theory, I should desire to study it further and long before making up my mind. But I do not conceive that to be my duty, because I strongly believe that my agreement or disagreement has nothing to do with the right of a majority to embody their opinions in law. It is settled by various decisions of this court that state constitutions and state laws may regulate life in many ways which we as legislators might think as injudicious or if you like as tyrannical as this, and which equally with this interfere with the liberty to contract. Sunday laws and usury laws are ancient examples. A more modern one is the prohibition of lotteries. The liberty of the citizen to do as he likes so long as he does not interfere with the liberty of others to do the same, which has been a shibboleth for some well-known writers, is interfered with by school laws, by the Post Office, by every state or municipal institution which takes his money for purposes thought desirable, whether he likes it or not. The Fourteenth Amendment does not enact Mr. Herbert Spencer's Social Statics. The other day we sustained the Massachusetts vaccination law. *Jacobson* v. *Massachusetts*, 197 U.S. 11. United States and state statutes and decisions cutting down the liberty to contract by way of combination are familiar to this court. *Northern Securities Co.* v. *United States*, 193 U.S. 197. Two years ago we upheld the prohibition of sales of stock on margins or for future delivery in the constitution of California. *Otis* v. *Parker*, 187 U.S. 606. The decision sustaining an eight hour law for miners is still recent. *Holden* v. *Hardy*, 169 U.S. 366. Some of these laws embody convictions or prejudices which judges are likely to share. Some may not. But a constitution is not intended to em-

body a particular economic theory, whether of paternalism and the organic relation of the citizen to the State or of *laissez faire*. It is made for people of fundamentally differing views, and the accident of our finding certain opinions natural and familiar or novel and even shocking ought not to conclude our judgment upon the question whether statutes embodying them conflict with the Constitution of the United States.

... I think that the word liberty in the Fourteenth Amendment is perverted when it is held to prevent the natural outcome of a dominant opinion, unless it can be said that a rational and fair man necessarily would admit that the statute proposed would infringe fundamental principles as they have been understood by the traditions of our people and our law. It does not need research to show that no such sweeping condemnation can be passed upon the statute before us. A reasonable man might think it a proper measure on the score of health. Men whom I certainly could not pronounce unreasonable would uphold it as a first instalment of a general regulation of the hours of work. Whether in the latter aspect it would be open to the charge of inequality I think it unnecessary to discuss.

Adkins v. Children's Hospital

261 U.S. 525 (1923)

In 1918, Congress passed a law setting minimum wages for women and children in the District of Columbia. As in other cases, the question was one of balancing the police power of Congress to regulate health and safety with the right of individuals to conduct their own affairs without legislative interference. Children's Hospital and a female elevator operator at a hotel brought this case to prevent enforcement of the act by Jesse C. Adkins and the two other members of a wage board.

MR. JUSTICE SUTHERLAND delivered the opinion of the Court.

The question presented for determination by these appeals is the constitutionality of the Act of September 19, 1918, providing for the fixing of minimum wages for women and children in the District of Columbia. 40 Stat. 960, c. 174. *[The act authorized a three-member wage board to investigate wages for women and minors and to order changes in wages after giving public notice and holding a public hearing. Questions of fact determined by the board could not be appealed.]*

The statute now under consideration is attacked upon the ground that it authorizes an unconstitutional interference with the freedom of contract included within the guaranties of the due process

clause of the Fifth Amendment. That the right to contract about one's affairs is a part of the liberty of the individual protected by this clause, is settled by the decisions of this Court and is no longer open to question.... Within this liberty are contracts of employment of labor: In making such contracts, generally speaking, the parties have an equal right to obtain from each other the best terms they can as the result of private bargaining.

... But freedom of contract is, nevertheless, the general rule and restraint the exception; and the exercise of legislative authority to abridge it can be justified only by the existence of exceptional circumstances. *[Justice Sutherland reviews cases in which the Court upheld statutes fixing rates and charges to be exacted on businesses impressed with a public interest;*

statutes relating to contracts for the performance of public work; statutes prescribing the character, methods, and time for payment of wages; and statutes fixing hours of labor.]

In the *Muller Case* the validity of an Oregon statute, forbidding the employment of any female in certain industries more than ten hours during any one day was upheld. The decision proceeded upon the theory that the difference between the sexes may justify a different rule respecting hours of labor in the case of women than in the case of men. It is pointed out that these consist in differences of physical structure, especially in respect of the maternal functions, and also in the fact that historically woman has always been dependent upon man, who has established his control by superior physical strength.... In view of the great—not to say revolutionary—changes which have taken place since that utterance, in the contractual, political and civil status of women, culminating in the Nineteenth Amendment, it is not unreasonable to say that these differences have now come almost, if not quite, to the vanishing point. In this aspect of the matter, while the physical differences must be recognized in appropriate cases, and legislation fixing hours or conditions of work may properly take them into account, we cannot accept the doctrine that women of mature age, *sui juris,* require or may be subjected to restrictions upon their liberty of contract which could not lawfully be imposed in the case of men under similar circumstances....

If now, in the light furnished by the foregoing exceptions to the general rule forbidding legislative interference with freedom of contract, we examine and analyze the statute in question, we shall see that it differs from them in every material respect. It is not a law dealing with any business charged with a public interest or with public work, or to meet and tide over a temporary emergency. It has nothing to do with the character, methods or periods of wage payments. It does not prescribe hours of labor or conditions under which labor is to be done. It is not for the protection of persons under legal disability or for the prevention of fraud. It is simply and exclusively a price-fixing law, confined to adult women (for we are not now considering the provisions relating to minors), who are legally as capable of contracting for themselves as men....

The standard furnished by the statute for the guidance of the board is so vague as to be impossible of practical application with any reasonable degree of accuracy. What is sufficient to supply the necessary cost of living for a woman worker and maintain her in good health and protect her morals is obviously not a precise or unvarying sum—not even approximately so. The amount will depend upon a variety of circumstances: the individual temperament, habits of thrift, care, ability to buy necessaries intelligently, and whether the woman live alone or with her family. To those who practice economy, a given sum will afford comfort, while to those of contrary habit the same sum will be wholly inadequate.... The relation between earnings and morals is not capable of standardization. It cannot be shown that well paid women safeguard their morals more carefully than those who are poorly paid....

It is said that great benefits have resulted from the operation of such statutes, not alone in the District of Columbia but in the several States, where they have been in force. A mass of reports, opinions of special observers and students of the subject, and the like, has been brought before us in support of this statement, all of which we have found interesting but only mildly persuasive....

Finally, it may be said that if, in the interest of the public welfare, the police power may be invoked to justify the fixing of a minimum wage, it may, when the public welfare is thought to require it, be invoked to justify a maximum wage. The power to fix high wages connotes, by like course of reasoning, the power to fix low wages. If, in the face of the guaranties of the Fifth Amendment, this form of legislation shall be legally justified, the field for the operation of the police power will have been widened to a great and dangerous degree....

It follows from what has been said that the act in question passes the limit prescribed by the Constitution, and, accordingly, the decrees of the court below are

Affirmed.

Mr. Justice Brandeis took no part in the consideration or decision of these cases.

Mr. Chief Justice Taft, dissenting.

. . .

Legislatures in limiting freedom of contract between employee and employer by a minimum wage proceed on the assumption that employees, in the class receiving least pay, are not upon a full level of equality of choice with their employer and in their necessitous circumstances are prone to accept pretty much anything that is offered. They are peculiarly subject to the overreaching of the harsh and greedy employer. The evils of the sweating system and of the long hours and low wages which are characteristic of it are well known. Now, I agree that it is a disputable question in the field of political economy how far a statutory requirement of maximum hours or minimum wages may be a useful remedy for these evils, and whether it may not make the case of the oppressed employee worse than it was before. But it is not the function of this Court to hold congressional acts invalid simply because they are passed to carry out economic views which the Court believes to be unwise or unsound. [Chief Justice Taft cites earlier cases in which the Court upheld legislation setting maximum hours.]

... I assume that the conclusion in this case rests on the distinction between a minimum of wages and a maximum of hours in the limiting of liberty to contract. I regret to be at variance with the Court as to the substance of this distinction. In absolute freedom of contract the one term is as important as the other, for both enter equally into the consideration given and received, a restriction as to one is not any greater in essence than the other, and is of the same kind. One is the multiplier and the other the multiplicand.

If it be said that long hours of labor have a more direct effect upon the health of the employee than the low wage, there is very respectable authority from close observers, disclosed in the record and in the literature on the subject quoted at length in the briefs, that they are equally harmful in this regard. Congress took this view and we can not say it was not warranted in so doing....

I am not sure from a reading of the opinion whether the Court thinks the authority of *Muller* v. *Oregon* is shaken by the adoption of the Nineteenth Amendment. The Nineteenth Amendment did not change the physical strength or limitations of women upon which the decision in *Muller* v. *Oregon* rests....

I am authorized to say that MR. JUSTICE SANFORD concurs in this opinion.

MR. JUSTICE HOLMES, dissenting.

The question in this case is the broad one, Whether Congress can establish minimum rates of wages for women in the District of Columbia with due provision for special circumstances, or whether we must say that Congress has no power to meddle with the matter at all.... When so many intelligent persons, who have studied the matter more than any of us can, have thought that the means are effective and are worth the price, it seems to me impossible to deny that the belief reasonably may be held by reasonable men....

The earlier decisions upon the same words in the Fourteenth Amendment began within our memory and went no farther than an unpretentious assertion of the liberty to follow the ordinary callings. Later that innocuous generality was expanded into the dogma, Liberty of Contract. Contract is not specially mentioned in the text that we have to construe. It is merely an example of doing what you want to do, embodied in the word liberty. But pretty much all law consists in forbidding men to do some things that they want to do, and contract is no more exempt from law than other acts....

I confess that I do not understand the principle on which the power to fix a minimum for the wages of women can be denied by those who admit the power to fix a maximum for their hours of work. I fully assent to the proposition that here as elsewhere the distinctions of the law are distinctions of degree, but I perceive no difference in the kind or degree of interference with liberty, the only matter with which we have any concern, between the one case and the other. The bargain is equally affected whichever half you regulate. *Muller* v. *Oregon*, I take it, is as good law today as it was in 1908. It will need more than the Nineteenth Amendment to convince me that there are no differences between men and women, or that legislation cannot take those differences into account....

West Coast Hotel Co. v. Parrish

300 U.S. 379 (1937)

This case overruled *Adkins* v. *Children's Hospital* (1923) and, with it, the doctrine that courts can continually second-guess legislative judgments about the need for statutes governing minimum wages, maximum hours, and other aspects of industrial working conditions. Similarly, this case rejects the exalted notion of "liberty of contract," which presupposed an equality of power between employer and employee to work out a mutually satisfactory contract. The issue before the Court in this case was a statute of the state of Washington providing for the establishment of minimum wages for women. Elsie Parrish, an employee of the West Coast Hotel Company, sued to recover wages owed her under the state law.

MR. CHIEF JUSTICE HUGHES delivered the opinion of the Court.

· · ·

The appellant relies upon the decision of this Court in *Adkins* v. *Children's Hospital*, 261 U.S. 525, which held invalid the District of Columbia Minimum Wage Act, which was attacked under the due process clause of the Fifth Amendment....

... The Supreme Court of Washington has upheld the minimum wage statute of that State. It has decided that the statute is a reasonable exercise of the police power of the State. In reaching that conclusion the state court has invoked principles long established by this Court in the application of the Fourteenth Amendment. The state court has refused to regard the decision in the *Adkins* case as determinative and has pointed to our decisions both before and since that case as justifying its position. We are of the opinion that this ruling of the state court demands on our part a reëxamination of the *Adkins* case. The importance of the question, in which many States having similar laws are concerned, the close division by which the decision in the *Adkins* case was reached, and the economic conditions which have supervened, and in the light of which the reasonableness of the exercise of the protective power of the State must be considered, make it not only appropriate, but we think imperative, that in deciding the present case the subject should receive fresh consideration.

· · ·

The principle which must control our decision is not in doubt. The constitutional provision invoked is the due process clause of the Fourteenth Amendment governing the States, as the due process clause invoked in the *Adkins* case governed Congress. In each case the violation alleged by those attacking minimum wage regulation for women is deprivation of freedom of contract. What is this freedom? The Constitution does not speak of freedom of contract. It speaks of liberty and prohibits the deprivation of liberty without due process of law. In prohibiting that deprivation the Constitution does not recognize an absolute and uncontrollable liberty. Liberty in each of its phases has its history and connotation. But the liberty safeguarded is liberty in a social organization which requires the protection of law against the evils which menace the health, safety, morals and welfare of the people. Liberty under the Constitution is thus necessarily subject to the restraints of due process, and regulation which is reasonable in relation to its subject and is adopted in the interests of the community is due process....

The point that has been strongly stressed that adult employees should be deemed competent to make their own contracts was decisively met nearly forty years ago in *Holden* v. *Hardy, supra*, where we pointed out the inequality in the footing of the parties....

· · ·

It is manifest that this established principle is peculiarly applicable in relation to the employment of women in whose protection the State has a special interest. That phase of the subject received elaborate consideration in *Muller* v. *Oregon* (1908), 208 U.S. 412, where the constitutional authority of the State to limit the working hours of women was sustained. *[After reviewing the dissents of Justice Holmes and Chief Justice Taft in* Adkins, *and citing cases after* Adkins *that upheld state statutes on economic regulation, the Court concludes:]*

With full recognition of the earnestness and vigor which characterize the prevailing opinion in the *Adkins* case, we find it impossible to reconcile that ruling with these well-considered declarations. What can be closer to the public interest than the health of women and their protection from unscrupulous and overreaching employers? And if the protection of women is a legitimate end of the exercise of state power, how can it be said that the requirement of the payment of a minimum wage fairly fixed in order to meet the very necessities of existence is not an admissible means to that end? The legislature of the State was clearly entitled to consider the situation of women in employment, the fact that they are in the class receiving the least pay, that their bargaining power is relatively weak, and that they are the ready victims of those who would take advantage of their necessitous circumstances....

... We may take judicial notice of the unparalleled demands for relief which arose during the recent period of depression and still continue to an alarming extent despite the degree of economic recovery which has been achieved.... The community is not bound to provide what is in effect a subsidy for unconscionable employers....

Our conclusion is that the case of *Adkins* v. *Children's Hospital, supra,* should be, and it is, overruled. The judgment of the Supreme Court of the State of Washington is

Affirmed.

MR. JUSTICE SUTHERLAND, dissenting:

MR. JUSTICE VAN DEVANTER, MR. JUSTICE MCREYNOLDS, MR. JUSTICE BUTLER and I think the judgment of the court below should be reversed.

. . .

The suggestion that the only check upon the exercise of the judicial power, when properly invoked, to declare a constitutional right superior to an unconstitutional statute is the judge's own faculty of self-restraint, is both ill considered and mischievous. Self-restraint belongs in the domain of will and not of judgment. The check upon the judge is that imposed by his oath of office, by the Constitution and by his own conscientious and informed convictions; and since he has the duty to make up his own mind and adjudge accordingly, it is hard to see how there could be any other restraint....

It is urged that the question involved should now receive fresh consideration, among other reasons, because of "the economic conditions which have supervened"; but the meaning of the Constitution does not change with the ebb and flow of economic events. We frequently are told in more general words that the Constitution must be construed in the light of the present. If by that it is meant that the Constitution is made up of living words that apply to every new condition which they include, the statement is quite true. But to say, if that be intended, that the words of the Constitution mean today what they did not mean when written — that is, that they do not apply to a situation now to which they would have applied then — is to rob that instrument of the essential element which continues it in force as the people have made it until they, and not their official agents, have made it otherwise.

... Women today stand upon a legal and political equality with men. There is no longer any reason why they should be put in different classes in respect of their legal right to make contracts; nor should they be denied, in effect, the right to compete with men for work paying lower wages which men may be willing to accept. And it is an arbitrary exercise of the legislative power to do so....

Ferguson v. Skrupa

372 U.S. 726 (1963)

For a period of about four or five decades, ending in 1937, the Supreme Court overturned dozens of statutes enacted by Congress and state legislatures to ameliorate the conditions of industrialization. Laws establishing minimum wages and maximum hours, regulating child labor, and governing other aspects of industrial society were struck down. In this decision, the Court explains that such matters in the future will be left essentially to legislatures, not courts. Frank C. Skrupa, in the business of "debt adjusting," brought this action against the Attorney General of Kansas, William M. Ferguson.

MR. JUSTICE BLACK delivered the opinion of the Court.

In this case, properly here on appeal under 28 U.S.C. § 1253, we are asked to review the judgment of a three-judge District Court enjoining, as being in violation of the Due Process Clause of the Fourteenth Amendment, a Kansas statute making it a misdemeanor for any person to engage "in the business of debt adjusting" except as an incident to "the lawful practice of law in this state." The statute defines "debt adjusting" as "the making of a contract, express or implied, with a particular debtor whereby the debtor agrees to pay a certain amount of money periodically to the person engaged in the debt ad-

justing business who shall for a consideration distribute the same among certain specified creditors in accordance with a plan agreed upon."

The complaint, filed by appellee Skrupa doing business as "Credit Advisors," alleged that Skrupa was engaged in the business of "debt adjusting" as defined by the statute, that his business was a "useful and desirable" one, that his business activities were not "inherently immoral or dangerous" or in any way contrary to the public welfare, and that therefore the business could not be "absolutely prohibited" by Kansas. The three-judge court heard evidence by Skrupa tending to show the usefulness and desirability of his business and evidence by the state officials tending to show that "debt adjusting" lends itself to grave abuses against distressed debtors, particularly in the lower income brackets, and that these abuses are of such gravity that a number of States have strictly regulated "debt adjusting" or prohibited it altogether....

The only case discussed by the court below as support for its invalidation of the statute was *Commonwealth* v. *Stone,* 191 Pa. Super. 117, 155 A.2d 453 (1959), in which the Superior Court of Pennsylvania struck down a statute almost identical to the Kansas act involved here.... [T]he Pennsylvania court relied heavily on *Adams* v. *Tanner,* 244 U.S. 590 (1917), which held that the Due Process Clause forbids a State to prohibit a business which is "useful" and not "inherently immoral or dangerous to public welfare."

Both the District Court in the present case and the Pennsylvania court in *Stone* adopted the philosophy of *Adams* v. *Tanner,* and cases like it, that it is the province of courts to draw on their own views as to the morality, legitimacy, and usefulness of a particular business in order to decide whether a statute bears too heavily upon that business and by so doing violates due process. Under the system of government created by our Constitution, it is up to legislatures, not courts, to decide on the wisdom and utility of legislation. There was a time when the Due Process Clause was used by this Court to strike down laws which were thought unreasonable, that is, unwise or incompatible with some particular economic or social philosophy. In this manner the Due Process Clause was used, for example, to nullify laws prescribing maximum hours for work in bakeries, *Lochner* v. *New York,* 198 U.S. 45 (1905), outlawing "yellow dog" contracts, *Coppage* v. *Kansas,* 236 U.S. 1 (1915), setting minimum wages for women, *Adkins* v. *Children's Hospital,* 261 U.S. 525 (1923), and fixing the weight of loaves of bread, *Jay Burns Baking Co.* v. *Bryan,* 264 U.S. 504 (1924). This intrusion by the judiciary into the realm of legislative value judgments was strongly objected to at the time, particularly by Mr. Justice Holmes and Mr. Justice Brandeis....

The doctrine that prevailed in *Lochner, Coppage, Adkins, Burns,* and like cases—that due process authorizes courts to hold laws unconstitutional when they believe the legislature has acted unwisely—has long since been discarded. We have returned to the original constitutional proposition that courts do not substitute their social and economic beliefs for the judgment of legislative bodies, who are elected to pass laws....

... We conclude that the Kansas Legislature was free to decide for itself that legislation was needed to deal with the business of debt adjusting. Unquestionably, there are arguments showing that the business of debt adjusting has social utility, but such arguments are properly addressed to the legislature, not to us. We refuse to sit as a "superlegislature to weigh the wisdom of legislation," and we emphatically refuse to go back to the time when courts used the Due Process Clause "to strike down state laws, regulatory of business and industrial conditions, because they may be unwise, improvident, or out of harmony with a particular school of thought." Nor are we able or willing to draw lines by calling a law "prohibitory" or "regulatory." Whether the legislature takes for its textbook Adam Smith, Herbert Spencer, Lord Keynes, or some other is no concern of ours. The Kansas debt adjusting statute may be wise or unwise. But relief, if any be needed, lies not with us but with the body constituted to pass laws for the State of Kansas....

Reversed.

MR. JUSTICE HARLAN concurs in the judgment on the ground that this state measure bears a rational relation to a constitutionally permissible objective. See *Williamson* v. *Lee Optical Co.,* 348 U.S. 483, 491.

CONCLUSIONS

The protection of economic rights is not the province solely of the courts. Legislators and executives (at both the national and state levels) make the initial determination in balancing the rights of property owners against the interests of communities and society. The historical record demonstrates that when the judiciary invokes artificial doctrines to prevent legislative action ("liberty of contract" and other slogans), the persistence of social and political pressures has been sufficient, over time, to prevail. The main struggle over economic rights is fought out within the political branches through the electoral process. Aside from a few pivotal decisions, courts generally play a marginal role at the very edges of these conflicts.

Judicial deference to legislatures is again being challenged and may lead to some changes. In the legal arena there has been renewed interest in litigating issue of economic liberty, reflected in the rise of the Law and Economics field and by interest groups with the primary purpose of litigating against state and federal regulation of business. Beyond increased use of litigation strategies by such long-standing organizations as the Chamber of Commerce, new groups have become active, including the Washington Legal Foundation. Its Web site identifies these priorities: "free-enterprise principles, responsible government, [and] property rights." The organization actively engages in lawsuits and administrative/regulatory proceedings to promote those principles.

An artificial line between property rights and human rights continues to be drawn. With forceful prose, Justice Stewart attempted to join the two concepts: "[T]he dichotomy between personal liberties and property rights is a false one. Property does not have rights. People have rights. The right to enjoy property without unlawful deprivation, no less than the right to speak or the right to travel, is in truth a 'personal' right, whether the 'property' in question be a welfare check, a home, or a savings account. In fact, a fundamental interdependence exists between the personal right to liberty and the personal right in property. Neither could have meaning without the other." Lynch v. Household Finance Corp., 405 U.S. 538, 552 (1972).

NOTES AND QUESTIONS

1. In *Calder v. Bull*, Justices Chase and Iredell held different views on the role of "natural justice" as a limitation on governmental power. Is natural justice a constitutional or a philosophical concept? If the former, what is its source? If the latter, what are its limits? Would a "philosophical" concept be judicially enforceable? Is natural justice a synonym for substantive due process? If not, what are the differences? In your view, how does judicial resort to natural justice differ from *Lochnerizing*, if at all?

2. Chief Justice Taney's opinion in *Charles River Bridge* represented a dramatic departure from the Marshall Court's interpretation of the Contract Clause. In your view, which approach better promotes economic development in the United States? Is one approach a more accurate reflection of the constitutional norms that govern property?

3. In his opinion for the Court in *Blaisdell*, Chief Justice Hughes spoke of a distinction between "altering" and "impairing" the obligation of contracts. What is the difference? Do you agree with Hughes that alteration does not constitute impairment? Why or why not? Did the Court in *Blaisdell* have a realistic alternative to upholding the Minnesota statute? What would have been the economic and social consequences of finding the statute to be unconstitutional?

4. The *Blaisdell* Court held that emergencies do not create power. Can you articulate a constitutional theory to defend that view? May constitutional provisions, such as the Contract Clause, be suspended to meet an emergency? If so, which branch of government possesses that authority? What are the limits to such a power?

5. Can you explain the doctrine of a "business affected with a public interest"? Did the Court in *Munn v. Illinois* provide an adequate explanation of the doctrine? Which businesses are not "affected with a public interest?"

6. In light of *Kelo*, what criteria should be applied to satisfy the Fifth Amendment's requirement of a "public" use? Is the Court's reasoning in *Kelo* consistent with its reasoning in *Midkiff*?

SELECTED READINGS

ACKERMAN, BRUCE. Private Property and the Constitution. New Haven, Conn.: Yale University Press, 1977.

BERGER, LAWRENCE. "A Policy Analysis of the Taking Problem." 49 New York University Law Review 165 (1974).

BLUME, LAWRENCE, AND DANIEL L. RUBINFELD. "Compensation for Takings: An Economic Analysis." 72 California Law Review 569 (1984).

BRIGHAM, JOHN. "Property & the Supreme Court: Do the Justices Make Sense?" 16 Polity 242 (1983).

CALLIES, DAVID L., et al. Cases and Materials on Land Use. St. Paul, Minn.: West Group, 1999.

————, ed. Takings: Land-Development Conditions and Regulatory Takings after *Dolan* and *Lucas.* Section of State and Local Government Law, American Bar Association, 1996.

COHEN, FELIX S. "Dialogue on Private Property." 9 Rutgers Law Review 357 (1954).

DUNHAM, ALLISON. "Griggs v. Allegheny County in Perspective: Thirty Years of Supreme Court Expropriation Law." 1962 Supreme Court Review 63.

ELY, JAMES W., JR. The Guardian of Every Other Right: A Constitutional History of Property Rights. New York: Oxford University Press, 1992.

EPSTEIN, RICHARD A. Takings: Private Property and the Power of Eminent Domain. Cambridge, Mass.: Harvard University Press, 1985.

————. Skepticism and Freedom: A Modern Case for Classical Liberalism. Chicago: University of Chicago Press, 2003.

————. "Taking Stock of Takings: An Author's Retrospective," 15 William and Mary Bill of Rights Journal 407 (2006).

HALE, ROBERT L. "The Supreme Court and the Contract Clause." 57 Harvard Law Review 512, 621, 852 (1944).

HORWITZ, MORTON J. "The Transformation in the Conception of Property in American Law." 40 University of Chicago Law Review 248 (1973).

HUMBACH, JOHN A. "A Unifying Theory for the Just-Compensation Cases: Takings, Regulation and Public Use." 34 Rutgers Law Review 243 (1982).

JOHNSON, CORWIN W. "Compensation for Invalid Land-Use Regulations." 15 Georgia Law Review 559 (1981).

LERNER, MAX. "The Supreme Court and American Capitalism." 42 Yale Law Journal 668 (1933).

LEVY, LEONARD W. "Property As a Human Right." 5 Constitutional Commentary 169 (1988).

McCLOSKEY, ROBERT G. "Economic Due Process and the Supreme Court: An Exhumation and Reburial." 1962 Supreme Court Review 34.

MANDELKER, DANIEL R. "Land Use Takings: The Compensation Issue." 8 Hastings Constitutional Law Quarterly 491 (1981).

MELTZ, ROBERT, DWIGHT H. MERRIAM, AND RICHARD M. FRANK. The Takings Issue. Washington, D.C.: Island Press. 1999.

MENDELSON, WALLACE. "B.F. Wright on the Contract Clause: A Progressive Misreading of the Marshall-Taney Era," 38 Western Political Quarterly 262 (1985).

MICHELMAN, FRANK I. "Property, Utility, and Fairness: Comments on the Ethical Foundations of 'Just Compensation' Law." 80 Harvard Law Review 1165 (1967).

OAKES, JAMES L. "'Property Rights' in Constitutional Analysis Today." 56 Washington Law Review 583 (1981).

REICH, CHARLES A. "The New Property." 73 Yale Law Journal 733 (1964).

ROSE, CAROL M. "Mahon Reconsidered: Why the Takings Issue Is Still a Muddle." 57 Southern California Law Review 561 (1984).

SALLET, JONATHAN B. "Regulatory 'Takings' and Just Compensation: The Supreme Court's Search for a Solution Continues." 18 Urban Lawyer 635 (1986).

SAX, JOSEPH L. "Takings and the Police Power." 74 Yale Law Journal 36 (1964).

————. "Takings, Private Property, and Public Rights." 81 Yale Law Journal 149 (1971).

STOEBUCK, WILLIAM B. "Police Power, Takings, and Due Process." 37 Washington and Lee Law Review 1057 (1980).

WRIGHT, BENJAMIN F., JR. The Contract Clause of the Constitution. Cambridge, Mass.: Harvard University Press, 1938.

10

Efforts to Curb the Court

Justice Stone once chided his brethren: "the only check upon our own exercise of power is our own sense of self-restraint." United States v. Butler, 297 U.S. 1, 79 (1936). While that is an important check, it is by no means the only one. Judges act within a political environment that constantly tests the reasonableness and acceptability of their rulings. Courts issue the "last word" only for an instant, for after the release of an opinion the process of interaction begins: with Congress, the President, executive agencies, states, professional associations, law journals, and the public at large.

Earlier chapters identified some of the constraints that operate on the judiciary: the President's power to appoint; the Senate's power to confirm; congressional powers over the purse, impeachment, and court jurisdiction; the force of public opinion, the press, and scholarly studies. Other restraints, covered in this chapter, include constitutional amendments, statutory reversals, changing the number of Justices (court packing), withdrawing jurisdiction, and noncompliance with court rulings.

Court-curbing periods at the national level often emerge when the judiciary nullifies statutes passed by Congress. The judiciary can also create enemies by *upholding* legislation, such as the broad nationalist rulings issued by Chief Justice John Marshall. To restrain the courts, members of Congress introduce a variety of legislative bills and constitutional amendments. Hearings are held to explore ways to curb the judiciary. State legislatures prepare petitions of protest; state judges pass resolutions of "concern," if not condemnation. Citizens pass initiatives, propositions, and take other positions on constitutional issues. To reduce the tension, the federal judiciary may decide to conduct a partial and possibly graceful retreat.

Judicial-congressional confrontations were especially sharp between 1858 and 1869 (reflecting the *Dred Scott* case and congressional efforts to protect Reconstruction legislation), 1935 and 1937 (reacting to the Court's nullification of New Deal legislation), and 1955 and 1959 (triggered by decisions involving desegregation, congressional investigations, and national security).[1] A new round of court-curbing efforts began in the late 1970s to challenge judicial rulings on school prayer, school busing, abortion, and affirmative action.

The judiciary is most likely to be out of step with Congress or the President during periods of electoral and partisan realignment, when the country is undergoing sharp shifts in political directions while the courts retain the orientation of an age gone by.[2] During earlier periods, attacks on the judiciary generally came from liberal groups: Jeffersonians, Jacksonians, Radical Republicans, LaFollette Republicans, and New Deal Democrats. Conservatives dominated the 1955–59 confrontation and have inspired most of the court-curbing efforts since then.

---

1. See Stuart S. Nagel, "Court-Curbing Periods in American History," 18 Vand. L. Rev. 925 (1965). For a review of proposals to remedy judicial activism, see Charles Grove Haines, The American Doctrine of Judicial Supremacy 467–99 (1932).

2. Richard Funston, "The Supreme Court and Critical Elections," 69 Am. Pol. Sci. Rev. 795 (1975); David Adamany, "Legitimacy, Realigning Elections, and the Supreme Court," 1973 Wisc. L. Rev. 790.

A. CONSTITUTIONAL AMENDMENTS

Whenever two-thirds of both Houses of Congress deem it necessary, they may propose amendments to the Constitution. Ratification requires three-fourths of the states. Alternatively, two-thirds of the states may call a convention for constitutional amendment, but thus far all successful amendments have been initiated by Congress. The process of amending the Constitution is extraordinarily difficult and time-consuming. On only four occasions has Congress successfully used constitutional amendments to reverse Supreme Court decisions.

The Eleventh Amendment responded to *Chisholm* v. *Georgia*, 2 U.S. (2 Dall.) 419 (1793), which decided that a state could be sued in federal court by a plaintiff from another state. The lower house of the Georgia legislature adopted the modest proposal that any federal marshal attempting to enforce that ruling would be guilty of a felony and hanged until death "without the benefit of the clergy." To protect states from a flood of costly citizen suits, Congress quickly passed a constitutional amendment. Although a sufficient number of states ratified it by 1795, not until 1798 did President John Adams notify Congress that the amendment was effective. The Eleventh Amendment reads: "The Judicial power of the United States shall not be construed to extend to any suit in law or equity, commenced or prosecuted against one of the United States by Citizens of another State, or by Citizens or Subjects of any Foreign States."

The Fourteenth Amendment nullified the Supreme Court's decision in *Dred Scott* v. *Sandford*, 60 U.S. (19 How.) 393 (1857), which held that blacks as a class were not citizens protected under the Constitution. After the nation had fought a bloody civil war, North against South, the Fourteenth Amendment was ratified in 1868. Section 1 provides: "All persons born or naturalized in the United States and subject to the jurisdiction thereof, are citizens of the United States and of the State wherein they reside." *Dred Scott* had been partially reversed by statute in 1862 when Congress passed legislation to prohibit slavery in the territories. 12 Stat. 432.

The Sixteenth Amendment overruled *Pollock* v. *Farmers' Loan and Trust Co.*, 158 U.S. 601 (1895), which struck down a federal income tax. The need to finance national expansion and new international responsibilities, combined with a desire to reduce the dependence on high tariffs as the main source of revenue, triggered the drive for a constitutional amendment. Ratified in 1913, the Sixteenth Amendment gave Congress the power "to lay and collect taxes on incomes, from whatever source derived, without apportionment among the several States, and without regard to any census or enumeration."

The Twenty-sixth Amendment was ratified in 1971 to overturn *Oregon* v. *Mitchell*, 400 U.S. 112 (1970), a Supreme Court decision of the previous year that had voided a congressional effort to lower the minimum voting age in state elections to 18. Proponents of lowering the voting age argued that if 18-year-olds could be drafted to fight in wars, they were old enough to vote in elections. As a way to encourage youths to participate constructively in the political process and to avoid the cost and confusion of a dual registration system of 18 years for national elections and 21 years for state and local elections, Congress sent a constitutional amendment to the states. In record time, three months later, a sufficient number of states ratified this language: "The right of citizens of the United States, who are eighteen years of age or older, to vote shall not be denied or abridged by the United States or any State on account of age."

Other Amendment Efforts

Other constitutional amendments, driven by seemingly irresistible political forces, have fallen by the wayside. A successful amendment process requires an extraordinary combination of social, economic, and political forces. If any one of these factors is absent, an amendment may fail. For example, Congress made a concerted effort in 1964 to amend the Constitution to overturn the Supreme Court's decisions in the reapportionment and school prayer cases. Because of delays by House committees and filibusters on the Senate side, these efforts proved fruitless.

Debate on Equal Rights Amendment

[During House debate in 1970 and 1971, Congress-woman Martha Griffiths used the proposed Equal Rights Amendment as a vehicle for attacking the Supreme Court for its failure to address laws and practices that discriminated against women. These debates helped provoke the Court to act in Reed v. Reed, 404 U.S. 71 (1971).]

Mrs. GRIFFITHS.... We will show you that the Supreme Court which has readily moved to change the boundaries of your District and the boundaries of your school district has on not one single occasion granted to women the basic protection of the fifth or 14th amendment. The only right guaranteed to women today by the Constitution of the United States is the right to vote and to hold public office.

It is time, Mr. Speaker, that in this battle with the Supreme Court, that this body and the legis-latures of the States come to the aid of women by passing this amendment....

Mr. Speaker, this is not a battle between the sexes — nor a battle between this body and women. This body and State legislatures have supported women. This is a battle with the Supreme Court of the United States.

... Let me repeat again and again that the States, their legislatures and frequently their courts or Federal district courts have shown more sense than the Supreme Court ever has....

Mr. Chairman, what the equal rights amendment seeks to do, and all it seeks to do, is to say to the Supreme Court of the United States, "Wake up! This is the 20th century. Before it is over, judge women as individual human beings. They, too, are entitled to the protection of the Constitution, the basic fundamental law of this country."

SOURCE: 116 Cong. Rec. 28000, 28004, 28005 (1970); 117 Cong. Rec. 35323 (1971).

Even when Congress reacts against a Court decision by clearing an amendment for ratification by the states, the hurdles are immense. After the Supreme Court in 1918 and 1922 denied Congress the right to regulate child labor conditions, opponents of the Court rulings tried unsuccessfully to reverse them by constitutional amendment. Hammer v. Dagenhart, 247 U.S. 251 (1918); Bailey v. Drexel Furniture Co., 259 U.S. 20 (1922). In 1924 both Houses of Congress passed a constitutional amendment to give Congress the power to "limit, regulate and prohibit the labor of persons under 18 years of age." By 1937 only 28 of the necessary 36 states had ratified the amendment. The issue became moot after Congress regulated child labor through the Fair Labor Standards Act of 1938 and the Supreme Court upheld the statute three years later. United States v. Darby, 312 U.S. 100 (1941).

Unsuccessful constitutional amendments can sometimes prod the Court to address neglected issues. In 1970 the House of Representatives passed the Equal Rights Amendment. After Senate action, the language sent to the states for ratification read: "Equality of rights under the law shall not be denied or abridged by the United States or by any State on account of sex." The ERA was never ratified, even with an extension by Congress to June 30, 1982, but the debate on the amendment had an obvious impact on the Court. Congresswoman Martha Griffiths, during debate in October 1971, said that the whole purpose of the ERA was to tell the Supreme Court "Wake up! This is the 20th century." 117 Cong. Rec. 35323 (1971). A month later the Court invalidated an Idaho law that preferred men over women in administering estates, the first time in its history that the Court had struck down sex discrimination on constitutional grounds (see box).

Once the Constitution is successfully amended to overturn a Court decision, there is no guarantee that the judiciary will interpret the amendment consistent with the intent of the framers and ratifiers. Although the Thirteenth, Fourteenth, and Fifteenth Amendments were meant to overturn *Dred Scott* and protect the rights of blacks, such decisions as *The Civil Rights Cases,* 109 U.S. 3 (1883) and *Plessy* v. *Ferguson,* 163 U.S. 537 (1896), were more in line with racial attitudes that flourished before the Civil War.

In addition to constitutional amendments aimed at particular decisions, other proposals attempt to curb the Court's strength by imposing procedural requirements. These amendments have never been successful. Of recurring interest are the following: requiring more than a majority of Justices to strike down a statute; subjecting the Court's decisions to another tribunal, such as the Senate or a judicial body consisting of a judge from each state; submitting the Court's decisions to popular referenda; allowing Congress by two-thirds vote to override a Court decision just as it does a presidential veto; and making laws held unconstitutional by the Court valid if reenacted by Congress.

Other amendments are directed at the Court's tenure and qualifications: allowing the removal of Supreme Court Justices and other federal judges by majority vote of each House of Congress; restricting the term of a Justice to a set number of years; having Justices retire at the age of 75; requiring direct election from the judicial districts; itemizing the qualifications for Justices, such as requiring prior judicial service in the highest court of a state or excluding anyone who has, within the preceding five years, served in the executive or legislative branch; and vesting the appointment of Justices in judges from the highest state courts.[3] Although unsuccessful in every case, these amendments serve the purpose of venting popular and professional resentment toward Court decisions and may even temper future rulings.

The Court held in 1921 that constitutional amendments must be ratified within some reasonable time after their submission to the states. Ratification "must be sufficiently contemporaneous in that number of States to reflect the will of the people in all sections at relatively the same period." Dillon v. Gloss, 256 U.S. 368, 375 (1921). However, in 1939 the Court declined to be the judge of what constituted a reasonable period for ratification. Coleman v. Miller, 307 U.S. 433, 452 (1939). In 1992 Congress agreed that 202 years were not too long to ratify a constitutional amendment proposed in 1789. That language, now the Twenty-seventh Amendment, reads: "No law, varying the compensation for the services of the Senators and Representatives, shall take effect, until an election of Representatives shall have intervened."

B. STATUTORY REVERSALS

When decisions turn on the interpretation of federal statutes, Congress may overturn a ruling simply by passing a new statute to clarify legislative intent. The private sector often uses Congress as an "appellate court" to reverse judicial interpretations of a statute. At a congressional hearing in 1959, Congressman Wilbur Mills leaned across the witness table and told a company president: "It seems that it is becoming more and more almost a full-time job of the Congress to correct the Supreme Court's desire to legislate." The company president, seeking to have a major Supreme Court decision modified to his advantage, nodded his agreement. Emmette S. Redford, et al., Politics and Government in the United States 518 (1965).

In 1969 the Supreme Court struck down a joint operating agreement by two newspapers on the ground that it violated the Antitrust Act. Citizen Publishing Co. v. United States, 394 U.S. 131 (1969). Congress responded within a year with the Newspaper Preservation Act, specifically exempting from the Act any authorizing agreement needed to prevent newspapers from going out of business. 84 Stat. 466 (1970).

Judicial-legislative conversations helped shape the meaning of the Freedom of Information Act (FOIA). In one case, 33 members of the House of Representatives went to court to obtain documents prepared for President Nixon concerning an underground nuclear test. In 1973 the Supreme Court decided that it had no authority to examine the documents *in camera* to sift out "non-secret compo-

---

3. Maurice S. Culp, "A Survey of the Proposals to Limit or Deny the Power of Judicial Review by the Supreme Court of the United States," 4 Ind. L. J. 386 (1929); Shelden D. Elliott, "Court-Curbing Proposals in Congress," 33 Notre Dame Lawyer 597, 606 (1958).

nents" for their release. EPA v. Mink, 410 U.S. 73 (1973). Congress passed legislation a year later to authorize federal courts to examine sensitive records in judges' chambers. 88 Stat. 1562, § 4(B) (1974).

The *Grove City* Confrontation

Another successful congressional effort concerned the case of *Grove City College* v. *Bell,* 465 U.S. 555 (1984). Title IX of the Education Amendments of 1972 prohibited sex discrimination in any education program or activity that received federal financial assistance. After the Reagan administration had issued statements indicating that its interpretation of Title IX was not as broad as rulings from previous administrations, the House of Representatives on November 16, 1983, passed a resolution by a vote of 414–8 opposing the administration's position. The resolution stated the sense of the House that Title IX and regulations issued pursuant to the title "should not be amended or altered in any manner which will lessen the comprehensive coverage of such statute in eliminating gender discrimination throughout the American educational system." The resolution, of course, was not legally binding, but it was passed because the Supreme Court was about to hear oral argument on the *Grove City* case. As Congressman Paul Simon noted: "Passing this resolution the House can send the Court a signal that we believe that no institution should be allowed to discriminate on the basis of sex if it receives Federal funds." 129 Cong. Rec. 33105 (1983).

The issue before the Court was whether Title IX required federal funds to be terminated only for specific programs in which discrimination occurs or for the entire educational institution. The Supreme Court adopted the narrow interpretation. Justices Brennan and Marshall dissented in part, stating that the Court was ignoring congressional intent for institution-wide coverage. Within four months the House of Representatives, by a vote of 375–32, passed legislation to amend not only Title IX but also three other statutes to adopt broad coverage of the antidiscrimination provisions. 130 Cong. Rec. 18880 (1984). (See reading.) The Senate resisted action that year, and subsequent efforts were complicated by questions of church-state and abortion. Finally, in 1988, Congress was able to forge a compromise. President Reagan vetoed the measure, but both Houses overrode the veto to enact the broader coverage for civil rights that had been rejected in *Grove City.*

Continued Challenges

In 1988, Congress passed two other statutes to reverse the Supreme Court. In one decision, the Court ruled that federal employees could be sued for common law torts committed on the job. They were not entitled to absolute immunity from lawsuit. However, the Court remarked: "Congress is in the best position to provide guidance for the complex and often highly empirical inquiry into whether absolute immunity is warranted in a particular context." Westfall v. Erwin, 484 U.S. 292, 300 (1988). Congress passed legislation to overturn this decision by protecting federal employees from personal liability for common law torts committed within the scope of their employment. The statute provides the injured person with a remedy against the United States government. Thus, compensation would come from the U.S. Treasury, not the employee's pocketbook. 102 Stat. 4563 (1988).

The other statutory reversal in 1988 concerned a Supreme Court decision that accepted the definition of the Veterans Administration that alcoholism results from "willful misconduct" rather than from a disease. For those who regarded the Court's position as erroneous, they were advised that their arguments would be "better presented to Congress than to the courts." Traynor v. Turnage, 485 U.S. 535 (1988). Legislation enacted by Congress recognized that veterans seeking education or rehabilitation would not be denied those benefits under the willful-misconduct standard. 102 Stat. 4170, § 109 (1988).

The Jencks Bill

These cases involve matters of statutory interpretation, an area in which Congress can ultimately prevail. However, even in cases where constitutional rights are present, Congress may pass legislation to modify a Court ruling. A 1957 case involved access by defendants to government files bearing on their trial. On the basis of statements by two informers for the FBI, the government prosecuted Clifford Jencks for failing to state that he was a member of the Communist Party. He asked that the FBI reports be turned over to the trial judge for examination to determine whether they had value in impeaching the statements of the two informers. The Supreme Court went beyond Jencks' request by ordering the government to produce for *his* inspection all FBI reports "touching the events and activities" at issue in the trial. Jencks v. United States, 353 U.S. 657, 668 (1957). The Court specifically rejected the option of producing government documents only to the trial judge for his determination of relevancy and materiality. Id. at 669.

In their concurrence, Justices Burton and Harlan believed that Jencks was only entitled to have the records submitted to the trial judge. A dissent by Justice Clark agreed that the documents should be delivered solely to the trial judge. In a remarkable statement he incited Congress to act: "Unless the Congress changes the rule announced by the Court today, those intelligence agencies of our Government engaged in law enforcement may as well close up shop, for the Court has opened their files to the criminal and thus afforded him a Roman holiday for rummaging through confidential information as well as vital national secrets."

The Court announced its decision on June 3, 1957. Both Houses of Congress quickly held hearings and reported remedial legislation. The Jencks Bill (after much redrafting) passed the Senate by voice vote on August 26 and cleared the House on August 27, 351 to 17. The conference report was adopted with huge majorities: 74–2 in the Senate and 315–0 in the House. The bill became law on September 2, 1957. The statute provides that in any federal criminal prosecution, no statement or report in the possession of the government "which was made by a Government witness or prospective Government witness (other than the defendant) to an agent of the Government shall be the subject of subpena, discovery, or inspection unless said witness has testified on direct examination in the trial of the case." If a witness testifies, statements may be delivered to the defendant for examination and use unless the United States claims that the statement contains irrelevant matter, in which case the statement shall be inspected by the court *in camera*. The judge may excise irrelevant portions of the statement before submitting it to the defendant. 71 Stat. 595 (1957); 18 U.S.C. § 3500 (1994).

Contemporary Reversals

Congress has resorted to statutory reversals with greater frequency in recent years. A single statute in 1991 overturned or modified nine Supreme Court decisions (see the heading "Civil Rights Act of 1991" in Section E of Chapter 15). In 1995, Congress passed legislation to overturn the Supreme Court's opinion in *Dole* v. *United Steelworkers of America*, 494 U.S. 26 (1990), which had restricted OMB's authority to review and countermand agency regulations. The new legislation (P.L. 104-13) made all paperwork requirements subject to OMB review. In 2008, Congress took steps to overturn several Supreme Court decisions regarding people with disabilities. The House approved a bill 402 to 17 to make it easier for workers to prove discrimination. Both Houses were active in considering legislation to overturn a Court decision regarding a pay discrimination suit brought by Lilly Ledbetter. Ledbetter v. Goodyear Tire & Rubber Co., 550 U.S. ____ (2007).

Statutory Reversal: *Grove City*

After the Supreme Court announced *Grove City College* v. *Bell* on February 28, 1984, which restricted the reach of congressional prohibitions on sex discrimination, the House quickly passed legislation that year to overturn the Court's statutory interpretation. Senate action was delayed and complicated by questions of church-state and abortion. Finally, in 1988 the Senate acted and the legislation was sent to President Reagan. Both Houses had the votes to override his veto and enact this statutory reversal. The Senate debate below is taken from 134 Cong. Rec. 97 (1988).

Mr. KENNEDY. Mr. President, today the Senate begins consideration of the Civil Rights Restoration Act, one of the most important civil rights measures in recent years. A broad, bipartisan coalition of 56 Senators is sponsoring the bill. Our goal is to reverse the 1984 Supreme Court decision in Grove City College versus Bell, which permits tax dollars to be spent in support of discrimination.

The moment is ripe for Congress to renew its commitment to civil rights. The historic struggle to secure these rights for all Americans has known both triumph and tragedy.

Over the past 200 years, the American people have worked hard to make the promises of the Constitution a reality for all of our citizens. The harsh fact remains, however, that discrimination still prevents too many of our citizens from enjoying the American dream.

Despite the 1954 Supreme Court decision in Brown versus Board of Education, subsequent predictions about the demise of racial segregation proved grossly premature. Faith in what the Brown case would accomplish swiftly turned to frustration and then cynicism. It took inspiration and leadership from Presidents Eisenhower and Kennedy, Martin Luther King Jr., and other great leaders to advance the legislation that has achieved so much in the past two decades.

Twenty-four summers ago, Congress distinguished itself by passing the landmark Civil Rights Act of 1964. In enacting this monumental measure, we initiated a new assault against the injustices which pervaded America's social fabric and political order. One of the most significant components of the 1964 legislation is title VI, which prohibits discrimination based on race, color, or national origin in any "program or activity" which receives Federal aid.

In terms of eradicating racial injustice, the success of title VI surpassed our expectations. Under its impact, many engines of discrimination began grinding to a halt. Faced with the prospect of losing Federal aid, schools, hospitals, and State and local governments had no choice but to dismantle their discriminatory practices. For example, black enrollment in colleges increased by 92 percent in the decade of the 1970's.

Influenced by a new national awareness, Congress in the 1970's grew sensitive to additional groups which suffer from the effects of prejudice and discrimination. In this climate, title VI emerged as a prime model for new initiatives. In 1972, Congress enacted title IX, which prohibits sex discrimination in educational programs or activities receiving Federal aid. In 1973, Congress adopted section 504 of the Rehabilitation Act, which prevents the recipients of Federal funds from discriminating against the disabled. And the Age Discrimination Act of 1975 was written into law to guarantee the same protection for the elderly.

Each of these statutes achieved remarkable results. Under title IX, the participation of women in high school and college athletic activities has soared. And their achievements have soared, too, including the extraordinary successes of American women in the summer and winter Olympic games. Equally impressive is the record for section 504, which has brought disabled citizens into the mainstream of American life by dismantling the barriers to education and employment of the handicapped.

But suddenly, in 1984, much of the progress against discrimination in each of these areas was placed at risk by the decision of the Supreme Court in the Grove City College case. In that case, a divided court interpreted the antidiscrimination language in title IX extremely narrowly. Since the only Federal money reaching the college was in the form of student aid, the Court concluded that only the financial aid office was covered by the law. The rest of the college was left free to deny equal opportunities to women.

The decision affects all of the civil rights statutes which prohibit discrimination in federally funded programs or activities, since each of these statutes is identical to the phrasing which the Supreme Court interpreted in the Grove City case. If this decision is permitted to stand, millions of female, minority, disabled, and senior citizens will be denied simple, basic protections.

Repercussions from the decision proved to be swift and substantial. Within a matter of weeks, the Department of Education's Office of Civil Rights dropped 18 antidiscrimination cases in higher education and 4 cases in elementary and secondary education. To date, 674 pending cases have been closed or suspended by the Department of Education.

... [T]he sponsors of this legislation have stated and restated our intention to do nothing more than restore the status quo which existed before the Supreme Court decision in the Grove City College case. The legislative history of the civil rights laws shows that broad coverage is consistent with the original intent of Congress. That construction has been followed by past Democratic and Republican administrations alike, and it deserves to be restored so that we can keep the faith of the four great statutes that protect the basic rights of millions of Americans to be free from federally subsidized discrimination.

Our goal is clear and our legislation is straight-forward. The bill adds no new operative language to the four civil rights laws. It merely adds a definition of "program or activity" which restores the meaning that these terms had prior to the Grove City College decision.

C. COURT PACKING

Congress has altered the number of Justices on the Supreme Court throughout its history. Congress authorized six Justices in 1789, lowered that to five in 1801, returned the number to six a year later, and increased the size of the Court in subsequent years to keep pace with the creation of new circuits. Since 1869 the number of Justices has remained fixed at nine. Appointments to the Court have often produced marked changes in judicial policy, as witnessed by the abrupt shift in the Legal Tender Cases from 1870 to 1871. In none of these earlier examples was the alteration of court size linked so blatantly to changing judicial policy as in FDR's court-packing plan.

In his inaugural address in 1933, Franklin D. Roosevelt struck a confident note for presidential-judicial relations. He said that the Constitution "is so simple and practical that it is possible always to meet extraordinary needs by changes in emphasis and arrangement without loss of essential form." Privately, he tempered that public optimism with the knowledge that most members of the Supreme Court were conservative and business-oriented.

Black Monday

Presidential hopes were routed on "Black Monday," May 27, 1935, when the Supreme Court unanimously struck down the National Industrial Recovery Act (NIRA). Schechter Corp. v. United States, 295 U.S. 495 (1935). On that same day it ruled that Presidents could remove members of independent regulatory commissions only by following the statutory reasons for removal, and it held unconstitutional a statute for the relief of farm mortgagors. Humphrey's Executor v. United States, 295 U.S. 602 (1935); Louisville Bank v. Radford, 295 U.S. 555 (1935). Feeling betrayed by the liberal members on the Court, Roosevelt asked plaintively: "Well, where was Ben Cardozo? And what about old Isaiah [Brandeis]?"[4] Direct attacks on the Court were shelved after the public reacted unfavorably to Roosevelt's sneering accusation at a press conference that the Justices had adopted a "horse-and-buggy definition of interstate commerce." At a cabinet meeting in December 1935, Roosevelt reviewed several methods of restraining the Court. The notion of packing the Court, Interior Secretary Harold Ickes recorded in his diary, "was a distasteful idea." 1 The Secret Diary of Harold L. Ickes 495 (1953).

Roosevelt's patience was tested again on January 6, 1936, when the Court struck down the processing tax in the Agricultural Adjustment Act. The ruling divided the Court, 6 to 3, with Justice Stone penning a stinging dissent. He reminded the other Justices that they were not the only branch of government assumed to have the capacity to govern. United States v. Butler, 297 U.S. at 87. This time there appeared to be a groundswell of public support for adding younger Justices more attuned to the temper of the times. Yet Roosevelt bided his time, not wanting to give his opponents in an election year the opportunity to rally behind the Constitution and the Court. Other decisions in 1936, striking down federal and state laws, provided extra incentives to curb the Court. Some of those decisions attracted three or four dissents.[5] The climate for curbing the Court was encouraged by the national popularity of The Nine Old Men (1936), a caustic portrait of the Justices written by Drew Pearson and Robert Allen. Peppered by such chapters as "The Lord High Executioners," the book charged that "jus-

---

4. William E. Leuchtenburg, "The Origins of Franklin D. Roosevelt's 'Court-Packing' Plan," 1966 Sup. Ct. Rev. 347, 357.

5. Jones v. SEC, 298 U.S. 1 (1936) (Cardozo, Brandeis, and Stone dissenting); St. Joseph Stock Yards Co. v. United States, 298 U.S. 38 (1936) (Cardozo, Brandeis, and Stone dissenting in part); Carter v. Carter Coal Co., 298 U.S. 238 (1936); Morehead v. New York ex rel. Tipaldo, 298 U.S. 587 (1936) (Hughes, Brandeis, Stone, and Cardozo dissenting).

tice has no relation whatsoever to popular will. Administrations may come and go, the temper of the people may reverse itself, economic conditions may be revolutionalized, the Nine Old Men sit on."

Roosevelt's landslide victory in 1936, capturing all but two states, paved the way for a direct assault on the Court. Constitutional amendments seemed to him wholly impracticable. They were difficult to frame and nearly impossible to pass. Statutory remedies, such as requiring a unanimous or 8-to-1 decision in the Supreme Court to invalidate a law, were of doubtful constitutionality. After rejecting a number of alternatives, he considered court packing the only feasible solution.

Roosevelt Shows His Hand

Working closely with his Attorney General and Solicitor General, but without the advice of congressional leaders, Roosevelt ordered the preparation of a draft bill. The President would be authorized to nominate Justices to the Supreme Court whenever an incumbent over the age of 70 declined to resign or retire. The same procedure would apply to lower courts, limiting the number of additional appointments to 50 and setting the maximum size of the Supreme Court at 15. Under this scenario, Roosevelt could name as many as six new Justices to the Supreme Court.

When he submitted his proposal to Congress on February 5, 1937, he attempted to disguise it primarily as an economy and efficiency measure. Additional Justices would help relieve the delay and congestion he claimed resulted from aged or infirm judges. FDR's "indirection" (a euphemism for his deception and deviousness) offended some potential supporters. Roosevelt soon revealed his real purpose: to pack the Supreme Court with liberal Justices. In a "fireside chat" on March 9, 1937, he told the country that he wanted a Supreme Court that "will enforce the Constitution as written." But a mechanical application of that document by six additional Justices would not alleviate the problem Roosevelt faced. Later in that address he called for judges "who will bring to the Courts a present-day sense of the Constitution." He wanted "younger men who have had personal experience and contact with modern facts and circumstances." More concretely, he promised to appoint Justices "who will not undertake to override the judgment of the Congress on legislative policy." The result of this reform, he said plainly, would be a "reinvigorated, liberal-minded Judiciary."

Repudiation by the Senate

The Senate Judiciary Committee denounced Roosevelt's bill. Its report methodically and mercilessly shreds the bill's premises, structure, content, and motivation. This searing indictment constituted an extraordinary determination on the part of the committee to pulverize Roosevelt's creation and bury it forever. The first of six reasons for rejecting the plan bluntly noted: "the bill does not accomplish any one of the objectives for which it was originally offered." S. Rept. No. 711, 75th Cong., 1st Sess., 3 (1937). Among other points in this scathing attack, the committee said that the courts "with the oldest judges have the best records in the disposition of business." The bill called for retirement only for judges who had served for ten years (penalizing not age itself but age combined with experience). Nothing in the bill prevented Roosevelt from nominating someone 69 years and eleven months of age without prior judicial service. The result could be a Court of 15 members, all of them older than 70 and with no means of altering its composition. To the committee, the bill had one purpose and one purpose only: to apply force to the judiciary.

The committee condemned the bill as a "needless, futile, and utterly dangerous abandonment of constitutional principle." The report's harsh language (see reading) was designed to repudiate the bill so emphatically "that its parallel will never again be presented to the free representatives of the free people of America." The committee's position was reinforced by a letter from Chief Justice Hughes stating that the Court was "fully abreast of its work" and there was "no congestion of cases upon our calendar" (see box on next page).

A number of unexpected developments sealed the fate of the court-packing bill. Senate Majority

Chief Justice Hughes Writes to Congress

March 21, 1937

Hon. Burton K. Wheeler
United States Senate
Washington, D.C.

My Dear Senator Wheeler: In response to your inquiries, I have the honor to present the following statement with respect to the work of the Supreme Court:

1. The Supreme Court is fully abreast of its work. When we rose on March 15 (for the present recess) we had heard argument in cases in which certiorari had been granted only 4 weeks before—February 15.

During the current term, which began last October and which we call "October term, 1936", we have heard argument on the merits in 150 cases (180 numbers) and we have 28 cases (30 numbers) awaiting argument. We shall be able to hear all these cases, and such others as may come up for argument, before our adjournment for the term. There is no congestion of cases upon our calendar.

This gratifying condition has been obtained for several years. We have been able for several terms to adjourn after disposing of all cases which are ready to be heard. [*Hughes supplies statistics for six years on total cases on docket (original and appellate), cases disposed of during term, and cases remaining on dockets.*]

7. An increase in the number of Justices of the Supreme Court, apart from any question of policy, which I do not discuss, would not promote the efficiency of the Court. It is believed that it would impair that efficiency so long as the Court acts as a unit. There would be more judges to hear, more judges to confer, more judges to discuss, more judges to be convinced and to decide....

I understand that it has been suggested that with more Justices the Court could hear cases in divisions. It is believed that such a plan would be impracticable. A large proportion of the cases we hear are important and a decision by a part of the Court would be unsatisfactory.

I may also call attention to the provisions of article III, section 1, of the Constitution that the judicial power of the United States shall be vested "in one Supreme Court" and in such inferior courts as the Congress may from time to time ordain and establish. The Constitution does not appear to authorize two or more Supreme Courts or two or more parts of a supreme court functioning in effect as separate courts.

On account of the shortness of time I have not been able to consult with the members of the Court generally with respect to the foregoing statement, but I am confident that it is in accord with the views of the Justices. I should say, however, that I have been able to consult with Mr. Justice Van Devanter and Mr. Justice Brandeis, and I am at liberty to say that the statement is approved by them.

I have the honor to remain,
Respectfully yours,

Charles E. Hughes
Chief Justice of the Supreme Court

SOURCE: S. Rept. No. 711, 75th Cong., 1st Sess. 38–40 (1937).

Leader Joe Robinson, who Roosevelt hoped would steer the bill through the Senate, died on July 14 after a week of debate in the sweltering capital. By that time the Court had already begun to modify some of its earlier rulings. On March 29, 1937, it upheld a state law establishing a minimum wage law for women, basically reversing a decision handed down ten months earlier.[6] This reversal occurred because of a change in position by Justice Roberts, or what has been called the "switch in time that saved nine." However, before FDR submitted his court-packing plan Roberts had already broken with

---

6. West Coast Hotel Co. v. Parrish, 300 U.S. 379 (1937), overturning Adkins v. Children's Hospital, 261 U.S. 525 (1923) and "distinguishing" (in fact reversing) Morehead v. New York ex rel. Tipaldo, 298 U.S. 587 (1936).

his doctrinaire laissez-faire colleagues. He wrote the opinion for a 5–4 Court in *Nebbia* v. *New York*, 291 U.S. 502 (1934), upholding a New York price-setting statute. With his support, the Court was prepared to sustain minimum-wage legislation in the fall of 1936 but had delayed its ruling because of Justice Stone's illness. Late in 1936, Roberts had voted with the liberals to affirm a state unemployment insurance law.[7]

Other decisions in 1937 confirmed that the Court had become more accepting of New Deal programs. Roosevelt remarked with obvious relish: "The old minority of 1935 and 1936 had become the majority of 1937—without a single new appointment of a justice!"[8] Because Congress finally passed legislation early in 1937 to provide full judicial pay during retirement, Justice Van Devanter stepped down on June 2, 1937, giving Roosevelt his first chance in more than four years to nominate a Justice to the Supreme Court. Other retirements were imminent. Within a matter of months, the need for the court-packing plan had evaporated. President Roosevelt would be able to "reorganize" the Court through the regular constitutional process.

FDR's Court-Packing Plan: Senate Report

President Franklin D. Roosevelt submitted to Congress on February 5, 1937, a proposal for "judicial reorganization." In actual fact, the plan would have allowed him to pack the Supreme Court and lower federal courts with liberal judges. With top-heavy majorities in both Houses, he hoped for quick passage. His hopes were permanently dashed on June 7, when the Senate Judiciary Committee reported the bill adversely and so excoriated the President's idea that any parallels to it would "never again be presented to the free representatives of the free people of America." S. Rept. No. 711, 75th Cong., 1st Sess. (1937).

The Committee on the Judiciary, to whom was referred the bill (S. 1392) to reorganize the judicial branch of the Government, after full consideration, having unanimously amended the measure, hereby report the bill adversely with the recommendation that it do not pass....

THE ARGUMENT

The committee recommends that the measure be rejected for the following primary reasons:

I. The bill does not accomplish any one of the objectives for which it was originally offered.

II. It applies force to the judiciary and in its initial and ultimate effect would undermine the independence of the courts.

III. It violates all precedents in the history of our Government and would in itself be a dangerous precedent for the future.

IV. The theory of the bill is in direct violation of

the spirit of the American Constitution and its employment would permit alteration of the Constitution without the people's consent or approval; it undermines the protection our constitutional system gives to minorities and is subversive of the rights of individuals.

V. It tends to centralize the Federal district judiciary by the power of assigning judges from one district to another at will.

VI. It tends to expand political control over the judicial department by adding to the powers of the legislative and executive departments respecting the judiciary.

· · ·

BILL FAILS OF ITS PURPOSE

In the first place, as already pointed out, the bill does not provide for any increase of personnel un-

---

7. W. H. H. Chamberlin, Inc. v. Andrews, 299 U.S. 515, decided November 23, 1936. The Court was equally divided. For Roberts' vote, see John W. Chambers, "The Big Switch: Justice Roberts and the Minimum-Wage Cases," 10 Labor Hist. 44, 57 (1969). See also Felix Frankfurter, "Mr. Justice Roberts," 104 U. Pa. L. Rev. 311 (1955); 2 Merlo J. Pusey, Charles Evans Hughes 757 (1963). For a challenge to Roberts' recollection of key events in 1936, see Clement E. Vose, Constitutional Change: Amendment Politics and Supreme Court Litigation Since 1900, 228–34 (1972).

8. 6 Public Papers and Addresses of Franklin D. Roosevelt lxviii (1941). See also Virginian Ry. v. Federation, 300 U.S. 515 (1937); Wright v. Vinton Branch, 300 U.S. 440 (1937); NLRB v. Jones & Laughlin, 301 U.S. 1 (1937); NLRB v. Fruehauf Co., 301 U.S. 49 (1937); NLRB v. Clothing Co., 301 U.S. 58 (1937); Steward Machine Co. v. Davis, 301 U.S. 548 (1937); Helvering v. Davis, 301 U.S. 619 (1937).

less judges of retirement age fail to resign or retire. Whether or not there is to be an increase of the number of judges, and the extent of the increase if there is to be one, is dependent wholly upon the judges themselves and not at all upon the accumulation of litigation in any court. To state it another way the increase of the number of judges is to be provided, not in relation to the increase of work in any district or circuit, but in relation to the age of the judges and their unwillingness to retire.

In the second place, as pointed out in the President's message, only 25 of the 237 judges serving in the Federal courts on February 5, 1937, were over 70 years of age. Six of these were members of the Supreme Court at the time the bill was introduced.... Moreover, the facts indicate that the courts with the oldest judges have the best records in the disposition of business....

QUESTION OF AGE NOT SOLVED

The next question is to determine to what extent "the persistent infusion of new blood" may be expected from this bill.

... The man on the bench may be 80 years of age, but this bill will not authorize the President to appoint a new judge to sit beside him unless he has served as a judge for 10 years. In other words, age itself is not penalized; the penalty falls only when age is attended with experience.

No one should overlook the fact that under this bill the President, whoever he may be and whether or not he believes in the constant infusion of young blood in the courts, may nominate a man 69 years and 11 months of age to the Supreme Court, or to any court, and, if confirmed, such nominee, if he never had served as a judge, would continue to sit upon the bench unmolested by this law until he had attained the ripe age of 79 years and 11 months.

We are told that "modern complexities call also for a constant infusion of new blood in the courts, just as it is needed in executive functions of the Government and in private business." Does this bill provide for such? The answer is obviously no....

THE BILL APPLIES FORCE TO THE JUDICIARY

The [bill] applies force to the judiciary. It is an attempt to impose upon the courts a course of action, a line of decision which, without that force, without that imposition, the judiciary might not adopt.

Can there be any doubt that this is the purpose of the bill? Increasing the personnel is not the object of this measure; infusing young blood is not the object; for if either one of these purposes had been in the minds of the proponents, the drafters would not have written the following clause to be found on page 2, lines 1 to 4, inclusive:

"*Provided*, That no additional judge shall be appointed hereunder if the judge who is of retirement age dies, resigns, or retires prior to the nomination of such additional judge."

... For the protection of the people, for the preservation of the rights of the individual, for the maintenance of the liberties of minorities, for maintaining the checks and balances of our dual system, the three branches of the Government were so constituted that the independent expression of honest difference of opinion could never be restrained in the people's servants and no one branch could overawe or subjugate the others. That is the American system. It is immeasurably more important, immeasurably more sacred to the people of America, indeed, to the people of all the world than the immediate adoption of any legislation however beneficial....

A PRECEDENT OF LOYALTY TO THE CONSTITUTION

. . .

This is the first time in the history of our country that a proposal to alter the decisions of the court by enlarging its personnel has been so boldly made. Let us meet it. Let us now set a salutary precedent that will never be violated. Let us, of the Seventy-fifth Congress, in words that will never be disregarded by any succeeding Congress, declare that we would rather have an independent Court, a fearless Court, a Court that will dare to announce its honest opinions in what it believes to be the defense of the liberties of the people, than a Court that, out of fear or sense of obligation to the appointing power, or factional passion, approves any measure we may enact. We are not the judges of the judges. We are not above the Constitution.

Even if every charge brought against the so-called "reactionary" members of this Court be true, it is far better that we await orderly but inevitable change of personnel than that we impatiently overwhelm them with new members....

SUMMARY

We recommend the rejection of this bill as a needless, futile, and utterly dangerous abandonment of constitutional principle.

It was presented to the Congress in a most intricate form and for reasons that obscured its real purpose.

It would not banish age from the bench nor abolish divided decisions.

It would not affect the power of any court to hold laws unconstitutional nor withdraw from any judge the authority to issue injunctions.

It would not reduce the expense of litigation nor speed the decision of cases.

It is a proposal without precedent and without justification.

It would subjugate the courts to the will of Congress and the President and thereby destroy the in-dependence of the judiciary, the only certain shield of individual rights....

Its ultimate operation would be to make this Government one of men rather than one of law, and its practical operation would be to make the Constitution what the executive or legislative branches of the Government choose to say it is — an interpretation to be changed with each change of administration.

It is a measure which should be so emphatically rejected that its parallel will never again be presented to the free representatives of the free people of America.

D. WITHDRAWING JURISDICTION

During the past several decades, Congress has been under strong pressure to withdraw the Supreme Court's jurisdiction to hear appeals in cases of abortion, school busing, school prayer, and other issues on the conservatives' "social agenda." This strategy is based on language in Article III of the Constitution: "The Supreme Court shall have appellate jurisdiction, both as to law and fact, with such exceptions, and under such regulations, as the Congress shall make." The Exceptions Clause, it is argued, gives Congress plenary power to determine the Court's appellate jurisdiction.

Although this approach appears to be grounded on constitutional language, the Exceptions Clause must be read in concert with other provisions in the Constitution. An aggressive use of the Exceptions Clause by Congress would make an exception the rule and deny citizens access to the Supreme Court to vindicate constitutional rights. Stripping the Supreme Court of jurisdiction to hear certain issues would vest ultimate judicial authority in the lower federal and state courts, producing contradictory and conflicting legal doctrines.

A more radical proposal would prevent even the lower federal courts from ruling on specific social issues. Under Article III, the judicial power is vested in a Supreme Court "and in such inferior Courts as the Congress may from time to time ordain and establish." Because Congress creates the lower courts, it may by statute confer, define, and withdraw jurisdiction. Sheldon v. Sill, 49 U.S. (8 How.) 441, 449 (1850). Although Congress has withdrawn jurisdiction to adjudicate certain issues, the exercise of that power "is subject to compliance with at least the requirements of the Fifth Amendment. That is to say, while Congress has the undoubted power to give, withhold, and restrict the jurisdiction of courts other than the Supreme Court, it must not so exercise that power as to deprive any person of life, liberty, or property without due process of law or to take private property without just compensation." Battaglia v. General Motors Corp., 169 F.2d 254, 257 (2d Cir. 1948), cert. denied, 335 U.S. 887 (1948). To deny the lower federal courts jurisdiction to hear claims arising under the Constitution would upset the system of checks and balances, alter the balance of power between the national government and the states, and strengthen the force of majority rule over individual rights (see reading on ABA report).

Withdrawing appellate jurisdiction from the Supreme Court and withdrawing jurisdiction from the lower federal courts would also undercut the Supremacy Clause in Article VI, which states that the Constitution and federal laws "made in Pursuance thereof ... shall be the supreme Law of the Land; and the Judges in every State shall be bound thereby, any Thing in the Constitution or Laws of any State to the contrary notwithstanding." In 1982 the chief justices of the highest state courts issued a unanimous resolution expressing "serious concerns" about bills introduced in Congress to give the states sole authority to decide certain social issues. Among other objections, the chief justices pointed out that the result of such legislation would be contrary to what conservatives professed to be their goal. Instead of overturning Supreme Court decisions, they would be "cast in stone" when state judges continued to honor their oaths to obey the federal Constitution and to give full force (pursuant to the Supremacy Clause) to Supreme Court precedents. The practical effect, therefore, would be to place a body of legal doctrine outside the reach of federal courts or state courts either to alter or overrule. 128 Cong. Rec. 689–90 (1982).

Members of Congress have also attempted to use their power to enforce the Fourteenth Amendment as a lever to alter the jurisdiction of the federal courts. Section 5 of the Fourteenth Amendment gives Congress the power "to enforce, by appropriate legislation," the provisions of that Amendment. In 1981 the Senate Judiciary Committee held hearings on a bill that looked to Section 5 as the vehicle for overturning the Supreme Court's 1973 abortion decision. The hearings covered the scope of Section 5, the issue of whether Congress would be exercising judgments over "facts" or "law," and a possible shift of balance of power between the national government and the states (see reading).

The *McCardle* Case

In a number of early decisions, the Supreme Court recognized the power of Congress to make exceptions and to regulate the Court's appellate jurisdiction.[9] For example, in 1847 the Court stated that it possessed "no appellate power in any case, unless conferred upon it by act of Congress; nor can it, when conferred be exercised in any other form, or by any other mode of proceeding than that which the law prescribes." Barry v. Mercein, 5 How. 103, 119 (1847). These early decisions defined the congressional power too broadly, as will be shown.

The leading case for empowering Congress to withdraw appellate jurisdiction from the Supreme Court is *Ex parte McCardle* (1869). In 1868 Congress withdrew the Court's jurisdiction to review circuit court judgments on habeas corpus actions. The clear purpose was to prevent the Court from deciding a case on the constitutionality of the Reconstruction military government in the South, even though the Court had already heard oral argument in the case of William McCardle. He had been held in custody awaiting trial by military commission, charged with publishing articles that incited "insurrection, disorder, and violence." Under an act of February 5, 1867, he petitioned a federal circuit court for the writ of habeas corpus. The writ was issued, directing the military commander to deliver McCardle to a federal marshal. After the commander complied with the writ (having denied that the restraint was unlawful), the circuit court rejected McCardle's petition.

At that point McCardle appealed to the Supreme Court. On February 17, 1868, the Court dismissed the government's argument that the Court lacked jurisdiction to hear the case. 73 U.S. (6 Wall.) 318 (1868). The case was argued March 2, 3, 4, and 9. However, before the Court could meet in conference to decide the case, Congress passed legislation to nullify McCardle's relief under the act of February 5, 1867. The new legislation provided that the portion of the 1867 statute that authorized an appeal from the judgment of the circuit court to the Supreme Court, "or the exercise of any such jurisdiction by said Supreme Court on appeals which have been or may hereafter be taken, be, and the same is, hereby repealed." 15 Stat. 44 (1868). Congress wanted to sweep McCardle's case from the docket, fearing that the Court might use it to invalidate the Reconstruction laws.

In a unanimous opinion upholding the repeal statute, Chief Justice Chase stated that the Court was "not at liberty to inquire into the motives of the legislature. We can only examine into its power under the Constitution; and the power to make exceptions to the appellate jurisdiction of this court is given by express words." EX PARTE McCARDLE, 74 U.S. (7 Wall.) 506, 514 (1869). The Court dismissed the case for want of jurisdiction. The Court might have used Section 14 of the Judiciary Act

---

9. Wiscart v. Dauchy, 3 Dall. 321 (1796); Durousseau v. United States, 10 U.S. (6 Cr.) 306 (1810); Daniels v. Railroad Co., 70 U.S. (3 Wall.) 250, 254 (1866).

Congress Responds to *Milligan*

[James Falconer Wilson, floor manager of this bill for the House Judiciary Committee, explains why Congress had not only the authority but also the obligation to respond to the Court's decision in Ex parte Milligan*]:*

Mr. WILSON, of Iowa....

The object of this part of the bill cannot be mistaken. It is alleged that the President of the United States, in regard to the various matters here enumerated, has acted without authority of law, and that all who have been in any manner associated with him, as instruments in rendering effective his acts, proclamations, and orders, are guilty of infractions of the law, for which they may be indicted, convicted, punished, and subjected to civil actions for the recovery of damages. Many officers and soldiers of the United States have already been made defendants in civil and criminal actions for acts which it is proposed to cover by the broad mantle of this bill....

[Wilson reviews congressional and judicial precedents that support the pending bill.] The legislative and judicial action of the Government presents no difficulty in this regard until we reach the recent decision of the Supreme Court in the Milligan case, and even that case interposes no real and valid objection to the passage of this bill. It is true that a majority of the court, in the opinion announced by Mr. Justice Davis, declares that Congress could grant no power to try, in the State of Indiana, a citizen in civil life, in nowise connected with the military service, by a court-martial or military commission, and in so far as this goes the court stands in opposition to this bill. But this is a piece of judicial impertinence which we are not bound to respect. No such question was before the court in the Milligan case, and that tribunal wandered beyond the record in treating of it. Its discussion by the court was out of place, uncalled for, and wholly unjustifiable....

The purpose of the bill is very plainly indicated in its terms, and that is to deprive the civil courts of the United States of all jurisdiction in relation to the acts of military commissions and courts-martial.

SOURCE: Congressional Globe, 39th Cong., 2d Sess. 1484, 1487 (1867).

of 1789 to review habeas corpus actions. 1 Stat. 81–82, § 14. To do that in the face of the repeal statute would have invited a major collision with Congress. The House of Representatives had already passed legislation to require a two-thirds majority of the Court to invalidate a federal statute, and some of the more rambunctious Radicals wanted to trim the power of the Supreme Court.

There is some question whether Congress acted under the Exceptions Clause, even though it forms the basis for the Court's decision. Congress may have merely repealed a special statutory right of access that it had previously granted. As the Court noted a year later, Congress did not repeal alternative rights of access, such as under the Judiciary Act of 1789 and later statutes that expanded the writ of habeas corpus. Ex parte Yerger, 75 U.S. (8 Wall.) 85, 101–02 (1869).

During this same period, Congress passed legislation to remove from federal and state courts their jurisdiction to hear other cases arising from the Civil War. The legislation responded to the Supreme Court's decision in *Ex parte Milligan* (1866), holding that military courts could not function in states where federal courts had been open and operating. Although cases were already pending with regard to the conduct of U.S. officials during and immediately after the war, Congress gave indemnity to all officials who implemented presidential proclamations from March 4, 1861, to June 30, 1866, with respect to martial law and military trials. The statute adds: "And no civil court of the United States, or of any State, or of the District of Columbia, or of any district or territory of the United States, shall have or take jurisdiction of, or in any manner reverse any of the proceedings had or acts done as aforesaid...." 14 Stat. 432, 433 (1867). Legislative debate underscored the determination of Congress to limit the jurisdiction of the courts (see box).

Refinements to *McCardle*

McCardle remains in a shadowy realm, surrounded by conflicting cases that both limit and legitimate congressional power under the Exceptions Clause. Shortly after *McCardle,* the Supreme Court decided *United States* v. *Klein* (1872), which involved a congressional attempt to use the appropriations power to nullify the President's power to pardon. The Court said that Congress had exceeded its authority, first by trying to limit a presidential power granted by the Constitution, and second by preventing a presidential pardon or amnesty from being admitted as evidence in court. The statute was meant to strip the Supreme Court of its jurisdiction over such cases. The Court agreed that the Exceptions Clause gave Congress the power to deny the right of appeal in a particular class of cases, but it could not withhold appellate jurisdiction "as a means to an end" if the end was forbidden under the Constitution. In this case, the effect of withholding appellate jurisdiction was to prescribe impermissible rules of decision for the judiciary in a pending case. 80 U.S. (13 Wall.) 128, 146 (1872).

Other considerations place limits on the Exceptions Clause. For example, Congress could not extend certain rights and then attempt, through the Exceptions Clause, to exclude a particular race or religious group. Such actions would violate the Due Process Clause and the First Amendment. As noted by Laurence H. Tribe, Congress could not deny access to federal courts "to all but white Anglo-Saxon Protestants, or to all who voted in the latest election for a losing candidate." 127 Cong. Rec. 13360 (1981).

The Supreme Court has announced in cases following *McCardle* and *Klein* that its appellate jurisdiction "is confined within such limits as Congress sees fit to prescribe." The "Francis Wright," 105 U.S. 381, 385 (1881). However, the establishment of exceptions and regulations must give "due regard to all the provisions of the Constitution." United States v. Bitty, 208 U.S. 393, 399–400 (1908). For district and appellate courts, Congress "may give, withhold or restrict such jurisdiction at its discretion, provided it be not extended beyond the boundaries fixed by the Constitution." Kline v. Burke Const. Co., 260 U.S. 226, 234 (1922). Precisely what those boundaries are is never said, which is probably prudent. The Court has allowed Congress to limit the availability of certain judicial remedies, such as prohibiting district courts from issuing injunctions to control labor disputes or the enforcement of price regulations. Lauf v. E.G. Shinner & Co., 303 U.S. 323 (1938); Lockerty v. Phillips, 319 U.S. 182 (1942).

Contemporary Issues

An appropriations bill enacted in 1989 raised a possible violation of *Klein.* The bill stated that Congress determined and directed that the management of forests covered by previous legislation was "adequate consideration for the purpose of meeting the statutory requirements" that were the basis for two pending lawsuits. The Ninth Circuit held that the language in the appropriations bill was unconstitutional under *Klein* because it attempted to direct courts to reach a particular decision. A unanimous Supreme Court disagreed, concluding that the language in the appropriations bill merely changed the law underlying the litigation. Robertson v. Seattle Audubon Soc., 503 U.S. 429 (1992).

Although not technically an issue of withdrawing jurisdiction, in 1995 the Supreme Court referred to the *Klein* and *Seattle Audubon* cases in determining that Congress cannot pass legislation that has the effect of reopening cases that had been dismissed in response to a Supreme Court ruling. The congressional statute was considered a violation of separation of powers. Plaut v. Spendthrift Farm, Inc., 514 U.S. 211 (1995).

A 1996 decision by the Supreme Court directly concerned a possible challenge to the Exceptions Clause. In a unanimous opinion, the Court upheld a congressional statute that placed limits on prisoners who seek to make successive habeas petitions to the Court. After the first appeal, prisoners would need the approval of a three-judge panel before presenting a habeas petition to a trial judge. Felker v. Turpin, 518 U.S. 651 (1996).

These precedents cannot be read to justify the exclusion of whole areas of constitutional law from the Supreme Court.[10] The mere existence of a power does not mean that it may be used without limit. Such a construction runs counter to basic principles of constitutionalism, separation of powers, and checks and balances. The President has the "power" to withhold documents and appropriations, but we live under a system that recognizes limits on executive privilege and impoundment. The Court has the "power" to declare presidential and congressional acts unconstitutional, but it can exercise that power effectively only by acknowledging the limits imposed on it by the political system. The use of the Exceptions Clause must take due regard of an independent judiciary, the Supremacy Clause, and the constitutional rights available to citizens.

Disputes from 2004 to 2008

Twice in 2004 the House voted to strip federal courts of their ability to rule on the constitutionality of certain issues. On July 22, the House voted 233 to 194 to limit federal court jurisdiction over questions under the Defense of Marriage Act (DOMA). The bill language, cross-referencing to DOMA, reads: "No court created by Act of Congress shall have any jurisdiction, and the Supreme Court shall have no appellate jurisdiction, to hear or decide any question pertaining to the interpretation of, or the validity under the Constitution of, section 1738C or this section." 150 Cong. Rec. H6561-69, 6580-13 (daily ed. July 22, 2004); H. Rept. No. 108-614, 108th Cong., 2d sess. (2004). The Senate took no action on the bill.

The second House effort involved the emotional issue of placing the words "under God" in the Pledge of Allegiance. Although the Supreme Court in *Elk Grove Unified School Dist.* v. *Newdow* (2004) had held that the plaintiff in this case lacked standing to challenge the constitutionality of this language in the Pledge, the House decided that federal courts should have no future opportunities to rule on the issue. On September 23, voting 247 to 173, the House barred federal courts from hearing this type of Pledge case. The bill language: "No court created by Act of Congress shall have any jurisdiction, and the Supreme Court shall have no appellate jurisdiction, to hear or decide any question pertaining to the interpretation of, or the validity under the Constitution of, the Pledge of Allegiance, as defined in section 4 of title 4, or its recitation." The limitation would not apply to the Superior Court of the District of Columbia or the District of Columbia Court of Appeals. 150 Cong. Rec. H7391-95, 7451-78 (daily ed. Sept. 22–23, 2004); H. Rept. No. 108-691, 108th Cong., 2d Sess. (2004). The Senate did not act on that measure either.

In 2005 and 2006, Congress took several steps in an effort to strip federal courts of jurisdiction to hear cases brought by detainees held at the U.S. naval base in Guantánamo Bay, Cuba. The first appeared in the Detainee Treatment Act of 2005, which placed restrictions on the jurisdiction of federal courts to hear habeas petitions filed by the detainees. P.L. 109-148, 119 Stat. 2741-43 (2005). However, the Supreme Court in *Hamdan v. Rumsfeld* (2006) interpreted the statutory language narrowly to permit the detainee in this case to have his appeal heard and decided by the Court. In response, Congress adopted more specific language in the Military Commissions Act of 2006. Section 7 provides that no federal court "shall have jurisdiction to hear or consider an application for a writ of habeas corpus filed by or on behalf of an alien detained by the United States who has been determined by the United States to have been properly detained as an enemy combatant or is awaiting such de-

---

10. For studies cautioning unbounded use of the Exceptions Clause, see Lawrence Gene Sager, "The Supreme Court, 1980 Term — Foreword: Constitutional Limitations on Congress' Authority to Regulate the Jurisdiction of the Federal Courts," 95 Harv. L. Rev. 17 (1981); Leonard G. Ratner, "Congressional Power over the Appellate Jurisdiction of the Supreme Court," 109 U. Pa. L. Rev. 157 (1960); and Henry M. Hart, Jr., "The Power of Congress to Limit the Jurisdiction of Federal Courts: An Exercise in Dialectic," 66 Harv. L. Rev. 1362 (1953).

termination." The D.C. Circuit would have exclusive jurisdiction to determine the validity of any *final decision* rendered by a military commission.

On June 12, 2008, the Supreme Court held that the procedures in the Detainee Treatment Act and the Military Commissions Act, regarding the right of detainees to have their cases heard by federal courts, operated as an unconstitutional suspension of the writ of habeas corpus. The Court emphasized the importance of habeas as a check on arbitrary and unlawful restraint by the executive branch. Boumediene v. Bush, 553 U.S. ____ (2008).

Jurisdiction-Stripping Proposals: ABA Report

Congress has authority under Article III of the Constitution to regulate the jurisdiction of federal district and appellate courts and to make "exceptions" to the appellate jurisdiction of the Supreme Court. That authority, however, must be placed in the context of other constitutional principles and restrictions, an issue discussed below by the Association of the Bar of the City of New York, "Jurisdiction-Stripping Proposals in Congress: The Threat to Judicial Constitutional Review," December 1981. Footnotes omitted.

... There are pending in both houses of Congress at least 25 bills that, if enacted and upheld as constitutional, would have the effect of scrapping the federal courts' historical role in the system of checks and balances. These bills ... would divest the federal courts of all original and appellate jurisdiction to hear cases relating to (1) the constitutionality of programs of "voluntary" prayer in the public schools or other public places, (2) the constitutionality of laws or regulations affecting abortions, (3) busing as a remedy for school segregation, and (4) the constitutionality of treating men and women differently in connection with the armed forces or the draft. One bill, H.R. 114, may be read to go even further—to eliminate all federal judicial review of state court decisions.

In this Report, we do not address the merits of the various federal court decisions on these subjects that have prompted the proposed legislation, nor do we analyze the individual bills in detail. Rather, we address a question that is raised by all such proposals: Is the elimination of federal court jurisdiction to hear constitutional claims a lawful and appropriate response to judicial decisions of which a current majority in Congress disapproves? That question is fundamental to the structure of our government because, if Congress can legitimately curtail the federal courts' jurisdiction to hear constitutional claims concerning such specific issues as school prayer, abortion, and desegregation, then there is no principled limitation on Congress' power effectively to eliminate the judicial branch as a check on the other branches of the federal government or the states. By enacting any of the present bills, Congress would necessarily be claiming the power, should it so choose, to forbid the federal courts to hear *any* claim

asserted under the Bill of Rights or under any other provision of the Constitution.

Although most of the proponents of these bills generally style themselves as "conservatives," our review of the historical record reveals that their proposals are *radical* in the most extreme sense of that word. They would not only cast doubt upon the abortion, school prayer, and busing decisions of the past few years, but two centuries of historical development and constitutional doctrine. For the reasons set forth below, we conclude that this radical departure from the system of checks and balances that has served our nation well for the past two centuries is unwise and probably unconstitutional....

Article III of the Constitution does grant Congress power to regulate the jurisdiction of the federal courts.... But, as the following analysis shows, this power cannot fairly be construed to permit Congress to deprive the courts of jurisdiction to hear claims arising under the Constitution itself, particularly on an issue-by-issue basis. If Congress' power were so extensive, it would undo the elaborate system of checks and balances that the Framers of the Constitution so carefully crafted. First, it would upset the checks and balances among the three coordinate branches of the federal government, eliminating the judiciary as a check upon unconstitutional actions of the political branches by the simple expedient of removing their jurisdiction to consider challenges to such actions. Second, it would disrupt the allocation of power between the federal government and the states, by eliminating the power of the federal judiciary to restrain acts of the states that violate the Constitution. Third, and perhaps most significant, it would alter the constitutional balance between individual rights and majority will, since the judiciary is the only organ of government that is institutionally suited to protect the rights that our Constitution guarantees to individuals against the wishes of a strong-willed majority.

Another serious objection to legislation of the sort currently proposed is that it is undesirable to deal with complex and controversial social issues, particularly those of constitutional dimension, by eliminating the opportunity for full airing and debate in the federal judiciary. Indeed, one of the ironies of the present bills is that the constitutional interpretations with which the bills' sponsors differ would remain frozen as the supreme law of the land forever, binding upon the state courts under the Supremacy Clause and the doctrine of *stare decisis,* without any possibility of change through the evolution of legal thought or a change in judicial (particularly Supreme Court) personnel....

Human Life Bill: Senate Hearings

In response to the Supreme Court's abortion decision in *Roe* v. *Wade,* 410 U.S. 113 (1973), members of Congress looked for ways to overturn the ruling. Possible approaches: define *person* in the Fourteenth Amendment to include life beginning at conception, allow states to enact antiabortion laws, and prevent lower federal courts from striking down those state laws. Members looked for authority to Section 5 of the Fourteenth Amendment, under which Congress may "enforce, by appropriate legislation, the provisions of this article." This approach was defended by Stephen H. Galebach, attorney for Covington & Burling, and opposed by Professor Laurence H. Tribe of the Harvard Law School. "The Human Life Bill," hearings before the Senate Committee on the Judiciary, 97th Cong., 1st Sess. (1981).

STEPHEN H. GALEBACH:

In its 1973 abortion decision, the Supreme Court declared that it was unable to determine whether unborn children were human beings. The Court also held that unborn children were not persons within the meaning of the 14th amendment and that a woman's right to privacy took precedence over the State's right to protect potential life until a fetus had become viable.

The Supreme Court thus left unresolved the fundamental question of whether unborn children are human beings. The answer to this question necessarily influences the proper resolution of the abortion issue. However, if the Supreme Court is unable to decide when human life begins, who can make that decision? I submit that under the Constitution, Congress can make that decision.

The 5th and 14th amendments to the Constitution provide that no person may be deprived of life without due process of law. The 14th amendment expressly authorizes Congress to enforce its protections by appropriate legislation.

If Congress examines the question the Supreme Court was unable to answer and concludes that unborn children are human beings, then the Court's conclusion that they are not persons would be subject to change, and Congress would have the power to enforce the 14th amendment by declaring that unborn children are persons within the meaning of that amendment.

In my law review article, I explained the constitutional justification of the human life bill in terms of two leading theories advanced by Supreme Court Justices concerning the power of Congress to enforce 14th amendment rights.

The first theory is found in Justice Brennan's majority opinion in the landmark case of *Katzenbach* v. *Morgan.* Under this theory, Congress has broad power to define the scope and meaning of the 14th amendment rights so long as it acts to expand those rights.

The second theory is found in Justice Harlan's dissenting opinion in *Katzenbach* v. *Morgan.* Justice Harlan took a narrower view of Congress power, allowing Congress to make legislative findings that influence constitutional determinations, but reserving to the Court the authority to make the ultimate constitutional decision.

The majority opinion in *Katzenbach* v. *Morgan* is controversial because it confers on Congress such broad power to redefine the 14th amendment rights and to force its view on the Supreme Court. There is serious question whether the Court would or should reaffirm such a broad precedent today.

However, the constitutionality of the human life bill does not depend on the validity of such a broad theory of Congress power. The narrow enforcement power described by Justice Harlan is sufficient to justify the human life bill.

... The key sentence in Justice Harlan's opinion in *Katzenbach* v. *Morgan* is as follows:

"To the extent 'legislative facts' are relevant to a judicial determination, Congress is well equipped to investigate them, and such determinations are of course entitled to due respect."

According to this theory, congressional findings influence the Supreme Court, but do not necessarily control the Court's decisions. For example, in the 1965 and 1970 Voting Rights Acts, Congress influenced the Supreme Court to conclude that literacy tests for voting were racially discriminatory, even though in 1959 the Court held them not to be discriminatory. The Supreme Court was not persuaded, on the other hand, by Congress finding that equal protection requires the extension of voting rights to 18-year-olds in State elections.

· · ·

... [T]he Supreme Court will have to reevaluate the proper balance between the privacy right and the right to life of unborn children. The Supreme Court will still have the final say. The human life bill does not dictate what the result must be. All the bill does is ask the Court to look at the issue again in light of Congress' answer to the question that the Court said it could not resolve, namely, when does human life begin.

LAURENCE H. TRIBE:

The fact that a question is profound and important does not mean that Government must tell us how to answer it. The whole point of the Supreme Court's decision in 1973 was not simply one of judicial incapacity, for right after the Court said that it was unable to answer the question of when human life begins, the Court explained that what it really meant was that no State, by adopting its own answer to that question—choosing one theory of life rather than another—could be permitted to override the fundamental right of the pregnant woman to give an answer for herself.

One may disagree with that view. One may disagree with the view that this fundamental question

must be left to the woman. However, if one disagrees with that view, one is not disagreeing on a question of fact—What is the fetus? What is a human being?—but on a basic proposition of constitutional law.

The only way to undo a proposition of constitutional law announced by the Court is by constitutional amendment, not by legislative redefinition of constitutional language and not by waving the magic wand of section 5 of the 14th amendment and saying, "We will now inform the Court as to what the fertilized ovum is." ...

Let me close with a concern that I have that would persist even if this law were to be upheld, even if it were deemed to be constitutional.

I believe that S. 158 is inherently and unavoidably defective as measured by its own aims. I think the chairman stated the reasonable aims in a way that I found almost compelling when he said that we are simply trying to return to the States a matter that perhaps ought never to have been taken over by the Federal Government in the first place. If these matters are divisive, if they are unclear, why try to resolve them nationally? Why not decentralize?

However, observe that that is not, despite its intentions, what this law does. To begin with, on the matter of State and local funding for abortions, the law leaves States no choice. In Massachusetts and in California, the State constitutions require public funds to be expended without discrimination against abortion. Under this law, spending on abortion would be forbidden because that would, if this law were upheld, amount to State action which destroys the lives of persons.

To that degree at least, the matter is suddenly nationalized and not restored to its condition as it was in 1973. ...

It seems to me this measure is clearly unconstitutional. That it would be so held by the Supreme Court is not a matter of guesswork. It is not a responsible thing, however well-intentioned, for this Congress to do. I would regard it as a very sad day were this very serious, difficult issue to become the occasion for futile confrontation between the Congress and the Supreme Court, with a predictable outcome—one that would not enhance respect for either body, and one that would not advance the cause either of women or of unborn life.

Ex Parte McCardle

74 U.S. (7 Wall.) 506 (1869)

William H. McCardle, a Southern editor, had been arrested under the Reconstruction Acts and tried before a military commission for publishing articles considered incendiary and libelous. After his petition for a writ of habeas corpus was denied by a federal circuit court in Mississippi, the Supreme Court accepted jurisdiction and held oral argument. It was widely speculated that the Court might hold the Reconstruction Acts unconstitutional. Congress had begun the impeachment of President Andrew Johnson, partly for his opposition to the Reconstruction Acts. To prevent a decision on the constitutionality of the Reconstruction Acts, Congress passed legislation to withdraw the appellate jurisdiction of the Supreme Court in McCardle's case.

The CHIEF JUSTICE delivered the opinion of the court.

The first question necessarily is that of jurisdiction; for, if the act of March, 1868, takes away the jurisdiction defined by the act of February, 1867, it is useless, if not improper, to enter into any discussion of other questions.

It is quite true, as was argued by the counsel for the petitioner, that the appellate jurisdiction of this court is not derived from acts of Congress. It is, strictly speaking, conferred by the Constitution. But it is conferred "with such exceptions and under such regulations as Congress shall make."

It is unnecessary to consider whether, if Congress had made no exceptions and no regulations, this court might not have exercised general appellate jurisdiction under rules prescribed by itself. For among the earliest acts of the first Congress, at its first session, was the act of September 24th, 1789, to establish the judicial courts of the United States. That act provided for the organization of this court; and prescribed regulations for the exercise of its jurisdiction.

The source of that jurisdiction, and the limitations of it by the Constitution and by statute, have been on several occasions subjects of consideration here. In the case of *Durousseau* v. *The United States,* particularly, the whole matter was carefully examined, and the court held, that while "the appellate powers of this court are not given by the judicial act, but are given by the Constitution," they are, nevertheless, "limited and regulated by that act, and by such other acts as have been passed on the subject." The court said, further, that the judicial act was an exercise of the power given by the Constitution to Congress "of making exceptions to the appellate jurisdiction of the Supreme Court." "They have described affirmatively," said the court, "its jurisdiction, and this affirmative description has been understood to imply a negation of the exercise of such appellate power as is not comprehended within it."

The principle that the affirmation of appellate jurisdiction implies the negation of all such jurisdiction not affirmed having been thus established, it was an almost necessary consequence that acts of Congress, providing for the exercise of jurisdiction, should come to be spoken of as acts granting jurisdiction, and not as acts making exceptions to the constitutional grant of it.

The exception to appellate jurisdiction in the case before us, however, is not an inference from the affirmation of other appellate jurisdiction. It is made in terms. The provision of the act of 1867, affirming the appellate jurisdiction of this court in cases of *habeas corpus* is expressly repealed. It is hardly possible to imagine a plainer instance of positive exception.

We are not at liberty to inquire into the motives of the legislature. We can only examine into its power under the Constitution; and the power to make exceptions to the appellate jurisdiction of this court is given by express words.

What, then, is the effect of the repealing act upon the case before us? We cannot doubt as to this. Without jurisdiction the court cannot proceed at all in any cause. Jurisdiction is power to declare the law, and when it ceases to exist, the only function remaining to the court is that of announcing the fact and dismissing the cause. And this is not less clear upon authority than upon principle.

Several cases were cited by the counsel for the petitioner in support of the position that jurisdiction of this case is not affected by the repealing act. But none of them, in our judgment, afford any support to it. They are all cases of the exercise of judicial power by the legislature, or of legislative interference with courts in the exercising of continuing jurisdiction.

On the other hand, the general rule, supported by the best elementary writers, is, that "when an act of the legislature is repealed, it must be considered, except as to transactions past and closed, as if it never existed." And the effect of repealing acts upon suits under acts repealed, has been determined by the adjudications of this court. The subject was fully considered in *Norris* v. *Crocker,* and more recently in *Insurance Company* v. *Ritchie.* In both of these cases it was held that no judgment could be rendered in a suit after the repeal of the act under which it was brought and prosecuted.

It is quite clear, therefore, that this court cannot proceed to pronounce judgment in this case, for it has no longer jurisdiction of the appeal; and judicial duty is not less fitly performed by declining ungranted jurisdiction than in exercising firmly that which the Constitution and the laws confer.

Counsel seemed to have supposed, if effect be given to the repealing act in question, that the whole appellate power of the court, in cases of *habeas corpus,* is denied. But this is an error. The act of 1868 does not except from that jurisdiction any cases but appeals from Circuit Courts under the act of 1867. It does not affect the jurisdiction which was previously exercised.

The appeal of the petitioner in this case must be

Dismissed for want of jurisdiction.

E. NONCOMPLIANCE

In a masterful phrase, rendered almost hypnotic by its elegance, Justice Jackson said: "We are not final because we are infallible, but we are infallible only because we are final." Brown v. Allen, 344 U.S. 443, 540 (1953). The historical record demonstrates convincingly that the Supreme Court is neither infallible nor final. The lack of finality is evident in the fluid quality of its decisions, reshaped over the years by all three branches. Furthermore, the Court often experiences substantial difficulty in obtaining full compliance with decisions when they are handed down. Noncompliance is a direct threat to the Court's dignity, authority, legitimacy, and reputation (see reading "Sustaining Public Confidence").

In theory, judicial opinions are binding on the public and the other branches of government. In practice, judicial opinions are implemented with varying degrees of fidelity by local and federal officials. Noncompliance sometimes results from deliberate evasion, as in the South's "massive resistance" to the desegregation cases. Unintentional violations may also occur, but they can be relieved by adequate education and clear judicial rulings. Between these two positions are various shades of avoidance and evasion.

In 1983 the Supreme Court held that the "legislative veto," used by Congress for 50 years to control executive actions, was unconstitutional. INS v. Chadha, 462 U.S. 919 (1983). Over the following years, however, Congress passed more than 400 additional legislative vetoes, all signed into law by Presidents Reagan, Bush I, Clinton, and Bush II. Moreover, Congress continued to exercise other instruments of control that are the functional equivalent of the legislative veto. Although the Court had announced one of the most important separation of powers cases of all time, the practical effect was not nearly as sweeping as the Court's decision (see readings on legislative veto in Chapter 6).

One source of noncompliance is poor communication of judicial opinions. Scholars have found that most people do not know or understand decisions rendered by the courts. Instead, the public receives abbreviated interpretations, often erroneous, from the media and local officials. For a variety of reasons, the media have difficulty providing adequate coverage of the courts.

Second, the sheer force of inertia limits compliance. Court decisions must pass through the perceptual screens of citizens who believe that current practices can persist with only slight modifications. A half century after *Engel* v. *Vitale* (1962), which struck down state-sponsored prayers in public schools, school authorities continue to set aside time during the day for students to say prayers (see reading). Local officials may prefer to reinterpret judicial decisions on church-state separation to minimize the level of conflict and dissension within their communities.[11]

---

11. Kenneth M. Dolbeare and Phillip E. Hammond, The School Prayer Decisions: From Court Policy to Local Practice (1971); Frank J. Sorauf, "*Zorach* v. *Clauson:* The Impact of a Supreme Court Decision," 53 Am. Pol. Sci. Rev. 777 (1959); Gordon Patric, "The Impact of a Court Decision: Aftermath of the McCollum Case," 6 J. Pub. L. 455 (1957).

Justice Thurgood Marshall Encourages Lower Courts to Protect Rights More Expansively than Supreme Court

Dissenting in *Bell* v. *Wolfish* (1979), a case involving the rights of prisoners, Justice Marshall argued that the lower courts were correct the first time when they concluded that pretrial detainees should not be subjected to certain procedures (such as body-cavity searches) while in jail awaiting trial. As part of his responsibilities for supervising the Second Circuit (which had been reversed in this case), Marshall gave an address before the judges of that circuit and said that he "can only hope that district and appellate judges will read the [Court's] decision narrowly." His conclusion produced gasps from the audience: "Ill-conceived reversals should be considered as no more than temporary interruptions." The New York Times, May 28, 1979, at A1, A11.

As noted by political scientist Sotirios Barber: "Justice Marshall's remarks attracted an unusual amount of public attention, for this was not the kind of talk one usually hears from members of the Supreme Court.... Surely, a measure of shock was understandable; here was a top judicial official appearing to exhort the judges of his circuit to take advantage of whatever opportunities they might have to undermine the will of the Supreme Court. Justice Marshall knew that his advice could have an effect on the course of decision in the lower courts." Sotirios A. Barber, On What the Constitution Means 3 (1984).

Lower-Court Implementation

Decisions by the Supreme Court and federal appellate courts are filtered through U.S. district courts and state courts. Lower courts, legislatures, and administrators have a number of ways to avoid full compliance. Lower courts can reinterpret rulings. Parties can relitigate to delay implementation or appeal to legislators to reverse a ruling that turns on statutory interpretation. When the Supreme Court reverses a lower court decision, it may remand the case for disposition "not inconsistent with this opinion." In this new round, the litigant who found success at the Supreme Court level may lose out in the lower courts. 67 Harv. L. Rev. 1251 (1954). For a specific example of this surprise reversal, see the box in Section G of Chapter 1.

If the Court's opinion is a patchwork quilt, stitched together from disparate strands of conflicting views in the majority, the leeway for lower courts and elected officials will be substantial. Ambiguities can result from "inadvertence, or because of a deliberate fudging or vagueness built into the opinion to secure the support of a wavering colleague." Davis & Reynolds, 1974 Duke L. J. 59, 71. When the Supreme Court is unable to muster a majority of Justices behind a decision and instead merely releases a plurality opinion, a confused message is sent to lower courts (state and federal) and to the legislative and executive branches.

Judges in the lower courts have substantial latitude in applying Supreme Court doctrines. Justice Thurgood Marshall, after dissenting in a case that reversed the Second Circuit, later met with the judges from that circuit and urged them to read the Court's decision narrowly (see box). In 1985 Justice Brennan said that the Court's rulings on *Miranda*-type cases "have led nearly every lower court to reject its simplistic reasoning." Oregon v. Elstad, 470 U.S. 298, 320 (1985) (dissenting opinion). He pointed out that the Court's reasoning "is sufficiently obscured and qualified as to leave state and federal courts with continued authority to combat obvious flouting by the authorities of the privilege against self-incrimination. I am confident that lower courts will exercise this authority responsibly, as they have for the most part prior to this Court's intervention." Id. at 346.

After the Supreme Court handed down its Desegregation Decision in 1954, lower court judges followed different paths in implementing the ruling. Some were faithful; others were defiant or evasive. Many federal judges were torn between the edict of the High Court and the sentiments and customs of their local communities. It has been said that the Constitution is what the Supreme Court says it is, but Supreme Court decisions often mean what district courts say they mean. Jack W. Peltason, Federal Courts in the Political Process 14 (1955).

Sustaining Public Confidence

In *Baker* v. *Carr*, 369 U.S. 186 (1962), the Supreme Court accepted jurisdiction to decide the politically volatile issue of legislative reapportionment. Justice Frankfurter, who had written the Court's opinion in *Colegrove* v. *Green*, 328 U.S. 549 (1946), describing reapportionment as "of a peculiarly political nature and therefore not meet for judicial determination," dissented in *Baker*. Although he proved to be a false prophet by overstating the difficulties of judicial remedies to malapportionment, his dissent explains that the Court's ultimate authority is not its status as the "court of last resort" but rather its ability to sustain public confidence in the moral force of its opinions.

MR. JUSTICE FRANKFURTER, whom MR. JUSTICE HARLAN joins, dissenting.

The Court today reverses a uniform course of decision established by a dozen cases, including one by which the very claim now sustained was unanimously rejected only five years ago. The impressive body of rulings thus cast aside reflected the equally uniform course of our political history regarding the relationship between population and legislative representation—a wholly different matter from denial of the franchise to individuals because of race, color, religion or sex. Such a massive repudiation of the experience of our whole past in asserting destructively novel judicial power demands a detailed analysis of the role of this Court in our constitutional scheme. Disregard of inherent limits in the effective exercise of the Court's "judicial Power" not only presages the futility of judicial intervention in the essentially political conflict of forces by which the relation between population and representation has time out of mind been and now is determined. It may well impair the Court's position as the ultimate organ of "the supreme Law of the Land" in that vast range of legal problems, often strongly entangled in popular feeling, on which this Court must pronounce. The Court's authority—possessed of neither the purse nor the sword—ultimately rests on sustained public confidence in its moral sanction. Such feeling must be nourished by the Court's complete detachment, in fact and in appearance, from political entanglements and by abstention from injecting itself into the clash of political forces in political settlements.

... [T]here is not under our Constitution a judicial remedy for every political mischief, for every undesirable exercise of legislative power. The Framers carefully and with deliberate forethought refused so to enthrone the judiciary. In this situation, as in others of like nature, appeal for relief does not belong here. Appeal must be to an informed, civically militant electorate. In a democratic society like ours, relief must come through an aroused popular conscience that sears the conscience of the people's representatives. In any event there is nothing judicially more unseemly nor more self-defeating than for this Court to make *in terrorem* pronouncements, to indulge in merely empty rhetoric, sounding a word of promise to the ear, sure to be disappointing to the hope.

Prayers in Public Schools

In *Engel* v. *Vitale*, 370 U.S. 421 (1962), the Supreme Court struck down state-sponsored prayers in public schools. Nevertheless, school authorities across the nation permitted prayers to continue, sometimes by acquiescing to the initiatives of individual teachers, sometimes by directly intervening to assure a daily prayer. The following extracts are from an article by David E. Rosenbaum, "Prayer in Many Schoolrooms Continues Despite '62 Ruling," *The New York Times*, March 11, 1984, Section 1, pp. 1, 32.

The 31 children in Alvenia P. Hunter's second-grade class at the Pratt Elementary School in Birmingham, Ala., began the school day Thursday as they do every day, by bowing their heads for prayer.

In unison, they recited: "O, help me please each day to find new ways of just being kind. At home, at work, at school and play, please help me now and every day. Amen."

Mrs. Hunter's class is one of many across the nation where, despite the Supreme Court's prohibition of organized prayer in the schools more than 20 years ago, students continue to recite prayers, sing hymns or read the Bible aloud.

Many more students observe a period of silence in which they can pray if they want, a practice the Supreme Court has neither upheld nor rejected.

There is no organized worship in most of the country's public schools. In the main, educators have accepted the Supreme Court's doctrine that prayer prescribed by government or led by a teacher, a government employee, violates the First Amendment sanction against "establishment of religion." ...

A spot check of schools in communities from coast to coast last week revealed practices ranging from that in Iowa, where few schools had organized prayers even before the Supreme Court outlawed them in 1962, a practice that continues, to that in North Carolina, where a survey found regular prayer recitation and Bible readings in 39 of the state's 100 counties.

Mrs. Hunter, who has been a teacher for 18 years, said she had never heard an objection to her classroom prayer from a parent or a principal. "I believe in doing things right," she said. "I have been given the strength to come here and the ability to teach. This way I am thanking my God for enabling me to come here to work."

Louis Dale, president of the Birmingham School Board, said that the board had an official policy against organized prayer in the schools but that the policy was not enforced. He said he was personally of two minds about the matter.

. . .

In some places, parents who complained about prayers in the schools have been ostracized, or worse.

Three years ago, two mothers sued to stop organized prayers in the schools in Little Axe, Okla., a rural community southeast of Oklahoma City. One of the women, JoAnn Bell, a member of the Church of the Nazarene, argued that other people should not tell her children how to pray. She said last week that after she won her suit in Federal court, she was beaten by a school worker and her home was set afire, so she moved.

F. CONSTITUTIONAL DIALOGUES

"Judicial sacrosanctity" can be a useful rallying cry to protect the independence of the courts from external attacks. The concept is a powerful talisman for warding off major court-curbing efforts, such as court-packing or the withdrawal of appellate jurisdiction. However, it is ineffective in preventing Congress from passing laws to reverse statutory interpretations by the courts. No one doubts the right of Congress to pass legislation that overturns what it considers to be judicial misinterpretations of statutes. But even when the courts render a constitutional interpretation, it is usually only a matter of time before Congress prevails. Through changes in the composition of courts or adjustments in the attitudes of judges who continue to sit, a determined majority in Congress is likely to have its way. At some point a similar statute, struck down in the past as unconstitutional, will find acceptance in the courts. That pattern has been evident in such areas as commerce, federalism, and civil rights.

Do these congressional challenges to the Court threaten to usurp judicial responsibilities? If the Constitution could be interpreted in mechanical fashion, left unchanged over the years and with few dissenting or even concurring opinions, and if the record revealed precious few instances of the Court reversing itself, this argument might have merit. But if the function of the Supreme Court is to apply the general language of the Constitution to changing needs, and if the Constitution is developmental rather than static in meaning, there can be no doubt about the propriety of legislation that prompts the Court to reconsider its decisions.

When the Supreme Court struck down the first effort by Congress to regulate child labor, Congress shifted the basis for national legislation from the commerce power to the taxing power. That effort was also invalidated by the Supreme Court. By 1938 Congress had returned to the commerce power, and this time the legislation was upheld by a unanimous court. United States v. Darby, 312 U.S. 100 (1941). Similar examples can be cited. Congress decided to pass the Civil Rights Act of 1964, despite its apparent collision with the *Civil Rights Cases* of 1883. This conflict between judicial doctrine and legislative aspirations did not prevent Congress from acting. It avoided a direct confrontation with the judiciary by basing the statute not only on the Fourteenth Amendment but also on the Commerce Clause. The Supreme Court promptly upheld the Act as a valid exercise of congressional power. Heart of Atlanta Motel v. United States, 379 U.S. 241 (1964); Katzenbach v. McClung, 379 U.S. 294 (1964).

The "Continuing Colloquy"

Through what Alexander Bickel once called the Court's "continuing colloquy" with the political branches and society at large, the judiciary's search for constitutional principles can be reconciled with democratic values. Bickel, The Least Dangerous Branch 240 (1962). An open dialogue between Congress and the courts is a more fruitful avenue for constitutional interpretation than simply believing that the judiciary possesses superior skills and authority.

No one doubts that Congress, like the Court, can reach unconstitutional results. As Justice Brennan said in a 1983 dissent: "Legislators, influenced by the passions and exigencies of the moment, the pressure of constituents and colleagues, and the press of business, do not always pass sober constitutional judgment on every piece of legislation they enact." Marsh v. Chambers, 463 U.S. 783, 814 (1983). Yet if we count the times that Congress has been "wrong" about the Constitution and compare those lapses with the occasions when the Court has been "wrong" by its own later admissions, the results make a compelling case for legislative confidence and judicial modesty. George Anastaplo has noted that "in the great crises over the past two hundred years, when Congress and the Supreme Court have differed on major issues, Congress has been correct." Center Magazine, November/December 1986, at 15.

There is no justification for deferring automatically to the judiciary because of its doctrinal announcements and political independence. Each decision by a court is subject to scrutiny and rejection by private citizens and public officials. What is "final" at one stage of political development may be reopened at some later date, leading to revisions, fresh interpretations, and reversals of Court decisions. Through this process of interaction among the branches, all three institutions are able to expose weaknesses, hold excesses in check, and gradually forge a consensus on constitutional issues. Also through that process, the public has an opportunity to add a legitimacy and a meaning to what might otherwise be an alien and short-lived document.

Arguments for Judicial Finality

At certain moments in U.S. constitutional history, there has been a compelling need for an authoritative and binding decision by the Supreme Court. The unanimous ruling in 1958, signed by each Justice, was essential in dealing with the Little Rock crisis. Cooper v. Aaron, 358 U.S. 1 (1958). Another unanimous decision in 1974 disposed of the confrontation between President Nixon and the judiciary regarding the Watergate tapes. United States v. Nixon, 418 U.S. 683 (1974). These moments are rare. Usually the Court makes a series of exploratory movements followed by backing and filling — a necessary and sensible tactic for resolving constitutional issues that have profound political, social, and economic ramifications.

For the most part, Court decisions are tentative and reversible like other political events. The Court is not the Constitution. To accept the two as equivalent is to relinquish individual responsibility and the capacity for self-government. Popular sovereignty should not be made subordinate to judicial supremacy. Constitutional determinations are not exclusively for the courts. Individuals outside the courts have their own judgments to make. They cannot abdicate the duty to think for themselves. What is constitutional or unconstitutional must be left for citizens to explore, ponder, and come to terms with. Attorney General Edwin Meese III presented a controversial speech in 1986, in which he challenged the belief that the Constitution is equivalent to Supreme Court decisions (see reading).

Chief Justice Warren Disputes Judicial Supremacy

Whatever may be the correct view of the specific holding of these cases [regarding the rights of Japanese-Americans during World War II], their importance for present purposes lies in a more general consideration. These decisions demonstrate dramatically that there are some circumstances in which the Court will, in effect, conclude that it is simply not in a position to reject descriptions by the Executive of the degree of military necessity. Thus, in a case like *Hirabayashi*, only the Executive is qualified to determine whether, for example, an invasion is imminent....

The consequence of the limitations under which the Court must sometimes operate in this area is that other agencies of government must bear the primary responsibility for determining whether specific actions they are taking are consonant with our Constitution. To put it another way, the fact that the Court rules in a case like *Hirabayashi* that a given program is constitutional, does not necessarily answer the question whether, in a broader sense, it actually is....

In concluding, I must say that I have, of course, not touched upon every type of situation having some relation to our military establishment which the Court considers. Those to which I have pointed might suggest to some that the Court has at times exceeded its role in this area. My view of the matter is the opposite. I see how limited is the role that the courts can truly play in protecting the heritage of our people against military supremacy. In our democracy it is still the Legislature and the elected Executive who have the primary responsibility for fashioning and executing policy consistent with the Constitution. Only an occasional aberration from norms of operation is brought before the Court by some zealous litigant. Thus we are sometimes provided with opportunities for reiterating the fundamental principles on which our country was founded and has grown mighty. But the day-to-day job of upholding the Constitution really lies elsewhere. It rests, realistically, on the shoulders of every citizen.

SOURCE: Earl Warren, "The Bill of Rights and the Military," 37 N.Y.U. L. Rev. 181, 192–93, 202 (1962).

The "finality" of Supreme Court decisions was examined during Senate hearings in 1986 on William Rehnquist's nomination as Chief Justice and a year later on Anthony Kennedy's nomination as Associate Justice. Their attitudes were fundamentally different (see reading).

An "activist" member of the judiciary, Earl Warren, explained the limits of the courts. In times of political stress, the courts may acquiesce to actions that we later deplore. Commenting on the Court's role in upholding the treatment of Japanese-Americans during World War II, he said: "the fact that the Court rules in a case like *Hirabayashi* that a given program is constitutional, does not necessarily answer the question whether, in a broader sense, it actually is." The underlying message: a judicial failure to strike down a governmental action does not mean that constitutional standards have been followed. The habit of looking automatically to the courts to protect constitutional liberties is ill-advised. Warren concluded that under our political system the judiciary must play a limited role: "In our democracy it is still the Legislature and the elected Executive who have the primary responsibility for fashioning and executing policy consistent with the Constitution" (see box).

The belief in judicial supremacy imposes a burden that the Court cannot carry. It sets up expectations that invite disappointment if not disaster. A President once reassured his country in an inaugural address that an issue deeply dividing the nation "legitimately belongs to the Supreme Court of the United States, before whom it is now pending, and will, it is understood, be speedily and finally settled." The President was James Buchanan. The case about to be decided: *Dred Scott* v. *Sandford*.[12]

---

12. Judicial supremacy on constitutional issues was recently endorsed by Larry Alexander and Frederick Schauer, "On Extrajudicial Constitutional Interpretation," 110 Harv. L. Rev. 1359 (1997). For a rebuttal, see Neal Devins and Louis Fisher, "Judicial Exclusivity and Political Instability," 84 Va. L. Rev. 83 (1998). See also: Devins and Fisher, The Democratic Constitution (2004).

In her book, *The Majesty of the Law* (2003), Justice Sandra Day O'Connor examined the assertion that the judiciary's word on the meaning of the Constitution is final. She said that if "one looks at the history of the Court, the country, and the Constitution over a very long period, the relationship appears to be more of a dialogue than a series of commands." As to the Court's decision in *Roe v. Wade*, she points out that it did not end the debate over abortion rights: "A nation that docilely and unthinkingly approved every Supreme Court decision as infallible and immutable would, I believe, have severely disappointed our founders" (pp. 44, 45).

The Last-Word Doctrine

Although constitutional law and constitutional values have never been monopolized by the courts over the past two centuries, many scholars, judges, reporters and other observers continue to say that the Supreme Court has the final word on constitutional disputes. Such statements fail to address the following realities.

1. The fact that the Supreme Court upholds the constitutionality of a measure, as when it sustained the U.S. Bank in *McCulloch,* places no obligation on executive and legislative branches to agree with that judgment. Congress was free to discontinue the Bank. If it passed legislation to renew it, President Jackson was within his rights to veto the bill. A decision by the Supreme Court did not relieve the other branches of their duty or freedom to reach independent interpretations.

2. A decision by the Supreme Court that a certain practice is not prohibited by the Constitution, such as the use of search warrants in *Zurcher* v. *Stanford Daily* (1978) or access to bank records in *United States* v. *Miller* (1976), does not prevent the other branches from passing legislation to prohibit or restrict these practices. Rights unprotected by the courts may be secured by Congress and the President.

3. When the Supreme Court concludes that an action has no constitutional protection in the federal courts — for example, distributing petitions in a shopping center, as in *PruneYard Shopping Center* v. *Robins* (1980) — the states are not inhibited in any way from protecting those actions through their own constitutional interpretations. Decisions by the Supreme Court set a floor, or minimum, for constitutional rights. States may exceed those rights through independent interpretations of their own constitutions and unique cultures.

4. Many constitutional issues are resolved through rules of evidence, statutes, customs, and accommodations — a common-law method of settling disputes. Through these techniques, institutions outside the courts play a decisive role in shaping not only constitutional values but [**also**] constitutional doctrines.

5. There are occasions when Supreme Court rulings strike such a discordant note in the body politic that they will be tested again and again with new variations on the same theme. Court decisions are entitled to respect, not adoration. When the Court issues its judgment, we should not suspend ours. These challenges and collisions help keep the constitutional dialogue open and vigorous. In the search for a harmony between constitutional law and self-government, we all participate.

6. It is unrealistic to expect the Court to "settle" an important issue at a single stroke. Typically, the Court tackles one slice of an issue, leaving the rest for subsequent court decisions and nonjudicial actions. Justice Ginsburg put it this way: "In our system of adjudication, matters seldom can be fully settled 'on the basis of one or two cases'; they generally 'require a closer working out,' often involving responses by, or a continuing dialogue with, other branches of government, the States, or the private sector." Ginsburg, 83 Geo. L. J. 2119, 2125 (1995), citing language from Roscoe Pound.

7. The Court generally announces broad guidelines: "undue burden," "compelling governmental interest," "narrowly tailored," "all deliberate speed," and "prurient" material. It is up to elected officials (and juries) to apply those general principles to particular cases. The Court defines the edges; nonjudicial actors fill in the important middle.

8. Through the use of threshold doctrines and prudential considerations, the courts often duck constitutional issues and leave them to the regular political process. For example, the meaning of the

Statement and Account Clause for covert spending by the intelligence community is decided by the legislative and executive branches.

9. Judicial decisions are not pure creative acts. They build on precedents and values established by other actors, both at the national and state levels. Long before *Gideon* v. *Wainwright*, many states had decided that due process required that attorneys be appointed to represent indigent defendants. Federal courts often look for guidance to state practices and congressional judgments.

10. In many cases the Court does have finality, of a sort. In the summer of 1998, when Chief Justice Rehnquist turned down a White House effort to prevent the Office of Independent Counsel from questioning Secret Service agents about Monica Lewinsky's visits to President Clinton, within two hours the agents were called to testify in the grand jury room. However, Congress may reopen the issue by enacting legislation that gives Secret Service agents greater privilege not to testify about presidential activities. Thus, there are interim points of finality. On complex and overarching issues, like abortion, affirmative action, religious freedom, and the death penalty, there is no finality until a consensus is reached by all of the branches and society at large.

In 2008, Linda Greenhouse summed up 30 years of legal reporting for the *New York Times*. What she witnessed over that period was not a Supreme Court occupying a dominant position in deciding constitutional law, but rather Justices engaged "in the ceaseless American dialogue about constitutional values." Judicial rulings were not accepted as the "final voice" about a dispute. Elected leaders at the national and state level could respond by trying to do indirectly what the Court had just said it could not do directly, producing a "constitutional Ping-Pong match." The Court, she cautioned, "can only do so much. It can lead, but the country does not necessarily follow." The Court often found itself following nonjudicial decisions. It "ratifies or consolidates changes rather than propelling it." As a result, Justices "live in constant dialogue with other institutions, formal and informal." Judicial rulings can collide with policies adopted by legitimate participants outside the Court. On those occasions "it is often the court that eventually retreats when it finds itself out of sync with the prevailing mood." Linda Greenhouse, "2,691 Decisions," New York Times, July 13, 2008, WK 1, 4.

Is the Supreme Court the Constitution?

On October 21, 1986, Attorney General Edwin Meese III presented an address at Tulane University called "The Law of the Constitution." He referred to the Constitution as fundamental law, capable of change only by constitutional amendment, and contrasted that "higher law" to the body of law developed by the Supreme Court. He quoted from constitutional historian Charles Warren that "however the Court may interpret the provisions of the Constitution, it is still the Constitution which is the law, not the decisions of the Court." Meese's address sent shock waves across the country. Some columnists called the speech a "stink bomb" that showed disrespect for the Court. One newspaper column claimed that the speech invited anarchy. Other commentators predicted "enormous chaos" if Meese's view ever prevailed. His speech provides an important backdrop for the next reading, which is a colloquy between Senator Arlen Specter and Judge Anthony Kennedy on the Court's authority and power to issue the "final word" in constitutional law.

. . .

Since becoming Attorney General, I have had the pleasure to speak about the Constitution on several occasions. I have tried to examine it from many angles. I have discussed its moral foundations. I have also addressed on separate occasions its great structural principles—federalism and separation of powers. Tonight I would like to look at it from yet another perspective and try to develop further some of the views that I have already expressed. Specifically, I would like to consider a distinction that is essential to maintaining our limited form of government. That is the necessary distinction between the Constitution and constitutional law. The two are not synonymous.

What, then, is this distinction?

The Constitution is—to put it simply but, one hopes, not simplistically—the Constitution. It is a document of our most fundamental law. It begins "We the People of the United States, in Order to form a more perfect Union ..." and ends up, some 6,000 words later, with the 26th Amendment. It creates the institutions of our government, it enumerates the powers those institutions may wield, and it cordons off certain areas into which government may not enter. It prohibits the national authority, for example, from passing *ex post facto* laws while it prohibits the states from violating the obligations of contracts.

The Constitution is, in brief, the instrument by which the consent of the governed—the fundamental requirement of any legitimate government—is transformed into a government complete with "the powers to act and a structure designed to make it act wisely or responsibly." Among its various "internal contrivances" (as James Madison called them) we find federalism, separation of powers, bicameralism, representation, an extended commercial republic, an energetic executive, and an independent judiciary. Together, these devices form the machinery of our popular form of government and secure the rights of the people. The Constitution, then, is the Constitution, and as such it is, in its own words, "the supreme Law of the Land."

Constitutional law, on the other hand, is that body of law which has resulted from the Supreme Court's adjudications involving disputes over constitutional provisions or doctrines. To put it a bit more simply, constitutional law is what the Supreme Court says about the Constitution in its decisions resolving the cases and controversies that come before it.

And in its limited role of offering judgment, the Court has had a great deal to say. In almost two hundred years, it has produced nearly 500 volumes of *Reports* of cases. While not all these opinions deal with constitutional questions, of course, a good many do. This stands in marked contrast to the few, slim paragraphs that have been added to the original Constitution as amendments. So, in terms of sheer bulk, constitutional law greatly overwhelms the Constitution. But in substance, it is meant to support and not overwhelm the Constitution whence it is derived.

And this body of law, this judicial handiwork, is, in a fundamental way, unique in our scheme. For the Court is the only branch of our government that routinely, day in and day out, is charged with the awesome task of addressing the most basic, the most enduring political questions: What *is* due process of law? How *does* the idea of separation of powers affect the Congress in certain circumstances? And so forth. The answers the Court gives are very important to the stability of the law so necessary for good government. But as constitutional historian Charles Warren once noted, what's most important to remember is that "however the Court may interpret the provisions of the Constitution, it is still the Constitution which is the law, not the decisions of the Court."

By this, of course, Charles Warren did not mean that a constitutional decision by the Supreme Court lacks the character of law. Obviously it does have binding quality: It binds the parties in a case and also the executive branch for whatever enforcement is necessary. But such a decision does not establish a "supreme Law of the Land" that is binding on all persons and parts of government, henceforth and forevermore.

This point should seem so obvious as not to need elaboration. Consider its necessity in particular reference to the Court's own work. The Supreme Court would face quite a dilemma if its own constitutional decisions really were "the supreme Law of the Land" binding on all persons and governmental entities, including the Court itself, for then the Court would not be able to change its mind. It could not overrule itself in a constitutional case. Yet we know that the Court has done so on numerous occasions....

... If a constitutional decision is not the same as the Constitution itself, if it is not binding in the same way that the Constitution is, we as citizens may respond to a decision we disagree with. As Lincoln in effect pointed out, we can make our responses through the presidents, the senators, and the representatives we elect at the national level. We can also make them through those we elect at the state and local levels....

Once we understand the distinction between constitutional law and the Constitution, once we see that constitutional decisions need not be seen as the last words in constitutional construction, once we comprehend that these decisions do not necessarily determine future public policy—once we see all of this, we can grasp a correlative point: that constitutional interpretation is not the business of the Court only, but also, and properly, the business of all branches of government....

... [A]s Justice Felix Frankfurter once said, "The ultimate touchstone of constitutionality is the Constitution itself and not what we have said about it."

The "Finality" of Supreme Court Decisions: Senate Hearings

During the hearings in 1986 on the nomination of William Hubbs Rehnquist as Chief Justice of the U.S. Supreme Court, Senator Arlen Specter referred to the "binding precedent" of *Marbury* v. *Madison* (1803). Specter claimed that the Supreme Court "is the final arbiter, the final decisionmaker of what the Constitution means." Asked whether he agreed with that assessment, Rehnquist responded: "Unquestionably" (p. 187 of Rehnquist's 1986 hearings). A year later, when Senator Specter put that same question to Anthony M. Kennedy during his confirmation hearings for appointment as Associate Justice of the U.S. Supreme Court, Kennedy did not agree that the Court is the final arbiter of all constitutional issues. Instead, Kennedy develops an interesting picture of the constant interaction between the Court and the political branches (pp. 221–225 of Kennedy's 1987 hearings).

Senator SPECTER. There was a comment in a speech you made before the Los Angeles Patent Lawyers Association back in February of 1982, which I would like to call to your attention and ask you about.

Quote: As I have pointed out, the Constitution, in some of its most critical aspects, is what the political branches of the government have made it, whether the judiciary approves or not.

By making that statement, you didn't intend to undercut, to any extent at all, your conviction that the Supreme Court of the United States has the final word on the interpretation of the Constitution?

Judge KENNEDY. That is my conviction. And I think that the Court has an important role to play in umpiring disputes between the political branches.

Senator SPECTER. What did you mean by that, that in most critical aspects, it is what the political branches of the government have made it, whether the judiciary approves or not?

Judge KENNEDY. I was thinking in two different areas. One in this area of separation of powers and the growth of the office of the presidency. The courts just have had nothing to do with that.

Second, and even more importantly, is the shape of federalism. It seems to me that the independence of the States, or their nonindependence, as the case may be, is really largely now committed to the Congress of the United States, in the enactment of its grants-in-aid programs, and in the determination whether or not to impose conditions that the States must comply with in order to receive federal monies; that kind of thing.

Senator SPECTER. Well, this is a very important subject. And I want to refer you to a comment which was made by Attorney General Meese in a speech last year at Tulane, and ask for your reaction to it.

He said this:

"But as constitutional historian Charles Warren once noted, what is most important to remember is that, quote, however the Court may interpret the provisions of the Constitution, it is still the Constitution which is the law, not the decisions of the Court.

"By this, of course, Charles Warren did not mean that a constitutional decision by the Supreme Court lacks the character of law. Obviously it does have binding quality. It binds the parties in a case, and also the executive branch for whatever enforcement is necessary.

"But such a decision does not establish a supreme law of the land that is binding on all persons and parts of government henceforth and evermore."

Do you agree with that?

Judge KENNEDY. Well, I am not sure—I am not sure I read that entire speech. But if we can just take it as a question, whether or not I agree that the decisions of the Supreme Court are or are not the law of the land. They are the law of the land, and they must be obeyed.

I am somewhat reluctant to say that in all circumstances each legislator is immediately bound by the full consequences of a Supreme Court decree.

Senator SPECTER. Why not?

Judge KENNEDY. Well, as I have indicated before, the Constitution doesn't work very well if there is not a high degree of voluntary compliance, and, in the school desegregation cases, I think, it was not permissible for any school board to refuse to implement *Brown* v. *Board of Education* immediately.

On the other hand, without specifying what the situations are, I can think of instances, or I can accept the proposition that a chief executive or a Congress might not accept as doctrine the law of the Supreme Court.

Senator SPECTER. Well, how can that be if the Supreme Court is to have the final word?

Judge KENNEDY. Well, suppose that the Supreme Court of the United States tomorrow morning in a sudden, unexpected development were to overrule in *New York Times* v. *Sullivan*. Newspapers no longer have protection under the libel laws. Could you, as a legislator, say I think that decision is constitutionally wrong and I want to have legislation to change it? I think you could. And I think you should.

Senator SPECTER. Well, there could be legislation—

Judge KENNEDY. And I think you could make that judgment as a constitutional matter.

Senator SPECTER. Well, there could be legislation in the hypothetical you suggest which would give the newspapers immunity for certain categories of writings.

Judge KENNEDY. But I think you could stand up on the floor of the U.S. Senate and say I am introducing this legislation because in my view the Supreme Court of the United States is 180 degrees wrong under the Constitution. And I think you would be fulfilling your duty if you said that.

Senator SPECTER. Well, you can always say it, but the issue is whether or not I would comply with it.

Judge KENNEDY. Well, I am just indicating that it doesn't seem to me that just because the Supreme Court has said it legislators cannot attempt to affect its decision in legitimate ways.

Senator SPECTER. Well, but the critical aspect about the final word that the Supreme Court has is that there is a significant school of thought in this country that the Supreme Court does not have the final word. That the President has the authority to interpret the Constitution as the President chooses and the Congress has the authority to interpret the Constitution as the Congress chooses, and there is separate but equal and the Supreme Court does not have the final word.

And, if *Marbury* v. *Madison* is to have any substance, then it seems to me that we do have to recognize the Supreme Court as the final arbiter of the Constitution, just as rockbed.

Judge KENNEDY. Well, as I have indicated earlier in my testimony, I think it was a landmark in constitutional responsibility for the Presidents in the *Youngstown* case and the *Nixon* case to instantly comply with the Court's decisions. I think that was an exercise of the constitutional obligation on their part. I have no problem with that at all.

Senator SPECTER. Well, there has been compliance because it has been accepted that the Supreme Court is the final arbiter. I just want to be sure that you agree with that proposition.

Judge KENNEDY. Yes, but there just may be instances in which I think it is consistent with constitutional morality to challenge those views. And I am

not saying to avoid those views or to refuse to obey a mandate.

Senator SPECTER. Well, I think it is fine to challenge them. You can challenge them by constitutional amendment, you can challenge by taking another case to the Supreme Court. But, as long as the Court has said what the Court concludes the Constitution means, then I think it is critical that there be an acceptance that that is the final word.

Judge KENNEDY. I would agree with that as a general proposition. I am not sure there are not exceptions.

Senator SPECTER. But you can't think of any at the moment?

Judge KENNEDY. Not at the moment.

Senator SPECTER. Okay. If you do think of any between now and the time we vote, would you let me know?

Judge KENNEDY. I will let you know, Senator.

Senator SPECTER. Let me pick up some specific issues on executive power and refer to a speech that you presented in Salzburg, Austria, back in November of 1980, where you talk about the extensive discretion saying, "The blunt fact is that American Presidents have in the past had a significant degree of discretion in defining their constitutional powers."

Then you refer to, "The President in the international sphere can commit us to a course of conduct that is all but irrevocable despite the authority of Congress to issue corrective instructions in appropriate cases." Then you refer to President Truman, saying he committed thousands of troops to Korea without a congressional declaration. And then you say, "My position has always been that as to some fundamental constitutional questions it is best not to insist on definitive answers."

And you say further, "I am not one who believes that all of the important constitutional declarations of most important constitutional evolutions come from pronouncements of the courts."

And, without asking you for a specific statement on the War Powers Act, that is a matter of enormous concern that engulfs us with frequency. Major questions arise under the authority of the Congress to require notice from the President on covert operations coming out of the Iran-contra hearings. What is the appropriate range of redress for the Congress? Do we cut off funding for military action in the Persian Gulf? Do we cut off funding for covert operations? Are these justiciable issues which we can expect the Supreme Court of the United States to decide?

Judge KENNEDY. Well, whether or not they are justiciable issues, of course, depends on the peculiar facts of the case, and I would not like to commit myself on that. But the very examples you gave indicate to me that there are within the political powers of the Congress, within its great arsenal of powers under article I of the Constitution, very strong remedies that it can take to bring a chief executive into compliance with its will, and this is the way the political system was designed to work.

The framers knew about fighting for turf. I don't think they knew that term, but they deliberately set up a system wherein each branch would compete somewhat with the other in an orderly constitutional fashion for control over key policy areas. And these are the kinds of things where the political branches of the government may have a judgment that is much better than that of the courts.

Senator SPECTER. But isn't it unrealistic, Judge Kennedy, to expect the Congress to respond by cutting off funds for U.S. forces in the Persian Gulf? If you accept the proposition that the President can act to involve us in war without a formal declaration, and the President and the Congress ought to decide those questions for themselves, isn't that pretty much an abdication of the Supreme Court's responsibility to be the arbiter and the interpreter of the Constitution?

Judge KENNEDY. Well, I don't know if it is an abdication of responsibility for a nominee not to say that under all circumstances he thinks the Court can decide that broad of an issue. If the issue is presented in a manageable judicial form, in a manageable form, I have no objection to the Court being the umpire between the branches.

On the other hand, I point out that having to rely on the courts may infer, or may imply an institutional weakness on the part of the Congress that is ultimately debilitating. It seems to me that in some instances Congress is better off standing on its own feet and making its position known and then its strength in the federal system will be greater than if it had relied on the assistance of the courts.

CONCLUSIONS

Judicial review fits our constitutional system because we like to fragment power. We feel safer with checks and balances, even when an unelected Court tells an elected legislature or elected President that they have overstepped. This very preference for fragmented power denies the Supreme Court an authoritative and final voice for deciding constitutional questions. We do not accept the concentration of legislative power in Congress or executive power in the President. For the same reason, we cannot permit constitutional interpretation to reside only in the courts. Supremacy in a single branch should be subordinate to the higher value placed on freedom, discourse, democracy, and limited government. The dialogue that takes place between the Court, elected government, and the American people is not merely inevitable and a conspicuous part of our history. It is also constructive and stabilizing because this dynamic adds to public understanding and public support of constitutional values.

We all have a need to respect procedure and our institutions. Nevertheless, respect for the judiciary does not mean blind deference and an unwillingness by other actors to think independently and critically. Congress can respect the President's duties in foreign affairs without abdicating its own constitutionally assigned powers. The history of American law provides convincing evidence that national policies hammered out jointly by two or more branches is superior to singlehanded efforts by one branch. Each branch should be exposed to penetrating critiques from the other two. From such scrutiny no branch is immune.

NOTES AND QUESTIONS

1. Rulings on such controversial issues as abortion, school busing and school prayers, among others, have triggered calls for Congress to strip the Supreme Court of some of its appellate jurisdiction. Advocates of this strategy have invoked the Exceptions Clause of Article III. What are the implications of court-stripping? Consider the impact on efforts by citizens to vindicate their rights and liberties in the Supreme Court. How is due process affected? Would lower federal courts exercise the final "judicial word" on the meaning of the Constitution?

2. Did the Court surrender its "judicial power" in *Ex parte McCardle* when it upheld congressional legislation to withdraw the appellate jurisdiction of the Court in McCardle's case? Or was this a temporary, strategic retreat? Consider the distinction between "jurisdiction" and "judicial power." When does a case move from the realm of jurisdiction to the realm of judicial power?

3. In theory, judicial opinions are binding on the public and other branches of government. In practice, of course, judicial opinions are implemented with varying degrees of fidelity by governmental officials. In your view, what are the implications of noncompliance for the enterprise of constitutional government? Is the Rule of Law undermined? Are there circumstances in which noncompliance is permissible, even desirable, and perhaps warranted? If so, when, and why? Recall the reaction by the executive and legislative branches to the Court's ruling in *INS v. Chadha*.

4. Having come to the end of your course, you are in a position to assess the oft-quoted observation that the Supreme Court has the final word on constitutional disputes. Does that assertion capture the realities of constitutional dialogue in the United States? If not, how would you explain the American process of resolving constitutional issues?

SELECTED READINGS

ALEXANDER, LARRY, AND FREDERICK SCHAUER. "On Extrajudicial Constitutional Interpretation." 110 Harvard Law Review 1359 (1997).

BECKER, THEODORE L., AND MALCOLM M. FEELEY, eds. The Impact of Supreme Court Decisions. New York: Oxford University Press, 1973.

BRECKENRIDGE, ADAM CARLYLE. Congress Against the Court. Lincoln: University of Nebraska Press, 1970.

CULP, MAURICE S. "A Survey of the Proposals to Limit or Deny the Power of Judicial Review by the Supreme Court of the United States." 4 Indiana Law Journal 386, 474 (1929).

DEVINS, NEAL, AND LOUIS FISHER. "Judicial Exclusivity and Political Instability." 84 Virginia Law Review 83 (1998).

———. The Democratic Constitution. New York: Oxford University Press, 2004.

DEVINS, NEAL, AND KEITH E. WHITTINGTON, EDS. Congress and the Constitution. Durham: Duke University Press, 2005.

"Efforts in the Congress to Curtail the Federal Courts: Pro & Con." Congressional Digest, May 1982.

ELLIOTT, SHELDEN D. "Court-Curbing Proposals in Congress." 33 Notre Dame Lawyer 597 (1958).

ESKRIDGE, WILLIAM N, JR. "Overriding Supreme Court Statutory Interpretation Decisions." 101 Yale Law Journal 331 (1991).

FISHER, LOUIS. "One of the Guardians Some of the Time," in Is the Supreme Court the Guardian of the Constitution? (Robert A. Licht, ed. Washington, D.C.: American Enterprise Institute, 1993).

———. "Statutory Construction: Keeping a Respectful Eye on Congress," 53 SMU Law Review 49 (2000).

———. The Supreme Court and Congress: Rival Interpretations. Washington, D.C.: CQ Press, 2009.

GEYH, CHARLES GARDNER. When Courts and Congress Collide: The Struggle for Control of America's Judicial System. Ann Arbor: University of Michigan Press, 2006.

HALPER, THOMAS. "Supreme Court Responses to Congressional Threats: Strategy and Tactics." 19 Drake Law Review 292 (1970).

HANDBERG, ROGER, AND HAROLD F. HILL, JR. "Court Curbing, Court Reversals, and Judicial Review: The Supreme Court Versus Congress." 14 Law & Society Review 309 (1980).

HARRIGER, KATY J., ED. Separation of Powers: Documents and Commentary. Washington, D.C.: CQ Press, 2003.

HENSCHEN, BETH. "Statutory Interpretations of the Supreme Court: Congressional Responses." 11 American Politics Quarterly 441 (1983).

IGNAGNI, JOSEPH AND JAMES MEERNIK. "Explaining Congressional Attempts to Reverse Supreme Court Decisions." 47 Political Research Quarterly 353 (1994).

KYVIG, DAVID E. Explicit and Authentic Acts: Amending the U.S. Constitution, 1776–1995. Lawrence, Kansas: University Press of Kansas, 1996.

LEUCHTENBURG, WILLIAM E. "The Origins of Franklin D. Roosevelt's 'Court-Packing' Plan." 1966 Supreme Court Review 347.

LICHT, ROBERT A. Is the Supreme Court the Guardian of the Constitution? Washington, D.C.: American Enterprise Institute, 1993.

LYTLE, CLIFFORD M. "Congressional Response to Supreme Court Decisions in the Aftermath of the School Desegregation Cases." 12 Journal of Public Law 290 (1963).

McDowell, Gary L. Curbing the Courts: The Constitution and the Limits of Judicial Power. Baton Rouge: Louisiana State University Press, 1988.

Mckenna, Marian c. Franklin Roosevelt and the Great Constitutional War: The Court-Packing Crisis of 1937. New York: Fordham University Press, 2002.

Mikva, Abner J., and Jeff Bleich. "When Congress Overrules the Court." 79 California Law Review 729 (1991).

Murphy, Walter F. Congress and the Court. Chicago: University of Chicago Press, 1962.

———. "Lower Court Checks on Supreme Court Power." 53 American Political Science Review 1017 (1959).

Nagel, Stuart S. "Court-Curbing Periods in American History." 18 Vanderbilt Law Review 925 (1965).

Nichols, Egbert Ray, ed. Congress or the Supreme Court: Which Shall Rule America? New York: Noble and Noble, 1935.

Note. "Congressional Reversal of Supreme Court Decisions: 1945–1957." 71 Harvard Law Review 1324 (1958).

———. "Tension Between Judicial and Legislative Powers as Reflected in Confrontations Between Congress and the Courts." 13 Georgia Law Review 1513 (1979).

Paschal, Richard A. "The Continuing Colloquy: Congress and the Finality of the Supreme Court." 8 Journal of Law & Politics 143 (1991).

Pritchett, C. Herman. Congress Versus the Supreme Court: 1957–1960. Minneapolis: University of Minnesota Press, 1961.

Quirk, William J. Courts and Congress: America's Unwritten Constitution. New Brunswick, N.J.: Transaction Publishers, 2008.

Ross, William G. A Muted Fury: Populists, Progressives, and Labor Unions Confront the Courts, 1890–1937. Princeton, N.J.: Princeton University Press, 1994.

Schmidhauser, John R., and Larry L. Berg. The Supreme Court and Congress: Conflict and Interaction, 1945–1968. New York: The Free Press, 1972.

Solimine, Michael E. and James L. Walker. "The Next Word: Congressional Response to Supreme Court Statutory Decisions." 65 Temple Law Review 425 (1992).

Stumpf, Harry P. "Congressional Response to Supreme Court Rulings: The Interaction of Law and Politics." 14 Journal of Public Law 377 (1965).

Tushnet, Mark. Taking the Constitution Away from the Courts. Princeton, N.J.: Princeton University Press, 1999.

Vose, Clement E. Constitutional Change: Amendment Politics and Supreme Court Litigation Since 1900. Lexington, Mass.: D.C. Heath, 1972.

Warren, Charles. "Legislative and Judicial Attacks on the Supreme Court of the United States — A History of the Twenty-Fifth Section of the Judiciary Act." 47 American Law Review 1, 161 (1913).

Appendix 1

The Constitution of the United States

We the People of the United States, in Order to form a more perfect Union, establish Justice, insure domestic Tranquility, provide for the common defence, promote the general Welfare, and secure the Blessings of Liberty to ourselves and our Posterity, do ordain and establish this Constitution for the United States of America.

ARTICLE 1

Section 1.   All legislative Powers herein granted shall be vested in a Congress of the United States, which shall consist of a Senate and House of Representatives.

Section 2.   The House of Representatives shall be composed of Members chosen every second Year by the People of the several States, and the Electors in each State shall have the Qualifications requisite for Electors of the most numerous Branch of the State Legislature.

No Person shall be a Representative who shall not have attained to the Age of twenty five Years, and been seven Years a Citizen of the United States, and who shall not, when elected, be an Inhabitant of that State in which he shall be chosen.

[Representatives and direct Taxes shall be apportioned among the several States which may be included within this Union, according to their respective Numbers, which shall be determined by adding to the whole Number of free Persons, including those bound to Service for a Term of Years, and excluding Indians not taxed, three fifths of all other Persons.][1] The actual Enumeration shall be made within three Years after the first Meeting of the Congress of the United States, and within every subsequent Term of ten Years, in such Manner as they shall by Law direct. The Number of Representatives shall not exceed one for every thirty Thousand, but each State shall have at Least one Representative; and until such enumerations shall be made, the State of New Hampshire shall be entitled to chuse three, Massachusetts eight, Rhode-Island and Providence Plantations one, Connecticut five, New-York six, New Jersey four, Pennsylvania eight, Delaware one, Maryland six, Virginia ten, North Carolina five, South Carolina five, and Georgia three.

When vacancies happen in the Representation from any State, the Executive Authority thereof shall issue Writs of Election to fill such Vacancies.

The House of Representatives shall chuse their speaker and other Officers; and shall have the sole Power of Impeachment.

Section 3.   The Senate of the United States shall be composed of two Senators from each State, [chosen by the Legislature thereof,][2] for six Years; and each Senator shall have one Vote.

Immediately after they shall be assembled in Consequence of the first Election, they shall be divided as equally as may be into three Classes. The Seats of the Senators of the first Class shall be va-

---

1. Changed by Section 2 of the Fourteenth Amendment.
2. Changed by the Seventeenth Amendment.

cated at the Expiration of the second Year, of the second Class at the Expiration of the fourth Year, and of the third Class at the Expiration of the sixth Year, so that one third may be chosen every second Year; [and if Vacancies happen by Resignation, or otherwise, during the Recess of the Legislature of any State, the Executive thereof may make temporary Appointments until the next Meeting of the Legislature, which shall then fill such Vacancies.][3]

No Person shall be a Senator who shall not have attained to the Age of thirty Years, and been nine Years a Citizen of the United States, and who shall not, when elected, be an Inhabitant of that State for which he shall be chosen.

The Vice President of the United States shall be President of the Senate, but shall have no Vote, unless they be equally divided.

The Senate shall chuse their other Officers, and also a President pro tempore, in the Absence of the Vice President, or when he shall exercise the Office of President of the United States.

The Senate shall have the sole Power to try all Impeachments. When sitting for that Purpose, they shall be on Oath or Affirmation. When the President of the United States is tried, the Chief Justice shall preside: And no Person shall be convicted without the concurrence of two thirds of the Members present. Judgment in Cases of Impeachment shall not extend further than to removal from Office, and disqualification to hold and enjoy any Office of honor, Trust or Profit under the United States: but the Party convicted shall nevertheless be liable and subject to Indictment, Trial, Judgment and Punishment, according to law.

Section 4.   The Times, Places and Manner of holding Elections for Senators and Representatives, shall be prescribed in each State by the Legislature thereof; but the Congress may at any time by Law make or alter such Regulations, except as to the Places of chusing Senators.

The Congress shall assemble at least once in every Year, and such Meeting shall be [on the first Monday in December,][4] unless they shall by Law appoint a different Day.

Section 5.   Each House shall be the Judge of the Elections, Returns and Qualifications of its own Members, and a Majority of each shall constitute a Quorum to do business; but a smaller Number may adjourn from day to day, and may be authorized to compel the Attendance of absent Members, in such Manner, and under such Penalties as each House may provide.

Each House may determine the Rules of its Proceedings, punish its Members for disorderly Behaviour, and, with the Concurrence of two thirds, expel a Member.

Each House shall keep a Journal of its Proceedings, and from time to time publish the same, excepting such Parts as may in their Judgment require Secrecy; and the yeas and Nays of the Members of either House on any question shall, at the Desire of one fifth of those Present, be entered on the Journal.

Neither House, during the Session of Congress, shall, without the Consent of the other, adjourn for more than three days, nor to any other place than that in which the two Houses shall be sitting.

Section 6.   The Senators and Representatives shall receive a Compensation for their Services, to be ascertained by Law, and paid out of the Treasury of the United States. They shall in all Cases, except Treason, Felony and Breach of the Peace, be privileged from Arrest during their Attendance at the Session of their respective Houses, and in going to and returning from the same; and for any Speech or Debate in either House, they shall not be questioned in any other Place.

No Senator or Representative shall, during the Time for which he was elected, be appointed to any civil Office under the Authority of the United States, which shall have been created, or the Emoluments whereof shall have been encreased during such time; and no Person holding any Office under the United States, shall be a Member of either House during his Continuance in Office.

---

3. Changed by the Seventeenth Amendment.
4. Changed by Section 2 of the Twentieth Amendment.

Section 7.   All Bills for raising Revenue shall originate in the House of Representatives; but the Senate may propose or concur with Amendments as on other Bills.

Every Bill which shall have passed the House of Representatives and the Senate, shall, before it become a Law, be presented to the President of the United States; If he approve he shall sign it, but if not he shall return it, with his Objections to that House in which it shall have originated, who shall enter the Objections at large on their Journal, and proceed to reconsider it. If after such Reconsideration two thirds of that House shall agree to pass the Bill, it shall be sent, together with the Objections, to the other House, by which it shall likewise be reconsidered, and if approved by two thirds of that House, it shall become a Law. But in all such Cases the Votes of both Houses shall be determined by yeas and Nays, and the Names of the Persons voting for and against the Bill shall be entered on the Journal of each House respectively. If any Bill shall not be returned by the President within ten Days (Sundays excepted) after it shall have been presented to him, the Same shall be a Law, in like Manner as if he had signed it, unless the Congress by their Adjournment prevent its Return, in which Case it shall not be a Law.

Every Order, Resolution, or Vote to which the Concurrence of the Senate and House of Representatives may be necessary (except on a question of Adjournment) shall be presented to the President of the United States; and before the Same shall take Effect, shall be approved by him, or being disapproved by him, shall be repassed by two thirds of the Senate and House of Representatives, according to the Rules and Limitations prescribed in the Case of a Bill.

Section 8.   The Congress shall have Power To lay and collect Taxes, Duties, Imposts and Excises, to pay the Debts and provide for the common Defence and general Welfare of the United States; but all duties, Imposts and Excises shall be uniform throughout the United States;

To borrow Money on the Credit of the United States;

To regulate Commerce with foreign Nations, and among the several States, and with the Indian Tribes;

To establish an uniform Rule of Naturalization, and uniform Laws on the subject of Bankruptcies throughout the United States;

To coin Money, regulate the Value thereof, and of foreign Coin, and fix the Standard of Weights and Measures;

To provide for the Punishment of counterfeiting the Securities and current Coin of the United States;

To establish Post Offices and post Roads;

To promote the Progress of Science and useful Arts, by securing for limited Times to Authors and Inventors exclusive Right to their respective Writings and Discoveries;

To constitute Tribunals inferior to the supreme Court;

To define and punish Piracies and Felonies committed on the high Seas, and Offences against the Law of Nations;

To declare War, grant Letters of Marque and Reprisal, and make rules concerning Captures on Land and Water;

To raise and support Armies, but no Appropriation of Money to that Use shall be for a longer Term than two Years;

To provide and maintain a Navy;

To make rules for the Government and Regulation of the land and naval Forces;

To provide for calling forth the Militia to execute the Laws of the Union, suppress Insurrections and repel Invasions;

To provide for organizing, arming, and disciplining, the Militia, and for governing such Part of them as may be employed in the Service of the United States, reserving to the States respectively, the Appointment of the Officers, and the Authority of training the Militia according to the discipline prescribed by Congress;

To exercise exclusive Legislation in all Cases whatsoever, over such District (not exceeding ten Miles square), as may, by Cession of particular States, and the Acceptance of Congress, become the Seat of the Government of the United States, and to exercise like Authority over all Places purchased by the Consent of the Legislature of the State in which the Same shall be for the Erection of Forts, Magazines, Arsenals, dock-Yards, and other needful Buildings; — And

To make all Laws which shall be necessary and proper for carrying into Execution the foregoing Powers, and all other Powers vested by this Constitution in the Government of the United States, or in any Department or Officer thereof.

Section 9.   The Migration or Importation of such Persons as any of the States now existing shall think proper to admit, shall not be prohibited by the Congress prior to the Year one thousand eight hundred and eight, but a Tax or duty may be imposed on such Importation, not exceeding ten dollars for each Person.

The Privilege of the Writ of Habeas Corpus shall not be suspended, unless when in Cases of Rebellion or Invasion the public Safety may require it.

No Bill of Attainder or ex post facto Law shall be passed.

[No Capitation, or other direct, Tax shall be laid, unless in Proportion to the Census or Enumeration herein before directed to be taken.][5]

No Tax or Duty shall be laid on Articles exported from any State.

No Preference shall be given by any Regulation of Commerce or Revenue to the Ports of one State over those of another: nor shall Vessels bound to, or from, one State, be obliged to enter, clear, or pay Duties in another.

No money shall be drawn from the Treasury, but in Consequence of Appropriations made by Law; and a regular Statement and Account of the Receipts and Expenditures of all public Money shall be published from time to time.

No Title of Nobility shall be granted by the United States: And no Person holding any Office of Profit or Trust under them, shall, without the Consent of the Congress, accept of any present, Emolument, Office, or Title, of any kind whatever, from any King, Prince, or foreign State.

Section 10.   No State shall enter into any Treaty, Alliance, or Confederation; grant Letters of Marque and Reprisal; coin Money; emit Bills of Credit; make any Thing but gold and silver Coin a Tender in Payment of Debts; pass any Bill of Attainder, ex post facto Law, or Law impairing the Obligation of Contracts, or grant any Title of Nobility.

No State shall, without the Consent of the Congress, lay any Imposts or Duties on Imports or Exports, except what may be absolutely necessary for executing it's inspection Laws: and the net Produce of all Duties and Imposts, laid by any State on Imports or Exports, shall be for the Use of the Treasury of the United States; and all such Laws shall be subject to the Revision and Controul of the Congress.

No State shall, without the Consent of Congress, lay any Duty of Tonnage, keep Troops, or Ships of War in time of Peace, enter into any Agreement or Compact with another State, or with a foreign Power, or engage in War, unless actually invaded, or in such imminent Danger as will not admit of delay.

ARTICLE II

Section 1.   The executive Power shall be vested in a President of the United States of America. He shall hold his Office during the Term of four Years, and, together with the Vice President, chosen for the same term, be elected, as follows

---

5. Changed by the Sixteenth Amendment.

Each State shall appoint, in such Manner as the Legislature thereof may direct, a Number of Electors, equal to the whole Number of Senators and Representatives to which the State may be entitled in the Congress: but no Senator or Representative, or Person holding an Office of Trust or Profit under the United States, shall be appointed an Elector.

[The Electors shall meet in their respective States, and vote by Ballot for two Persons, of whom one at least shall not be an Inhabitant of the same State with themselves. And they shall make a List of all the Persons voted for, and of the Number of Votes for each; which List they shall sign and certify, and transmit sealed to the Seat of the Government of the United States, directed to the President of the Senate. The President of the Senate shall, in the Presence of the Senate and House of Representatives, open all the Certificates, and the Votes shall then be counted. The Person having the greatest Number of Votes shall be the President, if such Number be a Majority of the whole Number of Electors appointed; and if there be more than one who have such Majority, and have an equal Number of Votes, then the House of Representatives shall immediately chuse by Ballot one of them for President: and if no Person have a Majority, then from the five highest on the List the said House shall in like Manner chuse the President. But in chusing the President, the Votes shall be taken by States, the Representation from each State having one Vote; A quorum for this Purpose shall consist of a Member or Members from two thirds of the States, and a Majority of all the States shall be necessary to a Choice. In every Case, after the Choice of the President, the Person having the greatest Number of Votes of the Electors shall be the Vice President. But if there should remain two or more who have equal Votes, the Senate shall chuse from them by Ballot the Vice President.][6]

The Congress may determine the Time of chusing the Electors, and the Day on which they shall give their Votes; which Day shall be the same throughout the United States.

No Person except a natural born Citizen, or a Citizen of the United States, at the time of the Adoption of this Constitution, shall be eligible to the Office of President; neither shall any Person be eligible to that Office who shall not have attained to the Age of thirty five Years, and been fourteen Years a Resident within the United States.

[In Case of the Removal of the President from Office, or of his Death, Resignation, or Inability to discharge the Powers and Duties of the said Office, the Same shall devolve on the Vice President, and the Congress may by Law provide for the Case of Removal, Death, Resignation or Inability, both of the President and Vice President, declaring what Officer shall then act as President, and such Officer shall act accordingly, until the Disability be removed, or a President shall be elected.][7]

The President shall, at stated Times, receive for his Services, a Compensation, which shall neither be increased nor diminished during the Period for which he shall have been elected, and he shall not receive within that Period any other Emolument from the United States, or any of them.

Before he enter on the Execution of his Office, he shall take the following Oath or Affirmation: —
"I do solemnly swear (or affirm) that I will faithfully execute the Office of President of the United States, and will to the best of my Ability, preserve, protect and defend the Constitution of the United States."

Section 2.   The President shall be Commander in Chief of the Army and Navy of the United States, and of the Militia of the several States, when called into the actual Service of the United States; he may require the Opinion, in writing, of the principal Officer in each of the executive Departments, upon any Subject relating to the Duties of their respective Offices, and he shall have Power to grant Reprieves and Pardons for Offences against the United States, except in Cases of Impeachment.

He shall have Power, by and with the Advice and Consent of the Senate, to make Treaties, provided

---

6. Changed by the Twelfth Amendment.
7. Changed by the Twenty-Fifth Amendment.

two thirds of the Senators present concur; and he shall nominate, and by and with the Advice and Consent of the Senate, shall appoint Ambassadors, other public Ministers and Consuls, Judges of the supreme Court, and all other Officers of the United States, whose Appointments are not herein otherwise provided for, and which shall be established by Law; but the Congress may by Law vest the Appointment of such inferior Officers, as they think proper, in the President alone, in the Courts of Law, or in the Heads of Departments.

The President shall have Power to fill up all Vacancies that may happen during the Recess of the Senate, by granting Commissions which shall expire at the End of their next Session.

Section 3.   He shall from time to time give to the Congress Information of the State of the Union, and recommend to their Consideration such Measures as he shall judge necessary and expedient; he may, on extraordinary Occasions, convene both Houses, or either of them, and in Case of Disagreement between them, with Respect to the Time of Adjournment, he may adjourn them to such Time as he shall think proper; he shall receive Ambassadors and other public Ministers; he shall take Care that the Laws be faithfully executed, and shall Commission all the Officers of the United States.

Section 4.   The President, Vice President and all civil Officers of the United States, shall be removed from Office on Impeachment for, and Conviction of, Treason, Bribery, or other High Crimes and Misdemeanors.

ARTICLE III

Section 1.   The judicial Power of the United States, shall be vested in one supreme Court, and in such inferior Courts as the Congress may from time to time ordain and establish. The Judges, both of the supreme and inferior Courts, shall hold their Offices during good Behaviour, and shall, at stated Times, receive for their Services, a Compensation, which shall not be diminished during their Continuance in Office.

Section 2.   The judicial Power shall extend to all Cases, in Law and Equity, arising under this Constitution, the Laws of the United States, and Treaties made, or which shall be made, under their Authority; — to all Cases affecting Ambassadors, other public Ministers and Consuls; — to all Cases of admiralty and maritime Jurisdiction; — to Controversies to which the United States shall be a Party; — to Controversies between two or more States; [between a State and Citizens of another State;][8] — between Citizens of different States; — between Citizens of the same State claiming Lands under Grants of different States, [and between a State, or the Citizens thereof, and foreign States, Citizens or Subjects.][9]

In all Cases affecting Ambassadors, other public Ministers and Consuls, and those in which a State shall be Party, the supreme Court shall have original Jurisdiction. In all the other Cases before mentioned, the supreme Court shall have appellate Jurisdiction, both as to Law and Fact, with such Exceptions, and under such Regulations as the Congress shall make.

The Trial of all Crimes, except in Cases of Impeachment, shall be by Jury; and such Trial shall be held in the State where the said Crimes shall have been committed; but when not committed within any State, the Trial shall be at such Place or Places as the Congress may by Law have directed.

Section 3.   Treason against the United States, shall consist only in levying War against them, or in adhering to their Enemies, giving them Aid and Comfort. No Person shall be convicted of Treason unless on the Testimony of two Witnesses to the same overt Act, or on Confession in open Court.

The Congress shall have Power to declare the Punishment of Treason, but no Attainder of Treason shall work Corruption of Blood, or Forfeiture except during the Life of the Person attainted.

---

8. Changed by the Eleventh Amendment.
9. Changed by the Eleventh Amendment.

ARTICLE IV

Section 1.   Full Faith and Credit shall be given in each State to the public Acts, Records, and judicial Proceedings of every other State. And the Congress may by general Laws prescribe the Manner in which such Acts, Records and Proceedings shall be proved, and the Effect thereof.

Section 2.   The Citizens of each State shall be entitled to all Privileges and Immunities of Citizens in the several States.

A Person charged in any State with Treason, Felony, or other Crime, who shall flee from Justice, and be found in another State, shall on Demand of the executive Authority of the State from which he fled, be delivered up, to be removed to the State having Jurisdiction of the Crime.

[No person held to Service or Labour in one State, under the Laws thereof, escaping into another, shall, in Consequence of any Law or Regulation therein, be discharged from such Service or Labour, but shall be delivered up on Claim of the Party to whom such Service or Labour may be due.][10]

Section 3.   New States may be admitted by the Congress into this Union; but no new State shall be formed or erected within the Jurisdiction of any other State; nor any State be formed by the Junction of two or more States, or Parts of States, without the Consent of the Legislatures of the States concerned as well as of the Congress.

The Congress shall have Power to dispose of and make all needful Rules and Regulations respecting the Territory or other Property belonging to the United States; and nothing in this Constitution shall be so construed as to Prejudice any Claims of the United States, or of any particular State.

Section 4.   The United States shall guarantee to every State in this Union a Republican Form of Government, and shall protect each of them against Invasion; and on Application of the Legislature, or of the Executive (when the Legislature cannot be convened) against domestic Violence.

ARTICLE V

The Congress, whenever two thirds of both Houses shall deem it necessary, shall propose Amendments to this Constitution, or, on the Application of the Legislatures of two thirds of the several States, shall call a Convention for proposing Amendments, which, in either Case, shall be valid to all Intents and Purposes, as Part of this Constitution, when ratified by the Legislatures of three fourths of the several States, or by Conventions in three fourths thereof, as the one or the other Mode of Ratification may be proposed by the Congress; Provided that no Amendment which may be made prior to the Year One thousand eight hundred and eight shall in any Manner affect the first and fourth Clauses in the Ninth Section of the first Article; and that no State, without its Consent, shall be deprived of its equal Suffrage in the Senate.

ARTICLE VI

All Debts contracted and Engagements entered into, before the Adoption of this Constitution, shall be as valid against the United States under this Constitution, as under the Confederation.

This Constitution, and the Laws of the United States which shall be made in Pursuance thereof; and all Treaties made, or which shall be made, under the Authority of the United States, shall be the supreme Law of the Land; and the Judges in every State shall be bound thereby, any Thing in the Constitution or Laws of any State to the Contrary notwithstanding.

The Senators and Representatives before mentioned, and the Members of the several State Legislatures, and all executive and judicial Officers, both of the United States and of the several States, shall be bound by Oath or Affirmation, to support this Constitution; but no religious Test shall ever be re-

---

10. Changed by the Thirteenth Amendment.

quired as a Qualification to any Office or public Trust under the United States.

ARTICLE VII

The Ratification of the Conventions of nine States, shall be sufficient for the Establishment of this Constitution between the States so ratifying the Same.

AMENDMENTS

(The first 10 Amendments were ratified December 15, 1791, and form what is known as the "Bill of Rights")

AMENDMENT 1

Congress shall make no law respecting an establishment of religion, or prohibiting the free exercise thereof; or abridging the freedom of speech, or of the press; or the right of the people peaceably to assemble, and to petition the Government for a redress of grievances.

AMENDMENT 2

A well regulated Militia, being necessary to the security of a free State, the right of the people to keep and bear Arms, shall not be infringed.

AMENDMENT 3

No Soldier shall, in time of peace be quartered in any house, without the consent of the Owner, nor in time of war, but in a manner to be prescribed by law.

AMENDMENT 4

The right of the people to be secure in their persons, houses, papers, and effects, against unreasonable searches and seizures, shall not be violated, and no Warrants shall issue, but upon probable cause, supported by Oath or affirmation, and particularly describing the place to be searched, and the persons or things to be seized.

AMENDMENT 5

No person shall be held to answer for a capital, or otherwise infamous crime, unless on a presentment or indictment of a Grand Jury, except in cases arising in the land or naval forces, or in the Militia, when in actual service in time of War or public danger; nor shall any person be subject for the same offence to be twice put in jeopardy of life or limb; nor shall be compelled in any criminal case to be a witness against himself, nor be deprived of life, liberty, or property, without due process of law; nor shall private property be taken for public use, without just compensation.

AMENDMENT 6

In all criminal prosecutions, the accused shall enjoy the right to a speedy and public trial, by an impartial jury of the State and district wherein the crime shall have been committed, which district shall have been previously ascertained by law, and to be informed of the nature and cause of the accusation; to be confronted with the witnesses against him; to have compulsory process for obtaining witnesses in his favor, and to have the Assistance of Counsel for his defence.

AMENDMENT 7

In Suits at common law, where the value in controversy shall exceed twenty dollars, the right of trial by jury shall be preserved, and no fact tried by a jury, shall be otherwise re-examined in any Court of the United States, than according to the rules of the common law.

AMENDMENT 8

Excessive bail shall not be required, nor excessive fines imposed, nor cruel and unusual punishments inflicted.

AMENDMENT 9

The enumeration in the Constitution, of certain rights, shall not be construed to deny or disparage others retained by the people.

AMENDMENT 10

The powers not delegated to the United States by the Constitution, nor prohibited by it to the States, are reserved to the States respectively, or to the people.

AMENDMENT 11
(Ratified February 7, 1795)

The Judicial power of the United States shall not be construed to extend to any suit in law or equity, commenced or prosecuted against one of the United States by Citizens of another State, or by Citizens or Subjects of any Foreign State.

AMENDMENT 12
(Ratified July 27, 1804)

The Electors shall meet in their respective states and vote by ballot for President and Vice-President, one of whom, at least, shall not be an inhabitant of the same state with themselves; they shall name in their ballots the person voted for as President, and in distinct ballots the person voted for as Vice-President, and they shall make distinct lists of all persons voted for as President, and of all persons voted for as Vice-President, and of the number of votes for each, which lists they shall sign and certify, and transmit sealed to the seat of the government of the United States, directed to the President of the Senate;—The President of the Senate shall, in the presence of the Senate and House of Representatives, open all the certificates and the votes shall then be counted;—The person having the greatest number of votes for President, shall be the President, if such number be a majority of the whole number of Electors appointed; and if no person have such majority, then from the persons having the highest numbers not exceeding three on the list of those voted for as President, the House of Representatives shall choose immediately, by ballot, the President. But in choosing the President, the votes shall be taken by states, the representation from each state having one vote; a quorum for this purpose shall consist of a member or members from two-thirds of the states, and a majority of all the states shall be necessary to a choice. [And if the House of Representatives shall not choose a President whenever the right of choice shall devolve upon them, before the fourth day of March next following, then the Vice-President shall act as President, as in the case of the death or other constitutional disability of the President. —]* The person having the greatest number of votes as Vice-President, shall be the Vice-President, if such number be a majority of the whole number of Electors appointed, and if no person have a majority, then from the two highest numbers on the list, the Senate shall choose the Vice-President; a quorum for the purpose shall consist of two-thirds of the whole number of Senators, and a majority of the whole number shall be necessary to a choice. But no person constitutionally ineligible to the office of President shall be eligible to that of Vice-President of the United States.

AMENDMENT 13
(Ratified December 6, 1865)

Section 1.   Neither slavery nor involuntary servitude, except as a punishment for crime whereof the party shall have been duly convicted, shall exist within the United States, or any place subject to their jurisdiction.

Section 2.   Congress shall have power to enforce this article by appropriate legislation.

AMENDMENT 14
(Ratified July 9, 1868)

Section 1.   All persons born or naturalized in the United States, and subject to the jurisdiction thereof, are citizens of the United States and of the State wherein they reside. No State shall make or enforce any law which shall abridge the privileges or immunities of citizens of the United States; nor shall any State deprive any person of life, liberty, or property, without due process of law; nor deny to any person within its jurisdiction the equal protection of the laws.

Section 2.   Representatives shall be apportioned among the several States according to their respective numbers, counting the whole number of persons in each State, excluding Indians not taxed. But when the right to vote at any election for the choice of electors for President and Vice President of the United States, Representatives in Congress, the Executive and Judicial officers of a State, or the members of the Legislature thereof, is denied to any of the male inhabitants of such State, being twenty-one years of age, and citizens of the United States, or in any way abridged, except for participation in rebellion, or other crime, the basis of representation therein shall be reduced in the proportion which the number of such male citizens shall bear to the whole number of male citizens twenty-one years of age in such State.

Section 3.   No person shall be a Senator or Representative in Congress, or elector of President and Vice President, or hold any office, civil or military, under the United States, or under any State, who, having previously taken an oath, as a member of Congress, or as an officer of the United States, or as a member of any State legislature, or as an executive or judicial officer of any State, to support the Constitution of the United States, shall have engaged in insurrection or rebellion against the same, or given aid or comfort to the enemies thereof. But Congress may by a vote of two-thirds of each House, remove such disability.

Section 4.   The validity of the public debt of the United States, authorized by law, including debts incurred for payment of pensions and bounties for services in suppressing insurrection or rebellion, shall not be questioned. But neither the United States nor any State shall assume or pay any debt or obligation incurred in aid of insurrection or rebellion against the United States, or any claim for the loss or emancipation of any slave; but all such debts, obligations and claims shall be held illegal and void.

Section 5.   The Congress shall have power to enforce, by appropriate legislation, the provisions of this article.

---

* Superseded by Section 3 of the Twentieth Amendment.

AMENDMENT 15
(Ratified February 3, 1870)

Section 1.   The right of citizens of the United States to vote shall not be denied or abridged by the United States or by any State on account of race, color, or previous condition of servitude.

Section 2.   The Congress shall have power to enforce this article by appropriate legislation.

AMENDMENT 16
(Ratified February 3, 1913)

The Congress shall have power to lay and collect taxes on incomes, from whatever source derived, without apportionment among the several States, and without regard to any census or enumeration.

AMENDMENT 17
(Ratified April 8, 1913)

The Senate of the United States shall be composed of two Senators from each State, elected by the people thereof for six years; and each Senator shall have one vote. The electors in each State shall have the qualifications requisite for electors of the most numerous branch of the State legislatures.

When vacancies happen in the representation of any State in the Senate, the executive authority of such State shall issue writs of election to fill such vacancies: *Provided,* That the legislature of any State may empower the executive thereof to make temporary appointments until the people fill the vacancies by election as the legislature may direct.

This amendment shall not be so construed as to affect the election or term of any Senator chosen before it becomes valid as part of the Constitution.

AMENDMENT 18
(Ratified January 16, 1919. Repealed December 5, 1933 by Amendment 21)

Section 1.   After one year from the ratification of this article the manufacture, sale, or transportation of intoxicating liquors within, the importation thereof into, or the exportation thereof from the United States and all territory subject to the jurisdiction thereof for beverage purposes is hereby prohibited.

Section 2.   The Congress and the several States shall have concurrent power to enforce this article by appropriate legislation.

Section 3.   This article shall be inoperative unless it shall have been ratified as an amendment to the Constitution by the legislatures of the several States as provided in the Constitution, within seven years from the date of the submission hereof to the States by the Congress.

AMENDMENT 19
(Ratified August 18, 1920)

The right of citizens of the United States to vote shall not be denied or abridged by the United States or by any State on account of sex.

Congress shall have power to enforce this article by appropriate legislation.

AMENDMENT 20
(Ratified January 23, 1933)

Section 1.   The terms of the President and Vice President shall end at noon on the 20th day of January, and the terms of Senators and Representatives at noon on the 3d day of January, of the years in which such terms would have ended if this article had not been ratified; and the terms of their successors shall then begin.

Section 2.   The Congress shall assemble at least once in every year, and such meeting shall begin at noon on the 3d day of January, unless they shall by law appoint a different day.

Section 3.   If, at the time fixed for the beginning of the term of the President, the President elect shall have died, the Vice President elect shall become President. If a President shall not have been chosen before the time fixed for the beginning of his term, or if the President elect shall have failed to qualify, then the Vice President elect shall act as President until a President shall have qualified; and the Congress may by law provide for the case wherein neither a President elect nor a Vice President elect shall have qualified, declaring who shall then act as President, or the manner in which one who is to act shall be selected, and such person shall act accordingly until a President or Vice President shall have qualified.

Section 4.   The Congress may by law provide for the case of the death of any of the persons from whom the House of Representatives may choose a President whenever the right of choice shall have devolved upon them, and for the case of the death of any of the persons from whom the Senate may choose a Vice President whenever the right of choice shall have devolved upon them.

Section 5.   Sections 1 and 2 shall take effect on the 15th day of October following the ratification of this article.

Section 6.   This article shall be inoperative unless it shall have been ratified as an amendment to the Constitution by the legislatures of three-fourths of the several States within seven years from the date of its submission.

AMENDMENT 21
(Ratified December 5, 1933)

Section 1.   The eighteenth article of amendment to the Constitution of the United States is hereby repealed.

Section 2.   The transportation or importation into any State, Territory, or possession of the United States for delivery or use therein of intoxicating liquors, in violation of the laws thereof, is hereby prohibited.

Section 3.   This article shall be inoperative unless it shall have been ratified as an amendment to the Constitution by conventions in the several States, as provided in the Constitution, within seven years from the date of the submission hereof to the States by the Congress.

AMENDMENT 22
(Ratified February 27, 1951)

Section 1.   No person shall be elected to the office of the President more than twice, and no person who has held the office of President, or acted as President, for more than two years of a term to which some other person was elected President shall be elected to the office of the President more than once. But this Article shall not apply to any person holding the office of President when this Article was proposed by the Congress, and shall not prevent any person who may be holding the office of President, or acting as President, during the term within which this Article becomes operative from holding the office of President or acting as President during the remainder of such term.

Section 2.   This article shall be inoperative unless it shall have been ratified as an amendment to the Constitution by the legislatures of three-fourths of the several States within seven years from the date of its submission to the States by the Congress.

AMENDMENT 23
(Ratified March 29, 1961)

Section 1. The District constituting the seat of Government of the United States shall appoint in such manner as the Congress may direct:

A number of electors of President and Vice President equal to the whole number of Senators and Representatives in Congress to which the District would be entitled if it were a State, but in no event more than the least populous State; they shall be in addition to those appointed by the States, but they shall be considered, for the purposes of the election of President and Vice President, to be electors appointed by a State; and they shall meet in the District and perform such duties as provided by the twelfth article of amendment.

Section 2. The Congress shall have power to enforce this article by appropriate legislation.

AMENDMENT 24
(Ratified January 23, 1964)

Section 1. The right of citizens of the United States to vote in any primary or other election for President or Vice President, for electors for President or Vice President, or for Senator or Representative in Congress, shall not be denied or abridged by the United States or any State by reason of failure to pay any poll tax or other tax.

Section 2. The Congress shall have power to enforce this article by appropriate legislation.

AMENDMENT 25
(Ratified February 10, 1967)

Section 1. In case of the removal of the President from office or of his death or resignation, the Vice President shall become President.

Section 2. Whenever there is a vacancy in the office of the Vice President, the President shall nominate a Vice President who shall take office upon confirmation by a majority vote of both Houses of Congress.

Section 3. Whenever the President transmits to the President pro tempore of the Senate and the Speaker of the House of Representatives his written declaration that he is unable to discharge the powers and duties of his office, and until he transmits to them a written declaration to the contrary, such powers and duties shall be discharged by the Vice President as Acting President.

Section 4. Whenever the Vice President and a majority of either the principal officers of the executive departments or of such other body as Congress may by law provide, transmit to the President pro tempore of the Senate and the Speaker of the House of Representatives their written declaration that the President is unable to discharge the powers and duties of his office, the Vice President shall immediately assume the powers and duties of the office as Acting President.

Thereafter, when the President transmits to the President pro tempore of the Senate and the Speaker of the House of Representatives his written declaration that no inability exists, he shall resume the powers and duties of his office unless the Vice President and a majority of either the principal officers of the executive department or of such other body as Congress may by law provide, transmit within four days to the President pro tempore of the Senate and the Speaker of the House of Representatives their written declaration that the President is unable to discharge the powers and duties of his office. Thereupon Congress shall decide the issue, assembling within forty-eight hours for that purpose if not in session. If the Congress, within twenty-one days after receipt of the latter written declaration, or, if Congress is not in session, within twenty-one days after Congress is required to assemble, determines by two-thirds vote of both Houses that the President is unable to discharge the powers and duties of his office, the Vice President shall continue to discharge the same as Acting President; otherwise, the President shall resume the powers and duties of his office.

AMENDMENT 26
(Ratified July 1, 1971)

Section 1.   The right of citizens of the United States, who are eighteen years of age or older, to vote shall not be denied or abridged by the United States or by any State on account of age.

Section 2.   The Congress shall have the power to enforce this article by appropriate legislation.

AMENDMENT 27
(Ratified May 7, 1992)

No law, varying the compensation for the services of the Senators and Representatives, shall take effect, until an election of Representatives shall have intervened.

Appendix 2

Justices of the Supreme Court (1789–2008)

Year	Chief Justice	Associate Justices								
1789	Jay	Rutledge	Cushing	Wilson	Blair					
1790	Jay	Rutledge	Cushing	Wilson	Blair	Iredell				
1791	Jay	Johnson	Cushing	Wilson	Blair	Iredell				
1793	Jay	Paterson	Cushing	Wilson	Blair	Iredell				
1795	Rutledge	Paterson	Cushing	Wilson	Blair	Iredell				
1796	Ellsworth	Paterson	Cushing	Wilson	Chase	Iredell				
1798	Ellsworth	Paterson	Cushing	Washington	Chase	Iredell				
1799	Ellsworth	Paterson	Cushing	Washington	Chase	Moore				
1801	Marshall	Paterson	Cushing	Washington	Chase	Moore				
1804	Marshall	Paterson	Cushing	Washington	Chase	Johnson				
1806	Marshall	Livingston	Cushing	Washington	Chase	Johnson				
1807	Marshall	Livingston	Cushing	Washington	Chase	Johnson	Todd			
1811	Marshall	Livingston	Story	Washington	Duvall	Johnson	Todd			
1823	Marshall	Thompson	Story	Washington	Duvall	Johnson	Todd			
1826	Marshall	Thompson	Story	Washington	Duvall	Johnson	Trimble			
1829	Marshall	Thompson	Story	Washington	Duvall	Johnson	McLean			
1830	Marshall	Thompson	Story	Baldwin	Duvall	Johnson	McLean			
1835	Marshall	Thompson	Story	Baldwin	Duvall	Wayne	McLean			
1836	Taney	Thompson	Story	Baldwin	Barbour	Wayne	McLean			
1837	Taney	Thompson	Story	Baldwin	Barbour	Wayne	McLean	McKinley		Catron
1841	Taney	Thompson	Story	Baldwin	Daniel	Wayne	McLean	McKinley		Catron
1845	Taney	Nelson	Woodbury	Baldwin	Daniel	Wayne	McLean	McKinley		Catron
1846	Taney	Nelson	Woodbury	Grier	Daniel	Wayne	McLean	McKinley		Catron
1851	Taney	Nelson	Curtis	Grier	Daniel	Wayne	McLean	McKinley		Catron
1853	Taney	Nelson	Curtis	Grier	Daniel	Wayne	McLean	Campbell		Catron
1858	Taney	Nelson	Clifford	Grier	Daniel	Wayne	McLean	Campbell		Catron
1862	Taney	Nelson	Clifford	Grier	Miller	Wayne	Swayne	Davis		Catron
1863	Taney	Nelson	Clifford	Grier	Miller	Wayne	Swayne	Davis	Field	Catron
1864	Chase	Nelson	Clifford	Grier	Miller	Wayne	Swayne	Davis	Field	Catron
1865	Chase	Nelson	Clifford	Grier	Miller	—	Swayne	Davis	Field	Catron
1867	Chase	Nelson	Clifford	Grier	Miller	—	Swayne	Davis	Field	—
1870	Chase	Nelson	Clifford	Strong	Miller	Bradley	Swayne	Davis	Field	
1872	Chase	Hunt	Clifford	Strong	Miller	Bradley	Swayne	Davis	Field	
1874	Waite	Hunt	Clifford	Strong	Miller	Bradley	Swayne	Davis	Field	
1877	Waite	Hunt	Clifford	Strong	Miller	Bradley	Swayne	Harlan	Field	
1880	Waite	Hunt	Clifford	Woods	Miller	Bradley	Swayne	Harlan	Field	
1881	Waite	Hunt	Gray	Woods	Miller	Bradley	Matthews	Harlan	Field	
1882	Waite	Blatchford	Gray	Woods	Miller	Bradley	Matthews	Harlan	Field	
1888	Fuller	Blatchford	Gray	Lamar	Miller	Bradley	Matthews	Harlan	Field	
1889	Fuller	Blatchford	Gray	Lamar	Miller	Bradley	Brewer	Harlan	Field	
1890	Fuller	Blatchford	Gray	Lamar	Brown	Bradley	Brewer	Harlan	Field	
1892	Fuller	Blatchford	Gray	Lamar	Brown	Shiras	Brewer	Harlan	Field	
1893	Fuller	Blatchford	Gray	Jackson	Brown	Shiras	Brewer	Harlan	Field	
1894	Fuller	White	Gray	Jackson	Brown	Shiras	Brewer	Harlan	Field	
1895	Fuller	White	Gray	Peckham	Brown	Shiras	Brewer	Harlan	Field	
1898	Fuller	White	Gray	Peckham	Brown	Shiras	Brewer	Harlan	McKenna	
1902	Fuller	White	Holmes	Peckham	Brown	Shiras	Brewer	Harlan	McKenna	
1903	Fuller	White	Holmes	Peckham	Brown	Day	Brewer	Harlan	McKenna	
1906	Fuller	White	Holmes	Peckham	Moody	Day	Brewer	Harlan	McKenna	
1909	Fuller	White	Holmes	Lurton	Moody	Day	Brewer	Harlan	McKenna	

1910	White	Van Devanter	Holmes	Lurton	Lamar	Day	Hughes	Harlan	McKenna
1912	White	Van Devanter	Holmes	Lurton	Lamar	Day	Hughes	Pitney	McKenna
1914	White	Van Devanter	Holmes	McReynolds	Lamar	Day	Hughes	Pitney	McKenna
1916	White	Van Devanter	Holmes	McReynolds	Brandeis	Day	Clarke	Pitney	McKenna
1921	Taft	Van Devanter	Holmes	McReynolds	Brandeis	Day	Clarke	Pitney	McKenna
1922	Taft	Van Devanter	Holmes	McReynolds	Brandeis	Butler	Sutherland	Pitney	McKenna
1923	Taft	Van Devanter	Holmes	McReynolds	Brandeis	Butler	Sutherland	Sanford	McKenna
1925	Taft	Van Devanter	Holmes	McReynolds	Brandeis	Butler	Sutherland	Sanford	Stone
1930	Hughes	Van Devanter	Holmes	McReynolds	Brandeis	Butler	Sutherland	Roberts	Stone
1932	Hughes	Van Devanter	Cardozo	McReynolds	Brandeis	Butler	Sutherland	Roberts	Stone
1937	Hughes	Black	Cardozo	McReynolds	Brandeis	Butler	Sutherland	Roberts	Stone
1938	Hughes	Black	Cardozo	McReynolds	Brandeis	Butler	Reed	Roberts	Stone
1939	Hughes	Black	Frankfurter	McReynolds	Douglas	Butler	Reed	Roberts	Stone
1940	Hughes	Black	Frankfurter	McReynolds	Douglas	Murphy	Reed	Roberts	Stone
1941	Stone	Black	Frankfurter	Byrnes	Douglas	Murphy	Reed	Roberts	Jackson
1943	Stone	Black	Frankfurter	Rutledge	Douglas	Murphy	Reed	Roberts	Jackson
1945	Stone	Black	Frankfurter	Rutledge	Douglas	Murphy	Reed	Burton	Jackson
1946	Vinson	Black	Frankfurter	Rutledge	Douglas	Murphy	Reed	Burton	Jackson
1949	Vinson	Black	Frankfurter	Minton	Douglas	Clark	Reed	Burton	Jackson
1953	Warren	Black	Frankfurter	Minton	Douglas	Clark	Reed	Burton	Jackson
1955	Warren	Black	Frankfurter	Minton	Douglas	Clark	Reed	Burton	Harlan
1956	Warren	Black	Frankfurter	Brennan	Douglas	Clark	Reed	Burton	Harlan
1957	Warren	Black	Frankfurter	Brennan	Douglas	Clark	Whittaker	Burton	Harlan
1958	Warren	Black	Frankfurter	Brennan	Douglas	Clark	Whittaker	Stewart	Harlan
1962	Warren	Black	Goldberg	Brennan	Douglas	Clark	White	Stewart	Harlan
1965	Warren	Black	Fortas	Brennan	Douglas	Clark	White	Stewart	Harlan
1967	Warren	Black	Fortas	Brennan	Douglas	Marshall	White	Stewart	Harlan
1969	Burger	Black	Fortas	Brennan	Douglas	Marshall	White	Stewart	Harlan
1970	Burger	Black	Blackmun	Brennan	Douglas	Marshall	White	Stewart	Harlan
1972	Burger	Powell	Blackmun	Brennan	Douglas	Marshall	White	Stewart	Rehnquist
1975	Burger	Powell	Blackmun	Brennan	Stevens	Marshall	White	Stewart	Rehnquist
1981	Burger	Powell	Blackmun	Brennan	Stevens	Marshall	White	O'Connor	Rehnquist
1986	Rehnquist	Powell	Blackmun	Brennan	Stevens	Marshall	White	O'Connor	Scalia
1988	Rehnquist	Kennedy	Blackmun	Brennan	Stevens	Marshall	White	O'Connor	Scalia
1990	Rehnquist	Kennedy	Blackmun	Souter	Stevens	Marshall	White	O'Connor	Scalia
1991	Rehnquist	Kennedy	Blackmun	Souter	Stevens	Thomas	White	O'Connor	Scalia
1993	Rehnquist	Kennedy	Blackmun	Souter	Stevens	Thomas	Ginsburg	O'Connor	Scalia
1994	Rehnquist	Kennedy	Breyer	Souter	Stevens	Thomas	Ginsburg	O'Connor	Scalia
2005	Roberts	Kennedy	Breyer	Souter	Stevens	Thomas	Ginsburg	O'Connor	Scalia
2006	Roberts	Kennedy	Breyer	Souter	Stevens	Thomas	Ginsburg	Alito	Scalia

Appendix 3

Glossary of Legal Terms

Abstention doctrine   Permits a federal court to relinquish jurisdiction where necessary to avoid needless friction with the state's administration of its own affairs.

Acquittal   Certifying the innocence of a person charged with a crime.

Advisory opinion   An opinion rendered by a court indicating how the court would rule on a matter; an interpretation of a law without binding effect. Federal courts do not issue advisory opinions.

Affidavit   A written statement of facts, made voluntarily and confirmed by oath or affirmation before a judge or magistrate.

Affirm   To declare that a lower court's judgment is valid and right. This is done by an appellate court.

Amicus curiae   "Friend of the court." A person or group, not a party to a case, that submits a brief detailing its views on a case.

Ante   "Before."

Appeal   A review by a superior court of an inferior court's decision. There may also be levels of appeal within an administrative agency.

Appellant   The party appealing a case.

Appellate jurisdiction   The power of an appellate court to review and revise the judicial action of an inferior court; distinguished from *original jurisdiction.*

Appellee   The party responding to a case brought by an appellant; sometimes called "respondent."

Arraignment   Bringing an accused before a court, stating the criminal charge against him or her and calling on him or her to enter a plea.

Article I court   See *legislative court.*

Article III court   See *constitutional court.*

Aver   In a pleading, to declare, assert, or allege.

Balancing test   A constitutional doctrine in which a court weighs an individual's rights with the rights or powers of the state.

Battery   The unlawful use of force, either bodily injury or offensive touching, against another person.

Bill of attainder   A legislative act that inflicts punishment without judicial proceeding.

Brandeis brief   A brief that includes, along with legal citations and principles, references to economic and social surveys. It takes its name from Louis D. Brandeis, who used such practices before joining the Supreme Court.

Brief   A written statement prepared by the counsel arguing a case in court.

Case   A general term for an action, cause, suit, or controversy, at law or in equity.

Case law   The aggregate of reported cases that forms a body of jurisdiction; distinguished from statutory law.

Case or controversy   A constitutional prerequisite, from Article III, that determines the justiciability of a question before a federal court.

Cause of action   The facts that give a person a right of judicial relief.

Certification, writ of   A method of taking a case from a federal appellate court to the Supreme Court. The appellate court may certify any question of law on which it requests instruction from the Court.

Certiorari, writ of   An order by the Supreme Court when it exercises discretion to hear an appeal. It may grant or deny "cert."

Circuit courts   Federal appellate courts with jurisdiction over several states.

Civil law   The body of law that is concerned with private rights and remedies; distinguished from *criminal law.*

Class action   A suit brought by a person or group of persons to represent the interests of a class.

Collateral estoppel The doctrine that prevents relitigation of the same issue in a suit upon a different claim or cause of action.

Common law The body of law that derives its authority from usages and customs or from court decrees regarding these usages and customs; distinguished from law created by legislative enactments (statutory law).

Compelling state interest The term used to uphold state action in the area of Equal Protection or First Amendment rights because of an overriding need for state action.

Concurrent powers Powers that may be exercised independently by Congress and state legislatures on the same subject matter.

Concurring opinion An opinion that agrees with the decision of the majority but offers separate reasons for reaching that decision.

Consent decree A decree entered by a judge expressing the consent of both parties in resolving their dispute; a contract by the parties made under the sanction of the court.

Constitutional court A court protected by Article III rights (life tenure and no diminution of salary). See *legislative court.*

Criminal law The body of law created to prevent harm to society; distinguished from *civil law.*

Curtilage The land and buildings immediately adjacent to a home.

Declaratory judgment A binding adjudication of the legal rights of litigants but with no award of relief.

De facto "In fact"; in reality; distinguished from *de jure.*

Defendant The party against whom relief is sought in an action or suit; the accused in a criminal case.

De jure "By law"; the result of official action; distinguished from *de facto.* For example, de jure segregation is mandated by law; de facto segregation exists but is not officially sanctioned.

Demurrer A defendant admits the facts of a complaint but states that they are insufficient to proceed upon or to oblige the defendant to answer.

De novo "From the beginning."

Dicta Expressions in a court opinion that go beyond the necessities of the case and are not binding. Singular is *dictum.* See *obiter dictum.*

Dissenting opinion A disagreement with the majority opinion. A dissent may or may not be accompanied by an opinion.

Distinguish A court's explanation of why a previous decision does not apply.

District courts Trial courts. Each state has one or more federal judicial districts.

Diversity jurisdiction The jurisdiction of federal courts over cases between citizens of different states.

Docket The list of cases set to be tried at a specified term.

Eo nomine "Under that name."

Eleemosynary Devoted to charity.

En banc The full bench of an appellate court, as distinguished from a panel of three judges.

Enjoin To require or command; specifically, to require a person to perform or desist from some act. See *injunction.*

Equity Justice administered according to fairness rather than the stricter rules of common law.

Estop To stop, bar, or prevent.

Exclusionary rule A rule that prohibits the introduction in a criminal trial of evidence obtained by illegal means, such as from a search or seizure that violates the Fourth Amendment.

Ex parte "On one side only"; by or for one party.

Ex post facto "After the fact."

Ex post facto law A law that inflicts punishment on a person for an act done which, at the time committed, was not illegal. This is forbidden by the U.S. Constitution.

Express Clear; definite; explicit; set forth in words; distinguished from *implied.*

Ex proprio vigore "By their own force."

Federal question A case arising under the U.S. Constitution, federal statutes, or treaties. It generally involves a significant or major issue.

Grand jury A jury of inquiry to hear accusations in criminal cases and find bills of indictment when it is satisfied that the accused should be tried. See *petit jury.*

Habeas corpus "You have the body." A writ commanding a law officer to bring a party before a court or judge. The purpose is to release someone from unlawful imprisonment.

Harmless error An error that is not prejudicial to the substantial rights of a person convicted. It does not provide grounds for granting a new trial.

Implied Not manifested by explicit and direct words. The meaning is gathered by necessary deduction; distinguished from *express*.

Inalienable rights Rights that are not capable of being surrendered without the consent of the person possessing such rights.

In camera "In chambers"; in private. In camera hearings occur in the judge's private chambers or when all spectators are excluded from the courtroom.

Indictment An accusation in writing presented by a grand jury. It charges the person named with an act that is a public offense.

In forma pauperis (I.F.P.) "In the character or manner of a pauper." Permission is given to a poor person to proceed without liability for court fees or costs.

Information An accusation against a person for some criminal offense. It differs from indictment in that it is presented by a public officer instead of by a grand jury.

Infra "Below."

Injunction A prohibitive remedy issued by a court that forbids the defendant to do some act.

In re "In the matter of."

Ipse dixit "He himself said it." A bare assertion resting on an individual's authority.

Judicial Conference The policy-making organization of the federal judiciary. Annual meetings consist of the Chief Justice of the United States, the chief judge of each judicial circuit, and a district judge from each judicial circuit.

Judicial council The meeting of judges of each circuit to assure expeditious and effective administration of the business of the courts.

Judicial review A court's authority to review the constitutionality of legislative and executive acts.

Jure belli "By the law of war."

Jurisdiction The authority, the right, or the power by which courts take cognizance of and decide cases. This term embraces every kind of judicial action.

Jurisprudence The philosophy of law; the science that treats the principles of law.

Jury A body of persons sworn to inquire into matters of fact and to declare the truth upon evidence laid before them.

Jus belli "The law of war."

Justiciable A matter appropriate for court review.

Legislative court Courts created by Congress (Article I courts) in contrast to those created by the Constitution (Article III courts). See *constitutional court*.

Litigant A party to a lawsuit.

Magistrate A person, such as a public civil officer, invested with executive or judicial power.

Mandamus "We command." The name of a writ issued from a court and commanding the performance of a particular act.

Mandatory jurisdiction The jurisdiction that a court must accept.

Moot A question is moot when it presents no actual controversy or where the issues have ceased to exist or have become academic or dead.

Motion An application made to a court or judge for the purpose of obtaining a rule or order.

Natural law A universal system of rules and principles that guide human conduct. It applies to all nations and people; distinguished from *positive law*. Also called "*jus naturale*."

Natural rights Rights that grow out of the nature of human beings; distinguished from rights created by *positive law*.

Obiter dictum "A remark by the way." A statement in an opinion that is not essential to the case at hand. Plural is *dicta*.

Order A direction of a court or judge made in writing but not included in the judgment.

Original jurisdiction The jurisdiction in the first instance; distinguished from *appellate jurisdiction*.

Overbreadth doctrine The requirement that a statute be aimed specifically at evils within the allowable area of governmental control. A statute cannot reach conduct that is constitutionally protected.

Per curiam   "By the court." An unsigned opinion reflecting a majority of the court.

Perjury   False, material statement under oath or equivalent affirmation.

Petitioner   The party filing a petition seeking action or relief from a court.

Petit jury   Trial jury; the ordinary jury to try civil or criminal action.

Plaintiff   The party bringing an action to obtain relief for a claimed injury.

Plurality opinion   An opinion of an appellate court that has the support of less than a majority of judges.

Police power   The power of government to protect the health, safety, welfare, and morals of its citizens.

Political question   An issue that must be resolved by the nonjudicial branches.

Positive law   A law enacted by a governmental body; distinguished from *natural law.*

Post   "After."

Preemption   The doctrine adopted by the U.S. Supreme Court holding that certain matters are of such a national character that federal laws take precedence over state laws.

Prima facie   "At first sight." A fact presumed to be true unless disproved by contrary evidence.

Pro se   "For himself." One who appears in court without legal representation.

Quash   To overthrow, vacate, annul; to make void.

Recuse   For a judge to disqualify himself or herself from hearing a case because of interest or prejudice.

Remand   To send a case back to a lower court with instructions to correct specified irregularities. This is done by an appellate court.

Respondent   One who answers. When the Supreme Court grants a writ of certiorari, the party seeking review is the petitioner and the party responding is the respondent.

Reverse   To overthrow or set aside. An appellate court may send a case back to a lower court with instructions to change the result reached.

Ripeness   The doctrine that requires a court to consider whether a case has matured or developed into a controversy worthy of adjudication.

Saving clause   The clause that returns to the states the power to enforce state laws not preempted by federal law. It is often used in federal statutes that preempt state action. Also refers to an exception for a particular provision in a statute that distinguishes it from the rest of the statute (see *severability clause,* which is a specific form of a saving clause).

Scienter   "Knowingly." Used to signify the defendant's guilty knowledge.

Seriatim   "One after another." Initially, each Justice of the Supreme Court prepared a separate opinion rather than have one Justice write for the majority.

Severability clause   Language in a statute providing that in the event one or more provisions are declared unconstitutional, the balance of the statute remains valid. Also called *separability clause.*

Standing   A position from which one may assert legal rights. To have standing to sue, a person must have a sufficient stake in a controversy to merit judicial resolution.

Stare decisis   "Stand by things decided." To abide by, or adhere to, decided cases.

State action   A term used to determine whether an action complained of has its source in state authority or policy.

Statutory law   Law created by legislative enactments.

Stay   To stop, arrest, or hold in abeyance.

Strict constructionism   A close or rigid reading and interpretation of a law or constitutional provision.

Sua sponte   "On its own initiative."

Sub nomine   "Under the name of."

Suborn   To procure or persuade another person to commit perjury.

Subpoena   "Under pain." A command to appear at a certain time and place. A *subpoena duces tecum* requires the production of books, papers, or objects. A *subpoena ad testificandum* requires testimony.

Sub silentio   "Under silence"; without notice taken.

Summary judgment   A short opinion written by the Court without receiving briefs or oral argument.

Supra   "Above."

Temporary restraining order (TRO)   An emergency remedy issued by a court until it can hear arguments or evidence on a controversy.

Three-judge court   A panel that combines federal district and appellate judges to expedite the review of a challenged action.

Trial court   The first court to consider litigation.

Trover   A remedy for any wrongful interference with or detention of the goods of another.

Ultra vires   "Beyond powers." Acts in excess of powers granted.

Underinclusiveness   The challenge that a statute is invalid because it limits benefits to a specified group rather than making them available to all groups.

Uttering   To circulate counterfeit notes.

Vacate   To annul; to set aside.

Vel non   "Or not." For example, the Court might say, "We now judge the merits vel non of this claim."

Venire   "To come." This is used in summoning a jury.

Vested rights   Rights so settled in a person that they cannot be taken or diminished without the person's consent.

Vicinage   Neighborhood; vicinity.

Voir dire   "To speak the truth." Preliminary examination by a court to determine competency and impartiality of a witness or juror.

Warrant   A writ issued by a judge or magistrate authorizing a law officer to make an arrest, a search, or a seizure or to perform other acts in the administration of justice. An *arrest warrant,* made on behalf of the state, commands a law enforcement officer to arrest a person and bring him before a magistrate. A *search warrant,* issued in writing by a judge or magistrate, directs a law enforcement officer to search for and seize specified property.

Writ   An order issued from a court requiring the performance of a specified act.

Appendix 4

How to Research the Law

When a bill passes Congress and is signed by the President, or is vetoed by the President and Congress overrides the veto, the bill is printed either as a public law or a private law. The latter series is reserved for legislation intended for the relief of private parties, especially bills dealing with claims against the United States, the waiver of claims by the government against individuals, and exceptions for individuals subject to certain immigration and naturalization requirements.

The enacted bill first appears as a "slip law." The heading indicates the public law number, date of approval, and bill number. For example, the Civil Rights Restoration Act of 1987, which originated as S. 557, was enacted on March 22, 1988, and designated Public Law 100-259 (the 259th public law of the One Hundredth Congress). The heading also indicates the volume and page in the *U.S. Statutes at Large,* where the public law will appear. For the Civil Rights Restoration Act of 1987, the citation is 102 Stat. 28 (Volume 102, page 28). At the end of the slip law is a convenient legislative history that refers to the House and Senate reports and floor debates that preceded the bill's enactment. Private laws are numbered by a separate series, also prefixed by the Congress. Thus, a bill for the relief of Miriama Jones, enacted October 28, 1978, was called Private Law 95-110.

Bound volumes, called the *U.S. Statutes at Large,* contain public laws, private laws, reorganization plans, joint resolutions, concurrent resolutions, and proclamations issued by the President. There is little practical difference between a bill and a joint resolution. Both forms of legislation must be presented to the President for his signature; both are legally binding. Concurrent resolutions, adopted by the House and the Senate, are not presented to the President and do not have the force of law. Nor are simple resolutions, adopted either by the House or the Senate.

Beginning with Volume 52 (1938), each volume of the *Statutes at Large* contains the laws enacted during a calendar year. After Volume 64, treaties and other international agreements were no longer printed in the *Statutes.* They are printed in a new series of volumes, published by the State Department, called *United States Treaties and Other International Agreements.* The documents first appear in pamphlet form numbered in the "Treaties and Other International Acts Series" (TIAS). Citations are usually given to both the TIAS number and the volume of *United States Treaties and Other International Agreements,* as in 30 UST 617, TIAS 9207 (1978).

Treaties may supersede prior conflicting statutes.[1] By virtue of Article VI, Section 2, the Constitution, statutes, and treaties are collectively called "the supreme Law of the Land." On the other hand, executive agreements cannot be "inconsistent with legislation enacted by Congress in the exercise of its constitutional authority."[2] In cases where executive agreements violate rights secured by the Constitution, they have been struck down by the courts.[3]

As laws are modified or repealed by subsequent enactments of Congress, the need arises for a publication that consolidates the permanent body of law. The first codification of U.S. laws, enacted June 22, 1874, appeared in the *Revised Statutes.* A second edition was published in 1878, followed by sup-

---

1. United States v. Schooner Peggy, 5 U.S. (1 Cr.) 103 (1801).
2. 11 Foreign Affairs Manual [FAM] 721.2(b)(3) (1974); United States v. Guy W. Capps, Inc., 204 F.2d 655, 660 (4th Cir. 1953), aff'd on other grounds, 348 U.S. 296 (1955).
3. Seery v. United States, 127 F.Supp. 601, 606 (Ct. Cl. 1955); Reid v. Covert, 354 U.S. 1, 16 (1956).

plements. In 1926 Congress passed a law to provide for a code intended to embrace the laws of the United States that are general and permanent in their character. The first volume, reflecting the laws in force as of December 7, 1925, was printed as Volume 44, Part I, of the *Statutes at Large.* This series is now known as the *United States Code.* New editions of the code appeared in 1934, 1940, 1946, 1952, 1958, 1964, 1970, 1976, 1982, 1988, and 1994. Supplements to the code are issued after each session of Congress. The code consists of fifty titles organized by subject matter (Agriculture, Highways, Money and Finance, and so forth). Index references are to title, section, and year, as in 7 U.S.C. 443 (1982) and 10 U.S.C. 1437 (Supp. IV, 1986).

Administrative Legislation

Unless superseded by federal statute or invalidated by the courts, presidential proclamations, executive orders, and regulations are other sources of law. Not until 1935 did Congress pass legislation to provide for the custody and publication of these administrative rules and pronouncements. This publication, the *Federal Register,* includes all presidential proclamations and executive orders that have general applicability and legal effect, as well as agency regulations and orders that prescribe a penalty. Based partly on the statutory authority vested in him by the Federal Register Act, President Franklin D. Roosevelt issued an executive order in 1936 that vested in the Bureau of the Budget (now Office of Management and Budget) the responsibility for reviewing all proposed executive orders and proclamations.[4]

The *Federal Register* is published daily, Monday through Friday, except for official holidays. A typical citation is 46 Fed. Reg. 36707 (1981). The rules, regulations, and orders that constitute the current body of administrative regulations are arranged under fifty titles (generally parallel to those of the *United States Code*) and printed as the *Code of Federal Regulations.* Citations are by title and section, as in 50 C.F.R. 17.13 (1980).

There is continuing controversy over the range and legal effect of executive orders and proclamations. Executive orders cannot supersede a statute or override contradictory congressional expressions,[5] but the latitude for presidential lawmaking is still substantial and a source of concern.[6] Proclamations also operate in a twilight zone of legality. When a statute prescribes a specific procedure and the President elects to follow a different course, a proclamation by him is illegal and void.[7] Proclamations have been upheld, however, with only tenuous ties to statutory authority.[8]

Constitutional Interpretation

As a general guide to constitutional powers, students can consult what has become known as the "Annotated Constitution." The actual title is *The Constitution of the United States of America: Analysis and Interpretation,* prepared periodically by the Congressional Research Service of the Library of Congress and printed as a Senate document. Edward S. Corwin wrote the 1952 edition, which is revised every ten years. Other basic sources include *The Records of the Federal Convention of 1787,* a four-volume

---

4. 49 Stat. 500, § 5 (1935). Roosevelt's Executive Order 7298, February 18, 1936, appeared too early for the first volume of the Federal Register. It is reprinted in James Hart, "The Exercise of Rule-Making Power," the President's Committee on Administrative Management 355 (1937).

5. Marks v. CIA, 590 F.2d 997, 1003 (D.C. Cir. 1978); Weber v. Kaiser Aluminum & Chemical Corp., 563 F.2d 216, 227 (5th Cir. 1977), rev'd on other grounds, Steelworkers v. Weber, 443 U.S. 193 (1979). The judiciary has struck down executive orders that exceed presidential authority; for example, Youngstown Co. v. Sawyer, 343 U.S. 579 (1952) and Panama Refining Co. v. Ryan, 293 U.S. 388, 433 (1935). See Louis Fisher, "Laws Congress Never Made," Constitution, Fall 1993, pp. 59–66.

6. Note, "Judicial Review of Executive Action in Domestic Affairs," 80 Colum. L. Rev. 1535 (1980); "Presidential Control of Agency Rulemaking: An Analysis of Constitutional Issues That May be Raised by Executive Order 12291," a Report Prepared for the Use of the House Committee on Energy and Commerce, 97th Cong., 1st Sess. (Comm. Print, June 15, 1981).

7. Schmidt Pritchard & Co. v. United States, 167 F.Supp. 272 (Cust. Ct. 1958); Carl Zeiss, Inc. v. United States, 76 F.2d 412 (Ct. Cust. & Pa. App. 1935).

8. United States v. Yoshida Intern., Inc., 526 F.2d 560 (Ct. Cust. & Pat. App. 1975); Louis Fisher, Constitutional Conflicts between Congress and the President 106–18 (1997).

work edited by Max Farrand and published by Yale University Press in 1937, and the *Federalist Papers* of Hamilton, Jay, and Madison, a prominent edition of which was published by Harvard University Press in 1966 under the guidance of Benjamin Fletcher Wright.

Other than brief accounts that appear in daily newspapers announcing major decisions by the Supreme Court, a researcher must rely on more specialized sources to keep track of legal interpretations—especially lower-court decisions. Decisions by federal district and appellate courts are fascinating for two reasons: (1) they are the first step in shaping constitutional and statutory law and (2) often they are the last step, for few of their rulings are reviewed by the Supreme Court.

This huge body of material is conveniently organized by the *United States Law Week,* which consists of four major sections: (1) a summary and analysis of major decisions, with page references to more extended treatment in the *Law Week;* (2) congressional and agency actions; (3) Supreme Court proceedings, including oral arguments before the Court, reviews granted, summary actions, reviews denied, cases recently filed, and special articles summarizing and analyzing the most significant Supreme Court opinions rendered for each term; and (4) Supreme Court opinions. The *Law Week* is published by the Bureau of National Affairs. Citations are by volume, page, and year, as in *Maher* v. *Roe,* 45 U.S.L.W. [or L.W.] 4787 (1977).

Two weekly newspapers, catering to the legal profession, are especially valuable. Both newspapers contain stories on appointments to the federal agencies, personnel actions, departmental politics, budget cutbacks, executive-legislative clashes, regulatory policy, and administrative law. They also regularly review the literature. *The National Law Journal* is published weekly by the New York Law Publishing Company. The *Legal Times of Washington* is published weekly by Legal Times of Washington. These periodicals contain incisive, sophisticated, and well-written accounts on current developments.

Supreme Court decisions are printed first in the form of "slip opinions." They may be purchased from the Government Printing Office and are usually available from libraries that serve as depositories for government documents. The full decisions are republished in paperbacks called "preliminary prints" and finally in bound volumes of the *United States Reports.* Citations take this form: *Ohio* v. *Roberts,* 448 U.S. 56 (1980), which indicates that the decision may be found in Volume 448, beginning on page 56.

The first ninety volumes of the *Reports* were named after court reporters. Volumes 1 through 4 (1790–1800) were named after Dallas. Later volumes, 5 through 90, carry the names of Cranch, Wheaton, Peters, Howard, Black, and Wallace. Volumes 91–107 (1875–1882) are designated "1 to 17 Otto" as well as "United States Reports 91–107." Reprints of Volumes 1 through 90 generally have a dual numbering system to the *Reports* and to court reporters, requiring such citations as *Marbury* v. *Madison,* 5 U.S. (1 Cr.) 137 (1803).

The full text of each Supreme Court decision also appears in the *Supreme Court Reporter,* issued by West Publishing Company. The citations for these decisions are in the form *Maryland* v. *Louisiana,* 101 S.Ct. 2114 (1981).

Another source of Supreme Court decisions is *United States Supreme Court Reports, Lawyers' Edition,* published by the Lawyers Co-Operative Publishing Company. A unique feature of the *Lawyers' Edition* is a summary of the arguments in each case for the majority of the Court and for justices who concur and dissent. The first series of the *Lawyers' Edition,* consisting of 100 volumes, covers the period from 1790 to 1956. There is now a second series. A typical citation is *Steagald* v. *United States,* 68 L.Ed. 2d 38 (1981).

Briefs and oral arguments to the Supreme Court, for major cases, are published in *Landmark Briefs and Arguments of the Supreme Court of the United States: Constitutional Law,* edited by Gerald Gunther and Gerhard Casper and published by University Publications of America.

Significant decisions by federal district courts are printed in the *Federal Supplement,* issued first in a paper edition and later in bound volumes. The citation shows the volume, page, state, and year, as in *United States* v. *Mandel,* 505 F.Supp. 189 (D. Md. 1981). The "D" in parentheses indicates that the decision occurred at the district court level. For decisions that are not reported in the *Federal Supple-*

ment, or in situations where immediate access to a decision is needed, a researcher may call the judge's chamber and receive a copy of the memorandum decision from a law clerk or filing clerk.

To follow appeals of district court decisions, the source is the *Federal Reporter,* consisting of two series. The first series (F. or Fed.) stopped with Volume 300; the second series (F.2d) ended with Volume 999. The *Federal Reporter* is now in its third series (F.3d). Typical citations are *Rowe v. Drohen,* 262 F. 15 (2d Cir. 1919) and *Romeo v. Youngberg,* 644 F.2d 147 (3d Cir. 1980). These decisions are initially available as slip opinions and in memorandum form either from the court or libraries.

Finding Citations

Various databases, including LEXIS and WESTLAW, are used to find citations to statutes, administrative legislation, and court decisions. *U.S. Code Congressional and Administrative News,* published by West, reprints the full text of public laws and selected House and Senate documents, as well as presidential proclamations, executive orders, presidential messages, and federal regulations. The *CIS/Index* provides citations to all congressional publications, including reports, hearings, and other legislative documents.

The "citator" or citation book tells the student whether a decision is still valid and authoritative. A decision by a lower court may be affirmed, reversed, or modified. *Shepard's Citations,* a widely used sourcebook, has spawned such words as *Shepardize* and *Shepardizing* to describe the process of determining the current state of the law. *Shepard's United States Citations* includes citations to Supreme Court decisions, U.S. statutes, treaties, and court rules for federal courts. *Shepard's Federal Citations,* covering decisions by federal courts below the Supreme Court, is issued in two series. One series covers the *Federal Supplement,* and the other the *Federal Reporter.*

DOJ and GAO

Many of the issues that come before the courts have been first explored by the Justice Department and the General Accounting Office. These analyses are published in *Official Opinions of the Attorneys General* and *Decisions of the Comptroller General.* Among his other duties, the Attorney General renders important opinions on legal issues presented to him by Presidents and departmental heads. Citations to these opinions are by volume, page, and year, as in 40 Ops. Att'y Gen. [or Op. A.G.] 469 (1946). A new series, called *Opinions of the Office of Legal Counsel,* is now available to record the memorandum opinions from the Office of Legal Counsel, which advises the President, the Attorney General, and other executive officers.

The Comptroller General determines the legality of payments of appropriated funds by federal officials. This function was vested in the Treasury Department from 1817 to 1921 but passed thereafter to the Comptroller General as the head of the newly created General Accounting Office. The decisions are cited as 49 Comp. Gen. 59 (1969). In 1969 the Comptroller General and the Attorney General disagreed completely about the legality of the Nixon administration's "Philadelphia Plan," designed to increase the number of minority workers in federally assisted contracts.[9] In this dispute the courts sided with the Attorney General's interpretation.[10]

General Literature

An indispensable guide to the literature is the *Index to Legal Periodicals,* published by the H.W. Wilson Company. Currently covering more than 400 legal periodicals, it indexes the articles under subject and author. Entries of special interest include administrative agencies, administrative law, administrative procedure, delegation of powers, discrimination, executive agreements, executive power,

---

9. 49 Comp. Gen. (1969); 42 Ops. Att'y Gen. 405 (1969).

10. Contractors Ass'n of Eastern Pa. v. Secretary of Labor, 442 F.2d 159 (3d Cir. 1971), cert. denied, 404 U.S. 854 (1971).

federalism, freedom of information, freedom of religion, freedom of speech, freedom of the press, government, judicial review, legislation, political science, politics, public finance, separation of powers, United States: Congress, United States: President, and United States: Supreme Court. Legal periodicals can also be accessed through *Current Law Index,* published by Information Access Company, and InfoTrac/LegalTrac Database, a computerized system offered by Information Access Company.

State Decisions

Decisions by state courts are reported in volumes published by each state. They are also published in seven regional reporters. For example, decisions by Connecticut, Delaware, the District of Columbia, Maine, Maryland, New Hampshire, New Jersey, Pennsylvania, Rhode Island, and Vermont appear in the *Atlantic Reporter.* The citation for the second series is A.2d. Other state court decisions appear in the following reporters, with citations given to the second series: *North Eastern Reporter* (N.E.2d; Illinois, Indiana, Massachusetts, New York, Ohio); *North Western Reporter* (N.W.2d; Iowa, Michigan, Minnesota, Nebraska, North Dakota, South Dakota, Wisconsin); *Pacific Reporter* (P.2d; Alaska, Arizona, California, Colorado, Hawaii, Idaho, Kansas, Montana, Nevada, New Mexico, Oklahoma, Oregon, Utah, Washington, Wyoming); *South Eastern Reporter* (S.E.2d; Georgia, North Carolina, South Carolina, Virginia, West Virginia); *Southern Reporter* (So.2d; Alabama, Florida, Louisiana, Mississippi); and *South Western Reporter* (S.W.2d; Arkansas, Kentucky, Missouri, Tennessee, Texas).

Table of Cases

Index